T0142157

Lecture Notes in Computer Science   **11217**

Commenced Publication in 1973
Founding and Former Series Editors:
Gerhard Goos, Juris Hartmanis, and Jan van Leeuwen

More information about this series at http://www.springer.com/series/7412

Vittorio Ferrari · Martial Hebert
Cristian Sminchisescu · Yair Weiss (Eds.)

Computer Vision – ECCV 2018

15th European Conference
Munich, Germany, September 8–14, 2018
Proceedings, Part XIII

 Springer

Editors
Vittorio Ferrari
Google Research
Zurich
Switzerland

Martial Hebert
Carnegie Mellon University
Pittsburgh, PA
USA

Cristian Sminchisescu
Google Research
Zurich
Switzerland

Yair Weiss
Hebrew University of Jerusalem
Jerusalem
Israel

ISSN 0302-9743   ISSN 1611-3349 (electronic)
Lecture Notes in Computer Science
ISBN 978-3-030-01260-1   ISBN 978-3-030-01261-8 (eBook)
https://doi.org/10.1007/978-3-030-01261-8

Library of Congress Control Number: 2018955489

LNCS Sublibrary: SL6 – Image Processing, Computer Vision, Pattern Recognition, and Graphics

This Springer imprint is published by the registered company Springer Nature Switzerland AG
The registered company address is: Gewerbestrasse 11, 6330 Cham, Switzerland

Foreword

It was our great pleasure to host the European Conference on Computer Vision 2018 in Munich, Germany. This constituted by far the largest ECCV event ever. With close to 2,900 registered participants and another 600 on the waiting list one month before the conference, participation more than doubled since the last ECCV in Amsterdam. We believe that this is due to a dramatic growth of the computer vision community combined with the popularity of Munich as a major European hub of culture, science, and industry. The conference took place in the heart of Munich in the concert hall Gasteig with workshops and tutorials held at the downtown campus of the Technical University of Munich.

One of the major innovations for ECCV 2018 was the free perpetual availability of all conference and workshop papers, which is often referred to as open access. We note that this is not precisely the same use of the term as in the Budapest declaration. Since 2013, CVPR and ICCV have had their papers hosted by the Computer Vision Foundation (CVF), in parallel with the IEEE Xplore version. This has proved highly beneficial to the computer vision community.

We are delighted to announce that for ECCV 2018 a very similar arrangement was put in place with the cooperation of Springer. In particular, the author's final version will be freely available in perpetuity on a CVF page, while SpringerLink will continue to host a version with further improvements, such as activating reference links and including video. We believe that this will give readers the best of both worlds; researchers who are focused on the technical content will have a freely available version in an easily accessible place, while subscribers to SpringerLink will continue to have the additional benefits that this provides. We thank Alfred Hofmann from Springer for helping to negotiate this agreement, which we expect will continue for future versions of ECCV.

September 2018

Horst Bischof
Daniel Cremers
Bernt Schiele
Ramin Zabih

Preface

Welcome to the proceedings of the 2018 European Conference on Computer Vision (ECCV 2018) held in Munich, Germany. We are delighted to present this volume reflecting a strong and exciting program, the result of an extensive review process. In total, we received 2,439 valid paper submissions. Of these, 776 were accepted (31.8%): 717 as posters (29.4%) and 59 as oral presentations (2.4%). All oral presentations were presented as posters as well. The program selection process was complicated this year by the large increase in the number of submitted papers, +65% over ECCV 2016, and the use of CMT3 for the first time for a computer vision conference. The program selection process was supported by four program co-chairs (PCs), 126 area chairs (ACs), and 1,199 reviewers with reviews assigned.

We were primarily responsible for the design and execution of the review process. Beyond administrative rejections, we were involved in acceptance decisions only in the very few cases where the ACs were not able to agree on a decision. As PCs, and as is customary in the field, we were not allowed to co-author a submission. General co-chairs and other co-organizers who played no role in the review process were permitted to submit papers, and were treated as any other author is.

Acceptance decisions were made by two independent ACs. The ACs also made a joint recommendation for promoting papers to oral status. We decided on the final selection of oral presentations based on the ACs' recommendations. There were 126 ACs, selected according to their technical expertise, experience, and geographical diversity (63 from European, nine from Asian/Australian, and 54 from North American institutions). Indeed, 126 ACs is a substantial increase in the number of ACs due to the natural increase in the number of papers and to our desire to maintain the number of papers assigned to each AC to a manageable number so as to ensure quality. The ACs were aided by the 1,199 reviewers to whom papers were assigned for reviewing. The Program Committee was selected from committees of previous ECCV, ICCV, and CVPR conferences and was extended on the basis of suggestions from the ACs. Having a large pool of Program Committee members for reviewing allowed us to match expertise while reducing reviewer loads. No more than eight papers were assigned to a reviewer, maintaining the reviewers' load at the same level as ECCV 2016 despite the increase in the number of submitted papers.

Conflicts of interest between ACs, Program Committee members, and papers were identified based on the home institutions, and on previous collaborations of all researchers involved. To find institutional conflicts, all authors, Program Committee members, and ACs were asked to list the Internet domains of their current institutions. We assigned on average approximately 18 papers to each AC. The papers were assigned using the affinity scores from the Toronto Paper Matching System (TPMS) and additional data from the OpenReview system, managed by a UMass group. OpenReview used additional information from ACs' and authors' records to identify collaborations and to generate matches. OpenReview was invaluable in refining conflict definitions and in generating quality matches. The only glitch is that, once the matches were generated, a small percentage of papers were unassigned because of discrepancies between the OpenReview conflicts and the conflicts entered in CMT3. We manually assigned these papers. This glitch is revealing of the challenge of using multiple systems at once (CMT3 and OpenReview in this case), which needs to be addressed in future.

After assignment of papers to ACs, the ACs suggested seven reviewers per paper from the Program Committee pool. The selection and rank ordering were facilitated by the TPMS affinity scores visible to the ACs for each paper/reviewer pair. The final assignment of papers to reviewers was generated again through OpenReview in order to account for refined conflict definitions. This required new features in the OpenReview matching system to accommodate the ECCV workflow, in particular to incorporate selection ranking, and maximum reviewer load. Very few papers received fewer than three reviewers after matching and were handled through manual assignment. Reviewers were then asked to comment on the merit of each paper and to make an initial recommendation ranging from definitely reject to definitely accept, including a borderline rating. The reviewers were also asked to suggest explicit questions they wanted to see answered in the authors' rebuttal. The initial review period was five weeks. Because of the delay in getting all the reviews in, we had to delay the final release of the reviews by four days. However, because of the slack included at the tail end of the schedule, we were able to maintain the decision target date with sufficient time for all the phases. We reassigned over 100 reviews from 40 reviewers during the review period. Unfortunately, the main reason for these reassignments was reviewers declining to review, after having accepted to do so. Other reasons included technical relevance and occasional unidentified conflicts. We express our thanks to the emergency reviewers who generously accepted to perform these reviews under short notice. In addition, a substantial number of manual corrections had to do with reviewers using a different email address than the one that was used at the time of the reviewer invitation. This is revealing of a broader issue with identifying users by email addresses that change frequently enough to cause significant problems during the timespan of the conference process.

The authors were then given the opportunity to rebut the reviews, to identify factual errors, and to address the specific questions raised by the reviewers over a seven-day rebuttal period. The exact format of the rebuttal was the object of considerable debate among the organizers, as well as with prior organizers. At issue is to balance giving the author the opportunity to respond completely and precisely to the reviewers, e.g., by including graphs of experiments, while avoiding requests for completely new material or experimental results not included in the original paper. In the end, we decided on the two-page PDF document in conference format. Following this rebuttal period, reviewers and ACs discussed papers at length, after which reviewers finalized their evaluation and gave a final recommendation to the ACs. A significant percentage of the reviewers did enter their final recommendation if it did not differ from their initial recommendation. Given the tight schedule, we did not wait until all were entered.

After this discussion period, each paper was assigned to a second AC. The AC/paper matching was again run through OpenReview. Again, the OpenReview team worked quickly to implement the features specific to this process, in this case accounting for the existing AC assignment, as well as minimizing the fragmentation across ACs, so that each AC had on average only 5.5 buddy ACs to communicate with. The largest number was 11. Given the complexity of the conflicts, this was a very efficient set of assignments from OpenReview. Each paper was then evaluated by its assigned pair of ACs. For each paper, we required each of the two ACs assigned to certify both the final recommendation and the metareview (aka consolidation report). In all cases, after extensive discussions, the two ACs arrived at a common acceptance decision. We maintained these decisions, with the caveat that we did evaluate, sometimes going back to the ACs, a few papers for which the final acceptance decision substantially deviated from the consensus from the reviewers, amending three decisions in the process.

We want to thank everyone involved in making ECCV 2018 possible. The success of ECCV 2018 depended on the quality of papers submitted by the authors, and on the very hard work of the ACs and the Program Committee members. We are particularly grateful to the OpenReview team (Melisa Bok, Ari Kobren, Andrew McCallum, Michael Spector) for their support, in particular their willingness to implement new features, often on a tight schedule, to Laurent Charlin for the use of the Toronto Paper Matching System, to the CMT3 team, in particular in dealing with all the issues that arise when using a new system, to Friedrich Fraundorfer and Quirin Lohr for maintaining the online version of the program, and to the CMU staff (Keyla Cook, Lynnetta Miller, Ashley Song, Nora Kazour) for assisting with data entry/editing in CMT3. Finally, the preparation of these proceedings would not have been possible without the diligent effort of the publication chairs, Albert Ali Salah and Hamdi Dibeklioğlu, and of Anna Kramer and Alfred Hofmann from Springer.

September 2018

Vittorio Ferrari
Martial Hebert
Cristian Sminchisescu
Yair Weiss

Organization

General Chairs

Horst Bischof — Graz University of Technology, Austria
Daniel Cremers — Technical University of Munich, Germany
Bernt Schiele — Saarland University, Max Planck Institute for Informatics, Germany
Ramin Zabih — CornellNYCTech, USA

Program Committee Co-chairs

Vittorio Ferrari — University of Edinburgh, UK
Martial Hebert — Carnegie Mellon University, USA
Cristian Sminchisescu — Lund University, Sweden
Yair Weiss — Hebrew University, Israel

Local Arrangements Chairs

Björn Menze — Technical University of Munich, Germany
Matthias Niessner — Technical University of Munich, Germany

Workshop Chairs

Stefan Roth — TU Darmstadt, Germany
Laura Leal-Taixé — Technical University of Munich, Germany

Tutorial Chairs

Michael Bronstein — Università della Svizzera Italiana, Switzerland
Laura Leal-Taixé — Technical University of Munich, Germany

Website Chair

Friedrich Fraundorfer — Graz University of Technology, Austria

Demo Chairs

Federico Tombari — Technical University of Munich, Germany
Joerg Stueckler — Technical University of Munich, Germany

Publicity Chair

Giovanni Maria   University of Catania, Italy
  Farinella

Industrial Liaison Chairs

Florent Perronnin   Naver Labs, France
Yunchao Gong   Snap, USA
Helmut Grabner   Logitech, Switzerland

Finance Chair

Gerard Medioni   Amazon, University of Southern California, USA

Publication Chairs

Albert Ali Salah   Boğaziçi University, Turkey
Hamdi Dibeklioğlu   Bilkent University, Turkey

Area Chairs

Kalle Åström   Lund University, Sweden
Zeynep Akata   University of Amsterdam, The Netherlands
Joao Barreto   University of Coimbra, Portugal
Ronen Basri   Weizmann Institute of Science, Israel
Dhruv Batra   Georgia Tech and Facebook AI Research, USA
Serge Belongie   Cornell University, USA
Rodrigo Benenson   Google, Switzerland
Hakan Bilen   University of Edinburgh, UK
Matthew Blaschko   KU Leuven, Belgium
Edmond Boyer   Inria, France
Gabriel Brostow   University College London, UK
Thomas Brox   University of Freiburg, Germany
Marcus Brubaker   York University, Canada
Barbara Caputo   Politecnico di Torino and the Italian Institute
                           of Technology, Italy
Tim Cootes   University of Manchester, UK
Trevor Darrell   University of California, Berkeley, USA
Larry Davis   University of Maryland at College Park, USA
Andrew Davison   Imperial College London, UK
Fernando de la Torre   Carnegie Mellon University, USA
Irfan Essa   GeorgiaTech, USA
Ali Farhadi   University of Washington, USA
Paolo Favaro   University of Bern, Switzerland
Michael Felsberg   Linköping University, Sweden

Sanja Fidler	University of Toronto, Canada
Andrew Fitzgibbon	Microsoft, Cambridge, UK
David Forsyth	University of Illinois at Urbana-Champaign, USA
Charless Fowlkes	University of California, Irvine, USA
Bill Freeman	MIT, USA
Mario Fritz	MPII, Germany
Jürgen Gall	University of Bonn, Germany
Dariu Gavrila	TU Delft, The Netherlands
Andreas Geiger	MPI-IS and University of Tübingen, Germany
Theo Gevers	University of Amsterdam, The Netherlands
Ross Girshick	Facebook AI Research, USA
Kristen Grauman	Facebook AI Research and UT Austin, USA
Abhinav Gupta	Carnegie Mellon University, USA
Kaiming He	Facebook AI Research, USA
Martial Hebert	Carnegie Mellon University, USA
Anders Heyden	Lund University, Sweden
Timothy Hospedales	University of Edinburgh, UK
Michal Irani	Weizmann Institute of Science, Israel
Phillip Isola	University of California, Berkeley, USA
Hervé Jégou	Facebook AI Research, France
David Jacobs	University of Maryland, College Park, USA
Allan Jepson	University of Toronto, Canada
Jiaya Jia	Chinese University of Hong Kong, SAR China
Fredrik Kahl	Chalmers University, USA
Hedvig Kjellström	KTH Royal Institute of Technology, Sweden
Iasonas Kokkinos	University College London and Facebook, UK
Vladlen Koltun	Intel Labs, USA
Philipp Krähenbühl	UT Austin, USA
M. Pawan Kumar	University of Oxford, UK
Kyros Kutulakos	University of Toronto, Canada
In Kweon	KAIST, South Korea
Ivan Laptev	Inria, France
Svetlana Lazebnik	University of Illinois at Urbana-Champaign, USA
Laura Leal-Taixé	Technical University of Munich, Germany
Erik Learned-Miller	University of Massachusetts, Amherst, USA
Kyoung Mu Lee	Seoul National University, South Korea
Bastian Leibe	RWTH Aachen University, Germany
Aleš Leonardis	University of Birmingham, UK
Vincent Lepetit	University of Bordeaux, France and Graz University of Technology, Austria
Fuxin Li	Oregon State University, USA
Dahua Lin	Chinese University of Hong Kong, SAR China
Jim Little	University of British Columbia, Canada
Ce Liu	Google, USA
Chen Change Loy	Nanyang Technological University, Singapore
Jiri Matas	Czech Technical University in Prague, Czechia

Yasuyuki Matsushita	Osaka University, Japan
Dimitris Metaxas	Rutgers University, USA
Greg Mori	Simon Fraser University, Canada
Vittorio Murino	Istituto Italiano di Tecnologia, Italy
Richard Newcombe	Oculus Research, USA
Minh Hoai Nguyen	Stony Brook University, USA
Sebastian Nowozin	Microsoft Research Cambridge, UK
Aude Oliva	MIT, USA
Bjorn Ommer	Heidelberg University, Germany
Tomas Pajdla	Czech Technical University in Prague, Czechia
Maja Pantic	Imperial College London and Samsung AI Research Centre Cambridge, UK
Caroline Pantofaru	Google, USA
Devi Parikh	Georgia Tech and Facebook AI Research, USA
Sylvain Paris	Adobe Research, USA
Vladimir Pavlovic	Rutgers University, USA
Marcello Pelillo	University of Venice, Italy
Patrick Pérez	Valeo, France
Robert Pless	George Washington University, USA
Thomas Pock	Graz University of Technology, Austria
Jean Ponce	Inria, France
Gerard Pons-Moll	MPII, Saarland Informatics Campus, Germany
Long Quan	Hong Kong University of Science and Technology, SAR China
Stefan Roth	TU Darmstadt, Germany
Carsten Rother	University of Heidelberg, Germany
Bryan Russell	Adobe Research, USA
Kate Saenko	Boston University, USA
Mathieu Salzmann	EPFL, Switzerland
Dimitris Samaras	Stony Brook University, USA
Yoichi Sato	University of Tokyo, Japan
Silvio Savarese	Stanford University, USA
Konrad Schindler	ETH Zurich, Switzerland
Cordelia Schmid	Inria, France and Google, France
Nicu Sebe	University of Trento, Italy
Fei Sha	University of Southern California, USA
Greg Shakhnarovich	TTI Chicago, USA
Jianbo Shi	University of Pennsylvania, USA
Abhinav Shrivastava	UMD and Google, USA
Yan Shuicheng	National University of Singapore, Singapore
Leonid Sigal	University of British Columbia, Canada
Josef Sivic	Czech Technical University in Prague, Czechia
Arnold Smeulders	University of Amsterdam, The Netherlands
Deqing Sun	NVIDIA, USA
Antonio Torralba	MIT, USA
Zhuowen Tu	University of California, San Diego, USA

Tinne Tuytelaars	KU Leuven, Belgium
Jasper Uijlings	Google, Switzerland
Joost van de Weijer	Computer Vision Center, Spain
Nuno Vasconcelos	University of California, San Diego, USA
Andrea Vedaldi	University of Oxford, UK
Olga Veksler	University of Western Ontario, Canada
Jakob Verbeek	Inria, France
Rene Vidal	Johns Hopkins University, USA
Daphna Weinshall	Hebrew University, Israel
Chris Williams	University of Edinburgh, UK
Lior Wolf	Tel Aviv University, Israel
Ming-Hsuan Yang	University of California at Merced, USA
Todd Zickler	Harvard University, USA
Andrew Zisserman	University of Oxford, UK

Technical Program Committee

Hassan Abu Alhaija	Peter Anderson	Arunava Banerjee
Radhakrishna Achanta	Juan Andrade-Cetto	Atsuhiko Banno
Hanno Ackermann	Mykhaylo Andriluka	Aayush Bansal
Ehsan Adeli	Anelia Angelova	Yingze Bao
Lourdes Agapito	Michel Antunes	Md Jawadul Bappy
Aishwarya Agrawal	Pablo Arbelaez	Pierre Baqué
Antonio Agudo	Vasileios Argyriou	Dániel Baráth
Eirikur Agustsson	Chetan Arora	Adrian Barbu
Karim Ahmed	Federica Arrigoni	Kobus Barnard
Byeongjoo Ahn	Vassilis Athitsos	Nick Barnes
Unaiza Ahsan	Mathieu Aubry	Francisco Barranco
Emre Akbaş	Shai Avidan	Adrien Bartoli
Eren Aksoy	Yannis Avrithis	E. Bayro-Corrochano
Yağız Aksoy	Samaneh Azadi	Paul Beardlsey
Alexandre Alahi	Hossein Azizpour	Vasileios Belagiannis
Jean-Baptiste Alayrac	Artem Babenko	Sean Bell
Samuel Albanie	Timur Bagautdinov	Ismail Ben
Cenek Albl	Andrew Bagdanov	Boulbaba Ben Amor
Saad Ali	Hessam Bagherinezhad	Gil Ben-Artzi
Rahaf Aljundi	Yuval Bahat	Ohad Ben-Shahar
Jose M. Alvarez	Min Bai	Abhijit Bendale
Humam Alwassel	Qinxun Bai	Rodrigo Benenson
Toshiyuki Amano	Song Bai	Fabian Benitez-Quiroz
Mitsuru Ambai	Xiang Bai	Fethallah Benmansour
Mohamed Amer	Peter Bajcsy	Ryad Benosman
Senjian An	Amr Bakry	Filippo Bergamasco
Cosmin Ancuti	Kavita Bala	David Bermudez

Achal Dave
Shalini De Mello
Teofilo deCampos
Joseph DeGol
Koichiro Deguchi
Alessio Del Bue
Stefanie Demirci
Jia Deng
Zhiwei Deng
Joachim Denzler
Konstantinos Derpanis
Aditya Deshpande
Alban Desmaison
Frédéric Devernay
Abhinav Dhall
Michel Dhome
Hamdi Dibeklioğlu
Mert Dikmen
Cosimo Distante
Ajay Divakaran
Mandar Dixit
Carl Doersch
Piotr Dollar
Bo Dong
Chao Dong
Huang Dong
Jian Dong
Jiangxin Dong
Weisheng Dong
Simon Donné
Gianfranco Doretto
Alexey Dosovitskiy
Matthijs Douze
Bruce Draper
Bertram Drost
Liang Du
Shichuan Du
Gregory Dudek
Zoran Duric
Pınar Duygulu
Hazım Ekenel
Tarek El-Gaaly
Ehsan Elhamifar
Mohamed Elhoseiny
Sabu Emmanuel
Ian Endres

Aykut Erdem
Erkut Erdem
Hugo Jair Escalante
Sergio Escalera
Victor Escorcia
Francisco Estrada
Davide Eynard
Bin Fan
Jialue Fan
Quanfu Fan
Chen Fang
Tian Fang
Yi Fang
Hany Farid
Giovanni Farinella
Ryan Farrell
Alireza Fathi
Christoph Feichtenhofer
Wenxin Feng
Martin Fergie
Cornelia Fermuller
Basura Fernando
Michael Firman
Bob Fisher
John Fisher
Mathew Fisher
Boris Flach
Matt Flagg
Francois Fleuret
David Fofi
Ruth Fong
Gian Luca Foresti
Per-Erik Forssén
David Fouhey
Katerina Fragkiadaki
Victor Fragoso
Jan-Michael Frahm
Jean-Sebastien Franco
Ohad Fried
Simone Frintrop
Huazhu Fu
Yun Fu
Olac Fuentes
Christopher Funk
Thomas Funkhouser
Brian Funt

Ryo Furukawa
Yasutaka Furukawa
Andrea Fusiello
Fatma Güney
Raghudeep Gadde
Silvano Galliani
Orazio Gallo
Chuang Gan
Bin-Bin Gao
Jin Gao
Junbin Gao
Ruohan Gao
Shenghua Gao
Animesh Garg
Ravi Garg
Erik Gartner
Simone Gasparin
Jochen Gast
Leon A. Gatys
Stratis Gavves
Liuhao Ge
Timnit Gebru
James Gee
Peter Gehler
Xin Geng
Guido Gerig
David Geronimo
Bernard Ghanem
Michael Gharbi
Golnaz Ghiasi
Spyros Gidaris
Andrew Gilbert
Rohit Girdhar
Ioannis Gkioulekas
Georgia Gkioxari
Guy Godin
Roland Goecke
Michael Goesele
Nuno Goncalves
Boqing Gong
Minglun Gong
Yunchao Gong
Abel Gonzalez-Garcia
Daniel Gordon
Paulo Gotardo
Stephen Gould

Venu Govindu
Helmut Grabner
Petr Gronat
Steve Gu
Josechu Guerrero
Anupam Guha
Jean-Yves Guillemaut
Alp Güler
Erhan Gündoğdu
Guodong Guo
Xinqing Guo
Ankush Gupta
Mohit Gupta
Saurabh Gupta
Tanmay Gupta
Abner Guzman Rivera
Timo Hackel
Sunil Hadap
Christian Haene
Ralf Haeusler
Levente Hajder
David Hall
Peter Hall
Stefan Haller
Ghassan Hamarneh
Fred Hamprecht
Onur Hamsici
Bohyung Han
Junwei Han
Xufeng Han
Yahong Han
Ankur Handa
Albert Haque
Tatsuya Harada
Mehrtash Harandi
Bharath Hariharan
Mahmudul Hasan
Tal Hassner
Kenji Hata
Soren Hauberg
Michal Havlena
Zeeshan Hayder
Junfeng He
Lei He
Varsha Hedau
Felix Heide

Wolfgang Heidrich
Janne Heikkila
Jared Heinly
Mattias Heinrich
Lisa Anne Hendricks
Dan Hendrycks
Stephane Herbin
Alexander Hermans
Luis Herranz
Aaron Hertzmann
Adrian Hilton
Michael Hirsch
Steven Hoi
Seunghoon Hong
Wei Hong
Anthony Hoogs
Radu Horaud
Yedid Hoshen
Omid Hosseini Jafari
Kuang-Jui Hsu
Winston Hsu
Yinlin Hu
Zhe Hu
Gang Hua
Chen Huang
De-An Huang
Dong Huang
Gary Huang
Heng Huang
Jia-Bin Huang
Qixing Huang
Rui Huang
Sheng Huang
Weilin Huang
Xiaolei Huang
Xinyu Huang
Zhiwu Huang
Tak-Wai Hui
Wei-Chih Hung
Junhwa Hur
Mohamed Hussein
Wonjun Hwang
Anders Hyden
Satoshi Ikehata
Nazlı Ikizler-Cinbis
Viorela Ila

Evren Imre
Eldar Insafutdinov
Go Irie
Hossam Isack
Ahmet Işcen
Daisuke Iwai
Hamid Izadinia
Nathan Jacobs
Suyog Jain
Varun Jampani
C. V. Jawahar
Dinesh Jayaraman
Sadeep Jayasumana
Laszlo Jeni
Hueihan Jhuang
Dinghuang Ji
Hui Ji
Qiang Ji
Fan Jia
Kui Jia
Xu Jia
Huaizu Jiang
Jiayan Jiang
Nianjuan Jiang
Tingting Jiang
Xiaoyi Jiang
Yu-Gang Jiang
Long Jin
Suo Jinli
Justin Johnson
Nebojsa Jojic
Michael Jones
Hanbyul Joo
Jungseock Joo
Ajjen Joshi
Amin Jourabloo
Frederic Jurie
Achuta Kadambi
Samuel Kadoury
Ioannis Kakadiaris
Zdenek Kalal
Yannis Kalantidis
Sinan Kalkan
Vicky Kalogeiton
Sunkavalli Kalyan
J.-K. Kamarainen

Martin Kampel
Kenichi Kanatani
Angjoo Kanazawa
Melih Kandemir
Sing Bing Kang
Zhuoliang Kang
Mohan Kankanhalli
Juho Kannala
Abhishek Kar
Amlan Kar
Svebor Karaman
Leonid Karlinsky
Zoltan Kato
Parneet Kaur
Hiroshi Kawasaki
Misha Kazhdan
Margret Keuper
Sameh Khamis
Naeemullah Khan
Salman Khan
Hadi Kiapour
Joe Kileel
Chanho Kim
Gunhee Kim
Hansung Kim
Junmo Kim
Junsik Kim
Kihwan Kim
Minyoung Kim
Tae Hyun Kim
Tae-Kyun Kim
Akisato Kimura
Zsolt Kira
Alexander Kirillov
Kris Kitani
Maria Klodt
Patrick Knöbelreiter
Jan Knopp
Reinhard Koch
Alexander Kolesnikov
Chen Kong
Naejin Kong
Shu Kong
Piotr Koniusz
Simon Korman
Andreas Koschan

Dimitrios Kosmopoulos
Satwik Kottur
Balazs Kovacs
Adarsh Kowdle
Mike Krainin
Gregory Kramida
Ranjay Krishna
Ravi Krishnan
Matej Kristan
Pavel Krsek
Volker Krueger
Alexander Krull
Hilde Kuehne
Andreas Kuhn
Arjan Kuijper
Zuzana Kukelova
Kuldeep Kulkarni
Shiro Kumano
Avinash Kumar
Vijay Kumar
Abhijit Kundu
Sebastian Kurtek
Junseok Kwon
Jan Kybic
Alexander Ladikos
Shang-Hong Lai
Wei-Sheng Lai
Jean-Francois Lalonde
John Lambert
Zhenzhong Lan
Charis Lanaras
Oswald Lanz
Dong Lao
Longin Jan Latecki
Justin Lazarow
Huu Le
Chen-Yu Lee
Gim Hee Lee
Honglak Lee
Hsin-Ying Lee
Joon-Young Lee
Seungyong Lee
Stefan Lee
Yong Jae Lee
Zhen Lei
Ido Leichter

Victor Lempitsky
Spyridon Leonardos
Marius Leordeanu
Matt Leotta
Thomas Leung
Stefan Leutenegger
Gil Levi
Aviad Levis
Jose Lezama
Ang Li
Dingzeyu Li
Dong Li
Haoxiang Li
Hongdong Li
Hongsheng Li
Hongyang Li
Jianguo Li
Kai Li
Ruiyu Li
Wei Li
Wen Li
Xi Li
Xiaoxiao Li
Xin Li
Xirong Li
Xuelong Li
Xueting Li
Yeqing Li
Yijun Li
Yin Li
Yingwei Li
Yining Li
Yongjie Li
Yu-Feng Li
Zechao Li
Zhengqi Li
Zhenyang Li
Zhizhong Li
Xiaodan Liang
Renjie Liao
Zicheng Liao
Bee Lim
Jongwoo Lim
Joseph Lim
Ser-Nam Lim
Chen-Hsuan Lin

Shih-Yao Lin
Tsung-Yi Lin
Weiyao Lin
Yen-Yu Lin
Haibin Ling
Or Litany
Roee Litman
Anan Liu
Changsong Liu
Chen Liu
Ding Liu
Dong Liu
Feng Liu
Guangcan Liu
Luoqi Liu
Miaomiao Liu
Nian Liu
Risheng Liu
Shu Liu
Shuaicheng Liu
Sifei Liu
Tyng-Luh Liu
Wanquan Liu
Weiwei Liu
Xialei Liu
Xiaoming Liu
Yebin Liu
Yiming Liu
Ziwei Liu
Zongyi Liu
Liliana Lo Presti
Edgar Lobaton
Chengjiang Long
Mingsheng Long
Roberto Lopez-Sastre
Amy Loufti
Brian Lovell
Canyi Lu
Cewu Lu
Feng Lu
Huchuan Lu
Jiajun Lu
Jiasen Lu
Jiwen Lu
Yang Lu
Yujuan Lu

Simon Lucey
Jian-Hao Luo
Jiebo Luo
Pablo Márquez-Neila
Matthias Müller
Chao Ma
Chih-Yao Ma
Lin Ma
Shugao Ma
Wei-Chiu Ma
Zhanyu Ma
Oisin Mac Aodha
Will Maddern
Ludovic Magerand
Marcus Magnor
Vijay Mahadevan
Mohammad Mahoor
Michael Maire
Subhransu Maji
Ameesh Makadia
Atsuto Maki
Yasushi Makihara
Mateusz Malinowski
Tomasz Malisiewicz
Arun Mallya
Roberto Manduchi
Junhua Mao
Dmitrii Marin
Joe Marino
Kenneth Marino
Elisabeta Marinoiu
Ricardo Martin
Aleix Martinez
Julieta Martinez
Aaron Maschinot
Jonathan Masci
Bogdan Matei
Diana Mateus
Stefan Mathe
Kevin Matzen
Bruce Maxwell
Steve Maybank
Walterio Mayol-Cuevas
Mason McGill
Stephen Mckenna
Roey Mechrez

Christopher Mei
Heydi Mendez-Vazquez
Deyu Meng
Thomas Mensink
Bjoern Menze
Domingo Mery
Qiguang Miao
Tomer Michaeli
Antoine Miech
Ondrej Miksik
Anton Milan
Gregor Miller
Cai Minjie
Majid Mirmehdi
Ishan Misra
Niloy Mitra
Anurag Mittal
Nirbhay Modhe
Davide Modolo
Pritish Mohapatra
Pascal Monasse
Mathew Monfort
Taesup Moon
Sandino Morales
Vlad Morariu
Philippos Mordohai
Francesc Moreno
Henrique Morimitsu
Yael Moses
Ben-Ezra Moshe
Roozbeh Mottaghi
Yadong Mu
Lopamudra Mukherjee
Mario Munich
Ana Murillo
Damien Muselet
Armin Mustafa
Siva Karthik Mustikovela
Moin Nabi
Sobhan Naderi
Hajime Nagahara
Varun Nagaraja
Tushar Nagarajan
Arsha Nagrani
Nikhil Naik
Atsushi Nakazawa

P. J. Narayanan
Charlie Nash
Lakshmanan Nataraj
Fabian Nater
Lukáš Neumann
Natalia Neverova
Alejandro Newell
Phuc Nguyen
Xiaohan Nie
David Nilsson
Ko Nishino
Zhenxing Niu
Shohei Nobuhara
Klas Nordberg
Mohammed Norouzi
David Novotny
Ifeoma Nwogu
Matthew O'Toole
Guillaume Obozinski
Jean-Marc Odobez
Eyal Ofek
Ferda Ofli
Tae-Hyun Oh
Iason Oikonomidis
Takeshi Oishi
Takahiro Okabe
Takayuki Okatani
Vlad Olaru
Michael Opitz
Jose Oramas
Vicente Ordonez
Ivan Oseledets
Aljosa Osep
Magnus Oskarsson
Martin R. Oswald
Wanli Ouyang
Andrew Owens
Mustafa Özuysal
Jinshan Pan
Xingang Pan
Rameswar Panda
Sharath Pankanti
Julien Pansiot
Nicolas Papadakis
George Papandreou
N. Papanikolopoulos

Hyun Soo Park
In Kyu Park
Jaesik Park
Omkar Parkhi
Alvaro Parra Bustos
C. Alejandro Parraga
Vishal Patel
Deepak Pathak
Ioannis Patras
Viorica Patraucean
Genevieve Patterson
Kim Pedersen
Robert Peharz
Selen Pehlivan
Xi Peng
Bojan Pepik
Talita Perciano
Federico Pernici
Adrian Peter
Stavros Petridis
Vladimir Petrovic
Henning Petzka
Tomas Pfister
Trung Pham
Justus Piater
Massimo Piccardi
Sudeep Pillai
Pedro Pinheiro
Lerrel Pinto
Bernardo Pires
Aleksis Pirinen
Fiora Pirri
Leonid Pischulin
Tobias Ploetz
Bryan Plummer
Yair Poleg
Jean Ponce
Gerard Pons-Moll
Jordi Pont-Tuset
Alin Popa
Fatih Porikli
Horst Possegger
Viraj Prabhu
Andrea Prati
Maria Priisalu
Véronique Prinet

Victor Prisacariu
Jan Prokaj
Nicolas Pugeault
Luis Puig
Ali Punjani
Senthil Purushwalkam
Guido Pusiol
Guo-Jun Qi
Xiaojuan Qi
Hongwei Qin
Shi Qiu
Faisal Qureshi
Matthias Rüther
Petia Radeva
Umer Rafi
Rahul Raguram
Swaminathan Rahul
Varun Ramakrishna
Kandan Ramakrishnan
Ravi Ramamoorthi
Vignesh Ramanathan
Vasili Ramanishka
R. Ramasamy Selvaraju
Rene Ranftl
Carolina Raposo
Nikhil Rasiwasia
Nalini Ratha
Sai Ravela
Avinash Ravichandran
Ramin Raziperchikolaei
Sylvestre-Alvise Rebuffi
Adria Recasens
Joe Redmon
Timo Rehfeld
Michal Reinstein
Konstantinos Rematas
Haibing Ren
Shaoqing Ren
Wenqi Ren
Zhile Ren
Hamid Rezatofighi
Nicholas Rhinehart
Helge Rhodin
Elisa Ricci
Eitan Richardson
Stephan Richter

Gernot Riegler
Hayko Riemenschneider
Tammy Riklin Raviv
Ergys Ristani
Tobias Ritschel
Mariano Rivera
Samuel Rivera
Antonio Robles-Kelly
Ignacio Rocco
Jason Rock
Emanuele Rodola
Mikel Rodriguez
Gregory Rogez
Marcus Rohrbach
Gemma Roig
Javier Romero
Olaf Ronneberger
Amir Rosenfeld
Bodo Rosenhahn
Guy Rosman
Arun Ross
Samuel Rota Bulò
Peter Roth
Constantin Rothkopf
Sebastien Roy
Amit Roy-Chowdhury
Ognjen Rudovic
Adria Ruiz
Javier Ruiz-del-Solar
Christian Rupprecht
Olga Russakovsky
Chris Russell
Alexandre Sablayrolles
Fereshteh Sadeghi
Ryusuke Sagawa
Hideo Saito
Elham Sakhaee
Albert Ali Salah
Conrad Sanderson
Koppal Sanjeev
Aswin Sankaranarayanan
Elham Saraee
Jason Saragih
Sudeep Sarkar
Imari Sato
Shin'ichi Satoh

Torsten Sattler
Bogdan Savchynskyy
Johannes Schönberger
Hanno Scharr
Walter Scheirer
Bernt Schiele
Frank Schmidt
Tanner Schmidt
Dirk Schnieders
Samuel Schulter
William Schwartz
Alexander Schwing
Ozan Sener
Soumyadip Sengupta
Laura Sevilla-Lara
Mubarak Shah
Shishir Shah
Fahad Shahbaz Khan
Amir Shahroudy
Jing Shao
Xiaowei Shao
Roman Shapovalov
Nataliya Shapovalova
Ali Sharif Razavian
Gaurav Sharma
Mohit Sharma
Pramod Sharma
Viktoriia Sharmanska
Eli Shechtman
Mark Sheinin
Evan Shelhamer
Chunhua Shen
Li Shen
Wei Shen
Xiaohui Shen
Xiaoyong Shen
Ziyi Shen
Lu Sheng
Baoguang Shi
Boxin Shi
Kevin Shih
Hyunjung Shim
Ilan Shimshoni
Young Min Shin
Koichi Shinoda
Matthew Shreve

Tianmin Shu
Zhixin Shu
Kaleem Siddiqi
Gunnar Sigurdsson
Nathan Silberman
Tomas Simon
Abhishek Singh
Gautam Singh
Maneesh Singh
Praveer Singh
Richa Singh
Saurabh Singh
Sudipta Sinha
Vladimir Smutny
Noah Snavely
Cees Snoek
Kihyuk Sohn
Eric Sommerlade
Sanghyun Son
Bi Song
Shiyu Song
Shuran Song
Xuan Song
Yale Song
Yang Song
Yibing Song
Lorenzo Sorgi
Humberto Sossa
Pratul Srinivasan
Michael Stark
Bjorn Stenger
Rainer Stiefelhagen
Joerg Stueckler
Jan Stuehmer
Hang Su
Hao Su
Shuochen Su
R. Subramanian
Yusuke Sugano
Akihiro Sugimoto
Baochen Sun
Chen Sun
Jian Sun
Jin Sun
Lin Sun
Min Sun

Qing Sun
Zhaohui Sun
David Suter
Eran Swears
Raza Syed Hussain
T. Syeda-Mahmood
Christian Szegedy
Duy-Nguyen Ta
Tolga Taşdizen
Hemant Tagare
Yuichi Taguchi
Ying Tai
Yu-Wing Tai
Jun Takamatsu
Hugues Talbot
Toru Tamak
Robert Tamburo
Chaowei Tan
Meng Tang
Peng Tang
Siyu Tang
Wei Tang
Junli Tao
Ran Tao
Xin Tao
Makarand Tapaswi
Jean-Philippe Tarel
Maxim Tatarchenko
Bugra Tekin
Demetri Terzopoulos
Christian Theobalt
Diego Thomas
Rajat Thomas
Qi Tian
Xinmei Tian
YingLi Tian
Yonghong Tian
Yonglong Tian
Joseph Tighe
Radu Timofte
Massimo Tistarelli
Sinisa Todorovic
Pavel Tokmakov
Giorgos Tolias
Federico Tombari
Tatiana Tommasi

Chetan Tonde
Xin Tong
Akihiko Torii
Andrea Torsello
Florian Trammer
Du Tran
Quoc-Huy Tran
Rudolph Triebel
Alejandro Troccoli
Leonardo Trujillo
Tomasz Trzcinski
Sam Tsai
Yi-Hsuan Tsai
Hung-Yu Tseng
Vagia Tsiminaki
Aggeliki Tsoli
Wei-Chih Tu
Shubham Tulsiani
Fred Tung
Tony Tung
Matt Turek
Oncel Tuzel
Georgios Tzimiropoulos
Ilkay Ulusoy
Osman Ulusoy
Dmitry Ulyanov
Paul Upchurch
Ben Usman
Evgeniya Ustinova
Himanshu Vajaria
Alexander Vakhitov
Jack Valmadre
Ernest Valveny
Jan van Gemert
Grant Van Horn
Jagannadan Varadarajan
Gul Varol
Sebastiano Vascon
Francisco Vasconcelos
Mayank Vatsa
Javier Vazquez-Corral
Ramakrishna Vedantam
Ashok Veeraraghavan
Andreas Veit
Raviteja Vemulapalli
Jonathan Ventura

Matthias Vestner
Minh Vo
Christoph Vogel
Michele Volpi
Carl Vondrick
Sven Wachsmuth
Toshikazu Wada
Michael Waechter
Catherine Wah
Jacob Walker
Jun Wan
Boyu Wang
Chen Wang
Chunyu Wang
De Wang
Fang Wang
Hongxing Wang
Hua Wang
Jiang Wang
Jingdong Wang
Jinglu Wang
Jue Wang
Le Wang
Lei Wang
Lezi Wang
Liang Wang
Lichao Wang
Lijun Wang
Limin Wang
Liwei Wang
Naiyan Wang
Oliver Wang
Qi Wang
Ruiping Wang
Shenlong Wang
Shu Wang
Song Wang
Tao Wang
Xiaofang Wang
Xiaolong Wang
Xinchao Wang
Xinggang Wang
Xintao Wang
Yang Wang
Yu-Chiang Frank Wang
Yu-Xiong Wang

Zhaowen Wang
Zhe Wang
Anne Wannenwetsch
Simon Warfield
Scott Wehrwein
Donglai Wei
Ping Wei
Shih-En Wei
Xiu-Shen Wei
Yichen Wei
Xie Weidi
Philippe Weinzaepfel
Longyin Wen
Eric Wengrowski
Tomas Werner
Michael Wilber
Rick Wildes
Olivia Wiles
Kyle Wilson
David Wipf
Kwan-Yee Wong
Daniel Worrall
John Wright
Baoyuan Wu
Chao-Yuan Wu
Jiajun Wu
Jianxin Wu
Tianfu Wu
Xiaodong Wu
Xiaohe Wu
Xinxiao Wu
Yang Wu
Yi Wu
Ying Wu
Yuxin Wu
Zheng Wu
Stefanie Wuhrer
Yin Xia
Tao Xiang
Yu Xiang
Lei Xiao
Tong Xiao
Yang Xiao
Cihang Xie
Dan Xie
Jianwen Xie

Jin Xie
Lingxi Xie
Pengtao Xie
Saining Xie
Wenxuan Xie
Yuchen Xie
Bo Xin
Junliang Xing
Peng Xingchao
Bo Xiong
Fei Xiong
Xuehan Xiong
Yuanjun Xiong
Chenliang Xu
Danfei Xu
Huijuan Xu
Jia Xu
Weipeng Xu
Xiangyu Xu
Yan Xu
Yuanlu Xu
Jia Xue
Tianfan Xue
Erdem Yörük
Abhay Yadav
Deshraj Yadav
Payman Yadollahpour
Yasushi Yagi
Toshihiko Yamasaki
Fei Yan
Hang Yan
Junchi Yan
Junjie Yan
Sijie Yan
Keiji Yanai
Bin Yang
Chih-Yuan Yang
Dong Yang
Herb Yang
Jianchao Yang
Jianwei Yang
Jiaolong Yang
Jie Yang
Jimei Yang
Jufeng Yang
Linjie Yang

Michael Ying Yang
Ming Yang
Ruiduo Yang
Ruigang Yang
Shuo Yang
Wei Yang
Xiaodong Yang
Yanchao Yang
Yi Yang
Angela Yao
Bangpeng Yao
Cong Yao
Jian Yao
Ting Yao
Julian Yarkony
Mark Yatskar
Jinwei Ye
Mao Ye
Mei-Chen Yeh
Raymond Yeh
Serena Yeung
Kwang Moo Yi
Shuai Yi
Alper Yılmaz
Lijun Yin
Xi Yin
Zhaozheng Yin
Xianghua Ying
Ryo Yonetani
Donghyun Yoo
Ju Hong Yoon
Kuk-Jin Yoon
Chong You
Shaodi You
Aron Yu
Fisher Yu
Gang Yu
Jingyi Yu
Ke Yu
Licheng Yu
Pei Yu
Qian Yu
Rong Yu
Shoou-I Yu
Stella Yu
Xiang Yu

Yang Yu
Zhiding Yu
Ganzhao Yuan
Jing Yuan
Junsong Yuan
Lu Yuan
Stefanos Zafeiriou
Sergey Zagoruyko
Amir Zamir
K. Zampogiannis
Andrei Zanfir
Mihai Zanfir
Pablo Zegers
Eyasu Zemene
Andy Zeng
Xingyu Zeng
Yun Zeng
De-Chuan Zhan
Cheng Zhang
Dong Zhang
Guofeng Zhang
Han Zhang
Hang Zhang
Hanwang Zhang
Jian Zhang
Jianguo Zhang
Jianming Zhang
Jiawei Zhang
Junping Zhang
Lei Zhang
Linguang Zhang
Ning Zhang
Qing Zhang

Quanshi Zhang
Richard Zhang
Runze Zhang
Shanshan Zhang
Shiliang Zhang
Shu Zhang
Ting Zhang
Xiangyu Zhang
Xiaofan Zhang
Xu Zhang
Yimin Zhang
Yinda Zhang
Yongqiang Zhang
Yuting Zhang
Zhanpeng Zhang
Ziyu Zhang
Bin Zhao
Chen Zhao
Hang Zhao
Hengshuang Zhao
Qijun Zhao
Rui Zhao
Yue Zhao
Enliang Zheng
Liang Zheng
Stephan Zheng
Wei-Shi Zheng
Wenming Zheng
Yin Zheng
Yinqiang Zheng
Yuanjie Zheng
Guangyu Zhong
Bolei Zhou

Guang-Tong Zhou
Huiyu Zhou
Jiahuan Zhou
S. Kevin Zhou
Tinghui Zhou
Wengang Zhou
Xiaowei Zhou
Xingyi Zhou
Yin Zhou
Zihan Zhou
Fan Zhu
Guangming Zhu
Ji Zhu
Jiejie Zhu
Jun-Yan Zhu
Shizhan Zhu
Siyu Zhu
Xiangxin Zhu
Xiatian Zhu
Yan Zhu
Yingying Zhu
Yixin Zhu
Yuke Zhu
Zhenyao Zhu
Liansheng Zhuang
Zeeshan Zia
Karel Zimmermann
Daniel Zoran
Danping Zou
Qi Zou
Silvia Zuffi
Wangmeng Zuo
Xinxin Zuo

Contents – Part XIII

Learning for Vision

Group Normalization

Yuxin Wu and Kaiming He[✉]

Facebook AI Research (FAIR), Menlo Park, USA
kaiminghe@fb.com

Abstract. Batch Normalization (BN) is a milestone technique in the development of deep learning, enabling various networks to train. However, normalizing along the batch dimension introduces problems—BN's error increases rapidly when the batch size becomes smaller, caused by inaccurate batch statistics estimation. This limits BN's usage for training larger models and transferring features to computer vision tasks including detection, segmentation, and video, which require small batches constrained by memory consumption. In this paper, we present Group Normalization (GN) as a simple alternative to BN. GN divides the channels into groups and computes within each group the mean and variance for normalization. GN's computation is independent of batch sizes, and its accuracy is stable in a wide range of batch sizes. On ResNet-50 trained in ImageNet, GN has 10.6% lower error than its BN counterpart when using a batch size of 2; when using typical batch sizes, GN is comparably good with BN and outperforms other normalization variants. Moreover, GN can be naturally transferred from pre-training to fine-tuning. GN can outperform its BN-based counterparts for object detection and segmentation in COCO, and for video classification in Kinetics, showing that GN can effectively replace the powerful BN in a variety of tasks. GN can be easily implemented by a few lines of code.

1 Introduction

Batch Normalization (Batch Norm or BN) [1] has been established as a very effective component in deep learning, largely helping push the frontier in computer vision [2,3] and beyond [4]. BN normalizes the features by the mean and variance computed within a (mini-)batch. This has been shown by many practices to ease optimization and enable very deep networks to converge. The stochastic uncertainty of the batch statistics also acts as a regularizer that can benefit generalization. BN has been a foundation of many state-of-the-art algorithms.

Despite its great success, BN exhibits drawbacks that are also caused by its distinct behavior of normalizing along the batch dimension. In particular, it is required for BN to work with a *sufficiently large batch size* (*e.g.*, 32 per worker[1] [1–3]). A small batch leads to inaccurate estimation of the batch statistics, and *reducing BN's batch size increases the model error dramatically* (Fig. 1).

---

[1] In the context of this paper, we use "batch size" to refer to the number of samples *per worker* (*e.g.*, GPU). BN's statistics are computed for each worker, but *not* broadcast across workers, as is standard in many libraries.

© Springer Nature Switzerland AG 2018
V. Ferrari et al. (Eds.): ECCV 2018, LNCS 11217, pp. 3–19, 2018.
https://doi.org/10.1007/978-3-030-01261-8_1

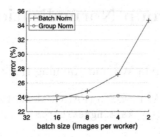

Fig. 1. ImageNet classification error *vs.* batch sizes. The model is ResNet-50 trained in the ImageNet training set using 8 workers (GPUs) and evaluated in the validation set. BN's error increases rapidly when reducing the batch size. GN's computation is independent of batch sizes, and its error rate is stable despite the batch size changes. GN has substantially lower error (by 10%) than BN with a batch size of 2.

As a result, many recent models [2,3,5–7] are trained with non-trivial batch sizes that are memory-consuming. The heavy reliance on BN's effectiveness to train models in turn prohibits people from exploring higher-capacity models that would be limited by memory.

The restriction on batch sizes is more demanding in computer vision tasks including detection [8–10], segmentation [10,11], video recognition [12,13], and other high-level systems built on them. E.g., the Fast/er and Mask R-CNN frameworks [8–10] use a batch size of 1 or 2 images because of higher resolution, where BN is "frozen" by transforming to a linear layer [3]; in video classification with 3D convolutions [12,13], the presence of spatial-temporal features introduces a trade-off between the temporal length and batch size. The usage of BN often requires these systems to compromise between the model design and batch sizes.

This paper presents Group Normalization (GN) as a simple alternative to BN. We notice that many classical features like SIFT [14] and HOG [15] are *group-wise* features and involve *group-wise normalization*. For example, a HOG vector is the outcome of several spatial cells where each cell is represented by a normalized orientation histogram. Analogously, we propose GN as a layer that divides channels into groups and normalizes the features within each group (Fig. 2). GN does not exploit the batch dimension, and its computation is independent of batch sizes.

GN behaves very stably over a wide range of batch sizes (Fig. 1). With a batch size of 2 samples, GN has 10.6% lower error than its BN counterpart for ResNet-50 [3] in ImageNet [16]. With a regular batch size, GN is comparably good as BN (with a gap of ∼0.5%) and outperforms other normalization variants [17–19]. Moreover, although the batch size may change, GN can naturally transfer from pre-training to fine-tuning. GN shows improved results *vs.* its BN counterpart on Mask R-CNN for COCO object detection and segmentation [20], and on 3D convolutional networks for Kinetics video classification [21]. The effectiveness of GN in ImageNet, COCO, and Kinetics demonstrates that GN is a competitive alternative to BN that has been dominant in these tasks.

There have been existing methods, such as Layer Normalization (LN) [17] and Instance Normalization (IN) [18] (Fig. 2), that also avoid normalizing along the batch dimension. These methods are effective for training sequential models (RNN/LSTM [22,23]) or generative models (GANs [24,25]). But as we will show by experiments, both LN and IN have limited success in visual recognition, for which GN presents better results. Conversely, GN could be used in place of LN and IN and thus is applicable for sequential or generative models. This is beyond the focus of this paper, but it is suggestive for future research.

2   Related Work

Normalization. Normalization layers in deep networks had been widely used before the development of BN. Local Response Normalization (LRN) [26–28] was a component in AlexNet [28] and following models [29–31]. LRN computes the statistics in a small neighborhood for each pixel.

Batch Normalization [1] performs more global normalization along the batch dimension (and as importantly, it suggests to do this for all layers). But the concept of "batch" is not always present, or it may change from time to time. For example, batch-wise normalization is not legitimate at inference time, so the mean and variance are pre-computed from the training set [1], often by running average; consequently, there is no normalization performed when testing. The pre-computed statistics may also change when the target data distribution changes [32]. These issues lead to inconsistency at training, transferring, and testing time. In addition, as aforementioned, reducing the batch size can have dramatic impact on the estimated batch statistics.

Several normalization methods [17–19,33,34] have been proposed to avoid exploiting the batch dimension. Layer Normalization (LN) [17] operates along the channel dimension, and Instance Normalization (IN) [18] performs BN-like computation but only for each sample (Fig. 2). Instead of operating on features, Weight Normalization (WN) [19] proposes to normalize the filter weights. These methods do not suffer from the issues caused by the batch dimension, but they have not been able to approach BN's accuracy in many visual recognition tasks. We compare with these methods in context of the remaining sections.

Addressing Small Batches. Ioffe [35] proposes Batch Renormalization (BR) that alleviates BN's issue involving small batches. BR introduces two extra parameters that constrain the estimated mean and variance of BN within a certain range, reducing their drift when the batch size is small. BR has better accuracy than BN in the small-batch regime. But BR is also batch-dependent, and when the batch size decreases its accuracy still degrades [35].

There are also attempts to *avoid* using small batches. The object detector in [36] performs synchronized BN whose mean and variance are computed across multiple GPUs. However, this method does not solve the problem of small batches; instead, it migrates the algorithm problem to engineering and hardware

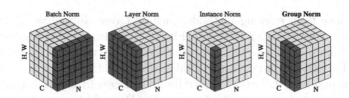

Fig. 2. Normalization methods. Each subplot shows a feature map tensor. The pixels in blue are normalized by the same mean and variance, computed by aggregating the values of these pixels. Group Norm is illustrated using a group number of 2. (Color figure online)

demands, using a number of GPUs proportional to BN's requirements. Moreover, the synchronized BN computation prevents using *asynchronous* solvers (ASGD [37]), a practical solution to large-scale training widely used in industry. These issues can limit the scope of using synchronized BN.

Instead of addressing the batch statistics computation (*e.g.*, [35,36]), our normalization method inherently avoids this computation.

Group-Wise Computation. *Group convolutions* have been presented by AlexNet [28] for distributing a model into two GPUs. The concept of *groups* as a dimension for model design has been more widely studied recently. The work of ResNeXt [7] investigates the trade-off between depth, width, and groups, and it suggests that a larger number of groups can improve accuracy under similar computational cost. MobileNet [38] and Xception [39] exploit *channel-wise* (also called "depth-wise") convolutions, which are group convolutions with a group number equal to the channel number. ShuffleNet [40] proposes a channel shuffle operation that permutes the axes of grouped features. These methods all involve dividing the channel dimension into groups. Despite the relation to these methods, GN does *not* require group convolutions. GN is a generic layer, as we evaluate in standard ResNets [3].

3   Group Normalization

The channels of visual representations are not entirely independent. Classical features of SIFT [14], HOG [15], and GIST [41] are *group-wise* representations by design, where each group of channels is constructed by some kind of histogram. These features are often processed by *group-wise normalization* over each histogram or each orientation. Higher-level features such as VLAD [42] and Fisher Vectors (FV) [43] are also group-wise features where a group can be thought of as the sub-vector computed with respect to a cluster.

Analogously, it is not necessary to think of deep neural network features as unstructured vectors. For example, for $conv_1$ (the first convolutional layer) of a network, it is reasonable to expect a filter and its horizontal flipping to exhibit similar distributions of filter responses on natural images. If $conv_1$ happens to approximately learn this pair of filters, or if the horizontal flipping (or other transformations) is made into the architectures by design [44, 45], then the corresponding channels of these filters can be normalized together.

The higher-level layers are more abstract and their behaviors are not as intuitive. However, in addition to orientations (SIFT [14], HOG [15], or [44, 45]), there are many factors that could lead to grouping, e.g., frequency, shapes, illumination, textures. Their coefficients can be interdependent. In fact, a well-accepted computational model in neuroscience is to normalize across the cell responses [46–49], "with various receptive-field centers (covering the visual field) and with various spatiotemporal frequency tunings" (p. 183, [46]); this can happen not only in the primary visual cortex, but also "throughout the visual system" [49]. Motivated by these works, we propose new generic group-wise normalization for deep neural networks.

Formulation. We first describe a general formulation of feature normalization, and then present GN in this formulation. A family of feature normalization methods, including BN, LN, IN, and GN, perform the following computation:

$$\hat{x}_i = \frac{1}{\sigma_i}(x_i - \mu_i). \tag{1}$$

Here x is the feature computed by a layer, and i is an index. In the case of 2D images, $i = (i_N, i_C, i_H, i_W)$ is a 4D vector indexing the features in (N, C, H, W) order, where N is the batch axis, C is the channel axis, and H and W are the spatial height and width axes.

μ and σ in (1) are the mean and standard deviation (std) computed by:

$$\mu_i = \frac{1}{m}\sum_{k \in \mathcal{S}_i} x_k, \quad \sigma_i = \sqrt{\frac{1}{m}\sum_{k \in \mathcal{S}_i}(x_k - \mu_i)^2 + \epsilon}, \tag{2}$$

with ϵ as a small constant. $\mathcal{S}_i$ is the set of pixels in which the mean and std are computed, and m is the size of this set. Many types of feature normalization methods mainly differ in how the set $\mathcal{S}_i$ is defined (Fig. 2), discussed as follows.

In **Batch Norm** [1], the set $\mathcal{S}_i$ is defined as:

$$\mathcal{S}_i = \{k \mid k_C = i_C\}, \tag{3}$$

where i_C (and k_C) denotes the sub-index of i (and k) along the C axis. This means that the pixels sharing the same channel index are normalized together, i.e., for each channel, BN computes μ and σ along the (N, H, W) axes. In **Layer Norm** [17], the set is:

$$\mathcal{S}_i = \{k \mid k_N = i_N\}, \tag{4}$$

meaning that LN computes μ and σ along the (C, H, W) axes for each sample. In **Instance Norm** [18], the set is:

$$\mathcal{S}_i = \{k \mid k_N = i_N, k_C = i_C\}. \tag{5}$$

```
def GroupNorm(x, gamma, beta, G, eps=1e-5):
    # x: input features with shape [N,C,H,W]
    # gamma, beta: learnable scale and offset, with shape [1,C,1,1]
    # G: number of groups for GN

    N, C, H, W = x.shape
    x = tf.reshape(x, [N, G, C // G, H, W])

    mean, var = tf.nn.moments(x, [2, 3, 4], keep_dims=True)
    x = (x - mean) / tf.sqrt(var + eps)

    x = tf.reshape(x, [N, C, H, W])

    return x * gamma + beta
```

Fig. 3. Python code of Group Norm based on TensorFlow.

meaning that IN computes μ and σ along the (H, W) axes for each sample and each channel. The relations among BN, LN, and IN are in Fig. 2.

As in [1], all methods of BN, LN, and IN learn a per-channel linear transform to compensate for the possible lost of representational ability:

$$y_i = \gamma \hat{x}_i + \beta, \qquad (6)$$

where γ and β are trainable scale and shift (indexed by i_C in all case, which we omit for simplifying notations).

Group Norm. A Group Norm layer computes μ and σ in $\mathcal{S}_i$ defined as:

$$\mathcal{S}_i = \{k \mid k_N = i_N, \lfloor \frac{k_C}{C/G} \rfloor = \lfloor \frac{i_C}{C/G} \rfloor\}. \qquad (7)$$

Here G is the number of groups, which is a pre-defined hyper-parameter ($G = 32$ by default). C/G is the number of channels per group. $\lfloor \cdot \rfloor$ is the floor operation, and "$\lfloor \frac{k_C}{C/G} \rfloor = \lfloor \frac{i_C}{C/G} \rfloor$" means that the indexes i and k are in the same group of channels, assuming each group of channels are stored in a sequential order along the C axis. GN computes μ and σ along the (H, W) axes and along a group of $\frac{C}{G}$ channels. The computation of GN is illustrated in Fig. 2 (rightmost), which is a simple case of 2 groups ($G = 2$) each having 3 channels.

Given $\mathcal{S}_i$ in Eq. (7), a GN layer is defined by Eqs. (1), (2) and (6). Specifically, the pixels in the same group are normalized together by the same μ and σ. GN also learns the per-channel γ and β.

Relation to Prior Work. LN, IN, and GN all perform independent computations along the batch axis. The two extreme cases of GN are equivalent to LN and IN (Fig. 2).

GN becomes LN [17] if we set the group number as $G = 1$. LN assumes *all* channels in a layer make "similar contributions" [17]. Unlike the case of fully-connected layers studied in [17], this assumption can be less valid with the presence of convolutions, as discussed in [17]. GN is less restricted than LN,

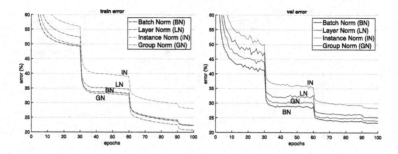

Fig. 4. Comparison of error curves with a batch size of **32 images**/GPU. We show the ImageNet training error (left) and validation error (right) *vs.* numbers of training epochs. The model is ResNet-50.

Table 1. Comparison of error rates with a batch size of **32 images**/GPU, on ResNet-50 in the ImageNet validation set. The error curves are in Fig. 4.

	BN	LN	IN	GN
val error (%)	**23.6**	25.3	28.4	24.1
Δ (*vs.* BN)	-	*1.7*	*4.8*	***0.5***

because each group of channels (instead of all of them) are assumed to subject to the shared mean and variance; the model still has flexibility of learning a different distribution for each group. This leads to improved representational power of GN over LN, as shown by the lower training and validation error in experiments (Fig. 4).

GN becomes IN [18] if we set the group number as $G = C$ (*i.e.*, one channel per group). But IN can only rely on the spatial dimension for computing the mean and variance and it misses the opportunity of exploiting the channel dependence.

Implementation. GN can be easily implemented by a few lines of code in PyTorch [50] and TensorFlow [51] where automatic differentiation is supported. Figure 3 shows the code based on TensorFlow. In fact, we only need to specify how the mean and variance ("moments") are computed, along the appropriate axes as defined by the normalization method.

4 Experiments

4.1 Image Classification in ImageNet

Implementation Details. As standard practice [3,52], we use 8 GPUs to train all models, and the batch mean and variance of BN are computed *within* each GPU. We use the method of [53] to initialize all convolutions for all models.

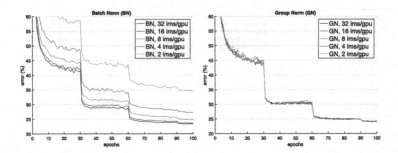

Fig. 5. Sensitivity to batch sizes. We show ResNet-50's validation error of BN (left) and LN (right) using a batch size of 32, 16, 8, 4, and 2 images/GPU.

Table 2. Sensitivity to batch sizes. We show ResNet-50's validation error (%) in ImageNet. The last row shows the differences between BN and GN. The error curves are in Fig. 5. This table is visualized in Fig. 1.

Batch size	32	16	8	4	2
BN	**23.6**	**23.7**	24.8	27.3	34.7
GN	24.1	24.2	**24.0**	**24.2**	**24.1**
△	*0.5*	*0.5*	*−0.8*	*−3.1*	*−10.6*

We use 1 to initialize all γ parameters, except for each residual block's last normalization layer where we initialize γ by 0 following [54] (such that the initial state of a residual block is identity). We use a weight decay of 0.0001 for all weight layers, including γ and β (following [52] but unlike [3,54]). We train 100 epochs for all models, and decrease the learning rate by 10× at 30, 60, and 90 epochs. During training, we adopt the data augmentation of [31] as implemented by [52]. We evaluate the top-1 classification error on the center crops of 224 × 224 pixels in the validation set. To reduce random variations, we report the median error rate of the final 5 epochs [54]. Other implementation details follow [52].

Our baseline is the ResNet trained with BN [3]. To compare with LN, IN, and GN, we replace BN with the specific variant. We use the same hyper-parameters for all models. We set $G = 32$ for GN by default.

Comparison of Feature Normalization Methods. We first experiment with a regular batch size of **32 images** (per GPU) [1,3]. BN works successfully in this regime, so this is a strong baseline to compare with. Figure 4 shows the error curves, and Table 1 shows the final results. *All* of these normalization methods are able to converge. LN has a small degradation of 1.7% comparing with BN. This is an encouraging result, as it suggests that normalizing along *all* channels (as done by LN) of a *convolutional* network is reasonably good. IN also makes the model converge, but is 4.8% worse than BN.

Table 3. Group division. We show ResNet-50's validation error (%) in ImageNet, trained with 32 images/GPU. (Left): a given number of groups. (Right): a given number of channels per group. The last rows show the differences with the best number.

# groups (G)							channels per group						
64	32	16	8	4	2	1 (=LN)	64	32	16	8	4	2	1 (=IN)
24.6	**24.1**	24.6	24.4	24.6	24.7	25.3	24.4	24.5	**24.2**	24.3	24.8	25.6	28.4
0.5	*-*	*0.5*	*0.3*	*0.5*	*0.6*	*1.2*	*0.2*	*0.3*	*-*	*0.1*	*0.6*	*1.4*	*4.2*

In this regime where BN works well, GN is able to approach BN's accuracy, with a decent degradation of 0.5% in the validation set. Actually, Fig. 4 (left) shows that GN has *lower training error* than BN, indicating that GN is effective for easing *optimization*. The slightly higher validation error of GN implies that GN loses some regularization ability of BN. This is understandable, because BN's mean and variance computation introduces uncertainty caused by the stochastic batch sampling, which helps regularization [1]. This uncertainty is missing in GN (and LN/IN). But it is possible that GN combined with a suitable regularizer will improve results. This can be a future research topic.

Small Batch Sizes. Although BN benefits from the stochasticity under some situations, its error increases when the batch size becomes smaller and the uncertainty gets bigger. We show this in Figs. 1, 5 and Table 2.

We evaluate batch sizes of 32, 16, 8, 4, 2 images per GPU. In all cases, the BN mean and variance are computed within each GPU and not synchronized. All models are trained in 8 GPUs. In this set of experiments, we adopt the linear learning rate scaling rule [54–56] to adapt to batch size changes—we use a learning rate of 0.1 [3] for the batch size of 32, and 0.1N/32 for a batch size of N. This linear scaling rule works well for BN if the total batch size changes (by changing the number of GPUs) but the per-GPU batch size does not change [54]. We keep the same number of training epochs for all cases (Fig. 5, x-axis). All other hyper-parameters are unchanged.

Figure 5 (left) shows that BN's error becomes considerably higher with small batch sizes. GN's behavior is more stable and insensitive to the batch size. Actually, Fig. 5 (right) shows that GN has very similar curves (subject to random variations) across a wide range of batch sizes from 32 to 2. For a batch size of 2, GN has **10.6%** lower error rate than its BN counterpart (24.1% *vs.* 34.7%).

These results indicate that the batch mean and variance estimation can be overly stochastic and inaccurate, especially when they are computed over 4 or 2 images. However, this stochasticity disappears if the statistics are computed from 1 image, in which case BN becomes similar to IN at training time. We see that IN has a better result (28.4%) than BN with a batch size of 2 (34.7%).

The robust results of GN in Table 2 demonstrate GN's strength. It allows to remove the batch size constraint imposed by BN, which can give considerably more memory (*e.g.*, 16× or more). This will make it possible to train

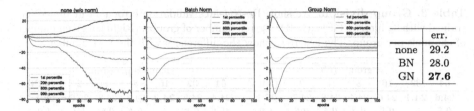

Fig. 6. Evolution of feature distributions of conv$_{5\_3}$'s output features (before normalization and ReLU) from VGG-16, shown as the $\{1, 20, 80, 99\}$ percentile of responses, with no normalization, BN, and GN. The table on the right shows the classification error (%) in ImageNet validation. Models are trained with 32 images/GPU.

higher-capacity models that would be otherwise bottlenecked by memory limitation. We hope this will create new opportunities in architecture design.

Comparison with Batch Renorm (BR). BR [35] introduces two extra parameters (r and d in [35]) that constrain the estimated mean and variance of BN. Their values are controlled by r_{max} and d_{max}. To apply BR to ResNet-50, we have carefully chosen these hyper-parameters, and found that $r_{max} = 1.5$ and $d_{max} = 0.5$ work best for ResNet-50. With a batch size of 4, ResNet-50 trained with BR has an error rate of 26.3%. This is better than BN's 27.3%, but still 2.1% higher than GN's 24.2%.

Group Division. Thus far all presented GN models are trained with a group number of $G = 32$. Next we evaluate different ways of dividing into groups. With a given fixed group number, GN performs reasonably well for all values of G we studied (Table 3, right panel). In the extreme case of $G = 1$, GN is equivalent to LN, and its error rate is higher than all cases of $G > 1$ studied.

We also evaluate fixing the number of channels per group (Table 3, left panel). Note that because the layers can have different channel numbers, the group number G can change across layers in this setting. In the extreme case of 1 channel per group, GN is equivalent to IN. Even if using as few as 2 channels per group, GN has substantially lower error than IN (25.6% *vs.* 28.4%). This result shows the effect of grouping channels when performing normalization.

Deeper Models. We have also compared GN with BN on ResNet-101 [3]. With a batch size of 32, our BN baseline of ResNet-101 has 22.0% validation error, and the GN counterpart has 22.4%, slightly worse by 0.4%. With a batch size of 2, GN ResNet-101's error is 23.0%. This is still a decently stable result considering the very small batch size, and it is 8.9% better than the BN counterpart's 31.9%.

Results and Analysis of VGG Models. To study GN/BN compared to *no normalization*, we consider VGG-16 [57] that can be healthily trained without

Table 4. Detection and segmentation results in COCO, using Mask R-CNN with the **ResNet-50 C4** backbone. BN* means BN is frozen.

Backbone	AP^{bbox}	AP^{bbox}_{50}	AP^{bbox}_{75}	AP^{mask}	AP^{mask}_{50}	AP^{mask}_{75}
C4, BN*	37.7	57.9	40.9	32.8	54.3	34.7
C4, GN	**38.8**	**59.2**	**42.2**	**33.6**	**55.9**	**35.4**

normalization layers. We apply BN or GN right after each convolutional layer. Figure 6 shows the evolution of the feature distributions of conv$_{5\_3}$ (the last convolutional layer). GN and BN behave *qualitatively similar*, while being substantially different with the variant that uses no normalization; this phenomenon is also observed for all other convolutional layers. This comparison suggests that performing normalization is essential for controlling the distribution of features.

For VGG-16, GN is *better* than BN by 0.4% (Fig. 6, right). This possibly implies that VGG-16 benefits less from BN's regularization effect, and GN (that leads to lower training error) is superior to BN in this case.

4.2 Object Detection and Segmentation in COCO

Next we evaluate fine-tuning the models for transferring to object detection and segmentation. These computer vision tasks in general benefit from higher-resolution input, so the batch size tends to be small in common practice (1 or 2 images/GPU [8–10,58]). As a result, BN is turned into a *linear* layer $y = \frac{\gamma}{\sigma}(x - \mu) + \beta$ where μ and σ are pre-computed from the pre-trained model and frozen [3]. We denote this as BN*, which in fact performs no normalization during fine-tuning. We have also tried a variant that fine-tunes BN (normalization is performed and not frozen) and found it works poorly (reducing $\sim$6 AP with a batch size of 2), so we ignore this variant.

We experiment on the Mask R-CNN baselines [10], implemented in the publicly available codebase of *Detectron* [59]. We use the end-to-end variant with the same hyper-parameters as in [59]. We replace BN* with GN during fine-tuning, using the corresponding models pre-trained from ImageNet.[2] During fine-tuning, we use a weight decay of 0 for the γ and β parameters, which is important for good detection results when γ and β are being tuned. We fine-tune with a batch size of 1 image/GPU and 8 GPUs.

The models are trained in the COCO `train2017` set and evaluated in the COCO `val2017` set (a.k.a `minival`). We report the standard COCO metrics of Average Precision (AP), AP$_{50}$, and AP$_{75}$, for bounding box detection (AP^{bbox}) and instance segmentation (AP^{mask}).

---

[2] Detectron [59] uses pre-trained models provided by the authors of [3]. For fair comparisons, we instead use the models pre-trained in this paper. The object detection and segmentation accuracy is statistically similar between these pre-trained models.

Table 5. Detection and segmentation results in COCO, using Mask R-CNN with **ResNet-50 FPN** and a 4conv1fc bounding box head. BN* means BN is frozen.

Backbone	box head w/	AP^{bbox}	AP^{bbox}_{50}	AP^{bbox}_{75}	AP^{mask}	AP^{mask}_{50}	AP^{mask}_{75}
FPN, BN*	-	38.6	59.5	41.9	34.2	56.2	36.1
FPN, BN*	GN	39.5	60.0	43.2	34.4	56.4	**36.3**
FPN, GN	GN	**40.0**	**61.0**	**43.3**	**34.8**	**57.3**	**36.3**

Table 6. Detection and segmentation results in COCO using Mask R-CNN and FPN. Here BN* is the default Detectron baseline [59], and GN is applied to the backbone, box head, and mask head. "long" means training with more iterations.

Backbone	AP^{bbox}	AP^{bbox}_{50}	AP^{bbox}_{75}	AP^{mask}	AP^{mask}_{50}	AP^{mask}_{75}
R50 BN*	38.6	59.8	42.1	34.5	56.4	36.3
R50 GN	40.3	61.0	44.0	35.7	57.9	37.7
R50 GN, long	**40.8**	**61.6**	**44.4**	**36.1**	**58.5**	**38.2**
R101 BN*	40.9	61.9	44.8	36.4	58.5	38.7
R101 GN	41.8	62.5	45.4	36.8	59.2	39.0
R101 GN, long	**42.3**	**62.8**	**46.2**	**37.2**	**59.7**	**39.5**

Results of C4 Backbone. Table 4 shows the comparison of GN *vs.* BN* on Mask R-CNN using a conv$_4$ backbone ("C4" [10]). This C4 variant uses ResNet's layers of up to conv$_4$ to extract feature maps, and ResNet's conv$_5$ layers as the Region-of-Interest (RoI) heads for classification and regression. As they are inherited from the pre-trained model, the backbone and head both involve normalization layers.

On this baseline, GN improves over BN* by 1.1 box AP and 0.8 mask AP. We note that the pre-trained GN model is slightly worse than BN in ImageNet (24.1% *vs.* 23.6%), but GN still outperforms BN* for fine-tuning. BN* creates inconsistency between pre-training and fine-tuning (frozen), which may explain the degradation.

Results of FPN Backbone. Next we compare GN and BN* on Mask R-CNN using a Feature Pyramid Network (FPN) backbone [60], the currently state-of-the-art framework in COCO. Unlike the C4 variant, FPN exploits all pre-trained layers to construct a pyramid, and appends randomly initialized layers as the head. In [60], the box head consists of two hidden fully-connected layers (2fc). We find that replacing the 2fc box head with 4conv1fc (similar to [61]) can better leverage GN. The resulting comparisons are in Table 5.

As a baseline, BN* has 38.6 box AP using the 4conv1fc head, on par with its 2fc counterpart using the same pre-trained model (38.5 AP). By adding GN to all convolutional layers of the box head (but still using the BN* backbone), we increase the box AP by 0.9 to 39.5 (2nd row, Table 5). This ablation shows that

Table 7. COCO models trained **from scratch** using Mask R-CNN and FPN.

from scratch	AP^{bbox}	AP$^{bbox}_{50}$	AP$^{bbox}_{75}$	AP^{mask}	AP$^{mask}_{50}$	AP$^{mask}_{75}$
R50 GN	39.5	59.8	43.6	35.2	56.9	37.6
R101 GN	41.0	61.1	44.9	36.4	58.2	38.7

a substantial portion of GN's improvement for detection is from *normalization in the head* (which is also done by the C4 variant). On the contrary, applying BN to the box head (that has 512 RoIs per image) does not provide satisfactory result and is ~9 AP worse—in detection, the batch of RoIs are sampled from the same image and their distribution is not *i.i.d.*, and the *non-i.i.d.* distribution is also an issue that degrades BN's batch statistics estimation [35]. GN does not suffer from this problem.

Next we replace the FPN backbone with the GN-based counterpart, *i.e.*, the GN pre-trained model is used during fine-tuning (3rd row, Table 5). Applying GN to the backbone *alone* contributes a 0.5 AP gain (from 39.5 to 40.0), suggesting that GN helps when transferring features.

Table 6 shows the full results of GN (applied to the backbone, box head, and mask head), compared with the Detectron baseline [59] based on BN*. Using the same hyper-parameters as [59], GN increases over BN* by a healthy margin. Moreover, we found that GN is not fully trained with the default schedule in [59], so we also tried increasing the iterations from 180k to 270k (BN* does not benefit from longer training). Our final ResNet-50 GN model ("long", Table 6) is **2.2** points box AP and **1.6** points mask AP better than its BN* variant.

Training Mask R-CNN from Scratch. GN allows us to easily investigate training object detectors *from scratch* (without any pre-training). We show the results in Table 7, where the GN models are trained for 270k iterations. To our knowledge, our numbers (**41.0** box AP and **36.4** mask AP) are the best *from-scratch* results in COCO reported to date; they can even compete with the ImageNet-pretrained results in Table 6. As a reference, with synchronous BN [36], a concurrent work [62] achieves a from-scratch result of 34.5 box AP using R50 and 36.3 using a specialized backbone.

4.3   Video Classification in Kinetics

Lastly we evaluate video classification in the Kinetics dataset [21]. This task is memory-demanding and imposes constraints on the batch sizes.

We experiment with Inflated 3D (I3D) convolutional networks [13]. We use the ResNet-50 I3D *baseline* as described in [63]. The models are pre-trained from ImageNet. For both BN and GN, we extend the normalization from over (H, W) to over (T, H, W), where T is the temporal axis. We train in the 400-class Kinetics training set and evaluate in the validation set. We report the top-1 and top-5 classification accuracy, using standard 10-clip testing that averages softmax scores from 10 clips regularly sampled.

We study two different temporal lengths: 32-frame and 64-frame input clips. The 32-frame clip is regularly sampled with a frame interval of 2 from the raw video, and the 64-frame clip is sampled continuously. The model is fully convolutional in spacetime, so the 64-frame variant consumes about 2× more memory. We study a batch size of 8 or 4 clips/GPU for the 32-frame variant, and 4 clips/GPU for the 64-frame variant due to memory limitation.

Results of 32-frame Inputs. Table 8 (col. 1, 2) shows the video classification accuracy in Kinetics using 32-frame clips. For the batch size of 8, GN is slightly worse than BN by 0.3% top-1 accuracy and 0.1% top-5. This shows that GN is competitive with BN when BN works well. For the smaller batch size of 4, GN's accuracy is kept similar (72.8 / 90.6 *vs.* 73.0 / 90.6), but is better than BN's 72.1 / 90.0. BN's accuracy is decreased by 1.2% when the batch size decreases from 8 to 4. Figure 7 shows the error curves. BN's error curves (left) have a noticeable gap when the batch size decreases from 8 to 4, while GN's error curves (right) are very similar.

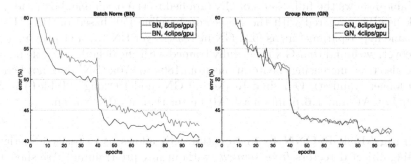

Fig. 7. Error curves in Kinetics with an input length of 32 frames. We show ResNet-50 I3D's validation error of BN (left) and GN (right) using a batch size of 8 and 4 clips/GPU. The monitored validation error is the 1-clip error under the same data augmentation as the training set, while the final validation accuracy in Table 8 is 10-clip testing without data augmentation.

Results of 64-frame Inputs. Table 8 (col. 3) shows the results of using 64-frame clips. In this case, BN has a result of 73.3 / 90.8. These appear to be acceptable numbers (*vs.* 73.3 / 90.7 of 32-frame, batch size 8), but *the trade-off between the temporal length (64 vs. 32) and batch size (4 vs. 8) could have been overlooked.* Comparing col. 3 and col. 2 in Table 8, we find that the temporal length actually has positive impact (+1.2%), but it is veiled by BN's negative effect of the smaller batch size.

GN does not suffer from this trade-off. The 64-frame variant of GN has 74.5 / 91.7 accuracy, showing healthy gains over its BN counterpart and all BN variants. GN helps the model benefit from temporal length, and the longer clip boosts the top-1 accuracy by 1.7% (top-5 1.1%) with the same batch size.

Table 8. Video classification in Kinetics: ResNet-50 I3D's top-1/5 accuracy (%).

Clip length	32	32	64
Batch size	8	4	4
BN	**73.3 / 90.7**	72.1 / 90.0	73.3 / 90.8
GN	73.0 / 90.6	**72.8 / 90.6**	**74.5 / 91.7**

The improvement of GN on detection, segmentation, and video classification demonstrates that GN is a strong alternative to the powerful and currently dominant BN technique in these tasks.

5   Discussion and Future Work

We have presented GN as an effective normalization layer without exploiting the batch dimension. We have evaluated GN's behaviors in a variety of applications. We note, however, that BN has been so influential that many state-of-the-art systems and their hyper-parameters have been designed for it, which may not be optimal for GN-based models. It is possible that re-designing the systems or searching new hyper-parameters for GN will give better results.

References

1. Ioffe, S., Szegedy, C.: Batch normalization: accelerating deep network training by reducing internal covariate shift. In: ICML (2015)
2. Szegedy, C., Vanhoucke, V., Ioffe, S., Shlens, J., Wojna, Z.: Rethinking the inception architecture for computer vision. In: CVPR (2016)
3. He, K., Zhang, X., Ren, S., Sun, J.: Deep residual learning for image recognition. In: CVPR (2016)
4. Silver, D., et al.: Mastering the game of go without human knowledge. Nature 550(7676), 354–359 (2017)
5. Szegedy, C., Ioffe, S., Vanhoucke, V.: Inception-v4, inception-resnet and the impact of residual connections on learning. In: ICLR Workshop (2016)
6. Huang, G., Liu, Z., van der Maaten, L., Weinberger, K.Q.: Densely connected convolutional networks. In: CVPR (2017)
7. Xie, S., Girshick, R., Dollár, P., Tu, Z., He, K.: Aggregated residual transformations for deep neural networks. In: CVPR (2017)
8. Girshick, R.: Fast R-CNN. In: ICCV (2015)
9. Ren, S., He, K., Girshick, R., Sun, J.: Faster R-CNN: towards real-time object detection with region proposal networks. In: NIPS (2015)
10. He, K., Gkioxari, G., Dollár, P., Girshick, R.: Mask R-CNN. In: ICCV (2017)
11. Long, J., Shelhamer, E., Darrell, T.: Fully convolutional networks for semantic segmentation. In: CVPR (2015)
12. Tran, D., Bourdev, L., Fergus, R., Torresani, L., Paluri, M.: Learning spatiotemporal features with 3D convolutional networks. In: ICCV (2015)

13. Carreira, J., Zisserman, A.: Quo vadis, action recognition? A new model and the kinetics dataset. In: CVPR (2017)
14. Lowe, D.G.: Distinctive image features from scale-invariant keypoints. In: IJCV (2004)
15. Dalal, N., Triggs, B.: Histograms of oriented gradients for human detection. In: CVPR (2005)
16. Russakovsky, O., et al.: ImageNet large scale visual recognition challenge. In: IJCV (2015)
17. Ba, J.L., Kiros, J.R., Hinton, G.E.: Layer normalization (2016). arXiv:1607.06450
18. Ulyanov, D., Vedaldi, A., Lempitsky, V.: Instance normalization: the missing ingredient for fast stylization (2016). arXiv:1607.08022
19. Salimans, T., Kingma, D.P.: Weight normalization: a simple reparameterization to accelerate training of deep neural networks. In: NIPS (2016)
20. Lin, T.-Y., et al.: Microsoft COCO: common objects in context. In: Fleet, D., Pajdla, T., Schiele, B., Tuytelaars, T. (eds.) ECCV 2014, Part V. LNCS, vol. 8693, pp. 740–755. Springer, Cham (2014). https://doi.org/10.1007/978-3-319-10602-1_48
21. Kay, W., et al.: The kinetics human action video dataset (2017). arXiv:1705.06950
22. Rumelhart, D.E., Hinton, G.E., Williams, R.J.: Learning representations by back-propagating errors. Nature **323**, 533–536 (1986)
23. Hochreiter, S., Schmidhuber, J.: Long short-term memory. Neural Comput. **9**(8), 1735–1780 (1997)
24. Goodfellow, I., et al.: Generative adversarial nets. In: NIPS (2014)
25. Isola, P., Zhu, J.Y., Zhou, T., Efros, A.A.: Image-to-image translation with conditional adversarial networks. In: CVPR (2017)
26. Lyu, S., Simoncelli, E.P.: Nonlinear image representation using divisive normalization. In: CVPR (2008)
27. Jarrett, K., Kavukcuoglu, K., LeCun, Y., et al.: What is the best multi-stage architecture for object recognition? In: ICCV (2009)
28. Krizhevsky, A., Sutskever, I., Hinton, G.: Imagenet classification with deep convolutional neural networks. In: NIPS (2012)
29. Zeiler, M.D., Fergus, R.: Visualizing and understanding convolutional networks. In: Fleet, D., Pajdla, T., Schiele, B., Tuytelaars, T. (eds.) ECCV 2014, Part I. LNCS, vol. 8689, pp. 818–833. Springer, Cham (2014). https://doi.org/10.1007/978-3-319-10590-1_53
30. Sermanet, P., Eigen, D., Zhang, X., Mathieu, M., Fergus, R., LeCun, Y.: Overfeat: integrated recognition, localization and detection using convolutional networks. In: ICLR (2014)
31. Szegedy, C., et al.: Going deeper with convolutions. In: CVPR (2015)
32. Rebuffi, S.A., Bilen, H., Vedaldi, A.: Learning multiple visual domains with residual adapters. In: NIPS (2017)
33. Arpit, D., Zhou, Y., Kota, B., Govindaraju, V.: Normalization propagation: a parametric technique for removing internal covariate shift in deep networks. In: ICML (2016)
34. Ren, M., Liao, R., Urtasun, R., Sinz, F.H., Zemel, R.S.: Normalizing the normalizers: comparing and extending network normalization schemes. In: ICLR (2017)
35. Ioffe, S.: Batch renormalization: towards reducing minibatch dependence in batch-normalized models. In: NIPS (2017)
36. Peng, C., et al.: MegDet: a large mini-batch object detector. In: CVPR (2018)
37. Dean, J., et al.: Large scale distributed deep networks. In: NIPS (2012)

38. Howard, A.G., et al.: MobileNets: efficient convolutional neural networks for mobile vision applications (2017). arXiv:1704.04861
39. Chollet, F.: Xception: deep learning with depthwise separable convolutions. In: CVPR (2017)
40. Zhang, X., Zhou, X., Lin, M., Sun, J.: ShuffleNet: an extremely efficient convolutional neural network for mobile devices. In: CVPR (2018)
41. Oliva, A., Torralba, A.: Modeling the shape of the scene: a holistic representation of the spatial envelope. In: IJCV (2001)
42. Jegou, H., Douze, M., Schmid, C., Perez, P.: Aggregating local descriptors into a compact image representation. In: CVPR (2010)
43. Perronnin, F., Dance, C.: Fisher kernels on visual vocabularies for image categorization. In: CVPR (2007)
44. Dieleman, S., De Fauw, J., Kavukcuoglu, K.: Exploiting cyclic symmetry in convolutional neural networks. In: ICML (2016)
45. Cohen, T., Welling, M.: Group equivariant convolutional networks. In: ICML (2016)
46. Heeger, D.J.: Normalization of cell responses in cat striate cortex. Vis. Neurosci. 9(2), 181–197 (1992)
47. Schwartz, O., Simoncelli, E.P.: Natural signal statistics and sensory gain control. Nat. Neurosci. 4(8), 819 (2001)
48. Simoncelli, E.P., Olshausen, B.A.: Natural image statistics and neural representation. Ann. Rev. Neurosci. 24(1), 1193–1216 (2001)
49. Carandini, M., Heeger, D.J.: Normalization as a canonical neural computation. Nat. Rev. Neurosci. 13(1), 51 (2012)
50. Paszke, A., et al.: Automatic differentiation in pytorch (2017)
51. Abadi, M., et al.: Tensorflow: a system for large-scale machine learning. In: Operating Systems Design and Implementation (OSDI) (2016)
52. Gross, S., Wilber, M.: Training and investigating Residual Nets (2016). https://github.com/facebook/fb.resnet.torch
53. He, K., Zhang, X., Ren, S., Sun, J.: Delving deep into rectifiers: surpassing human-level performance on imagenet classification. In: ICCV (2015)
54. Goyal, P., et al.: Accurate, large minibatch SGD: training ImageNet in 1 hour (2017). arXiv:1706.02677
55. Krizhevsky, A.: One weird trick for parallelizing convolutional neural networks (2014). arXiv:1404.5997
56. Bottou, L., Curtis, F.E., Nocedal, J.: Optimization methods for large-scale machine learning (2016). arXiv:1606.04838
57. Simonyan, K., Zisserman, A.: Very deep convolutional networks for large-scale image recognition. In: ICLR (2015)
58. Lin, T.Y., Goyal, P., Girshick, R., He, K., Dollár, P.: Focal loss for dense object detection. In: ICCV (2017)
59. Girshick, R., Radosavovic, I., Gkioxari, G., Dollár, P., He, K.: Detectron (2018). https://github.com/facebookresearch/detectron
60. Lin, T.Y., Dollár, P., Girshick, R., He, K., Hariharan, B., Belongie, S.: Feature pyramid networks for object detection. In: CVPR (2017)
61. Ren, S., He, K., Girshick, R., Zhang, X., Sun, J.: Object detection networks on convolutional feature maps. TPAMI 39(7), 1476–1481 (2017)
62. Li, Z., Peng, C., Yu, G., Zhang, X., Deng, Y., Sun, J.: DetNet: a backbone network for object detection (2018). arXiv:1804.06215
63. Wang, X., Girshick, R., Gupta, A., He, K.: Non-local neural networks. In: CVPR (2018)

Deep Expander Networks:
Efficient Deep Networks from Graph Theory

Ameya Prabhu[✉], Girish Varma, and Anoop Namboodiri

Center for Visual Information Technology, Kohli Center on Intelligent Systems,
IIIT Hyderabad, Hyderabad, India
ameya.pandurang.prabhu@gmail.com, {girish.varma,anoop}@iiit.ac.in,
https://github.com/DrImpossible/Deep-Expander-Networks

Abstract. Efficient CNN designs like ResNets and DenseNet were proposed to improve accuracy vs efficiency trade-offs. They essentially
increased the connectivity, allowing efficient information flow across layers. Inspired by these techniques, we propose to model connections
between filters of a CNN using graphs which are simultaneously sparse
and well connected. Sparsity results in efficiency while well connectedness can preserve the expressive power of the CNNs. We use a well-
studied class of graphs from theoretical computer science that satisfies
these properties known as Expander graphs. Expander graphs are used
to model connections between filters in CNNs to design networks called
X-Nets. We present two guarantees on the connectivity of X-Nets: Each
node influences every node in a layer in logarithmic steps, and the number of paths between two sets of nodes is proportional to the product of
their sizes. We also propose efficient training and inference algorithms,
making it possible to train deeper and wider X-Nets effectively.

Expander based models give a 4% improvement in accuracy on
MobileNet over grouped convolutions, a popular technique, which has
the same sparsity but worse connectivity. X-Nets give better performance
trade-offs than the original ResNet and DenseNet-BC architectures. We
achieve model sizes comparable to state-of-the-art pruning techniques
using our simple architecture design, without any pruning. We hope that
this work motivates other approaches to utilize results from graph theory
to develop efficient network architectures.

1 Introduction

Convolutional Neural Networks (CNNs) achieve state-of-the-art results in a variety of machine learning applications [1–4]. However, they are also computationally intensive and consume a large amount of computing power and runtime

---

A. Prabhu and G. Varma—Contributed equally to this work.

Electronic supplementary material The online version of this chapter (https://
doi.org/10.1007/978-3-030-01261-8_2) contains supplementary material, which is
available to authorized users.

© Springer Nature Switzerland AG 2018
V. Ferrari et al. (Eds.): ECCV 2018, LNCS 11217, pp. 20–36, 2018.
https://doi.org/10.1007/978-3-030-01261-8_2

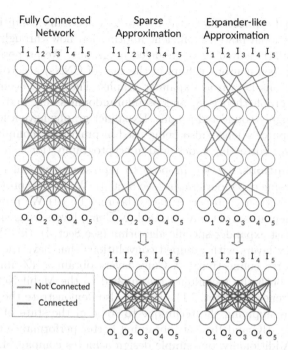

Fig. 1. Popular sparse approximations are agnostic to the global information flow in a network, possibly creating disconnected components. In contrast, expander graph-based models produce sparse yet highly connected networks.

memory. After the success of VGG Networks [5], there has been significant interest in designing compact neural network architectures due to the wide range of applications valuing mobile and embedded devices based use cases.

ResNet [6] and DenseNet-BC [3] directed the focus of efficient designs of convolutional layers on increasing connectivity. Additional connectivity with residual connections to previous layers provided efficient information flow through the network, enabling them to achieve an order of magnitude reduction in storage and computational requirements. We take inspiration from these approaches, to focus on designing highly connected networks. We explore making networks efficient by designing sparse networks that preserve connectivity properties. Recent architectures like MobileNet [7] improves the efficiency by an order of magnitude over a ResNet. However, in order to achieve this, they sparsify a network by removing several connections from a trained network, reducing their accuracies in the process. We ask a basic question: If we try to maximize the connectivity properties and information flow, can we achieve the same efficiency gains with minimal loss in accuracy? It is essential that the connections allow information to flow through the network easily. That is, each output node must at least have the capacity to be sensitive to features of previous layers. As we can see from Fig. 1, traditional model compression techniques such as pruning can aggravate the problem, since they can prune the neuron connections of a layer, while being agnostic of global connectivity of the network. A necessary condition for having good representational power is efficient information flow through the network, which is particularly suited to be modeled by graphs. We propose to make the connections between neurons (filters in the case of CNNs) according to specific graph constructions known as expander graphs. They have been widely studied in spectral graph theory [8] and pseudorandomness [9], and are known to be sparse but highly connected graphs. Expander graphs have a long history in theoretical computer science, also being used in practice in computer networks, constructing error correcting codes, and in cryptography (for a survey, see [10]).

Main Contributions: (i) We propose to represent neuronal connections in deep networks using expander graphs (see Sect. 3). We further prove that X-Nets have strong connectivity properties (see Theorem 1). (ii) We provide memory-efficient implementations of Convolutional (X-Conv) layers using sparse matrices and propose a fast expander-specific algorithm (see Sect. 4). (iii) We empirically compare X-Conv layers with grouped convolutions that have the same level of sparsity but worse connectivity. X-Conv layers obtain a 4% improvement in accuracy when both the techniques are applied to the MobileNet architecture trained on Imagenet (see Sect. 5.1). (iv) We also demonstrate the robustness of our approach by applying the technique to some of the state of the art models like DenseNet-BC and ResNet, obtaining better performance trade-offs (see Sect. 5.2). (v) Additionally, our simple design achieves comparable compression rates to even the state-of-the-art trained pruning techniques (see Sect. 5.3). (vi) Since we enforce the sparsity before the training phase itself, our models are inherently compact and faster to train compared to pruning techniques. We leverage this and showcase the performance of wider and deeper X-Nets (see Sect. 5.5).

2   Related Work

Our approach lies at the intersection of trained pruning techniques and efficient layer design techniques. We present a literature survey regarding both the directions in detail.

2.1   Efficient Layer Designs

Currently there is extensive interest in developing novel convolutional layers/blocks and effectively leveraging them to improve architectures like [7,11,12]. Such micro-architecture design is in a similar direction as our work. In contrast, approaches like [4] try to design the macro-architectures by connecting pre-existing blocks. Recent concurrent work has been on performing architecture searches effectively [13–16]. Our work is complementary to architecture search techniques as we can leverage their optimized macro-architectures.

Another line of efficient architecture design is Grouped Convolutions: which was first proposed in AlexNet [1], recently popularized by MobileNets [7] and

XCeption [17] architectures. This is currently a very active area of current research, with a lot of new concurrent work being proposed [18–20].

It is interesting to note that recent breakthroughs in designing accurate deep networks [3,6,21] were mainly by introducing additional connectivity to enable the efficient flow of information through deep networks. This enables the training of compact, accurate deep networks. These approaches, along with Grouped Convolutions are closely related to our approach.

2.2 Network Compression

Several methods have been introduced to compress pre-trained networks as well as train-time compression. Models typically range from low-rank decomposition [22–24] to network pruning [25–28].

There is also a major body of work that quantizes the networks at train-time to achieve efficiency [29–35]. The problem of pruning weights in train-time have been extensively explored [36,37] primarily from weight-level [38–41] to channel-level pruning [36,37,42]. Weight-level pruning has the highest compression rate while channel-level pruning is easier to practically exploit and has compression rates almost on par with the former. Hence, channel-level pruning is currently considered superior [42]. Channel-level pruning approaches started out with no guidance for sparsity [43] and eventually added constraints [44–46], tending towards more structured pruning.

However, to the best of our knowledge, this is the first attempt at constraining neural network connections by graph-theoretic approaches to improve deep network architecture designs. Note that we do not prune weights during training.

3   Approach

Recent breakthroughs in CNN architectures like ResNet [47] and DenseNet-BC [3] are ideas based on increasing connectivity, which resulted in better performance trade-offs. These works suggest that connectivity is an important property for improving the performance of deep CNNs. In that vein, we investigate ways of preserving connectivity between neurons while significantly sparsifying the connections between them. Such networks are expected to preserve accuracy (due to connectivity) while being runtime efficient (due to the sparsity). We empirically demonstrate this in the later sections.

3.1   Graphs and Deep CNNs

We model the connections between neurons as graphs. This enables us to leverage well-studied concepts from Graph Theory like Expander Graphs. Now, we proceed to formally describe the connection between graphs and Deep CNNs.

Linear Layer Defined by a Graph: Given a bipartite graph G with vertices U, V, the Linear layer defined by G, is a layer with $|U|$ input neurons, $|V|$ output neurons and each output neuron $v \in V$ is only connected to the neighbors given by G. Let the graph G be sparse, having only M edges. Then this layer has only M parameters as compared to $|V| \times |U|$, which is the size of typical linear layers.

Convolutional Layer Defined by a Graph: Let a Convolutional layer be defined as a bipartite graph G with vertices U, V and a window size of $c \times c$. This layer takes a 3D input with $|U|$ channels and produces a 3D output with $|V|$ channels. The output channel corresponding to a vertex $v \in V$ is computed only using the input channels corresponding the the neighbors of v. Let G be sparse, having only M edges. Hence the kernel of this convolutional layer has $M \times c \times c$ parameters as compared to $|V| \times |U| \times c \times c$, which is the number of parameters in a vanilla CNN layer.

3.2   Sparse Random Graphs

We want to constrain our convolutional layers to form a sparse graph G. Without any prior knowledge of the data distribution, we take inspiration from randomized algorithms and propose choosing the neighbours of every output neuron/channel uniformly and independently at random from the set of all its input channels. It is known that a graph G obtained in this way belongs to a well-studied category of graphs called Expander Graphs, known to be sparse but well connected.

Expander Graph: A bipartite expander with degree D and spectral gap γ, is a bipartite graph $G = (U, V, E)$ (E is the set of edges, $E \subseteq U \times V$) in which:

>   **(1) Sparsity:** Every vertex in V has only D neighbors in U. We will be using constructions with $D << |U|$. Hence the number of edges is only $D \times |V|$ as compared to $|U| \times |V|$ in a dense graph.
>   **(2) Spectral Gap:** The eigenvalue with the second largest absolute value λ of the adjacency matrix is bounded away from D (the largest eigenvalue). Formally $1 - \lambda/D \geq \gamma$.

Random Expanders: A random bipartite expander of degree D on the two vertex sets U, V, is a graph in which for every vertex $v \in V$, the D neighbors are chosen independently and uniformly from U. It is a well-known result in graph theory that such graphs have a large spectral gap ([9]). Similar to random expanders, there exist several explicit expander constructions. More details about explicit expanders can be found in the supplementary section. We now proceed to give constructions of deep networks that have connections defined by an expander graph.

Expander Linear Layer (X-Linear): The Expander Linear (X-Linear) layer is a layer defined by a random bipartite expander G with degree D. The expander graphs that we use have values of $D << |U|$, while having an expansion factor of $K \approx D$, which ensures that the layer still has good expressive power.

Expander Convolutional Layer (X-Conv): The Expander Convolutional (X-Conv) layer is a convolutional layer defined by a random bipartite expander graph G with degree D, where $D << |U|$.

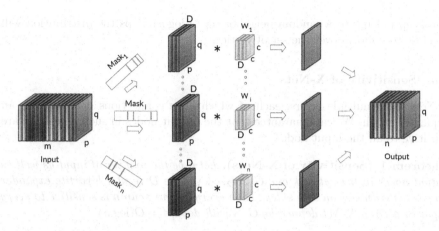

Fig. 2. The proposed fast convolution algorithm for X-Conv layer. We represent all the non-zero filters in the weight matrix of the X-Conv layer as a compressed dense matrix of D channels. The algorithm starts by selecting D channels from input (with replacement) using a mask created while initializing the model. The output is computed by convolving these selected channels with the compressed weight matrices.

Deep Expander Networks (X-Nets): Given expander graphs

$$G_1 = (V_0, V_1, E_1), G_2 = (V_1, V_2, E_2), \cdots, G_t = (V_{t-1}, V_t, E_t),$$

we define the Deep Expander Convolutional Network (Convolutional X-Net or simply X-Net) as a t layer deep network in which the convolutional layers are replaced by X-Conv layers and linear layers are replaced by X-Linear layers defined by the corresponding graphs.

3.3 Measures of Connectivity

In this subsection, we describe some connectivity properties of Expander graphs (see [9], for the proofs). These will be used to prove the properties of sensitivity and mixing of random walks in X-Nets.

Expansion: For every subset $S \subseteq V$ of size $\leq \alpha|V|$ ($\alpha \in (0,1)$ depends on the construction), let $N(S)$ be the set of neighbors. Then $|N(S)| \geq K|S|$ for $K \approx D$. That is, the neighbors of the vertices in S are almost distinct. It is known that random expanders have expansion factor $K \approx D$ (see Theorem 4.4 in [9]).

Small Diameter: The diameter of a graph is the length of the longest path among all shortest paths. If $G(U, V, E)$ is a D-regular expander with expansion factor $K > 1$ and diameter d, then $d \leq O(\log n)$. This bound on the diameter implies that for any pair of vertices, there is a path of length $O(\log n)$ in the graph.

Mixing of Random Walks: Random walks in the graph quickly converge to the uniform distribution over nodes of the graph. If we start from any vertex and keep moving to a random neighbor, in $O(\log n)$ steps the distribution will be close to uniform over the set of vertices.

3.4 Sensitivity of X-Nets

X-Nets have multiple layers, each of which have connections derived from an expander graph. We can guarantee that the output nodes in such a network are sensitive to all the input nodes.

Theorem 1 (Sensitivity of X-Nets). *Let n be the number of input as well as output nodes in the network and $G_1, G_2, \cdots, G_t$ be D regular bipartite expander graphs with n nodes on both sides. Then every output neuron is sensitive to every input in a Deep X-Net defined by G_i's with depth $t = O(\log n)$.*

Proof. For every pair of input and output (u, v), we show that there is a path in the X-Net. The proof is essentially related to the the fact that expander graphs have diameter $O(\log n)$. A detailed proof can be found in the supplementary material.

Next, we show a much stronger connectivity property known as mixing for the X-Nets. The theorem essentially says that the number of edges between subsets of input and output nodes is proportional to the product of their sizes. This result implies that the connectivity properties are uniform and rich across all nodes as well as subsets of nodes of the same size. Simply put, all nodes tend to have equally rich representational power.

Theorem 2 (Mixing in X-Nets). *Let n be the number of input as well as output nodes in the network and G be D regular bipartite expander graph with n nodes on both sides. Let S, T be subsets of input and output nodes in the X-Net layer defined by G. The number of edges between S and T is $\approx D|S||T|/n$.*

Proof. A detailed proof is provided in the supplementary material.

4 Efficient Algorithms

In this section, we present efficient algorithms of X-Conv layers. Our algorithms achieve speedups and save memory in the training as well as the inference phase. This enables one to experiment with significantly wider and deeper networks given memory and runtime constraints. We exploit the structured sparsity of expander graphs to design fast algorithms. We propose two methods of training X-Nets, both requiring substantially less memory and computational cost than their vanilla counterparts:

(1) Using Sparse Representations
(2) Expander-Specific Fast Algorithms.

Algorithm 1. Fast Algorithm for Convolutions in X-Conv Layer

1: For every vertex $v \in \{1, \cdots, n\}$, let $N(v,i)$ denote the ith neighbor of v ($i \in \{1, \cdots, D\}$).
2: Let K_v be the $c \times c \times D \times 1$ sized kernel associated with the vth output channel.
3: Let $O_v[x,y]$ be the output value of the vth channel at the position x, y.
4: **for** $v = 1$ to n **do**
5:     $O_v[x,y] = K_v * Mask_{N(v,1), \cdots N(v,D)}(I)[x,y]$.

4.1 Using Sparse Representation

The adjacency matrices of expander graphs are highly sparse for $D << n$. Hence, we can initialize a sparse matrix with non-zero entries corresponding to the edges of the expander graphs. Unlike most pruning techniques, the sparse connections are determined before training phase, and stay fixed. Dense-Sparse convolutions are easy to implement, and are supported by most deep learning libraries. CNN libraries like Cuda-convnet [48] support such random sparse convolution algorithms.

4.2 X-Net Based Fast Dense Convolution

Next, we present fast algorithms that exploit the sparsity of expander graphs.

X-Conv: In an X-Conv layer, every output channel is only sensitive to *out* rom input channels. We propose to use a mask to select D channels of the input, and then convolve with a $c \times c \times D \times 1$ kernel, obtaining a single channel per filter in the output. The mask is obtained by choosing D samples uniformly (without replacement) from the set $\{1, \cdots N\}$, where N is the number of input channels. The mask value is 1 for each of the selected D channels and 0 for others (see Algorithm 1). This is illustrated in Fig. 2. There has been recent work about fast CUDA implementations called Block-Sparse GPU Kernels [49], which can implement this algorithm efficiently.

5 Experiments and Results

In this section, we benchmark and empirically demonstrate the effectiveness of X-Nets on a variety of CNN architectures. Our code is available at: https://github.com/DrImpossible/Deep-Expander-Networks.

5.1 Comparison with Grouped Convolution

First, we compare our Expander Convolutions (X-Conv) against Grouped Convolutions (G-Conv). We choose G-Conv as it is a popular approach, on which a lot of concurrent works [18] have developed their ideas. G-Conv networks

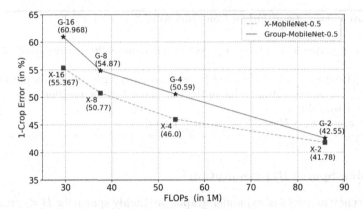

Fig. 3. Comparison between Grouped convolutions and X-Conv using MobileNet architecture trained on ImageNet. X-d or G-d represents the 1×1 conv layers are compressed by d times using X-Conv or Groups. We observe X-MobileNets beat Group-MobileNet by 4% in accuracy on increasing sparsity.

have the same sparsity as X-Conv networks but lack only the connectivity property. This will test whether increasing connectivity increases accuracy, i.e does a graph without good connectivity properties provides worse accuracy? We choose MobileNet as the base model for this experiment, since it is the state-of-the-art in efficient CNN architectures. We compare X-Conv against grouped convolutions using MobileNet-0.5 on the ImageNet classification task. We replace the 1×1 convolutional layers in MobileNet-0.5 with X-Conv layers forming X-MobileNet-0.5. Similarly, we replace them with G-Conv layers to form Group-MobileNet-0.5. Note that we perform this only in layers with most number of parameters (after the 8th layer as given in Table 1 of [7]). We present our results in Fig. 3. The reference original MobileNet-0.5 has an error of 36.6% with a cost of 150M FLOPs. Additional implementation details are given in the supplementary material.

We can observe that X-MobileNets beat Group-MobileNets by over 4% in terms of accuracy when we increase sparsity. This also demonstrates that X-Conv can be used to further improve the efficiency of even the most efficient architectures like MobileNet.

5.2 Comparison with Efficient CNN Architectures

In this section, we test whether Expander Graphs can improve the performance trade-offs even in state-of-the-art architectures such as DenseNet-BCs [3] and ResNets [47] on the ImageNet [50] dataset. We additionally train DenseNet-BCs on CIFAR-10 and CIFAR-100 [51] datasets to demonstrate the robustness of our approach across datasets.

Our X-ResNet-C-D is a D layered ResNet that has every layer except the first and last replaced by an X-Conv layer that compresses connections between it and the previous layer by a factor of C. We compare across various models

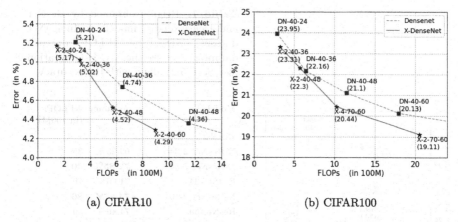

(a) CIFAR10   (b) CIFAR100

Fig. 4. We show the error as a function of #FLOPs during test-time (below) for DenseNet-BC with X-DenseNet-BCs on CIFAR10 and CIFAR100 datasets. We observe X-DenseNet-BCs achieve better performance tradeoffs over DenseNet-BC models. For each datapoint, we mention the X-C-D-G notation (see Sect. 5.2) along with the accuracy.

like ResNets-34,50,101. Similarly, our X-DenseNet-BC-C-D-G architecture has depth D, and growth rate G. We use DenseNet-BC-121-32,169-32,161-48,201-32 as base models. These networks have every layer except the first and last replaced by an X-Conv layer that compresses connections between it and the previous layer by a factor of C. More details are provided in the supplementary material.

5.3   Comparison with Pruning Techniques

We plot the performance tradeoff of X-ResNets against ResNets in Fig. 5. We achieve significantly better performance tradeoffs compared to the original model. More specifically, we can reduce the #FLOPs in ResNets by half while incurring only 1–1.5% decrease in accuracy. Also, we can compare models with similar #FLOPs or accuracy with the help of Table 1. We observe that X-ResNet-2-50 has 43% fewer FLOPs than ResNet-34, but achieves a 1% improvement in accuracy against it. Similarly, X-DenseNet-BC-2-161 has similar #FLOPs as DenseNet-BC-121, but achieves a 1% improvement in accuracy.

To further prove the robustness of our approach on DenseNet-BC, we test the same on CIFAR10 and CIFAR100, and plot the tradeoff curve in Fig. 4. We observe that we can achieve upto 33% compression keeping accuracy constant on CIFAR-10 and CIFAR-100 datasets.

We compare our approach with methods which prune the weights during or after training. Our method can be thought of as constraining the weight matrices with a well studied sparse connectivity pattern even before the training starts. This results in fast training for the compact X-Conv models, while the trained pruning techniques face the following challenges:

Table 1. Results obtained by ResNet and DenseNet-BC models on ImageNet dataset, ordered by #FLOPs or each datapoint, we use the X-C-D-G notation (see Sect. 5.2) along with the accuracy.

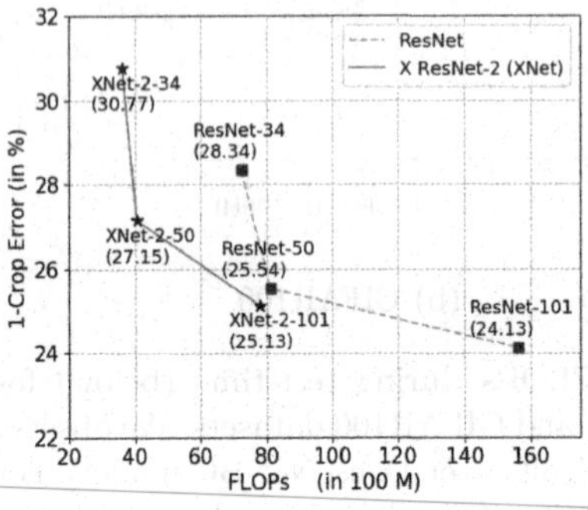

Fig. 5. We show the error as a function of #FLOPs to compare between ResNet and X-ResNet on the ImageNet dataset. We observe X-ResNets achieve better performance tradeoffs over original ResNet models.

Model	Accuracy	#FLOPs (in 100M)
ResNet		
X-ResNet-2-34	69.23%	35
X-ResNet-2-50	**72.85%**	**40**
ResNet-34	71.66%	70
X-ResNet-2-101	**74.87%**	**80**
ResNet-50	74.46%	80
ResNet-101	75.87%	160
DenseNet-BC		
X-DenseNet-BC-2-121	70.5%	28
X-DenseNet-BC-2-169	71.7%	33
X-DenseNet-BC-2-201	72.5%	43
X-DenseNet-BC-2-161	**74.3%**	**55**
DenseNet-BC-121	73.3%	55
DenseNet-BC-169	74.8%	65
DenseNet-BC-201	75.6%	85
DenseNet-BC-161	76.3%	110

(1) Slow initial training due to full dense model.
(2) Several additional phases of pruning and retraining.

Hence they achieve the compactness and runtime efficiency only in test time. Nevertheless we show similar sparsity can be achieved by our approach without explicitly pruning. We benchmark on VGG16 and AlexNet architectures since most previous results in the pruning literature have been reported on these architectures. In Table 2, we compare two X-VGG-16 models against existing pruning techniques. We achieve comparable accuracies to the previous state-of-the-art model with 50% fewer parameters and #FLOPs. Similarly, in Table 3 we compare X-AlexNet with trained pruning techniques on the Imagenet dataset. Despite having poor connectivity due to parameters being concentrated only in the last three fully connected layers, we achieve similar accuracy to AlexNet model using only 7.6M-9.7M parameters out of 61M, comparable to the state-of-the-art pruning techniques which have upto 3.4M-5.9M parameters. Additionally, it is possible to improve compression by applying pruning methods on our compact architectures, but pruning X-Nets is out of the scope of our current work.

Table 2. Comparison with other methods on CIFAR-10 dataset using VGG16 as the base model. We significantly outperform popular compression techniques, achieving similar accuracies with upto 13x compression rate.

Method	Accuracy	#Params	Training
Li et al. [37]	93.4%	5.4M	✗
Liu et al. [42]	93.8%	2.3M	✗
X-VGG16-1	93.4%	1.65M (9x)	✓
X-VGG16-2	93.0%	1.15M (13x)	✓
VGG16-Orig	94.0%	15.0M	-

Table 3. Comparison with other methods on ImageNet-2012 using AlexNet as the base model. We are able to achieve comparable accuracies using only 9.7M parameters.

Method	Accuracy	#Params	Training speedup?
Network pruning			
Collins et al. [52]	55.1%	15.2M	✗
Zhou et al. [45]	54.4%	14.1M	✗
Han et al. [31]	57.2%	6.7M	✗
Han et al. [31]	57.2%	6.7M	✗
Srinivas et al. [44]	56.9%	5.9M	✗
Guo et al. [41]	56.9%	3.4M	✗
X-AlexNet-1	55.2%	7.6M	✓
X-AlexNet-2	56.2%	9.7M	✓
AlexNet-Orig	57.2%	61M	-

5.4 Stability of Models

We give empirical evidence as well as a theoretical argument regarding the stability of our method. For the vanilla DNN training, the weights are randomly initialized, and randomized techniques like dropouts, augmentation are used. Hence there is some randomness present and is well accepted in DNN literature prior to our method. We repeat experiments on different datasets (Imagenet and CIFAR10) and architectures (VGG, DenseNet and MobileNet0.5) to empirically show that the accuracy of expander based models has variance similar to vanilla DNN training over multiple runs.

We repeated the experiments with independent sampling of random expanders on the VGG and DenseNet baselines on the CIFAR10 dataset. The results can be seen in Table 4. It is noted that the accuracy values changes only by less than 0.3% across runs and the standard deviation of expander method is also comparable to the vanilla DNN training.

Table 4. The accuracies (mean ± std-dev) of various models over 10 training runs on CIFAR-10 dataset.

MobileNet variant	Mean accuracy	Range (Max-Min)
Base	63.39%	0.11%
G2	57.45%	0.06%
X2	58.22%	0.14%
G4	49.41%	0.55%
X4	54.00%	0.53%
G8	45.13%	0.03%
X8	49.23%	0.60%
G16	39.03%	0.64%
X16	44.63%	0.18%

Table 5. The mean accuracy and range of variation over 2 runs of MobileNet0.5 variants on ImageNet dataset.

MobileNet variant	Mean accuracy	Range (Max-Min)
Base	63.39%	0.11%
G2	57.45%	0.06%
X2	58.22%	0.14%
G4	49.41%	0.55%
X4	54.00%	0.53%
G8	45.13%	0.03%
X8	49.23%	0.60%
G16	39.03%	0.64%
X16	44.63%	0.18%

We also repeated experiments of our main result, which is the comparison with grouped convolutions on ImageNet dataset. We rerun the experiment with MobileNet0.5 feature extractor twice with Groups and the expander method. As can be seen from Table 5, the accuracy variations are comparable between the two models, and it is less than 1%.

A theoretical argument also concludes that choosing random graphs doesn't degrade stability. It is a well known result (See Theorem 4.4 in [9]) in random graph theory, that graphs chosen randomly are well connected with overwhelmingly high probability (with only inverse exponentially small error, due to the Chernoff's Tail bounds) and satisfies the Expander properties. Hence the chance that for a specific run, the accuracy gets affected due to the selection of a particularly badly connected graph is insignificant.

5.5   Training Wider and Deeper Networks

Since X-Nets involve constraining the weight matrices to sparse connectivity patterns before training, the fast algorithms can make it possible to utilize memory and runtime efficiently in training phase. This makes it possible to train significantly deeper and wider networks. Note the contrast with pruning techniques, where it is necessary to train the full, bulky model, inherently limiting the range of models that can be compressed.

Wide-DenseNets[1] offered a better accuracy-memory-time trade-off. We increase the width and depth of these networks to train significantly wider and deeper networks. The aim is to study whether leveraging the effectiveness of

---

[1] https://github.com/liuzhuang13/DenseNet#wide-densenet-for-better-timeaccuracy-and-memoryaccuracy-tradeoff.

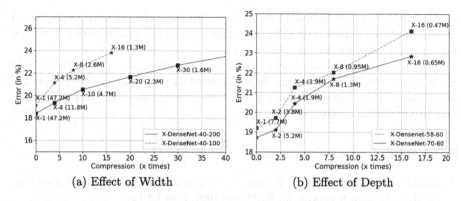

(a) Effect of Width   (b) Effect of Depth

Fig. 6. We show the performance tradeoff obtained on training significantly wider and deeper networks on CIFAR-100 dataset. Every datapoint is X-C specified along with the number of parameters, C being the compression factor. We show that training wider or deeper networks along with more compression using X-Nets achieve better accuracies with upto two-thirds of the total parameter and FLOPs on CIFAR-100 dataset.

X-Nets in this fashion can lead to better accuracies. We widen and deepen the DenseNet-BC-40-60 architecture, increasing the growth rate from 60 to 100 and 200 respectively and compare the effect of increasing width on these new models. Similarly, we increase the depth from 40 to 58 and 70 to obtain deeper networks. We benchmark these approaches using CIFAR-100 dataset and present the results in Fig. 6.

We have two interesting observations. First, the deeper X-DenseNet-BC-70-60 significantly outperforms X-DenseNet-BC-58-60 and wider X-DenseNet-40-200 outperforms X-DenseNet-BC-40-100 with fewer parameters for a wide range of C values (Expander degree).

The second interesting observation is the decreasing slope of the curves. This indicates that expander graph modeling seems to be effective on wider and deeper X-Nets i.e X-DenseNet-BC models suffer lesser penalty with increasing depth and width compression. This enables X-Nets to work at high compression rates of 30x, compressing DenseNet-BC-40-200 model from 19.9B FLOPs to 0.6B FLOPs with only 4.3% drop in accuracy. We hope this preliminary investigation holds significant value in alleviating the constraint of GPU memory and resources.

6   Conclusion

We proposed a new network layer architecture for deep networks using expander graphs that give strong theoretical guarantees on connectivity. The resulting architecture (X-Net) is shown to be highly efficient in terms of both computational requirements and model size. In addition to being compact and computationally efficient, the connectivity properties of the network allow us to achieve significant improvements over the state-of-the-art architectures in performance on a parameter or run-time budget. In short, we show that the use of principled approaches that sparsify a model while maintaining global information flows can help in developing efficient deep networks.

To the best of our knowledge, this is the first attempt at using theoretical results from graph theory in modeling connectivity to improve deep network architectures. We believe that the field of deep networks can gain significantly from other similar explorations.

References

1. Krizhevsky, A., Sutskever, I., Hinton, G.E.: Imagenet classification with deep convolutional neural networks. In: NIPS, pp. 1097–1105 (2012)
2. He, K., Zhang, X., Ren, S., Sun, J.: Identity mappings in deep residual networks. In: Leibe, B., Matas, J., Sebe, N., Welling, M. (eds.) ECCV 2016, Part IV. LNCS, vol. 9908, pp. 630–645. Springer, Cham (2016). https://doi.org/10.1007/978-3-319-46493-0_38
3. Huang, G., Liu, Z., Weinberger, K.Q., van der Maaten, L.: Densely connected convolutional networks. In: CVPR (2017)
4. Szegedy, C., et al.: Going deeper with convolutions. In: CVPR, pp. 1–9, June 2015
5. Simonyan, K., Zisserman, A.: Very deep convolutional networks for large-scale image recognition. CoRR abs/1409.1556 (2014)
6. He, K., Zhang, X., Ren, S., Sun, J.: Deep residual learning for image recognition. In: CVPR, June 2016
7. Howard, A.G., et al.: Mobilenets: efficient convolutional neural networks for mobile vision applications (2017). arXiv preprint: arXiv:1704.04861
8. Spielman, D.A.: Spectral graph theory and its applications. In: FOCS 2007, pp. 29–38, October 2007
9. Vadhan, S.P.: Pseudorandomness. Found. Trends Theoret. Comput. Sci. 7(13), 1–336 (2012)
10. Hoory, S., Linial, N., Wigderson, A.: Expander graphs and their applications. Bull. Am. Math. Soc. 43(4), 439–561 (2006)
11. Iandola, F.N., Han, S., Moskewicz, M.W., Ashraf, K., Dally, W.J., Keutzer, K.: Squeezenet: Alexnet-level accuracy with 50x fewer parameters and <0.5mb model size. In: ICLR (2017)
12. Hu, J., Shen, L., Sun, G.: Squeeze-and-excitation networks (2017). arXiv preprint: arXiv:1709.01507
13. Liu, H., Simonyan, K., Vinyals, O., Fernando, C., Kavukcuoglu, K.: Hierarchical representations for efficient architecture search (2017). arXiv preprint: arXiv:1711.00436
14. Zoph, B., Vasudevan, V., Shlens, J., Le, Q.V.: Learning transferable architectures for scalable image recognition (2017). arXiv preprint: arXiv:1707.07012
15. Zhong, Z., Yan, J., Liu, C.L.: Practical network blocks design with q-learning (2017). arXiv preprint: arXiv:1708.05552
16. Liu, C., et al.: Progressive neural architecture search (2017). arXiv preprint: arXiv:1712.00559
17. Chollet, F.: Xception: deep learning with depthwise separable convolutions. In: CVPR (2017)
18. Zhang, X., Zhou, X., Lin, M., Sun, J.: Shufflenet: an extremely efficient convolutional neural network for mobile devices (2017). arXiv preprint: arXiv:1707.01083

19. Sandler, M., Howard, A., Zhu, M., Zhmoginov, A., Chen, L.C.: Inverted residuals and linear bottlenecks: mobile networks for classification, detection and segmentation (2018). arXiv preprint: arXiv:1801.04381

20. Huang, G., Liu, S., van der Maaten, L., Weinberger, K.Q.: Condensenet: an efficient densenet using learned group convolutions (2017). arXiv preprint: arXiv:1711.09224

21. Xie, S., Girshick, R., Dollár, P., Tu, Z., He, K.: Aggregated residual transformations for deep neural networks. In: CVPR, pp. 5987–5995. IEEE (2017)

22. Sainath, T.N., Kingsbury, B., Sindhwani, V., Arisoy, E., Ramabhadran, B.: Low-rank matrix factorization for deep neural network training with high-dimensional output targets. In: ICASSP, pp. 6655–6659. IEEE (2013)

23. Novikov, A., Podoprikhin, D., Osokin, A., Vetrov, D.P.: Tensorizing neural networks. In: NIPS, pp. 442–450 (2015)

24. Masana, M., van de Weijer, J., Herranz, L., Bagdanov, A.D., Malvarez, J.: Domain-adaptive deep network compression. Network **16**, 30 (2017)

25. Blundell, C., Cornebise, J., Kavukcuoglu, K., Wierstra, D.: Weight uncertainty in neural networks. In: ICML (2015)

26. Liu, B., Wang, M., Foroosh, H., Tappen, M., Pensky, M.: Sparse convolutional neural networks. In: CVPR, pp. 806–814 (2015)

27. He, Y., Zhang, X., Sun, J.: Channel pruning for accelerating very deep neural networks. In: CVPR (2017)

28. Molchanov, P., Tyree, S., Karras, T., Aila, T., Kautz, J.: Pruning convolutional neural networks for resource efficient inference. In: ICLR (2017)

29. Rastegari, M., Ordonez, V., Redmon, J., Farhadi, A.: XNOR-Net: ImageNet classification using binary convolutional neural networks. In: Leibe, B., Matas, J., Sebe, N., Welling, M. (eds.) ECCV 2016, Part IV. LNCS, vol. 9908, pp. 525–542. Springer, Cham (2016). https://doi.org/10.1007/978-3-319-46493-0_32

30. Courbariaux, M., Bengio, Y.: Binarynet: training deep neural networks with weights and activations constrained to +1 or −1. In: ICML (2016)

31. Han, S., Mao, H., Dally, W.J.: Deep compression: compressing deep neural networks with pruning, trained quantization and huffman coding. In: ICLR (2016)

32. Wu, J., Leng, C., Wang, Y., Hu, Q., Cheng, J.: Quantized convolutional neural networks for mobile devices. In: CVPR, pp. 4820–4828 (2016)

33. Bagherinezhad, H., Rastegari, M., Farhadi, A.: LCNN: Lookup-based convolutional neural network. In: CVPR (2017)

34. Zhu, C., Han, S., Mao, H., Dally, W.J.: Trained ternary quantization. In: ICLR (2017)

35. Zhou, S., Wu, Y., Ni, Z., Zhou, X., Wen, H., Zou, Y.: Dorefa-net: training low bitwidth convolutional neural networks with low bitwidth gradients. In: ICLR (2016)

36. Wen, W., Wu, C., Wang, Y., Chen, Y., Li, H.: Learning structured sparsity in deep neural networks. In: NIPS, pp. 2074–2082 (2016)

37. Li, H., Kadav, A., Durdanovic, I., Samet, H., Graf, H.P.: Pruning filters for efficient convnets. In: ICLR (2017)

38. Lebedev, V., Lempitsky, V.: Fast convnets using group-wise brain damage. In: CVPR, pp. 2554–2564 (2016)

39. Scardapane, S., Comminiello, D., Hussain, A., Uncini, A.: Group sparse regularization for deep neural networks. Neurocomputing **241**, 81–89 (2017)

40. Srinivas, S., Babu, R.V.: Data-free parameter pruning for deep neural networks. In: BMVC (2015)

41. Guo, Y., Yao, A., Chen, Y.: Dynamic network surgery for efficient DNNs. In: NIPS, pp. 1379–1387 (2016)
42. Liu, Z., Li, J., Shen, Z., Huang, G., Yan, S., Zhang, C.: Learning efficient convolutional networks through network slimming. In: ICCV (2017)
43. Chen, W., Wilson, J., Tyree, S., Weinberger, K., Chen, Y.: Compressing neural networks with the hashing trick. In: ICML, pp. 2285–2294 (2015)
44. Srinivas, S., Subramanya, A., Babu, R.V.: Training sparse neural networks. In: CVPRW, pp. 455–462. IEEE (2017)
45. Zhou, H., Alvarez, J.M., Porikli, F.: Less is more: towards compact CNNs. In: Leibe, B., Matas, J., Sebe, N., Welling, M. (eds.) ECCV 2016, Part IV. LNCS, vol. 9908, pp. 662–677. Springer, Cham (2016). https://doi.org/10.1007/978-3-319-46493-0_40
46. Yoon, J., Hwang, S.J.: Combined group and exclusive sparsity for deep neural networks. In: ICML, pp. 3958–3966 (2017)
47. He, K., Sun, J.: Convolutional neural networks at constrained time cost. In: CVPR, pp. 5353–5360. IEEE (2015)
48. Krizhevsky, A.: Cuda-convnet: high-performance C++/CUDA implementation of convolutional neural networks (2012)
49. Gray, S., Radford, A., Kingma, D.P.: GPU kernels for block-sparse weights (2017). arXiv preprint: arXiv:1711.09224
50. Deng, J., Dong, W., Socher, R., Li, L.J., Li, K., Fei-Fei, L.: Imagenet: a large-scale hierarchical image database. In: CVPR 2009, pp. 248–255. IEEE (2009)
51. Krizhevsky, A., Hinton, G.: Learning multiple layers of features from tiny images (2009)
52. Collins, M.D., Kohli, P.: Memory bounded deep convolutional networks (2014). arXiv preprint: arXiv:1412.1442

Towards Realistic Predictors

Pei Wang and Nuno Vasconcelos[⊠]

Statistical and Visual Computing Lab, UC San Diego, San Diego, USA
{pew062,nvasconcelos}@ucsd.edu

Abstract. A new class of predictors, denoted realistic predictors, is defined. These are predictors that, like humans, assess the difficulty of examples, reject to work on those that are deemed too hard, but guarantee good performance on the ones they operate on. In this paper, we talk about a particular case of it, realistic classifiers. The central problem in realistic classification, the design of an inductive predictor of hardness scores, is considered. It is argued that this should be a predictor independent of the classifier itself, but tuned to it, and learned without explicit supervision, so as to learn from its mistakes. A new architecture is proposed to accomplish these goals by complementing the classifier with an auxiliary hardness prediction network (HP-Net). Sharing the same inputs as classifiers, the HP-Net outputs the hardness scores to be fed to the classifier as loss weights. Alternatively, the output of classifiers is also fed to HP-Net in a new defined loss, variant of cross entropy loss. The two networks are trained jointly in an adversarial way where, as the classifier learns to improve its predictions, the HP-Net refines its hardness scores. Given the learned hardness predictor, a simple implementation of realistic classifiers is proposed by rejecting examples with large scores. Experimental results not only provide evidence in support of the effectiveness of the proposed architecture and the learned hardness predictor, but also show that the realistic classifier always improves performance on the examples that it accepts to classify, performing better on these examples than an equivalent nonrealistic classifier. All of these make it possible for realistic classifiers to guarantee a good performance.

Keywords: Hardness score prediction · Realistic predictors

1 Introduction

Recent years have produced significant advances in computer vision, due to the introduction of deep convolutional neural networks. Like most other machine learning and computer vision models, they are trained to perform as well as possible on *every* example. In result, these models have no awareness of what they can and cannot do. This is unlike people, who have a sense of their limitations. Most humans can do certain things and do them well but, beyond these, will say 'sorry, I don't know how to do that'. Then they work on what they can do and gradually overcome their limitations. One could say that humans are *realistic predictors*, who would rather refuse tasks that are too hard than almost surely

© Springer Nature Switzerland AG 2018
V. Ferrari et al. (Eds.): ECCV 2018, LNCS 11217, pp. 37–53, 2018.
https://doi.org/10.1007/978-3-030-01261-8_3

fail. This is unlike most classifiers, who are *optimistic* and attempt to classify all examples, no matter how hard. This can be a problem for applications where incorrect decisions can have very negative consequences. For example, a significant problem for smart cars is that their vision systems offer no performance guarantees. For these applications, the vision system should guarantee that the error rate will not exceed some specifications, based on the scene, weather conditions, etc. Even more importantly, it should have a *reject* option, refusing to operate on instances that are too hard, preferring to bring the vehicle to a stop than risk accidents. Another beneficial example is that this new type of predictors could make use of computer use and human skilled labor effectively. In supervised learning, although many automatic annotation methods [23,30] have been proposed, no performance guarantee of their results leads to the fact that humans still need to annotate all collected billions of data in practice, like by Amazon Turk. Instead of annotating all data manually, it is undoubtedly efficient to let realistic models handle on easy examples so as to guarantee accuracy comparable to humans, and just leave the hard ones aside for human experts.

A pre-requisite of realistic classifiers is the ability to *self-assess,* i.e. predict the likelihood of success or failure. This is, however, not easy in the current classification settings. One possibility is to design classifiers with a reject option. For example, classifier cascades are composed of stages that implement a series of reject decisions, efficiently zooming in on image region containing the object to detect [28]. Neural network routing [20], where samples are processed by different network paths, according to their difficulty, is a neural variant of this idea. While increasing computational efficiency, these methods frequently degrade classification performance. They produce a classifier that is faster but usually less accurate than one without rejection options. Many procedures have also been proposed to account for example hardness during training. For instance, curriculum learning [4] suggests using easy samples first and hard samples latter. On the other hand, hard example mining [24] techniques seek examples on which a classifier does poorly, to improve its performance. The goal of these methods is not to produce a *hardness predictor*, which can be applied to examples *unseen* during training, but to improve classifier performance or enable faster optimization convergence. Instead, realistic predictions require *inductive* hardness predictors, capable of operating beyond the training set.

This is, in general, a non-trivial pursuit. The main challenge is that there is no ground truth to train such a predictor. Even when human supervision is available, the ranking of samples is onerous and the identification of easy and hard samples is difficult. This is partly because what is intuitively hard for humans is not guaranteed to be hard for algorithms, and vice versa. Figure 1 shows an example of easy and hard assessments produced by a classifier trained with different approaches. On a dataset of simple images, like MNIST, the hardness predictions are understandable to a human. One can say that easy samples are clearly written, close to prototypical digits, while hard samples are "in between" digits, e.g. "a 6 that looks like a 0," poorly executed digits, e.g. "a 6 that looks like an i" or "an open 0," etc. On the other hand, when the images are complex,

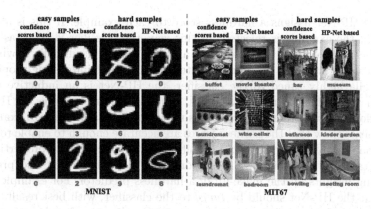

Fig. 1. Top 3 easiest and hardest examples on MNIST and MIT67 dataset according to different criteria. Ground truth labels are shown below each image. "Confidence score based" equates harder to smaller confidence scores. "HP-Net" refers to the ranking by the scores of the proposed hardness predictor.

as in the MIT67 scene dataset, it is too difficult to understand why the classifiers finds the displayed examples easy or hard. In fact, the problem is not even well defined in general, since different classifiers can have different ground-truth for easy and difficult. This is certainly the case for humans, whose difficulty assessments tend to be personal and vary over time, e.g. with experience. Hence, it appears that hardness predictors should be learned in an unsupervised manner, and *personalized,* i.e., classifier specific. On the other hand, it does not appear that they can be *self-referential,* i.e. the hardness predictions cannot be produced by the classifier itself. If this were possible, the classifiers could simply implement a reject option. However, experience with hard example mining suggests that this is not very reliable. While useful for gathering difficult examples, it can produce a significant percentage of examples that are not difficult. Given all this, it appears that, for realistic prediction, the classifier should rely on an *independent* hardness predictor. However, this predictor should be trained *without* explicit supervision, *tuned* to the classifier, and *learn* from its mistakes.

Motivated by this, we propose to implement the hardness predictor as an auxiliary network, which we call the auxiliary *hardness prediction network* (HP-Net). Its input is the example to be processed by the classifier and its output a hardness score. To learn from the classifiers mistakes, the HP-Net is trained *jointly* with it. The two networks are trained in an *adversarial* setting, that resembles that of generative adversarial networks (GANs). While the proposed architecture is not a GAN, the two networks are trained *alternately*. During classifier training, the hardness scores produced by the HP-Net are used as loss weights, assigning more weight to harder examples. This encourages the classifier to classify all examples as best as possible. During HP-Net training, the classifier softmax probabilities are used to tune the HP-Net, using a variant of the cross entropy loss function that elicits adversarial behavior. In this way, as the classifier learns to *improve* its predictions, the HP-Net *refines* its hardness scores. At test time, the HP-Net assigns a hardness score to each example. If this is above a threshold, the example is rejected. In this way, the classifier is never asked to produce class scores for examples that are deemed too hard. This is what we call *realism*. Overall, the proposed architecture has three interesting properties. First, while highly tuned to the classifier, the HP-Net is an inductive model that can be applied to unseen samples. Second, training requires no HP-Net supervision, priors, or hand-crafted rules regarding the nature of hard examples. Experiments show that the harness scores are accurate enough to enable realistic prediction, without compromise of classification accuracy. These properties are demonstrated by extensive evaluation on three datasets, which also provides interesting insights on the make-up of a hardness predictor. For example, they show that the HP-Net should be *tuned* to the classifier, with best results when the two networks have the *same* architecture. On the other hand, performance degrades substantially when the two networks have shared layers, showing that they are solving *fundamentally different* tasks. This is strong evidence against self-referential solutions. Finally, it is shown that classifier performance always increases upon restriction to easier examples. This enables the classifier to meet a specified error rate by simple control of the rejection threshold.

2 Related Work

Several criteria have been proposed to assess sample hardness. One possibility is to use task-specific criteria that leverage prior human knowledge [3,17,25,27]. For example, Ionescu *et al.* [27] define image difficulty as human response time for solving a visual search task. Another popular approach is the use of loss values [13,18,19,24], confidence scores [29], or the magnitude of the loss gradient [1,9,12,33]. These criteria are mostly used to increase the speed of optimization procedures such as stochastic gradient descent. They are sensible for hardness prediction, since small losses tend to correspond to easy samples and vice versa. On the other hand, two samples of equal loss can be classified correctly and incorrectly. For example, adversarial examples of high confidence score are not necessarily easy to classify [11,26]. To address this, Chang *et al.* [5] emphasize sample uncertainty when differentiating easy and hard examples. All these methods rely on handcrafted criteria for selecting and ranking examples. Similar networks with ours are proposed by [15,31] to learn the significant samples for deep reinforcement learning and noisy labeled data, but the classifiers depending on unstable hyper-parameters are not realistic ones. The proposed approach is more closely related to the method of McGill *et al.* [20], who add a 2-way junction to neural network layers to dynamically route easy samples for direct classification and hard samples to the next layer. Nevertheless, all these methods are self-referential, in the sense that a classifier is used to assess the hardness of the samples that it classifies. This is not easy, since hard samples are, by definition, those that the classifier makes mistakes on. We propose, instead, the use of an auxiliary predictor for this task, which learns from the classifier's mistakes.

Realistic prediction is closely related to the literature on failure prediction, where the goal is to build systems that can reliably predict the failures of a predictor. Jammalamadaka *et al.* [14] introduce evaluator algorithms to predict failures of human pose estimators, from features specific to this problem. Bansal *et al.* [2] characterize and group misclassified images using pre-selected attributes, with clustering algorithms that learn a semantic characterization of failure modes. Zhang *et al.* [32] reject probable failure samples with a binary SVM that predicts errors using 14 pre-defined kernels. Daftry *et al.* [6] define failure degree as the fraction of trajectories correctly predicted by an UAV and train a linear SVM to estimate it from the feature responses of a deep network trained for autonomous navigation. These methods rely on post-hoc analysis of the predictor performance, simply learning a regressor or classifier from its mistakes. Realistic prediction aims to go beyond this, by integrating the learning of hardness predictor and classifier, so as to guarantee optimal classifier performance on non-rejected examples. To the best of our knowledge, the proposed architecture is the first implementation of this idea. Our experiments also show that the features needed for classification are fundamentally different from those needed for difficulty prediction. This suggests that simply reading feature responses from the stages of a deep predictor [6] is sub-optimal even for failure prediction.

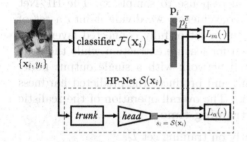

Fig. 2. Proposed architecture. $\mathcal{F}$ is the classifier, HP-Net the hardness predictor.

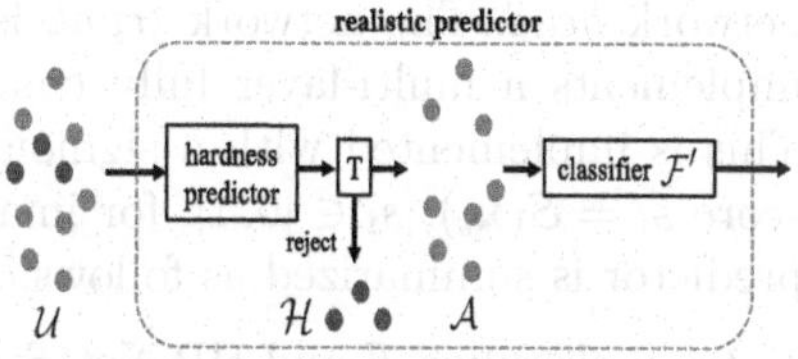

Fig. 3. Procedure of the realistic predictor.

3   Realistic Predictor Architecture

In this section, we introduce the proposed realistic predictor architecture.

3.1   Architecture

While realistic prediction is of interest for many computer vision tasks, in this work we focus on image classification into one of C classes. The operation of a realistic predictor is illustrated in Fig. 3. Consider a classifier $\mathcal{F}(\mathbf{x})$ faced with examples $\mathbf{x}_i$ from a universal example set $\mathcal{U}$. The classifier is denoted realistic if it rejects a subset of examples $\mathcal{H} \subset \mathcal{U}$ that it deems *too hard* so as to guarantee a certain performance on a subset of examples $\mathcal{A} = \mathcal{U} - \mathcal{H}$ that it agrees to classify. Example rejection is determined by thresholding a *hardness score,* which is assigned to each example $\mathbf{x}$ by an auxiliary *hardness predictor* $\mathcal{S}(\mathbf{x})$, denoted the HP-Net. Note that, at inference time, $\mathcal{S}(\mathbf{x})$ predicts the hardness of *unseen test examples.* It must, therefore, be an inductive predictor, e.g. it does not suffice to assign weights to examples during training.

In the failure prediction literature, the classifier $\mathcal{F}$ is first learned from a training set $\mathcal{D} = \{(\mathbf{x}_i, y_i)\}_{i=1}^{N}$, where $\mathcal{D} \subset \mathcal{U}$, y_i is the ground truth label of image $\mathbf{x}_i$, and N the number of training samples. Upon training, a failure predictor is then learned from its performance on the training set, i.e. from the set $\{\mathbf{x}_i, y_i, \hat{y}_i\}$, where $\hat{y}_i$ is the class prediction for sample $\mathbf{x}_i$. While this failure predictor could be used to implement the HP-Net of realistic prediction, this would fail to guarantee that $\mathcal{F}$ has optimal performance on the set $\mathcal{A}$ of accepted examples. One simple solution would be to use the failure predictor to reject training examples and then fine-tune $\mathcal{F}$ on those remaining. This, however, would make the failure predictor sub-optimal for the fine-tuned $\mathcal{F}$. To prevent these problems, we propose to learn $\mathcal{F}$ and $\mathcal{S}$ *jointly,* as illustrated in Fig. 2.

The classifier $\mathcal{F}$ can be any convolutional neural network (CNN), usually containing a number of convolutional layers followed by fully connected layers. Its final layer implements a softmax function with C outputs, outputting a probability distribution $\mathbf{p}_i = \mathcal{F}(\mathbf{x}_i)$ in response to sample $\mathbf{x}_i$. The HP-Net has a similar structure. For notational convenience, we divide it into a set of convolution layers, the network *trunk,* and a set of fully connected layers, the network *head.* The network *trunk* is used for feature extraction while the *head* implements a multi-layer fully connected network with a single output node. This is implemented with a sigmoid unit and produces the predicted hardness score $s_i = \mathcal{S}(\mathbf{x}_i)$, $s_i \in [0, 1]$, for image $\mathbf{x}_i$. The overall operation of the realistic predictor is summarized as follows. At **training time,**

1. train classifier $\mathcal{F}$ and HP-Net $\mathcal{S}$ jointly on training set $\mathcal{D}$.
2. run $\mathcal{S}$ on $\mathcal{D}$ and eliminate hard examples, to create realistic training set $\mathcal{D}'$.
3. learn realistic classifier $\mathcal{F}'$ on $\mathcal{D}'$, with $\mathcal{S}$ fixed.
4. output pair $\mathcal{S}$, $\mathcal{F}'$.

At **test time,** run test example $\mathbf{x}$ by $\mathcal{S}$, reject hard examples, classify remaining with $\mathcal{F}'$. In all cases, $\mathbf{x}$ rejected if $\mathcal{S}(\mathbf{x}) > T$, for some threshold T.

3.2 Adversarial Cross Entropy Loss Function

The joint training of the classifier and HP-Net requires a loss function that induces the desired complimentary functions in the two networks. As is common in the literature, the classifier is trained by cross-entropy minimization. Denoting the one-hot code of ground truth label y_i by $\mathbf{y}_i$, the loss of sample $\{\mathbf{x}_i, y_i\}$ is $l(\mathbf{p}_i, \mathbf{y}_i) = -\mathbf{y}_i^T \log \mathbf{p}_i = -\sum_{c=1}^{C} y_i^c \log p_i^c = -\log p_i^{\bar{c}}$, where $p_i^{\bar{c}}$ is entry of $\mathbf{p}_i$ corresponding to the ground truth label location. The cross-entropy loss

$$L(\mathcal{D}) = -\sum_{i=1}^{N} \log p_i^{\bar{c}} \tag{1}$$

treats each sample equally. As is common in the cost-sensitive learning literature, we replace this with

$$L_m(\mathcal{D}) = -\sum_{i=1}^{N} s_i \log p_i^{\overline{c}}. \tag{2}$$

where $s_i \in [0,1]$ is the hardness score of example $\mathbf{x}_i$, produced by the HP-Net. This makes harder examples (larger s_i) more important, while easier examples (lower s_i) are given less importance. In this way, the classifier is encouraged to learn from as many hard examples as possible and only reject examples that require an unreasonable amount of effort or expertise. This aims to reflect the behavior of a motivated human, who will attempt to learn as much as realistically possible about a problem and reject tasks that exceeds his or her expertise.

To encourage the HP-Net to produce scores s_i proportional to the difficulty of the corresponding samples, the HP-Net is trained with the loss function

$$L_a(\mathcal{D}) = -\sum_{i=1}^{N} \{p_i^{\overline{c}} \log(1 - s_i) + (1 - p_i^{\overline{c}}) \log s_i\}, \tag{3}$$

where $s_i, p_i^{\overline{c}} \in [0,1]$. This is the binary cross entropy loss but with reversed semantics. It measures the cross-entropy between the distributions $(p_i^{\overline{c}}, 1 - p_i^{\overline{c}})$ and $(1 - s_i, s_i)$. Its minimization is equivalent to minimizing the Kullback-Leibler divergence between the two distributions and has a minimum when $s_i = 1 - p_i^{\overline{c}}$. This encourages large scores for poorly classified samples (low $p_i^{\overline{c}}$) and small scores for well classified samples. It can, thus, be seen as an adversarial loss that measures sample hardness, while sharing the appealing properties of the cross-entropy. These can be seen in Fig. 4, which shows a surface plot of the argument of the summation in (3). Note that this is always positive and has global minimum at the configurations $s_i = 1, p_i^{\overline{c}} = 0$ and $s_i = 0, p_i^{\overline{c}} = 1$. Hence, it encourages binary hardness scores. It is also smooth, penalizing heavily the configurations inconsistent with a hardness score ($s_i = p_i^{\overline{c}} = 0$ and $s_i = p_i^{\overline{c}} = 1$).

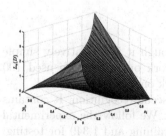

Fig. 4. HP-Net loss surface.

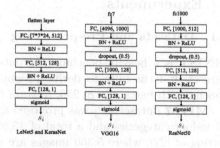

Fig. 5. Detailed structure of different *head* networks.

3.3   Training Strategy

Our attempts to optimize the complete architecture of Fig. 2, using the combined loss function $L(\mathcal{D}) = L_m(\mathcal{D}) + L_a(\mathcal{D})$, produced mixed results. We have experienced difficulties to guarantee convergence of the learning procedure. It is not totally clear why at this point, we leave this for future research. Instead, we found it much easier to optimize the classifier and the HP-Net alternately. Specifically, the HP-Net is first frozen and the classifier updated. The classifier is then frozen and the HP-Net updated. The process is iterated until convergence. Note that the consistency of convergence of this process is quite intuitive. Given the classifier, the optimization of the HP-Net encourages predictions $s_i = 1 - p_i^{\bar{c}}$. Given these scores, the classifier then emphasizes the samples on which it did poorly, i.e. produced a low $p_i^{\bar{c}}$. This increases $p_i^{\bar{c}}$. In the next iteration, s_i decreases, becoming closer to $p_i^{\bar{c}}$. As $p_i^{\bar{c}}$ increases, the example acquires a smaller weight s_i and is ignored by the learning algorithm. Hence, the algorithm "puts away" the well classified examples and focuses on the poorly classified ones.

This is similar to boosting algorithms [8,21], but has one fundamental difference. While, in boosting, the classifier reweights the examples by how well it performs on them, the proposed architecture uses an alternate predictor. Similarly, the procedure has some similarities to generative adversarial networks (GANs) [10] in the sense that there is an adversarial relationship between the classifier and hardness predictor. When the classifier produces bad predictions, the HP-Net generates an adversarial signal that encourages it to produce better predictions. Hence, the HP-Net can be seen as a signal generator that attempts to "confuse" the classifier into thinking that all samples are easy. This is similar to the GAN generator, which attempts to confuse the discriminator, rendering it unable to distinguish real from fake examples. Under this interpretation, the proposed architecture can be seen as an unsupervised generator of hardness scores. However, it is not a GAN. It is also not clear that formulating it as a GAN would add more clarity to its convergence, given the well known convergence issues surrounding GANs [10].

4   Experiments

4.1   Datasets and Pre-processing

MNIST is a heavily benchmarked dataset. Although it is a relatively simple dataset, it is usefully to derive insights on network operation. We used 100 epochs, with batch size of 256, to train the network on this dataset.

MIT67 dataset [22] was proposed for indoor scene recognition. It contains 67 indoor categories and a total of 15,620 images. We follow the experimental setting of [22], where 5,360 images are used for training and 1,340 for testing. On this dataset, we fine-tune a pre-trained network, trained on ImageNet. The number of epochs is set to 50. Batch sizes 32 and 64 are used for VGG and ResNet.

ImageNet LSVRC 2012 [7] contains 1,000 classes with 1.2 million training images, 50,000 validation images, and 100,000 test images. Our evaluation is conducted on the validation set. On these two datasets, we adopt the same data augmentation and pre-processing of the previous studies [16]. Each RGB image pixel is scaled to $[0,1]$ with mean value subtracted and standard variance divided. Then scale and aspect ratio augmentation are applied to the processed images. The 224×224 crop is sampled from augmented images or random horizontal flips. Since, on this dataset, we used a pre-trained network, only 5 epochs are used. Again, batch sizes of 32, 64 batch are used for VGG, ResNet.

4.2 Setup

To study the impact of various network configurations, we consider several strategies for combining networks: simple classifier with complex HP-Net, complex classifier with simple HP-Net, simple classifier with simple HP-Net and complex classifier with complex HP-Net. On MNIST, LeNet5 is used as simple network and kerasNet, a network proposed by keras[1] as the complex one. On MIT67 and ImageNet, VGG16 and ResNet50 are used as simple and complex networks respectively. Additionally, we study the setting where classifier and HP-Net have the same structure and shared convolutional layer weights.

For notational convenience, we use 'A-B(-s)' to represent that A is used as classifier and B as HP-Net. If the '-s' added, A and B have shared weights. For the HP-Net, we also varied the structure of the network *head*. Three basic structures, shown in Fig. 5, are used: 'flatten layer', 'fc7' and 'fc1000' represent the flatten layer, fc7 layer and fc1000 layer of kerasNet, VGG16 and ResNet50 respectively. 'FC, [M1,M2]' represents a fully connected layer of M1 inputs and M2 outputs, 'BN' a batch normalization layer, and 'ReLU' a layer of rectified linear units.

The networks are trained using SGD with a momentum of 0.9. On MNIST, the initial learning rate is set to 0.1, 1e-3 for the classifier and HP-Net, respectively. On the other datasets, it is set to 1e-3, 1e-4 for two networks, for all of the models discussed herein, respectively. The learning rate is reduced by 5% after each epoch on MNIST, and is divided by 10 after every 10 epochs on MIT67, and 1 epoch on ImageNet.

4.3 Learning to Predict Hardness Scores

We start by presenting some results that provide some intuition on the joint learning of classifier and hardness predictor. Figure 6 shows (1) the evolution of distribution of scores produced by the HP-Net, and (2) the test set accuracy of the classifier as a function of training iteration, on MNIST and MIT67. These results were produced with the kerasNet-kerasNet network on MNIST and VGG16-VGG16 on MIT67. On MIT67, we only show the first 20 epochs because there is little change after that. Note that, as classification accuracy increases,

---

[1] https://github.com/keras-team/keras/blob/master/examples/cifar10_cnn.py.

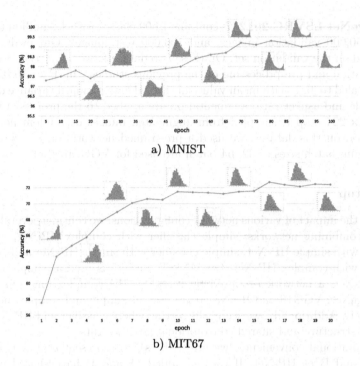

Fig. 6. Evolution of classification accuracy and distribution of hardness scores during training.

the bulk of the mass of the hardness score distribution moves from right to left. This shows that the predicted scores decrease gradually as training progresses. As the classifier updates its predictions, the HP-Net refines its hardness scores to reflect this improvement. This, in turn, encourages the classifier to focus on the harder examples, as in hard example mining. Over training iterations, the hardness predictor learns that samples initially considered hard are not hard after all. This enables it to make good predictions even for unseen examples. The process resembles human learning, which focuses on gradually harder examples that are eventually mastered and found easy.

4.4   Image Recognition Without Rejection

We next consider image recognition results. LeNet5 and kerasNet are used as baseline on MNIST, VGG16 and ResNet50 on MIT67 and ImageNet. All baseline results are based on our experiments, and could differ slightly from results published by their authors. Table 1 summarizes the classification results, enabling a number of conclusions. First, the addition of the HP-Net can produce a slight performance decrease of the classifier on the entire dataset. In fact, this happened for all mixed models (different architectures for HP-Net and classifier) and when the networks are the same and share weights. Note that these numbers are for

Table 1. Image recognition accuracy comparison among all model combinations

Classifier	HP-Net	Shared weights	MNIST	MIT67	ImageNet	
					top 1	top 5
LeNet5			99.0%	—	—	—
kerasNet			99.0%	—	—	—
LeNet5	kerasNet		98.4%	—	—	—
kerasNet	LeNet5		98.2%	—	—	—
LeNet5	LeNet5		99.1%	—	—	—
kerasNet	kerasNet	s	97.9%	—	—	—
kerasNet	kerasNet		**99.2%**	—	—	—
AlexNet [34]			—	56.8%	—	—
CaffeNet [35]			—	56.8%	—	—
GoogleNet [34]			—	59.5%	—	—
VGG16	ResNet50		—	67.9%	65.6%	87.3%
ResNet50	VGG16		—	72.7%	70.4%	90.0%
VGG16			—	72.2%	71.6%	90.3%
VGG16	VGG16	s	—	67.6%	70.9%	89.9%
VGG16	VGG16		—	72.3%	73.3%	91.2%
ResNet50			—	75.6%	76.1%	92.8%
ResNet50	ResNet50	s	—	73.2%	75.9%	92.7%
ResNet50	ResNet50		—	**75.8%**	**76.4%**	**93.0%**

classification *on the entire dataset*. They do not imply that the classifier does not have improved performance on the examples that are accepted by the HP-Net. This will be analyzed below. However, and somewhat surprisingly, when the HP-Net is based on the same model as the classifier, the performance of the latter on the entire dataset improves by some amount. This is likely due to the hard example mining aspect of the procedure. The re-weighting of hard examples with large weights allows the classifier to improve on these. Although the goal of realistic prediction is not to improve image classification performance on all samples, it is interesting to see that the classifier outperforms the baselines.

Second, on all datasets, best performances occur when the classifier and the HP-Net have the same architecture. Combinations with simpler and more complex HP-Nets than the classifier have weaker performance. This is evidence that the hardness predictor has to be *tuned* to the classifier. Third, when this holds, different models can lead to variations of performance. On MNIST, there is no obvious difference between LeNet5 and the more complex kerasNet. This is probably because baseline performance is already saturated. On the other hand, on MIT67, ResNet50-ResNet50 outperforms VGG16-VGG16 by 3.5%. For the larger scale ImageNet, the increase in accuracy is 3.1% when the ResNet50 is adopted. Finally, when the convolutional layers are shared, all classifiers have

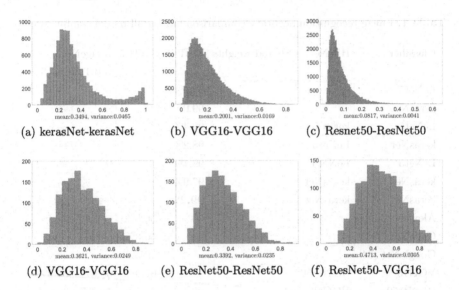

(a) kerasNet-kerasNet   (b) VGG16-VGG16   (c) Resnet50-ResNet50

(d) VGG16-VGG16   (e) ResNet50-ResNet50   (f) ResNet50-VGG16

Fig. 7. The distribution of predicted hardness scores on different settings. Sub-figure (a) is the results on MNIST; (b), (c) are on the ImageNet; The last three are on the MIT67.

slightly weaker performances on all datasets. This is interesting, given the best performance of identical models. While the two networks must be identical, sharing weights leads to a significant performance decrease. This shows that the networks are solving *fundamentally different tasks*, and argues against self-referential solutions based on a single network, such as boosting.

Overall, this section shows that realistic prediction does not have to sacrifice recognition performance even when no examples are rejected. This, however, requires careful selection of classifier and HP-Net architectures.

4.5   Hardness Score Predictions on Test Set

We next analyze the hardness scores produced by the various models. Figure 7 presents the test set distribution of the scores learned by various network combinations. The mean and variance of each distribution are shown below it. The distributions produced by the different networks are consistent with the classification performances in Table 1. Plots (a)–(e), relative to configurations with equal models, assign small scores (less than 0.5) to most test examples. On the other hand, the ResNet50-VGG16 configuration produces a more uniform distribution, of larger mean value. Its lower classification performance has been learned by the hardness predictor, which assigns a larger score to many examples. Note also that, for the two network combinations tested on ImageNet (plots (b)) and (c)), the ResNet50-ResNet50 configuration produces a distribution sharper than that of the VGG16-VGG16 and more concentrated on the neighborhood of 0. This shows that the ResNet50 hardness predictor is more *confident* on the outcome of the classification of the test samples. The hardness predictor, meanwhile, has learned that ResNet is a better model.

4.6   Realistic Predictors

We finish with an evaluation of realistic predictions, based on three classifiers. The first, denoted $\mathcal{C}$, uses a standard (non-realistic) predictor. The second, denoted $\mathcal{F}$, is the realistic predictor produced by the training procedure, without fine-tuning to accepted examples. These two classifiers are trained on the entire training set. Finally, the third, denoted $\mathcal{F}'$, is obtained by fine tuning $\mathcal{F}$ on the training examples accepted by the hardness predictor $\mathcal{S}$. Two strategies are also compared for the rejection of examples. In both cases, a threshold T is found such that $p\%$ of the training examples are rejected. The first strategy is the self-referential strategy of rejecting examples based on the classifier confidence level. Example $\mathbf{x}_i$ is rejected if $\max_c p_i^c < T$, where p_i^c is the softmax output for class c. The second strategy leverages the HP-Net: $\mathbf{x}_i$ is rejected if $\mathcal{S}(\mathbf{x}_i) > T$. Note that only the first strategy is possible for classifier $\mathcal{C}$, which is learned without an HP-Net.

Table 2. Performances of different methods when removing some hard samples

MIT67 (top 1 accuracy, mean(variance); VGG16-VGG16 architecture)							
Classifier	Rejection	0%	5%	10%	15%	20%	25%
$\mathcal{C}$	$\max_c p_i^c < T$	72.2(1.5)	73.1(0.0)	75.6(0.0)	77.5(0.0)	81.0(0.0)	83.0(0.0)
$\mathcal{F}$	$\max_c p_i^c < T$	72.3(1.6)	72.9(0.0)	75.4(0.0)	77.1(0.0)	80.8(0.0)	83.0(0.0)
$\mathcal{F}'$	$\max_c p_i^c < T$	72.3(1.6)	73.4(0.0)	75.8(0.0)	77.2(0.0)	**81.3**(0.0)	**83.1**(0.0)
$\mathcal{F}$	$\mathcal{S}(x) > T$	72.3(1.6)	75.0(0.0)	76.0(0.0)	77.5(0.0)	80.7(0.0)	82.6(0.0)
$\mathcal{F}'$	$\mathcal{S}(x) > T$	**72.3**(1.6)	**75.4**(0.0)	**76.6**(0.0)	**77.9**(0.0)	81.1(0.0)	82.9(0.0)
ImageNet (top 5 accuracy, mean(variance); VGG16-VGG16 architecture)							
		0%	5%	10%	15%	20%	25%
$\mathcal{C}$	$\max_c p_i^c < T$	90.3(0.0)	91.1(0.0)	92.2(0.0)	93.1(0.0)	93.8(0.0)	**95.1**(0.0)
$\mathcal{F}$	$\max_c p_i^c < T$	91.2(0.5)	91.0(0.0)	92.2(0.0)	93.0(0.0)	93.8(0.0)	95.0(0.0)
$\mathcal{F}'$	$\max_c p_i^c < T$	91.2(0.5)	91.2(0.0)	92.4(0.0)	93.1(0.0)	93.7(0.0)	**95.1**(0.0)
$\mathcal{F}$	$\mathcal{S}(x) > T$	91.2(0.5)	91.8(0.0)	92.5(0.0)	93.1(0.0)	93.8(0.0)	94.8(0.0)
$\mathcal{F}'$	$\mathcal{S}(x) > T$	**91.2**(0.5)	**91.9**(0.0)	**92.5**(0.0)	**93.2**(0.0)	**93.8**(0.0)	95.0(0.0)

Table 2 compares the performances of all classifiers and rejection strategies, as a function of the rejection percentage p. A few observations can be made. First, the performance of the realistic predictors is always superior to that of the standard classifier $\mathcal{C}$. As is the case for humans, by refusing to classify hard examples realistic predictors have better performance on those they classify. Second, the rejection by $\mathcal{S}(x) > T$ outperforms standard rejection ($\max_c p_i^c < T$) almost in all settings. The gains can be quite significant, especially as p decreases, e.g. 2.3 points of top 1 performance for $p = 5\%$. This shows that it is important to learn the hardness predictor jointly with the classifier and that the commonly used self-referential confidence scores are not enough to guarantee good hardness predictions. Finally, when the hardness predictions are based on the HP-Net, there is little difference between the top 1 accuracy of the realistic predictor $\mathcal{F}$ trained on the whole training set and that ($\mathcal{F}'$) fine-tunned on accepted examples only. This shows that $\mathcal{F}$ is truly a realistic predictor, capable of close to optimal performance on the accepted examples without any finetuning.

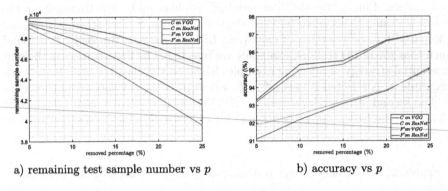

a) remaining test sample number vs p b) accuracy vs p

Fig. 8. Comparison between realistic predictors and standard predictors on ImageNet.

Figure 8 illustrates more results and additionally compares the performance of the realistic predictor $\mathcal{F}'$ to the standard $\mathcal{C}$ over different network configurations (VGG16-VGG16 and ResNet50-ResNet50) on ImageNet. The realistic predictor $\mathcal{F}'$ implemented with the weaker VGG model approaches the performance of the original classifier implemented with the stronger ResNet model. This shows that, even though the VGG cannot learn everything that the ResNet can (i.e. it is not as *smart* as the ResNet), it can *guarantee* the same performance by rejecting some examples. In this case, the VGG passes the 2% rejection performance of the ResNet by rejecting around 10% test examples and the performance of the ResNet on the full test set by rejecting 5% test examples. On the other hand, in order to guarantee a target performance, the realistic predictor can accept and classify more examples than standard non-realistic predictor. For instance, to a target accuracy 93.2%, the ResNet $\mathcal{F}'$ only need to reject less than 2% samples, but for $\mathcal{C}$, it has to reject about 5% samples. In summary, while better models always have better performance, a realistic predictor can provide performance guarantees "above its pay-grade" by refusing to classify examples where it is likely to fail. This applies even to the best models. On ImageNet the superior ResNet is able to improve its performance from 93% to 97% by rejecting about 10% of the examples. While part of this is due to the fact that the examples are indeed easier, the gain is much larger than for the original predictor, which only increases its performance to 95%. The ability to predict which examples are hard, through the hardness predictor, and adapt to them enables this gain.

5   Conclusion

In this work, we have proposed a new class of classifiers, denoted realistic classifiers. These are classifiers that, like humans, assess the difficulty of examples, reject to classify those that are deemed too hard, but guarantee good performance on the ones they classify. The central problem in realistic classification, the design of an inductive predictor of hardness scores, has been then considered. It was argued that this should be a predictor independent of the classifier itself, but tuned to it, and jointly learned, so as to learn from its mistakes. A new architecture has been proposed to accomplished these goals by complementing the classifier with an auxiliary prediction network (HP-Net). The two networks are trained in an adversarial setting, that resembles that of generative adversarial networks (GANs). Experimental results have provided evidence in support of this architecture. While best results were achieved when the HP-Net has the identical architecture to the classifier, sharing weights between the two considerably degraded classification performance. This shows that, while the hardness predictor must be tuned to the classifier, the two solve fundamentally different tasks. Extensive classification experiments have also shown that the realistic classifier always improves performance on the examples that it accepts to classify, performing better on these examples than an equivalent nonrealistic classifier.

References

1. Alain, G., Lamb, A., Sankar, C., Courville, A., Bengio, Y.: Variance reduction in SGD by distributed importance sampling. In: International Conference on Learning Representations (2016)
2. Bansal, A., Farhadi, A., Parikh, D.: Towards transparent systems: semantic characterization of failure modes. In: Fleet, D., Pajdla, T., Schiele, B., Tuytelaars, T. (eds.) ECCV 2014, Part VI. LNCS, vol. 8694, pp. 366–381. Springer, Cham (2014). https://doi.org/10.1007/978-3-319-10599-4_24
3. Basu, S., Christensen, J.: Teaching classification boundaries to humans. In: AAAI Conference on Artificial Intelligence (2013)
4. Bengio, Y., Louradour, J., Collobert, R., Weston, J.: Curriculum learning. In: International Conference on Machine Learning, pp. 41–48. ACM (2009)
5. Chang, H.S., Learned-Miller, E., McCallum, A.: Active bias: training more accurate neural networks by emphasizing high variance samples. In: Advances in Neural Information Processing Systems, pp. 1003–1013 (2017)
6. Daftry, S., Zeng, S., Bagnell, J.A., Hebert, M.: Introspective perception: learning to predict failures in vision systems. In: IEEE International Conference on Intelligent Robots and Systems, pp. 1743–1750. IEEE (2016)
7. Deng, J., Dong, W., Socher, R., Li, L.J., Li, K., Fei-Fei, L.: Imagenet: a large-scale hierarchical image database. In: IEEE Conference on Computer Vision and Pattern Recognition, pp. 248–255. IEEE (2009)

8. Freund, Y., Schapire, R.E., et al.: Experiments with a new boosting algorithm. In: International Conference on Machine Learning, vol. 96, pp. 148–156 (1996)
9. Gao, J., Jagadish, H., Ooi, B.C.: Active sampler: light-weight accelerator for complex data analytics at scale. In: Advances in Neural Information Processing Systems (2016)
10. Goodfellow, I., et al.: Generative adversarial nets. In: Advances in Neural Information Processing Systems, pp. 2672–2680 (2014)
11. Goodfellow, I.J., Shlens, J., Szegedy, C.: Explaining and harnessing adversarial examples. CoRR abs/1412.6572 (2014)
12. Gopal, S.: Adaptive sampling for SGD by exploiting side information. In: International Conference on Machine Learning, pp. 364–372 (2016)
13. Hinton, G.E.: To recognize shapes, first learn to generate images. Progr. Brain Res. **165**, 535–547 (2007)
14. Jammalamadaka, N., Zisserman, A., Eichner, M., Ferrari, V., Jawahar, C.V.: Has my algorithm succeeded? An evaluator for human pose estimators. In: Fitzgibbon, A., Lazebnik, S., Perona, P., Sato, Y., Schmid, C. (eds.) ECCV 2012, Part III. LNCS, vol. 7574, pp. 114–128. Springer, Heidelberg (2012). https://doi.org/10.1007/978-3-642-33712-3_9
15. Kim, T.H., Choi, J.: Screenernet: learning curriculum for neural networks (2018). arXiv preprint: arXiv:1801.00904
16. Krizhevsky, A., Sutskever, I., Hinton, G.E.: Imagenet classification with deep convolutional neural networks. In: Advances in Neural Information Processing Systems, pp. 1097–1105 (2012)
17. Lapedriza, A., Pirsiavash, H., Bylinskii, Z., Torralba, A.: Are all training examples equally valuable? (2013). arXiv preprint: arXiv:1311.6510
18. Lin, T.Y., Goyal, P., Girshick, R., He, K., Dollár, P.: Focal loss for dense object detection. In: IEEE International Conference on Computer Vision (2017)
19. Loshchilov, I., Hutter, F.: Online batch selection for faster training of neural networks. In: International Conference on Learning Representations Workshop (2016)
20. McGill, M., Perona, P.: Deciding how to decide: dynamic routing in artificial neural networks. In: International Conference on Machine Learning, pp. 2363–2372 (2017)
21. Moghimi, M., Belongie, S.J., Saberian, M.J., Yang, J., Vasconcelos, N., Li, L.J.: Boosted convolutional neural networks. In: British Machine Vision Conference (2016)
22. Quattoni, A., Torralba, A.: Recognizing indoor scenes. In: IEEE Conference on Computer Vision and Pattern Recognition, pp. 413–420. IEEE (2009)
23. Shin, H.C., Roberts, K., Lu, L., Demner-Fushman, D., Yao, J., Summers, R.M.: Learning to read chest x-rays: recurrent neural cascade model for automated image annotation. In: The IEEE Conference on Computer Vision and Pattern Recognition, June 2016
24. Shrivastava, A., Gupta, A., Girshick, R.: Training region-based object detectors with online hard example mining. In: IEEE Conference on Computer Vision and Pattern Recognition, pp. 761–769 (2016)
25. Spitkovsky, V.I., Alshawi, H., Jurafsky, D.: Baby steps: how "less is more" in unsupervised dependency parsing. In: NIPS: Grammar Induction, Representation of Language and Language Learning, pp. 1–10 (2009)
26. Szegedy, C., et al.: Intriguing properties of neural networks (2013). arXiv preprint: arXiv:1312.6199

27. Tudor Ionescu, R., Alexe, B., Leordeanu, M., Popescu, M., Papadopoulos, D.P., Ferrari, V.: How hard can it be? Estimating the difficulty of visual search in an image. In: IEEE Conference on Computer Vision and Pattern Recognition, pp. 2157–2166 (2016)

28. Viola, P., Jones, M.: Rapid object detection using a boosted cascade of simple features. In: IEEE Conference on Computer Vision and Pattern Recognition, vol. 1, p. I (2001)

29. Wang, X., Luo, Y., Crankshaw, D., Tumanov, A., Yu, F., Gonzalez, J.E.: IDK cascades: fast deep learning by learning not to overthink (2017). arXiv preprint: arXiv:1706.00885

30. Wu, B., Chen, W., Sun, P., Liu, W., Ghanem, B., Lyu, S.: Tagging like humans: diverse and distinct image annotation. In: The IEEE Conference on Computer Vision and Pattern Recognition (2018)

31. Xiao, T., Xia, T., Yang, Y., Huang, C., Wang, X.: Learning from massive noisy labeled data for image classification. In: Proceedings of the IEEE Conference on Computer Vision and Pattern Recognition, pp. 2691–2699 (2015)

32. Zhang, P., Wang, J., Farhadi, A., Hebert, M., Parikh, D.: Predicting failures of vision systems. In: CVPR (2014)

33. Zhao, P., Zhang, T.: Stochastic optimization with importance sampling for regularized loss minimization. In: International Conference on Machine Learning, pp. 1–9 (2015)

34. Zhou, B., Lapedriza, A., Khosla, A., Oliva, A., Torralba, A.: Places: a 10 million image database for scene recognition. IEEE Trans. Pattern Anal. Mach. Intell. (2017)

35. Zhou, B., Lapedriza, A., Xiao, J., Torralba, A., Oliva, A.: Learning deep features for scene recognition using places database. In: Advances in Neural Information Processing Systems, pp. 487–495 (2014)

Learning SO(3) Equivariant Representations with Spherical CNNs

Carlos Esteves[1]([✉]), Christine Allen-Blanchette[1], Ameesh Makadia[2], and Kostas Daniilidis[1]

[1] GRASP Laboratory, University of Pennsylvania, Philadelphia, USA
{machc,allec,kostas}@seas.upenn.edu
[2] Google, Menlo Park, USA
makadia@google.com

Abstract. We address the problem of 3D rotation equivariance in convolutional neural networks. 3D rotations have been a challenging nuisance in 3D classification tasks requiring higher capacity and extended data augmentation in order to tackle it. We model 3D data with multivalued spherical functions and we propose a novel spherical convolutional network that implements exact convolutions on the sphere by realizing them in the spherical harmonic domain. Resulting filters have local symmetry and are localized by enforcing smooth spectra. We apply a novel pooling on the spectral domain and our operations are independent of the underlying spherical resolution throughout the network. We show that networks with much lower capacity and without requiring data augmentation can exhibit performance comparable to the state of the art in standard retrieval and classification benchmarks.

1 Introduction

One of the reasons for the tremendous success of convolutional neural networks (CNNs) is their equivariance to translations in euclidean spaces and the resulting invariance to local deformations. Invariance with respect to other nuisances has been traditionally addressed with data augmentation while non-euclidean inputs like point-clouds have been approximated by euclidean representations like voxel spaces. Only recently, equivariance has been addressed with respect to other groups [1,2] and CNNs have been proposed for manifolds or graphs [3–5].

Equivariant networks retain information about group actions on the input and on the feature maps throughout the layers of a network. Because of their special structure, feature transformations are directly related to spatial transformations of the input. Such equivariant structures yield a lower network capacity in terms of unknowns than alternatives like the Spatial Transformer [6] where a canonical transformation is learnt and applied to the original input.

In this paper, we are primarily interested in analyzing 3D data for alignment, retrieval or classification. Volumetric and point cloud representations have

---

http://github.com/daniilidis-group/spherical-cnn

© Springer Nature Switzerland AG 2018
V. Ferrari et al. (Eds.): ECCV 2018, LNCS 11217, pp. 54–70, 2018.
https://doi.org/10.1007/978-3-030-01261-8_4

yielded translation and scale invariant approaches: Normalization of translation and scale can be achieved by setting the object's origin to its center and constraining its extent to a fixed constant. However, 3D rotations remain a challenge to current approaches (Fig. 2 illustrates how classification performance for conventional methods suffers when arbitrary rotations are introduced).

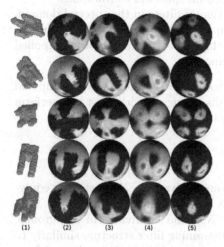

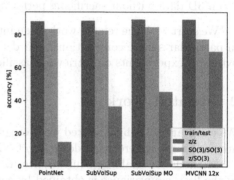

Fig. 1. Columns: (1) input, (2) initial spherical representation, (3–5) learned feature maps. Activations of chair legs illustrate rotation equivariance.

Fig. 2. ModelNet40 classification for point cloud [7], volumetric [8], and multi-view [9] methods. The significant drop in accuracy illustrates that conventional methods do not generalize to arbitrary (SO(3)/SO(3)) and unseen orientations (z/SO(3)).

In this paper, we model 3D-data with spherical functions valued in $\mathbb{R}^n$ and introduce a novel equivariant convolutional neural network with spherical inputs (Fig. 1 illustrates the equivariance). We clarify the difference between convolution that has spherical outputs and correlation that has outputs in the rotation group $\mathbf{SO}(3)$ and we apply exact convolutions that yield zonal filters, i.e. filters with constant values along the same latitude. Convolutions cannot be applied with spatially-invariant impulse responses (masks), but can be exactly computed in the spherical harmonic domain through pointwise multiplication. To obtain localized filters, we enforce a smooth spectrum by learning weights only on few anchor frequencies and interpolating between them, yielding, as additional advantage, a number of weights independent of the spatial resolution.

It is natural then to apply pooling in the spectral domain. Spectral pooling has the advantage that it retains equivariance while spatial pooling on the sphere is only approximately equivariant. We also propose a weighted averaging pooling where the weights are proportional to the cell area. The only reason to return to the spatial domain is the rectifying nonlinearity, which is a pointwise operator.

We perform 3D retrieval, classification, and alignment experiments. Our aim is to show that we can achieve near state of the art performance with a much lower network capacity, which we achieve for the SHREC'17 [10] contest and ModelNet40 [11] datasets.

Our main contributions can be summarized as follows:

- We propose the first neural network based on spherical convolutions.
- We introduce pooling and parameterization of filters in the spectral domain, with enforced spatial localization and capacity independent of the resolution.
- Our network has much lower capacity than non-spherical networks applied on 3D data without sacrificing performance.

We start with the related work, then introduce the mathematics of group and in particular sphere convolutions, and details of our network. Last, we perform extensive experiments on retrieval, classification, and alignment.

2 Related Work

We will start describing related work on group equivariance, in particular equivariance on the sphere, then delve into CNN representations for 3D data.

Methods for enabling equivariance in CNNs can be divided in two groups. In the first, equivariance is obtained by constraining filter structure similarly to Lie generator based approaches [12,13]. Worral et al. [14] use filters derived from the complex harmonics achieving both rotational and translational equivariance. The second group requires the use of a filter orbit which is itself equivariant to obtain group equivariance. Cohen and Welling [1] convolve with the orbit of a learned filter and prove the equivariance of group-convolutions and preservation of rotational equivariance in the presence of rectification and pooling. Dieleman et al. [15] process elements of the image orbit individually and use the set of outputs for classification. Gens and Domingos [16] produce maps of finite-multiparameter groups, Zhou et al. [17] and Marcos et al. [18] use a rotational filter orbit to produce oriented feature maps and rotationally invariant features, and Lenc and Vedaldi [19] propose a transformation layer which acts as a group-convolution by first permuting then transforming by a linear filter.

Recently, a body of work on Graph Convolutional Networks (GCN) has emerged. There are two threads within this space, spectral [20–22] and spatial [23–25]. These approaches learn filters on irregular but structured graph representations. These methods differ from ours in that we are looking to explicitly learn equivariant and invariant representations for 3D-data modeled as spherical functions under rotation. While such properties are difficult to construct for general manifolds, we leverage the group action of rotations on the sphere.

Most similar to our approach and developed in parallel[1] is [5], which uses spherical correlation to map spherical inputs to features on $\mathbf{SO}(3)$, then processed with a series of convolutions on $\mathbf{SO}(3)$. The main difference is that we

---

[1] The first version of this work was submitted to CVPR on 11/15/2017, shortly after we became aware of Cohen et al. [5] ICLR submission on 10/27/2017.

use spherical convolutions, which are potentially one order of magnitude faster, with smaller (one fewer dimension) filters and feature maps. In addition, we enforce smoothness in the spectral domain that results in better localization of the receptive fields on the sphere and we perform pooling in two different ways, either as a low-pass in the spectral domain or as a weighted averaging in the spatial domain. Moreover, our method outperforms [5] in the SHREC'17 benchmark.

Spherical representations for 3D-data are not novel and have been used for retrieval tasks before the deep learning era [26,27] because of their invariance properties and efficient implementation of spherical correlation [28]. In 3D deep learning, the most natural adaptation of 2D methods was to use a voxel-grid representation of the 3D object and amend the 2D CNN framework to use collections of 3D filters for cascaded processing in the place of conventional 2D filters. Such approaches require a tremendous amount of computation to achieve very basic voxel resolution and need a much higher capacity.

Several attempts have been made to use CNNs to produce discriminative representations from volumetric data. 3D ShapeNets [11] and VoxNet [29] propose a fully-volumetric network with 3D convolutional layers followed by fully-connected layers. Qi *et al.* [8] observe significant overfitting when attempting to train the aforementioned end-to-end and choose to amend the technique using subvolume classification as an auxiliary task, and also propose an alternate 3D CNN which learns to project the volumetric representation to a 2D representation, then processed using a conventional 2D CNN architecture. Even with these adaptations, Qi *et al.* [8] are challenged by overfitting and suggest augmentation in the form of orientation pooling as a remedy. Qi *et al.* [7] also present an attempt to train a neural network that operates directly on point clouds. Currently, the most successful approaches are view-based, operating in rendered views of the 3D object [8,9,30,31]. The high performance of these methods is in part due to the use of large pre-trained 2D CNNs (on ImageNet, for instance).

3 Preliminaries

3.1 Group Convolution

Consideration of symmetries, in particular rotational symmetries, naturally evokes notions of the Fourier Transform. In the context of deriving rotationally invariant representations, the Fourier Transform is particularly appealing since it exhibits invariance to rotational deformations up to phase (a truly invariant representation can be achieved through application of the modulus operator).

To leverage this property for 3D shape analysis, it is necessary to construct a rotationally equivariant representation of our 3D input. For a group G and function $f : E \to F$, f is said to be equivariant to transformations $g \in G$ when

$$f(g \circ x) = g' \circ f(x), \quad x \in E \tag{1}$$

where g acts on elements of E and g' is the corresponding group action which transforms elements of F. If $E = F$, $g = g'$. A straightforward example of an equivariant representation is an orbit. For an object x, its orbit $O(x)$ with respect to the group G is defined

$$O(x) = \{g \circ x \mid \forall g \in G\}. \tag{2}$$

Through this example it is possible to develop an intuition into the equivariance of the group convolution; convolution can be viewed as the inner-products of some function f with all elements of the orbit of a "flipped" filter h. Formally, the group convolution is defined as

$$(f \star_G h)(x) = \int_{g \in G} f(g \circ \eta)h(g^{-1} \circ x)\, dg, \tag{3}$$

where η is typically a canonical in the domain of f (e.g. the origin if $E = \mathbb{R}^n$, or I_n if $E = \mathbf{SO}(n)$). The familiar convolution on the plane is a special case of the group convolution with the group $G = \mathbb{R}^2$ with addition,

$$(f \star h)(x) = \int_{g \in \mathbb{R}^2} f(g \circ \eta)h(g^{-1} \circ x)\, dg = \int_{g \in \mathbb{R}^2} f(g)h(x - g)\, dg. \tag{4}$$

The group convolution can be shown to be equivariant. For any $\alpha \in G$,

$$((\alpha^{-1} \circ f) \star_G h)(x) = (\alpha^{-1} \circ (f \star_G h))(x). \tag{5}$$

3.2   Spherical Harmonics

Following directly the preliminaries above, we can define convolution of spherical signal f by a spherical filter h with respect to the group of 3D rotations $\mathbf{SO}(3)$:

$$(f \star_G h)(x) = \int_{g \in \mathbf{SO}(3)} f(g\eta)h(g^{-1}x)\, dg, \tag{6}$$

where η is north pole on the sphere.

To implement (6), it is desirable to sample the sphere with well-distributed and compact cells with transitivity (rotations exist which bring cells into coincidence). Unfortunately, such a discretization does not exist [32]. Neither the familiar sampling by latitude and longitude nor the uniformly distributed sampling according to Platonic solids satisfies all constraints. These issues are compounded with the eventual goal of performing cascaded convolutions on the sphere.

To circumvent these issues, we choose to evaluate the spherical convolution in the spectral domain. This is possible as the machinery of Fourier analysis has extended the well-known convolution theorem to functions on the sphere: the Spherical Fourier transform of a convolution is the pointwise product of Spherical Fourier transforms (see [33,34] for further details). The Fourier transform and its inverse are defined on the sphere as follows [33]:

$$f = \sum_{0 \leq \ell \leq b} \sum_{|m| \leq \ell} \hat{f}_m^\ell Y_m^\ell, \tag{7}$$

$$\hat{f}^\ell_m = \int_{S^2} f(x)\overline{Y^\ell_m}dx, \tag{8}$$

where b is the bandwidth of f, and Y^ℓ_m are the spherical harmonics of degree ℓ and order m. We refer to (8) as the Spherical Fourier Transform (SFT), and to (7) as its inverse (ISFT). Revisiting (6), letting $y = (f \star_G h)(x)$, the spherical convolution theorem [34] gives us

$$\hat{y}^\ell_m = 2\pi\sqrt{\frac{4\pi}{2\ell+1}}\hat{f}^\ell_m\hat{h}^\ell_0, \tag{9}$$

To compute the convolution of a signal f with a filter h, we first expand f and h into their spherical harmonic basis (8), second compute the pointwise product (9), and finally invert the spherical harmonic expansion (7).

It is important to note that this definition of spherical convolution is unique from spherical correlation which produces an output response on **SO**(3). Convolution here can be seen as marginalizing the angle responsible for rotating the filter about its north pole, or equivalently considering zonal filters on the sphere.

3.3   Practical Considerations and Optimizations

To evaluate the SFT, we use equiangular samples on the sphere according to the sampling theorem of [34]

$$\hat{f}^\ell_m = \frac{\sqrt{2\pi}}{2b}\sum_{j=0}^{2b-1}\sum_{k=0}^{2b-1} a^{(b)}_j f(\theta_j,\phi_k)\overline{Y^\ell_m}(\theta_j,\phi_k), \tag{10}$$

where $\theta_j = \pi j/2b$ and $\phi_k = \pi k/b$ form the sampling grid, and $a^{(b)}_j$ are the sample weights. Note that all the required operations are matrix pointwise multiplications and sums, which are differentiable and readily available in most automatic differentiation frameworks. In our direct implementation, we precompute all needed Y^ℓ_m, which are stored as constants in the computational graph.

Separation of Variables: We also implement a potentially faster SFT based on separation of variables as shown in [34]. Expanding Y^ℓ_m in (10), we obtain

$$\hat{f}^\ell_m = \sum_{j=0}^{2b-1}\sum_{k=0}^{2b-1} a^{(b)}_j f(\theta_j,\phi_k)q^\ell_m P^\ell_m(\cos\theta_j)e^{-im\phi_k}$$

$$= q^\ell_m\sum_{j=0}^{2b-1} a^{(b)}_j P^\ell_m(\cos\theta_j)\sum_{k=0}^{2b-1} f(\theta_j,\phi_k)e^{-im\phi_k}, \tag{11}$$

where P^ℓ_m is the associated Legendre polynomial, and q^ℓ_m a normalization factor. The inner sum can be computed using a row-wise Fast Fourier Transform and what remains is an associated Legendre transform, which we compute directly. The same idea is done for the ISFT. We found that this method is faster when $b \geq 32$. There are faster algorithms available [34,35], which we did not attempt.

Leveraging Symmetry: For real-valued inputs, $\hat{f}^\ell_{-m} = (-1)^m \overline{\hat{f}^\ell_m}$ (this follows from $\overline{Y^\ell_{-m}} = (-1)^m Y^\ell_m$). We thus need only compute half the coefficients ($m > 0$). Furthermore, we can rewrite the SFT and ISFT to avoid expensive complex number support or multiplication:

$$f = \sum_{0 \leq \ell \leq b} \left(\hat{f}^\ell_0 Y^\ell_0 + \sum_{m=1}^{\ell} 2\,\mathrm{Re}(\hat{f}^\ell_m)\mathrm{Re}(Y^\ell_m) - 2\,\mathrm{Im}(\hat{f}^\ell_m)\mathrm{Im}(Y^\ell_m) \right). \qquad (12)$$

4   Method

Figure 3 shows an overview of our method. We define a block as one spherical convolutional layer, followed by optional pooling, and nonlinearity. A weighted global average pooling is applied at the last layer to obtain an invariant descriptor. This section details the architectural design choices.

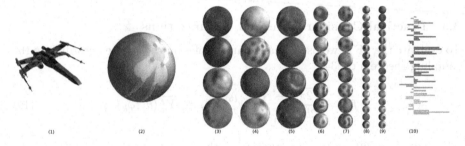

Fig. 3. Overview of our method. From left to right: a 3D model (1) is mapped to a spherical function (2), which passes through a sequence of spherical convolutions, nonlinearities and pooling, resulting in equivariant feature maps (3–9). We show only a few channels per layer. A global weighted average pooling of the last feature map results in a descriptor invariant to rotation (10), which can be used for classification or retrieval. The input spherical function (2) may have multiple channels, in this picture we show the distance to intersection representation.

4.1   Spectral Filtering

In this section, we define the filter parameterization. One possible approach would be to define a compact support around one of the poles and learn the values for each discrete location, setting the rest to zero. The downside of this approach is that there are no guarantees that the filter will be bandlimited. If it is not, the SFT will be implicitly bandlimiting the signal, which causes a discrepancy between the parameters and the actual realization of the filters.

To avoid this problem, we parameterize the filters in the spectral domain. In order to compute the convolution of a function f and a filter h, only the SFT coefficients of order $m = 0$ of h are used. In the spatial domain, this implies that for any h, there is always a zonal filter (constant value per latitude) h_z, such that $\forall y$, $y * h = y * h_z$. Thus, it only makes sense to learn zonal filters.

The spectral parameterization is also faster because it eliminates the need to compute the filter SFT, since the filters are defined in the spectral domain, which is the same domain where the convolution computed.

Non-localized Filters: A first approach is to parameterize the filters by all SFT coefficients of order $m = 0$. For example, given 32×32 inputs, the maximum bandwidth is $b = 16$, so there are 16 parameters to be learned $(\hat{h}_0^0, \dots \hat{h}_0^{15})$. A downside is that the filters may not be local; however, locality may be learned.

Localized Filters: From Parseval's theorem and the derivative rule from Fourier analysis we can show that spectral smoothness corresponds to spatial decay. This is used in the construction of graph-based neural networks [36], and also applies to the filters spanned by the family of spherical harmonics of order zero $(m = 0)$.

To obtain localized filters, we parameterize the spectrum with anchor points. We fix n uniformly spaced degrees ℓ_i and learn the correspondent coefficients $f_0^{\ell_i}$. The coefficients for the missing degrees are then obtained by linear interpolation, which enforces smoothness. A second advantage is that the number of parameters per filter is independent of the input resolution. Figure 4 shows some filters learned by our model; the right side filters are obtained imposing locality.

Fig. 4. Filters learned in the first layer. The filters are zonal. *Left:* 16 nonlocalized filters. *Right:* 16 localized filters. Nonlocalized filters are parameterized by all spectral coefficients (16, in the example). Even though locality is not enforced, some filters learn to respond locally. Localized filters are parameterized by a few points of the spectrum (4, in the example), the rest of the spectrum is obtained by interpolation.

4.2 Pooling

The conventional spatial max pooling used in CNNs has two drawbacks in Spherical CNNs: (1) need an expensive ISFT to convert back to spatial domain, and (2) equivariance is not completely preserved, specially because of unequal cell areas from equiangular sampling. Weighted average pooling (WAP) takes into account the cell areas to mitigate the latter, but is still affected by the former.

We introduce the spectral pooling (SP) for Spherical CNNs. If the input has bandwidth b, we remove all coefficients with degree larger or equal than $b/2$ (effectively, a lowpass box filter). Such operation is known to cause ringing artifacts, which can be mitigated by previous smoothing, although we did not find any performance advantage in doing so. Note that spectral pooling was proposed before for conventional CNNs [37].

We found that spectral pooling is significantly faster, reduces the equivariance error, but also reduces classification accuracy. The choice between SP and WAP is application-dependent. For example, our experiments show SP is more suitable for shape alignment, while WAP is better for classification and retrieval. Table 5 shows the performance for each method.

4.3   Global Pooling

In fully convolutional networks, it is usual to apply a global average pooling at the last layer to obtain a descriptor vector, where each entry is the average of one feature map. We use the same idea; however, the equiangular spherical sampling results in cells of different areas, so we compute a weighted average instead, where a cell's weight is the sine of its latitude. We denote it Weighted Global Average Pooling (WGAP). Note that the WGAP is invariant to rotation, therefore the descriptor is also invariant. Figure 5 shows such descriptors.

An alternative to this approach is to use the magnitude per degree of the SFT coefficients; formally, if the last layer has bandwidth b and $\hat{f}^\ell = [\hat{f}^\ell_{-\ell}, \hat{f}^\ell_{-\ell+1}, \ldots, \hat{f}^\ell_\ell]$, then $d = \left[\left\|\hat{f}^0\right\|, \left\|\hat{f}^1\right\|, \ldots \left\|\hat{f}^{b-1}\right\|\right]$ is an invariant descriptor [33]. We denote this approach as MAG-L (magnitude per degree ℓ). We found no difference in classification performance when using it (see Table 5).

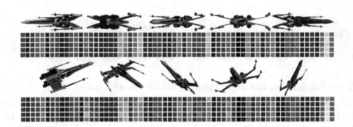

Fig. 5. Our model learns descriptors that are nearly invariant to input rotations. From top to bottom: azimutal rotations and correspondent descriptors (one per row), arbitrary rotations and correspondent descriptors. The invariance error is negligible for azimuthal rotations; since we use equiangular sampling, the cell area varies with the latitude, and rotations around z preserve latitude. Arbitrary rotations brings a small invariance error, for reasons detailed in Sect. 5.5.

4.4   Architecture

Our main architecture has two branches, one for distances and one for surface normals. This performs better than having two input channels and slightly better than having two separate voting networks for distance and normals. Each branch has 8 spherical convolutional layers, and $16, 16, 32, 32, 64, 64, 128, 128$ channels per layer. Pooling and feature concatenation of one branch into the other is performed when the number of channels increase. WGAP is performed after the last layer, which is then projected into the number of classes.

5 Experiments

The greatest advantage of our model is inherent equivariance to $SO(3)$; we focus the experiments in problems that benefit from it; namely, shape classification and retrieval in arbitrary orientations, and shape alignment.

We chose problems related to 3D shapes due to the availability of large datasets and published results on them; our method would also be applicable to any kind of data that can be mapped to the sphere (e.g. panoramas).

5.1 Preliminaries

Ray-Mesh Intersection: 3D shapes are usually represented by mesh or voxel grid, which need to be converted to spherical functions. Note that the conversion function itself must be equivariant to rotations; our learned representation will not be equivariant if the input is pre-processed by a non-equivariant function.

Given a mesh or voxel grid, we first find the bounding sphere and its center. Given a desired resolution n, we cast $n \times n$ equiangular rays from the center, and obtain the intersections between each ray and the mesh/voxel grid. Let d_{jk} be the distance from the center to the farthest point of intersection, for a ray at direction (θ_j, ϕ_k). The function on the sphere is given by $f(\theta_j, \phi_k) = d_{jk}, 1 \le j, k \le n$.

For mesh inputs, we also compute the angle α between the ray and the surface normal at the intersecting face, giving a second channel $f(\theta_j, \phi_k) = [d, \sin \alpha]$.

Note that this representation is suitable for star-shaped objects, defined as objects that contain an interior point from where the whole boundary is visible. Moreover, the center of the bounding sphere must be one of such points. In practice, we do not check if these conditions hold – even if the representation is ambiguous or non-invertible, it is still useful.

Training: We train using ADAM, for 48 epochs, initial learning rate of 10^{-3}, which is divided by 5 on epochs 32 and 40.

We make use of data augmentation for training, performing rotations, anisotropic scaling and mirroring on the meshes, and adding jitter to the bounding sphere center when constructing the spherical function. Note that, even though our learned representation is equivariant to rotations, augmenting the inputs with rotations is still beneficial due to interpolation and sampling effects.

5.2 3D Object Classification

This section shows classification performance on ModelNet40 [11]. Three modes are considered: (1) trained and tested with azimuthal rotations (z/z), (2)

Table 1. ModelNet40 classification accuracy per instance. Spherical CNNs are robust to arbitrary rotations, even when not seen during training, while also having one order of magnitude fewer parameters and faster training.

Method	z/z	SO3/SO3	z/SO3	params	inp. size
PointNet [7]	89.2	83.6	14.7	3.5M	2048×3
PointNet++ [38]	89.3	85.0	28.6	1.7M	1024×3
VoxNet [29]	83.0	73.0	-	0.9M	30^3
SubVolSup [8]	88.5	82.7	36.6	17M	30^3
SubVolSup MO [8]	89.5	85.0	45.5	17M	20×30^3
MVCNN 12x [9]	89.5	77.6	70.1	99M	12×224^2
MVCNN 80x [9]	**90.2**	86.0	-[a]	99M	80×224^2
RotationNet 20x [30]	**92.4**	80.0	20.2	58.9M	20×224^2
Ours	88.9	**86.9**	**78.6**	**0.5M**	$\mathbf{2 \times 64^2}$

[a] The 80 views are not restricted to azimuthal, hence cannot be compared (acc: 81.5%).

trained and tested with arbitrary rotations (**SO**(3)/**SO**(3)), and (3) trained with azimuthal and tested with arbitrary rotations (z/**SO**(3)).

Table 1 shows the results. All competing methods suffer a sharp drop in performance when arbitrary rotations are present, even if they are seen during training. Our model is more robust, but there is a noticeable drop for mode 3, attributed to sampling effects. Since we use equiangular sampling, the cell area varies with latitude. Rotations around z preserve latitude, so regions at same height are sampled at same resolution during training, but not during test. We believe this can be improved by using equal-area spherical sampling.

We evaluate competing methods using default settings of their published code. The volumetric [8] and point cloud based [7,38] methods cannot generalize to unseen orientations (z/**SO**(3)). The multi-view [9,30] methods can be seen as a brute force approach to equivariance; and MVCNN [9] generalizes to unseen orientations up to a point. Yet, the Spherical CNN outperforms it, even with orders of magnitude fewer parameters and faster training. Interestingly, RotationNet [30], which holds the current state-of-the-art on ModelNet40 classification, fails to generalize to unseen rotations, despite being multi-view based.

Equivariance to **SO**(3) is unneeded when only azimuthal rotations are present (z/z); the full potential of our model is not exercised in this case.

5.3   3D Object Retrieval

We run retrieval experiments on ShapeNet Core55 [39], following the SHREC'17 3D shape retrieval rules [10], which includes random **SO**(3) perturbations.

The network is trained for classification on the 55 core classes (we do not use the subclasses), with an extra in-batch triplet loss (from [40]) to encourage descriptors to be close for matching categories and far for non-matching.

The invariant descriptor is used with a cosine distance for retrieval. We first compute a threshold per class that maximizes the training set F-score. For test set retrieval, we return elements whose distances are below their class threshold and include all elements classified as the same class as the query. Table 2 shows the results. Our model matches the state of the art performance (from [41]), with significantly fewer parameters, smaller input size, and no pre-training.

Table 2. SHREC'17 perturbed dataset results. We show precision, recall and mean average precision. *micro* average is adjusted by category size, *macro* is not. The sum of *micro* and *macro* mAP is used for ranking. We match the state of the art even with significantly fewer parameters, smaller input resolution, and no pre-training. Top results are bold, runner-ups italic.

	micro			macro			Total		
	P@N	R@N	mAP	P@N	R@N	mAP	score	input size	params
Furuya [41]	**0.814**	0.683	0.656	**0.607**	0.539	**0.476**	**1.13**	126×10^3	8.4M
Ours	*0.717*	*0.737*	*0.685*	*0.450*	*0.550*	*0.444*	**1.13**	2×64^2	**0.5M**
Tatsuma [42]	0.705	**0.769**	**0.696**	0.424	**0.563**	0.418	*1.11*	38×224^2	3M
Cohen [5]	0.701	0.711	0.676	-	-	-	-	6×128^2	*1.4M*
Zhou [31]	0.660	0.650	0.567	0.443	0.508	0.406	0.97	50×224^2	36M

5.4 Shape Alignment

Our learned equivariant feature maps can be used for shape alignment using spherical correlation. Given two shapes from the same category (not necessarily the same instance), under arbitrary orientations, we run them through the network and collect the feature maps at some layer. We compute the correlation between each pair of corresponding feature maps, and add the results. The maximum value of the correlation function (which takes inputs on $SO(3)$) corresponds to the rotation that aligns both shapes [28].

Features from deeper layers are richer and carry semantic value, but are at lower resolution. We run an experiment to determine the performance of the shape alignment per layer, while also comparing with the spherical correlation done at the network inputs (not learned).

We select categories from Model-Net10 that do not have rotational symmetry so that the ground truth rotation is unique and the angular error is measurable. These categories are: *bed, sofa, toilet, chair*. Only entries from the test set are used. Results are in Table 3, while Fig. 6 shows some examples. Results show that the learned features are superior to the handcrafted

Table 3. Shape alignment median angular error in degrees. The intermediate learned features are best suitable for this task.

	bed	chair	sofa	toilet
input	91.63	111.47	12.15	21.65
conv2	85.64	21.10	14.47	14.95
conv4	**12.73**	**14.63**	**10.03**	**11.03**
conv6	16.70	18.92	15.83	17.62

spherical shape representation for this task, and best performance is achieved by using intermediate layers. The resolution at conv4 is 32 × 32, which corresponds to cell dimensions up to 11.25 deg, so we cannot expect errors much lower than this.

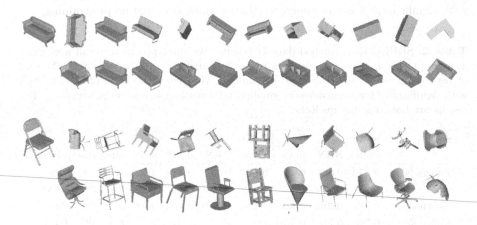

Fig. 6. Shape alignment for two categories. We align shapes by running spherical correlation of their feature maps. The semantic features learned can be used to align shapes from the same class even with large appearance variation. *1st and 3rd rows:* reference shape, followed by queries from the same category. *2nd and 4th rows:* Corresponding aligned shapes. Last column shows failure cases.

5.5   Equivariance Error Analysis

Even though spherical convolutions are equivariant to **SO**(3) for bandlimited inputs, and spectral pooling preserves bandlimit, there are other factors that may introduce equivariance errors. We quantify these effects in this section.

We feed each entry in the test set and one random rotation to the network, then apply the same rotation to the feature maps and measure the average relative error. Table 4 shows the results. The pointwise nonlinearity does not preserve bandlimit, and cause equivariance errors (rows 1, 4). The mesh to sphere map is only approximately equivariant, which can be mitigated with larger input dimensions (*input* column for rows 1, 5). Error is smaller when the input is bandlimited (rows 1, 7). Spectral pooling is exactly equivariant, while maxpooling introduces higher frequencies and has larger error than WAP (rows 1, 2, 3). Error for an untrained model demonstrates that the equivariance is by design and not learned (row 6). Note that the error is smaller because the learned filters are usually high-pass, which increase the pointwise relative error. A linear model with bandlimited inputs has zero equivariance error, as expected (row 8).

Note that even conventional planar CNNs will exhibit a degree of translational equivariance error introduced by max pooling and discretization.

Table 4. Equivariance error. Error is zero for bandlimited inputs and linear layers.

	Configuration					Error per layer						
	res.	blim.	pool	linear	trained	input	conv1	conv2	conv3	conv4	conv5	conv6
1. baseline	64^2	no	WAP	no	yes	0.05	0.11	0.12	0.14	0.16	0.17	0.15
2. maxpool	64^2	no	max	no	yes	0.05	0.11	0.12	0.14	0.18	0.19	0.15
3. specpool	64^2	no	SP	no	yes	0.05	0.11	0.12	0.10	0.10	0.09	0.08
4. linear	64^2	no	WAP	yes	yes	0.05	0.12	0.13	0.15	0.14	0.12	0.04
5. lowres	32^2	no	WAP	no	yes	0.09	0.15	0.18	0.21	0.21	0.21	0.20
6. untrained	64^2	no	WAP	no	no	0.05	0.09	0.07	0.07	0.11	0.07	0.04
7. blim	64^2	yes	WAP	no	yes	0.00	0.10	0.11	0.11	0.15	0.14	0.04
8. blim/lin/sp	64^2	yes	SP	yes	yes	0.00	0.01	0.01	0.00	0.00	0.00	0.00

5.6   Ablation Study

In this section we evaluate numerous variations of our method to determine the sensitivity to design choices. First, we are interested in assessing the effects from our contributions SP, WAP, WGAP, and localized filters. Second, we are interested in understanding how the network size affects performance. Results show that the use of WAP, WGAP, and localized filters significantly improve performance, and also that further performance improvements can be achieved with larger networks. In summary, factors that increase bandwidth (e.g. max-pooling) also increase equivariance error and may reduce accuracy. Global operations in early layers (e.g. non-local filters) escape the receptive field and reduce accuracy.

Table 5. Ablation study. Spherical CNN accuracy on rotated ModelNet40. We compare various types of pooling, filter localization and network sizes.

inp. res.	pool	global pool	localized	params	details	acc. [%]
64×64	WAP	WGAP	yes	0.49M	best	**86.9**
64×64	WAP	MAG-L	yes	0.54M		86.9
64×64	SP	WGAP	yes	0.49M		85.8
64×64	max	WGAP	yes	0.49M		86.7
64×64	avg	WGAP	yes	0.49M		86.7
64×64	WAP	avg	yes	0.49M		86.4
64×64	WAP	WGAP	no	0.49M		85.9
32×32	WAP	WGAP	yes	0.39M		85.0
32×32	WAP	WGAP	yes	0.69M	deeper	85.6
32×32	WAP	WGAP	yes	1.06M	wider	85.5
32×32	WAP	WGAP	yes	0.12M	narrower	83.8

6   Conclusion

We presented Spherical CNNs, which leverage spherical convolutions to achieve equivariance to $SO(3)$ perturbations. The network is applied to 3D object classification, retrieval, and alignment, but has potential applications in spherical images such as panoramas, or any data that can be represented as a spherical function. We show that our model can naturally handle arbitrary input orientations, requiring relatively few parameters and small input sizes.

Acknowledgments. We are grateful for support through the following grants: NSF-DGE-0966142 (IGERT), NSF-IIP-1439681 (I/UCRC), NSF-IIS-1426840, NSF-IIS-1703319, NSF MRI 1626008, ARL RCTA W911NF-10-2-0016, ONR N00014-17-1-2093, and by Honda Research Institute.

References

1. Cohen, T.S., Welling, M.: Group equivariant convolutional networks (2016). arXiv preprint: arXiv:1602.07576
2. Worrall, D.E., Garbin, S.J., Turmukhambetov, D., Brostow, G.J.: Harmonic networks: deep translation and rotation equivariance. In: Proceedings of the IEEE Conference on Computer Vision and Pattern Recognition (CVPR), vol. 2 (2017)
3. Bruna, J., Szlam, A., LeCun, Y.: Learning stable group invariant representations with convolutional networks (2013). arXiv preprint: arXiv:1301.3537
4. Bronstein, M.M., Bruna, J., LeCun, Y., Szlam, A., Vandergheynst, P.: Geometric deep learning: going beyond Euclidean data. IEEE Signal Process. Mag. **34**(4), 18–42 (2017)
5. Cohen, T.S., Geiger, M., Khler, J., Welling, M.: Spherical CNNs. In: International Conference on Learning Representations (2018)
6. Jaderberg, M., Simonyan, K., Zisserman, A., et al.: Spatial transformer networks. In: Advances in Neural Information Processing Systems, pp. 2017–2025 (2015)
7. Qi, C.R., Su, H., Mo, K., Guibas, L.J.: Pointnet: deep learning on point sets for 3D classification and segmentation. In: Proceedings of the Computer Vision and Pattern Recognition (CVPR), vol. 1(2), p. 4. IEEE (2017)
8. Qi, C.R., Su, H., Nießner, M., Dai, A., Yan, M., Guibas, L.J.: Volumetric and multi-view CNNs for object classification on 3D data. In: 2016 IEEE Conference on Computer Vision and Pattern Recognition, CVPR 2016, Las Vegas, NV, USA, pp. 5648–5656, 27–30 June 2016
9. Su, H., Maji, S., Kalogerakis, E., Learned-Miller, E.: Multi-view convolutional neural networks for 3D shape recognition. In: Proceedings of the IEEE International Conference on Computer Vision, pp. 945–953 (2015)
10. Savva, M., et al.: Shrec'17 track: large-scale 3D shape retrieval from shapenet core55. In: 10th Eurographics workshop on 3D Object retrieval, pp. 1–11 (2017)
11. Wu, Z., et al.: 3D shapenets: a deep representation for volumetric shapes. In: IEEE Conference on Computer Vision and Pattern Recognition, CVPR 2015, Boston, MA, USA, pp. 1912–1920, 7–12 June 2015
12. Segman, J., Rubinstein, J., Zeevi, Y.Y.: The canonical coordinates method for pattern deformation: theoretical and computational considerations. IEEE Trans. Pattern Anal. Mach. Intell. **14**(12), 1171–1183 (1992)

13. Hel-Or, Y., Teo, P.C.: Canonical decomposition of steerable functions. In: Proceedings of the 1996 IEEE Computer Society Conference on Computer Vision and Pattern Recognition, CVPR 1996, pp. 809–816. IEEE (1996)
14. Worrall, D.E., Garbin, S.J., Turmukhambetov, D., Brostow, G.J.: Harmonic networks: deep translation and rotation equivariance (2016). arXiv preprint: arXiv:1612.04642
15. Dieleman, S., Willett, K.W., Dambre, J.: Rotation-invariant convolutional neural networks for galaxy morphology prediction. Mon. Not. R. Astron. Soc. **450**(2), 1441–1459 (2015)
16. Gens, R., Domingos, P.M.: Deep symmetry networks. In: Advances in Neural Information Processing Systems, pp. 2537–2545 (2014)
17. Zhou, Y., Ye, Q., Qiu, Q., Jiao, J.: Oriented response networks. In: The IEEE Conference on Computer Vision and Pattern Recognition (CVPR), July 2017
18. Marcos, D., Volpi, M., Komodakis, N., Tuia, D.: Rotation equivariant vector field networks. CoRR (2016)
19. Lenc, K., Vedaldi, A.: Understanding image representations by measuring their equivariance and equivalence. In: Proceedings of the IEEE Conference on Computer Vision and Pattern Recognition, pp. 991–999 (2015)
20. Bruna, J., Zaremba, W., Szlam, A., LeCun, Y.: Spectral networks and locally connected networks on graphs (2013). arXiv preprint: arXiv:1312.6203
21. Defferrard, M., Bresson, X., Vandergheynst, P.: Convolutional neural networks on graphs with fast localized spectral filtering. In: Advances in Neural Information Processing Systems, pp. 3844–3852 (2016)
22. Kipf, T.N., Welling, M.: Semi-supervised classification with graph convolutional networks (2016). arXiv preprint: arXiv:1609.02907
23. Boscaini, D., Masci, J., Rodolà, E., Bronstein, M.: Learning shape correspondence with anisotropic convolutional neural networks. In: Advances in Neural Information Processing Systems, pp. 3189–3197 (2016)
24. Masci, J., Boscaini, D., Bronstein, M., Vandergheynst, P.: Geodesic convolutional neural networks on Riemannian manifolds. In: Proceedings of the IEEE International Conference on Computer Vision Workshops, pp. 37–45 (2015)
25. Monti, F., Boscaini, D., Masci, J., Rodolà, E., Svoboda, J., Bronstein, M.M.: Geometric deep learning on graphs and manifolds using mixture model CNNs (2016). arXiv preprint: arXiv:1611.08402
26. Frome, A., Huber, D., Kolluri, R., Bülow, T., Malik, J.: Recognizing objects in range data using regional point descriptors. In: Pajdla, T., Matas, J. (eds.) ECCV 2004, Part III. LNCS, vol. 3023, pp. 224–237. Springer, Heidelberg (2004). https://doi.org/10.1007/978-3-540-24672-5_18
27. Kazhdan, M., Funkhouser, T.: Harmonic 3D shape matching. In: ACM SIGGRAPH 2002 Conference Abstracts and Applications, p. 191. ACM (2002)
28. Makadia, A., Daniilidis, K.: Spherical correlation of visual representations for 3D model retrieval. Int. J. Comput. Vis. **89**(2), 193–210 (2010)
29. Maturana, D., Scherer, S.: Voxnet: a 3D convolutional neural network for real-time object recognition. In: 2015 IEEE/RSJ International Conference on Intelligent Robots and Systems, IROS 2015, Hamburg, Germany, 28 September–2 October 2015, pp. 922–928 (2015)
30. Kanezaki, A., Matsushita, Y., Nishida, Y.: Rotationnet: joint object categorization and pose estimation using multiviews from unsupervised viewpoints. In: Proceedings of IEEE International Conference on Computer Vision and Pattern Recognition (CVPR) (2018)

31. Bai, S., Bai, X., Zhou, Z., Zhang, Z., Jan Latecki, L.: Gift: a real-time and scalable 3D shape search engine. In: Proceedings of the IEEE Conference on Computer Vision and Pattern Recognition, pp. 5023–5032 (2016)
32. Thurston, W.P.: Three-Dimensional Geometry and Topology, vol. 1. Princeton University Press, Princeton (1997)
33. Arfken, G.: Mathematical Methods for Physicists, vol. 2. Academic Press, London (1966)
34. Driscoll, J.R., Healy, D.M.: Computing fourier transforms and convolutions on the 2-sphere. Adv. Appl. Math. 15(2), 202–250 (1994)
35. Healy, D.M., Rockmore, D.N., Kostelec, P.J., Moore, S.: Ffts for the 2-sphere-improvements and variations. J. Fourier Anal. Appl. 9(4), 341–385 (2003)
36. Bruna, J., Zaremba, W., Szlam, A., LeCun, Y.: Spectral networks and locally connected networks on graphs. CoRR (2013)
37. Rippel, O., Snoek, J., Adams, R.P.: Spectral representations for convolutional neural networks. CoRR (2015)
38. Qi, C.R., Yi, L., Su, H., Guibas, L.J.: Pointnet++: deep hierarchical feature learning on point sets in a metric space. In: Advances in Neural Information Processing Systems, pp. 5105–5114 (2017)
39. Chang, A.X., et al.: Shapenet: An information-rich 3D model repository. CoRR (2015)
40. Schroff, F., Kalenichenko, D., Philbin, J.: Facenet: a unified embedding for face recognition and clustering. In: Proceedings of the IEEE Conference on Computer Vision and Pattern Recognition, pp. 815–823 (2015)
41. Furuya, T., Ohbuchi, R.: Deep aggregation of local 3D geometric features for 3D model retrieval. In: BMVC (2016)
42. Tatsuma, A., Aono, M.: Multi-fourier spectra descriptor and augmentation with spectral clustering for 3D shape retrieval. Vis. Comput. 25(8), 785–804 (2009)

Poster Session

Learnable PINs: Cross-modal Embeddings for Person Identity

Arsha Nagrani$^{(\boxtimes)}$ (ID), Samuel Albanie (ID), and Andrew Zisserman (ID)

VGG, Department of Engineering Science, Oxford, UK
{arsha,albanie,az}@robots.ox.ac.uk

Abstract. We propose and investigate an identity sensitive joint embedding of face and voice. Such an embedding enables cross-modal retrieval from voice to face and from face to voice.

We make the following four contributions: first, we show that the embedding can be learnt from videos of talking faces, without requiring any identity labels, using a form of cross-modal self-supervision; second, we develop a curriculum learning schedule for hard negative mining targeted to this task that is essential for learning to proceed successfully; third, we demonstrate and evaluate cross-modal retrieval for identities unseen and unheard during training over a number of scenarios and establish a benchmark for this novel task; finally, we show an application of using the joint embedding for automatically retrieving and labelling characters in TV dramas.

Keywords: Joint embedding · Cross-modal
Multi-modal · Self-supervised · Face recognition
Speaker identification · Metric learning

1 Introduction

Face and voice recognition, both non-invasive and easily accessible biometrics, are the tools of choice for a variety of tasks. State of the art methods for face recognition use face embeddings generated by a deep convolutional neural network [38,40,45] trained on a large-scale dataset of labelled faces [9,18,23]. A similar path for generating a voice embedding is followed in the audio community for speaker recognition [13,32,34,52]. However, even though a person can be identified by their face or their voice, these two 'modes' have been treated quite independently – could they not be considered jointly?

To that end, the objective of this paper is to learn a *joint* embedding of faces and voices, and to do so using a virtually free and limitless source of

---

A. Nagrani and S. Albanie—Equal contribution.

Electronic supplementary material The online version of this chapter (https://doi.org/10.1007/978-3-030-01261-8_5) contains supplementary material, which is available to authorized users.

© Springer Nature Switzerland AG 2018
V. Ferrari et al. (Eds.): ECCV 2018, LNCS 11217, pp. 73–89, 2018.
https://doi.org/10.1007/978-3-030-01261-8_5

unlabelled training data – videos of human speech or 'talking faces' – in an application of cross-modal self-supervision. The key idea is that a subnetwork for faces and a subnetwork for voice segments can be trained jointly to predict whether a face corresponds to a voice or not, and that training data for this task is freely available: the positives are faces and voice segments acquired from the same 'talking face' in a video, the negatives are a face and voice segment from different videos.

What is the motivation for learning such a joint embedding? First, a joint embedding of the modalities enables cross-modal retrieval – a person's face can retrieve face-less voice segments, and their voice can retrieve still photos and speech-less video segments. Second, this may in fact be how humans internalise identity. A highly-influential cognitive model due to the psychologists Bruce and Young [6] proposed that 'person identity nodes' or 'PINs' are a portion of associative memory holding identity-specific semantic codes that can be accessed via the face, the voice, or other modalities: and hence are entirely abstracted from the input modality.

It is worth first considering if a joint embedding is even possible. Certainly, if we task a network with learning a joint embedding then it is likely to succeed on the training data – since arbitrary associations can be learnt even from unrelated data [51]. However, if the relationship between face and voice is completely arbitrary, and the network has 'memorised' the training data then we would expect chance behaviour for cross-modal retrieval of identities that were *unseen and unheard* during training. It is unlikely that the relationship between face and voice is completely arbitrary, because we would expect some dependence between gender and the face/voice, and age and the face/voice [33]. Somewhat surprisingly, the experiments show that employing cross-modal retrieval on the joint embeddings for unseen-unheard identities achieves matches that go beyond gender and age.

In this paper we make the following four contributions. First, in Sect. 3, we propose a network architecture for jointly embedding face and voice, and a training loss for learning from unlabelled videos from YouTube. Second, in Sect. 4, we develop a method for curriculum learning that uses a single parameter to control the difficultly of the within-batch hard negatives. Scheduling the difficulty of the negatives turns out to be a crucial factor for learning the joint embedding in an unsupervised manner. Third, in Sect. 7, we evaluate the learnt embedding for unseen-unheard identities over a number of scenarios. These include using the face and voice embedding for cross-modal verification, and '1 in N' cross-modal retrieval where we beat the current state of the art [33]. Finally, in Sect. 8, we show an application of the learnt embedding to one-shot learning of identities for character labelling in a TV drama. This again evaluates the embeddings on unseen-unheard identities.

2   Related Work

Cross-modal Embeddings: The relationship between visual content and audio has been researched in several different contexts, with common applications being generation, matching and retrieval [25,28,30]. The primary focus of this work, however, is to construct a shared representation, or joint embedding of the two modalities. While joint embeddings have been researched intensively for images and text, [5,16,17,27,48], they have also started to gain traction for audio and vision [1,4,36,43]. There are several ways in which this embedding may be learned—we take inspiration from a series of works that exploit audio-visual correspondence as a form of self-supervised learning [2,37]. It is also possible to learn the embedding via cross-modal distillation [1,4,20] in which a trained model (the "teacher") transfers its knowledge in one modality to a second model (the "student") in another to produce aligned representations.

Of particular relevance is a recent work [3] that learns a joint embedding between visual frames and sound segments for musical instruments, singing and tools. Our problem differs from theirs in that ours is one of fine grained recognition: we must learn the subtle differences between pairs of faces or pairs of voices; whereas [3] must learn to distinguish between different types of instruments by their appearance and sound. We also note a further challenge; human speech exhibits considerable variability that results not only from *extrinsic* factors such as background chatter, music and reverberation, but also from *intrinsic* factors, which are variations in speech from the same speaker such as the lexical content of speech (the exact words being spoken), emotion and intonation [34]. A person identity-sensitive embedding must achieve invariance to both sets of factors.

Cross-modal Learning with Faces and Voices: In biometrics, an active research area is the development of multimodal recognition systems which seek to make use of the *complementary* signal components of facial images and speech [7, 24], in order to achieve better performance than systems using a single modality, typically through the use of feature fusion. In contrast to these, our goal is to exploit the *redundancy* of the signal that is common to both modalities, to facilitate the task of cross-modal retrieval. Le and Odobez [29] try to instill knowledge from face embeddings to improve speaker diarisation results, however their focus is only to achieve better audio embeddings.

In our earlier work [33] we established, by using a forced matching task, that strong correlations exist between faces and voices belonging to the same identity. These occur as a consequence of cross-modal biometrics such as gender, age, nationality and others, which affect both facial appearance and the sound of the voice. This paper differs from [33] in two key aspects. First, while [33] used identity labels to train a discriminative model for matching, we approach the problem in an *unsupervised* manner, learning directly from videos without labels. Second, rather than training a model restricted to the task of matching, we instead learn a *joint* embedding between faces and voices. Unlike [33], our learnt representation is no longer limited to forced matching, but can instead be used for other tasks such as cross-modal verification and retrieval.

3   Learning Joint Embeddings

Our objective is to learn functions $f_\theta(x_f) : \mathbb{R}^F \to \mathbb{R}^E$ and $g_\phi(x_v) : \mathbb{R}^V \to \mathbb{R}^E$ which map faces and voices of the same identity in $\mathbb{R}^F$ and $\mathbb{R}^V$ respectively onto

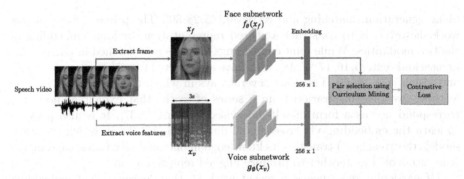

Fig. 1. Learning a joint embedding between faces and voices. Positive face-voice pairs are extracted from speech videos and fed into a two-stream architecture with a face subnetwork $f_\theta(x_f)$ and a voice subnetwork $g_\phi(x_v)$, each producing 256-D embeddings. A curriculum-based mining schedule is used to select appropriate negative pairs which are then trained using a contrastive loss.

nearby points in a shared coordinate space $\mathbb{R}^E$. To this end, we instantiate $f_\theta(x_f)$ and $g_\phi(x_v)$ as convolutional neural networks and combine them to form a two-stream architecture comprising a face subnetwork and a voice subnetwork (see Fig. 1). To learn the parameters of f_θ and g_ϕ, we sample a set $\mathcal{P}$ of training pairs $\{x_f, x_v\}$, each consisting of a face image x_f and a speech segment x_v and attach to each pair an associated label $y \in \{0,1\}$, where $y = 0$ if x_f and x_v belong to different identities (henceforth a negative pair) and $y = 1$ if both belong to the same identity (a positive pair). We employ a contrastive loss [11,19] on the paired data $\{(x_{f_i}, x_{v_j}, y_{i,j})\}$, which seeks to optimise f_θ and g_ϕ to minimise the distance between the embeddings of positive pairs and penalises the negative pair distances for being smaller than a margin parameter α. Concretely, the cost function is defined as:

$$\mathcal{L} = \frac{1}{|\mathcal{P}|} \sum_{(i,j)\in p} y_{i,j} D_{i,j}^2 + (1 - y_{i,j}) \max\{0, \alpha - D_{i,j}\}_+^2 \tag{1}$$

where $(i,j) \in p$ is used to indicate $(x_{f_i}, x_{v_j}, y_{i,j}) \in \mathcal{P}$ and $D_{i,j}$ denotes the Euclidean distance between normalised embeddings, $D_{i,j} = \|\frac{f_\theta(x_{f_i})}{\|f_\theta(x_{f_i})\|_2} - \frac{g_\phi(x_{v_j})}{\|g_\phi(x_{v_j})\|_2}\|_2$. Details of the architectures for each subnetwork are provided in Sect. 6.1.

3.1 Generating Face-Voice Pairs

Obtaining Speaking Face Tracks: In contrast to previous audio-visual self-supervised works that seek to exploit naturally synchronised data [2,4], simply extracting audio and video frames at the same time is not sufficient to obtain pairs of faces and voice samples (of the same identity) required to train the contrastive loss described in Eq. 1. Even for a given video tagged as content that may contain a talking human, a short sample from the associated audio may not contain any speech, and in cases when speech is present, there is no guarantee that the speaker of the audio is visible in the frame (e.g. in the case of 'reaction shots', flashbacks and dubbing of videos [35]). Furthermore, even when the face of the speaker is present there may be more than one face occupying the frame.

We address these issues by using SyncNet [12], an unsupervised method that obtains speaking face-tracks from video automatically. SyncNet consists of a two-stream convolutional neural network which estimates the correlation between the audio track and the mouth motion of the video. This allows the video to be accurately segmented into *speaking face-tracks*—contiguous groupings of face detections from the video of the *speaker*.

Selecting Face-Voice Pairs: Given a collection of speaking face-tracks, we can then construct a collection of labelled training pairs with the following simple labelling algorithm. We define face and voice segments extracted from the *same* face-track as *positive pairs* and define face and voice segments extracted from *different* face-tracks as *negative pairs* (this approach was also taken for single modality in [14]).

Since our objective is to learn embeddings that place identities together, rather than capturing synchronous, intrinsic factors (such as emotion expressions, or lexical content), we do not constrain the face associated with a positive pair to be temporally aligned with the audio. Instead it is sampled uniformly from the speaking face-track, preventing the model from learning to use synchronous clues to align the embeddings (see Fig. 2). We next describe the procedure for pair selection during training.

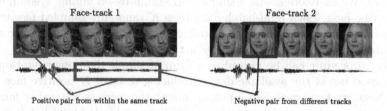

Face-track 1   Face-track 2

Positive pair from within the same track   Negative pair from different tracks

Fig. 2. Generating positive and negative face/voice pairs (Sect. 3.1). To prevent the embeddings from learning to encode synchronous nuisance factors, the frame for the positive face is not temporally aligned with the sequence for the voice.

4   The Importance of Curriculum-Based Mining

One of the key challenges associated with learning embeddings via contrastive losses is that as the dataset gets larger the number of possible pairs grows quadratically. In such a scenario, the network rapidly learns to correctly map the easy examples, but hard positive and negative mining [12,21,42,44,49] is often required to improve performance further. In the context of our task, a neural network of sufficient capacity quickly learns to embed faces and voices of differing genders far apart—samples from different genders then become "easy" negative pairs. Since gender forms only one of the many components that make up identity, we would like to ensure that the embeddings also learn to encode other factors. However, as we do not know the identities of the speaker face-tracks a priori, we cannot enforce sampling of gender-matched negative pairs. We tackle this issue with a hard negative mining approach that does not require knowledge of the identities during training.

When used in the unsupervised setting, hard negative selection is a somewhat delicate process, particularly when networks are trained from scratch. If the negative samples are too hard, the network will focus disproportionally on outliers, and may struggle to learn a meaningful embedding. In our setting, the hardest negatives are particularly dangerous, since they may in fact correspond to false negative labels (in which a voice and a face of the *same* identity has been sampled by chance from different speaking face-tracks)[1].

4.1 Controlling the Difficulty of Mined Negatives

Standard online hard example mining (OHEM) techniques [21,41] sample the hardest positive and negative pairs within a minibatch. However, in our setting hard positive mining may be of limited value since we do not expect the video data to exhibit significant variability within speaking face-tracks. If the hardest negative example within each mini-batch is selected, training with large batches leads to an increased risk of outliers or false negatives (i.e. pairs labelled as negatives which are actually positives), both of which will lead to poor learning dynamics. We therefore devise a simple curriculum-based mining system, which we describe next. Each mini-batch comprises K randomly sampled face-tracks. For each face-track we construct a positive pair by uniformly sampling a single frame x_f, and uniformly sampling a three second audio segment x_v. This sampling procedure can be viewed as a form of simple data augmentation and makes good use of the available data, producing a set of K positive face-voice pairs. Next, we treat each face input x_f among the pairs as an *anchor face* and select an *appropriately hard* negative sample from within the mini-batch. This is achieved by computing the distances between its corresponding face embedding and all voice embeddings with the exception of its directly paired voice, leading to a total of $K - 1$ potential negatives. The potential negatives are then ranked in descending order based on their distance to the anchor face (with the last element being the hardest negative in the batch), and the appropriate negative is chosen according to a 'negative difficulty parameter' τ. This parameter simply corresponds to the percentile of the ranked negatives: $\tau = 1$ is the hardest negative, $\tau = 0.5$ the median, and $\tau = 0$ the easiest. This parameter τ can be tuned just like a learning rate. In practice, we found that a schedule that selects easier

---

[1] For a given face image and voice sampled from different speaking face-tracks, the false negative rate of the labelling diminishes as the number of identities represented in the videos grows.

negatives during early epochs of training, and harder negatives for later epochs to be particularly effective[2]. While selecting the appropriate negative, we also ensure that the distance between the anchor face to the threshold negative is larger than the distance between the anchor face and the positive face, (following the semi-hard negative mining procedure outlined in [40]). Pseudocode for the mining procedure is provided in Appendix A and the effect of our curriculum mining procedure on training is examined in more detail in the ablation analysis (Appendix B.1), demonstrating that it plays an important role in achieving good performance.

5   Dataset

We learn the joint face-voice embeddings on VoxCeleb [34], a large-scale dataset of audio-visual human speech video extracted 'in the wild' from YouTube. The dataset contains over $100,000$ segmented *speaking face-tracks* obtained using SyncNet [12] from over 20k challenging videos. The speech audio is naturally degraded with background noise, laughter, and varying room acoustics, while the face images span a range of lighting conditions, image quality and pose variations (see Fig. 5 for examples of face images present in the dataset). VoxCeleb also contains labels for the identities of the celebrities, which, we stress, are not used while learning the joint embeddings. We make use of the labels only for the purposes of analysing the learned representations – they allow us to evaluate their properties numerically and visualise their structure (e.g. Fig. 4). We use two train/test splits for the purpose of this task. The first split is provided with the dataset, and consists of disjoint videos from the same set of speakers. This can be used to evaluate data from identities seen and heard during training. We also create a second split which consists of 100 randomly selected disjoint identities for validation, and 250 disjoint identities for testing. We train the model using the intersection of the two training sets, allowing us to evaluate on both test sets, the first one for seen-heard identities, and the second for unseen-unheard identities. The statistics of the dataset are given in Table 1.

6   Experiments

We experiment with two initialisation techniques, training from scratch (where the parameters for both subnetworks are initialised randomly) and using pre-trained subnetworks. In the latter formulation, both the subnetworks are initialised using weights trained for identification within a single modality. We also experiment with a teacher-student style architecture, where the face subnetwork

---

[2] It is difficult to tune this parameter based on the loss alone, since a stagnating loss curve is not necessarily indicative of a lack of progress. As the network improves its performance at a certain difficulty, it will be presented with more difficult pairs and continue to incur a high loss. Hence we observe the mean distance between positive pairs in a minibatch, mean distance between negative pairs in the minibatch, and mean distance between *active* pairs (those that contribute to the loss term) in the minibatch, and found that it was effective to increase τ by 10% every two epochs, starting from 30% up until 80%, and keeping it constant thereafter.

Table 1. Dataset statistics. Note the identity labels are not used at any point during training. SH: Seen-heard. US-UH: Unseen-unheard. The identities in the unseen-unheard test set are disjoint from those in the train set.

	Train	Test(S-H)	Val(US-UH)	Test(US-UH)
# speaking face-tracks	105,751	4,505	12,734	30,496
# identities	901	901	100	250

is initialised with pretrained weights which are frozen during training (teacher) and the voice subnetwork is trained from scratch (student), however we found that this leads to a drop in performance (an analysis is provided in Appendix B.2). We use weights pretrained for identity on the VGG-face dataset for the face subnetwork, and weights pretrained for speaker identification on the VoxCeleb dataset for the voice subnetwork.

6.1 Network Architectures and Implementation Details

Face Subnetwork: The face subnetwork is implemented using the VGG-M [10] architecture, with batch norm layers [22] added after every convolutional layer. The input to the face subnetwork is an RGB image, cropped from the source frame to include only the face region and resized to 224×224. The images are augmented using random horizontal flipping, brightness and saturation jittering, but we do not extract random crops from within the face region. The final fully connected layer of the VGG-M architecture is reduced to produce a single 256-D embedding for every face input. The embeddings are then L2-normalised before being passed into the pair selection layer for negative mining (Sect. 4).

Voice Subnetwork: The audio subnetwork is implemented using the VGG-Vox architecture [34], which is a modified version of VGG-M suitable for speaker recognition, also incorporating batch norm. The input is a short-term amplitude spectrogram, extracted from three seconds of raw audio using a 512-point FFT (following the approach in [34]), giving spectrograms of size 512×300. At train-time, the three second segment of audio is chosen randomly from the entire audio segment. Mean and variance normalisation is performed on every frequency bin of the spectrogram. Similarly to the face subnetwork, the dimensionality of the final fully connected layer is reduced to 256, and the 256-D voice embeddings are L2-normalised. At test time, the entire audio segment is evaluated using average pooling in an identical manner to [34].

The lightweight VGG-M inspired architectures described above have the benefit of computational efficiency and in practice we found that they performed reasonably well for our task. We note that either subnetwork could be replaced with a more computationally intensive trunk architecture without modification to our method.

Training Procedure: The networks are trained on three Titan X GPUs for 50 epochs using a batch-size of 256. We use SGD with momentum (0.9), weight decay $(5E - 4)$ and a logarithmically decaying learning rate (initialised to 10^{-2} and decaying to 10^{-8}). We experimented with different values of the margin for the contrastive loss $(0.2, 0.4, 0.6, 0.8)$ and found that a margin of 0.6 was optimal.

7   Evaluation

7.1   Cross-Modal Verification

We evaluate our network on the task of *cross-modal verification*, the objective of which is to determine whether two inputs from different modalities are semantically aligned. More specifically, given a face input and a speech segment, the goal is to determine if they belong to the same identity. Since there are no available benchmarks for this task, we create two evaluation protocols for the VoxCeleb dataset, one for *seen-heard* identities and one for *unseen-unheard* identities. For each evaluation benchmark test pairs are randomly sampled, $30,496$ pairs from unseen-unheard identities and $18,020$ pairs from seen-heard identities (a description of the evaluation protocol is in Appendix C) using the identity labels provided by VoxCeleb: positives are faces and voices of the same identity, and negative pairs are from differing identities.

Table 2. Cross-modal Verification: Results are reported for an untrained model (with random weights), as well as for the two initialisations described in Sect. 6.

	AUC %	EER %
Seen-Heard		
Random	50.3	49.8
Scratch	73.8	34.1
Pretrained	87.0	21.4
Unseen-Unheard		
Random	50.1	49.9
Scratch	63.5	39.2
Pretrained	78.5	29.6

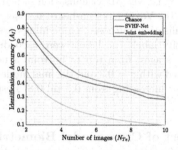

Fig. 3. N-way forced matching: We compare our joint embedding to SVHF-Net [33]. Our method comfortably beats the current state of the art for all values of N.

The results for cross-modal verification are reported in Table 2. We use standard metrics for verification, i.e area under the ROC curve (AUC) and equal error rate (EER). As can be seen from the table, the model learned from scratch performs significantly above random, even for unseen-unheard identities, providing evidence to support the hypothesis that it is, in fact, possible to learn a joint embedding for faces and voices with no explicit identity supervision. A visualisation of the embeddings is provided in Fig. 4, where we observe that the embeddings form loose groups of clusters based on identity. Initialising the model with two pretrained subnetworks brings expected performance gains and also performs surprisingly well for unseen-unheard identities, a task that is even difficult for humans to perform. Previous work has shown that on the less challenging forced matching task (selecting from two faces given a voice), human performance is around 80% [33].

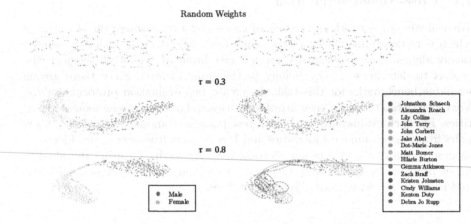

Fig. 4. t-SNE [31] visualisation of learnt embeddings for *faces only* from 15 identities from the VoxCeleb seen-heard test set. The model is trained entirely from scratch. For visualisation purposes, embeddings are coloured with (left) gender labels and (right) identity labels (no labels were used during training). The embeddings are shown for three stages, from top to bottom; a non-trained network (random weights), a model trained with $\tau = 0.3$ and the final model trained using our curriculum learning schedule, with τ increasing from 0.3 till 0.8. Best viewed in colour. (Color figure online)

Effect of Cross-modal Biometrics: In this section we examine the effect of specific latent properties (age, gender and nationality) which influence both face and voice. We evaluate the model by sampling negative test pairs while holding constant each of the following demographic criteria: gender (G), nationality (N) and age (A). Gender and nationality labels are obtained from Wikipedia. Since the age of a speaker could vary over different videos, we apply an age classifier [39] to the face frames (extracted at 1 fps) and average the age predictions over each video (see Appendix D for more details) (Table 3).

We find that gender is the most influential demographic factor. Studies in biology and evolutionary perception [47,50] also show that other more subtle factors such as hormone levels during puberty affect both face morphology and voice pitch, eg. lower voice pitch correlating with a stronger jawline. However since these factors are harder to quantify, we leave this analysis for future work.

Searching for Shortcuts (bias): As a consequence of their high modelling capacity, CNNs are notorious for learning to exploit biases that enables them to minimise the learning objective with trivial solutions (see [15] for an interesting

Table 3. Analysis of cross-modal biometrics under varying demographics: Results are reported for both seen-heard and unseen-unheard identities using AUC: Area Under Curve. Chance performance is 50%.

Demographic criteria	Random	G	N	A	GNA
Unseen-unheard (AUC %)	78.5	61.1	77.2	74.9	58.8
Seen-heard (AUC %)	87.0	74.2	85.9	86.6	74.0

discussion in the context of unsupervised learning). While we are careful to avoid correlations due to lexical content and emotion, there may be other low level correlations in the audio and video data that the network has learned to exploit. To probe the learned models for bias, we construct two additional evaluation sets. In both sets, negative pairs are selected following the same strategy as for the original evaluation set (they are faces and voices of different identities). However, we now sample positives pairs for the bias evaluation test sets as follows. For the first test set we sample positive pairs from the *same speaking face-track*, as opposed to sampling pairs from the same identity across all videos and speaking face-tracks (as done in our original evaluation set), and for the second test set we sample positive pairs from the *same video*. We then evaluate the performance of the model trained from scratch on the task of cross-modal verification. We obtain results that are slightly better when positive pairs are always from the same video (AUC: 74.5, EER: 33.8) vs (AUC:73.8, EER: 34.1, Table 2) on the original test set, but with minimal further improvement when they are constrained to belong to the same track (AUC: 74.6, EER: 33.6). This suggests that audio and faces taken from the same video have small additional correlations beyond possessing the same identity which the network has learned to exploit. For example, it is likely that blurry low quality videos are often accompanied by low quality audio, and that faces from professionally shot studio interviews often occur with high quality audio. While these signals are unavoidable artefacts of working with datasets collected 'in the wild', the difference in performance is slight, providing some measure of confidence that the network is relying primarily on identity to solve the task.

7.2 Cross-modal Retrieval with Varying Gallery Size

The learned joint embedding also enables cross-modal retrieval. Given a single query from one modality, the goal is to retrieve all semantically matching templates from another modality (here the set of all possible templates is referred to as the *gallery set*). This can be done for both the F-V formulation (using a face to retrieve voices of the same identity) and the V-F formulation (using a voice segment to retrieve matching faces). Since there are limited baselines available for this task, we instead perform a variant of cross-modal retrieval to allow us to compare with previous work [33] (which we refer to as SVHF-Net), which represents the current state of the art for matching faces and voices. In [33], a forced matching task is used to select the *single* semantically matching template from N options in another modality, and the SVHF-Net is trained directly to perform this task. Unlike this work where we learn a joint embedding, SVHF-Net consists of a concatenation layer which allows comparison of the two modalities, i.e. learnt representations in each modality are not aligned. In order to compare our method to SVHF-Net, a query set is made using all the available test samples in a particular modality. For example for the V-F formulation (used in [33]), we use all the voice segments in our unseen-unheard test set. A gallery of size N is then created for each query – a gallery consists of a single positive face and N-1 negative faces from different identities. We adopt a simple method to perform the task: the query embedding is compared directly to the embeddings of all the faces in the gallery using the Euclidean distance, and the closest embedding is chosen as the retrieved result. We compare to SVHF-Net directly on our test set, for values $N = 2$ to 10. A comparison of the results is given in Fig. 3.

We observe that learning a joint embedding and using this embedding directly to match faces and voices, outperforms previous work [33] for all values of N. In addition, note that in contrast to the SVHF-Net [33] which cannot be used if there is more than one matching sample in the gallery set, our joint embedding can be used directly to provide a ranking. In addition to the numerical results for the V-F formulation (this is the formulation used by [33]) we present qualitative results for both the V-F and face to voice (F-V) formulations in Fig. 5.

Fig. 5. Qualitative results for cross-modal *forced matching* (selecting the matching template from N samples). We show results for $N = 10$. A query sample from one modality is shown on the left, and 10 templates from the other modality are shown on the right. For each formulation, we show four successful predictions, with the matching template highlighted in green (top four rows in each set) and one failure case (bottom row in each set) with the ground truth highlighted in green and the model prediction in red. Best viewed zoomed in and in colour. (Color figure online)

8   One-Shot Learning for TV Show Character Retrieval

One shot retrieval in TV shows is the extremely challenging task of recognising all appearances of a character in a TV show or feature film, with only a single face image as a query. This is difficult because of the significant visual variation of character appearances in a TV show caused by pose, illumination, size, expression and occlusion, which can often exceed those due to identity. Recently there has been a growing interest in the use of the audio-track to aid identification [8,35,46] which comes for free with multimedia videos. However, because face and voice representations are usually not aligned, in prior work the query face cannot be directly compared to the audio track, necessitating the use of complex fusion systems to combine information from both modalites. For example, [8] use clustering on face-tracks and diarised speaker segments after a round of human annotation for both, [35] use confidence labels from one modality to provide supervsion for the other modality, and [46] fuse the outputs of a face recognition model, and a clothing model, with a GMM-based speaker model. With a joint embedding, however, the query face image can be compared directly to the audio track, leading to an extremely simple solution which we describe below.

Method: For this evaluation, we use the tracks and labels provided by [35] for episode 1 of the TV series 'Sherlock'. In order to demonstrate the effectiveness of using voice information as well, we use only the 336 speaking face-tracks from the episode, which are often the most difficult to classify visually due to large variations in head pose (it is extremely rare for the speaker to look directly at the camera during a conversation). We demonstrate our method on the retrieval of the two most frequently appearing characters, Sherlock and John, from among all the other 17 classes in the episode (16 principal characters and a single class for all the background characters).

A single query face is selected randomly for Sherlock and for John, and an embedding computed for the query using our face representation. Each face-track from the set of total tracks is then split into frames, and embeddings for each face detection are computed using our learned face representation, giving a 256-D vector for each face. The vectors are then averaged over all frames, leading to a single 256-D embedding for every track. Audio segments are also extracted for each track, and an embedding computed using our learned voice representation, giving a 256-D vector for each track in a similar fashion.

Because our representations are aligned, for each track, we can compare both the visual track and the audio track embeddings directly to the features of the query image, using L2 Euclidean distance. The tracks are then ranked according to this final score. We report results for 3 cases, retrieval using visual embeddings alone, retrieval using audio embeddings alone, and a simple fusion method where we take the maximum score out of the two (i.e. we pick the score of the modality that is closest in distance to the query image). Note, none of the identities in the episode are in the VoxCeleb training set, this test is for unseen-unheard identities. As can be seen from Table 4, using information from both modalities provides a slight improvement over using face or speech alone. Such a fusion method is useful for cases when one modality is a far stronger cue, e.g. when the face is too small or dark, or for extreme poses where the voice can still be clear [35]. On the other hand facial appearance scores can be higher when voice segments are corrupted with crosstalk, background effects, music, laughter, or other noise. We note that a superior fusion strategy could be applied in order to better exploit this complementary information from both modalities (e.g. an attention based strategy) and we leave this for future work.

Table 4. One-shot retrieval results: Retrieval from amongst 17 categories, 16 principal characters and 1 class for all the background characters. A higher AUC is better.

	Sherlock (AUC %)	John (AUC %)
Face only	35.0	44.6
Voice only	28.7	37.2
Max fusion	**37.5**	**45.4**

Fig. 6. Results of one-shot retrieval for speaking face-tracks from the TV series 'Sherlock'. A single query image and the top 5 retrieved results are shown. For each query we show tracks retrieved using only the face embeddings of the tracks (F only), and using both the face and voice embeddings (FV max). The middle frame of each retrieved track is shown. Note how FV fusion allows more profile faces to be retrieved – row 2, second and fourth frames, and row 4, third ranked frame. Face detections are green for correctly retrieved faces and red otherwise. Best viewed in colour. (Color figure online)

9   Conclusion

We have demonstrated the somewhat counter-intuitive result – that face and voice can be jointly embedded and enable cross-modal retrieval for unseen and unheard identities. We have also shown an application of this joint embedding to character retrieval in TV shows. Other possible applications include biometric security, for example a face in video footage can be directly compared to an existing dataset which is in another modality, e.g. a scenario where only voice data is stored because it was obtained from telephone conversations. The joint embedding could also be used to check whether the face in a video actually matches the voice, as part of a system to detect tampering (e.g. detecting 'Deepfakes' [26]).

Identity is more than just the face. Besides voice, identity is also in a person's gait, the way the face moves when speaking (a preliminary exploration is provided in Appendix E), the way expressions form, etc. So, this work can be extended to include more cues – in accord with the original abstraction of a PIN.

Acknowledgements. The authors gratefully acknowledge the support of EPSRC CDT AIMS grant EP/L015897/1 and the Programme Grant Seebibyte EP/M013774/1. The authors would also like to thank Judith Albanie for helpful suggestions.

References

1. Albanie, S., Nagrani, A., Vedaldi, A., Zisserman, A.: Emotion recognition in speech using cross-modal transfer in the wild. In: Proceedings of the 2018 ACM on Multimedia Conference. ACM (2018)
2. Arandjelovic, R., Zisserman, A.: Look, listen and learn. In: ICCV, pp. 609–617. IEEE (2017)
3. Arandjelović, R., Zisserman, A.: Objects that sound (2017). arXiv preprint: arXiv:1712.06651
4. Aytar, Y., Vondrick, C., Torralba, A.: Soundnet: learning sound representations from unlabeled video. In: NIPS, pp. 892–900 (2016)
5. Barnard, K., et al.: Matching words and pictures. J. Mach. Learn. Res. **3**, 1107–1135 (2003)
6. Bruce, V., Young, A.: Understanding face recognition. Br. J. Psychol. **77**(3), 305–327 (1986)
7. Brunelli, R., Falavigna, D.: Person identification using multiple cues. IEEE Trans. Pattern Anal. Mach. Intell. **17**(10), 955–966 (1995)
8. Budnik, M., Poignant, J., Besacier, L., Quénot, G.: Automatic propagation of manual annotations for multimodal person identification in TV shows. In: 2014 12th International Workshop on Content-Based Multimedia Indexing (CBMI), pp. 1–4. IEEE (2014)
9. Cao, Q., Shen, L., Xie, W., Parkhi, O.M., Zisserman, A.: Vggface2: a dataset for recognising faces across pose and age. In: Proceedings of the International Conference on Automatic Face and Gesture Recognition (2018)
10. Chatfield, K., Lempitsky, V., Vedaldi, A., Zisserman, A.: The devil is in the details: an evaluation of recent feature encoding methods. In: Proceedings of BMVC (2011)
11. Chopra, S., Hadsell, R., LeCun, Y.: Learning a similarity metric discriminatively, with application to face verification. In: Proceedings of CVPR, vol. 1, pp. 539–546. IEEE (2005)
12. Chung, J.S., Zisserman, A.: Out of time: automated lip sync in the wild. In: Chen, C.-S., Lu, J., Ma, K.-K. (eds.) ACCV 2016, Part II. LNCS, vol. 10117, pp. 251–263. Springer, Cham (2017). https://doi.org/10.1007/978-3-319-54427-4_19
13. Chung, J.S., Nagrani, A., Zisserman, A.: Voxceleb2: deep speaker recognition. In: INTERSPEECH (2018)
14. Cinbis, R.G., Verbeek, J., Schmid, C.: Unsupervised metric learning for face identification in TV video. In: 2011 IEEE International Conference on Computer Vision (ICCV), pp. 1559–1566. IEEE (2011)

15. Doersch, C., Gupta, A., Efros, A.A.: Unsupervised visual representation learning by context prediction. In: Proceedings of the IEEE International Conference on Computer Vision, pp. 1422–1430 (2015)
16. Duygulu, P., Barnard, K., de Freitas, J.F.G., Forsyth, D.A.: Object recognition as machine translation: learning a lexicon for a fixed image vocabulary. In: Heyden, A., Sparr, G., Nielsen, M., Johansen, P. (eds.) ECCV 2002, Part IV. LNCS, vol. 2353, pp. 97–112. Springer, Heidelberg (2002). https://doi.org/10.1007/3-540-47979-1_7
17. Gordo, A., Larlus, D.: Beyond instance-level image retrieval: Leveraging captions to learn a global visual representation for semantic retrieval. In: IEEE Conference on Computer Vision and Pattern Recognition (CVPR) (2017)
18. Guo, Y., Zhang, L., Hu, Y., He, X., Gao, J.: MS-Celeb-1M: challenge of recognizing one million celebrities in the real world. Electron. Imaging **2016**(11), 1–6 (2016)
19. Hadsell, R., Chopra, S., LeCun, Y.: Dimensionality reduction by learning an invariant mapping. In: CVPR, vol. 2, pp. 1735–1742. IEEE (2006)
20. Harwath, D., Torralba, A., Glass, J.: Unsupervised learning of spoken language with visual context. In: Advances in Neural Information Processing Systems, pp. 1858–1866 (2016)
21. Hermans, A., Beyer, L., Leibe, B.: In defense of the triplet loss for person re-identification (2017). arXiv preprint: arXiv:1703 07737
22. Ioffe, S., Szegedy, C.: Batch normalization: accelerating deep network training by reducing internal covariate shift (2015). arXiv preprint: arXiv:1502.03167
23. Kemelmacher-Shlizerman, I., Seitz, S.M., Miller, D., Brossard, E.: The megaface benchmark: 1 million faces for recognition at scale. In: Proceedings of the IEEE Conference on Computer Vision and Pattern Recognition, pp. 4873–4882 (2016)
24. Khoury, E., El Shafey, L., McCool, C., Günther, M., Marcel, S.: Bi-modal biometric authentication on mobile phones in challenging conditions. Image Vis. Comput. **32**(12), 1147–1160 (2014)
25. Kidron, E., Schechner, Y.Y., Elad, M.: Pixels that sound. In: IEEE Computer Society Conference on Computer Vision and Pattern Recognition, CVPR 2005, vol. 1, pp. 88–95. IEEE (2005)
26. Kim, H., et al.: Deep video portraits. In: SIGGRAPH (2018)
27. Kiros, R., Salakhutdinov, R., Zemel, R.S.: Unifying visual-semantic embeddings with multimodal neural language models (2014). arXiv preprint: arXiv:1411.2539
28. Lampert, C.H., Krömer, O.: Weakly-paired maximum covariance analysis for multimodal dimensionality reduction and transfer learning. In: Daniilidis, K., Maragos, P., Paragios, N. (eds.) ECCV 2010, Part II. LNCS, vol. 6312, pp. 566–579. Springer, Heidelberg (2010). https://doi.org/10.1007/978-3-642-15552-9_41
29. Le, N., Odobez, J.M.: Improving speaker turn embedding by cross-modal transfer learning from face embedding (2017). arXiv preprint: arXiv:1707.02749
30. Li, D., Dimitrova, N., Li, M., Sethi, I.K.: Multimedia content processing through cross-modal association. In: Proceedings of the Eleventh ACM International Conference on Multimedia, pp. 604–611. ACM (2003)
31. van der Maaten, L., Hinton, G.: Visualizing data using t-SNE. J. Mach. Learn. Res. **9**, 2579–2605 (2008)
32. McLaren, M., Ferrer, L., Castan, D., Lawson, A.: The speakers in the wild (SITW) speaker recognition database. In: Interspeech, pp. 818–822 (2016)
33. Nagrani, A., Albanie, S., Zisserman, A.: Seeing voices and hearing faces: cross-modal biometric matching. In: Proceedings of CVPR (2018)
34. Nagrani, A., Chung, J.S., Zisserman, A.: Voxceleb: a large-scale speaker identification dataset. In: INTERSPEECH (2017)

35. Nagrani, A., Zisserman, A.: From benedict cumberbatch to sherlock holmes: character identification in TV series without a script. In: Proceedings of BMVC (2017)
36. Ngiam, J., Khosla, A., Kim, M., Nam, J., Lee, H., Ng, A.Y.: Multimodal deep learning. In: Proceedings of the 28th International Conference on Machine Learning (ICML 2011), pp. 689–696 (2011)
37. Owens, A., Wu, J., McDermott, J.H., Freeman, W.T., Torralba, A.: Ambient sound provides supervision for visual learning. In: Leibe, B., Matas, J., Sebe, N., Welling, M. (eds.) ECCV 2016, Part I. LNCS, vol. 9905, pp. 801–816. Springer, Cham (2016). https://doi.org/10.1007/978-3-319-46448-0_48
38. Parkhi, O.M., Vedaldi, A., Zisserman, A.: Deep face recognition. In: Proceedings of BMVC (2015)
39. Rothe, R., Timofte, R., Van Gool, L.: Deep expectation of real and apparent age from a single image without facial landmarks. Int. J. Comput. Vis. **126**, 144–157 (2018)
40. Schroff, F., Kalenichenko, D., Philbin, J.: Facenet: a unified embedding for face recognition and clustering. In: Proceedings of CVPR (2015)
41. Shrivastava, A., Gupta, A., Girshick, R.: Training region-based object detectors with online hard example mining. In: Proceedings of the IEEE Conference on Computer Vision and Pattern Recognition, pp. 761–769 (2016)
42. Song, H.O., Xiang, Y., Jegelka, S., Savarese, S.: Deep metric learning via lifted structured feature embedding. In: 2016 IEEE Conference on Computer Vision and Pattern Recognition (CVPR), pp. 4004–4012. IEEE (2016)
43. Srivastava, N., Salakhutdinov, R.R.: Multimodal learning with deep Boltzmann machines. In: Advances in Neural Information Processing Systems, pp. 2222–2230 (2012)
44. Sung, K.K.: Learning and example selection for object and pattern detection (1996)
45. Taigman, Y., Yang, M., Ranzato, M., Wolf, L.: Deepface: closing the gap to human-level performance in face verification. In: Proceedings of CVPR, pp. 1701–1708 (2014)
46. Tapaswi, M., Bäuml, M., Stiefelhagen, R.: "Knock! knock! who is it?" probabilistic person identification in tv-series. In: 2012 IEEE Conference on Computer Vision and Pattern Recognition (CVPR), pp. 2658–2665. IEEE (2012)
47. Thornhill, R., Møller, A.P.: Developmental stability, disease and medicine. Biol. Rev. **72**, 497–548 (1997)
48. Wang, L., Li, Y., Lazebnik, S.: Learning deep structure-preserving image-text embeddings. In: Proceedings of the IEEE Conference on Computer Vision and Pattern Recognition, pp. 5005–5013 (2016)
49. Wang, X., Gupta, A.: Unsupervised learning of visual representations using videos (2015). arXiv preprint: arXiv:1505.00687
50. Wells, T., Baguley, T., Sergeant, M., Dunn, A.: Perceptions of human attractiveness comprising face and voice cues. Arch. Sex. Behav. **42**, 805–811 (2013)
51. Zhang, C., Bengio, S., Hardt, M., Recht, B., Vinyals, O.: Understanding deep learning requires rethinking generalization (2016). arXiv preprint: arXiv:1611.03530
52. Zhang, C., Koishida, K., Hansen, J.H.: Text-independent speaker verification based on triplet convolutional neural network embeddings. IEEE/ACM Trans. Audio Speech Lang. Process. **26**(9), 1633–1644 (2018)

Separating Reflection and Transmission Images in the Wild

Patrick Wieschollek[1,2]([✉]), Orazio Gallo[1], Jinwei Gu[1], and Jan Kautz[1]

[1] NVIDIA, Santa Clara, CA, USA
mail@patwie.com
[2] University of Tübingen, Tübingen, Germany

Abstract. The reflections caused by common semi-reflectors, such as glass windows, can impact the performance of computer vision algorithms. State-of-the-art methods can remove reflections on synthetic data and in controlled scenarios. However, they are based on strong assumptions and do not generalize well to real-world images. Contrary to a common misconception, real-world images are challenging even when polarization information is used. We present a deep learning approach to separate the reflected and the transmitted components of the recorded irradiance, which *explicitly* uses the polarization properties of light. To train it, we introduce an accurate synthetic data generation pipeline, which simulates realistic reflections, including those generated by curved and non-ideal surfaces, non-static scenes, and high-dynamic-range scenes.

1 Introduction

Computer vision algorithms generally rely on the assumption that the value of each pixel is a function of the radiance of a single area in the scene. Semi-reflectors, such as typical windows or glass doors, break this assumption by creating a superposition of the radiance of two different objects: the one behind the surface and the one that is reflected. It is virtually impossible to avoid semi-reflectors in man-made environments, as can be seen in Fig. 2(a), which shows a typical downtown area. Any multi-view stereo or SLAM algorithm would be hard-pressed to produce accurate reconstructions on this type of images.

Several methods exist that attempt to separate the reflection and transmission layers. At a semi-reflective surface, the observed image can be modeled as a linear combination of the reflection and the transmission images: $I_o = \alpha_r I_r + \alpha_t I_t$. The inverse problem is ill-posed as it requires estimating multiple unknowns from a single observation. A solution, therefore, requires additional priors or data. Indeed, previous works rely on assumptions about the appearance of the reflection (*e.g.*, it is blurry), about the shape and orientation of the surface (*e.g.*, it is perfectly flat and exactly perpendicular to the principal axis

---

Electronic supplementary material The online version of this chapter (https://doi.org/10.1007/978-3-030-01261-8_6) contains supplementary material, which is available to authorized users.

© Springer Nature Switzerland AG 2018
V. Ferrari et al. (Eds.): ECCV 2018, LNCS 11217, pp. 90–105, 2018.
https://doi.org/10.1007/978-3-030-01261-8_6

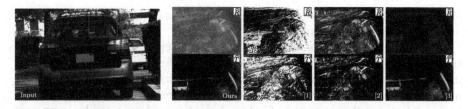

Fig. 1. Glass surfaces are virtually unavoidable in real-world pictures. Our approach to separate the reflection and transmission layers, works even for general, curved surfaces, which break the assumptions of state-of-the-art methods. In this example, only our method can correctly estimate both reflection $\widehat{R}$ (the tree branches) and transmission $\widehat{T}$ (the car's interior).

Fig. 2. Depending on the ratio between transmitted and reflected radiance, a semi-reflector may produce no reflections ❶, pure reflections ❷, or a mix of the two, which can vary smoothly ❸, or abruptly ❺. The local curvature of the surface can also affect the appearance of the reflection ❹. The last two, ❹ and ❺, are all but uncommon, as shown in (b).

of the camera), and others. Images taken in the wild, however, regularly break even the most basic of these assumptions, see Fig. 2(b), causing the results of state-of-the-art methods [2–4] to deteriorate even on seemingly simple cases, as shown in Fig. 1, which depicts a fairly typical real-world scene.

One particularly powerful tool is is polarization: images captured through a polarizer oriented at different angles offer additional observations. Perhaps surprisingly, however, our analysis of the state-of-the-art methods indicates that the quality of the results degrades significantly when moving from synthetic to real data, *even when using polarization*. This is due to the simplifying assumptions that are commonly made, but also to an inherent issue that is all too often neglected: a polarizer's ability to attenuate reflections greatly depends on the viewing angle [5]. The attenuation is maximal at an angle called the Brewster angle, θ_B. However, even when part of a semi-reflector is imaged at θ_B, the angle of incidence in other areas is sufficiently different from θ_B to essentially void the effect of the polarizer, as clearly shown in Fig. 3. Put differently, because of the limited signal-to-noise ratio, for certain regions in the scene, *the additional observations may not be independent.*

We present a deep-learning method capable of separating the reflection and transmission components of images captured *in the wild*. The success of the method stems from our two main contributions. First, rather than requiring a network to learn the reflected and transmitted images directly from the observations, we leverage the properties of light polarization and use a residual representation, in which the input images are projected onto the canonical polarization angles (Sects. 3.1 and 3.2). Second, we design an image-based data generator that faithfully reproduces the image formation model (Sect. 3.3).

We show that our method can successfully separate the reflection and transmission layers even in challenging cases, on which previous works fail. To further validate our findings, we capture the Urban Reflections Dataset, a polarization-based dataset of reflections in urban environments that can be used to test reflection removal algorithms on realistic images. Moreover, to perform a thorough evaluation against state-of-the-art methods whose implementation is not publicly available, we re-implemented several representative methods. As part of our contribution, we release those implementations for others to be able to compare against their own methods [1].

2   Related Work

There is a rich literature of methods dealing with semi-reflective surfaces, which can be organized in three main categories based on the assumptions they make.

Single-image methods can leverage gradient information to solve the problem. Levin and Weiss, for instance, require manual input to separate gradients of the reflection and the transmission [6]. Methods that are fully automated can distinguish the gradients of the reflected and transmitted images by leveraging the defocus blur [7]: reflections can be blurry because the subject behind the semi-reflector is much closer than the reflected image [4], or because the camera is focused at infinity and the reflected objects are close to the surface [8]. Moreover, for the case of double-pane or thick windows, the reflection can appear "doubled" [9], and this can be used to separate it from the transmitted image [10]. While these methods show impressive results, their assumptions are stringent and do not generalize well to real-world cases, causing them to fail on common cases.

Multiple images captured from different viewpoints can also be used to remove reflections. Several methods propose different ways to estimate the relative motion of the reflected and transmitted image, which can be used to separate them [11–15]. It is important to note that these methods assume static scenes— the motion is the apparent motion of the reflected layer relative to the transmitted layer, not scene motion. Other than that, these methods make assumptions that are less stringent than those made by single-image methods. Nonetheless, these algorithms work well when reflected and transmitted scenes are shallow in terms of depth, so that their velocity can be assumed uniform. For the case of spatially and temporally varying mixes, Kaftory and Zeevi propose to use sparse component analysis instead [16].

Multiple images captured under different polarization angles offer a third venue to tackle this problem. Assuming that images taken at different polarization angles offer independent measurements of the same scene, reflection and transmission can be separated using independent component analysis [17–19]. An additional prior that can be leveraged is given by double reflections, when the semi-reflective surface generates them [9]. Under ideal conditions, and leveraging polarization information, a solution can also be found in closed form [2,3]. In our experiments, we found that most of the pictures captured in unconstrained settings break even the well-founded assumptions used by these papers, as shown in Fig. 2.

3   Method

We address the problem of layer decomposition by leveraging the ability of a semi-reflector to polarize the reflected and transmitted layers differently. Capturing multiple polarization images of the same scene, then, offers partially independent observations of the two layers. To use this information, we take a deep learning approach. Since the ground truth for this problem is virtually impossible to capture, we synthesize it. As for any data-driven approach, the realism of the training data is paramount to the quality of the results. In this section, after reviewing the image formation model, we give an overview of our approach, we discuss the limitations of the assumptions that are commonly made, and how we address them in our data generation pipeline. Finally, we describe the details of our implementation.

3.1   Polarization, Reflections, and Transmissions

Consider two points, P_R and P_T such that P_R', the reflection of P_R, lies on the line of sight of P_T, and assume that both emit unpolarized light, see Fig. 3. After being reflected or transmitted, unpolarized light becomes polarized by an amount that depends on θ, the *angle of incidence* (AOI).

At point P_S, the intersection of the line of sight and the surface, the total radiance L is a combination of the reflected radiance L_R, and the transmitted radiance L_T. Assume we place a linear polarizer with polarization angle ϕ in front of the camera. If we integrate over the exposure time, the intensity at *each pixel* x is

$$I_\phi(x) = \alpha(\theta, \phi_\perp, \phi) \cdot \frac{I_R(x)}{2} + (1 - \alpha(\theta, \phi_\perp, \phi)) \cdot \frac{I_T(x)}{2}, \qquad (1)$$

where the mixing coefficient $\alpha(\cdot) \in [0, 1]$, the angle of incidence $\theta(x) \in [0, \pi/2]$, the p–polarization direction [2] $\phi_\perp(x) \in [-\pi/4, \pi/4]$, and the reflected and transmitted images *at the semi-reflector*, $I_R(x)$ and $I_T(x)$, are all unknown.

At the Brewster angle, θ_B, the reflected light is completely polarized along $\phi_\perp$, *i.e.* in the direction perpendicular to the incidence plane[1], and the transmitted light along $\phi_\parallel$, the direction parallel to the plane of incidence. The angles $\phi_\perp$ and $\phi_\parallel$ are called the *canonical* polarization angles. In the unique condition in which $\theta(x) = \theta_B$, two images captured with the polarizer at the canonical polarization angles offer independent observations that are sufficient to disambiguate between I_R and I_T. Unless the camera or the semi-reflector are at infinity, however, $\theta(x) = \theta_B$ only holds for few points in the scene, if any, as shown in Fig. 3. To complicate things, for curved surfaces, $\theta(x)$ varies non-linearly with x. Finally, even for arbitrarily many acquisitions at different polarization angles, ϕ_j, the problem remains ill-posed as each observation I_{ϕ_j} adds new pixel-wise unknowns $\alpha(\theta, \phi_\perp, \phi_j)$.

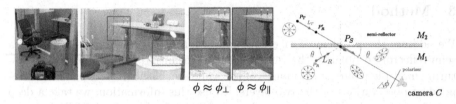

Fig. 3. A polarizer attenuates reflections when they are viewed at the Brewster angle $\theta = \theta_B$. For the scene shown on the left, we manually selected the two polarization directions that maximize and minimize reflections respectively. Indeed, the reflection of the plant is almost completely removed. However, only a few degrees away from the Brewster angle, the polarizer has little to no effect, as is the case for the reflection of the book on the right.

3.2   Recovering R and T

When viewed through a polarizer oriented along direction ϕ, I_R and I_T, which are the reflected and transmitted images *at the semi-reflector*, produce image I_ϕ at the sensor. Due to differences in dynamic range, as well as noise, in some regions the reflection may dominate I_ϕ, or vice versa, see Sect. 3.3. Without hallucinating content, one can only aim at separating R and T, which we define to be the observable reflected and transmitted components. For instance, T may be zero in regions where R dominates, even though I_T may be greater than zero in those regions. To differentiate them from the ground truth, we refer to our estimates as $\widehat{R}$ and $\widehat{T}$.

To recover $\widehat{R}$ and $\widehat{T}$, we use an encoder-decoder architecture, which has been shown to be particularly effective for a number of tasks, such as image-to-image translation [20], denoising [21], or deblurring [22]. Learning to estimate $\widehat{R}$ and $\widehat{T}$ directly from images taken at arbitrary polarization angles does not produce

---

[1] The incidence plane is defined by the direction in which the light is traveling and the semi-reflector's normal.

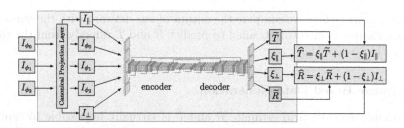

Fig. 4. Our encoder-decoder network architecture with ResNet blocks includes a Canonical Projection Layer, which projects the input images onto the canonical polarization directions, and uses a residual parametrization for $\widehat{T}$ and $\widehat{R}$.

satisfactory results. One main reason is that parts of the image may be pure reflections, thus yielding no information about the transmission, and vice versa.

To address this issue, we turn to the polarization properties of reflected and transmitted images. Recall that R and T are maximally attenuated, though generally not completely removed, at $\phi_\parallel$ and $\phi_\perp$ respectively. The canonical polarization angles depend on the geometry of the scene, and are thus hard to capture directly. However, we note that an image $I_\phi(x)$ can be expressed as [3]:

$$I_\phi(x) = I_\perp(x)\cos^2(\phi - \phi_\perp(x)) + I_\parallel(x)\sin^2(\phi - \phi_\perp(x)). \qquad (2)$$

Since Eq. 2 has three unknowns, $I_\perp$, $\phi_\perp$, and $I_\parallel$, we can use three different observations of the same scene, $\{I_{\phi_i}(x)\}_{i=\{0,1,2\}}$, to obtain a linear system that allows to compute $I_\perp(x)$ and $I_\parallel(x)$. To further simplify the math we capture images such that $\phi_i = \phi_0 + i \cdot \pi/4$.

For efficiency, we implement the projection onto the canonical views as a network layer in TensorFlow. The canonical views and the actual observations are then stacked in a 15-channel tensor and used as input to our network. Then, instead of training the network to learn to predict $\widehat{R}$ and $\widehat{T}$, we train it to learn the *residual* reflection and transmission layers. More specifically, we train the network to learn an 8-channel output, which comprises the residual images $\widetilde{T}(x)$, $\widetilde{R}(x)$, and the two single-channel weights $\xi_\parallel(x)$ and $\xi_\perp(x)$. Dropping the dependency on pixel x for clarity, we can then compute:

$$\widehat{R} = \xi_\perp\widetilde{R} + (1 - \xi_\perp)I_\perp \qquad \text{and} \qquad \widehat{T} = \xi_\parallel\widetilde{T} + (1 - \xi_\parallel)I_\parallel. \qquad (3)$$

While $\xi_\perp$ and $\xi_\parallel$ introduce two additional unknowns per pixel, they significantly simplify the prediction task in regions where the canonical projections are already good predictors of $\widehat{R}$ and $\widehat{T}$. We use an encoder-decoder with skip connections [23] that consists of three down-sampling stages, each with two ResNet blocks [24]. The corresponding decoder mirrors the encoding layers using a transposed convolution with two ResNet blocks. We use an ℓ_2 loss on $\widehat{R}$ and $\widehat{T}$. We also tested ℓ_1 and a combination of ℓ_1 and ℓ_2, which did not yield significant improvements.

The use of the canonical projection layer, as well as the parametrization of residual images is key for the success of our method. We show this in the

Supplementary, where we compare the output of our network with the output of the exact same architecture trained to predict $\widehat{R}$ and $\widehat{T}$ directly from the three polarization images $I_{\phi_i}(x)$.

3.3   Image-Based Data Generation

The ground truth data to estimate $\widehat{R}$ and $\widehat{T}$ is virtually impossible to capture in the wild. Recently, Wan *et al.* released a dataset for single-image reflection removal [25], but it does not offer polarization information. In principle, Eq. 1 could be used directly to generate, from any two images, the data we need. The term α in the equation, however, hides several subtleties and nonidealities. For instance, previous polarization-based works use it to synthesize data by assuming uniform AOI, perfectly flat surfaces, comparable power for the reflected and transmitted irradiance, or others. This generally translates to poor results on images captured in the wild: Figs. 1 and 2 show common scenes that violate all of these assumptions.

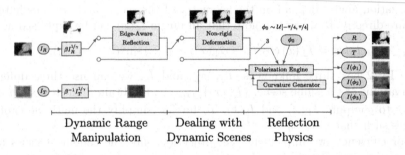

Fig. 5. Our image-based data generation procedure. We apply several steps to images I_R and I_T simulating reflections in most real-world scenarios (Sect. 3.3).

We propose a more accurate synthetic data generation pipeline, see Fig. 5. Our pipeline starts from two randomly picked images from the PLACE2 dataset [26], I_R and I_T, which we treat as the image of reflected and transmitted scene *at the surface*. From those, we model the behaviors observed in real-world data, which we describe as we "follow" the path of the photons from the scene to the camera.

Dynamic Range Manipulation at the Surface. To simulate realistic reflections, the dynamic range (DR) of the transmitted and reflected images *at the surface* must be significantly different. This is because real-world scenes are generally high-dynamic-range (HDR). Additionally, the light intensity at the surface drops with the distance from the emitting object, further expanding the combined DR. However, our inputs are low-dynamic-range images because a large dataset of HDR images is not available. We propose to artificially manipulate the DR of the inputs so as to match the appearance of the reflections we observe in real-world scenes.

Going back to Fig. 3 (right), we note that for regions where $L_T \approx L_R$, a picture taken without a polarizer will capture a smoothly varying superposition of the images of P_R and P_T (Fig. 2 ❸). For areas of the surface where $L_R \gg L_T$, however, the total radiance is $L \approx L_R$, and the semi-reflector essentially acts as a mirror (Fig. 2 ❷). The opposite situation is also common (Fig. 2 ❶). To allow for these distinct behaviors, we manipulate the dynamic range of the input images with a random factor $\beta \sim \mathcal{U}[1, K]$:

$$\tilde{I}_R = \beta I_R^{1/\gamma} \quad \text{and} \quad \tilde{I}_T = \frac{1}{\beta} I_T^{1/\gamma}, \tag{4}$$

where $1/\gamma$ linearizes the gamma-compressed inputs[2]. We impose that $K > 1$ to compensate for the fact that a typical glass surface transmits a much larger portion of the incident light than it reflects[3].

Images $\tilde{I}_R$ and $\tilde{I}_T$ can reproduce the types of reflections described above, but are limited to those cases for which $L_R - L_T$ changes smoothly with P_S. However, as shown in Fig. 2 ❺, the reflection can drop abruptly following the boundaries of an object. This may happen when an object is much closer than the rest of the scene, or when its radiance is larger than the surrounding objects. To properly model this behavior, we treat it as a type of reflection on its own, which we apply to a random subset of the image whose range we have already expanded. Specifically, we set to zero the regions of the reflection or transmission layer, whose intensity is below $T = \text{mean}(\tilde{I}_R + \tilde{I}_T)$, similarly to the method proposed by Fan et al. [4].

Dealing with Dynamic Scenes. Our approach requires images captured under three different polarization angles. While cameras that can simultaneously capture multiple polarization images exist [27–29], they are not widespread. To date, the standard way to capture different polarization images is sequential; this causes complications for non-static scenes. As mentioned in Sect. 2, if multiple pictures are captured from different locations, the relative motion between the transmitted and reflected layers can help disambiguate them. Here, however, "non-static" refers to the scene itself, such as is the case when a tree branch moves between the shots. Several approaches were proposed that can deal with dynamic scenes in the context of stack-based photography [30]. Rather than requiring some pre-processing to fix artifacts due to small scene changes at inference time, however, we propose to synthesize training data that simulates them, such as local, non-rigid deformations. We first define a regular grid over a patch, and then we perturb each one of the grid's anchors by (dx, dy), both sampled

---

[2] Approximating the camera response function with a gamma function does not affect the accuracy of our results, as we are not trying to produce data that is radiometrically accurate with respect to the original scenes.

[3] At an angle of incidence of $\pi/4$, for instance, a glass surface reflects less than 16% of the incident light.

from a Gaussian with variance σ_{NR}^2, which is also drawn randomly for each patch. We then interpolate the position of the rest of the pixels in the patch. For each input patch, we generate three different images, one per polarization angle. We only apply this processing to a subset of the synthesized images—the scene is not always dynamic. Figure 6(a) and (b) show an example of original and distorted patch respectively.

Geometry of the Semi-Reflective Surface. The images synthesized up to this point can be thought of as the irradiance of the unpolarized light at the semi-reflector. After bouncing off of, or going through, the surface, light becomes polarized as described in Sect. 3.1. The effect of a linear polarizer placed in front of the camera and oriented at a given polarization angle, depends on the angle of incidence (AOI) of the *specific* light ray. Some previous works assume this angle to be uniform over the image, which is only true if the camera is at infinity, or if the surface is flat.

We observe that real-world surfaces are hardly ever perfectly flat. Many common glass surfaces are in fact designed to be curved, as is the case of car windows, see Fig. 1. Even when the surfaces are meant to be flat, the imperfections of the glass manufacturing process introduce local curvatures, see Fig. 2 ❹.

At training time, we could generate unconstrained surface curvatures to account for this observation. However, it would be difficult to sample realistic surfaces. Moreover, the computation of the AOI from the surface curvature may be non-trivial. As a regularizer, we propose to use a parabola. When the patches are synthesized, we just sample four parameters: the camera position C, a point on the surface P_S, a segment length, ℓ, and the convexity as ± 1, Fig. 6(c). Since the segment is always mapped to the same output size, this parametrization allows to generate a number of different, realistic curvatures. Additionally, because we use a parabola, we can quickly compute the AOI in closed form, from the sample parameters, see Supplementary.

3.4 Implementation Details

From the output of the pipeline described so far, the simulated AOI, and a random polarization angle ϕ_0, the polarization engine generates three observations with polarization angles separated by $\pi/4$, see Fig. 5. In practice, the polarizer angles ϕ_i will be inaccurate for real data due to the manual adjustments of the polarizer rotation. We account for this by adding noise within $\pm 4°$ to each polarizer angle ϕ_i. Additionally we set $\beta \sim \mathcal{U}[1, 2.8]$. The input for our neural network is $\mathbb{R}^{B \times 128 \times 128 \times 9}$ when trained on 128×128 patches, where $B = 32$ is the batch size. We trained the model from scratch with a learning rate $5 \cdot 10^{-3}$ using ADAM. See the Supplementary for more details about the architecture. The colors of the network predictions might be slightly desaturated [4,31,32]. We use a parameter-free color-histogram matching against one of the observations to obtain the final results.

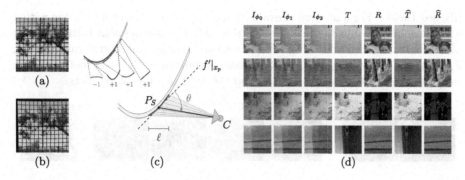

Fig. 6. Examples of our non-rigid motion deformation (a, b) and a curved surface-generator given the camera position, C, a surface-point, P_S, length, ℓ, and the convexity ± 1 (c). Randomly sampled training data (d) with synthesized observations I_{ϕ_0}, I_{ϕ_1}, I_{ϕ_2} from the ground truth data T and R, and estimates $\widehat{T}$, $\widehat{R}$.

4 Experiments

In this section we evaluate our method and data modeling pipeline on both synthetic and real data. For the latter, we introduce the Urban Reflections Dataset (URD), a new dataset of images containing semi-reflectors captured with polarization information. A fair evaluation can only be done against other polarization-based methods, which use multiple images. However, we also compare against single-image methods for completeness.

The Urban Reflections Dataset (URD). For practical relevance, we compile a dataset of 28 high-resolution RAW images (24MP) that are taken in urban environments using two different consumer cameras (Alpha 6000 and Canon EOS 7D, both ASP-C sensors), and which we make publicly available. The Supplementary shows all the pictures in the dataset. This dataset includes examples taken with a wide aperture, and while focusing on the plane of the semi-reflector, thus meeting the assumptions of Fan *et al.* [4].

4.1 Numerical Performance Evaluation

Due to the need for ground-truth, a large-scale numerical evaluation can only be performed on synthetic data. For this task we take two datasets, the VOC2012 [33] and the PLACE2 [26] datasets. A comparison with state-of-the-art methods shows that our method outperforms the second best method by a significant margin in terms of PSNR: ~ 2

Table 1. Cross-validation on synthetic data. Best results in bold.

Method	PASCAL VOC 2012		PLACE2	
	RMSE	PSNR	RMSE	PSNR
Farid *et al.* [17]	0.401	7.93	0.380	8.38
Kong *et al.* [3]	0.160	15.88	0.156	16.12
Schechner *et al.* [2]	0.085	21.34	0.086	21.27
Fan *et al.* [4]	0.080	21.89	0.084	21.48
Ours	**0.064**	**23.83**	**0.066**	**23.58**

dB, see Table 1. For a numerical evaluation on real data, we set up a scene with a glass surface and objects causing reflections. After capturing polarization images of the scene, we removed the glass and captured the ground truth transmission, T_{gt}. Figure 7 shows the transmission images estimated by different methods. Our method achieves the highest PSRN, and the least amount of artifacts.

Fig. 7. By removing the semi-reflector, we can capture the ground truth transmission, T_{gt}, optically.

4.2   Effect of Data Modeling

We also thoroughly validate our data-generation pipeline. Using both synthetic and real data, we show that the proposed non-rigid deformation (NRD) procedure and the local curvature generation (LCG) are effective and necessary. To do this, we train our network until convergence on three types of data: data generated only with the proposed dynamic range manipulation, DR for short, data generated with DR + NRD, and data generated with DR + NRD + LCG.

We evaluate these three models on a hold-out synthetic validation set that features all the transformations from Fig. 5. The table in Fig. 8 shows that the PSNR drops significantly when only part of our pipeline is used to train the network. Unfortunately, a numerical evaluation is only possible when the ground truth is available. However, Fig. 8 shows the output of the three models on the real image from Fig. 1. The benefits of using the full pipeline are apparent.

A visual inspection of Fig. 1 allows to appreciate that, thanks to our ability to deal with curved surfaces and dynamic scenes, we achieve better performance than the state-of-the-art methods.

4.3   Evaluation on Real-World Examples

We extensively evaluate our method against previous work on the proposed URD. For fairness towards competing methods, which make stronger assumptions or expect different input data, we slightly adapt them, or run them multiple times with different parameters retaining only the best result. Due to space constraints, Fig. 10 only shows seven of the results. We refer the reader to the Supplementary for the rest of the results and for a detailed explanation about how we adapted previous methods. One important remark is in order. Although the images we use include opaque objects, $i.e.$ the semi-reflector does not cover the whole picture, the methods against which we compare are local: applying the different algorithms to the whole image and cropping a region is equivalent to applying the same algorithms to the cropped region directly, Fig. 9.

Model	PSNR
DR	28.17 dB
DR+NRD	30.44 dB
DR+NRD+LCG	31.18 dB

Fig. 8. Our reflection estimation (left) on a real-world curved surface and synthetic data (right Table) using the same network architecture trained on different components of our data pipeline. Only when using the full pipeline (DR+NRD+LCG) the reflection layer is estimated correctly. Note how faint the reflection is in the inputs (bottom row).

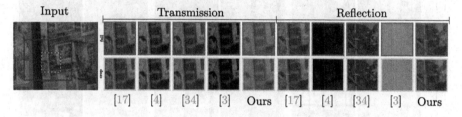

Fig. 9. Applying the different algorithms to the whole image and cropping a region ('full') is equivalent to applying the same algorithms to the cropped region directly ('crop').

Figure 10, *Curved Window* shows a challenging case in which the AOI is significantly different from θ_B across the whole image, thus limiting the effect of the polarizer in all of the inputs. Moreover, the glass surface is slanted and locally curved, which breaks several of the assumptions of previous works. As a result, other methods completely fail at estimating the reflection layer, the transmission layer, or both. On the contrary, our method separates $\widehat{T}$ and $\widehat{R}$ correctly, with only a slight halo of the reflection in $\widehat{T}$. In particular, notice the contrast of the white painting with the stars, as compared with other methods. While challenging, this scene is far from uncommon.

Figure 10, *Bar* shows another result on which our method performs significantly better than most related works. On this example, the method by Schechner *et al.* [2] produces results comparable to ours. However, recall that, to be fair towards their method, we exhaustively search the parameter space and hand-pick the best result. Another thing to note is that our method may introduce artifacts in a region for which there is little or no information about the reflected or transmitted layer in any of the inputs, such as the case in the region marked with the red square on our $\widehat{T}$.

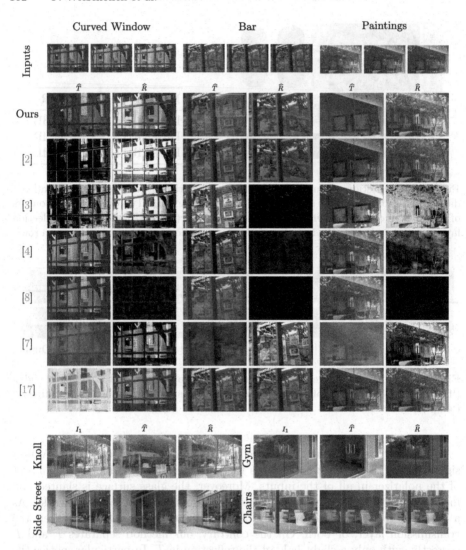

Fig. 10. Results on typical real-world scenes. Top pane: comparison with state-of-the-art methods, bottom pane: additional results. More results are given in the Supplementary.

We also show an additional comparison showing the superiority of our method (Fig. 10, *Paintings*) and a few more challenging cases. We note that in a few examples, our method may fail at removing part of the "transmitted" objects from $\widehat{R}$, as is the case in Fig. 10, *Chairs*.

User Study. Since we do not have the ground truth for real data, we evaluate our method against previous results by means of a thorough user study. We asked 43 individuals not involved with the project, to rank our results against the state-of-the-art [2–4,7,17]. In our study, we evaluate $\hat{R}$ and $\hat{T}$ as two separate tasks, because different methods may perform better on one or the other. For each task, the subjects were shown the three input polarization images, and the results of each method on the same screen, in randomized order. They were given the task to rank the results 1–6,

Table 2. Result from the user study. We report the average recall-rate for each method.

Method	Transmission		Reflection	
	$R@1$	$R@2$	$R@1$	$R@2$
Ours	**0.46**	**0.65**	**0.34**	**0.54**
[2]	0.14	0.38	0.23	0.40
[3]	0.11	0.27	0.09	0.20
[4]	0.06	0.17	0.08	0.20
[7]	0.08	0.21	0.10	0.29
[17]	0.06	0.13	0.15	0.37

which took, on average, 35 min per subject. We measure the recall rate in ranking, $R@k$, *i.e.* the fraction of times a method ranks among the top-k results. Table 2 reports the recall-rates. Two conclusions emerge from analyzing the table. First, and perhaps expected, polarization-based methods outperform the other methods. Second, our method ranks higher than related works by a significant margin.

5   Conclusion

Separating the reflection and transmission layers from images captured *in the wild* is still an open problem, as state-of-the-art methods fail on many real-world images. Rather than learning to estimate the reflection and the transmission directly from the observations, we propose a deep learning solution that leverages the properties of polarized light: it uses a Canonical Projection Layer, and it learns the residuals of the reflection and transmission relative to the canonical images. Another key ingredient to the success of our method is the definition of an image-synthesis pipeline that can accurately reproduce typical nonidealities observed in everyday pictures. We also note that the non-rigid deformation procedure that we propose can be used for other stack-based methods where non-static scenes may be an issue. To evaluate our method, we also propose the Urban Reflection Dataset, which we will make available upon publication. Using this dataset, we extensively compare our method against a number of related works, both visually and by means of a user study, which confirms that our approach is superior to the state-of-the-art methods. Finally, the code for most of the existing methods that separate reflection and transmission is not available: to perform an accurate comparison, we re-implemented representative, state-of-the-art works, and make our implementation of those algorithms available to the community, to enable more comparisons.

Acknowledgments. We thank the reviewers for their feedback, in particular the reviewer who suggested the experiment in Fig. 7, Hendrik P.A. Lensch for the fruitful discussions, and the people who donated half hour of their lives to take our survey.

References

1. Project Website (2018). http://research.nvidia.com/publication/2018-09_Separating-Reflection-and
2. Schechner, Y.Y., Shamir, J., Kiryati, N.: Polarization and statistical analysis of scenes containing a semireflector. J. Opt. Soc. Am. **17**(2), 276–284 (2000)
3. Kong, N., Tai, Y.W., Shin, J.S.: A physically-based approach to reflection separation: from physical modeling to constrained optimization. IEEE Trans. Pattern Anal. Mach. Intell. (TPAMI) **36**(2), 209–221 (2014)
4. Fan, Q., Yang, J., Hua, G., Chen, B., Wipf, D.: A generic deep architecture for single image reflection removal and image smoothing. In: Proceedings of the IEEE International Conference on Computer Vision (ICCV), pp. 3258–3267 (2017)
5. Collett, E.: Field Guide to Polarization. SPIE Press, Bellingham (2005)
6. Levin, A., Weiss, Y.: User assisted separation of reflections from a single image using a sparsity prior. IEEE Trans. Pattern Anal. Mach. Intell. (TPAMI), 29(9) (2007)
7. Li, Y., Brown, M.S.: Single image layer separation using relative smoothness. In: Proceedings of the IEEE Conference on Computer Vision and Pattern Recognition (CVPR), pp. 2752–2759 (2014)
8. Arvanitopoulos, D.N., Achanta, R., Süsstrunk, S.: Single image reflection suppression. In: Proceedings of the IEEE Conference on Computer Vision and Pattern Recognition (CVPR), pp. 1752–1760 (2017)
9. Diamant, Y., Schechner, Y.Y.: Overcoming visual reverberations. In: Proceedings of the IEEE Conference on Computer Vision and Pattern Recognition (CVPR), pp. 1–8 (2008)
10. Shih, Y., Krishnan, D., Durand, F., Freeman, W.T.: Reflection removal using ghosting cues. In: Proceedings of the IEEE Conference on Computer Vision and Pattern Recognition (CVPR), pp. 3193–3201 (2015)
11. Li, Y., Brown, M.S.: Exploiting reflection change for automatic reflection removal. In: Proceedings of the IEEE International Conference on Computer Vision (ICCV), pp. 2432–2439 (2013)
12. Xue, T., Rubinstein, M., Liu, C., Freeman, W.T.: A computational approach for obstruction-free photography. ACM Trans. Graph. (SIGGRAPH) **34**(4), 79 (2015)
13. Szeliski, R., Avidan, S., Anandan, P.: Layer extraction from multiple images containing reflections and transparency. In: Proceedings of the IEEE Conference on Computer Vision and Pattern Recognition (CVPR), p. 1246 (2000)
14. Guo, X., Cao, X., Ma, Y.: Robust separation of reflection from multiple images. In: Proceedings of the IEEE Conference on Computer Vision and Pattern Recognition (CVPR), pp. 2187–2194 (2014)
15. Han, B.J., Sim, J.Y.: Reflection removal using low-rank matrix completion. In: Proceedings of the IEEE Conference on Computer Vision and Pattern Recognition (CVPR) (2017)
16. Kaftory, R., Zeevi, Y.Y.: Blind separation of time/position varying mixtures. IEEE Trans. Image Process. (TIP) **22**(1), 104–118 (2013)
17. Farid, H., Adelson, E.H.: Separating reflections and lighting using independent components analysis. In: Proceedings of the IEEE Conference on Computer Vision and Pattern Recognition (CVPR), vol. 1, pp. 262–267 (1999)
18. Barros, A.K., Yamamura, T., Ohnishi, N.: Separating virtual and real objects using independent component analysis. IEICE Trans. Inf. Syst. **84**(9), 1241–1248 (2001)

19. Bronstein, A.M., Bronstein, M.M., Zibulevsky, M., Zeevi, Y.Y.: Sparse ICA for blind separation of transmitted and reflected images. Int. J. Imaging Syst. Technol. **15**(1), 84–91 (2005)
20. Isola, P., Zhu, J.Y., Zhou, T., Efros, A.A.: Image-to-image translation with conditional adversarial networks. In: Proceedings of the IEEE Conference on Computer Vision and Pattern Recognition (CVPR) (2017)
21. Mao, X., Shen, C., Yang, Y.: Image restoration using very deep convolutional encoder-decoder networks with symmetric skip connections. In: Advances in Neural Information Processing Systems (NIPS) (2016)
22. Wieschollek, P., Schölkopf, M.H.B., Lensch, H.P.A.: Learning blind motion deblurring. In: Proceedings of the IEEE International Conference on Computer Vision (ICCV) (2017)
23. Ronneberger, O., Fischer, P., Brox, T.: U-Net: Convolutional networks for biomedical image segmentation (2015). arXiv preprint arXiv:1505.04597
24. He, K., Zhang, X., Ren, S., Sun, J.: Deep residual learning for image recognition. In: Proceedings of the IEEE Conference on Computer Vision and Pattern Recognition (CVPR) (2016)
25. Wan, R., Shi, B., Duan, L.Y., Tan, A.H., Kot, A.C.: Benchmarking single-image reflection removal algorithms. In: Proceedings of the IEEE International Conference on Computer Vision (ICCV) (2017)
26. Zhou, B., Lapedriza, A., Khosla, A., Oliva, A., Torralba, A.: Places: A 10 million image database for scene recognition. IEEE Trans. Pattern Anal. Mach. Intell. (TPAMI) (2017)
27. Fluxdata.   http://www.fluxdata.com/products/fd-1665p-imaging-polarimeter. Accessed 10 Jul 2018
28. Ricoh. https://www.ricoh.com/technology/tech/051_polarization.html. Accessed 10 Jul 2018
29. Polarcam (2018). https://www.4dtechnology.com/products/polarimeters/polar cam/
30. Gallo, O., Sen, P.: Stack-based algorithms for HDR capture and reconstruction. High Dynamic Range Video. Elsevier, Oxford (2016)
31. Wieschollek, P., Schölkopf, B., Lensch, H.P.A., Hirsch, M.: End-to-end learning for image burst deblurring. In: Proceedings of the Asian Conference on Computer Vision (ACCV) (2016)
32. Kim, J., Kwon Lee, J., Mu Lee, K.: Accurate image super-resolution using very deep convolutional networks. In: Proceedings of the IEEE Conference on Computer Vision and Pattern Recognition (CVPR) (2016)
33. Everingham, M., Van Gool, L., Williams, C.K.I., Winn, J., Zisserman, A.: The PASCAL Visual Object Classes Challenge (VOC 2012) Results (2012). http://www.pascal-network.org/challenges/VOC/voc2012/workshop/index.html
34. Schechner, Y.Y., Kiryati, N., Shamir, J.: Separation of transparent layers by polarization analysis. In: Proceeding of the Scandinavian Conference on Image Analysis (1999)

Object Level Visual Reasoning in Videos

Fabien Baradel[1(✉)], Natalia Neverova[2], Christian Wolf[1,3], Julien Mille[4], and Greg Mori[5]

[1] Université Lyon, INSA Lyon, CNRS, LIRIS, 69621 Villeurbanne, France
{fabien.baradel,christian.wolf}@liris.cnrs.fr
[2] Facebook AI Research, Paris, France
nneverova@fb.com
[3] INRIA, CITI Laboratory, Villeurbanne, France
[4] Laboratoire d'Informatique de l'Univ. de Tours,
INSA Centre Val de Loire, 41034 Blois, France
julien.mille@insa-cvl.fr
[5] Simon Fraser University, Vancouver, Canada
mori@cs.sfu.ca

Abstract. Human activity recognition is typically addressed by detecting key concepts like global and local motion, features related to object classes present in the scene, as well as features related to the global context. The next open challenges in activity recognition require a level of understanding that pushes beyond this and call for models with capabilities for fine distinction and detailed comprehension of interactions between actors and objects in a scene. We propose a model capable of learning to reason about semantically meaningful spatio-temporal interactions in videos. The key to our approach is a choice of performing this reasoning at the object level through the integration of state of the art object detection networks. This allows the model to learn detailed spatial interactions that exist at a semantic, object-interaction relevant level. We evaluate our method on three standard datasets (Twenty-BN Something-Something, VLOG and EPIC Kitchens) and achieve state of the art results on all of them. Finally, we show visualizations of the interactions learned by the model, which illustrate object classes and their interactions corresponding to different activity classes.

Keywords: Video understanding · Human-object interaction

1 Introduction

The field of video understanding is extremely diverse, ranging from extracting highly detailed information captured by specifically designed motion capture

---

Electronic supplementary material The online version of this chapter (https://doi.org/10.1007/978-3-030-01261-8_7) contains supplementary material, which is available to authorized users.

© Springer Nature Switzerland AG 2018
V. Ferrari et al. (Eds.): ECCV 2018, LNCS 11217, pp. 106–122, 2018.
https://doi.org/10.1007/978-3-030-01261-8_7

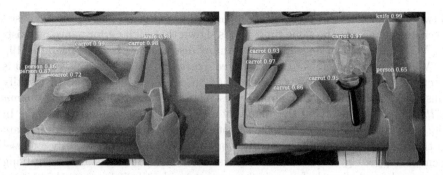

Fig. 1. Humans can understand what happened in a video ("the leftmost carrot was chopped by the person") given only a pair of frames. Along these lines, the goal of this work is to explore the capabilities of higher-level *reasoning* in neural models operating at the semantic level of objects and interactions.

systems [30] to making general sense of videos from the Web [1]. As in the domain of image recognition, there exist a number of large-scale video datasets [6,11–13,21,24], which allow the training of high-capacity deep learning models from massive amounts of data. These models enable detection of key cues present in videos, such as global and local motion, various object categories and global scene-level information, and often achieve impressive performance in recognizing high-level, abstract concepts in the wild.

However, recent attention has been directed toward a more thorough understanding of human-focused activity in diverse internet videos. These efforts range from atomic human actions [13] to fine-grained object interactions [12] to everyday, commonly occurring human-object interactions [11]. This returns us to a human-centric viewpoint of activity recognition where it is not only the presence of certain objects/scenes that dictate the activity present, but the manner, order, and effects of human interaction with these scene elements that are necessary for understanding. In a sense, this is akin to the problems in current 3D human activity recognition datasets [30], but requires the more challenging reasoning and understanding of diverse environments common to internet video collections.

Humans are able to infer what happened in a video given only a few sample frames. This faculty is called *reasoning* and is a key component of human intelligence. As an example we can consider the pair of images in Fig. 1, which shows a complex situation involving articulated objects (human, carrots and knife), the change of location and composition of objects. For humans it is straightforward to draw a conclusion on what happened (a carrot was chopped by the human). Humans have this extraordinary ability of performing visual reasoning on very complicated tasks while it remains unattainable for contemporary computer vision algorithms [10,34].

There have been a number of attempts to equip neural models with reasoning abilities by training them to solve Visual Question Answering (VQA) problems. Among proposed solutions are prior-less data normalization [25], structuring networks to model relationships [29,40] as well as more complex attention based mechanisms [17]. At the same time, it was shown that high performance on existing VQA datasets can be achieved by simply discovering biases in the data [19].

We extend these efforts to *object level reasoning in videos*. Since a video is a temporal sequence, we leverage time as an explicit causal signal to identify causal object relations. Our approach is related to the concept of the *"arrow of the time"* [26] involving the "one-way direction" or "asymmetry" of time. In Fig. 1 the knife was used before the carrot switched over to the chopped-up state on the right side. For a video classification problem, we want to identify a causal event A happening in a video that affects its label B. But instead of identifying this causal event directly from pixels we want to identify it from an object level perspective.

Following this hypothesis we propose to make a bridge between object detection and activity recognition. Object detection allows us to extract low-level information from a scene with all the present object instances and their semantic meanings. However, detailed activity understanding requires reasoning over these semantic structures, determining which objects were involved in interactions, of what nature, and what were the results of these. To compound problems, the semantic structure of a scene may change during a video (e.g. a new object can appear, a person may make a move from one point to another one of the scene).

We propose an **Object Relation Network** (ORN), a neural network module for reasoning between detected semantic object instances through space and time. The ORN has potential to address these issues and conduct relational reasoning over object interactions for the purpose of activity recognition. A set of object detection masks ranging over different object categories and temporal occurrences is input to the ORN. The ORN is able to infer pairwise relationships between objects detected at varying different moments in time.

Code and object masks predictions will be publicly available[1].

2   Related Work

Action Recognition. Pre-deep learning approaches in action recognition focused on handcrafted spatio-temporal features including space-time interest points like SIFT-3D, HOG3D, IDT and aggregated them using bag-of-words techniques. Some hand-crafted representations, like dense trajectories [39], still give competitive performance and are frequently combined with deep learning.

In the recent past, work has shifted to deep learning. Early attempts adapt 2D convolutional networks to videos through temporal pooling and 3D convolutions [2,37]. 3D convolutions are now widely adopted for activity recognition with the introduction of feature transfer by inflating pre-trained 2D convolutional kernels from image classification models trained on ImageNet/ILSVRC [28] through 3D kernels [6]. The downside of 3D kernels is their computational complexity

---

[1] https://github.com/fabienbaradel/object_level_visual_reasoning.

and the large number of learnable parameters, leading to the introduction of 2.5D kernels, i.e. separable filters in the form of a 2D spatial kernel followed by a temporal kernel [41]. An alternative to temporal convolutions are Recurrent Neural Networks (RNNs) in their various gated forms (GRUs, LSTMs) [8,16].

Karpathy et al. [18] presented a wide study on different ways of connecting information in spatial and temporal dimensions through convolutions and pooling. On very general datasets with coarse activity classes they have showed that there was a small margin between classifying individual frames and classifying videos with more sophisticated temporal aggregation.

Simoyan et al. [32] proposed a widely adopted two-stream architecture for action recognition which extracts two different streams, one processing raw RGB input and one processing pre-computed optical flow images.

In slightly narrower settings, prior information on the video content can allow more fine-grained models. Articulated pose is widely used in cases where humans are guaranteed to be present [30]. Pose estimation and activity recognition as a joint (multi-task) problem has recently shown to improve both tasks [23].

Attention models are a way to structure deep networks in an often generic way. They are able to iteratively focus attention to specific parts in the data without requiring prior knowledge about part or object positions. In activity recognition, they have gained some traction in recent years, either as soft-attention on articulated pose (joints) [33], on feature map cells [31,36], on time [42] or on parts in raw RGB input through differentiable crops [3].

When raw video data is globally fed into deep neural networks, they focus on extracting spatio-temporal features and perform aggregations. It has been shown that these techniques fail on challenging fine-grained datasets, which require learning long temporal dependencies and human-object interactions. A concentrated effort has been made to create large scale datasets to overcome these issues [11–13,21].

Relational Reasoning. Relational reasoning is a well studied field for many applications ranging from visual reasoning [29] to reasoning about physical systems [4]. Battaglia et al. [4] introduce a fully-differentiable network physics engine called Interaction Network (IN). IN learns to predict several physical systems such as gravitational systems, rigid body dynamics, and mass-spring systems. It shows impressive results; however, it learns from a virtual environment, which provides access to virtually unlimited training examples. Following the same perspective, Santoro et al. [29] introduced Relation Network (RN), a plug-in module for reasoning in deep networks. RN shows human-level performance in Visual Question Answering (VQA) by inferring pairwise "object" relations. However, in contrast to our work, the term "object" in [29] does not refer to semantically meaningful entities, but to discrete cells in feature maps. The number of interactions therefore grows with feature map resolutions, which makes it difficult to scale. Furthermore, a recent study [19] has shown that some of these results are subject to dataset bias and do not generalize well to small changes in the settings of the dataset.

In the same line, a recent work [35] has shown promising results on discovering objects and their interactions in an unsupervised manner using training examples from virtual environments. In [38], attention and relational modules are combined on a graph structure. From a different perspective, [25] show that relational reasoning can be learned for visual reasoning in a data driven way without any prior using conditional batch normalization with a feature-wise affine transformation based on conditioning information. In an opposite approach, a strong structural prior is learned in the form of a complex attention mechanism: in [17], an external memory module combined with attention processes over input images and text questions, performing iterative reasoning for VQA.

While most of the discussed work has been designed for VQA and for predictions on physical systems and environments, extensions have been proposed for video understanding. Reasoning in videos on a mask or segmentation level has been attempted for video prediction [22], where the goal was to leverage semantic information to be able predict further into the future. Zhou et al. [5] have recently shown state-of-the-art performance on challenging datasets by extending Relation Network to video classification. Their chosen entities are frames, on which they employ RN to reason on a temporal level only through pairwise frame relations. The approach is promising, but restricted to temporal contextual information without an understanding on a local object level, which is provided by our approach.

3   Object-Level Visual Reasoning in Space and Time

Our goal is to extract multiple types of cues from a video sequence: interactions between predicted objects and their semantic classes, as well as local and global motion in the scene. We formulate this objective as a neural architecture with two heads: an *activity head* and an *object head*. Figure 2 gives a functional overview of the model. Both heads share common features up to a certain layer shown in red in the figure. The *activity head*, shown in orange in the figure, is a CNN-based architecture employing convolutional layers, including spatio-temporal convolutions, able to extract global motion features. However, it is not able to extract information from an object level perspective. We leverage the *object head* to perform reasoning on the relationships between predicted object instances.

Our main contribution is a new structured module called **Object Relation Network** (ORN), which is able to perform spatio-temporal reasoning between detected object instances in the video. ORN is able to reason by modeling how objects move, appear and disappear and how they interact between two frames.

In this section, we will first describe our main contribution, the ORN network. We then provide details about object instance features, about the activity head, and finally about the final recognition task. In what follows, lowercase letters denote 1D vectors while uppercase letters are used for 2D and 3D matrices or higher order tensors. We assume that the input of our system is a video of T frames denoted by $\mathbf{X}_{1:T} = (\mathbf{X}_t)_{t=1}^{T}$ where $\mathbf{X}_t$ is the RGB image at timestep t. The goal is to learn a mapping from $\mathbf{X}_{1:T}$ to activity classes $\mathbf{y}$.

3.1 Object Relation Network

ORN (Object Relation Network) is a module for reasoning between semantic objects through space and time. It captures object moves, arrivals and interactions in an efficient manner. We suppose that for each frame t, we have a set of objects k with associated features $\mathbf{o}_t^k$. Objects and features are detected and computed by the object head described in Sect. 3.2.

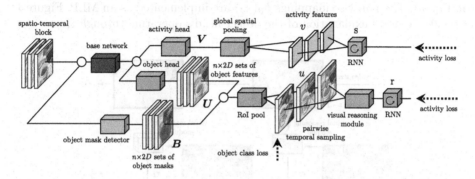

Fig. 2. A functional overview of the model. A global convolutional model extracts features and splits into two heads trained to predict, respectively activity classes and object classes. The latter are predicted by pooling over object instance masks, which are predicted by an additional convolutional model. The object instances are passed through a visual reasoning module. (Color figure online)

Reasoning about activities in videos is inherently temporal, as activities follow the *arrow of time* [26], i.e. the causality of the time dimension imposes that past actions have consequences in the future but *not* vice-versa. We handle this by sampling: running a process over time t, and for each instant t, sampling a second frame t' with $t' < t$. Our network reasons on objects which interact between pairs of frames and their corresponding sets of objects $\mathbf{O}_{t'} = \left\{ \mathbf{o}_{t'}^k \right\}_{k=1}^{K'}$ and $\mathbf{O}_t = \left\{ \mathbf{o}_t^k \right\}_{k=1}^{K}$. The goal is to learn a general function defined on the set of all input objects from the combined set of both frames:

$$\mathbf{g}_t = g(\mathbf{o}_{t'}^1, \dots, \mathbf{o}_{t'}^{K'}, \mathbf{o}_t^1, \dots, \mathbf{o}_t^K). \tag{1}$$

The objects in this set are unordered, aside for the frame they belong to.

Inspired by relational networks [29], we chose to directly model inter-frame interactions between pairs of objects (j, k) and leave modeling of higher-order interactions to the output space of the mappings h_θ and the global mapping f_ϕ:

$$\mathbf{g}_t = \sum_{j,k} h_\theta(\mathbf{o}_{t'}^j, \mathbf{o}_t^k) \tag{2}$$

It is interesting to note that $h_\theta(\cdot)$ could have been evaluated over arbitrary cliques, like singletons and triplets—this has been evaluated in the experimental section. In order to better directly model long-range interactions, we make the global mapping $f_\phi(\cdot, \cdot)$ recurrent, which leads to the following form:

$$\mathbf{r}_t = f_\phi(\mathbf{g}_t, \mathbf{r}_{t-1}) \tag{3}$$

where $\mathbf{r}_t$ represents the recurrent *object reasoning state* at time t and $\mathbf{g}_t$ is the global inter-frame interaction inferred at time t such as described in Eq. 2. In practice, this is implemented as a GRU, but for simplicity we omitted the gates in Eq. (3). The pairwise mappings $h_\theta(\cdot, \cdot)$ are implemented as an MLP. Figure 3 provides a visual explanation of the object head's operating through time.

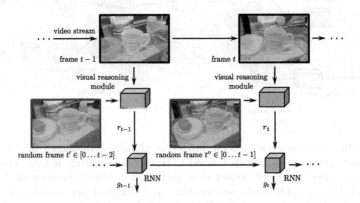

Fig. 3. ORN in the object head operating on detected instances of objects.

Our proposed ORN differs from [29] in three main points:

Objects have a semantic definition — we model relationships with respect to semantically meaningful entities (object instances) instead of feature map cells which do not have a semantically meaningful spatial extent. We will show in the experimental section that this is a key difference.

Objects are selected from different frames — we infer object pairwise relations only between objects present in two different sets. This is a key design choice which allows our model to reason about changes in object relationships over time.

Long range reasoning — integration of the object relations over time is recurrent by using a RNN for $f_\phi(\cdot)$. Since reasoning from a full sequence cannot be done by inferring the relations between two frames, $f_\phi(\cdot)$ allows long range reasoning on sequences of variable length.

3.2 Object Instance Features

The object features $\mathbf{O}_t = \left\{ \mathbf{o}_t^k \right\}_{k=1}^{K}$ for each frame t used for the ORN module described above are computed and collected from local regions predicted by a mask predictor. Independently for each frame $\mathbf{X}_t$ of the input data block, we predict object instances as binary masks $\mathbf{B}_t^k$ and associated object class predictions $\mathbf{c}_t^k$, a distribution over C classes. We use Mask-RCNN [14], which is able to detect objects in a frame using region proposal networks [27] and produces a high quality segmentation mask for each object instance.

The objective is to collect features for each object instance, which jointly describe its appearance, the change in its appearance over time, and its shape, i.e. the shape of the binary mask. In theory, appearance could also be described by pooling the feature representation learned by the mask predictor (Mask R-CNN). However, in practice we choose to pool features from the dedicated *object head* such as shown in Fig. 2, which also include motion through the spatio-temporal convolutions shared with the activity head:

$$\mathbf{u}_t^k = \text{ROI-Pooling}(\mathbf{U}_t, \mathbf{B}_t^k) \tag{4}$$

where $\mathbf{U}_t$ is the feature map output by the *object head*, $\mathbf{u}_t^k$ is a D-dimensional vector of appearance and appearance change of object k.

Shape information from the binary mask $\mathbf{B}_t^k$ is extracted through the following mapping function: $\mathbf{b}_t^k = g_\phi(\mathbf{B}_t^k)$, where $g_\phi(\cdot)$ is a MLP. Information about object k in image $\mathbf{X}_t$ is given by a concatenation of appearance, shape, and object class: $\mathbf{o}_t^k = [\, \mathbf{b}_t^k \ \ \mathbf{u}_t^k \ \ \mathbf{c}_t^k \,]$.

3.3 Global Motion and Context

Current approaches in video understanding focus on modeling the video from a high-level perspective. By a stack of spatio-temporal convolution and pooling they focus on learning global scene context information. Effective activity recognition requires integration of both of these sources: global information about the entire video content in addition to relational reasoning for making fine distinctions regarding object interactions and properties.

In our method, local low-level reasoning is provided through object head and the ORN module such as described above in Sect. 3.1. We complement this representation by high-level context information described by $\mathbf{V}_t$ which are feature outputs from the activity head (orange block in Fig. 2).

We use spatial global average pooling over $\mathbf{V}_t$ to output T D-dimensional feature vectors denoted by $\mathbf{v}_t$, where $\mathbf{v}_t$ corresponds to the context information of the video at timestep t.

We model the dynamics of the context information through time by employing a RNN $f_\gamma(\cdot)$ given by:

$$\mathbf{s}_t = f_\gamma(\mathbf{v}_t, \mathbf{s}_{t-1}) \tag{5}$$

where $\mathbf{s}$ is the hidden state of $f_\gamma(\cdot)$ and gives cues about the evolution of the context though time.

3.4 Recognition

Given an input video sequence $\mathbf{X}_{1:T}$, the two different streams corresponding to the activity head and the object head result in the two representations $\mathbf{h}$

and $\mathbf{r}$, respectively where $\mathbf{h} = \sum_t \mathbf{h}_t$ and $\mathbf{r} = \sum_t \mathbf{r}_t$. Each representation is the hidden state of the respective GRU, which were described in the preceding subsections. Recall that $\mathbf{h}$ provides the global motion context while $\mathbf{r}$ provides the object reasoning state output by the ORN module. We perform independent linear classification for each representation:

$$\mathbf{y}^1 = \mathbf{W}\,\mathbf{h} \tag{6}$$

$$\mathbf{y}^2 = \mathbf{Z}\,\mathbf{r} \tag{7}$$

where $\mathbf{y}^1, \mathbf{y}^2$ correspond to the logits from the *activity head* and the *object head*, respectively, and $\mathbf{W}$ and $\mathbf{Z}$ are trainable weights (including biases). The final prediction is done by averaging logits $\mathbf{y}^1$ and $\mathbf{y}^2$ followed by softmax activation.

4 Network Architectures and Feature Dimensions

The input RGB images $\mathbf{X}_t$ are of size $\mathbf{R}^{3 \times W \times H}$ where W and H correspond to the width and height and are of size 224 each. The object and activity heads (orange and green in Fig. 2) are a joint convolutional neural network with Resnet50 architecture pre-trained on ImageNet/ILSVRC [28], with Conv1 and Conv5 blocks being inflated to 2.5D convolutions [41] (3D convolutions with a separable temporal dimension). This choice has been optimized on the validation set, as explained in Sect. 6 and shown in Table 5.

The last *conv5* layers have been split into two different heads (activity head and object head). The intermediate feature representations $\mathbf{U}_t$ and $\mathbf{V}_t$ are of dimensions $2048 \times T \times 7 \times 7$ and $2048 \times T \times 14 \times 14$, respectively. We provide a higher spatial resolution for the feature maps $\mathbf{U}_t$ of the object head to get more precise local descriptors. This can be done by changing the stride of the initial *conv5* layers from 2 to 1. Temporal convolutions have been configured to keep the same time temporal dimension through the network.

Global spatial pooling of activity features results in a 2048 dimensional feature vector fed into a GRU with 512 dimensional hidden state $\mathbf{s}_t$. ROI-Pooling of object features results in 2048 dimensional feature vectors $\mathbf{u}_t^k$. The encoder of the binary mask is a MLP with one hidden layer of size 100 and outputs a mask embedding $\mathbf{b}_t^k$ of dimension 100. The number of object classes is 80, which leads in total to a 2229 dimensional object feature vector $\mathbf{o}_t^k$.

The non-linearity $h_\theta(\cdot)$ is implemented as an MLP with 2 hidden layers each with 512 units and produces an 512 dimensional output space. $f_\phi(\cdot)$ is implemented as a GRU with a 256 dimension hidden state $\mathbf{r}_t$. We use ReLU as the activation function after each layer for each network.

5 Training

We train the model with two different losses:

$$\mathcal{L} = \mathcal{L}_1\Big(\frac{\hat{\mathbf{y}}^1 + \hat{\mathbf{y}}^2}{2}, \mathbf{y}\Big) + \sum_t \sum_k \mathcal{L}_2(\hat{\mathbf{c}}_t^k, \mathbf{c}_t^k). \tag{8}$$

where $\mathcal{L}_1$ and $\mathcal{L}_2$ are the cross-entropy loss. The first term corresponds to supervised activity class losses comparing two different activity class predictions to the class ground truth: $\hat{\mathbf{y}}^1$ is the prediction of the activity head, whereas $\hat{\mathbf{y}}^2$ is the prediction of the object head, as given by Eqs. (6) and (7), respectively.

The second term is a loss which pushes the features $\mathbf{U}$ of the object towards representations of the semantic object classes. The goal is to obtain features related to, both, motion (through the layers shared with the activity head), as well as object classes. As ground-truth object classes are not available, we define the loss as the cross-entropy between the class label $\mathbf{c}_t^k$ predicted by the mask predictor and a dedicated linear class prediction $\hat{\mathbf{c}}_t^k$ based on features $\mathbf{u}_t^k$, which, as we recall, are RoI-pooled from $\mathbf{U}$:

$$\mathbf{c}_t^k = \mathbf{R}\,\mathbf{u}_t^k \tag{9}$$

where $\mathbf{R}$ trainable parameters (biases integrated) learned end-to-end together with the other parameters of the model.

We found that first training the object head only and then the full network was performing better. A ResNet50 network pretrained on ImageNet is modified by inflating some of its filters to 2.5 convolutions (3D convolutions with the time dimension separated), as described in Sect. 4; then by fine-tuning.

We train the model using the Adam optimizer [20] with an initial learning rate of 10^{-4} on 30 epochs and use early-stopping criterion on the validation set for hyper-parameter optimization. Training takes $\sim$50 min per epoch on 4 Titan XP GPUs with clips of 8 frames.

6   Experimental Results

We evaluated the method on three standard datasets, which represent difficult fine-grained activity recognition tasks: the Something-Something dataset, the VLOG dataset and the recently released EPIC Kitchens dataset.

Something-Something (SS) is a recent video classification dataset with 108,000 example videos and 157 classes [12]. It shows humans performing different actions with different objects, actions and objects being combined in different ways. Solving SS requires common sense reasoning and the state-of-the-art methods in activity recognition tend to fail, which makes this dataset challenging.

VLOG is a multi-label binary classification of human-object interactions recently released with 114,000 videos and 30 classes [11]. Classes correspond to objects, and labels of a class are 1 if a person has touched a certain object during the video, otherwise they are 0. It has recently been shown, that state-of-the-art video based methods [6] are outperformed on VLOG by image based methods like ResNet-50 [15], although these video methods outperform image based ResNet-50 on large-scale video datasets like the Kinetics dataset [6]. This suggests a gap between traditional datasets like Kinetics and the fine-grained dataset VLOG, making it particularly difficult.

Table 1. Results on Hand/Semantic Object Interaction Classification (Average precision in % on the test set) on VLOG dataset. R50 and I3D implemented by [11].

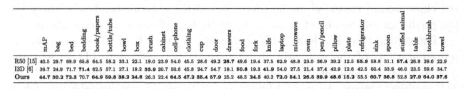

	mAP	bag	bed	bedding	book/papers	bottle/tube	bowl	box	brush	cabinet	cell-phone	clothing	cup	door	drawers	food	fork	knife	laptop	microwave	oven	pen/pencil	pillow	plate	refrigerator	sink	spoon	stuffed animal	table	toothbrush	towel
R50 [15]	40.5	29.7	68.9	65.8	64.5	58.2	33.1	22.1	19.0	23.9	54.0	45.5	28.6	49.2	28.7	49.6	19.4	37.5	62.9	48.8	23.0	36.9	39.2	12.5	55.9	58.8	31.1	57.4	26.8	39.6	22.9
I3D [6]	39.7	24.9	71.7	71.4	62.5	57.1	27.1	19.2	33.9	20.7	50.6	45.8	24.7	54.7	19.1	50.8	19.3	41.9	54.0	27.5	21.4	37.4	42.9	12.6	42.5	60.4	33.9	46.0	23.5	59.6	34.7
Ours	44.7	30.2	72.3	70.7	64.9	59.8	38.2	24.6	26.3	22.4	64.5	47.2	35.4	57.9	25.2	48.5	24.5	40.2	72.0	54.1	26.5	39.9	48.6	15.2	53.5	60.7	36.8	52.8	27.9	64.0	37.6

EPIC Kitchens (EPIC) is an egocentric video dataset recently released containing 55 hours recording of daily activities [7]. This is the largest in first-person vision and the activities performed are non-scripted, which makes the dataset very challenging and close to real world data. The dataset is densely annotated and several tasks exist such as object detection, action recognition and action prediction. We focus on action recognition with 39'594 action segments in total and 125 actions classes (i.e. verbs). Since the test set is not available yet we conducted our experiments on the training set (28'561 videos). We use the videos recorded by person 01 to person 25 for training (22'675 videos) and define the validation set as the remaining videos (5'886 videos).

For all datasets we rescale the input video resolution to 256×256. While training, we crop space-time blocks of 224×224 spatial resolution and L frames, with $L = 8$ for the SS dataset and $L = 4$ for VLOG and EPIC. We do not perform any other data augmentation. While training we extract L frames from the entire video by splitting the video into L sub-sequences and randomly sampling one frame per sub-sequence. The output sequence of size L is called a *clip*. A clip aims to represent the full video with less frames. For testing we aggregate results of 10 clips. We use *lintel* [9] for decoding video on the fly.

The ablation study is done by using the train set as training data and we report the result on the validation set. We compare against other state-of-the-art approaches on the test set. For the ablation studies, we slightly decreased the computational complexity of the model: the base network (including activity and object heads) is a ResNet-18 instead of ResNet-50, a single clip of 4 frames is extracted from a video at test time.

Comparison with Other Approaches. Table 1 shows the performance of the proposed approach on the VLOG dataset. We outperform the state of the art on this challenging dataset by a margin of ≈ 4.2 points (44.7% accuracy against 40.5% by [15]). As mentioned above, traditional video approaches tend to fail on this challenging fine-grained dataset, providing inferior results. Table 3 shows performance on SS where we outperform the state of the art given by very recent methods (+2.3 points). On EPIC we re-implement standard baselines and report results on the validation set (Table 4) since the test set is not available. Our full method reports an accuracy of 40.89 and outperforms baselines by a large margin ($\approx +6.4$ and $\approx +7.9$ points respectively for against CNN-2D and I3D based on a ResNet-18).

Table 2. Ablation study with ResNet-18 backbone. Results in %: Top-1 accuracy for EPIC and SS datasets, and mAP for VLOG dataset.

Method	Object type	EPIC		VLOG		SS	
		obj. head	2 heads	obj. head	2 heads	obj. head	2 heads
Baseline	–	–	*38.33*	–	*35.03*	–	*31.31*
ORN	pixel	23.71	38.83	14.40	35.18	2.51	31.43
ORN	**COCO**	**29.94**	**40.89**	**27.14**	**37.49**	10.26	**32.12**
ORN-mlp	COCO	28.15	39.41	25.40	36.35	–	–
ORN	COCO-visual	28.45	38.92	22.92	35.49	–	–
ORN	COCO-shape	21.92	37.16	7.18	35.39	–	–
ORN	COCO-class	21.96	37.75	13.40	35.94	–	–
ORN	COCO-intra	29.25	38.10	26.78	36.28	–	–
ORN clique-1	COCO	28.25	40.18	26.48	36.71	–	–
ORN clique-3	COCO	22.61	37.67	27.05	36.04	–	–

Effect of Object-Level Reasoning. Table 2 shows the importance of reasoning on the performance of the method. The baseline corresponds to the performance obtained by the activity head trained alone (inflated ResNet, in the ResNet-18 version for this table). No object level reasoning is present in this baseline. The proposed approach (third line) including an object head and the ORN module gains 0.8, 2.5 and 2.4 points compared to our baseline respectively on SS, on EPIC and on VLOG. This indicates that the reasoning module is able to extract complementary features compared to the activity head.

Using *semantically defined objects* proved to be important and led to a gain of 2 points on EPIC and 2.3 points on VLOG for the full model (6/12.7 points using the object head only) compared to an extension of Santoro *et al.* [29] operating on pixel level. This indicates importance of object level reasoning. The gain on SS is smaller (0.7 point with the full model and 7.8 points with the object head only) and can be explained by the difference in spatial resolution of the videos. Object detections and predictions of the binary masks are done using the initial video resolution. The mean video resolution for VLOG is 660×1183 and for EPIC is 640×480 against 100×157 for SS. Mask-RCNN has been trained on images of resolution 800×800 and thus performs best on higher resolutions. The quality of the object detector is important for leveraging object level understanding then for the rest of the ablation study we focus on EPIC and VLOG datasets.

The function f_ϕ in Eq. (3) is an important design choice in our model. In our proposed model, f_ϕ is recurrent over time to ensure that the ORN module captures long range reasoning over time, as shown in Eq. (3). Removing the recurrence in this equation leads to an MLP instead of a (gated) RNN, as evaluated in row 4 of Table 2. Performance decreases by 1.1 point on VLOG and 1.4 points on EPIC. The larger gap for EPIC compared to VLOG and can arguably be explained by the fact that in SS actions cover the whole video, while solving

Table 3. Experimental results on the Something-Something dataset (classification accuracy in % on the test set).

Methods	Top1
C3D + Avg [12]	21.50
I3D [12]	27.63
MultiScale TRN [5]	33.60
Ours	**35.97**

Table 4. Experimental results on the EPIC Kitchens dataset (accuracy in % on the validation set – methods with * have been re-implemented).

Methods	Top1
R18 [15]*	32.05
I3D-18 [6]*	34.20
Ours	**40.89**

Table 5. Effect of the CNN architecture (choice of kernel inflations) on a single head ResNet-18 network. Accuracy in % on the validation set of Something-Something is shown. 2.5D kernels are separable kernels: 2D followed by a 1D temporal.

Conv1			Conv2			Conv3			Conv4			Conv5			Aggreg		SS
2D	3D	2.5D	2D	3D	2.5D	2D	3D	2.5D	2D	3D	2.5D	2D	3D	2.5D	GAP	RNN	
✓	–	–	✓	–	–	✓	–	–	✓	–	–	✓	–	–	✓	–	15.73
✓	–	–	✓	–	–	✓	–	–	✓	–	–	✓	–	–	–	✓	15.88
–	✓	–	–	✓	–	–	✓	–	–	✓	–	–	✓	–	✓	–	31.42
–	–	✓	–	–	✓	–	–	✓	–	–	✓	–	–	✓	✓	–	27.58
✓	–	–	✓	–	–	✓	–	–	✓	–	–	–	✓	–	✓	–	31.28
✓	–	–	✓	–	–	✓	–	–	–	✓	–	–	✓	–	✓	–	32.06
✓	–	–	✓	–	–	–	✓	–	–	✓	–	–	✓	–	✓	–	32.25
✓	–	–	✓	–	–	✓	–	–	✓	–	–	–	–	✓	✓	–	31.31
✓	–	–	✓	–	–	✓	–	–	–	–	✓	–	–	✓	✓	–	32.79
✓	–	–	✓	–	–	–	–	✓	–	–	✓	–	–	✓	✓	–	**33.77**
–	✓	–	✓	–	–	✓	–	–	✓	–	–	✓	–	–	✓	–	28.71
–	✓	–	–	✓	–	✓	–	–	✓	–	–	✓	–	–	✓	–	31.42
–	–	✓	✓	–	–	✓	–	–	✓	–	–	✓	–	–	✓	–	20.05
–	–	✓	–	–	✓	✓	–	–	✓	–	–	✓	–	–	✓	–	22.52

VLOG requires detecting the right moment when the human-object interaction occurs and thus long range reasoning plays a less important role.

Visual features extracted from object regions are the most discriminative, however object shapes and labels also provide complementary information. Finally, the last part of Table 2 evaluates the effect of the cliques size for modeling the interactions between objects and show that pairwise cliques outperform cliques of size 1 and 3.

CNN Architecture and Kernel Inflations. The convolutional architecture of the model was optimized over the validation set of the SS dataset, as shown in Table 5. The architecture itself (in terms of numbers of layers, filters etc.)

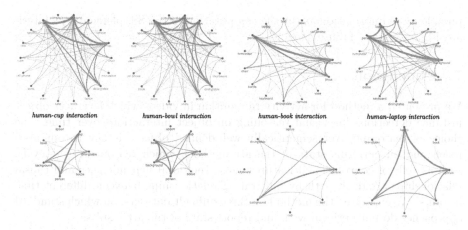

Fig. 4. Example of object pairwise interactions learned by our model on VLOG for four different classes. Objects co-occurrences are at the top and learned pairwise objects interactions are at the bottom. Line thickness indicates learned importance of a given relation. Interactions have been normalized by the object co-occurrences.

Fig. 5. Examples of failure cases – (a) small sized objects (on the left). Our model detects a *cell phone* and a *person* but fails to detect *hand-cell-phone contact*; (b) confusion between semantically similar objects (on the right). The model falsly predicts *hand-cup contact* instead of *hand-glass-contact* even though the *wine glass* is detected.

is determined by pre-training on image classification. We optimized the choice of filter inflations from 2D to 2.5D or 3D for several convolutional blocks. This has been optimized for the single head model and using a ResNet-18 variant to speed up computation. Adding temporal convolutions increases performance up to 100% w.r.t. to pure 2D baselines. This indicates, without surprise, that motion is a strong cue. Inflating kernels to 2.5D on the input side and on the output side provided best performances, suggesting that temporal integration is required at a very low level (motion estimation) as well as on a very high level, close to reasoning. Our study also corroborates recent research in activity recognition, indicating that 2.5D kernels provide a good trade-off between high-capacity and learnable numbers of parameters. Finally temporal integration via RNN outperforms global average pooling over space and time.

Visualizing the Learned Object Interactions. Figure 4 shows visualizations of the pairwise object relationships the model learned from data, in particular from the VLOG dataset. Each graph is computed for a given activity class, we provide more information about the computation in the Supplementary Materials. Figure 5 shows failure cases.

7   Conclusion

We presented a method for activity recognition in videos which leverages object instance detections for visual reasoning on object interactions over time. The choice of reasoning over semantically well-defined objects is key to our approach and outperforms state of the art methods which reason on grid-levels, such as cells of convolutional feature maps. Temporal dependencies and causal relationships are dealt with by integrating relationships between different time instants. We evaluated the method on three difficult datasets, on which standard approaches do not perform well, and report state-of-the-art results.

Acknowledgements. This work was funded by grant Deepvision (ANR-15-CE23-0029, STPGP-479356-15), a joint French/Canadian call by ANR & NSERC.

References

1. Abu-El-Haija, S., et al.: Youtube-8m: a large-scale video classification benchmark. arXiv preprint arxiv:1609.08675 (2016)
2. Baccouche, M., Mamalet, F., Wolf, C., Garcia, C., Baskurt, A.: Sequential deep learning for human action recognition. In: Salah, A.A., Lepri, B. (eds.) HBU 2011. LNCS, vol. 7065, pp. 29–39. Springer, Heidelberg (2011). https://doi.org/10.1007/978-3-642-25446-8_4
3. Baradel, F., Wolf, C., Mille, J., Taylor, G.: Glimpse clouds: human activity recognition from unstructured feature points. In: CVPR (2018)
4. Battaglia, P.W., Pascanu, R., Lai, M., Rezende, D.J., Kavukcuoglu, K.: Interaction networks for learning about objects, relations and physics. In: NIPS (2016)
5. Bolei, Z., Andonian, A., Oliva, A., Torralba, A.: Temporal relational reasoning in videos. In: Ferrari, V., Hebert, M., Sminchisescu, C., Weiss, Y. (eds.) ECCV 2018, Part I. LNCS, vol. 11205, pp. 831–846. Springer, Cham (2018)
6. Carreira, J., Zisserman, A.: Quo vadis, action recognition? A new model and the kinetics dataset. In: CVPR (2017)
7. Damen, D., et al.: Scaling egocentric vision: the epic-kitchens dataset. In: ECCV (2018, to appear)
8. Donahue, J., et al.: Long-term recurrent convolutional networks for visual recognition and description. In: CVPR (2015)
9. Duke, B.: Lintel: Python video decoding (2018). https://github.com/dukebw/lintel
10. Fleuret, F., Li, T., Dubout, C., Wampler, E.K., Yantis, S., Geman, D.: Comparing machines and humans on a visual categorization test. Proc. Natl. Acad. Sci. U.S.A. **108**(43), 17621–5 (2011)
11. Fouhey, D.F., Kuo, W., Efros, A.A., Malik, J.: From lifestyle vlogs to everyday interactions. In: CVPR (2018)
12. Goyal, R., et al.: The "something something" video database for learning and evaluating visual common sense. In: ICCV (2017)
13. Gu, C., et al.: AVA: a video dataset of spatio-temporally localized atomic visual actions. arXiv preprint arXiv:1705.08421 (2017)

14. He, K., Gkioxari, G., Dollar, P., Girshick, R.: Mask R-CNN. In: ICCV (2017)
15. He, K., Zhang, X., Ren, S., Sun, J.: Deep residual learning for image recognition. In: CVPR (2016)
16. Hochreiter, S., Schmidhuber, J.: Long short-term memory. Neural Comput. **9**(8), 1735–1780 (1997)
17. Hudson, D., Manning, C.: Compositional attention networks for machine reasoning. In: ICLR (2018)
18. Karpathy, A., Toderici, G., Shetty, S., Leung, T., Sukthankar, R., Fei-Fei, L.: Large-scale video classification with convolutional neural networks. In: CVPR (2014)
19. Kim, J., Ricci, M., Serre, T.: Not-So-CLEVR: visual relations strain feedforward neural networks. arXiv preprint arXiv:1802.03390 (2018)
20. Kingma, D., Ba, J.: Adam: a method for stochastic optimization. In: ICML (2015)
21. Krishna, R., et al.: Visual genome: connecting language and vision using crowd-sourced dense image annotations. Int. J. Comput. Vis. (IJCV) **123**, 32–73 (2017)
22. Luc, P., Neverova, N., Couprie, C., Verbeek, J., LeCun, Y.: Predicting deeper into the future of semantic segmentation. In: ICCV (2017)
23. Luvizon, D., Picard, D., Tabia, H.: 2D/3D pose estimation and action recognition using multitask deep learning. In: CVPR (2018)
24. Monfort, M., et al.: Moments in time dataset: one million videos for event understanding. arXiv preprint arXiv:1801.03150 (2018)
25. Perez, E., Vries, H.D., Strub, F., Dumoulin, V., Courville, A.: Learning visual reasoning without strong priors. In: ICML Machine Learning in Speech and Language Processing Workshop (2017)
26. Pickup, L.C., et al.: Seeing the arrow of time. In: CVPR (2014)
27. Ren, S., He, K., Girshick, R., Sun, J.: Faster R-CNN: towards real-time object detection with region proposal networks. In: NIPS (2015)
28. Russakovsky, O., et al.: Imagenet large scale visual recognition challenge. IJCV **115**(3), 211–252 (2015)
29. Santoro, A., et al.: A simple neural network module for relational reasoning. In: NIPS (2017)
30. Shahroudy, A., Liu, J., Ng, T.T., Wang, G.: NTU RGB+D: a large scale dataset for 3D human activity analysis. In: CVPR (2016)
31. Sharma, S., Kiros, R., Salakhutdinov, R.: Action recognition using visual attention. In: ICLR Workshop (2016)
32. Simonyan, K., Zisserman, A.: Two-stream convolutional networks for action recognition in videos. In: NIPS (2014)
33. Song, S., Lan, C., Xing, J., Zeng, W., Liu, J.: An end-to-end spatio-temporal attention model for human action recognition from skeleton data. In: AAAI (2016)
34. Stabinger, S., Rodríguez-Sánchez, A., Piater, J.: 25 years of CNNs: can we compare to human abstraction capabilities? In: Villa, A.E.P., Masulli, P., Pons Rivero, A.J. (eds.) ICANN 2016. LNCS, vol. 9887, pp. 380–387. Springer, Cham (2016). https://doi.org/10.1007/978-3-319-44781-0_45
35. van Steenkiste, S., Chang, M., Greff, K., Schmidhuber, J.: Relational neural expectation maximization: unsupervised discovery of objects and their interactions. In: ICLR (2018)
36. Sun, L., Jia, K., Chen, K., Yeung, D., Shi, B.E., Savarese, S.: Lattice long short-term memory for human action recognition. In: ICCV (2017)
37. Tran, D., Bourdev, L., Fergus, R., Torresani, L., Paluri, M.: Learning spatiotemporal features with 3D convolutional networks. In: ICCV (2015)
38. Velikovi, P., Cucurull, G., Casanova, A., Romero, A., Li , P., Bengio, Y.: Graph attention networks. In: ICLR (2018)

39. Wang, H., Kläser, A., Schmid, C., Liu, C.L.: Action Recognition by Dense Trajectories. In: CVPR (2011)
40. Watters, N., Zoran, D., Weber, T., Battaglia, P., Pascanu, R., Tacchetti, A.: Visual interaction networks: learning a physics simulator from video. In: NIPS (2017)
41. Xie, S., Sun, C., Huang, J., Tu, Z., Murphy, K.: Rethinking spatiotemporal feature learning for video understanding. arXiv preprint arxiv:1712.04851 (2017)
42. Yeung, S., Russakovsky, O., Jin, N., Andriluka, M., Mori, G., Fei-Fei, L.: Every moment counts: dense detailed labeling of actions in complex videos. arXiv preprint arXiv:1507.05738 (2015)

Maximum Margin Metric Learning
over Discriminative Nullspace
for Person Re-identification

T. M. Feroz Ali[✉][iD] and Subhasis Chaudhuri

Indian Institute of Technology Bombay, Mumbai, India
{ferozalitm,sc}@ee.iitb.ac.in

Abstract. In this paper we propose a novel metric learning framework
called Nullspace Kernel Maximum Margin Metric Learning (NK3ML)
which efficiently addresses the small sample size (SSS) problem inherent in person re-identification and offers a significant performance gain
over existing state-of-the-art methods. Taking advantage of the very high
dimensionality of the feature space, the metric is learned using a maximum margin criterion (MMC) over a discriminative nullspace where all
training sample points of a given class map onto a single point, minimizing the within class scatter. A kernel version of MMC is used to obtain a
better between class separation. Extensive experiments on four challenging benchmark datasets for person re-identification demonstrate that the
proposed algorithm outperforms all existing methods. We obtain 99.8%
rank-1 accuracy on the most widely accepted and challenging dataset
VIPeR, compared to the previous state of the art being only 63.92%.

Keywords: Person re-identification · Metric learning
Small sample size problem

1 Introduction

Person re-identification (re-ID) is the task of matching the image of pedestrians
across spatially non overlapping cameras, even if the pedestrian identities are
unseen before. It is a very challenging task due to large variations in illumination, viewpoint, occlusion, background and pose changes. Supervised methods
for re-ID generally include two stages: computing a robust feature descriptor and
learning an efficient distance metric. Various feature descriptors like SDALF [10],
LOMO [23] and GOG [31] have improved the efficiency to represent a person. But
feature descriptors are unlikely to be completely invariant to large variations in
the data collection process and hence the second stage for person re-identification
focusing on metric learning is very important. They learn a discriminative metric
space to minimize the intra-person distance while maximizing the inter-person
distance. It has been shown that learning a good distance metric can drastically
improve the matching accuracy in re-ID. Many efficient metric learning methods
have been developed for re-ID in the last few years, for e.g., XQDA [23], KISSME

© Springer Nature Switzerland AG 2018
V. Ferrari et al. (Eds.): ECCV 2018, LNCS 11217, pp. 123–141, 2018.
https://doi.org/10.1007/978-3-030-01261-8_8

[19], LFDA [36]. However, most of these methods suffer from the small sample size (SSS) problem inherent in re-ID since the feature dimension is often very high.

Recent deep learning based methods address feature computation and metric learning jointly for an improved performance. However, their performance depends on the availability of manually labeled large training data, which is not possible in the context of re-ID. Hence we refrain from discussing deep learning based methods in this paper, and concentrate on the following problem: given a set of image features, can we design a good discriminant criterion for improved classification accuracy for cases when the number of training samples per class is very minimal and the testing identities are unseen during training. Our application domain is person re-identification.

In this paper we propose a novel metric learning framework called Nullspace Kernel Maximum Margin Metric Learning (NK3ML) which efficiently addresses the SSS problem and provide better performance compared to the state-of-the-art approaches for re-ID. The discriminative metric space is learned using a maximum margin criterion over a discriminative nullspace. In the learned metric space, the samples of distinct classes are separated with maximum margin while keeping the samples of same class collapsed to a single point (i.e., zero intra-class variance) to maximize the separability in terms of Fisher criterion.

1.1 Related Methods

Most existing person re-identification methods try to build robust feature descriptors and learn discriminative distance metrics. For feature descriptors, several works have been proposed to capture the invariant and discriminative properties of human images [10,12,18,23,26,31,52,59]. Specifically, GOG [31] and LOMO [23] descriptors have shown impressive robustness against illumination, pose and viewpoint changes.

For recognition purposes, many metric learning methods have been proposed recently [6,15,19,23,36,51,54,61,62]. Most of the metric learning methods in re-ID originated elsewhere and are applied with suitable modification for overcoming the additional challenges in re-identification. Köstinger et al. proposed an efficient metric called KISSME [19] using log likelihood ratio test of two Gaussian distributions. Hirzer et al. [15] used a relaxed positive semi definite constraint of the Mahalanobis metric. Zheng et al. proposed PRDC [62] where the metric is learned to maximize the probability of a pair of true match having a smaller distance than that of a wrong match pair. As an improvement for KISSME [19], Liao et al. proposed XQDA [23] to learn a more discriminative distance metric and a low-dimensional subspace simultaneously. In [36], Pedagadi et al. successfully applied Local Fisher Discriminant Analysis (LFDA) [44] which is a variant of Fisher discriminant analysis to preserve the local structure.

Most metric learning methods based on Fisher-type criterion suffer from the small sample size (SSS) problem [14,61]. The dimensionality of various efficient feature descriptors like LOMO [23] and GOG [31] are in ten thousands and too high compared to the number of samples typically available for training. This makes the within class scatter matrix singular. Some methods use matrix regularization [23,25,31,36,51] or unsupervised dimensionality reduction [19,36] to overcome the singularity which makes them less discriminative and suboptimal. Also these methods typically have a number of free parameters to tune.

Recently, Null Foley-Sammon Transform (NFST) [3,14,61] has gained increasing attention in computer vision applications. NFST was proposed in [61] to address the SSS problem in re-ID. They find a transformation which collapses the intra class training samples into a single point. By restricting the between class variance to be non zero, they maximize the Fisher discriminant criterion without the need of using any regularization or unsupervised dimensionality reduction.

In this paper, we first identify a serious limitation of NFST, i.e. though NFST minimizes the intra-class distance to zero for all training data, it fails to maximize the inter class distance and has serious consequences creating suboptimality in generalizing the discrimination for test data samples when the test sample does not map to the corresponding singular points. Secondly, we propose a novel metric learning framework called Nullspace Kernel Maximum Margin Metric Learning (NK3ML). The method learns a discriminative metric subspace to maximize the inter-class distance as well as minimize the intra-class distance to zero. NK3ML efficiently addresses the suboptimality of NFST in generalizing the discrimination to test data samples also. In particular, NK3ML first take advantage of NFST to find a low dimensional discriminative nullspace to collapse the intra class samples into a single point. Later NK3ML utilizes a secondary metric learning framework to learn a discriminant subspace using the nullspace to maximally separate the inter-class distance. NK3ML also uses a nonlinear mapping of the discriminative nullspace into an infinite dimensional space using an appropriate kernel to further increase the maximum attainable margin between the inter class samples. The proposed NK3ML does not require regularization nor unsupervised dimensionality reduction and efficiently addresses the SSS problem as well as the suboptimality of NFST in generalizing the discrimination for test data samples. The proposed NK3ML has a closed from solution and has no free parameters to tune.

We first explain NFST in Sect. 2. Later we present NK3ML in Sect. 3 and the experimental results in Sect. 4.

2   Null Foley-Sammon Transform

2.1   Foley-Sammon Transform

The objective of Foley-Sammon Transform (FST) [34,38] is to learn optimal discriminant vectors $\mathbf{w} \in \mathbb{R}^d$ that maximize the *Fisher criterion* $J_F(\mathbf{w})$ under orthonormal constraints:

$$J_F(\mathbf{w}) = \frac{\mathbf{w}^T \mathbf{S}_b \mathbf{w}}{\mathbf{w}^T \mathbf{S}_w \mathbf{w}}. \tag{1}$$

$\mathbf{S}_w$ represents the *within class scatter matrix* and $\mathbf{S}_b$ the *between class scatter matrix*. $\mathbf{x} \in \mathbb{R}^d$ are the data samples with classes $\mathcal{C}_1, \ldots, \mathcal{C}_c$ where c is the total number of classes. Let n be the total number of samples and n_i the number of samples in class C_i. FST tries to maximize the between class distance and minimize the within class distance simultaneously by maximizing the Fisher criterion.

The optimal discriminant vectors of FST are generated using the following steps. The first discriminant vector $\mathbf{w}_1$ of FST is the unit vector that maximizes $J_F(\mathbf{w}_1)$. If $\mathbf{S}_w$ is nonsingular, the solution becomes a conventional eigenvalue problem: $\mathbf{S}_w^{-1}\mathbf{S}_b\mathbf{w} = \lambda\mathbf{w}$, and can be solved by the normalized eigenvector of $\mathbf{S}_w^{-1}\mathbf{S}_b$ corresponding to its largest eigenvalue. The ith discriminant vector $\mathbf{w}_i$ of FST is calculated by the following optimization problem with orthonormality constraints:

$$\underset{||\mathbf{w}_i||=1, \mathbf{w}_i^T\mathbf{w}_j=0}{\text{maximize}} \quad \{J_F(\mathbf{w}_i)\} \quad j = 1, \ldots, i-1. \tag{2}$$

A major drawback of FST is that it cannot be directly applied when $\mathbf{S}_w$ becomes singular in small sample size (SSS) problems. The SSS problem occures when $n < d$. Common solutions include adding regularization term to $\mathbf{S}_w$ or reducing the dimensionality using PCA, which makes them suboptimal.

2.2   Null Foley-Sammon Transform

The suboptimality due to SSS problem in FST is overcome in an efficient way using Null Foley-Sammon Transform (NFST). The objective of NFST is to find orthonormal discriminant vectors satisfying the following set of constraints:

$$\mathbf{w}^T\mathbf{S}_w\mathbf{w} = 0, \quad \mathbf{w}^T\mathbf{S}_b\mathbf{w} > 0. \tag{3}$$

Each discriminant vector $\mathbf{w}$ should satisfy zero within-class scatter and positive between-class scatter. This leads to $J_F(\mathbf{w}) \to \infty$ and thus NFST tries to attain the best separability in terms of Fisher criterion. Such a vector $\mathbf{w}$ is called *Null Projecting Direction* (NPD). The zero within-class scatter ensures that the transformation using NPDs collapse the intra-class training samples into a single point.

Obtaining Null Projecting Directions: We explain how to obtain the Null Projecting Direction (NPD) of NFST. The total class scatter matrix $\mathbf{S}_t$ is defined as $\mathbf{S}_t = \mathbf{S}_b + \mathbf{S}_w$. We also have $\mathbf{S}_t = \frac{1}{n}\mathbf{P}_t\mathbf{P}_t^T$, where $\mathbf{P}_t$ consists of zero mean data $\mathbf{x}_1 - \mathbf{m}, \ldots, \mathbf{x}_n - \mathbf{m}$ as its columns. Let $\mathbf{Z}_t$ and $\mathbf{Z}_w$ be the null space of $\mathbf{S}_t$ and $\mathbf{S}_w$ respectively. Let $\mathbf{Z}_t^\perp$ represent orthogonal complement of $\mathbf{Z}_t$. Note the lemmas [14].

Lemma 1: Let $\mathbf{A}$ be a positive semidefinite matrix. Then $\mathbf{w}^T A\mathbf{w} = 0$ iff $A\mathbf{w} = 0$.

Lemma 2: If $\mathbf{w}$ is an NPD, then $\mathbf{w} \in (\mathbf{Z}_t^\perp \cap \mathbf{Z}_w)$.

Lemma 3: For small sample size (SSS) case, there exists exactly $c - 1$ NPDs, c being the number of classes.

In order to obtain the NPDs, we first obtain vectors from the space $\mathbf{Z}_t^\perp$. From this space, we next obtain vectors that also satisfy $\mathbf{w} \in \mathbf{Z}_w$. A set of orthonormal vectors can be obtained from the resultant vectors which form the NPDs.

Based on the lemmas, $\mathbf{Z}_t$ can be solved as:

$$\begin{aligned} \mathbf{Z}_t &= \{\mathbf{w} \mid \mathbf{S}_t \mathbf{w} = 0\} = \{\mathbf{w} \mid \mathbf{w}^T \mathbf{S}_t \mathbf{w} = 0\} \\ &= \{\mathbf{w} \mid (\mathbf{P}_t^T \mathbf{w})^T (\mathbf{P}_t^T \mathbf{w}) = 0\} = \{\mathbf{w} \mid \mathbf{P}_t^T \mathbf{w} = 0\}. \end{aligned} \tag{4}$$

Thus $\mathbf{Z}_t$ is the null space of $\mathbf{P}_t^T$. So $\mathbf{Z}_t^\perp$ is the row space of $\mathbf{P}_t^T$, which is the column space of $\mathbf{P}_t$. Therefore $\mathbf{Z}_t^\perp$ is the subspace spanned by zero mean data. $\mathbf{Z}_t^\perp$ can be represented using an orthonormal basis $\mathbf{Q} = (\theta_1, \ldots, \theta_{n-1})$, where n is the total number of samples. The basis $\mathbf{Q}$ can be obtained using Gram-Schmidt orthonormalization procedure. Any vector in $\mathbf{Z}_t^\perp$ can hence be represented as:

$$\mathbf{w} = \beta_1 \theta_1 + \ldots + \beta_{n-1} \theta_{n-1} = \mathbf{Q}\boldsymbol{\beta}. \tag{5}$$

A vector $\mathbf{w}$, satisfying Eq. (5) for any $\boldsymbol{\beta}$, belongs to $\mathbf{Z}_t^\perp$. Now we have to find those specific $\boldsymbol{\beta}$ which ensures $\mathbf{w} \in \mathbf{Z}_w$. They can be found by substituting (5) in the condition for $\mathbf{w} \in \mathbf{Z}_w$ as follows:

$$\begin{aligned} 0 = \mathbf{S}_w \mathbf{w} &= \mathbf{w}^T \mathbf{S}_w \mathbf{w} = (\mathbf{Q}\boldsymbol{\beta})^T \mathbf{S}_w (\mathbf{Q}\boldsymbol{\beta}) \\ &= \boldsymbol{\beta}^T (\mathbf{Q}^T \mathbf{S}_w \mathbf{Q}) \boldsymbol{\beta} = \mathbf{Q}^T \mathbf{S}_w \mathbf{Q}\boldsymbol{\beta}. \end{aligned} \tag{6}$$

Hence $\boldsymbol{\beta}$ can be solved by finding the null space of $\mathbf{Q}^T \mathbf{S}_w \mathbf{Q}$. The set of solutions $\{\boldsymbol{\beta}\}$ can be chosen orthonormal. Since the dimension of $\mathbf{w} \in (\mathbf{Z}_t^\perp \cap \mathbf{Z}_w)$ is $c - 1$ [14], we get $c - 1$ solutions for $\boldsymbol{\beta}$. The $c - 1$ NPDs can now be computed using (5). Since $\mathbf{Q}$ and $\{\boldsymbol{\beta}\}$ are orthonormal, the resulting NPDs are also orthonormal. The projection matrix $\mathbf{W}_N \in \mathbb{R}^{d \times (c-1)}$ of NFST now constitutes of the $c - 1$ NPDs as its columns.

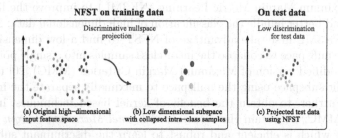

Fig. 1. Illustration of the suboptimality in NFST. Each color corresponds to distinct classes. (Color figure online)

3   Nullspace Kernel Maximum Margin Metric Learning

Methods based on Fisher criterion, in general, learn the discriminant vectors using the training samples so that the vectors generalize well for the test data also in terms of separability of classes. NFST [3,14] was proposed in [61] to address the SSS problem in re-ID. They find a transformation by collapsing the intra-class samples into a single point. We identify a serious limitation of NFST. Maximizing $J_F(\mathbf{w})$ in Eq. (1) by making the denominator to zero, does not allow to make use of the information contained in the numerator. As illustrated in Fig. 1, the mapped singular points in the NFST projected space for two different classes may be quite close. Thus, when a test data is projected into this NFST nullspace, it no longer maps to the same singular point. Rather, it maps to a point close to the above point. But this projected point may be closer to the singular point for the other class and misclassification takes place. Under the NFST formulation, one has no control on this aspect as one makes $\mathbf{w}^T \mathbf{S}_w \mathbf{w} = 0$, but $\mathbf{w}^T \mathbf{S}_b \mathbf{w}$ may also be very small instead of being large, and the classification performance may be very poor.

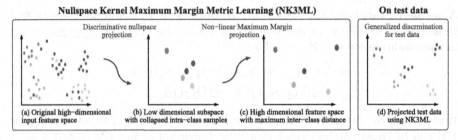

Fig. 2. Illustration of our method NK3ML. Each color corresponds to distinct classes. (Color figure online)

In this paper we propose a metric learning framework, namely, Nullspace Kernel Maximum Margin Metric Learning (NK3ML) to improve the limitation of NFST and better handle the classification of high dimensional data. As shown in Fig. 2, NK3ML first take advantage of NFST to find a low dimensional discriminative nullspace to collapse the intra-class samples into a single point. Later it uses a modified version of Maximum Margin Criterion (MMC) [20] to learn a discriminant subspace using the nullspace to maximally separate the inter-class distance. Further, to obtain the benefit of kernel based techniques, instead of using the MMC, we obtain the *Normalized Kernel Maximum margin criterion* (NKMMC) which is efficient and robust to learn the discriminant subspace to maximize the distances among the classes. NK3ML can efficiently address the suboptimality of NFST in enhancing the discrimination to test data samples also.

3.1 Maximum Margin Criterion

Maximum margin criterion (MMC) [20,21] is an efficient way to learn a discriminant subspace which maximize the distances between classes. For the separability of classes $\mathcal{C}_1, \ldots, \mathcal{C}_c$, the maximum margin criterion is defined as

$$J = \frac{1}{2} \sum_{i=1}^{c} \sum_{j=1}^{c} p_i p_j d(\mathcal{C}_i, \mathcal{C}_j), \tag{7}$$

where the inter-class margin (or distance) of class $\mathcal{C}_i$ and $\mathcal{C}_j$ is defined as

$$d(\mathcal{C}_i, \mathcal{C}_j) = d(\mathbf{m}_i, \mathbf{m}_j) - s(\mathcal{C}_i) - s(\mathcal{C}_j), \tag{8}$$

and $d(\mathbf{m}_i, \mathbf{m}_j)$ represents the squared Euclidean distance between mean vectors $\mathbf{m}_i$ and $\mathbf{m}_j$ of classes $\mathcal{C}_i$ and $\mathcal{C}_j$, respectively. $s(\mathcal{C}_i)$ is the scatter of class $\mathcal{C}_i$, estimated as $s(\mathcal{C}_i) = tr(\mathbf{S}_i)$ where $\mathbf{S}_i$ is the within class scatter matrix of class $\mathcal{C}_i$. The inter-class margin can be solved to get $d(\mathcal{C}_i, \mathcal{C}_j) = tr(\mathbf{S}_b - \mathbf{S}_w)$. A set of r unit linear discriminant vectors $\{\mathbf{v}_k \in \mathbb{R}^d | k = 1, \ldots, r\}$ is learned such that they maximize J in the projected subspace. If $\mathbf{V} \in \mathbb{R}^{d \times r}$ is the projection matrix, the MMC criterion becomes $J(\mathbf{V}) = tr(\mathbf{V}^T(\mathbf{S}_b - \mathbf{S}_w)\mathbf{V})$. The optimization problem can be equivalently written as:

$$\begin{aligned} \underset{\mathbf{v}_k}{\text{maximize}} \quad & \sum_{k=1}^{r} \mathbf{v}_k^T(\mathbf{S}_b - \mathbf{S}_w)\mathbf{v}_k, \\ \text{subject to} \quad & \mathbf{v}_k^T \mathbf{v}_k = 1, \qquad k = 1, \ldots, r. \end{aligned} \tag{9}$$

The optimal solutions are obtained by finding the normalized eigenvectors of $\mathbf{S}_b - \mathbf{S}_w$ corresponding to its first r largest eigenvectors.

3.2 Kernel Maximum Margin Criterion

Kernels methods are well known techniques to learn non-linear discriminant vectors. They use an appropriate non-linear function $\mathbf{\Phi}(\mathbf{z})$ to map the input data $\mathbf{z}$ to a higher dimensional feature space $\mathcal{F}$ and find discriminant vectors $\mathbf{v}_k \in \mathcal{F}$. Given n training data samples and a kernel function $k(\mathbf{z}_i, \mathbf{z}_j) = \langle \mathbf{\Phi}(\mathbf{z}_i), \mathbf{\Phi}(\mathbf{z}_j) \rangle$, we can calculate the kernel matrix $\mathbf{K} \in \mathbb{R}^{n \times n}$. The matrix $\mathbf{K}_i \in \mathbb{R}^{n \times n_i}$ for the ith class with n_i samples is $(\mathbf{K}_i)_{pq} := k(\mathbf{z}_p, \mathbf{z}_q^{(i)})$. As every discriminant vector $\mathbf{v}_k$ lies in the span of the mapped data samples, it can be expressed in the form $\mathbf{v}_k = \sum_{j=1}^{n} (\boldsymbol{\alpha}_k)_j \mathbf{\Phi}(\mathbf{z}_j)$, where $(\boldsymbol{\alpha}_k)_j$ is the jth element of the vector $\boldsymbol{\alpha}_k \in \mathbb{R}^n$, which constitutes the expansion coefficients of $\mathbf{v}_k$. The optimization problem proposed for Kernel Maximum Margin Criterion (KMMC) [20] is:

$$\begin{aligned} \underset{\boldsymbol{\alpha}_k}{\text{maximize}} \quad & \sum_{k=1}^{r} \boldsymbol{\alpha}_k^T(\mathbf{M} - \mathbf{N})\boldsymbol{\alpha}_k, \\ \text{subject to} \quad & \boldsymbol{\alpha}_k^T \boldsymbol{\alpha}_k = 1, \end{aligned} \tag{10}$$

where $\mathbf{N} := \sum_{i=1}^{c} \frac{1}{n} \mathbf{K}_i(\mathbf{I}_{n_i} - \frac{1}{n_i} \mathbf{1}_{n_i} \mathbf{1}_{n_i}^T)\mathbf{K}_i^T$, $\mathbf{I}_{n_i}$ is $(n_i \times n_i)$ identity matrix; $\mathbf{1}_{n_i}$ is n_i dimensional vector of ones and $\mathbf{M} = \sum_{i=1}^{c} \frac{1}{n_i}(\tilde{\mathbf{m}}_i - \tilde{\mathbf{m}})(\tilde{\mathbf{m}}_i - \tilde{\mathbf{m}})^T$; $\tilde{\mathbf{m}} := \frac{1}{n} \sum_{i=1}^{c} n_i \tilde{\mathbf{m}}_i$ and $(\tilde{\mathbf{m}}_i)_j := \frac{1}{n_i} \sum_{\mathbf{z} \in \mathcal{C}_i} k(\mathbf{z}, \mathbf{z}_j)$. The optimal solutions are the normalized eigenvectors of $(\mathbf{M} - \mathbf{N})$, corresponding to its first r largest eigenvalues.

3.3   NK3ML

The kernalized optimization problem given in (10) obtained by KMMC [20] does not enforce normalization of discriminant vectors in the feature space, but rather uses normalization constraint on eigenvector expansion coefficient vector α_k. In NK3ML, we require the discriminant vectors obtained by KMMC to be normalized, i.e., $v_k^T v_k = 1$. The normalized discriminant vectors are important to preserve the shape of the distribution of data. Hence we derive *Normalized Kernel Maximum Margin Criterion* (NKMMC) as follows. We rewrite the discriminant vector v_k as:

$$v_k = \sum_{j=1}^{n} (\alpha_k)_j \Phi(z_j) = \Big[\Phi(z_1) \; \Phi(z_2) \; \dots \; \Phi(z_n) \Big] \alpha_k. \tag{11}$$

Then normalization constraint becomes

$$\Big(\sum_{j=1}^{n} (\alpha_k)_j \Phi(z_j) \Big)^T \Big(\sum_{j=1}^{n} (\alpha_k)_j \Phi(z_j) \Big) = 1$$

$$\Rightarrow \qquad \alpha_k^T K \alpha_k = 1. \tag{12}$$

where K is the kernel matrix. The optimization problem in (10) can now be reformulated to enforce normalized discriminant vectors as follows.

$$\begin{aligned} \underset{\alpha_k}{\text{maximize}} \quad & \sum_{k=1}^{r} \alpha_k^T (M - N) \alpha_k, \\ \text{subject to} \quad & \alpha_k^T K \alpha_k = 1. \end{aligned} \tag{13}$$

We introduce a Lagrangian to solve the above problem.

$$\mathcal{L}(\alpha_k, \lambda_k) = \sum_{k=1}^{r} \alpha_k^T (M - N) \alpha_k + \lambda_k (\alpha_k^T K \alpha_k - 1), \tag{14}$$

where λ_k is the Lagrangian multiplier. The Lagrangian $\mathcal{L}$ has to be maximized with respect to α_k and the multipliers λ_k. The derivatives of $\mathcal{L}$ with respect to α_k should vanish at the stationary point.

$$\begin{aligned} \frac{\partial \mathcal{L}(\alpha_k, \lambda_k)}{\partial \alpha_k} &= (M - N - \lambda_k K) \alpha_k = 0 \quad \forall \, k = 1, \dots, r \\ &\Rightarrow (M - N) \alpha_k = \lambda_k K \alpha_k. \end{aligned} \tag{15}$$

This is a generalized eigenvalue problem. λ_k's are the generalized eigenvalues and α_k's the generalized eigenvectors of $(M - N)$ and K. The objective function at this stationary point is given as:

$$\sum_{k=1}^{r} \alpha_k^T (M - N) \alpha_k = \sum_{k=1}^{r} \lambda_k \alpha_k^T K \alpha_k = \sum_{k=1}^{r} \lambda_k. \tag{16}$$

Hence the objective function in NKMMC is maximized by the *generalized* eigenvectors corresponding to the first r generalized eigenvalues of $(\mathbf{M} - \mathbf{N})$ and $\mathbf{K}$. We choose all the eigenvectors with positive eigenvalues, since they ensure maximum inter-class margin, i.e., the samples of different classes are well separated in the direction of these eigenvectors. It should be noted that our NKMMC has a different solution from that of original KMMC [20], since KMMC uses standard eigenvectors of $\mathbf{M} - \mathbf{N}$.

NFST is first used to learn the discriminant vectors using the training data $\{\mathbf{x}\}$. The discriminants of NFST form the projection matrix $\mathbf{W}_N$. Each training data sample $\mathbf{x} \in \mathbb{R}^d$ is projected as

$$\mathbf{z} = \mathbf{W}_N^T \mathbf{x}. \tag{17}$$

Each projected data sample $\mathbf{z} \in \mathbb{R}^{c-1}$ now lies in the discriminative nullspace of NFST. Now we use all the projected data $\{\mathbf{z}\}$ for learning the secondary distance metric using NKMMC.

Any general feature vector $\widetilde{\mathbf{x}} \in \mathbb{R}^d$ can be projected onto the discriminant vector $\mathbf{v}_k$ of NK3ML in two steps:
Step 1: Project $\widetilde{\mathbf{x}}$ onto the nullspace of NFST to get $\widetilde{\mathbf{z}}$:

$$\widetilde{\mathbf{z}} = \mathbf{W}_N^T \widetilde{\mathbf{x}}. \tag{18}$$

Step 2: Project the $\widetilde{\mathbf{z}}$ onto the discriminant vector $\mathbf{v}_k$ of NKMMC:

$$\mathbf{v}_k^T \Phi(\widetilde{\mathbf{z}}) = \Big(\sum_{j=1}^n (\boldsymbol{\alpha}_k)_j \boldsymbol{\Phi}(\mathbf{z}_j) \Big)^T \Phi(\widetilde{\mathbf{z}}) = \sum_{j=1}^n (\boldsymbol{\alpha}_k)_j k(\mathbf{z}_j, \widetilde{\mathbf{z}}). \tag{19}$$

The proposed NK3ML does not require any regularization or unsupervised dimensionality reduction and can efficiently address the SSS problem as well as the suboptimality of NFST in generalizing the discrimination for test data samples. The NK3ML has a closed form solution and no free parameters to tune. The only issue to be decided is what kernel to be used. In effect what the proposed method does is to project the data into the NFST nullspace, where the dimensionality of the feature space is reduced to force all points belonging to a given class to a single point. In the second stage, the dimensionality is increased by using an appropriate kernel in conjunction with NKMMC, thereby allowing us to enhance the between class distance. This provides a better margin while classifying the test samples.

4   Experimental Results

Parameter Settings: There are no free parameters to tune in NK3ML, unlike most state-of-the-art methods which have to carefully tune their parameters to attain their best results. In all the experiments, we use the RBF kernel whose kernel width is set to be the root mean squared pairwise distance among the samples.

Table 1. Comparison of NK3ML with baselines on GRID and PRID450S datasets

Methods	GRID		PRID450S	
	Rank1	Rank10	Rank1	Rank10
WHOS + NK3ML	21.20	55.60	50.67	88.09
WHOS + NFST	18.64	52.32	42.58	77.07
WHOS + KNFST	21.12	54.32	45.87	85.78
WHOS + XQDA	18.72	52.56	43.38	77.91
LOMO + NK3ML	18.24	43.76	60.62	91.96
LOMO + NFST	17.04	42.64	58.84	89.42
LOMO + KNFST	14.88	41.28	59.47	91.96
LOMO + XQDA	16.56	41.84	59.78	90.09
GOG + NK3ML	26.96	57.52	68.04	95.07
GOG + NFST	24.88	58.00	67.60	94.18
GOG + KNFST	24.88	53.28	64.80	94.00
GOG + XQDA	24.80	58.40	68.00	94.36

Fig. 3. Sample images of PRID450S dataset. Images with the same column corresponds to the same identities.

Datasets: The proposed NK3ML is evaluated on four popular benchmark datasets: PRID450S [37], GRID [27], CUHK01 [22] and VIPeR [12], respectively contains 450, 250, 971, and 632 identities captured in two disjoint camera views. CUHK01 contains two images for each person in one camera view and all other datasets contain just one image. Quite naturally, these datasets constitute the extreme examples of SSS. Following the conventional experimental setup [1,5,23,31,35,52], each dataset is randomly divided into training and test sets, each having half of the identities. During testing, the probe images are matched against the gallery. In the test sets of all datasets, except GRID, the number of probe images and gallery images are equal. The test set of GRID has additional 775 gallery images that do not belong to the 250 identities. The procedure is repeated 10 times and the average rank scores are reported.

Features: Most existing methods use a fixed feature descriptor for all datasets. Such an approach is less efficient to represent the intrinsic characteristics of each dataset. Hence in NK3ML, we use specific set of feature descriptors for each dataset. We choose from the standard feature descriptors GOG [31] and WHOS [26]. We also use an improved version of LOMO [23] descriptor, which we call *LOMO**. We generate it by concatenating the LOMO features generated using YUV and RGB color spaces separately.

Method of Comparison: We use only the available data in each dataset for training. No separate pre-processing of the features or images (such as domain adaptation/body parts detection), or post-processing of the classifier has been used in the study. There has been some efforts on using even the test data for re-ranking of re-ID results [1,2,63] to boost up the accuracy. But these techniques being not suitable for any real time applications, we refrain from using such supplementary methods in our proposal.

Table 2. Comparison with state-of-the-art results on (a) GRID and (b) PRID450S dataset. The best and second best scores are shown in red and blue, respectively. The methods with a * signifies pre/post-processing based methods

(a) GRID dataset

Methods	Rank1	Rank10	Rank20
MtMCML[28]	14.08	45.84	59.84
KNFST[61]	14.88	41.28	50.88
PolyMap[6]	16.30	46.00	57.60
LOMO+XQDA[23]	16.56	41.84	52.40
MLAPG[24]	16.64	41.20	52.96
KEPLER[30]	18.40	50.24	61.44
DR-KISS[45]	20.60	51.40	62.60
SSSVM[54]	22.40	51.28	61.20
SCSP[5]	24.24	54.08	65.20
GOG+XQDA[31]	**24.80**	**58.40**	**68.88**
NK3ML(Ours)	27.20	60.96	71.04
*SSDAL[43]	22.40	48.00	58.40
*SSM[1]	27.20	61.12	70.56
*OL-MANS[64]	30.16	49.20	59.36

(b) PRID450S dataset

Methods	Rank1	Rank10	Rank20
WARCA[16]	24.58	-	-
SCNCD[52]	41.60	79.40	87.80
CSL[39]	44.40	82.20	89.80
TMA[29]	52.89	85.78	93.33
KNFST[61]	59.47	91.96	96.53
LOMO+XQDA[23]	59.78	90.09	95.29
SSSVM[54]	60.49	88.58	93.60
GOG+XQDA[31]	**68.00**	**94.36**	**97.64**
NK3ML(Ours)	73.42	96.31	98.58
*Semantic[41]	44.90	77.50	86.70
*SSM[1]	72.98	96.76	99.11

4.1 Comparison with Baselines

In Table 1, we compare the performances of NK3ML with the baseline metric learning methods. As NK3ML is proposed as an improvement to address the limitations of NFST, we first compare the performance of NK3ML with NFST. For fair comparison with NFST, we also use its kernalized version KNFST [61]. KNFST is also the state-of-the-art metric learning method applied for LOMO descriptor. For uniformity, all metric learning methods are evaluated using the same standard feature descriptors LOMO [23], WHOS [26] and GOG [31]. We also compare with Cross-view Quadratic Discriminant Analysis (XQDA) [31] which is the state of the art metric learning method for GOG descriptor. XQDA is also successfully applied with LOMO in many cases [23]. We use GRID and PRID450S datasets for comparison with the baselines. GRID is a pretty difficult person re-identification dataset having poor image quality with large variations in pose and illuminations, which makes it very challenging to obtain good matching accuracies. PRID450S is also a challenging dataset due to the partial occlusion, background interference and viewpoint changes. From the results in Table 1, it can be seen that NK3ML provides significant performance gains against all the baselines for all the standard feature descriptors (Fig. 3).

Comparison with NFST: NK3ML provides a good performance gain against NFST. In particular for PRID450S dataset, when compared using WHOS, NK3ML provides an improvement of 8.09% at rank-1 and 11.02% at rank-10. Similar gain can also be seen while using LOMO and GOG features for both GRID and PRID450S datasets.

Table 3. Comparison with state-of-the-art results on CUHK01 dataset using (a) single-shot and (b) multi-shot settings. ** corresponds to deep learning based methods

(a) single-shot

Methods	Rank1	Rank10	Rank20
MLFL[59]	34.30	65.00	75.00
LOMO+XQDA[23]	50.00	83.40	89.51
KNFST[61]	52.80	84.97	91.07
CAMEL[53]	57.30	-	-
GOG+XQDA[31]	**57.89**	**86.25**	**92.14**
WARCA[16]	58.34	-	-
NK3ML(Ours)	67.09	91.85	95.92
*Semantic[41]	32.70	64.40	76.30
*MetricEnsemble[35]	53.40	84.40	90.50
**TPC[8]	53.70	91.00	96.30
**Quadruplet[7]	62.55	89.71	-
*DLPAR[56]	72.30	94.90	97.20

(b) multi-shot

Methods	Rank1	Rank10	Rank20
11-Graph[17]	50.10	-	-
LOMO+XQDA[23]	61.98	89.30	93.62
CAMEL[53]	62.70	-	-
MLAPG[24]	64.24	90.84	94.92
SSSVM[54]	65.97	-	-
KNFST[61]	66.07	91.56	95.64
GOG+XQDA[31]	**67.28**	**91.77**	**95.93**
NK3ML(Ours)	76.77	95.58	98.02
**DGD[50]	66.60	-	-
*OLMANS[64]	68.44	92.67	95.88
*SHaPE[2]	76.00	-	-
*Spindle[55]	79.90	97.10	98.60

Comparison with KNFST: In spite of KNFST being the state-of-the-art metric learning method for LOMO descriptor, NK3ML outperforms KNFST with a significant difference. In GRID dataset, NK3ML gains 3.36% in rank-1 and 2.48% in rank-10. Similar improvements are seen for other features also for both datasets.

Comparison with XQDA: For GOG descriptor, XQDA is the state of the art metric learning method. At rank-1, NK3ML gains 2.16% in GRID. Similarly, it gains 7.29% at rank-1 in PRID450S using WHOS descriptor.

Based on the above comparisons, it may be concluded that NK3ML attains a much better margin over NFST as expected from the theory. Also NK3ML outperforms KNFST and XQDA for all aforementioned standard feature descriptors.

4.2   Comparison with State-of-the-Art

In the performance comparison of NK3ML with the state-of-the-art methods, we also report the accuracies of pre/post processing methods on separate rows for completeness. As mentioned previously, direct comparisons of our results with pre/post processing methods are not advisable. However, even if such a comparison is made, we still have accuracies that are best or comparable to the best existing techniques on most of the evaluated datasets. Moreover, our approach is general enough to be easily integrated with the existing pre/post processing methods to further increase their accuracy.

Experiments on GRID Dataset: We use GOG and LOMO* as the feature descriptor for GRID. Table 2a shows the performance comparison of NK3ML. GOG + XQDA [31] reports the best performance of 24.8% at rank-1 till date. NK3ML achieves an accuracy of 27.20% at rank-1, outperforming GOG+XQDA by 2.40%. At rank-1, NK3ML also outperforms all the post processing methods except OL-MANS [64], which uses the test data and train data together to learn a better similarity function. However, the penalty for misclassification at rank-1, if any, severely affects the rank-N performance for OL-MANS. NK3ML outperforms OL-MANS by 11.76% at rank-10 and 11.68% at rank-20.

Experiments on PRID450S Dataset: GOG and LOMO* are used as the feature descriptor for PRID450S. NK3ML provides the best performances at all ranks, as shown in Table 2b. Especially, it provides an improvement margin of 5.42% in rank-1 compared to the second best method GOG+XQDA [31]. At rank-1, NK3ML also outperforms all the post processing based methods. SSM [1] incorporates XQDA as the metric learning method. As analyzed in Sect. 4.1, since NK3ML outperforms XQDA, it can be anticipated that even the re-ranking methods like SSM can benefit from NK3ML.

Table 4. Comparison with state-of-the-art results on VIPeR dataset. RN means Rank-N accuracy

Methods	Ref	R1	R10	R20	Methods	Ref	R1	R10	R20
ELF[12]	ECCV2008	12.0	44.0	61.0	SSSVM[54]	CVPR2016	42.1	84.3	91.9
PCCA[32]	CVPR2012	19.3	64.9	80.3	**TPC[8]	CVPR2016	47.8	84.8	91.1
KISSME[19]	CVPR2012	19.6	62.2	77.0	GOG+XQDA[31]	CVPR2016	49.7	88.7	94.5
LFDA[36]	CVPR2013	24.2	67.1	-	SCSP[5]	CVPR2016	53.5	91.5	96.7
eSDC[58]	CVPR2013	26.7	62.4	76.4	**SCNN[46]	ECCV2016	37.8	66.9	-
SalMatch[57]	ICCV2013	30.2	-	-	**Shi et al.[40]	ECCV2016	40.9	-	-
MLFL[59]	CVPR2014	29.1	66.0	79.9	l1-graph[17]	ECCV2016	41.5	-	-
rPCCA[51]	ECCV2014	22.0	71.0	85.3	**S-LSTM[47]	ECCV2016	42.4	79.4	-
kLFDA[51]	ECCV2014	32.3	79.7	90.9	*SSDAL[43]	ECCV2016	43.5	81.5	89.0
SCNCD[52]	ECCV2014	37.8	81.2	90.4	*TMA[29]	ECCV2016	48.2	87.7	93.5
PolyMap[6]	CVPR2015	36.8	83.7	91.7	*SSM[1]	CVPR2017	53.7	91.5	96.1
LOMO+XQDA[23]	CVPR2015	40.0	80.5	91.1	*Spindle[55]	CVPR2017	53.8	83.2	92.1
*Semantic[41]	CVPR2015	41.6	86.2	95.1	CAMEL[53]	ICCV2017	30.9	-	-
QALF[60]	CVPR2015	30.2	62.4	73.8	*MuDeep	ICCV2017	43.0	85.8	-
CSL[39]	ICCV2015	34.8	82.3	91.8	*OLMANS[64]	ICCV2017	45.0	85.0	93.6
MLAPG[24]	ICCV2015	40.7	82.3	92.4	*DLPAR[56]	ICCV2017	48.7	85.1	93.0
*DCIA[11]	ICCV2015	**63.9**	87.5	-	*PDC[42]	ICCV2017	51.3	84.2	91.5
**DGD[50]	CVPR2016	38.6	-	-	*SHAPE[2]	ICCV2017	62.0	-	-
KNFST[61]	CVPR2016	42.3	82.9	92.1	NK3ML	Ours	99.8	100	100

Experiments on CUHK01 Dataset: We use GOG and LOMO* as the features for CUHK01. Each person of the dataset has two images in each camera view. Hence we report comparison with both single-shot and multi-shot settings in Tables 3a and b. NK3ML provides the state-of-the-art performances in all ranks. For single-shot setting, it outperforms the current best method GOG+XQDA [31] with a high margin of 9.20%. Similarly for multi-shot setting, NK3ML improves the accuracy by 9.49% for rank-1 over GOG+XQDA. At rank-1, NK3ML outperforms almost all of the pre/post processing based methods also, except DLPAR [56] in single-shot setting, and Spindle [55] and SHaPE [2] for multi-shot setting. However, note that Spindle and DLPAR uses other camera domain information for training, and SHaPE is a re-ranking technique to aggregate scores from multiple metric learning methods. Also note that NK3ML even outperforms the deep learning based methods (see Table 4 also), emphasizing the limitation of deep learning based methods in re-ID systems with minimal training data.

Experiments on VIPeR Dataset: Concatenated GOG, LOMO* and WHOS are used as the features for VIPeR. It is the most widely accepted benchmark for person re-ID. It is a very challenging dataset as it contains images captured from outdoor environment with large variations in background, illumination and viewpoint. An enormous number of algorithms have reported results on VIPeR, with most of them reporting an accuracy below 50% at rank-1, as shown in Table 4. Even with the deep learning and pre/post processing re-ID methods, the best reported result for rank-1 is only 63.92% by DCIA [11]. On the contrary, NK3ML provides unprecedented improvement over these methods and attains a 99.8% rank-1 accuracy. The superior performance of NK3ML is due to its capability to enhance the discriminability even for the test data by simultaneously providing the maximal separation between the classes as well as minimizing the within class distance to the least value of zero.

Table 5. Comparison of execution time (in seconds) on VIPeR dataset

Methods	NK3ML	NFST	KNFST	XQDA	MLAPG	kLFDA	MFA	rPCCA
Training	1.64	1.47	0.37	1.35	12.10	4.10	3.68	23.98
Testing	0.37	0.34	0.33	0.34	0.13	4.13	3.99	3.74

4.3   Computational Requirements

We compare the execution time of NK3ML with other metric learning methods including NFST [61], KNFST [61], XQDA [23,31], MLAPG [24], kLFDA [51], MFA [51] and rPCCA [51] on VIPeR dataset. The details are shown in Table 5. The training time is calculated for the 632 samples in the training set, and the testing time is calculated for all the 316 queries in the test set. The training and testing time are averaged over 10 random trials. All methods are implemented in MATLAB on a PC with an Intel i7-6700 CPU@3.40 GHz and 32 GB memory. The testing time for NK3ML is 0.37 s for the set of 316 query images (0.0012 s per query), which is adequate for real time applications.

4.4   Application in Another Domain

In order to evaluate the applicability of NK3ML on other object verification problems also, we conduct experiments using LEAR ToyCars [33] dataset. It contains a total of 256 images of 14 distinct cars and trucks. The images have

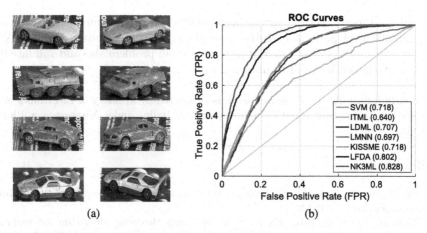

Fig. 4. ToyCars dataset (a) Sample images (b) ROC curves and EER comparisons.

wide variations in pose, illumination and background. The objective is to verify if a given pair of images are similar or not, even if they are *unseen* before. The training set has 7 distinct objects, provided as 1185 similar pairs and 7330 dissimilar pairs. The remaining 7 objects are used in the test set with 1044 similar pairs and 6337 dissimilar pairs. We use the feature representation from [19], which uses LBP with HSV and Lab histograms.

We compare the performance of NK3ML with the state-of-the-art metric learning methods including KISSME [19], ITML [9], LDML [13], LMNN [48,49], LFDA [36,44] and SVM [4]. Note that NK3ML and LMNN need the true class labels (not the similar/dissimilar pairs) for training. The proposed NK3ML learned a six dimensional subspace. For fair comparisons, we use the same features and learn an equal dimensional subspace for all the methods. We plot the Receiver Operator Characteristic (ROC) curves of the methods in Fig. 4, with the Equal Error Rate (EER) shown in parenthesis. NK3ML outperforms all other methods with a good margin. This experiment re-emphasizes that NK3ML is efficient to generalize well for unseen objects. Moreover, it indicates that NK3ML has the potential for other object verification problems also, apart from person re-identification.

5   Conclusions

In this work we presented a novel metric learning framework to efficiently address the small training sample size problem inherent in re-ID systems due to high dimensional data. We identify the suboptimality of NFST in generalizing to the test data. We provide a solution that minimizes the intra-class distance of training samples trivially to zero, as well as maximizes the inter-class distance to a much higher margin so that the learned discriminant vectors are effective in terms of generalization of the classifier performance for the test data also. Experiments on various challenging benchmark datasets show that our method outperforms the state-of-the-art metric learning approaches. Especially, our method attains near human level perfection in the most widely accepted dataset VIPeR. We evaluate our method on another object verification problem also and validate its efficiency to generalize well to unseen data.

Acknowledgement. This research work is supported by Ministry of Electronics and Information Technology (MeitY), Government of India, under Visvesvaraya Ph.D. Scheme.

References

1. Bai, S., Bai, X., Tian, Q.: Scalable person re-identification on supervised smoothed manifold. In: CVPR (2017)
2. Barman, A., Shah, S.K.: Shape: a novel graph theoretic algorithm for making consensus-based decisions in person re-identification systems. In: ICCV (2017)
3. Bodesheim, P., Freytag, A., Rodner, E., Kemmler, M., Denzler, J.: Kernel null space methods in novelty detection. In: CVPR (2013)
4. Chang, C.C., Lin, C.J.: LIBSVM: a library for support vector machines. ACM Trans. Intell. Syst. Technol. **2**(3), 27:1–27:27 (2011)
5. Chen, D., Yuan, Z., Chen, B., Zheng, N.: Similarity learning with spatial constraints for person re-identification. In: CVPR (2016)
6. Chen, D., Yuan, Z., Hua, G., Zheng, N., Wang, J.: Similarity learning on an explicit polynomial kernel feature map for person re-identification. In: CVPR (2015)
7. Chen, W., Chen, X., Zhang, J., Huang, K.: Beyond triplet loss: a deep quadruplet network for person re-identification. In: CVPR (2017)
8. Cheng, D., Gong, Y., Zhou, S., Wang, J., Zheng, N.: Person re-identification by multi-channel parts-based CNN with improved triplet loss function. In: CVPR (2016)
9. Davis, J.V., Kulis, B., Jain, P., Sra, S., Dhillon, I.S.: Information-theoretic metric learning. In: ICML (2007)
10. Farenzena, M., Bazzani, L., Perina, A., Cristani, M., Murino, V.: Person re-identification by symmetry-driven accumulation of local features. In: CVPR (2010)
11. Garcia, J., Martinel, N., Micheloni, C., Gardel, A.: Person re-identification ranking optimisation by discriminant context information analysis. In: ICCV (2015)
12. Gray, D., Tao, H.: Viewpoint invariant pedestrian recognition with an ensemble of localized features. In: Forsyth, D., Torr, P., Zisserman, A. (eds.) ECCV 2008. LNCS, vol. 5302, pp. 262–275. Springer, Heidelberg (2008). https://doi.org/10.1007/978-3-540-88682-2_21
13. Guillaumin, M., Verbeek, J., Schmid, C.: Is that you? Metric learning approaches for face identification. In: ICCV (2009)
14. Guo, Y., Wu, L., Lu, H., Feng, Z., Xue, X.: Null Foley-Sammon transform. Pattern Recognit. **39**(11), 2248–2251 (2006)
15. Hirzer, M., Roth, P.M., Köstinger, M., Bischof, H.: Relaxed pairwise learned metric for person re-identification. In: Fitzgibbon, A., Lazebnik, S., Perona, P., Sato, Y., Schmid, C. (eds.) ECCV 2012. LNCS, vol. 7577, pp. 780–793. Springer, Heidelberg (2012). https://doi.org/10.1007/978-3-642-33783-3_56
16. Jose, C., Fleuret, F.: Scalable metric learning via weighted approximate rank component analysis. In: Leibe, B., Matas, J., Sebe, N., Welling, M. (eds.) ECCV 2016. LNCS, vol. 9909, pp. 875–890. Springer, Cham (2016). https://doi.org/10.1007/978-3-319-46454-1_53

17. Kodirov, E., Xiang, T., Fu, Z., Gong, S.: Person re-identification by unsupervised ℓ_1 graph learning. In: Leibe, B., Matas, J., Sebe, N., Welling, M. (eds.) ECCV 2016. LNCS, vol. 9905, pp. 178–195. Springer, Cham (2016). https://doi.org/10.1007/978-3-319-46448-0_11

18. Kviatkovsky, I., Adam, A., Rivlin, E.: Color invariants for person reidentification. IEEE TPAMI **35**(7), 1622–1634 (2013)

19. Kstinger, M., Wohlhart, P., Hirzer, H., Roth, P.M., Bischof, H.: Large scale metric learning from equivalence constraints. In: CVPR (2012)

20. Li, H., Jiang, T., Zheng, K.: Efficient and robust feature extraction by maximum margin criterion. In: NIPS (2004)

21. Li, H., Jiang, T., Zheng, K.: Efficient and robust feature extraction by maximum margin criterion. IEEE TNN **17**(1), 157–165 (2006)

22. Li, W., Zhao, R., Wang, X.: Human reidentification with transferred metric learning. In: Lee, K.M., Matsushita, Y., Rehg, J.M., Hu, Z. (eds.) ACCV 2012. LNCS, vol. 7724, pp. 31–44. Springer, Heidelberg (2013). https://doi.org/10.1007/978-3-642-37331-2_3

23. Liao, S., Hu, Y., Zhu, X., Li, S.Z.: Person re-identification by local maximal occurrence representation and metric learning. In: CVPR (2015)

24. Liao, S., Li, S.Z.: Efficient PSD constrained asymmetric metric learning for person re-identification. In: ICCV (2015)

25. Lisanti, G., Masi, I., Bimbo, A.D.: Matching people across camera views using kernel canonical correlation analysis. In: Proceedings of the International Conference on Distributed Smart Cameras. ACM (2014)

26. Lisanti, G., Masi, I., Bimbo, A.D.: Person re-identification by iterative re-weighted sparse ranking. IEEE TPAMI (2014)

27. Loy, C.C., Xiang, T., Gong, S.: Multi-camera activity correlation analysis. In: CVPR (2009)

28. Ma, L., Yang, X., Tao, D.: Person re-identification over camera networks using multi-task distance metric learning. IEEE TIP **23**(8), 3656–3670 (2014)

29. Martinel, N., Das, A., Micheloni, C., Roy-Chowdhury, A.K.: Temporal model adaptation for person re-identification. In: Leibe, B., Matas, J., Sebe, N., Welling, M. (eds.) ECCV 2016. LNCS, vol. 9908, pp. 858–877. Springer, Cham (2016). https://doi.org/10.1007/978-3-319-46493-0_52

30. Martinel, N., Micheloni, C., Foresti, G.L.: Kernelized saliency-based person re-identification through multiple metric learning. IEEE TIP **24**(12), 5645–5658 (2015)

31. Matsukawa, T., Okabe, T., Suzuki, E., Sato, Y.: Hierarchical Gaussian descriptor for person re-identification. In: CVPR (2016)

32. Mignon, A., Jurie, F.: PCCA: A new approach for distance learning from sparse pairwise constraints. In: CVPR (2012)

33. Nowak, E., Jurie, F.: Learning visual similarity measures for comparing never seen objects. In: CVPR (2007)

34. Okada, T., Tomita, S.: An optimal orthonormal system for discriminant analysis. Pattern Recognit. **18**(2), 139–144 (1985)

35. Paisitkriangkrai, S., Shen, C., van den Hengel, A.: Learning to rank in person re-identification with metric ensembles. In: CVPR (2015)

36. Pedagadi, S., Orwell, J., Velastin, S., Boghossian, B.: Local Fisher discriminant analysis for pedestrian re-identification. In: CVPR (2013)

37. Roth, P.M., Hirzer, M., Köstinger, M., Beleznai, C., Bischof, H.: Mahalanobis distance learning for person re-identification. In: Gong, S., Cristani, M., Yan, S., Loy, C. (eds.) Person Re-Identification. Advances in Computer Vision and Pattern Recognition. Springer, London (2014). https://doi.org/10.1007/978-1-4471-6296-4_12
38. Sammon Jr., J.: An optimal discriminant plane. IEEE Trans. Comput. **100**(9), 826–829 (1970)
39. Shen, Y., Lin, W., Yan, J., Xu, M., Wu, J., Wang, J.: Person re-identification with correspondence structure learning. In: ICCV (2015)
40. Shi, H., et al.: Embedding deep metric for person re-identification: a study against large variations. In: Leibe, B., Matas, J., Sebe, N., Welling, M. (eds.) ECCV 2016. LNCS, vol. 9905, pp. 732–748. Springer, Cham (2016). https://doi.org/10.1007/978-3-319-46448-0_44
41. Shi, Z., Hospedales, T.M., Xiang, T.: Transferring a semantic representation for person re-identification and search. In: CVPR (2015)
42. Su, C., Li, J., Zhang, S., Xing, J., Gao, W., Tian, Q.: Pose-driven deep convolutional model for person re-identification. In: ICCV (2017)
43. Su, C., Zhang, S., Xing, J., Gao, W., Tian, Q.: Deep attributes driven multi-camera person re-identification. In: Leibe, B., Matas, J., Sebe, N., Welling, M. (eds.) ECCV 2016. LNCS, vol. 9906, pp. 475–491. Springer, Cham (2016). https://doi.org/10.1007/978-3-319-46475-6_30
44. Sugiyama, M.: Local Fisher discriminant analysis for supervised dimensionality reduction. In: ICML (2006)
45. Tao, D., Guo, Y., Song, M., Li, Y., Yu, Z., Tang, Y.Y.: Person re-identification by dual-regularized kiss metric learning. IEEE TIP **25**(6), 2726–2738 (2016)
46. Varior, R.R., Haloi, M., Wang, G.: Gated siamese convolutional neural network architecture for human re-identification. In: Leibe, B., Matas, J., Sebe, N., Welling, M. (eds.) ECCV 2016. LNCS, vol. 9912, pp. 791–808. Springer, Cham (2016). https://doi.org/10.1007/978-3-319-46484-8_48
47. Varior, R.R., Shuai, B., Lu, J., Xu, D., Wang, G.: A siamese long short-term memory architecture for human re-identification. In: Leibe, B., Matas, J., Sebe, N., Welling, M. (eds.) ECCV 2016. LNCS, vol. 9911, pp. 135–153. Springer, Cham (2016). https://doi.org/10.1007/978-3-319-46478-7_9
48. Weinberger, K.Q., Blitzer, J., Saul, L.K.: Distance metric learning for large margin nearest neighbor classification. In: NIPS (2006)
49. Weinberger, K.Q., Saul, L.K.: Fast solvers and efficient implementations for distance metric learning. In: ICML (2008)
50. Xiao, T., Li, H., Ouyang, W., Wang, X.: Learning deep feature representations with domain guided dropout for person re-identification. In: CVPR (2016)
51. Xiong, F., Gou, M., Camps, O., Sznaier, M.: Person re-identification using kernel-based metric learning methods. In: Fleet, D., Pajdla, T., Schiele, B., Tuytelaars, T. (eds.) ECCV 2014. LNCS, vol. 8695, pp. 1–16. Springer, Cham (2014). https://doi.org/10.1007/978-3-319-10584-0_1
52. Yang, Y., Yang, J., Yan, J., Liao, S., Yi, D., Li, S.Z.: Salient color names for person re-identification. In: Fleet, D., Pajdla, T., Schiele, B., Tuytelaars, T. (eds.) ECCV 2014. LNCS, vol. 8689, pp. 536–551. Springer, Cham (2014). https://doi.org/10.1007/978-3-319-10590-1_35
53. Yu, H.X., Wu, A., Zheng, W.S.: Cross-view asymmetric metric learning for unsupervised person re-identification. In: ICCV (2017)
54. Zhang, Y., Li, B., Lu, H., Irie, A., Ruan, X.: Sample-specific SVM learning for person re-identification. In: CVPR (2016)

55. Zhao, H., et al.: Spindle net: person re-identification with human body region guided feature decomposition and fusion. In: CVPR (2017)
56. Zhao, L., Li, X., Zhuang, Y., Wang, J.: Deeply-learned part-aligned representations for person re-identification. In: ICCV (2017)
57. Zhao, R., Ouyang, W., Wang, X.: Person re-identification by salience matching. In: ICCV (2013)
58. Zhao, R., Ouyang, W., Wang, X.: Unsupervised salience learning for person re-identification. In: CVPR (2013)
59. Zhao, R., Ouyang, W., Wang., X.: Learning mid-level filters for person re-identification. In: CVPR (2014)
60. Zheng, L., Wang, S., Tian, L., He, F., Liu, Z., Tian, Q.: Query-adaptive late fusion for image search and person reidentification. In: CVPR (2015)
61. Zheng, L., Xiang, T., Gong, S.: Learning a discriminative null space for person re-identification. In: CVPR (2016)
62. Zheng, S., Gong, S., Xiang, T.: Person re-identification by probabilistic relative distance comparison. In: CVPR (2011)
63. Zhong, Z., Zheng, L., Cao, D., Li, S.: Re-ranking person re-identification with k-reciprocal encoding. In: CVPR (2017)
64. Zhou, J., Yu, P., Tang, W., Wu, Y.: Efficient online local metric adaptation via negative samples for person re-identification. In: ICCV (2017)

Incremental Multi-graph Matching via Diversity and Randomness Based Graph Clustering

Tianshu Yu[1], Junchi Yan[2], Wei Liu[3], and Baoxin Li[1(✉)]

[1] Arizona State University, Tempe, USA
{tianshuy,baoxin.li}@asu.edu
[2] Shanghai Jiao Tong University, Shanghai, China
yanjunchi@sjtu.edu.cn
[3] Tencent AI Lab, Shenzhen, China
wl2223@columbia.edu

Abstract. Multi-graph matching refers to finding correspondences across graphs, which are traditionally solved by matching all the graphs in a single batch. However in real-world applications, graphs are often collected incrementally, rather than once for all. In this paper, we present an incremental multi-graph matching approach, which deals with the arriving graph utilizing the previous matching results under the global consistency constraint. When a new graph arrives, rather than re-optimizing over all graphs, we propose to partition graphs into subsets with certain topological structure and conduct optimization within each subset. The partitioning procedure is guided by the diversity within partitions and randomness over iterations, and we present an interpretation showing why these two factors are essential. The final matching results are calculated over all subsets via an intersection graph. Extensive experimental results on synthetic and real image datasets show that our algorithm notably improves the efficiency without sacrificing the accuracy.

Keywords: Multi-graph matching · Incremental graph matching
Determinantal point process · Graph clustering

1 Introduction

Graph matching (GM), which refers to the problem of finding common vertex correspondences over a set of graphs by exploring both unary (vertex) and pairwise (edge) affinity, is a fundamental problem in computer vision and is known to be NP-hard [1]. Compared with vector data, expressive graph representation is often more welcomed when structural relation need to be considered. Due to its robustness against noise, GM has been adopted in various vision applications e.g. scene understanding [2], visual tracking [3], and object recognition [4], etc.

Though proven successful in exploiting structural data, two-graph matching still suffers from the inherent local ambiguity, which on one hand leads to

© Springer Nature Switzerland AG 2018
V. Ferrari et al. (Eds.): ECCV 2018, LNCS 11217, pp. 142–158, 2018.
https://doi.org/10.1007/978-3-030-01261-8_9

non-smooth and difficult optimization problem. On the other hand, the affinity objective can be biased from ground truth correspondence. Though learning the affinity function [5] can mitigate such an issue, bringing more graphs for joint matching can be a more natural and effective way to dismiss local bias [6,7].

However, rather than being obtained at one time, graphs are often collected over time in practice, e.g. photos taken by street-view vehicle, video from surveillance camera, newly discovered protein v.s. existing protein. For this setting, the naive strategy by treating the old batch and new graphs as a new batch for matching from scratch is inefficient. Given previous matching results, the problem arises for how to utilize existing matchings to accelerate new matchings or even enhance the accuracy. Despite the practical importance, little effort has been made to address this online setting, which is the focus of this paper.

In contrast to the vast literature on offline multi-graph matching [7–14], the paper is tailored to the online setting with the following contributions:

- To our best knowledge, this is one of the first works for addressing the problem of incremental matching of multiple graphs.
- Compared with the offline baselines, our method can achieve or even improve the matching accuracy while notably decreases the computing cost.
- We present interpretation to the proposed structure and mechanism, which can be treated as a more general framework to [6] and [7].

2   Related Works

Due to its importance and fundamentality, extensive work on graph matching have been performed and thoroughly reviewed in a recent survey [15]. We categorize the representative work by the following perspectives.

2.1   Affinity Function Model

Graph matching incorporates both unary *node-to-node*, and second-order, or even higher-order, *(hyper)edge-to-(hyper)edge* structural similarities. In its traditional setting, whereby no higher-order affinity is considered [16–20], the two graph matching problem can be formulated as a quadratic assignment problem (QAP) [1], being well-known NP-complete [21]. More recent work on hypergraph matching further explores the higher-order (and mostly third-order) in affinity function modeling [22–26] at the cost of increased time and space complexity, whereby tensor marginalization is often used.

In contrast to the above methods whereby the affinity function is predefined regardless their order or attribute layer, learning is adopted to adapt the affinity function to different settings [5,16,19]. Supervised [5] and unsupervised [16] learning paradigm have been explored to improve the matching accuracy. However, either learning based or learning-free affinity function modeling cannot completely address the inherent ambiguity and noise in two-graph matching.

2.2   Solvers and Techniques

In the past decades there have emerged various GM solvers. A large body of literature are devoted to the study of different relaxation techniques, in order to mitigate the hard combinatorial problem in nature. Typical relaxations include (i) doubly-stochastic relaxation on the matching matrix [17,27,28]; (ii) Semidefinite-programming (SDP) [29,30]; (iii) spectral relaxations [27,31]. From the optimization perspective, different continuation methods [17,32,33] are widely adopted.

Different from these continuous relaxation methods which involves a post-processing step to binarize the final result, several methods tend to directly compute the solution in discrete assignment space. Sampling based methods [34, 35] directly generate discrete solutions via Monte Carlo Sampling. More recently, [36] devises a tailored Tabu search for graph matching.

Our approach involves iteratively solving pairwise matching. We depart from the above techniques, and follow a binarization-free composition based technique [7] to derive pairwise matchings which has been proved efficient and effective.

2.3   Multi-graph Matching

Beyond two-graph matching, an emerging line of work tend to address the matching problem for multiple graphs jointly. These works [9–11,13,37–41] are motivated by the fact that: (i) in real cases, it is more often that multiple graphs are available and needed for matching; (ii) the availability to a batch of graphs provides global information to enable robust model against local noise.

Employing an independent two-graph matching method for each pair of graphs may result in the so-called cycle-inconsistency issue. Consider one toy example, for graph $\mathcal{G}_i$, $\mathcal{G}_j$, $\mathcal{G}_k$ of equal size with no outlier. The three naive matching solutions $\mathbf{X}_{ij}$, $\mathbf{X}_{ik}$, $\mathbf{X}_{kj}$ obtained independently from each pair of graphs, may lead to cycle-inconsistency: $\mathbf{X}_{ij} \neq \mathbf{X}_{ik}\mathbf{X}_{kj}$ as illustrated in [9].

To address this issue, various multi-graph matching models are proposed incorporating the so-called consistency either in an iterative or a one-shot manner. We follow the survey [15] to categorize these works in the following two folds.

Iterative methods [6,7,9–11] seek to find a tradeoff between affinity and consistency scores. In general, the authors write out the objective for multi-graph matching by adding up pairwise affinity terms $\{\text{vec}(\mathbf{X})^\top \mathbf{K}\text{vec}(\mathbf{X})\}_{i,j=1}^N$, and the pairwise matchings $\{\mathbf{X}\}_{i,j=1}^N$ are iteratively updated whereby in each iteration the cycle-consistency constraints are strictly, or gradually satisfied. Specifically, [6,9] enforce the strict cycle-consistency constraint $\mathbf{X}_{ij} = \mathbf{X}_{ib}\mathbf{X}_{bj}$ over the whole iterative variable updating procedure. As a result, the matching accuracy may degenerate due to the inherent sensitivity to the starting point and updating rotating order. Such idea is also employed in [10] for extending two-graph matching method – Graduated Assignment [17] to multi-graph case. In contrast, a more flexible and robust mechanism is devised in [7,11], whereby the consistency is gradually added over iterations.

One-shot methods [39,40] try to enforce overall consistency as a post-step given the putative two-graph matchings. However, since the affinity information is totally discarded in the consistency enforcement procedure, these methods suffer from the sensitivity to the quality of putative matchings as initialization. In [42], the first-order affinity is utilized together with the consistency constraint, to improve robustness on real images. However, higher-order information is neglected.

Based on the above two lines of methods, the authors in [12] present a formulation where the affinity among graphs is encoded by a matrix stacked by the vectorized attributes of graphs, and the variables are reduced to a set of non-redundant bases inherent free from the consistency constraint. In [13], a tensor representation based approach for multi-graph matching is presented.

However, all the aforementioned work ignore an important setting, whereby the graphs arrive in a sequential way and online matching is needed. In fact the problem of online or incremental matching of graphs is nontrivial and existing methods may not be readily generalized to handle this new problem.

To our best knowledge, this is one of the first works for explicitly addressing the graph matching problem in an online fashion, whereby an incremental matching technique is presented. Experimental results show our solver can notably outperform the traditional multi-graph matching methods.

3   Preliminaries

We consider the case of one-to-one bijection matching. This setting has its technical consideration as cycle consistency constraint requires sizes of graphs to be identical. While most existing multi-graph matching methods employ such setting [11,14,25,39,42], unbalanced graph sizes can be handled by introducing dummy nodes or slack variables as in [18]. In case of bijection, a matching between graph $\mathcal{G}_i$ and $\mathcal{G}_j$ can be expressed via a permutation matrix $\mathbf{X}_{ij} \in \{0,1\}^{n \times n}$, where n is the number of vertices in each graph. Given the affinity matrix $\mathbf{K}_{ij} \in \mathcal{R}^{n^2 \times n^2}$ encoding the vertex and edge similarities on diagonal and off diagonal respectively (see more detailed definition for $\mathbf{K}_{ij}$ in prior art [6]), the matching objective between graph $\mathcal{G}_i$ and $\mathcal{G}_j$ can be compactly defined as:

$$\max_{\mathbf{x}} \mathcal{E}_{ij} = \mathbf{x}_{ij}^T \mathbf{K}_{ij} \mathbf{x}_{ij}$$
$$\text{s.t.}\ \ \mathbf{H}\mathbf{x}_{ij} = \mathbf{1}, \mathbf{x}_{ij} \in \{0,1\}^{n^2} \tag{1}$$

where $\mathbf{x}_{ij} = \text{vec}(\mathbf{X}_{ij})$ is the column-wise vectorized formation of $\mathbf{X}_{ij}$. $\mathbf{H}$ is a selection matrix enforcing the matching to be one-to-one. Due to the combinatorial nature, to obtain the optimal solution for $\mathcal{E}_{ij}$ is in general NP-hard, and it is often relaxed into continuous domain by replacing the constraint $\mathbf{x}_{ij} \in \{0,1\}^{n^2}$ with $\mathbf{x}_{ij} \in [0,1]^{n^2}$ for efficient and approximate optimization [18,27,31].

Beyond two-graph matching, multi-graph matching has recently received extensive attention, which is a process of simultaneously finding pairwise matchings between all given graphs to maximize the overall affinity score $\mathcal{E} = \sum_{i,j} \mathcal{E}_{ij}$.

A naive approach is to solve each two-graph matching problem by maximizing each $\mathcal{E}_{ij}$ independently. However, this can lead to a fact that one matching solution $\mathbf{X}_{ij}$ does not agree with another solution derived by an alternative path: $\mathbf{X}_{ij} = \mathbf{X}_{ik}\mathbf{X}_{kj}$. To address this, cycle consistency [7] is proposed to constrain the matching results to be cycle consistent, which emphasizes any two matching paths between graph $\mathcal{G}_i$ and $\mathcal{G}_j$ should derive similar correspondence. For efficiency and simplicity, in this paper we follow the widely used first-order consistency over graph $\mathcal{G}_k$ as in [6,7], which is defined as:

$$\mathcal{C}_k = 1 - \frac{\sum_i \sum_{j>i} \|\mathbf{X}_{ij} - \mathbf{X}_{ik}\mathbf{X}_{kj}\|_F/2}{nN(N-1)/2} \in (0,1] \tag{2}$$

where N is the number of graphs, and $\|\cdot\|_F$ refers to the Frobenius norm. This equation measures how much a direct matching agrees to another matching via an intermediate graph. Thus the overall consistency over all graphs becomes:

$$\mathcal{C} = \frac{1}{N} \sum_k \mathcal{C}_k \tag{3}$$

By adding $\mathcal{C}$ as a regularizer to affinity score, multi-graph matching with consistency regularization yields to optimize:

$$\mathcal{E}^{\mathrm{mgm}} = \lambda\mathcal{E} + (1-\lambda)\mathcal{C} \tag{4}$$

where λ is a controlling parameter. As this objective is significantly different to those which are optimized using analytical or gradient-based methods, a heuristic multi-graph matching method over $\mathcal{E}^{\mathrm{mgm}}$ is introduced in [7], in which the matching in previous iteration is replaced by the product of two permutation matrices on the path $\mathbf{X}'_{ij} = \mathbf{X}_{ik}\mathbf{X}_{kj}$ if $\mathcal{E}^{\mathrm{mgm}}$ ascends. For its effectiveness and efficiency, we employ this strategy in part of our method.

As an extension of offline multi-graph matching, incremental multi-graph matching tries to match the $N+1$th arriving graph when previous matchings of N graphs have been computed. It is desired that one can reuse the previous matching results when one or a few new graphs arrive. A naive way is to take the previous solution for N graphs as starting point for iterative updating with the $N+1$ graph no matter what existing multi-graph matching method is used, under the expectation that the results obtained from N graphs can serve as better initialization than random guess and speedup the convergence. However, one still has to compute all $N+1$ matchings $\mathbf{X}_{ij}$ each time a new graph arrives.

4   Proposed Approach

4.1   Concepts for Hypergraph Topology

Before going into the details, it is worthwhile to mention some definitions here. A hypergraph $\mathfrak{G}$ consists of multiple graphs and the pairwise matchings between them. Mathematically, a hypergraph is defined as (also sketched in Fig. 1):

$$\mathfrak{G} = \{\{\mathcal{G}_1, ..., \mathcal{G}_N\}, \{\mathcal{M}_{ij}\}\}, \quad i,j \in \{1, ..., N\} \quad i \neq j \tag{5}$$

where $\mathcal{M}_{ij}$ is the matching between $\mathcal{G}_i$ and $\mathcal{G}_j$. For hypergraph, there is a complex that covers the corresponding structure. Given an index subset $u \subseteq \{1, ..., N\}$, we re-number the index as $u = \{l_1, ..., l_k\}$. Then a sub-hypergraph $\mathfrak{G}_u$ contains a subset of k graphs and its matchings induced by the index set u:

$$\mathfrak{G}_u = \{\{\mathcal{G}_{l_1}, ..., \mathcal{G}_{l_k}\}, \{\mathcal{M}_{l_i l_j}\}\}, \quad l_i, l_j \in u, \quad l_i \neq l_j \qquad (6)$$

According to the topology of hypergraph $\mathfrak{G}$ which is a fully connected structure, matchings are calculated between each pair of individual graphs. As the amount of such matchings is combinatorial to the number of graphs, it could be computationally intensive. However, if we can reduce the size of the hypergraph, the computational cost will be mitigated significantly. This fact motivates the idea to partition a hypergraph into several sub-hypergraphs, conduct optimization on each subset and merge all the matching results. Figure 1 demonstrates a general view of our method. We will detail the algorithm and give an intuitive interpretation in the following sections.

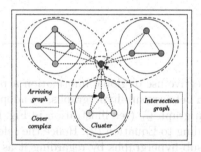

Fig. 1. The hypergraph with a petal-shape topology and its cover complex. There are 10 existing graphs and an arriving graph. Note that: (i) graphs are re-clustered into k partitions overlapped by the intersection graph over iterations; (ii) at each iteration, the intersection graph is re-selected from all graphs which is not necessarily the new graph; (iii) the partitions are clustered by the criterion of randomness and diversity under a given cluster number (here $k = 3$).

4.2 Algorithm Details

As shown in Algorithm 1, a method called Incremental Multi-Graph Matching via randomness and diversity based graph clustering (abbr. **IMGM**) is proposed.

In general, the method consists of (i) intersection graph selection and exclusion; (ii) randomness and diversity based graph clustering without the intersection graph; (iii) matching propagation along the intersection graph. These steps are performed iteratively and illustrated in Fig. 1.

(1) Selecting Intersection Graph Shared by Sub-hypergraphs. Applying multi-graph matching within each sub-hypergraph cannot guarantee the global cycle consistency, because there is no link between different sub-hypergraphs

---

Algorithm 1. Incremental multi-graph matching via randomness and diversity based graph clustering (IMGM)

1: **function** IMGM($\mathbf{S}, \mathfrak{G}, \mathfrak{N}$)   ▷ $\mathbf{S}$ - Similarity, $\mathfrak{G}$ - Hypergraph, $\mathcal{G}_N$ - New graph
2:    **for** each new graph $\mathcal{G}_N$: **do**
3:        $\mathfrak{G} = \mathfrak{G} \cup \{\mathcal{G}_N\}$
4:        Find intersection graph v by maximizing Equation (2) based on updated $\mathbb{X}$
5:        Update similarity $\mathbf{S}$ by Equation (1) based on updated $\mathbb{X}$
6:        Partition $\mathfrak{G} \setminus v$ into d clusters using k-DPP based on $\mathbf{S}$, or random partition
7:        **for** $u = 1, \ldots, d$ **do**
8:            Generate sub-hypergraph $\mathfrak{G}_u$ induced by u-th cluster
9:            $\mathfrak{G}_u = \mathfrak{G}_u \cup \{\mathcal{G}_v\}$
10:            Construct cover using $\mathfrak{G}_u, \quad u = 1, \ldots, U$
11:            Apply CAO^{PC} (or other multi-graph matching solvers) to obtain $\mathbb{X}_u$
12:        **end for**
13:        **for** $i \in \mathcal{I}_{u_1}, j \in \mathcal{I}_{u_2}, \quad i, j \neq v$ **do**
14:            $\mathbf{X}_{ij} = \mathbf{X}_{iv}\mathbf{X}_{vj}$ ▷ Construct length-two path through new graph
15:            $\mathbb{X} = \cup \mathbb{X}_u \cup \{\mathbf{X}_{ij}\}$
16:        **end for**
17:    **end for**
18:    **return** $\mathbb{X}$
19: **end function**

---

which also limit the effective use of global information across all the graphs. To establish the connection between sub-hypergraphs, we adopt the criterion in [6,7] to select an intersection graph $\mathcal{G}_v$ (see illustration in Fig. 1) by maximizing the consistency score according to Equation (2). Hence the reference graph becomes the intersection of all sub-hypergraphs by regarding it as belonging to each of the sub-hypergraphs. The resulting topology of the hypergraph is petal-shape, as shown in Fig. 1 (note the resulting clusters are overlapped to each other by the intersection graph). As a result, to obtain a cycle-consistent hypergraph $\mathfrak{G}$ for multi-graph matching, one only needs to consider the cycle consistency constraint within each sub-hypergraph.

(2) Clustering Sub-hypergraphs by Randomness and Diversity. We focus on two desirable properties for partitioning/clustering hypergraph in our setting: diversity (in iteration) and randomness (over iterations). We first describe the general idea as follows:

For the first property, traditional clustering methods partition data into several collections to aggregate *similar* objects and separate *dissimilar* ones. However, this strategy does not fit with our case, and the intuitive idea is that it is difficult to match two dissimilar graphs from two clusters via an intersection graph. Hence we adopt the policy that encourages diversity in each cluster, and the hope is that each cluster is representative for the whole hypergraph.

The second property, on the other hand, emphasizes the relative randomness of the partitions over iterations. If the partitions are fixed at each iteration, the optimization may fall into local optima and has less chance to escape.

In this sense, the matching solution will converge in early iterations and not evolve along with the graph sequence. To introduce randomness, we expect that the partition can change to some extent from iteration to iteration, such that the heuristic procedure can explore more solution space.

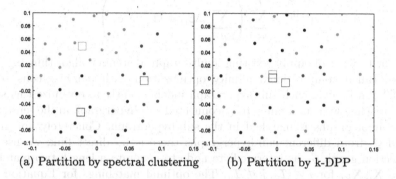

(a) Partition by spectral clustering   (b) Partition by k-DPP

Fig. 2. Partitioning results using spectral clustering with *similarity* (left) and proposed DPP procedure with *diversity* (right) on 40 graphs. Graphs are converted to 2-D points by Multi-Dimensional Scaling [45] with pairwise affinity score. Square markers are the centroids of each cluster.

Based on the above observations, we introduce two specific ways for partitioning at and over iterations: random sampling and determinantal point process (DPP) [43]. Since random sampling is trivial, we explain more about DPP partitioning in the following. DPP sampling relies on computation of similarity $\mathbf{S}_{ij}$ of any pair of graphs i and j. To this end, we at first introduce the optimal energy $\mathbf{S}_{ij} = \mathcal{E}_{ij}$ as a measurement when $i \neq j$. For $i = j$, we let $\mathbf{S}_{ii} = 1.1 \times \max_{i,j,i \neq j} \mathcal{E}_{ij}$ without loss of generality. Then we let $\mathbf{S}_{ij} = \mathbf{S}_{ij} - \min_{i,j,i \neq j} \mathcal{E}_{ij}$. For N graphs with d partitions, we first compute the size of each partition by using N/d and rounding it properly. We then apply d times of k-DPP [44] to obtain the partitions. Readers are referred to [44] for more details about k-DPP. We visualize such partitioning strategies in Fig. 2. This example contains 40 graphs and the 2-D points are obtained by Multi-Dimensional Scaling [45]. The square box corresponds to each cluster centroid. One can see the centroids in the left panel are more scattered than those in the right panel. The points within a cluster in the left panel are closer to each other, while the points within a partition in the right panel span the whole space as much as possible.

Remarks. One may argue the adoption of dissimilarity based spectral clustering which can also generate scattered points in each cluster. However, this approach is deterministic causing the partition in each iteration frozen. Another alternative is using random sampling to form each cluster, while the drawback is the diversity in each cluster cannot be effectively ensured. In fact, DPP can ensure the diversity in each cluster at each iteration as well as the randomness over iterations due to its inherent stochastic nature.

(3) Propagating Matching along the Intersection. Specifically, for each cluster u with graph sample index set $\mathcal{I}_u$, by treating the reference graph as the intersection graph that forms the petal-shape topology we define a new objective for incremental matching:

$$\mathcal{E}^{\text{inc}} = \sum_{u=1}^{U} \left(\sum_{i,j \in \mathcal{I}_u} \lambda \mathcal{E}_{ij} + (1-\lambda)\mathcal{C}_u \right) \tag{7}$$

In fact, we can apply existing multi-graph matching algorithm e.g. the method called compositional affinity optimization with pairwise consistency (CAO^{PC}) in [7] over each sub-hypergraph independently to optimize this score function. Then we can obtain a fully-connected sub-hypergraph in the sense that each pair of graphs is matched in the sub-hypergraph. Concretely, for graph $\mathcal{G}_i$ and $\mathcal{G}_j$ from different sub-hypergraphs there is no direct link, we use the intersection graph $\mathcal{G}_k$ as intermediate node to generate a length-two matching $\mathbf{X}_{ij} = \mathbf{X}_{ik}\mathbf{X}_{kj}$ for $i \in \mathcal{I}_u, j \notin \mathcal{I}_u$. The optimal matchings for Equation (7), together with the generated matchings via the intersection graph, are denoted by $\mathbb{X} = \{\mathbf{X}_{ij}^*\}$ which can also be used as the starting point for matching next new graph.

Remarks. Figure 1 demonstrates the topology generated from our algorithm. Each solid circle corresponds to a partition, while optimization is conducted within each dashed ellipse. In each dashed ellipse, we densely calculate matchings of each pair of graphs with consistency regularization.

4.3   Further Discussion

Complexity. The complexity of CAO^{PC} is $O(N^3 n^3 + N^2 \tau_{pair})$, where N and n are the numbers of the graphs and vertices, respectively. τ_{pair} refers to the complexity of the selected graph matching solver. In k-DPP sampling, an eigen-decomposition and a projection procedure are involved, with complexity $O(N^3)$ and $O(N^2)$, respectively. If the hypergraph is clustered into d partitions, and w.l.g. equal size for each partition, the complexity of CAO-PC step of IMGM becomes $O(N^3 n^3/d^2 + N^2 \tau_{pair})$. In this case, the complexity of k-DPP partitioning is $O(N^3/d^2)$. It is easily seen that the clustering and cover topology can reduce the complexity significantly. In general, the complexity of the proposed algorithm with k-DPP partitioning becomes $O(N^3 n^3/d^2 + N^2 \tau_{pair} + N^3/d^2)$.

Topological Interpretation. The complex concept for offline multi-graph matching has been discussed in [14], and the authors have proven that under the following conditions the hypergraph $\mathfrak{G}$ is cycle-consistent: (1) Each sub-hypergraph (not including $\mathfrak{G}$ itself) is cycle-consistent; (2) Each pair of sub-hypergraph is joint normal; (3) The cover complex of the hypergraph is topologically simply connected. Though the assumption in these statements is ideal, it still provides hints showing why our algorithm works. Since the proposed topological structure assures that, once cycle-consistency is reached out in each partition, the holistic cycle-consistency derived from intersection graph will be satisfied accordingly. Furthermore we provide an explicit strategy on how to construct such a topology which is not covered in [14].

Alternative Topology. First we observe that the topology of the proposed method can be viewed as a generalized versions of [6] and [7]. If the size of the partitions is the same as the number of graphs, our method becomes [6]. On the other hand, if there is only one partition, our method degenerates to [7]. In this sense, our topology leverages the previous two structures, thus can reach out a good balance between accuracy and efficiency. Besides, other topologies sufficing the three conditions stated in previous paragraph can also be proposed, as long as the matching can be propagated through intersection graph (e.g., line or circle structure). We leave these variations to future work.

5   Experiments

Performance Evaluation Criteria. We impose three popular measurements [6,7] to evaluate the performance of algorithms: accuracy, affinity score and consistency (abbreviated as acc, scr and con, respectively). $acc = 1 - \sum_{i,j} \|\mathbf{X}_{ij}^* - \mathbf{X}_{ij}^{GT}\|_F^2 / nN^2 \in [0,1]$ refers to the matching accuracy by comparing solution $\mathbf{X}_{ij}^*$ to ground-truth matching $\mathbf{X}_{ij}^{GT}$. $scr = \frac{1}{N^2} \sum_{i,j} \frac{vec(\mathbf{X}_{ij}^*)^T \mathbf{K}_{ij} vec(\mathbf{X}_{ij}^*)}{vec(\mathbf{X}_{ij}^{GT})^T \mathbf{K}_{ij} vec(\mathbf{X}_{ij}^{GT})}$ calculates the overall affinity score. $con = \mathcal{C}$ referring to Eq. 3. Note scr can be above 1 – recall the affinity function can be biased rendering an incorrect matching leads to a higher affinity score than the one by ground truth matching.

Comparing Methods and Settings. As there is little existing multi-graph matching algorithm in an incremental fashion, we devise two baselines by extending the CAO^{PC} algorithm in [7] and Consistent Matching algorithm in [6]. To this end, we reuse the matching result $\mathbb{X}$ in the previous iteration as a starting point, and incorporate the arriving graph $\mathcal{G}_N$ in the current iteration for another round of batch based multi-graph matching. We term these two baselines **incremental CAO** and **incremental ConMatch**. We also employ **raw CAO^{PC}** which calculates matching from scratch without using the previous result. Permutation synchronization (**mSync**) [39], which processes the matchings to fulfill the cycle consistency, is also adopted for comparison. The proposed algorithms equipped with DPP and random sampling for graph clustering over iterations, are termed as **IMGM-D** and **IMGM-R**, respectively. All initial pairwise matchings are obtained using Reweighted Random Walk [18] which has been proved an effective and stable two-graph matching solver.

5.1   On Synthetic Random Graph

We follow [7,9] to implement tests on synthetic data, in which the pairwise affinity scores are randomly generated with Gaussion deformation perturbation. For each trial, a reference graph with node count $n_R = 10$ is created, by assigning a weight q_{ab}^R for edge (a, b) uniformly sampled from $[0, 1]$. Then a Gaussian noise $\mu \sim \mathcal{N}(0, \epsilon)$ is added as $q_{ab}^D = q_{ab}^R + \mu$ to generate a destination graph. The edge density of graphs is adjusted according to density parameter ρ. The edge affinity is thus calculated by $\mathbf{K}_{ac;bd} = \exp(-\frac{(q_{ab}-q_{cd})^2}{\sigma^2})$. We test different combinations of numbers of base graphs N_B and arriving graphs N_A. Three settings of such combinations is conducted as $(N_B, N_A) \in \{(25, 15), (30, 20), (35, 25)\}$. We keep to partition the hypergraph into 2 sub-hypergraphs in all tests (if not otherwise specified) and conduct 50 times for each test and calculate the average performance. We let $\rho = 0.9$, $\epsilon = 0.15$ and $\sigma^2 = 0.05$. The testing results are demonstrated in the first three rows of Fig. 3. To evaluate of impact different partition size d, we conduct an additional test with $(N_B, N_A) = (30, 20)$ with $d \in \{2, 3, 4\}$. This test consists of 100 times of independent trials. The results for this additional test are shown in the last row of Fig. 3, where DPP and Rnd correspond to IMGM-D and IMGM-R, respectively.

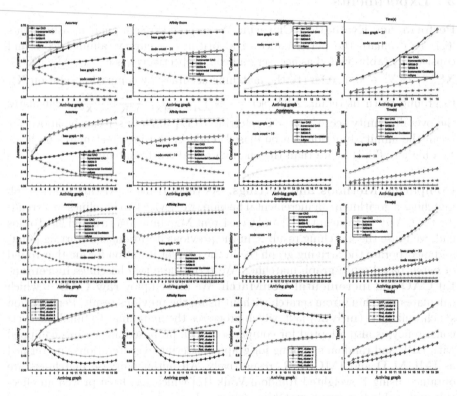

Fig. 3. Performance on synthetic data w.r.t. accumulated arriving graph count. Base graph number from top to bottom: 25, 30, 35, 30.

As one can see, when the size of base graphs is 25, our algorithm outperforms raw CAO in accuracy, and is very close to incremental CAO. When the size increases to 30, IMGM outperforms incremental CAO when more graphs arrive. In either case, raw CAO, incremental ConMatch and mSync have much lower accuracy. When there are 35 base graphs, both IMGM-D and IMGM-R outperform all other algorithms significantly, achieving state-of-the-art performance. Further, IMGM-D has a more stable accuracy growth along with arriving graphs. We can also observe that our algorithm reaches better global consistency than CAO-based methods. This is due to the fact that the matchings across sub-hypergraphs are generated via an intermediate graph, thus have higher consistency score. It should be noted that the matching accuracy of incremental ConMatch decreases along with graph sequence. This is because the topology of this algorithm does not evolve along with arriving graphs (there is always only one cluster), therefore randomness is missing from iteration to iteration. Notably, we also observe about 3 to 4 times of speedup compared to CAO algorithms. From the bottom row, one can observe that a larger cluster size d generally accelerates the computation and enhances the consistency. However, larger d results in accuracy drop – perhaps due to the cluster becomes too small to explore the joint matching effectively. Hence we need to find a trade-off between accuracy and efficiency controlled by d (see complexity analysis in Sect. 4.3). Last but not least, we also observe IMGM-D can often converge more quickly than IMGM-R, which compensates the additional overhead of performing DPP.

5.2   On Real Images: CMU Sequence

The CMU pose dataset[1] consists of two image sequences. One is CMU house with 111 frames and 30 landmarks, and the other is CMU hotel with 101 frames and 30 landmarks. Each sequence contains an object gradually changing its poses. This dataset is widely tested in [7,18,42]. We use this dataset to evaluate the performance under partial similarity and outlier nodes. To this end, we follow the settings in [7] by selecting 10 inlier points in each frame, and randomly choose 4 points from the remaining landmarks in each frame rendering the matching more challenging. The graphs are constructing with sparse delaunay triangulation on both inliers and outliers following the method in [7]. The affinity is generated by $\mathbf{K}_{ac;bd} = \exp(-\frac{(q_{ab}-q_{cd})^2}{\sigma^2})$, where q_{ab} measures the Euclidean distance between point a and b normalized to $[0,1]$ by dividing the largest edge length. The diagonal elements of the affinity corresponding to node similarity are set to 0 as previous test. For each trail, we randomly sample $N_B = 30$ frames as base graphs, then randomly sample $N_A = 20$ frames from the remaining frames as arriving graphs. We conduct 20 times of single trial and calculate the average performance. Let $\sigma^2 = 0.05$. The performance curves are shown in Fig. 4.

On the hotel sequence, IMGM-D method achieves significant accuracy superiority against the other compared algorithms. In the house sequence test, IMGM-D performs competitively to state-of-the-art algorithms. Though the change of

---

[1]   http://vasc.ri.cmu.edu/idb/html/motion/.

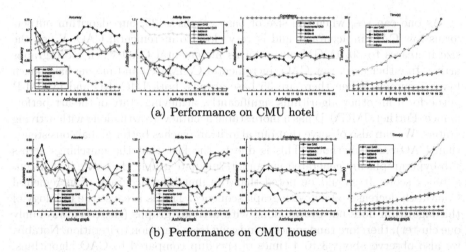

(a) Performance on CMU hotel

(b) Performance on CMU house

Fig. 4. Performance on CMU sequence w.r.t. accumulated arriving graph count.

relative positions of landmarks is not severe across graphs, the outlier points hinder the matching algorithms as disturbing edges may appear along with outliers. The stable performance demonstrates the robustness of the proposed algorithm, especially IMGM-D, against outliers. The algorithms show similar behavior as in synthetic test on the metrics other than accuracy. Thus we only present accuracy in the next Willow-ObjectClass data test.

5.3   On Real Images: Willow-ObjectClass

The Willow-ObjectClass dataset is collected and released in [5], which consists of 5 classes of images collected from Caltech-256 and PASCAL07: 109 Face, 66 Winebottle, 50 Duck, 40 Car and 40 Motorbike images. All images are taken from natural scenes. For each image, 10 landmark points on the corresponding object are manually labelled. We select Winebottle, Duck and Car in our experiment with splits (N_B, N_A) of $(30, 20)$, $(30, 20)$ and $(25, 15)$, respectively. For Winebottle (or namely Bottle), as $N_B + N_A < 66$, we following the setting in previous test to randomly sample 50 images in each trial. For the resting two objects, we randomly permute all images. 4 SIFT feature points on the background are randomly selected as outliers. We still employ sparse delaunay triangulation to construct the adjacency graph. Then the affinity is calculated as $\mathbf{K}_{ac;bd} = \beta \mathbf{K}_{ac;bd}^{\text{len}} + (1 - \beta)\mathbf{K}_{ac;bd}^{\text{ang}}$ taking into account both edge length and angle similarity, where $\beta \in [0, 1]$ is a controlling parameter. While the definition of $\mathbf{K}_{ac;bd}^{\text{len}}$ is the same as used for the CMU sequence test, $\mathbf{K}_{ac;bd}^{\text{ang}}$ measures difference of the absolute angles between edge (a, b) and (c, d). The diagonal elements of affinity matrix are all set to 0 as before. $\beta = 0.9$ in this test. We conduct 20 times of independent trial and the mean accuracy is shown in Fig. 5.

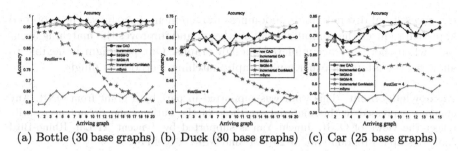

(a) Bottle (30 base graphs) (b) Duck (30 base graphs) (c) Car (25 base graphs)

Fig. 5. Accuracy on matching objects from Willow-ObjectClass dataset.

When there are more base graphs in Winebottle and Duck tests, IMGM-D outperforms the selected counterparts on most arriving graphs. On the other hand, in Car test with fewer base graphs, the proposed method gradually adapts the problem along with arriving graphs, and reaches competitive performance.

5.4 Discussion

We observe that the proposed method outperforms all peer algorithms when the size of graphs is sufficiently large. This may be due to the following two reasons. On one hand, the diversity in a sub-hypergraph must be sufficiently representative of the whole graph space, which is barely satisfied when the number of graphs is too small. On the other hand, the partitioning procedure is capable of restricting the unreliability within a sub-hypergraph imposed by "outlier" graph, which may be propagated to all matching results if a whole batch optimization is employed. We also observe that, as the algorithm in [7] works on permutation matrices, if the partitions are stable along time, the matching solution after a period within each sub-hypergraph may fall into a permutation sub-group, and will not evolve any further. On the contrary, by imposing randomness in partitions, our algorithm can escape from poor local optima. Last but not least, we observe IMGM-D performs closely to IMGM-R on our synthetic test, and outperforms IMGM-R on all the real-world image tests. We conjecture this is due to the fact that for synthetic data, they are generated based on a shared base structure (with additional slight noise). However, the natural image data has a more complex distribution in their graph structure which can be better captured by diversity-based clustering.

6 Conclusion

In this paper, we present an incremental multi-graph matching approach called IMGM, which takes previous matchings and arriving graph as input, and performs optimization over a cycle-consistent topological structure. To the best of our knowledge, this is the first attempt to solve graph matching incrementally. We also analyze the functional topological structure of hypergraph and interpret the necessity of diversity and randomness in incremental settings. The proposed approach reduces the computational overhead, and improves the matching accuracy when there has accumulated enough graphs. Our paradigm is flexible to allow for the adoption other multi-graph matching methods as plugin.

Acknowledgement. This work was supported in part by a grant from ONR. Any opinions expressed in this material are those of the authors and do not necessarily reflect the views of ONR. Junchi Yan is supported by Tencent AI Lab Rhino-Bird Joint Research Program (No. JR201804) and NSFC 61602176.

References

1. Loiola, E.M., de Abreu, N.M., Boaventura-Netto, P.O., Hahn, P., Querido, T.: A survey for the quadratic assignment problem. EJOR **176**(2), 657–690 (2007)
2. Wang, W., Lin, W., Chen, Y., Wu, J., Wang, J., Sheng, B.: Finding coherent motions and semantic regions in crowd scenes: a diffusion and clustering approach. In: Fleet, D., Pajdla, T., Schiele, B., Tuytelaars, T. (eds.) ECCV 2014. LNCS, vol. 8689, pp. 756–771. Springer, Cham (2014). https://doi.org/10.1007/978-3-319-10590-1_49
3. Nie, W., et al.: Single/cross-camera multiple-person tracking by graph matching. Neurocomputing **139**, 220–232 (2014)
4. Duchenne, O., Joulin, A., Ponce, J.: A graph-matching kernel for object categorization. In: ICCV, pp. 1792–1799 (2011)
5. Cho, M., Alahari, K., Ponce, J.: Learning graphs to match. In: ICCV (2013)
6. Yan, J., Wang, J., Zha, H., Yang, X.: Consistency-driven alternating optimization for multigraph matching: a unified approach. IEEE Trans. Image Process. **24**(3), 994–1009 (2015)
7. Yan, J., Cho, M., Zha, H., Yang, X., Chu, S.: Multi-graph matching via affinity optimization with graduated consistency regularization. TPAMI **38**(6), 1228–1242 (2016)
8. Williams, M.L., Wilson, R.C., Hancock, E.: Multiple graph matching with bayesian inference. Pattern Recognit. Lett. **18**(11–13), 1275–1281 (1997)
9. Yan, J., Tian, Y., Zha, H., Yang, X., Zhang, Y., Chu, S.: Joint optimization for consistent multiple graph matching. In: ICCV, pp. 1649–1656 (2013)
10. Sole-Ribalta, A., Serratosa, F.: Graduated assignment algorithm for multiple graph matching based on a common labeling. IJPRAI **27**(01), 1350001 (2013)
11. Yan, J., Li, Y., Liu, W., Zha, H., Yang, X., Chu, S.M.: Graduated consistency-regularized optimization for multi-graph matching. In: Fleet, D., Pajdla, T., Schiele, B., Tuytelaars, T. (eds.) ECCV 2014. LNCS, vol. 8689, pp. 407–422. Springer, Cham (2014). https://doi.org/10.1007/978-3-319-10590-1_27
12. Yan, J., Xu, H., Zha, H., Yang, X., Liu, H., Chu, S.: A matrix decomposition perspective to multiple graph matching. In: ICCV, pp. 199–207 (2015)
13. Shi, X., Ling, H., Hu, W., Xing, J., Zhang, Y.: Tensor power iteration for multi-graph matching. In: CVPR, pp. 5026–5070 (2016)
14. Hu, N., Thibert, B., Guibas, L.: Distributable consistent multi-graph matching. In: CVPR (2018)
15. Yan, J., Yin, X., Lin, W., Deng, C., Zha, H., Yang, X.: A short survey of recent advances in graph matching. In: ICMR, pp. 167–174 (2016)

16. Leordeanu, M., Sukthankar, R., Hebert, M.: Unsupervised learning for graph matching. Int. J. Comput. Vis. **96**(1), 28–45 (2012)
17. Gold, S., Rangarajan, A.: A graduated assignment algorithm for graph matching. TPAMI **18**(4), 377–388 (1996)
18. Cho, M., Lee, J., Lee, K.M.: Reweighted random walks for graph matching. In: Daniilidis, K., Maragos, P., Paragios, N. (eds.) ECCV 2010. LNCS, vol. 6315, pp. 492–505. Springer, Heidelberg (2010). https://doi.org/10.1007/978-3-642-15555-0_36
19. Caetano, T., McAuley, J., Cheng, L., Le, Q., Smola, A.J.: Learning graph matching. TPAMI **31**(6), 1048–1058 (2009)
20. Egozi, A., Keller, Y., Guterman, H.: A probabilistic approach to spectral graph matching. TPAMI **35**(1), 18–27 (2013)
21. Garey, M.R., Johnson, D.S.: Computers and Intractability. A Guide to the Theory of NP-Completeness. Freeman and Co., New York (1990)
22. Zass, R., Shashua, A.: Probabilistic graph and hypergraph matching. In: CVPR (2008)
23. Chertok, M., Keller, Y.: Efficient high order matching. TPAMI (2010)
24. Duchenne, O., Bach, F., Kweon, I., Ponce, J.: A tensor-based algorithm for high-order graph matching. TPAMI (2011)
25. Yan, J., Zhang, C., Zha, H., Liu, W., Yang, X., Chu, S.: Discrete hyper-graph matching. In: CVPR (2015)
26. Ngoc, Q., Gautier, A., Hein, M.: A flexible tensor block coordinate ascent scheme for hypergraph matching. In: CVPR, pp. 5270–5278 (2015)
27. Leordeanu, M., Hebert, M.: A spectral technique for correspondence problems using pairwise constraints. In: ICCV, vol. 2, pp. 1482–1489 (2005)
28. Leordeanu, M., Hebert, M., Sukthankar, R.: An integer projected fixed point method for graph matching and map inference. In: NIPS, pp. 1114–1122 (2009)
29. Torr, P.H.S.: Solving markov random fields using semidefinite programmin. In: AISTATS (2003)
30. Schellewald, C., Schnörr, C.: Probabilistic subgraph matching based on convex relaxation. In: Rangarajan, A., Vemuri, B., Yuille, A.L. (eds.) EMMCVPR 2005. LNCS, vol. 3757, pp. 171–186. Springer, Heidelberg (2005). https://doi.org/10.1007/11585978_12
31. Cour, T., Srinivasan, P., Shi, J.: Balanced graph matching. In: NIPS, pp. 313–320 (2006)
32. Zaslavskiy, M., Bach, F.R., Vert, J.P.: A path following algorithm for the graph matching problem. TPAMI **31**(12), 2227–2242 (2009)
33. Zhou, F., Torre, F.: Factorized graph matching. TPAMI (2016)
34. Lee, J., Cho, M., Lee, K.: A graph matching algorithm using data-driven Markov chain Monte Carlo sampling. In: ICPR, pp. 2816–2819 (2010)
35. Suh, Y., Cho, M., Lee, K.M.: Graph matching via sequential Monte Carlo. In: Fitzgibbon, A., Lazebnik, S., Perona, P., Sato, Y., Schmid, C. (eds.) ECCV 2012. LNCS, vol. 7574, pp. 624–637. Springer, Heidelberg (2012). https://doi.org/10.1007/978-3-642-33712-3_45
36. Adamczewski, K., Suh, Y., Lee, K.: Discrete tabu search for graph matching. In: ICCV (2015)
37. Solé-Ribalta, A., Serratosa, F.: Models and algorithms for computing the common labelling of a set of attributed graphs. CVIU **115**(7), 929–945 (2011)
38. Huang, Q., Zhang, G., Gao, L., Hu, S., Butscher, A., Guibas, L.: An optimization approach for extracting and encoding consistent maps in a shape collection. ACM Trans. Graph. (TOG) **31**(6), 167 (2012)

39. Pachauri, D., Kondor, R., Vikas, S.: Solving the multi-way matching problem by permutation synchronization. In: NIPS, pp. 1860–1868 (2013)
40. Chen, Y., Leonidas, G., Huang, Q.: Matching partially similar objects via matrix completion. In: ICML (2014)
41. Zhang, Q., Song, X., Shao, X., Zhao, H., Shibasaki, R.: Object discovery: soft attributed graph mining. TPAMI **38**(3), 532–545 (2016)
42. Zhou, X., Zhu, M., Daniilidis, K.: Multi-image matching via fast alternating minimization. In: ICCV (2015)
43. Kulesza, A., Taskar, B.: Determinantal point processes for machine learning. Found. Trends® Mach. Learn. **5**(2–3), 123–286 (2012)
44. Kulesza, A., Taskar, B.: k-DPPs: Fixed-size determinantal point processes. In: ICML, pp. 1193–1200 (2011)
45. Mardia, K.V.: Some properties of clasical multi-dimesional scaling. Commun. Stat. Theory Methods **7**(13), 1233–1241 (1978)

Visual Text Correction

Amir Mazaheri[(✉)] and Mubarak Shah[(✉)]

Center for Research in Computer Vision, University of Central Florida, Orlando, USA
amirmazaheri@knights.ucf.edu , shah@crcv.ucf.edu

Abstract. This paper introduces a new problem, called *Visual Text Correction (VTC)*, i.e., finding and replacing an inaccurate word in the textual description of a video. We propose a deep network that can simultaneously detect an inaccuracy in a sentence, and fix it by replacing the inaccurate word(s). Our method leverages the semantic interdependence of videos and words, as well as the short-term and long-term relations of the words in a sentence. Our proposed formulation can solve the VTC problem employing an End-to-End network in two steps: (1) Inaccuracy detection, and (2) correct word prediction. In detection step, each word of a sentence is reconstructed such that the reconstruction for the inaccurate word is maximized. We exploit both Short Term and Long Term Dependencies employing respectively Convolutional N-Grams and LSTMs to reconstruct the word vectors. For the correction step, the basic idea is to simply substitute the word with the maximum reconstruction error for a better one. The second step is essentially a classification problem where the classes are the words in the dictionary as replacement options. Furthermore, to train and evaluate our model, we propose an approach to automatically construct a large dataset for the VTC problem. Our experiments and performance analysis demonstrates that the proposed method provides very good results and also highlights the general challenges in solving the VTC problem. To the best of our knowledge, this work is the first of its kind for the Visual Text Correction task.

1 Introduction

Text Correction (TC) has been a major application of Natural Language Processing (NLP). Text Correction can be in form of a single word auto-correction system, which notifies the user of misspelled words and suggests the most similar word, or an intelligent system that recommends the next word of an inchoate sentence. In this paper, we formulate a new type of Text Correction problem named *Visual Text Correction* (**VTC**). In VTC, given a video and an inaccurate textual description in terms of a sentence about the video, the task is to fix the inaccuracy of the sentence.

The inaccuracy can be in form of a phrase or a single word, and it may cause grammatical errors, or an inconsistency in context of the given video. For example, the word "car" in the sentence: "He is swimming in a car" is causing

© Springer Nature Switzerland AG 2018
V. Ferrari et al. (Eds.): ECCV 2018, LNCS 11217, pp. 159–175, 2018.
https://doi.org/10.1007/978-3-030-01261-8_10

Inaccurate Sentence: Someone shakes his hand.

Inaccuracy Detection: Someone shakes his hand

Corrected Sentence: Someone shakes his head

Fig. 1. One inaccurate sentence example for a given video. The VTC task is to find the inaccuracy and replace it with a correct word.

a textual inconsistency and the word "*hand*" is causing an inaccuracy in the context of the video (See Fig. 1).

To formalize the problem, let sentence $S = [w_1, w_2, ..., w_N]$ consisting of N words be an accurate description of the video V, where $w_i \in \{0,1\}^{|V|}$, and $|V|$ is the number of words in our dictionary. For an inaccurate sentence $\tilde{S} = [\tilde{w}_1, \tilde{w}_2, ..., \tilde{w}_N]$, the VTC task is to find the inaccurate word $\tilde{w}_{t^*}$ where $1 \le t^* \le N$ and also to estimate the replacement word w_t. There can be several inaccurate words in a sentence; However, we train our system using sentences with just one inaccurate word. Nonetheless, we show that our trained network can be applied to sentences with multiple inaccurate words.

Our proposed formulation can solve the VTC problem employing an End-to-End network in two steps: (1) Inaccuracy detection, and (2) correct word prediction. Figure 2 shows the proposed framework of our approach. During the first step, we detect the inaccuracy by reconstruction, that is, we embed each word into a continuous vector, and reconstruct a word vector for each of the words in the sentence based on its neighboring words. A large distance between the reconstructed vector and the actual word vector implies an inaccurate word. For the second step, the basic idea is to simply substitute the word with the maximum reconstruction error for a better one. The second step is essentially a classification problem where the classes are the words in the dictionary as replacement options.

1.1 Motivations

Why Visual Text Correction?: We believe that the VTC is very challenging and is a demanding problem to solve. During the last few years, the integration of computer vision and natural language processing (NLP) has received a lot of attention, and excellent progress has been made. Problems like Video Caption Generation, Visual Question Answering, etc., are prominent examples of this progress. With this paper, we start a new line of research which has many potential applications of VTC in real-world systems such as caption auto correction for video sharing applications and social networks, false tolerant text-based video retrieval systems, automatic police report validation, etc.

Why is VTC challenging?: Given a large number of words in a dictionary, many different combinations of words can take place in a sentence. For example, there are $\binom{|V|}{3}$ possible triplet combinations of words from a dictionary of size

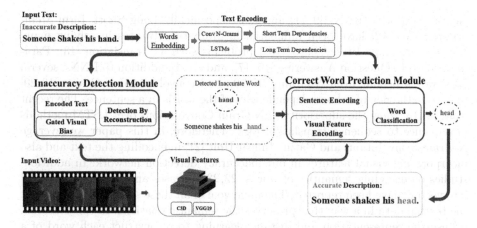

Fig. 2. Proposed framework for Visual Text Correction. The goal is to find and replace the inaccurate word in the descriptive sentence of a given video. There are two main modules: (1) The Inaccuracy Detection module finds the inaccurate word, and (2) the Correct Word Prediction module predicts an accurate word as a substitution. Both of these modules use the encoded text and visual features. The Inaccuracy Detection uses Visual Gating Bias to detect an inaccuracy and the Word Prediction Modules uses an efficient method to encode a sentence and visual features to predict the correct word.

$|V|$, which makes pre-selection of all possible correct combinations impractical. Also, in many cases, even a meaningful combination of words may result in an incorrect or inconsistent sentence. Furthermore, sentences can vary in length, and the inaccuracy can be in the beginning, middle or at the end of a sentence. Last but not least, a VTC approach must find the inaccuracy and also choose the best replacement to fix it. The video can provide useful information in addition to text since some words of the sentence, like verbs and nouns, need to be consistent with the video semantics like objects and actions present in the video.

1.2 Contributions

The contribution of this paper is three-fold. First, we introduce the novel VTC problem. Second, we propose a principled approach to solve the VTC problem by decomposing the problem into inaccurate word detection and correct word prediction steps. We propose a novel sentence encoder and a gating method to fuse the visual and textual inputs. Third, we offer an efficient way to build a large dataset to train our deep network and conduct experiments. We also show that our method is applicable to sentences with multiple inaccuracies.

2 Related Work

In the past few years Deep Convolutional Neural Networks (CNNs) [1–4] have been demonstrated to be very useful in solving numerous Computer Vision problems like object detection [5,6], action classification [7,8]. Similarly, Recurrent

Neural Networks (RNN) [9–11] and more specifically Long Short Term Memories(LSTM) [12] have been influential in dramatic advances in solving many Natural Language Processing (NLP) problems such as Translation [13], Paraphrasing [14], Question Answering [15–17], and etc. In addition to RNNs, several NLP works benefit from N-Grams [18,19], and convolutional N-Grams [13,20] to encode the neighborhood dependencies of the words in a sentence. The recent work in [13] show the superiority of N-Gram Convolutions over LSTM methods in sequence to sequence translation task. Therefore, in this paper we leverage N-Grams convolutions and Gating Linear Unit [21] in encoding the text and also incorporating visual features in our inaccuracy detection network. In addition, studies on encoding semantics of words [22,23], phrases and documents [24,25] into vectors have been reported. The main goal of all these studies is to represent the textual data in a way that preserves the semantic relations. In this research, we use the representation and distance learning to reconstruct each word of a sentence and find the inaccurate word based on the reconstruction error.

NLP and CV advances have motivated a new generation of problems, which are at the intersection of NLP and CV. Image/Video captioning [26–28] is to generate a description sentence about a given image/video. Visual Question Answering (VQA) [29,30,30–34] is to find the answer of a given question about a given image. In the captioning task, any correct sentence about the image/video can be acceptable, but in VQA, the question can be about specific details of the visual input. There are different types of the VQA problems, like multiple choice question answering [35], Textbook Question Answering (TQA) [36], Visual Dialogue [36], Visual Verification [37], Fill In the Blank (FIB) [28,38,39], etc. In addition to several types of questions in each of aforementioned works, different kinds of inputs have been used. Authors in [35] introduced a dataset of movie clips with the corresponding subtitles (conversations between actors) and questions about each clip. TQA [36] is a more recent form of VQA, where the input is a short section of elementary school textbooks including multiple paragraphs, figures, and a few questions about each. The aim of Visual Dialogue [36] is to keep a meaningful dialogue about a given photo, where a dialogue is a sequence of questions asked by a user followed by answers provided by system. Visual Knowledge Extraction [37] problem is to verify statements by a user (e.g. "Do horses fly?") from web crawled images.

Fill-In-the-Blank (FIB) [28,38,39] is the most related to our work. FIB is a Question Answering task, where the question comes in the form of an incomplete sentence. In the FIB task, the position of the blank word in each sentence is given and the aim is to find the correct word to fill in the blank. Although FIB is somehow similar to the proposed VTC task, it is not straightforward to correct an inaccurate sentence with a simple FIB approach. In FIB problem the position of the blank is given, however in VTC it is necessary to find the inaccurate word in the sentence first and then substitute it with the correct word.

Traditional TC tasks like grammatical and spelling correction have a rich literature in NLP. For instance, the authors in [40] train a Bayesian network to find the correct misspelled word in a sentence. Other line of works like [41,42], try to rephrase a sentence to fix a grammatical abnormality. In contrast to works in [40,41,41–43], there is no misspelled word in our problem, and we solve the VTC problem even for cases when the grammatical structure of the sentence is correct. Also, reordering the words of a sentence [42] cannot be the solution to our problem, since we need to detect and replace a single word while preserving the structure of the sentence. Moreover, this is the first work to employ the videos in the Textual Correction task.

3   Approach

To formulate the VTC problem, assume $\widetilde{\mathcal{S}} = [\widetilde{w}_1, \widetilde{w}_2, ..., \widetilde{w}_N]$ is a given sentence for the video $\mathcal{V}$. Our aim is to find the index of the incorrect word, t^*, and correct it with $w^*_{t^*}$ as follows:

$$(t^*, w^*_{t^*}) = \underset{1 \le t \le N, w_t \in \beta}{\arg\max} \; p((t, w_t) | \widetilde{\mathcal{S}}, \mathcal{V}), \tag{1}$$

where $w_i \in \{0,1\}^{|V|}$ is an one-hot vector representing the $i'th$ word of the sentence, $|V|$ is the size of our dictionary and N is the length of the sentence. Also, $\beta \subseteq V$ represents the set of all potential substitution words. Since t^* and $w^*_{t^*}$ are sequentially dependent, we decompose the Eq. 1 into two sub-tasks: Inaccurate word detection as:

$$t^* = \underset{1 \le t \le N}{\arg\max} \; p(t | \widetilde{\mathcal{S}}, \mathcal{V}), \tag{2}$$

and the accurate word $w^*_{t^*}$ prediction as:

$$w^*_{t^*} = \underset{w \in \beta}{\arg\max} \; p(w | \widetilde{\mathcal{S}}, \mathcal{V}, t^*). \tag{3}$$

3.1   Inaccuracy Detection

We propose detection by reconstruction method to find the most inaccurate word in a sentence, leveraging the semantic relationship between the words in a sentence. In our approach, each word of a sentence is reconstructed such that the reconstruction for the inaccurate word is maximized. For this purpose, we build embedded word vector $x_i \in \mathbb{R}^{d_x}$ for each corresponding word w_i using a trainable lookup table $\theta_x \in \mathbb{R}^{|V| \times d_x}$. We exploit both Short Term and Long Term Dependencies employing respectively Convolutional N-Grams and LSTMs to reconstruct the word vectors.

Short-Term Dependencies: Convolutional N-Gram networks [13] capture the *short-term* dependencies of each word surrounding. Sentences can vary in length, and a proper model should not be confused easily by long sentences. The main advantage of N-Gram approach is its robustness to disrupting words in long sentences, since it considers just a neighboring block around each word.

Let $X = [x_1; x_2; \ldots; x_N]$ be the stacked vectors representing embedded word vectors. Since the location of each word provides extra information about the correctness of that word in a sentence, we combine it with word vectors X. We denote $p_t \in \mathbb{R}^{d_x}$ as an embedded vector associated to the t'th *position* of each sentence, which is one row of the trainable matrix, $P \in \mathbb{R}^{N \times d_x}$. We use p_t values as gates for the corresponding word vectors x_t for each sentence and get final combination I as:

$$I_t = x_t \odot \sigma(p_t), \tag{4}$$

where $\odot$ denotes element-wise multiplication, and $I \in \mathbb{R}^{N \times d_x}$ is the input to a 1-D convolution with $2d_x$ filters and receptive field size of m. We call the resulting activation vectors $C \in \mathbb{R}^{N \times 2d_x}$. Furthermore, we use Gated Linear Units (GLU) [21] as the non-linear activation function. First, we split the C matrix in half along its depth dimension:

$$\begin{aligned} [A, B] &= C, \\ \Phi &= A \odot \sigma(B), \end{aligned} \tag{5}$$

where $A, B \in \mathbb{R}^{N \times d_x}$, and $\Phi = [\phi_1; \phi_2; \ldots; \phi_N]$, and $\phi_i \in \mathbb{R}^{d_x}$. The idea is to use the B matrix as gates for the matrix A. An open gate lets the input pass, and a close gate changes the input to zero. By stacking multiple 1-D convolutions and GLU activation functions the model goes deeper and the receptive field becomes larger. The output, Φ, from each layer is the input, I, for the next layer. We call the final output Φ, from the last Convolutional N-Grams layer, $\hat{X}^C \in \mathbb{R}^{N \times d_x}$. In Fig. 3, we illustrate one layer of the N-Grams encoding.

Long-Term Dependencies: Recurrent networks, and specifically LSTMs, have been successfully used to capture the *long-term* relations in sequences. Long-term relations are beneficial to comprehend the meaning of a text and also to find the possible inaccuracies. To reconstruct a word vector based on the rest of the sentence using LSTMs, we define a left fragment and a right fragment for each word in a sentence. The left fragment starts from the first word of the sentence to one word before the word under consideration; and the right fragment is from the last word of the sentence to one word after the word under consideration in a reverse order. We encode each of the left and right fragments with a LSTM and extract the last hidden state vector of the LSTM as the encoded fragment:

$$\hat{x}_t^R = W_c \times [u_t^l | u_t^r], \tag{6}$$

where $u_t^{l/r} \in \mathbb{R}^h$ are the encoded vectors of left/right fragments of the t'th word, and $W_c \in \mathbb{R}^{d_x \times 2h}$ is a trainable matrix to transform the $[u_t^l | u_t^r]$ into the $\hat{x}_t^R$.

Detection Module: We design a module to learn the distance between an actual word vector x_t and the reconstructed $\hat{x}_t$ as explained above. This module

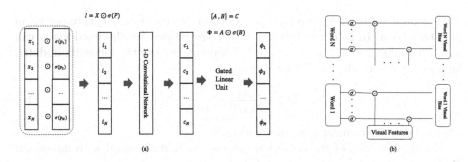

Fig. 3. (a) One layer of Convolutional Text Encoding which captures the neighboring relationships. To extend one layer to multiple layers, we simply consider the ϕ_i vectors as I_i for the next layer. (b) Our proposed Visual Gating Bias process. Given each word vector, we filter out some parts of a given visual feature through a gating process.

learns to assign a larger distance to the inaccurate words and reconstruct the predictions as follows:

$$\mathcal{D}_t = W_d \times \left(\frac{\hat{x}_t}{\|\hat{x}_t\|} \odot \frac{x_t}{\|x_t\|} \right), \tag{7}$$

where $W_d \in \mathbb{R}^{1 \times d_x}$, and $\mathcal{D}_t$ is a scalar. $\hat{x}_t$ is the output of the text encoding; namely, $\hat{x}_t = \hat{x}_t^C$ for Convolutional N-Grams or $\hat{x}_t = \hat{x}_t^R$ in case of Recurrent Networks. Next, we combine both as a vector $\hat{x}_t = \hat{x}_t^R + \hat{x}_t^C$ to capture both long term and short term dependencies of a sentence. We design our distance module as a single layer network for simplicity; however, it can be a deeper network.

Visual Features as Gated Bias: Visual features can contribute in finding the inaccuracy in a video description; however, it can be very challenging since some words may not correspond to any visible form or shape (e.g. 'weather'), while some others may correspond to distinct visual appearances (e.g. 'cat'). We introduce a gating model to incorporate the visual features to measure the inconsistency of each word. The main idea is to find a dynamic vector for the visual features which changes for each word as follows (see Fig. 3):

$$\Psi_{\mathcal{V}} = W_v \times \Omega(\mathcal{V}), \tag{8}$$

where $\Omega(\mathcal{V}) \in \mathcal{R}^{d_v}$ is the visual feature vector, and $W_v \in \mathcal{R}^{d_x \times d_v}$ is a transformation matrix for the visual features. We build the visual bias v_t for each word vector x_t:

$$v_t = \frac{\Psi_{\mathcal{V}}}{\|\Psi_{\mathcal{V}}\|} \odot \sigma([W_g \times x_t]), \tag{9}$$

and $W_g \in \mathcal{R}^{d_x \times d_x}$ is transformation matrix, and $\|.\|$ denotes L2-Norm of a vector. The Sigmoid ($\sigma(.)$) operator bounds its input into $(0, 1)$. It makes the model capable of refusing or accepting visual features dynamically for each word in a sentence.

The most intuitive way to incorporate the V vectors in Eq. 7, is to use them as a bias term. In fact, the features which are refused by the word gates will have zero value and will act as neutral. Therefore, we use the following updated form of Eq. 7 with the video contribution:

$$\mathcal{D}_t = W_d \times (\frac{\hat{x}_t}{\|\hat{x}_t\|} \odot \frac{x_t}{\|x_t\|} \oplus v_t), \tag{10}$$

where $\oplus$ denotes element-wise summation.

For the last step of the detection process, we find the word with maximum $\mathcal{D}$ value:

$$t^* = \arg\max_{1 \leq t \leq N} (\mathcal{D}_t). \tag{11}$$

Detection Loss: We use the cross-entropy as detection loss function. Given the ground-truth one-hot vector $y \in \{0,1\}^N$, which indicates the inaccurate word, and the $T^* = softmax(D)$ as probabilities, we compute the detection loss l_d.

3.2 Correct Word Prediction

The second stage of our proposed method to solve the VTC problem is to predict a substitute word for the inaccurate word. Proposed correct word prediction consists of three sub-modules: 1- Text Encoder, 2- Video Encoder, and 3- Inference sub-modules.

Text Encoder: This sub-module must encode the input sentence in such a way that the network be able to predict the correct word for the t^*'th word. We leverage the reconstructed word vectors $\hat{x}_t$ in Eq. 7, since these vectors are rich enough to detect an inaccuracy by reconstruction error. We can feed the output of inaccuracy detection, t^*, to our accurate word prediction network; however, the *argmax* operator in Eq. 11 is not differentiable and prevents us to train our model End-to-End. To resolve this issue, we approximate the Eq. 11 by vector $T^* = Softmax(D)$, which consists of probabilities of each of N words being incorrect in the sentence. We build the encoded text vector q_t:

$$q_t = tanh(W_q \times \hat{x}_t), \tag{12}$$

where $W_q \in \mathbb{R}^{d_q \times d_x}$ is trainable matrix. $q_t \in \mathbb{R}^{d_q}$ is in fact a hypothetical representation of the textual description. To be more specific, q_t is the encoded sentence, assuming that the word t is the incorrect word, which is to be replaced by a blank, according to the Eq. 12. Finally, the **textual representation** $u_q \in \mathbb{R}^{d_q}$, is formulated as a weighted sum over all q_t vectors:

$$u_q = \sum_{t=1}^{N} T_t^* q_t. \tag{13}$$

Note that, due to the "$tanh(.)$" operator in Eq. 12, both q_t and u_q vectors have bounded values.

Video Encoding: We leverage the video information to find the accurate word for t^*'th word of a sentence. While the textual information can solely predict a word for each location, visual features can help it to predict a better word based on the video, since the correct word can have a specific visual appearance. We extract the visual feature vector $\Omega(\mathcal{V})$ and compute our video encoding using a fully-connected layer:

$$u_\mathcal{V} = tanh(W_\mathcal{V} \times \Omega(\mathcal{V})), \tag{14}$$

where $W_\mathcal{V} \in \mathbb{R}^{d_q \times d_v}$, and $u_\mathcal{V} \in \mathbb{R}^{d_q}$ is our visual representation, which has bounded values. For simplicity, we have used just one layer video encoding; however, it can be a deeper and more complicated network.

Inference: For the inference, we select the correct substitute word from the dictionary. In fact, this amounts to a classification problem, where the classes are the words and the inputs are the textual representation and the visual features:

$$w_{t^*}^* = \arg\max_{w \in \beta}(W_i \times [u_q + u_\mathcal{V}]), \tag{15}$$

where $W_i \in \mathbb{R}^{|\beta| \times d_q}$. Finally, we use cross-entropy to compute the correct word prediction loss, namely l_f. The total loss for our VTC method is $l = l_f + l_d$ and we train both sub-tasks together.

4   Dataset and Experiments

4.1   Dataset

In this section, we describe our visual text correction dataset and the method to generate it. The main idea behind our approach to build a dataset for the VTC task is to remove one word from each sentence and substitute it with an inaccurate word; however, there are several challenges to address in order to build a realistic dataset. Here, we list a few and also propose our approach to address those challenges.

Our goal is to build a large dataset with a variety of videos with textual descriptions. We require that the vocabulary of the dataset and the number of video samples be large enough to train a deep network; hence we choose "Large Scale Movie Description Challenge (LSMDC)" dataset [38,44], which is one of the largest video description datasets available. Also, LSMDC has been annotated for "Video Fill In the Blank (FIB)" task. In FIB dataset, each video description contains one or more blanks, which needs to be filled in. For the VTC problem, we introduce inaccurate word in place of the blanks in FIB dataset. If there is more than one blanks in a sentence of the FIB dataset, we generate multiple examples of that sentence.

Note that there are some important points related to selection of the replacement words, which we need to keep in mind. First, there shouldn't be a high correlation between the original and replacement words. For example, if we exchange the word "car" with "bicycle" frequently, any method will be biased and will always suggest replacing "bicycle" with "car" in all sentences. Second, we want our sentences to look natural even after the word substitution. Therefore, the replacement word should have the same "Part Of Speech" (POS) tag. For example, a singular verb is better to be replaced by another singular verb.

It is costly to manually annotate and select the replacement words for each sample, because of the significant number of videos, and the vast vocabulary of the dataset. Also, it is hard for the human annotators to prevent the correlation between the original and replacement words. We have considered all the mentioned points to build our dataset. Following we describe how we build a proper dataset for the VTC problem.

Random Placement: In this approach, for each annotated blank in the LSMDC-FIB dataset, we place a randomly selected word from dictionary. This approach evidently is the most straightforward and simple way to introduce the incorrect word. However, in this method, a bias towards some specific words may exist, since the selected inaccurate words may not follow the natural distribution of the words in the dictionary. For example, we have many words with less than 4 or 5 occurrences in total. By Random Placement approach, rare words and the words with high frequencies have the same chance to show up as an inaccurate word. This increases the rate of "inaccurate occurrences to accurate occurrences" for some specific words. This imbalanced dataset allows any method to detect the inaccuracy just based on the word itself not the word in the context. Also, since replacement and original words may not take the same POS tag, Random Placement approach cannot meet one of the requirements mentioned above.

POS and Natural Distribution: Due to the weaknesses of the Random Placement, we introduce a more sophisticated approach that selects the inaccurate words from a set of words with the same tag as the original (or accurate) word. We first extract the POS tags of all the words from all the sentences using Natural Language Toolkit (NLTK) [45], resulting in 32 tags. Let S_r be the set of all the words that takes the tag r ($1 \leq r \leq 32$) at least once in the training sentences. To find a replacement for the annotated blank word w with the tag r in a sentence, we draw a sample from S_r and use it as the inaccurate word. Obviously, some tags are more common than the others in natural language and as a result the incorrect words are similarly the same.

To draw a sample from a set, we use the distribution of the words in all sentences. As a result, the words with more occurrences in the training set have more chance to be appeared as an inaccurate word. Therefore, the rate of incorrect to correct appearances of different words are close to each other. With this approach, we prevent the rare words to be chosen as the inaccurate word frequently and vice versa.

4.2   Results

Detection Experiments: In this subsection, we present our results for detection module and examine our method with various settings. The results are summarized in Table 1. Following we explain each experiment in more details.

Random guess is to select one of the words in the sentence randomly as the inaccurate word. In *Text Only Experiments* part of Table 1, we compare all the blind experiments, where no visual features are used to detect the inaccuracy. *Vanilla LSTM* uses a simple LSTM to directly produce the $\mathcal{D}_t$ (Eq. 7) out of its hidden state using a fully connected layer.

One-Way Long-Term Dependencies uses just u_l in Eq. 6. *Long-Term Dependencies* experiment uses Recurrent Neural Networks method explained in Sect. 3.1. *Convolutional N-Grams w/o Position Embedding* uses just Convolutional N-Grams, however, without the contribution of the positions of each word explained in Sect. 3.1 while *Convolutional N-Grams* is the complete explained module in Sect. 3.1. These two experiments show the effectiveness of our proposed words position gating, and finally, *Convolutional N-Grams + Long-Term Dependencies* uses the combination of Convolutional N-Grams and RNNs as mentioned in Sect. 3.1. The last experiment reveals the contribution of both short-term and long-term dependencies of words in a sentence for the TC task.

To further study the strength of our method to detect the wrong words, we compare our method with a *Commercial Web-App*[1]. This application can detect structural or grammatical errors in text. We provide 600 random samples from the test set to the web application and examine if it can detect the inaccuracy. In Table 1, we show the comparison between our method and the aforementioned web application. This experiment shows the superiority of our results and also the quality of our generated dataset.

In *Video and Text Experiments* part of the Table 1, we show experiments with both video and text. **Visual Gated Bias** experiment shows the capability of our proposed formulation to leverage the visual features in the detection sub-task. To show the superiority of our visual gating method, we conduct *Visual Feature Concatenation* experiment. In this experiment, we combine the visual feature vector $\Omega(\mathcal{V})$ with each of the vectors x_t and $\hat{x}_t$ in Eq. 7 using concatenation and a fully connected layer. For these experiments, we have used the pre-trained C3D [8] to compute the $\Omega(\mathcal{V})$.

4.3   Correction Experiments

In Table 2, we provide our results for the correction task. Note that, the correction task is composed of both inaccurate word detection and correct word predictions sub-tasks; thus, a correct answer for a given test sample must have the exact position of the inaccurate word and also the true word prediction $((t^*, w_{t^*}^*)$ in Eq. 1).

Our Model - Just Text experiment demonstrates our method performance with only textual information. *Our Model With C3D Features* uses both video

---

[1] www.grammarly.com.

Table 1. Detection experiments results. for these experiments we just evaluate the ability of different models to localize the inaccurate word.

Method	Accuracy (%)
Random	8.3
Text Only Experiments	
Commercial Web-App	18.8
Vanilla LSTM	28.0
One-Way Long-Term Dependencies	58.0
Long-Term Dependencies	67.2
Conv N-Grams w/o Position Embedding	66.8
Conv N-Grams	69.0
Conv N-Grams + Long-Term Dependencies	72.5
Video and Text Experiments	
Conv N-Grams + Long-Term Dependencies + Visual Feature Concatenation	72.8
Conv N-Grams + Long-Term Dependencies + Visual Gated Bias	**74.5**

and text, with C3D [8] features as visual features. Similarly, *Our Model With VGG19 Features* shows the results when VGG19 [46] features are the visual input. In *Our Pre-trained Detection Model + Pre-Trained FIB* [39] experiment we use our best detection model from Table 1 to detect an inaccurate word. We remove the inaccurate word and make an incomplete sentence with one blank. Then, we use one of the pre-trained state of the art FIB methods [39], which uses two staged Bi-LSTMs (LR/RL LSTMs) for text encoding + C3D and VGG19 features + temporal and spatial attentions, to find the missing word of the incomplete sentence. We show the superiority of our method which has been trained End-to-End. In both of detection (Table 2) and correction (Table 1) tasks, there are accuracy improvements after including visual features. We also report the Mean-Average-Precision (MAP) metric, to have a comprehensive comparison. To measure the MAP, we compute $N \times |\beta|$ scores for all the possible $(t^*, w^*_{t^*})$.

4.4 Multiple Inaccuracies

Here, we show that our method is capable of to be generalized to sentences with more than one inaccurate words. We conduct a new experiment with multiple inaccuracies in the test sentences and show the results in Table 3. In fact, we replace all the annotated blank words in the LSMDC-FIB test sentences with an inaccurate word. We assume that the number of inaccuracies, k, is given for each test sample, but the model needs to locate them. To select the inaccuracies in each sentence, we use the LSMDC-FIB dataset annotations. Note that in training we use sentences that contain just one inaccurate word,

Table 2. Text Correction Experiments Results. For the correction task, a model needs to successfully locate the inaccurate word and provides the correct substitution.

Method	Accuracy (%)	MAP (%)
Random	0.04	$\simeq 0$
Vanilla LSTM - Just Text	17.2	17.7
Our Model - Just Text	35.2	36.9
Our Pre-trained Detection Model + Pre-Trained FIB [39]	36.0	38.6
Our Model With C3D Features	38.6	39.8
Our Model With VGG19 Features	38.8	40.1
Our Model With VGG19 + C3D Features	**38.9**	**40.7**

Table 3. Detection and Correction results for sentences with multiple inaccuracies. Two types of Accuracy evaluations are provided. (1) Word-Based (WB) Accuracy: All correctly fixed incorrect words are counted independently. (2) Sentence-Based (SB) Accuracy: All inaccurate words in a sentence must be fixed correctly. Similarly, two types of MAP is reported: (1) WB-MAP, in which, one AP per each incorrect word is computed. (2) SB-MAP, in which, one AP per each sentence, including all the k incorrect words, is computed. k represents the number of inaccuracies in each sentence.

k =	1	2	3	4	All	1	2	3	4	All
# Of Test Samples	1805	4856	5961	520	30349	1805	2428	1987	130	9575
Detection	WB-Acc. (%)					SB-Acc. (%)				
Vanilla LSTM - Just Text	59	63	67	68	66	59	37	27	18	36
Our Method - Just Text	80	81	80	80	80	80	65	48	37	59
Our Method - Text + Video	**85**	**83**	**83**	**82**	**83**	**85**	**68**	**54**	**39**	**63**
Correction	WB-Acc. (%)					SB-Acc. (%)				
Our Method - Just Text	19	12	12	11	3	19	2	$\simeq 0$	$\simeq 0$	5
Our Method - Text + Video	**24**	**18**	**17**	**17**	**18**	**24**	**4**	$\simeq 0$	$\simeq 0$	**7**
Correction	WB-MAP (%)					SB-MAP (%)				
Our Method - Just Text	30	14	10	**8**	12	30	15	11	9	17
Our Method - Text + Video	**35**	**17**	**11**	7	**14**	**35**	**18**	**12**	**10**	**19**

similar to previous experiments. During the test time, we modify the Eq. 11 to $t^*_{i=1,..,k} = arg\,kmax(\mathcal{D}_t)$, where $arg\,kmax$ returns the top k inaccurate word candidates. Number of inaccurate words in our test set sentences reaches up to 10 words. However, in Table 3, we show the detection results for sentences with each $k \leq 4$ value separately, and also the overall accuracy for all the k values.

4.5   Qualitative Results

We show a few VTC examples in Fig. 4. For each sample, we show frames of a video and corresponding sentence with an inaccuracy. We provide the qualitative results for each example using our "Just Text" and "Text + Video" methods. We show two columns for the detection and correct word prediction. The green and red colors respectively indicate true and false outputs. Note that, for the VTC task, just a good detection or prediction is not enough. Both of these sub-tasks are needed to solve the VTC problem. For example, the left bottom example in Fig. 4 shows a failure case for both "Just Text", and "Text + Video", although the predicted word is correct using "Text + Video".

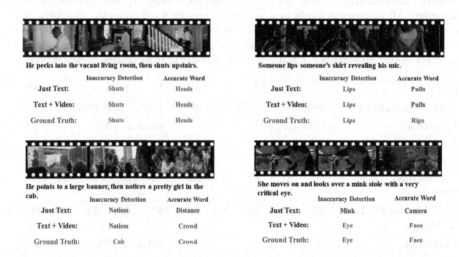

Fig. 4. Here we show four samples of our test results. For each sample, we show a video and an inaccurate sentence, the detected inaccurate word, and the predicted accurate word for substitution. The green color indicates a correct result while the red color shows a wrong result. (Color figure online)

5   Conclusion

We have presented a new formulation of text correction problem, where the goal is to find an inaccuracy in a video description, and fix it by replacing the inaccurate word. We propose a novel approach to leverage both textual and visual features to detect and fix the inaccurate sentences, and we show the superior results are obtained our approach. Moreover, we introduce an approach to generate a suitable dataset for VTC problem. Our proposed method provides a strong baseline for inaccuracy detection and correction tasks for sentences with one or multiple inaccuracies. We believe that our work is a step forward in the research related to intersection of Natural Language Processing and Computer Vision. We hope that this work lead to more exciting future researches in VTC.

Acknowledgments. This material is based upon work supported by the National Science Foundation under Grant No. 1741431. Any opinions, findings, and conclusions or recommendations expressed in this material are those of the author(s) and do not necessarily reflect the views of the National Science Foundation.

References

1. Krizhevsky, A., Sutskever, I., Hinton, G.E.: Imagenet classification with deep convolutional neural networks. In: NIPS (2012)
2. Simonyan, K., Zisserman, A.: Very deep convolutional networks for large-scale image recognition. arXiv preprint arXiv:1409.1556 (2014)
3. Szegedy, C., Liu, W., Jia, Y., Sermanet, P., Reed, S., Anguelov, D., Erhan, D., Vanhoucke, V., Rabinovich, A.: Going deeper with convolutions. In: CVPR (2015)
4. He, K., Zhang, X., Ren, S., Sun, J.: Deep residual learning for image recognition. arXiv preprint arXiv:1512.03385 (2015)
5. Deng, J., Dong, W., Socher, R., Li, L.J., Li, K., Fei-Fei, L.: Imagenet: A large-scale hierarchical image database. In: CVPR (2009)
6. He, K., Zhang, X., Ren, S., Sun, J.: Deep residual learning for image recognition. In: Proceedings of the IEEE Conference on Computer Vision and Pattern Recognition, pp. 770–778 (2016)
7. Soomro, K., Zamir, A.R., Shah, M.: Ucf101: A dataset of 101 human actions classes from videos in the wild. arXiv preprint arXiv:1212.0402 (2012)
8. Tran, D., Bourdev, L., Fergus, R., Torresani, L., Paluri, M.: Learning spatiotemporal features with 3D convolutional networks. In: ICCV (2015)
9. Schuster, M., Paliwal, K.K.: Bidirectional recurrent neural networks. IEEE Trans. Signal Process. **45**(11), 2673–2681 (1997)
10. Hochreiter, S., Schmidhuber, J.: Long short-term memory. Neural Comput. **9**(8), 1735–1780 (1997)
11. Chung, J., Gulcehre, C., Cho, K., Bengio, Y.: Empirical evaluation of gated recurrent neural networks on sequence modeling. arXiv preprint arXiv:1412.3555 (2014)
12. Malinowski, M., Rohrbach, M., Fritz, M.: Ask your neurons: a neural-based approach to answering questions about images. In: CVPR (2015)
13. Gehring, J., Auli, M., Grangier, D., Yarats, D., Dauphin, Y.N.: Convolutional sequence to sequence learning. arXiv preprint arXiv:1705.03122 (2017)
14. Chen, D.L., Dolan, W.B.: Collecting highly parallel data for paraphrase evaluation. In: Proceedings of the 49th Annual Meeting of the Association for Computational Linguistics: Human Language Technologies-Volume 1, Association for Computational Linguistics, pp. 190–200 (2011)
15. Bordes, A., Usunier, N., Chopra, S., Weston, J.: Large-scale simple question answering with memory networks. arXiv preprint arXiv:1506.02075 (2015)

16. Kumar, A., Irsoy, O., Su, J., Bradbury, J., English, R., Pierce, B., Ondruska, P., Gulrajani, I., Socher, R.: Ask me anything: dynamic memory networks for natural language processing. arXiv preprint arXiv:1506.07285 (2015)
17. Weston, J., Chopra, S., Bordes, A.: Memory networks. arXiv preprint arXiv:1410.3916 (2014)
18. Zhang, H., Chiang, D.: Kneser-Ney smoothing on expected counts
19. Chen, S.F., Goodman, J.: An empirical study of smoothing techniques for language modeling. In: Proceedings of the 34th Annual Meeting on Association for Computational Linguistics, Association for Computational Linguistics, pp. 310–318 (1996)
20. Kalchbrenner, N., Grefenstette, E., Blunsom, P.: A convolutional neural network for modelling sentences. arXiv preprint arXiv:1404.2188 (2014)
21. Dauphin, Y.N., Fan, A., Auli, M., Grangier, D.: Language modeling with gated convolutional networks. arXiv preprint arXiv:1612.08083 (2016)
22. Mikolov, T., Chen, K., Corrado, G., Dean, J.: Efficient estimation of word representations in vector space. arXiv preprint arXiv:1301.3781 (2013)
23. Mikolov, T., Sutskever, I., Chen, K., Corrado, G.S., Dean, J.: Distributed representations of words and phrases and their compositionality. In: NIPS, pp. 3111–3119 (2013)
24. Le, Q., Mikolov, T.: Distributed representations of sentences and documents. In: Proceedings of the 31st International Conference on Machine Learning (ICML 2014), pp. 1188–1196 (2014)
25. Dai, A.M., Olah, C., Le, Q.V.: Document embedding with paragraph vectors. arXiv preprint arXiv:1507.07998 (2015)
26. Vinyals, O., Toshev, A., Bengio, S., Erhan, D.: Show and tell: A neural image caption generator. In: CVPR (2015)
27. Johnson, J., Karpathy, A., Fei-Fei, L.: Densecap: Fully convolutional localization networks for dense captioning. arXiv preprint arXiv:1511.07571 (2015)
28. Yu, Y., Ko, H., Choi, J., Kim, G.: End-to-end concept word detection for video captioning, retrieval, and question answering. In: Proceedings of the IEEE Conference on Computer Vision and Pattern Recognition, pp. 3165–3173 (2017)
29. Antol, S., Agrawal, A., Lu, J., Mitchell, M., Batra, D., Lawrence Zitnick, C., Parikh, D.: VQA: Visual question answering. In: ICCV (2015)
30. Ren, M., Kiros, R., Zemel, R.: Exploring models and data for image question answering. In: NIPS (2015)
31. Malinowski, M., Fritz, M.: A multi-world approach to question answering about real-world scenes based on uncertain input. In: NIPS (2014)
32. Agrawal, A., Lu, J., Antol, S., Mitchell, M., Zitnick, C.L., Batra, D., Parikh, D.: Vqa: Visual question answering. arXiv preprint arXiv:1505.00468 (2015)
33. Xiong, C., Merity, S., Socher, R.: Dynamic memory networks for visual and textual question answering. arXiv preprint arXiv:1603.01417 (2016)
34. Zhang, P., Goyal, Y., Summers-Stay, D., Batra, D., Parikh, D.: Yin and yang: Balancing and answering binary visual questions. arXiv preprint arXiv:1511.05099 (2015)
35. Tapaswi, M., Zhu, Y., Stiefelhagen, R., Torralba, A., Urtasun, R., Fidler, S.: Movieqa: Understanding stories in movies through question-answering. In: CVPR (2016)
36. Nadeem, F., Ostendorf, M.: Language based mapping of science assessment items to skills. In: Proceedings of the 12th Workshop on Innovative Use of NLP for Building Educational Applications, pp. 319–326 (2017)
37. Sadeghi, F., Divvala, S.K., Farhadi, A.: VisKE: Visual knowledge extraction and question answering by visual verification of relation phrases. In: CVPR (2015)

38. Maharaj, T., Ballas, N., Courville, A., Pal, C.: A dataset and exploration of models for understanding video data through fill-in-the-blank question-answering. arXiv preprint arXiv:1611.07810 (2016)
39. Mazaheri, A., Zhang, D., Shah, M.: Video fill in the blank using LR/RL LSTMS with spatial-temporal attentions. In: ICCV 2017 (2017)
40. Mays, E., Damerau, F.J., Mercer, R.L.: Context based spelling correction. Inf. Process. Manag. **27**(5), 517–522 (1991)
41. Wu, C.H., Liu, C.H., Harris, M., Yu, L.C.: Sentence correction incorporating relative position and parse template language models. IEEE Trans. Audio Speech Lang. Process. **18**(6), 1170–1181 (2010)
42. Wagner, R.A.: Order-N correction for regular languages. Commun. ACM **17**(5), 265–268 (1974)
43. Suhm, B., Myers, B., Waibel, A.: Multimodal error correction for speech user interfaces. ACM Trans. Comput. Hum. Interact. **8**(1), 60–98 (2001)
44. Rohrbach, A., Rohrbach, M., Tandon, N., Schiele, B.: A dataset for movie description. In: CVPR (2015)
45. Loper, E., Bird, S.: NLTK: The natural language toolkit. In: Proceedings of the ACL-02 Workshop on Effective tools and methodologies for teaching natural language processing and computational linguistics-Volume 1, Association for Computational Linguistics, pp. 63–70 (2002)
46. Simonyan, K., Zisserman, A.: Very deep convolutional networks for large-scale image recognition. CoRR abs/1409.1556 (2014)

Generalizing a Person Retrieval Model Hetero- and Homogeneously

Zhun Zhong[1,2], Liang Zheng[2,3], Shaozi Li[1(✉)], and Yi Yang[2]

[1] Cognitive Science Department, Xiamen University, Xiamen, China
zhunzhong007@gmail.com, szlig@xmu.edu.cn
[2] Centre for Artificial Intelligence, University of Technology Sydney,
Ultimo, Australia
liangzheng06@gmail.com, yee.i.yang@gmail.com
[3] Research School of Computer Science, Australian National University,
Canberra, Australia

Abstract. Person re-identification (re-ID) poses unique challenges for unsupervised domain adaptation (UDA) in that classes in the source and target sets (domains) are entirely different and that image variations are largely caused by cameras. Given a labeled source training set and an unlabeled target training set, we aim to improve the generalization ability of re-ID models on the target testing set. To this end, we introduce a Hetero-Homogeneous Learning (HHL) method. Our method enforces two properties simultaneously: (1) camera invariance, learned via positive pairs formed by unlabeled target images and their camera style transferred counterparts; (2) domain connectedness, by regarding source/target images as negative matching pairs to the target/source images. The first property is implemented by *homogeneous* learning because training pairs are collected from the same domain. The second property is achieved by *heterogeneous* learning because we sample training pairs from both the source and target domains. On Market-1501, DukeMTMC-reID and CUHK03, we show that the two properties contribute indispensably and that very competitive re-ID UDA accuracy is achieved. Code is available at: https://github.com/zhunzhong07/HHL.

Keywords: Person re-identification · Unsupervised domain adaptation

1 Introduction

Given a query, person re-identification (re-ID) aims to retrieve the same person from a database collected by different cameras from the query. Despite the dramatic performance improvement obtained by the convolutional neural network (CNN), it is reported that deep re-ID models trained on the source domain may have a large performance drop on the target domain [7,10]. The main reason is that the data distribution of the source domain is usually different from the target domain. In this paper, we consider the setting of unsupervised domain

© Springer Nature Switzerland AG 2018
V. Ferrari et al. (Eds.): ECCV 2018, LNCS 11217, pp. 176–192, 2018.
https://doi.org/10.1007/978-3-030-01261-8_11

adaptation (UDA), in which during training we are provided with labeled source training images and unlabeled target training images. Performance is evaluated on the target testing database.

Unsupervised domain adaptation [16,26,37], which has been studied extensively in image classification, object detection and semantic segmentation, faces new challenges in the context of person re-ID. On the one hand, the source and target domains in person re-ID have entirely different classes (person identities), while in generic UDA, the source and target share the same set of classes. On the other hand, a critical factor that leads to domain variance in person re-ID can be clearly identified, *i.e.*, the disparities of cameras. Even in the unlabeled target domain, camera information, *i.e.*, the camera by which an image is captured, is known. However, it remains unknown in the UDA community how to effectively leverage the camera information for person re-ID.

In this paper, our design is motivated in two aspects, closely associated with the new challenges mentioned above. First, a critical part of our motivation arises from the *intra-domain* image variations caused by different camera configurations. This perspective is largely overlooked in recent methods addressing the UDA problem in person re-ID. These recent works either concentrate on content-preserving source-target translation models [7,39] or employ both the attribute and identity labels to learn a transferable model [38]. To our knowledge, these methods only consider the overall *inter-domain* differences, but do not explicitly consider the *intra-domain* image style variations caused by different camera configurations. In fact, the *intra-domain* camera style difference is a critical influencing factor for person re-ID, because during testing, the query and its ground truth matches are captured by different cameras. Without considering the fine-grained *intra-domain* image variations, a transfer learning model trained on the source set will probably only capture the overall data bias between the two domains and have problems when encountering the large *intra-domain* image variations in target domain testing set.

Second, we consider the prior that the source and target sets have entirely different classes/identities, so a source image and a target image naturally form a negative training pair. A similar idea has been explored by Deng *et al.* [7]. However, the two papers differ in the purpose of using this prior. In [7], Deng *et al.* use the negative pairs to improve the image-image translation model, so that the generated images will largely preserve their identity label, a desirable property for UDA. In comparison, we directly use these negative pairs to learn person embeddings within a triplet loss formulation.

With the two considerations, we propose a new unsupervised domain adaptation method, named **H**etero-**H**omogeneous **L**earning (HHL), for the person re-ID task. HHL is constructed without target supervision, *i.e.*, we do not require laborious manual annotations such as identities in the target set. In fact, the construction of HHL requires a source set (identity labels given), a target set (without identity labels), and the camera information for each image in the target set. Here, we emphasize that the camera ID for each target image can be obtained along with the raw videos: it suffices to simply record the ID of the camera capturing the videos. Therefore, we call the construction of HHL "without target supervision", or in the most strict way "with extremely weak target supervision".

In our method, HHL underpins constraints at two properties. First, we constrain to learn person embeddings which are robust to camera variances in the target domain. To achieve this *camera invariance* property in an unsupervised fashion, positive training pairs are generated by image-image translation, viewing each camera as an individual style. Second, in order to endow *domain connectedness* to the system, we learn the underlying structures between source and target domains using negative training pairs sampled from the source and target sets, respectively. In this paper, imposing the camera invariance property is a *homogeneous learning* process because training images are from the same domain. Imposing the domain connectedness property implies a *heterogeneous learning* procedure because the training samples are from two domains. The two properties produce a positive pair homogeneously and a negative pair heterogeneously, which, bridged by an anchor image to be fed into a triplet loss training.

To summarize, this paper is featured in the three aspects. First, a Hetero-Homogeneous Learning (HHL) scheme is introduced. Through a triplet loss, it brings about camera invariance and domain connectedness to the system, which are essential properties towards an effective UDA approach in person re-ID. Second, HHL is a new method for training sample construction in UDA. It is robust to parameter changes. The insights and indispensability of camera invariance and domain connectedness are validated through experimental studies. Third, we report new state-of-the-art UDA accuracy on the Market-1501, CUHK03 and DukeMTMC-reID datasets.

2   Related Work

Unsupervised Domain Adaptation. Our work is closely related to unsupervised domain adaptation (UDA) where the target domain is unlabeled. Most of the previous methods try to align the source to the target domain by reducing the divergence of feature distributions [11,26,35–37,41]. These methods are motivated by the theory stating that the error for the target domain is bounded by the difference between domains [2]. CORAL [35] aligns the mean and covariance of source domain and target domain distributions and achieves promising results in various visual recognition tasks. Further, deep CORAL [36] extends the approach by incorporating the CORAL loss into deep model. There exist many methods which aim at providing pseudo-labels to unlabeled samples. Several methods utilize similarity of features to give pseudo-labels to unlabeled target samples [31,33]. In [33], an approach is presented to estimate the labels of unlabeled samples by using the k-nearest neighbors. Then, the predicted labels are leveraged to learn the optimal deep feature. Alternatively, many methods try to predict labels to unlabeled samples by leveraging the predictions of a classifier and retraining the classifier with both labeled samples and pseudo-labeled samples, which is called co-training [50]. The underlying assumption of these methods is that high-confidence prediction is a mostly correct class for an unlabeled sample. In [4], the idea of co-training is applied to domain adaptation by gradually adding the target samples of high-confidence predictions to the training set. Saito *et al.* [32] propose to generate pseudo-labels for target domain samples through three classifiers asymmetrically and train the final classifier with predicted labels.

Recently, Many Generative Adversarial Networks (GAN) [12] based domain adaptation approaches focus on learning a generator network that transforms samples in the pixel space from one domain to another [3,16,24]. CyCADA [16] adapts representations at both the pixel-level and feature-level via pixel cycle-consistency and semantic losses, it achieves high performance on both digit recognition and semantic segmentation. Most of existing unsupervised domain adaptation methods assume that class labels are the same across domains, while the person identities (classes) of different re-ID datasets are totally different. Hence, the approaches mentioned above fail to be utilized directly for the problem of unsupervised domain adaptation in person re-ID.

Unsupervised Person re-ID. Hand-craft features can be directly applied for unsupervised person re-ID, for example, ELF [13], LOMO [23], and SDALF [1], which aim to design or learn robust feature for person re-ID. These methods often ignore the distribution of samples in the dataset and fail to perform well on large-scale dataset. Benefit from the remarkable success of deep learning [8,9,14,21,27], recent works [10,25,40] attempt to predict pseudo-labels to unlabeled samples based on the deep learning framework. Fan *et al.* [10] propose an unsupervised re-ID approach for iteratively applying k-means clustering to assign labels to unlabeled samples and fine-tuning the deep re-ID model on the target domain. Liu *et al.* [25] estimate labels with k-reciprocal nearest neighbors [29] and iteratively learn features for unsupervised video re-ID. Wu *et al.* [40] propose a progressive sampling method to gradually predict reliable pseudo labels and update deep model for one-shot video-based re-ID.

Few works [7,17,28,38,39] have studied on unsupervised domain adaptation for re-ID. Peng *et al.* [28] propose to learn a discriminative representation for target domain based on asymmetric multi-task dictionary learning. Deng *et al.* [7] learn a similarity preserving generative adversarial network based on CycleGAN [49] to translate images from source domain to target domain. The translated images are utilized to train re-ID model in a supervised way. In [38], a transferable model is proposed to jointly learn attribute-semantic and identity discriminative feature representation for target domain. These approaches aim at reducing the gap between source domain and target domain on either the image-level space [7,39] or feature-level space [17,28,38], while overlook the image style variations caused by different cameras in target domain. In this work, we explicitly consider the intra-domain image variations caused by cameras to learn discriminative re-ID model for target domain.

3   Proposed Method

Problem Definition. For unsupervised domain adaptation in person re-ID, we have a labeled source set $\{X_s, Y_s\}$ consisting of N_s person images. Each image x_s corresponds to a label y_s, where $y_s \in \{1, 2, ..., M_s\}$, and M_s is the number of identities. We also have N_t unlabeled target images from unlabeled target set $\{X_t\}$. The identity of each target image x_t in $\{X_t\}$ is unknown. The goal of this paper is to leverage both labeled source training images and unlabeled target training images to learn discriminative embeddings for target testing set.

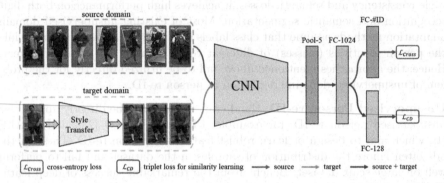

Fig. 1. The framework of the proposed approach. It consists of two loss functions: (1) cross-entropy loss for classification, which learned by labeled source samples; (2) triplet loss for similarity learning, which imposes camera invariance and domain connectedness to the model and learned through labeled source samples, unlabeled target samples and cameras style transferred samples.

3.1   Baseline Configuration

We use ResNet-50 [14] as backbone and follow the training strategy in [48] which fine-tunes on the ImageNet [6] pre-trained model. We discard the last 1,000-dim fully connected (FC) layer and add two FC layers. The output of the first FC layer is 1,024-dim named as "FC-1024", followed by batch normalization [18], ReLU and Dropout [34]. The output of the second FC layer, named as "FC-#ID" is M_s-dim, where M_s is the number of identities (classes) in the labeled training set.

Given the labeled training images, an effective strategy is to learn the ID-discriminative embedding (IDE) [44] for person re-ID. The cross-entropy loss is employed by casting the training process as a classification problem. The cross-entropy loss is written as,

$$\mathcal{L}_{Cross} = -\frac{1}{n_s} \sum_{i=1}^{n_s} \log p_i(y),$$
$$(1)$$

where n_s is the number of labeled training images in a batch, $p_i(y)$ is the predicted probability of the input belonging to ground-truth class y. We name this model as **baseline** throughout this paper.

The IDE-based methods [44, 46, 47] achieve good performance on fully labeled datasets, but often fail to generalize to a new target set. Next, we will describe the Hetero-Homogeneous Learning (HHL) approach to improve the transferability of the baseline.

3.2   Network Architecture

The network used in this paper is shown in Fig. 1. It has two branches. The first branch is the same with the **baseline**, which is an identification task. The second branch is different from the first branch in two aspects: (1) a 128-dim FC layer named "FC-128" is used instead of the "FC-#ID" layer; (2) a triplet loss is used instead of the cross-entropy loss. Therefore, our network has two loss functions, a cross-entropy loss for classification and a triplet loss for similarity learning. For similarity learning, we employ the triplet loss used in [15], which is formulated as,

$$\mathcal{L}_T(X) = \sum_{x_a, x_p, x_n} [m + D_{x_a, x_p} - D_{x_a, x_n}], \ \forall \ x_a, x_p, x_n \in X, \qquad (2)$$

where X represents images in a training batch, x_a is an anchor point. x_p is a hardest (farthest) sample in the same class with x_a, and x_n is a hardest (closest) sample of a different class to x_a. m is a margin parameter and $D(\cdot)$ is the Euclidean distance between two images in the embedding space. We use the output of FC-128 as the embedding feature and set m to 0.3. Note that during re-ID testing, we use the output of Pool-5 (2,048-dim) as person descriptor.

3.3   Camera Invariance Learning

The variation of image style caused by cameras is a critical influencing factor during person re-ID testing procedure. To achieve the camera invariance property in target domain, we impose the camera invariance constraint by learning with both unlabeled target images and their counterparts containing the same person but with different camera styles.

In order to generate new target images that more or less preserve the person identity and reflect the style of another camera, we employ the CamStyle approach [48] to learn camera style transfer model in the target set. Different from [48] which uses CycleGAN [49] for image-image translation, we build CamStyle based on StarGAN [5]. This is because StarGAN allows us to train multi-camera image-image translation with a single model, while CycleGAN needs to train a translation model for each pair of cameras. Suppose we have C cameras in the target set. We first train a StarGAN model which enables image-image translation between every camera pair. With the learned StarGAN model, for a real image $x_{t,j}$ collected by camera j ($j \in 1, 2, ..., C$) in the target set, we generate C fake (camera style transferred) images $x_{t^*,1}, x_{t^*,2}, ..., x_{t^*,C}$ which more or less contain the same person with $x_{t,j}$ but whose styles are similar to camera $1, 2, ..., C$, respectively. Note that the C images include the one transferred to the style of camera j, that is, the style of the real image $x_{t,j}$. Examples of real images and fake images generated by CamStyle [48] are shown in Fig. 2.

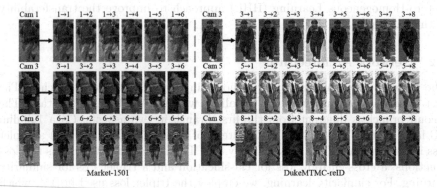

Fig. 2. Examples of camera style transfer on Market-1501 and DukeMTMC-reID. An image collected by a certain camera is transferred to the style of other cameras. In this process, the identity information is preserved to some extent. The real image and its corresponding fake images are assumed to belong to the same class during training.

To learn camera invariant person embeddings for the target set, we view $x_{t,j}$ and its corresponding fake images $x_{t^*,1}, x_{t^*,2}, ..., x_{t^*,C}$ as belonging to the same class. We view all the other images as belonging to a different class with $x_{t,j}$. For simplicity, we omit the subscript of camera. Specifically, we compute a triplet loss through the unlabeled target domain samples $\{x_t^i\}_{i=1}^{n_t}$ and their corresponding camera transferred samples $\{x_{t^*}^i\}_{i=1}^{n_t^*}$. The loss function of camera invariance learning can be written as,

$$\mathcal{L}_C = \mathcal{L}_T(\{x_t^i\}_{i=1}^{n_t} \cup \{x_{t^*}^i\}_{i=1}^{n_t^*}), \tag{3}$$

where n_t is the number of real target images in a training batch, and n_t^* is the number of camera style transferred samples. In our experiment, we generate C fake images for each real target image, i.e. $n_t^*/n_t = C$, where C is the number of cameras. In a training batch, x_t^i is randomly selected from the target set, and we assume that $x_t^1, x_t^2, ..., x_t^{n_t}$ as belonging to different classes. Technically speaking, this assumption is incorrect, because each target training class has several images, and it may well be the case that two images of the same class are selected into the training batch. That being said, we will show in Sect. 3.6 and Fig. 3 that our assumption does not affect the performance noticeably.

3.4 Domain Connectedness Learning

In person re-ID, different domains have completely different classes/identities, so a source image and a target image naturally form a negative training pair.

With this prior, we propose to endow domain connectedness to the system by regarding source/target images as negative matching pairs to the target/source images. Given an anchor image from the source, we use source domain labels to construct a positive pair. We then choose a target domain image to form a negative pair with the anchor. Formally, given the labeled source domain samples $\{x_s^i\}_{i=1}^{n_s}$ and the unlabeled target domain samples $\{x_t^i\}_{i=1}^{n_t}$, the loss function of domain connectedness learning can be defined as,

$$\mathcal{L}_D = \mathcal{L}_T(\{x_s^i\}_{i=1}^{n_s} \cup \{x_t^i\}_{i=1}^{n_t}), \tag{4}$$

where n_s is the number of source images, and n_t is the number of target images. In this loss function, since the identities of target images do not overlap with the identities in source domain, each source image and each target image form a negative pair. Therefore, the relationship between the source and target samples is considered, so that the communication and the underlying structures between two domains can be achieved to some extent.

3.5 Hetero-Homogeneous Learning

In this paper, we argue that camera invariance and domain connectedness are complementary properties towards an effective UDA system for person re-ID. To this end, we propose to jointly learn camera invariance and domain connectedness using a single loss in a training batch. Specifically, a training batch contains labeled source images $\{x_s^i\}_{i=1}^{n_s}$, unlabeled real target images $\{x_t^i\}_{i=1}^{n_t}$, and their corresponding fake images $\{x_{t*}^i\}_{i=1}^{n_t^*}$. The triplet loss function of camera invariance learning and domain connectedness learning can be written as,

$$\mathcal{L}_{CD} = \mathcal{L}_T(\{x_s^i\}_{i=1}^{n_s} \cup \{x_t^i\}_{i=1}^{n_t} \cup \{x_{t*}^i\}_{i=1}^{n_t^*}). \tag{5}$$

In this loss function, we enforce two properties simultaneously: (1) camera invariance, learned through real target images and its corresponding fake images; (2) domain connectedness, mapping the source and target samples into shared feature space by regarding source/target samples (including their camera style transferred samples) as negative matching pairs to the target/source samples.

Finally, the overall loss function (Fig. 1) in a training batch is expressed as,

$$\mathcal{L}_{HHL} = \mathcal{L}_{Cross} + \beta \mathcal{L}_{CD}, \tag{6}$$

where β is the weight of the joint camera invariance and domain connectedness loss. We name this learning method "Hetero-Homogeneous learning (HHL)" because of the heterogeneous sample selection scheme of domain connectedness learning, and because of the homogeneous sample selection scheme of camera invariance learning. Also, we note that the cross-entropy loss is indispensable in Eq. 6, which provides a basic discriminative ability *learned on the source only*. Without the cross-entropy loss, the system will be harmed significantly.

3.6   Discussion

Why Use Camera Style Transfer? In Table 1, we compare the distance between images that undergoes different data augmentation method, *i.e.* random cropping, random flipping and camera style transfer. It is clearly that, the re-ID model trained on source set is robust to random cropping and random flipping on target set, but is sensitive to image variations caused by cameras. Therefore, the change of image style caused by different cameras on target set is a key influencing factor that should be explicitly considered in person re-ID UDA.

Table 1. The average distance between two images that undergo different data augmentation techniques. We use the baseline re-ID model (Sect. 3.1) trained on the source set to extract image descriptors (Pool-5, 2,048-dim) on the target set.

Source	Target	Random Crop	Random Flip	CamStyle Transfer
Duke	Market-1501	0.049	0.034	**0.485**
Market-1501	Duke	0.059	0.044	**0.614**

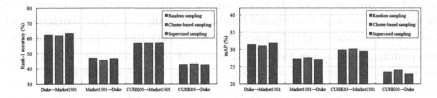

Fig. 3. Comparison of different sampling strategies on the target set, including random sampling, cluster-based sampling and supervised sampling. Rank-1 accuracy and mAP are reported. We set $\beta = 0.5$, $n_t = 16$. We find that different sampling methods achieve very similar results. So for simplicity, we use random sampling throughout the paper.

How to Sample Training Images from Target Domain? We compare three sampling strategies, (1) random sampling, we randomly sample n_t target images in each mini-batch and assign non-overlap randomly identity for each image, *i.e.* each image has a different identity in a mini-batch; (2) cluster-based sampling, at begin of each training epoch, we apply k-means to cluster target images into n_t clusters based on currently learned re-ID model, and sample one image from each cluster to compose training data of target domain in a mini-batch. The cluster-based sampling strategy could effectively avoid to sample the same identity in a mini-batch; (3) supervised sampling, assume that we are provided with labeled target set, we randomly select n_t images in a supervised way ensuring that each target image comes from a different identity. The comparison of different sampling strategies is shown in Fig. 3. It is clearly that random sampling yields quite approximate results with the other two strategies. It is because of the probability of images to be the same identities is very low when sampling few images from target set including a large number of images and identities. Therefore, we use random sampling in this paper.

4 Experiment

4.1 Datasets

We evaluate our method on three re-ID datasets which are considered as large-scale in the community, *i.e.*, Market-1501 [43], DukeMTMC-reID [30,45], and CUHK03 [22]. **Market-1501** [43] contains 32,668 labeled images of 1,501 identities collected from 6 cameras. For evaluation, 12,936 images from 751 identities are used for training, and 19,732 images from 750 identities plus some distractors form the gallery/database. Moreover, 3,368 hand-drawn bounding boxes from 750 identities are used as queries to retrieve the corresponding person images in the database. We use the single-query evaluation in our experiment. **DukeMTMC-reID** [45] has 8 cameras and 36,411 labeled images belonging to 1,404 identities. Similar to the division of Market-1501, the dataset contains 16,522 training images from 702 identities, 2,228 query images from another 702 identities and 17,661 gallery images. **CUHK03** [22] contains 14,096 images of 1,467 identities. Each identity is captured from two cameras. The dataset has two train/test settings: using labeled bounding boxes and using DPM detected bounding boxes. We use the detected setting because it is more challenging and closer to practical scenarios. Note that images in CUHK03 do not have camera labels, so we cannot perform *camera invariance learning*. Therefore, we only use CUHK03 as the *source domain* instead of the *target domain*. We use the conventional rank-n accuracy and mean average precision (mAP) for evaluation on all datasets. Example persons of different re-ID datasets are shown in Fig. 4.

Market-1501   DukeMTMC-reID   CUHK03

Fig. 4. Example images of the Market-1501, DukeMTMC-reID and CUHK03 datasets. Images in each column represent the same identity/class collected from different cameras. We observe that the image style of the three datasets is very different and that within each dataset, the image style of different cameras is different as well.

4.2   Experiment Settings

Camera Style Transfer Model. Given a target set collected by C cameras, we use StarGAN [5] to train an image-image translation model to transfer images between every camera pair. We follow the same architecture as [5]. Specifically, the generator contains 2 convolutional layer, 6 residual blocks and 2 transposed convolution layers, while the discriminator is the same as PatchGANs [19]. The input images are resized to 128 × 64. In training, we use the Adam optimizer [20] with $\beta_1 = 0.5$ and $\beta_2 = 0.999$. Two data augmentation methods, random flipping and random cropping, are employed. The learning rate is 0.0001 for both generator and discriminator at the first 100 epochs and linearly decays to zero in the remaining 100 epochs. In camera style transfer, for each image in the target set, we generate C style-transferred images (including the one transferred to the camera style of the original real image). These C fake images are regarded as containing the same person with original real image.

Re-ID Model Training. To train the re-ID model, we employ the training strategy in [48]. Specifically, we keep the aspect ratio of input images and resize them to 256×128. For data augmentation, random cropping and random flipping are applied. Dropout probability is set to 0.5. Learning rate is initialized to 0.1 for the classification layer and to 0.01 for the rest of the layers. Learning rate is divided by 10 after 40 epochs. We set the mini-batch size of source images to 128 and 64 for IDE and triplet loss, respectively. The model is trained with the SGD optimizer in a total of 60 epochs. In testing, we extract the output of the 2,048-dim Pool-5 layer as the image descriptor and use the Euclidean distance to compute the similarity between the query and database images.

4.3   Important Parameters

We evaluate two important parameters, *i.e.* the weight of the triplet loss β and the number of real target images n_t in a batch. When evaluating one parameter, we fix the other one. Results are shown in Figs. 5 and 6, respectively.

Weight of the Triplet Loss. When $\beta = 0$, our method reduces to the baseline (with cross-entropy loss only, Sect. 3.1). It is clearly shown that, our approach significantly improves the baseline at all values. The rank-1 accuracy and mAP improve with the increase of β and achieve the best results when β is between 0.4 to 0.8.

Number of the Real Target Images in a Training Batch. When $n_t = 0$, only source images are used for training the re-ID model with IDE and triplet loss, so our method reduces to "baseline+$\mathcal{L}_T$". From Fig. 5, we observe that when increasing the number of real target images and their corresponding camera style transferred samples in a training batch, our method consistently outperforms "baseline+$\mathcal{L}_T$". Performance becomes stable after $n_t = 16$.

Based on the above analysis, our method is robust to parameters changes. In the following experiment, we set $\beta = 0.5$ and $n_t = 16$.

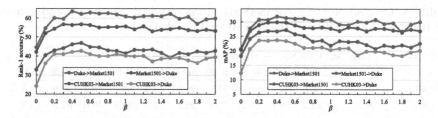

Fig. 5. Sensitivity to parameter β (weight of the triplet loss) in Eq. 6. We fix $n_t = 16$.

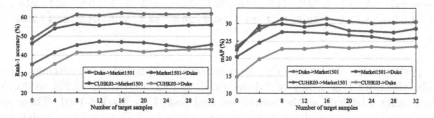

Fig. 6. Sensitivity to the number of real target images n_t in a batch. β is fixed to 0.5.

4.4 Evaluation

Baseline Accuracy. We present results of the baselines (see Sect. 3.1) in Tables 2 and 3. When trained and tested both on the target set, high accuracy can be observed. However, performance drops significantly when the model is trained on the source set and directly deployed on the target set. For example, the baseline model trained and tested on Market-1501 yields a rank-1 accuracy of 83.8%, but drops to 44.6% when trained on DukeMTMC-reID and tested on Market-1501. The reason is the data distribution bias among datasets.

Effectiveness of Domain Connectedness Learning Over Baseline. Because the loss function of domain connectedness learning in Eq. 4 includes both source labeled samples and unlabeled target samples, we first add triplet loss with source samples into baseline (Basel.+$\mathcal{L}_T$). As shown in Tables 2 and 3,

Table 2. Methods comparison using Duke/Market as source, and using Market/Duke as target. S: labeled source set, T: labeled target set, T^u: unlabeled target set.

Methods	Train set	Duke → Market-1501					Market-1501 → Duke				
		R-1	R-5	R-10	R-20	mAP	R-1	R-5	R-10	R-20	mAP
Basel.	T	83.8	93.3	95.6	97.1	66.3	72.3	84.1	88.1	90.9	53.5
Basel.	S	44.6	62.5	69.6	76.5	20.6	32.9	49.5	54.8	61.7	16.9
Basel.+$\mathcal{L}_T$	S	48.6	66.4	73.3	78.9	23.5	35.1	50.7	57.6	64.0	20.5
Basel.+$\mathcal{L}_D$	S+T^u	49.8	67.8	74.5	80.5	23.8	36.8	52.3	59.1	64.9	21.1
Basel.+$\mathcal{L}_C$	S+T^u	60.6	77.1	83.0	87.6	28.5	42.5	56.8	62.9	67.9	22.1
Basel.+$\mathcal{L}_{CD}$	S+T^u	**62.2**	**78.8**	**84.0**	**88.3**	**31.4**	**46.9**	**61.0**	**66.7**	**71.9**	**27.2**

Table 3. Comparison of various methods on unsupervised domain adaptation from CUHK03 to Market-1501 and DukeMTMC-reID (Duke).

Methods	Train set	CUHK03 → Market-1501					CUHK03 → Duke				
		R-1	R-5	R-10	R-20	mAP	R-1	R-5	R-10	R-20	mAP
Basel.	T	83.8	93.3	95.6	97.1	66.3	72.3	84.1	88.1	90.9	53.5
Basel.	S	42.2	59.1	66.1	73.8	20.3	24.3	38.2	45.0	51.9	12.3
Basel.+$\mathcal{L}_T$	S	46.1	63.8	71.1	78.1	22.5	28.4	43.4	49.6	55.9	14.8
Basel.+$\mathcal{L}_D$	S+T^u	48.9	66.7	74.6	79.6	23.3	29.2	44.5	50.7	57.5	15.7
Basel.+$\mathcal{L}_C$	S+T^u	53.6	71.0	77.6	82.7	25.6	40.9	55.9	60.9	66.2	20.8
Basel.+$\mathcal{L}_{CD}$	S+T^u	**56.8**	**74.7**	**81.4**	**86.3**	**29.8**	**42.7**	**57.5**	**64.2**	**69.1**	**23.4**

the performance of "Basel.+$\mathcal{L}_T$" is consistently improved in all settings. Specially, the rank-1 accuracy of "Basel.+$\mathcal{L}_T$" is increased from 42.2% to 46.1% when using CUHK03 as the source set and tested on Market-1501. Then, we inject domain connectedness learning into "Basel.+$\mathcal{L}_T$" by adding unlabeled target samples into triplet loss. Comparison to "Basel.+$\mathcal{L}_T$", when tested on Market-1501, "Basel.+$\mathcal{L}_D$" leads to +1.2% and +2.8% improvement in rank-1 accuracy when using Duke and CUHK03 as the source set, respectively.

Effectiveness of Camera Invariance Learning Over Baseline. We verify the effectiveness of camera invariance learning over baseline in Tables 2 and 3. It is clear that, "Basel.+$\mathcal{L}_C$" significantly outperforms the baseline in all settings. For example, when tested on Market-1501, "Basel.+$\mathcal{L}_C$" gives rank-1 accuracy of 60.6% when using Duke as source set. This is +16% higher than the baseline in rank-1 accuracy. Similar improvement is observed when tested on DukeMTMC-reID. The consistent improvement indicates that camera invariance learning is critical for improving the discriminate ability in target domain.

Benefit of Hetero-Homogeneous Learning. We study the benefit of hetero-homogeneous learning in Tables 2 and 3. The "Basel.+$\mathcal{L}_{CD}$" achieves higher performance than the model trained independently with camera invariance learning (Basel.+$\mathcal{L}_C$) or domain connectedness learning (Basel.+$\mathcal{L}_D$). For example, when Market-1501 is the target set, the "Basel.+$\mathcal{L}_{CD}$" obtains rank-1 accuracy in 56.8% by using CUHK03 as source set, surpassing the "Basel.+$\mathcal{L}_D$" and "Basel.+$\mathcal{L}_C$" by +7.9% and +3.2%, respectively. Similar improvement is observed in other settings, indicating that camera invariance and domain connectedness are indispensable to improve the transferability of the re-ID model in UDA.

4.5   Comparison with the State-of-the-Art Methods

We compare our method with the state-of-the-art unsupervised learning methods. Table 4 presents the comparison when Market-1501/Duke is the source set and Duke/Market-1501 is the target. We compare with two hand-crafted features, *i.e.* BoW [43] and LOMO [23], three unsupervised methods, including

Table 4. Unsupervised person re-ID performance comparison with state-of-the-art methods.

Methods	Duke → Market-1501				Market-1501 → Duke			
	R-1	R-5	R-10	mAP	R-1	R-5	R-10	mAP
LOMO [23]	27.2	41.6	49.1	8.0	12.3	21.3	26.6	4.8
Bow [43]	35.8	52.4	60.3	14.8	17.1	28.8	34.9	8.3
UMDL [28]	34.5	52.6	59.6	12.4	18.5	31.4	37.6	7.3
PTGAN [39]	38.6	-	66.1	-	27.4	-	50.7	-
PUL [10]	45.5	60.7	66.7	20.5	30.0	43.4	48.5	16.4
SPGAN [7]	51.5	70.1	76.8	22.8	41.1	56.6	63.0	22.3
CAMEL [42]	54.5	-	-	26.3	-	-	-	-
SPGAN+LMP [7]	57.7	75.8	82.4	26.7	46.4	62.3	**68.0**	26.2
TJ-AIDL [38]	58.2	74.8	81.1	26.5	44.3	59.6	65.0	23.0
HHL	**62.2**	**78.8**	**84.0**	**31.4**	**46.9**	**61.0**	66.7	**27.2**

Table 5. Unsupervised person re-ID performance comparison with state-of-the-art methods when trained on CUHK03.

Methods	CUHK03 → Market-1501					CUHK03 → Duke				
	R-1	R-5	R-10	R-20	mAP	R-1	R-5	R-10	R-20	mAP
PTGAN [39]	31.5	-	60.2	-	-	17.6	-	38.5	-	-
PUL [10]	41.9	57.3	64.3	70.5	18.0	23.0	34.0	39.5	44.2	12.0
SPGAN [7]	42.3	-	-	-	19.0	-	-	-	-	-
HHL	**56.8**	**74.7**	**81.4**	**86.3**	**29.8**	**42.7**	**57.5**	**64.2**	**69.1**	**23.4**

CAMEL [42], PUL [10], and UMDL [28], and three unsupervised domain adaptation approaches, including PTGAN [39], SPGAN [7] and TJ-AIDL [38]. The two hand-crafted features are directly applied on target testing set without training. Both features fail obtain competitive results. With training on target set, unsupervised methods obtain higher results than hand-crafted features. For example, CAMEL [42] achieves 54.4% rank-1 accuracy when using DukeMTMC-reID as source set and tested on Market-1501 (multi-query setting). Comparing with unsupervised domain adaptation methods, our method is superior. Specifically, when tested on Market-1501, our results are higher than all the competing methods, achieving **rank-1 accuracy = 62.2% and mAP = 31.4%**. For example, comparing with the recently published TJ-AIDL method [38], our results are higher by +4.0% in rank-1 accuracy and +4.9% in mAP. When tested on DukeMTMC-reID, our method achieves **rank-1 accuracy = 46.9% and mAP = 27.2%**, higher than previous methods as well. So this paper sets a new state of the art on Duke → Market-1501 and yields competitive results on Market-1501 → Duke.

Table 5 presents comparisons of methods using CUHK03 as the source set. Our method outperforms the state-of-the-art methods by a large margin. Specifically, HHL yields an mAP of 29.8% when Market-1501 is the target set. This is higher than SPGAN [7] (19.0%) by +10.8%.

5   Conclusion

In this paper, we present Hetero-Homogeneous Learning (HHL), a new unsupervised domain adaptation approach for person re-identification (re-ID). Taking advantage of the unique challenges of UDA approaches in the context of person re-ID, we propose to learn camera invariance and domain connectedness simultaneously to obtain more generalized person embeddings on the target domain. Experiment conducted on Market-1501, DukeMTMC-reID and CUHK03 confirms that our approach achieves very competitive performance compared with the state of the art.

Acknowledgements. This work is supported by the National Nature Science Foundation of China (No. 61572409, No. U1705286 & No. 61571188), Fujian Province 2011Collaborative Innovation Center of TCM Health Management, Collaborative Innovation Center of Chinese Oolong Tea Industry-Collaborative Innovation Center (2011) of Fujian Province, Fund for Integration of Cloud Computing and Big Data, Innovation of Science and Education, the Data to Decisions CRC (D2D CRC) and the Cooperative Research Centres Programme. Zhun Zhong thanks Wenjing Li for encouragement.

References

1. Bazzani, L., Cristani, M., Murino, V.: Symmetry-driven accumulation of local features for human characterization and re-identification. CVIU (2013)
2. Ben-David, S., et al.: A theory of learning from different domains. Mach. Learn. **79**, 151–175 (2010)
3. Bousmalis, K., Silberman, N., Dohan, D., Erhan, D., Krishnan, D.: Unsupervised pixel-level domain adaptation with generative adversarial networks. In: CVPR (2017)
4. Chen, M., Weinberger, K.Q., Blitzer, J.: Co-training for domain adaptation. In: Advances in Neural Information Processing Systems, pp. 2456–2464 (2011)
5. Choi, Y., et al.: Stargan: unified generative adversarial networks for multi-domain image-to-image translation. In: CVPR (2018)
6. Deng, J., et al.: Imagenet: a large-scale hierarchical image database. In: CVPR (2009)
7. Deng, W., et al.: Image-image domain adaptation with preserved self-similarity and domain-dissimilarity for person re-identification. In: CVPR (2018)
8. Dong, X., Yan, Y., Ouyang, W., Yang, Y.: Style aggregated network for facial landmark detection. In: CVPR (2018)
9. Dong, X., et al.: Supervision-by-Registration: an unsupervised approach to improve the precision of facial landmark detectors. In: CVPR (2018)
10. Fan, H., Zheng, L., Yang, Y.: Unsupervised person re-identification: Clustering and fine-tuning. arXiv preprint arXiv:1705.10444 (2017)

11. Ganin, Y., et al.: Domain-adversarial training of neural networks. JMLR (2016)
12. Goodfellow, I., et al.: Generative adversarial nets. In: NIPS (2014)
13. Gray, D., Tao, H.: Viewpoint invariant pedestrian recognition with an ensemble of localized features. In: Forsyth, D., Torr, P., Zisserman, A. (eds.) ECCV 2008. LNCS, vol. 5302, pp. 262–275. Springer, Heidelberg (2008). https://doi.org/10.1007/978-3-540-88682-2_21
14. He, K., Zhang, X., Ren, S., Sun, J.: Deep residual learning for image recognition. In: CVPR (2016)
15. Hermans, A., Beyer, L., Leibe, B.: In defense of the triplet loss for person re-identification. arXiv preprint arXiv:1703.07737 (2017)
16. Hoffman, J., et al.: Cycada: cycle-consistent adversarial domain adaptation. arXiv preprint arXiv:1711.03213 (2017)
17. Hu, J., Lu, J., Tan, Y.P.: Deep transfer metric learning. In: CVPR (2015)
18. Ioffe, S., Szegedy, C.: Batch normalization: accelerating deep network training by reducing internal covariate shift. In: ICML (2015)
19. Isola, P., Zhu, J.Y., Zhou, T., Efros, A.A.: Image-to-image translation with conditional adversarial networks. In: CVPR (2017)
20. Kingma, D., Ba, J.: Adam: a method for stochastic optimization. In: ICLR (2015)
21. Krizhevsky, A., Sutskever, I., Hinton, G.E.: Imagenet classification with deep convolutional neural networks. In: NIPS (2012)
22. Li, W., Zhao, R., Xiao, T., Wang, X.: Deepreid: deep filter pairing neural network for person re-identification. In: CVPR (2014)
23. Liao, S., Hu, Y., Zhu, X., Li, S.Z.: Person re-identification by local maximal occurrence representation and metric learning. In: CVPR (2015)
24. Liu, M.Y., Tuzel, O.: Coupled generative adversarial networks. In: NIPS (2016)
25. Liu, Z., Wang, D., Lu, H.: Stepwise metric promotion for unsupervised video person re-identification. In: ICCV (2017)
26. Long, M., Cao, Y., Wang, J., Jordan, M.: Learning transferable features with deep adaptation networks. In: ICML (2015)
27. Luo, Y., Zheng, Z., Zheng, L., Guan, T., Yu, J., Yang, Y.: Macro-micro adversarial network for human parsing. In: Ferrari, V., Hebert, M., Sminchisescu, C., Weiss, Y. (eds.) ECCV 2018, Part IX. LNCS, vol. 11217, pp. 424–440. Springer, Cham (2018)
28. Peng, P., et al.: Unsupervised cross-dataset transfer learning for person re-identification. In: CVPR (2016)
29. Qin, D., Gammeter, S., Bossard, L., Quack, T., Van Gool, L.: Hello neighbor: Accurate object retrieval with k-reciprocal nearest neighbors. In: CVPR (2011)
30. Ristani, E., Solera, F., Zou, R., Cucchiara, R., Tomasi, C.: Performance measures and a data set for multi-target, multi-camera tracking. In: ECCVW (2016)
31. Rohrbach, M., Ebert, S., Schiele, B.: Transfer learning in a transductive setting. In: NIPS (2013)
32. Saito, K., Ushiku, Y., Harada, T.: Asymmetric tri-training for unsupervised domain adaptation. arXiv preprint arXiv:1702.08400 (2017)
33. Sener, O., Song, H.O., Saxena, A., Savarese, S.: Learning transferrable representations for unsupervised domain adaptation. In: NIPS (2016)
34. Srivastava, N., Hinton, G.E., Krizhevsky, A., Sutskever, I., Salakhutdinov, R.: Dropout: a simple way to prevent neural networks from overfitting. JMLR (2014)
35. Sun, B., Feng, J., Saenko, K.: Return of frustratingly easy domain adaptation. In: AAAI (2016)

36. Sun, B., Saenko, K.: Deep CORAL: correlation alignment for deep domain adaptation. In: Hua, G., Jégou, H. (eds.) ECCV 2016. LNCS, vol. 9915, pp. 443–450. Springer, Cham (2016). https://doi.org/10.1007/978-3-319-49409-8_35

37. Tzeng, E., Hoffman, J., Zhang, N., Saenko, K., Darrell, T.: Deep domain confusion: maximizing for domain invariance. arXiv preprint arXiv:1412.3474 (2014)

38. Wang, J., Zhu, X., Gong, S., Li, W.: Transferable joint attribute-identity deep learning for unsupervised person re-identification. In: CVPR (2018)

39. Wei, L., Zhang, S., Gao, W., Tian, Q.: Person transfer GAN to bridge domain gap for person re-identification. In: CVPR (2018)

40. Wu, Y., et al.: Exploit the unknown gradually: One-shot video-based person re-identification by stepwise learning. In: CVPR (2018)

41. Yan, H., et al.: Mind the class weight bias: weighted maximum mean discrepancy for unsupervised domain adaptation. In: CVPR (2017)

42. Yu, H., Wu, A., Zheng, W.S.: Cross-view asymmetric metric learning for unsupervised person re-identification. In: ICCV (2017)

43. Zheng, L., et al.: Scalable person re-identification: a benchmark. In: ICCV (2015)

44. Zheng, L., Yang, Y., Hauptmann, A.G.: Person re-identification: Past, present and future. arXiv preprint arXiv:1610.02984 (2016)

45. Zheng, Z., Zheng, L., Yang, Y.: Unlabeled samples generated by gan improve the person re-identification baseline in vitro. In: ICCV (2017)

46. Zhong, Z., Zheng, L., Cao, D., Li, S.: Re-ranking person re-identification with k-reciprocal encoding. In: CVPR (2017)

47. Zhong, Z., Zheng, L., Kang, G., Li, S., Yang, Y.: Random erasing data augmentation. arXiv preprint arXiv:1708.04896 (2017)

48. Zhong, Z., Zheng, L., Zheng, Z., Li, S., Yang, Y.: Camera style adaptation for person re-identification. In: CVPR (2018)

49. Zhu, J.Y., Park, T., Isola, P., Efros, A.A.: Unpaired image-to-image translation using cycle-consistent adversarial networks. In: ICCV (2017)

50. Zhu, X.: Semi-supervised learning literature survey. Technical report, University of Wisconsin-Madison (2005)

Domain Adaptation Through Synthesis for Unsupervised Person Re-identification

Sławomir Bąk[1](✉) ⓘD, Peter Carr[1], and Jean-François Lalonde[2] ⓘD

[1] Argo AI, Pittsburgh, PA 15222, USA
{sbak,pcarr}@argo.ai
[2] Université Laval, Quebec City G1V 0A6, Canada
jflalonde@gel.ulaval.ca

Abstract. Drastic variations in illumination across surveillance cameras make the person re-identification problem extremely challenging. Current large scale re-identification datasets have a significant number of training subjects, but lack diversity in lighting conditions. As a result, a trained model requires fine-tuning to become effective under an unseen illumination condition. To alleviate this problem, we introduce a new synthetic dataset that contains hundreds of illumination conditions. Specifically, we use 100 virtual humans illuminated with multiple HDR environment maps which accurately model realistic indoor and outdoor lighting. To achieve better accuracy in unseen illumination conditions we propose a novel domain adaptation technique that takes advantage of our synthetic data and performs fine-tuning in a completely unsupervised way. Our approach yields significantly higher accuracy than semi-supervised and unsupervised state-of-the-art methods, and is very competitive with supervised techniques.

Keywords: Synthetic · Identification · Unsupervised Domain adaptation

1 Introduction

Even over the course of just a few minutes, a person can look surprisingly different when observed by different cameras at different locations. Indeed, her visual appearance can vary drastically due to changes in her pose, to the different illumination conditions, and to the camera configurations and viewing angles. To further complicate things, she may be wearing the same shirt as another, unrelated person, and could thus easily be confused.

The task of person re-identification tackles the challenge of finding the same subject across a network of non-overlapping cameras. Most effective state-of-the-art algorithms employ supervised learning [25–27,46,51], and require thousands

Electronic supplementary material The online version of this chapter (https://doi.org/10.1007/978-3-030-01261-8_12) contains supplementary material, which is available to authorized users.

© Springer Nature Switzerland AG 2018
V. Ferrari et al. (Eds.): ECCV 2018, LNCS 11217, pp. 193–209, 2018.
https://doi.org/10.1007/978-3-030-01261-8_12

Fig. 1. Sample images from our **SyRI** dataset: the same 3D character rendered in various HDR environment maps. The dataset provides 100 virtual humans rendered in 140 realistic illumination conditions.

of labeled images for training. With novel deep architectures, we are witnessing an exponential growth of large scale re-identification datasets [25,48]. Recent re-identification benchmarks have focused on capturing large numbers of identities, which allows the models to increase their discriminative capabilities [43]. Unfortunately, current re-identification datasets lack significant diversity in the number of lighting conditions, since they are usually limited to a relatively small number of cameras (the same person is registered under a handful of illumination conditions). Models trained on these datasets are thus biased to the illumination conditions seen during training. One can increase the model generalization by merging multiple re-identification datasets into a single dataset and training the network as joint single-task learning [43]. In this approach, the learned models show generalization properties but only upon fine-tuning [2]. This is because the merged datasets contain tens of different lighting conditions, which might not be sufficient to generalize. To apply the previously trained model to a new set of cameras, we need to annotate hundreds of subjects in each camera, which is a tedious process and does not scale to real-world scenarios.

In this work, we introduce the *Synthetic Person Re-Identification* (**SyRI**) dataset. Employing a game engine, we simulate the appearance of hundreds of subjects under different realistic illumination conditions, including indoor and outdoor lighting (see Fig. 1). We first carefully designed 100 virtual humans based on 3D scans of real people. These digital humans are then rendered using realistic backgrounds and lighting conditions captured in a variety of high dynamic range (HDR) environment maps. We use HDR maps as the virtual light source and background plate when rendering the 3D virtual scenes. With the increased diversity in lighting conditions, the learned re-identification models gain additional generalization properties, thus performing significantly better in unseen lighting conditions.

To further improve recognition performance, we propose a novel **three-step domain adaptation technique**, which translates our dataset to the target conditions by employing cycle-consistent adversarial networks [52]. Since the cycle-consistent formulation often produces semantic shifts (the color of clothing may change drastically during translation), we propose an additional regularization term to limit the magnitude of the translation [37], as well as an additional masking technique to force the network to focus on the foreground object. The translated images are then used to fine-tune the model to the specific lighting conditions. In summary, our main contributions are:

- We introduce a new dataset with 100 virtual humans rendered with 140 HDR environment maps. We demonstrate how this dataset can increase generalization capabilities of trained models in unseen illumination conditions without fine-tuning.
- We improve re-identification accuracy in an unsupervised fashion using a novel three-step domain adaptation technique. We use cycle-consistency translation with a new regularization term for preserving identities. The translated synthetic images are used to fine-tune the re-identification model for a specific target domain.

2   Related Work

Person Re-identification: Most successful person re-identification approaches employ supervised learning [3,22,23]. This includes novel deep architectures and the debate as to whether the triplet or multi-classification loss is more effective for training re-identification networks [3,16,43]. Larger architectures have improved accuracy, but also increased the demand for larger re-identification datasets [12,47,48]. However all of these approaches require fine-tuning [2,47] to become effective in unseen target illumination conditions, which is infeasible for large camera networks. To overcome this scalability issue, semi-supervised and unsupervised methods have been proposed [20,21,35]. This includes transfer learning [18,35,49] and dictionary learning [1,10,28]. However, without labeled data, these techniques usually look for feature invariance, which reduces discriminativity, and makes the methods uncompetitive with supervised techniques.

Synthetic Data: Recently, data synthesis and its application for training deep neural architectures has drawn increasing attention [37]. It can potentially generate unlimited labeled data. Many computer vision tasks have already been successfully tackled with synthetic data: human pose estimation [36], pedestrian detectors [7,14,19] and semantic segmentation [30,34]. The underlying challenge when training with synthetic visual data is to overcome the significant differences between synthetic and real image statistics. With increasing capacity of neural networks, there is a risk that the network will learn details only present in synthetic data and fail to generalize to real images. One solution is to focus on rendering techniques to make synthetic images appear more realistic. However, as the best renderers are not differentiable, the loss from the classifier cannot be directly back-propagated, thus leaving us with simple sampling strategies [19]. Instead, we take an approach closer to [37]: rather than optimizing renderer parameters, we cast the problem as a domain adaptation task. In our case, the domain adaptation performs two tasks simultaneously: (1) makes the synthetic images look more realistic and (2) minimizes the domain shift between the source and the target illumination conditions.

Domain Adaptation: Typically, domain adaptation is a way of handling dataset bias [40]. Not surprisingly, domain adaptation is also used to minimize the visual gap betwen synthetic and real images [37]. Often this shift between distributions of the source and target domain is measured by the distance between

Fig. 2. Example HDR environment maps used to relight virtual humans.
The environment maps capture a wide variety of realistic indoor (left) and outdoor
(right) lighting conditions. The images have been tonemapped for display purposes
with $\gamma = 2.2$. Please zoom-in for more details.

the source and target subspace representations [8]. Thus, many techniques focus
on learning feature space transformations to align the source and the target
domains [18,41]. This enables knowledge transfer (*e.g.* how to perform a particular task) between the two domains. Recently, adversarial training has achieved
impressive results not only in image generation [11], but also in unsupervised
domain adaptation [9]. In this work, we are inspired by a recent approach for
unsupervised image-to-image translation [52], where the main goal is to learn the
mapping between images, rather than maximizing the performance of the model
in particular task. Given our synthesized images and the domain translation, we
are able to hallucinate labeled training data in the target domain that can be
used for fine-tuning (adaptation).

3   SyRI Dataset

Given sufficient real data covering all possible illumination variations, we should
be able to learn re-identification models that have good generalization capabilities without the need for fine-tuning. Unfortunately, gathering and annotating
such a dataset is prohibitive. Instead, we propose training with synthesized data.
The underlying challenge is to create photo-realistic scenes with realistic lighting conditions. Rather than hand-crafting the illumination conditions, we use
High Dynamic Range (HDR) environment maps [5]. These can be seen as 360°
panoramas of the real world that contain accurate lighting information, and can
be used to relight virtual objects and provide realistic backgrounds.

Environment Maps. To accurately model realistic lighting, a database of 140
HDR environment maps was acquired. First, 40 of those environment maps were
gathered from several sources online[1]. Further, we also captured an additional
100 environment maps. A Canon 5D Mark III camera with a Sigma 8 mm fisheye
lens was mounted on a tripod equipped with panoramic tripod head. 7 brack-
eted exposures were shot at 60° increments, for a total of 42 RAW photos per

---

[1] The following online sources were used: http://gl.ict.usc.edu/Data/HighResProbes/,
  http://dativ.at/lightprobes,   http://www.unparent.com/photos_probes.html,
  http://www.hdrlabs.com/sibl/archive.html.

panorama. The resulting set of photos were automatically merged and stitched into a 22 f-stop HDR 360° environment map using the PTGui Pro commercial software. Our dataset represents a wide variety of indoor and outdoor environments, such as offices, theaters, shopping malls, museums, classrooms, hallways, corridors, etc. Figure 2 shows example environment maps from our dataset.

3D Virtual Humans and Animations. Our 3D virtual humans are carefully designed with *Adobe Fuse CC* that provides 3D content, including body scans of real people with customizable body parts and clothing. We generate 100 character prototypes, where we customize body shapes, clothing, material textures and colors (see Fig. 3). These characters are then animated using rigs to obtain realistic looking walking poses.

Rendering. We use *Unreal Engine 4* to achieve real-time rendering speeds. To relight our 3D virtual humans, the HDR environment map is texture mapped on a large sphere surrounding the scene. This sphere is then used as a the sole light source (light emitter) to render the scene. We position a 3D character at the center of the sphere. The character is animated using either a male or female walking rig, depending on the model gender. We also add a rotation animation to acquire multiple viewpoints of each subject. The camera position is matched with existing re-identification datasets. Each subject is rendered twice under the same HDR map rotating the sphere about its vertical axis by two random angles. This effectively provides two different backgrounds and lighting conditions for each environment map. We render 2-second videos at 30 fps as the character is being rotated. In the end, we render 100 (subjects) × 140 (environment maps) × 2 (rotations) × 2 (seconds) × 30 (fps) = 1,680,000 frames. Both the rendered dataset as well as the Unreal Engine project that will allow a user to render more data are going to be made publicly available.

Fig. 3. Sample 3D virtual humans from **SyRI** dataset.

4   Method

We cast person re-identification as a domain adaptation problem, where the domain is assumed to be an illumination condition (*i.e.*, a camera-specific lighting). Our objective is to find an effective and unsupervised strategy for performing person re-identification under the target illumination condition.

For training, we assume we have access to M real source domains $\mathbf{R} = \{R_1 \dots R_M\}$, where each $R_m = \{x_i, y_i\}_{i=1}^{Z_{R_m}}$ consists of Z_{R_m} real images x_i

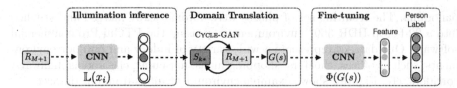

Fig. 4. Unsupervised Domain Adaptation. Given unlabelled input images from target domain R_{M+1}, we first select the closest synthetic domain S_{k*} through illumination inference. Afterwards, images from the selected domain S_{k*} are translated by $G : S_{k*} \rightarrow R_{M+1}$ to better resemble the input images in R_{M+1}. Finally, the translated synthetic images $G(s)$ along with their known identities are used to fine-tune the re-identification network $\Phi(\cdot)$.

and their labels y_i (person's identity); and N source synthetic domains $\mathbf{S} = \{S_1 \dots S_N\}$, where each $S_n = \{s_i, y_i\}_{i=1}^{Z_{S_n}}$ consists of Z_{S_n} synthetic images s_i and their labels y_i (3D character's identity). In our case $N \gg M$ as we have access to hundreds of different illumination conditions (see Sect. 3). Our ultimate goal is to perform re-identification in unknown target domain $R_{M+1} = \{x_i\}_{i=1}^{Z_{R_{M+1}}}$ for which we do not have labels.

4.1   Joint Learning of Re-identification Network

We first learn a generic image feature representation for person re-identification. The feature extractor $\Phi(\cdot)$ is a Convolutional Neural Network (CNN) trained to perform multi-classification task, *i.e.* given a cropped image of a person, the CNN has to predict the person's identity. We propose to merge all domains $\mathbf{R}$ and $\mathbf{S}$ into a single large dataset and train the network jointly from scratch. We adopt the CNN model from [43]. To learn discriminative and generalizable features, the number of classes during training has to be significantly larger than the dimensionality of the last hidden layer (feature layer). In our case the training set consists of 3K+ classes (identities) and the feature layer has been fixed to 256 dimensions.

One could assume that with our new dataset, the pre-trained model should generalize well in novel target conditions. Although synthetic data helps (see Sect. 5.1), there is still a significant performance gap between the pre-trained model and its fine-tuned version on the target domain. We believe there are two reasons for this gap: (1) our dataset does not cover all possible illumination conditions, and (2) there is a gap between synthetic and real image distributions [37]. This motivates the investigation of domain adaptation techniques that can potentially address both issues: making the synthetic images looking more realistic, as well as minimizing the shifts between source and target illumination conditions.

4.2 Domain Adaptation

We formulate domain adaptation as the following three-step process, as illustrated in Fig. 4.

1. **Illumination inference**: find the closest illumination condition (domain $S_{k*} \in \mathbf{S}$) for a given input R_{M+1}.
2. **Domain translation**: translate domain S_{k*} to R_{M+1}, by learning G, $G : S_{k*} \to R_{M+1}$ while preserving a 3D character's identity from $s \in S_{k*}$.
3. **Fine-tuning**: update $\Phi(\cdot)$ with the translated domain $G(s)$.

Illumination Inference. Domain adaptation is commonly called a visual dataset bias problem. Dataset bias was compellingly demonstrated in computer vision by the *name the dataset* game of Torralba and Efros [40]. They trained a classifier to predict which dataset an image originated from, illustrating that visual datasets are biased samples of the visual world. In this work, we employ a similar idea to identify the synthetic domain $S_{k*} \in \mathbf{S}$ that is closest to the target domain R_{M+1}. To do so, we train a CNN classifier that takes an input image and predicts which illumination condition the image was rendered with. In our case, the classifier has to classify the image into one of $N = 140$ classes (the number of different environment maps in our synthetic dataset). We used Resnet-18 [15] pretrained on ImageNet and fine-tuned to perform illumination classification. Given the trained classifier, we take a set of test images from R_{M+1} and predict the closest lighting condition by

$$k^* = \arg\max_{k \in \{1...N\}} \sum_{i=1}^{Z_{R_{M+1}}} \Delta\big(\mathbb{L}(x_i), k\big), \quad \text{s.t.} \quad \Delta\big(\mathbb{L}(x_i), k\big) = \begin{cases} 1, & L(x_i) = k \\ 0, & \text{otherwise} \end{cases}. \quad (1)$$

Here, k corresponds to domain class, $\mathbb{L}(x_i)$ is the class predicted by the CNN classifier and Δ is a counting function. We use this formulation to find S_{k*}: the synthetic illumination condition that is most similar to the target domain R_{M+1} (*i.e.* requiring the minimum amout of domain shift). S_{k*} will be used to translate images from S_{k*} to R_{M+1} while preserving each 3D character's identity.

Domain Translation. Given two domains S and R (for convenience we skip sub-indices here) and the training samples $s_i \in S$ and $x_i \in R$, our objective is to learn a mapping function $G : S \to R$. As we do not have corresponding pairs between our synthetic and real domains, G is fairly unconstrained and standard procedures will lead to the well-known problem of mode collapse (all input images map to the same output image). To circumvent this problem, we adapt the technique of [52], where rather than learning a single mapping $G : S \to R$, we exploit the property that translation should be *cycle-consistent*. In other words there should exist the opposite mapping $F : R \to S$, where G and F are inverses of each other.

We train both mappings G and F simultaneously, and use two *cycle consistency losses* to regularize the training: $s \to G(s) \to F(G(s)) \approx s$ and $x \to$

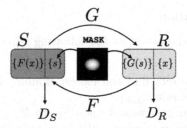

Fig. 5. Semantic Shift Regularization. The Cycle-GAN loss only applies to $F(G(s))$ and $G(F(x))$. There is no constraint on what $G()$ and $F()$ can do individually, which can result in drastic color changes. We incorporate an additional regularization loss requiring s and $G(s)$ to be similar. The loss should only apply to the foreground (to preserve identity), since the target camera may have a very different background than the synthetic data.

$F(x) \rightarrow G(F(x)) \approx x$. G and F are generator functions, where G tries to generate images $G(s)$ that look similar to images from domain R, and F generates images $F(x)$ that should look like images from domain S. Additionally, two adversarial discriminators D_S and D_R are trained, where D_S tries to discriminate between images $\{s\}$ and translated images $\{F(x)\}$; and analogously D_R aims to distinguish between $\{x\}$ and $\{G(s)\}$ (see Fig. 5).

The training objective contains *adversarial losses* [11] for both G and F, as well as two *cycle consistency losses*. The *adversarial loss* for G is defined as

$$\mathcal{L}_{GAN}(G, D_R, S, R) = \mathbb{E}_{x \sim p_{data}(x)}[\log D_R(x)] + \mathbb{E}_{s \sim p_{data}(s)}[\log(1 - D_R(G(s)))], \tag{2}$$

and we can analogously define *adversarial loss* for F, *i.e.* $\mathcal{L}_{GAN}(F, D_S, R, S)$. Both *cycle consistency losses* can be expressed as

$$\mathcal{L}_{cyc}(G, F) = \mathbb{E}_{s \sim p_{data}(s)}[||F(G(s)) - s||_1] + \mathbb{E}_{x \sim p_{data}(x)}[||G(F(x)) - x||_1]. \tag{3}$$

The final objective is

$$\mathcal{L}_{CycleGAN}(G, F, D_S, D_R) = \mathcal{L}_{GAN}(G, D_R, S, R) + \mathcal{L}_{GAN}(F, D_S, R, S) + \lambda_1 \mathcal{L}_{cyc}(G, F), \tag{4}$$

where λ_1 controls the relative importance of the *cycle consistency losses*.

Semantic Shift Regularization. In the above formulation, there is no constraint that the color distribution of the generated image $G(s)$ should be close to instance s. With large capacity models, the approach can map the colors within s to any distribution, as long as this distribution is indistinguishable from the emperical distribution within R ($F(x)$ will learn the inverse mapping). In our application, the color of a person's shirt (*e.g.* red) can drastically switch under $G(s)$ (*e.g.* to blue) as long as $F(G(S))$ is able to reverse this process (see Fig. 8). This semantic shift corrupts the training data, since a synthetic image and its corresponding domain translated variant could look very different (*e.g.* the labels are not consistent). Semantic shift can occur because the *cycle-consistency* loss does not regulate the amount by which the domains can be shifted.

As mentioned in [52], one can adopt the technique from [39] and introduce an additional loss that forces the network to learn an identity mapping when samples from the target domain are provided as input to the generator, *i.e.* $\mathcal{L}_{id}(G, F) = \mathbb{E}_{x \sim p_{data}(x)}[||G(x) - x||_1] + \mathbb{E}_{s \sim p_{data}(s)}[||F(s) - s||_1]$. Although, this loss helps to some degree, many subjects still exhibited drastic shifts in appearance.

Alternatively, we can integrate the loss from [37] which ensures the translated synthetic image is not too different from the original synthetic image *i.e.* $\mathcal{L}_{Ref}(G) = \mathbb{E}_{s \sim p_{data}(s)}[||G(s) - s||_1]$. We found this loss often leads to artifacts in the translated synthetic images, since the regularization does not distinguish between background/foreground. In practice, only the appearance of the person needs to be preserved. The background of synthetic image could be very different than what appears in the real images captured by the target camera.

To circumvent this issue, we apply a masking function which forces the network to focus on the foreground region

$$\mathcal{L}_{Mask}(G) = \mathbb{E}_{s \sim p_{data}(s)}\Big[\left\|(G(s) - s) * \mathbf{m}\right\|_1\Big], \tag{5}$$

where $\mathbf{m}$ is a mask that encourages the mapping to preserve the appearance only near to the center (see Fig. 5). Because re-identification datasets have well cropped images, the foreground region is typically in the middle of the bounding box, with the background around the periphery. Therefore, we pre-define a soft matte that resembles a 2D Gaussian kernel.

Our full objective loss is

$$\begin{aligned}\mathcal{L}_{our}(G, F, D_S, D_R) = \mathcal{L}_{GAN}(G, D_R, S, R) + \mathcal{L}_{GAN}(F, D_S, R, S) \\ + \lambda_1 \mathcal{L}_{cyc}(G, F) + \lambda_2 \mathcal{L}_{id}(G, F) + \lambda_3 \mathcal{L}_{Mask}(G),\end{aligned} \tag{6}$$

where $\lambda_1 = \lambda_2 = 10$ and $\lambda_3 = 5$ in our experiments (See Fig. 6).

Fine-Tuning. Given our re-identification network (see Sect. 4.1), we can fine-tune its feature extraction process to specialize for images generated from $G(s)$, which is our approximation of data coming from target domain (test camera). In practice, when we need to fine-tune our representation to a set of cameras, for every camera we identify its closest synthetic domain S_{k*} through our illumination inference, and then use it to learn a generator network that can transfer synthetic images to the given camera domain. The transferred synthetic images $G(s) : s \in S_{k*}$ are then used for fine-tuning the re-identification network, thus maximizing the performance of $\Phi(G(s))$.

5 Experiments

We carried out experiments on 5 datasets: **VIPeR** [13], **iLIDS** [50], **CUHK01** [24], **PRID2011** [17] and **Market-1501** [48]. To learn a generic feature extrac-

Fig. 6. Domain translation results for VIPeR (left) and PRID (right) datasets. From top to bottom: domain images $s \in S_{k*}$, translated images $G(s)$, target images $x \in R_{M+1}$.

tor we used two large scale re-identification datasets: **CUHK03** [25] and **DukeMTMC4ReID** [12,33], and our **SyRI** dataset. Re-identification performance is reported using rank-1 accuracy of the CMC curve [13].

Datasets: VIPeR contains 632 image pairs of pedestrians captured by two outdoor cameras. Large variations in lighting conditions, in background and in viewpoint are present. PRID2011 consists of person images recorded from two non-overlapping static surveillance cameras. Characteristic challenges of this dataset are extreme illumination conditions. There are two camera views containing 385 and 749 identities, respectively. Only 200 people appear in both cameras. i-LIDS consists of 476 images with 119 individuals. The images come from airport surveillance cameras. This dataset is challenging due to many occlusions. CUHK01 consists of 3,884 images of 971 identities. There are two images per identity, per camera. The first camera captures the side view of pedestrians and the second camera captures the front or back view. Market-1501 contains 1501 identities, registered by at most 6 cameras. All the images were cropped by an automatic pedestrian detector, resulting in many inaccurate detections.

Evaluation Protocol: We generate probe/gallery images accordingly to the settings in [43]: VIPeR: 316/316; CUHK01: 486/486; i-LIDS: 60/60; and PRID2011: 100/649, where we follow a single shot setting [31]. For Market-1501 we employ the protocol from [44], where 750 test identities are used in a single query setting.

5.1 Generalization Properties

In this experiment, we train two feature extractors: one with only real images **R** containing CUHK03 and DukeMTMC4ReID images (in total 3279 identities); and the other one with both real and our synthetic images **R + S** (our **SyRI** dataset provides additional 100 identities but under 140 illumination

Table 1. CMC rank-1 accuracy. The base model **R** is only trained on real images from auxiliary re-identification datasets. Adding synthetic images **S** improves the performance. Fine-tuning $(\mathbf{R} + \mathbf{S}^*)$ to the training data of a specific dataset implies the maximum performance that could be expected with the correct synthetic data. Adapting the synthetic data to the target domain leads to significant gains, depending on the combination of semantic shift regularizations. Compared with state-of-the-art unsuperivsed techniques, our approach yields significantly higher accuracy on 4 of the 5 datasets. We achieve competitive performance to state-of-the-art on CUHK01

	METHOD	VIPeR	CUHK01	iLIDS	PRID	Market
Unsupervised	State-of-the-art	38.5 [42]	**57.3** [44]	49.3 [32]	34.8 [42]	58.2 [42]
	R	32.3	41.6	51.0	7.0	44.7
	R + S	36.4	49.5	54.8	15.0	54.3
	CYCLEGAN	37.0	49.9	53.9	33.0	55.4
	CYCLEGAN+$\mathcal{L}_{id}$	39.9	54.0	55.9	40.0	63.1
	CYCLEGAN+$\mathcal{L}_{Ref}$	41.1	48.4	56.1	28.0	57.5
	OURS	**43.0**	54.9	**56.5**	**43.0**	**65.7**
	$\mathbf{R} + \mathbf{S}^*$	49.4	71.4	63.2	65.0	83.9

conditions, for a total of 3379 identities). For **S** we used 4 randomly sampled images per illumination condition per identity, which results in 56,000 images $(4 \times 140 \times 100)$. Table 1 reports the performance comparison of these models on various target datasets. First, we evaluate the performance of the models directly on the target datasets without fine-tuning (fully unsupervised scenario, compare rows **R** and **R + S**, respectively). Adding our synthetic dataset significantly increases the re-identification performance. The row marked with * are the results after fine-tuning on the actual target datasets (e.g. in VIPeR column we fine-tune the model only on VIPeR dataset). It represents the maximum performance we expect to achieve if we could somehow hallucinate the perfect set of domain translated synthetic training images. These results indicate that the performance of supervised methods (using additional real data directly from the target domain) is still significantly better than unsupervised methods using domain adaptation. Interestingly, although adding our synthetic dataset doubled the performance on PRID2011, the lighting conditions in this dataset are so extreme that the gap to the supervised model is still significant. Similar findings have been reported in [2,42].

5.2 Illumination Inference

We carry out experiments to evaluate the importance of the illumination inference step. To do so, we compare the proposed *illumination estimator* to a random selection of the target illumination condition S_{k*}. After the illumination condition is selected, the proposed domain translation is applied. Table 2 illustrates the comparison on multiple dataset. We report minimum performance obtained by random procedure (MIN), the average across 10 experiments (RANDOM),

Table 2. Impact of illumination inference. The selection of the right illumination condition for the domain translation improves the recognition performance

Method	VIPeR	CUHK01	iLIDS	PRID	Market
R + S	36.4	49.5	54.8	15.0	54.3
Min	35.2	50.4	55.1	29.0	58.1
Random	38.9	51.2	56.1	36.0	60.9
Our	**43.0**	**54.9**	**56.5**	**43.0**	**65.7**

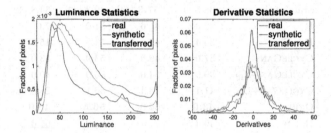

Fig. 7. Comparison of image statistics. Domain translation decreases the gap between synthetic and real image statistics.

and the average using our illumination inference. The results demonstrate that reasoning about illumination greatly improves the recognition performance. Our illumination condition estimator ensures that the source illumination is the closest to the target domain, thus facilitating the domain translation task.

5.3 Image Statistics of SyRI

The effect of domain translation is reflected in the underlying image statistics (see Fig. 7). The statistics of real and synthetic images are derived from a single camera from the VIPeR dataset and its corresponding camera in our SyRI dataset (selected by illumination inference). After passing through the generator function learned during domain translation ($G(s)$), the statistics of the translated images are much closer to the statistics of real images.

5.4 Domain Adaptation

Table 1 reports the performance of *CycleGAN* with different regularization terms. Domain translation without any regularization term between s and $G(s)$ can deteriorate performance (compare **R + S** and CycleGAN for iLIDS). We suspect this is due to the previously mentioned semantic shift (see Fig. 8). Adding identity mapping $\mathcal{L}_{id}$ makes significant improvement on both visual examples and re-identification performance. Replacing $\mathcal{L}_{id}$ with $\mathcal{L}_{Ref}$ can lower performance and tends to produce artifacts (notice artificial green regions in Fig. 8 for CUHK01). For CUHK01 and PRID datasets there are significant drops

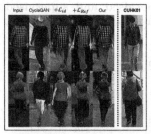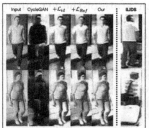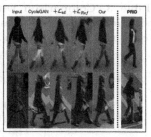

Fig. 8. Comparison of different regularization terms for translating synthetic images to a target domain. Representative image pairs for CUHK01, iLIDS and PRID datasets have been selected. Notice that CycleGAN without any regularization tends to have semantic shifts, *e.g.* for CUHK01 blue color of the t-shirt changed to red.

in the performance when using $\mathcal{L}_{Ref}$ regularization. Unlike [37], our images have distinct foreground/background regions. Background is not useful for re-identification, and it's influecen in the loss function should be minimial. Incorporating our mask makes significant improvements—especially for datasets where images are less tightly cropped, such as PRID. In this case, adding synthetic data improved performance from 7% to 15%. Our domain adaptation technique boosts the performance to 43.0% rank1-accuracy. We surpass the current state-of-the-art results by 8.2%.

5.5 Comparison with State-of-the-Art Methods

We divide the state-of-the-art approaches into unsupervised and supervised techniques as well as methods that employ hand-crafted features (including graph-learning GL [20] and transfer learning TL [20]) and embeddings learned with Convolutional Neural Newtworks (CNN) (including source identity knowledge transfer learning CAMEL [44] and attribute knowledge transfer TJ-AIDL [42]). Table 3 illustrates that: (1) our three-step domain adaptation technique outperforms the state-of-the-art unsupervised techniques—on 4 of the 5 datasets, we outperform the state-of-the-art results by large margins: 5.1%, 7.2%, 8.2% and 7.5% on VIPeR, iLIDS, PRID and Market, respectively; on CUHK01 we achieve competitive performance to CAMEL [44] (2.4% performance gap), but CAMEL performs significantly worse than our approach on VIPeR and Market. Compared with other augmentation techniques (*e.g.* SPGAN [6]), our illumination inference step ensures that the source illumination, chosen from a large number of options in our SyRI dataset, is closest to the target domain. (2) When compared to unsupervised hand-crafted based approaches, the performance margins for rank-1 are even larger: 11.5%, 13.9%, 7.2% and 18% on VIPeR, CUHK01, iLIDS and PRID, respectively. (3) Our approach is also very competitive with the best supervised techniques—regardless of the dataset. This confirms the effectiveness of the proposed solution, which does not require any human supervision and thus scales to large camera networks.

Table 3. Comparison with state-of-the-art unsupervised and supervised techniques. The best scores for unsupervised methods are shown in **bold**. The best scores of supervised methods are highlighted in red

		METHOD	VIPeR	CUHK01	iLIDS	PRID	Market
Unsupervised	Hand-craft	GL [20]	33.5	41.0	–	25.0	–
		DLLAP [21]	29.6	28.4	–	21.4	–
		TSR [35]	27.7	23.3	–	–	–
		TL [32]	31.5	27.1	49.3	24.2	–
	CNN	SSDAL [38]	37.9	–	–	20.1	39.4
		CAMEL [44]	30.9	**57.3**	–	–	54.5
		SPGAN [6]	–	–	–	–	57.7
		TJ-AIDL [42]	38.5	–	–	34.8	58.2
		Ours	**43.0**	54.9	**56.5**	**43.0**	**65.7**
Supervised	Hand-craft	LOMO+XQDA[27]	40.0	63.2	–	26.7	–
		Ensembles[31]	45.9	53.4	50.3	17.9	–
		Null Space[45]	42.2	64.9	–	29.8	55.4
		Gaussian+XQDA [29]	49.7	57.8	–	–	66.5
	CNN	Triplet Loss[4]	47.8	53.7	60.4	22.0	–
		FT-JSTL+DGD[43]	38.6	66.6	64.6	64.0	73.2
		SpindleNeT[46]	53.8	79.9	66.3	67.0	76.9

6   Conclusion

Re-identification datasets contain many identities, but rarely have a substantial number of different lighting conditions. In practice, this lack of diversity limits the generalization performance of learned re-identification models on new unseen data. Typically, the networks must be fine-tuned in a supervised manner using data collected for each target camera pair, which is infeasible at scale. To solve this issue, we propose a new synthetic dataset of virtual people rendered in indoor and outdoor environments. Given example unlabelled images from a test camera, we develop an illumination condition estimator to select the most appropriate subset of our synthesized images to use for fine-tuning a pre-trained re-identification model. Our approach is ideal for large scale deployments, since no labelled data needs to be collected for each target domain.

We employ a deep network to modify the subset of synthesized images (selected by the illumination estimator) so that they more closely resemble images from the test domain (see Fig. 6). To accomplish this, we use the recently introduced cycle-consistent adversarial architecture and integrate an additional regularization term to ensure the learned domain shift (between synthetic and real images) does not result in generating unrealistic training examples (*e.g.* drastic changes in color). Because re-identification images have distinct foreground/background regions, we also incorporate a soft matte to help the network focus on ensuring the foreground region is correctly translated to the target domain. Extensive experiments on multiple datasets (see Table 3) show that our approach outperforms other unsupervised techniques, often by a large margin.

References

1. Aharon, M., Elad, M., Bruckstein, A.: K-SVD: an algorithm for designing overcomplete dictionaries for sparse representation. IEEE Trans. Signal Process. **54**(11), 4311–4322 (2006)
2. Bak, S., Carr, P.: One-shot metric learning for person re-identification. In: CVPR, June 2017
3. Chen, W., Chen, X., Zhang, J., Huang, K.: Beyond triplet loss: a deep quadruplet network for person re-identification. In: CVPR, July 2017
4. Cheng, D., Gong, Y., Zhou, S., Wang, J., Zheng, N.: Person re-identification by multi-channel parts-based CNN with improved triplet loss function. In: CVPR, June 2016
5. Debevec, P.: Rendering synthetic objects into real scenes: bridging traditional and image-based graphics with global illumination and high dynamic range photography. In: Proceedings of ACM SIGGRAPH, pp. 189–198 (1998)
6. Deng, W., Zheng, L., Kang, G., Yang, Y., Ye, Q., Jiao, J.: Image-image domain adaptation with preserved self-similarity and domain-dissimilarity for person re-identification. In: CVPR (2018)
7. Dibra, E., Maye, J., Diamanti, O., Siegwart, R., Beardsley, P.: Extending the performance of human classifiers using a viewpoint specific approach. In: WACV (2015)
8. Fernando, B., Habrard, A., Sebban, M., Tuytelaars, T.: Unsupervised visual domain adaptation using subspace alignment. In: ICCV (2013)
9. Ganin, Y., Lempitsky, V.: Unsupervised domain adaptation by backpropagation. In: ICML (2015)
10. Gao, S., Tsang, I.W.H., Chia, L.T., Zhao, P.: Local features are not lonely–laplacian sparse coding for image classification. In: CVPR (2010)
11. Goodfellow, I., et al.: Generative adversarial nets. In: NIPS (2014)
12. Gou, M., Karanam, S., Liu, W., Camps, O., Radke, R.J.: DukeMTMC4ReID: a large-scale multi-camera person re-identification dataset. In: CVPRW (2017)
13. Gray, D., Brennan, S., Tao, H.: Evaluating appearance models for recognition, reacquisition, and tracking. In: PETS (2007)
14. Hattori, H., Boddeti, Y.V.N., Kitani, K.M., Kanade, T.: Learning scene-specific pedestrian detectors without real data. In: CVPR (2015)
15. He, K., Zhang, X., Ren, S., Sun, J.: Deep residual learning for image recognition. In: CVPR, June 2016
16. Hermans, A., Beyer, L., Leibe, B.: In defense of the triplet loss for person re-identification. arxiv (2017)
17. Hirzer, M., Beleznai, C., Roth, P.M., Bischof, H.: Person re-identification by descriptive and discriminative classification. In: Heyden, A., Kahl, F. (eds.) SCIA 2011. LNCS, vol. 6688, pp. 91–102. Springer, Heidelberg (2011). https://doi.org/10.1007/978-3-642-21227-7_9
18. Hu, J., Lu, J., Tan, Y.P.: Deep transfer metric learning. In: CVPR (2015)
19. Huang, S., Ramanan, D.: Expecting the unexpected: training detectors for unusual pedestrians with adversarial imposters. In: CVPR (2017)
20. Kodirov, E., Xiang, T., Fu, Z., Gong, S.: Person re-identification by unsupervised ℓ_1 graph learning. In: Leibe, B., Matas, J., Sebe, N., Welling, M. (eds.) ECCV 2016. LNCS, vol. 9905, pp. 178–195. Springer, Cham (2016). https://doi.org/10.1007/978-3-319-46448-0_11

21. Kodirov, E., Xiang, T., Gong, S.: Dictionary learning with iterative laplacian regularisation for unsupervised person re-identification. In: BMVC (2015)

22. Li, D., Chen, X., Zhang, Z., Huang, K.: Learning deep context-aware features over body and latent parts for person re-identification. In: CVPR, July 2017

23. Li, S., Bak, S., Carr, P., Wang, X.: Diversity regularized spatiotemporal attention for video-based person re-identification. In: CVPR, June 2018

24. Li, W., Zhao, R., Wang, X.: Human reidentification with transferred metric learning. In: Lee, K.M., Matsushita, Y., Rehg, J.M., Hu, Z. (eds.) ACCV 2012. LNCS, vol. 7724, pp. 31–44. Springer, Heidelberg (2013). https://doi.org/10.1007/978-3-642-37331-2_3

25. Li, W., Zhao, R., Xiao, T., Wang, X.: DeepReID: Deep filter pairing neural network for person re-identification. In: CVPR (2014)

26. Li, Z., Chang, S., Liang, F., Huang, T., Cao, L., Smith, J.: Learning locally-adaptive decision functions for person verification. In: CVPR (2013)

27. Liao, S., Hu, Y., Zhu, X., Li, S.Z.: Person re-identification by local maximal occurrence representation and metric learning. In: CVPR (2015)

28. Liu, X., Song, M., Tao, D., Zhou, X., Chen, C., Bu, J.: Semi-supervised coupled dictionary learning for person re-identification. In: CVPR, June 2014

29. Matsukawa, T., Okabe, T., Suzuki, E., Sato, Y.: Hierarchical gaussian descriptor for person re-identification. In: CVPR, June 2016

30. McCormac, J., Handa, A., Leutenegger, S., Davison, A.J.: SceneNet RGB-D: can 5m synthetic images beat generic imagenet pre-training on indoor segmentation? In: ICCV, October 2017

31. Paisitkriangkrai, S., Shen, C., van den Hengel, A.: Learning to rank in person re-identification with metric ensembles. In: CVPR (2015)

32. Peng, P., et al.: Unsupervised cross-dataset transfer learning for person re-identification. In: CVPR, June 2016

33. Ristani, E., Solera, F., Zou, R., Cucchiara, R., Tomasi, C.: Performance measures and a data set for multi-target, multi-camera tracking. In: Hua, G., Jégou, H. (eds.) ECCV 2016. LNCS, vol. 9914, pp. 17–35. Springer, Cham (2016). https://doi.org/10.1007/978-3-319-48881-3_2

34. Ros, G., Sellart, L., Materzynska, J., Vazquez, D., Lopez, A.: The SYNTHIA dataset: a large collection of synthetic images for semantic segmentation of urban scenes. In: CVPR (2016)

35. Shi, Z., Hospedales, T.M., Xiang, T.: Transferring a semantic representation for person re-identification and search. In: CVPR (2015)

36. Shotton, J., et al.: Efficient human pose estimation from single depth images. TPAMI 35(12), 2821–2840 (2013)

37. Shrivastava, A., Pfister, T., Tuzel, O., Susskind, J., Wang, W., Webb, R.: Learning from simulated and unsupervised images through adversarial training. In: CVPR (2017)

38. Su, C., Zhang, S., Xing, J., Gao, W., Tian, Q.: Deep attributes driven multi-camera person re-identification. In: Leibe, B., Matas, J., Sebe, N., Welling, M. (eds.) ECCV 2016. LNCS, vol. 9906, pp. 475–491. Springer, Cham (2016). https://doi.org/10.1007/978-3-319-46475-6_30

39. Taigman, Y., Polyak, A., Wolf, L.: Unsupervised cross-domain image generation. In: arXiv preprint (2016)

40. Torralba, A., Efros, A.A.: Unbiased look at dataset bias. In: CVPR (2011)

41. Tzeng, E., Hoffman, J., Darrell, T., Saenko, K.: Simultaneous deep transfer across domains and tasks. In: ICCV (2015)

42. Wang, J., Zhu, X., Gong, S., Li, W.: Transferable joint attribute-identity deep learning for unsupervised person re-identification. In: CVPR (2018)
43. Xiao, T., Li, H., Ouyang, W., Wang, X.: Learning deep feature representations with domain guided dropout for person re-identification. In: CVPR (2016)
44. Yu, H.X., Wu, A., Zheng, W.S.: Cross-view asymmetric metric learning for unsupervised person re-identification. In: ICCV (2017)
45. Zhang, L., Xiang, T., Gong, S.: Learning a discriminative null space for person re-identification. In: CVPR (2016)
46. Zhao, H., et al.: Spindle net: person re-identification with human body region guided feature decomposition and fusion. In: CVPR (2017)
47. Zheng, L., et al.: MARS: a video benchmark for large-scale person re-identification. In: Leibe, B., Matas, J., Sebe, N., Welling, M. (eds.) ECCV 2016. LNCS, vol. 9910, pp. 868–884. Springer, Cham (2016). https://doi.org/10.1007/978-3-319-46466-4_52
48. Zheng, L., Shen, L., Tian, L., Wang, S., Wang, J., Tian, Q.: Scalable person re-identification: a benchmark. In: ICCV (2015)
49. Zheng, W.S., Gong, S., Xiang, T.: Towards open-world person re-identification by one-shot group-based verification. IEEE Trans. Pattern Anal. Mach. Intell. **38**(3), 591–606 (2016)
50. Zheng, W.S., Gong, S., Xiang, T.: Associating groups of people. In: BMVC (2009)
51. Zheng, W.S., Gong, S., Xiang, T.: Person re-identification by probabilistic relative distance comparison. In: CVPR (2011)
52. Zhu, J.Y., Park, T., Isola, P., Efros, A.A.: Unpaired image-to-image translation using cycle-consistent adversarial networks. In: ICCV (2017)

SOD-MTGAN: Small Object Detection via Multi-Task Generative Adversarial Network

Yancheng Bai[1,2], Yongqiang Zhang[1,3(✉)], Mingli Ding[3], and Bernard Ghanem[1]

[1] Visual Computing Center, King Abdullah University of Science and Technology, Thuwal, Saudi Arabia
baiyancheng20@gmail.com, bernard.ghanem@kaust.edu.sa
[2] Institute of Software, Chinese Academy of Sciences (CAS), Beijing, China
[3] School of Electrical Engineering and Automation, Harbin Institute of Technology, Harbin, China
{zhangyongqiang,dingml}@hit.edu.cn

Abstract. Object detection is a fundamental and important problem in computer vision. Although impressive results have been achieved on large/medium sized objects in large-scale detection benchmarks (*e.g.* the COCO dataset), the performance on small objects is far from satisfactory. The reason is that small objects lack sufficient detailed appearance information, which can distinguish them from the background or similar objects. To deal with the small object detection problem, we propose an end-to-end multi-task generative adversarial network (MTGAN). In the MTGAN, the generator is a super-resolution network, which can up-sample small blurred images into fine-scale ones and recover detailed information for more accurate detection. The discriminator is a multi-task network, which describes each super-resolved image patch with a real/fake score, object category scores, and bounding box regression off-sets. Furthermore, to make the generator recover more details for easier detection, the classification and regression losses in the discriminator are back-propagated into the generator during training. Extensive experiments on the challenging COCO dataset demonstrate the effectiveness of the proposed method in restoring a clear super-resolved image from a blurred small one, and show that the detection performance, especially for small sized objects, improves over state-of-the-art methods.

Keywords: Small object detection · Super-resolution · Multi-task Generative adversarial network · COCO

1 Introduction

Object detection is a fundamental and important problem in computer vision. It is usually a key step towards many real-world applications, including image

---

Y. Bai and Y. Zhang—Equal contribution.

© Springer Nature Switzerland AG 2018
V. Ferrari et al. (Eds.): ECCV 2018, LNCS 11217, pp. 210–226, 2018.
https://doi.org/10.1007/978-3-030-01261-8_13

retrieval, intelligent surveillance, autonomous driving, etc. Object detection has been extensively studied over the past few decades and huge progress has been made with the emergence of deep convolutional neural networks. Currently, there are two main frameworks for CNN-based object detection: (i) the one-stage framework, such as YOLO [27] and SSD [24], which applies an object classifier and regressor in a dense manner without objectness pruning; and (ii) the two-stage framework, such as Faster-RCNN [29], RFCN [3] and FPN [22], which extracts object proposals followed by per-proposal classification and regression.

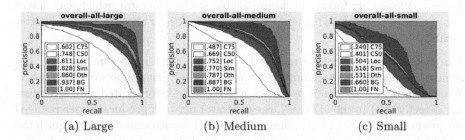

(a) Large   (b) Medium   (c) Small

Fig. 1. The overall error analysis of the performance of the FPN detector [22] over all categories on the large, medium, and small subsets of the COCO dataset [23], respectively. The plots in each sub-image are a series of precision-recall curves under different evaluation settings defined in [23]. From the comparisons, we can see that there is a large gap between the performance of small and large/medium sized objects.

Object detectors of both frameworks have achieved impressive results on objects of large/medium size in large-scale detection benchmarks (*e.g.* the COCO dataset [23]) as shown in Fig. 1(a) and (b). However, the performance on small sized objects (defined as in [23]) is far from satisfactory as shown in Fig. 1(c). From the comparisons, we can see that there is a large gap between the performance of small and large/medium sized objects. The main difficulty for small object detection (SOD) is that small objects lack appearance information needed to distinguish them from background (or similar categories) and to achieve better localization. To achieve better detection performance on these small objects, SSD [24] exploits the intermediate *conv* feature maps to represent small objects. However, the shallow fine-grained *conv* feature maps are less discriminative, which leads to many false positive results. On the other hand, FPN [22] uses the feature pyramid to represent objects at different scales, in which low-resolution feature maps with strong semantic information are up-sampled and fused with the high-resolution feature maps with weak semantic information. However, up-sampling might generate artifacts, which can degrade detection performance.

To deal with the SOD problem, we propose a unified end-to-end convolutional neural network based on the classical generative adversarial network (GAN) framework, which can be incorporated into any existing detector. Following the structure of the seminal GAN work [9,21], there are two sub-networks in our model: a generator network and a discriminator network. In the generator, a super-resolution network (SRN) is introduced to up-sample a small object image to a larger scale. Compared to directly resizing the image with bilinear interpolation, SRN can generate images of higher quality and less artifacts at large up-scaling factors (4× in our current implementation). In the discriminator, we introduce the classification and regression branches for the task of object detection. The real and generated super-resolved images pass through the discriminator network that *jointly* distinguishes whether they are real or generated high-resolution images, determines which classes they belong to, and refines the predicted bounding boxes. More importantly, the classification and regression losses are further back-propagated to the generator, which encourages the generator to produce higher quality images for easier classification and better localization.

Contributions. This paper makes the following three main contributions. **(1)** A novel unified end-to-end multi-task generative adversarial network (MTGAN) for small object detection is proposed, which can be incorporated with any existing detector. **(2)** In the MTGAN, the generator network produces super-resolved images and the multi-task discriminator network is introduced to distinguish the real high-resolution images from fake ones, predict object categories, and refine bounding boxes, simultaneously. More importantly, the classification and regression losses are back-propagated to further guide the generator network to produce super-resolved images for easier classification and better localization. **(3)** Finally, we demonstrate the effectiveness of MTGAN within the object detection pipeline, where detection performance improves a lot over several state-of-the-art baseline detectors, primarily for small objects.

2   Related Work

2.1   General Object Detection

As a classic topic, numerous object detection systems have been proposed during the past decade or so. Traditional object detection methods are based on handcrafted features and the deformable part model (DPM). Due to the limited representation of handcrafted features, traditional object detectors register subpar performance, particularly on small sized objects.

In recent years, superior performance in image classification and scene recognition has been achieved with the resurgence of deep neural networks including CNNs [19,32,34]. Similarly, the performance of object detection has been significantly boosted due to richer appearance and spatial representations, which are learned by CNNs [7] from large scale image datasets. Currently, a CNN-based object detector can be simply categorized as belonging to one of two frameworks: the two stage framework and the one stage framework. The region-based CNN (RCNN) [7] can be considered as a milestone of the two stage framework for object detection and it has achieved state-of-the-art detection performance. Each region proposal is processed separately in RCNN [7], which is very time-consuming. After that, ROI-Pooling is introduced in Fast-RCNN [6], which can share the computation between the proposal extraction and classification steps, thus improving the efficiency greatly. By learning both these stages end-to-end, Faster RCNN [29] has registered further improvement in both detection performance and computational efficiency. However, all detectors of this framework show unsatisfactory performance on small objects in the COCO benchmark, since they do not have any explicit strategy to deal with such objects. To detect small objects better, FPN [22] combines the low-resolution, semantically strong features with high-resolution, semantically weak features via a top-down pathway and lateral connections, in which the learned *conv* feature maps are expected to contain strong semantic information for small objects. Because of this, FPN shows superior performance over Faster RCNN for the task of detecting small objects. However, the low-resolution feature maps in FPN are up-sampled to create the feature pyramid, a process which tends to introduce artifacts into the features and consequently degrades detection performance. Compared to FPN, our proposed method employs the super-resolution network to generate images with high-resolution (4× up-scaling) from images with low-resolution, thus, avoiding the artifact problem caused by the up-sampling operator in FPN.

In the one stage framework, the detector directly classifies anchors into specific classes and regresses bounding boxes in a dense manner. For example, in SSD [24] (a typical one-stage detector), the low-level intermediate *conv* feature maps of high-resolution are used to detect small objects. However, these *conv* features usually only capture basic visual patterns void of strong semantic information, which may lead to many false positive results. Compared to SSD-like detectors, our discriminator uses deep strong semantic features to better represent small objects, thus, reducing the false positive rate.

2.2 Generative Adversarial Networks

In the seminal work [9], the generative adversarial network (GAN) is introduced to generate realistic-looking images from random noise inputs. GANs have achieved impressive results in image generation [4], image editing [35], representation learning [25], image super-resolution [21] and style transfer [16]. Recently, GANs have been successfully applied to super-resolution (SRGAN) [21], leading to impressive and promising results. Compared to super-resolution on natural images, images of specific objects in the COCO benchmark for example are full of diversity (*e.g.* blur, pose and illumination), thus, making the super-resolution process on these images much more challenging. In fact, the super-resolution images generated by SRGAN are blurred especially for low-resolution small objects, which is not helpful to train an accurate object classifier. To alleviate this problem, we introduce novel losses into the loss function of the generator, *i.e.* the classification and regression losses are back-propagated to the generator network in our proposed MTGAN, which further guides the generator to reconstruct finer super-resolved images for easier classification and better localization.

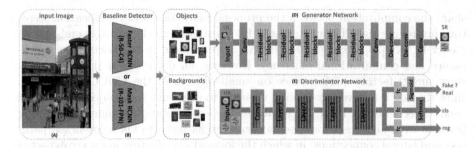

Fig. 2. The pipeline of the proposed small object detection system (SOD-MTGAN).
(A) The images are fed into the network. (B) The baseline detector can be any type
of detector (*e.g.* Faster RCNN [29], FPN [22], or SSD [24]). It is used to crop positive
(*i.e.* objects) and negative (*i.e.* background) examples from input images for training
the generator and discriminator networks, or generate regions of interest (ROIs) for
testing. (C) The positive and negative examples (or ROIs) are generated by off-the-shelf
detectors. (D) The generator sub-network reconstructs a super-resolved version ($4\times$ up-
scaling) of the low-resolution input image. (D) The discriminator network distinguishes
the real from the generated high-resolution images, predicts the object categories, and
regresses the object locations, simultaneously. The discriminator network can use any
typical architecture like AlexNet [20], VGGNet [32] or ResNet [12] as the backbone
network. We use ResNet-50 or ResNet-101 in our experiments.

3   MTGAN for Small Object Detection

In this section, we introduce the proposed method in detail. First, we give a
brief description of the classical GAN network to lay the context for describing
our proposed Multi-Task GAN (MTGAN) for small object detection. Then, the
whole architecture of our framework is described (refer to Fig. 2 for an illustration). Finally, we present each part of our MTGAN network and define the loss
functions for training the generator and discriminator, respectively.

3.1   GAN

GAN [9] learns a generator network G and a discriminator network D simultaneously via an adversarial process. The training process alternately optimizes
the generator and discriminator, which are in competition with each other. The
generator G is trained to produce samples to fool the discriminator D, and D is
trained to distinguish real from fake images produced by G. The GAN loss to
be optimized is defined as follows:

$$\mathcal{L}_{GAN}(G, D) = \mathbb{E}_{x \sim p_{data}(x)}[\log D_\theta(x)] + \mathbb{E}_{z \sim p_z(z)}[\log(1 - D_\theta(G_\omega(z)))], \quad (1)$$

where z is random noise, x denotes the real data, θ and ω denote the parameters
of D and G respectively. Here, G tries to minimize the objective function, while
D tries to maximize it as Eq. (2):

$$\arg \min_G \max_D \mathcal{L}_{GAN}(G, D) \quad (2)$$

Table 1. The architecture of the generator and discriminator network. "conv" and "layer*" represent the convolutional layer, "x5" denotes a residual block which has 5 convolutional layers, "de-conv" means a up-sampling convolutional layer, "2x" denotes up-sampling by a factor of 2, and "fc" indicates a fully connected layer. Note that we only post the architecture of the discriminator network with ResNet-50.

	Generator					Discriminator (ResNet-50)						
Layer	conv	conv x5	conv	de-conv	de-conv	conv	conv	layer1	layer2	layer3	layer4	fc
Kernel Num.	64	64	64	256	256	3	64	128	256	512	1024	3
Kernel Size	9	3	3	3	3	9	3	1	1	1	1	-
Stride	1	1	1	2x	2x	1	2	1	2	2	2	-

Similar to [9,21], we design a generator network G_w, which is optimized in an alternating manner with discriminator network D_θ seeking to jointly solve the super-resolution, object classification, and bounding box regression problems for small object detection. Therefore, the overall loss is defined as follows:

$$\arg\min_w \max_\theta \mathbb{E}_{(I^{HR},u,v)\sim p_{train}(I^{HR},u,v)}[\log D_\theta(I^{HR},u,v)]+ \\ \mathbb{E}_{(I^{LR},u,v)\sim p_G(I^{LR},u,v)}[\log(1-D_\theta(G_w(I^{LR}),u,v))], \quad (3)$$

where I^{LR} and I^{HR} denote low-resolution and high-resolution images, respectively. u is the class label and v is the ground-truth bounding-box regression target. Unlike [9], the input of our generator is a low-resolution image rather than random noise. Compared to [21], we have multiple tasks in the discriminator, where we distinguish the generated super-resolved images vs. real high-resolution images, classify the object category, and regress the object location jointly. Specifically, the general idea behind Eq. (3) is that it allows one to train a generator G with the goal of fooling a differentiable discriminator D that is trained to distinguish super-resolved images from real high-resolution images. Furthermore, our method (SOD-MTGAN) extends classical SRGAN [21] by adding two more parallel branches to classify the categories and regress the bounding boxes of candidate ROI images. Moreover, the classification loss and regression loss in the discriminator are back-propagated to the generator to further promote it to produce super-resolved images that are also suitable for easier classification and better localization. In the following subsection, we introduce the architecture of the MTGAN and the training losses in detail.

3.2 Network Architecture

Our generator takes low-resolution images as input, instead of random noise, and outputs super-resolved images. For the purpose of object detection, the discriminator is designed to distinguish generated super-resolved images from real high-resolution images, classify the object categories, and regress the location jointly.

Generator Network (G_w). As shown in Table 1 and Fig. 2, we adopt a deep CNN architecture which has shown effectiveness for image de-blurring in [13] and face detection in [1]. Different from [13], our generator includes up-sampling layers (*i.e.* de-conv in Table 1). There are two up-sampling fractionally-strided *conv* layers, three conv layers, and five residual blocks in the network. Particularly, in these residual blocks, we use two *conv* layers with 3×3 kernels and 64 feature maps followed by batch-normalization layers [15] and parametric ReLU [11] as the activation function. Each de-convolutional layer consists of learned kernels, which up-samples a low-resolution image to a $2\times$ super-resolved image, which is usually better than re-sizing the same image by an interpolation method [5,17,33].

Our generator first up-samples low-resolution small images, which include both object and background candidate ROI images, to $4\times$ super-resolved images via the de-convolutional layers, and then performs convolution to produce corresponding clear images. The outputs of the generator (clear super-resolved images) are easier for the discriminator to classify as fake or real and to perform object detection (*i.e.* object classification and bounding-box regression).

Discriminator Network (D_θ). We employ ResNet-50 or ResNet-101 [12] as our backbone network in the discriminator, and Table 1 shows the architecture of the ResNet-50 network. We add three parallel fc layers behind the last average pooling layer of the backbone network, which play the role of distinguishing the real high-resolution images from the generated super-resolved images, classifying object categories, and regressing bounding boxes, respectively. For this specific task, the first fc layer (called fc_{GAN}) uses a sigmoid loss function [26], while the classification fc layer (called fc_{cls}) and regression fc layer (called fc_{reg}) use the softmax and smooth $L1$ loss [6] functions, respectively.

The input of the discriminator is a high-resolution ROI image, and the output of the fc_{GAN} branch is the probability (p_{GAN}) of the input image being a real image, the output of fc_{cls} branch is the probability ($p_{cls} = (p_0, ..., p_K)$) of the input image being each of $K+1$ object categories, and the output of fc_{reg} branch is the bounding-box regression offsets ($t = (t_x, t_y, t_w, t_h)$) for the ROI candidate.

3.3   Overall Loss Function

We adopt the pixel-wise and adversarial losses from some state-of-the-art GAN approaches [16,21] to optimize our generator. In contrast to [21], we remove the feature matching loss to decrease the computational complexity without sacrificing much in generation performance. Furthermore, we introduce the classification and regression losses into the generator objective function to drive the generator network to recover fine details from small scale images for easier detection.

Pixel-wise Loss. The input of our generator network is small ROI images instead of random noise [9]. A natural and simple way to enforce the output of the generator (*i.e.* the super-resolved images) to be close to the ground-truth images is by minimizing the pixel-wise MSE loss, and it is computed as Eq. (4):

$$L_{MSE}(w) = \frac{1}{N} \sum_{i=1}^{N} \|G_w(I_i^{LR}) - I_i^{HR}\|^2, \tag{4}$$

where I_i^{LR}, $G_w(I_i^{LR})$ and I_i^{HR} denote small low-resolution images, generated super-resolved images, and real high-resolution images, respectively. G represents the generator network, and w denotes its parameters. However, it is known that the solution to the MSE optimization problem usually lacks high-frequency content, which results in blurred images with overly smooth texture.

Adversarial Loss. To achieve more realistic results, we introduce the adversarial loss [21] to the objective loss, defined as Eq. (5):

$$L_{adv} = \frac{1}{N} \sum_{i=1}^{N} \log(1 - D_\theta(G_w(I_i^{LR}))) \tag{5}$$

The adversarial loss encourages the network to generate sharper high-frequency details so as to fool the discriminator D. In Eq. (5), $D_\theta(G_w(I_i^{LR}))$ denotes the probability of the resolved image $G_w(I_i^{LR})$ being a real high-resolution image.

Classification Loss. In order to complete the task of object detection and to make the generated images easier to classify, we introduce the classification loss to the overall objective. Let $\{I_i^{LR}, i=1,2,\ldots,N\}$ and $\{I_i^{HR}, i=1,2,\ldots,N\}$ denote low-resolution images and real high-resolution images respectively, and $\{u_i, i=1,2,\ldots,N\}$ represent their corresponding labels, where $u_i \in \{0,\ldots,K\}$ indicates the object category. As such, we formulate the classification loss as:

$$L_{cls}(p,u) = \frac{1}{N} \sum_{i=1}^{N} -(\log(D_{cls}(G_w(I_i^{LR}))) + \log(D_{cls}(I_i^{HR}))) \tag{6}$$

where $p_{I_i^{LR}} = D_{cls}(G_w(I_i^{LR}))$ and $p_{I_i^{HR}} = D_{cls}(I_i^{HR}))$ denote the probabilities of the generated super-resolved image and the real high-resolution image belonging to the true category u_i, respectively.

In our method, our classification loss plays two roles. First, it guides the discriminator to learn a classifier that classifies high-resolution images, albeit generated super-resolved and real high-resolution images, as real or fake. Second, it promotes the generator to recovery sharper images for easier classification.

Regression Loss. To enable more accurate localization, we also introduce a bounding box regression loss [6] to the objective function, defined in Eq. (7):

$$L_{reg}(t,v) = \frac{1}{N} \sum_{i=1}^{N} \sum_{j \in \{x,y,w,h\}} [u_i \geq 1](S_{L_1}(t_{i,j}^{HR} - v_{i,j}) + S_{L_1}(t_{i,j}^{SR} - v_{i,j})) \tag{7}$$

in which,

$$S_{L_1}(x) = \begin{cases} 0.5x^2 & \text{if } |x| < 1 \\ |x| - 0.5 & \text{otherwise} \end{cases} \tag{8}$$

where $v_i = (v_{i,x}, v_{i,y}, v_{i,w}, v_{i,h})$ denotes a tuple of the true bounding-box regression target, and $t_i = (t_{i,x}, t_{i,y}, t_{i,w}, t_{i,h})$ denotes the predicted regression tuple. t_i^{HR} and t_i^{SR} denote the tuples for the i-th real high-resolution and generated super-resolved images, respectively. The bracket indicator function $[u_i \geq 1]$ equals to 1 when $u_i \geq 1$ and 0 otherwise. For a more detailed description of the regression loss, we refer the reader to [6].

Similar to the classification loss, our regression loss also has two purposes. First, it encourages the discriminator to regress the location of the object candidates cropped from the baseline detector. Second, it promotes the generator to produce super-resolved images with fine details for more accurate localization.

Objective Function. Based on the above analysis, we combine the adversarial loss in Eq. (5), classification loss in Eq. (6) and regression loss in Eq. (7) with the pixel-wise MSE loss in Eq. (4). As such, our GAN network can be trained by optimizing the objective function in Eq. (9):

$$
\begin{aligned}
\max_{\theta} \min_{w} \quad & \frac{1}{N} \sum_{i-1}^{N} \alpha(\log(1 - D_\theta(G_w(I_i^{LR}))) + \log D_\theta(I_i^{HR})) \\
& + \frac{1}{N} \sum_{i=1}^{N} -\beta(\log(D_{cls}(G_w(I_i^{LR}))) + \log(D_{cls}(I_i^{HR}))) \\
& + \frac{1}{N} \sum_{i=1}^{N} \gamma \sum_{j \in \{x,y,w,h\}} [u_i \geq 1](\mathrm{S}_{L_1}(t_{i,j}^{HR} - v_{i,j}) + \mathrm{S}_{L_1}(t_{i,j}^{SR} - v_{i,j})) \\
& + \frac{1}{N} \sum_{i=1}^{N} \|G_w(I_i^{LR}) - I_i^{HR}\|^2
\end{aligned}
\tag{9}
$$

where α, β, and γ are weights trading off the different terms. These weights are cross-validated in our experiments.

Directly optimizing Eq. (9) with respect to w for updating generator G makes w diverge to infinity rapidly, since large w always makes the objective attain a large loss. For better behavior, we optimize the objective function in a fixed point optimization manner, as done in previous GAN work [16,21]. Specifically, we optimize for the parameter w of generator G while keeping the discriminator D fixed and then update its parameter θ keeping the generator fixed. Below are the resulting two sub-problems that are iteratively optimized as:

$$
\begin{aligned}
\min_{w} \quad & \frac{1}{N} \sum_{i=1}^{N} (\alpha \log(1 - D_\theta(G_w(I_i^{LR}))) - \beta \log(D_{cls}(G_w(I_i^{LR})))) \\
& + \frac{1}{N} \sum_{i=1}^{N} \gamma \sum_{j \in \{x,y,w,h\}} [u_i \geq 1]\mathrm{S}_{L_1}(t_{i,j}^{SR} - v_{i,j}) + \frac{1}{N} \sum_{i=1}^{N} \|G_{w1}(I_i^{LR}) - I_i^{HR}\|^2
\end{aligned}
\tag{10}
$$

and

$$\min_{\theta} \quad \frac{1}{N}\sum_{i=1}^{N} -\alpha(\log(1 - D_{\theta}(G_w(I_i^{LR}))) + \log D_{\theta}(I_i^{HR}))$$

$$+ \frac{1}{N}\sum_{i=1}^{N} -\beta(\log(D_{cls}(G_w(I_i^{LR}))) + \log(D_{cls}(I_i^{HR}))) \qquad (11)$$

$$+ \frac{1}{N}\sum_{i=1}^{N} \gamma \sum_{j\in\{x,y,w,h\}} [u_i \geq 1](S_{L_1}(t_{i,j}^{HR} - v_{i,j}) + S_{L_1}(t_{i,j}^{SR} - v_{i,j}))$$

The loss function of generator G in Eq. (10) consists of adversarial loss Eq. (5), MSE loss Eq. (4), classification loss Eq. (6) and regression loss Eq. (7), which enforce that the reconstructed images be similar to real, object specific, and localizable high-resolution images with high-frequency details. Compared to the previous GANs, we add the classification and regression losses of generated super-resolved object images to the generator loss. By introducing these two losses, the super-resolved images recovered from the generator network are more realistic than those optimized by only using the adversarial and MSE losses.

The loss function of discriminator D in Eq. (11) introduces the classification loss Eq. (6) and the regression loss Eq. (7). The function of classification loss is to classify the categories of the real high-resolution and generated super-resolved images, which is parallel to the basic formulation of GAN [9] to distinguish real or generated high-resolution images. In the field of small object detection, as we all know, a few pixel drift may make the predicted bounding-boxes fail to fulfill the evaluation criteria. Therefore, we introduce the regression loss (regression branch) into the discriminator network for better localization.

4   Experiments

In this section, we validate our proposed SOD-MTGAN detector on a challenging public object detection benchmark (*i.e.* COCO dataset [23]), where includes some ablation studies and comparisons against other state-of-the-art detectors.

4.1   Training and Validation Datasets

We use the COCO dataset [23] for all experiments. As stated in [23], there are more small objects than large/medium objects in the dataset, approximately 41% of objects are small ($area < 32^2$). Therefore, we use this dataset for training and validating the proposed method. For the object detection task, there are 125 K images taken in natural settings and of everyday life (*i.e.* objects with much diversity). 80 K/40 K/5 K of the data is randomly selected for training, validation, and testing, respectively. Following previous works [2,22], we use the union of 80 k training images and a subset of 35 k validation images (*trainval135k*) for training, and report ablation results on the remaining 5 k validation images (*minival*).

Table 2. The detection performance (AP) of our proposed method SOD-MTGAN against the baseline methods on the COCO *minival* subset. The AP performance of Faster RCNN [29] and Mask-RCNN [10] are provided by [8]. Obviously, SOD-MTGAN outperforms the baseline methods, especially on the small subset where the AP performance increases more than 1.5%.

Methods	Backbone	AP	AP_{50}	AP_{75}	AP_S	AP_M	AP_L
Faster-RCNN (Baseline)	ResNet-50-C4	36.5	57.3	39.3	18.4	40.6	50.6
SOD-MTGAN (Ours)	ResNet-50	**37.2**	**57.7**	**40.2**	**19.9**	**41.1**	**51.2**
Mask-RCNN (Baseline)	ResNet-101-FPN	40.9	61.9	44.8	23.5	44.2	53.9
SOD-MTGAN (Ours)	ResNet-101	**41.5**	**62.5**	**45.4**	**25.1**	**44.6**	**54.1**

During evaluation, the COCO dataset is divided into three subsets (small, medium, and large) based on the areas of objects. The medium and large subsets contain objects with an area larger than 32^2 and 96^2 pixels, respectively, while the small subset contains objects with an area less than 32^2 pixels. In this paper, we focus on small object detection using our proposed MTGAN network. We report the final detection performance using the standard COCO metrics, which include AP (averaged over all IoU thresholds, *i.e.* [0.5:0.05:0.95]), AP_{50}, AP_{75} and AP_S, AP_M, AP_L (AP at different scales).

4.2 Implementation Details

In the generator network, we set the trade-off weights $\alpha = 0.001$, $\beta = \gamma = 0.01$. The generator network is trained from scratch and the weights in each layer are initialized with a zero-mean Gaussian distribution with standard deviation 0.02, and the biases are initialized with 0. To avoid undesirable local optima, we first train an MSE-based SR network to initialize the generator network. For the discriminator network, we employ the ResNet-50 or ResNet-101 [12] model pre-trained on ImageNet as our backbone network and add three parallel *fc* layers as described in Sect. 3.2. The *fc* layers are initialized by a zero-mean Gaussian distribution with standard deviation 0.1, and biases initialized with 0.

Our baseline detectors are based on Faster RCNN with ResNet50-C4 [12] and FPN with ResNet101 [22]. All hyper-parameters of the baseline detectors are adopted from the setup in [10]. For training our generator and discriminator networks, we crop positive and negative ROI examples from COCO [23] *trainval135k* set with our baseline detectors. The corresponding low-resolution images are generated by down-sampling the high-resolution images using bicubic interpolation with a factor 4. During testing, 100 ROIs are cropped by our baseline detector and then fed to our MTGAN network to produce final detection.

During training, we use the Adam optimizer [18] for the generator and the SGD optimizer for the discriminator network. The learning rate for SGD is initially set to 0.01 and then reduced by a factor of 10 after every $40k$ mini-batches. Training is terminated after a maximum of $80k$ iterations. We alternately update the generator and discriminator network as in [9]. Our system is implemented in PyTorch, and the source code will be made publicly available.

4.3   Ablation Studies

We first compare our proposed method with the baseline detectors to prove the effectiveness of the MTGAN for small object detection. Moreover, we verify the positive influence of the regression branch in the discriminator network by comparing the AP performance with/without this branch. Finally, to validate the contribution of each loss (adversarial, classification, and regression) in the loss function of the generator, we also conduct ablation studies by gradually adding each of them to the pixel-wise MSE loss. Unless otherwise stated, all the ablation studies use the ResNet-50 as the backbone network in the discriminator.

Influence of the Multi-task GAN (MTGAN). Table 2 (the 2nd vs. 3rd row and the 4th vs. 5th row) compares the performance of the baseline detectors against our method on the COCO *minival* subset. From Table 2, we observe that the performance of our MTGAN with ResNet-50 outperforms Faster-RCNN (the ResNet-50-C4 detector) by a sizable margin (*i.e.* 1.5% in AP) on the small subset. Similarly, MTGAN with ResNet-101 improves over the FPN detector with ResNet-101 by 1.6% in AP. The reason is that the baseline detectors perform the down-sampling operations (*i.e.* convolution with stride 2) when extracting *conv* feature maps. The small objects themselves contain limited information, and the majority of the detailed information will be lost after down-sampling. For example, if the input is a 16×16 pixel object ROI, the result is a 1×1 C4 feature map and nothing is preserved for the C5 feature map. These limited *conv* feature maps degrade the detection performance for such small objects. In contrast, our method up-samples the low-resolution image to a fine scale, thus, recovering the detailed information and making detection possible. Figure 3 shows some super-resolved images generated by our MTGAN generator.

Influence of the Regression Branch. As shown in Fig. 1, imperfect localization is one of the main sources of detection error. This especially the case for small sized objects, where small shifts in their bounding boxes lead to failed detections when the standard strict evaluation criteria are used. The regression branch in the discriminator can further refine bounding boxes and lead to more accurate localization. From Table 3 (1st and 5th row), we see that the AP performance on the small object subset improves by 0.9% when the regression branch is added, thus, demonstrating its effectiveness on the detection pipeline.

Influence of the Adversarial Loss. Table 3 (the 2nd and 5th row) shows that the AP on the small subset drops by 0.5% without the adversarial loss. The reason is that the generated images without adversarial loss are over-smooth and lack high frequency information, which is important for object detection. To encourage the generator to produce high-quality images for better detection, we use the adversarial loss to train our generator network.

Fig. 3. Some examples of super-resolved images generated by our MTGAN network from small low-resolution patches. The first column of each image group depicts the original low-resolution image, which is upsampled 4× for visualization. The second column is the ground truth high-resolution image, while the third column is the corresponding super-resolved image generated by our generator network.

Table 3. Performance of our SOD-MTGAN model trained with and without the regression branch, adversarial loss, classification loss, and regression loss on the COCO *minival* subset. "reg+" indicates the regression branch in the discriminator, "adv" denotes the adversarial loss in Eq. (5), "cls" represents the classification loss in Eq. (6), and "reg" indicates the regression loss in Eq. (7).

Methods	AP	AP_{50}	AP_{75}	AP_S	AP_M	AP_L
w/o reg+ branch	36.7	57.5	39.8	19.0	40.9	49.9
w/o adv loss	37.0	57.6	40.0	19.4	41.0	51.0
w/o cls loss	36.8	57.6	39.9	19.2	41.1	50.3
w/o reg loss	36.7	57.6	39.7	19.1	41.1	50.2
SOD-MTGAN (Ours)	**37.2**	**57.7**	**40.2**	**19.9**	**41.2**	**51.2**

Influence of the Classification Loss. From Table 3 (the 3rd and 5th row), we see that the AP performance increases by about 1% on the small subset when the classification loss is incorporated. Clearly, this validates the claim that the classification loss promotes the generator to recover finer detailed information for better classification. In doing so, the discriminator can exploit the fine details to predict the correct category of the ROI images.

Influence of the Regression Loss. As shown in Table 3 (the 4th and 5th row), the AP performance increases by nearly 1% on the small subset by using the regression loss to train the generator network. Similar to the classification loss, the regression loss drives the generator to recover some fine details for better localization. The increased AP demonstrates the necessity of the regression loss in the generator loss function.

Table 4. The performance (AP) of the proposed SOD-MTGAN detector and other state-of-the-art methods on COCO $test-dev$ subset. "+++" denotes the more complex training/test stages, which includes multi-scale train/test, horizontal flip train/test and OHEM [30] in the Faster RCNN.

Methods	Backbone	AP	AP_{50}	AP_{75}	AP_S	AP_M	AP_L
SSD512 [24]	VGG16	26.8	46.5	27.8	9.0	28.9	41.9
YOLO9000 [28]	Darknet-19	21.6	44.0	19.2	5.0	22.4	35.5
Faster RCNN+++ [12]	ResNet-101-C4	34.9	55.7	37.4	15.6	38.7	50.9
FPN [22]	ResNet-101-FPN	36.2	59.1	39.0	18.2	39.0	48.2
G-RMI [14]	Inception-ResNet-v2	34.7	55.5	36.7	13.5	38.1	52.0
TDM [31]	Inception-ResNet-v2-TDM	36.8	57.7	39.7	16.2	39.8	52.1
Mask RCNN [10]	ResNeXt-101-FPN	39.8	62.3	43.4	22.1	43.2	51.2
SOD-MTGAN (Ours)	ResNet-101	**41.4**	**63.2**	**45.4**	**24.7**	**44.2**	**52.6**

Fig. 4. Qualitative results of the SOD-MTGAN detector. Green and red boxes denote the ground-truths and the results of our method. Best seen in color and zoomed in. (Color figure online)

4.4 State-of-the-Art Comparison

We compare our proposed method (SOD-MTGAN) with several state-of-the-art object detectors [10,12,14,22,24,28,31] on the COCO $test - dev$ subset. Table 4 lists the performance of every detector, from which we conclude that our method surpasses all other state-of-the-art methods on all subsets. More importantly, our SOD-MTGAN achieves the highest performance (24.7%) on the small subset, outperforming the second best object detector by about 3%. This AP improvement is most notable for the small object subset, which clearly demonstrates the effectiveness of our method on small object detection.

4.5 Qualitative Results

Figure 4 shows some detection results generated by the proposed SOD-MTGAN detector. We observe that our method successfully finds almost all the objects, even though some ones are very small. This demonstrates the effectiveness of our detector on the small object detection problem. Figure 4 shows some failure cases including some false negative and positive results, which indicate that there is still room for progress in further improving small object detection performance.

5   Conclusion

In this paper, we propose an end-to-end multi-task GAN (MTGAN) to detect small objects in unconstrained scenarios. In the MTGAN, the generator upsamples the small blurred ROI images to fine-scale clear images, which are passed through the discriminator for classification and bounding box regression. To recover detailed information for better detection, the classification and regression losses in the discriminator are propagated back to the generator. Extensive experiments on the COCO dataset demonstrate that our detector improves state-of-the-art AP performance in general, where the largest improvement is observed for small sized objects.

Acknowledgments. This work was supported mainly by the King Abdullah University of Science and Technology (KAUST) Office of Sponsored Research and by Natural Science Foundation of China, Grant No. 61603372.

References

1. Bai, Y., Zhang, Y., Ding, M., Ghanem, B.: Finding tiny faces in the wild with generative adversarial network. In: CVPR, June 2018
2. Bell, S., Zitnick, C.L., Bala, K., Girshick, R.: Inside-outside net: Detecting objects in context with skip pooling and recurrent neural networks. In: CVPR (2016)
3. Dai, J., Li, Y., He, K., Sun, J.: R-FCN: object detection via region-based fully convolutional networks. In: NIPS, pp. 379–387 (2016)
4. Denton, E.L., Chintala, S., Szlam, A., Fergus, R.: Deep generative image models using a laplacian pyramid of adversarial networks. In: Advances in Neural Information Processing Systems 28, pp. 1486–1494. Curran Associates, Inc. (2015). http://papers.nips.cc/paper/5773-deep-generative-image-models-using-a-laplacian-pyramid-of-adversarial-networks.pdf
5. Dong, C., Loy, C.C., Tang, X.: Accelerating the super-resolution convolutional neural network. In: Leibe, B., Matas, J., Sebe, N., Welling, M. (eds.) ECCV 2016. LNCS, vol. 9906, pp. 391–407. Springer, Cham (2016). https://doi.org/10.1007/978-3-319-46475-6_25
6. Girshick, R.: Fast R-CNN. In: ICCV, pp. 1440–1448. IEEE (2015)
7. Girshick, R., Donahue, J., Darrell, T., Malik, J.: Rich feature hierarchies for accurate object detection and semantic segmentation. In: CVPR, pp. 580–587 (2014)
8. Girshick, R., Radosavovic, I., Gkioxari, G., Dollár, P., He, K.: Detectron. https://github.com/facebookresearch/detectron (2018)
9. Goodfellow, I., et al.: Generative adversarial nets. In: Advances in Neural Information Processing Systems 27, pp. 2672–2680. Curran Associates, Inc. (2014). http://papers.nips.cc/paper/5423-generative-adversarial-nets.pdf
10. He, K., Gkioxari, G., Dollar, P., Girshick, R.: Mask R-CNN. In: CVPR, pp. 2961–2969 (2017)

11. He, K., Zhang, X., Ren, S., Sun, J.: Delving deep into rectifiers: surpassing human-level performance on imagenet classification. In: ICCV, pp. 1026–1034 (2015)
12. He, K., Zhang, X., Ren, S., Sun, J.: Deep residual learning for image recognition. In: CVPR, June 2016
13. Hradiš, M., Kotera, J., Zemcík, P., Šroubek, F.: Convolutional neural networks for direct text deblurring. In: Xianghua Xie, M.W.J., Tam, G.K.L. (eds.) BMVC, pp. 6.1–6.13 (2015)
14. Huang, J., et al.: Speed/accuracy trade-offs for modern convolutional object detectors. In: IEEE CVPR (2017)
15. Ioffe, S., Szegedy, C.: Batch normalization: accelerating deep network training by reducing internal covariate shift. In: ICML, pp. 448–456 (2015)
16. Isola, P., Zhu, J.Y., Zhou, T., Efros, A.A.: Image-to-image translation with conditional adversarial networks. In: CVPR, pp. 1125–1134 (2017)
17. Kim, J., Kwon Lee, J., Mu Lee, K.: Accurate image super-resolution using very deep convolutional networks. In: CVPR, June 2016
18. Kingma, D.P., Ba, J.: Adam: a method for stochastic optimization. CoRR abs/1412.6980 (2014)
19. Krizhevsky, A., Sutskever, I., Hinton, G.E.: Imagenet classification with deep convolutional neural networks. In: NIPS, pp. 1097–1105 (2012)
20. Krizhevsky, A., Sutskever, I., Hinton, G.E.: Imagenet classification with deep convolutional neural networks. In: Pereira, F., Burges, C.J.C., Bottou, L., Weinberger, K.Q. (eds.) Advances in Neural Information Processing Systems 25, pp. 1097–1105. Curran Associates, Inc. (2012). http://papers.nips.cc/paper/4824-imagenet-classification-with-deep-convolutional-neural-networks.pdf
21. Ledig, C., et al.: Photo-realistic single image super-resolution using a generative adversarial network. In: CVPR, pp. 4681–4690 (2017)
22. Lin, T.Y., et al.: Feature pyramid networks for object detection. In: CVPR, vol. 1, p. 4 (2017)
23. Lin, T.-Y., et al.: Microsoft COCO: common objects in context. In: Fleet, D., Pajdla, T., Schiele, B., Tuytelaars, T. (eds.) ECCV 2014. LNCS, vol. 8693, pp. 740–755. Springer, Cham (2014). https://doi.org/10.1007/978-3-319-10602-1_48
24. Liu, W., et al.: SSD: single shot multibox detector. In: Leibe, B., Matas, J., Sebe, N., Welling, M. (eds.) ECCV 2016. LNCS, vol. 9905, pp. 21–37. Springer, Cham (2016). https://doi.org/10.1007/978-3-319-46448-0_2
25. Mathieu, M.F., et al.: Disentangling factors of variation in deep representation using adversarial training. In: Advances in Neural Information Processing Systems 29, pp. 5040–5048. Curran Associates, Inc. (2016). http://papers.nips.cc/paper/6051-disentangling-factors-of-variation-in-deep-representation-using-adversarial-training.pdf
26. Radford, A., Metz, L., Chintala, S.: Unsupervised representation learning with deep convolutional generative adversarial networks. CoRR abs/1511.06434 (2015)
27. Redmon, J., Divvala, S., Girshick, R., Farhadi, A.: You only look once: Unified, real-time object detection. In: CVPR, pp. 779–788 (2016)
28. Redmon, J., Farhadi, A.: Yolo9000: Better, faster, stronger. In: CVPR, pp. 6517–6525. IEEE (2017)
29. Ren, S., He, K., Girshick, R., Sun, J.: Faster R-CNN: towards real-time object detection with region proposal networks. In: NIPS, pp. 91–99 (2015)
30. Shrivastava, A., Gupta, A., Girshick, R.: Training region-based object detectors with online hard example mining. In: CVPR, pp. 761–769 (2016)
31. Shrivastava, A., Sukthankar, R., Malik, J., Gupta, A.: Beyond skip connections: Top-down modulation for object detection. CoRR abs/1612.06851 (2016)

32. Simonyan, K., Zisserman, A.: Very deep convolutional networks for large-scale image recognition. CoRR abs/1409.1556 (2014)
33. Wang, Z., Liu, D., Yang, J., Han, W., Huang, T.: Deep networks for image super-resolution with sparse prior. In: ICCV, December 2015
34. Zhou, B., Lapedriza, A., Xiao, J., Torralba, A., Oliva, A.: Learning deep features for scene recognition using places database. In: NIPS, pp. 487–495 (2014)
35. Zhu, J.-Y., Krähenbühl, P., Shechtman, E., Efros, A.A.: Generative visual manipulation on the natural image manifold. In: Leibe, B., Matas, J., Sebe, N., Welling, M. (eds.) ECCV 2016. LNCS, vol. 9909, pp. 597–613. Springer, Cham (2016). https://doi.org/10.1007/978-3-319-46454-1_36

Facial Expression Recognition
with Inconsistently Annotated Datasets

Jiabei Zeng[1(✉)], Shiguang Shan[1,2,3], and Xilin Chen[1,2]

[1] Key Lab of Intelligent Information Processing of Chinese Academy of Sciences
(CAS), Institute of Computing Technology, CAS, Beijing 100190, China
{jiabei.zeng,sgshan,xlchen}@ict.ac.cn
[2] University of Chinese Academy of Sciences, Beijing 100190, China
[3] CAS Center for Excellence in Brain Science and Intelligence Technology,
Beijing, China

Abstract. Annotation errors and bias are inevitable among different facial expression datasets due to the subjectiveness of annotating
facial expressions. Ascribe to the inconsistent annotations, performance
of existing facial expression recognition (FER) methods cannot keep
improving when the training set is enlarged by merging multiple datasets.
To address the inconsistency, we propose an Inconsistent Pseudo Annotations to Latent Truth (IPA2LT) framework to train a FER model from
multiple inconsistently labeled datasets and large scale unlabeled data. In
IPA2LT, we assign each sample more than one labels with human annotations or model predictions. Then, we propose an end-to-end LTNet with
a scheme of discovering the latent truth from the inconsistent pseudo
labels and the input face images. To our knowledge, IPA2LT serves as
the first work to solve the training problem with inconsistently labeled
FER datasets. Experiments on synthetic data validate the effectiveness
of the proposed method in learning from inconsistent labels. We also
conduct extensive experiments in FER and show that our method outperforms other state-of-the-art and optional methods under a rigorous
evaluation protocol involving 7 FER datasets.

1 Introduction

Facial expressions convey varied and nuanced meanings. Automatically recognizing facial expression is important to understand human's behaviors and interact with them. During the last decades, the community has made promising
progresses in building datasets and developing methods for facial expression
recognition (FER). Datasets have sprung up for both in-the-lab and in-the-wild
facial expressions, such as CK+[20], MMI [28], Oulu-CASIA [33], SFEW/AFEW
[7], AffectNet [22], EmotioNet [2], RAF-DB [16], and others. Based on these
datasets, lots of FER approaches are proposed and achieve the state-of-the-art
performance [4,14,18,25,27,30,34].

However, errors and bias of human annotations exist among different
datasets. As been known, it is subjective to classify the face expression into

© Springer Nature Switzerland AG 2018
V. Ferrari et al. (Eds.): ECCV 2018, LNCS 11217, pp. 227–243, 2018.
https://doi.org/10.1007/978-3-030-01261-8_14

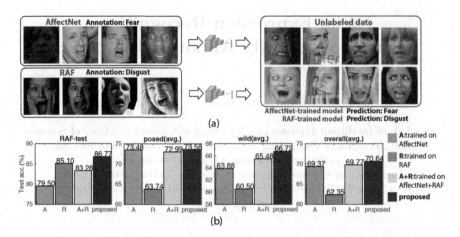

Fig. 1. (a) Inconsistent predictions due to the annotations bias in AffectNet and RAF. (b) Test accuracy on different datasets with varied combination of training data.

several emotional categories. Human's understanding of facial expressions varies with different cultures, living environments, and other experiences. Although the human coders are claimed to be trained before the annotation tasks [16,30], the bias of annotations is inevitable among different datasets, because teams from different backgrounds would have different criterions in controlling the quality of the released datasets. The annotation bias results in two main issues: (1) FER systems are easy to heritage the recognition bias from the training dataset. Figure 1(a) shows examples of the inconsistent predictions caused by the annotation bias in AffectNet and RAF datasets. The faces presented on the left have similar expressions but they are labeled as "fear" in AffectNet and as "disgust" in RAF. As a consequence, the two models trained from AffectNet and RAF have inconsistent predictions on the unlabeled images presented on the right. They are predicted as "fear" by the AffectNet-trained model but as "disgust" by the RAF-trained one. (2) It is difficult to accumulate the benefit of different datasets by simply merging them as a whole during the training process. Figure 1(b) shows the test accuracy on different test sets with varied combination of training data. As can be seen, models trained from the most data are not sufficient to be the best one. On RAF-test, the model trained from the union of AffectNet and RAF(A+R) has lower test accuracy than the one trained from RAF only. On posed facial expression data, model A+R performs worse than the one from AffectNet only.

To address the issues, we propose a 3-step framework to build a FER system on inconsistently annotated datasets. We name the framework as Inconsistent Pseudo Annotations to Latent Truth (IPA2LT) because it tags multiple labels for each image with the human annotations or predicted pseudo labels, and then learns a FER model to fit the latent truth from the inconsistent pseudo labels. Figure 2 illustrates the main idea of the IPA2LT framework. IPA2LT

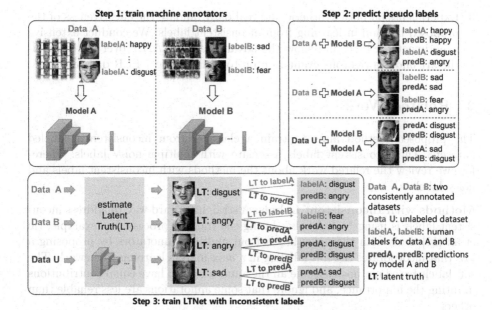

Fig. 2. Three steps in the proposed Inconsistent Pseudo Annotations to Latent Truth (IPA2LT) framework.

consists of three steps. It first trains two machine annotators from data A and B respectively. The predictions by machine annotators and the human annotations are probably to be inconsistent. They are used as multiple labels for each image in several human labeled datasets as well as the large scale unlabeled data. Unlabeled data serves as the bridge between data A and B by sharing the same machine annotators with them. Then, IPA2LT trains a Latent Truth Net (LTNet) to discover the latent true label. LTNet is end-to-end trainable and therefore it can estimate the latent truth depending on both the input face image and the inconsistent labels. During the inference, the learned LTNet is applied to estimate the true label for a new face. Our contributions are summarized as follows:

1. We propose a relatively unexplored problem: how to learn a classifier from more than one datasets with different annotation preferences. To the best of our knowledge, it is the first work that addresses the annotation inconsistency in different FER datasets.
2. We introduce a IPA2LT framework to train a FER model from multiple inconsistently labeled datasets and the large scale unlabeled data. In the framework, we propose an end-to-end trainable LTNet[1] embedded with a scheme of discovering the latent truth given multiple observed(or predicted) labels and the input face images.

---

[1] Code available at https://github.com/dualplus/LTNet.

3. Experiments on both synthetic and real data validate the effectiveness of the proposed method in learning from inconsistent labels. We conduct extensive experiments in FER and show the advantages of IPA2LT over the state-of-the-art under a rigorous evaluation protocol involving 7 FER datasets.

2   Related Work

The proposed method aims to train a classifier from inconsistently labeled datasets. The inconsistent labels associate with multiple noisy labels. Therefore we review the related work about the methods with inconsistent labels and noisy labels.

Methods with Inconsistent Labels: A straightforward way to address inconsistent labels is using "soft labels" during the training process. For example, He et al. [11] dealt with the noisy labels from multiple annotators by proposing a loss that incorporates the soft labeling in a max-margin learning framework. The soft labels based methods assume all the annotations to have equal contributions in rating the importance, and ignore that some annotations are less reliable than others.

Another typical way is the ones in estimating the ground truth in crowdsourcing [35]. These works estimate the latent truth from different annotators using EM algorithm. As early as 1979, Dawid and Skene [5] proposed to solve the labeling task with k different categories by assuming each worker to be associated with a $k \times k$ confusion matrix, where the (l, c)-th entry represents the probability that a sample in class l is labeled as class c by the worker. The EM-based methods have had empirical success in determining the labels in crowdsourcing [3,19,32,36]. Considering the label qualities from different annotators, methods are proposed to iteratively qualify the annotators and estimate the latent truths, such as using Gaussian Mixture Model and Bayesian Information Criterion [31], Chinese restaurant process [23], and other probabilistic frameworks.

However, the methods in crowdsourcing focus on estimating the ground truth of the samples that already have a set of inconsistent annotations. They ignore the mapping between the latent truth and the input data and make few efforts on learning a predictor to estimate labels for unseen samples. We focus on training the predictor for unseen samples and capture the relations between the input data and the true labels.

Methods with Noisy Labels: To address the noisy labels, numbers of methods were proposed. One idea is to leverage a small set of clean data. The clean data is used to assess the quality of the labels during the training process [6,17,29], or to train the feature extractors [1], or to estimate the distribution of noisy labels [26]. For example, Li et al. [17] proposed a unified distillation framework using information from a small clean dataset and label relations in knowledge graph, to hedge the risk of learning from noisy labels. Veit et al. [29] comprised a multi-task network that jointly learns to clean the noisy annotations and to classify the images. Azadi et al. [1] selected reliable images by an auxiliary image regularization for deep CNNs with noisy labels. The CNN feature extractor was trained from a set of clean data. Sukhbaatar and Fergus [26] introduced an extra layer into the network to adapt the network outputs to match the noisy label distribution and they estimated the layer's parameters from clean and noisy data.

Other methods do not need a set of clean data but assume extra constrains or distributions on the noisy labels [21], such as proposing losses for randomly flipped labels [24], regularizing the deep networks on corrupted labels by a Metor-Net [13], augmenting the prediction objective with the similarities and improving the learner iteratively using bootstrapping [15], and other approaches that introducing constrains. As a very similar work to the proposed LTNet, Goldberger and Ben-Reuven [9] modeled the noise by a softmax layer that connects the correct labels to the noisy ones. They presented a neural-network approach that optimizes the same likelihood function as optimized by the EM algorithm. LTNet differs from this work, as well as other methods with noisy labels, by that we consider each sample having several annotations rather than one for each. Therefore, we can discover the noise patterns from the multiple anotations.

3   Proposed Method

3.1   IPA2LT Framework

We propose an Inconsistent Pseudo Annotations to Latent Truth (IPA2LT) framework to train a FER model from multiple inconsistently labeled datasets. IPA2LT leverages large scale unlabeled data as well as several human labeled datasets. In IPA2LT, each sample has more than one annotations, including the observed or predicted ones. With the inconsistent pseudo annotations, IPA2LT builds an end-to-end network LTNet to fit the latent truth.

Figure 2 illustrates the 3-step IPA2LT framework. Let us suppose that we are given two human labeled datasets A and B, and the unlabeled data U. Note that the IPA2LT framework is flexible to be adapted to more than two human labeled datasets. As can be seen in the Step 1 in Fig. 2, IPA2LT trains two machine coders (M_A and M_B) from the two datasets A and B, respectively. In Step 2, IPA2LT makes pseudo annotations for both the human labeled and unlabeled data using the predictions by machine coders. Specifically, we predict data A using M_B and thus data A has two sets of labels, i.e., the human annotated one and the M_B-predicted one. Similarly, data B has two sets labels as the human annotated one and the M_A-predicted one. We also estimate two sets of labels for the large scale unlabeled data U using M_A and M_B, respectively. Then, each sample has two labels that are probably inconsistent. In Step 3, IPA2LT trains an end-to-end Latent Truth Net (LTNet) to discover the latent truth considering the inconsistent labels and the input images. A scheme of discovering the latent truth is embedded in LTNet. During the inference, the learned LTNet can be used to estimate the true label for a new face image.

The first two steps can be complemented easily by adopting any classification methods as the machine coders and using them to predict the pseudo labels.

Yet, it is non-trivial to train a model that fits the latent truth provided multiple inconsistent annotations. To achieve this, we propose an end-to-end trainable LTNet that is embedded with a scheme of discovering the latent truths from multiple observed (or predicted) labels and the input images.

3.2 Formulation of LTNet

Inconsistent annotations are caused by the labeling preference bias of different annotators when they are labeling a set of data. Each annotator has a coder-specific bias in assigning the samples to some categories. Mathematically speaking, let $\mathcal{X} = \{\mathbf{x}_i, \ldots, \mathbf{x}_N\}$ denote the data, $\mathbf{y}^c = [y_1^c, \ldots, y_N^c]$ the annotations by coder c. Inconsistent annotations assume that

$$P(y_n^i|\mathbf{x}_n) \neq P(y_n^j|\mathbf{x}_n), \forall \mathbf{x}_n \in \mathcal{X}, i \neq j \tag{1}$$

where $P(y^i|\mathbf{x}_n)$ denotes the probability distribution that coder i annotates sample $\mathbf{x}_n$.

LTNet assumes that each sample $\mathbf{x}_n$ has a latent truth y_n. Without the loss of generality, let us suppose that LTNet classifies $\mathbf{x}_n$ into category i with probability $P(y_n = i|\mathbf{x}_n; \Theta)$, where Θ denotes the network parameters. If $\mathbf{x}_n$ has a ground truth of i, coder c has an opportunity of $\tau_{ij}^c = P(y_n^c = j|y_n = i)$ to annotate $\mathbf{x}_n$ as j, where y_n^c is the annotation of sample $\mathbf{x}_n$ by coder c. Then, the sample $\mathbf{x}_n$ is annotated as label j by coder c with a probability of:

$$P(y_n^c = j|\mathbf{x}_n; \Theta) = \sum_{i=1}^{L} P(y_n^c = j|y_n = i)P(y_n = i|\mathbf{x}_n; \Theta), \tag{2}$$

where L is the number of categories and $\sum_j^L P(y_n^c = j|y_n = i) = \sum_j^L \tau_{ij}^c = 1$.

Given the annotations from C different coders on data $\mathcal{X}$, LTNet aims to maximize the loglikelihood of the observed annotations as:

$$\max_{\Theta, \mathbf{T}^1, \cdots, \mathbf{T}^C} \log\left(P(\mathbf{y}^1, \mathbf{y}^2, \cdots, \mathbf{y}^C|\mathcal{X}; \Theta)\right), \tag{3}$$

where $\mathbf{y}^c = [y_1^c, y_2^c, \cdots, y_N^c]^\top$ is the annotations by coder c on the N samples in $\mathcal{X}$. $\mathbf{T}^c = [\tau_{ij}^c]_{L \times L}$ denotes the transition matrix with rows summed to 1. The loglikelihood is computed as:

$$\log\left(P(\mathbf{y}^1, \cdots, \mathbf{y}^C|\mathcal{X}; \Theta)\right) = \log\left(\prod_{n=1}^{N}\prod_{c=1}^{C} P(y_n^c|\mathbf{x}_n; \Theta)\right)$$

$$= \sum_{n=1}^{N}\sum_{c=1}^{C}\sum_{j=1}^{L} \mathbf{1}(y_n^c = j)\log\left(\tau_{ij}^c P(y_n = i|\mathbf{x}_n; \Theta)\right) \tag{4}$$

where $\mathbf{1}(\cdot)$ is the indicating function. It equals to 1 if the condition in the bracket holds and equals to 0 otherwise.

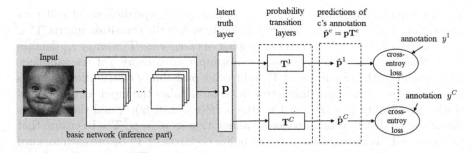

Fig. 3. Architecture of the end-to-end trainable LTNet. Each row of the transition matrix **T** is constrained to be summed to 1.

3.3 Solutions to the Objective Function of LTNet

The objective function (3) aims to find the transition matrics $\mathbf{T}^1, \cdots, \mathbf{T}^c$ and the optimal parameters Θ that are used to compute the latent truths for the input data $\mathcal{X}$.

It is difficult to optimize (3) because it is NP hard. An intuitive approach is to solve (3) in two separate steps: estimate the latent truth using Dawid&Skene's EM algorithm [5] and then train the network with the estimated labels. The EM algorithm alternatively optimizes the latent truth $\{y_n\}_{n=1}^N$ and the transition matrices $\mathbf{T}^c, \forall c \in \{1, \cdots, C\}$ by maximizing:

$$\max_{\{y_n\}_{n=1}^N, \mathbf{T}^1, \cdots, \mathbf{T}^C} \log P(\mathbf{y}^1, \mathbf{y}^2, \cdots, \mathbf{y}^C), \qquad (5)$$

where $P(\mathbf{y}^1, \mathbf{y}^2, \cdots, \mathbf{y}^C) = \prod_{n=1}^N \prod_{c=1}^C \prod_{j=1}^C \left(\tau_{ij}^c P(y_n = i)\right)^{1(y_n^c = j)}$. During the E-step in each iteration of EM algorithm, we fix the transition matrices $\mathbf{T}^c, \forall c \in \{1, \cdots, C\}$ and compute the expectation of latent truth $\{y_n\}_{n=1}^N$. During the M-step, we fix the latent truth $\{y_n\}_{n=1}^N$ and optimize the transition matrices $\mathbf{T}^c, \forall c \in \{1, \cdots, C\}$. After several iterations in EM algorithm, we can have the estimated latent truth for each sample. Then, we train a convolution neural network for FER, whose parameters are Θ, to fit the estimated latent truth.

The 2-step solution estimates the latent truth and learns the classifier parameters separately. It ignores the relations between the input images and the latent truths. The latent truth should also be determined according to the raw images rather than only to the annotations by multiple coders. To this end, we integrate the Dawid&Skene's [5] and the CNN into an end-to-end trainable architecture LTNet.

Figure 3 illustrates the architecture of LTNet. LTNet takes facial images as inputs and estimates the latent truths' probability distribution **p** through a basic deep convolution neural network. Then, rather than minimizing the discrepancy between the estimated truths and the observed labels directly, LTNet predicts each coder's annotation and minimizes the discrepancy between the predicted and observed annotations. Specifically, the estimated truths are passed through a coder-specific probability transition layer to get the predictions of coder c's annotation. Coder c's probability transition layer has the transition matrix $\mathbf{T}^c \in \mathbb{R}^{L \times L}$ as parameters, where L is the number of categories. $\mathbf{T}^c$'s entry τ_{ij}^c denotes the probability that coder c annotates a sample as category j if the sample is with ground truth i. Each row of $\mathbf{T}^c$ indicates a probability distribution and thus is summed to 1. The probability transition layer takes the input as the ground truths' probability $\mathbf{p} = [P(y = 1|\mathbf{x}, \Theta), \cdots, P(y = L|\mathbf{x}, \Theta)]^\top$, and then outputs the predicted distribution of coder c's annotation as $\hat{\mathbf{p}}^c = \mathbf{p}^\top \mathbf{T}^c$. To ensure that each row of $\mathbf{T}^c$ is summed to 1, we normalize each row of $\mathbf{T}^c$ before each forward process. Note that other tricks can be adopted to keep $\mathbf{T}^c$'s rows summed to 1 as well. For example, the probability transition layers can take the row of $\mathbf{T}^c$ as the output of soft-max operation on a L-dimensional vector.

Finally, parameters in LTNet is learned by minimizing the cross-entropy loss of the predicted and observed annotations for each coder as:

$$\min_{\Theta, \{\mathbf{T}^1, \cdots, \mathbf{T}^C\}} \quad -\sum_{n=1}^{N} \sum_{c=1}^{C} \sum_{k=1}^{L} \mathbf{1}(y_n^c = k) \log(\hat{p}_n^c(k)) \tag{6}$$

$$s.t. \quad \sum_{j}^{L} \tau_{ij}^c = 1, \forall i = 1, \ldots, L \tag{7}$$

where N is the number of samples, C is the number of coders, and L is the number of categories. τ_{ij}^c is the element of $\mathbf{T}^c$. y_n^c is the annotation of the n-th sample by coder c. $\hat{\mathbf{p}}_n^c = [\hat{p}_n^c(1), \cdots, \hat{p}_n^c(L)]^\top$ denotes the predicted distribution of coder c's annotation on the n-th sample. Solving (6) is equivalent to solving the objective function (3). LTNet can be optimized by back-propagation methods.

4   Experiments

4.1   Evaluations on Synthetic Inconsistently Labeled Data

Data: The synthetic data was builded from the widely used CIFAR-10 dataset, which contained 60,000 tiny images in 10 categories. In CIFAR-10, 10000 images (1000 image/category) were chosen as the test part and the others were the training part. We synthesized 3 pieces of inconsistent annotations for the training samples by randomly revising 20%, 30%, and 40% of the corrected labels, respectively. The artificial noisy labels were distributed uniformly in different categories. The test set remained clean and was used to evaluate the approaches in our experiments.

Comparison to Other Methods: We compared LTNet with 3 types of methods: (i) basic CNNs trained on a single set of noisy labels; (ii) basic CNNs trained on all the 3 pieces of noisy labels with different label selecting strategy, i.e., simply mixing all the labels or selecting the majority ratings as labels; and (iii) state-of-the-art methods that address inconsistent or noisy labels, i.e., AIR [1], NAL [9], EM+CNN [5,32]. In AIR, we trained a CNN from the mixture of the

Table 1. Test accuracy on CIFAR-10 with noisy labels

Training data	Methods	Test Acc.(%)
clean	*basic CNN*	*87.43*
40% noise (A)	basic CNN	62.50
30% noise (B)	basic CNN	68.70
20% noise (C)	basic CNN	75.15
mixture of ABC	basic CNN	84.04
mixture of ABC	AIR [1]	76.37
mixture of ABC	NAL [9] (re-implementation)	84.41
majority ratings of ABC	basic CNN	82.95
inconsistent annotations	EM+CNN (majority init. [5])	77.65
inconsistent annotations	EM+CNN (spectral init. [32])	78.82
inconsistent annotations	LTNet (proposed)	**87.23**

noisy labels and used the features from the trained CNN to do the afterward L_{12}-norm regularization. In NAL, we regarded the mixture of the three noisy sets as a whole. EM+CNN is similar to the 2-step solution in Sect. 3.3, where we used EM algorithms to estimate the latent truth, and then trained a CNN on the latent truth. In our experiments, we used two ways to initialize the EM algorithm, i.e., majority rating [5] and spectral method [32]. The source code for AIR and EM are downloaded from the authors' website. NAL was re-implemented by ourselves. No other datasets were used to pre-train or initialize the models in all of the experiments.

The test accuracy of all the methods are shown in Table 1. We also report the test accuracy of the basic CNN trained on clean data. As can be seen in Table 1, whichever methods are used, using all the inconsistently labeled sets boosts the performance of the models using a single noisy set. Because the multiple annotations, although being inconsistent, convey more correct information than a single set of noisy labels.

Within the methods trained on mixture data, we observe that the end-to-end methods (e.g., basic CNN on mixture data or majority ratings, NAL, LTNet) are significantly better than the step-by-step methods (e.g., AIR, EM+CNN). A viable explanation is that the end-to-end methods can intrinsically capture the relations between the input image and inconsistent labels. But the step-by-step methods separately capture the relations between the input images and the estimated labels, and the relations between the latent truths and inconsistent labels. Among all the end-to-end methods, the proposed LTNet achieves the highest test accuracy and has a comparable performance to the CNN trained from clean data.

To further investigate the methods, we plot the test accuracy curve during the training iterations in Fig. 4(a). The x-axis is the iteration number during the training process. As can be seen, the test accuracy curves of LTNet, CNN (clean

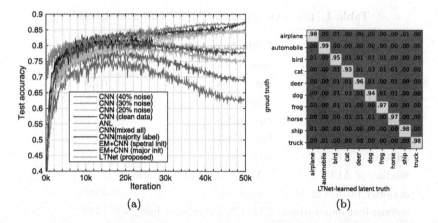

(a)   (b)

Fig. 4. (a) Test accuracy curve of different methods during the training process. (b) Confusion matrix between the true labels and LTNet-learned latent truths. The LTNet is trained from the mixture of data with 20%, 30%, and 40% noises.

data), CNN (mixed all), and ANL keep increasing during the training, while those of CNN (with 40%, 30%, or 20% noisy labels) and EM+CNN (spectral or major init) reach a peak value and then decrease as the training iterates. Because the latter methods are unable to distinguish the incorrect label information from the noisy labels or estimated ground truth. That is also why the latter methods have lower test accuracy than the former methods in Table 1.

Latent Truth Learning: To investigate that if LTNet can discover the latent truth given multiple inconsistent labels, we illustrate the confusion matrix between the ground truth labels and the LTNet-learned latent truth in Fig. 4(b). As can be seen, the diagonal values are larger than 0.9 and most of them are larger than 0.95. The average agreement between the true labels and LTNet-learned latent truth is 0.964. Note that the LTNet was trained on the images with three sets of noisy labels. The noise percentages are 20%, 30%, and 40%, respectively. The average agreement between the ground truth and the three noisy labels is 0.7. If we plot confusion matrix between the true labels and the three noisy labels, the diagonal values should be about 0.8, 0.7, and 0.6 respectively. The high agreement between the ground truth and LTNet-learned latent truth indicates that LTNet is competent in discovering the latent truth from several inconsistent and noisy labels.

4.2 Evaluations on Facial Expression Datasets

To validate the effectiveness of the proposed method in the real-world FER application, we first compared it with the state-of-the-art methods. Since errors and bias exist in the annotations of different FER datasets, we adopted a rigorous cross-dataset evaluation protocol and evaluated the methods by their average performance on 7 different datasets covering both in-the-wild and in-the-lab (posed) facial expression. Then, we analyzed the inconsistent labels in FER datasets using the proposed method.

Data: Both human annotated data and unlabeled data were used in the experiments. The annotated data includes three FER datasets in-the-wild (RAF [16], AffectNet [22], and SFEW [7]) and four in-the-lab ones (CK+[20], CFEE [8], MMI [28], and Oulu-CASIA [33]).

The in-the-wild datasets contain facial expression in real world with various poses, illuminations, intensities, and other uncontrolled conditions. Both RAF and AffectNet have images downloaded from the web search engines. **RAF** [16] contains 12,271 training samples and 3,068 test samples annotated with six basic emotional categories (anger, disgust, fear, happy, sad, surprise) and neutral. Images in RAF were labeled by 315 human coders and the final annotations were determined through the crowdsourcing techniques. **AffectNet** [22] contains around 400,000 annotated images and each image is labeled by only one human coder. It includes 5,000 labeled images in 10 categories as the validation set. We selected around 280,000 images as training samples and 3,500 images as validation ones with neutral and six basic emotions. **SFEW** [7] contains images from movies annotated with neutral or one of the six basic emotions. It has 879 training samples and 406 validation samples.

The in-the-lab datasets record the facial expression in controlled environment and they usually contain posed expression. **CK+**[20] contains 593 sequences from 123 subjects, of which only 327 are annotated with 7 emotion labels (six basic emotions and contempt). We only used the ones with basic emotion labels and select the first frame of each sequence as neutral face and the last peak frame as the emotional face. Hence, 636 images were selected in total. **CFEE** [8] contains 230 subjects with 22 images each. For each subject, we selected 7 images with the six basic emotions and the neutral face. **MMI** [28] contains 30 subjects with 213 videos. For each video, we selected the first 2 images as neutral faces and the middle one third part as emotional faces. **Oulu-CASIA** [33] contains 80 subjects with 480 videos. We also selected the first 2 images as neutral faces and the last two fifth part as emotional faces.

The unlabeled data consists of the un-annotated part of AffectNet (around 700,000 images) and a collection of unlabeled facial images downloaded from Bing (around 500,000 images).

Experiment Settings: To evaluate the methods' generalization ability on data under the unseen condition, cross-dataset evaluation protocol was applied for SFEW, CK+, CFEE, MMI, and Oulu-CASIA datasets. In other words, only the training part of AffectNet (AffTr) and RAF (RAFTr) datasets and the unlabeled data were utilized to learn the models.

In our experiments, we adopted a 80-layer Residual Network [10] as the basic network. In the proposed IPA2LT framework, we first trained two basic models M_A and M_R from AffTr and RAFTr, respectively. Then, we used M_A to predict on RAFTr as well as the unlabeled data. Similarly, we assigned another set of annotations for AffTr and unlabeled data using M_R. The estimated annotations and the human annotations constituted the inconsistent labels, from which we

Table 2. Test accuracy (%) of different methods on different test sets with both the in-the-wild and in-the-lab facial expressions. (**Bold**: best. <u>Underline</u>: second best.)

Methods	Test sets									
	in-the-wild			Posed				Average		
	RAF (te.)	AffectNet (val.)	SFEW (tr+val)	CK+	CFEE	MMI	Oulu-CASIA	wild	posed	overall
AffTr (base)	79.50	56.51	55.64	91.04	**76.09**	**65.32**	61.49	63.88	<u>73.48</u>	69.37
RAFTr (base)	85.10	44.66	51.75	79.87	64.41	58.17	52.50	60.50	63.74	62.35
AffTr+RAFTr (base)	83.28	<u>56.57</u>	56.58	**92.45**	76.09	62.90	60.50	65.48	72.99	69.77
E2E-FC	23.99	24.00	22.33	51.73	26.52	22.25	31.28	23.44	32.95	28.87
AIR [1]	67.37	54.23	49.88	43.87	64.47	59.64	47.03	57.16	53.75	55.21
NAL [9]	84.22	55.97	**58.13**	91.20	75.84	64.71	61.00	**66.11**	73.19	<u>70.15</u>
IPA2LT (EM [5]+CNN)	<u>85.30</u>	**57.31**	54.94	86.64	72.48	63.11	59.95	65.85	70.54	68.53
IPA2LT (LTNet)	**86.77**	55.11	**58.29**	<u>91.67</u>	<u>76.02</u>	<u>65.61</u>	<u>61.02</u>	**66.72**	**73.58**	**70.64**

trained the LTNet. Parameters in LTNet arc initialized by pre-training them on the union the dataset AffTr and RAFTr. The transition layer is initialized by a close-to-identity-matrix. It is computed by adding an identity matrix and a random matrix with each entry positive. Then, each row of the initial matrix is normalized to have a sum 1. We do not initialize the probability transition matrix by the identity matrix because the identity matrix has all the non-diagonal entries as 0, which will not be updated during the training process.

The proposed LTNet was implemented under the framework of Caffe [12]. Stochastic gradient decent method was used to optimize the parameters. The momentum was 0.9 and the weight decay was 0.0005. The learning rate was initialized as 0.00001 and decreased with "poly" policy. Parameters γ and power for the learning rate policy was 0.1 and 0.5. The max iteration was set as 300,000.

Comparison with the State-of-the-Art: We compared the proposed method with models trained from either or both of AffTr and RAFTr, and the state-of-the-art methods addressing noisy or inconsistent labels. Table 2 presents the test accuracy of the methods on different test datasets.

When compared to the models that are directly trained from either or both of AffTr and RAFTr, the proposed IPA2LT framework with LTNet, denoted as IPA2LT (LTNet), achieves the highest average test accuracy on in-the-wild, posed, and the overall facial expressions datasets. The consistent improvements indicate that the proposed methods cut the edge by exploring the inconsistent labels in an end-to-end training manner.

In E2E-FC, we replaced the probability transition layers in Fig. 3 with a fully connected layer that are category general but coder specific. The performance of E2E-FC is low because the probability distribution constrain is very crucial in LTNet. With the probability distribution constrain, the last second layer in LTNet can be interpreted as the hidden truth by a probability distribution.

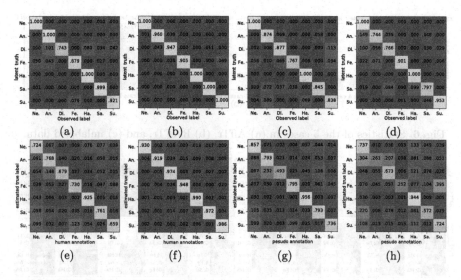

Fig. 5. The LTNet-learned transition matrices (top row) and the confusion matrices counted from the estimated truth and human/predicted annotations (bottom row). The top row shows transition matrices for coder (a) AffectNet, (b) RAF, (c) AffectNet-trained model, and (d) RAF-trained model. The bottom row shows statistics on dataset (e) AffectNet, (f) RAF, (g) Unlabeled data annotated by AffectNet-trained model, and (h) Unlabeled data annotated by RAF-trained model.

However, without the constrain, the outputs of the last second layer of E2E-FC are not essentially the reflections of the hidden truth.

AIR [1] and NAL [9] are methods that address noisy labels. In the experiments of AIR and NAL, we considered the union of AffTr and RAFTr with their human annotations as a set of noisy training data. As can be seen in Table 2, both AIR and NAL have lower test accuracy than IPA2LT (LTNet). Because AIR and NAL did not consider the annotation bias of different annotators.

We also investigated the two solutions to discover the latent truth by comparing IPA2LT (EM+CNN) and IPA2LT (LTNet). For IPA2LT(EM+CNN), we used the 2-step solution in Sect. 3.3 to estimate the latent truth. Results in Table 2 show that LTNet outperforms EM+CNN, because EM+CNN estimates the latent truth and trains the network separately, ignoring the relations between the input facial images and the given inconsistent labels.

Analysis of the Inconsistent Labels in FER: To investigate whether the LTNet has learned a reasonable latent truth, we analyzed the inconsistent labels by plotting the LTNet-learned transition matrices and the confusion matrices computed from the estimated truth and the observed annotations in Fig. 5. The top row shows the transition matrices for different coders. The bottom row shows the confusion matrices computed from different datasets. Although the LTNet-learned transition matrices have larger diagonal values than the confusion matrices from statistics, the two rows of matrices have similar patterns. Both

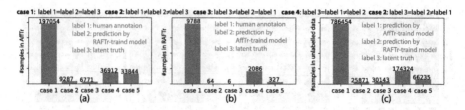

Fig. 6. Statistics of the 5 cases in (a) AffTr, (b) RAFTr, and (c) unlabeled data.

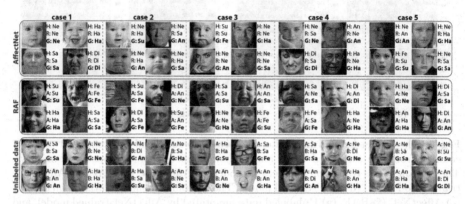

Fig. 7. Examples from the 5 cases in AffectNet, RAF, and the unlabeled data. (H: human annotation, A: prediction by AffTr-trained model, R: prediction by RAFTr-trained model, G: LTNet-learned truth. Ne: neutral, An: anger, Di: disgust, Fe: fear, Ha: happy, Sa: sad, and Su: surprise.)

the transition matrix and confusion matrix with RAF dataset have the closest to 1 diagonal values. It means that the human annotations of RAF are the most reliable. That is reasonable because RAF determines a label from tens of human coders while AffectNet has only one coder each image and the unlabeled data is labeled by the trained models. We can also see from Fig. 5(c), (d), (g), and (h) that annotations by the trained models are the least reliable.

We counted the images that have consistent and inconsistent annotations in AffTr, RAFTr, and the unlabeled data. Figure 6 plots the statistics of samples in different cases. Case 1 contains samples with consistent human annotation, latent truth, and model-predicted labels. In Case 2, all the three annotations are different from each other. In Case 3, the latent truth differs from the other two while the other two are the same. In Case 4 and 5, the latent truth agrees with one but differs from the other. Majority of the samples have consistent labels and very few of them have a latent truth that differs from both the other two labels. As can be seen from Fig. 6(c) that the latent truth agrees more with the predictions from the AffTr-trained model, because AffTr contains much more samples than RAFTr and leads to a more robust FER model. Figure 7 shows some samples from the 5 cases in the three datasets. As can be seen, the estimated truth is reasonable whatever the other two labels are.

5 Conclusions

This paper proposed a IPA2LT framework to solve a relatively unexplored problem, i.e., how to learn a classifier from more than one datasets with inconsistent labels. To our knowledge, it is the first work to address the annotation inconsistency in different facial expression datasets. In the IPA2LT framework, we proposed an end-to-end trainable network LTNet embedded with a scheme of discovering the latent truth from multiple inconsistent labels and the input images. Experiments on both the synthetic and real data validate the effectiveness and advantages of the proposed method over other state-of-the-art methods that deal with noisy or inconsistent labels.

Acknowledgement. We gratefully acknowledge the supports from National Key R&D Program of China (grant 2017YFA0700800), National Natural Science Foundation of China (grant 61702481), and External Cooperation Program of CAS (grant GJHZ1843).

References

1. Azadi, S., Feng, J., Jegelka, S., Darrell, T.: Auxiliary image regularization for deep cnns with noisy labels. In: ICLR (2016)
2. Benitez-Quiroz, C.F., Srinivasan, R., Martinez, A.M., et al.: Emotionet: an accurate, real-time algorithm for the automatic annotation of a million facial expressions in the wild. In: CVPR, pp. 5562–5570 (2016)
3. Chen, X., Lin, Q., Zhou, D.: Optimistic knowledge gradient policy for optimal budget allocation in crowdsourcing. In: ICML, pp. 64–72 (2013)
4. Chu, W.S., De la Torre, F., Cohn, J.F.: Selective transfer machine for personalized facial expression analysis. IEEE Trans. Pattern Anal. Mach. Intell. **39**(3), 529–545 (2017)
5. Dawid, A.P., Skene, A.M.: Maximum likelihood estimation of observer error-rates using the EM algorithm. Appl. Stat., 20–28 (1979)
6. Dehghani, M., Severyn, A., Rothe, S., Kamps, J.: Avoiding your teacher's mistakes: training neural networks with controlled weak supervision. arXiv preprint arXiv:1711.00313 (2017)
7. Dhall, A., Goecke, R., Lucey, S., Gedeon, T.: Static facial expression analysis in tough conditions: Data, evaluation protocol and benchmark. In: ICCV Workshops, pp. 2106–2112 (2011)
8. Du, S., Tao, Y., Martinez, A.M.: Compound facial expressions of emotion. Proc. Nat. Acad. Sci. **111**(15), E1454–E1462 (2014)
9. Goldberger, J., Ben-Reuven, E.: Training deep neuralnetworks using a noise adaptation layer. In: ICLR (2017)
10. He, K., Zhang, X., Ren, S., Sun, J.: Deep residual learning for image recognition. In: CVPR, pp. 770–778 (2016)
11. Hu, N., Englebienne, G., Lou, Z.: Kr02se, B.: Learning to recognize human activities using soft labels. IEEE Trans. Pattern Anal. Mach. Intell. **39**(10), 1973–1984 (2017)
12. Jia, Y., et al.: Caffe: convolutional architecture for fast feature embedding. arXiv preprint arXiv:1408.5093 (2014)

13. Jiang, L., Zhou, Z., Leung, T., Li, L.J., Fei-Fei, L.: Mentornet: regularizing very deep neural networks on corrupted labels. arXiv preprint arXiv:1712.05055 (2017)
14. Jung, H., Lee, S., Yim, J., Park, S., Kim, J.: Joint fine-tuning in deep neural networks for facial expression recognition. In: ICCV, pp. 2983–2991 (2015)
15. Reed, S.: Training deep neural networks on noisy labels with bootstrapping. In: ICLR Workshops, pp. 1–11 (2015)
16. Li, S., Deng, W., Du, J.: Reliable crowdsourcing and deep locality-preserving learning for expression recognition in the wild. In: CVPR, pp. 2584–2593 (2017)
17. Li, Y., et al.: Learning from noisy labels with distillation. In: CVPR, pp. 1910–1918 (2017)
18. Liu, P., Han, S., Meng, Z., Tong, Y.: Facial expression recognition via a boosted deep belief network. In: CVPR, pp. 1805–1812 (2014)
19. Liu, Q., Peng, J., Ihler, A.T.: Variational inference for crowdsourcing. In: NIPS, pp. 692–700 (2012)
20. Lucey, P., et al.: The extended cohn-kanade dataset (ck+): a complete dataset for action unit and emotion-specified expression. In: CVPR Workshops (2010)
21. Mnih, V., Hinton, G.E.: Learning to label aerial images from noisy data. In: ICML, pp. 567–574 (2012)
22. Mollahosseini, A., Hasani, B., Mahoor, M.H.: Affectnet: A database for facial expression, valence, and arousal computing in the wild. IEEE Trans. Affect. Comput. **PP**(99), 1 (2017)
23. Moreno, P.G., Artés-Rodríguez, A., Teh, Y.W., Perez-Cruz, F.: Bayesian nonparametric crowdsourcing. J. Mach. Learn. Res. (2015)
24. Natarajan, N., Dhillon, I.S., Ravikumar, P.K., Tewari, A.: Learning with noisy labels. In: NIPS, pp. 1196–1204 (2013)
25. Pantic, M.: Facial expression recognition. In: Encyclopedia of biometrics, pp. 400–406. Springer (2009)
26. Sukhbaatar, S., Fergus, R.: Learning from noisy labels with deep neural networks. arXiv preprint arXiv:1406.2080 (2014)
27. Tian, Y., Kanade, T., Cohn, J.F.: Facial expression recognition. In: Handbook of Face Recognition, pp. 487–519. Springer, London (2011). https://doi.org/10.1007/978-0-85729-932-1_19
28. Valstar, M.F., Pantic, M.: Induced disgust, happiness and surprise: an addition to the MMI facial expression database. In: International Conference on Language Resources and Evaluation, Workshop on EMOTION, pp. 65–70 (2010)
29. Veit, A., Alldrin, N., Chechik, G., Krasin, I., Gupta, A., Belongie, S.: Learning from noisy large-scale datasets with minimal supervision. In: CVPR (2017)
30. Zeng, Z., Pantic, M., Roisman, G.I., Huang, T.S.: A survey of affect recognition methods: audio, visual, and spontaneous expressions. IEEE Trans. Pattern Anal. Mach. Intell. **31**(1), 39–58 (2009)
31. Zhang, P., Obradovic, Z.: Learning from inconsistent and unreliable annotators by a Gaussian mixture model and bayesian information criterion. In: Joint European Conference on Machine Learning and Knowledge Discovery in Databases, pp. 553–568 (2011)
32. Zhang, Y., Chen, X., Zhou, D., Jordan, M.I.: Spectral methods meet em: a provably optimal algorithm for crowdsourcing. J. Mach. Learn. Res. **17**(1), 3537–3580 (2016)
33. Zhao, G., Huang, X., Taini, M., Li, S.Z., Pietikäinen, M.: Facial expression recognition from near-infrared videos. Image Vis. Comput. **29**(9), 607–619 (2011)
34. Zhao, X., et al.: Peak-piloted deep network for facial expression recognition. In: Leibe, B., Matas, J., Sebe, N., Welling, M. (eds.) ECCV 2016. LNCS, vol. 9906, pp. 425–442. Springer, Cham (2016). https://doi.org/10.1007/978-3-319-46475-6_27

35. Zheng, Y., Li, G., Li, Y., Shan, C., Cheng, R.: Truth inference in crowdsourcing: Is the problem solved? Proc. VLDB Endow. **10**(5), 541–552 (2017)
36. Zhou, D., Liu, Q., Platt, J., Meek, C.: Aggregating ordinal labels from crowds by minimax conditional entropy. In: ICML, pp. 262–270 (2014)

Stroke Controllable Fast Style Transfer with Adaptive Receptive Fields

Yongcheng Jing[1,2], Yang Liu[1,2], Yezhou Yang[3], Zunlei Feng[1,2], Yizhou Yu[4],
Dacheng Tao[5], and Mingli Song[1,2(✉)]

[1] College of Computer Science and Technology, Zhejiang University,
Hangzhou, China
brooksong@zju.edu.cn
[2] Alibaba-Zhejiang University Joint Institute of Frontier Technologies,
Hangzhou, China
[3] Arizona State University, Tempe, USA
[4] Deepwise AI Lab, Beijing, China
[5] UBTECH Sydney AI Centre, SIT, FEIT, University of Sydney, Sydney, Australia

Abstract. The Fast Style Transfer methods have been recently proposed to transfer a photograph to an artistic style in real-time. This task involves controlling the stroke size in the stylized results, which remains an open challenge. In this paper, we present a stroke controllable style transfer network that can achieve continuous and spatial stroke size control. By analyzing the factors that influence the stroke size, we propose to explicitly account for the receptive field and the style image scales. We propose a StrokePyramid module to endow the network with adaptive receptive fields, and two training strategies to achieve faster convergence and augment new stroke sizes upon a trained model respectively. By combining the proposed runtime control strategies, our network can achieve continuous changes in stroke sizes and produce distinct stroke sizes in different spatial regions within the same output image.

Keywords: Neural Style Transfer · Adaptive receptive fields

1 Introduction

Rendering a photograph with a given artwork style has been a long-standing research topic [15,17,31,33]. Conventionally, the task of style transfer is usually studied as a generalization of texture synthesis [8,9,11]. Based on the recent progress in visual texture modelling [12], Gatys *et al.* firstly propose an algorithm

Project page: http://yongchengjing.com/StrokeControllable

Electronic supplementary material The online version of this chapter (https://doi.org/10.1007/978-3-030-01261-8_15) contains supplementary material, which is available to authorized users.

V. Ferrari et al. (Eds.): ECCV 2018, LNCS 11217, pp. 244–260, 2018.
https://doi.org/10.1007/978-3-030-01261-8_15

(a) Content&Style (b) Stroke Size #1 (c) Stroke Size #2 (d) Stroke Size #3 (e) Mixed Strokes

Fig. 1. Stylized results with different stroke sizes. All these results are produced by one single model in real-time using our proposed algorithm.

that exploits Convolutional Neural Network (CNN) to recombine the content of a given photograph and the style of an artwork, and reconstruct a visually plausible stylized image, known as the process of Neural Style Transfer [13]. Since the seminal work of Gatys *et al.*, Neural Style Transfer has been attracting wide attention from both academia and industry [1,3,23,25,30]. However, the algorithm of Gatys *et al.* is based on iterative image optimizations and leads to a slow optimization process for each pair of content and style. To tackle this issue, several algorithms have been proposed to speed up the style transfer process, called the Fast Style Transfer in the literature [14,29].

The current Fast Style Transfer approaches can be categorized into three classes, Per-Style-Per-Model (PSPM) [19,24,34,35], Multiple-Style-Per-Model (MSPM) [2,7,26,39], and Arbitrary-Style-Per-Model (ASPM) [18,27]. The gist of PSPM is to train a feed-forward style-specific generator and to produce a corresponding stylized result with a forward pass. MSPM improves the efficiency by further incorporating multiple styles into one single generator. ASPM aims at transferring an arbitrary style through only one single model.

There is a trade-off between efficiency and quality for all such Fast Style Transfer algorithms [18,27]. In terms of quality, PSPM is usually regarded to produce more appealing stylized results [18,35]. However, PSPM is not flexible in terms of controlling perceptual factors (*e.g.*, style-content tradeoff, color control, spatial control). Among these perceptual factors, strokes are one of the most important geometric primitives to characterize an artwork, as shown in Fig. 1. In reality, for the same texture, different artists have their own way to place different sizes of strokes as a reflection of their unique "styles" (*e.g.*, Monet and Pollock). To achieve different stroke sizes with PSPM, one possible solution is to train multiple models, which is time and space consuming. Another solution is to resize the input image to different scales, which will inevitably hurt the quality of stylization. None of these solutions, however, can achieve continuous stroke size control or produce distinct stroke sizes in different spatial regions without trading off quality and efficiency.

In this paper, we propose a stroke controllable Fast Style Transfer algorithm that can incorporate multiple stroke sizes into one single model and achieves flexible continuous stroke size control and spatial stroke size control. By analyzing the factors that influence the stroke size in stylized results, we propose to explicitly account for both the receptive field and the style image scale. To this end, we propose a *StrokePyramid* module to endow the network with adaptive receptive fields and different stroke sizes are learned with different receptive fields. We then introduce a progressive training strategy to make the network converge faster and an incremental training strategy to learn new stroke sizes upon a trained model. By combining two proposed runtime control techniques which are continuous stroke size control and spatial stroke size control, our network can produce distinct stroke sizes in different outputs or different spatial regions within the same output image.

In summary, our work has three primary contributions: (1) We analyze the factors that influence the stroke size in stylized results, and propose that both the receptive field and the style image scale should be considered for stroke size control in most cases. (2) We propose a stroke controllable style transfer network and two corresponding training strategies in order to achieve faster convergence and augment new stroke sizes upon a trained model respectively. (3) We present two runtime control strategies to empower our single model with the ability of producing continuous changes in stroke size and distinct stroke sizes in different spatial regions within the same output image. To the best of our knowledge, this is the first style transfer network that achieves continuous stroke size control and spatial stroke size control.

2   Related Work

We briefly review here perceptual factors in Fast Style Transfer as well as the involving regulating receptive field in neural networks.

Controlling Perceptual Factors in Fast Style Transfer. Stroke size control belongs to the domain of controlling perceptual factors during stylization. In this field, several significant works are recently presented. However, there are few efforts devoted to controlling stroke size during Fast Style Transfer. In [14], Gatys *et al.* study the color control and spatial control for Fast Style Transfer. Lu *et al.* further extend Gatys *et al.*'s work to meaningful spatial control by incorporating semantic content, achieving the so-called Fast Semantic Style Transfer [29]. Another related work is Wang *et al.*'s algorithm which aims to learn large brush strokes for high-resolution images [36]. They find that current Fast Style Transfer algorithms fail to paint large strokes in high-resolution images and propose a coarse-to-fine architecture to solve this problem. Note that the work in [36] is intrinsically different from this paper as one single pre-trained model in [36] still produces one stroke size for the same input image. A concurrent work in [39] also explores the issue of stroke size control. Compared with [39], our work has the benefits of flexible continuous and spatial stroke size control.

Regulating Receptive Field in Neural Networks. The receptive field is one of the basic concepts in convolutional neural networks, which refers to a region of the input image that one neuron is responsive to. It can affect the performance of the networks and becomes a critical issue in many tasks (*e.g.*,

Content & Style   LRF Result   SRF Result   Content & Style   LRF Result   SRF Result

Fig. 2. Results of learning the same size of large strokes with large and small receptive fields, respectively. LRF represents the result produced with a large receptive field and SRF represents the result produced with a small receptive field. Content images are credited to flickr users *Kevin Robson* and *b togol.*

semantic segmentation [40], image parsing). To regulate the receptive field, [38] proposes the operation of dilated convolution (also called atrous convolution in [4]), which supports the expansion of receptive field by setting different dilation values and is widely used in many generation tasks like [10,16]. Another work in [5] further proposes a deformable convolution which augments the sampling locations in regular convolution with additional offsets. Furthermore, Wei *et al.* [37] propose a learning-based receptive field regulating method which is to inflate or shrink feature maps automatically.

3   Pre-analysis

We start by reviewing the concept of the stroke size. Consider an image in style transfer as a composition of a series of small stroke textons, which are referred as the fundamental geometric micro-structures in images [20,41]. The stroke size of an image can be defined as the average scale of the composed stroke textons.

In the deep neural network based Fast Style Transfer, three factors are found to influence the stroke size, namely the scale of the style image [36], the receptive field in the loss network [14], and the receptive field in the generative network.

The objective style is usually learned by matching the style image's gram-based statistics [13] in style transfer algorithms, which are computed over the feature maps from the pre-trained VGG network [32]. These gram-based statistics are scale-sensitive, *i.e.*, they contain the scale information of the given style image. One reason for this characteristic is that the VGG features vary with the image scale. We also find that for other style statistics (*e.g.*, BN-based statistics in [25]), it reaches the same conclusion. Therefore, given the same content image, generative networks trained with different scales of the style image can produce different stroke sizes.

Although the stroke in stylized results usually becomes larger with the increase of the style image scale, this is infeasible when the style image is scaled to a high resolution (*e.g.*, 3000 × 3000 pixels [14]). The reason for this problem is that a neuron in pre-trained VGG loss network can only affect a region with the receptive field size in the input image. When the stroke texton is much larger than the fixed receptive field in VGG loss network, there is no visual difference between a large and larger stroke texton in a relatively small region.

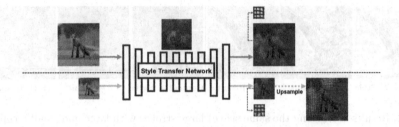

Fig. 3. The feed-forward process of Fast Style Transfer. For the same size of regions in the outputs of both small and large input images respectively, their stroke sizes are almost the same. The content image is credited to flickr user *BillChenSF*.

Apart from these above two factors, we further find that the receptive field size in the generative network also has influence on the stroke size. In Fig. 2, we change the receptive field size in the generative network and other factors remain the same. It is noticeable that a larger stroke size is produced with a larger receptive field for some styles. To explain this result, we interpret the training process of the generative network as teaching the convolutional kernels to paint a pre-defined size of stroke textons in each region with the size of receptive field. Therefore, given two different sizes of input images, the kernels of a trained network paint almost the same size of stroke textons in the same size of regions, as shown in Fig. 3. In particular, when the receptive field in a generative network is smaller than the stroke texton, the kernels can only learn to paint a part of the whole stroke texton in each region, which influences the stroke size. Hence, for a large stroke size, the network needs larger receptive fields to learn the global stroke configuration. For a small stroke size, the network only needs to learn local features.

To sum up, both the scale of the style image and the receptive field in the generative network should generally be considered for stroke size control. As the style image is not high-resolution in most cases, the influence of the receptive field in the loss network is not considered in this work.

4   Proposed Approach

4.1   Problem Formulation

Assume that $\mathcal{T}_i \in \mathbb{T}$ denotes the stroke size of an image, $\mathbb{T}$ denotes the set of all stroke sizes, and $I^{\mathcal{T}_i}$ represents an image I with the stroke size $\mathcal{T}_i$. The problem studied in this paper is to incorporate different stroke sizes $\mathcal{T}_i \in \mathbb{T}$ into the feed-forward fast neural style transfer model. Firstly, we formulate the feed-forward stylization process as:

$$g(I_c) = I_o, \quad I_o \sim p(I_o | I_c, I_s), \tag{1}$$

where g is the trained generator. And the target statistic $p(I_o)$ of the output image I_o is characterized by two components, which are the semantic content

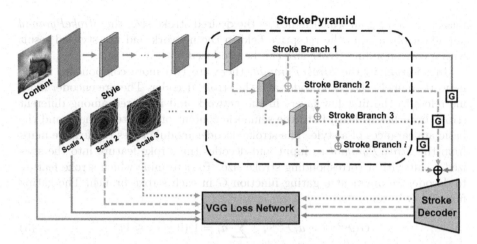

Fig. 4. An overview of our network architecture with the *StrokePyramid*. It consists of several stroke branches with gating functions. Each stroke branch corresponds to a specific stroke size.

statistics derived from the input image I_c, and the visual style statistics derived from the style image I_s.

Our feed-forward style transfer process for producing multiple stroke sizes can then be modeled as:

$$g'(I_c, \mathcal{T}_i) = I_o^{\mathcal{T}_i}, \quad I_o^{\mathcal{T}_i} \sim p(I_o^{\mathcal{T}_i}|I_c, I_s, \mathcal{T}_i) \; (\mathcal{T}_i \in \mathbb{T}). \tag{2}$$

We aim to enable one single generator g' to produce stylized results with multiple stroke sizes $\mathcal{T}_i \in \mathbb{T}$ for the same content image I_c.

4.2   Network Architecture

Based on the analysis in Sect. 3, to incorporate different stroke sizes into one single model, we propose to design a network with adaptive receptive fields and each receptive field is used to learn a corresponding size of stroke. The network architecture of our proposed approach is depicted in Fig. 4.

Our network consists of three components. At the core of our network, a *StrokePyramid* module is proposed to decompose the network into several stroke branches. Each branch has a larger receptive field than the previous branch through progressively growing convolutional filters. In this way, our network also encourages *stroke consistency* (which refers to the consistency of stroke orientation, configuration, *etc.*) between adjacent stroke size control results which should differ only in stroke sizes. By handling different stroke branches, the *StrokePyramid* can regulate the receptive field in the generative network. With different receptive fields, the network learns to paint strokes with different sizes. In particular, to better preserve the desired size of strokes, larger strokes are learned with larger receptive fields, as explained in Sect. 3. During the testing phase, given a signal which indicates the desired stroke size, the *StrokePyramid* automatically adapts the receptive field in the network and the stylized result with a corresponding stroke size can be produced.

In addition to the *StrokePyramid*, there are two more components in the network, namely the pre-encoder and the stroke decoder. The pre-encoder module refers to the first few layers in the network and is shared among different stroke branches to learn both the semantic content of a content image and the basic appearances of a style. The stroke decoder module takes the feature maps from the *StrokePyramid* as input and decodes the stroke feature into the stylized result with a corresponding stroke size. To determine which stroke feature to decode, we augment a gating function G in each stroke branch. The gating function G is defined as

$$G(\mathcal{F}^{\mathcal{B}_{s_i}}) = a_i \mathcal{F}^{\mathcal{B}_{s_i}}, \quad \sum_i a_i = 1 \ (0 \le a_i \le 1), \tag{3}$$

where $\mathcal{F}^{\mathcal{B}_{s_i}}$ is the output feature map of the branch $\mathcal{B}_{s_i}$ in the *StrokePyramid*, which corresponds to the stroke size $\mathcal{T}_i$. For the selection of a, at the training stage, a_i is binary. More specifically, $a_i = 1$ when $i = k$ (*i.e.*, the selected stroke branch to be trained is $\mathcal{B}_{s_k}$). Otherwise, $a_i = 0$ when $i \ne k$. At the testing stage, a_i can be fractional, which is the basis of our continuous stroke size control.

All the stroke features from the *StrokePyramid* need to go through the gating function and then be fed into the stroke decoder Dec to be decoded into the output result $I_o^{\mathcal{T}_k}$ with the desired stroke size:

$$Dec(\sum_i G(\mathcal{F}^{\mathcal{B}_{s_i}})) = I_o^{\mathcal{T}_k}. \tag{4}$$

4.3   Loss Function

Semantic Loss. The semantic loss is defined to preserve the semantic information in the content image, which is formulated as the Euclidean distance between the content image I_c and the output stylized image I_o in the feature space of the VGG network [13].

Assume that $\mathcal{F}^l(I) \in \mathbb{R}^{C \times H \times W}$ represents the feature map at layer l in VGG network with a given image I, where C, H and W denote the number of channels, the height and width of the feature map respectively. The semantic content loss is then defined as:

$$\mathcal{L}_c = \sum_{l \in \{l_c\}} \|\mathcal{F}^l(I_c) - \mathcal{F}^l(I_o)\|^2, \tag{5}$$

where $\{l_c\}$ represents the set of VGG layers used to compute the content loss.

Stroke Loss. The visual style statistics can be well represented by the correlations between filter responses of the style image I_s in different layers of pre-trained VGG network. These feature correlations can be obtained by computing the Gram matrix over the feature map at a certain layer in VGG network. As the gram-based statistic is scale-sensitive, representations of different stroke sizes can be obtained by simply resizing the given style image.

By reshaping $\mathcal{F}^l(I)$ into $\mathcal{F}^l(I)' \in \mathbb{R}^{C \times (H \times W)}$, the Gram matrix $\mathcal{G}(\mathcal{F}^l(I)') \in \mathbb{R}^{C \times C}$ over feature map $\mathcal{F}^l(I)'$ can be computed as:

$$\mathcal{G}(\mathcal{F}^l(I_s)') = [\mathcal{F}^l(I_s)'][\mathcal{F}^l(I_s)']^T. \tag{6}$$

The stroke loss for size $\mathcal{T}_k$ can be therefore defined as:

$$\mathcal{L}_{\mathcal{T}_k} = \sum_{l \in \{l_s\}} \|\mathcal{G}(\mathcal{F}^l(\mathcal{R}(I_s, \mathcal{T}_k))') - \mathcal{G}(\mathcal{F}^l(I_o^{\mathcal{B}_{s_k}})')\|^2, \tag{7}$$

where $\mathcal{R}$ represents the function that resizes the style image to an appropriate scale according to the desired stroke size $\mathcal{T}_k$, and $I_o^{\mathcal{B}_{s_k}}$ represents the output of the k-th stroke branch. $\{l_s\}$ is the set of VGG layers used for style loss.

The total loss for stroke branch $\mathcal{B}_{s_k}$ is then written as:

$$\mathcal{L}_{\mathcal{B}_{s_k}} = \alpha \mathcal{L}_c + \beta_k \mathcal{L}_{\mathcal{T}_k} + \gamma \mathcal{L}_{tv}, \tag{8}$$

where α, β and γ are balancing factors. $\mathcal{L}_{tv}$ is a total variation regularization loss to encourage smoothness in the generated images.

4.4 Training Strategies

Progressive Training. To train different stroke branches in one single network, we propose a progressive training strategy. This training strategy stems from the intuition that the training of the latter stroke branch benefits from the knowledge of the previously learned branches. Taken this into consideration, the network learns different stroke sizes with different stroke branches progressively. Assume that the number of the stroke sizes to be learned is K. For every K iterations, the network firstly updates the first stroke branch in order to learn the smallest size of stroke. Then, based on the learned knowledge of the first branch, the network uses the second stroke branch to learn the second stroke size with a corresponding scale of the style image. In particular, since the second stroke branch grows the convolutional filters on the basis of the first stroke branch, the updated components in the previous iteration are also adjusted. Similarly, the following stroke branches are updated with the same progressive process. In the next K iterations, the network repeats the above progressive process, since we need to ensure that the network preserves the previously learned stroke sizes.

Incremental Training. We also propose a flexible incremental training strategy to efficiently augment new stroke sizes upon a trained model. Given a new desired stroke size, instead of learning from scratch, our algorithm incrementally learns the new stroke size by adding one single layer as a new stroke branch in the *StrokePyramid*. The position of the augmented layer depends on the previously learned stroke sizes and their corresponding receptive fields. By fixing other network components and only updating the augmented layer, the network learns to paint a new size of strokes on the basis of the previously learned stroke features and thus can reach convergence quickly.

4.5   Runtime Control Strategies

Continuous Stroke Size Control. One of the advantages of our algorithm over previous approaches is that our algorithm can endow one single model with the ability of finer continuous stroke size control. We propose a stroke interpolation strategy to exploit our architecture to interpolate between trained stroke sizes in the feature embedding space, instead of training with tons of style image scales.

Given a content image I_c, we assume that $\mathcal{F}^{\mathcal{B}_{sm}}$ and $\mathcal{F}^{\mathcal{B}_{sn}}$ are two output feature maps in the *StrokePyramid*, which can be decoded into the stylized results with two stroke sizes $I_o^{\mathcal{T}_m}$ and $I_o^{\mathcal{T}_n}$ respectively. The interpolated feature $\mathcal{F}^{\mathcal{B}_{\tilde{s}}}$ can then be obtained by controlling the gating functions in Fig. 4 to interpolate between output feature maps in the *StrokePyramid*:

$$\mathcal{F}^{\mathcal{B}_{\tilde{s}}} = a_m \mathcal{F}^{\mathcal{B}_{sm}} + (1 - a_m)\mathcal{F}^{\mathcal{B}_{sn}}. \tag{9}$$

By gradually changing the value of a_m and feeding the obtained $\mathcal{F}^{\mathcal{B}_{\tilde{s}}}$ into the stroke decoder module, stylized results with arbitrary intermediate stroke sizes $I_o^{\tilde{\mathcal{T}}}$ can be produced.

To our knowledge, none of previous approaches considers this much finer continuous stroke size control. However, from our point of view, there may be some possible solutions which can be derived from current approaches: (1) Directly interpolate between stylized results with different stroke sizes in the pixel space. (2) Design a network with different encoders but a shared decoder, and train each encoder and shared decoder jointly with different style image scales. Then interpolate between two representations from the encoders. (3) Rescale the style image and use ASPM methods to produce the corresponding results.

However, our algorithm outperforms these solutions in the following aspects correspondingly: (1) We manipulate the interpolation in the feature embedding space to achieve perceptually superior results [6,19]. (2) Our stroke representations are obtained with different receptive fields in the *StrokePyramid*. As explained and verified in Sect. 3 and Fig. 2, our stroke representations are perceptually better than those obtained with the same receptive field. In addition, the results of our proposed *StrokePyramid* are more consistent in stroke orientations and configurations during stroke size control. The comparison results can be found in the supplementary material. (3) ASPM compromises on visual quality and is generally not effective at producing fine strokes and details. Our algorithm outperforms ASPM in terms of quality and also stylization speed.

Spatial Stroke Size Control. Previously, in the community of Fast Style Transfer, stylized results usually have almost the same stroke size across the whole image, which is impractical in the real case. Our algorithm supports mixed stroke sizes in different spatial regions and also with only one single model. In this way, the contrast information in stylized results can be enhanced.

Our spatial stroke size control is achieved by feeding masked content image through different corresponding stroke branches by controlling the gating functions, and then combining these stylized results. The mask can be obtained either by manual labelling or forwarding the content image through a pre-trained semantic segmentation network, *e.g.*, DeepLabv2 [4]. By further combining our continuous stroke size control strategy, our algorithm provides practitioners a much finer control over the stylized results.

5   Experiment

5.1   Implementation Details

Our proposed network is trained on MS-COCO dataset [28]. All the images are cropped and resized to 512×512 pixels before training. We adopt the Adam optimizer [22] during training. The pre-trained VGG-19 network [32] is selected as the loss network and $\{relu1\_1, relu2\_1, relu3\_1, relu4\_1, relu5\_1\}$ are used as the style layers and $relu4\_2$ is used as the content layer. By default, the number of initially learned stroke sizes is set to 3 to ensure the ability of stroke decoder, and the scales are 256, 512, and 768 for different stroke sizes for all styles in our experiment. More information can be found in the supplementary material.

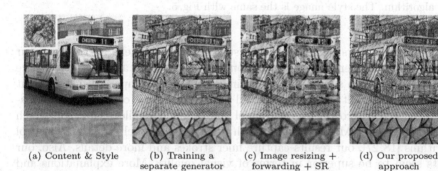

(a) Content & Style   (b) Training a   (c) Image resizing +   (d) Our proposed
                           separate generator   forwarding + SR   approach

Fig. 5. Quality comparison of our proposed algorithm and aforementioned two possible stroke control solutions in Sect. 4. SR represents the image super-resolution technique [21]. The images in the second line represent the zoom regions in the red frames. (Color figure online)

5.2   Qualitative Evaluation

Comparison with Previous Solutions. Sample results of our algorithm and two aforementioned possible solutions are shown in Fig. 5 (Fig. 5(b) is produced by [19]). Our algorithm achieves comparable results with the first possible solution in Fig. 5(b) regarding quality while preserving the flexibility of the second possible solution in Fig. 5(c). Figure 6 shows sample results of our algorithm and other Fast Style Transfer algorithms. Compared with [19,35], our results with different stroke sizes are more consistent in stroke orientations and stroke configurations (the positions of the blue strokes in Fig. 6). The stroke orientations and configurations in [19,35]'s results are more random, since they use different

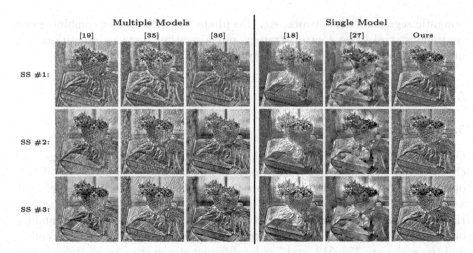

Fig. 6. Some example results of different stroke sizes (SS) produced by our algorithm and other Fast Style Transfer algorithms. Each column represents the results of the same algorithm. The style image is the same with Fig. 5.

encoder-decoder pairs to learn different stroke sizes separately. By contrast, our *StrokePyramid* can encourage *stroke consistency* between adjacent stroke size control results which should differ only in stroke sizes. Compared with [36], our algorithm can exploit one single trained model to achieve continuous and spatial stroke size control. Also, our model size is much smaller than [36], which is 0.99 MB *vs* 32.2 MB. Compared with other single-model stroke size control algorithms [18,27], our results capture finer strokes and more details. Also, our results seem to be superior in terms of visual quality. More explanations and comparison results can be found in the supplementary material.

Runtime User Controls. In Fig. 7, we show sample results of our proposed continuous stroke size control strategy. Our network is trained with three scales of the style image as default and we do the stroke interpolation between them to obtain totally six stroke sizes. The test content image is never seen during training. We also demonstrate the results of [18,27] for comparison, as explained in Sect. 4.5. We compare the results of different algorithms both globally and locally. Globally, our algorithm seems to achieve superior performance in terms of visual quality. Locally, compared with [18,27], our algorithm is more effective at producing fine strokes and preserving details. In addition, as shown in Fig. 8, the absolute differences of our adjacent continuous stroke size control results have a much clearer stroke contour, which indicates that most strokes in our results increase or decrease in size together during continuous stroke size control. We have also produced a sample video to demonstrate our continuous stroke size control in the supplementary material. Figure 9 demonstrates the results of our spatial stroke size control strategy. Our spatial stroke size control is realized with only one single model. Compared with Fig. 9(c), controlling the stroke size

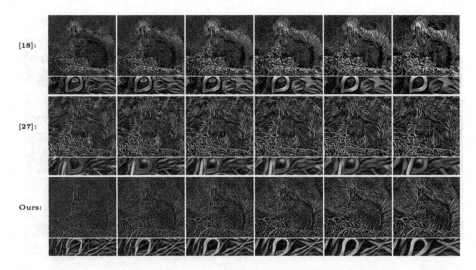

Fig. 7. Results of continuous stroke size control. We zoom in on the same region (red frame) to observe the variations of stroke sizes. Our algorithm produces finer strokes and details. The content and style image can be found in Fig. 4. (Color figure online)

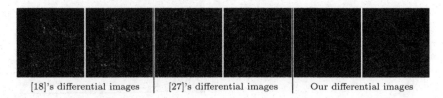

[18]'s differential images | [27]'s differential images | Our differential images

Fig. 8. Results of the absolute differences of adjacent images in each row of Fig. 7.

in different spatial regions can enhance the contrast of stylized images and make AI-Created Art much closer to Human-Created Art.

5.3 Quantitative Evaluation

For the quantitative evaluation, we focus on three evaluation metrics, which are: training curves during progressive training and incremental training; average content and style loss for test content images; training time for our single model and corresponding generating time for results with different stroke sizes.

Training Curve Analysis. To demonstrate the effectiveness of our progressive training strategy, we record the stroke losses when learning several sizes of strokes progressively and learning different strokes individually. The result is shown in Fig. 10(a). The reported loss values were averaged over 15 randomly selected batches of content images. It can be observed that the network which progressively learns multiple stroke sizes converges relatively faster than the one which learns only one single stroke size individually. The result indicates that

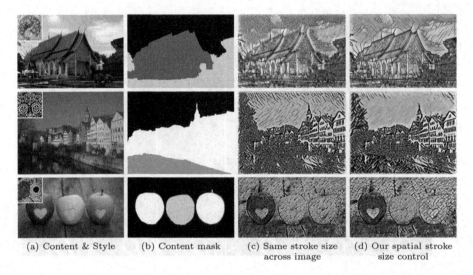

(a) Content & Style   (b) Content mask   (c) Same stroke size   (d) Our spatial stroke
                                                across image   size control

Fig. 9. Our algorithm allows flexible spatial stroke size control during stylization. The result produced by our single model can have mixed stroke sizes, which is more consistent with an artist's artwork in reality.

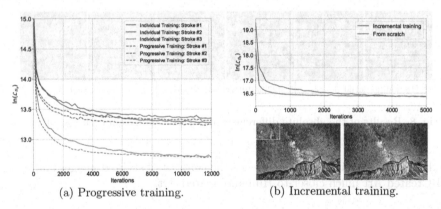

(a) Progressive training.   (b) Incremental training.

Fig. 10. Training curve comparisons of the training strategies. The bottom left and right images in (b) are the results of incremental training and training from scratch.

during progressive training, the latter stroke branch benefits from the learned knowledge of the previous branches, and can even improve the training of previous branches through a shared network component in turn. To validate our stroke incremental training strategy, we present both the training curves of the incremental training and training from scratch in Fig. 10(b). While achieving comparable stylization quality, incrementally learning a stroke can significantly speed up the training process compared to learning from scratch.

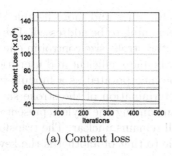
(a) Content loss

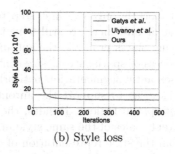
(b) Style loss

Fig. 11. Comparisons of the average content and style loss of our algorithm with state-of-the-art Neural Style Transfer algorithms.

Average Loss Analysis. To measure how well the loss function is minimized, we compare the average content and style loss of our algorithm with other style transfer methods. The recorded values are averaged over 100 content images and 5 style images. For each style, we calculate the average loss of the three stroke sizes. As shown in Fig. 11, the average style loss of our algorithm is similar to [35], and our average content loss is slightly lower than [35]. This indicates that our algorithm achieves comparable or slightly better performance than [35] regarding the ability to minimize the loss function.

Speed and Model Size Analysis. Fully training one single model with three stroke sizes takes about 2 h on a single NVIDIA Quadro M6000. For generating time, it takes averagely 0.09 seconds to stylize an image with size 1024 × 1024 on the same GPU using our algorithm. Since our network architecture is similar with [19,35] but with a shorter path for some stroke sizes, our algorithm can be on average faster than [19,35], and further faster than Wang et al.'s algorithm, Huang and Belongie's algorithm and Li et al.'s algorithm according to the speed analysis in [18,27,36]. The size of our model on disk is 0.99 MB.

6 Discussion and Conclusion

In this paper, we introduce a fine and flexible stroke size control approach for Fast Style Transfer. Without trading off quality and efficiency, our algorithm is the first to achieve continuous and spatial stroke size control with one single model. Our idea can also be directly applied to MSPM methods. For the application in the real world, our work provides a new tool for practitioners to inject their own artistic preferences into style transfer results, which can be directly applied in the production software and entertainment. Regarding the significance of our work for the larger vision community beyond style transfer, our work takes one step in the direction of learning adaptive receptive fields in the human vision system and primarily validates its significance in style transfer. In the future, we hope to further explore the use of learning adaptive receptive fields to benefit the larger vision community, e.g., multi-scale deep image aesthetic assessment, deep image compression, deep image colorization, etc.

Our work is only the first step towards the finer and more flexible stroke size control, and there are still some issues remaining to be addressed. The most interesting one is probably the automatic spatial stroke size control in one shot. The process of spatial stroke size control will be more efficient and user-friendly if the semantic segmentation network can be incorporated as a module in our network, so as to support the automatic determination of the stroke sizes for different spatial regions. Besides, the relations among the style representations of different scales of the same style image still remains unclear. The transformation from the style representation of one scale to that of another is the key to a more flexible stroke size control.

Acknowledgments. The first two authors contributed equally. Mingli Song is the corresponding author. This work is supported by National Key Research and Development Program (2016YFB1200203), National Natural Science Foundation of China (61572428, U1509206), Fundamental Research Funds for the Central Universities (2017FZA5014) and Key Research, Development Program of Zhejiang Province (2018C01004) and ARC FL-170100117, DP-180103424 of Australia.

References

1. Chen, D., Liao, J., Yuan, L., Yu, N., Hua, G.: Coherent online video style transfer. In: Proceedings of the IEEE International Conference on Computer Vision (2017)
2. Chen, D., Yuan, L., Liao, J., Yu, N., Hua, G.: Stylebank: an explicit representation for neural image style transfer. In: Proceedings of the IEEE Conference on Computer Vision and Pattern Recognition (2017)
3. Chen, D., Yuan, L., Liao, J., Yu, N., Hua, G.: Stereoscopic neural style transfer. In: Proceedings of the IEEE Conference on Computer Vision and Pattern Recognition (2018)
4. Chen, L.C., Papandreou, G., Kokkinos, I., Murphy, K., Yuille, A.L.: Deeplab: semantic image segmentation with deep convolutional nets, atrous convolution, and fully connected CRFs. IEEE Trans. Pattern Anal. Mach. Intell. (2017)
5. Dai, J., et al.: Deformable convolutional networks. In: Proceedings of the IEEE International Conference on Computer Vision (2017)
6. Dosovitskiy, A., Brox, T.: Generating images with perceptual similarity metrics based on deep networks. In: Advances in Neural Information Processing Systems, pp. 658–666 (2016)
7. Dumoulin, V., Shlens, J., Kudlur, M.: A learned representation for artistic style. In: International Conference on Learning Representations (2017)
8. Efros, A.A., Freeman, W.T.: Image quilting for texture synthesis and transfer. In: Proceedings of the 28th Annual Conference on Computer Graphics and Interactive Techniques, pp. 341–346. ACM (2001)
9. Elad, M., Milanfar, P.: Style transfer via texture synthesis. IEEE Trans. Image Process. **26**(5), 2338–2351 (2017)
10. Fan, Q., Chen, D., Yuan, L., Hua, G., Yu, N., Chen, B.: Decouple learning for parameterized image operators. In: Ferrari, V., Hebert, M., Sminchisescu, C., Weiss, Y. (eds.) ECCV 2018, Part XIII. LNCS, vol. 11217, pp. 455–471. Springer, Cham (2018)

11. Frigo, O., Sabater, N., Delon, J., Hellier, P.: Split and match: example-based adaptive patch sampling for unsupervised style transfer. In: Proceedings of the IEEE Conference on Computer Vision and Pattern Recognition, pp. 553–561 (2016)
12. Gatys, L.A., Ecker, A.S., Bethge, M.: Texture synthesis using convolutional neural networks. In: Advances in Neural Information Processing Systems, pp. 262–270 (2015)
13. Gatys, L.A., Ecker, A.S., Bethge, M.: Image style transfer using convolutional neural networks. In: Proceedings of the IEEE Conference on Computer Vision and Pattern Recognition, pp. 2414–2423 (2016)
14. Gatys, L.A., Ecker, A.S., Bethge, M., Hertzmann, A., Shechtman, E.: Controlling perceptual factors in neural style transfer. In: Proceedings of the IEEE Conference on Computer Vision and Pattern Recognition (2017)
15. Gooch, B., Gooch, A.: Non-Photorealistic Rendering. A. K. Peters Ltd., Natick (2001)
16. He, M., Chen, D., Liao, J., Sander, P.V., Yuan, L.: Deep exemplar-based colorization. ACM Transactions on Graphics (Proc. of Siggraph 2018) (2018)
17. Hertzmann, A., Jacobs, C.E., Oliver, N., Curless, B., Salesin, D.H.: Image analogies. In: Proceedings of the 28th Annual Conference on Computer Graphics and Interactive Techniques, pp. 327–340. ACM (2001)
18. Huang, X., Belongie, S.: Arbitrary style transfer in real-time with adaptive instance normalization. In: Proceedings of the IEEE International Conference on Computer Vision (2017)
19. Johnson, J., Alahi, A., Fei-Fei, L.: Perceptual losses for real-time style transfer and super-resolution. In: Leibe, B., Matas, J., Sebe, N., Welling, M. (eds.) ECCV 2016. LNCS, vol. 9906, pp. 694–711. Springer, Cham (2016). https://doi.org/10.1007/978-3-319-46475-6_43
20. Julesz, B., et al.: Textons, the elements of texture perception, and their interactions. Nature 290(5802), 91–97 (1981)
21. Kim, J., Kwon Lee, J., Mu Lee, K.: Accurate image super-resolution using very deep convolutional networks. In: Proceedings of the IEEE Conference on Computer Vision and Pattern Recognition, pp. 1646–1654 (2016)
22. Kingma, D., Ba, J.: Adam: a method for stochastic optimization. In: International Conference on Learning Representations (2015)
23. Li, C., Wand, M.: Combining Markov random fields and convolutional neural networks for image synthesis. In: Proceedings of the IEEE Conference on Computer Vision and Pattern Recognition, pp. 2479–2486 (2016)
24. Li, C., Wand, M.: Precomputed real-time texture synthesis with markovian generative adversarial networks. In: European Conference on Computer Vision, pp. 702–716 (2016)
25. Li, Y., Wang, N., Liu, J., Hou, X.: Demystifying neural style transfer. In: Proceedings of the Twenty-Sixth International Joint Conference on Artificial Intelligence, IJCAI-17, pp. 2230–2236 (2017). https://doi.org/10.24963/ijcai.2017/310, https://doi.org/10.24963/ijcai.2017/310
26. Li, Y., et al.: Diversified texture synthesis with feed-forward networks. In: Proceedings of the IEEE Conference on Computer Vision and Pattern Recognition (2017)
27. Li, Y., et al.: Universal style transfer via feature transforms. In: Advances in Neural Information Processing Systems (2017)
28. Lin, T.-Y., et al.: Microsoft COCO: common objects in context. In: Fleet, D., Pajdla, T., Schiele, B., Tuytelaars, T. (eds.) ECCV 2014. LNCS, vol. 8693, pp. 740–755. Springer, Cham (2014). https://doi.org/10.1007/978-3-319-10602-1_48

29. Lu, M., et al.: Decoder network over lightweight reconstructed feature for fast semantic style transfer. In: Proceedings of the IEEE International Conference on Computer Vision (2017)

30. Prisma Labs, I. Prisma: turn memories into art using artificial intelligence (2016). http://prisma-ai.com

31. Rosin, P., Collomosse, J.: Image and Video-Based Artistic Stylisation, vol. 42. Springer Science & Business Media, London (2012)

32. Simonyan, K., Zisserman, A.: Very deep convolutional networks for large-scale image recognition. arXiv preprint arXiv:1409.1556 (2014)

33. Strothotte, T., Schlechtweg, S.: Non-Photorealistic Computer Graphics: Modeling, Rendering, and Animation. Morgan Kaufmann, San Francisco (2002)

34. Ulyanov, D., Lebedev, V., Vedaldi, A., Lempitsky, V.: Texture networks: feed-forward synthesis of textures and stylized images. In: International Conference on Machine Learning, pp. 1349–1357 (2016)

35. Ulyanov, D., Vedaldi, A., Lempitsky, V.: Improved texture networks: maximizing quality and diversity in feed-forward stylization and texture synthesis. In: Proceedings of the IEEE Conference on Computer Vision and Pattern Recognition (2017)

36. Wang, X., Oxholm, G., Zhang, D., Wang, Y.F.: Multimodal transfer: A hierarchical deep convolutional neural network for fast artistic style transfer. In: Proceedings of the IEEE Conference on Computer Vision and Pattern Recognition (2017)

37. Wei, Z., Sun, Y., Wang, J., Lai, H., Liu, S.: Learning adaptive receptive fields for deep image parsing network. In: Proceedings of the IEEE Conference on Computer Vision and Pattern Recognition, pp. 2434–2442 (2017)

38. Yu, F., Koltun, V.: Multi-scale context aggregation by dilated convolutions. In: International Conference on Learning Representations (2016)

39. Zhang, H., Dana, K.: Multi-style generative network for real-time transfer. arXiv preprint arXiv:1703.06953 (2017)

40. Zhang, H., et al.: Context encoding for semantic segmentation. In: Proceedings of the IEEE Conference on Computer Vision and Pattern Recognition (2018)

41. Zhu, S.C., Guo, C.E., Wang, Y., Xu, Z.: What are textons? Int. J. Comput. Vis. **62**(1), 121–143 (2005)

Towards End-to-End License Plate Detection and Recognition: A Large Dataset and Baseline

Zhenbo Xu[1,2] , Wei Yang[1(✉)] , Ajin Meng[1,2], Nanxue Lu[1,2], Huan Huang[2],
Changchun Ying[2], and Liusheng Huang[1]

[1] School of Computer Science and Technology,
University of Science and Technology of China, Hefei, China
qubit@ustc.edu.cn
[2] Xingtai Financial Holdings Group Co., Ltd., Hefei, Anhui, China

Abstract. Most current license plate (LP) detection and recognition approaches are evaluated on a small and usually unrepresentative dataset since there are no publicly available large diverse datasets. In this paper, we introduce CCPD, a large and comprehensive LP dataset. All images are taken manually by workers of a roadside parking management company and are annotated carefully. To our best knowledge, CCPD is the largest publicly available LP dataset to date with over 250k unique car images, and the only one provides vertices location annotations. With CCPD, we present a novel network model which can predict the bounding box and recognize the corresponding LP number simultaneously with high speed and accuracy. Through comparative experiments, we demonstrate our model outperforms current object detection and recognition approaches in both accuracy and speed. In real-world applications, our model recognizes LP numbers directly from relatively high-resolution images at over 61 fps and 98.5% accuracy.

Keywords: Object detection · Object recognition
Object segmentation · Convolutional neural network

1 Introduction

License plate detection and recognition (LPDR) is essential in Intelligent Transport System and is applied widely in many real-world surveillance systems, such as traffic monitoring, highway toll station, car park entrance and exit management. Extensive researches have been made for faster or more accurate LPDR.

However, challenges for license plate (LP) detection and recognition still exist in uncontrolled conditions, such as rotation (about 20° onwards), snow or fog

Electronic supplementary material The online version of this chapter (https://doi.org/10.1007/978-3-030-01261-8_16) contains supplementary material, which is available to authorized users.

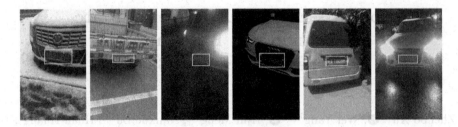

Fig. 1. Sample images from CCPD. Each image above is labelled with its bounding box (the yellow border) and four vertices location (four red dots). Other annotations are omitted here for simplicity. (Color figure online)

weather, distortions, uneven illumination, and vagueness. Most papers concerning LPDR [1–10] often validate their approaches on extremely limited datasets (less than 3,000 unique images), thus might work well only under some controlled conditions. Current datasets for LPDR (see Tables 1 and 2) either lack in quantity (less than 10k images) or diversity (collected from fixed surveillance cameras) because an artificial collection of LP pictures requires a lot of manpower. However, uncontrolled conditions are common in real world. A truly reliable LPDR system should function well in these cases. To aid in better benchmarking LPDR approaches, we present our Chinese City Parking Dataset (CCPD).

CCPD collects data from roadside parking in all the streets of one provincial capital in China where residuals own millions of cars. Each parking fee collector (PFC) works on one street from 07:30 AM to 10:00 PM every day regardless of weather conditions. For each parking bill, the collector is required to take a picture of the car with an Android handheld POS machine and manually annotates the exact LP number. It is worth noting that images from handheld devices exhibit strong variations due to the uncertain position and shooting angle of handheld devices, as well as varying illuminations and different backgrounds at different hours and on different streets (see Fig. 1). Each image in CCPD has detailed annotations in several aspects concerning the LP: (i) LP number. (ii) LP bounding box. (iii) Four vertices locations. (iv) Horizontal tilt degree and vertical tilt degree [11]. (v) Other relevant information like the LP area, the degree of brightness, the degree of vagueness and so on. Details about those annotations are explained in Sect. 3.

Most papers [3–7] separate LPDR into two stages (detection · recognition) or three stages (detection · segmentation · character recognition) and process the LP image step by step. However, separating detection from recognition is detrimental to the accuracy and efficiency of the entire recognition process. An imperfect bounding box prediction given by detection methods might make a part of the LP missing, and thus results in the subsequent recognition failure. Moreover, operations between different stages such as extracting and resizing the LP region for recognition are always accomplished by less efficient CPU, making LP recognition slower. Given these two observations, we come to the intuition that the LP recognition stage can exploit convolutional features extracted in the

LP detection stage for recognizing LP characters. Following that, we design a novel architecture named Roadside Parking net (RPnet) for accomplishing LP detection and recognition in a single forward pass. It's worth noting that we are not the first to design an end-to-end deep neural network which can localize LPs and recognize the LP number simultaneously. However, exploiting Region Proposal Network and Bi-directional Recurrent Neural Networks, the end-to-end model put forward by Li *et al.* [12] is not efficient as it needs 0.3 s to accomplish the recognition process on a Titan X GPU. By contrast, based on a simpler and more elegant architecture, RPnet can run at more than 60 fps on a weaker NVIDIA Quadro P4000.

Both CCPD and the code for training and evaluating RPnet are available under the open-source MIT License at: https://github.com/detectRecog/CCPD.

To summarize, this paper makes the following contributions:

- We introduce CCPD, the largest and the most diverse publicly available dataset for LPDR to date. CCPD provides over 250k unique car images with detailed annotations, nearly two orders of magnitude more images than other diverse LP datasets.
- We propose a novel network architecture for unified LPDR named RPnet which can be trained end-to-end. As feature maps are shared for detection and recognition and losses are optimized jointly, RPnet can detect and recognize LPs more accurately and at a faster speed.
- By evaluating state-of-the-art detection and recognition models on CCPD, we demonstrate our proposed model outperforms other approaches in both accuracy and speed.

2   Related Work

Our work is related to prior art in two aspects: publicly available datasets (as shown in Tables 1 and 2), and existing algorithms on LPDR. Except for [12] which proposed a unified deep neural network to accomplish LPDR in one step, most works separate LP detection from LP recognition.

2.1   Datasets for LPDR

Most datasets for LPDR [13–15] usually collect images from traffic monitoring systems, highway toll station or parking lots. These images are always under even sunlight or supplementary light sources and the tilt angle of LPs does not exceed 20°.

Caltech [13] and Zemris [14] collected less than 700 images from high-resolution cameras on the road or freeways and thus had little variations on distances and tilt degrees. The small volume of images is not sufficient to cover various conditions. Therefore, those datasets are not convincing to evaluate LP detection algorithms. Different from previous datasets, Azam *et al.* [10] and Hsu *et al.* [16] pointed out researches on LP detection under hazardous conditions were scarce and specifically looked for images in various conditions like great tilt angles, blurriness, weak illumination, and bad weather. Compared with CCPD, the shooting distance of these images varies little and the number of images is limited.

Current datasets for LP recognition usually collect extracted LP images and annotate their corresponding LP numbers. As shown in Table 2, SSIG [17] and UFPR [3] captured images by cameras on the road. These images were collected on a sunny day and rarely had tilted LPs. Before we introducing CCPD, ReId [15] is the largest dataset for LP recognition with 76k extracted LPs and annotations. However, gathered from surveillance cameras on highway toll gates, images in ReId are relatively invariant in tilt angles, distances, and illuminations. Lack of either quantity or variance, current datasets are not convincing enough to comprehensively evaluate LP recognition algorithms.

Table 1. A comparison of publicly available datasets for LP detection and CCPD. Var denotes variations.

	Zemris [14]	Azam [10]	AOLPE [16]	CCPD
Year	2002	2015	2017	2018
Number of images	510	850	4200	250k
Var in distance	✗	✗	✗	✓
Var in tilt degrees	✗	✓	✓	✓
Var in blur	✗	✓	✓	✓
Var in illumination	✓	✓	✓	✓
Var in weather	✓	✓	✓	✓
Annotations	✗	✗	✓	✓

Table 2. A comparison of publicly available datasets for LP recognition and CCPD. Var denotes variations.

	SSIG [17]	ReId [15]	UFPR [3]	CCPD
Year	2015	2017	2018	2018
Number of LPs	2000	76k	4500	250k
Var in tilt degrees	✗	✗	✗	✓
Var in blur	✗	✓	✓	✓
Var in illumination	✗	✗	✗	✓
Char dataset	✓	✗	✗	✓
Vertices annotation	✗	✗	✗	✓

2.2   LP Detection Algorithms

LP detection algorithms can be roughly divided into traditional methods and neural network models.

Traditional LP detection methods always exploit the abundant edge information [18–24] or the background color features [25,26]. Hsieh *et al.* [19] utilized morphology method to reduce the number of candidates significantly and thus speeded up the plate detection process. Yu *et al.* [21] proposed a robust method based on wavelet transform and empirical mode decomposition analysis to locate a LP. In [22] the authors analyzed vertical edge gradients to select true plate regions. Wang *et al.* [23] exploited cascade AdaBoost classifier and a voting mechanism to elect plate candidates. In [27] a new pattern named Local Structure Patterns was introduced to detect plate regions. Moreover, based on the observation that the LP background always exhibits a regular color appearance, many works utilize HSI (Hue, Saturation, Intensity) color space to filter out the LP area. Deb *et al.* [25] applied HSI color model to detect candidate regions and achieve 89% accuracy on 90 images. In [26] the authors also exploited a color checking module to help find LP regions.

Recent progress on Region-based Convolutional Neural Network [28] stimulates wide applications [3,4,12,16] of popular object detection models on LP detection problem. Faster-RCNN [29] utilizes a region proposal network which can generate high-quality region proposals for detection and thus detects objects more accurately and quickly. SSD [30] completely eliminates proposal generation and subsequent pixel or feature resampling stages and encapsulates all computation in a single network. YOLO [31] and its improved version [32] frame object detection as a regression problem to spatially separated bounding boxes and associated class probabilities.

2.3 LP Recognition Algorithms

LP Recognition can be classified into two categories: (i) segmentation-free methods. (ii) segment first and then recognize the segmented pictures. The former [33,34] usually utilizes LP character features to extract plate characters directly to avoid segmentation or delivers the LP to an optical character recognition (OCR) system [35] or a convolutional neural network [15] to perform the recognition task. For the latter, the LP bounding box should be determined and shape correction is applied before segmentation. Various features of LP characters can be utilized for segmentation like Connected components analysis (CCA) [36] and character-specific extremal regions [37]. After segmentation, current high-performance methods always train a deep convolutional neural network [38] or utilize features around LP characters like SIFT [39].

3   CCPD Overview

In this section, we introduce CCPD – a large, diverse and carefully annotated LP dataset.

3.1 Data Creation and Privacy Concerns

CCPD collects images from a city parking management company in one provincial capital in China where car owners own millions of vehicles. The company employs over 800 PFCs each of which charges the parking fee on a specific street. Each parking fee order not only records LP number, cost, parking time and so on, but also requires PFC to take a picture of the car from the front or the rear as a proof. PFCs basically have no holidays and usually work from early morning (07:30 AM) to almost midnight (10:00 PM). Therefore, CCPD has images under diverse illuminations, environments in different weather. Moreover, as the only requirement for taking photos is containing the LP, PFC may shoot from various positions and angles and even makes a slight tremor. As a result, images in CCPD are taken from different positions and angles and are even blurred.

Apart from the LP number, each image in CCPD has many other annotations. The most difficult part is annotating the four vertices locations. To accomplish this task, we first manually labelled the four vertices locations over 10k images. Then we designed a network for locating vertices from a small image of LP regions and exploited the 10k images and some data augmentation strategies to train it. Then, after training this network well, we combined a detection module and this network to automatically annotate the four vertices locations of each image. Finally, we hired seven part-time workers to correct these annotations in two weeks. Details about the annotation process are provided in the supplementary material.

In order to avoid leakage of residents' privacy, CCPD removes records other than the LP number of each image and selects images from discrete days and in different streets. In addition, all image metadata including device information, GPS location, etc., is cleared and privacy regions like human faces are blurred.

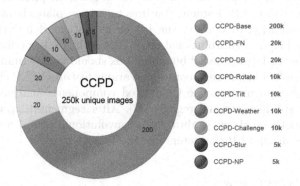

Fig. 2. CCPD layout.

3.2 Dataset Splits and Statistics

CCPD provides over 250k unique LP images with detailed annotations. The resolution of each image is 720 (Width) × 1160 (Height) × 3 (Channels). In practice, this resolution is enough to guarantee that the LP in each image is legible. The average size of each file is about 200 KB (a total of over 48.0 GB for the entire dataset).

Table 3. Descriptions of different sub-datasets in CCPD.

	Description
CCPD-Base	The only common feature of these photos is the inclusion of a license plate
CCPD-DB	Illuminations on the LP area are dark, uneven or extremely bright
CCPD-FN	The distance from the LP to the shooting location is relatively far or near
CCPD-Rotate	Great horizontal tilt degree ($20°\sim 50°$) and the vertical tilt degree varies from $-10°$ to $10°$
CCPD-Tilt	Great horizontal tilt degree ($15°\sim 45°$ degrees) and vertical tilt degree ($15°\sim 45°$)
CCPD-Blur	Blurry largely due to hand jitter while taking pictures
CCPD-Weather	Images taken on a rainy day, snow day or fog day
CCPD-Challenge	The most challenging images for LPDR to date
CCPD-NP	Images of new cars without a LP

Each image in CCPD is labelled in the following aspects:

- LP number. Each image in CCPD has only one LP. Each LP number is comprised of a Chinese character, a letter, and five letters or numbers. The LP number is an important metric for recognition accuracy.
- LP bounding box. The bounding box label contains (x, y) coordinates of the top left and bottom right corner of the bounding box. These two points can be utilized to locate the minimum bounding rectangle of LP.
- Four vertices locations. This annotation contains the exact (x, y) coordinates of the four vertices of LP in the whole image. As the shape of the LP is basically a quadrilateral, these vertices location can accurately represent the borders of the LP for object segmentation.
- Horizontal tilt degree and vertical tilt degree. As explained in [11], the horizontal tilt degree is the angle between LP and the horizontal line. After the 2D rotation, the vertical tilt degree is the angle between the left border line of LP and the horizontal line.
- Other information concerning the LP like the area, the degree of brightness and the degree of vagueness.

Current diverse LPDR datasets [10,16,40] usually contains less than 5k images. After dividing these challenging images into different categories [40], some categories contains less than 100 images. Based on this observation, we select images under different conditions to build several sub-datasets for CCPD from millions of LP images. The distribution of sub-datasets in CCPD is shown in the Fig. 2. Descriptions of these sub-datasets are shown in Table 3. Statistics and samples of these sub-datasets are provided in the supplementary material.

We further add **CCPD-Characters** which contains at least 1000 extracted images for each possible LP character. CCPD-Characters is designed for training neural networks to recognize segmented character images. More character images can be automatically extracted by utilizing annotations of images in CCPD.

4 The Roadside Parking Net (RPnet)

In this section, we introduce our proposed LP detection and recognition framework, called RPnet, and discuss the associated training methodology.

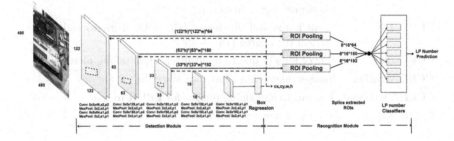

Fig. 3. The overall structure of our RPnet. It consists of ten convolutional layers with ReLU and Batch Normalization, several MaxPooling layers with Dropout and several components composed of fully connected layers. Given an input RGB image, in a single forward computation, RPnet predicts the LP bounding box and the corresponding LP number at the same time. RPnet first exploits the Box Regression layer to predict the bounding box. Then, refer to the relative position of the bounding box in each feature map, RPnet extracts ROIs from several already generated feature maps, combine them after pooling them to the same width and height (16 * 8), and feeds the combined features maps to the subsequent Classifiers.

4.1 Model

RPnet, as shown in Fig. 3, is composed of two modules. The first module is a deep convolutional neural network with ten convolutional layers to extract different level feature maps from the input LP image. We name this module 'the detection module'. The detection module feeds the feature map output by the last convolutional layer to three sibling fully-connected layers which we name 'the box predictor' for bounding box prediction. The second module, named 'the recognition module', exploits region-of-interest (ROI) pooling layers [28] to extract feature maps of interest and several classifiers to predict the LP number of the LP in the input image. The entire module is a single, unified network for LP detection and recognition.

Using a popular terminology 'attention' [41] in neural networks, the detection module serves as the 'attention' of this unified network. It tells the recognition module where to look. Then the recognition module extracts the ROI from shared feature maps and predicts the LP number.

Feature Extraction. RPnet extracts features from the input image by all the convolutional layers in the detection module. As the number of layers increases, the number of channels increases and the size of the feature map decreases progressively. The later feature map has higher level features extracted and thus is more beneficial for recognizing the LP and predicting its bounding box. Suppose the center point x-coordinate, the center point y-coordinate, the width, and the height of the bounding box are b_x, b_y, b_w, b_h respectively. Let W and H be the width and the height of the input image. The bounding box location cx, cy, w, h satisfies:

$$cx = \frac{b_x}{W} \quad cy = \frac{b_y}{H} \quad w = \frac{b_w}{W} \quad h = \frac{b_h}{H}, \quad 0 < cx, cy, w, h < 1$$

Multi-layer Feature Maps for Recognition. Empirically feature maps from different layers within a network are empirically known to have different receptive field sizes [42]. Moreover, previous works such as [43] have shown that using feature maps from the lower layers can improve semantic segmentation quality because the lower layers capture more fine details of the input objects. Similarly, feature maps from relatively lower layers also matter for recognizing LP characters as, just like the object borders in semantic segmentation, the area of the LP is expected to be very small relative to the entire image. After the detection module accomplishes the computation of all convolutional layers, the box predictor outputs the bounding box location (cx, cy, w, h). For a feature layer of size $m x n$ with p channels, as shown in Fig. 3, the recognition module extracts feature maps in the bounding box region of size $(m * h) * (n * w)$ with p channels. By default, RPnet extracts feature maps at the end of three low-level layers: the second, fourth, sixth convolutional layer. The sizes of extracted feature maps are $(122 * h) * (122 * w) * 64$, $(63 * h) * (63 * w) * 160$, $(33 * h) * (33 * w) * 192$. In practice, extracting feature maps from higher convolutional layers makes recognition process slower and offers little help in improving the recognition accuracy. After these feature maps are extracted, RPnet exploits ROI Pooling layers to convert each extracted feature into a feature map with a fixed spatial extent of $P_H * P_W$ (e.g., $8 * 16$ in this paper). Afterwards, these three resized feature maps $8 * 16 * 64$, $8 * 16 * 160$ and $8 * 16 * 192$ are concatenated to one feature map of size $8 * 16 * 416$ for LP number classification.

4.2   Training

RPnet can be trained end-to-end on CCPD and accomplishes LP bounding box detection and LP number recognition in a single forward. The training involves choosing suitable loss functions for detection performance and recognition performance, as well as pre-training the detection module before training RPnet end-to-end.

Training Objective. The RPnet training objective can be divided into two parts: the localization loss (loc) and the classification loss (cls). Let N be the size of a mini-batch in training. The localization loss (see Eq. (1)) is a Smooth L1 loss [28] between the predicted box (pb) and the ground truth box (gb). Let the ground-truth seven LP numbers be $gn_i(1 \leq i \leq 7)$. $pn_i(1 \leq i \leq 7)$ denotes predictions for the seven LP characters and each LP character prediction pn_i contains nc_i float numbers, each representing the possibility of belonging to a specific character class. The classification loss (see Eq. (2)) is a cross-entropy loss. With the joint optimization of both localization and classification losses, the extracted features would have richer information about LP characters. Experiments show that both detection and recognition performance can be enhanced by jointly optimizing these two losses.

$$L_{loc}(pb, gb) = \sum_{N} \sum_{m \in \{cx, cy, w, h\}} smooth_{L1}(pb^m - gb^m) \tag{1}$$

$$L_{cls}(pn, gn) = \sum_{N} \sum_{1 \leq i \leq 7} \{-pn_i[gn_i] + log(\sum_{1 \leq j \leq nc_i} exp(pn_i[j]))\} \tag{2}$$

$$L(pb, pn, gb, gn) = \frac{1}{N}(L_{loc}(pb, gb) + L_{cls}(pn, gn)) \tag{3}$$

Pre-training Detection Module. Before training PRnet end-to-end, the detection module must provide a reasonable bounding box prediction (cx, cy, w, h). A reasonable prediction (cx, cy, w, h) must meet $0 < cx, cy, w, h < 1$ and might try to meet $\frac{w}{2} \leq cx \leq 1 - \frac{w}{2}, \frac{h}{2} \leq cy \leq 1 - \frac{h}{2}$, thus can represent a valid ROI and guide the recognition module to extract feature maps. Unlike most object detection related papers [29,31] which pre-train their convolutional layers on ImageNet [44] to make these layers more representative, we pre-train the detection module from scratch on CCPD as the data volume of CCPD is large enough and, for locating a single object such as a license plate, parameters pre-trained on ImageNet are not necessarily better than training from scratch. In practice, the detection module always gives a reasonable bounding box prediction after being trained 300 epochs on the training set.

5   Evaluations

In this section, we conduct experiments to compare RPnet with state-of-the-art models on both LP detection performance and LP recognition performance.

Furthermore, we explore the effect of extracting features maps from different layers on the final recognition accuracy.

All data comes from our proposed CCPD, the largest publicly available annotated LP Dataset to date. All our training tasks are accomplished on a GPU server with 8 CPU (Intel(R) Xeon(R) CPU E5-2682 v4 @ 2.50 GHz), 60 GB RAM and one Nvidia GPU (Tesla P100 PCIe 16 GB). All our evaluation tasks are finished on desktop PCs with eight 3.40 GHz Intel Core i7-6700 CPU, 24 GB RAM and one Quadro P4000 GPU.

5.1 Data Preparation

As aforementioned in Sect. 3, CCPD-Base consists of approximately 200k unique images. We divide CCPD-Base into two equal parts. One as the default training set, another as the default evaluation set. In addition, several sub-datasets (CCPD-DB, CCPD-FN, CCPD-Rotate, CCPD-Tilt, CCPD-Weather, CCPD-Challenge) in CCPD are also exploited for detection and recognition performance evaluation. Apart from Cascade classifier [45], all models used in experiments rely on GPU and are fine-tuned on the training set. For models without default data augmentation strategies, we augment the training data by randomly sampling four times on each image to increase the training set by five times. More details are provided in the supplementary material.

We did not reproduce our experiments on other datasets because most current available LP datasets [13–15] are not as diverse as CCPD and their data volume is far fewer than CCPD. Thus, detection accuracy or recognition accuracy on other datasets might not be as convincing as on CCPD. Moreover, we also did not implement approaches not concerning machine learning like [8] because in practice, when evaluated on a large-scale dataset, methods based on machine learning always perform better.

Table 4. LP detection precision (percentage) of state-of-the-art detection models on each test set. AP denotes average precision in the whole test set and FPS denotes frames per second.

	FPS	AP	Base (100k)	DB	FN	Rotate	Tilt	Weather	Challenge
Cascade classifier [45]	32	47.2	55.4	49.2	52.7	0.4	0.6	51.5	27.5
SSD300 [30]	40	94.4	99.1	89.2	84.7	**95.6**	**94.9**	83.4	**93.1**
YOLO9000 [32]	42	93.1	98.8	89.6	<u>77.3</u>	93.3	91.8	84.2	88.6
Faster-RCNN [29]	15	92.9	98.1	92.1	83.7	91.8	89.4	81.8	83.9
TE2E [12]	3	94.2	98.5	91.7	83.8	95.1	94.5	83.6	93.1
RPnet	**61**	**94.5**	**99.3**	89.5	85.3	94.7	93.2	**84.1**	92.8

5.2   Detection

Detection Accuracy Metric. We follow the standard protocol in object detection Intersection-over-Union (IoU) [12].

The bounding box is considered to be correct if and only if its IoU with the ground-truth bounding box is more than 70% ($IoU > 0.7$). All models are fine-tuned on the same 100k training set.

We set a higher IoU boundary in the detection accuracy metric than TE2E [12] because a higher boundary can filter out imperfect bounding boxes and thus better evaluates the detection performance. The results are shown in Table 4. Cascade classifier has difficulty in precisely locating LPs and thus performs badly under a high IoU threshold and it is not robust when dealing with tilted LPs. Concluded from the low detection accuracy 77.3% on CCPD-FN, YOLO has a relatively bad performance on relatively small/large object detection. Benefited from the joint optimization of detection and recognition, the performance of both RPnet and TE2E surpasses Faster-RCNN and YOLO9000. However, RPnet can recognize twenty times faster than TE2E. Moreover, by analysing the bounding boxes predicted by SSD, we found these boxes wrap around LPs very tightly. Actually, when the IoU threshold is set higher than 0.7, SSD achieves the highest accuracy. The reason might be that the detection loss is not the only training objective of RPnet. For example, a little imperfect bounding box (slightly smaller than the ground-truth one) might be beneficial for more correct LP recognition.

Table 5. LP recognition precision (percentage) on each test set. Apart from TE2E and RPnet, we append a high-performance model to other object detection models for subsequent LP recognition. HC denotes Holistic-CNN [15].

	FPS	AP	Base (100k)	DB	FN	Rotate	Tilt	Weather	Challenge
Cascade classifier + HC	29	58.9	69.7	67.2	69.7	0.1	3.1	52.3	30.9
SSD300 + HC	35	95.2	98.3	96.6	**95.9**	88.4	91.5	87.3	83.8
YOLO9000 + HC	36	93.7	98.1	96.0	88.2	84.5	88.5	87.0	80.5
Faster-RCNN+ HC	13	92.8	97.2	94.4	90.9	82.9	87.3	85.5	76.3
TE2E	3	94.4	97.8	94.8	94.5	87.9	92.1	86.8	81.2
RPnet	**61**	**95.5**	**98.5**	**96.9**	94.3	**90.8**	**92.5**	**87.9**	**85.1**

5.3   Recognition

Recognition Accuracy Metric. A LP recognition is correct if and only if the IoU is greater than 0.6 and all characters in the LP number are correctly recognized.

To our knowledge, before us, TE2E [12] is the only end-to-end network for LPDR. Apart from TE2E and our RPnet, in our evaluations we combine state-of-the-art detection models with a state-of-the-art recognition model named Holistic-CNN [15] as comparisons to TE2E and RPnet. We fine-tuned Holistic-CNN on the training set produced by extracting the LP region from the same

Fig. 4. Detection and recognition results on CCPD with our RPnet model. Each image is the smaller license plate area extracted from the original resolution 720 (Width) × 1160 (Height) × 3 (Channels).

100k images according to their ground-truth bounding box. On the test set produced in a similar manner, Holistic-CNN can recognize over 200 small LP region images per second with a 98.5% accuracy.

As shown in Table 5, these combined models can achieve high recognition speed (36 fps) and high recognition accuracy (95.2%). As a result of precise LP bounding boxes predicted by SSD, the model combining SSD and Holistic-CNN achieves up to 95.2% average precision on CCPD. However, by sharing feature maps between the detection module and recognition module, RPnet achieves a much faster recognition rate 61 FPS and a slightly higher recognition accuracy 95.5%.

In addition, it's worth noting that nearly all evaluated models fail to perform well on CCPD-Rotate, CCPD-Weather, and especially CCPD-Challenge. Difficulties of detection and recognition on these three sub-datasets are partly resulted from the scarce of LPs under these conditions in training data. Their low performances partly demonstrate that by classifying LPs into different sub-categories, CCPD can evaluate LPDR algorithms more comprehensively.

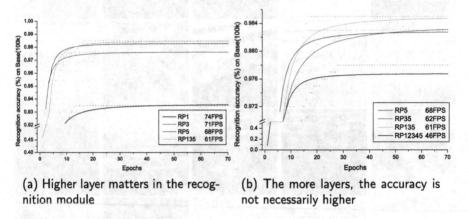

(a) Higher layer matters in the recognition module

(b) The more layers, the accuracy is not necessarily higher

Fig. 5. Performance analysis on extracting feature maps from different layers or multiple layers. FPS denotes frames per second.

5.4 Model Analysis

Samples of detection and recognition results produced by evaluating RPnet on CCPD are shown in Fig. 4. To understand RPnet better, we carried out some controlled experiments to examine how each layer affects performance. For all variants of RPnet in experiments, we use the same settings and input size as the original RPnet, except for specified changes.

Higher Layer Matters in the Recognition Module. We number ten convolutional layers in RPnet $C_i, 0 \leq i \leq 9$. Therefore, the original RPnet described in Sect. 4 can be denoted RP135 because it extracts feature maps from C_1, C_3, C_5 for LP character recognition. Similarly, we implement RP1, RP3, and RP5 where feature maps are extracted from only one specific layer. The results are shown in Fig. 5(a). Among these four models, RP1 only reaches the lowest accuracy 93.5%, while all other models achieve an accuracy higher than 97.5%. From RP1 to RP5, with the higher layer is exploited for feature extraction, the recognition accuracy increases and the epochs needed for fitting decreases. With a single layer C_5 for feature extraction, RP5 achieves almost the same accuracy as RP135. Though lower layers can improve semantic segmentation quality, higher order features seem to be more useful for recognition tasks.

Feature Extraction from More Layers Not Necessarily Increases the Accuracy. Based on the knowledge that the sixth convolutional layer C_5 might have a greater impact on the recognition accuracy, we trained two new models RP35 and RP12345 for performance analysis which also exploits C_5 and has different number of layers for feature extraction. As shown in Fig. 5(b), from RP5 to RP35 to RP135, the number of layers for feature extraction increases and the recognition accuracy that can be achieved also increases. However, with five layers for feature extraction, RP12345 not only introduces significantly more recognition time, but its accuracy decreased. Extracting features from too many layers and not having enough neurons for analysing might lead to poor generalization.

6 Conclusions

In this paper, we present a large-scale and diverse license plate dataset named CCPD and a novel network architecture named RPnet for unified license plate detection and recognition. Images in CCPD are annotated carefully and are classified into different categories according to different features of LPs. The great data volume (250k unique images), data diversity (eight different categories), and detailed annotations make CCPD a valuable dataset for object detection, object recognition, and object segmentation. Extensive evaluations on CCPD demonstrate our proposed RPnet outperforms state-of-the-art approaches both in speed and accuracy. Currently, RPnet has been put into practice for road-side parking services. Its accuracy and speed significantly surpass other existing commercial license plate recognition systems.

Acknowledgments. This work was supported by the National Natural Science Foundation of China (No. 61572456) and the Anhui Province Guidance Funds for Quantum Communication and Quantum Computers.

References

1. Xie, L., Ahmad, T., Jin, L., Liu, Y., Zhang, S.: A new CNN-based method for multi-directional car license plate detection. IEEE Trans. Intell. Transp. Syst. **19**, 507–517 (2018)
2. Al-Shemarry, M.S., Li, Y., Abdulla, S.: Ensemble of adaboost cascades of 3L-LBPs classifiers for license plates detection with low quality images. Expert Syst. Appl. **92**, 216–235 (2018)
3. Laroca, R., et al.: A robust real-time automatic license plate recognition based on the yolo detector (2018). arXiv preprint: arXiv:1802.09567
4. Montazzolli, S., Jung, C.: Real-time Brazilian license plate detection and recognition using deep convolutional neural networks. In: 2017 30th SIBGRAPI Conference on Graphics, Patterns and Images (SIBGRAPI), pp. 55–62 (2017)
5. Selmi, Z., Halima, M.B., Alimi, A.M.: Deep learning system for automatic license plate detection and recognition. In: 2017 14th IAPR International Conference on Document Analysis and Recognition (ICDAR), vol. 1, pp. 1132–1138. IEEE (2017)
6. Rizvi, S.T.H., Patti, D., Björklund, T., Cabodi, G., Francini, G.: Deep classifiers-based license plate detection, localization and recognition on GPU-powered mobile platform. Future Internet **9**(4), 66 (2017)
7. Masood, S.Z., Shu, G., Dehghan, A., Ortiz, E.G.: License plate detection and recognition using deeply learned convolutional neural networks (2017). arXiv preprint: arXiv:1703.07330

8. Yuan, Y., Zou, W., Zhao, Y., Wang, X., Hu, X., Komodakis, N.: A robust and efficient approach to license plate detection. IEEE Trans. Image Process. **26**(3), 1102–1114 (2017)
9. Cheang, T.K., Chong, Y.S., Tay, Y.H.: Segmentation-free vehicle license plate recognition using convnet-RNN (2017). arXiv preprint: arXiv:1701.06439
10. Azam, S., Islam, M.M.: Automatic license plate detection in hazardous condition. J. Vis. Commun. Image Represent. **36**, 172–186 (2016)
11. Zhang, Z., Yin, S.: Hough transform and its application in vehicle license plate tilt correction. Comput. Inf. Sci. **1**(3), 116 (2008)
12. Li, H., Wang, P., Shen, C.: Towards end-to-end car license plates detection and recognition with deep neural networks (2017). arXiv preprint: arXiv:1709.08828
13. Caltech: Caltech Licese Plate Dataset. http://www.vision.caltech.edu/html-files/archive.html
14. Zemris: Zemris License Plate Dataset. http://www.zemris.fer.hr/projects/LicensePlates/hrvatski/rezultati.shtml
15. Špaňhel, J., Sochor, J., Juránek, R., Herout, A., Maršík, L., Zemčík, P.: Holistic recognition of low quality license plates by CNN using track annotated data. In: 2017 14th IEEE International Conference on Advanced Video and Signal Based Surveillance (AVSS), pp. 1–6. IEEE (2017)
16. Hsu, G.S., Ambikapathi, A., Chung, S.L., Su, C.P.: Robust license plate detection in the wild. In: 2017 14th IEEE International Conference on Advanced Video and Signal Based Surveillance (AVSS), pp. 1–6. IEEE (2017)
17. Gonçalves, G.R., da Silva, S.P.G., Menotti, D., Schwartz, W.R.: Benchmark for license plate character segmentation. J. Electron. Imaging **25**(5), 1–5 (2016)
18. Haralick, R.M., Sternberg, S.R., Zhuang, X.: Image analysis using mathematical morphology. IEEE Trans. Pattern Anal. Mach. Intell. PAMI **9**(4), 532–550 (1987)
19. Hsieh, J.W., Yu, S.H., Chen, Y.S.: Morphology-based license plate detection from complex scenes. In: Proceedings of the 16th International Conference on Pattern Recognition, vol. 3, pp. 176–179. IEEE (2002)
20. Wu, H.H.P., Chen, H.H., Wu, R.J., Shen, D.F.: License plate extraction in low resolution video. In: 18th International Conference on Pattern Recognition, ICPR 2006, vol. 1, pp. 824–827. IEEE (2006)
21. Yu, S., Li, B., Zhang, Q., Liu, C., Meng, M.Q.H.: A novel license plate location method based on wavelet transform and emd analysis. Pattern Recogn. **48**(1), 114–125 (2015)
22. Saha, S., Basu, S., Nasipuri, M., Basu, D.K.: License plate localization from vehicle images: an edge based multi-stage approach. Int. J. Recent Trends Eng. **1**(1), 284–288 (2009)
23. Wang, R., Sang, N., Huang, R., Wang, Y.: License plate detection using gradient information and cascade detectors. Optik Int. J. Light Electron Opt. **125**(1), 186–190 (2014)
24. Bachchan, A.K., Gorai, A., Gupta, P.: Automatic license plate recognition using local binary pattern and histogram matching. In: Huang, D.-S., Jo, K.-H., Figueroa-García, J.C. (eds.) ICIC 2017, Part II. LNCS, vol. 10362, pp. 22–34. Springer, Cham (2017). https://doi.org/10.1007/978-3-319-63312-1_3
25. Deb, K., Jo, K.H.: HSI color based vehicle license plate detection. In: International Conference on Control, Automation and Systems, ICCAS 2008, pp. 687–691. IEEE (2008)
26. Yao, Z., Yi, W.: License plate detection based on multistage information fusion. Inf. Fusion **18**, 78–85 (2014)

27. Lee, Y., Song, T., Ku, B., Jeon, S., Han, D.K., Ko, H.: License plate detection using local structure patterns. In: 2010 Seventh IEEE International Conference on Advanced Video and Signal Based Surveillance (AVSS), pp. 574–579. IEEE (2010)
28. Girshick, R.: Fast R-CNN (2015). arXiv preprint: arXiv:1504.08083
29. Ren, S., He, K., Girshick, R., Sun, J.: Faster R-CNN: towards real-time object detection with region proposal networks. In: Advances in Neural Information Processing Systems, pp. 91–99 (2015)
30. Liu, W., et al.: SSD: single shot MultiBox detector. In: Leibe, B., Matas, J., Sebe, N., Welling, M. (eds.) ECCV 2016, Part I. LNCS, vol. 9905, pp. 21–37. Springer, Cham (2016). https://doi.org/10.1007/978-3-319-46448-0_2
31. Redmon, J., Divvala, S., Girshick, R., Farhadi, A.: You only look once: unified, real-time object detection. In: Proceedings of the IEEE Conference on Computer Vision and Pattern Recognition, pp. 779–788 (2016)
32. Redmon, J., Farhadi, A.: Yolo9000: better, faster, stronger (2016). arXiv preprint: arXiv:1612.08242
33. Ho, W.T., Lim, H.W., Tay, Y.H.: Two-stage license plate detection using gentle adaboost and SIFT-SVM. In: First Asian Conference on Intelligent Information and Database Systems, ACIIDS 2009, pp. 109–114. IEEE (2009)
34. Duan, T.D., Du, T.H., Phuoc, T.V., Hoang, N.V.: Building an automatic vehicle license plate recognition system. In: Proceedings of the International Conference on Computer Science RIVF, pp. 59–63 (2005)
35. Yousef, K.M.A., Al-Tabanjah, M., Hudaib, E., Ikrai, M.: Sift based automatic number plate recognition. In: 2015 6th International Conference on Information and Communication Systems (ICICS), pp. 124–129. IEEE (2015)
36. Maglad, K.W.: A vehicle license plate detection and recognition system. J. Comput. Sci. 8(3), 310 (2012)
37. Gou, C., Wang, K., Yao, Y., Li, Z.: Vehicle license plate recognition based on extremal regions and restricted Boltzmann machines. IEEE Trans. Intell. Transp. Syst. 17(4), 1096–1107 (2016)
38. Ciregan, D., Meier, U., Schmidhuber, J.: Multi-column deep neural networks for image classification. In: 2012 IEEE Conference on Computer Vision and Pattern Recognition (CVPR), pp. 3642–3649. IEEE (2012)
39. Abdel-Hakim, A.E., Farag, A.A.: CSIFT: a SIFT descriptor with color invariant characteristics. In: 2006 IEEE Computer Society Conference on Computer Vision and Pattern Recognition (CVPR 2006), vol. 2, pp. 1978–1983 (2006)
40. Anagnostopoulos, C.N.E., Anagnostopoulos, I.E., Psoroulas, I.D., Loumos, V., Kayafas, E.: License plate recognition from still images and video sequences: a survey. IEEE Trans. Intell. Transp. Syst. 9(3), 377–391 (2008)
41. Chorowski, J.K., Bahdanau, D., Serdyuk, D., Cho, K., Bengio, Y.: Attention-based models for speech recognition. In: Advances in Neural Information Processing Systems, pp. 577–585 (2015)
42. Zhou, B., Khosla, A., Lapedriza, A., Oliva, A., Torralba, A.: Object detectors emerge in deep scene CNNs (2014). arXiv preprint arXiv:1412.6856
43. Long, J., Shelhamer, E., Darrell, T.: Fully convolutional networks for semantic segmentation. In: Proceedings of the IEEE conference on Computer Vision and Pattern Recognition, pp. 3431–3440 (2015)
44. Russakovsky, O., et al.: Imagenet large scale visual recognition challenge. Int. J. Comput. Vis. 115(3), 211–252 (2015)
45. Wang, S.Z., Lee, H.J.: A cascade framework for a real-time statistical plate recognition system. IEEE Trans. Inf. Forensics Secur. 2(2), 267–282 (2007)

Learning Warped Guidance for Blind Face Restoration

Xiaoming Li[1], Ming Liu[1], Yuting Ye[1], Wangmeng Zuo[1(✉)],
Liang Lin[2], and Ruigang Yang[3]

[1] School of Computer Science and Technology, Harbin Institute of Technology,
Harbin, China
{csxmli,wmzuo}@hit.edu.cn, csmliu@outlook.com, yeyuting.jlu@gmail.com
[2] School of Data and Computer Science, Sun Yat-sen University, Guangzhou, China
linliang@ieee.org
[3] Department of Computer Science, University of Kentucky, Lexington, USA
ryang@cs.uky.edu

Abstract. This paper studies the problem of blind face restoration from an unconstrained blurry, noisy, low-resolution, or compressed image (i.e., degraded observation). For better recovery of fine facial details, we modify the problem setting by taking both the degraded observation and a high-quality guided image of the same identity as input to our guided face restoration network (GFRNet). However, the degraded observation and guided image generally are different in pose, illumination and expression, thereby making plain CNNs (e.g., U-Net) fail to recover fine and identity-aware facial details. To tackle this issue, our GFRNet model includes both a warping subnetwork (WarpNet) and a reconstruction subnetwork (RecNet). The WarpNet is introduced to predict flow field for warping the guided image to correct pose and expression (i.e., warped guidance), while the RecNet takes the degraded observation and warped guidance as input to produce the restoration result. Due to that the ground-truth flow field is unavailable, landmark loss together with total variation regularization are incorporated to guide the learning of Warp-Net. Furthermore, to make the model applicable to blind restoration, our GFRNet is trained on the synthetic data with versatile settings on blur kernel, noise level, downsampling scale factor, and JPEG quality factor. Experiments show that our GFRNet not only performs favorably against the state-of-the-art image and face restoration methods, but also generates visually photo-realistic results on real degraded facial images.

Keywords: Face hallucination · Blind image restoration · Flow field

Electronic supplementary material The online version of this chapter (https://doi.org/10.1007/978-3-030-01261-8_17) contains supplementary material, which is available to authorized users.

1 Introduction

Face restoration aims to reconstruct high quality face image from degraded observation for better display and further analyses [4,5,8,9,17,32,49,52–54,59]. In the ubiquitous imaging era, imaging sensors are embedded into many consumer products and surveillance devices, and more and more images are acquired under unconstrained scenarios. Consequently, low quality face images cannot be completely avoided during acquisition and communication due to the introduction of low-resolution, defocus, noise and compression. On the other hand, high quality face images are sorely needed for human perception, face recognition [42] and other face analysis [1] tasks. All these make face restoration a very challenging yet active research topic in computer vision.

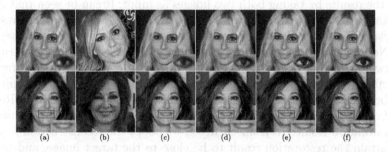

| | | | | | |
| (a) | (b) | (c) | (d) | (e) | (f) |

Fig. 1. Restoration results on real low quality images: (a) real low quality image, (b) guided image, and the results by (c) U-Net [43] by taking low quality image as input, (d) U-Net [43] by taking both guided image and low quality image as input, (e) our GFRNet without landmark loss, and (f) our full GFRNet model. Best viewed by zooming in the screen.

Many studies have been carried out to handle specific face restoration tasks, such as denoising [2,3], hallucination [4,5,8,17,32,49,52–54,59] and deblurring [9]. Most existing methods, however, are proposed for handling a single specific face restoration task in a non-blind manner. In practical scenario, it is more general that both the degradation types and degradation parameters are unknown in advance. Therefore, more attentions should be given to blind face restoration. Moreover, most previous works produce the restoration results purely relying on a single degraded observation. It is worth noting that the degradation process generally is highly ill-posed. By learning a direct mapping from degraded observation, the restoration result inclines to be over-smoothing and cannot faithfully retain fine and identity-aware facial details.

In this paper, we study the problem of guided blind face restoration by incorporating the degraded observation and a high-quality guided face image. Without loss of generality, the guided image is assumed to have the same identity with the degraded observation, and is frontal with eyes open. We note that such guided restoration setting is practically feasible in many real world applications.

For example, most smartphones support to recognize and group the face images according to their identities[1]. In each group, the high quality face image can thus be exploited to guide the restoration of low quality images. In film restoration, it is also encouraging to use the high quality portrait of an actor to guide the restoration of low-resolution and corrupted face images of the same actor from an old film. For these tasks, further incorporation of guided image not only can ease the difficulty of blind restoration, but also is helpful in faithfully recovering fine and identity-aware facial details.

Guided blind face restoration, however, cannot be addressed well by simply taking the degraded observation and guided image as input to plain convolutional networks (CNNs), due to that the two images generally are of different poses, expressions and lighting conditions. Figure 1(c) shows the results obtained using the U-Net [43] by only taking degraded observation as input, while Fig. 1(d) shows the results by taking both two images as input. It can be seen that direct incorporation of guided image brings very limited improvement on the restoration result. To tackle this issue, we develop a guided face restoration network (GFRNet) consisting of a warping subnetwork (WarpNet) and a reconstruction subnetwork (RecNet). Here, the WarpNet is firstly deployed to predict a flow field for warping the guided image to obtain the warped guidance, which is required to have the same pose and expression with degraded observation. Then, the RecNet takes both degraded observation and warped guidance as input to produce the final restoration result. To train GFRNet, we adopt the reconstruction learning to constrain the restoration result to be close to the target image, and further employ the adversarial learning for visually realistic restoration.

Nonetheless, even though the WarpNet can be end-to-end trained with reconstruction and adversarial learning, we empirically find that it cannot converge to the desired solution and fails to align the guided image to the correct pose and expression. Figure 1(e) gives the results of our GFRNet trained by reconstruction and adversarial learning. One can see that its improvement over U-Net is still limited, especially when the degraded observation and guided images are distinctly different in pose. Moreover, the ground-truth flow field is unavailable, and the target and guided images may be of different lighting conditions, making it infeasible to directly use the target image to guide the WarpNet learning. Instead, we adopt the face alignment method [57] to detect the face landmarks of the target and guided images, and then introduce the landmark loss as well as the total variation (TV) regularizer to train the WarpNet. As in Fig. 1(f), our full GFRNet achieves the favorable visual quality, and is effective in recovering fine facial details. Furthermore, to make the learned GFRNet applicable to blind face restoration, our model is trained on the synthetic data generated by a general degradation model with versatile settings on blur kernel, noise level, downsampling scale factor, and JPEG quality factor.

Extensive experiments are conducted to evaluate the proposed GFRNet for guided blind face restoration. The proposed GFRNet achieves significant performance gains over the state-of-the-art restoration methods in quantitative metrics

---

[1] https://support.apple.com/HT207103.

and visually perceptual quality as well as real degraded image. Moreover, our GFRNet also performs favorably on real degraded images as shown in Fig. 1(f).To sum up, the main contribution of this work includes:

- The GFRNet architecture for guided blind face restoration, which includes a warping subnetwork (WarpNet) and a reconstruction subnetwork (RecNet).
- The incorporation of landmark loss and TV regularization for training the WarpNet.
- The promising results of GFRNet on both synthetic and real face images.

2 Related Work

Recent years have witnessed the unprecedented success of deep learning in many image restoration tasks such as super-resolution [11,24,28], denoising [46,55], compression artifact removal [10,12], compressed sensing [22,26,34], and deblurring [7,27,36,37]. As to face images, several CNN architectures have been developed for face hallucination [5,8,17,59], and the adversarial learning is also introduced to enhance the visual quality [52,53]. Most of these methods, however, are suggested for non-blind restoration and are restricted by the specialized tasks. Benefitted from the powerful modeling capability of deep CNNs, recent studies have shown that it is feasible to train a single model for handling multiple instantiations of degradation (e.g., different noise levels) [35,55]. As for face hallucination, Yu et al. [53,54] suggest one kind of transformative discriminative networks to super-resolve different unaligned tiny face images. Nevertheless, blind restoration is a more challenging problem and requires to learn a single model for handling all instantiations of one or more degradation types.

Most studies on deep blind restoration are given to blind deblurring, which aims to recover the latent clean image from noisy and blurry observation with unknown degradation parameters. Early learning-based or CNN-based blind deblurring methods [7,45,48] usually follow traditional framework which includes a blur kernel estimation stage and a non-blind deblurring stage. With the rapid progress and powerful modeling capability of CNNs, recent studies incline to bypass blur kernel estimation by directly training a deep model to restore clean image from degraded observation [16,27,36–38]. As to blind face restoration, Chrysos and Zafeiriou [9] utilize a modified ResNet architecture to perform face deblurring, while Xu et al. [49] adopt the generative adversarial network (GAN) framework to super-resolve blurry face image. It is worth noting that the success of such kernel-free end-to-end approaches depends on both the modeling capability of CNN and the sufficient sampling on clean images and degradation parameters, making it difficult to design and train. Moreover, the highly ill-posed degradation further increases the difficulty of recovering the correct fine details only from degraded observation [31]. In this work, we elaborately tackle this issue by incorporating a high quality guided image and designing appropriate network architecture and learning objective.

Several learning-based and CNN-based approaches are also developed for color-guided depth image enhancement [15,18,29], where the structural interdependency between intensity and depth image is modeled and exploited to reconstruct high quality depth image. For guided depth image enhancement, Hui et al. [18] present a CNN model to learn multi-scale guidance, while Gu et al. [15] incorporate weighted analysis representation and truncated inference for dynamic guidance learning. For general guided filtering, Li et al. [29] construct CNN-based joint filters to transfer structural details from guided image to reconstructed image. However, these approaches assume that the guided image is spatially well aligned with the degraded observation. Due to that the guided image and degraded observation usually are different in pose and expression, such assumption generally does not hold true for guided face restoration. To address this issue, a WarpNet is introduced in our GFRNet to learn a flow field for warping the guided image to the desired pose and expression.

Recently, spatial transformer networks (STNs) are suggested to learn a spatial mapping for warping an image [21], and appearance flow networks (AFNs) are presented to predict a dense flow field to move pixels [13,58]. Deep dense flow networks have been applied to view synthesis [40,58], gaze manipulation [13], expression editing [50], and video frame synthesis [33]. In these approaches, the target image is required to have the similar lighting condition with the input image to be warped, and the dense flow networks can thus be trained via reconstruction learning. However, in our guided face restoration task, the guided image and the target image usually are of different lighting conditions, making it less effective to train the flow network via reconstruction learning. Moreover, the ground-truth dense flow field is not available, further increasing the difficulty to train WarpNet. To tackle this issue, we use the face alignment method [57] to extract the face landmarks of guided and target images. Then, the landmark loss and TV regularization are incorporated to facilitate the WarpNet training.

3   Proposed Method

This section presents our GFRNet to recover high quality face image from degraded observation with unknown degradation. Given a degraded observation I^d and a guided image I^g, our GFRNet model produces the restoration result $\hat{I} = \mathcal{F}(I^d, I^g)$ to approximate the ground-truth target image I. Without loss of generality, I^g and I are of the same identity and image size 256×256. Moreover, to provide richer guidance information, I^g is assumed to be of high quality, frontal, non-occluded with eyes open. Nonetheless, we empirically find that our GFRNet is robust when the assumption is violated. For simplicity, we also assume I^d has the same size with I^g. When such assumption does not hold, e.g., in face hallucination, we simply apply the bicubic scheme to upsample I^d to the size of I^g before inputting it to the GFRNet.

In the following, we first describe the GFRNet model as well as the network architecture. Then, a general degradation model is introduced to generate synthetic training data. Finally, we present the model objective of our GFRNet.

3.1   Guided Face Restoration Network

The degraded observation I^d and guided image I^g usually vary in pose and expression. Directly taking I^d and I^g as input to plain CNNs generally cannot achieve much performance gains over taking only I^d as input (See Fig. 1(c) and (d)). To address this issue, the proposed GFRNet consists of two subnetworks: (i) the warping subnetwork (WarpNet) and (ii) reconstruction subnetwork (Rec-Net).

Figure 2 illustrates the overall architecture of our GFRNet. The WarpNet takes I^d and I^g as input to predict the flow field for warping guided image,

$$\Phi = \mathcal{F}_w(I^d, I^g; \Theta_w), \tag{1}$$

where Θ_w denotes the WarpNet model parameters. With Φ, the output pixel value of the warped guidance I^w at location (i, j) is given by

$$I_{i,j}^w = \sum_{(h,w) \in \mathcal{N}} I_{h,w}^g \max(0, 1 - |\Phi_{i,j}^y - h|) \max(0, 1 - |\Phi_{i,j}^x - w|), \tag{2}$$

where $\Phi_{i,j}^x$ and $\Phi_{i,j}^y$ denote the predicted x and y coordinates for the pixel $I_{i,j}^w$, respectively. $\mathcal{N}$ stands for the 4-pixel neighbors of $(\Phi_{i,j}^x, \Phi_{i,j}^y)$. From Eq. (2), we note that I^w is subdifferentiable to Φ [21]. Thus, the WarpNet can be end-to-end trained by minimizing the losses defined either on I^w or on Φ.

The predicted warping guidance I^w is expected to have the same pose and expression with the ground-truth I. Thus, the RecNet takes I^d and I^w as input to produce the final restoration result,

$$\hat{I} = \mathcal{F}_r(I^d, I^w; \Theta_r), \tag{3}$$

where Θ_r denotes the RecNet model parameters.

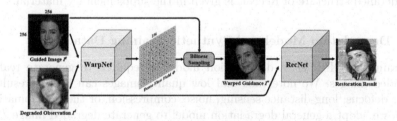

Fig. 2. Overview of our GFRNet. The WarpNet takes the degraded observation I^d and guided image I^g as input to predict the dense flow field Φ, which is adopted to deform I^g to the warped guidance I^w. I^w is expected to be spatially well aligned with I. Thus the RecNet takes I^w and I^d as input to produce the restoration result $\hat{I}$.

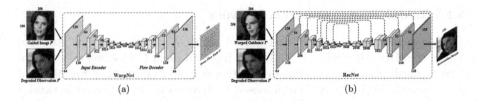

Fig. 3. The network architectures of (a) WarpNet and (b) RecNet.

Warping Subnetwork (WarpNet). The WarpNet adopts the encoder-decoder structure (see Fig. 3(a)) and is comprised of two major components:

- The <u>input encoder</u> extracts feature representation from I^d and I^g, consisting of eight convolution layers and each one with size 4×4 and stride 2.
- The <u>flow decoder</u> predicts the dense flow field for warping I^g to the desired pose and expression, consisting of eight deconvolution layers.

Except the first layer in encoder and the last layer in decoder, all the other layers adopt the convolution-BatchNorm-ReLU form. The detailed structure of WarpNet is given in the supplementary material.

Reconstruction Subnetwork (RecNet). For the RecNet, the input (I^d and I^w) are of the same pose and expression with the output ($\hat{I}$), and thus the U-Net can be adopted to produce the final restoration result $\hat{I}$. The RecNet also includes two components, i.e., an encoder and a decoder (see Fig. 3(b)). The encoder and decoder of RecNet are of the same structure with those adopted in WarpNet. To circumvent the information loss, the i-th layer is concatenated to the $(L-i)$-th layer via skip connections (L is the depth of the U-Net), which has been demonstrated to benefit the rich and fine details of the generated image [20]. The detailed structure of RecNet is given in the supplementary material.

3.2   Degradation Model and Synthetic Training Data

To train our GFRNet, a degradation model is required to generate realistic degraded images. We note that real low quality images can be the results of either defocus, long-distance sensing, noise, compression, or their combinations. Thus, we adopt a general degradation model to generate degraded image $I^{d,s}$,

$$I^{d,s} = ((I \otimes \mathbf{k}_\varrho) \downarrow_s + \mathbf{n}_\sigma)_{JPEG_q}, \tag{4}$$

where $\otimes$ denotes the convolution operator. $\mathbf{k}_\varrho$ stands for the Gaussian blur kernel with the standard deviation ϱ. $\downarrow_s$ denotes the downsampling operator with scale factor s. $\mathbf{n}_\sigma$ denotes the additive white Gaussian noise (AWGN) with the noise level σ. $(\cdot)_{JPEG_q}$ denotes the JPEG compression operator with quality factor q.

In our general degradation model, $(I \otimes \mathbf{k}_\varrho) \downarrow_s + \mathbf{n}_\sigma$ characterizes the degradation caused by long-distance acquisition, while $(\cdot)_{JPEG_q}$ depicts the degradation caused by JPEG compression. We also note that Xu et al. [49] adopt the degradation model $(I \otimes \mathbf{k}_\varrho + \mathbf{n}_\sigma) \downarrow_s$. However, to better simulate the long-distance image acquisition, it is more appropriate to add the AWGN on the downsampled image. When $s \neq 1$, the degraded image $I^{d,s}$ is of different size with the ground-truth I. So we use bicubic interpolation to upsample $I^{d,s}$ with scale factor s, and then take $I^d = (I^{d,s}) \uparrow_s$ and I^g as input to our GFRNet.

In the following, we explain the parameter settings for these operations:

- **Blur kernel.** In this work, only the isotropic Gaussian blur kernel $\mathbf{k}_\varrho$ is considered to model the defocus effect. We sample the standard deviation of Gaussian blur kernel from the set $\varrho \in \{0, 1 : 0.1 : 3\}$, where 0 indicates no blurring.
- **Downsampler.** We adopt the bicubic downsampler as [5,8,17,49,59]. The scale factor s is sampled from the set $s \in \{1 : 0.1 : 8\}$.
- **Noise.** As for the noise level σ, we adopt the set $\sigma \in \{0 : 1 : 7\}$ [49].
- **JPEG compression.** For economic storage and communication, JPEG compression with quality factor q is further operated on the degraded image, and we sample q from the set $q \in \{0, 10 : 1 : 40\}$. When $q = 0$, the image is only losslessly compressed.

By including $\varrho = 0$, $s = 1$, $\sigma = 0$ and $q = 0$ in the set of degradation parameters, the general degradation model can simulate the effect of either the defocus, long-distance acquisition, noising, compression or their versatile combinations.

Given a ground-truth image I_i together with the guided image I_i^g, we can first sample ϱ_i, s_i, σ_i and q_i from the parameter set, and then use the degradation model to generate a degraded observation I_i^d. Furthermore, the face alignment method [57] is adopted to extract the landmarks $\{(x_j^{I_i}, y_j^{I_i})|_{j=1}^{68}\}$ for I_i and $\{(x_j^{I_i^g}, y_j^{I_i^g})|_{j=1}^{68}\}$ for I_i^g. Therefore, we define the synthetic training set as $\mathcal{X} = \{(I_i, I_i^g, I_i^d, \{(x_j^{I_i}, y_j^{I_i})|_{j=1}^{68}\}, \{(x_j^{I_i^g}, y_j^{I_i^g})|_{j=1}^{68}\})|_{i=1}^{N}\}$, where N denotes the number of samples.

3.3 Model Objective

Losses on Restoration Result $\hat{I}$. To train our GFDNet, we define the reconstruction loss on the restoration result $\hat{I}$, and the adversarial loss is further incorporated on $\hat{I}$ to improve the visual perception quality.

Reconstruction Loss. The reconstruct loss is used to constrain the restoration result $\hat{I}$ to be close to the ground-truth I, which includes two terms. The first term is the ℓ_2 loss defined as the squared Euclidean distance between $\hat{I}$ and I, i.e., $\ell_r^0(I, \hat{I}) = \|I - \hat{I}\|^2$. Due to the inherent irreversibility of image restoration, only the ℓ_2 loss inclines to cause over-smoothing result. Following [23], we define the second term as the perceptual loss on the pre-trained VGG-Face [41]. Denote by ψ the VGG-Face network, $\psi_l(I)$ the feature map of the l-th convolution layer. The perceptual loss on the l-th layer (i.e., Conv-4 in this work) is defined as

$$\ell_p^{\psi,l}(I, \hat{I}) = \frac{1}{C_l H_l W_l} \left\| \psi_l(\hat{I}) - \psi_l(I) \right\|_2^2 \tag{5}$$

where C_l, H_l and W_l denote the channel numbers, height and width of the feature map, respectively. Finally, we define the reconstruction loss as

$$\mathcal{L}_r(I, \hat{I}) = \lambda_{r,0} \ell_r^0(I, \hat{I}) + \lambda_{r,l} \ell_p^{\psi,l}(I, \hat{I}), \tag{6}$$

where $\lambda_{r,0}$ and $\lambda_{r,l}$ are the tradeoff parameters for the ℓ_2 and the perceptual losses, respectively.

Adversarial Loss. Following [19,30], both global and local adversarial losses are deployed to further improve the perceptual quality of the restoration result. Let $p_{data}(I)$ be the distribution of ground-truth image, $p_d(I^d)$ be the distribution of degraded observation. Using the global adversarial loss [14] as an example, the adversarial loss can be formulated as,

$$\ell_{a,g} = \min_\Theta \max_D \mathbb{E}_{I \sim p_{data}(I)}[\log D(I)] + \mathbb{E}_{I^d \sim p_d(I^d)}[\log(1 - D(\mathcal{F}(I^d, I^g; \Theta)))], \tag{7}$$

where $D(I)$ denotes the global discriminator which predicts the possibility that I is from the distribution $p_{data}(I)$. $\mathcal{F}(I^d, I^g; \Theta)$ denotes the restoration result by our GFRNet with the model parameters $\Theta = (\Theta_w, \Theta_r)$.

Following the conditional GAN [20], the discriminator has the same architecture with pix2pix [20], and takes the degraded observation, guided image and restoration result as the input. The network is trained in an adversarial manner, where our GFRNet is updated by minimizing the loss $\ell_{a,g}$ while the discriminator is updated by maximizing $\ell_{a,g}$. To improve the training stability, we adopt the improved GAN [44], and replace the labels 0/1 with the smoothed 0/0.9 to reduce the vulnerability to adversarial examples. The local adversarial loss $\ell_{a,l}$ adopts the same settings with the global one but its discriminator is defined only on the minimal bounding box enclosing all facial landmarks. To sum up, the overall adversarial loss is defined as

$$\mathcal{L}_a = \lambda_{a,g} \ell_{a,g} + \lambda_{a,l} \ell_{a,l}. \tag{8}$$

where $\lambda_{a,g}$ and $\lambda_{a,l}$ are the tradeoff parameters for the global and local adversarial losses, respectively.

Losses on Flow Field Φ. Although the WarpNet can be end-to-end trained based on the reconstruction and adversarial losses, it cannot be learned to correctly align I^w with I in terms of pose and expression (see Fig. 7). In [13,50], the appearance flow network is trained by minimizing the MSE loss between the output and the ground-truth of the warped image. But for guided face restoration, I generally has different illumination with I^g, and cannot serve as the ground-truth of the warped image. To circumvent this issue, we present the landmark loss as well as the TV regularization to facilitate the learning of WarpNet.

Landmark Loss. Using the face alignment method TCDCN [57], we detect the 68 landmarks $\{(x_j^{I^g}, y_j^{I^g})|_{j=1}^{68}\}$ for I^g and $\{(x_j^{I}, y_j^{I})|_{j=1}^{68}\}$ for I. In order to align I^w and I, it is natural to require that the landmarks of I^w are close to those of I, i.e., $\Phi^x(x_j^{I}, y_j^{I}) \approx x_j^{I^g}$ and $\Phi^y(x_j^{I}, y_j^{I}) \approx y_j^{I^g}$. Thus, the landmark loss is defined as

$$\ell_{lm} = \sum_i (\Phi_x(x_i^{I}, y_i^{I}) - x_i^{I^g})^2 + (\Phi_y(x_i^{I}, y_i^{I}) - y_i^{I^g})^2. \tag{9}$$

All the coordinates (including x, y, Φ_x and Φ_y) are normalized to range $[-1, 1]$.

TV Regularization. The landmark loss can only be imposed on the locations of the 68 landmarks. For better learning WarpNet, we further take the TV regularization into account to require that the flow field should be spatially smooth. Given the 2D dense flow field (f_x, f_y), the TV regularizer is defined as

$$\ell_{TV} = \|\nabla_x \Phi_x\|^2 + \|\nabla_y \Phi_x\|^2 + \|\nabla_x \Phi_y\|^2 + \|\nabla_y \Phi_y\|^2, \tag{10}$$

where ∇_x (∇_y) denotes the gradient operator along the $x(y)$ coordinate.

Combining landmark loss with TV regularizer, we define the flow loss as

$$\mathcal{L}_{flow} = \lambda_{lm}\ell_{lm} + \lambda_{TV}\ell_{TV}, \tag{11}$$

where λ_{lm} and λ_{TV} denote the tradeoff parameters for landmark loss and TV regularizer, respectively.

Overall Objective. Finally, we combine the reconstruction loss, adversarial loss, and flow loss to give the overall objective,

$$\mathcal{L} = \mathcal{L}_r + \mathcal{L}_a + \mathcal{L}_{flow}. \tag{12}$$

4   Experimental Results

Extensive experiments are conducted to assess our GFRNet for guided blind face restoration. Peak Signal-to-Noise Ratio (PSNR) and structural similarity (SSIM) indices are adopted for quantitative evaluation with the related state-of-the-arts (including image super-resolution, deblurring, denoising, compression artifact removal and face hallucination). As for qualitative evaluation, we illustrate the results by our GFRNet and the competing methods. Results on real low quality images are also given to evaluate the generalization ability of our GFRNet. More results can be found in the supplementary material. More results and the code are available at: https://github.com/csxmli2016/GFRNet.

4.1   Dataset

We adopt the CASIA-WebFace [51] and VggFace2 [6] datasets to constitute our training and test sets. The WebFace contains 10,575 identities and each has about 46 images with the size 256×256. The VggFace2 contains 9,131 identities and each has an average of 362 images with different sizes. The images in the two datasets are collected in the wild and cover a large range of pose, age, illumination and expression. For each identity, at most five high quality images are selected, in which a frontal image with eyes open is chosen as the guided image and the others are used as the ground-truth to generate degraded observations. By this way, we build our training set of 20,273 pairs of ground-truth and guided images from the VggFace2 training set. Our test set includes two subsets: (i) 1,005 pairs from the VggFace2 test set, and (ii) 1,455 pairs from WebFace. In addition, 200 pairs from Web-face are chosen as a validation set, which are not included in training and testing. The images whose identities have appeared in our training set are excluded from the test set. Furthermore, low quality images are also excluded in training and testing, which include: (i) low-resolution images, (ii) images with large occlusion, (iii) cartoon images, and (iv) images with obvious artifacts. The face region of each image in VGGFace2 is cropped and resized to 256×256 based on the bounding box detected by MTCNN [56]. All training and test images are not aligned to keep their original pose and expression. Facial landmarks of the ground-truth and guided images are detected by TCDCN [57] and are only used in training.

4.2 Training Details and Parameter Setting

Our model is trained using the Adam algorithm [25] with the learning rate of 2×10^{-4}, 2×10^{-5}, 2×10^{-6} and $\beta_1 = 0.5$. In each learning rate, the model is trained until the reconstruction loss on validation set becomes non-decreasing. Then a smaller learning rate is adopted to further fine-tune the model. The tradeoff parameters are set as $\lambda_{r,0} = 100$, $\lambda_{r,l} = 0.001$, $\lambda_{a,g} = 1$, $\lambda_{a,l} = 0.5$, $\lambda_{lm} = 10$, and $\lambda_{TV} = 1$. We first pre-train the WarpNet for 5 epochs by minimizing the flow loss $\mathcal{L}_{flow}$, and then both WarpNet and RecNet are end-to-end trained by using the objective $\mathcal{L}$. The batch size is 1 and the training is stopped after 100 epochs. Data augmentation such as flipping is also adopted during training.

4.3 Results on Synthetic Images

Table 1 lists the PSNR and SSIM results on the two test subsets, where our GFRNet achieves significant performance gains over all the competing methods. Using the 4× SR on WebFace as an example, in terms of PSNR, our GFRNet outperforms other methods by at least 3.5 dB. Since guided blind face restoration remains an uninvestigated issue in literature, we compare our GFRNet with several relevant state-of-the-arts, including three non-blind image super-resolution (SR) methods (SRCNN [11], VDSR [24], SRGAN [28]), three blind deblurring methods (DCP [39], DeepDeblur [36], DeblurGAN [27]), two denoising methods (DnCNN [55], MemNet [46]), one compression artifact removal method (ARCNN [10]), three non-blind face hallucination (FH) methods (CBN [59], WaveletSRNet [17], TDAE [54]), and two blind FH methods (SCGAN [49], MCGAN [49]). To keep consistent with the SR and FH methods, only two scale factors, i.e., 4 and 8, are considered for the test images. As for non-SR methods,

Table 1. Quantitative results on two test subsets. Numbers in the parentheses indicate SSIM and the remaining represents PSNR (dB). The best results are highlighted in red and second best ones except our GFRNet variants are highlighted in blue.

Methods		VggFace2 [6]				WebFace [51]			
		4×		8×		4×		8×	
SR	SRCNN [11]	24.57	(.842)	22.30	(.802)	26.11	(.872)	23.50	(.842)
	VDSR [24]	25.36	(.858)	22.50	(.807)	26.60	(.884)	23.65	(.847)
	SRGAN [28]	25.85	(.911)	23.01	(.874)	27.65	(.941)	24.49	(.913)
	MSRGAN	26.55	(.906)	23.45	(.862)	28.10	(.934)	24.92	(.908)
Deblur	DCP [39]	24.42	(.894)	21.54	(.848)	24.97	(.895)	23.05	(.887)
	DeepDeblur [36]	26.31	(.917)	22.97	(.873)	28.13	(.934)	24.63	(.910)
	DeblurGAN [27]	24.65	(.889)	22.06	(.846)	24.63	(.910)	23.38	(.896)
	MDeblurGAN	25.32	(.918)	22.46	(.867)	29.41	(.952)	23.49	(.900)
Denoise	DnCNN [55]	26.73	(.920)	23.29	(.877)	28.35	(.933)	24.75	(.912)
	MemNet [46]	26.85	(.923)	23.31	(.877)	28.57	(.934)	24.77	(.909)
	MDnCNN	27.05	(.925)	23.33	(.879)	29.40	(.942)	24.84	(.912)
AR	ARCNN [10]	22.05	(.863)	20.84	(.827)	23.39	(.876)	20.47	(.858)
	MARCNN	25.43	(.923)	23.16	(.876)	28.40	(.938)	25.15	(.914)
Non-blind FH	CBN [59]	24.52	(.867)	21.84	(.817)	25.43	(.899)	23.10	(.852)
	WaveletSR [17]	25.66	(.909)	20.87	(.831)	27.10	(.937)	21.63	(.869)
	TDAE [54]	-	(-)	20.19	(.729)	-	(-)	20.24	(.741)
Blind FH	SCGAN [49]	25.16	(.905)	-	-	26.37	(.923)	-	-
	MCGAN [49]	25.26	(.912)	-	-	26.35	(.931)	-	-
Ours	Ours(−WG)	25.97	(.915)	22.91	(.838)	28.73	(.928)	24.76	(.884)
	Ours(−WG2)	27.20	(.932)	23.22	(.863)	29.45	(.945)	25.93	(.914)
	Ours(−W)	26.03	(.923)	23.29	(.843)	29.66	(.934)	25.20	(.897)
	Ours(−W2)	27.25	(.933)	23.24	(.864)	29.73	(.948)	25.95	(.917)
	Ours(−F)	26.61	(.927)	23.17	(.863)	31.43	(.920)	26.00	(.922)
	Ours(R)	27.90	(.943)	24.05	(.890)	31.46	(.962)	26.88	(.922)
	Ours(Full)	28.55	(.947)	24.10	(.898)	32.31	(.973)	27.21	(.935)

we take the bicubic upsampling result as the input to the model. To handle 8× SR for SRCNN [11] and VDSR [24], we adopt the strategy in [47] by applying the 2× model to the result produced by the 4× model. For SCGAN [49] and MCGAN [49], only the 4× models are available. For TDAE [54], only the 8× model is available.

Quantitative Evaluation. It is worth noting that the promising performance of our GFRNet cannot be solely attributed to the use of our training data and the simple incorporation of guided image. To illustrate this point, we retrain four competing methods (i.e., SRGAN, DeblurGAN, DnCNN, and ARCNN) by using our training data and taking both degraded observation and guided image as input. For the sake of distinction, the retrained models are represented as MSRGAN, MDeblurGAN, MDnCNN, MARCNN. From Table 1, the retrained models do achieve better PSNR and SSIM results than the original ones, but still perform inferior to our GFRNet with a large margin, especially on WebFace.

Therefore, the performance gains over the retrained models should be explained by the network architecture and model objective of our GFRNet.

Qualitative Evaluation. In Fig. 4, we select three competing methods with top quantitative performance, and compare their results with those by our GFRNet. It is obvious that our GFRNet is more effective in restoring fine details while suppressing visual artifacts. In comparison with the competing methods, the results by GFRNet are visually photo-realistic and can correctly recover more fine and identity-aware details especially in eyes, nose, and mouth regions. More results of all competing methods are included in the supplementary material.

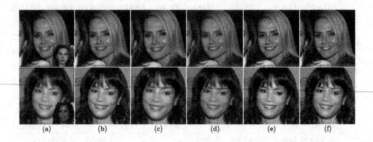

Fig. 4. The 4× SR results: (a) synthetic low quality image (Close-up in right bottom is the guided image), (b) MDnCNN [55], (c) MARCNN [10], (d) MDeblurGAN [27], (e) Ours, and (f) ground-truth.

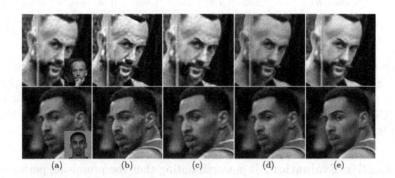

Fig. 5. Restoration results on real low quality images with different poses: (a) real low quality images (Close-up in right bottom is the guided image), (b) MDnCNN [55], (c) MARCNN [10], (d) MDeblurGAN [27], and (e) Ours.

4.4   Results on Real Low Quality Images

Figure 5 further shows the results on real low quality images by MDnCNN [55], MARCNN [10], MDeblurGAN [27], and our GFRNet. The real images are selected from VGGFace2 with the resolution lower than 60×60. Even the degradation is unknown, our method yields visually realistic and pleasing results in face region with more fine details, while the competing methods can only achieve moderate improvement on visual quality.

4.5   Ablative Analysis

Two groups of ablative experiments are conducted to assess the components of our GFRNet. First, we consider five variants of our GFRNet: (i) Ours($Full$): the full GFRNet, (ii) Ours($-F$): GFRNet by removing the flow loss $\mathcal{L}_{flow}$, (iii) Ours($-W$): GFRNet by removing WarpNet (RecNet takes both I^d and I^g as input), (iv) Ours($-WG$): GFRNet by removing WarpNet and guided image (RecNet only takes I^d as input), and (v) Ours(R): GFRNet by using a random I^g with different identity to I^d. Table 1 also lists the PSNR and SSIM results of these variants, and we have the following observations. (i) All the three components, i.e., guided image, WarpNet and flow loss, contribute to the performance improvement. (ii) GFRNet cannot be well trained without the help of flow loss. As a result, although Ours($-F$) outperforms Ours($-W$) in most cases, sometimes Ours($-W$) can perform slightly better than Ours($-F$) by average PSNR, e.g., for $8\times$ SR on VggFace2. (iii) It is worth noting that GFRNet with random guidance (i.e., Ours(R)) achieves the second best results, indicating that GFRNet is robust to the misuse of identity. Figures 1 and 6 give the restoration results by GFRNet variants. Ours($Full$) can generate much sharper and richer details, and achieves better perceptual quality than its variants. Moreover, Ours(R) also achieves the second best performance in qualitative results, but it may introduce the fine details of the other identity to the result (e.g., eye regions in Fig. 6(h)). Furthermore, to illustrate the effectiveness of flow loss, Fig. 7 shows the warped guidance by Ours($Full$) and Ours($-F$). Without the help of flow loss, Ours($-F$) cannot converge to stable solution and results in unreasonable warped guidance. In contrast, Ours($Full$) can correctly align guided image to the desired pose and expression, indicating the necessity and effectiveness of flow loss.

In addition, it is noted that the parameters of Ours($Full$) are nearly two times of Ours($-W$) and Ours($-WG$). To show that the gain of Ours($Full$) does not come from the increase of parameter number, we include two other variants of GFRNet, i.e., Ours($-W2$) and Ours($-WG2$), by increasing the channels of Ours($-W$) and Ours($-WG$) to 2 times, respectively. From Table 1, in terms of PSNR, Ours($Full$) also outperforms Ours($-W2$) and Ours($-WG2$). Instead of the increase of model parameters, the performance improvement of Ours($Full$) should be mainly attributed to the incorporation of both WarpNet and flow loss.

292   X. Li et al.

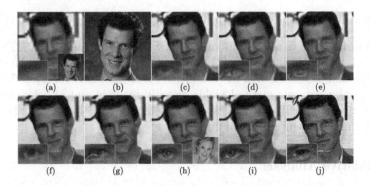

Fig. 6. Restoration results of our GFRNet variants: (a) input, (b) guided image. (c) Ours($-WG$), (d) Ours($-WG2$), (e) Ours($-W$), (f) Ours($-W2$), (g) Ours($-F$), (h) Ours(R) (Close-up in right bottom is the random guided image), (i) Ours($Full$), and (j) ground-truth. Best viewed by zooming in the screen.

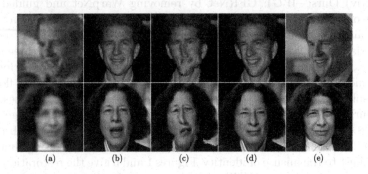

Fig. 7. Warped guidance by Ours($Full$) and Ours($-F$): (a) input, (b) guided image, (c) Ours($-F$), (d) Ours($Full$), and (e) ground-truth.

5   Conclusion

In this paper, we present a guided blind face restoration model, i.e., GFRNet, by taking both the degraded observation and a high-quality guided image from the same identity as input. Besides the reconstruction subnetwork, our GFRNet also includes a warping subnetwork (WarpNet), and incorporates the landmark loss as well as TV regularizer to align the guided image to the desired pose and expression. To make our GFRNet be applicable to blind restoration, we further introduce a general image degradation model to synthesize realistic low quality face image. Quantitative and qualitative results show that our GFRNet not only performs favorably against the relevant state-of-the-arts but also generates visually pleasing results on real low quality face images.

Acknowledgments. This work was supported in part by the National Natural Science Foundation of China under grant Nos. 61671182 and 61471146.

References

1. Andreu, Y., López-Centelles, J., Mollineda, R.A., García-Sevilla, P.: Analysis of the effect of image resolution on automatic face gender classification. In: IEEE International Conference Pattern Recognition, pp. 273–278. IEEE (2014)
2. Anwar, S., Huynh, C., Porikli, F.: Combined internal and external category-specific image denoising. In: British Machine Vision Conference (2017)
3. Anwar, S., Porikli, F., Huynh, C.P.: Category-specific object image denoising. IEEE Trans. Image Process. **26**(11), 5506–5518 (2017)
4. Baker, S., Kanade, T.: Hallucinating faces. In: IEEE International Conference on Automatic Face and Gesture Recognition, pp. 83–88. IEEE (2000)
5. Cao, Q., Lin, L., Shi, Y., Liang, X., Li, G.: Attention-aware face hallucination via deep reinforcement learning. In: IEEE Conference on Computer Vision and Pattern Recognition, pp. 690–698. IEEE (2017)
6. Cao, Q., Shen, L., Xie, W., Parkhi, O.M., Zisserman, A.: Vggface2: a dataset for recognising faces across pose and age (2017). arXiv preprint: arXiv:1710.08092
7. Chakrabarti, A.: A neural approach to blind motion deblurring. In: Leibe, B., Matas, J., Sebe, N., Welling, M. (eds.) ECCV 2016, Part III. LNCS, vol. 9907, pp. 221–235. Springer, Cham (2016). https://doi.org/10.1007/978-3-319-46487-9_14
8. Chen, Y., Tai, Y., Liu, X., Shen, C., Yang, J.: FSRNet: end-to-end learning face super-resolution with facial priors (2017). arXiv preprint: arXiv:1711.10703
9. Chrysos, G.G., Zafeiriou, S.: Deep face deblurring. In: IEEE Conference on Computer Vision and Pattern Recognition Workshops, pp. 2015–2024. IEEE (2017)
10. Dong, C., Deng, Y., Change Loy, C., Tang, X.: Compression artifacts reduction by a deep convolutional network. In: IEEE International Conference on Computer Vision, pp. 576–584. IEEE (2015)
11. Dong, C., Loy, C.C., He, K., Tang, X.: Learning a deep convolutional network for image super-resolution. In: Fleet, D., Pajdla, T., Schiele, B., Tuytelaars, T. (eds.) ECCV 2014, Part IV. LNCS, vol. 8692, pp. 184–199. Springer, Cham (2014). https://doi.org/10.1007/978-3-319-10593-2_13
12. Galteri, L., Seidenari, L., Marco, B., Alberto, B.D.: Deep generative adversarial compression artifact removal. In: IEEE International Conference on Computer Vision, pp. 4826–4835. IEEE (2017)
13. Ganin, Y., Kononenko, D., Sungatullina, D., Lempitsky, V.: DeepWarp: photorealistic image resynthesis for gaze manipulation. In: Leibe, B., Matas, J., Sebe, N., Welling, M. (eds.) ECCV 2016, Part II. LNCS, vol. 9906, pp. 311–326. Springer, Cham (2016). https://doi.org/10.1007/978-3-319-46475-6_20
14. Goodfellow, I.J., et al.: Generative adversarial networks. In: Advances in Neural Information Processing Systems, vol. 3, pp. 2672–2680 (2014)
15. Gu, S., Zuo, W., Guo, S., Chen, Y., Chen, C., Zhang, L.: Learning dynamic guidance for depth image enhancement. In: IEEE Conference on Computer Vision and Pattern Recognition, pp. 3769–3778. IEEE (2017)
16. Hradiš, M., Kotera, J., Zemčík, P., Šroubek, F.: Convolutional neural networks for direct text deblurring. In: British Machine Vision Conference (2015)
17. Huang, H., He, R., Sun, Z., Tan, T.: Wavelet-SRNet: a wavelet-based CNN for multi-scale face super resolution. In: IEEE International Conference on Computer Vision, pp. 1689–1697. IEEE (2017)
18. Hui, T.-W., Loy, C.C., Tang, X.: Depth map super-resolution by deep multi-scale guidance. In: Leibe, B., Matas, J., Sebe, N., Welling, M. (eds.) ECCV 2016, Part III. LNCS, vol. 9907, pp. 353–369. Springer, Cham (2016). https://doi.org/10.1007/978-3-319-46487-9_22

19. Iizuka, S., Simo-Serra, E., Ishikawa, H.: Globally and locally consistent image completion. ACM Trans. Graph. **36**(4), 107:1–107:14 (2017)
20. Isola, P., Zhu, J.Y., Zhou, T., Efros, A.A.: Image-to-image translation with conditional adversarial networks. In: IEEE Conference on Computer Vision and Pattern Recognition, pp. 1125–1134. IEEE (2016)
21. Jaderberg, M., Simonyan, K., Zisserman, A., Kavukcuoglu, K.: Spatial transformer networks. In: Advances in Neural Information Processing Systems, pp. 2017–2025 (2015)
22. Jin, K.H., McCann, M.T., Froustey, E., Unser, M.: Deep convolutional neural network for inverse problems in imaging. IEEE Trans. Image Process. **26**(9), 4509–4522 (2017)
23. Johnson, J., Alahi, A., Fei-Fei, L.: Perceptual losses for real-time style transfer and super-resolution. In: Leibe, B., Matas, J., Sebe, N., Welling, M. (eds.) ECCV 2016, Part II. LNCS, vol. 9906, pp. 694–711. Springer, Cham (2016). https://doi.org/10. 1007/978-3-319-46475-6_43
24. Kim, J., Lee, J.K., Lee, K.M.: Accurate image super-resolution using very deep convolutional networks. In: IEEE Conference on Computer Vision and Pattern Recognition, pp. 1646–1654. IEEE (2016)
25. Kingma, D., Ba, J.: Adam: a method for stochastic optimization (2014). arXiv preprint: arXiv:1412.6980
26. Kulkarni, K., Lohit, S., Turaga, P., Kerviche, R., Ashok, A.: Reconnet: non-iterative reconstruction of images from compressively sensed measurements. In: IEEE Conference on Computer Vision and Pattern Recognition, pp. 449–458. IEEE (2016)
27. Kupyn, O., Budzan, V., Mykhailych, M., Mishkin, D., Matas, J.: DeblurGAN: blind motion deblurring using conditional adversarial networks (2017). arXiv preprint: arXiv:1711.07064
28. Ledig, C., et al.: Photo-realistic single image super-resolution using a generative adversarial network. In: IEEE Conference on Computer Vision and Pattern Recognition, pp. 4681–4690. IEEE (2017)
29. Li, Y., Huang, J.-B., Ahuja, N., Yang, M.-H.: Deep joint image filtering. In: Leibe, B., Matas, J., Sebe, N., Welling, M. (eds.) ECCV 2016, Part IV. LNCS, vol. 9908, pp. 154–169. Springer, Cham (2016). https://doi.org/10.1007/978-3-319-46493-0_10
30. Li, Y., Liu, S., Yang, J., Yang, M.H.: Generative face completion. In: IEEE Conference on Computer Vision and Pattern Recognition, pp. 3911–3919. IEEE (2017)
31. Lin, Z., He, J., Tang, X., Tang, C.K.: Limits of learning-based superresolution algorithms. Int. J. Comput. Vis. **80**(3), 406–420 (2008)
32. Liu, C., Shum, H.Y., Freeman, W.T.: Face hallucination: theory and practice. Int. J. Comput. Vis. **75**(1), 115–134 (2007)
33. Liu, Z., Yeh, R.A., Tang, X., Liu, Y., Agarwala, A.: Video frame synthesis using deep voxel flow. In: IEEE International Conference on Computer Vision, pp. 4463–4471. IEEE (2017)
34. Lucas, A., Iliadis, M., Molina, R., Katsaggelos, A.K.: Using deep neural networks for inverse problems in imaging: beyond analytical methods. IEEE Signal Process. Mag. **35**(1), 20–36 (2018)
35. Mao, X.J., Shen, C., Yang, Y.B.: Image denoising using very deep fully convolutional encoder-decoder networks with symmetric skip connections (2016). arXiv preprint: arXiv:1603.09056

36. Nah, S., Kim, T.H., Lee, K.M.: Deep multi-scale convolutional neural network for dynamic scene deblurring. In: IEEE Conference on Computer Vision and Pattern Recognition, pp. 3883–3891. IEEE (2017)
37. Nimisha, T., Singh, A.K., Rajagopalan, A.: Blur-invariant deep learning for blind-deblurring. In: IEEE Conference on Computer Vision and Pattern Recognition, pp. 4752–4760. IEEE (2017)
38. Noroozi, M., Chandramouli, P., Favaro, P.: Motion deblurring in the wild. In: Roth, V., Vetter, T. (eds.) GCPR 2017. LNCS, vol. 10496, pp. 65–77. Springer, Cham (2017). https://doi.org/10.1007/978-3-319-66709-6_6
39. Pan, J., Sun, D., Pfister, H., Yang, M.H.: Blind image deblurring using dark channel prior. In: IEEE Conference on Computer Vision and Pattern Recognition, pp. 1628–1636. IEEE (2016)
40. Park, E., Yang, J., Yumer, E., Ceylan, D., Berg, A.C.: Transformation-grounded image generation network for novel 3d view synthesis. In: IEEE Conference on Computer Vision and Pattern Recognition, pp. 3500–3509. IEEE (2017)
41. Parkhi, O.M., Vedaldi, A., Zisserman, A.: Deep face recognition. In: British Machine Vision Conference, pp. 41.1–41.12 (2015)
42. Phillips, P.J., et al.: Overview of the face recognition grand challenge. In: IEEE Conference on Computer Vision and Pattern Recognition, pp. 947–954. IEEE (2005)
43. Ronneberger, O., Fischer, P., Brox, T.: U-Net: convolutional networks for biomedical image segmentation. In: Navab, N., Hornegger, J., Wells, W.M., Frangi, A.F. (eds.) MICCAI 2015, Part III. LNCS, vol. 9351, pp. 234–241. Springer, Cham (2015). https://doi.org/10.1007/978-3-319-24574-4_28
44. Salimans, T., Goodfellow, I., Zaremba, W., Cheung, V., Radford, A., Chen, X.: Improved techniques for training gans. In: Advances in Neural Information Processing Systems, pp. 2234–2242 (2016)
45. Schuler, C.J., Hirsch, M., Harmeling, S., Schölkopf, B.: Learning to deblur. IEEE Trans. Pattern Anal. Mach. Intell. 38(7), 1439–1451 (2016)
46. Tai, Y., Yang, J., Liu, X., Xu, C.: MemNet: a persistent memory network for image restoration. In: International Conference on Computer Vision, pp. 4549–4557. IEEE (2017)
47. Tuzel, O., Taguchi, Y., Hershey, J.R.: Global-local face upsampling network (2016). arXiv preprint: arXiv:1603.07235
48. Xiao, L., Wang, J., Heidrich, W., Hirsch, M.: Learning high-order filters for efficient blind deconvolution of document photographs. In: Leibe, B., Matas, J., Sebe, N., Welling, M. (eds.) ECCV 2016, Part III. LNCS, vol. 9907, pp. 734–749. Springer, Cham (2016). https://doi.org/10.1007/978-3-319-46487-9_45
49. Xu, X., Sun, D., Pan, J., Zhang, Y., Pfister, H., Yang, M.H.: Learning to super-resolve blurry face and text images. In: IEEE International Conference on Computer Vision, pp. 251–260. IEEE (2017)
50. Yeh, R., Liu, Z., Goldman, D.B., Agarwala, A.: Semantic facial expression editing using autoencoded flow (2016). arXiv preprint: arXiv:1611.09961
51. Yi, D., Lei, Z., Liao, S., Li, S.Z.: Learning face representation from scratch (2014). arXiv preprint: arXiv:1411.7923
52. Yu, X., Porikli, F.: Ultra-resolving face images by discriminative generative networks. In: Leibe, B., Matas, J., Sebe, N., Welling, M. (eds.) ECCV 2016, Part V. LNCS, vol. 9909, pp. 318–333. Springer, Cham (2016). https://doi.org/10.1007/978-3-319-46454-1_20

53. Yu, X., Porikli, F.: Face hallucination with tiny unaligned images by transformative discriminative neural networks. In: AAAI Conference on Artificial Intelligence, pp. 4327–4333 (2017)
54. Yu, X., Porikli, F.: Hallucinating very low-resolution unaligned and noisy face images by transformative discriminative autoencoders. In: IEEE Conference on Computer Vision and Pattern Recognition, pp. 3760–3768. IEEE (2017)
55. Zhang, K., Zuo, W., Chen, Y., Meng, D., Zhang, L.: Beyond a Gaussian denoiser: residual learning of deep CNN for image denoising. IEEE Trans. Image Process. **26**(7), 3142–3155 (2017)
56. Zhang, K., Zhang, Z., Li, Z., Qiao, Y.: Joint face detection and alignment using multitask cascaded convolutional networks. IEEE Signal Process. Lett. **23**(10), 1499–1503 (2016)
57. Zhang, Z., Luo, P., Loy, C.C., Tang, X.: Learning deep representation for face alignment with auxiliary attributes. IEEE Trans. Pattern Anal. Mach. Intell. **38**(5), 918–930 (2016)
58. Zhou, T., Tulsiani, S., Sun, W., Malik, J., Efros, A.A.: View synthesis by appearance flow. In: Leibe, B., Matas, J., Sebe, N., Welling, M. (eds.) ECCV 2016, Part IV. LNCS, vol. 9908, pp. 286–301. Springer, Cham (2016). https://doi.org/10.1007/978-3-319-46493-0_18
59. Zhu, S., Liu, S., Loy, C.C., Tang, X.: Deep cascaded Bi-network for face hallucination. In: Leibe, B., Matas, J., Sebe, N., Welling, M. (eds.) ECCV 2016, Part V. LNCS, vol. 9909, pp. 614–630. Springer, Cham (2016). https://doi.org/10.1007/978-3-319-46454-1_37

Face De-spoofing: Anti-spoofing
via Noise Modeling

Amin Jourabloo, Yaojie Liu$^{(\boxtimes)}$, and Xiaoming Liu

Department of Computer Science and Engineering, Michigan State University,
East Lansing, USA
{jourablo,liuyaoj1,liuxm}@msu.edu

Abstract. Many prior face anti-spoofing works develop discriminative models for recognizing the subtle differences between live and spoof faces. Those approaches often regard the image as an indivisible unit, and process it holistically, without explicit modeling of the spoofing process. In this work, motivated by the noise modeling and denoising algorithms, we identify a new problem of face de-spoofing, for the purpose of anti-spoofing: inversely decomposing a spoof face into a spoof noise and a live face, and then utilizing the spoof noise for classification. A CNN architecture with proper constraints and supervisions is proposed to overcome the problem of having no ground truth for the decomposition. We evaluate the proposed method on multiple face anti-spoofing databases. The results show promising improvements due to our spoof noise modeling. Moreover, the estimated spoof noise provides a visualization which helps to understand the added spoof noise by each spoof medium.

Keywords: Face anti-spoofing · Generative model · CNN
Image decomposition

1 Introduction

With the increasing influence of smart devices in our daily lives, people are seeking for secure and convenient ways to access their personal information. Biometrics, such as face, fingerprint, and iris, are widely utilized for person authentication due to their intrinsic distinctiveness and convenience to use. Face, as one of the most popular modalities, has received increasing attention in the academia and industry in the recent years (e.g., iPhone X). However, the attention also brings a growing incentive for hackers to design biometric presentation attacks (PA), or spoofs, to be authenticated as the genuine user. Due to the almost no-cost access to the human face, the spoof face can be as simple as a printed photo paper (i.e., print attack) and a digital image/video (i.e., replay attack), or as complicated as a 3D Mask and facial cosmetic makeup. With proper handling,

---

A. Jourabloo and Y. Liu—Denotes equal contribution by the authors.

© Springer Nature Switzerland AG 2018
V. Ferrari et al. (Eds.): ECCV 2018, LNCS 11217, pp. 297–315, 2018.
https://doi.org/10.1007/978-3-030-01261-8_18

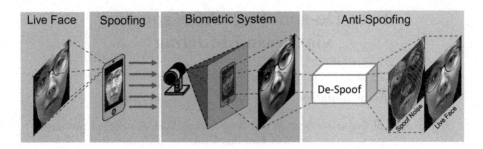

Fig. 1. The illustration of face spoofing and anti-spoofing processes. De-spoofing process aims to estimate a spoof noise from a spoof face and reconstruct the live face. The estimated spoof noise should be discriminative for face anti-spoofing.

those spoofs can be visually very close to the genuine user's live face. As a result, these call for the need of developing robust face anti-spoofing algorithms.

As the most common spoofs, print attack and replay attack have been well studied previously, from different perspectives. The cue-based methods aim to detect liveness cues [1,2] (e.g., eye blinking, head motion) to classify live videos. But these methods can be fooled by video replay attacks. The texture-based methods attempt to compare texture difference between live and spoof faces, using pre-defined features such as LBP [3,4], HOG [5,6]. Similar to texture-based methods, CNN-based methods [2,7,8] design a unified process of feature extraction and classification. With a softmax loss based binary supervision, they have the risk of overfitting on the training data. Regardless of the perspectives, almost all the prior works treat face anti-spoofing as a *black box* binary classification problem. In contrast, we propose to open the black box by modeling the process of how a spoof image is generated from its original live image.

Our approach is motivated by the classic image de-X problems, such as image de-noising and de-blurring [9–12]. In image de-noising, the corrupted image is regarded as a degradation from the additive noise, e.g., salt-and-pepper noise and white Gaussian noise. In image de-blurring, the uncorrupted image is degraded by motion, which can be described as a process of convolution. Similarly, in face anti-spoofing, the spoof image can be viewed as a re-rendering of the live image but with some "special" noise from the spoof medium and the environment. Hence, the natural question is, *can we recover the underlying live image when given a spoof image, similar to image de-noising?*

Yes. This paper shows "how" to do this. We call the process of decomposing a spoof face to the spoof noise pattern and a live face as *Face De-spoofing*, shown in Fig. 1. Similar to the previous de-X works, the degraded image $\mathbf{x} \in \mathbb{R}^m$ can be formulated as a function of the original image $\hat{\mathbf{x}}$, the degradation matrix $\mathbf{A} \in \mathbb{R}^{m \times m}$ and an additive noise $\mathbf{n} \in \mathbb{R}^m$.

$$\mathbf{x} = \mathbf{A}\hat{\mathbf{x}} + \mathbf{n} = \hat{\mathbf{x}} + (\mathbf{A} - \mathbb{I})\hat{\mathbf{x}} + \mathbf{n} = \hat{\mathbf{x}} + N(\hat{\mathbf{x}}), \tag{1}$$

where $N(\hat{\mathbf{x}}) = (\mathbf{A} - \mathbb{I})\hat{\mathbf{x}} + \mathbf{n}$ is the image-dependent noise function. Instead of solving $\mathbf{A}$ and $\mathbf{n}$, we decide to estimate $N(\hat{\mathbf{x}})$ directly since it is more solvable under the deep learning framework [13–17]. Essentially, by estimating $N(\hat{\mathbf{x}})$ and $\hat{\mathbf{x}}$, we aim to peel off the spoof noise and reconstruct the original live face. Likewise, if given a live face, face de-spoofing model should return itself plus *zero* noise. Note that our face de-spoofing is designed to handle paper attack, replay attack and possibly make-up attack, but our experiments are limited to the first two PAs. The benefits of face de-spoofing are twofold: (1) it reverses, or undoes, the spoofing generation process, which helps us to model and visualize the spoof noise pattern of different spoof mediums. (2) the spoof noise itself is discriminative between live and spoof images and hence is useful for face anti-spoofing.

While face de-spoofing shares the same challenges as other image de-X problems, it has a few distinct difficulties to conquer:

No Ground Truth: Image de-X works often use synthetic data where the original undegraded image could be used as ground truth for supervised learning. In contrast, we have no access to $\hat{\mathbf{x}}$, which is the corresponding live face of a spoof face image.

No Noise Model: There is no comprehensive study and understanding about the spoof noise. Hence it is not clear how we can constrain the solution space to *faithfully* estimate the spoof noise pattern.

Diverse Spoof Mediums: Each type of spoofs utilizes different spoof mediums for generating spoof images. Each spoof medium represents a specific type of noise pattern.

To address these challenges, we propose several constraints and supervisions based on our prior knowledge and the conclusions from a case study (in Sect. 3.1). Given that a live face has no spoof noise, we impose the constraint that $N(\hat{\mathbf{x}})$ of a live image is *zero*. Based on our study, we assume that the spoof noise of a spoof image is ubiquitous, i.e., it exists everywhere in the spatial domain of the image; and is repetitive, i.e., it is the spatial repetition of certain noise in the image. The repetitiveness can be encouraged by maximizing the high-frequency magnitude of the estimated noise in the Fourier domain.

With such constraints and auxiliary supervisions proposed in [18], a novel CNN architecture is presented in this paper. Given an image, one CNN is designed to synthesize the spoof noise pattern and reconstruct the corresponding live image. In order to examine the reconstructed live image, we train another CNN with auxiliary supervision and a GAN-like discriminator in an end-to-end fashion. These two networks are designed to ensure the quality of the reconstructed image regarding its discriminativeness between live and spoof, and the visual plausibility of the synthesized live image.

To summarize, the main contributions of this work include:

- We offer a new perspective for detecting the spoofing face from print attack and replay attack by inversely decomposing a spoof face image into the live face and the spoofing noise, without having the ground truth of either.
- A novel CNN architecture is proposed for face de-spoofing, where appropriate constraints and auxiliary supervisions are imposed.

- We demonstrate the value of face de-spoofing by its contribution to face anti-spoofing and the visualization of the spoof noise patterns.

2 Prior Work

We review the most relevant prior works to ours from two perspectives: texture-based face anti-spoofing and de-X problems.

Texture-Based Face Anti-spoofing. Texture analysis is widely adopted in face anti-spoofing as well as other computer vision tasks [19,20], where defining an effective feature representation is the key endeavor. Early works apply the hand-crafted feature descriptors, such as LBP [3,4,21], HoG [5,6], SIFT [22] and SURF [23], to project the faces to a low-dimension embedding. However, those hand-crafted features are not specifically designed to capture the subtle differences in the spoofing faces, and thus the embedding may not be discriminative. In addition, those features may not be robust to variations such as illumination, pose, and etc. To overcome some of these difficulties, researchers tackle the problem in different domains, such as HSV and YCbCr color space [24,25], temporal domain [26–29] and Fourier spectrum [30].

Heading into the deep learning era, researchers aim to build deep models for a higher accuracy. Most of the CNN works treat face anti-spoofing as a binary classification problem and apply the softmax loss function. Compared to hand-crafted features, such models [29] achieve remarkable improvements in the intra-testing (i.e., train and test within the same dataset). However, during the cross-testing (i.e., train and test in different datasets), these CNN models exhibit a poor generalization ability due to the overfitting to training data. Atoum et al. [31] and Liu et al. [18] observe the overfitting issue of the softmax loss, and both propose novel auxiliary-driven loss functions instead of softmax to supervise the CNN. These works bring us the insight that we need to involve the domain knowledge to solve face anti-spoofing.

To the best of our knowledge, all the previous methods are discriminative models. There are only a few papers [2,22] trying to categorize the types and properties of the spoof noise pattern, such as color distortion and moiré pattern. In this work, we analyze the properties of spoof noise and design a GAN-fashion generative model [32] to estimate the spoof noise pattern and peel it off the spoof image. We believe by decomposing the spoof image, CNN can analyze the spoof noise more directly and effectively, and gain more knowledge in tackling face anti-spoofing.

De-X Problems. De-X problems, such as de-noising, de-blurring, de-mosaicing, super-resolution and inpainting [13–17,33–38], are classic low-level vision problems that remove the degradation effect or artifacts from the image. General de-noising works assume additive Gaussian noise and researchers propose non-local filters [33] or CNNs [13,34] to exploit the inherent similarity within the images. For de-mosaicing and super-resolution, many models, such as ResNet in [14,15] and joint models in [16,17,35], are learnt from the given pairs of low-quality input and high-quality ground truth. In image inpainting, users mark

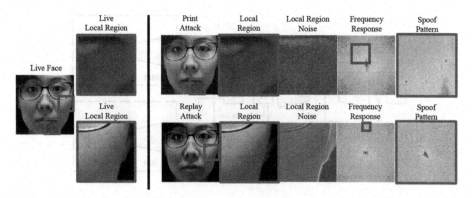

Fig. 2. The illustration of the spoof noise pattern. **Left:** live face and its local regions. **Right:** Two registered spoofing faces from print attack and replay attack. For each sample, we show the local region of the face, intensity difference to the live image, magnitude of 2D FFT, and the local peaks in the frequency domain that indicates the spoof noise pattern. Best viewed electronically.

the area to inpaint in a mask map and apply the filling based on the existing patch texture and the overall view structure in the unmasked region [36,37,39].

One advantage of existing de-X problems is that most of the image degradation can be easily synthesized. This brings two benefits: (1) it provides the model training with the input degraded samples and *golden* ground-truth original images for supervision. (2) it is easy to synthesize a large amount of data for training and evaluation. On the contrary, degradation due to spoofing is versatile, complex, and subtle. It consists of 2-stage degradation: one from the spoof medium (e.g., paper and digital screen), and the other from the interaction of the spoof medium with the imaging environment. Each stage includes a large number of variations, such as medium type, illumination, non-rigid deformation and sensor types. Combination of these variations makes the overall degradation varies greatly. As a result, it is almost impossible to mimic realistic spoofing by synthesizing a degradation, which is a distinct challenge of face de-spoofing compared to the conventional de-X problems.

Without the ground truth of the degraded image, face de-spoofing becomes a very challenging problem. In this work, we propose an encoder-decoder architecture with novel loss functions and supervisions to solve the de-spoofing problem.

3   Face De-spoofing

In this section, we start with a case study of spoof noise pattern, which demonstrates a few important characteristics of the noise. This study motivates us to design the novel CNN architecture that will be presented in Sect. 3.2.

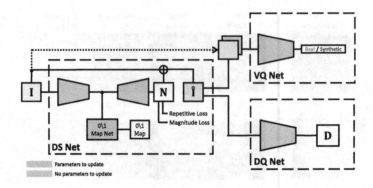

Fig. 3. The proposed network architecture.

3.1 A Case Study of Spoof Noise Pattern

The core task of face de-spoofing is to estimate the spoofing-relevant noise pattern in the given face image. Despite the strength of using a CNN model, we are still facing the challenge of learning *without* the ground truth of the noise pattern. To address this challenge, we would like to first carry out a case study on the noise pattern with the objectives of answering the following questions: (1) is Eq. 1 a good modeling of the spoof noise? (2) what characteristics does the spoof noise hold?

Let us denote a genuine face as $\hat{\mathbf{I}}$. By using printed paper or video replay on digital devices, the attacker can manufacture a spoof image $\mathbf{I}$ from $\hat{\mathbf{I}}$. Considering no non-rigid deformation between $\mathbf{I}$ and $\hat{\mathbf{I}}$, we summarize the degradation from $\hat{\mathbf{I}}$ to $\mathbf{I}$ as the following steps:

1. **Color distortion:** Color distortion is due to a narrower color gamut of the spoof medium (e.g. LCD screen or Toner Cartridge). It is a projection from the original color space to a tinier color subspace. This noise is dependent on the color intensity of the subject, and hence it may apply as a degradation matrix to the genuine face $\mathbf{I}$ during the degradation.
2. **Display artifacts:** Spoof mediums often use several nearby dots/sensors to approximate one pixel's color, and they may also display the face differently than the original size. Approximation and down-sampling procedure would cause a certain degree of high-frequency information loss, blurring, and pixel perturbation. This noise may also apply as a degradation matrix due to its subject dependence.
3. **Presenting artifacts:** When presenting the spoof medium to the camera, the medium interacts with the environment and brings several artifacts, including reflection and transparency of the surface. This noise may apply as an additive noise.
4. **Imaging artifacts:** Imaging lattice patterns such as screen pixels on the camera's sensor array (e.g. CMOS and CCD) would cause interference of light. This effect leads to aliasing and creates moiré pattern, which appears

in replay attack and some print attack with strong lattice artifacts. This noise may apply as an additive noise.

These four steps show that the spoof image $\mathbf{I}$ can be generated via applying degradation matrices and additive noises to $\hat{\mathbf{I}}$, which is basically conveyed by Eq. 1. As expressed by Eq. 1, the spoof image is the summation of the live image and image-dependent noise. To further validate this model, we show an example in Fig. 2. Given a high-quality live image, we carefully produce two spoof images via print and replay attack, with minimal non-rigid deformation. After each spoof image is registered with the live image, the live image becomes the *ground truth* live image if we would perform de-spoofing on the spoof image. This allows us to compute the difference between the live and spoof images, which is the noise pattern $N(\hat{\mathbf{I}})$. To analyze its frequency properties, we perform FFT on the spoof noise and show the 2D shifted magnitude response.

In both spoof cases, we observe a high response in the low-frequency domain, which is related to color distortion and display artifacts. In print attack, *repetitive* noise in Step 3 leads to a few "peak" responses in the high-frequency domain. Similarly, in the replay attack, visible moiré pattern reflects as several spurs in the low-frequency domain, and the lattice pattern that causes the moiré pattern is represented as peaks in the high-frequency domain. Moreover, spoof patterns are uniformly distributed in the image domain due to the uniform texture of the spoof mediums. And the high response of the repetitive pattern in the frequency domain exactly demonstrates that it appears widely in the image and thus can be viewed as ubiquitous.

Under this ideal registration, the comparison between live and spoof images provides us a basic understanding of the spoof noise pattern. It is a type of texture that has the characteristics of **repetitive** and **ubiquitous**. Based on this modeling and noise characteristics, we design a network to estimate the noise *without* the access to the precisely registered ground truth live image, as this case study has.

3.2   De-Spoof Network

Network Overview: Figure 3 shows the overall network architecture of our proposed method. It consists of three parts: De-Spoof Net (DS Net), Discriminative Quality Net (DQ Net), and Visual Quality Net (VQ Net). DS Net is designed to estimate the spoof noise pattern $\mathbf{N}$ (i.e. the output of $N(\hat{\mathbf{I}})$) from the input image $\mathbf{I}$. The live face $\hat{\mathbf{I}}$ then can be reconstructed by subtracting the estimated noise $\mathbf{N}$ from the input image $\mathbf{I}$. This reconstructed image $\hat{\mathbf{I}}$ should be both visually appealing and indeed live, which will be safeguarded by the DQ Net and VQ Net respectively. All networks can be trained in an end-to-end fashion. The details of the network structure are shown in Table 1.

As the core part, DS Net is designed as an encoder-decoder structure with the input $\mathbf{I} \in \mathbb{R}^{256 \times 256 \times 6}$. Here the 6 channels are RGB + HSV color space, following the suggestion in [31]. In the encoder part, we first stack 10 convolutional layers with 3 pooling layers. Inspired by the residual network [40], we follow by a short-cut connection: concatenating the responses from *pool*1-1, *pool*1-2 with *pool*1-3,

304   A. Jourabloo et al.

Table 1. The network structure of DS Net, DQ Net and VQ Net. Each convolutional layer is followed by an exponential linear unit (ELU) and batch normalization layer. The input image size for DS Net is $256 \times 256 \times 6$. All the convolutional filters are 3×3. 0\1 Map Net is the bottom-left part, i.e., conv1-10, conv1-11, and conv1-12.

DS Net (Encoder Part)			DS Net (Decoder Part)			DQ Net			VQ Net		
Layer	Chan./Stri.	Outp. Size	Layer	Chan./Stri.	Outp. Size	Layer	Chan./Stri.	Outp. Size	Layer	Chan./Stri.	Outp. Size
Input image			Input pool1-1+pool1-2+pool1-3			Input {image,live}			Input {image,live}		
conv1-0	24/1	256	resize	-/-	256	conv3-0	64/1	256			
conv1-1	20/1	256	conv2-1	28/1	256	conv3-1	128/1	256	conv4-1	24/2	256
conv1-2	25/1	256	conv2-2	24/1	256	conv3-2	196/1	256	conv4-2	20/2	256
conv1-3	20/1	256				conv3-3	128/1	256	pool4-1	-/2	128
pool1-1	-/2	128				pool3-1	-/2	128			
conv1-4	20/1	128	conv2-3	20/1	256	conv3-4	128/1	128	conv4-3	20/1	128
conv1-5	25/1	128	conv2-4	20/1	256	conv3-5	196/1	128	conv4-4	16/1	128
conv1-6	20/1	128				conv3-6	128/1	128	pool4-2	-/2	64
pool1-2	-/2	64				pool3-2	-/2	64			
conv1-7	20/1	64	conv2-5	20/1	256	conv3-7	128/1	64	conv4-5	12/1	64
conv1-8	25/1	64	conv2-6	16/1	256	conv3-8	196/1	64	conv4-6	6/1	64
conv1-9	20/1	64				conv3-9	128/1	64	pool4-3	-/2	32
pool1-3	-/2	32				pool3-3	-/2	32			
short-cut connection pool1-1+pool1-2+pool1-3						short-cut connection pool3-1+pool3-2+pool3-3			vectorize		1024
conv1-10	28/1	32	conv2-7	16/1	256	conv3-10	128/1	32	fc4-1	1/1	100
conv1-11	16/1	32	conv2-8	6/1	256	conv3-11	64/1	32	dropout	-	0.2%
conv1-12	1/1	32	live	(image - conv2-8)		conv3-12	1/1	32	fc4-2	1/1	2

and then sending them to *conv*1-10. This operation helps us to pass the feature responses from different scales to the later stages and ease the training procedure. Going through 3 more convolution layers, the responses $\mathbf{F} \in \mathbb{R}^{32 \times 32 \times 32}$ from *conv*1-12 are the feature representation of the spoof noise patterns. The higher magnitudes the responses have, the more spoofing-perceptible the input is.

Out from the encoder, the feature representation $\mathbf{F}$ is fed into the decoder to reconstruct the spoof noise pattern. $\mathbf{F}$ is directly resized to the input spatial size 256×256. It introduces no extra grid artifacts, which exist in the alternative approach of using a deconvolutional layer. Then, we pass the resized $\mathbf{F}$ to several convolutional layers to reconstruct the noise pattern $\mathbf{N}$. According to Eq. 1, the reconstructed live image can be retrieved by: $\hat{\mathbf{x}} = \mathbf{x} - N(\hat{\mathbf{x}}) = \mathbf{I} - \mathbf{N}$.

Each convolutional layer in the DS Net is equipped with exponential linear unit (ELU) and batch normalization layers. To supervise the training of DS Net, we design multiple loss functions: losses from DQ Net and VQ Net for the image quality, 0\1 map loss, and noise property losses. We introduce these loss functions in Sects. 3.3 and 3.4.

3.3   DQ Net and VQ Net

While we do not have the ground truth to supervise the estimated spoof noise pattern, it is possible to supervise the reconstructed live image, which implicitly guides the noise estimation. To estimate a good-quality spoof noise, the reconstructed live image should be quantitatively and visually recognized as live. For this purpose, we propose two networks in our architecture: Discriminative Quality Net (DQ Net) and Visual Quality Net (VQ Net). The VQ Net aims to guarantee the reconstructed live face is photorealistic. The DQ Net is proposed to guarantee the reconstructed face would indeed be considered as live, based on the judgment of a pre-trained face anti-spoofing network. The details of our proposed architecture are shown in Table 1.

Discriminative Quality Net: We follow the state-of-the-art network architecture of face anti-spoofing [18] to build our DQ Net. It is a fully convolutional network with three filter blocks and three additional convolutional layers. Each block consists of three convolutional layers and one pooling layer. The feature maps after each pooling layer are resized and stacked to feed into the following convolutional layers. Finally, DQ Net is supervised to estimate the pseudo-depth **D** of an input face, where **D** for the live face is the depth of the face shape and **D** for the spoof face is a zero map as a flat surface. We adopt the 3D face alignment algorithm in [41] to estimate the face shape and render the depth via Z-Buffering.

Similar to the previous work [42], DQ Net is pre-trained to obtain the semantic knowledge of live faces and spoofing faces. And during the training of DS Net, the parameters of DQ Net are fixed. Since the reconstructed images $\hat{\mathbf{I}}$ are live images, the corresponding pseudo-depth **D** should be the depth of the face shape. The backpropagation of the error from DQ Net guides the DS Net to estimate the spoof noise pattern which should be subtracted from the input image,

$$J_{DQ} = \left\| \text{CNN}_{DQ}(\hat{\mathbf{I}}) - \mathbf{D} \right\|_1, \tag{2}$$

where CNN_{DQ} is a fixed network and **D** is the depth of the face shape.

Visual Quality Net: We deploy a GAN to verify the visual quality of the estimated live image $\hat{\mathbf{I}}$. Given both the real live image $\mathbf{I}_{\text{live}}$ and the synthesized live image $\hat{\mathbf{I}}$, VQ Net is trained to distinguish between $\mathbf{I}_{\text{live}}$ and $\hat{\mathbf{I}}$. Meanwhile, DS Net tries to reconstruct photorealistic live images where the VQ Net would classify them as non-synthetic (or real) images. The VQ Net consists of 6 convolutional layers and a fully connected layer with a 2D vector as the output, which represents the probability of the input image to be real or synthetic. In each iteration during the training, the VQ Net is evaluated with two batches, in the first one, the DS Net is fixed and we update the VQ Net,

$$J_{VQ_{train}} = -\mathbb{E}_{\mathbf{I} \in \mathcal{R}} \log(\text{CNN}_{VQ}(\mathbf{I})) - \mathbb{E}_{\mathbf{I} \in \mathcal{S}} \log(1 - \text{CNN}_{VQ}(\text{CNN}_{DS}(\mathbf{I}))), \tag{3}$$

where $\mathcal{R}$ and $\mathcal{S}$ are the sets of real and synthetic images respectively. In the second batch, the VQ Net is fixed and the DS Net is updated,

$$J_{VQ_{test}} = -\mathbb{E}_{\mathbf{I} \in \mathcal{S}} \log(\text{CNN}_{VQ}(\text{CNN}_{DS}(\mathbf{I}))). \tag{4}$$

3.4 Loss Functions

The main challenge for spoof modeling is the lack of the ground truth for the spoof noise pattern. Since we have concluded some properties about the spoof noise in Sect. 3.1, we can leverage them to design several novel loss functions to constrain the convergence space. First, we introduce magnitude loss to enforce the spoof noise of the live image to be zero. Second, zero\one map loss is used to demonstrate the ubiquitousness of the spoof noise. Third, we encourage the repetitiveness property of spoof noise via repetitive loss. We describe three loss functions as the following:

Magnitude Loss: The spoof noise pattern for the live images is zero. The magnitude loss can be utilized to impose the constraint for the estimated noise. Given the estimated noise $\mathbf{N}$ and reconstructed live image $\hat{\mathbf{I}} = \mathbf{I} - \mathbf{N}$ of an original live image $\mathbf{I}$, we have,

$$J_m = \|\mathbf{N}\|_1. \tag{5}$$

Zero\One Map Loss: To learn discriminative features in the encoder layers, we define a sub-task in the DS Net to estimate a zero-map for the live faces and an one-map for the spoof. Since this is a per *pixel* supervision, it is also a constraint of ubiquitousness on the noise. Moreover, 0\1 map enables the receptive field of each pixel to cover a local area, which helps to learn generalizable features for this problem. Formally, given the extracted features $\mathbf{F}$ from an input face image $\mathbf{I}$ in the encoder, we have,

$$J_z = \|\mathrm{CNN}_{01map}(\mathbf{F}; \Theta) - \mathbf{M}\|_1, \tag{6}$$

where $\mathbf{M} \in \mathbf{0}^{32\times32}$ or $\mathbf{M} \in \mathbf{1}^{32\times32}$ is the zero\one map label.

Repetitive Loss: Based on the previous discussion, we assume the spoof noise pattern to be repetitive, because it is generated from the repetitive spoof medium. To encourage the repetitiveness, we convert the estimated noise $\mathbf{N}$ to the Fourier domain and compute the maximum value in the high-frequency band. The existence of high peak is indicative of the repetitive pattern. We would like to maximize this peak for spoof images, but minimize it for live images, as the following loss function:

$$J_r = \begin{cases} -\max(H(\mathcal{F}(\mathbf{N}), k)), & \mathbf{I} \in Spoof \\ \|\max(H(\mathcal{F}(\mathbf{N}), k))\|_1, & \mathbf{I} \in Live \end{cases},$$

where $\mathcal{F}$ is the Fourier transform operator, H is an operator for masking the low-frequency domain of an image, i.e., setting a $k \times k$ region in the center of the shifted 2D Fourier response to zero.

Finally, the total loss function in our training is the weighted summation of the aforementioned loss functions and the supervisions for the image qualities,

$$J_T = J_z + \lambda_1 J_m + \lambda_2 J_r + \lambda_3 J_{DQ} + \lambda_4 J_{VQ_{test}}, \tag{7}$$

where $\lambda_1, \lambda_2, \lambda_3, \lambda_4$ are the weights. During the training, we alternate between optimizing Eqs. 7 and 3.

Table 2. The accuracy of different outputs of the proposed architecture and their fusions.

Method	0\1 map	Spoof noise	Depth map	Fusion (Spoof noise, Depth map)		Fusion of all three outputs	
				Maximum	Average	Maximum	Average
APCER	2.50	1.70	1.66	1.70	1.27	1.70	1.27
BPCER	2.52	1.70	1.68	1.73	1.73	1.73	1.73
ACER	2.51	1.70	1.67	1.72	1.50	1.72	1.50

4 Experimental Results

4.1 Experimental Setup

Databases. We evaluate our work on three face anti-spoofing databases, with print and replay attacks: Oulu-NPU [43], CASIA-MFSD [44] and Replay-Attack [45]. Oulu-NPU [43] is a high-resolution database, considering many real-world variations. Oulu-NPU also includes 4 testing protocols: Protocol 1 evaluates on the illumination variation, Protocol 2 examines the influence of different spoof medium, Protocol 3 inspects the effect of different camera devices and Protocol 4 contains all the challenges above, which is close to the scenario of cross testing. CASIA-MFSD [44] contains videos with resolution 640×480 and 1280×720. Replay-Attack [45] includes videos of 320×240. These two databases are often used for cross testing [2].

Parameter Setting. We implement our method in Tensorflow [46]. Models are trained with the batch size of 6 and the learning rate of 3e−5. We set the $k = 64$ in the repetitive loss and set λ_1 to λ_4 in Eq. 7 as $3, 0.005, 0.1$ and 0.016, respectively. DQ Net is trained separately and remains fixed during the update of DS Net and VQ Net, but all sub-networks are trained with the same and respective data in each protocol.

Evaluation Metrics. To compare with previous methods, we use Attack Presentation Classification Error Rate ($APCER$) [47], Bona Fide Presentation Classification Error Rate ($BPCER$) [47] and, $ACER = (APCER + BPCER)/2$ [47] for the intra testing on Oulu-NPU, and Half Total Error Rate ($HTER$) [48], half of the summation of FAR and FRR, for the cross testing between CASIA-MFSD and Replay-Attack.

4.2 Ablation Study

Using Oulu-NPU Protocol 1, we perform three studies on the effect of score fusing, the importance of each loss function, and the influence of image resolution and blurriness.

Different Fusion Methods. In the proposed architecture, three outputs can be utilized for classification: the norms of either the 0\1 map, the spoof noise pattern or the depth map. Because of the discriminativeness enabled by our learning, we can simply use a rudimentary classifier like L-1 norm. Note that a more advance classifier is applicable and would likely lead to higher performance.

Table 3. ACER of the proposed method with different image resolutions and blurriness. To create blurry images, we apply Gaussian filters with different kernel sizes to the input images.

Metric \ Resolution	256 × 256	128 × 128	64 × 64
APCER	1.27	2.27	5.24
BPCER	1.73	3.36	5.30
ACER	1.50	3.07	5.27

Metric \ Blurriness	1 × 1	3 × 3	5 × 5	7 × 7	9 × 9
APCER	1.27	2.29	3.12	3.95	4.79
BPCER	1.73	2.50	3.33	4.16	5.00
ACER	1.50	2.39	3.22	4.06	4.89

Table 2 shows the performance of each output and their fusion with maximum and average. It shows that the fusion of spoof noise and depth map achieves the best performance. However, adding the 0\1 map scores do not improve the accuracy since it contains the same information as the spoof noise. Hence, for the rest of experiments, we report performance from the average fusion of the spoof noise $\mathbf{N}$ and the depth map $\hat{\mathbf{D}}$, i.e., $score = (\|\mathbf{N}\|_1 + \left\|\hat{\mathbf{D}}\right\|_1)/2$.

Advantage of Each Loss Function. We have three main loss functions in our proposed architecture. To shows the effect of each loss function, we train a network with each loss excluded one by one. By disabling the magnitude loss, the 0\1 map loss and the repetitive loss, we obtain the ACERs 5.24, 2.34 and 1.50, respectively. To further validate the repetitive loss, we perform an experiment on high-resolution images by changing the network input to the cheek region of the original 1080P resolution. The ACER of the network with the repetitive loss is 2.92 but the network without cannot converge.

Resolution and Blurriness. As shown in the ablation study of repetitive loss, the image quality is critical for achieving a high accuracy. The spoof noise pattern may not be detected in the low-resolution or motion-blurred images. The testing results on different image resolutions and blurriness are shown in Table 3. These results validate that the spoof noise pattern is less discriminative for the lower-resolution or blurry images, as the high-frequency part of the input images contains most of the spoof noise pattern.

4.3 Experimental Comparison

To show the performance of our proposed method, we present our accuracy in the intra testing of Oulu-NPU and the cross testing on CASIA and Replay-Attack.

Intra Testing. We compare our intra testing performance on all 4 protocols of Oulu-NPU. Table 4 shows the comparison of our method and the best 3 out of 18 previous methods [18,49]. Our proposed method achieves promising results on all protocols. Specifically, we outperform the previous state of the art by a large margin in Protocol 4, which is the most challenging protocol, and similar to cross testing.

Table 4. The intra testing results on 4 protocols of Oulu-NPU.

Protocol	Method	APCER (%)	BPCER (%)	ACER (%)
1	CPqD [49]	2.9	10.8	6.9
	GRADIANT [49]	1.3	12.5	6.9
	Auxiliary [18]	1.6	**1.6**	1.6
	Ours	**1.2**	1.7	**1.5**
2	MixedFASNet [49]	9.7	2.5	6.1
	Ours	4.2	4.4	4.3
	Auxiliary [18]	2.7	2.7	2.7
	GRADIANT	**3.1**	**1.9**	**2.5**
3	MixedFASNet	5.3 ± 6.7	7.8 ± 5.5	6.5 ± 4.6
	GRADIANT	$\mathbf{2.6 \pm 3.9}$	5.0 ± 5.3	3.8 ± 2.4
	Ours	4.0 ± 1.8	3.8 ± 1.2	3.6 ± 1.6
	Auxiliary [18]	2.7 ± 1.3	$\mathbf{3.1 \pm 1.7}$	$\mathbf{2.9 \pm 1.5}$
4	Massy_HNU [49]	35.8 ± 35.3	8.3 ± 4.1	22.1 ± 17.6
	GRADIANT	$\mathbf{5.0 \pm 4.5}$	15.0 ± 7.1	10.0 ± 5.0
	Auxiliary [18]	9.3 ± 5.6	10.4 ± 6.0	9.5 ± 6.0
	Ours	5.1 ± 6.3	$\mathbf{6.1 \pm 5.1}$	$\mathbf{5.6 \pm 5.7}$

Cross Testing. We perform cross testing between CASIA-MFSD [44] and Replay-Attack [45]. As shown in Table 5, our method achieves the competitive performance on the cross testing from CASIA-MFSD to Replay-Attack. However, we achieve a worse HTER compared to the best performing methods from Replay Attack to CASIA-MFSD. We hypothesize the reason is that images of CASIA-MFSD are of much higher resolution than those of Replay Attack. This shows that the model trained with higher-resolution data can generalize well on lower-resolution testing data, but not the other way around. This is one limitation of the proposed method, and worthy further research.

4.4 Qualitative Experiments

Spoof Medium Classification. The estimated spoof noise pattern of the test images can be used for clustering them into different groups and each group represents one spoof medium. To visualize the results, we use t-SNE [52] for dimension reduction. The t-SNE projects the noise $\mathbf{N} \in \mathbb{R}^{256 \times 256 \times 6}$ to 2 dimensions by best preserving the KL divergence distance. Figure 4 shows the distributions of the testing videos on Oulu-NPU Protocol 1. The left image shows that the noise of live is well-clustered, and the noise of spoof is subject dependent, which is consistent with our noise assumption. To obtain a better visualization, we utilize the high pass filter to extract the high-frequency information of noise pattern for dimension reduction. The right image shows that the high frequency

Table 5. The HTER of different methods for the cross testing between the CASIA-MFSD and the Replay-Attack databases. We mark the top-2 performances in bold.

Method	Train	Test	Train	Test
	CASIA MFSD	Replay attack	Replay attack	CASIA MFSD
Motion [4]	50.2%		47.9%	
LBP-TOP [4]	49.7%		60.6%	
Motion-Mag [50]	50.1%		47.0%	
Spectral cubes [51]	34.4%		50.0%	
CNN [8]	48.5%		45.5%	
LBP [24]	47.0%		39.6%	
Colour Texture [25]	30.3%		**37.7%**	
Auxiliary [18]	**27.6%**		**28.4%**	
Ours	**28.5%**		41.1%	

Table 6. The confusion matrices of spoof mediums classification based on spoof noise pattern.

Predicted / Actual	live	print	display
live	59	1	0
print	0	88	32
display	13	8	99

Predicted / Actual	live	print1	print2	display1	display2
live	59	0	1	0	0
print1	0	41	2	11	6
print2	0	34	11	9	6
display1	10	6	0	13	31
display2	8	7	0	6	39

part has more subject independent information about the spoof type and can be utilized for classification of the spoof medium.

To further show the discriminative power of the estimated spoof noise, we divide the testing set of Protocol 1 to training and testing parts and train an SVM classifier for spoof medium classification. We train two models, a three-class classifier (live, print and display) and a five-class classifier (live, print1, print2, display1 and display2), and they achieve the classification accuracy of 82.0% and 54.3% respectively, shown in Table 6. Most classification errors of the five-class model are within the same spoof medium. This result is noteworthy given that no label of spoof medium type is provided during the learning of the spoof noise model. Yet the estimated noise actually carries appreciable information regarding the medium type; hence we can observe reasonable results of spoof medium classification. This demonstrates that the estimated noise contains spoof medium information and indeed we are moving toward estimating the faithful spoof noise residing in each spoof image. In the future, if the performance of spoof medium classification improves, this could bring new impact to applications such as forensic.

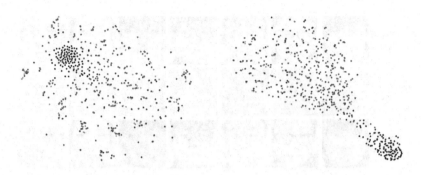

Fig. 4. The 2D visualization of the estimated spoof noise for test videos on Oulu-NPU Protocol 1. Left: the estimated noise, Right: the high-frequency band of the estimated noise, *Color code* used: *black*=live, *green*=printer1, *blue*=printer2, *magenta*=display1, *red*=display2. (Color figure online)

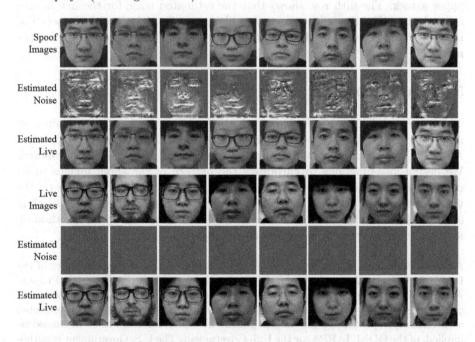

Fig. 5. The visualization of input images, estimated spoof noises and estimated live images for test videos of Protocol 1 of Oulu-NPU database. The first four columns in the first row are paper attacks and the second four are the replay attacks. For a better visualization, we magnify the noise by 5 times and add the value with 128, to show both positive and negative noise.

Successful and Failure Cases. We show several success and failure cases in Figs. 5 and 6. Figure 5 shows that the estimated spoof noises are similar within each medium but different from the other mediums. We suspect that the yellowish color in the first four columns is due to the stronger color distortion in the

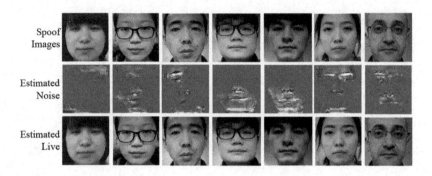

Fig. 6. The failure cases for converting the spoof images to the live ones.

paper attack. The fifth row shows that the estimated noise for the live images is nearly zero. For the failure cases, we only have a few false positive cases. The failures are due to undesired noise estimation which will motivate us for further research.

5   Conclusions

This paper introduces a new perspective for solving the face anti-spoofing by inversely decomposing a spoof face into the live face and the spoof noise pattern. A novel CNN architecture with multiple appropriate supervisions is proposed. We design loss functions to encourage the pattern of the spoof images to be ubiquitous and repetitive, while the noise of the live images should be zero. We visualize the spoof noise pattern which can help to have a deeper understanding of the added noise by each spoof medium. We evaluate the proposed method on multiple widely-used face anti-spoofing databases.

Acknowledgment. This research is based upon work supported by the Office of the Director of National Intelligence (ODNI), Intelligence Advanced Research Projects Activity (IARPA), via IARPA R&D Contract No. 2017-17020200004. The views and conclusions contained herein are those of the authors and should not be interpreted as necessarily representing the official policies or endorsements, either expressed or implied, of the ODNI, IARPA, or the U.S. Government. The U.S. Government is authorized to reproduce and distribute reprints for Governmental purposes notwithstanding any copyright annotation thereon.

References

1. Pan, G., Sun, L., Wu, Z., Lao, S.: Eyeblink-based anti-spoofing in face recognition from a generic webcamera. In: ICCV. IEEE (2007)
2. Patel, K., Han, H., Jain, A.K.: Cross-database face antispoofing with robust feature representation. In: You, Z. (ed.) CCBR 2016. LNCS, vol. 9967, pp. 611–619. Springer, Cham (2016). https://doi.org/10.1007/978-3-319-46654-5_67

3. de Freitas Pereira, T., Anjos, A., De Martino, J.M., Marcel, S.: LBP-TOP based countermeasure against face spoofing attacks. In: Park, J.-I., Kim, J. (eds.) ACCV 2012, Part I. LNCS, vol. 7728, pp. 121–132. Springer, Heidelberg (2013). https://doi.org/10.1007/978-3-642-37410-4_11

4. de Freitas Pereira, T., Anjos, A., De Martino, J.M., Marcel, S.: Can face anti-spoofing countermeasures work in a real world scenario? In: ICB. IEEE (2013)

5. Komulainen, J., Hadid, A., Pietikainen, M.: Context based face anti-spoofing. In: BTAS. IEEE (2013)

6. Yang, J., Lei, Z., Liao, S., Li, S.Z.: Face liveness detection with component dependent descriptor. In: ICB. IEEE (2013)

7. Li, L., Feng, X., Boulkenafet, Z., Xia, Z., Li, M., Hadid, A.: An original face anti-spoofing approach using partial convolutional neural network. In: 2016 6th International Conference on Image Processing Theory Tools and Applications (IPTA). IEEE (2016)

8. Yang, J., Lei, Z., Li, S.Z.: Learn convolutional neural network for face anti-spoofing (2014). arXiv preprint: arXiv:1408.5601

9. Dong, C., Loy, C.C., He, K., Tang, X.: Learning a deep convolutional network for image super-resolution. In: Fleet, D., Pajdla, T., Schiele, B., Tuytelaars, T. (eds.) ECCV 2014, Part IV. LNCS, vol. 8692, pp. 184–199. Springer, Cham (2014). https://doi.org/10.1007/978-3-319-10593-2_13

10. Jourabloo, A., Feghahati, A., Jamzad, M.: New algorithms for recovering highly corrupted images with impulse noise. Sci. Iranica 19(6), 1738–1745 (2012)

11. Kulkarni, K., Lohit, S., Turaga, P., Kerviche, R., Ashok, A.: Reconnet: non-iterative reconstruction of images from compressively sensed measurements. In: CVPR. IEEE (2016)

12. Pathak, D., Krahenbuhl, P., Donahue, J., Darrell, T., Efros, A.A.: Context encoders: feature learning by inpainting. In: CVPR. IEEE (2016)

13. Lefkimmiatis, S.: Non-local color image denoising with convolutional neural networks. In: CVPR. IEEE (2017)

14. Tai, Y., Yang, J., Liu, X., Xu, C.: Memnet: a persistent memory network for image restoration. In: ICCV. IEEE (2017)

15. Tai, Y., Yang, J., Liu, X.: Image super-resolution via deep recursive residual network. In: CVPR. IEEE (2017)

16. Zhou, R., Achanta, R., Süsstrunk, S.: Deep residual network for joint demosaicing and super-resolution (2018). arXiv preprint: arXiv:1802.06573

17. Gharbi, M., Chaurasia, G., Paris, S., Durand, F.: Deep joint demosaicking and denoising. ACM Trans. Graph. 35(6), 191 (2016)

18. Liu, Y., Jourabloo, A., Liu, X.: Learning deep models for face anti-spoofing: binary or auxiliary supervision. In: CVPR. IEEE (2018)

19. Krizhevsky, A., Sutskever, I., Hinton, G.E.: Imagenet classification with deep convolutional neural networks. In: NIPS (2012)

20. Jourabloo, A., Liu, X.: Pose-invariant face alignment via CNN-based dense 3D model fitting. Int. J. Comput. Vis. 124(2), 187–203 (2017)

21. Määttä, J., Hadid, A., Pietikäinen, M.: Face spoofing detection from single images using micro-texture analysis. In: ICJB. IEEE (2011)

22. Patel, K., Han, H., Jain, A.K.: Secure face unlock: spoof detection on smartphones. IEEE Trans. Inf. Forens. Secur. 11(10), 2268–2283 (2016)

23. Boulkenafet, Z., Komulainen, J., Hadid, A.: Face antispoofing using speeded-up robust features and fisher vector encoding. IEEE Signal Process. Lett. 24(2), 141–145 (2017)

24. Boulkenafet, Z., Komulainen, J., Hadid, A.: Face anti-spoofing based on color texture analysis. In: ICIP. IEEE (2015)
25. Boulkenafet, Z., Komulainen, J., Hadid, A.: Face spoofing detection using colour texture analysis. IEEE Trans. Inf. Forens. Secur. **11**(8), 1818–1830 (2016)
26. Siddiqui, T.A., et al.: Face anti-spoofing with multifeature videolet aggregation. In: ICPR. IEEE (2016)
27. Bao, W., Li, H., Li, N., Jiang, W.: A liveness detection method for face recognition based on optical flow field. In: IASP. IEEE (2009)
28. Feng, L., et al.: Integration of image quality and motion cues for face anti-spoofing: a neural network approach. J. Vis. Commun. Image Represent. **38**, 451–460 (2016)
29. Xu, Z., Li, S., Deng, W.: Learning temporal features using LSTM-CNN architecture for face anti-spoofing. In: IAPR Asian Conference. IEEE (2015)
30. Li, J., Wang, Y., Tan, T., Jain, A.K.: Live face detection based on the analysis of fourier spectra. In: Biometric Technology for Human Identification. SPIE (2004)
31. Atoum, Y., Liu, Y., Jourabloo, A., Liu, X.: Face anti-spoofing using patch and depth-based CNNs. In: ICJB. IEEE (2017)
32. Tran, L., Yin, X., Liu, X.: Disentangled representation learning GAN for pose-invariant face recognition. In: CVPR. IEEE (2017)
33. Buades, A., Coll, B., Morel, J.M.: A non-local algorithm for image denoising. In: CVPR. IEEE (2005)
34. Zhang, H., Sindagi, V., Patel, V.M.: Image de-raining using a conditional generative adversarial network (2017). arXiv preprint: arXiv:1701.05957
35. Zhang, H., Patel, V.M.: Densely connected pyramid dehazing network. In: CVPR. IEEE (2018)
36. Criminisi, A., Pérez, P., Toyama, K.: Region filling and object removal by exemplar-based image inpainting. IEEE Trans. Image Process. **13**(9), 1200–1212 (2004)
37. Bertalmio, M., Vese, L., Sapiro, G., Osher, S.: Simultaneous structure and texture image inpainting. IEEE Trans. Image Process. **12**(8), 882–889 (2003)
38. Chen, Y., Tai, Y., Liu, X., Shen, C., Yang, J.: FSRNet: end-to-end learning face super-resolution with facial priors. In: CVPR. IEEE (2018)
39. Liu, Y., Shu, C.: A comparison of image inpainting techniques. In: Sixth International Conference on Graphic and Image Processing (ICGIP 2014). SPIE (2015)
40. He, K., Zhang, X., Ren, S., Sun, J.: Deep residual learning for image recognition. In: CVPR. IEEE (2016)
41. Liu, Y., Jourabloo, A., Ren, W., Liu, X.: Dense face alignment. In: ICCVW. IEEE (2017)
42. Johnson, J., Alahi, A., Fei-Fei, L.: Perceptual losses for real-time style transfer and super-resolution. In: Leibe, B., Matas, J., Sebe, N., Welling, M. (eds.) ECCV 2016, Part II. LNCS, vol. 9906, pp. 694–711. Springer, Cham (2016). https://doi.org/10.1007/978-3-319-46475-6_43
43. Boulkenafet, Z., Komulainen, J., Li, L., Feng, X., Hadid, A.: OULU-NPU: a mobile face presentation attack database with real-world variations. In: FG. IEEE (2017)
44. Zhang, Z., Yan, J., Liu, S., Lei, Z., Yi, D., Li, S.Z.: A face antispoofing database with diverse attacks. In: ICB. IEEE (2012)
45. Chingovska, I., Anjos, A., Marcel, S.: On the effectiveness of local binary patterns in face anti-spoofing. IEEE (2012)
46. Abadi, M., Agarwal, A., et al.: TensorFlow: large-scale machine learning on heterogeneous systems (2015)
47. ISO/IEC JTC 1/SC 37 Biometrics: Information technology biometric presentation attack detection part 1: Framework. International organization for standardization (2016). https://www.iso.org/obp/ui/iso

48. Bengio, S., Mariéthoz, J.: A statistical significance test for person authentication. In: Proceedings of Odyssey 2004: The Speaker and Language Recognition Workshop (2004)

49. Boulkenafet, Z.: A competition on generalized software-based face presentation attack detection in mobile scenarios. In: ICJB. IEEE (2017)

50. Bharadwaj, S., Dhamecha, T.I., Vatsa, M., Singh, R.: Computationally efficient face spoofing detection with motion magnification. In: CVPRW. IEEE (2013)

51. Pinto, A., Pedrini, H., Schwartz, W.R., Rocha, A.: Face spoofing detection through visual codebooks of spectral temporal cubes. IEEE Trans. Image Process. **24**(12), 4726–4740 (2015)

52. van der Maaten, L., Hinton, G.: Visualizing data using t-SNE. J. Mach. Learn. Res. **9**, 2579–2605 (2008)

Unsupervised Hard Example Mining from Videos for Improved Object Detection

SouYoung Jin[✉], Aruni RoyChowdhury, Huaizu Jiang, Ashish Singh,
Aditya Prasad, Deep Chakraborty, and Erik Learned-Miller

College of Information and Computer Sciences,
University of Massachusetts, Amherst, USA
{souyoungjin,arunirc,hzjiang,ashishsingh,
aprasad,dchakraborty,elm}@cs.umass.edu

Abstract. Important gains have recently been obtained in object detection by using training objectives that focus on *hard negative* examples, i.e., negative examples that are currently rated as positive or ambiguous by the detector. These examples can strongly influence parameters when the network is trained to correct them. Unfortunately, they are often sparse in the training data, and are expensive to obtain. In this work, we show how large numbers of hard negatives can be obtained *automatically* by analyzing the output of a trained detector on video sequences. In particular, detections that are *isolated in time*, i.e., that have no associated preceding or following detections, are likely to be hard negatives. We describe simple procedures for mining large numbers of such hard negatives (and also hard *positives*) from unlabeled video data. Our experiments show that retraining detectors on these automatically obtained examples often significantly improves performance. We present experiments on multiple architectures and multiple data sets, including face detection, pedestrian detection and other object categories.

Keywords: Object detection · Face detection · Pedestrian detection
Semi-supervised learning · Hard negative mining

1 Introduction

Detection is a core computer vision problem that has seen major advances in the last few years due to larger training sets, improved architectures, end-to-end training, and improved loss functions [13,41,42,67]. In this work, we consider

S. Jin and A. RoyChowdhury—Equally contributed.

Electronic supplementary material The online version of this chapter (https://doi.org/10.1007/978-3-030-01261-8_19) contains supplementary material, which is available to authorized users.

V. Ferrari et al. (Eds.): ECCV 2018, LNCS 11217, pp. 316–333, 2018.
https://doi.org/10.1007/978-3-030-01261-8_19

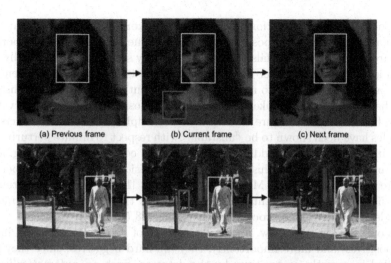

Fig. 1. Detector flicker in videos. Three consecutive frames from a video are shown for face and pedestrian detection. On the top row, the boxes show face detections from the Faster R-CNN [42] (trained on WIDER face) [25,61]. On the bottom row are detections from the same detector trained on the Caltech pedestrian dataset [12]. Yellow boxes show true positives and red boxes show false positives. For the true positives, the same object is detected in all three frames whereas for the false positives, the detection is *isolated* – it occurs neither in the previous nor the subsequent frame. These detections that are "isolated in time" frequently turn out to be false positives, and hence provide important sources of hard negative training data for detectors. (Color figure online)

another direction for improving detectors – by dramatically expanding the number of hard examples available to the learner. We apply the method to several different detection problems (including face and pedestrian), a variety of architectures, and multiple data sets, showing significant gains in a variety of settings.

Many discriminative methods are more influenced by challenging examples near the boundary of a classifier than easy examples that have low loss. Some classifiers, such as support vector machines, are completely determined by examples near the classifier boundary (the "support vectors") [45]. More recent techniques that emphasize examples near the boundary include general methods such as *active bias* [8], which re-weights examples according to the variance of their posteriors during training. In the context of class imbalance in training object detectors, on-line hard example mining (OHEM) [46] and the *focal loss* [33] were designed to emphasize hard examples.

In this paper, we introduce simple methods for automatically mining both hard negatives and hard positives from videos using a previously trained detector. To illustrate, Fig. 1 shows a sequence of consecutive video frames from two videos containing a face and a pedestrian respectively. The results of the Faster R-CNN detector (trained for each class) run on each frame are marked as rectangles, with true positives as yellow boxes and false positives as red boxes. Notice that false positives are neither preceded nor followed by a detection. We refer to such isolated-in-time detections as **detector flickers** and postulate that these are usually caused by false positives rather than true positives.[1] This hypothesis stems from the idea that a false positive, caused by something that usually does not look like a face (or other target object), such as a hand, only momentarily causes a detector network to respond positively, but that small deviations from these hard negatives will likely not register as positives. Similar observations can be found in the literature on adversarial examples, where many adversarial examples have been shown to be "unstable" with respect to minute perturbations of the image [3,36,37]. In addition, leveraging the continuity of labelling across space and time has a long history in computer vision. Spatial label dependencies are widely modeled by Markov random fields [18] and conditional random fields [53], while the smoothness of labels across time is a staple of tracking methods and other video processing algorithms [28,50,59].

As our experiments show, a large percentage of detector flickers are indeed false positives, and more importantly, they are hard negatives, since they were identified incorrectly as positives by the detector. Such an *automatically generated training set* of hard negatives can be used to fine-tune a detector, often leading to improved performance. Similar benefits are gained from fine-tuning with *hard positives*, which are obtained in an analogous fashion from cases where a consistently detected object "flickers off" in an isolated frame. While these flickers are relatively rare, it is inexpensive to run a modern detector on many hours of unlabeled video, generating essentially unlimited numbers of hard examples. Being an unsupervised process, training sets gathered automatically in this fashion do include some noise. Nevertheless, our experiments show that significant improvements can be gleaned by retraining detectors using these noisy hard examples. An alternative to gathering such hard examples automatically is, of course, to obtain them manually. However, the rarity of false positives for modern detectors makes this process extremely expensive. Doing this manually requires that every positive detection be examined for validity. With typical false positive rates around one per 1000 images, this process requires the examination of 1000 images per false positive, making it prohibitively expensive.

2   Related Work

Convolutional neural networks have recently been applied to achieve state-of-the-art results in object detection [6,19–21,32,34,40,41]. Many of these object detectors have been re-purposed for other tasks such as face detection [15,29,39,60], [23,25,31,57,62,63,66] and pedestrian detection [6,7,14,22,30,64,65], achieving impressive results [12,24,61].

Hard Negatives in Detection. Massive class imbalance is an issue with sliding-window-style object detectors—being densely applied over an image, such models see far more "easy" negative samples from background regions than

---

[1] Note we are *not* claiming that most false positives will be isolated, but only that flickers are likely to be false positives, a very different statement.

positive samples from regions containing an object. Some form of hard negative mining is used by most successful object detectors to account for this imbalance [10,11,16,19–21,33,46,51,55,64]. Early approaches include *bootstrapping* [52] for training SVM-based object detectors [10,16], where false positive detections were added to the set of background training samples in an incremental fashion. Other methods [11,44] apply a pre-trained detector on a larger dataset to mine false positives and then re-train.

Hard negative mining has also improved the performance of deep learning based models [19,33,35,46,47,55,64]. Shrivastava *et al.* [46] proposed an *Online Hard Example Mining* (OHEM) procedure,training using only high-loss region proposals. This technique, originally applied to the Fast R-CNN detector [19], yielded significant gains on the PASCAL and MS-COCO benchmarks. Lin *et al.* [33] propose the *focal loss* to down-weight the contribution of easy examples and train a single-stage, multi-scale network [32]. The A-Fast-RCNN [56] does adversarial generation of hard examples using occlusions and deformations. While similar to our work, our model is trained with hard examples from *real* images and variations are not limited to occlusion and spatial deformations. Zhang *et al.* [64] show that effective bootstrapping of hard negatives, using a boosted decision forest [2,17], significantly improves over a Faster R-CNN baseline for *pedestrian detection*. Recent *face detection* methods, such as Wan *et al.* [55] and Sun *et al.* [51], have also used the bootstrapping of hard negatives to improve the performance of CNN-based detectors—a pre-trained Faster R-CNN is used to mine hard negatives; then the model is re-trained. However, these methods require a human-annotated dataset of suitable size. Our unsupervised approach does not rely upon bounding-box annotations and thus can be trained upon potentially unlimited data.

Semi-supervised Learning. Using mixtures of labeled and unlabeled data is known as *semi-supervised learning* [4,9,58]. Rosenberg *et al.* [43] ran a trained object detector on unlabeled data and then trained on a subset of this noisy labeled data in an incremental re-training procedure. In Kalal *et al.* [27], constraints based on video object trajectories are used to correct patch labels of a random forest classifier; these corrected samples are used for re-training. Tang *et al.* [54] adapt still-image object detectors to video by selecting training samples from unlabeled videos, based on the consistency between detections and tracklets, and then follow an iterative procedure that selects the easy examples from videos and hard examples from images to re-train the detector. Rather than adapting to the video domain, we seek to improve detector performance on the source domain by selecting hard examples from videos. Singh *et al.* [48] gather discriminative regions from weakly-labeled images and then refine their bounding-boxes by incorporating tracking information from weakly-labeled videos.

3   Mining Hard Examples from Videos

This section discusses methods for automatically mining hard examples from videos, including data collection (Sect. 3.1), our hard negative mining algorithm

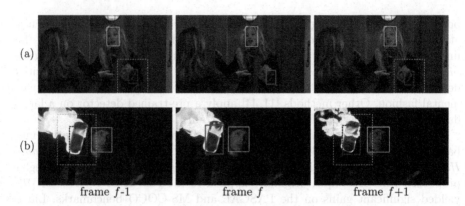

frame f-1   frame f frame f+1

Fig. 2. Mining hard negatives from detector-flicker. The solid boxes denote detections, and the dashed boxes are associated with the tracking algorithm. Given all of the high-confidence **face detections** in a video (yellow boxes), the proposed algorithm generates a **tracklet** (blue *dashed* boxes) for the **current detection** (red box in frame f) by applying template matching within the **search regions** of the adjacent frames (cyan *dashed* boxes). As there are no matching detections in adjacent frames for the current detection (*i.e.* no yellow box matches the blue dashed boxes in frames $f-1$ or $f+1$), it is correctly considered to be an "isolated detection" and added to the set of *hard negatives*. The remaining detections in frame f, which are temporally consistent, are added to the set of *pseudo-positives*. (Color figure online)

(Sect. 3.2), statistics of recovered hard negatives (Sect. 3.3) and extension to hard positives (Sect. 3.4). Details of re-training the detector on these new samples are in the Experiments section (Sect. 4.1).

3.1   Video Collection

To mine hard examples for face detection, we used 101 videos from sitcoms, each with a duration of 21–25 min and a full-length movie of 1 h 47 min, *"Hannah and her sisters"* [38]. Further, we performed YouTube searches with keywords based on: *public address*, *debate society*, *orchestra performance*, *choir practice* and *courtroom*, downloading 89 videos of durations ranging from 10 to 25 min. We obtained videos that were expected to feature a large number of human faces in various scenes, reflecting the everyday settings of our face benchmarks. Similarly, for pedestrian detection, we collected videos from YouTube by searching with the two key phrases: *driving cam videos* and *walking videos*. We obtained 40 videos with an average duration of about 30 min.

3.2   Hard Negative Mining

Running a pre-trained face detector on every frame of a video gives us a large set of detections with noisy labels. We crucially differ here from recent bootstrapping approaches [51,55] by (a) using large amounts of *unlabeled* data available on the web instead of relying only on the limited fully-supervised training data from WIDER Face [61] or Caltech Pedestrians [12], and (b) having a novel filtering criterion on the noisy labels obtained from the detector that retains the hard negative examples and minimizes noise in the obtained labels.

The raw detections from a video were thresholded at a relatively high confidence score of 0.8. For every detection in a frame, we formed a short tracklet by performing template matching in adjacent frames, within a window of ± 5 frames—the bounding box of the current detection was enlarged by 100 pixels and this region was searched in adjacent frames for the best match using normalized cross correlation (NCC). To account for occlusions, we put a threshold on the NCC similarity score (set as 0.5) to reject cases where there was a lot of appearance-change between frames. Now in each frame, if the maximum intersection-over-union (IoU) between the tracklet prediction and detections in the adjacent frames was below 0.2, we considered it to be an isolated detection resulting from **detector flicker**. These isolated detections were taken as *hard negatives*. The detections that *were* found to be consistent with adjacent frames were considered to have a high probability of being true predictions and were termed *pseudo-positives*. For the purpose of creating the re-training set, we kept only those frames that had at least one pseudo-positive detection in addition to one or more hard negatives. Illustrative examples of this procedure are shown in Fig. 2, where we visualize only the previous and next frames for simplicity.

3.3 Results of Automatic Hard Negative Mining

Our initial mining experiments were performed using a standard Faster R-CNN detector trained on WIDER Face [61] for faces and Caltech [12] for pedestrians. We collected 13,888 video frames for faces, where each frame contains at least one pseudo-positive and one hard negative (detector flicker). To verify the quality of our automatically mined hard negatives, we randomly sampled 511 hard negatives for inspection. 453 of them are true negatives, while 16 samples are true positives, and 42 samples are categorized as *ambiguous*, which correspond extreme head pose or severe occlusions. The precision for true negatives is 88.65% and precision for true negatives plus *ambiguous* is 96.87%.

For pedestrians, we collected 14,967 video frames. We manually checked 328 automatically mined hard negatives, where 244 of them are true negatives and 21 belong to *ambiguous*. The precision for true negatives is 74.48% and precision for true negatives plus *ambiguous* is 82.18%.

To further validate our method on an existing fully-annotated video dataset, we used the Hannah dataset [38], which has every frame annotated with face bounding boxes. Here, out of 234 mined hard negatives, 187 were true negatives, resulting in a precision of 79.91%. We note that the annotations on the Hannah movie are not always consistent and involve a significant domain shift from WIDER. Considering the fact no human supervision is provided, the mined face hard negatives are consistently of high quality across various domains.

3.4 Extension to Hard Positive Mining

In principle, the same concept for using detector flickers can be directly applied to obtaining **hard positives**. The idea is to look for "off-flickers" of a detector in a video tracklet – given a series of detections of an object in a video, such as a face, we can search for single frames that have no detections but are surrounded by detections on either side. Of course, these could be caused by short-duration occlusions, for example, but a large percentages of these "off-flickers" are hard positives, as in Fig. 3. We generate tracklets using the method from [26] and show results incorporating hard positives on pedestrian and face detection in the experiments section. The manually calculated purity over 300 randomly sampled frames was 94.46% for faces and 83.13% for pedestrians.

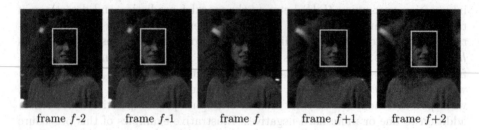

frame f-2   frame f-1   frame f frame f+1   frame f+2

Fig. 3. Hard positive samples. Given a sequence of video frames, the face of the actor is consistently detected except at frame f. Such isolated "off-flickers" can be harvested in an unsupervised fashion to form a set of *hard positives*.

4   Experiments

We evaluate our method on face and pedestrian detection and perform ablation studies analyzing the effect of the hard examples. For pedestrians, we show results on the Caltech dataset [12], while for face detection, we show results on the WIDER Face [61] dataset.

The Caltech Pedestrian Dataset [12] consists of videos taken from a vehicle driving through urban traffic, with about 350k annotated bounding-boxes from 250k video frames.

The WIDER dataset consists of 32,203 images having 393,703 labeled faces in challenging situations of scale, pose and occlusion. The evaluation set of WIDER is divided into *easy*, *medium*, and *hard* sets according to the detection scores of object proposals from EdgeBox [67]. From easy to hard, the faces get smaller and more crowded.

4.1 Retraining Detectors with Mined Hard Examples

We experimented with two ways to leverage our mined *hard negative* samples. In our initial experiments, a single mini-batch is formed by including one image from the original labeled training dataset and another image sampled from our automatically-mined hard negative video frames. In this way, positive region proposals are sampled from the original training dataset image, based on manual annotation, while negative region proposals are sampled from both the original dataset image and the mined hard negative video frame. Thus, we can *explicitly* force the network to focus on the hard negatives from the mined video frame. However, this method did not produce better results in our initial experiments. An alternate approach was found to be more effective – we simply provided the *pseudo-positives* in the mined video frames as true object annotations during training and *implicitly* allowed the network to pick the hard-negatives. The inclusion of video frames with *hard positives* is more straightforward – we can simply treat them as additional images with object annotations at training time. The models were fine-tuned with and without OHEM, and we consistently chose the setting that gave the best validation results. While OHEM would increase the likelihood of hard negatives being selected in a mini-batch, it would also place extra emphasis on any mislabels in the hard examples. This would magnify the effect of a small amount of label noise and can in some cases decrease the overall performance.

4.2 Ablation Settings

In addition to the comparisons to the baseline Faster R-CNN detectors, we conduct various ablation studies on the Caltech Pedestrian and WIDER Face datasets to address the effectiveness of hard example mining.

Effect of Training Iterations. To account for the possible situation where simply training the baseline model longer may result in a gain in performance, we create another baseline by fine-tuning the original model for additional iterations with a lower learning rate, matching the number of training iterations used in our hard example trained models. We refer to this model as "w/ more iterations".

Effect of Additional Video Frames. Unlike the baseline detector, our fine-tuned models use additional video frames for training. It's possible that just using the high-confidence detection results on unlabeled video frames as *pseudo-groundtruths* during training is sufficient to boost performance, without correcting the hard negatives using our detector flicker approach. Therefore we train another detector, "Flickers as Positives", starting from the baseline model, that takes exactly same training set as our hard negative model, but where *all* the high-confidence detections on the video frames are used as positive labels.

Effect of Automatically Mined Hard Examples. We include the results from our proposed method of considering detector flickers as hard negatives and hard positives separately – "Flickers as HN" and "Flickers as HP". Finally, we report results from fine-tuning the detector on the union of both types of hard examples (Flickers as HN + HP).

4.3   Pedestrian Detection

For our `baseline` model, we train the VGG16-based **Faster R-CNN** object detector [42] with OHEM [46] for 150K iterations on the **Caltech Pedestrian** training dataset [12]. We used *all* the frames from set00-set05 (which constitute the training set), irrespective of whether they are flagged as "reasonable" or not by the Caltech meta-data. Following Zhang *et al.* [64], we set the IoU ratio for RPN training to 0.5, while all the other experimental settings are identical to [42]. The number of labeled Caltech images is 128,419 and our mining provides 14,967 hard negative and 42,914 hard positive frames. We fine-tune the baseline model with hard examples and the annotated examples from the Caltech Pedestrian *training* dataset, with a fixed learning rate of 0.0001 for 60K iterations, using OHEM. We evaluate our model on the Caltech Pedestrian testing dataset under the *reasonable* condition.

The ROC curves of various settings of our models are shown in Fig. 4(a). Fine-tuning the existing detector for more iterations gives a modest reduction in log average miss rate, from 23.83% to 22.4%. Using all detections without correcting the hard negatives (`Flickers as Pos`) also gives a small improvement – the extra training data, although noisy, still has some positive contribution during fine-tuning. Our proposed model, fine-tuned with the mined hard negatives (`Flickers as HN`), has a log average miss rate of **18.78%**, which outperforms the `baseline` model by **5.05%**. Fine-tuning with hard positives (`Flickers as HP`) also shows an improvement of **4.39%** over the baseline. Combining both hard positives and hard negatives results in the best performance of **18.72%** log average miss rate.

In Fig. 4(b) we report results using the state-of-the-art **SDS-RCNN** [5] pedestrian detector[2]. Every 3rd frame is sampled from the Caltech dataset for training the original detector [5], and we keep this setting in our experiments. For SDS-RCNN, there are 42,782 labeled training images while the mining gives us 2,191 hard negative and 177,563 hard positive frames. The inclusion of hard negatives in training (`Flickers as HN`) improves the performance of SDS-RCNN in the low False Positives regime compared to the baseline – the detector learns to eliminate a number of false detections, thereby increasing precision, but it also ends up hurting the recall. Including mined hard positives (`Flickers as HP`) we get the best performance of **8.71%** log average miss rate, outperforming the model using both the mined hard negative and positive samples (`Flickers as HP + HN`), which gets 9.12%.

4.4   Face Detection

We adopt the Faster R-CNN framework, using VGG16 as the backbone network. We first train a baseline detector starting from an ImageNet pre-trained model, with a fixed learning rate of 0.001 for 80K iterations using the SGD optimizer,

---

[2] Running the authors' released code from https://github.com/garrickbrazil/SDS-RCNN.

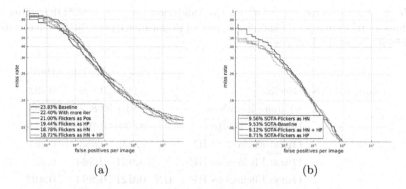

(a)   (b)

Fig. 4. Results on the **Caltech Pedestrian** dataset [12] in *reasonable* condition. (a) Faster R-CNN results: using hard negative samples (`Flickers as HN`) and hard positive samples (`Flickers as HP`) improve the performance over the baseline in; using a combination of both gives the best performance. (b) State-of-the-art SDS-RCNN results: `Flickers as HN` improves the original SDS-RCNN results only in the low false positive regime, while `Flickers as HP` gives the best results.

where the momentum is 0.9 and weight decay is 0.0005. For hard negatives, the model is fine-tuned for 50k iterations with learning rate 0.0001. For hard positives, and the combination of both types of hard examples, we train longer for 150k iterations. Following the **WIDER Face** protocol, we report Average Precision (AP) values in Table 1 on the three splits – 'Easy', 'Medium' and 'Hard'. OHEM is not used as it was empirically observed to decrease performance.

Fine-tuning the baseline model for more iterations improves performance slightly on the Easy and Medium splits. Naively considering all the high confidence detections as true positives (`Flickers as Positives`) degrades performance substantially across all splits. Hard negative mining, `Flickers as HN`, slightly outperforms the baseline Faster R-CNN detector (`w/ more iterations`) on the Medium and Hard splits, retaining the same performance of 0.907 AP on the Easy split. Using the mined hard positives, `Flickers as HP`, we observe a significant gain in performance on all three splits. Using both hard positives and hard negatives jointly (`Flickers as HP + HN`) improves over using hard negatives and the baseline, but the improvement is less than the gains from `Flickers as HP`.

For faces, we additionally experimented with the recent RetinaNet [33] detector as a second high-performance baseline model. Unfortunately, inclusion of the unlabeled data hurt performance slightly using this model, despite the reasonably high purity of the mined examples. While the purity of our mined examples is high, it is not perfect. These incorrect samples would be strongly emphasized by the focal loss used in RetinaNet. Thus, it is possible that while RetinaNet outperforms the Faster R-CNN on standard benchmarks, it may be more susceptible to label noise and thus not a good candidate for our method. In the future, we will investigate different values of the focal loss parameter to see whether this can mitigate the effects of label noise.

326   S. Jin et al.

Table 1. Average precision (AP) on the validation set of the **WIDER Face** [61] benchmark. Including hard examples improves performance over the baseline, with HP and HP+HN giving the best results.

		Easy	Medium	Hard
Faster R-CNN	Baseline	0.907	0.850	0.492
	w/ more iterations	0.910	0.852	0.493
	Flickers as Positives	0.829	0.790	0.434
	Ours: Flickers as HN	0.909	0.853	0.494
	Ours: Flickers as HP	**0.921**	**0.864**	0.492
	Ours: Flickers as HP + HN	**0.921**	**0.864**	**0.497**

Fig. 5. Examples of hard negatives. Visualization of mined hard negatives for faces (*top row*) and pedestrians (*bottom row*). Red boxes denote the "detection-flicker cases" among the high confidence detections (green boxes). (Color figure online)

5   Discussion

In this section, we discuss some further applications and extensions to our proposed hard example mining method.

On the Entropy of the False Positive Distribution. In mining thousands of hard negatives from unlabeled video, we noticed a striking pattern in the hard negatives of face detectors. A large percentage of false positives were generated by a few types of objects. Specifically, a large percentage of hard negatives in face detectors seem to stem from human hands, ears, and the torso/chest area. Since it appears that a large percentage of the false positives in face detection are the result of a relatively small number of phenomena, this could explain the significant gains realized by modeling hard negatives. In particular, characterizing the distribution of hard negatives, and learning to avoid them, may involve a relatively small set of hard negatives (Figs. 5 and 6).

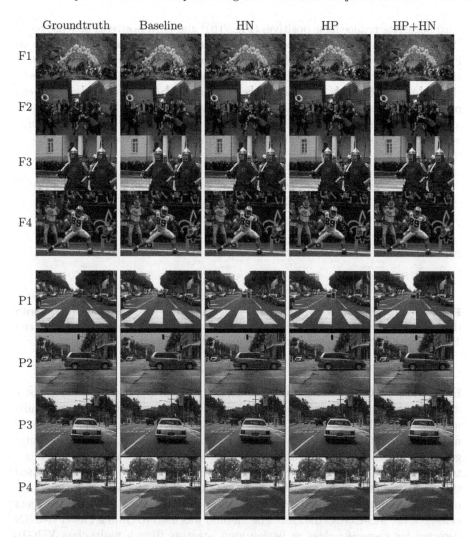

Fig. 6. Qualitative comparison. Faster R-CNN detections for faces (F1-4) and pedestrians (P1-4).The detector fine-tuned with hard negatives (HN) reduces false positives compared to the Baseline (F-1,3,4; P-1,2,3), but can sometimes lower the recall (P4). Hard positives (HP) increases recall (F2, P4) but can also introduce false positives (F4). Using both (HP+HN) the detector is usually able to achieve a good balance.

Effect of Domain Shift on FDDB. The FDDB dataset [24] is comprised of 5,171 annotated faces in a set of 2,845 images taken from a subset of the Face in the Wild dataset. The images and the annotation style of FDDB have a significant *domain shift* from WIDER Face, which are discussed in Jamal et al. [1]. Figure 7 compares our method with the Faster R-CNN baseline on FDDB, using the trained models from our experiments on WIDER Face (Sect. 4.4). Although hard negatives reduce false positives (Fig. 7(b)) and hard positives increase recall (Fig. 7(c)), the performance does not consistently improve over the baseline on FDDB. We hypothesize that the large amounts of new training data result in shifting the original detector further away from the target FDDB domain, and this domain shift leads to a loss in performance. This may not have hurt our performance as much on WIDER Face because the domain shift between the relatively unconstrained WIDER images and our videos downloaded from YouTube was not severe enough to subsume the advantages from the hard examples.

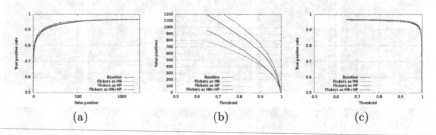

(a)   (b)   (c)

Fig. 7. Results on **FDDB**. (a) ROC curves comparing our hard example methods with the baseline Faster R-CNN detector; (b–c) separate plots showing False Positives and True Positive Rate with varying thresholds on detection score.

Extension to Other Classes. The simplicity of our approach makes it easily extensible to other categories in a one-versus-rest setting. YouTube is a promising source of videos for various MS-COCO or PASCAL categories; mining hard negatives after that is fully automatic. To demonstrate this, we selected categories from MS-COCO and ran experiments to check if inclusion of hard negatives improves the baseline performance of a Faster R-CNN detector. We used the training method deployed by Sonntag et al. [49], which allows for a convenient fine-tuning of the VGG16-based Faster R-CNN model on specific object classes of the MS-COCO dataset. The method was used to train a Faster R-CNN detector for a specific class vs background, starting from a multi-class VGG16 classifier pre-trained on Image-Net categories. This baseline detector was then used to mine hard negatives from downloaded YouTube videos of that category and then re-trained on the union of the new data and the original labeled training data. We show results for two categories: *dogs* and *trains*. A held out subset of the MS-COCO validation set was used for validating training hyper-parameters and the remainder of the validation data was used for evaluation.

For the *dog* category, the labeled data was divided into train/val/test splits of 3041/177/1521 images. We manually selected and downloaded about 22 h of dog videos from YouTube. We used the baseline dog detector to obtain detections on about 15 h (1,296,000 frames at 24 fps) of dog videos. The hard negative mining algorithm was then run at a detector confidence threshold of 0.8. This yielded 2611 frames with at least one hard negative and one positive detection. The baseline model was then fine-tuned for 30k iterations on the union of the labeled MS-COCO data and the hard negatives. The hyper-parameters and best model were selected using a validation set. Similar experiments with *trains* were performed, with train/val/test splits of 2464/157/1281 images. The results are summarized in the Table 2, where inclusion of hard negatives is observed to improve the baseline detector in both cases.

Table 2. Results on augmenting Faster R-CNN detectors with hard negatives for '*dog*' and '*train*' categories on MS-COCO.

Category	Model	Training iterations	Training hyperparams	Validation set AP	Test set AP
Dog	Baseline	29000	LR : 1e-3 for 10k, 1e-4 for 10k-20k, 1e-5 for 20k-29k	26.9	25.3
	Flickers as HN	22000	LR : 1e-4 for 15k, 1e-5 for 15k-22k	28.1	26.4
Train	Baseline	26000	LR : 1e-3, stepsize: 10k, lr-decay: 0.1	33.9	33.2
	Flickers as HN	24000	LR : 1e-3, stepsize: 10k, lr-decay: 0.1	35.4	33.7

6   Conclusion

This work leverages an existing phenomenon – detector flicker in videos – to mine hard negatives and hard positives at scale in an unsupervised manner. The usefulness of this method for improving an object detector is demonstrated on standard benchmarks for two well-known tasks – face and pedestrian detection, using various detector architectures and supported by several ablation studies. The simplicity of our hard example mining approach makes it widely applicable to a variety of practical scenarios – YouTube is a promising source of videos for almost any category and mining hard examples is a fully automatic procedure.

Acknowledgment. This research is based in part upon work supported by the Office of the Director of National Intelligence (ODNI), Intelligence Advanced Research Projects Activity (IARPA) under contract number 2014-14071600010 and in part on research sponsored by the Air Force Research Laboratory and DARPA under agreement number FA8750-18-2-0126. The views and conclusions contained herein are those of the authors and should not be interpreted as necessarily representing the official policies or endorsements, either expressed or implied, of ODNI, IARPA, the Air Force Research Laboratory and DARPA or the U.S. Government. The U.S. Government is authorized to reproduce and distribute reprints for Governmental purpose notwithstanding any copyright annotation thereon.

References

1. Abdullah Jamal, M., Li, H., Gong, B.: Deep face detector adaptation without negative transfer or catastrophic forgetting. In: The IEEE Conference on Computer Vision and Pattern Recognition (CVPR), June 2018
2. Appel, R., Fuchs, T., Dollár, P., Perona, P.: Quickly boosting decision trees-pruning underachieving features early. In: International Conference on Machine Learning, pp. 594–602 (2013)
3. Athalye, A., Sutskever, I.: Synthesizing robust adversarial examples (2017). arXiv preprint: arXiv:1707.07397
4. Blum, A., Mitchell, T.: Combining labeled and unlabeled data with co-training. In: Proceedings of the Eleventh Annual Conference on Computational Learning Theory, pp. 92–100. ACM (1998)
5. Brazil, G., Yin, X., Liu, X.: Illuminating pedestrians via simultaneous detection & segmentation (2017). arXiv preprint: arXiv:1706.08564
6. Cai, Z., Fan, Q., Feris, R.S., Vasconcelos, N.: A unified multi-scale deep convolutional neural network for fast object detection. In: Leibe, B., Matas, J., Sebe, N., Welling, M. (eds.) ECCV 2016, Part IV. LNCS, vol. 9908, pp. 354–370. Springer, Cham (2016). https://doi.org/10.1007/978-3-319-46493-0_22
7. Cai, Z., Saberian, M., Vasconcelos, N.: Learning complexity-aware cascades for deep pedestrian detection. In: Proceedings of the IEEE International Conference on Computer Vision, pp. 3361–3369 (2015)
8. Chang, H.S., Learned-Miller, E., McCallum, A.: Active bias: training more accurate neural networks by emphasizing high variance samples. In: Advances in Neural Information Processing Systems, pp. 1003–1013 (2017)
9. Chapelle, O., Scholkopf, B., Zien, A.: Semi-supervised learning. IEEE Trans. Neural Netw. **20**(3), 542 (2009). (chapelle, o. et al. (eds.); 2006) [book reviews]
10. Dalal, N., Triggs, B.: Histograms of oriented gradients for human detection. In: CVPR, pp. 886–893 (2005). https://doi.org/10.1109/CVPR.2005.177
11. Dollár, P., Tu, Z., Perona, P., Belongie, S.: Integral channel features (2009)
12. Dollár, P., Wojek, C., Schiele, B., Perona, P.: Pedestrian detection: a benchmark. In: IEEE Conference on Computer Vision and Pattern Recognition, CVPR 2009, pp. 304–311. IEEE (2009)
13. Dollár, P., Zitnick, C.L.: Fast edge detection using structured forests. IEEE Trans. Pattern Anal. Mach. Intell. **37**(8), 1558–1570 (2015). https://doi.org/10.1109/TPAMI.2014.2377715
14. Du, X., El-Khamy, M., Lee, J., Davis, L.: Fused DNN: a deep neural network fusion approach to fast and robust pedestrian detection. In: 2017 IEEE Winter Conference on Applications of Computer Vision (WACV), pp. 953–961. IEEE (2017)
15. Farfade, S.S., Saberian, M.J., Li, L.: Multi-view face detection using deep convolutional neural networks. In: ICMR, pp. 643–650 (2015). https://doi.org/10.1145/2671188.2749408
16. Felzenszwalb, P.F., Girshick, R.B., McAllester, D., Ramanan, D.: Object detection with discriminatively trained part-based models. IEEE Trans. Pattern Anal. Mach. Intell. **32**(9), 1627–1645 (2010)
17. Friedman, J., Hastie, T., Tibshirani, R., et al.: Additive logistic regression: a statistical view of boosting (with discussion and a rejoinder by the authors). Ann. Stat. **28**(2), 337–407 (2000)
18. Geman, S., Graffigne, C.: Markov random field image models and their applications to computer vision. In: Proceedings of the International Congress of Mathematicians, vol. 1, p. 2 (1986)

19. Girshick, R.B.: Fast R-CNN. In: ICCV, pp. 1440–1448 (2015). https://doi.org/10. 1109/ICCV.2015.169
20. Girshick, R.B., Donahue, J., Darrell, T., Malik, J.: Rich feature hierarchies for accurate object detection and semantic segmentation. In: CVPR, pp. 580–587 (2014). https://doi.org/10.1109/CVPR.2014.81
21. He, K., Zhang, X., Ren, S., Sun, J.: Spatial pyramid pooling in deep convolutional networks for visual recognition. In: Fleet, D., Pajdla, T., Schiele, B., Tuytelaars, T. (eds.) ECCV 2014, Part III. LNCS, vol. 8691, pp. 346–361. Springer, Cham (2014). https://doi.org/10.1007/978-3-319-10578-9_23
22. Hosang, J., Omran, M., Benenson, R., Schiele, B.: Taking a deeper look at pedestrians. In: Proceedings of the IEEE Conference on Computer Vision and Pattern Recognition, pp. 4073–4082 (2015)
23. Hu, P., Ramanan, D.: Finding tiny faces. In: 2017 IEEE Conference on Computer Vision and Pattern Recognition (CVPR), pp. 1522–1530. IEEE (2017)
24. Jain, V., Learned-Miller, E.: FDDB: a benchmark for face detection in unconstrained settings. Technical report UM-CS-2010-009, University of Massachusetts, Amherst (2010)
25. Jiang, H., Learned-Miller, E.: Face detection with the faster R-CNN. In: 2017 12th IEEE International Conference on Automatic Face & Gesture Recognition (FG 2017), pp. 650–657. IEEE (2017)
26. Jin, S., Su, H., Stauffer, C., Learned-Miller, E.: End-to-end face detection and cast grouping in movies using Erdos-Renyi clustering. In: ICCV (2017)
27. Kalal, Z., Matas, J., Mikolajczyk, K.: PN learning: bootstrapping binary classifiers by structural constraints. In: 2010 IEEE Conference on Computer Vision and Pattern Recognition (CVPR), pp. 49–56. IEEE (2010)
28. Kläser, A., Marszałek, M., Schmid, C., Zisserman, A.: Human focused action localization in video. In: Kutulakos, K.N. (ed.) ECCV 2010, Part I. LNCS, vol. 6553, pp. 219–233. Springer, Heidelberg (2012). https://doi.org/10.1007/978-3-642-35749-7_17
29. Li, H., Lin, Z., Shen, X., Brandt, J., Hua, G.: A convolutional neural network cascade for face detection. In: CVPR, pp. 5325–5334 (2015). https://doi.org/10. 1109/CVPR.2015.7299170
30. Li, J., Liang, X., Shen, S., Xu, T., Feng, J., Yan, S.: Scale-aware fast R-CNN for pedestrian detection. IEEE Trans. Multimed. **20**, 985–996 (2017)
31. Li, Y., Sun, B., Wu, T., Wang, Y., Gao, W.: Face detection with end-to-end integration of a convnet and a 3D model. ECCV abs/1606.00850 (2016). http://dblp. uni-trier.de/db/journals/corr/corr1606.html#LiSWW016
32. Lin, T.Y., Dollár, P., Girshick, R., He, K., Hariharan, B., Belongie, S.: Feature pyramid networks for object detection. In: CVPR, vol. 1, p. 4 (2017)
33. Lin, T.Y., Goyal, P., Girshick, R., He, K., Dollár, P.: Focal loss for dense object detection (2017). arXiv preprint: arXiv:1708.02002
34. Liu, W., et al.: SSD: single shot multibox detector. In: Leibe, B., Matas, J., Sebe, N., Welling, M. (eds.) ECCV 2016, Part I. LNCS, vol. 9905, pp. 21–37. Springer, Cham (2016). https://doi.org/10.1007/978-3-319-46448-0_2
35. Loshchilov, I., Hutter, F.: Online batch selection for faster training of neural networks (2015). arXiv preprint: arXiv:1511.06343
36. Lu, J., Sibai, H., Fabry, E., Forsyth, D.: No need to worry about adversarial examples in object detection in autonomous vehicles (2017). arXiv preprint: arXiv:1707.03501
37. Luo, Y., Boix, X., Roig, G., Poggio, T., Zhao, Q.: Foveation-based mechanisms alleviate adversarial examples (2015). arXiv preprint: arXiv:1511.06292

38. Ozerov, A., Vigouroux, J.R., Chevallier, L., Pérez, P.: On evaluating face tracks in movies. In: 2013 20th IEEE International Conference on Image Processing (ICIP), pp. 3003–3007. IEEE (2013)
39. Ranjan, R., Patel, V.M., Chellappa, R.: A deep pyramid deformable part model for face detection. In: BTAS, pp. 1–8. IEEE (2015). http://dblp.uni-trier.de/db/conf/btas/btas2015.html#RanjanPC15
40. Redmon, J., Divvala, S., Girshick, R., Farhadi, A.: You only look once: unified, real-time object detection. In: Proceedings of the IEEE Conference on Computer Vision and Pattern Recognition, pp. 779–788 (2016)
41. Ren, S., He, K., Girshick, R., Sun, J.: Faster R-CNN: towards real-time object detection with region proposal networks. IEEE Trans. Pattern Anal. Mach. Intell. **1**(6), 1137–1149 (2016)
42. Ren, S., He, K., Girshick, R.B., Sun, J.: Faster R-CNN: towards real-time object detection with region proposal networks. In: NIPS, pp. 91–99 (2015). http://papers.nips.cc/paper/5638-faster-r-cnn-towards-real-time-object-detection-with-region-proposal-networks
43. Rosenberg, C., Hebert, M., Schneiderman, H.: Semi-supervised self-training of object detection models (2005)
44. Rowley, H.A., Baluja, S., Kanade, T.: Neural network-based face detection. IEEE Trans. Pattern Anal. Mach. Intell. **20**(1), 23–38 (1998)
45. Schölkopf, B., Smola, A.J.: Learning with Kernels: Support Vector Machines, Regularization, Optimization, and Beyond. MIT Press, Cambridge (2002)
46. Shrivastava, A., Gupta, A., Girshick, R.: Training region-based object detectors with online hard example mining. In: Proceedings of the IEEE Conference on Computer Vision and Pattern Recognition, pp. 761–769 (2016)
47. Simo-Serra, E., Trulls, E., Ferraz, L., Kokkinos, I., Moreno-Noguer, F.: Fracking deep convolutional image descriptors. CoRR, abs/1412.6537 2 (2014)
48. Singh, K.K., Xiao, F., Lee, Y.J.: Track and transfer: watching videos to simulate strong human supervision for weakly-supervised object detection. In: CVPR, vol. 1, p. 2 (2016)
49. Sonntag, D., et al.: Fine-tuning deep cnn models on specific MS COCO categories (2017). arXiv preprint: arXiv:1709.01476
50. Stalder, S., Grabner, H., Van Gool, L.: Cascaded confidence filtering for improved tracking-by-detection. In: Daniilidis, K., Maragos, P., Paragios, N. (eds.) ECCV 2010, Part I. LNCS, vol. 6311, pp. 369–382. Springer, Heidelberg (2010). https://doi.org/10.1007/978-3-642-15549-9_27
51. Sun, X., Wu, P., Hoi, S.C.: Face detection using deep learning: an improved faster RCNN approach (2017). arXiv preprint: arXiv:1701.08289
52. Sung, K.K., Poggio, T.: Learning and example selection for object and pattern detection (1994)
53. Sutton, C., McCallum, A.: An Introduction to Conditional Random Fields for Relational Learning. Introduction to Statistical Relational Learning, vol. 2. MIT Press, Cambridge (2006)
54. Tang, K., Ramanathan, V., Fei-Fei, L., Koller, D.: Shifting weights: adapting object detectors from image to video. In: Advances in Neural Information Processing Systems, pp. 638–646 (2012)
55. Wan, S., Chen, Z., Zhang, T., Zhang, B., Wong, K.K.: Bootstrapping face detection with hard negative examples (2016). arXiv preprint: arXiv:1608.02236
56. Wang, X., Shrivastava, A., Gupta, A.: A-fast-RCNN: hard positive generation via adversary for object detection (2017)

57. Wang, Y., Ji, X., Zhou, Z., Wang, H., Li, Z.: Detecting faces using region-based fully convolutional networks (2017). arXiv preprint: arXiv:1709.05256
58. Weston, J.: Large-scale semi-supervised learning
59. Yang, B., Nevatia, R.: An online learned CRF model for multi-target tracking. In: 2012 IEEE Conference on Computer Vision and Pattern Recognition (CVPR), pp. 2034–2041. IEEE (2012)
60. Yang, S., Luo, P., Loy, C.C., Tang, X.: From facial parts responses to face detection: a deep learning approach. In: ICCV, pp. 3676–3684 (2015). https://doi.org/10.1109/ICCV.2015.419
61. Yang, S., Luo, P., Loy, C.C., Tang, X.: WIDER FACE: a face detection benchmark. In: CVPR (2016)
62. Yu, J., Jiang, Y., Wang, Z., Cao, Z., Huang, T.: Unitbox: an advanced object detection network. In: Proceedings of the 2016 ACM on Multimedia Conference, pp. 516–520. ACM (2016)
63. Zhang, K., Zhang, Z., Li, Z., Qiao, Y.: Joint face detection and alignment using multitask cascaded convolutional networks. IEEE Signal Process. Lett. 23(10), 1499–1503 (2016)
64. Zhang, L., Lin, L., Liang, X., He, K.: Is faster R-CNN doing well for pedestrian detection? In: Leibe, B., Matas, J., Sebe, N., Welling, M. (eds.) ECCV 2016, Part II. LNCS, vol. 9906, pp. 443–457. Springer, Cham (2016). https://doi.org/10.1007/978-3-319-46475-6_28
65. Zhang, S., Benenson, R., Omran, M., Hosang, J., Schiele, B.: How far are we from solving pedestrian detection? In: Proceedings of the IEEE Conference on Computer Vision and Pattern Recognition, pp. 1259–1267 (2016)
66. Zhang, S., Zhu, X., Lei, Z., Shi, H., Wang, X., Li, S.Z.: S^{3}FD: single shot scale-invariant face detector (2017). arXiv preprint: arXiv:1708.05237
67. Zitnick, C.L., Dollár, P.: Edge boxes: locating object proposals from edges. In: Fleet, D., Pajdla, T., Schiele, B., Tuytelaars, T. (eds.) ECCV 2014, Part V. LNCS, vol. 8693, pp. 391–405. Springer, Cham (2014). https://doi.org/10.1007/978-3-319-10602-1_26

BiSeNet: Bilateral Segmentation Network for Real-Time Semantic Segmentation

Changqian Yu[1], Jingbo Wang[2], Chao Peng[3], Changxin Gao[1(✉)],
Gang Yu[3], and Nong Sang[1]

[1] National Key Laboratory of Science and Technology on Multispectral Information
Processing, School of Automation, Huazhong University of Science and Technology,
Wuhan, China
{changqian_yu,cgao,nsang}@hust.edu.cn
[2] Key Laboratory of Machine Perception, Peking University, Beijing, China
wangjingbo1219@pku.edu.cn
[3] Megvii Inc. (Face++), Beijing, China
{pengchao,yugang}@megvii.com

Abstract. Semantic segmentation requires both rich spatial information and sizeable receptive field. However, modern approaches usually compromise spatial resolution to achieve real-time inference speed, which leads to poor performance. In this paper, we address this dilemma with a novel Bilateral Segmentation Network (BiSeNet). We first design a Spatial Path with a small stride to preserve the spatial information and generate high-resolution features. Meanwhile, a Context Path with a fast downsampling strategy is employed to obtain sufficient receptive field. On top of the two paths, we introduce a new Feature Fusion Module to combine features efficiently. The proposed architecture makes a right balance between the speed and segmentation performance on Cityscapes, CamVid, and COCO-Stuff datasets. Specifically, for a 2048×1024 input, we achieve 68.4% Mean IOU on the Cityscapes test dataset with speed of 105 FPS on one NVIDIA Titan XP card, which is significantly faster than the existing methods with comparable performance.

Keywords: Real-time semantic segmentation
Bilateral Segmentation Network

1 Introduction

The research of semantic segmentation, which amounts to assign semantic labels to each pixel, is a fundamental task in computer vision. It can be broadly applied to the fields of augmented reality devices, autonomous driving, and video surveillance. These applications have a high demand for efficient inference speed for fast interaction or response.

C. Yu and J. Wang—Equal Contribution.

© Springer Nature Switzerland AG 2018
V. Ferrari et al. (Eds.): ECCV 2018, LNCS 11217, pp. 334–349, 2018.
https://doi.org/10.1007/978-3-030-01261-8_20

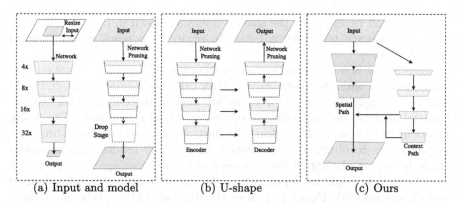

(a) Input and model   (b) U-shape   (c) Ours

Fig. 1. Illustration of the architectures to speed up and our proposed approach. (a) presents the cropping or resizing operation on the input image and the lightweight model with pruning channels or dropping stages. (b) indicates the U-shape structure. (c) demonstrates our proposed Bilateral Segmentation Network (BiSeNet). The black dash line represents the operations which damage the spatial information, while the red dash line represents the operations which shrink the receptive field. The green block is our proposed Spatial Path (SP). In the network part, each block represents the feature map of different down-sampling size. And the length of the block represents the spatial resolution, while the thickness is on behalf of the number of channels. (Color figure online)

Recently, the algorithms [1,17,25,39] of real-time semantic segmentation have shown that there are mainly three approaches to accelerate the model. (1) [34,39] try to restrict the input size to reduce the computation complexity by cropping or resizing. Though the method is simple and effective, the loss of spatial details corrupts the predication especially around boundaries, leading to the accuracy decrease on both metrics and visualization. (2) Instead of resizing the input image, some works prune the channels of the network to boost the inference speed [1,8,25], especially in the early stages of the base model. However, it weakens the spatial capacity. (3) For the last case, ENet [25] proposes to drop the last stage of the model in pursuit of an extremely tight framework. Nevertheless, the drawback of this method is obvious: since the ENet abandons the downsampling operations in the last stage, the receptive field of the model is not enough to cover large objects, resulting in a poor discriminative ability. Overall, all of the above methods compromise the accuracy to speed, which is inferior in practice. Figure 1(a) gives the illustration.

To remedy the loss of spatial details mentioned above, researchers widely utilize the U-shape structure [1,25,35]. By fusing the hierarchical features of the backbone network, the U-shape structure gradually increases the spatial resolution and fills some missing details. However, this technique has two drawbacks. (1) The complete U-shape structure can reduce the speed of the model due to the introduction of extra computation on high-resolution feature maps. (2) More importantly, most spatial information lost in the pruning or cropping cannot be easily recovered by involving the shallow layers as shown in Fig. 1(b). In other words, the U-shape technique is better to regard as a relief, rather than an essential solution.

Based on the above observation, we propose the Bilateral Segmentation Network (BiSeNet) with two parts: *Spatial Path* (SP) and *Context Path* (CP). As their names imply, the two components are devised to confront with the loss of spatial information and shrinkage of receptive field respectively. The design philosophy of the two paths is clear. For *Spatial Path*, we stack only three convolution layers to obtain the 1/8 feature map, which retains affluent spatial details. In respect of *Context Path*, we append a global average pooling layer on the tail of a lightweight model [8], where the receptive field is the maximum of the backbone network. Figure 1(c) shows the structure of these two components.

In pursuit of better accuracy without loss of speed, we also research the fusion of two paths and refinement of final prediction and propose Feature Fusion Module (FFM) and Attention Refinement Module (ARM) respectively. As our following experiments show, these two extra components can further improve the overall semantic segmentation accuracy on both Cityscapes [9], CamVid [2], and COCO-Stuff [3] benchmarks.

Our main contributions are summarized as follows:

- We propose a novel approach to decouple the function of spatial information preservation and receptive field offering into two paths. Specifically, we propose a Bilateral Segmentation Network (BiSeNet) with a Spatial Path (SP) and a Context Path (CP).
- We design two specific modules, Feature Fusion Module (FFM) and Attention Refinement Module (ARM), to further improve the accuracy with acceptable cost.
- We achieve impressive results on the benchmarks of Cityscapes, CamVid, and COCO-Stuff. More specifically, we obtain the results of 68.4% on the Cityscapes test dataset with the speed of 105 FPS.

2   Related Work

Recently, lots of approaches based on FCN [22] have achieved the *state-of-the-art* performance on different benchmarks of the semantic segmentation task. Most of these methods are designed to encode more spatial information or enlarge the receptive field.

Spatial Information: The convolutional neural network (CNN) [16] encodes high-level semantic information with consecutive down-sampling operations. However, in the semantic segmentation task, the spatial information of the image is crucial to predicting the detailed output. Modern existing approaches devote to encode affluent spatial information. DUC [32], PSPNet [40], DeepLab v2 [5], and Deeplab v3 [6] use the dilated convolution to preserve the spatial size of the feature map. Global Convolution Network [26] utilizes the "large kernel" to enlarge the receptive field.

U-Shape Method: The U-shape structure [1,10,22,24,27] can recover a certain extent of spatial information. The original FCN [22] network encodes different level features by a skip-connected network structure. Some methods employ their specific refinement structure into U-shape network structure. [1,24] create a U-shape network structure with the usage of deconvolution layers. U-net [27] introduces the useful skip connection network structure for this task. Global Convolution Network [26] combines the U-shape structure with "large kernel". LRR [10] adopts the Laplacian Pyramid Reconstruction Network. RefineNet [18] adds multi-path refinement structure to refine the prediction. DFN [36] designs a channel attention block to achieve the feature selection. However, in the U-shape structure, some lost spatial information cannot be easily recovered.

Context Information: Semantic segmentation requires context information to generate a high-quality result. The majority of common methods enlarge the receptive field or fuse different context information. [5,6,32,37] employ the different dilation rates in convolution layers to capture diverse context information. Driven by the image pyramid, multi-scale feature ensemble is always employed in the semantic segmentation network structure. In [5], an "ASPP" module is proposed to capture context information of different receptive field. PSPNet [40] applies a "PSP" module which contains several different scales of average pooling layers. [6] designs an "ASPP" module with global average pooling to capture the global context of the image. [38] improves the neural network by a scale adaptive convolution layer to obtain an adaptive field context information. DFN [36] adds the global pooling on the top of the U-shape structure to encode the global context.

Attention Mechanism: Attention mechanism can use the high-level information to guide the feed-forward network [23,31]. In [7], the attention of CNN depends on the scale of the input image. In [13], they apply channel attention to recognition task and achieve the *state-of-the-art*. Like the DFN [36], they learn the global context as attention and revise the features.

Real Time Segmentation: Real-time semantic segmentation algorithms require a fast way to generate the high-quality prediction. SegNet [1] utilizes a small network structure and the skip-connected method to achieve a fast speed. E-Net [25] designs a lightweight network from scratch and delivers an extremely high speed. ICNet [39] uses the image cascade to speed up the semantic segmentation method. [17] employs a cascade network structure to reduce the computation in "easy regions". [34] designs a novel two-column network and spatial sparsity to reduce computation cost. Differently, our proposed method employs a lightweight model to provide sufficient receptive field. Furthermore, we set a shallow but wide network to capture adequate spatial information.

3   Bilateral Segmentation Network

In this section, we first illustrate our proposed Bilateral Segmentation Network (BiSeNet) with Spatial Path and Context Path in detail. Furthermore,

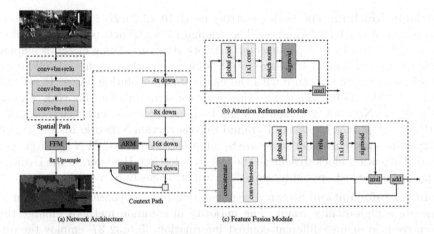

Fig. 2. An overview of the Bilateral Segmentation Network. (a) Network Architecture. The length of block indicates the spatial size, while the thickness represents the number of channels. (b) Components of the Attention Refinement Module (ARM). (c) Components of the Feature Fusion Module (FFM). The read line represents we take this process only when testing.

we elaborate on the effectiveness of these two paths correspondingly. Finally, we demonstrate how to combine the features of these two paths with Feature Fusion Module and the whole architecture of our BiSeNet.

3.1 Spatial Path

In the task of semantic segmentation, some existing approaches [5,6,32,40] attempt to preserve the resolution of the input image to encode enough spatial information with dilated convolution, while a few approaches [5,6,26,40] try to capture sufficient receptive field with pyramid pooling module, atrous spatial pyramid pooling or "large kernel". These methods indicate that the spatial information and the receptive field are crucial to achieving high accuracy. However, it is hard to meet these two demands simultaneously. Especially, in the case of real-time semantic segmentation, existing modern approaches [1,25,39] utilize small input image or lightweight base model to speed up. The small size of the input image loses the majority of spatial information from the original image, while the lightweight model damages spatial information with the channel pruning.

Based on this observation, we propose a Spatial Path to preserve the spatial size of the original input image and encode affluent spatial information. The Spatial Path contains three layers. Each layer includes a convolution with $stride = 2$, followed by batch normalization [15] and ReLU [11]. Therefore, this path extracts the output feature maps that is 1/8 of the original image. It encodes rich spatial information due to the large spatial size of feature maps. Figure 2(a) presents the details of the structure.

3.2   Context Path

While the Spatial Path encodes affluent spatial information, the Context Path is designed to provide sufficient receptive field. In the semantic segmentation task, the receptive field is of great significance for the performance. To enlarge receptive field, some approaches have taken advantage of the pyramid pooling module [40], atrous spatial pyramid pooling [5,6] or "large kernel" [26]. However, these operations are computation demanding and memory consuming, which result in the low speed.

With the consideration of the large receptive field and efficient computation simultaneously, we propose the Context Path. The Context Path utilizes lightweight model and global average pooling [5,6,21] to provide large receptive field. In this work, the lightweight model, like Xception [8], can downsample the feature map fast to obtain large receptive field, which encodes high level semantic context information. Then we add a global average pooling on the tail of the lightweight model, which can provide the maximum receptive field with global context information. Finally, we combine the up-sampled output feature of global pooling and the features of the lightweight model. In the lightweight model, we deploy U-shape structure [1,25,35] to fuse the features of the last two stages, which is an incomplete U-shape style. Figure 2(c) shows the overall perspective of the Context Path.

Attention Refinement Module: In the Context Path, we propose a specific Attention Refinement Module (ARM) to refine the features of each stage. As Fig. 2(b) shows, ARM employs global average pooling to capture global context and computes an attention vector to guide the feature learning. This design can refine the output feature of each stage in the Context Path. It integrates the global context information easily without any up-sampling operation. Therefore, it demands negligible computation cost.

3.3   Network Architecture

With the Spatial Path and the Context Path, we propose BiSeNet for real-time semantic segmentation as illustrated in Fig. 2(a).

We use the pre-trained Xception model as the backbone of the Context Path and three convolution layers with stride as the Spatial Path. And then we fuse the output features of these two paths to make the final prediction. It can achieve real-time performance and high accuracy at the same time. First, we focus on the practical computation aspect. Although the Spatial Path has large spatial size, it only has three convolution layers. Therefore, it is not computation intensive. As for the Context Path, we use a lightweight model to down-sample rapidly. Furthermore, these two paths compute concurrently, which considerably increase the efficiency. Second, we discuss the accuracy aspect of this network. In our paper, the Spatial Path encodes rich spatial information, while the Context Path provides large receptive field. They are complementary to each other for higher performance.

Feature Fusion Module: The features of the two paths are different in level of feature representation. Therefore, we can not simply sum up these features. The spatial information captured by the Spatial Path encodes mostly rich detail information. Moreover, the output feature of the Context Path mainly encodes context information. In other words, the output feature of Spatial Path is low level, while the output feature of Context Path is high level. Therefore, we propose a specific Feature Fusion Module to fuse these features.

Given the different level of the features, we first concatenate the output features of Spatial Path and Context Path. And then we utilize the batch normalization [15] to balance the scales of the features. Next, we pool the concatenated feature to a feature vector and compute a weight vector, like SENet [13]. This weight vector can re-weight the features, which amounts to feature selection and combination. Figure 2(c) shows the details of this design.

Loss Function: In this paper, we also utilize the auxiliary loss function to supervise the training of our proposed method. We use the principal loss function to supervise the output of the whole BiSeNet. Moreover, we add two specific auxiliary loss functions to supervise the output of the Context Path, like deep supervision [35]. All the loss functions are Softmax loss, as Eq. 1 shows. Furthermore, we use the parameter α to balance the weight of the principal loss and auxiliary loss, as Eq. 2 presents. The α in our paper is equal to 1. The joint loss makes optimizer more comfortable to optimize the model.

$$loss = \frac{1}{N} \sum_i L_i = \frac{1}{N} \sum_i -log \left(\frac{e^{p_i}}{\sum_j e^{p_j}} \right) \tag{1}$$

where p is the output prediction of the network.

$$L(X;W) = l_p(X;W) + \alpha \sum_{i=2}^{K} l_i(X_i;W) \tag{2}$$

where l_p is the principal loss of the concatenated output. X_i is the output feature from stage i of Xception model. l_i is the auxiliary loss for stage i. The K is equal to 3 in our paper. The L is the joint loss function. Here, we only use the auxiliary loss in the training phase.

4   Experimental Results

We adopt a modified Xception model [8], Xception39, into the real-time semantic segmentation task. Our implementation code will be made publicly available.

We evaluate our proposed BiSeNet on Cityscapes [9], CamVid [2] and COCO-Stuff [3] benchmarks. We first introduce the datasets and the implementation protocol. Next, we describe our speed strategy in comparison with other methods in detail. And then we investigate the effects of each component of our proposed approach. We evaluate all performance results on the Cityscapes validation set. Finally, we report the accuracy and speed results on Cityscapes,

CamVid and COCO-Stuff datasets compared with other real-time semantic segmentation algorithms.

Cityscapes: The Cityscapes [9] is a large urban street scene dataset from a car perspective. It contains 2,975 fine annotated images for training and another 500 images for validation. In our experiments, we only use the fine dataset. For testing, it offers 1,525 images without ground-truth for fair comparison. These images all have a resolution of 2,048 × 1,024, in which each pixel is annotated to pre-defined 19 classes.

CamVid: The CamVid [2] is another street scene dataset from the perspective of a driving automobile. It contains 701 images in total, in which 367 for training, 101 for validation and 233 for testing. The images have a resolution of 960 × 720 and 11 semantic categories.

COCO-Stuff: The COCO-Stuff [3] augments all 164,000 images of the popular COCO [20] dataset, out of which 118,000 images for training, 5,000 images for validation, 20,000 images for test-dev and 20,000 images for test-challenge. It covers 91 stuff classes and 1 class 'unlabeled'.

4.1 Implementation Protocol

In this section, we elaborate our implementation protocol in detail.

Network: We apply three convolutions as Spatial Path and Xception39 model for Context Path. And then we use Feature Fusion Module to combine the features of these two paths to predict the final results. The output resolution of Spatial Path and the final prediction are 1/8 of the original image.

Training Details: We use mini-batch stochastic gradient descent (SGD) [16] with batch size 16, momentum 0.9 and weight decay $1e^{-4}$ in training. Similar to [5,6,21], we apply the "poly" learning rate strategy in which the initial rate is multiplied by $(1 - \frac{iter}{max\_iter})^{power}$ each iteration with power 0.9. The initial learning rate is $2.5e^{-2}$.

Data Augmentation: We employ the mean subtraction, random horizontal flip and random scale on the input images to augment the dataset in training process. The scales contains {0.75, 1.0, 1.5, 1.75, 2.0}. Finally, we randomly crop the image into fix size for training.

4.2 Ablation Study

In this subsection, we detailedly investigate the effect of each component in our proposed BiSeNet step by step. In the following experiments, we use Xception39 as the base network and evaluate our method on the Cityscapes validation dataset [9].

Table 1. Accuracy and parameter analysis of our baseline model: Xception39 and Res18 on Cityscapes validation dataset. Here we use FCN-32s as the base structure. FLOPS are estimated for input of $3 \times 640 \times 360$.

Method	BaseModel	FLOPS	Parameters	Mean IOU (%)
FCN-32s	Xception39	185.5M	1.2M	60.78
FCN-32s	Res18	8.3G	42.7M	61.58

Baseline: We use the Xception39 network pretrained on ImageNet dataset [28] as the backbone of Context Path. And then we directly up-sample the output of the network as original input image, like FCN [22]. We evaluate the performance of the base model as our baseline, as shown in Table 1.

Table 2. Speed analysis of the U-shape-8s and the U-shape-4s on one NVIDIA Titan XP card. Image size is W × H.

Method	NVIDIA Titan XP						Mean IOU (%)
	640×360		1280×720		1920×1080		
	ms	fps	ms	fps	ms	fps	
U-shape-8s	3	413.7	6	189.8	12	86.7	66.01
U-shape-4s	4	322.9	9	114	17	61.1	66.13

Ablation for U-shape: We propose the Context Path to provide sufficient receptive field, where we use a lightweight model, Xception39, as the backbone of Context Path to down-sample quickly. Simultaneously, we use the U-shape structure [1, 25, 35] to combine the features of the last two stage in Xception39 network, called U-shape-8s, rather than the standard U-shape structure, called U-shape-4s. The number represents the down-sampling factor of the output feature, as shown in Fig. 2. The reason to use U-shape-8s structure is twofold. First, the U-shape structure can recover a certain extent of spatial information and spatial size. Second, the U-shape-8s structure is faster compared to the U-shape-4s, as shown in Table 2. Therefore, we use the U-shape-8s structure, which improves the performance from 60.79% to 66.01%, as shown in Table 2.

Ablation for Spatial Path: As Sect. 1 stated, existing modern approaches of real-time semantic segmentation task face the challenge of lost of spatial information. Therefore, we propose a Spatial Path to preserve the spatial size and capture rich spatial information. The Spatial Path contains three convolutions with *stride* = 2, followed by batch normalization [15] and ReLU [11]. This improves the performance from 66.01% to 67.42%, as shown in Table 3. The Spatial Path encodes abundant details of spatial information. Figure 3 shows that the BiSeNet can obtain more detailed spatial information, e.g. some traffic signs.

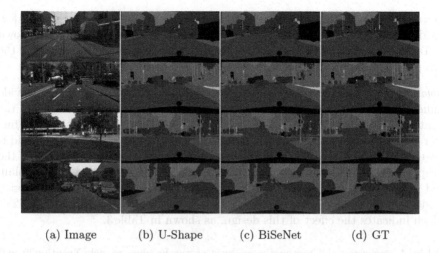

(a) Image   (b) U-Shape   (c) BiSeNet   (d) GT

Fig. 3. Example results of the output before adding the Spatial Path and after adding the Spatial Path. The output BiSeNet has more detail information than the output of U-shape.

Table 3. Detailed performance comparison of each component in our proposed BiSeNet. **CP:** Context Path; **SP:** Spatial Path; **GP:** global average pooling; **ARM:** Attention Refinement Module; **FFM:** Feature Fusion Module.

Method	Mean IOU (%)
CP	66.01
CP+SP(Sum)	66.82
CP+SP(FFM)	67.42
CP+SP(FFM)+GP	68.42
CP+SP(FFM)+ARM	68.72
CP+SP(FFM)+GP+ARM	71.40

Ablation for Attention Refinement Module: For further improving the performance, we specially design an Attention Refinement Module (ARM). This module contains a global average pooling to encode a ouput feature into a vector. Then we utilize a convolution, batch normalization [15] and ReLU unit [11] to compute the attention vector. The original feature will be re-weighted by the attention vector. For the original feature, it is easy to capture the global context information without the complex up-sample operation. The effect of the ARM is presented in Table 3.

Ablation for Feature Fusion Module: Based on the Spatial Path and Context Path, we need to fuse the output features of these two paths. With the consideration of the different levels of the features, low level for the features of Spatial Path and high level for the Context Path, we propose the Feature Fusion Module to combine these features effectively. First, we evaluate the effect of a straightforward sum of these features and our proposed Feature Fusion Module, as shown in Table 3. The gap of the comparison performance explains the features of the two paths belong to different levels in turn.

Ablation for Global Average Pooling: We expect the Context Path can provide sufficient receptive field. Although the original Xception39 model can cover the most region of input image theoretically, we still enlarge the receptive field further with global average pooling [21]. This can ensure the valid receptive field is large enough. In this paper, we add the global average pooling at the tail of the Xception39 model. Then, we up-sample the output of the global average pooling and sum up this feature with the output of the last stage in the Xception39 model, like DFN [36]. This improves the performance from 67.42% to 68.42%, which indicates the effect of this design, as shown in Table 3.

Table 4. Accuracy and parameter analysis of our baseline model: Xception39 and Res18 on Cityscapes validation dataset. Here we use FCN-32s as the base structure. FLOPS are estimated for input of $3 \times 640 \times 360$.

Method	BaseModel	GFLOPS	Parameters
SegNet [1]	VGG16 [29]	286.0	29.5M
ENet [25]	From scratch	3.8	0.4M
Ours	Xception39	2.9	5.8M
Ours	Res18	10.8	49.0M

Table 5. Speed comparison of our method against other *state-of-the-art* methods. Image size is W × H. The *Ours*[1] and *Ours*[2] are the BiSeNet based on Xception39 and Res18 model.

Method	NVIDIA Titan X						NVIDIA Titan XP					
	640×360		1280×720		1920×1080		640×360		1280×720		1920×1080	
	ms	fps	ms	fps	ms	fps	ms	fps	ms	fps	ms	fps
SegNet [1]	69	14.6	289	3.5	637	1.6	-	-	-	-	-	-
ENet [25]	7	135.4	21	46.8	46	21.6	-	-	-	-	-	-
Ours[1]	5	**203.5**	12	**82.3**	24	**41.4**	4	**285.2**	8	**124.1**	18	**57.3**
Ours[2]	8	129.4	21	47.9	43	23	5	205.7	13	78.8	29	34.4

4.3   Speed and Accuracy Analysis

In this section, we first analysis the speed of our algorithm. Then we report our final results on Cityscapes [9], CamVid [2] and COCO-Stuff [3] benchmarks compared with other algorithms.

Speed Analysis: Speed is a vital factor of an algorithm especially when we apply it in practice. We conduct our experiments on different settings for thorough comparison. First, we show our status of FLOPS and parameters in Table 4. The FLOPS and parameters indicate the number of operations to process images of this resolution. For a fair comparison, we choose the 640 × 360 as the resolution of the input image. Meanwhile, Table 5 presents the speed comparison between our method with other approaches on different resolutions of input images and different hardware benchmarks. Finally, we report our speed and corresponding accuracy results on Cityscapes test dataset. From Table 6, we can find out our method achieves significant progress against the other methods both in speed and accuracy. In the evaluation process, we first scale the input image of 2048 × 1024 resolution into the 1536 × 768 resolution for testing the speed and accuracy. Meanwhile, we compute the loss function with the online bootstrapping strategy as described in [33]. In this process, we don't employ any testing technology, like multi-scale or multi-crop testing.

Table 6. Accuracy and speed comparison of our method against other *state-of-the-art* methods on Cityscapes test dataset. We train and evaluate on NVIDIA Titan XP with 2048 × 1024 resolution input. "-" indicates that the methods didn't give the corresponding speed result of the accuracy.

Method	BaseModel	Mean IOU (%)		FPS
		val	*test*	
SegNet [1]	VGG16	-	56.1	-
ENet [25]	From scratch	-	58.3	-
SQ [30]	SqueezeNet [14]	-	59.8	-
ICNet [39]	PSPNet50 [40]	67.7	69.5	30.3
DLC [17]	Inception-ResNet-v2	-	71.1	-
Two-column Net [34]	Res50	74.6	72.9	14.7
Ours	Xception39	69.0	68.4	**105.8**
Ours	Res18	**74.8**	**74.7**	65.5

Accuracy Analysis: Actually, our BiSeNet can also achieve higher accuracy result against other non-real-time semantic segmentation algorithms. Here, we will show the accuracy result on Cityscapes [9], CamVid [2] and COCO-Stuff [3] benchmarks. Meanwhile, to ensure the validity of our method, we also employ it on different base models, such as the standard ResNet18 and ResNet101 [12]. Next, we will elaborate on some training details.

Cityscapes: As shown in Table 7, our method also achieves an impressing result on different models. For improving the accuracy, we take randomly take 1024 × 1024 crop as input. The Fig. 4 presents some visual examples of our results.

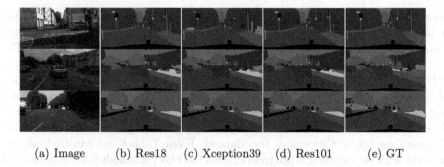

(a) Image   (b) Res18   (c) Xception39   (d) Res101   (e) GT

Fig. 4. Example results of the BiSeNet based on Xception39, Res18, and Res101 model on Cityscapes dataset.

Table 7. Accuracy comparison of our method against other *state-of-the-art* methods on Cityscapes test dataset. "-" indicates that the methods didn't give the corresponding result.

Method	BaseModel	Mean IOU (%)	
		val	test
DeepLab [4]	VGG16 [29]	-	63.1
FCN-8s [22]	VGG16	-	65.3
Adelaide [19]	VGG16	-	66.4
Dilation10 [37]	VGG16	68.7	67.1
LRR [10]	VGG16	70.0	69.7
DeepLab-v2+CRF [5]	Res101	71.4	70.4
RefineNet [18]	Res101	-	73.6
DUC [32]	Res152	76.7	76.1
PSPNet [40]	Res101	-	<u>78.4</u>
Ours	Xception39	72.0	71.4
Ours	Res18	<u>78.6</u>	77.7
Ours	Res101	**80.3**	**78.9**

CamVid: The Table 8 shows the statistic accuracy result on CamVid dataset. For testing, we use the training dataset and validation dataset to train our model. Here, we use 960×720 resolution for training and evaluation.

COCO-Stuff: We also report our accuracy results on COCO-Stuff validation dataset in Table 9. In the training and validation process, we crop the input into 640×640 resolution. For a fair comparison, we don't adopt the multi-scale testing.

Table 8. Accuracy result on CamVid test dataset. $Ours^1$ and $Ours^2$ indicate the model based on Xception39 and Res18 network.

Method	Building	Tree	Sky	Car	Sign	Road	Pedestrian	Fence	Pole	Sidewalk	Bicyclist	Mean IOU (%)
SegNet-Basic	75.0	84.6	91.2	82.7	36.9	93.3	55.0	47.5	44.8	74.1	16.0	n/a
SegNet	88.8	87.3	92.4	82.1	20.5	97.2	57.1	49.3	27.5	84.4	30.7	55.6
ENet	74.7	77.8	95.1	82.4	51.0	95.1	67.2	51.7	35.4	86.7	34.1	51.3
$Ours^1$	82.2	74.4	91.9	80.8	42.8	93.3	53.8	49.7	25.4	77.3	50.0	65.6
$Ours^2$	83.0	75.8	92.0	83.7	46.5	94.6	58.8	53.6	31.9	81.4	54.0	**68.7**

Table 9. Accuracy result on COCO-Stuff validation dataset.

Method	BaseModel	Mean IOU (%)	Pixel Accuracy (%)
Deeplab-v2	VGG-16	24.0	58.2
Ours	Xception39	22.8	59.0
Ours	Res18	28.1	63.2
Ours	Res101	**31.3**	**65.5**

5 Conclusions

Bilateral Segmentation Network (BiSeNet) is proposed in this paper to improve the speed and accuracy of real-time semantic segmentation simultaneously. Our proposed BiSeNet contains two paths: Spatial Path (SP) and Context Path (CP). The Spatial Path is designed to preserve the spatial information from original images. And the Context Path utilizes the lightweight model and global average pooling [6,21,40] to obtain sizeable receptive field rapidly. With the affluent spatial details and large receptive field, we achieve the result of 68.4% Mean IOU on Cityscapes [9] test dataset at 105 FPS.

Acknowledgment. This work was supported by the Project of the National Natural Science Foundation of China No. 61433007 and No. 61401170.

References

1. Badrinarayanan, V., Kendall, A., Cipolla, R.: SegNet: a deep convolutional encoder-decoder architecture for image segmentation. IEEE Trans. Pattern Anal. Mach. Intell. **39**(12), 2481–2495 (2017)
2. Brostow, G.J., Shotton, J., Fauqueur, J., Cipolla, R.: Segmentation and recognition using structure from motion point clouds. In: Forsyth, D., Torr, P., Zisserman, A. (eds.) ECCV 2008, Part I. LNCS, vol. 5302, pp. 44–57. Springer, Heidelberg (2008). https://doi.org/10.1007/978-3-540-88682-2_5
3. Caesar, H., Uijlings, J., Ferrari, V.: Coco-stuff: thing and stuff classes in context. In: IEEE Conference on Computer Vision and Pattern Recognition (2018)
4. Chen, L.C., Papandreou, G., Kokkinos, I., Murphy, K., Yuille, A.L.: Semantic image segmentation with deep convolutional nets and fully connected CRFs. In: ICLR (2015)

5. Chen, L.C., Papandreou, G., Kokkinos, I., Murphy, K., Yuille, A.L.: Deeplab: semantic image segmentation with deep convolutional nets, atrous convolution, and fully connected CRFs (2016). arXiv:1606.00915

6. Chen, L.C., Papandreou, G., Schroff, F., Adam, H.: Rethinking atrous convolution for semantic image segmentation (2017). arXiv:1706.05587

7. Chen, L.C., Yang, Y., Wang, J., Xu, W., Yuille, A.L.: Attention to scale: scale-aware semantic image segmentation. In: IEEE Conference on Computer Vision and Pattern Recognition (2016)

8. Chollet, F.: Xception: deep learning with depthwise separable convolutions. In: IEEE Conference on Computer Vision and Pattern Recognition (2017)

9. Cordts, M., et al.: The cityscapes dataset for semantic urban scene understanding. In: IEEE Conference on Computer Vision and Pattern Recognition (2016)

10. Ghiasi, G., Fowlkes, C.C.: Laplacian pyramid reconstruction and refinement for semantic segmentation. In: Leibe, B., Matas, J., Sebe, N., Welling, M. (eds.) ECCV 2016, Part III. LNCS, vol. 9907, pp. 519–534. Springer, Cham (2016). https://doi.org/10.1007/978-3-319-46487-9_32

11. Glorot, X., Bordes, A., Bengio, Y.: Deep sparse rectifier neural networks. In: International Conference on Artificial Intelligence and Statistics, pp. 315–323 (2011)

12. He, K., Zhang, X., Ren, S., Sun, J.: Deep residual learning for image recognition. In: IEEE Conference on Computer Vision and Pattern Recognition (2016)

13. Hu, J., Shen, L., Sun, G.: Squeeze-and-excitation networks (2017). arXiv:1709.01507

14. Iandola, F.N., Moskewicz, M.W., Ashraf, K., Han, S., Dally, W.J., Keutzer, K.: Squeezenet: Alexnet-level accuracy with 50x fewer parameters and <0.5MB model size (2016). arXiv:1602.07360

15. Ioffe, S., Szegedy, C.: Batch normalization: accelerating deep network training by reducing internal covariate shift. In: International Conference on Machine Learning, pp. 448–456 (2015)

16. Krizhevsky, A., Sutskever, I., Hinton, G.E.: Imagenet classification with deep convolutional neural networks. In: Neural Information Processing Systems (2012)

17. Li, X., Liu, Z., Luo, P., Loy, C.C., Tang, X.: Not all pixels are equal: difficulty-aware semantic segmentation via deep layer cascade. In: IEEE Conference on Computer Vision and Pattern Recognition (2017)

18. Lin, G., Milan, A., Shen, C., Reid, I.: Refinenet: multi-path refinement networks with identity mappings for high-resolution semantic segmentation. In: IEEE Conference on Computer Vision and Pattern Recognition (2017)

19. Lin, G., Shen, C., van den Hengel, A., Reid, I.: Efficient piecewise training of deep structured models for semantic segmentation. In: IEEE Conference on Computer Vision and Pattern Recognition (2016)

20. Lin, T.-Y., et al.: Microsoft COCO: common objects in context. In: Fleet, D., Pajdla, T., Schiele, B., Tuytelaars, T. (eds.) ECCV 2014, Part V. LNCS, vol. 8693, pp. 740–755. Springer, Cham (2014). https://doi.org/10.1007/978-3-319-10602-1_48

21. Liu, W., Rabinovich, A., Berg, A.C.: Parsenet: looking wider to see better. In: ICLR (2016)

22. Long, J., Shelhamer, E., Darrell, T.: Fully convolutional networks for semantic segmentation. In: IEEE Conference on Computer Vision and Pattern Recognition (2015)

23. Mnih, V., Heess, N., Graves, A., et al.: Recurrent models of visual attention. In: Neural Information Processing Systems (2014)

24. Noh, H., Hong, S., Han, B.: Learning deconvolution network for semantic segmentation. In: IEEE International Conference on Computer Vision (2015)

25. Paszke, A., Chaurasia, A., Kim, S., Culurciello, E.: Enet: a deep neural network architecture for real-time semantic segmentation (2016). arXiv:1606.02147

26. Peng, C., Zhang, X., Yu, G., Luo, G., Sun, J.: Large kernel matters-improve semantic segmentation by global convolutional network. In: IEEE Conference on Computer Vision and Pattern Recognition (2017)

27. Ronneberger, O., Fischer, P., Brox, T.: U-Net: convolutional networks for biomedical image segmentation. In: Navab, N., Hornegger, J., Wells, W.M., Frangi, A.F. (eds.) MICCAI 2015, Part III. LNCS, vol. 9351, pp. 234–241. Springer, Cham (2015). https://doi.org/10.1007/978-3-319-24574-4_28

28. Russakovsky, O., et al.: ImageNet large scale visual recognition challenge. Int. J. Comput. Vis. **115**(3), 211–252 (2015). https://doi.org/10.1007/s11263-015-0816-y

29. Simonyan, K., Zisserman, A.: Very deep convolutional networks for large-scale image recognition. In: ICLR (2015)

30. Treml, M., et al.: Speeding up semantic segmentation for autonomous driving. In: Neural Information Processing Systems Workshop (2016)

31. Wang, F., et al.: Residual attention network for image classification. In: IEEE Conference on Computer Vision and Pattern Recognition (2017)

32. Wang, P., et al.: Understanding convolution for semantic segmentation. In: IEEE Conference on Computer Vision and Pattern Recognition (2017)

33. Wu, Z., Shen, C., van den Hengel, A.: High-performance semantic segmentation using very deep fully convolutional networks (2016). arXiv preprint: arXiv:1604.04339

34. Wu, Z., Shen, C., van den Hengel, A.: Real-time semantic image segmentation via spatial sparsity (2017). arXiv:1712.00213

35. Xie, S., Tu, Z.: Holistically-nested edge detection. In: IEEE International Conference on Computer Vision (2015)

36. Yu, C., Wang, J., Peng, C., Gao, C., Yu, G., Sang, N.: Learning a discriminative feature network for semantic segmentation. In: IEEE Conference on Computer Vision and Pattern Recognition (2018)

37. Yu, F., Koltun, V.: Multi-scale context aggregation by dilated convolutions. In: ICLR (2016)

38. Zhang, R., Tang, S., Zhang, Y., Li, J., Yan, S.: Scale-adaptive convolutions for scene parsing. In: IEEE International Conference on Computer Vision, pp. 2031–2039 (2017)

39. Zhao, H., Qi, X., Shen, X., Shi, J., Jia, J.: ICNet for real-time semantic segmentation on high-resolution images (2017) arXiv:1704.08545

40. Zhao, H., Shi, J., Qi, X., Wang, X., Jia, J.: Pyramid scene parsing network. In: IEEE Conference on Computer Vision and Pattern Recognition (2017)

Pose Proposal Networks

Taiki Sekii(✉)

Konica Minolta, Inc., Osaka, Japan
`taiki.sekii@konicaminolta.com`

Abstract. We propose a novel method to detect an unknown number of articulated 2D poses in real time. To decouple the runtime complexity of pixel-wise body part detectors from their convolutional neural network (CNN) feature map resolutions, our approach, called *pose proposal networks*, introduces a state-of-the-art single-shot object detection paradigm using grid-wise image feature maps in a bottom-up pose detection scenario. Body part proposals, which are represented as region proposals, and limbs are detected directly via a single-shot CNN. Specialized to such detections, a bottom-up greedy parsing step is probabilistically redesigned to take into account the global context. Experimental results on the MPII Multi-Person benchmark confirm that our method achieves 72.8% mAP comparable to state-of-the-art bottom-up approaches while its total runtime using a GeForce GTX1080Ti card reaches up to 5.6 ms (180 FPS), which exceeds the bottleneck runtimes that are observed in state-of-the-art approaches.

Keywords: Human pose estimation · Object detection

1 Introduction

The problem of detecting humans and simultaneously estimating their articulated poses (which we refer to as *poses*) as shown in Fig. 1 has become an important and highly practical task in computer vision thanks to recent advances in deep learning. While this task has broad applications in fields such as sports analysis and human-computer interaction, its test-time computational cost can still be a bottleneck in real-time systems. Human pose estimation is defined as the localization of anatomical keypoints or landmarks (which we refer to as *parts*) and is tackled using various methods, depending on the final goals and the assumptions made:

- The use of single or sequential images as input;
- The use (or not) of depth information as input;

Electronic supplementary material The online version of this chapter (https://doi.org/10.1007/978-3-030-01261-8_21) contains supplementary material, which is available to authorized users.

© Springer Nature Switzerland AG 2018
V. Ferrari et al. (Eds.): ECCV 2018, LNCS 11217, pp. 350–366, 2018.
https://doi.org/10.1007/978-3-030-01261-8_21

- The localization of parts in a 2D or 3D space; and
- The estimation of single- or multi-person poses.

This paper focuses on multi-person 2D pose estimation from a 2D still image. In particular, we do not assume that the ground truth location and scale of the person instances are provided and, therefore, need to detect an unknown number of poses, *i.e.*, we need to achieve *human pose detection*. In this more challenging setting, referred to as "in the wild," we pursue an end-to-end, detection framework that can perform in real-time.

(a)   (b)   (c)   (d)

Fig. 1. Sample multi-person pose detection results by the ResNet-18-based *PPN*. Part bounding boxes (b) and limbs (c) are directly detected from input images (a) using single-shot CNNs and are parsed into individual people (d) (*cf.* Sect. 3).

Previous approaches [1–13] can be divided into the following two types: one detects person instances first and then applies single-person pose estimators to each detection and the other detects parts first and then parses them into each person instance. These are called as *top-down* and *bottom-up* approaches, respectively. Such state-of-the-art methods show competitive results in both runtime and accuracy. However, the runtime of top-down approaches is proportional to the number of people, making real-time performance a challenge, while bottom-up approaches require bottleneck parts association procedures that extract contextual cues between parts and parse part detections into individual people. In addition, most state-of-the-art techniques are designed to predict pixel-wise[1] part confidence maps in the image. These maps force convolutional neural networks (CNNs) to extract feature maps with higher resolutions, which are indispensable for maintaining robustness, and the acceleration of the architectures (*e.g.*, shrinking the architectures) is interfered depending on the applications.

In this paper, to decouple the runtime complexity of the human pose detection from the feature map resolution of the CNNs and improve the performance,

---

[1] We also use the term "pixel-wise" to refer to the downsampled part confidence maps.

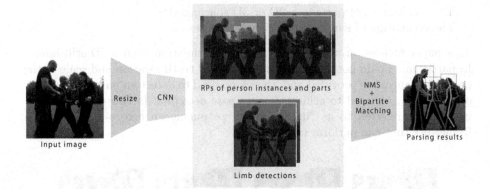

Fig. 2. Pipeline of our proposed approach. Pose proposals are generated by parsing RPs of person instances and parts into individual people with limb detections (*cf.* Sect. 3).

we rely on a state-of-the-art single-shot object detection paradigm that roughly extracts grid-wise object confidence maps in the image using relatively smaller CNNs. We benefit from region proposal (RP) frameworks[2] [14–17] and reframe the human pose detection as an object detection problem, regressing from image pixels to RPs of person instances and parts, as shown in Fig. 2. In addition, instead of the previous parts association designed for pixel-wise part proposals, our framework directly detects limbs[3] using single-shot CNNs and generates pose proposals from such detections via a novel, probabilistic greedy parsing step in which the global context is taken into account. Part RPs are defined as bounding box detections whose sizes are proportional to the person scales and can be supervised using just the common keypoint annotations. The entire architecture is constructed from a single, fully CNN with relatively lower-resolution feature maps and is optimized end-to-end directly using a loss function designed for pose detection performance; we call this architecture the *pose proposal network* (PPN).

2 Related Work

We will briefly review some of the recent progress in single- and multi-person pose estimations to put our contributions into context.

Single-Person Pose Estimation. The majority of early classic approaches for single-person pose estimation [18–23] assumed that the person dominates the image content and that all limbs are visible. These approaches primarily pursued

---

[2] We use the term "RP frameworks" to refer broadly to CNN-based methods that predict a fixed set of bounding boxes depending on the input image sizes.

[3] We refer to part pairs as limbs for clarity, despite the fact that some pairs are not human limbs (*e.g.*, faces).

the modeling of structures together with the articulation of single-person body parts and their appearances in the image under various concepts such as pictorial structure models [18,19], hierarchical models [22], and non-tree models [20,21, 23]. Since the appearance of deep learning-based models [24–26] that make the problem tractable, the benchmark results have been successively updated by various base architectures, such as convolutional pose machines (CPMs) [27], residual networks (ResNets) [11,28], and stacked hourglass networks (SHNs) [29]. These models focus on strong part detectors that take into account the large, detailed spatial context and are used as fundamental part detectors in both state-of-the-art single- [30–33] and multi-person contexts [1,2,9].

Multi-person Pose Estimation. The performance of top-down approaches [2–4,7,10,12] depends on human detectors and pose estimators; therefore, it has improved according to the performance of these detectors and estimators. More recently, to achieve efficiency and higher robustness, recent methods have tended to share convolutional layers between the human detectors and pose estimators by introducing spatial transformer networks [2,34] or RoIAlign [4].

Conversely, standard bottom-up approaches [1,6,8,9,11,13] rely less on human detectors and instead detect poses by finding groups or pairs of part detections, which occur in consistent geometric configurations. Therefore, they are not affected by the limitations of human detectors. Recent bottom-up approaches use CNNs not only to detect parts but also to directly extract contextual cues between parts from the image, such as image-conditioned pairwise terms [6], part affinity fields (PAFs) [1], and associative embedding (AE) [9].

The state-of-the-art methods in both top-down and bottom-up approaches achieve real-time performance. Their "primitives" of the part proposals are pixel points. However, our method differs from such approaches in that our primitives are grid-wise bounding box detections in which the part scale information is encoded. Our reduced grid-wise part proposals allow shallow CNNs to directly detect limbs which can be represented with at most a few dozen patterns for each part proposal. Specialized for these detections, a greedy parsing step is probabilistically redesigned to encode the global context. Therefore, our method does not need time-consuming, pixel-wise feature extraction or parsing steps, and its total runtime, as a result, exceeds the bottleneck runtimes that are observed in state-of-the-art approaches.

3   Method

Human pose detection is achieved via the following steps.

1. Resize an input image to the input size of the CNN.
2. Run forward propagation of the CNN and obtain RPs of person instances and parts and limb detections.
3. Perform non-maximum suppression (NMS) for these RPs.
4. Parse the merged RPs into individual people and generate pose proposals.

Figure 2 depicts the pipeline of our framework. Section 3.1 describes RP detections of person instances and parts and limb detections, which are used in steps 2 and 3. Section 3.2 describes step 4.

3.1 PPNs

We take advantage of YOLO [15,16], one of the RP frameworks, and apply its concept to the human pose detection task. The PPNs are constructed from a single CNN and produce a fixed-size collection of RPs for each detection target (person instances or each part) over the input image. The CNN divides the input image into a $H \times W$ grid, each cell of which corresponds to an image block, and produces a set of RP detections $\{\mathcal{B}_k^i\}_{k \in \mathcal{K}}$ for each grid cell $i \in \mathcal{G} = \{1, \ldots, H \times W\}$. Here, $\mathcal{K} = \{0, 1, \ldots, K\}$ is the set of indices of the detection targets, and K is the number of parts. The index of the class representing the overall person instances (the person instance class) is given by $k = 0$ in $\mathcal{K}$.

$\mathcal{B}_k^i$ encodes the two probabilities taking into consideration the confidence of the bounding box and the coordinates, width, and height of the bounding box, as shown in Fig. 3, and is given by

$$\mathcal{B}_k^i = \left\{ p(R|k,i), p(I|R,k,i), o_{x,k}^i, o_{y,k}^i, w_k^i, h_k^i \right\}, \tag{1}$$

where R and I are binary random variables. Here, $p(R|k,i)$ is a probability that represents the grid cell i "responsible" for detections of k. If the center of a ground truth bounding box of k falls into a grid cell, that grid cell is "responsible" for detections of k. $p(I|R,k,i)$ is a conditional probability that represents how well the bounding box predicted in i fits k and is supervised by the intersection over union (IoU) between the predicted bounding box and the ground truth bounding box.

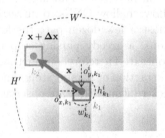

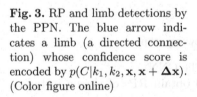

Fig. 3. RP and limb detections by the PPN. The blue arrow indicates a limb (a directed connection) whose confidence score is encoded by $p(C|k_1, k_2, \mathbf{x}, \mathbf{x} + \boldsymbol{\Delta}\mathbf{x})$. (Color figure online)

Fig. 4. Parts association defined as bipartite matching sub-problems. Matchings are decomposed and solved for every pair of detection targets that constitute limbs (*e.g.*, they are separately computed for (k_0, k_1) and for (k_1, k_2)).

The $\left(o_{x,k}^i, o_{y,k}^i \right)$ coordinates represent the center of the bounding box relative to the bounds of the grid cell with the scale normalized by the length of the cells.

w_k^i and h_k^i are normalized by the image width and height, respectively. The bounding boxes of person instances can be represented as rectangles around the entire body or the head. Unlike previous pixel-wise part detectors, parts are grid-wise detected in our method and the box sizes are supervised proportional to the person scales, $e.g.$, one-fifth of the length of the upper body or half the head segment length. The ground truth boxes supervise these predictions regarding the bounding boxes.

Conversely, for each grid cell i located at $\mathbf{x}$, the CNN also produces a set of limb detections, $\{C_{k_1 k_2}\}_{(k_1, k_2) \in \mathcal{L}}$, where $\mathcal{L}$ is a set of pairs of indices of detection targets that constitute limbs. $C_{k_1 k_2}$ encodes a set of probabilities that represents the presence of each limb and is given by

$$C_{k_1 k_2} = \{p(C|k_1, k_2, \mathbf{x}, \mathbf{x} + \mathbf{\Delta x})\}_{\mathbf{\Delta x} \in \mathcal{X}}, \tag{2}$$

where C is a binary random variable. $p(C|k_1, k_2, \mathbf{x}, \mathbf{x} + \mathbf{\Delta x})$ encodes the presence of a limb represented as a directed connection from the bounding box of k_1 predicted in $\mathbf{x}$ to that of k_2 predicted in $\mathbf{x} + \mathbf{\Delta x}$, as shown in Fig. 3. Here, we assume that all the limbs from $\mathbf{x}$ reach only the local $H' \times W'$ area centered on $\mathbf{x}$ and define $\mathcal{X}$ as a set of finite displacements from $\mathbf{x}$, which is given by

$$\mathcal{X} = \{\mathbf{\Delta x} = (\Delta x, \Delta y) | \, |\Delta x| \leq W' \wedge |\Delta y| \leq H'\}. \tag{3}$$

Here, $\mathbf{\Delta x}$ is a position relative to $\mathbf{x}$ and, therefore, $p(C|k_1, k_2, \mathbf{x}, \mathbf{x} + \mathbf{\Delta x})$ can be independently estimated at each grid cell using CNNs thanks to their characteristic of translation invariance.

Each of the above mentioned predictions corresponds to each channel in the depth of the output 3D tensor produced by the CNN. Finally, the CNN outputs an $H \times W \times \{6(K + 1) + H'W'|\mathcal{L}|\}$ tensor. During training, we optimize the following, multi-part loss function:

$$
\begin{aligned}
&\lambda_{\text{resp.}} \sum_{i \in \mathcal{G}} \sum_{k \in \mathcal{K}} \left\{ \delta_k^i - \hat{p}(R|k, i) \right\}^2 \\
&+ \lambda_{\text{IoU}} \sum_{i \in \mathcal{G}} \sum_{k \in \mathcal{K}} \delta_k^i \left\{ (p(I|R, k, i) - \hat{p}(I|R, k, i) \right\}^2 \\
&+ \lambda_{\text{coor.}} \sum_{i \in \mathcal{G}} \sum_{k \in \mathcal{K}} \delta_k^i \left\{ (o_{x,k}^i - \hat{o}_{x,k}^i)^2 + (o_{y,k}^i - \hat{o}_{y,k}^i)^2 \right\} \\
&+ \lambda_{\text{size}} \sum_{i \in \mathcal{G}} \sum_{k \in \mathcal{K}} \delta_k^i \left\{ \left(\sqrt{w_k^i} - \sqrt{\hat{w}_k^i}\right)^2 + \left(\sqrt{h_k^i} - \sqrt{\hat{h}_k^i}\right)^2 \right\} \\
&+ \lambda_{\text{limb}} \sum_{i \in \mathcal{G}} \sum_{\mathbf{\Delta x} \in \mathcal{X}} \sum_{(k_1, k_2) \in \mathcal{L}} \max(\delta_{k_1}^i, \delta_{k_2}^j) \left\{ \delta_{k_1}^i \delta_{k_2}^j - \hat{p}(C|k_1, k_2, \mathbf{x}, \mathbf{x} + \mathbf{\Delta x}) \right\}^2,
\end{aligned} \tag{4}
$$

where $\delta_k^i \in \{1, 0\}$ is a variable that indicates if i is responsible for the k of only a single person, j is the index of a grid cell located at $\mathbf{x} + \mathbf{\Delta x}$, and $(\lambda_{\text{resp.}}, \lambda_{\text{IoU}}, \lambda_{\text{coor.}}, \lambda_{\text{size}}, \lambda_{\text{limb}})$ are the weights for each loss.

3.2 Pose Proposal Generation

Overview. Applying standard NMS using an IoU threshold for the RPs of each detection target, we can obtain the fixed-size, merged RP subsets. Then, in the condition where both true and false positives of multiple people are contained in these RPs, pose proposals are generated by matching and associating the RPs between the detection targets that constitute limbs. This parsing step corresponds to a K-dimensional matching problem that is known to be NP hard [35], and many relaxations exist.

In this paper, inspired by [1], we introduce two relaxations capable of real-time generation of consistent matches. First, a minimal number of edges are chosen to obtain a spanning tree skeleton of articulated poses, whose nodes and edges represent the merged RP subsets of the detection targets and the limb detections between them, respectively, rather than using the complete graph. This tree consists of directed edges and, its root nodes belong to the person instance class. Second, the matching problem is further decomposed into a set of bipartite matching sub-problems, and the matching in adjacent tree nodes is determined independently, as shown in Fig. 4. Cao *et al.* [1] demonstrated that such a minimal greedy inference well approximates the global solution at a fraction of the computational cost and concluded that the relationship between nonadjacent tree nodes can be implicitly modeled in their pairwise part association scores, which the CNN estimates. In contrast to their approach, in order to use relatively shallow CNNs whose receptive fields are narrow and reduce the computational cost, we propose a probabilistic, greedy parsing algorithm that takes into account the relationship between nonadjacent tree nodes.

Confidence Scores. Given the merged RPs of the detection targets, we define a confidence score for the detection of the n-th RP of k as follows:

$$D_k^n = p(R|k, n)p(I|R, k, n). \tag{5}$$

Each probability on the right-hand side of Eq. (5) is encoded by $\mathcal{B}_k^i$ in Eq. (1). $n \in \mathcal{N} = \{1, \ldots, N\}$, where N is the number of merged RPs of each detection target. In addition, the confidence score of the limb, *i.e.*, the directed connection from the n_1-th RP of k_1 predicted at $\mathbf{x}$ to the n_2-th RP of k_2 predicted at $\mathbf{x} + \boldsymbol{\Delta}\mathbf{x}$, is defined by making use of Eq. (2) as follows:

$$E_{k_1 k_2}^{n_1 n_2} = p(C|k_1, k_2, \mathbf{x}, \mathbf{x} + \boldsymbol{\Delta}\mathbf{x}). \tag{6}$$

Parts Association. Parts association, which uses pairwise part association scores, can be generally defined as an optimal assignment problem for the set of all the possible connections,

$$\mathcal{Z} = \left\{ Z_{k_1 k_2}^{n_1 n_2} | (k_1, k_2) \in \mathcal{L}, n_1 \in \mathcal{N}_1, n_2 \in \mathcal{N}_2 \right\}, \tag{7}$$

which maximizes the confidence score that approximates the joint probability over all possible limb detections,

$$F = \prod_{\mathcal{L}} \prod_{\mathcal{N}_1} \prod_{\mathcal{N}_2} \left(E_{k_1 k_2}^{n_1 n_2} \right)^{Z_{k_1 k_2}^{n_1 n_2}}. \tag{8}$$

Here, $Z_{k_1 k_2}^{n_1 n_2}$ is a binary variable that indicates whether the n_1-th RP of k_1 and the n_2-th RP of k_2 are connected and satisfies

$$\sum_{\mathcal{N}_1} Z_{k_1 k_2}^{n_1 n_2} = 1 \wedge \sum_{\mathcal{N}_2} Z_{k_1 k_2}^{n_1 n_2} = 1,$$

$$\forall n_1 \in \mathcal{N}_1, \forall n_2 \in \mathcal{N}_2. \tag{9}$$

Using Eq. (9) ensures that no multiple edges share a node, *i.e.*, that an RP is not connected to different multiple RPs. In this graph-matching problem, the nodes of the graph are all the merged RPs of the detection targets, the edges are all the possible connections between the RPs, which constitute the limbs, and the confidence scores of the limb detections give the weights for the edges. Our goal is to find a matching in the bipartite graph as a subset of the edges chosen with maximum weight.

In our improved parts association with the abovementioned two relaxations, person instances are used as a root part, and the proposals of each part are assigned to person instance proposals along the route on the pose graph. Bipartite matching sub-problems are defined for each respective pair (k_1, k_2) of detection targets that constitute the limbs so as to find the optimal assignment for the set of connections between k_1 and k_2,

$$\mathcal{Z}_{k_1 k_2} = \left\{ Z_{k_1 k_2}^{n_1 n_2} | n_1 \in \mathcal{N}_1, n_2 \in \mathcal{N}_2 \right\}, \tag{10}$$

where

$$\{\mathcal{Z}_{k_1 k_2}\}_{(k_1, k_2) \in \mathcal{L}} = \mathcal{Z}. \tag{11}$$

We obtain the optimal assignment $\hat{\mathcal{Z}}_{k_1 k_2}$ as follows:

$$\hat{\mathcal{Z}}_{k_1 k_2} = \underset{\mathcal{Z}_{k_1 k_2}}{\arg \max} \, F_{k_1 k_2}, \tag{12}$$

where

$$F_{k_1 k_2} = \prod_{\mathcal{N}_1} \prod_{\mathcal{N}_2} \left(S_{k_1 k_2}^{n_1 n_2} \right)^{Z_{k_1 k_2}^{n_1 n_2}}. \tag{13}$$

Here, the nodes of k_1 are closer to those of the person instances on the route of the graph than those of k_2 and

$$S_{k_1 k_2}^{n_1 n_2} = \begin{cases} D_{k_1}^{n_1} E_{k_2 k_1}^{n_2 n_1} D_{k_2}^{n_2} & \text{if } k_1 = 0, \\ S_{k_0 k_1}^{\hat{n}_0 n_1} E_{k_2 k_1}^{n_2 n_1} D_{k_2}^{n_2} & \text{otherwise.} \end{cases} \tag{14}$$

$k_0 \neq k_2$ indicates that another detection target is connected to k_1. $\hat{n}_0$ is the index of the RPs of k_0, which is connected to the n_1-th RP of k_1 and satisfies

$$Z_{k_0 k_1}^{\hat{n}_0 n_1} = 1. \tag{15}$$

This optimization using Eq. (14) needs to be calculated from the parts connected to the person instances. We can use the Hungarian algorithm [36] to obtain the optimal matching. Finally, with all the optimal assignments, we can assemble the connections that share the same RPs into full-body poses of multiple people.

The difference between F in Eq. (8) and $F_{k_1 k_2}$ in Eq. (13) is that the confidence scores for the RPs and the limb detections on the route from the nodes of the person instances on the graph are considered in the matching using Eq. (12). This leads to a global context for wider image regions than the receptive fields of the CNN is taken into account in the parsing. In Sect. 4, we show detailed comparison results, demonstrating that our improved parsing approximates the global solution well when using shallow CNNs.

4   Experiments

4.1   Dataset

We evaluated our approach on the challenging, public "MPII Human Pose" dataset [37], which includes approximately 25 K images containing over 40 K annotated people (three-quarters of which are available for training). For a fair comparison, we followed the official evaluation protocol and used the publicly available evaluation scripts[4] for self-comparison on the validation set used in [1].

First, the "Single-Person" subset, containing only sufficiently separated people, was used to evaluate the pure performance of the proposed part RP representation. This subset contains a set of 6908 people, and the approximate locations and scales of each person are available. For the evaluation on this subset, we used the standard "Percentage of Correct Keypoints" evaluation metric (PCKh) whose matching threshold is defined as half the head segment length.

Second, to evaluate the full performance of the PPN for human pose detection in the wild, we used the "Multi-Person" subset, which contains a set of 1758 groups of multiple overlapping people in highly articulated poses with a variable number of parts. These groups are taken from the test set as outlined in [11]. In this subset, even though the regions that each group occupies and the mean scales of all the people in each group are available, no information is provided concerning the number of people or the scales of the individual people. For the evaluation on this subset, we used the evaluation metric outlined by Pishchulin et al. [11], calculating the average precision (AP) of the part detections.

4.2   Implementation

Setting of the RPs. As shown in Fig. 2, the RPs of person instances and those of parts are defined as square detections centered on the head and on each part, respectively. These lengths are defined as twice the head segment length for person instances and as half the head segment length for parts. Therefore, all ground truth boxes can be computed from two given head keypoints. For limb detections, the two head keypoints are defined as being connected to person

---

[4]   http://human-pose.mpi-inf.mpg.de.

instances and the other connections are defined similar to those in [1]. Therefore, $|\mathcal{L}|$ is set to 15.

Architecture. As the base architecture, we use an 18-layer standard ResNet pre-trained on the ImageNet 1000-class competition dataset [38]. The average-pooling layer and the fully connected layer in this architecture are replaced with three additional new convolutional layers. In this setting, the output grid cell size of the CNN on the image, which is described in Sect. 3.1, corresponds to 32×32 px^2 and $(H, W) = (12, 12)$ for the normalized 384×384 input size of the CNN used in the training. This grid cell size on the image is fairly large compared to those of previous pixel-wise part detectors (usually 4×4 px^2 or 8×8).

The last added convolutional layer uses a linear activation function and the other added layers use the following leaky rectified linear activation:

$$\phi(u) = \begin{cases} u & \text{if } u > 0, \\ 0.1u & \text{otherwise.} \end{cases} \tag{16}$$

All the added layers use a 1-px stride, and the weights are all randomly initialized. The first layer in the added layers uses batch normalization. The filter sizes and the number of filters of the added layers other than the last layer are set to 3×3 and 512, respectively. In the last layer, the filter size is set to 1×1, and, as described in Sect. 3.1, the number of filters is set to $6(K+1) + H'W'|\mathcal{L}| = 1311$, where (H', W') is set to $(9, 9)$. K is set to 15, which is similar to the values used in [1].

Training. During training, in order to have normalized 384×384 input samples, we first resized the images to make the samples roughly the same scale (*w.r.t.* 200 px person height) and cropped or padded the image according to the center positions and the rough scale estimations provided in the dataset. Then, we randomly augmented the data with rotation degrees in $[-40, 40]$, an offset perturbation, and horizontal flipping in addition to scaling with factors in $[0.35, 2.5]$ for the multi-person task and in $[1.0, 2.0]$ for the single-person task.

$(\lambda_{\text{resp.}}, \lambda_{\text{IoU}}, \lambda_{\text{coor.}}, \lambda_{\text{size}})$ in Eq. (4) are set to $(0.25, 1, 5, 5)$, and λ_{limb} is set to 0.5 in the multi-person task and to 0 in the single-person task. The entire network is trained using SGD for 260 K iterations in the multi-person task and for 130 K iterations in the single-person task with a batch size of 22, a momentum of 0.9, and a weight decay of 0.0005 on two GPUs. 260K iterations on two GPUs roughly correspond to 422 epochs of the training set. The learning rate l is linearly decreased depending on the number of iterations, m, calculated as follows:

$$l = 0.007(1 - m/260,000). \tag{17}$$

Training takes approximately 1.8 days using a machine with two GeForce GTX1080Ti cards, a 3.4 GHz Intel CPU, and 64 GB RAM.

Testing. During the testing of our method, the images were resized such that the mean scales for the target people corresponded to 1.43 in the multi-person task and to 1.3 in the single-person task. Then, they were cropped around the target people. The accuracies of previous approaches are taken from the original papers or are reproduced using their publicly available evaluation codes. During the timings of all the approaches including the baselines, the images were resized with each of the mean resolutions used when they were evaluated. The timings are reported using the same single GPU card and deep learning framework (Caffe [39]) on the machine described above averaged over the batch sizes with which each method performs the fastest. Our detection steps other than forward propagation by CNNs are run on the CPU.

4.3 Human Part Detection

We compare part detections by the PPN with several, pixel-wise part detectors used by state-of-the-art methods in both single-person and multi-person contexts. Predictions with pixel-wise detectors and those of the PPN are the maximum activating locations of the heatmap for a given part and the locations of the maximum activating RPs of each part, respectively.

Tables 1 and 2 compare the PCKh performance and the speeds of the PPN and other detectors on the single-person test set and lists the properties of the networks used in each approach. Note that [6] proposes part detectors while dealing with multi-person pose estimation. They use the same ResNet-based architecture as the PPN, which is several times deeper (152 layers) than ours and is different from ours only in that the network is massive to produce pixel-wise part proposals. We found that the speed and FLOP count (multiply-adds) of our detector overwhelm all others and are at least 11 times faster even when considering its slightly (several percent) lower PCKh. In particular, the fact that the PPN achieves a comparable PCKh to that of the ResNet-based part detector [6] using the same architecture as ours demonstrates that the part RPs effectively work as the part primitives when exploring the speed/accuracy trade-off.

Table 1. Pose estimation results on the MPII Single-Person test set.

Method	Architecture	Head	Shoulder	Elbow	Wrist	Hip	Knee	Ankle	PCKh
Ours	ResNet-18	97.9	95.3	89.1	83.5	87.9	82.7	76.2	88.1
SHN [29]	Custom	**98.2**	**96.3**	**91.2**	**87.1**	**90.1**	**87.4**	**83.6**	**90.9**
DeeperCut [6]	ResNet-152	96.8	95.2	89.3	84.4	88.4	83.4	78.0	88.5
CPM [27]	Custom	97.7	94.5	88.3	83.4	87.9	81.9	78.3	87.9

Table 2. The properties of the networks on the MPII Single-Person test set.

Method	PCKh	Architecture	Input size	Output size	FLOPs	Num. param	FPS
Ours	88.1	ResNet-18	384 × 384	12 × 12	6G	16M	**388**
SHN [29]	**90.9**	Custom	256 × 256	64 × 64	30G	34M	19
DeeperCut [6]	88.5	ResNet-152	344 × 344	43 × 43	37G	66M	34
CPM [27]	87.9	Custom	368 × 368	46 × 46	175G	31M	9

4.4   Human Pose Detection

Tables 3 and 4 compare the mean AP (mAP) performance between the full implementation of the PPN and previous approaches on the same subset of 288 testing images, as in [11], and on the entire multi-person test set. An illustration of the predictions made by our method can be seen in Fig. 7. Note that [1] is trained using unofficial masks of unlabeled persons (reported as *w/* or *w/o masks* in Fig. 6) and ranks with a favorable margin of a few percent mAP according to the original paper and that our method can be adjusted by replacing the base architecture with the 50- and 101-layer ResNets. Despite rough part detections, the deepest mode of our method (reported as *w/ ResNet-101*) achieves the top performance for upper body parts. The total runtime of this fast PPN reaches up to 5.6 ms (180 FPS) that exceeds the state-of-the-art bottleneck runtime described below. The runtime of the forward propagation with the CNN and the

Table 3. Pose estimation results of a subset of 288 images on the MPII Multi-Person test set.

Method	Head	Shoulder	Elbow	Wrist	Hip	Knee	Ankle	U.Body	L.Body	mAP
Ours w/ ResNet-18	94.0	91.6	80.7	68.1	75.0	65.5	61.3	83.6	67.8	76.6
Ours w/ ResNet-50	**95.6**	**92.5**	82.4	73.6	76.2	71.1	64.1	86.0	71.5	**79.4**
Ours w/ ResNet-101	95.2	92.2	**83.2**	73.8	74.8	71.3	63.4	**86.1**	71.3	79.1
ArtTrack [5]	92.2	91.3	80.8	71.4	**79.1**	72.6	**67.8**	83.9	73.2	79.3
PAF [1]	92.9	91.3	82.3	72.6	76.0	70.9	66.8	84.8	72.2	79.0
RMPE [2]	89.4	88.5	81.0	**75.4**	73.7	**75.4**	66.5	83.6	**73.5**	78.6
DeeperCut [6]	92.1	88.5	76.4	67.8	73.6	68.7	62.3	81.2	68.9	75.6
AE [9]	91.5	87.2	75.9	65.4	72.2	67.0	62.1	80.0	67.9	74.5

Table 4. Pose estimation results on the entire MPII Multi-Person test set.

Method	Head	Shoulder	Elbow	Wrist	Hip	Knee	Ankle	U.Body	L.Body	mAP
Ours w/ ResNet-18	93.2	89.0	74.9	62.4	72.2	62.6	55.4	79.9	63.6	72.8
Ours w/ ResNet-50	93.7	90.1	78.0	68.0	74.9	67.2	59.3	82.5	67.5	75.9
Ours w/ ResNet-101	**93.9**	**90.2**	**79.0**	68.7	74.8	68.7	60.5	**83.0**	68.6	76.6
AE [9]	92.1	89.3	78.9	69.8	**76.2**	71.6	64.7	82.5	71.3	**77.5**
RMPE [2]	88.4	86.5	78.6	**70.4**	74.4	**73.0**	**65.8**	81.0	**71.8**	76.7
PAF [1]	91.2	87.6	77.7	66.8	75.4	68.9	61.7	80.8	68.7	75.6
ArtTrack [5]	88.8	87.0	75.9	64.9	74.2	68.8	60.5	79.2	67.9	74.3
KLj*r [8]	89.8	85.2	71.8	59.6	71.1	63.0	53.5	76.6	62.4	70.6
DeeperCut [6]	89.4	84.5	70.4	59.3	68.9	62.7	54.6	75.9	62.4	70.0

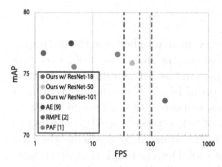
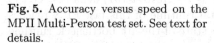
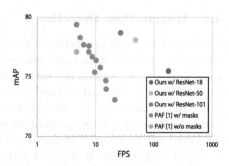

Fig. 5. Accuracy versus speed on the MPII Multi-Person test set. See text for details.

Fig. 6. Accuracy versus speed on the MPII Multi-Person validation set.

parsing step are 4 ms and 0.3 ms, respectively. The remaining runtime (1.3 ms) is mostly consumed by part proposal NMS.

Figure 5 is a scatterplot that visualizes the mAP performances and speeds of our method and the top-3 approaches reported using their publicly available implementation or from the original papers. The colored dot lines, each of which corresponds to one of previous approaches, denote limits of speed in total processing as speed for processing other than the forward propagation of CNNs such as resizing of CNN feature maps [1,2,9], grouping of parts [1,9], and NMS in human detection [2] or for part proposals [1,9] (The colors represent each method). Such bottleneck steps were optimized or were accelerated by GPUs to a certain extent. Improving the base architectures without the loss of accuracy will not help each state-of-the-art approach exceed their speed limits without leaving redundant pixel-wise or top-down strategies. It is also clear that all CNN-based methods significantly degrade when their accelerated speed reaches the speed limits. Our method is more than an order of magnitude faster compared with the state-of-the-art methods on average and can pass through the abovementioned bottleneck speed limits.

In addition, to compare our method with state-of-the-art methods in more detail, we reproduced the state-of-the-art bottom-up approach [1] based on its publicly available evaluation code and accelerated it by adjusting the number of multi-stage convolutions and scale search. Figure 6 is a scatterplot that visualizes the mAP performance and speeds of both our method and the method proposed in [1], which is adjusted with several patterns. In general, we observe that our method achieves faster and more accurate predictions on an average. The above comparisons with previous approaches indicate that our method can minimize the computational cost of the overall algorithm when exploring the speed/accuracy trade-off.

Table 5 lists the mAP performances of several different versions of our method. First, when $p(I|R, k, i)$ in Eq. (1), which is not estimated by the pixel-wise part detectors, is ignored in our approach (*i.e.*, when $p(I|R, k, i)$ is replaced

Table 5. Quantitative comparison for different versions of the proposed method on the MPII Multi-Person validation set.

Method	Architecture	Head	Shoulder	Elbow	Wrist	Hip	Knee	Ankle	mAP
Full.	ResNet-18	92.8	90.7	78.8	66.9	77.0	63.5	58.4	75.5
w/o scale		88.6	88.0	75.6	64.6	74.2	60.8	55.3	72.4
w/o glob.		91.8	90.1	77.7	63.9	76.7	61.5	51.7	73.3
Full.	ResNet-50	93.8	91.9	81.4	71.5	77.6	69.8	60.3	78.1
w/o scale		91.1	89.4	79.4	68.9	75.8	67.1	59.7	75.9
w/o glob.		93.3	92.2	81.4	69.7	77.8	70.2	58.1	77.5
Full.	ResNet-101	93.4	91.2	81.8	72.2	78.8	70.5	62.9	78.7
w/o scale		91.6	90.0	80.1	70.4	78.5	68.8	62.9	77.5
w/o glob.		93.2	91.6	81.8	71.0	79.6	70.5	61.4	78.4

Fig. 7. Qualitative pose estimation results by the ResNet-18-based PPN on MPII test images.

by 1), and when our NMS follows the previous pixel-wise scheme that finds the maxima on part confidence maps (reported as *w/o scale*), the performance deteriorates from that of the full implementation (reported as *Full.*). This indicates that the speed/accuracy trade-off is improved by additional information regarding the part scales obtained from the fact that the part proposals are bounding boxes. Second, when only the local context is taken into account in parts association (reported as *w/o glob.*), *i.e.*, $S_{k_0 k_1}^{\hat{n}_0 n_1}$ is replaced by $D_{k_1}^{n_1}$ in Eq. (14), the performance of our shallowest architecture, *i.e.*, ResNet-18, deteriorates further than the deepest one, *i.e.*, ResNet-101 (-2.2% vs -0.3%). This indicates that our context-aware parse works effectively for shallow CNNs.

4.5   Limitations

Our method can predict one RP for each detection target for every grid cell, and therefore this spatial constraint limits the number of nearby people that our model can predict within each grid cell. This causes our method to struggle with groups of people, such as crowded scenes, as shown in Fig. 8(c). Specifically, we observe that our approach will perform poorly on the "COCO" dataset [40] that contains large scale variations such as small people in close proximity. Even though a solution to this problem is to enlarge the input size of the CNN, this in turn causes the speed/accuracy trade-off to degrade, depending on its applications.

(a)   (b)   (c)   (d)

Fig. 8. Common failure cases: (a) rare pose or appearance, (b) false parts detection, (c) missing parts detection in crowded scenes, and (d) wrong connection associating parts from two persons.

5   Conclusions

We proposed a method to detect people and simultaneously estimate their 2D articulated poses from a 2D still image. Our principal innovations to improve speed/accuracy trade-offs are to introduce a state-of-the-art single-shot object detection paradigm to a bottom-up pose detection scenario and to represent part proposals as RPs. In addition, limbs are detected directly with CNNs, and a greedy parsing step is probabilistically redesigned for such detections to encode the global context. Experimental results on the MPII Human Pose dataset confirm that our method has comparable accuracy to state-of-the-art bottom-up approaches and is much faster, while providing an end-to-end training framework[5]. In future studies, to improve the performance for the spatial constraints caused by rough grid-wise predictions, we plan to explore an algorithm to harmonize the high-level and low-level features obtained from state-of-the-art architectures in both part detection and parts association.

References

1. Cao, Z., Simon, T., Wei, S.E., Sheikh, Y.: Realtime multi-person 2D pose estimation using part affinity fields. In: CVPR (2017)
2. Fang, H.S., Xie, S., Tai, Y.W., Lu, C.: RMPE: Regional multi-person pose estimation. In: ICCV (2017)

---

[5] For the supplementary material and videos, please visit: http://taikisekii.com.

3. Gkioxari, G., Hariharan, B., Girshick, R., Malik, J.: Using k-poselets for detecting people and localizing their keypoints. In: CVPR (2014)
4. He, K., Gkioxari, G., Dollár, P., Girshick, R.: Mask R-CNN. In: ICCV (2017)
5. Insafutdinov, E., et al.: ArtTrack: Articulated multi-person tracking in the wild. In: CVPR (2017)
6. Insafutdinov, E., Pishchulin, L., Andres, B., Andriluka, M., Schiele, B.: DeeperCut: a deeper, stronger, and faster multi-person pose estimation model. In: Leibe, B., Matas, J., Sebe, N., Welling, M. (eds.) ECCV 2016. LNCS, vol. 9910, pp. 34–50. Springer, Cham (2016). https://doi.org/10.1007/978-3-319-46466-4_3
7. Iqbal, U., Gall, J.: Multi-person pose estimation with local joint-to-person associations. In: Hua, G., Jégou, H. (eds.) ECCV 2016. LNCS, vol. 9914, pp. 627–642. Springer, Cham (2016). https://doi.org/10.1007/978-3-319-48881-3_44
8. Levinkov, E., et al.: Joint graph decomposition and node labeling: Problem, algorithms, applications. In: CVPR (2017)
9. Newell, A., Huang, Z., Deng, J.: Associative embedding: End-to-end learning for joint detection and grouping. In: NIPS (2017)
10. Papandreou, G., et al.: Towards accurate multi-person pose estimation in the wild. In: CVPR (2017)
11. Pishchulin, L., et al.: DeepCut: Joint subset partition and labeling for multi person pose estimation. In: CVPR (2016)
12. Pishchulin, L., Jain, A., Andriluka, M., Thormählen, T., Schiele, B.: Articulated people detection and pose estimation: Reshaping the future. In: CVPR (2012)
13. Varadarajan, S., Datta, P., Tickoo, O.: A greedy part assignment algorithm for real-time multi-person 2D pose estimation (2017). arXiv preprint arXiv:1708.09182
14. Liu, W., et al.: SSD: Single shot multibox detector. In: Leibe, B., Matas, J., Sebe, N., Welling, M. (eds.) ECCV 2016. LNCS, vol. 9905, pp. 21–37. Springer, Cham (2016). https://doi.org/10.1007/978-3-319-46448-0_2
15. Redmon, J., Divvala, S., Girshick, R., Farhadi, A.: You only look once: Unified, real-time object detection. In: CVPR (2016)
16. Redmon, J., Farhadi, A.: YOLO9000: Better, faster, stronger. In: CVPR (2017)
17. Ren, S., He, K., Girshick, R., Sun, J.: Faster R-CNN: Towards real-time object detection with region proposal networks. PAMI 39(6), 1137–1149 (2017)
18. Andriluka, M., Roth, S., Schiele, B.: Pictorial structures revisited: People detection and articulated pose estimation. In: CVPR (2009)
19. Felzenszwalb, P.F., Huttenlocher, D.P.: Pictorial structures for object recognition. IJCV 61(1), 55–79 (2005)
20. Lan, X., Huttenlocher, D.P.: Beyond trees: common-factor models for 2D human pose recovery. In: ICCV (2005)
21. Sigal, L., Black, M.J.: Measure locally, reason globally: Occlusion-sensitive articulated pose estimation. In: CVPR (2006)
22. Tian, Y., Zitnick, C.L., Narasimhan, S.G.: Exploring the spatial hierarchy of mixture models for human pose estimation. In: Fitzgibbon, A., Lazebnik, S., Perona, P., Sato, Y., Schmid, C. (eds.) ECCV 2012. LNCS, vol. 7576, pp. 256–269. Springer, Heidelberg (2012). https://doi.org/10.1007/978-3-642-33715-4_19
23. Wang, Y., Mori, G.: Multiple tree models for occlusion and spatial constraints in human pose estimation. In: Forsyth, D., Torr, P., Zisserman, A. (eds.) ECCV 2008. LNCS, vol. 5304, pp. 710–724. Springer, Heidelberg (2008). https://doi.org/10.1007/978-3-540-88690-7_53
24. Chen, X., Yuille, A.L.: Articulated pose estimation by a graphical model with image dependent pairwise relations. In: NIPS (2014)

25. Toshev, A., Szegedy, C.: DeepPose: Human pose estimation via deep neural networks. In: CVPR (2014)

26. Tompson, J., Jain, A., LeCun, Y., Bregler, C.: Joint training of a convolutional network and a graphical model for human pose estimation. In: NIPS (2014)

27. Wei, S.E., Ramakrishna, V., Kanade, T., Sheikh, Y.: Convolutional pose machines. In: CVPR (2016)

28. He, K., Zhang, X., Ren, S., Sun, J.: Deep residual learning for image recognition. In: CVPR (2016)

29. Newell, A., Yang, K., Deng, J.: Stacked hourglass networks for human pose estimation. In: Leibe, B., Matas, J., Sebe, N., Welling, M. (eds.) ECCV 2016. LNCS, vol. 9912, pp. 483–499. Springer, Cham (2016). https://doi.org/10.1007/978-3-319-46484-8_29

30. Bulat, A., Tzimiropoulos, G.: Human pose estimation via convolutional part heatmap regression. In: Leibe, B., Matas, J., Sebe, N., Welling, M. (eds.) ECCV 2016. LNCS, vol. 9911, pp. 717–732. Springer, Cham (2016). https://doi.org/10.1007/978-3-319-46478-7_44

31. Chen, Y., Shen, C., Wei, X.S., Liu, L., Yang, J.: Adversarial PoseNet: A structure-aware convolutional network for human pose estimation. In: ICCV (2017)

32. Chu, X., Yang, W., Ouyang, W., Ma, C., Yuille, A.L., Wang, X.: Multi-context attention for human pose estimation. In: CVPR (2017)

33. Yang, W., Li, S., Ouyang, W., Li, H., Wang, X.: Learning feature pyramids for human pose estimation. In: ICCV (2017)

34. Jaderberg, M., Simonyan, K., Zisserman, A., Kavukcuoglu, K.: Spatial transformer networks. In: NIPS (2015)

35. West, D.B.: Introduction to graph theory. Featured Titles for Graph Theory Series. Prentice Hall, Upper Saddle River (2001)

36. Kuhn, H.W.: The hungarian method for the assignment problem. Nav. Res. Logist. Q. 2(1–2), 83–97 (1955)

37. Andriluka, M., Pishchulin, L., Gehler, P., Schiele, B.: 2D human pose estimation: New benchmark and state of the art analysis. In: CVPR (2014)

38. Russakovsky, O.: ImageNet large scale visual recognition challenge. IJCV 115(3), 211–252 (2015)

39. Jia, Y., et al.: Caffe: Convolutional architecture for fast feature embedding. In: MM. ACM (2014)

40. Lin, T.Y., et al.: Microsoft COCO: Common objects in context (2014). arXiv preprint arXiv:1405.0312

Less Is More: Picking Informative Frames for Video Captioning

Yangyu Chen[1], Shuhui Wang[2(✉)], Weigang Zhang[3], and Qingming Huang[1,2]

[1] University of Chinese Academy of Science, Beijing 100049, China
yangyu.chen@vipl.ict.ac.cn, qmhuang@ucas.ac.cn
[2] Key Laboratory of Intelligent Information Processing, Institute of Computing Technology, CAS, Beijing 100190, China
wangshuhui@ict.ac.cn
[3] Harbin Institute of Technology, Weihai 264200, China
wgzhang@hit.edu.cn
https://yugnaynehc.github.io/picknet

Abstract. In video captioning task, the best practice has been achieved by attention-based models which associate salient visual components with sentences in the video. However, existing study follows a common procedure which includes a frame-level appearance modeling and motion modeling on equal interval frame sampling, which may bring about redundant visual information, sensitivity to content noise and unnecessary computation cost. We propose a plug-and-play **PickNet** to perform informative frame picking in video captioning. Based on a standard encoder-decoder framework, we develop a reinforcement-learning-based procedure to train the network sequentially, where the reward of each frame picking action is designed by maximizing visual diversity and minimizing discrepancy between generated caption and the ground-truth. The rewarded candidate will be selected and the corresponding latent representation of encoder-decoder will be updated for future trials. This procedure goes on until the end of the video sequence. Consequently, a compact frame subset can be selected to represent the visual information and perform video captioning without performance degradation. Experiment results show that our model can achieve competitive performance across popular benchmarks while only 6–8 frames are used.

1 Introduction

Human are born with the ability to identify useful information and filter redundant information. In biology, this mechanism is called sensory gating [6], which describes neurological processes of filtering out unnecessary stimuli in the brain from all possible environmental stimuli, thus prevents an overload of redundant information in the higher cortical centers of the brain. This cognitive mechanism is essentially consistent with a huge body of researches in computer vision [13].

As one of the strong evidences practicing on visual sensory gating, attention is introduced to identify the salient visual regions with high objectness and

© Springer Nature Switzerland AG 2018
V. Ferrari et al. (Eds.): ECCV 2018, LNCS 11217, pp. 367–384, 2018.
https://doi.org/10.1007/978-3-030-01261-8_22

meaningful visual patterns of an image [21,48]. It has also been established on videos that contains consecutive image frames. Existing study follows a common procedure which includes a frame-level appearance modeling and motion modeling on equal interval frame sampling, say, every 3 frames or 5 frames [29]. Visual features and motion features are extracted on the selected frame subset one by one, and they are all fed into the learning stage. Similar to image, the video attention is recognized as a spatial-temporal saliency that identifies both salient objects and their motion trajectories [27]. It is also recognized as the word-frame association learned by sparse coding [41] or gaze-guided attention learning [45], which is a de-facto frame weighting mechanism. This mechanism also benefits many downstream tasks such as visual captioning and visual question answering for image and video [12,20,43].

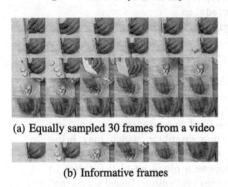

(a) Equally sampled 30 frames from a video

(b) Informative frames

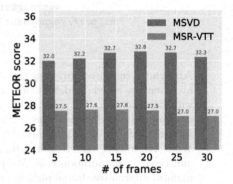

Fig. 1. An illustration of the temporal redundancy in video. Video always contains many redundant information. The whole video can be represented by a small portion of frames (b), while equally sampled frames still contain redundant information (a).

Fig. 2. The best METEOR score on the validation set of MSVD and MSR-VTT when using different number of equally sampled frames. The standard encoder-decoder model is used to generate captions.

Despite of the success on bridging vision and language achieved by existing attention-based methods, there still exists critical issues to be addressed as follows.

– **Frame Selection Perspective.** As shown in Fig. 1(a), there are many frames with duplicated and redundant visual appearance information selected with equal interval frame sampling. This will also involve remarkable computation expenditures and less performance gain as the information from the input is not appropriately sampled. For example, it takes millions of floating point calculation to extract a frame-level visual feature for a moderate-sized CNN model. Moreover, there is no guarantee that all the frames selected by equal interval sampling contain meaningful information, so it tends to be more sensitive to content noise such as motion blur, occlusion and object zoom-out.

- **Downstream Video Captioning Task Perspective.** Previous attention-based models mostly identify the spatial layout of visual saliency, but the temporal redundancy existing in neighboring frames remains unsolved as all the frames are taken into consideration. This may lead to an unexpected information overload on the visual-linguistic correlation analysis model. For example, the dense-captioning-based strategy [14,17,27] can potentially describe images/videos in finer levels of detail by captioning many visual regions within an image/video-clip. With an increasing number of frames, many highly similar visual regions will be generated and the problem will become prohibitive as the search space of sequence-to-sequence association becomes extremely large. We have conducted a preliminary study to investigate how many frames is enough for video captioning on two benchmarks. As shown in Fig. 2, using more frames may not always lead to better performance, since sampling more frames may be prone to contain noisy information, and makes the training procedure more difficult.

- **Human Perception Perspective.** The vision-to-language technique can be applied to depict ambient information for human, such as describing the road conditions through voice broadcast for drivers. Based on existing video captioning methods, a naive way for generating such descriptions for endless visual streaming is to sample frames in every fixed time interval. However, it is problematic to determine an appropriate interval. If the interval is too long, some useful information may be missed and lead to wrong description. If the interval is too short, repeated descriptions will be generated as the visual content may not change largely, which is annoying for drivers as they focus on the change of surroundings. Therefore, it is necessary to explore a more appropriate strategy to capture informative frames and produce meaningful descriptions.

To deal with the above issues, we propose PickNet to perform informative frame picking for video captioning. Specifically, the base model for visual-linguistic association in video captioning is a standard encoder-decoder framework [2]. We develop a reinforcement-learning-based procedure to train the network sequentially, where the reward of each frame picking action is designed by considering both visual and textual cues. From visual perspective, we maximize the diversity between current picked frame candidate and the selected frames. From textual perspective, we minimize the discrepancy between the generated caption and the ground truth using current picked candidate. The rewarded candidate will be selected and the corresponding latent representation of encoder-decoder will be updated for future trials. This procedure goes on until the end of the video sequence. Consequently, a compact frame subset can be selected to represent the visual information and perform video captioning without performance degradation.

To the best of our knowledge, this is the first study on online task-driven frame selection for video captioning. Different from the previous work [46] that summarizing the video before video captioning, our method selects frames under **partially observed** settings and **do not need any auxiliary annotation or**

information. It is very essential for real-world applications, since the video summarization annotations are subjective and expensive, and there is no trimmed video to summarize in real-world applications, but only endless visual streams. In fact, our framework can go beyond the encoder-decoder framework in video captioning task, and serves as a complementary building block for other state-of-the-art solutions. It can also be adapted by other task-specific objectives for video analysis. In summary, the merits of our PickNet include:

- **Flexibility.** We design a plug-and-play reinforcement-learning-based PickNet to pick informative frames for video captioning. A compact frame subset can be selected to represent the visual information and perform video captioning without performance degradation.
- **Efficiency.** The architecture can largely cut down the usage of convolution operations. It makes our method more applicable for real-world video processing.
- **Effectiveness.** Experiment shows that our model can achieve comparable or even better performance compared to state-of-the-art while only a small number of frames are used.

2   Related Works

2.1   Visual Captioning

The visual captioning is the task translating visual contents into natural language. Early to 2002, Kojima *et al.* [16] proposed the first video captioning system for describing human behavior. From then on, a series of image and video captioning studies have been conducted. Early approaches tackle this problem using bottom-up paradigm [8,9,18,40], which first generate descriptive words of an image by attribute learning and object recognition, then combine them by language models which fit predicted words to predefined sentence templates. With the development of neural networks and deep learning, modern captioning systems are based on CNN, RNN and the encoder-decoder architecture [35,36].

An active branch of captioning is utilizing the attention mechanism to weigh the input features. For image captioning, the mechanism is typically in the form of spatial attention. Xu *et al.* [39] first introduced an attention-based model that automatically learn to fix its gaze on salient objects while generating the corresponding words in the output sequence. For video captioning, the temporal attention is added. Yao *et al.* [41] took into account both the local and global temporal structure of videos to produce descriptions, and their model is learned to automatically select the most relevant temporal segments given the text-generating RNN. However, the attention-based methods, especially temporal attention, are operated on full observed condition, which is not suitable in some real world applications, such as blind navigation. Our method do not require the global information of videos, which is more effective in these applications.

2.2   Frame Selection

Selecting informative video frames is the most studied in the field of video summarization. This problem may be formulated as image searching. For example, Song et al. [32] considered images related to the video title that can serve as a proxy for important visual concepts, so they developed a co-archetypal analysis technique that learns canonical visual concepts shared between video and images, and used it to summarize videos. Other researchers use sparse learning to deal with this problem. Zhao et al. [47] proposed to learn a dictionary from given video using group sparse coding, and the summary video was then generated by combining segments that cannot be sparsely reconstructed using the learned dictionary.

Some video analysis task cooperates with frame selection mechanism. For example, in action detection, Yeung et al. [42] designed a policy network to directly predict the temporal bounds of actions, which decreased the cost of processing the whole video, and improved the detection performance. However, the prediction made by this method is in the form of normalized global position, which requires the knowledge of the video length, making it unable to deal with real video streams. Different from the above methods, our model selects frames based on both semantic and visual information, and does not need to know the global length of video.

3   Method

Our method can be viewed as inserting the play-and-plug PickNet into the standard encoder-decoder for video captioning. The PickNet sequentially picks informative frames to generate a compact frame subset which properly represent the visual information of input video. And the encoder-decoder uses this subset to generate sentence description about the video.

3.1   Preliminary

Like most of video captioning methods, our model is built on the encoder-decoder-based sentence generator. In this subsection, we briefly introduce this building block.

Encoder. Given an input video, we use a recurrent video encoder which takes a sequence of visual features $(x_1, x_2, \ldots, x_n)$ as input and outputs a fixed size vector v as the representation of this video. The encoder is built on top of a Long Short-Term Memory (LSTM) [11] unit, which has been widely used for video encoding, since it is known to properly deal with long range temporal dependencies. Different from vanilla recurrent neural network unit, LSTM introduces a memory cell c which maintains the history of the inputs observed up to a time-step. The update operations on memory cell are controlled by input gate i_t that controls how the current input should be added into memory cell, forget

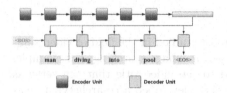

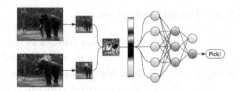

Fig. 3. The encode-decode procedure for video captioning.

Fig. 4. The PickNet uses the flattened difference gray-scale image as input and produces a Bernoulli distribution to indicate picking the current frame or not.

gate $\mathbf{f}_t$ that controls what the current memory cell $\mathbf{c}_t$ will forget from the previous memory $\mathbf{c}_{t-1}$, and output gate $\mathbf{o}_t$ that controls how the current memory cell should be passed as output. These gates all take the combination of the frame feature $\mathbf{x}_t$ and the previous hidden state $\mathbf{h}_{t-1}$ as input, and the sigmoid activation is used to avoid gradient vanishing or exploding. The hidden state $\mathbf{h}$ and memory cell $\mathbf{c}$ are initialized to zero vector. And the last hidden state $\mathbf{h}_T$ is used as the final encoded video representation $\mathbf{v}$.

Decoder and Sentence Generation. Once the representation of the video has been generated, the recurrent decoder can employ it to generate the corresponding description. At every time-step of the decoding phase, the decoder unit uses the encoded vector $\mathbf{v}$, previous generated one-hot representation word $\mathbf{w}_{t-1}$ and previous internal state $\mathbf{p}_{t-1}$ as input, and outputs a new internal state $\mathbf{p}_t$. Like [2], our decoder unit is the Gated Recurrent Unit (GRU) [5], a simplified version of LSTM, which is good at language decoding. The output of GRU is modulated via two sigmoid gates: a reset gate $\mathbf{r}_t$ which determines how the previous internal state should be dropped to generate the next outputs, and an update gate $\mathbf{z}_t$ which controls how much information of the previous internal state should be preserved. A softmax function is applied on $\mathbf{p}_t$ to compute the probability of producing certain word at current time-step:

$$p_\omega(\mathbf{w}_t|\mathbf{w}_{t-1}, \mathbf{w}_{t-2}, ..., \mathbf{w}_1, \mathbf{v}) = \mathbf{w}_t^T \text{softmax}(W_p \mathbf{p}_t), \tag{1}$$

where W_p is used to project the output of the decoder to the dictionary space and ω denotes all parameters of the encoder-decoder. Also, the internal state $\mathbf{p}$ is initialized to zero vector. We use the greedy decode routine to generate every word. It means that at every time-step, we choose the word that has the maximal $p_\omega(\mathbf{w}_t|\mathbf{w}_{t-1}, \mathbf{w}_{t-2}, ..., \mathbf{w}_1, \mathbf{v})$ as the current output word. Specifically, we use a special token <BOS> as $\mathbf{w}_0$ to start the decoding, and when the decoder generates another special token <EOS>, the decoding procedure is terminated.

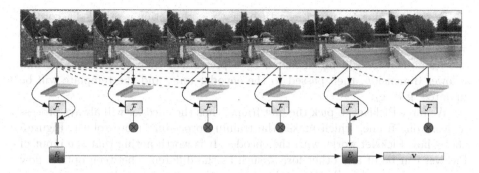

Fig. 5. A typical frame picking and encoding procedure of our framework. $\mathcal{F}$ denotes PickNet. E is the encoder unit and **v** is the encoded video representation. The design choice is the balance between processing time and computation cost. The system can simultaneously extract convolutional features and decide whether to pick the frame or not at each time-step. If it decides not to pick the frame at certain time-step, the convolutional neural network can stop early to save computation cost.

3.2 Our Approach

Architecture. The PickNet aims to select informative video content without knowing the global information. It means that the pick decision can only be based on the current observation and the history, which makes it more difficult than video summarization tasks. The more challenging issue is, we do not have supervision information to guide the learning of PickNet in video captioning tasks. Therefore, we formulate the problem as a reinforcement learning task, *i.e.*, given an input image sequence sampled from a video, the agent should select a subset of them under certain policy to retain video content as much as possible. Here, we use PickNet to produce the picking policy. Figure 4 shows the architecture of PickNet.

Considering the computation efficiency, we use a simple two-layer feedforward neural network as the prototype of PickNet. The network has two outputs, which indicate the probabilities to pick or drop the current observed frame. We model the frame picking process as the glance-and-compare operation. For each input frame $\mathbf{z}_t$, we first convert the colored image into grayscale image, and then resize it into a smaller image $\mathbf{g}_t$, which can be viewed as a "glance" of current frame. Then we subtract the current glance $\mathbf{g}_t$ by the glance of the last picked frame $\tilde{\mathbf{g}}$, to get a grayscale difference image $\mathbf{d}_t$; this can be seen as the "compare". Finally we flatten the 2D grayscale difference image into a 1D fixed size vector, and feed it to PickNet to produce a Bernoulli distribution that the pick decision is sampled from:

$$\mathbf{s}_t = W_2(\max(W_1\text{vec}(\mathbf{d}_t) + \mathbf{b}_1, \mathbf{0})) + \mathbf{b}_2 \tag{2}$$

$$p_\theta(a_t|\mathbf{z}_t, \tilde{\mathbf{g}}) \sim \text{softmax}(\mathbf{s}_t), \tag{3}$$

where W_* are learned weight matrices and $\mathbf{b}_*$ are learned bias vectors.

During training, we use stochastic policy, *i.e.*, the action is sampled according to Equation (3). When testing, the policy becomes determined, hence the action with higher probability is chosen. If the policy decides to pick the current frame, the frame feature will be extracted by a pretrained CNN and embedded into a lower dimension, then passed to the encoder unit, and the template will be updated: $\tilde{\mathbf{g}} \leftarrow \mathbf{g}_t$.

We force PickNet to pick the first frame, thus the encoder will always process at least one frame, which makes the training procedure more robust. Figure 5 shows how PickNet works with the encoder. It is worth noting that the input of PickNet can be of any other forms, such as the difference between optical flow maps, which may handle the motion information more properly.

Rewards. The design of rewards is very essential to reinforcement learning. For the purpose of picking informative video frames, we consider two parts for the reward: the language reward and visual diversity reward.

Language Reward. First of all, the picked frames should contain rich semantic information, which can be used to effectively generate language description. In the video captioning task, it is natural to use the evaluated language metrics as the language reward. Here, we choose CIDEr [33] score. Given a set of picked frames $\mathcal{V}_i$ for video v_i and a collection of human generated reference sentences $S_i = \{s_{ij}\}$, the goal of CIDEr is to measure the similarity of the machine generated sentence c_i to a majority of how most people describe the video. So the language reward r_l is defined as:

$$r_l(\mathcal{V}_i, S_i) = \text{CIDEr}(c_i, S_i) \tag{4}$$

Visual Diversity Reward. Also, we want the picked frames that have good diversity in visual features. Using only language reward may miss some important visual information, so we introduce the visual diversity reward r_v. For all the selected frame features $\{\mathbf{x}_k \in \mathbb{R}^D\}$, we use the pairwise cosine distance to construct the visual diversity reward:

$$r_v(\mathcal{V}_i) = \frac{2}{N_p(N_p - 1)} \sum_{k=1}^{N_p-1} \sum_{m>k}^{N_p} (1 - \frac{\mathbf{x}_k^{\mathbf{T}} \mathbf{x}_m}{\|\mathbf{x}_k\|_2 \|\mathbf{x}_m\|_2}), \tag{5}$$

where N_p is the number of picked frames, $\|\cdot\|_2$ is the 2-norm of a vector.

Picks Limitation. If the number of picked frames is too large or too small, it may lead to poor performances in either efficiency or effectiveness. So we assign a negative reward to discourage this situations. Empirically, we set the minimum picked number $N_{\min}$ as 3, which stands for beginning, highlight and ending. The maximum picked number $N_{\max}$ is initially set as the $\frac{1}{2}$ of total frame number, and will be shrunk down along with the training process, until decreased to a minimum value τ.

In summary, we merge the two parts of reward, and the final reward can be written as

$$r(\mathcal{V}_i) = \begin{cases} \lambda_l r_l(\mathcal{V}_i, S_i) + \lambda_v r_v(\mathcal{V}_i) & \text{if } N_{\min} \leq N_p \leq N_{\max} \\ R^- & \text{otherwise,} \end{cases} \qquad (6)$$

where λ_* is the weighting hyper-parameters and R^- is the penalty.

3.3   Training

The training procedure is splitted into three stages. The first stage is to pretrain the encoder-decoder. We call it *supervision* stage. In the second stage, we fix the encoder-decoder and train PickNet by reinforcement learning. It is called *reinforcement* stage. And the final stage is the joint training of PickNet and the encoder-decoder. We call it *adaptation* stage. We use standard back-propagation to train the encoder-decoder, and REINFORCE [37] to train PickNet.

Supervision Stage. When training the encoder-decoder, traditional method maximizes the likelihood of the next ground-truth word given previous ground-truth words using back-propagation. However, this approach causes the *exposure bias* [25], which results in error accumulation during generation at test time, since the model has never been exposed to its own predictions. In order to alleviate this phenomenon, the schedule sampling [3] procedure is used, which feeds back the model's own predictions and slowly increases the feedback probability during training. We use SGD with cross entropy loss to train the encoder-decoder. Given the ground-truth sentences $\mathbf{y} = (\mathbf{y}_1, \mathbf{y}_2, \dots, \mathbf{y}_m)$, the loss is defined as:

$$L_X(\omega) = -\sum_{t=1}^{m} \log(p_\omega(\mathbf{y}_t | \mathbf{y}_{t-1}, \mathbf{y}_{t-2}, \dots \mathbf{y}_1, \mathbf{v})), \qquad (7)$$

where $p_\omega(\mathbf{y}_t | \mathbf{y}_{t-1}, \mathbf{y}_{t-2}, \dots \mathbf{y}_1, \mathbf{v})$ is given by the parametric model in Equation (1).

Reinforcement Stage. In this stage, we fix the encoder-decoder and treat it as the *environment*, which can produce language reward to reinforce PickNet. The goal of training is to minimize the negative expected reward:

$$L_R(\theta) = -\mathbb{E}[r(\mathcal{V}_i)] = -\mathbb{E}_{\mathbf{a}^s \sim p_\theta}[r(\mathbf{a}^s)], \qquad (8)$$

where θ denotes all parameters of PickNet, p_θ is the learned policy parameterized by Eq. (3), and $\mathbf{a}^s = (a_1^s, a_2^s, \dots, a_T^s)$ is the action sequence, in which a_t^s is the action sampled from the learned policy at the time step t. s is a superscript to indicate a certain sampling sequence. $a_t^s = 1$ means frame t will be picked. The relation between $\mathcal{V}_i$ and $\mathbf{a}^s$ is:

$$\mathcal{V}_i = \{\mathbf{x}_t | a_t^s = 1 \wedge \mathbf{x}_t \in v_i\}, \qquad (9)$$

i.e., $\mathcal{V}_i$ are the picked frames from input video v_i following the action sequence $\mathbf{a}^s$.

We train PickNet by using REINFORCE algorithm, which is based on the observation that the gradient of a non-differentiable expected reward can be computed as follows:

$$\nabla_\theta L_R(\theta) = -\mathbb{E}_{\mathbf{a}^s \sim p_\theta} \left[r(\mathbf{a}^s) \nabla_\theta \log p_\theta(\mathbf{a}^s) \right]. \tag{10}$$

Using the chain rule, the gradient can be rewritten as:

$$\nabla_\theta L_R(\theta) = \sum_{t=1}^{n} \frac{\partial L_R(\theta)}{\partial \mathbf{s}_t} \frac{\partial \mathbf{s}_t}{\partial \theta} = \sum_{t=1}^{n} -\mathbb{E}_{\mathbf{a}^s \sim p_\theta} r(\mathbf{a}^s)(p_\theta(a_t^s) - \mathbf{1}_{a_t^s}) \frac{\partial \mathbf{s}_t}{\partial \theta}, \tag{11}$$

where $\mathbf{s}_t$ is the input to the softmax function. In practice, the gradient can be approximated using a single Monte-Carlo sample $\mathbf{a}^s = (a_1^s, a_2^s, \ldots, a_n^s)$ from p_θ:

$$\nabla_\theta L_R(\theta) \approx -\sum_{t=1}^{n} r(\mathbf{a}^s)(p_\theta(a_t^s) - \mathbf{1}_{a_t^s}) \frac{\partial \mathbf{s}_t}{\partial \theta}. \tag{12}$$

When using REINFORCE to train the policy network, we need to estimate a baseline reward b to diminish the variance of gradients. Here, the *self-critical* [26] strategy is used to estimate b. In brief, the reward obtained by current model under inferencing used at test stage, denoted as $r(\hat{\mathbf{a}})$, is treated as the baseline reward. Therefore, the final gradient expression is:

$$\nabla_\theta L_R(\theta) \approx -(r(\mathbf{a}^s) - r(\hat{\mathbf{a}})) \sum_{t=1}^{n} (p_\theta(a_t^s) - \mathbf{1}_{a_t^s}) \frac{\partial \mathbf{s}_t}{\partial \theta}. \tag{13}$$

Adaptation Stage. After the first two stages, the encoder-decoder and PickNet are well pretrained, but there exists a gap between them because the encoder-decoder use the full video frames as input while PickNet just selects a portion of frames. So we need a joint training stage to integrate this two parts together. However, the pick action is not differentiable, so the gradients introduced by cross-entropy loss can not flow into PickNet. Hence, we follow the approximate joint training scheme. In each iteration, the forward pass generates frame picks which are treated just like fixed picks when training the encoder-decoder, and the backward propagation and REINFORCE updates are performed as usual. It acts like performing dropout in time sequence, which can improve the versatility of the encoder-decoder.

4 Experimental Setup

4.1 Datasets

We evaluate our model on two widely used video captioning benchmark datasets: the Microsoft Video Description (MSVD) [4] and the MSR Video-to-Text (MSR-VTT) [38].

Microsoft Video Description (MSVD). The Microsoft Video Description is also known as YoutubeClips. It contains 1,970 Youtube video clips, each labeled with around 40 English descriptions collected by Amazon Mechanical Turks. As done in previous works [34], we split the dataset into three parts: the first 1,200 videos for training, then the followed 100 videos for validation and the remaining 670 videos for test. This dataset mainly contains short video clips with a single action, and the average duration is about 9 seconds. So it is very suitable to use only a portion of frames to represent the full video.

MSR Video-to-Text (MSR-VTT). The MSR Video-to-Text is a large-scale benchmark for video captioning. It provides 10,000 video clips, and each video is annotated with 20 English descriptions and category tag. Thus, there are 200,000 video-caption pairs in total. This dataset is collected from a commercial video search engine and so far it covers the most comprehensive categories and diverse visual contents. Following the original paper, we split the dataset in contiguous groups of videos by index number: 6,513 for training, 497 for validation and 2,990 for test.

4.2 Metrics

We employ four popular metrics for evaluation: BLEU [24], ROUGE$_L$ [19], METEOR [1] and CIDEr. As done in previous video captioning works, we use METEOR and CIDEr as the main comparison metrics. In addition, Microsoft COCO evaluation server has implemented these metrics and released evaluation functions[1], so we directly call such evaluation functions to test the performance of video captioning. Also, the CIDEr reward is computed by these functions.

4.3 Video Preprocessing

First, we sample equally-spaced 30 frames for every video, and resize them into 224×224 resolution. Then the images are encoded with the final convolutional layer of ResNet152 [10], which results in a set of 2,048-dimensional vectors. Most video captioning models use motion features to improve performance. However, we **only use the appearance features** in our model, because extracting motion features is very time-consuming, which deviates from our purpose that cutting down the computation cost for video captioning, and the appearance feature is enough to represent video content when the redundant or noisy frames are filtered by our PickNet.

4.4 Text Preprocessing

We tokenize the labeled sentences by converting all words to lowercases and then utilizing the word_tokenize function from NLTK toolbox to split sentences into words and remove punctuation. Then, the word with frequency less than 3 is

---

[1] https://github.com/tylin/coco-caption.

removed. As a result, we obtain the vocabulary with 5,491 words from MSVD and 13,064 words from MSR-VTT. For each dataset, we use the one-hot vector (1-of-N encoding, where N is the size of vocabulary) to represent each word.

4.5   Implementation Details

We use the validation set to tune some hyperparameters of our framework. The learning rates for three training stages are set to 3×10^{-4}, 3×10^{-4} and 1×10^{-4}, respectively. The training batchsize is 128 for MSVD and 256 for MSR-VTT, while each stage is trained up to 50 epoches and the best model is used to initialize the next stage. The minimum value of maximum picked frames τ is set to 7, and the penalty R^- is -1. To regularize the training and avoid over-fitting, we apply the well known regularization technique Dropout with retain probability 0.5 on the input and output of the encoding LSTMs and decoding GRUs. Embeddings for video features and words have size 512, while the sizes of all recurrent hidden states are empirically set to 1,024. For PickNet, the size of glance is 56×56, and the size of hidden layer is 1,024. The Adam [15] optimizer is used to update all the parameters.

5   Results and Discussion

Figure 6 gives some example results on the test sets of two datasets. As it can be seen, our PickNet can select informative frames, so the rest of our model can use these selected frames to generate reasonable descriptions. In short, two characteristics of picked frames can be found. The first characteristic is that the picked frames are concise and highly related to the generated descriptions, and the second one is that the adjacent frames may be picked to represent action. In order to demonstrate the effectiveness of our framework, we compare our approach with some state-of-the-art methods on the two datasets, and analyze the learned picks of PickNet in consequent sections.

Ours: a cat is playing with a dog
GT: a dog is playing with a cat

Ours: a person is solving a rubik's cube
GT: person playing with toy

Fig. 6. Example results on MSVD (left) and MSR-VTT (right). The green boxes indicate picked frames. (Best viewed in color and zoom-in. Frames are organized from left to right, then top to bottom in temporal order.) (Color figure online)

Table 1. Experiment results on MSVD. All values are reported as percentage(%). L denotes using language reward and V denotes using visual diversity reward. k is set to the average number of picks $\bar{N}_p$ on MSVD. ($\bar{N}_p \approx 6$)

Model	BLEU4	ROUGE-L	METEOR	CIDEr	Time
Previous Work					
LSTM-E [23]	45.3	–	31.0	–	5x
p-RNN [44]	49.9	–	32.6	65.8	5x
HRNE [22]	43.8	–	33.1	–	33x
BA [2]	42.5	–	32.4	63.5	12x
Baseline Models					
Full	44.8	68.5	31.6	69.4	5x
Random	35.6	64.5	28.4	49.2	2.5x
k-means (k = 6)	45.2	68.5	32.4	70.9	1x
Hecate [31]	43.2	67.4	31.7	68.8	1x
Our Models					
PickNet (V)	46.3	69.3	32.3	75.1	1x
PickNet (L)	49.9	69.3	32.9	74.7	1x
PickNet (V+L)	**52.3**	**69.6**	**33.3**	**76.5**	1x

Table 2. Experiment results on MSR-VTT. All values are reported as percentage(%). C denotes using the provided category information. k is set to the average number of picks $\bar{N}_p$ on MSR-VTT. ($\bar{N}_p \approx 8$)

Model	BLEU4	ROUGE-L	METEOR	CIDEr	Time
Previous Work					
ruc-uva [7]	38.7	58.7	26.9	45.9	4.5x
Aalto [28]	39.8	59.8	26.9	45.7	4.5x
DenseVidCap [27]	41.4	61.1	28.3	48.9	10.5x
MS-RNN [30]	39.8	59.3	26.1	40.9	10x
Baseline Models					
Full	36.8	59.0	26.7	41.2	3.8x
Random	31.3	55.7	25.2	32.6	1.9x
k-means (k = 8)	37.8	59.1	26.9	41.4	1x
Hecate [31]	37.3	59.1	26.6	40.8	1x
Our Models					
PickNet (V)	36.9	58.9	26.8	40.4	1x
PickNet (L)	37.3	58.9	27.0	41.9	1x
PickNet (V+L)	39.4	59.7	27.3	42.3	1x
PickNet (V+L+C)	41.3	59.8	27.7	44.1	1x

5.1 Comparison with the State-of-the-arts

We compare our approach on MSVD with four state-of-the-art approaches for video captioning: LSTM-E [23], p-RNN [44], HRNE [22] and BA [2]. LSTM-E uses a visual-semantic embedding to generate better captions. p-RNN use both temporal and spatial attention. BA uses a hierarchical encoder while HRNE uses a hierarchical decoder to describe videos. All of these methods use motion features (C3D or optical flow) and extract visual features frame by frame. Besides, we report the performance of our baseline models, which include using all the sampled frames, and using some straightforward picking strategies. In order to compare our PickNet with general picking policies, we conduct trials that pick frames by randomly selecting and k-means clustering, respectively. Specially, to compare with video summarization methods, we choose Hecate [31] to produce frame level summarization and use it to generate captions. For analyzing the effect of different rewards, we conduct some ablation studies on them. As it can be noticed in Table 1, our method improves plain techniques and achieves the state-of-the-art performance on MSVD. This result outperforms the most recent state-of-the-art method by a considerable margin of $\frac{76.5-65.8}{65.8} \approx 16.3\%$ on the CIDEr metric. Further, we try to compare the time efficiency among these approaches. However, most of state-of-the-art methods do not release executable codes, so the accurate performance may not be available. Instead, we estimate the running time by the complexity of visual feature extractors and the number of processed frames. Thanks to the PickNet, our captioning model is 5–33 times faster than other methods.

On MSR-VTT, we compare four state-of-the-art approaches: ruc-uva [7], Aalto [28], DenseVidCap [27] and MS-RNN [30]. ruc-uva incorporates the encoder-decoder with two new stages called early embedding which enriches input with tag embeddings, and late reranking which re-scores generated sentences in terms of their relevance to a specific video. Aalto first trains two models which are separately based on attribute and motion features, and then trains a evaluator to choose the best candidate generated by the two captioning model. DenseVidCap generates multiple sentences with regard to video segments and uses a winner-take-all scheme to produce the final description. MS-RNN uses a multi-modal LSTM to model the uncertainty in videos to generate diverse captions. Compared with these methods, our method can be simply trained in end-to-end fashion, and does not rely upon any auxiliary information. The performance of these approaches and that of our solution is reported in Table 2. We observe that our approach is able to achieve competitive result even **without utilizing attribute information**, while other methods take advantage of attributes and auxiliary information sources. Also, our model is the **fastest** among the compared methods. For fairly demonstrating the effectiveness of our method, we embed the provided category information into our language model, and better accuracy can be achieved (PickNet (V+L+C) in Table 2). It is also worth noting that the PickNet can be easily integrated with the compared methods, since none of them incorporated with frame selection algorithm. For example, DenseVidCap generates region-sequence candidates based on equally sampled frames. It can alternatively utilize PickNet to reduce the time for generating candidates by cutting down the number of selected frames.

5.2   Analysis of Learned Picks

We collect statistics on the properties of our PickNet. Figure 7 shows the distributions of the number and position of picked frames on the test sets of MSVD and MSR-VTT. As observed in Fig. 7(a), in the vast majority of the videos, less than 10 frames are picked. It implies that in most case only $\frac{10}{30} \approx 33.3\%$ frames

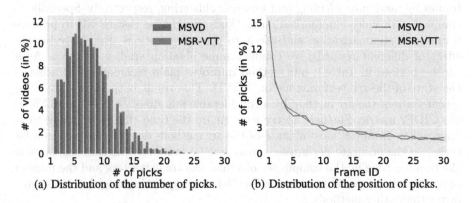

(a) Distribution of the number of picks.   (b) Distribution of the position of picks.

Fig. 7. Statistics on the behavior of our PickNet.

are necessary to be encoded for captioning videos, which can largely reduce the computation cost. Specifically, the average number of picks is around 6 for MSVD and 8 for MSR-VTT. Looking at the distributions of position of picks in Fig. 7(b), we observe a pattern of *power law distribution*, *i.e.*, the probability of picking a frame is reduced as time goes by. It is reasonable since most videos are single-shot and the anterior frames are sufficient to represent the whole video.

a cat is playing → **a rabbit is playing** → **a rabbit is being petted**
→ **a person is petting a rabbit** ×3

Fig. 8. An example of online video captioning.

5.3 Captioning for Streaming Video

One of the advantage of our method is that it can be applied to streaming video. Different from offline video captioning, captioning for streaming video requires the model to tackle with unbounded video and generate descriptions immediately when the visual information has changed, which meets the demand of practical applications. For this online setting, we first sample frames at 1fps, and then sequentially feed the sampled frames to PickNet. If certain frame is picked, the pretrained CNN will be used to extract visual features of this frame. After that, the encoder will receive this feature, and produce a new encoded representation of the video stream up to current time. Finally, the decoder will generate a description based on the encoded representation. Figure 8 demonstrates an example of online video captioning with the picked frames and corresponding descriptions. As it is shown, the descriptions will be more appropriate and more determined as the informative frames are picked.

6   Conclusion

In this work, we design a plug-and-play reinforcement-learning-based PickNet to select informative frames for the task of video captioning, which achieves promising performance on effectiveness, efficiency and flexibility on popular benchmarks. This architecture can largely cut down the usage of convolution operations by picking only 6–8 frames for a video clip, while other video analysis methods usually require more than 40 frames. This property makes our method more applicable for real-world video processing. The proposed PickNet has a good flexibility and could be potentially employed to other video-related applications, such as video classification and action detection, which will be further addressed in our future work.

Acknowledgment. This work was supported in part by National Natural Science Foundation of China: 61672497, 61332016, 61620106009, 61650202 and U1636214, in part by National Basic Research Program of China (973 Program): 2015CB351802 and in part by Key Research Program of Frontier Sciences of CAS: QYZDJ-SSW-SYS013.

References

1. Banerjee, S., Lavie, A.: Meteor: an automatic metric for MT evaluation with improved correlation with human judgments. In: ACL, pp. 65–72 (2005)
2. Baraldi, L., Grana, C., Cucchiara, R.: Hierarchical boundary-aware neural encoder for video captioning. In: CVPR, pp. 3185–3194 (2017)
3. Bengio, S., Vinyals, O., Jaitly, N., Shazeer, N.: Scheduled sampling for sequence prediction with recurrent neural networks. In: NIPS, pp. 1171–1179 (2015)
4. Chen, D.L., Dolan, W.B.: Collecting highly parallel data for paraphrase evaluation. In: ACL, pp. 190–200 (2011)
5. Cho, K., et al.: Learning phrase representations using RNN encoder-decoder for statistical machine translation. In: EMNLP, pp. 1724–1734 (2014)
6. Cromwell, H.C., Mears, R.P., Wan, L., Boutros, N.N.: Sensory gating: a translational effort from basic to clinical science. Clinical EEG Neurosci. **39**(2), 69–72 (2008)
7. Dong, J., Li, X., Lan, W., Huo, Y., Snoek, C.G.M.: Early embedding and late reranking for video captioning. In: ACM Multimedia, pp. 1082–1086 (2016)
8. Fang, H., et al.: From captions to visual concepts and back. In: CVPR, pp. 1473–1482 (2015)
9. Farhadi, A., Hejrati, M., Sadeghi, M.A., Young, P., Rashtchian, C., Hockenmaier, J., Forsyth, D.: Every picture tells a story: Generating sentences from images. In: ECCV, pp. 15–29 (2010)
10. He, K., Zhang, X., Ren, S., Sun, J.: Deep residual learning for image recognition. In: CVPR, pp. 770–778 (2016)
11. Hochreiter, S., Schmidhuber, J.J.J.: Long short-term memory. Neural Comput. **9**(8), 1735–1780 (1997)
12. Hori, C., Hori, T., Lee, T.Y., Sumi, K., Hershey, J.R., Marks, T.K.: Attention-based multimodal fusion for video description. In: ICCV, pp. 4203–4212 (2017)
13. Itti, L., Koch, C., Niebur, E.: A model of saliency-based visual attention for rapid scene analysis. IEEE Trans. Pattern Anal. Mach. Intell. **20**(11), 1254–1259 (1998)
14. Johnson, J., Karpathy, A., Fei-Fei, L.: Densecap: Fully convolutional localization networks for dense captioning. In: CVPR, pp. 4565–4574 (2016)
15. Kingma, D.P., Ba, J.L.: Adam: a method for stochastic optimization. In: ICLR (2015)
16. Kojima, A., Tamura, T., Fukunaga, K.: Natural language description of human activities from video images based on concept hierarchy of actions. IJCV **50**(2), 171–184 (2002)
17. Krause, J., Johnson, J., Krishna, R., Fei-Fei, L.: A hierarchical approach for generating descriptive image paragraphs. In: CVPR, pp. 3337–3345 (2017)
18. Kulkarni, G., et al.: Baby talk: Understanding and generating image descriptions. In: CVPR, pp. 1601–1608 (2011)
19. Lin, C.Y.: Rouge: A package for automatic evaluation of summaries. In: ACL (2004)
20. Lu, J., Yang, J., Batra, D., Parikh, D.: Hierarchical co-attention for visual question answering. In: NIPS, pp. 289–297 (2016)

21. Mnih, V., Heess, N., Graves, A., Kavukcuoglu, K.: Recurrent models of visual attention. In: NIPS, pp. 2204–2212 (2014)
22. Pan, P., Xu, Z., Yang, Y., Wu, F., Zhuang, Y.: Hierarchical recurrent neural encoder for video representation with application to captioning. In: CVPR, pp. 1029–1038 (2016)
23. Pan, Y., Mei, T., Yao, T., Li, H., Rui, Y.: Jointly modeling embedding and translation to bridge video and language. In: CVPR, pp. 4594–4602 (2016)
24. Papineni, K., Roukos, S., Ward, T., Zhu, W.J.: Bleu: a method for automatic evaluation of machine translation. In: ACL, pp. 311–318 (2002)
25. Ranzato, M., Chopra, S., Auli, M., Zaremba, W.: Sequence level training with recurrent neural networks. In: ICLR (2016)
26. Rennie, S.J., Marcheret, E., Mroueh, Y., Ross, J., Goel, V.: Self-critical sequence training for image captioning. In: CVPR, pp. 1179–1195 (2017)
27. Shen, Z., et al.: Weakly supervised dense video captioning. In: CVPR, pp. 5159–5167 (2017)
28. Shetty, R., Laaksonen, J.: Frame-and segment-level features and candidate pool evaluation for video caption generation. In: ACM Multimedia, pp. 1073–1076 (2016)
29. Simonyan, K., Zisserman, A.: Two-stream convolutional networks for action recognition in videos. In: NIPS, pp. 568–576 (2014)
30. Song, J., Guo, Y., Gao, L., Li, X., Hanjalic, A., Shen, H.T.: From deterministic to generative: multi-modal stochastic RNNs for video captioning. arXiv (2017)
31. Song, Y., Redi, M., Vallmitjana, J., Jaimes, A.: To click or not to click: automatic selection of beautiful thumbnails from videos. In: CIKM, pp. 659–668 (2016)
32. Song, Y., Vallmitjana, J., Stent, A., Jaimes, A.: Tvsum: Summarizing web videos using titles. In: CVPR, pp. 5179–5187 (2015)
33. Vedantam, R., Zitnick, C.L., Parikh, D.: Cider: consensus-based image description evaluation. In: CVPR, pp. 4566–4575 (2015)
34. Venugopalan, S., Rohrbach, M., Darrell, T., Donahue, J., Saenko, K., Mooney, R.: Sequence to sequence - video to text. In: ICCV, pp. 4534–4542 (2015)
35. Wang, B., Ma, L., Zhang, W., Liu, W.: Reconstruction network for video captioning. In: CVPR, pp. 7622–7631 (2018)
36. Wang, J., Jiang, W., Ma, L., Liu, W., Xu, Y.: Bidirectional attentive fusion with context gating for dense video captioning. In: CVPR, pp. 7190–7198 (2018)
37. Williams, R.J.: Simple statistical gradient-following algorithms for connectionist reinforcement learning. Mach. Learn. **8**(3–4), 229–256 (1992)
38. Xu, J., Mei, T., Yao, T., Rui, Y.: Msr-vtt: A large video description dataset for bridging video and language. In: CVPR, pp. 5288–5296 (2016)
39. Xu, K., et al.: Show, attend and tell: neural image caption generation with visual attention. In: ICML, pp. 2048–2057 (2015)
40. Yang, Y., Teo, C.L., Daumé III, H., Aloimonos, Y.: Corpus-guided sentence generation of natural images. In: EMNLP, pp. 444–454 (2011)
41. Yao, L., Cho, K., Ballas, N., Paí, C., Courville, A.: Describing videos by exploiting temporal structure. In: ICCV, pp. 4507–4515 (2015)
42. Yeung, S., Russakovsky, O., Mori, G., Fei-Fei, L.: End-to-end learning of action detection from frame glimpses in videos. In: CVPR, pp. 2678–2687 (2016)
43. You, Q., Jin, H., Wang, Z., Fang, C., Luo, J.: Image captioning with semantic attention. In: CVPR, pp. 4651–4659 (2016)
44. Yu, H., Wang, J., Huang, Z., Yang, Y., Xu, W.: Video paragraph captioning using hierarchical recurrent neural networks. In: CVPR, pp. 4584–4593 (2016)

45. Yu, Y., et al.: Supervising neural attention models for video captioning by human gaze data. In: CVPR, pp. 6119–6127 (2017)
46. Zeng, K., Chen, T., Niebles, J.C., Sun, M.: Title generation for user generated videos. In: ECCV, pp. 609–625 (2016)
47. Zhao, B., Xing, E.P.: Quasi real-time summarization for consumer videos. In: CVPR, pp. 2513–2520 (2014)
48. Zheng, H., Fu, J., Mei, T.: Look closer to see better: Recurrent attention convolutional neural network for fine-grained image recognition. In: CVPR, pp. 4476–4484 (2017)

Cross-Modal and Hierarchical Modeling
of Video and Text

Bowen Zhang[1], Hexiang Hu[1], and Fei Sha[2(✉)]

[1] Deptartment of Computer Science, University of Southern California,
Los Angeles, CA 90089, USA
{zhan734,hexiangh}@usc.edu
[2] Netflix, 5808 Sunset Blvd, Los Angeles, CA 90028, USA
fsha@netflix.com

Abstract. Visual data and text data are composed of information at
multiple granularities. A video can describe a complex scene that is composed of multiple clips or shots, where each depicts a semantically coherent event or action. Similarly, a paragraph may contain sentences with
different topics, which collectively conveys a coherent message or story. In
this paper, we investigate the modeling techniques for such hierarchical
sequential data where there are correspondences across multiple modalities. Specifically, we introduce hierarchical sequence embedding (HSE), a
generic model for embedding sequential data of different modalities into
hierarchically semantic spaces, with either explicit or implicit correspondence information. We perform empirical studies on large-scale video and
paragraph retrieval datasets and demonstrated superior performance by
the proposed methods. Furthermore, we examine the effectiveness of our
learned embeddings when applied to downstream tasks. We show its
utility in zero-shot action recognition and video captioning.

Keywords: Hierarchical sequence embedding · Video text retrieval
Video description generation · Action recognition · Zero-shot transfer

1 Introduction

Recently, there has been an intensive interest in multi-modal learning of vision
+ language. A few challenging tasks have been proposed: visual semantic
embedding (VSE) [5,15,16], image captioning [12,21,37,42], and visual question
answering (VQA) [2,3,47]. To jointly understand these two modalities of data
and make inference over them, the main intuition is that different types of data
can share a common semantic representation space. Examples are embedding

---

B. Zhang and H. Hu—Equally Contributed
On leave from University of Southern California (feisha@usc.edu)

Electronic supplementary material The online version of this chapter (https://
doi.org/10.1007/978-3-030-01261-8_23) contains supplementary material, which is
available to authorized users.

V. Ferrari et al. (Eds.): ECCV 2018, LNCS 11217, pp. 385–401, 2018.
https://doi.org/10.1007/978-3-030-01261-8_23

images and the visual categories [7], embedding images and texts for VSE [16], and embedding images, questions, and answers for VQA [11]. Once embedded into this common (vector) space, similarity and distances among originally heterogeneous data can be captured by learning algorithms.

While there has been a rich study on how to discover this shared semantic representation on structures such as images, noun phrases (visual object or action categories) and sentences (such as captions, questions, answers), less is known about how to achieve so on more complex structures such as videos and paragraphs of texts[1]. There are conceptual challenges: while complex structured data can be mapped to vector spaces (for instance, using deep architectures [8,18]), it is not clear whether the intrinsic structures in those data's original format, after being transformed to the vectorial representations, still maintain their correspondence and relevance across modalities.

Take the dense video description task as an example [17]. The task is to describe a video which is made of short, coherent and meaningful clips. (Note that those clips could overlap temporally.) Due to its narrowly focused semantic content, each clip is then describable with a sentence. The description for the whole video is then a paragraph of texts with sentences linearly arranged in order. Arguably, a corresponding pair of video and its descriptive paragraph can be embedded into a semantic space where their embeddings are close to each other, using a vanilla learning model by ignoring the boundaries of clips and sentences and treating as a sequence of continually flowing visual frames and words. However, for such a modeling strategy, it is opaque that if and how the correspondences at the "lower level" (*i.e.* clips versus sentences) are useful in either deriving the embeddings or using the embeddings to perform downstream tasks such as video or text retrieval.

Addressing these deficiencies, we propose a novel cross-modal learning approach to model both videos and texts jointly. The main idea is schematically illustrated in Fig. 1. Our approach is mindful of the intrinsic hierarchical structures of both videos and texts, and models them with hierarchical sequence learning models such as GRUs [4]. However, as opposed to methods which disregard low-level correspondences, we exploit them by deriving loss functions to ensure the embeddings for the clips and sentences are also in accordance in their own (shared) semantic space. Those low-level embeddings in turn strengthen the desiderata that videos and paragraphs are embedded coherently. We demonstrate the advantages of the proposed model in a range of tasks including video and text retrieval, zero-shot action recognition and video description.

The rest of the paper is organized as follows. In Sect. 2, we discuss related work. We describe our proposed approach in Sect. 3, followed by extensive experimental results and ablation studies in Sect. 4. We conclude in Sect. 5.

---

[1] We use paragraphs and documents interchangeably throughout this work.

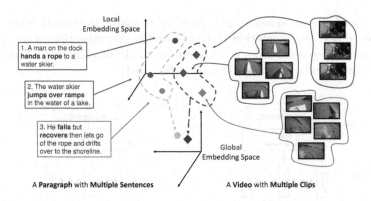

Fig. 1. Conceptual diagram of our approach for cross-modal modeling of video and texts. The main idea is to embed both low-level (clips and sentences) and high-level (video and paragraph) in their own semantic spaces coherently. As shown in the figure, the 3 sentences (and the corresponding 3 clips) are mapped into a local embedding space where the corresponding pairs of clips and sentences are placed close to each other. As a whole, the videos and the paragraphs are mapped into a global semantic space where their embeddings are close. See Fig. 3 and texts for details.

2   Related Work

Hierarchical Sequence Embedding Models. Embedding images, videos, and textual data has been very popular with the rise of deep learning. The most related works to ours are [19] and [25]. The former models the paragraph using a hierarchical auto-encoder for text modeling [19], and the later uses a hierarchical RNN for videos and a one-layer RNN for caption generation. In contrast, our work models both modalities hierarchically and learn the parameters by leveraging the correspondences across modalities. Works motivated by other application scenarios usually explore hierarchical modeling in one modality [24,43,45].

Cross-modal Embedding Learning. There has been a rich history to learn embeddings for images and smaller linguistic units (such as words and noun phrases). DeViSE [7] learns to align the latent embeddings of visual data and names of the visual object categories. ReViSE [34] uses auto-encoders to derive embeddings for images and words which allow them to leverage unlabeled data. In contrast to previous methods, our approach models both videos and texts hierarchically, bridging the embeddings at different granularities using discriminative loss computed on corresponded pairs (*i.e.* videos vs. paragraphs).

Action Recognition in Videos. Deep learning has brought significant improvement to video understanding [6,30,33,38,41,44] on large-scale action recognition datasets [9,14,31] in the past decade. Most of them [6,30,38] employed deep convolutional neural network to learn appearance feature and motion information respectively. Based on the spatial-temporal feature from these video modeling methods, we learn video semantic embedding to match the holistic video representation to text representation. To evaluate the generalization of our learned video semantic representation, we evaluate the model directly on the challenging action recognition benchmark. (Details in Sect. 4.4)

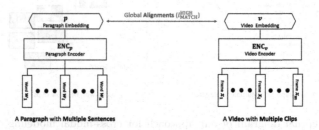

Fig. 2. Flat sequence modeling of videos and texts, ignoring the hierarchical structures in either and regarding the video (paragraph) as a sequence of frames (words).

3   Approach

We begin by describing the problem settings and introducing necessary notations. We then describe the standard sequential modeling technique, ignoring the hierarchical structures in the data. Finally, we describe our approach.

3.1   Settings and Notations

We are interested in modeling videos and texts that are paired in correspondence In the later section, we describe how to generalize this where there is no one to one correspondence.

A video v has n clips (or subshots), where each clip c_i contains n_i frames. Each frame is represented by a visual feature vector x_{ij}. This feature vector can be derived in many ways, for instance, by feeding the frame (and its contextual frames) to a convolution neural net and using the outputs from the penultimate layer. Likewise, we assume there is a paragraph of texts describing the video. The paragraph p contains n sentences, one for each video clip. Let s_i denote the ith sentence and w_{ij} the feature for the jth word out of n_i' words. We denote by $\mathcal{D} = \{(v_k, p_k)\}$ a set of corresponding videos and text descriptions.

We compute a clip vector embedding c_i from the frame features $\{x_{ij}\}$, and a sentence embedding s_i from the word features $\{w_{ij}\}$. From those, we derive v and p, the embedding for the video and the paragraph, respectively.

3.2   Flat Sequence Modeling

Many sequence-to-sequence (SEQ2SEQ) methods leverage the encoder-decoder structure [22,32] to model the process of transforming from the input sequence to the output sequence. In particular, the encoder, which is composed of a layer of long short-term memory units (LSTMs) [10] or Gated Recurrent Units (GRUs) [4], transforms the input sequence into a vector as the embedding $\boldsymbol{h}$. The similarly constructed decoder takes $\boldsymbol{h}$ as input and outputs another sequence.

The original SEQ2SEQ methods do not consider the hierarchical structures in videos or texts. We refer the embeddings as *flat sequence embedding* (FSE):

$$\boldsymbol{v} = \text{ENC}_v(\{\boldsymbol{x}_{ij}\}), \quad \boldsymbol{p} = \text{ENC}_p(\{\boldsymbol{w}_{ij}\}), \tag{1}$$

Figure 2 schematically illustrates this idea. We measure how well the videos and the texts are aligned by the following cosine similarity

$$\text{MATCH}(v, p) = \boldsymbol{v}^{\top}\boldsymbol{p}/\|\boldsymbol{v}\|\|\boldsymbol{p}\| \tag{2}$$

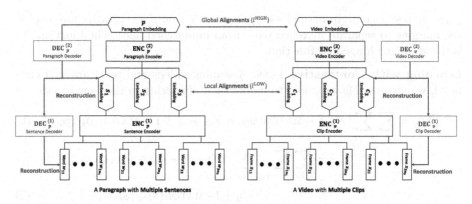

Fig. 3. Hierarchical cross-modal modeling of videos and texts. We differ from previous works [19,25] in two aspects (components in red color): layer-wise reconstruction through decoders, and matching at both global and local levels. See texts for details.

3.3 Hierarchical Sequence Modeling

One drawback of flat sequential modeling is that the LSTM/GRU layer needs to have a sufficient number of units to model well the potential long-range dependency among video frames (or words). This often complicates learning as the optimization becomes difficult [26].

We leverage the hierarchical structures in those data to overcome this deficiency: a video is made of clips which are made of frames. In parallel, a paragraph of texts is made of sentences which in turn are made of words. Similar ideas have been explored in [19,25] and other previous works. The basic idea is illustrated in Fig. 3, where we also add components in red color to highlight our extensions.

Hierarchical Sequence Embedding. Given the hierarchical structures in Fig. 3, we can compute the embeddings using the forward paths

$$
\begin{aligned}
\boldsymbol{c}_i &= \text{ENC}_v^{(1)}(\{\boldsymbol{x}_{ij}, j = 1, 2, \mathsf{n}_i\}), \quad \boldsymbol{v} = \text{ENC}_v^{(2)}(\{\boldsymbol{c}_i\}) \\
\boldsymbol{s}_i &= \text{ENC}_p^{(1)}(\{\boldsymbol{w}_{ij}, j = 1, 2, \mathsf{n}_i'\}), \quad \boldsymbol{p} = \text{ENC}_p^{(2)}(\{\boldsymbol{s}_i\})
\end{aligned}
\tag{3}
$$

Learning with Discriminative Loss. For videos and texts have strong correspondences where clips and sentences are paired, we optimize the encoders such that videos and texts are matched. To this end, we define two loss functions, corresponding to the matching at the low-level and the high-level respectively:

$$\ell_{\text{MATCH}}^{\text{HIGH}} = \sum_k \sum_{k' \neq k} [\alpha + \text{MATCH}(\boldsymbol{v}_k, \boldsymbol{p}_k) - \text{MATCH}(\boldsymbol{v}_{k'}, \boldsymbol{p}_k)]_+$$

$$+ [\alpha + \text{MATCH}(\boldsymbol{v}_k, \boldsymbol{p}_k) - \text{MATCH}(\boldsymbol{v}_k, \boldsymbol{p}_{k'})]_+ \quad (4)$$

$$\ell_{\text{MATCH}}^{\text{LOW}} = \sum_k \sum_i \sum_{(k',i') \neq (k,i)} [\beta + \text{MATCH}(\boldsymbol{c}_{ki}, \boldsymbol{s}_{ki}) - \text{MATCH}(\boldsymbol{c}_{k'i'}, \boldsymbol{s}_{ki})]_+$$

$$+ [\beta + \text{MATCH}(\boldsymbol{c}_{ki}, \boldsymbol{s}_{ki}) - \text{MATCH}(\boldsymbol{c}_{ki}, \boldsymbol{s}_{k'i'})]_+ \quad (5)$$

These losses are margin-based losses [29] where α and β are positive numbers as the margins to separate matched pairs from unmatched ones. The function $[\cdot]_+$ is the standard hinge loss function.

Learning with Contrastive Loss. Assuming videos and texts are well clustered, we use the following loss to model their clustering in their own space.

$$\ell_{\text{CLUSTER}}^{\text{HIGH}} = \sum_k \sum_{k' \neq k} [\gamma + 1 - \text{MATCH}(\boldsymbol{v}_{k'}, \boldsymbol{v}_k)]_+ + [\gamma + 1 - \text{MATCH}(\boldsymbol{p}_{k'}, \boldsymbol{p}_k)]_+ \quad (6)$$

$$\ell_{\text{CLUSTER}}^{\text{LOW}} = \sum_k \sum_i \sum_{(k',i') \neq (k,i)} [\eta + 1 - \text{MATCH}(\boldsymbol{c}_{k'i'}, \boldsymbol{c}_{ki})]_+$$

$$+ [\eta + 1 - \text{MATCH}(\boldsymbol{s}_{k'i'}, \boldsymbol{s}_{ki})]_+ \quad (7)$$

Note that the self-matching values $\text{MATCH}(\boldsymbol{v}_k, \boldsymbol{v}_k)$ and $\text{MATCH}(\boldsymbol{p}_k, \boldsymbol{p}_k)$ are 1 by definition. This loss can be computed on videos and texts alone and does not require them being matched.

Learning with Unsupervised Layer-wise Reconstruction Loss. Thus far, the matching loss focuses on matching across modality. The clustering loss focuses on separating between video/text data so that they do not overlap. None of them, however, focuses on the *quality* of the modeling data itself. In what follows, we propose a layer-wise reconstruction loss – when minimized, this loss ensures the learned video/text embedding faithfully preserves information in the data.

We first introduce a set of layer-wise decoders for both videos and texts. The key idea is to pair the encoders with decoders so that each pair of functions is an auto-encoder. Specifically, the decoder is also a layer of LSTM/GRU units, generating sequences of data. Thus, at the level of video (or paragraph), we will have a decoder to generate clips (or sentences). And at the level of clips (or sentences), we will have a decoder to generate frames (or words). Concretely, we would like to minimize the difference between what are generated by the decoders and what are computed by encoders on the data. Let

$$\{\hat{\boldsymbol{c}}_i\} = \text{DEC}_v^{(2)}(\boldsymbol{v}), \{\hat{\boldsymbol{s}}_i\} = \text{DEC}_p^{(2)}(\boldsymbol{p}) \quad (8)$$

be the two (high-level) decoders for videos and texts respectively. And similarly, for the decoder at the low-level

$$\{\hat{\boldsymbol{x}}_{ij}\} = \text{DEC}_v^{(1)}(\hat{\boldsymbol{c}}_i), \{\hat{\boldsymbol{w}}_{ij}\} = \text{DEC}_p^{(1)}(\hat{\boldsymbol{s}}_i) \tag{9}$$

where the low-level decoders take each *generated* clip and sentence embeddings as inputs and output sequences of generated frame and word embeddings.

$$\ell_{\text{RECONSTRUCT}}(v, p) = \sum_i \{\|\hat{\boldsymbol{c}}_i - \boldsymbol{c}_i\|_2^2 + \frac{1}{n_i} \sum_j \|\hat{\boldsymbol{x}}_{ij} - \boldsymbol{x}_{ij}\|_2^2\}$$

$$+ \sum_i \{\|\hat{\boldsymbol{s}}_i - \boldsymbol{s}_i\|_2^2 + \frac{1}{n_i'} \sum_j \|\hat{\boldsymbol{w}}_{ij} - \boldsymbol{w}_{ij}\|_2^2\} \tag{10}$$

Using those generated embeddings, we can construct a loss function characterizing how well the encoders encode the data pair (v, p) (see Eq. 10).

3.4 Final Learning Objective and Its Extensions

The final learning objective is to balance all those loss quantities

$$\ell = \ell^{\text{HIGH}} + \ell^{\text{LOW}} + \tau \sum_k \ell_{\text{RECONSTRUCT}}(\boldsymbol{v}_k, \boldsymbol{p}_k) \tag{11}$$

where the high-level and low-level losses are defined as

$$\ell^{\text{HIGH}} = \ell_{\text{MATCH}}^{\text{HIGH}} + \ell_{\text{CLUSTER}}^{\text{HIGH}}, \quad \ell^{\text{LOW}} = \ell_{\text{MATCH}}^{\text{LOW}} + \ell_{\text{CLUSTER}}^{\text{LOW}} \tag{12}$$

In our experiments, we will study the contribution by each term.

Learning Under Weak Correspondences. Our idea can be also extended to the common setting where only high-level alignments are available. In fact, high-level coarse alignments of data are easier and more economical to obtain, compared to fine-grained alignments between each sub-level sentence and video clip.

Since we do not have enough information to define the low-level matching loss $\ell_{\text{MATCH}}^{\text{LOW}}$ exactly, we resort to approximation. We first define an averaged matching over all pairs of clips and sentences for a pair of video and paragraph

$$\overline{\text{MATCH}}(v, p) = \frac{1}{nm} \sum_{c_i} \sum_{s_j} \text{MATCH}(\boldsymbol{c}_i, \boldsymbol{s}_j) \tag{13}$$

where we relax the assumption that there is precisely the same number of sentences and clips. We use this averaged quantity to approximate the low-level matching loss

$$\tilde{\ell}_{\text{MATCH}}^{\text{LOW}} = \sum_k \sum_{k' \neq k} [\beta' + \overline{\text{MATCH}}(\boldsymbol{v}_k, \boldsymbol{p}_k) - \overline{\text{MATCH}}(\boldsymbol{v}_{k'}, \boldsymbol{p}_k)]_+$$

$$+ [\beta' + \overline{\text{MATCH}}(\boldsymbol{v}_k, \boldsymbol{p}_k) - \overline{\text{MATCH}}(\boldsymbol{v}_k, \boldsymbol{p}_{k'})]_+ \tag{14}$$

This objective will push a clip embedding closer to the embeddings of the sentences belonging to the corresponding video (and vice versa for sentences to the corresponding video). A more refined approximation involving a soft assignment of matching can also be derived, which will be left for future work.

4 Experiments

We evaluate and demonstrate the advantage of learning hierarchical cross-modal embedding with our proposed approach on several tasks: (i) large-scale video-paragraph retrieval (Sect. 4.2), (ii) down-stream tasks such as video captioning (Sect. 4.3), and (iii) action recognition (Sect. 4.4).

4.1 Experiment Setups

Datasets. We evaluate on three large-scale video datasets: (1) `ActivityNet Dense Caption` [17]. This variant of ActivityNet contains densely labeled temporal segments for 10,009 training and 4,917/4,885 (val1/val2) validation videos. Each video contains multiple clips and a corresponding paragraph with sentences aligned to the clips. In all our retrieval experiments, we follow the setting in [17] and report retrieval metrics such as recall@k (k=1,5,50) and median rank (MR). Following [17] we use ground-truth clip proposals as input for our main results. In addition, we also study our algorithm with a heuristic proposal method (see Sect. 4.2). In the main text, we report all results on validation set 1 (val1). Please refer to the Supp. Material for the results on val2. For video caption experiment, we follow [17] and evaluate on the validation set (val1 and val2). Instead of using action proposal method, ground-truth video segmentation is used for training and evaluation. Performances are reported in Bleu@K, METEOR and CIDEr.
(2) `DiDeMo` [1]. The original goal of DiDeMo dataset is to locate the temporal segments that correspond to unambiguous natural language descriptions in a video. We re-purpose it for the task of video and paragraph retrieval. It contains 10,464 videos, 26,892 video clips and 40,543 sentences. The training, validation and testing split contain 8,395, 1,065 and 1,004 videos and corresponding paragraphs, respectively. Each video clip may correspond to one or many sentences. For the video and paragraph retrieval task, paragraphs are constructed by concatenating all sentences that corresponding to one video. Similar to the setting in ActivityNet, we use the ground-truth clip proposals as input.
(3) `ActivityNet Action Recognition` [9]. We use ActivityNet V1.3 for aforementioned off-the-shelf action recognition. The dataset contains 14,950 untrimmed videos with 200 action classes, which is split into training and validation set. Training and validation set have 10,024 and 4,926 videos, respectively. Among all 200 action classes, 189 of the action classes have been covered by the vocabulary extracted from the paragraph corpus and 11 of the classes are unseen.

Baselines and Our Methods. We use the FSE method (as described in Sect. 3.1) as a baseline model. It ignores the clip and sentence structures in the videos and paragraphs. We train a one-layer GRU directly on the extracted frame/word features and take their outputs as the embedding representing each modality. Results with C3D features are also included (see Table 1).

Our method has two variants: when $\tau = 0$, the method (HSE[τ=0]) simplifies to a stacked/hierarchical sequence models as used in [19,25] except that they do not consider cross-modal learning with cross-modal matching loss while we do. We consider this as a very strong baseline. When $\tau \neq 0$, the HSE takes full advantage of layer-wise reconstruction with multiple decoders, at different levels of the hierarchy. In our experiments, this method gives the best results.

Implementation Details. Following the settings of [17], we extract the C3D features [33] pretrained on Sports-1M dataset [13] for raw videos in ActivityNet. PCA is then used to reduce the dimensionality of the feature to 500. To verify the generalization of our model across different sets of visual feature, as well as leveraging the state-of-the-art video models, we also employed recently proposed TSN-Inception V3 network [38] pre-trained on Kinetics [14] dataset to extract visual features. Similarly, we extract TSN-Inception V3 feature for videos in Didemo dataset. We do not fine-tuning the convolutional neural network on the video along the training to reduce the computational cost. For word embedding, we use 300 dimension GloVe [27] features pre-trained on 840B common web-crawls. In all our experiments, we use GRU as sequence encoders. For HSE, we choose $\tau = 0.0005$ from tuning this hyper-parameter on the val2 set of ActivityNet retrieval dataset. The same τ value is used for experiments on DiDeMo, without further tuning. (More details in the Supp. Material)

Table 1. Video paragraph retrieval on ActivityNet (val1). Standard deviation from 3 random seeded experiments are also reported.

	Paragraph $\Rightarrow$ Video				Video $\Rightarrow$ Paragraph			
	R@1	R@5	R@50	MR	R@1	R@5	R@50	MR
C3D Feature with Dimensionality Reduction [33]								
LSTM-YT [35]	0.0	4.0	24.0	102.0	0.0	7.0	38.0	98.0
NO CONTEXT [36]	5.0	14.0	32.0	78.0	7.0	18.0	45.0	56.0
DENSE online[17]	10.0	32.0	60.0	36.0	17.0	34.0	70.0	33.0
DENSE full[17]	14.0	32.0	65.0	34.0	18.0	36.0	74.0	32.0
FSE	12.6±0.4	33.2±0.3	77.6±0.3	12.0	11.5±0.5	31.8±0.3	77.7±0.3	13.0
HSE[τ=0]	32.8±0.3	62.3±0.4	90.5±0.1	3.0	32.0±0.6	62.5±0.5	90.5±0.3	3.0
HSE[τ=5e-4]	32.7±0.7	63.2±0.4	90.8±0.2	3.0	32.8±0.4	63.2±0.2	91.2±0.3	3.0
Inception-V3 pre-trained on Kinetics [38]								
FSE	18.2±0.2	44.8±0.4	89.1±0.3	7.0	16.7±0.8	43.1±1.1	88.4±0.3	7.3
HSE[τ=0]	43.9±0.6	75.8±0.2	96.9±0.3	2.0	43.3±0.6	75.3±0.6	96.6±0.2	2.0
HSE[τ=5e-4]	44.4±0.5	76.7±0.3	97.1±0.1	2.0	44.2±0.6	76.7±0.3	97.0±0.3	2.0

4.2 Results on Video-Paragraph Retrieval

In this section, we first compare our proposed approach to the state-of-the-art algorithms, and then perform ablation studies on variants of our method, to evaluate the proposed learning objectives.

Main Results. We reported our results on ActivityNet Dense Caption val1 set and DiDeMo test set as Tables 1 and 2, respectively. For both C3D and Inception V3 feature, we observed performances on our hierarchical models improved the previous state-of-the-art result by a large margin (on Recall@1, over $\sim 15\%$ improvement with C3D and $\sim 30\%$ improvement with InceptionV3). DENSE full [17], which models the flat sequences of clips, outperforms our FSE baseline as they augment each segment embedding with a weighted aggregated context embedding. However, it fails to model more complex temporal structures of video and paragraph, which leads to inferior performance to our HSE models.

Comparing to our flat baseline model, both HSE[τ=0] and HSE[τ = 5e-4] improve performances over all metrics in retrieval. It implies that hierarchical mod-

Table 2. Video paragraph retrieval on DiDeMo dataset. S2VT method is re-implemented for retrieval task.

	Paragraph $\Rightarrow$ Video				Video $\Rightarrow$ Paragraph			
	R@1	R@5	R@50	MR	R@1	R@5	R@50	MR
S2VT [36]	11.9	33.6	76.5	13.0	13.2	33.6	76.5	15.0
FSE	13.9±0.7	36.0±0.8	78.9±1.6	11.0	13.1±0.5	33.9±0.4	78.0±0.8	12.0
HSE[τ=0]	**30.2**±0.8	**60.5**±1.1	91.8±0.7	**3.3**	29.4±0.4	58.9±0.7	91.9±0.6	3.7
HSE[τ=5e-4]	29.7±0.2	60.3±0.9	**92.4**±0.3	**3.3**	**30.1**±1.2	**59.2**±0.9	**92.1**±0.5	**3.0**

Table 3. Ablation studies on the learning objectives.

Dataset		ℓ^{LOW}	Paragraph $\Rightarrow$ Video			Video $\Rightarrow$ Paragraph		
			R@1	R@5	R@50	R@1	R@5	R@50
ActivityNet	HSE[τ=0]	✗	41.8±0.4	74.1±0.6	96.6±0.1	40.5±0.4	73.9±0.6	96.3±0.1
		WEAK	42.6±0.4	74.8±0.3	96.7±0.1	41.3±0.2	74.7±0.4	96.5±0.1
		STRONG	43.9±0.6	75.8±0.2	96.9±0.3	43.3±0.6	75.3±0.6	96.6±0.2
	HSE[τ=5e-4]	✗	42.5±0.3	74.8±0.1	96.9±0.0	41.6±0.2	74.7±0.6	96.6±0.1
		WEAK	43.0±0.6	75.2±0.4	96.9±0.1	41.5±0.1	75.2±0.6	96.8±0.2
		STRONG	44.4±0.5	76.7±0.3	97.1±0.1	44.2±0.6	76.7±0.3	97.0±0.3
DiDeMo	HSE[τ=0]	✗	27.1±1.9	59.1±0.4	92.2±0.3	27.3±1.0	57.6±0.5	91.3±1.2
		WEAK	28.0±0.8	58.9±0.5	91.4±0.6	28.3±0.3	58.5±0.6	91.2±0.3
		STRONG	30.2±0.8	60.5±1.1	91.8±0.7	29.4±0.4	58.9±0.7	91.9±0.6
	HSE[τ=5e-4]	✗	28.1±0.8	59.5±1.1	91.7±0.7	28.2±0.8	58.1±0.5	90.9±0.5
		WEAK	28.7±2.1	59.1±0.2	91.6±0.7	28.3±0.8	59.2±0.6	91.1±0.1
		STRONG	29.7±0.2	60.3±0.9	92.4±0.3	30.1±1.2	59.2±0.9	92.1±0.5

eling can effectively capture the structure information and relationships over clips and sentences among videos and paragraphs. Moreover, we observe that HSE[τ = 5e-4] consistently improves over HSE[τ=0] across most retrieval metrics on both datasets. This attributes the importance of our layer-wise reconstruction objectives, which suggests that better generalization performances.

Low-level Loss is Beneficial. Tables 1 and 2 have shown results with optimizing both low-level and high-level objectives. In Table 3, we further performed ablation studies on the learning objectives. Note that rows with ✗ represent learning without low-level loss ℓ^{LOW}. In all scenarios, joint learning with both low-level and high-level correspondences improves the retrieval performance.

Learning with Weak Correspondences at Low-level. As mentioned in Sect. 3, our method can be extended to learn the low-level embedding with weak correspondence. We evaluate its effectiveness on both ActivityNet and DiDeMo datasets. Performance are listed in Table 3. Note that for the rows of "weak", no auxiliary alignments between sentences and clips are available during training.

Clearly, including low-level loss with weak correspondence (ie, correspondence only at the high-level) obtained superior performances when compared to models that do not include low-level loss at all. On several occasions, it even attains the same competitive result as including low-level loss with strong correspondences at the clip/sentence levels.

Table 4. Performance of using proposal instead of ground truth on ActivityNet dataset

Proposal Method	# Segments	P ⇒ V		V ⇒ P		Precision	Recall
		R@1	R@5	R@1	R@5		
HSE + SSN	-	10.4	31.9	10.8	31.7	1.5	17.1
HSE + UNIFORM	1	18.0	45.5	16.5	44.9	63.2	31.1
	2	20.0	48.9	18.4	47.6	61.8	46.0
	3	20.0	48.6	18.2	47.9	55.3	50.6
	4	20.5	49.3	18.7	48.1	43.2	45.5
HSE + GROUND TRUTH	-	44.4	76.7	44.2	76.7	100.0	100.0
FSE	-	18.2	44.8	16.7	43.1	-	-

Learning with Video Proposal Methods. As using ground-truth temporal segments of videos is not a natural assumption, we perform experiments to validate the effectiveness of our method with proposal methods. Specifically, we experiment with two different proposal approaches: SSN [46] pre-trained on ActivityNet action proposal and a heuristic uniform proposal. For uniform proposal of K segments, we meant naturally segmenting a video into K non-overlapping and equal-length temporal segments.

The results are summarized in Table 4 (with columns of precision and recall being the performance metrics of the proposal methods). There are two main conclusions from these results: (1) The segments of Dense Caption dataset deviate significantly from the action proposals, therefore a pre-trained action proposal algorithm performs poorly. (2) Even with heuristic proposal methods, the performance of HSE is mostly better than (or comparable with) FSE. We leave to future work on identifying stronger methods for proposals.

Retrieval with Incomplete Video and Paragraph. In this section, we investigate the correlation between the number of observed clips and sentences and models' performance of video and paragraph retrieval. In this experiment, we gradually increase the number of clips and sentences observed by our model during the testing and obtained the Fig. 4, on ActivityNet. When the video/paragraph contains fewer clips/sentences than the number of observations we required, we take all those available clips/sentences for computing the video/paragraph embedding. (On average 3.65 clips/sentences per video/paragraph)

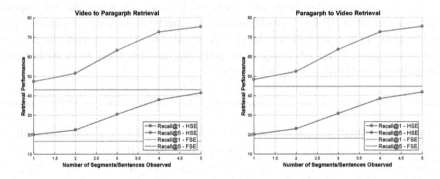

Fig. 4. Retrieval performance improves given more observed clips/sentences.

From Fig. 4, we note that increasing the number of the observed clips and sentences leads to improved performance results in retrievals. We can see that when observing only one clip and sentence, our model already outperforms the previous state-of-the-art method as well as our baseline FSE that observes the entire sequence. With observing less than the average length of clips and sentences, our learned model can achieve $\sim 70\%$ of the final performance.

4.3   Results on Video Captioning

Setups. In addition to the video paragraph retrieval, we evaluate our learned embeddings for video captioning. Specifically, we follow [17] and train a caption model [37] on top of the pre-trained video embeddings. Similar to [17], we concatenate the clip-level feature with contextual video-level feature, and build a two-layer LSTM as a caption generator. We randomly initialized the word embedding as well as LSTM and trained the model for 25 epochs with learning rate of 0.001. We use the ground-truth proposal throughout training and evaluation following the setting of [17,20]. During testing, beam search is used with beam=5. Results are reported in Table 5.

Table 5. Results for video captioning on ActivityNet

	B@1	B@2	B@3	B@4	M	C
LSTM-YT [35]	18.2	7.4	3.2	1.2	6.6	14.9
S2VT [36]	20.4	9.0	4.6	2.6	7.9	21.0
HRNN [43]	19.5	8.8	4.3	2.5	8.0	20.2
DENSE [17]	26.5	13.5	7.1	4.0	9.5	24.6
DVC [20]	19.6	9.9	4.6	1.6	10.3	25.2
FSE	17.9	8.2	3.6	1.7	8.7	32.1
HSE[τ=0]	19.6	9.4	4.2	2.0	9.2	39.5
HSE[τ=5e-4]	19.8	9.4	4.3	2.1	9.2	39.8

Table 6. Results for action recognition on ActivityNet (low-level embeddings)

	Zero-Shot Transfer		Train Classifier	
	Top-1	Top-5	Top-1	Top-5
FV-VAE [28]	-	-	78.6	-
TSN [39]	-	-	88.1	-
FSE	48.3	79.4	74.4	94.1
HSE[τ=0]	50.2	84.4	74.7	94.3
HSE[τ=5e-4]	51.4	83.8	75.3	94.3
RANDOM	0.5	2.5	0.5	2.5

Results. We observe that our proposed model outperforms baseline over most metrics. Meanwhile, HSE also improves over previous approaches such as LSTM-YT, S2VT, and HRNN on B@2, METEOR, and CIDEr by a margin. HSE achieves comparable results with DVC in all criterions. However, both HSE and HSE[τ=0] failed to obtain close performance to DENSE [17]. This may due to the fact that DENSE [17] carefully learns to aggregate the context information of a video clip for producing high-quality caption, while optimized for video-paragraph retrieval our embedding model does not equip with such capability. However, it is worth noting that our model obtains higher CIDEr score compared to all existing methods. We empirically observe that fine-tuning the pre-trained video embedding does not lead to further performance improvement.

4.4   Results on Action Recognition

To evaluate the effectiveness of our model, we take the off-the-shelf clip-level embeddings trained on video-paragraph retrieval for action recognition (on ActivityNet with non-overlapping training and validation data). We use two action recognition settings to evaluate, namely **zero-shot transfer** and **classification**.

Setups. In the **zero-shot** setting, we directly evaluate our low-level embedding model learned in the video and text retrieval, via treating the phrases of actions as sentences and use the sentence-level encoder to encode the action embedding. We take the raw video and apply clip-level video encoder to extract the feature for retrieving actions. No re-training is performed and all models have no access to the actions' data distribution. Note though action are not directly used as sentences during the training, some are available as verbs in the vocabulary. Meanwhile, as we are using pre-trained word vector (GloVe), it allows the transfer to unseen actions. In the **classification** setting, we discriminatively train a simple classifier to measure the classification accuracy. Concretely, a one-hidden-layer Multi-Layer Perceptron (MLP) is trained on the clip-level embeddings. We do not fine-tune the pre-trained clip-level video embedding here.

Results. We report results of above two settings on the ActivityNet validation set (see Table 6). We observe that our learned low-level embeddings allow superior zero-shot transfer to action recognition, without accessing any training data. This indicates that semantics of actions are indeed well reserved in the learned embedding models. More interestingly, we can see that both HSE[$\tau=0$] and HSE improve the performance over FSE. It shows that our hierarchical modeling of video benefits not only high-level embedding but also low-level embedding. A similar trend is also observed in the classification setting. Our method achieves comparable performance to the state-of-the-art video modeling approach such as FV-VAE [28]. Note TSN [39] is fully supervised thus not directly comparable.

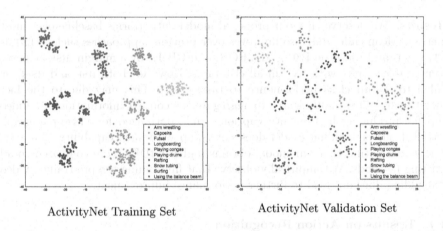

| ActivityNet Training Set | ActivityNet Validation Set |

Fig. 5. T-SNE visualization of off-the-shelf video embedding of HSE on ActivityNet v1.3 training and validation set. Points are marked with its action classes.

4.5   Qualitative Results

We use t-SNE [23] to visualize our results in the video to paragraph and paragraph to video retrieval task. Figure 5 shows that the proposed method can cluster the embedding of videos with regard to its action classes. To further explain the retrieval quality, we provide qualitative visualization in the Supp. Material.

5   Conclusion

In this paper, we propose a novel cross-modal learning approach to model videos and texts jointly, which leverages the intrinsic hierarchical structures of both videos or texts. Specifically, we consider the correspondences of videos and texts at multiple granularities, and derived loss functions to align the embeddings for the paired clips and sentences, as well as paired video and paragraph in accordance in their own semantic spaces. Another important component of our model is layer-wise reconstruction, which ensures that learned embeddings capture video (paragraph) and clips (words) at different levels. Moreover, we further extend our learning objective so that it allows to handle a more generalized learning scenario where only video paragraph correspondence exists. We demonstrate the advantage of our proposed model in a range of tasks including video and text retrieval, zero-shot action recognition and video caption.

Acknowledgments. We appreciate the feedback from the reviewers. This work is partially supported by NSF IIS-1065243, 1451412, 1513966/ 1632803/1833137, 1208500, CCF-1139148, a Google Research Award, an Alfred P. Sloan Research Fellowship, gifts from Facebook and Netflix, and ARO# W911NF-12-1-0241 and W911NF-15-1-0484.

References

1. Hendricks, L.A., Wang, O., Shechtman, E., Sivic, J., Darrell, T., Russell, B.: Localizing moments in video with natural language. In: ICCV, pp. 5804–5813 (2017)
2. Antol, S., et al.: Vqa: Visual question answering. In: ICCV, pp. 2425–2433 (2015)
3. Chao, W.L., Hu, H., Sha, F.: Being negative but constructively: lessons learnt from creating better visual question answering datasets. In: NAACL-HLT, pp. 431–441 (2018)
4. Chung, J., Gulcehre, C., Cho, K., Bengio, Y.: Empirical evaluation of gated recurrent neural networks on sequence modeling (2014). arXiv preprint arXiv:1412.3555
5. Collell, G., Moens, M.F.: Is an image worth more than a thousand words? on the fine-grain semantic differences between visual and linguistic representations. In: COLING, pp. 2807–2817 (2016)
6. Feichtenhofer, C., Pinz, A., Zisserman, A.: Convolutional two-stream network fusion for video action recognition. In: CVPR, pp. 1933–1941 (2016)
7. Frome, A., Corrado, G.S., Shlens, J., Bengio, S., Dean, J., Mikolov, T., et al.: Devise: a deep visual-semantic embedding model. In: NIPS, pp. 2121–2129 (2013)
8. He, K., Zhang, X., Ren, S., Sun, J.: Deep residual learning for image recognition. In: CVPR, pp. 770–778 (2016)
9. Heilbron, F.C., Escorcia, V., Ghanem, B., Niebles, J.C.: Activitynet: a large-scale video benchmark for human activity understanding. In: CVPR, pp. 961–970
10. Hochreiter, S., Schmidhuber, J.: Long short-term memory. Neural Comput. **9**(8), 1735–1780 (1997)
11. Hu, H., Chao, W.L., Sha, F.: Learning answer embeddings for visual question answering. In: CVPR, pp. 5428–5436 (2018)
12. Karpathy, A., Fei-Fei, L.: Deep visual-semantic alignments for generating image descriptions. In: CVPR, pp. 3128–3137 (2015)

13. Karpathy, A., Toderici, G., Shetty, S., Leung, T., Sukthankar, R., Fei-Fei, L.: Large-scale video classification with convolutional neural networks. In: CVPR, pp. 1725–1732 (2014)
14. Kay, W., Carreira, J., Simonyan, K., Zhang, B., Hillier, C., Vijayanarasimhan, S., Viola, F., Green, T., Back, T., Natsev, P., et al.: The kinetics human action video dataset (2017). arXiv preprint arXiv:1705.06950
15. Kiela, D., Bottou, L.: Learning Image Embeddings using Convolutional Neural Networks for Improved Multi-Modal Semantics. In: EMNLP, pp. 36–45 (2014)
16. Kiros, R., Salakhutdinov, R., Zemel, R.S.: Unifying visual-semantic embeddings with multimodal neural language models (2014). arXiv preprint arXiv:1411.2539
17. Krishna, R., Hata, K., Ren, F., Fei-Fei, L., Niebles, J.C.: Dense-captioning events in videos. In: ICCV, pp. 706–715 (2017)
18. Krizhevsky, A., Sutskever, I., Hinton, G.E.: Imagenet classification with deep convolutional neural networks. In: NIPS, pp. 1106–1114 (2012)
19. Li, J., Luong, M.T., Jurafsky, D.: A hierarchical neural autoencoder for paragraphs and documents. In: ACL, pp. 1106–1115 (2015)
20. Li, Y., Yao, T., Pan, Y., Chao, H., Mei, T.: Jointly localizing and describing events for dense video captioning. In: CVPR, pp. 7492–7500 (2018)
21. Lin, T.Y., et al.: Microsoft coco: Common objects in context. In: ECCV, pp. 740–755 (2014)
22. Luong, M.T., Pham, H., Manning, C.D.: Effective approaches to attention-based neural machine translation. In: EMNLP, pp. 1412–1421 (2015)
23. Maaten, L.V.D., Hinton, G.: Visualizing data using t-SNE. JMLR 9, 2579–2605 (2008)
24. Niu, Z., Zhou, M., Wang, L., Gao, X., Hua, G.: Hierarchical multimodal lstm for dense visual-semantic embedding. In: ICCV, pp. 1899–1907 (2017)
25. Pan, P., Xu, Z., Yang, Y., Wu, F., Zhuang, Y.: Hierarchical recurrent neural encoder for video representation with application to captioning. In: CVPR, pp. 1029–1038 (2016)
26. Pascanu, R., Mikolov, T., Bengio, Y.: On the difficulty of training recurrent neural networks. In: ICML, pp. 1310–1318 (2013)
27. Pennington, J., Socher, R., Manning, C.D.: Glove: Global vectors for word representation. In: EMNLP, pp. 1532–1543 (2014)
28. Qiu, Z., Yao, T., Mei, T.: Deep quantization: Encoding convolutional activations with deep generative model. In: CVPR, pp. 4085–4094 (2017)
29. Schroff, F., Kalenichenko, D., Philbin, J.: Facenet: A unified embedding for face recognition and clustering. In: CVPR, pp. 815–823 (2015)
30. Simonyan, K., Zisserman, A.: Two-stream convolutional networks for action recognition in videos. In: NIPS, pp. 568–576 (2014)
31. Soomro, K., Zamir, A.R., Shah, M.: UCF101: A dataset of 101 human actions classes from videos in the wild (2012). arXiv preprint arXiv:1212.0402
32. Sutskever, I., Vinyals, O., Le, Q.V.: Sequence to sequence learning with neural networks. In: NIPS, pp. 3104–3112 (2014)
33. Tran, D., Bourdev, L., Fergus, R., Torresani, L., Paluri, M.: Learning spatiotemporal features with 3D convolutional networks. In: ICCV, pp. 4489–4497 (2015)
34. Tsai, Y.H.H., Huang, L.K., Salakhutdinov, R.: Learning robust visual-semantic embeddings. In: ICCV, pp. 3591–3600 (2017)
35. Venugopalan, S., Rohrbach, M., Donahue, J., Mooney, R., Darrell, T., Saenko, K.: Sequence to sequence-video to text. In: ICCV, pp. 4534–4542 (2015)

36. Venugopalan, S., Xu, H., Donahue, J., Rohrbach, M., Mooney, R., Saenko, K.: Translating videos to natural language using deep recurrent neural networks. In: NAACL-HLT, pp. 1494–1504 (2015)
37. Vinyals, O., Toshev, A., Bengio, S., Erhan, D.: Show and tell: a neural image caption generator. In: CVPR, pp. 3156–3164 (2015)
38. Wang, L., et al.: Temporal segment networks: Towards good practices for deep action recognition. In: ECCV, pp. 20–36 (2016)
39. Wang, L., et al.: Temporal segment networks for action recognition in videos (2017). arXiv preprint arXiv:1705.02953
40. Wang, L., Li, Y., Lazebnik, S.: Learning deep structure-preserving image-text embeddings. In: CVPR, pp. 5005–5013 (2016)
41. Wu, C.Y., Zaheer, M., Hu, H., Manmatha, R., Smola, A.J., Krähenbühl, P.: Compressed video action recognition. In: CVPR (2018)
42. Xu, K., Ba, J., Kiros, R., Cho, K., Courville, A., Salakhudinov, R., Zemel, R., Bengio, Y.: Show, attend and tell: Neural image caption generation with visual attention. In: ICML, pp. 2048–2057 (2015)
43. Yu, H., Wang, J., Huang, Z., Yang, Y., Xu, W.: Video paragraph captioning using hierarchical recurrent neural networks. In: CVPR, pp. 4584–4593 (2016)
44. Zhang, B., Wang, L., Wang, Z., Qiao, Y., Wang, H.: Real-time action recognition with enhanced motion vector cnns. In: CVPR, pp. 2718–2726 (2016)
45. Zhang, K., Chao, W.L., Sha, F., Grauman, K.: Video summarization with long short-term memory. In: ECCV, pp. 766–782 (2016)
46. Zhao, Y., Xiong, Y., Wang, L., Wu, Z., Tang, X., Lin, D.: Temporal action detection with structured segment networks. In: ICCV, pp. 2933–2942 (2017)
47. Zhu, Y., Groth, O., Bernstein, M., Fei-Fei, L.: Visual7w: Grounded question answering in images. In: CVPR, pp. 4995–5004 (2016)

Tracking Emerges by Colorizing Videos

Carl Vondrick[(✉)], Abhinav Shrivastava, Alireza Fathi, Sergio Guadarrama,
and Kevin Murphy

Google Research, Mountain View, USA
vondrick@google.com

Abstract. We use large amounts of unlabeled video to learn models for
visual tracking without manual human supervision. We leverage the natural temporal coherency of color to create a model that learns to colorize
gray-scale videos by copying colors from a reference frame. Quantitative
and qualitative experiments suggest that this task causes the model to
automatically learn to track visual regions. Although the model is trained
without any ground-truth labels, our method learns to track well enough
to outperform the latest methods based on optical flow. Moreover, our
results suggest that failures to track are correlated with failures to colorize, indicating that advancing video colorization may further improve
self-supervised visual tracking.

Keywords: Colorization · Self-supervised learning · Tracking · Video

1 Introduction

Visual tracking is integral for video analysis tasks across recognition, geometry, and interaction. However, collecting the large-scale tracking datasets necessary for high performance often requires extensive effort that is impractical and
expensive. We believe a promising approach is to learn to track without human
supervision by instead leveraging large amounts of raw, unlabeled video.

We propose video colorization as a self-supervised learning problem for visual
tracking. However, instead of trying to predict the color directly from the gray-
scale frame, we constrain the colorization model to solve this task by learning to
copy colors from a reference frame. Although this may appear to be a roundabout
way to colorize video, it requires the model to learn to internally point to the
right region in order to copy the right colors. Once the model is trained, the
learned "pointing" mechanism acts as a tracker across time. Figure 1 illustrates
our problem setup.

Experiments and visualizations suggest that, although the network is trained
without ground-truth labels, a mechanism for tracking automatically emerges.
After training on unlabeled video collected from the web [1], the model is able to
track any segmented region specified in the first frame of a video [2]. It can also
track human pose given keypoints annotated in an initial frame [3]. While there
is still no substitute for cleanly labeled supervised data, our colorization model

© Springer Nature Switzerland AG 2018
V. Ferrari et al. (Eds.): ECCV 2018, LNCS 11217, pp. 402–419, 2018.
https://doi.org/10.1007/978-3-030-01261-8_24

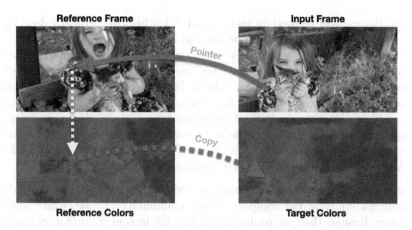

Fig. 1. Self-supervised Tracking: We capitalize on large amounts of unlabeled video to learn a self-supervised model for tracking. The model learns to predict the target colors for a gray-scale input frame by pointing to a colorful reference frame, and copying the color channels. Although we train without ground-truth labels, experiments and visualizations suggest that tracking emerges automatically in this model.

learns to track video segments and human pose well enough to outperform the latest methods based on optical flow. Breaking down performance by motion type suggests that the colorization model is more robust than optical flow for many natural complexities, such as dynamic backgrounds, fast motion, and occlusions.

A key feature of our model is that we do not require any labeled data during training. Our hypothesis, which our experiments support, is that learning to colorize video will cause a tracker to internally emerge, which we can directly apply to downstream tracking tasks without additional training nor fine-tuning. Moreover, we found that the failures from our tracker are often correlated with failures to colorize the video, which suggests that further improving our video colorization model can advance progress in self-supervised tracking.

The main contribution of this paper is to show that learning to colorize video causes tracking to emerge. The remainder of this paper describes this contribution in detail. In Sect. 2, we first review related work in self-supervised learning and tracking. In Sect. 3, we present our approach to use video colorization as a supervisory signal for learning to track. By equipping the model with a pointing mechanism into a reference frame, we learn an explicit representation that we can use for new tracking tasks without further training. In Sect. 4, we show several experiments to analyze our method. Since annotating videos is expensive and tracking has many applications in robotics and graphics, we believe learning to track with self-supervision can have a large impact.

2   Related Work

Self-supervised Learning: Our paper builds upon a growing body of work to train visual models without human supervision. A common approach is to leverage the natural context in images and video in order to learn deep visual representations [4–16], which can be used as a feature space for training classifiers for down-stream tasks, such as object detection. Other approaches include interaction with an environment to learn visual features [17–19], which is useful for applications in robotics. A related but different line of work explores how to learn geometric properties or cycle consistencies with self-supervision, for example for motion capture or correspondence [20–24]. We also develop a self-supervised model, but our approach focuses on visual tracking in video for segmentation and human pose. Moreover, our method is trained directly on natural data without the use of computer generated graphics [22,23].

Colorization: The task of colorizing gray-scale images has been the subject of significant study in the computer vision community [25–34], which inspired this paper. Besides the core problem of colorizing images, colorization has been shown to be a useful side task to learn representations for images without supervision [9,10]. The task of colorization also been explored in the video domain [35,36] where methods can explicitly incorporate optical flow to provide temporal coherency or learn to propagate color [37]. In this paper, we do not enforce temporal coherency; we instead leverage it to use video colorization as a proxy task for learning to track.

Video Segmentation: One task that we use our tracker for is video segmentation where the task is to densely label object instances in the video. Methods for video segmentation are varied, but can generally be classified into whether they start with an object of interest [38–41] or not [42–45]. The task is challenging, and state-of-the-art approaches typically use a large amount of supervision to achieve the best results [46–48], such as from ImageNet [49], MS-COCO [50], and DAVIS [2]. We instead learn to track from just unlabeled video.

Tracking without Labels: We build off pioneering work for learning to segment videos without labels [51–53]. However, rather than designing a tracking objective function by hand, we show that there is a self-supervised learning problem that causes the model to automatically learn tracking on its own. Consequently, our model is a *generic tracking method* that is applicable to multiple video analysis problems and not limited to just video segmentation. The same trained model can track segments, track key points, colorize video, and transfer any other annotation from the first frame to the rest of the video, without any fine-tuning or re-training. To highlight that our tracker is generic, we show results for three materially different tracking tasks (colorization, video segmentation, keypoint tracking). Moreover, our approach is fast, tracks multiple objects, and does not require training on the testing frames, making our approach fairly practical for large-scale video analysis tasks.

Note on Terminology: There is some disagreement in the tracking literature on terms, and we wish to clarify our nomenclature. In tracking, there are two common tasks. In task A, we are given the labels for the first frame. In task B, we are not given a labeled initial frame. The literature typically calls task A "semi-supervised" and task B "unsupervised" referring to whether the initial

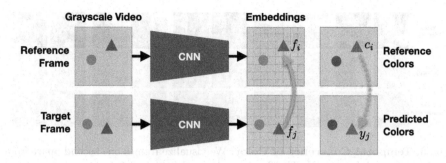

Fig. 2. Model Overview: Given gray-scale frames, the model computes low-dimensional embeddings for each location with a CNN. Using softmax similarity, the model points from the target frame into the reference frame embeddings (solid yellow arrow). The model then copies the color back into the predicted frame (dashed yellow arrow). After learning, we use the pointing mechanism as a visual tracker. Note that the model's pointer is soft, but for illustrations purposes we draw it as a single arrow.

frame is labeled or not. The confusing terminology is that, in both cases, you are allowed to train with supervised data, even for the unsupervised task. In this paper, our goal is to *learn only from unlabeled video*. At test time, we tackle task A, which specifies the region of interest to track. However, we call our method unsupervised because we do not learn with any labeled data.

3   Self-supervised Tracking

We first describe how to train our model for video colorization, then discuss how to use it for tracking. See Fig. 2 for a high level illustration of our model.

3.1   Model

Let $c_i \in \mathbb{R}^d$ be the true color for pixel i in the reference frame, and let $c_j \in \mathbb{R}^d$ be the true color for a pixel j in the target frame. We denote $y_j \in \mathbb{R}^d$ as the model's prediction for c_j. The model predicts y_j as a linear combination of colors in the reference frame:

$$y_j = \sum_i A_{ij} c_i \tag{1}$$

where A is a similarity matrix between the target and reference frame such that the rows sum to one. Several similarity metrics are possible. We use inner product similarity normalized by softmax:

$$A_{ij} = \frac{\exp\left(f_i^T f_j\right)}{\sum_k \exp\left(f_k^T f_j\right)} \tag{2}$$

Fig. 3. Temporal Coherence of Color: We visualize frames one second apart from the Kinetics training set [1]. The first row shows the original frames, and the second row shows the *ab* color channels from *Lab* space. The third row quantizes the color space into discrete bins and perturbs the colors to make the effect more pronounced. Unlabeled video from the web often has temporally coherent color, which provides excellent, large-scale training data for learning visual trackers. The last column shows an exception where a green light is turned on. Figure best viewed in color. (Color figure online)

where $f_i \in \mathbb{R}^D$ is a low-dimensional embedding for pixel i that is estimated by a convolutional neural network. Since we are computing distances between all pairs, the similarity matrix is potentially large. However, because color is fairly low spatial frequency, we can operate with lower resolution video frames allowing us to calculate and store all pairs on commodity hardware.

Similarity in color space does not imply that the embeddings are similar. Due to the softmax, the model only needs to point to one reference pixel in order to copy a color. Consequently, if there are two objects with the same color, the model does not constrain them to have the same embedding. This property enables the model to track multiple objects of the same color (which experiments show happens).

Our model uses a pointing mechanism similar to attention networks [54], matching networks [55], and pointer networks [56]. However, our approach is unsupervised and we train the model for the purpose of using the underlying pointer mechanism as a visual tracker. Our model points within a single training example rather than across training examples.

3.2   Learning

Our approach leverages the assumption during training that color is generally temporally stable. Clearly, there are exceptions, for example colorful lights can turn on and off. However, in practice, unlabeled video from the public web often has temporally stable color, which provides excellent, large-scale training data for learning to track. Figure 3 visualizes the coherency of color from a few videos on the Kinetics video dataset [1].

We use a large dataset of unlabeled videos for learning. We train the parameters of the model θ such that the predicted colors y_j are close to the target colors c_j across the training set:

$$\min_{\theta} \sum_{j} \mathcal{L}\left(y_j, c_j\right) \tag{3}$$

where $\mathcal{L}$ is the loss function. Since video colorization is a multi-modal problem [30], we use the cross-entropy categorical loss after quantizing the color-space into discrete categories. We quantize by clustering the color channels across our dataset using k-means (we use 16 clusters). We optimize Eq. 3 using stochastic gradient descent.

3.3   Inference

After learning, we have a model that can compute a similarity matrix A for a pair of target and reference frames. Given an initially labeled frame from a held-out video, we use this pointer to propagate labels throughout the video. To do this, we exploit the property that our model is non-parametric in the label space. We simply re-use Eq. 1 to propagate, but instead of propagating colors, we propagate distributions of categories. Since the rows of A sum to one, Eq. 1 can be interpreted as a mixture model where A is the mixing coefficients. We will describe how to use this model for two different types of tasks: segment tracking and key-point tracking.

Segment Tracking: To track segments, we re-interpret $c_i \in \mathbb{R}^d$ as a vector indicating probabilities for d categories. Note d can change between learning/inference. In segmentation, the categories correspond to instances. We treat the background as just another category. The initial frame labels c_i will be one-hot vectors (since we know the ground truth for the first frame), but the predictions c_j in subsequent frames will be soft, indicating the confidence of the model. To make a hard decision, we can simply take the most confident category.

Keypoints Tracking: Unlike colors and segmentation, keypoints are often sparse, but our model can still track them. We convert keypoints into a dense representation where $c_i \in \mathbb{R}^d$ is a binary vector indicating whether a keypoint is located at pixel i, if any. In this case, d corresponds to the number of keypoints in the initial frame. We then proceed as we did in the segmentation case.

Adjusting Temperature: Eq. 1 predicts a target label with a weighted average of all the labels in the reference frame. If the pointer is not confident, this can lead to blurry predictions over time, an effect also reported by [30]. To compensate for this, we can adjust the "temperature" of the softmax so that it makes more confident predictions. We simply divide the pre-softmax activations by a constant temperature T during inference. Setting $T = 1$ leaves the softmax distribution unchanged from training. We found $T = 0.5$ works well for inference.

Variable Length Videos: During inference, we will be required to process long videos. We adopt a recursive approach in which we always propagate the labels given a window of previous N frames (we use $N = 3$). Initially the window will contain the ground truth; later it will contain the model's predictions.

Reference Frame   Future Frame (gray)   Predicted Color   True Color

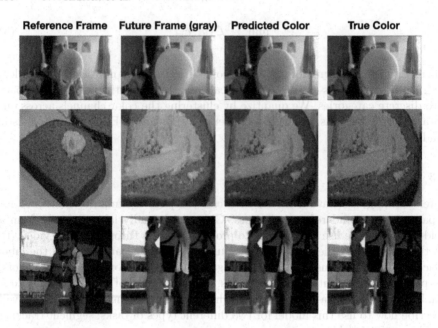

Fig. 4. Video Colorization: We show video colorization results given a colorful reference frame. Our model learns to copy colors over many challenging transformations, such as butter spreading or people dancing. Best viewed in color. (Color figure online)

3.4   Implementation Details

We use a 3D convolutional network to produce 64-dimensional embeddings. For efficiency, the network predicts a down-sampled feature map of 32×32 for each of the input frames. We use a ResNet-18 network architecture [57] on each input frame, followed by a five layer 3D convolutional network. Note that to give the features global spatial information, we encode the spatial location as a two-dimensional vector in the range $[-1, 1]$ and concatenate this to the features between the ResNet-18 and the 3D convolutional network.

The inputs to the model are four gray-scale video frames down-sampled to 256×256. We use the first three frames as reference frames, and the fourth frame as the target frame. The model pulls colors/labels from all three reference frames. We pre-process the inputs to the network by scaling the intensities to be in the range $[-1, 1]$, which is naturally near zero mean. We use a frame rate of 6 frames-per-second in learning and the full frame rate in inference. To quantize the color space, we convert the videos in the training set into Lab space, take the ab color channels, and cluster them with k-means. We represent the color of each pixel as a one-hot vector corresponding to the nearest cluster centroid.

We train our model for 400,000 iterations. We use a batch size of 32, and the Adam optimizer [58]. We use a learning rate of 0.001 for the first 60,000 iterations and reduce it to 0.0001 afterwards. The model is randomly initialized with Gaussian noise. Please see Appendix ?? for more implementation details including network architecture.

4   Experiments

The goal of our experiments to analyze how well a tracker can automatically emerge from our video colorization task. We first describe our experimental setup and baselines, then show two applications on video segmentation and human pose tracking. Finally, we visualize the embeddings learned by the model and analyze how to improve the tracker further.

4.1   Experimental Setup

We train our model on the training set from Kinetics [1]. Since our model learns from unlabeled video, we discard the labels. The Kinetics dataset is a large, diverse collection of 300, 000 videos from YouTube. We evaluate the model on the standard testing sets of other datasets depending on the task. Since we are analyzing how well trackers emerge from video colorization, we compare against the following unsupervised baselines:

Identity: Since we are given labels for the initial testing frame, we have a baseline that assumes the video is static and repeats the initial label.

Optical Flow: We use state-of-the-art methods in optical flow as a baseline. We experimented with two approaches. Firstly, we tried a classical optical flow implementation that is unsupervised and not learning based [59]. Secondly, we also use a learning based approach that learns from synthetic data [23]. In both cases, we estimate between frames and warp the initial labels to produce the predicted labels. We label a pixel as belonging to a category if the warped score is above a threshold. We experimented with several thresholds, and use the threshold that performs the best. We explored both recursive and non-recursive strategies, and report the strategy that works the best. Unless otherwise stated, we use the best performing optical flow based off FlowNet2 [23].

Single Image Colorization: We evaluated how well computing similarity from the embeddings of a single image colorization model [30] work instead of our embeddings. Note this task is not designed nor originally intended for tracking by the authors. However, it allows us to quantify the difference between video and image colorization. To make this baseline, we train our model with the image colorization loss of [30]. We then follow the same tracking procedure, except using the features from the penultimate layer of the single image model for calculating similarity.

Supervised Models: To analyze the gap between our self-supervised model and fully supervised approaches, we also consider the best available supervised approaches [46,47]. Note that these methods train on ImageNet, COCO segmentations, DAVIS, and even fine tune on the first frame of the test set.

4.2   Video Colorization

Figure 4 shows example video colorization results given a reference frame, which is the task the model is originally trained on. We use the Kinetics validation set (not seen during training). The model learns to copy colors even across many challenging transformations, for example butter spreading on toast and people deforming as they dance. Since the model must copy colors from the reference frame, this suggests that the model may be robust to many difficult tracking situations. The rest of the section analyzes this tracking mechanism.

4.3   Video Segmentation

We analyze our model on video segmentation with the DAVIS 2017 validation set [2] where the initial segmentation mask is given and the task is to predict the segmentation in the rest of the video. We follow the standard evaluation protocol using the validation set with the provided code and report two metrics that score segment overlap and boundary accuracy. The videos in DAVIS 2017 are challenging and consist of multiple objects that undergo significant deformation, occlusion, and scale change with cluttered backgrounds.

Table 1 shows the performance on video segmentation. Our approach outperforms multiple methods in optical flow estimation. While the estimation of optical flow is often quite strong, warping the previous segment is challenging due to occlusion and motion blur. In contrast, our approach may excel because it also learns the warping mechanism end-to-end on video that contains an abundance of these challenging effects.

We analyze how performance varies with the length of the video in Fig. 5. Our approach maintains consistent performance for longer time periods than optical flow. While optical flow works well in short time intervals, errors tend to accumulate over time. Our approach also has drift, but empirically colorization

Table 1. Video Segmentation Results. We show performance on the DAVIS 2017 validation set for video segmentation. Higher numbers (which represent mean overlap) are better. We compare against several baselines that do not use any labeled data during learning. Interestingly, our model learns a strong enough tracker to outperform optical flow based methods, suggesting that the model is learning useful motion and instance features. However, we still cannot yet match heavily supervised training.

Method	Supervised?	Segment	Boundary
Identity		22.1	23.6
Single Image Colorization		4.7	5.2
Optical Flow (Coarse-to-Fine) [59]		13.0	15.1
Optical Flow (FlowNet2) [23]		26.7	25.2
Ours		34.6	32.7
Fully Supervised [46, 47]	✓	55.1	62.1

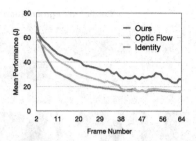

Fig. 5. Performance vs. Time: We plot video segmentation average performance versus time in the video. Our approach (red) maintains more consistent performance for longer time periods than optical flow (orange). For long videos, optical flow on average degrades to the identity baseline. Since videos are variable length, we plot up to the median video length.

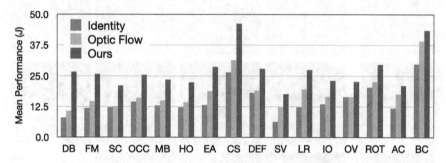

Fig. 6. Performance by Attribute: We show the average performance broken down by attributes that describe the type of motion in the video. The attributes come from Table 1 of [60]. We sort the attributes by relative gain over optical flow.

appears to learn more robust models. For long videos, optical flow based tracking eventually degrades to the identity baseline while ours remain relatively stronger for longer. The identity baseline, as expected, has a quick fall off as objects begin to move and deform.

We breakdown performance by video attributes in Fig. 6. Our model tends to excel over optical flow for videos that have dynamic backgrounds (DB) and fast motion (FM), which are traditionally challenging situations for optical flow. Since our approach is trained end-to-end on videos that also have these artifacts, this suggests the model may be learning to handle the effects internally. Our model also shows strengths at cases involving occlusion (OCC) and motion blur (MB), which are difficult for optical flow because matching key-points is difficult under these conditions. Since color is low-frequency, it is not as affected by blur and occlusion during training. The most challenging situations for both our model and optical flow are due to scale variation (SV).

To get a sense of the predicted segmentations, Fig. 7 shows a few example videos and the predicted segmentations from our method. Our model can suc-

Inputs   **Predicted Segmentations**

Time ──▶

Fig. 7. Example Video Segmentations: We show results from our self-supervised model on the task of video segmentation. Colors indicate different instances. Although the model is trained without ground truth labels, the model can still propagate segmentations throughout videos. The left column shows the input frame and input masks to the model, and the rest show the predictions. Results suggest that the model is generally robust to intra-class variations, such as deformations, and occlusions. The model often handles multiple objects and cluttered backgrounds. Best viewed in color. We provide videos of results online at https://goo.gl/qjHyPK (Color figure online)

Table 2. Human Pose Tracking (no supervision): We show performance on the JHMDB validation set for tracking human pose. PCK@X is the Probability of Correct Keypoint at a threshold of X (higher numbers are better). At a strict threshold, our model tracks key-points with a similar performance as optical flow, suggesting that it is learning some motion features. At relaxed thresholds, our approach outperforms optical flow based methods, suggesting the errors caused by our model are less severe.

Method	PCK@.1	PCK@.2	PCK@.3	PCK@.4	PCK@.5
Identity	43.1	64.5	76.0	83.5	88.5
Optical Flow (FlowNet2) [23]	45.2	62.9	73.5	80.6	85.5
Ours	45.2	69.6	80.8	87.5	91.4

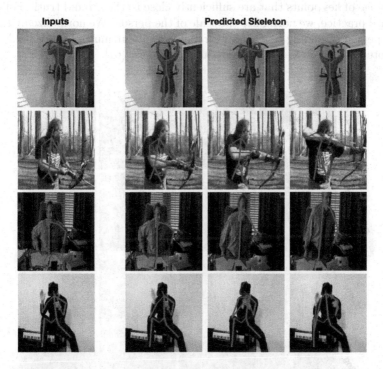

Fig. 8. Human Pose Tracking: We show results from our self-supervised model for tracking human pose key-points. Although the model is trained without ground truth labels, the model can propagate skeletons labeled in the first frame throughout the rest of the video. Best viewed in color. (Color figure online)

cessfully track multiple instances throughout the video, even when the objects are spatially near and have similar colors, for example the scene where multiple people are wearing similar white coats (third row). To quantify this, we analyze performance only on the videos with multiple objects (ranging from two to five objects). Under this condition, our model scores 31.0 on segment overlap (J) versus 19.1 for the optical flow based approach, suggesting our method still obtains strong performance with multiple objects. Finally, our model shows robustness to large deformations (second row) as well as large occlusions (second to last row). Typical failures include small objects and lack of fine-grained details.

4.4 Pose Tracking

We experiment on human pose tracking with the JHMDB dataset [3]. During testing, we are given an initial frame labeled with human keypoints and the task is to predict the keypoints in the subsequent frames. This task is challenging because it requires fine-grained localization of keypoints when people undergo deformation. We use the standard PCK metric from [61] which measures the percentage of keypoints that are sufficiently close to the ground truth. Following standard practice, we normalize the scale of the person. We normalize by the size of the person bounding box, and we report results at multiple threshold values X denoted as PCK@X. For more details, please see [61].

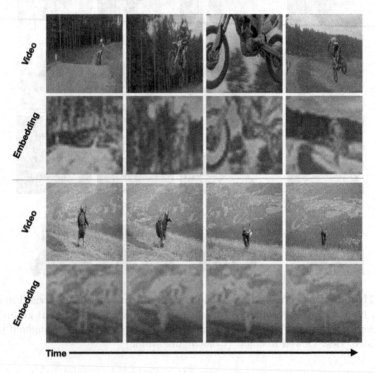

Fig. 9. Visualizing the Learned Embedding: We project the embeddings into 3 dimensions using PCA and visualize it as an RGB image. Similar colors illustrate the similarity in embedding space. Notice that the learned embeddings are stable over time even with significant deformation and viewpoint change. Best viewed in color. (Color figure online)

Fig. 10. Colorization vs. Tracking: We show a few failures case where we do not correctly track the object, and the model also fails to propagate the colors (red arrows). This suggest that improving video colorization may translate into further improvements for self-supervised visual trackers. Best viewed in color. (Color figure online)

Table 2 shows the performance of our tracker versus baselines for tracking human pose given an initially labeled frame. At the most strict evaluation threshold, our model obtains similar performance to optical flow, suggesting that our model may be learning some motion features. At more relaxed thresholds, our model outperforms optical flow. This shows that the errors from optical flow tend to be more extreme than the errors from our tracker, even when the localization is not perfect. Moreover, the optical flow method is trained on large amounts of synthetic data, while our approach only requires video that is naturally available.

Figure 8 shows qualitative results from our model on tracking human keypoints. The model often can track large motions fairly well, such as the second and third row. Typical failures from the model are due to occlusion since a keypoint cannot be recovered once it disappears from the frame.

4.5 Analysis of the Model and Its Failure Modes

Since our model is trained on large amounts of unlabeled video, we are interested in gaining insight into what the model internally learns. Figure 9 visualizes the embeddings f_i learned by our model by projecting them down to three dimensions using PCA and plotting it as an RGB image. The results show that nearest neighbors in the learned embedding space tend to correspond to object instances, even over significant deformations and viewpoint changes.

While our experiments show that these embeddings are useful for tracking, there are still failures. For example, Fig. 10 shows predicted segmentations from our tracker and the corresponding predicted colors. Moreover, we find that many of the failures to track are also failures to colorize. To quantify this correlation, if any, we use the odds ratio between the two events of tracker failure and colorization failure. If the events are independent, we expect the odds ratio to be 1. However, the odds ratio is 2.3, suggesting moderate association. This suggests that there is still "juice" left in the video colorization signal for learning to track. We expect that building more accurate models for video colorization will translate into tracking improvements.

5   Conclusion

This paper shows that the task of video colorization is a promising signal for learning to track without requiring human supervision. Our experiments show that learning to colorize video by pointing to a colorful reference frame causes a visual tracker to automatically emerge, which we leverage for video segmentation and human pose tracking. Moreover, our results suggest that improving the video colorization task may translate into improvements in self-supervised tracking. Since there is an abundance of unlabeled video in full color, video colorization appears to be a powerful signal for self-supervised learning of video models.

References

1. Kay, W., et al.: The kinetics human action video dataset (2017). arXiv preprint arXiv:1705.06950
2. Pont-Tuset, J., Caelles, S., Perazzi, F., Montes, A., Maninis, K.K., Chen, Y., Van Gool, L.: The 2017 davis challenge on video object segmentation (2017). arXiv preprint arXiv:1803.00557
3. Jhuang, H., Gall, J., Zuffi, S., Schmid, C., Black, M.J.: Towards understanding action recognition. In: International Conference on Computer Vision (ICCV), pp. 3192–3199, December 2013
4. Doersch, C., Gupta, A., Efros, A.A.: Unsupervised visual representation learning by context prediction. In: Proceedings of the IEEE International Conference on Computer Vision, pp. 1422–1430 (2015)
5. Owens, A., Wu, J., McDermott, J.H., Freeman, W.T., Torralba, A.: Ambient sound provides supervision for visual learning. In: Leibe, B., Matas, J., Sebe, N., Welling, M. (eds.) ECCV 2016. LNCS, vol. 9905, pp. 801–816. Springer, Cham (2016). https://doi.org/10.1007/978-3-319-46448-0_48
6. Jayaraman, D., Grauman, K.: Learning image representations tied to ego-motion. In: Proceedings of the IEEE International Conference on Computer Vision, pp. 1413–1421 (2015)
7. Doersch, C., Zisserman, A.: Multi-task self-supervised visual learning. In: The IEEE International Conference on Computer Vision (ICCV) (2017)
8. Wang, X., He, K., Gupta, A.: Transitive invariance for self-supervised visual representation learning (2017). arXiv preprint arXiv:1708.02901
9. Zhang, R., Isola, P., Efros, A.A.: Split-brain autoencoders: Unsupervised learning by cross-channel prediction. In: CVPR, vol. 1, no. 2, p. 5 (2017)
10. Larsson, G., Maire, M., Shakhnarovich, G.: Colorization as a proxy task for visual understanding. In: CVPR. Vol. 2, August 2017
11. Pathak, D., Krahenbuhl, P., Donahue, J., Darrell, T., Efros, A.A.: Context encoders: Feature learning by inpainting. In: Proceedings of the IEEE Conference on Computer Vision and Pattern Recognition, pp. 2536–2544 (2016)
12. Wang, X., Gupta, A.: Unsupervised learning of visual representations using videos (2015). arXiv preprint arXiv:1505.00687

13. Vondrick, C., Pirsiavash, H., Torralba, A.: Generating videos with scene dynamics. In: Advances In Neural Information Processing Systems, pp. 613–621 (2016)
14. Noroozi, M., Favaro, P.: Unsupervised learning of visual representations by solving jigsaw puzzles. In: Leibe, B., Matas, J., Sebe, N., Welling, M. (eds.) ECCV 2016. LNCS, vol. 9910, pp. 69–84. Springer, Cham (2016). https://doi.org/10.1007/978-3-319-46466-4_5
15. Pathak, D., Girshick, R., Dollár, P., Darrell, T., Hariharan, B.: Learning features by watching objects move. In: CVPR, vol. 1, no. 2, p. 7 (2017)
16. Isola, P., Zhu, J.Y., Zhou, T., Efros, A.A.: Image-to-image translation with conditional adversarial networks (2017). arXiv preprint
17. Pinto, L., Gandhi, D., Han, Y., Park, Y.-L., Gupta, A.: The curious robot: learning visual representations via physical interactions. In: Leibe, B., Matas, J., Sebe, N., Welling, M. (eds.) ECCV 2016. LNCS, vol. 9906, pp. 3–18. Springer, Cham (2016). https://doi.org/10.1007/978-3-319-46475-6_1
18. Agrawal, P., Nair, A.V., Abbeel, P., Malik, J., Levine, S.: Learning to poke by poking: experiential learning of intuitive physics. In: Advances in Neural Information Processing Systems, pp. 5074–5082 (2016)
19. Wu, J., Lim, J.J., Zhang, H., Tenenbaum, J.B., Freeman, W.T.: Physics 101: Learning physical object properties from unlabeled videos. In: BMVC, Vol. 2, p. 7 (2016)
20. Tung, H.Y., Tung, H.W., Yumer, E., Fragkiadaki, K.: Self-supervised learning of motion capture. In: Advances in Neural Information Processing Systems, pp. 5242–5252 (2017)
21. Zhou, T., Brown, M., Snavely, N., Lowe, D.G.: Unsupervised learning of depth and ego-motion from video. In: CVPR. vol. 2, p. 7 (2017)
22. Zhou, T., Krahenbuhl, P., Aubry, M., Huang, Q., Efros, A.A.: Learning dense correspondence via 3d-guided cycle consistency. In: Proceedings of the IEEE Conference on Computer Vision and Pattern Recognition, pp. 117–126 (2016)
23. Ilg, E., Mayer, N., Saikia, T., Keuper, M., Dosovitskiy, A., Brox, T.: Flownet 2.0: evolution of optical flow estimation with deep networks. In: IEEE Conference on Computer Vision and Pattern Recognition (CVPR), vol. 2 (2017)
24. Zhou, T., Tulsiani, S., Sun, W., Malik, J., Efros, A.A.: View synthesis by appearance flow. In: Leibe, B., Matas, J., Sebe, N., Welling, M. (eds.) ECCV 2016. LNCS, vol. 9908, pp. 286–301. Springer, Cham (2016). https://doi.org/10.1007/978-3-319-46493-0_18
25. Welsh, T., Ashikhmin, M., Mueller, K.: Transferring color to greyscale images. In: ACM Transactions on Graphics (TOG). vol. 21, pp. 277–280. ACM (2002)
26. Gupta, R.K., Chia, A.Y.S., Rajan, D., Ng, E.S., Zhiyong, H.: Image colorization using similar images. In: Proceedings of the 20th ACM International Conference on Multimedia, pp. 369–378 ACM (2012)
27. Liu, X., Wan, L., Qu, Y., Wong, T.T., Lin, S., Leung, C.S., Heng, P.A.: Intrinsic colorization. In: ACM Transactions on Graphics (TOG). vol. 27, pp. 152 ACM (2008)
28. Chia, A.Y.S., Zhuo, S., Gupta, R.K., Tai, Y.W., Cho, S.Y., Tan, P., Lin, S.: Semantic colorization with internet images. In: ACM Transactions on Graphics (TOG). vol. 30, p. 156 ACM (2011)
29. Deshpande, A., Rock, J., Forsyth, D.: Learning large-scale automatic image colorization. In: Proceedings of the IEEE International Conference on Computer Vision, pp. 567–575 (2015)
30. Zhang, R., Isola, P., Efros, A.A.: Colorful image colorization. In: Leibe, B., Matas, J., Sebe, N., Welling, M. (eds.) ECCV 2016. LNCS, vol. 9907, pp. 649–666. Springer, Cham (2016). https://doi.org/10.1007/978-3-319-46487-9_40

31. Larsson, G., Maire, M., Shakhnarovich, G.: Learning representations for automatic colorization. In: Leibe, B., Matas, J., Sebe, N., Welling, M. (eds.) ECCV 2016. LNCS, vol. 9908, pp. 577–593. Springer, Cham (2016). https://doi.org/10.1007/978-3-319-46493-0_35

32. Guadarrama, S., Dahl, R., Bieber, D., Norouzi, M., Shlens, J., Murphy, K.: Pixcolor: Pixel recursive colorization (2017). arXiv preprint arXiv:1705.07208

33. Iizuka, S., Simo-Serra, E., Ishikawa, H.: Let there be color!: joint end-to-end learning of global and local image priors for automatic image colorization with simultaneous classification. ACM Trans. Graph. (TOG) **35**(4), 110 (2016)

34. Ironi, R., Cohen-Or, D., Lischinski, D.: Colorization by example. In: Rendering Techniques. Citeseer, pp. 201–210 (2005)

35. Yatziv, L., Sapiro, G.: Fast image and video colorization using chrominance blending. IEEE Trans. Image Process. **15**(5), 1120–1129 (2006)

36. Heu, J.H., Hyun, D.Y., Kim, C.S., Lee, S.U.: Image and video colorization based on prioritized source propagation. In: 16th IEEE International Conference on Image Processing (ICIP), pp. 465–468. IEEE (2009)

37. Liu, S., Zhong, G., De Mello, S., Gu, J., Yang, M.H., Kautz, J.: Switchable temporal propagation network (2018). arXiv preprint arXiv:1804.08758

38. Badrinarayanan, V., Galasso, F., Cipolla, R.: Label propagation in video sequences. In: IEEE Conference on Computer Vision and Pattern Recognition (CVPR), pp. 3265–3272. IEEE (2010)

39. Ramakanth, S.A., Babu, R.V.: Seamseg: video object segmentation using patch seams. In: CVPR, vol. 2 (2014)

40. Vijayanarasimhan, S., Grauman, K.: Active frame selection for label propagation in videos. In: Fitzgibbon, A., Lazebnik, S., Perona, P., Sato, Y., Schmid, C. (eds.) ECCV 2012. LNCS, vol. 7576, pp. 496–509. Springer, Heidelberg (2012). https://doi.org/10.1007/978-3-642-33715-4_36

41. Perazzi, F., Wang, O., Gross, M., Sorkine-Hornung, A.: Fully connected object proposals for video segmentation. In: Proceedings of the IEEE International Conference on Computer Vision, pp. 3227–3234 (2015)

42. Grundmann, M., Kwatra, V., Han, M., Essa, I.: Efficient hierarchical graph-based video segmentation. In: IEEE Conference on Computer Vision and Pattern Recognition (CVPR), pp. 2141–2148. IEEE (2010)

43. Xu, C., Corso, J.J.: Evaluation of super-voxel methods for early video processing. In: IEEE Conference on Computer Vision and Pattern Recognition (CVPR), pp. 1202–1209. IEEE (2012)

44. Brox, T., Malik, J.: Object segmentation by long term analysis of point trajectories. In: Daniilidis, K., Maragos, P., Paragios, N. (eds.) ECCV 2010. LNCS, vol. 6315, pp. 282–295. Springer, Heidelberg (2010). https://doi.org/10.1007/978-3-642-15555-0_21

45. Fragkiadaki, K., Zhang, G., Shi, J.: Video segmentation by tracing discontinuities in a trajectory embedding. In: IEEE Conference on Computer Vision and Pattern Recognition (CVPR), pp. 1846–1853. IEEE (2012)

46. Yang, L., Wang, Y., Xiong, X., Yang, J., Katsaggelos, A.K.: Efficient video object segmentation via network modulation (2018). arXiv preprint arXiv:1802.01218

47. Caelles, S., Maninis, K.K., Pont-Tuset, J., Leal-Taixé, L., Cremers, D., Van Gool, L.: One-shot video object segmentation. In: CVPR 2017. IEEE (2017)

48. Perazzi, F., Khoreva, A., Benenson, R., Schiele, B., Sorkine-Hornung, A.: Learning video object segmentation from static images. In: Computer Vision and Pattern Recognition, vol. 2, no. 7 (2017)

49. Deng, J., Dong, W., Socher, R., Li, L.J., Li, K., Fei-Fei, L.: Imagenet: a large-scale hierarchical image database. In: IEEE Conference on Computer Vision and Pattern Recognition, CVPR 2009, pp. 248–255. IEEE (2009)

50. Lin, T.-Y., Maire, M., Belongie, S., Hays, J., Perona, P., Ramanan, D., Dollár, P., Zitnick, C.L.: Microsoft COCO: common objects in context. In: Fleet, D., Pajdla, T., Schiele, B., Tuytelaars, T. (eds.) ECCV 2014. LNCS, vol. 8693, pp. 740–755. Springer, Cham (2014). https://doi.org/10.1007/978-3-319-10602-1_48

51. Faktor, A., Irani, M.: Video segmentation by non-local consensus voting. In: BMVC, vol. 2, August 2014

52. Märki, N., Perazzi, F., Wang, O., Sorkine-Hornung, A.: Bilateral space video segmentation. In: Proceedings of the IEEE Conference on Computer Vision and Pattern Recognition, pp. 743–751 (2016)

53. Khoreva, A., Benenson, R., Ilg, E., Brox, T., Schiele, B.: Lucid data dreaming for multiple object tracking (2017). arXiv preprint arXiv:1703.09554

54. Bahdanau, D., Cho, K., Bengio, Y.: Neural machine translation by jointly learning to align and translate (2014). arXiv preprint arXiv:1409.0473

55. Vinyals, O., Blundell, C., Lillicrap, T., Wierstra, D., et al.: Matching networks for one shot learning. In: Advances in Neural Information Processing Systems, pp. 3630–3638 (2016)

56. Vinyals, O., Fortunato, M., Jaitly, N.: Pointer networks. In: Advances in Neural Information Processing Systems, pp. 2692–2700 (2015)

57. He, K., Zhang, X., Ren, S., Sun, J.: Deep residual learning for image recognition. In: Proceedings of the IEEE Conference on Computer Vision and Pattern Recognition, pp. 770–778 (2016)

58. Kingma, D.P., Ba, J.: Adam: A method for stochastic optimization (2014). arXiv preprint arXiv:1412.6980

59. Liu, C., et al.: Beyond pixels: exploring new representations and applications for motion analysis. PhD thesis, Massachusetts Institute of Technology (2009)

60. Perazzi, F., Pont-Tuset, J., McWilliams, B., Van Gool, L., Gross, M., Sorkine-Hornung, A.: A benchmark dataset and evaluation methodology for video object segmentation. In: Proceedings of the IEEE Conference on Computer Vision and Pattern Recognition, pp. 724–732 (2016)

61. Yang, Y., Ramanan, D.: Articulated human detection with flexible mixtures of parts. IEEE Trans. Pattern Anal. Mach. Intell. 35(12), 2878–2890 (2013)

SkipNet: Learning Dynamic Routing in Convolutional Networks

Xin Wang[1(✉)], Fisher Yu[1], Zi-Yi Dou[2], Trevor Darrell[1],
and Joseph E. Gonzalez[1]

[1] University of California, Berkeley, USA
xinw@berkeley.edu
[2] Nanjing University, Nanjing, China

Abstract. While deeper convolutional networks are needed to achieve maximum accuracy in visual perception tasks, for many inputs shallower networks are sufficient. We exploit this observation by learning to skip convolutional layers on a per-input basis. We introduce SkipNet, a modified residual network, that uses a gating network to selectively skip convolutional blocks based on the activations of the previous layer. We formulate the dynamic skipping problem in the context of sequential decision making and propose a hybrid learning algorithm that combines supervised learning and reinforcement learning to address the challenges of non-differentiable skipping decisions. We show SkipNet reduces computation by $30-90\%$ while preserving the accuracy of the original model on four benchmark datasets and outperforms the state-of-the-art dynamic networks and static compression methods. We also qualitatively evaluate the gating policy to reveal a relationship between image scale and saliency and the number of layers skipped.

1 Introduction

A growing body of research in convolutional network design [10,18,28] reveals a clear trend: *deeper networks are more accurate*. Consequently, the best-performing image recognition networks have hundreds of layers and tens of millions of parameters. These very deep networks come at the expense of increased prediction cost and latency. However, a network that doubles in depth may only improve prediction accuracy by a few percentage points. While these small improvements can be critical in real-world applications, their incremental nature suggests that the majority of images do not require the doubling in network depth and that the optimal depth depends on the input image.

In this paper, we introduce SkipNets (see Fig. 1) which are modified residual networks with gating units that dynamically select which layers of a convolutional neural network should be skipped during inference. We frame the dynamic

Electronic supplementary material The online version of this chapter (https://doi.org/10.1007/978-3-030-01261-8_25) contains supplementary material, which is available to authorized users.

V. Ferrari et al. (Eds.): ECCV 2018, LNCS 11217, pp. 420–436, 2018.
https://doi.org/10.1007/978-3-030-01261-8_25

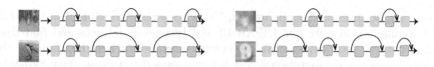

Fig. 1. The SkipNet learns to skip convolutional layers on a per-input basis. More layers are executed for challenging images (top) than easy images (bottom)

skipping problem as a sequential decision problem in which the outputs of previous layers are used to decide whether to bypass the subsequent layer. The objective in the dynamic skipping problem is then to skip as many layers as possible while retaining the accuracy of the full network. Not only can skipping policies significantly reduce the average cost of model inference they also provide insight into the diminishing return and role of individual layers.

While conceptually simple, learning an efficient skipping policy is challenging. To achieve a reduction in computation while preserving accuracy, we need to correctly bypass the unnecessary layers in the network. This inherently discrete decision is not differentiable, and therefore precludes the application of gradient based optimization. While some [2,30,31] have proposed soft approximations, we show that the subsequent hard thresholding required to reduce computation results in low accuracy.

Recent works [4,23] explored the application of reinforcement learning (RL) to learn hard decision gates. While promising, in our experiments we show that these RL based techniques are brittle, often getting stuck in poor local minima and producing networks that are not competitive with the state-of-the-art. One can also apply the reparametrization techniques [16,21], however, these approaches often find suboptimal policies partly due to the approximation error introduced by the relaxation (detailed in later sections).

We explore several SkipNet designs and introduce a hybrid learning algorithm which combines supervised learning with reinforcement learning to address the challenges of non-differentiable skipping decisions. We explicitly assign a gating module to each group of layers. The gating module maps the previous layer activations to the binary decision to skip or execute the subsequent layer. We train the gating module in two stages. First, we use a soft-max relaxation of the binary skipping decisions by adopting the reparameterization trick [16,21], and train the layers and gates jointly with standard cross entropy loss used by the original model. Then, we treat the probabilistic gate outputs as an initial skipping policy and use REINFORCE [34] to refine the policy without relaxation. In the latter stage, we jointly optimize the skipping policy and prediction error to stabilize the exploration process.

We evaluate SkipNets, using ResNets [10] as the base models, on the CIFAR-10, CIFAR-100, SVHN and ImageNet datasets. We show that, with the hybrid learning procedure, SkipNets learn skipping policies that significantly reduce model inference costs (50% on the CIFAR-10 dataset, 37% on the CIFAR-100 dataset, 86% on the SVHN dataset and 30% on the ImageNet dataset) while preserving accuracy. We compare SkipNet with several state-of-the-art models and techniques on both the CIFAR-10 and ImageNet datasets and find that SkipNet consistently outperforms the previous methods on both benchmarks. By manipulating the computational cost hyper-parameter, we show how SkipNets can be tuned for different computation constraints. Finally, we study the skipping behavior of the learned skipping policy and reveal the relation between image scale and saliency and the number of layers skipped. Our code is available at https://github.com/ucbdrive/skipnet.

2   Related Work

Accelerating existing convolutional networks has been a central problem in real-world deployments and several complementary approaches have been proposed. Much of this work focuses on model compression [5,9,12,20] through the application of weight sparsification, filter pruning, vector quantization, and distillation [13] to transfer knowledge to shallower networks. These methods are applied after training the initial networks and they are usually used as post-processing. Also, these optimized networks do not dynamically adjust the model complexity in response to the input. While these approaches are complimentary, we show SkipNet outperforms existing static compression techniques.

Several related efforts [6,8,29] explored dynamically scaling computation through early termination. Graves [8] explored halting in recurrent networks to save computational cost. Figurnov et al. [6] and Teerapittayanon et al. [29] proposed the use of early termination in convolutional networks. Closest to our work, Figurnov et al. [6] studied early termination in each group of blocks of ResNets. In contrast, SkipNet does not exit early but instead conditionally bypasses individual layers based on the output of the proceeding layers which we show results in a better accuracy to cost trade-off.

Another line of work [1,22,32] explores cascaded model composition. This work builds on the observation that many images can be accurately labeled with smaller models. Bolukabasi et al [1] train a termination policy for cascades of pre-trained models arranged in order of increasing costs. This standard cascaded approach fails to reuse features across classifiers and requires substantial storage overhead. Similar to the work on adaptive time computation, Bolukabasi et al. [1] also explore early termination within the network. However, in many widely used architectures (e.g., ResNet) layers are divided into groups; with some layers being more critical than others (Fig. 10a). The in-network cascading work by [1] is unable to bypass some layers while executing subsequent layers in future groups. SkipNets explore selecting layers within the network in a combinatorial way leading to a search space that is a superset of cascading.

The gating modules in SkipNets act as regulating gates for groups of layers. They are related to the gating designs in recurrent neural networks (RNN) [3,14,27]. Hochreiter et al. [14] propose to add gates to an RNN so that the network can keep important memory in network states, while Srivastava et al. [27] introduce similar techniques to convolutional networks to learn deep image representation. Both [3] and [26] apply gates to other image recognition problems. These proposed gates are "soft" in the sense that the gate outputs are continuous, while our gates are "hard" binary decisions. We show in our experiments that "hard" gating is preferable to "soft" gating for dynamic networks.

3   SkipNet Model Design

SkipNets are convolutional networks in which individual layers are selectively included or excluded for a given input. The per-input selection of layers is accomplished using small gating networks that are interposed between layers. The gating networks map the output of the previous layer or group of layers to a binary decision to execute or bypass the subsequent layer or group of layers as illustrated in Fig. 2.

More precisely, let $\mathbf{x}^i$ be the input and $F^i(\mathbf{x}^i)$ be the output of the ith layer or group of layers, then we define the output of the gated layer (or group of layers) as:

$$\mathbf{x}^{i+1} = G^i(\mathbf{x}^i)F^i(\mathbf{x}^i) + (1 - G^i(\mathbf{x}^i))\mathbf{x}^i, \tag{1}$$

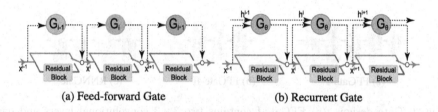

(a) Feed-forward Gate   (b) Recurrent Gate

Fig. 2. We study SkipNets with two gating designs. (a) Each residual block has a unique gating module and gate parameters. (b) A unified recurrent gate is shared across blocks

where $G^i(\mathbf{x}^i) \in \{0, 1\}$ is the gating function for layer i. In order for Eq. 1 to be well defined, we require $F^i(\mathbf{x}^i)$ and $\mathbf{x}^i$ to have the same dimensions. This requirement is satisfied by commonly used residual network architectures where

$$\mathbf{x}^{i+1}_{\text{ResNet}} = F^i(\mathbf{x}^i_{\text{ResNet}}) + \mathbf{x}^i_{\text{ResNet}}, \tag{2}$$

and can be addressed by pooling $\mathbf{x}^i$ to match the dimensions of $F^i(\mathbf{x}^i)$.

The gating network design needs to be both sufficiently expressive to accurately determine which layers to skip while also being computationally cheap. To address this trade-off between accuracy and computational cost we explore a range of gating network designs (Sect. 3.1) spanning feed-forward convolutional architectures to recurrent networks with varying degrees of parameter sharing. In either case, estimating the gating network parameters is complicated by the discrete gate decisions and the competing goals of maximizing accuracy and

minimizing cost. To learn the gating network we introduce a two stage training algorithm that combines supervised pre-training (Sect. 3.3) with based policy
optimization (Sect. 3.2) using a hybrid reward function that combines prediction
accuracy with the computational cost.

3.1   Gating Network Design

In this paper, we evaluate two feed-forward convolutional gate designs (Fig. 2a).
The *FFGate-I* (Fig. 3a) design is composed of two 3×3 convolutional layers
with stride of 1 and 2 respectively followed by a global average pooling layer and
a fully connected layer to output a single dimension vector. To reduce the gate
computation, we add a 2×2 max pooling layer prior to the first convolutional
layer. The overall computational cost of FFGate-I is roughly 19% of the residual
blocks [10] used in this paper. As a computationally cheaper alternative, we also
introduce the *FFGate-II* (Fig. 3b), consisting of one 3×3 stride 2 convolutional
layer followed by the same global average pooling and fully connected layers
as *FFGate-I*. The computational cost of *FFGate-II* is 12.5% of the cost of the
residual block. In our experiments, we use *FFGate-II* for networks with more
than 100 layers and *FFGate-I* for shallower networks.

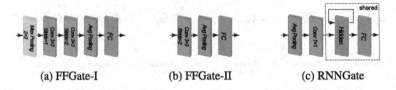

(a) FFGate-I   (b) FFGate-II   (c) RNNGate

Fig. 3. Gate designs. (a) FFGate-I contains two 3×3 convolutional layers and has
roughly 19% of the computation of the residual block. (b) FFGate-II is composed of
one convolutional layer with stride of 2 and has about 12.5% of the computation of
residual blocks. (c) RNNGate contains a one-layer LSTM with both input and hidden
unit size of 10. The cost of the RNNGate is negligible at 0.04% of the cost of the
residual blocks.

The feed-forward gate design is still relatively costly to compute and does not
leverage the decisions from previous gates. Therefore, we introduce a *recurrent
gate* (RNNGate) design (Fig. 3c) which enables parameter sharing and allows
gates to re-use computation across stages. We first apply global average pooling
on the input feature map of the gates and then linearly project the feature to the
input size of 10. We adopt a single layer *Long Short Term Memory* [14] (LSTM)
with hidden unit size of 10. At each gate, we project the LSTM output to a
one-dimensional vector to compute the final gate decision. Compared to the cost
of computing residual blocks, the cost of this recurrent gate design is negligible
(roughly 0.04% of the computation of residual blocks).

In our later experiments, we find that the recurrent gate dominates the feed-forward gates in both prediction accuracy and computation cost. We also evaluated simpler feed-forward gate designs without convolution layers and while these matched the computation cost of the recurrent gates the prediction accuracy suffered. We conjecture that the recurrent gate design better captures the cross-layer dependencies.

3.2 Skipping Policy Learning with Hybrid RL

During inference the most likely action is taken from the probability distribution encoded by each gate: *the layer is skipped or executed*. This inherently *discrete* and therefore non-differentiable decision process creates unique challenges for how we train SkipNets. A natural approximation, similar to that used in Highway Networks [27], would be to use differentiable soft-max decisions during training and then revert to hard decisions during inference. While this approach enables gradient based training, it results in poor prediction accuracy (Sect. 4.3) as the network parameters are not optimized for the subsequent hard-gating during inference. We therefore explore the use of reinforcement learning to learn the model parameters for the non-differentiable decision process.

Because SkipNets make a sequence of discrete decisions, one at each gated layer, we frame the task of estimating the gating function in the context of policy optimization through reinforcement learning. We define the skipping policy:

$$\pi(\mathbf{x}^i, i) = \mathbb{P}(G^i(\mathbf{x}^i) = g_i) \tag{3}$$

as a function from the input $\mathbf{x}^i$ to the probability distribution over the gate action g_i to execute ($g_i = 1$) or skip ($g_i = 0$) layer i. We define a sample sequence of gating decisions drawn from the skipping policy starting with input $\mathbf{x}$ as:

$$\mathbf{g} = [g_1, \ldots, g_N] \sim \pi_{F_\theta}, \tag{4}$$

where $F_\theta = [F_\theta^1, \ldots, F_\theta^N]$ is the sequence of network layers (including the gating modules) parameterized by θ and $\mathbf{g} \in \{0,1\}^N$. The overall objective is defined as

$$\min \mathcal{J}(\theta) = \min \mathbb{E}_{\mathbf{x}} \mathbb{E}_{\mathbf{g}} L_\theta(\mathbf{g}, \mathbf{x})$$

$$= \min \mathbb{E}_{\mathbf{x}} \mathbb{E}_{\mathbf{g}} \left[\mathcal{L}(\hat{y}(\mathbf{x}, F_\theta, \mathbf{g}), y) - \frac{\alpha}{N} \sum_{i=1}^{N} R_i \right], \tag{5}$$

where $R_i = (1 - g_i)C_i$ is the reward of each gating module. The constant C_i is the cost of executing F^i and the term $(1 - g_i)C_i$ reflects the reward associated with *skipping* F^i. In our experiments, all F^i have the same cost and so we set $C_i = 1$. Finally α is a tuning parameter that allows us to trade-off the competing goals of minimizing the prediction loss and maximizing the gate rewards.

To optimize this objective, we can derive the gradients with respect to θ as follows. We define $\pi_{F_\theta}(\mathbf{x}) = p_\theta(\mathbf{g}|\mathbf{x})$, $\mathcal{L} = \mathcal{L}(\hat{y}(\mathbf{x}, F_\theta, \mathbf{g}), y)$ and $r_i = -[\mathcal{L} - \frac{\alpha}{N}\sum_{j=i}^{N} R_j]$.

$$\nabla_\theta \mathcal{J}(\theta) = \mathbb{E}_\mathbf{x} \nabla_\theta \sum_\mathbf{g} p_\theta(\mathbf{g}|\mathbf{x}) L_\theta(\mathbf{g}, \mathbf{x})$$

$$= \mathbb{E}_\mathbf{x} \sum_\mathbf{g} p_\theta(\mathbf{g}|\mathbf{x}) \nabla_\theta \mathcal{L} + \mathbb{E}_\mathbf{x} \sum_\mathbf{g} p_\theta(\mathbf{g}|\mathbf{x}) \nabla_\theta \log p_\theta(\mathbf{g}|\mathbf{x}) L_\theta(\mathbf{g}, \mathbf{x})$$

$$= \mathbb{E}_\mathbf{x} \mathbb{E}_\mathbf{g} \nabla_\theta \mathcal{L} - \mathbb{E}_\mathbf{x} \mathbb{E}_\mathbf{g} \sum_{i=1}^{N} \nabla_\theta \log p_\theta(g_i|\mathbf{x}) r_i. \qquad (6)$$

The first part of Eq. 6 corresponds to the supervised learning loss while the second part corresponds to the REINFORCE [34] gradient where r_i is the cumulative future rewards associated the gating modules. We refer to this combined reinforcement learning and supervised learning procedure as *hybrid reinforcement learning*. In practice, we may relax the reward $\hat{r}_i = -\left[\beta\mathcal{L} - \frac{\alpha}{N}\sum_{j=i}^{N} R_j\right]$ to scale down the influence of the prediction loss as this hybrid reinforcement learning is followed by the supervised pre-training that will be discussed in the next section. We set $\beta = \frac{\alpha}{N}$ in our experiments on ImageNet and $\beta = 1$ for other datasets.

3.3   Supervised Pre-training

Optimizing Eq. 5 starting from random parameters also consistently produces models with poor prediction accuracy (Sect. 4.3). We conjecture that the reduced ability to learn is due to the interaction between policy learning and image representation learning. The gating policy can over-fit to early features limiting future feature learning.

To provide an effective supervised initialization procedure we introduce a form of supervised pre-training that combines hard-gating during the forward pass with *soft-gating* during backpropagation. We relax the gate outputs $G(\mathbf{x})$ in Eq. 1 to continuous values (i.e. approximating $G(\mathbf{x})$ by $S(\mathbf{x}) \in [0, 1]$). We round the output gating probability of the skipping modules in the forward pass. During backpropagation we use the soft-max approximation [16, 21] and compute the gradients with respect to soft-max outputs. The relaxation procedure is summarized by:

$$G_{\text{relax}}(\mathbf{x}) = \begin{cases} \mathbb{I}(S(\mathbf{x}) \geq 0.5), & \text{forward pass} \\ S(\mathbf{x}), & \text{backward pass} \end{cases}, \qquad (7)$$

where $\mathbb{I}(\cdot)$ is the indicator function. This hybrid form of supervised pre-training is able to effectively leverage labeled data to initialize model parameters for both the base network and the gating networks. After supervised pre-training we then apply the REINFORCE algorithm to refine the model and gate parameters improving prediction accuracy and further reducing prediction cost. Our two stage hybrid algorithm is given in Algorithm 1.

Algorithm 1. Hybrid Learning Algorithm (HRL+SP)

Input: A set of images $\mathbf{x}$ and labels $\mathbf{y}$
Output: Trained SkipNet
1. Supervised pre-training (Sect. 3.3)
   $\theta_{SP} \leftarrow \mathrm{SGD}(L_{\mathrm{Cross\text{-}Entropy}}, \mathrm{SkipNet\text{-}}G_{\mathrm{relax}}(\mathbf{x}))$
2. Hybrid reinforcement learning (Sect. 3.2)
   Initialize θ_{HRL+SP} with θ_{SP}
   $\theta_{HRL+SP} \leftarrow \mathrm{REINFORCE}(\mathcal{J}, \mathrm{SkipNet\text{-}}G(\mathbf{x}))$

---

4   Experiments

We evaluate a range of SkipNet architectures and our proposed training procedure on four image classification benchmarks: CIFAR-10/100 [17], SVHN [24] and ImageNet 2012 [25]. We construct SkipNets from ResNet models [10] by introducing hard gates between residual blocks. In Sect. 4.1, we evaluate the performance of SkipNets with both gate designs and compare SkipNets with the state-of-the-art models including dynamic networks and static compression networks which are also complementary approaches to our methods. We also compare our approach with baselines inspired by [15] to demonstrate the effectiveness of the learned skipping policy. In Sect. 4.2, we decipher the dynamic essence of SkipNets with extensive qualitative study and analysis to reveal the relation between image scale and saliency and number of layers skipped. In Sect. 4.3, we discuss the effectiveness of the proposed learning algorithm and gating designs.

Datasets: Table 1 summarizes the statistics of datasets used in this paper. We follow the common data augmentation scheme (mirroring/shifting) that is adopted for CIFAR and ImageNet datasets [7,19,33]. For the SVHN dataset, we use both the training and provided extra dataset for training and did not perform data augmentation [15]. For preprocessing, we normalize the data with the channel means and standard deviations.

Table 1. Dataset statistics

Dataset	# Train	# Test	# Classes
CIFAR-10	50k	10k	10
CIFAR-100	50k	10k	100
SVHN	604k[a]	26k	10
ImageNet	1.28m	50k	1k

[a] 531,131 of the images are extra images of SVHN for additional training.

Table 2. ResNets (R for short) Accuracy

Model	CIFAR-10	CIFAR-100	SVHN	Model	ImageNet
R-38	92.50%	68.54%	97.94%	R-34	73.30%
R-74	92.95%	70.64%	97.92%	R-50	76.15%
R-110	93.60%	71.21%	98.09%	R-101	77.37%
R-152	-	-	98.14%	-	-

Models: For CIFAR and SVHN, we use the ResNet [10] architecture with $6n+2$ stacked weighted layers for our base models and choose $n = \{6, 12, 18, 25\}$ to construct network instances with depth of $\{38, 74, 110, 152\}$. For ImageNet, we evaluate ResNet-34, ResNet-50 and ResNet-101 as described in [10]. We denote our model at depth x by SkipNet-x. In addition, we add +SP and +HRL to indicate whether supervised pre-training or hybrid reinforcement learning were used. If no modifier is provided then we conduct the full two stage training procedure. Finally we will also use +FFGate and +RNNGate to indicate which gating design is being used. If not specified, RNNGate is used. We summarize the accuracy of the base models in Table 2. In later sections, we demonstrate SkipNets can preserve the same accuracy (within a variance of 0.5%).

Training: Our two-stage training procedure combines supervised pre-training and policy refinement with hybrid reinforcement learning. In the first stage, we adopt the same hyper-parameters used in [10] for CIFAR and ImageNet and [15] for SVHN.

For the policy refining stage, we use the trained models as initialization and optimize them with the same optimizer with decreased learning rate of 0.0001 for all datasets. We train a fixed number of iterations (10k iterations for the CIFAR datasets, 50 epochs for the SVHN dataset and 40 epochs for the ImageNet dataset) and report the test accuracy evaluated at termination. The training time of the supervised pre-training stage is roughly the same as training the original models without gating. Our overall training time is slightly longer with an increase of about 30–40%.

4.1 SkipNet Performance Evaluation

In this subsection, we first provide the overall computation reduction of SkipNets on four benchmark datasets to demonstrate SkipNet achieves the primary goal of reducing computation while preserving full network prediction accuracy. We also show that by adjusting α, SkipNet can meet different computational cost and accuracy requirements. For horizontal comparison, we show SkipNet outperforms a set of state-of-the-art dynamic network and static compression techniques on both ImageNet and CIFAR-10.

Computation Reduction While Preserving Full Network Accuracy: Figs. 4 and 5a show the computation cost (including the computation of the gate networks), measured in *floating point operations* (FLOPs), of the original ResNets and SkipNets with both feed-forward and recurrent gate designs with α tuned to match the same accuracy (variance less than 0.5%). The trade-off between accuracy and computational cost will be discussed later. Following [10], we only consider the multiply-adds associated with convolution operations as others have negligible impact on cost.

We observe that the hybrid reinforcement learning (HRL) with supervised pre-training (SkipNet+HRL+SP) is able to substantially reduce the cost of computation. Overall, for the deepest model on each dataset, SkipNet-110+HRL+SP

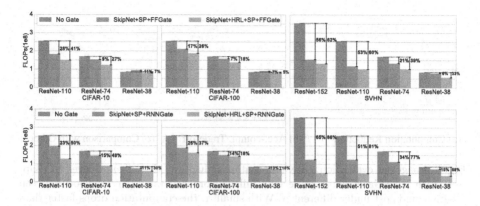

Fig. 4. Computation reduction of SkipNet+SP and SkipNet+HRL+SP with feed-forward gates and recurrent gates while preserving the full network accuracy. The computation cost includes the computation of gates. We are able to reduce computation costs by 50%, 37% and 86% of the deepest models on the CIFAR-10, 100 and SVHN data. Compared to using SP only, fine-tuning with HRL can gain another 10% or more computation reduction. Since feed-forward gates are more expensive, SkipNets with recurrent gates generally achieve greater cost savings

with recurrent gates reduces computation on the CIFAR-10 and CIFAR-100 datasets by 50% and 37% respectively. The largest SkipNet-152+HRL+SP model with recurrent gates reduces computation on the SVHN dataset by 86%. On the ImageNet data, the SkipNet-101+HRL+SP using recurrent gates is able to reduce computation by 30%. Interestingly, as noted earlier, even in the absence of the cost regularization in the objective, the supervised pre-training of the SkipNet architecture consistently results in reduced prediction costs. One way to explain it is that the shallower network is easier to train and thus more favorable. We also observe that deeper networks tend to experience greater cost reductions which supports our conjecture that only a small fraction of inputs require extremely deep networks.

Trade-Off Computational Cost and Accuracy: Eq. 5 introduces the hyper-parameter α to balance the computational cost and classification accuracy. In Fig. 5b we plot the accuracy against the average number of skipped layers for different values of α from 0.0 to 4.0 on ImageNet. We observe similar patterns on other datasets and details can be found in the supplementary material. By adjusting α, one can trade-off computation and accuracy to meet various computation or accuracy requirements.

Comparison with State-of-the-art Models: We compare SkipNet with existing state-of-the-art models on both ImageNet (Fig. 5c) and CIFAR-10 (Fig. 6c). The SACT and ACT models proposed by [6] are adaptive computation time models that attempt to terminate computation early in each group

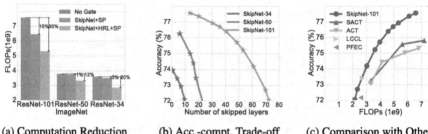

(a) Computation Reduction   (b) Acc.-compt. Trade-off   (c) Comparison with Others

Fig. 5. ImageNet evaluation. (a) Computation reduction (12 - 30%) achieved by Skip-Nets with RNNGates while preserving full network accuracy. (b) Trade-off between accuracy and cost under different α. With small α, the computation drops faster than the decrease of accuracy. (c) Comparison of SkipNet with state-of-the-art models. Skip-Net consistently outperforms existing approaches on both benchmarks under various trade-off between computational cost and prediction accuracy

of blocks of ResNets (Sect. 2). In addition, we compare SkipNet with static compression techniques: PEFC [20] and LCCL [5] which are also complementary approaches to our method.

As shown in Fig. 5c, SkipNet-101 outperforms SACT and ACT models by a large margin on the ImageNet benchmark even though they are using the recent more accurate pre-activation [11] ResNet-101 as the base model. We hypothesize that increased flexibility afforded by the skipping model formulation enables the SkipNet design to outperform SACT and ACT. Similar patterns can be observed on CIFAR-10 in Fig. 6c.[1]

For comparison with the static compression techniques, we plot the computation FLOPs and the accuracy of the compressed residual networks (may have different depths from what we used in this paper) in Fig. 5. Though the static compression techniques are complementary approaches, SkipNet performs similar to or better than these techniques. Note that, though LCCL [5] uses shallower and cheaper ResNets (34 layers on ImageNet and 20, 32, 44 layers on CIFAR-10), our approach still obtains comparable performance.

Comparison with Stochastic Depth Network Variant: Huang et al. [15] propose stochastic depth networks which randomly drop layers for a each training mini-batch and revert to using the full network for inference. The original goal of the stochastic depth model is to avoid gradient vanishing and speed up training. A natural variant of this model in order to reduce inference computation cost is to skip blocks randomly with a chosen ratio in both training and inference phases referred as *SDV*. We compare SkipNet to SDV on both the CIFAR-10 and CIFAR-100 datasets shown in Fig. 6a and b. SkipNet outperforms SDV by a large margin under networks with different depths.

---

[1] We obtain the CIFAR-10 results by running the code provided by the authors.

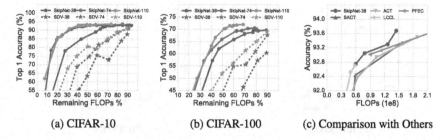

(a) CIFAR-10   (b) CIFAR-100   (c) Comparison with Others

Fig. 6. Comparison on CIFAR. (a) Comparison on CIFAR-10 with a variant of the stochastic depth model (SDV) that randomly drops blocks with chosen ratios during training and testing. The learned policy of SkipNet outperforms the baseline under various skipping ratios (b) Comparison on CIFAR-100 with SDV (c) Comparison of SkipNet with the state-of-the-art models on CIFAR-10. SkipNet is consistently matches or out-performs state-of-the-art models

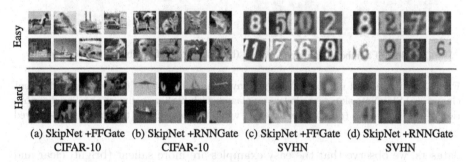

(a) SkipNet +FFGate   (b) SkipNet +RNNGate   (c) SkipNet +FFGate   (d) SkipNet +RNNGate
CIFAR-10   CIFAR-10   SVHN   SVHN

Fig. 7. Visualization of *easy* and *hard* images in the CIFAR-10 and SVHN with SkipNet-74. The top two rows are easy examples (with more than 15 layers skipped) and the bottom two rows are hard examples (with fewer than 8 layers skipped). Easy examples are brighter and clearer while hard examples tend to be dark and blurry

4.2 Skipping Behavior Analysis and Visualization

In this subsection, we investigate the key factors associated with the dynamic skipping and qualitatively visualize their behavior. We study the correlation between block skipping and the input images in the following aspects: (1) qualitative difference between images (2) the scale of the inputs and (3) prediction accuracy per category. We find that SkipNet skips more aggressively on inputs with smaller scales and on brighter and clearer images. Moreover, more blocks are skipped for classes with high accuracy.

Qualitative Difference Between Inputs: To better understand the learned skipping patterns, we cluster the images that SkipNets skip many layers (treated as *easy* examples) and keep many layers (treated as *hard* examples) in Fig. 7 for both CIFAR-10 and SVHN. Interestingly, we find that images within each cluster share similar characteristics with respect to saliency and clarity. On both

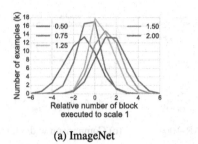 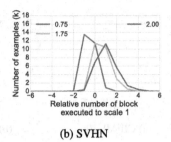

(a) ImageNet   (b) SVHN

Fig. 8. Distribution of number of blocks executed with multi-scale inputs. The x-axis is the relative number of blocks executed to scale 1 (#block kept at scale s - #block kept at scale 1). More blocks are executed for inputs with larger scales.

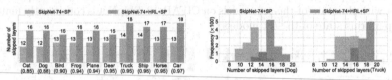

(a) Median of number of skipped layers   (b) Distribution of number of skipped layers

Fig. 9. Correlation of number of skipped layers and the level of complexity of different classes. (a) SkipNets skip more layers on classes with higher accuracy. (b) The distribution of the *hard* class (dogs) is left-skewed while the *easy* class (trucks) is right-skewed

datasets, we observe that the easy examples are more salient (bright, clear and with high contrast) while the hard examples are dark and blurry which are even hard for humans to recognize. These findings suggest that SkipNet can identify the visual difference of the inputs and skip layers accordingly.

Input Scales: We conjecture the input scale affects the skipping decisions of the gates. To verify this hypothesis, we conduct multi-scale testing of trained models on the ImageNet and SVHN datasets. We plot the distribution of the number of blocks of different input scales relative to the original scale 1 used in other experiments. We observe on both datasets that the distributions of smaller scales are skewed left (executing less blocks than the model with input scale 1) while the distributions of larger scales are skewed right (more block executed). This observation matches the intuition that inputs with larger scale require larger receptive field and thus need to execute more blocks. Another interpretation is that SkipNet dynamically selects layers with appropriate receptive field sizes for the given inputs with different input scales.

Prediction Accuracy per Category: We further study the correlation of skipping behaviors and the prediction accuracy per class on CIFAR-10. The conjecture is that the SkipNet skips more on easy classes (class with high accuracy, e.g., truck class) while skipping less on hard classes (class with low accuracy, e.g.,

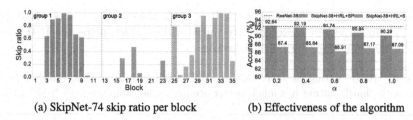

(a) SkipNet-74 skip ratio per block   (b) Effectiveness of the algorithm

Fig. 10. Visualization and analysis on CIFAR-10. (a) Visualization of the skipping ratio per block of SkipNet-74. The first and last few blocks are more critical in each group; group 2 is heavily utilized. (b) Accuracy of SkipNet-38+HRL+SP, SkipNet-38+HRL+S and SkipNet-38+RL with FFGates for different α values. SkipNet-38+RL (not plotted) can only achieve $\sim 10\%$ accuracy which indicates with pure RL, SkipNet fails to learn the correct feature representations. Moreover, the accuracy improves consistently with SP compared with random initialization.

cat and dog classes). We plot the median of number of skipped layers in each class for SkipNet+SP and SkipNet+HRL+SP in Fig. 9a. It shows that while all classes tend to skip more aggressively after applying HRL, SkipNets tend to skip more layers on easy classes. Figure 9b indicates that the distribution of hard classes (e.g. dog class) are skewed left, whereas easier classes (e.g. truck class) are skewed right as SkipNet tends to skip more layers on easier classes.

Skip Ratio of Different Blocks: We visualize the skip ratio of different blocks in SkipNet in Fig. 10a on CIFAR-10. Visualizations of SkipNets on other datasets (e.g. ImageNet, CIFAR-100) can be found in the supplementary material. The ResNet model can be divided into 3 groups where blocks in the same group have the same feature map size and tend to have similar functionality. Interestingly, we observe less skipping in group 2 than in groups 1 and 3 suggesting group 2 may be more critical to feature extraction.

4.3   SkipNet Design and Algorithm Analysis

Effectiveness of Hybrid Learning Algorithm: We compare the performances of SkipNet-38 trained using basic RL, hybrid RL from scratch (HRL+S), and hybrid RL plus supervised pre-training (HRL+SP) on CIFAR-10 in Fig. 10b. For SkipNet+HRL+S and SkipNet+RL, we train both networks for 80k iterations to match the total training steps of the two-stage training of Skip-Net+HRL+SP.

First, we were unable to train the model using the pure RL approach (SkipNet-38+RL accuracy was roughly 10%). This provides strong evidence for the importance of supervision in complex vision tasks. Second, SkipNet-38+HRL+SP consistently achieves higher accuracy than SkipNet-38+HRL+S. The accuracy of SkipNet-38+HRL+S is lower than the accuracy of the original

ResNet-38 model even with very small α. This suggests that supervised pre-training can provide a more effective initialization which helps the HRL stage to focus more on skipping policy learning.

Table 3. "Hard" gating *vs* "soft" gating. With similar computation, SkipNet (S for short) with "hard" gating has much better accuracy than SkipNet with "soft" gating.

Data	Model	Acc. (%)	FLOPs (1e8)	Data	Model	Acc.(%)	FLOPs (1e8)
	S-38-Hd	90.83	0.58		S-38-Hd	67.68	0.50
	S-38-St	66.67	0.61		S-38-St	21.70	0.62
CIFAR-10	S-74-Hd	92.38	0.92	CIFAR-100	S-74-Hd	67.79	0.61
	S-74-St	52.29	1.03		S-74-St	25.47	0.89
	S-110-Hd	88.11	0.18		S-110-Hd	63.66	0.96
	S-110-St	23.44	0.05		S-110-St	9.84	1.00

"Hard" Gating and "Soft" Gating Design: During supervised pre-training, we can either treat gate outputs as "hard" (Sect. 3.3) or "soft" (Sect. 3.2). For "soft" gating, continuous gating probabilities are adopted for training but discretized values are used for inference to achieve the desired computation reduction. In Table 3, we show the classification accuracy of SkipNet with "hard" (SkipNet-Hd) and "soft" gating (SkipNet-St) under similar computation cost[2]. SkipNet-Hd achieves much higher accuracy than SkipNet-St which may be due to the inconsistency between training and inference with soft gating.

5   Conclusion

We introduced SkipNet architecture that learns to dynamically skip redundant layers on a per-input basis, without sacrificing prediction accuracy. We framed the dynamic execution problem as a sequential decision problem. To address the inherent non-differentiability of dynamic execution, we proposed a novel hybrid learning algorithm which combines the strengths of supervised and reinforcement learning.

We evaluated the proposed approach on four benchmark datasets, showing that SkipNets reduce computation substantially while preserving the original accuracy. Compared to both state-of-the-art dynamic models and static compression techniques, SkipNets obtain better accuracy with lower computation. Moreover, we conducted a range of ablation study to further evaluate the proposed network architecture and algorithm.

The dynamic architectures offer the potential to be more computationally efficient and improve accuracy by specializing and reusing individual components. We believe that further study in this area will be critical to the long term progress in machine learning and computer vision.

---

[2] We tune SkipNet-Hd to match the computation of SkipNet-St.

Acknowledgements. We would like to thank the ECCV reviewers for their excellent feedback. This research was funded by the NSF CISE Expeditions Award CCF-1730628 and generous gifts from Alibaba, Amazon Web Services, Ant Financial, Arm, CapitalOne, Ericsson, Facebook, Google, Huawei, Intel, Microsoft, Scotiabank, Splunk and VMware.

References

1. Bolukbasi, T., Wang, J., Dekel, O., Saligrama, V.: Adaptive neural networks for efficient inference. In: Proceedings of the 34th International Conference on Machine Learning, pp. 527–536 (2017)
2. Chan, W., Jaitly, N., Le, Q., Vinyals, O.: Listen, attend and spell: A neural network for large vocabulary conversational speech recognition. In: IEEE International Conference on Acoustics, Speech and Signal Processing (ICASSP), pp. 4960–4964. IEEE (2016)
3. Dauphin, Y.N., Fan, A., Auli, M., Grangier, D.: Language modeling with gated convolutional networks. In: International Conference on Machine Learning, pp. 933–941 (2017)
4. Dhingra, B., Li, L., Li, X., Gao, J., Chen, Y.N., Ahmed, F., Deng, L.: Towards end-to-end reinforcement learning of dialogue agents for information access. In: Proceedings of the 55th Annual Meeting of the Association for Computational Linguistics, vol. 1, pp. 484–495 (2017)
5. Dong, X., Huang, J., Yang, Y., Yan, S.: More is less: a more complicated network with less inference complexity. In: Proceedings of the IEEE Conference on Computer Vision and Pattern Recognition, pp. 5840–5848 (2017)
6. Figurnov, M., et al.: Spatially adaptive computation time for residual networks. In: The IEEE Conference on Computer Vision and Pattern Recognition, July 2017
7. Goodfellow, I.J., Warde-Farley, D., Mirza, M., Courville, A., Bengio, Y.: Maxout networks. In: Proceedings of the 30th International Conference on Machine Learning, pp. III-1319 (2013)
8. Graves, A.: Adaptive computation time for recurrent neural networks. In: NIPS 2016 Deep Learning Symposium (2016)
9. Han, S., Mao, H., Dally, W.J.: Deep compression: compressing deep neural networks with pruning, trained quantization and huffman coding. In: International Conference on Learning Representations (2016)
10. He, K., Zhang, X., Ren, S., Sun, J.: Deep residual learning for image recognition. In: Proceedings of the IEEE conference on computer vision and pattern recognition, pp. 770–778 (2016)
11. He, K., Zhang, X., Ren, S., Sun, J.: Identity mappings in deep residual networks. In: European Conference on Computer Vision, pp. 630–645 (2016)
12. He, Y., Zhang, X., Sun, J.: Channel pruning for accelerating very deep neural networks. In: International Conference on Computer Vision (ICCV), vol. 2, p. 6 (2017)
13. Hinton, G., Vinyals, O., Dean, J.: Distilling the knowledge in a neural network. In: NIPS 2014 Deep Learning Workshop (2014)
14. Hochreiter, S., Schmidhuber, J.: Long short-term memory. Neural Comput. **9**(8), 1735–1780 (1997)
15. Huang, G., Sun, Y., Liu, Z., Sedra, D., Weinberger, K.Q.: Deep networks with stochastic depth. In: European Conference on Computer Vision, pp. 646–661 (2016)

16. Jang, E., Gu, S., Poole, B.: Categorical reparameterization with gumbel-softmax. In: International Conference on Learning Representations (2017)
17. Krizhevsky, A.: Learning multiple layers of features from tiny images. Technical report (2009)
18. Krizhevsky, A., Sutskever, I., Hinton, G.E.: Imagenet classification with deep convolutional neural networks. In: Advances in neural information processing systems, pp. 1097–1105 (2012)
19. Lee, C.Y., Gallagher, P.W., Tu, Z.: Generalizing pooling functions in convolutional neural networks: Mixed, gated, and tree. In: Artificial Intelligence and Statistics, pp. 464–472 (2016)
20. Li, H., Kadav, A., Durdanovic, I., Samet, H., Graf, H.P.: Pruning filters for efficient convnets. In: International Conference on Learning Representations (2017)
21. Maddison, C.J., Mnih, A., Teh, Y.W.: The concrete distribution: a continuous relaxation of discrete random variables. In: International Conference on Learning Representations (2017)
22. McGill, M., Perona, P.: Deciding how to decide: Dynamic routing in artificial neural networks. In: Proceedings of the 34th International Conference on Machine Learning, pp. 2363–2372 (2017)
23. Mnih, V., Heess, N., Graves, A., et al.: Recurrent models of visual attention. In: Advances in neural information processing systems, pp. 2204–2212 (2014)
24. Netzer, Y., Wang, T., Coates, A., Bissacco, A., Wu, B., Ng, A.Y.: Reading digits in natural images with unsupervised feature learning. In: NIPS workshop on deep learning and unsupervised feature learning, vol. 2011, p. 5 (2011)
25. Russakovsky, O., Deng, J., Su, H., Krause, J., Satheesh, S., Ma, S., Huang, Z., Karpathy, A., Khosla, A., Bernstein, M.: Imagenet large scale visual recognition challenge. Int. J. Comput. Vis. 115(3), 211–252 (2015)
26. Siam, M., Valipour, S., Jagersand, M., Ray, N.: Convolutional gated recurrent networks for video segmentation (2016). arXiv preprint arXiv:1611.05435
27. Srivastava, R.K., Greff, K., Schmidhuber, J.: Highway networks. In: ICML workshop on deep learning (2015)
28. Szegedy, C., Vanhoucke, V., Ioffe, S., Shlens, J., Wojna, Z.: Rethinking the inception architecture for computer vision. In: Proceedings of the IEEE Conference on Computer Vision and Pattern Recognition, pp. 2818–2826 (2016)
29. Teerapittayanon, S., McDanel, B., Kung, H.: Branchynet: Fast inference via early exiting from deep neural networks. In: 23rd International Conference on Pattern Recognition, pp. 2464–2469 (2016)
30. Vaswani, A., et al.: Attention is all you need. In: Advances in Neural Information Processing Systems, pp. 6000–6010 (2017)
31. Vinyals, O., Fortunato, M., Jaitly, N.: Pointer networks. In: Advances in Neural Information Processing Systems, pp. 2692–2700 (2015)
32. Vinyals, O., Fortunato, M., Jaitly, N.: Pointer networks. In: Advances in Neural Information Processing Systems, pp. 2692–2700 (2015)
33. Wan, L., Zeiler, M., Zhang, S., Cun, Y.L., Fergus, R.: Regularization of neural networks using dropconnect. In: Proceedings of the 30th International Conference on Machine Learning, pp. 1058–1066 (2013)
34. Williams, R.J.: Simple statistical gradient-following algorithms for connectionist reinforcement learning. Mach. Learn. 8(3–4), 229–256 (1992)

Person Search in Videos with One Portrait Through Visual and Temporal Links

Qingqiu Huang[1](✉) ⓘ, Wentao Liu[2,3] ⓘ, and Dahua Lin[1] ⓘ

[1] CUHK-SenseTime Joint Lab, The Chinese University of Hong Kong,
Shatin, Hong Kong
{hq016,dhlin}@ie.cuhk.edu.hk
[2] Department of Computer Science and Technology, Tsinghua University,
Beijing, China
[3] SenseTime Research, Beijing, China
liuwtwinter@gmail.com

Abstract. In real-world applications, *e.g.* law enforcement and video retrieval, one often needs to search a certain person in long videos with *just one portrait*. This is much more challenging than the conventional settings for person re-identification, as the search may need to be carried out in the environments different from where the portrait was taken. In this paper, we aim to tackle this challenge and propose a novel framework, which takes into account the identity invariance along a tracklet, thus allowing person identities to be propagated via both the visual and the temporal links. We also develop a novel scheme called *Progressive Propagation via Competitive Consensus*, which significantly improves the reliability of the propagation process. To promote the study of person search, we construct a large-scale benchmark, which contains 127K *manually annotated* tracklets from 192 movies. Experiments show that our approach remarkably outperforms mainstream person re-id methods, raising the mAP from 42.16% to 62.27% (Code at https://github.com/hqqasw/person-search-PPCC).

Keywords: Person search · Portrait · Visual and temporal
Progressive Propagation · Competitive Consensus

1 Introduction

Searching persons in videos is frequently needed in real-world scenarios. To catch a wanted criminal, the police may have to go through thousands of hours of videos collected from multiple surveillance cameras, probably with just a single

Electronic supplementary material The online version of this chapter (https://doi.org/10.1007/978-3-030-01261-8_26) contains supplementary material, which is available to authorized users.

V. Ferrari et al. (Eds.): ECCV 2018, LNCS 11217, pp. 437–454, 2018.
https://doi.org/10.1007/978-3-030-01261-8_26

portrait. To find the movie shots featured by a popular star, the retrieval system has to examine many hour-long films, with just a few facial photos as the references. In applications like these, the reference photos are often taken in an environment that is very different from the target environments where the search is conducted. As illustrated in Fig. 1, such settings are very challenging. Even state-of-the-art recognition techniques would find it difficult to reliably identify all occurrences of a person, facing the dramatic variations in pose, makeups, clothing, and illumination.

Fig. 1. Person re-id differs significantly from the person search task. The first row shows a typical example in person re-id from the *MARS dataset* [44], where the reference and the targets are captured under similar conditions. The second row shows an example from our person search dataset *CSM*, where the reference portrait is dramatically different from the targets that vary significantly in pose, clothing, and illumination.

It is noteworthy that two related problems, namely *person re-identification (re-id)* and *person recognition in albums*, have drawn increasing attention from the research community. However, they are substantially different from the problem of *person search with one portrait*, which we aim to tackle in this work. Specifically, in typical settings of person re-id [8,13,16,22,38,44,45], the queries and the references in the gallery set are usually captured under similar conditions, *e.g.* from different cameras along a street, and within a short duration. Even though some queries can be subject to issues like occlusion and pose changes, they can still be identifies via other visual cues, *e.g.* clothing. For person recognition in albums [43], one is typically given a diverse collection of gallery samples, which may cover a wide range of conditions and therefore can be directly matched to various queries. Hence, for both problems, the references in the gallery are often good representatives of the targets, and therefore the methods based on visual cues can perform reasonably well [1,3,4,14,15,22,39,43,44]. On the contrary, our task is to bridge a single portrait with a highly diverse set of samples, which is much more challenging and requires new techniques that go beyond visual matching.

To tackle this problem, we propose a new framework that propagates labels through both visual and temporal links. The basic idea is to take advantage of the *identity invariance* along a person trajectory, *i.e.* all person instances along a *continuous* trajectory in a video should belong to the same identity. The connections induced by tracklets, which we refer to as the *temporal links*, are complementary to the *visual links* based on feature similarity. For example, a trajectory can sometimes cover a wide range of facial images that can not be easily associated based on visual similarity. With both *visual* and *temporal* links incorporated, our framework can form a large connected graph, thus allowing the identity information to be propagated over a very diverse collection of instances.

While the combination of visual and temporal links provide a broad foundation for identity propagation, it remains a very challenging problem to carry out the propagation *reliably* over a large real-world dataset. As we begin with only a single portrait, a few wrong labels during propagation can result in catastrophic errors downstream. Actually, our empirical study shows that conventional schemes like linear diffusion [46, 47] even leads to substantially worse results. To address this issue, we develop a novel scheme called *Progressive Propagation via Competitive Consensus*, which performs the propagation *prudently*, spreading a piece of identity information only when there is high certainty.

To facilitate the research on this problem setting, we construct a dataset named *Cast Search in Movies (CSM)*, which contains $127K$ tracklets of 1218 cast identities from 192 movies. The identities of all the tracklets are *manually annotated*. Each cast identity also comes with a reference portrait. The benchmark is very challenging, where the person instances for each identity varies significantly in makeup, pose, clothing, illumination, and even age. On this benchmark, our approach get 63.49% and 62.27% mAP under two settings, Comparing to the 53.33% and 42.16% mAP of the conventional visual-matching method, it shows that only matching by visual cues can not solve this problem well, and our proposed framework – *Progressive Propagation via Competitive Consensus* can significantly raise the performance.

In summary, the main contributions of this work lie in four aspects: (1) We systematically study the problem of *person search in videos*, which often arises in real-world practice, but remains widely open in research. (2) We propose a framework, which incorporates both the visual similarity and the identity invariance along a tracklet, thus allowing the search to be carried out much further. (3) We develop the *Progressive Propagation via Competitive Consensus* scheme, which significantly improves the reliability of propagation. (4) We construct a dataset *Cast Search in Movies (CSM)* with $120K$ manually annotated tracklets to promote the study on this problem.

2   Related Work

Person Re-id. Person re-id [6, 7, 41], which aims to match pedestrian images (or tracklets) from different cameras within a short period, has drawn much attention in the research community. Many datasets [8, 13, 16, 22, 38, 44, 45] have been proposed to promote the research of re-id. However, the videos are captured by just several cameras in nearby locations within a short period. For example, the Airport [16] dataset is captured in an airport from 8 a.m. to 8 p.m. in one day. So the instances of the same identities are usually similar enough to identify by visual appearance although with occlusion and pose changes. Based on such characteristic of the data, most of the re-id methods focus on how to match a query and a gallery instance by visual cues. In early works, the matching process is splited into feature designing [9,11,26,27] and metric learning [17,23,28]. Recently, many deep learning based methods have been proposed to jointly handle the matching problem. *Li et al.* [22] and *Ahmed et al.* [1] designed siamese-based networks which employ a binary verification loss to train the parameters. *Ding et al.* [4] and *Cheng et al.* [3] exploit triple loss for training more discriminating feature. *Xiao et al.* [39] and *Zheng et al.* [44] proposed to learn features by classifying identities. Although the feature learning methods of re-id can be adopted for the Person Search with One Portrait problem, they are substantially different as the query and the gallery would have huge visual appearances gap in person search, which would make one-to-one matching fail.

Person Recognition in Photo Album. Person recognition [14,15,19,24,43] is another related problem, which usually focuses on the persons in photo album. It aims to recognize the identities of the queries given a set of labeled persons in gallery. *Zhang et al.* [43] proposed a Pose Invariant Person Recognition method (PIPER), which combines three types of visual recognizers based on ConvNets, respectively on face, full body, and poselet-level cues. The PIPA dataset published in [43] has been widely adopted as a standard benchmark to evaluate person recognition methods. *Oh et al.* [15] evaluated the effectiveness of different body regions, and used a weighted combination of the scores obtained from different regions for recognition. *Li et al.* [19] proposed a multi-level contextual model, which integrates person-level, photo-level and group-level contexts. But the person recognition is also quite different from the person search problem we aim to tackle in this paper, since the samples of the same identities in query and gallery are still similar in visual appearances and the methods mostly focus on recognizing by visual cues and context.

Person Search. There are some works that focus on person search problem. *Xiao et al.* [40] proposed a person search task which aims to search the corresponding instances in the images of the gallery without bounding box annotation. The associated data is similar to that in re-id. The key difference is that the bounding box is unavailable in this task. Actually it can be seen as a task to combine pedestrian detection and person re-id. There are some other works try to search person with different modality of data, such as language-based [21] and attribute-based [5,35], which focus on the application scenarios that are different from the portrait-based problem we aim to tackle in this paper.

Label Propogation. Label propagation (LP) [46,47], also known as Graph Transduction [30,32,37], is widely used as a semi-supervised learning method. It relies on the idea of building a graph in which nodes are data points (labeled and

Table 1. Comparing CSM with related datasets

Dataset	CSM	MARS[44]	iLIDS[38]	PRID[13]	Market[45]	PSD[40]	PIPA[43]
Task	Search	re-id	re-id	re-id	re-id	det.+re-id	recog.
Type	Video	Video	Video	Video	Image	Image	Image
Identities	1,218	1,261	300	200	1,501	8,432	2,356
Tracklets	127K	20K	600	400	-	-	-
Instances	11M	1M	44K	40K	32K	96K	63K

Fig. 2. Examples of *CSM* Dataset. In each row, the photo on the left is the query portrait and the following tracklets of are groud-truth tracklets of them in the gallery.

unlabeled) and the edges represent similarities between points so that labels can propagate from labeled points to unlabeled points. Different kinds of LP-based approaches have been proposed for face recognition [18,48], semantic segmentation [33], object detection [36], saliency detection [20] in the computer vision community. In this paper, We develop a novel LP-based approach called Progressive Propagation via Competitive Consensus, which differs from the conventional LP in two folds: (1) propagating by competitive consensus rather than linear diffusion, and (2) iterating in a progressive manner.

3   Cast Search in Movies Dataset

Whereas there have been a number of public datasets for person re-id [8,13, 16,22,38,44,45] and album-based person recognition [43]. But dataset for our task, namely person search with a single portrait, remains lacking. In this work, we constructed a large-scale dataset *Cast Search in Movies (CSM)* for this task. *CSM* comprises a *query set* that contains the portraits for 1,218 cast (the actors and actresses) and a *gallery set* that contains $127K$ tracklets (with $11M$ person instances) extracted from 192 movies.

We compare *CSM* with other datasets for person re-id and person recognition in Table 1. We can see that CSM is significantly larger, 6 times for tracklets and 11 times more instances than MARS [44], which is the largest dataset for person re-id to our knowledge. Moreover, CSM has a much wider range of tracklet durations (from 1 to 4686 frames) and instance sizes (from 23 to 557 pixels in height). Figure 2 shows several example tracklets as well as their corresponding portraits, which are very diverse in pose, illumination, and wearings. It can be seen that the task is very challenging (Fig. 3).

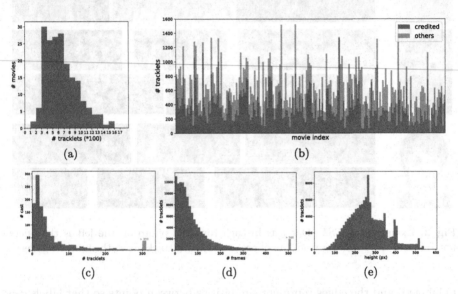

Fig. 3. Statistics of CSM dataset. (a): the tracklet number distribution over movies. (b): the tracklet number of each movie, both credited cast and "others". (c): the distribution of tracklet number over cast. (d): the distribution of length (frames) over tracklets. (e): the distribution of height (px) over tracklets.

Query Set. For each movie in *CSM*, we acquired the cast list from IMDB. For those movies with more than 10 cast, we only keep the top 10 according to the IMDB order, which can cover the main characters for most of the movies. In total, we obtained 1,218 cast, which we refer to as the *credited cast*. For each credited cast, we download a portrait from either its IMDB or TMDB homepage, which will serve as the query portraits in *CSM*.

Gallery Set. We obtained the tracklets in the gallery set through five steps:

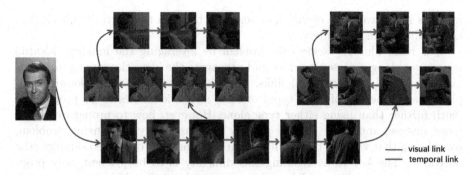

Fig. 4. Visual links and temporal links in our graph. We only keep one strongest link for each pair of tracklets. And we can see that these two kinds of links are complementary. The former allows the identity information to be propagated among those instances that are similar in appearance, while the latter allows the propagation along a continuous tracklet, in which the instances can look significantly different. With both types of links incorporated, we can construct a more connected graph, which allows the identities to be propagated much further.

1. *Detecting shots.* A movie is composed of a sequence of shots. Given a movie, we first detected the shot boundaries of the movies using a fast shot segmentation technique [2, 34], resulting in totally $200K$ shots for all movies. For each shot, we selected 3 frames as the *keyframes.*
2. *Annotating bounding boxes on keyframes.* We then *manually* annotated the person bounding boxes on keyframes and obtained around $700K$ bounding boxes.
3. *Training a person detector.* We trained a person detector with the annotated bounding boxes. Specifically, all the keyframes are partitioned into a training set and a testing set by a ratio 7:3. We then finetuned a Faster-RCNN [29] pre-trained on MSCOCO [25] on the training set. On the testing set, the detector gets around 91% mAP, which is good enough for tracklet generation.
4. *Generating tracklets.* With the person detector as described above, we performed per-frame person detection over all the frames. By concatenating the bounding boxes across frames with IoU > 0.7 *within each shot*, we obtained $127K$ tracklets from the 192 movies.
5. *Annotating identities.* Finally, we manually annotated the identities of all the tracklets. Particularly, each tracklet is annotated as one of the credited cast or as "others". Note that the identities of the tracklets in each movie are annotated independently to ensure high annotation quality with a reasonable budget. Hence, being labeled as "others" means that the tracklet does not belong to any credited cast of the corresponding movie.

4 Methodology

In this work, we aim to develop a method to find all the occurrences of a person in a long video, *e.g.* a movie, with just a single portrait. The challenge of this task lies in the vast gap of visual appearance between the portrait (query) and the candidates in the gallery.

Our basic idea to tackle this problem by leveraging the inherent *identity invariance* along a person tracklet and propagate the identities among instances via both visual and temporal links. The visual and temporal links are complementary. The use of both types of links allows identities to be propagated much further than using either type alone. However, how to propagate over a large, diverse, and noisy dataset reliably remains a very challenging problem, considering that we only begin with just a small number of labeled samples (the portraits). The key to overcoming this difficulty is to be *prudent*, only propagating the information which we are certain about. To this end, we propose a new propagation framework called *Progressive Propagation via Competitive Consensus*, which can effectively identify confident labels in a competitive way.

4.1 Graph Formulation

The propagation is carried out over a graph among person instances. Specifically, the propagation graph is constructed as follows. Suppose there are C cast in query set, M tracklets in gallery set, and the length of k-th tracklet (denoted by τ_k) is n_k, *i.e.* it contains n_k instances. The cast portraits and all the instances along the tracklets are treated as graph nodes. Hence, the graph contains $N = C + \sum_{k=1}^{M} n_k$ nodes. In particular, the identities of the C cast portraits are known, and the corresponding nodes are referred to as *labeled nodes*, while the other nodes are called *unlabled nodes*.

The propagation framework aims to propagate the identities from the labeled nodes to the unlabeled nodes through both *visual* and *temporal* links between them. The *visual links* are based on feature similarity. For each instance (say the i-th), we can extract a feature vector, denoted as $\mathbf{v}_i$. Each visual link is associated with an affinity value – the affinity between two instances $\mathbf{v}_i$ and $\mathbf{v}_j$ is defined to be their cosine similarity as $w_{ij} = \mathbf{v}_i^T \mathbf{v}_j / (\|\mathbf{v}_i\| \cdot \|\mathbf{v}_j\|)$. Generally, higher affinity value w_{ij} indicates that $\mathbf{v}_i$ and $\mathbf{v}_j$ are more likely to be from the same identity. The *temporal links* capture the *identity invariance* along a tracklet, *i.e.* all instances along a tracklet should share the same identity. In this framework, we treat the identity invariance as hard constraints, which is enforced via a *competitive consensus* mechanism.

For two tracklets with lengths n_k and n_l, there can be $n_k \cdot n_l$ links between their nodes. Among all these links, the strongest link, *i.e.* the one between the most similar pair, is the best to reflect the visual similarity. Hence, we only keep one strongest link for each pair of tracklets as shown in Fig. 4, which makes the propagation more reliable and efficient. Also, thanks to the temporal links, such reduction would not compromise the connectivity of the whole graph.

As illustrated in Fig. 4, the visual and temporal links are complementary. The former allows the identity information to be propagated among those instances that are similar in appearance, while the latter allows the propagation along a continuous trajectory, in which the instances can look significantly different. With only visual links, we can obtain clusters in the feature space. With only

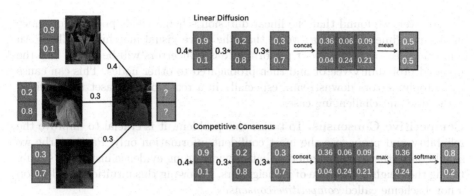

Fig. 5. An example to show the difference between competitive consensus and linear diffusion. There are four nodes here and their probability vectors are shown by their sides. We are going to propagate labels from the left nodes to the right node. However, two of its neighbor nodes are noise. The calculation process of linear diffusion and competitive consensus are shown on the right side. We can see that in a graph with much noise, our competitive consensus, which aims to propagate the most confident information, is more robust.

temporal links, we only have isolated tracklets. However, with both types of links incorporated, we can construct a more connected graph, which allows the identities to be propagated much further.

4.2 Propagating via Competitive Consensus

Each node of the graph is associated with a probability vector $\mathbf{p}_i \in \mathbb{R}^C$, which will be iteratively updated as the propagation proceeds. To begin with, we set the probability vector for each labeled node to be a one-hot vector indicating its label, and initialize all others to be zero vectors. Due to the identity invariance along tracklets, we enforce all nodes along a tracklet τ_k to share the same probability vector, denoted by $\mathbf{p}_{\tau_k}$. At each iteration, we traverse all tracklets and update their associated probability vectors one by one.

Linear Diffusion. Linear diffusion is the most widely used propagation scheme, where a node would update its probability vector by taking a linear combination of those from the neighbors. In our setting with identity invariance, the linear diffusion scheme can be expressed as follows:

$$\mathbf{p}_{\tau_k}^{(t+1)} = \sum_{j \in \mathcal{N}(\tau_k)} \alpha_{kj} \mathbf{p}_j^{(t)}, \quad \text{with } \alpha_{kj} = \frac{\tilde{w}_{kj}}{\sum_{j' \in \mathcal{N}(\tau_k)} \tilde{w}_{kj'}}. \tag{1}$$

Here, $\mathcal{N}(\tau_k) = \cup_{i \in \tau_k} \mathcal{N}_i$ is the set of all visual neighbors of those instances in τ_k. Also, $\tilde{w}_{kj}$ is the *affinity* of a neighbor node j to the tracklet τ_k. Due to the constraint that there is only one visual link between two tracklets (see Sect. 4.1), each neighbor j will be connected to just one of the nodes in τ_k, and $\tilde{w}_{kj}$ is set to the affinity between the neighbor j to that node.

However, we found that the linear diffusion scheme yields poor performance in our experiments, even far worse than the naive visual matching method. An important reason for the poor performance is that errors will be mixed into the updated probability vector and then propagated to other nodes. This can cause catastrophic errors downstream, especially in a real-world dataset that is filled with noise and challenging cases.

Competitive Consensus. To tackle this problem, it is crucial to improve the reliability and propagate the most confident information only. Particularly, we should only trust those neighbors that provide strong evidence instead of simply taking the weighted average of all neighbors. Following this intuition, we develop a novel scheme called *competitive consensus*.

When updating $\mathbf{p}_{\tau_k}$, the probability vector for the tracklet τ_k, we first collect the strongest evidence to support each identity c, from all the neighbors in $\mathcal{N}(\tau_k)$, as

$$\eta_k(c) = \max_{j \in \mathcal{N}(\tau_k)} \alpha_{kj} \cdot p_j^{(t)}(c), \tag{2}$$

where the normalized coefficient α_{kj} is defined in Eq. (1). Intuitively, an identity is *strongly* supported for τ_k if one of its neighbors assigns a high probability to it. Next, we turn the evidences for individual identities into a probability vector via a tempered softmax function as

$$p_{\tau_k}^{(t+1)}(c) = \exp(\eta_k(c)/T)/\sum_{c'=1}^{C} \exp(\eta_k(c')/T). \tag{3}$$

Here, T is a temperature the controls how much the probabilies concentrate on the strongest identity. In this scheme, all identities compete for getting high probability values in $\mathbf{p}_{\tau_k}^{(t+1)}$ by collecting the strongest supports from the neighbors. This allows the strongest identity to stand out.

Competitive consensus can be considered as a coordinate ascent method to solve Eq. 4, where we introduce a binary variable $z_{kj}^{(c)}$ to indicate whether the j-th neighbor is a trustable source for the class c for the k-th tracklet. Here, $\mathcal{H}$ is the entropy. The constraint means that one trustable source is selected for each class c and tracklet k.

$$\max \sum_{c=1}^{C} p_{\tau_k}^{(c)} \sum_{j \in \mathcal{N}(\tau_k)} \alpha_{kj} z_{kj}^{(c)} p_j^{(c)} + \sum_{c=1}^{C} \mathcal{H}(p_{\tau_k}^{(c)}) \quad s.t. \sum_{j \in \mathcal{N}(\tau_k)} z_{kj}^{(c)} = 1. \tag{4}$$

Figure 5 illustrates how linear diffusion and our competitive Consensus work. Experiments on CSM also show that competitive consensus significantly improves the performance of the person search problem.

4.3   Progressive Propagation

In conventional label propagation, labels of all the nodes would be updated until convergence. This way can be prohibitively expensive when the graph contains

Table 2. Train/Val/Test splits of CSM

	Movies	Cast	Tracklets	Credited tracklets
Train	115	739	79K	47K
Val	19	147	15K	8K
Test	58	332	32K	18K
Total	192	1,218	127K	73K

Table 3. Query/Gallery size

Setting	Query	Gallery
IN (per movie)	6.4	560.5
CROSS	332	17,927

a large number of nodes. However, for the person search problem, this is unnecessary – when we are very confident about the identity of a certain instance, we don't have to keep updating it.

Motivated by the analysis above, we propose a *progressive propagation* scheme to accelerate the propagation process. At each iteration, we will fix the labels for a certain fraction of nodes that have the highest confidence, where the confidence is defined to be the maximum probability value in $\mathbf{p}_i$. We found empirically that a simple freezing schedule, *e.g.* adding 10% of the instances to the label-frozen set, can already bring notable benefits to the propagation process.

Note that the progressive scheme not only reduces computational cost but also improves propagation accuracy. The reason is that without freezing, the noise and the uncertain nodes will keep affecting all the other nodes, which can sometimes cause additional errors. Experiments in Sect. 5.3 will show more details.

5 Experiments

5.1 Evaluation Protocol and Metrics of CSM

The 192 movies in CSM are partitioned into training (train), validation (val) and testing (test) sets. Statistics of these sets are shown in Table 2. Note that we make sure that there is no overlap between the cast of different sets. *i.e.* the cast in the testing set would not appear in training and validation. This ensures the reliability of the testing results.

Under the Person Search with One Portrait setting, one should rank all the tracklets in the gallery given a query. For this task, we use *mean Average Precision (mAP)* as the evaluation metric. We also report the recall of tracklet identification results in our experiments in terms of R@k. Here, we rank the identities for each tracklet according to their probabilities. R@k means the fraction of tracklets for which the correct identity is listed within the top k results.

We consider two test settings in the CSM benchmark named "search cast in a movie" (IN) and "search cast across all movies" (ACROSS). The setting "IN" means the gallery consists of just the tracklets from one movie, including the tracklets of the credited cast and those of "others". While in the "ACROSS" setting, the gallery comprises all the tracklets of credited cast in testing set. Here we exclude the tracklets of "others" in the "ACROSS" setting because "others" just means that it does not belong to any one of the credited cast of a particular movie rather than all the movies in the dataset as we have mentioned in Sect. 3. Table 3 shows the query/gallery sizes of each setting.

5.2   Implementation Details

We use two kinds of visual features in our experiments. The first one is the IDE feature [44] widely used in person re-id. The IDE descriptor is a CNN feature of the whole person instance, extracted by a Resnet-50 [12], which is pre-trained on ImageNet [31] and finetuned on the training set of CSM. The second one is the *face feature*, extracted by a Resnet-101, which is trained on MS-Celeb-1M [10]. For each instance, we extract its IDE feature and the face feature of the face region, which is detected by a face detector [42]. All the visual similarities in experiments are calculated by cosines similarity between the visual features.

Table 4. Results on CSM under two test settings

	IN				ACROSS			
	mAP	R@1	R@3	R@5	mAP	R@1	R@3	R@5
FACE	53.33	76.19	91.11	96.34	42.16	53.15	61.12	64.33
IDE	17.17	35.89	72.05	88.05	1.67	1.68	4.46	6.85
FACE+IDE	53.71	74.99	90.30	96.08	40.43	49.04	58.16	62.10
LP	8.19	39.70	70.11	87.34	0.37	0.41	1.60	5.04
PPCC-v	62.37	**84.31**	**94.89**	**98.03**	59.58	**63.26**	**74.89**	**78.88**
PPCC-vt	**63.49**	83.44	94.40	97.92	**62.27**	62.54	73.86	77.44

5.3   Results on CSM

We set up four baselines for comparison: (1) **FACE:** To match the portrait with the tracklet in the gallery by face feature similarity. Here we use the mean feature of all the instances in the tracklet to represent it. (2) **IDE:** Similar to FACE, except that the IDE features are used rather than the face features. (3) **IDE+FACE:** To combine face similarity and IDE similarity for matching, respectively with weights 0.8 and 0.2. (4) **LP:** Conventional label propagation with linear diffusion with both visual and temporal links. Specifically, we use face similarity as the visual links between portraits and candidates and the IDE similarity as the visual links between different candidates. We also consider two settings of the proposed Progressive Propagation via Competitive Consensus method. (5) **PPCC-v:** using only visual links. (6) **PPCC-vt:** the full config with both visual and temporal links.

From the results in Table 4, we can see that: (1) Even with a very powerful CNN trained on a large-scale dataset, matching portrait and candidates by visual cues cannot solve the person search problem well due to the big gap of visual appearances between the portraits and the candidates. Although face features are generally more stable than IDE features, they would fail when the faces are invisible, which is very common in real-world videos like movies. (2) Label propagation with linear diffusion gets very poor results, even worse than the matching-based methods. (3) Our approach raises the performance by a considerable margin. Particularly, the performance gain is especially remarkable on the more challenging "ACROSS" setting (62.27 with ours vs. 42.16 with the visual matching method).

Analysis on Competitive Consensus. To show the effectiveness of *Competitive Consensus*, we study different settings of the Competitive Consensus scheme in two aspects: (1) The max in Eq. (3) can be relaxed to top-k average. Here k indicates the number of neighbors to receive information from. When $k = 1$, it reduces to only taking the maximum, which is what we use in PPCC. Performances obtained with different k are shown in Fig. 6. (2) We also study on the "softmax" in Eq. (3) and compare results between different temperatures of it. The results are also shown in Fig. 6. Clearly, using smaller temperature of softmax significantly boosts the performance. This study supports what we have claimed when designing *Competitive Consensus*: we should only propagate the most confident information in this task.

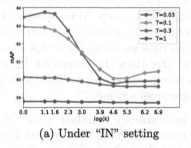
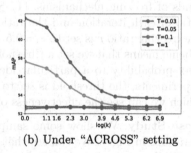

(a) Under "IN" setting   (b) Under "ACROSS" setting

Fig. 6. mAP of different settings of competitive consensus. Comparison between different temperatures(T) of softmax and different settings of k (in top-k average).

Table 5. Results of different updating schemes

	IN				ACROSS			
	mAP	R@1	R@3	R@5	mAP	R@1	R@3	R@5
Conventional	60.54	76.64	91.63	96.70	57.42	54.60	63.31	66.41
Threshold	62.51	81.04	93.61	97.48	61.20	61.54	72.31	76.01
Step	**63.49**	**83.44**	**94.40**	**97.92**	**62.27**	**62.54**	**73.86**	**77.44**

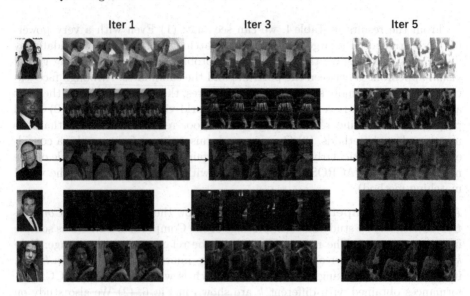

Fig. 7. Some samples that are correctly searched in different iterations.

Analysis on Progressive Propagation. Here we show the comparison between our progressive updating scheme and the conventional scheme that updates all the nodes at each iteration. For progressive propagation, we try two kinds of freezing mechanisms: (1) *Step* scheme means that we set the freezing ratio of each iteration and the ratio are raised step by step. More specifically, the freezing ratio r is set to $r = 0.5 + 0.1 \times$ iter in our experiment. (2) *Threshold* scheme means that we set a threshold, and each time we freeze the nodes whose max probability to a particular identity is greater than the threshold. In our experiments, the threshold is set to 0.5. The results are shown in Table 5, from which we can see the effectiveness of the progressives scheme.

Case Study. We show some samples that are correctly searched in different iterations in Fig. 7. We can see that the easy cases, which are usually with clear frontal faces, can be identified at the beginning. And after iterative propagation, the information can be propagated to the harder samples. At the end of the propagation, even some very hard samples, which are non-frontal, blurred, occluded and under extreme illumination, can be propagated a right identity.

6   Conclusion

In this paper, we studied a new problem named *Person Search in Videos with One Protrait*, which is challenging but practical in the real world. To promote the research on this problem, we construct a large-scale dataset *CSM*, which contains $127K$ tracklets of $1,218$ cast from 192 movies. To tackle this problem, we proposed a new framework that incorporates both visual and temporal links for identity propagation, with a novel *Progressive Propagation vis Competitive Consensus* scheme. Both quantitative and qualitative studies show the challenges of the problem and the effectiveness of our approach.

Acknowledgement. This work is partially supported by the Big Data Collaboration Research grant from SenseTime Group (CUHK Agreement No. TS1610626), the General Research Fund (GRF) of Hong Kong (No. 14236516).

References

1. Ahmed, E., Jones, M., Marks, T.K.: An improved deep learning architecture for person re-identification. In: Proceedings of the IEEE Conference on Computer Vision and Pattern Recognition, pp. 3908–3916 (2015)
2. Apostolidis, E., Mezaris, V.: Fast shot segmentation combining global and local visual descriptors. In: 2014 IEEE International Conference on Acoustics, Speech and Signal Processing (ICASSP), pp. 6583–6587. IEEE (2014)
3. Cheng, D., Gong, Y., Zhou, S., Wang, J., Zheng, N.: Person re-identification by multi-channel parts-based cnn with improved triplet loss function. In: Proceedings of the IEEE Conference on Computer Vision and Pattern Recognition, pp. 1335–1344 (2016)
4. Ding, S., Lin, L., Wang, G., Chao, H.: Deep feature learning with relative distance comparison for person re-identification. Pattern Recogn. **48**(10), 2993–3003 (2015)
5. Feris, R., Bobbitt, R., Brown, L., Pankanti, S.: Attribute-based people search: lessons learnt from a practical surveillance system. In: Proceedings of International Conference on Multimedia Retrieval, p. 153. ACM (2014)
6. Gheissari, N., Sebastian, T.B., Hartley, R.: Person reidentification using spatiotemporal appearance. In: 2006 IEEE Computer Society Conference on Computer Vision and Pattern Recognition, vol. 2, pp. 1528–1535. IEEE (2006)
7. Gong, S., Cristani, M., Yan, S., Loy, C.C. (eds.): Person Re-Identification. ACVPR. Springer, London (2014). https://doi.org/10.1007/978-1-4471-6296-4
8. Gou, M., Karanam, S., Liu, W., Camps, O., Radke, R.J.: DukeMTMC4ReID: a large-scale multi-camera person re-identification dataset. In: IEEE Conference on Computer Vision and Pattern Recognition Workshops (2017)
9. Gray, D., Tao, H.: Viewpoint invariant pedestrian recognition with an ensemble of localized features. In: Forsyth, D., Torr, P., Zisserman, A. (eds.) ECCV 2008. LNCS, vol. 5302, pp. 262–275. Springer, Heidelberg (2008). https://doi.org/10.1007/978-3-540-88682-2_21
10. Guo, Y., Zhang, L., Hu, Y., He, X., Gao, J.: Ms-celeb-1m: challenge of recognizing one million celebrities in the real world. Electron. Imaging **2016**(11), 1–6 (2016)
11. Hamdoun, O., Moutarde, F., Stanciulescu, B., Steux, B.: Person re-identification in multi-camera system by signature based on interest point descriptors collected on short video sequences. In: Second ACM/IEEE International Conference on Distributed Smart Cameras (ICDSC 2008), pp. 1–6. IEEE (2008)
12. He, K., Zhang, X., Ren, S., Sun, J.: Deep residual learning for image recognition. In: Proceedings of the IEEE Conference on Computer Vision and Pattern Recognition, pp. 770–778 (2016)

13. Hirzer, M., Beleznai, C., Roth, P.M., Bischof, H.: Person re-identification by descriptive and discriminative classification. In: Heyden, A., Kahl, F. (eds.) SCIA 2011. LNCS, vol. 6688, pp. 91–102. Springer, Heidelberg (2011). https://doi.org/10.1007/978-3-642-21227-7_9

14. Huang, Q., Xiong, Y., Lin, D.: Unifying identification and context learning for person recognition. In: Proceedings of the IEEE Conference on Computer Vision and Pattern Recognition, pp. 2217–2225 (2018)

15. Joon Oh, S., Benenson, R., Fritz, M., Schiele, B.: Person recognition in personal photo collections. In: Proceedings of the IEEE International Conference on Computer Vision, pp. 3862–3870 (2015)

16. Karanam, S., Gou, M., Wu, Z., Rates-Borras, A., Camps, O., Radke, R.J.: A systematic evaluation and benchmark for person re-identification: features, metrics, and datasets. arXiv preprint arXiv:1605.09653 (2016)

17. Koestinger, M., Hirzer, M., Wohlhart, P., Roth, P.M., Bischof, H.: Large scale metric learning from equivalence constraints. In: 2012 IEEE Conference on Computer Vision and Pattern Recognition (CVPR), pp. 2288–2295. IEEE (2012)

18. Kumar, V., Namboodiri, A.M., Jawahar, C.: Face recognition in videos by label propagation. In: 2014 22nd International Conference on Pattern Recognition (ICPR), pp. 303–308. IEEE (2014)

19. Li, H., Brandt, J., Lin, Z., Shen, X., Hua, G.: A multi-level contextual model for person recognition in photo albums. In: Proceedings of the IEEE Conference on Computer Vision and Pattern Recognition, pp. 1297–1305 (2016)

20. Li, H., Lu, H., Lin, Z., Shen, X., Price, B.: Inner and inter label propagation: salient object detection in the wild. IEEE Trans. Image Process. **24**(10), 3176–3186 (2015)

21. Li, S., Xiao, T., Li, H., Zhou, B., Yue, D., Wang, X.: Person search with natural language description. In: Proceedings of the CVPR (2017)

22. Li, W., Zhao, R., Xiao, T., Wang, X.: Deepreid: deep filter pairing neural network for person re-identification. In: Proceedings of the IEEE Conference on Computer Vision and Pattern Recognition, pp. 152–159 (2014)

23. Liao, S., Hu, Y., Zhu, X., Li, S.Z.: Person re-identification by local maximal occurrence representation and metric learning. In: Proceedings of the IEEE Conference on Computer Vision and Pattern Recognition, pp. 2197–2206 (2015)

24. Lin, D., Kapoor, A., Hua, G., Baker, S.: Joint people, event, and location recognition in personal photo collections using cross-domain context. In: Daniilidis, K., Maragos, P., Paragios, N. (eds.) ECCV 2010. LNCS, vol. 6311, pp. 243–256. Springer, Heidelberg (2010). https://doi.org/10.1007/978-3-642-15549-9_18

25. Lin, T.-Y., Maire, M., Belongie, S., Hays, J., Perona, P., Ramanan, D., Dollár, P., Zitnick, C.L.: Microsoft COCO: common objects in context. In: Fleet, D., Pajdla, T., Schiele, B., Tuytelaars, T. (eds.) ECCV 2014. LNCS, vol. 8693, pp. 740–755. Springer, Cham (2014). https://doi.org/10.1007/978-3-319-10602-1_48

26. Ma, B., Su, Y., Jurie, F.: Local descriptors encoded by fisher vectors for person re-identification. In: Fusiello, A., Murino, V., Cucchiara, R. (eds.) ECCV 2012. LNCS, vol. 7583, pp. 413–422. Springer, Heidelberg (2012). https://doi.org/10.1007/978-3-642-33863-2_41

27. Ma, B., Su, Y., Jurie, F.: Covariance descriptor based on bio-inspired features for person re-identification and face verification. Image Vis. Comput. **32**(6–7), 379–390 (2014)

28. Prosser, B.J., Zheng, W.S., Gong, S., Xiang, T., Mary, Q.: Person re-identification by support vector ranking. In: BMVC, vol. 2, p. 6 (2010)

29. Ren, S., He, K., Girshick, R., Sun, J.: Faster R-CNN: towards real-time object detection with region proposal networks. In: Advances in Neural Information Processing Systems, pp. 91–99 (2015)
30. Rohrbach, M., Ebert, S., Schiele, B.: Transfer learning in a transductive setting. In: Advances in nEural Information Processing Systems, pp. 46–54 (2013)
31. Russakovsky, O., et al.: Imagenet large scale visual recognition challenge. Int. J. Comput. Vis. **115**(3), 211–252 (2015)
32. Sener, O., Song, H.O., Saxena, A., Savarese, S.: Learning transferrable representations for unsupervised domain adaptation. In: Advances in Neural Information Processing Systems, pp. 2110–2118 (2016)
33. Sheikh, R., Garbade, M., Gall, J.: Real-time semantic segmentation with label propagation. In: Hua, G., Jégou, H. (eds.) ECCV 2016. LNCS, vol. 9914, pp. 3–14. Springer, Cham (2016). https://doi.org/10.1007/978-3-319-48881-3_1
34. Sidiropoulos, P., Mezaris, V., Kompatsiaris, I., Meinedo, H., Bugalho, M., Trancoso, I.: Temporal video segmentation to scenes using high-level audiovisual features. IEEE Trans. Circ. Syst. Video Technol. **21**(8), 1163–1177 (2011)
35. Su, C., Zhang, S., Xing, J., Gao, W., Tian, Q.: Deep attributes driven multi-camera person re-identification. In: Leibe, B., Matas, J., Sebe, N., Welling, M. (eds.) ECCV 2016. LNCS, vol. 9906, pp. 475–491. Springer, Cham (2016). https://doi.org/10.1007/978-3-319-46475-6_30
36. Tripathi, S., Belongie, S., Hwang, Y., Nguyen, T.: Detecting temporally consistent objects in videos through object class label propagation. In: 2016 IEEE Winter Conference on Applications of Computer Vision (WACV), pp. 1–9. IEEE (2016)
37. Wang, J., Jebara, T., Chang, S.F.: Graph transduction via alternating minimization. In: Proceedings of the 25th International Conference on Machine Learning, pp. 1144–1151. ACM (2008)
38. Wang, T., Gong, S., Zhu, X., Wang, S.: Person re-identification by discriminative selection in video ranking. IEEE Trans. Pattern Anal. Mach. Intell. **38**(12), 2501–2514 (2016)
39. Xiao, T., Li, H., Ouyang, W., Wang, X.: Learning deep feature representations with domain guided dropout for person re-identification. In: 2016 IEEE Conference on Computer Vision and Pattern Recognition (CVPR), pp. 1249–1258. IEEE (2016)
40. Xiao, T., Li, S., Wang, B., Lin, L., Wang, X.: Joint detection and identification feature learning for person search. In: 2017 IEEE Conference on Computer Vision and Pattern Recognition (CVPR), pp. 3376–3385. IEEE (2017)
41. Zajdel, W., Zivkovic, Z., Krose, B.: Keeping track of humans: have i seen this person before? In: Proceedings of the 2005 IEEE International Conference on Robotics and Automation, ICRA 2005. pp. 2081–2086. IEEE (2005)
42. Zhang, K., Zhang, Z., Li, Z., Qiao, Y.: Joint face detection and alignment using multitask cascaded convolutional networks. IEEE Sig. Process. Lett. **23**(10), 1499–1503 (2016)
43. Zhang, N., Paluri, M., Taigman, Y., Fergus, R., Bourdev, L.: Beyond frontal faces: improving person recognition using multiple cues. In: Proceedings of the IEEE Conference on Computer Vision and Pattern Recognition, pp. 4804–4813 (2015)
44. Zheng, L., et al.: MARS: a video benchmark for large-scale person re-identification. In: Leibe, B., Matas, J., Sebe, N., Welling, M. (eds.) ECCV 2016. LNCS, vol. 9910, pp. 868–884. Springer, Cham (2016). https://doi.org/10.1007/978-3-319-46466-4_52
45. Zheng, L., Shen, L., Tian, L., Wang, S., Wang, J., Tian, Q.: Scalable person re-identification: a benchmark. In: Proceedings of the IEEE International Conference on Computer Vision, pp. 1116–1124 (2015)

46. Zhou, D., Bousquet, O., Lal, T.N., Weston, J., Schölkopf, B.: Learning with local and global consistency. In: Advances in Neural Information Processing Systems, pp. 321–328 (2004)
47. Zhu, X., Ghahramani, Z.: Learning from labeled and unlabeled data with label propagation (2002)
48. Zoidi, O., Tefas, A., Nikolaidis, N., Pitas, I.: Person identity label propagation in stereo videos. IEEE Trans. Multimedia 16(5), 1358–1368 (2014)

Decouple Learning for Parameterized Image Operators

Qingnan Fan[1,3], Dongdong Chen[2], Lu Yuan[4], Gang Hua[4],
Nenghai Yu[2], and Baoquan Chen[1,5(✉)]

[1] Shandong University, Jinan, China
fqnchina@gmail.com
[2] University of Science and Technology of China, Hefei, China
cd722522@mail.ustc.edu.cn, ynh@ustc.edu.cn
[3] Beijing Film Academy, Beijing, China
[4] Microsoft Research, Beijing, China
{luyuan,ganghua}@microsoft.com
[5] Peking University, Beijing, China
baoquan@pku.edu.cn

Abstract. Many different deep networks have been used to approximate, accelerate or improve traditional image operators, such as image smoothing, super-resolution and denoising. Among these traditional operators, many contain parameters which need to be tweaked to obtain the satisfactory results, which we refer to as "parameterized image operators". However, most existing deep networks trained for these operators are only designed for one specific parameter configuration, which does not meet the needs of real scenarios that usually require flexible parameters settings. To overcome this limitation, we propose a new decouple learning algorithm to learn from the operator parameters to dynamically adjust the weights of a deep network for image operators, denoted as the *base* network. The learned algorithm is formed as another network, namely the *weight learning* network, which can be end-to-end jointly trained with the *base* network. Experiments demonstrate that the proposed framework can be successfully applied to many traditional parameterized image operators. We provide more analysis to better understand the proposed framework, which may inspire more promising research in this direction. Our codes and models have been released in https://github.com/fqnchina/DecoupleLearning.

1 Introduction

Image operators are fundamental building blocks for many computer vision tasks, such as image smoothing [16,42], super resolution [25,27] and denoising [33]. To

Q. Fan and D. Chen—Equal Contribution.

Electronic supplementary material The online version of this chapter (https://doi.org/10.1007/978-3-030-01261-8_27) contains supplementary material, which is available to authorized users.

V. Ferrari et al. (Eds.): ECCV 2018, LNCS 11217, pp. 455–471, 2018.
https://doi.org/10.1007/978-3-030-01261-8_27

obtain the desired results, many of these operators contain some parameters that need to be tweaked. We refer them as "parameterized image operators" in this paper. For example, parameters controlling the smoothness strength are widespread in most smoothing methods, and a parameter denoting the target upsampling scalar is always used in image super resolution.

Recently, many CNN based methods [16,25,44] have been proposed to approximate, accelerate or improve these parameterized image operators and achieved significant progress. However, we observe that the networks in these methods are often only trained for one specific parameter configuration, such as edge-preserving filtering [16] with a fixed smoothness strength, or super resolving low-quality images [25] with a particular downsampling scale. Many different models need to be retrained for different parameter settings, which is both storage-consuming and time-consuming. It also prohibits these deep learning solutions from being applicable and extendable to a much broader corpus of images.

In fact, given a specific network structure, when training separated networks for different parameter configurations $\overrightarrow{\gamma}_k$ as [16,25,44], the learned weights W_k are unconstrained and probably very different for each $\overrightarrow{\gamma}_k$. But can we find a common convolution weight space for different configurations by explicitly building their relationships? Namely, $W_k = h(\overrightarrow{\gamma}_k)$, where h can be a linear or non-linear function. In this way, we can adaptively change the weights of the single target network based on h in the runtime, thus enabling continuous parameter control.

To verify our hypothesis, we propose the first decouple learning framework for parameterized image operators by decoupling the weights from the target network structure. Specifically, we employ a simple *weight learning* network $\mathcal{N}_{weight}$ as h to directly learn the convolution weights of one task-oriented *base* network $\mathcal{N}_{base}$. These two networks can be trained end-to-end. During the runtime, the *weight learning* network will dynamically update the weights of the *base* network according to different input parameters, thus making the *base* network generate different objective results. This should be a very useful feature in scenarios where users want to adjust and select the most visually pleasant results interactively.

We justify the effectiveness of the proposed framework for many different types of applications, such as edge-preserving image filtering with different degrees of smoothness, image super resolution with different scales of blurring, and image denoising with different magnitudes of noise. We also demonstrate the extensibility of our proposed framework on multiple input parameters for a specific application, and combination of multiple different image processing tasks. Experiments show that the proposed framework is able to learn as good results as the one solely trained with a single parameter value.

As an extra bonus, the proposed framework makes it easy to analyze the underlying working principle of the trained task-oriented network by visualizing different parameters. The knowledge gained from this analysis may inspire more promising research in this area. To sum up, the contributions of this paper lie in the following three aspects.

- We propose the first decouple learning framework for parameterized image operators, where a *weight learning* network is learned to adaptively predict the weights for the task-oriented *base* network in the runtime.
- We show that the proposed framework can be learned to incorporate many different parameterized image operators and achieve very competitive performance with the one trained for a single specific parameter or operator.
- We provide a unique perspective to understand the working principle of the trained task-oriented network with some valuable analysis and discussion, which may inspire more promising research in this area.

2   Related Work

In the past decades, many different image operators have been proposed for low level vision tasks. Previous work [24,42,45,50] proposed different priors to smooth images while preserving salient structures. Some work [2,15] utilized the spatial relationship and redundancy to remove unpleasant noise in the image. Some other papers [37,39,46] aimed to recover a high-resolution image from a low-resolution image. Among them, many operators are allowed to tune some built-in parameters to obtain different results, which is the focus of this paper.

Recently, deep learning has been applied to many different tasks, like recognition [8,9,11,12,29,48,49], generation [28,30,35], and image to image translation [3–5,17,23,32]. For the aforementioned image operators, some methods like [16,31,44] are also proposed to approximate, accelerate and improve them. But their common limitation is that one model can only handle one specific parameter. To enable all other parameters, enormous different models need to be retrained, which is both storage-consuming and time-consuming. By contrast, our proposed framework allows us to input continuous parameters to dynamically adjust the weights of the task-oriented *base* network. Moreover, it can even be applied to multiple different parameterized operators with one single network.

Recently, Chen *et al.* [6] conducted a naive extension for parameterized image operators by concatenating the parameters as extra input channels to the network. Compared to their method, where both the network structure and weights maintain the same for different parameters, the weights of our *base* network are adaptively changed. Experimentally we find our framework outperforms their strategy by integrating multiple image operators. By decoupling the network structure and weights, our proposed framework also makes it easier to analyze the underlying working principle of the trained task-oriented network, rather than leaving it as a black box as in many previous works like [6].

Our method is also related to evolutionary computing and meta learning. Schmidhuber [36] suggested the concept of fast weights in which one network can produce context-dependent weight changes for a second network. Some other works [1,7,41] casted the design of an optimization algorithm as a learning problem, Recently, Ha *et al.* [22] proposed to use a static hypernetwork to generate weights for a convolutional neural network on MNIST and Cifar classification. They also leverage a dynamic hypernetwork to generate weights of recurrent networks for a variety of sequence modelling tasks. The purpose of their paper is to exploit weight sharing property across different convolution layers. But in our cases, we pay more attention to the common shared property among numerous input parameters and many different image operators.

3   Method

3.1   Problem Definition and Motivation

The input color image and the target parameterized image operators are denoted as $\mathcal{I}$ and $f(\overrightarrow{\gamma}, \mathcal{I})$ respectively. $f(\overrightarrow{\gamma}, \mathcal{I})$ transforms the content of $\mathcal{I}$ locally or globally without changing its dimension. $\overrightarrow{\gamma}$ denotes the parameters which determine the transform degree of f and may be a single value or a multi-value vector. For example, in L_0 smoothing [43], $\overrightarrow{\gamma}$ is the balance weight controlling the smoothness strength, while in RTV filter [45], it includes one more spatial gaussian variance. In most cases, f is a highly nonlinear process and solved by iterative optimization methods, which is very slow in runtime.

Our goal is to implement parameterized operator f with a base convolution network $\mathcal{N}_{base}$. In previous methods like [31,44], given a specific network structure of $\mathcal{N}_{base}$, separated networks are trained for different parameter configuration $\overrightarrow{\gamma}_k$. In this way, the learned weights $\overrightarrow{W}_k$ of these separated networks are highly unconstrained and probably very different. But intuitively, for one specific image operator, the weights $\overrightarrow{W}_k$ of different $\overrightarrow{\gamma}_k$ might be related. So retraining separated models is too redundant. Motivated by this, we try to find a common weight space for different $\overrightarrow{\gamma}_k$ by adding a mapping constraint: $\overrightarrow{W}_k = h(\overrightarrow{\gamma}_k)$, where h can be a linear or non-linear function.

In this paper, we directly learn h with another *weight learning* network $\mathcal{N}_{weight}$ rather than design it by handcraft. Assuming $\mathcal{N}_{base}$ is a fully convolutional network having a total of n convolution layers, we denote their weights as $\overrightarrow{W}_k = (W_1, W_2, ..., W_n)$ respectively, then

$$(W_1, W_2, ..., W_n) = \mathcal{N}_{weight}(\overrightarrow{\gamma}) \tag{1}$$

where the input of $\mathcal{N}_{weight}$ is $\overrightarrow{\gamma}$ and the outputs are these weight matrices. In the training stage, $\mathcal{N}_{base}$ and $\mathcal{N}_{weight}$ can be jointly trained. In the inference stage, given different input parameter $\overrightarrow{\gamma}$, $\mathcal{N}_{weight}$ will adaptively change the weights of the target base network $\mathcal{N}_{base}$, thus enabling continuous parameter control.

Besides the original input image $\mathcal{I}$, the computed edge maps are shown to be a very important input signal for the target *base* network in [16]. Therefore, we also pre-calculate the edge map E of $\mathcal{I}$ and concatenate it to the original image as an extra input channel:

$$E_{x,y} = \frac{1}{4} \sum_c (|\mathcal{I}_{x,y,c} - \mathcal{I}_{x-1,y,c}| + |\mathcal{I}_{x,y,c} - \mathcal{I}_{x+1,y,c}|$$
$$+ |\mathcal{I}_{x,y,c} - \mathcal{I}_{x,y-1,c}| + |\mathcal{I}_{x,y,c} - \mathcal{I}_{x,y+1,c}|) \tag{2}$$

where x, y are the pixel coordinates and c refers to the color channels.

To jointly train $\mathcal{N}_{base}$ and $\mathcal{N}_{weight}$, we simply use pixel-wise L2 loss in the RGB color space as [6] by default:

$$\mathcal{L} = \|\mathcal{N}_{base}(\mathcal{N}_{weight}(\overrightarrow{\gamma}), \mathcal{I}, E) - f(\overrightarrow{\gamma}, \mathcal{I})\|^2 \tag{3}$$

3.2 Network Structure

As shown in Fig. 1, our *base* network $\mathcal{N}_{base}$ follows a similar network structure as [16]. We employ 20 convolutional layers with the same 3×3 kernel size, among which the intermediate 14 layers are formed as residual blocks. Except the last convolution layer, all the former convolutional layers are followed by an instance normalization [40] layer and a ReLU layer. To enlarge the receptive field of $\mathcal{N}_{base}$, the third convolution layer downsamples the dimension of feature maps by $1/2$ using stride 2, and the third-to-last deconvolution layer (kernel size of 4×4) upsamples the downsampled feature maps to the original resolution symmetrically. In this way, the receptive field is effectively enlarged without losing too much image detail, and meanwhile the computation cost of intermediate layers is reduced. To further increase the receptive field, we also adopt dilated convolution [47] as [6], more detailed network structure can be found in the supplementary material.

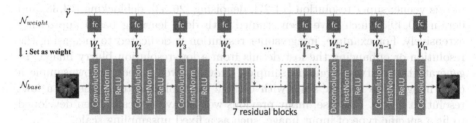

Fig. 1. Our system consists of two networks: the above *weight learning* network $\mathcal{N}_{weight}$ is designed to learn the convolution weights for the bottom *base* network $\mathcal{N}_{base}$. Given a parameterized image operator constraint by $\overrightarrow{\gamma}$, these two networks are jointly trained, and $\mathcal{N}_{weight}$ will dynamically update the weights of $\mathcal{N}_{base}$ for different $\overrightarrow{\gamma}$ in the inference stage.

In this paper, the *weight learning* network $\mathcal{N}_{weight}$ simply consists of 20 fully connected (fc) layers by default. The i_{th} fc layer is responsible to learn the weights W_i for the i_{th} convolutional layer, which can be written as following:

$$W_i = A_i \overrightarrow{\gamma} + B_i, \qquad \forall i \in \{1, 2, ..., 20\} \tag{4}$$

where A_i, B_i are the weight and bias of the i_{th} fc layer. Assuming the parameter $\overrightarrow{\gamma}$ has a dimension of m and W_i has a dimension of n_{wi}. The dimension of A_i and B_i would be $n_{wi} \times m$ and n_{wi} respectively.

Note in this paper, we don't intend to design an optimal network structure neither for the *base* network $\mathcal{N}_{base}$ nor the *weight learning* network $\mathcal{N}_{weight}$. On the contrary, we care more about whether it is feasible to learn the relationship of the weights of $\mathcal{N}_{base}$ and different parameter configurations $\overrightarrow{\gamma}$ even by such a simple *weight learning* network $\mathcal{N}_{weight}$.

4   Experiments

4.1   Choice of Image Operators

To evaluate the proposed framework on a broad scope of parameterized image operators, we leverage two representative types of image processing tasks: image filtering and image restoration. Within each of them, more than four popular operators are selected for detailed experiments.

Image Filtering. Here we employ six popular image filters, denoted as L_0 [42], WLS [18], RTV [45], RGF [50], WMF [51] and shock filter [34], which have been developed to work especially well for many different applications, such as image abstraction, detail exaggeration, texture removal and image enhancement. However, previous deep learning based approaches [16,31,44] are only able to deal with one single parameter value in one trained model, which is far from practical.

Image Restoration. The goal of image restoration is to recover a clear image from a corrupted image. In this paper we deal with four representative tasks in this venue: super resolution [14,27], denoising [26,33], deblocking [13,38] and derain [20,49], which have been studied with deep learning based approaches extensively. For example, image super resolution is dedicated to increasing the resolution or enhancing the lost details from a low-resolution blurry image. To generate the pairwise training samples, previous work used to downsample a clear image by a specific scale with bicubic interpolation to synthesize a low-resolution image. Likewise, many previous works have typically been developed to fit a specific type of input image, such as a fixed upsampling scale.

4.2   Implementation Details

Dataset. We take use of the 17k natural images in the PASCAL VOC dataset as the clear images to synthesize the ground truth training samples. The PASCAL VOC images are picked from Flicker, and consists of a wide range of viewing conditions. To evaluate our performance, 100 images from the dataset are randomly picked as the test data for the image filtering task. While for the restoration tasks, we take the well-known benchmark for each specific task for testing, which is specifically BSD100 (super resolution), BSD68 (denoise), LIVE1 (deblock), RAIN12 (derain). For the filtering task, we filter the natural images with the aforementioned algorithms to produce ground truth labels. As for the image restoration tasks, the clear natural image is taken as the target image while the synthesized corrupted image is used as input.

Parameter Sampling. To make our network able to handle various parameters, we generate training image pairs with a much broader scope of parameter values rather than a single one. We uniformly sample parameters in either the logarithm or the linear space depending on the specific application. Regarding the case of logarithm space, let l and u be the lower bound and upper bound of the parameter, the parameters are sampled as follows:

$$y = e^x, \text{ where } x \in [\ln l, \ln u] \tag{5}$$

In other words, we first uniformly sample x between $\ln l$ and $\ln u$, then map it back by the exponential function, similar to the one used in [6]. Note if the upper bound u is tens or even hundreds of times larger than the lower bound l, the parameters are sampled in the logarithm space to balance their magnitudes, otherwise they are sampled in the linear space.

Table 1. Quantitative absolute difference between the network trained with a *single* parameter value and *numerous* random values for each image smoothing filter.

Metric	L_0				WLS				RTV			
	λ	single	nume.	diff	λ	single	nume.	diff	λ	single	nume.	diff
PSNR	0.002	40.69	39.46	1.23	0.100	44.00	42.12	1.88	0.002	41.11	40.66	0.45
	0.004	38.96	38.72	0.24	0.215	43.14	42.64	0.50	0.004	40.91	41.10	0.19
	0.020	36.07	35.71	0.36	1.000	41.93	41.63	0.30	0.010	40.50	41.07	0.57
	0.093	33.08	31.92	1.16	4.641	39.42	39.64	0.22	0.022	41.07	40.77	0.30
	0.200	31.75	30.43	1.32	10.00	39.13	38.51	0.62	0.050	40.73	39.18	1.55
	ave.	36.11	35.25	**0.86**	ave.	41.52	40.91	**0.61**	ave.	40.86	40.55	**0.31**
SSIM	0.002	0.989	0.988	0.001	0.100	0.994	0.993	0.001	0.002	0.987	0.988	0.001
	0.004	0.986	0.987	0.001	0.215	0.993	0.993	0	0.004	0.989	0.990	0.001
	0.020	0.982	0.981	0.001	1.000	0.992	0.991	0.001	0.010	0.990	0.991	0.001
	0.093	0.977	0.973	0.004	4.641	0.987	0.989	0.002	0.022	0.992	0.992	0
	0.200	0.973	0.968	0.005	10.00	0.986	0.987	0.001	0.050	0.992	0.990	0.002
	ave.	0.981	0.979	**0.002**	ave.	0.990	0.990	**0**	ave.	0.990	0.990	**0**

4.3   Qualitative and Quantitative Comparison

Image Filtering. We first experiment with our framework on five image filters. To evaluate the performance of our proposed algorithm, we train one network for each parameter value (λ) in one filter, and also train a network jointly on continuous random values sampled from the filter's parameter range, which can be inferred from the λ column in Table 1. The performance of the two networks is evaluated on the test dataset with PSNR and SSIM error metrics. Since our goal is to measure the performance difference between these two strategies, we directly compute the absolute difference of their errors and demonstrate the results in Table 1. The results of the other two filters (RGF and WMF) are shown in the supplemental material due to space limitations.

As can be seen, though our proposed framework lags a little behind the one trained on a single parameter value, their difference is too small to be notice-able, especially for the SSIM error metric. Note that for each image filter, our algorithm only requires one jointly trained network, but previous methods need to train separate networks for each parameter value. Moreover even if the five filters are dedicated to different image processing applications, and varies a lot in their implementation details, our proposed framework is still able to learn all of them well, which verifies the versatility and robustness of our strategy.

Some visual results of our proposed framework are shown in Fig. 2. As can be seen, our single network trained on continuous random parameter values is capable of predicting high-quality smooth images of various strengths.

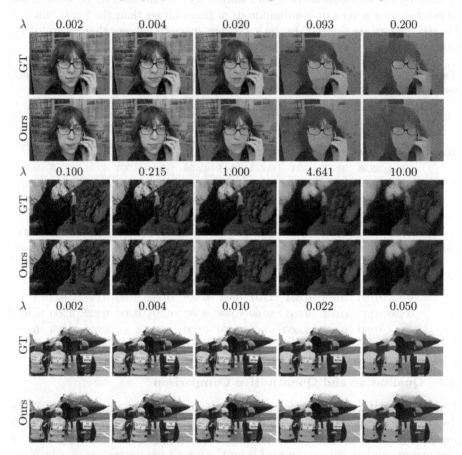

Fig. 2. Visual examples produced by our framework trained on continuous parameter settings of L_0 [42] (top), WLS [18] (middle) and RTV [45] (bottom) filters independently. Note all the smooth images for one filter are generated by a single network.

Image Restoration. We then evaluate the proposed framework on three popular image restoration tasks as shown in Table 2, which perform essentially different from image filtering. Unlike the above operators which employ the filtered images as target to learn, this task takes the clear images as the ground truth label while the corrupted images as input. That is to say, as for the former task, given an input image, our network learns different filtering effects, while regarding the latter one, our model learns to recover from different corrupted images.

Table 2. Quantitative absolute difference in PSNR and SSIM between the network trained on a *single* parameter value and *numerous* random values on the three image restoration tasks. Their parameters specifically mean downsampling scale (s), Gaussian standard deviation (σ) and JPEG quality (q).

Metric	Super resolution				Denoising				Deblock			
	s	single	nume.	diff	σ	single	nume.	diff	q	single	nume.	diff
PSNR	2	31.78	31.62	0.16	15	31.17	31.07	0.10	10	29.26	29.17	0.09
	3	28.78	28.76	0.02	25	28.94	28.98	0.04	20	31.49	31.43	0.06
	4	27.31	27.31	0	50	26.22	26.14	0.08				
	ave.	29.29	29.23	**0.06**	ave.	28.77	28.73	**0.04**	ave.	30.37	30.30	**0.07**
SSIM	2	0.894	0.892	0.002	15	0.881	0.883	0.002	10	0.817	0.817	0
	3	0.798	0.796	0.002	25	0.821	0.822	0.001	20	0.881	0.882	0.001
	4	0.728	0.726	0.002	50	0.722	0.718	0.004				
	ave.	0.806	0.804	**0.002**	ave.	0.808	0.807	**0.001**	ave.	0.849	0.849	**0**

As shown in Table 2, our results trained jointly on continuous random parameter values also show no big difference from the one trained solely on an individual parameter value, which further validate our algorithm in a broader image processing literature.

4.4 Extension to Multiple Input Parameters

Except for experimenting on a single input parameter, we also demonstrate our results on inputting multiple types of parameters, which is still very common for many image processing tasks.

In this section, we evaluate our performance on the famous texture removal tool RTV [45]. Likewise in previous experiments, we leverage λ which balances between the data prior term and smoothness term in its energy function as one parameter, and σ which controls the spatial scale for computing the windowed variation and is even more effective in removing textures. To generate the training samples, we randomly sample these two parameters. Therefore, the input parameter $\vec{\gamma}$ of the *weight learning* network is a two-element vector $[\lambda, \sigma]$.

To evaluate the performance of our network on this two dimensional parameter space compared with the single parameter setting case, we sample a few parameters along one dimension while fixing another as shown in Table 3. We can see that for most of the 10 parameter settings, all achieve very close results to the one trained with an individual parameter setting. This verifies the effectiveness of our proposed network on this more difficult case.

Table 3. Quantitative comparison between the network trained on a *single* parameter setting and *numerous* random settings under the condition of multiple input parameters. Their absolute difference is shown besides the value of *nume*. The results are tested by fixing one parameter while varying another.

RTV ($\lambda = 0.01$)			RTV ($\sigma = 3$)			
σ	single	nume.	diff	λ	single	nume.	diff
2	40.53	40.39	0.14	0.002	41.11	40.17	0.94
3	39.52	40.76	1.24	0.004	40.91	40.78	0.13
4	41.19	41.06	0.13	0.010	40.50	40.76	0.26
5	41.29	41.26	0.03	0.022	41.07	40.45	0.62
6	41.81	41.19	0.62	0.050	40.73	38.52	2.21
ave.	40.86	40.93	**0.06**	ave.	40.86	40.14	**0.72**

Table 4. Numerical results (PSNR (above) and SSIM (bottom)) of our proposed framework jointly trained over different number of image operators (#operators). "6/4" refers to the results jointly trained over either the front 6 filtering based approaches or the last 4 restoration tasks. "10" is the results of jointly training all 10 tasks.

#ope.	L_0	WLS	RTV	RGF	WMF	shock	SR	denoise	deblock	derain	ave.
1	35.25	40.91	40.55	37.74	38.40	37.88	29.13	28.70	30.21	29.86	**34.86**
6/4	33.54	38.02	37.69	35.90	36.46	35.27	28.89	28.67	30.10	30.32	**33.49**
10	33.09	37.34	36.89	35.26	35.69	33.57	28.58	28.43	29.76	30.30	**32.89**
1	0.979	0.991	0.990	0.984	0.980	0.987	0.804	0.804	0.847	0.893	**0.925**
6/4	0.972	0.983	0.982	0.976	0.970	0.979	0.797	0.800	0.842	0.893	**0.919**
10	0.967	0.980	0.978	0.973	0.966	0.970	0.791	0.792	0.838	0.890	**0.914**

4.5   Extension to Joint Training of Multiple Image Operators

Intuitively, another challenging case for our proposed framework is to incorporate multiple distinct image operators into a single learned neural network, which is much harder to be trained due to their different implementation details and purposes. To explore the potential of our proposed neural network, we experiment by jointly training over (*i*). 6 filtering based operators, (*ii*). 4 image restoration operators or (*iii*). all the 10 different operators altogether. To generate training images of each image operator, we sample random parameter values continuously within its parameter range. For the shock filter and derain task, we leverage its default parameter setting for training.

The input to the *weight learning* network now takes two parameters, one indicates the specific image operator while the other is the random parameter values assigned to the specified filter. These 10 image operators are denoted simply by 10 discrete values that range from 0.1 to 1.0 in the input parameter vector. Since the absolute parameter range may differ a lot from operator to operator, for example, [2,4] for super resolution and [0.002,0.2] for L_0 filter, we rescale the parameters in all the operators into the same numerical range to enable consistent back-propagated gradient magnitude.

As shown in Table 4, training on each individual image operator achieves the highest numerical score (#ope.=1), which is averaged over multiple different parameter settings just like in previous tables. While jointly training over either 6 image filters or 4 restoration tasks (#ope.=6/4), even for the case where all 10 image operators are jointly trained (#ope.=10), their average performance degrades but still achieves close results to the best score. It means with the same network structure, our framework is able to incorporate all these different image operators together into a single network without losing much accuracy.

Note that for the image restoration tasks, it is more meaningful not to specify parameters since in real life, users usually do not know the corruption degree of the input image. Therefore, we disable specifying parameters for the four restoration operators in this experiment. Surprisingly, we do not observe much performance degradation with this modification. Though it degrades the necessity of learning continuous parameter settings for image restoration tasks, it still makes a lot of sense by jointly training multiple image operators.

4.6 Comparison with State-of-the-art Image Operators

Note that we do not argue for the best performance in each specific task, since this is not the goal of this paper. Essentially, the performance on image operators is determined by the *base* network structure, which is not our contribution, but many others [16,31,44] which develop more complex and advanced networks on each specific task. Even if this is not our goal, we still provide comparisons to demonstrate that our general framework performs comparably or even better than many previous work (one operator with one parameter).

Regarding *image filtering*, the best performance is achieved by [16]. For the WLS filter example, with our simple and straightforward *base* network trained with continuous parameter settings, we achieve very comparable results with [16] (PSNR/SSIM: 41.07/0.991 *vs.* 41.39/0.994), which are superior to [31] (PSNR/SSIM: 38.29/0.983) and [44] (PSNR/SSIM: 33.92/0.963).

As for *image restoration*, our framework trained with all four image restoration tasks performs better than DerainNet [19] on the derain task (PSNR:30.32 vs 28.94 on RAIN12 dataset). And our model also achieves better PSNR (26.02) than many previous approaches BM3D [10] (25.62), EPLL [52](25.67), WNNM [21] (25.87) on the BSD68 dataset for the denoising task.

4.7 Understanding and Analysis

To better understand the *base* network $\mathcal{N}_{base}$ and the *weight learning* network $\mathcal{N}_{weight}$, we will conduct some analysis experiments in this section.

The Effective Receptive Field. In neuroscience, the receptive field is the particular region of the sensory space in which a stimulus will modify the firing of one specific neuron. The large receptive field is also known to be important for modern convolutional networks. Different strategies are proposed to increase the receptive field, such as deeper network structure or dilated convolution. Though the theoretical receptive field of one network may be very large, the real effective receptive field may vary with different learning targets. So how is the effective receptive field of $\mathcal{N}_{base}$ changed with different parameters $\overrightarrow{\gamma}$ and $\mathcal{I}$? Here we use L_0 smoothing [43] as the default example operator.

(a) Input image   (b) $\lambda = 0.01$ (c) $\lambda = 0.02$ (d) $\lambda = 0.03$ (e) $\lambda = 0.04$

Fig. 3. Effective receptive field of L_0 smoothing for different spatial positions and parameter λ. The top to bottom indicate the effective receptive field of a non-edge point, a moderate edge point, and a strong edge point.

In Fig. 3, we study the effective receptive field of a non-edge point, a moderate edge point, and a strong edge point with different smoothing parameters λ respectively. To obtain the effective receptive field for a specific spatial point p, we first feed the input image into the network to get the smoothing result, then propagate the gradients back to the input while masking out the gradient of all points except p. Only the points whose gradient value is large than $0.025 * grad_{max}$ ($grad_{max}$ is the maximum gradient value of input gradient) are considered within the receptive field and marked as green in Fig. 3. From Fig. 3, we observe three important phenomena: (1) For a non-edge point, the larger the smoothing parameter λ is, the larger the effective field is, and most effective points fall within the object boundary. (2) For a moderate edge point, its receptive field stays small until a relatively large smoothing parameter is used. (3) For a strong edge point, the effective receptive field is always small for all the different smoothing parameters. It means, on one hand, the *weight learning* network $\mathcal{N}_{weight}$ can dynamically change the receptive field of $\mathcal{N}_{base}$ based on different smoothing parameters. On the other hand, the *base* network $\mathcal{N}_{base}$ itself can also adaptively change its receptive field for different spatial points.

Decomposition of the Weight Learning Network. To help understand the connection between the *base* network $\mathcal{N}_{base}$ and the *weight learning* network $\mathcal{N}_{weight}$, we decompose the parameter vector $\overrightarrow{\gamma}$ and the weight matrix A_i into independent elements $\gamma_1, ..., \gamma_m$ and $A_{i0}, ..., A_{im}$ respectively, then:

$$(A_i \vec{\gamma} + B_i) \otimes x = \sum_{k=1}^{m} \gamma_k A_{ik} \otimes x + B_i \otimes x \tag{6}$$

where $\otimes$ denotes convolution operation, and m is the dimension of $\vec{\gamma}$. In other words, the one convolution layer, whose weights are learned with one single fc layer, is exactly equivalent to a multi-path convolution block as shown in Fig. 6. Learning the weight and bias of the single fc layer is equivalent to learning the common basic convolution kernels $B_i, A_{i1}, A_{i2}, ..., A_{im}$ in the convolution block.

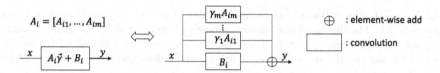

Fig. 4. Equivalent analysis of the connection between the *base* network $\mathcal{N}_{base}$ and the *weight learning* network $\mathcal{N}_{weight}$. One convolution layer whose weights are learnt by the fc layer is exactly equivalent to a multi-path convolution blocks.

Visualization of the Learned Convolution Weights. The learned convolution weights can be generally classified into two classes: kernels generated by different parameter values of a single image operator, and kernels generated by different image operators. We analyse both groups of kernels on the model trained on 10 image operators which is introduced in Subsect. 4.5. In this case, the input to the weight learning network takes two parameters, hence the learned convolution weights for a specific layer i in the base network should be,

$$W_i = \gamma_1 A_{i1} + \gamma_2 A_{i2} + B_i \tag{7}$$

where γ_1 refers to the input parameter value of a specific operator, and γ_2 indicates the type of the operator, which is defined by ten discrete numbers that range from "0.1" to "1.0" for different operators separately. A_{i1} and A_{i2} are its corresponding weights in the fully connected layer. Therefore, for a single image operator, $\gamma_2 A_{i2} + B_i$ is a fixed value and the only modification to its different parameter values is $\gamma_1 A_{i1}$, which scales a high-dimension value. That is to say, each time when one adjusts the operator parameter by γ_1, the learned convolution weights are only shifted to some extent in a fixed high-dimensional direction. Similar analysis also applies to the transformation of different operators.

We visualize the learned convolution kernels via t-SNE in Fig. 5. Each color indicates one image operator, and for each operator, we randomly generate 500 groups of convolution weights with different parameters. As can be seen, the distance of every two adjacent operator is almost the same, it shifts along the x dimension for a fixed distance. For a single filter, while adjusting the parameters continuously, the convolution weights shift along the y dimension. This figure just conforms to our analysis about the convolution weights in the high-dimensional space. It is very surprising that all different kinds of learned convolution weights

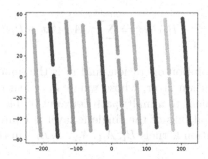

Fig. 5. T-SNE illustration of the learned weights of the 2nd convolution layer in the base network. The displayed convolution weights are generated by the jointly trained network with 10 image operators. Each color indicates one specific operator. We also observe similar visualized results for the other convolution layers. (Color figure online)

can be related with a high-dimensional vector, and the transformation between them can be represented by a very simple linear function.

As analyzed in the supplemental material, the solution space of an image processing task could be huge in the form of learned convolution kernels. Two exactly same results may be represented by very different convolution weights. The linear transformation in our proposed weight learning network actually connects all the different image operators and constrains their learned convolution weights in a limited high dimensional space.

5   Conclusion

In this paper, we propose the first decouple learning framework for parameterized image operators, where the weights of the task-oriented *base* network $\mathcal{N}_{base}$ are decoupled from the network structure and directly learned by another *weight learning* network $\mathcal{N}_{weight}$. These two networks can be easily end-to-end trained, and $\mathcal{N}_{weight}$ dynamically adjusts the weights of $\mathcal{N}_{base}$ for different parameters $\overrightarrow{\gamma}$ during the runtime. We show that the proposed framework can be applied to different parameterized image operators, such as image smoothing, denoising and super resolution, while obtaining comparable performance as the network trained for one specific parameter configuration. It also has the potential to jointly learn multiple different parameterized image operators within one single network. To better understand the working principle, we also provide some valuable analysis and discussions, which may inspire more promising research in this direction. More theoretical analysis is worthy of further exploration in the future.

Acknowledgement. This work was supported in part by: National 973 Program (2015CB352501), NSFC-ISF (61561146397), the Natural Science Foundation of China under Grant U1636201 and 61629301.

References

1. Andrychowicz, M., et al.: Learning to learn by gradient descent by gradient descent. In: Advances in Neural Information Processing Systems, pp. 3981–3989 (2016)
2. Buades, A., Coll, B., Morel, J.M.: A non-local algorithm for image denoising. In: IEEE Computer Society Conference on Computer Vision and Pattern Recognition, CVPR 2005, vol. 2, pp. 60–65. IEEE (2005)
3. Chen, D., Liao, J., Yuan, L., Yu, N., Hua, G.: Coherent online video style transfer. In: Proceedings of the International Conference on Computer Vision (ICCV) (2017)
4. Chen, D., Yuan, L., Liao, J., Yu, N., Hua, G.: Stylebank: an explicit representation for neural image style transfer. In: Proceedings of the CVPR, vol. 1, p. 4 (2017)
5. Chen, D., Yuan, L., Liao, J., Yu, N., Hua, G.: Stereoscopic neural style transfer. In: Proceedings of the IEEE Conference on Computer Vision and Pattern Recognition, vol. 10 (2018)
6. Chen, Q., Xu, J., Koltun, V.: Fast image processing with fully-convolutional networks. In: IEEE International Conference on Computer Vision, vol. 9 (2017)
7. Chen, Y., Hoffman, M.W., Colmenarejo, S.G., Denil, M., Lillicrap, T.P., de Freitas, N.: Learning to learn for global optimization of black box functions. In: International Conference on Machine Learning (2017)
8. Cheng, B., et al.: Robust emotion recognition from low quality and low bit rate video: a deep learning approach. In: 2017 Seventh International Conference on Affective Computing and Intelligent Interaction (ACII), pp. 65–70. IEEE (2017)
9. Cheng, B., Wei, Y., Shi, H., Feris, R., Xiong, J., Huang, T.: Revisiting RCNN: on awakening the classification power of faster RCNN. In: ECCV (2018)
10. Dabov, K., Foi, A., Katkovnik, V., Egiazarian, K.: Image denoising by sparse 3-D transform-domain collaborative filtering. IEEE Trans. Image Process. 16(8), 2080–2095 (2007)
11. Dai, X., Ng, J.Y.H., Davis, L.S.: FASON: first and second order information fusion network for texture recognition. In: IEEE Conference on Computer Vision and Pattern Recognition, pp. 7352–7360 (2017)
12. Dai, X., Singh, B., Zhang, G., Davis, L.S., Qiu Chen, Y.: Temporal context network for activity localization in videos. In: The IEEE International Conference on Computer Vision (ICCV) (2017)
13. Dong, C., Deng, Y., Change Loy, C., Tang, X.: Compression artifacts reduction by a deep convolutional network. In: Proceedings of the IEEE International Conference on Computer Vision, pp. 576–584 (2015)
14. Dong, C., Loy, C.C., He, K., Tang, X.: Learning a deep convolutional network for image super-resolution. In: Fleet, D., Pajdla, T., Schiele, B., Tuytelaars, T. (eds.) ECCV 2014. LNCS, vol. 8692, pp. 184–199. Springer, Cham (2014). https://doi.org/10.1007/978-3-319-10593-2_13
15. Elad, M., Aharon, M.: Image denoising via sparse and redundant representations over learned dictionaries. IEEE Trans. Image Process. 15(12), 3736–3745 (2006)
16. Fan, Q., Yang, J., Hua, G., Chen, B., Wipf, D.: A generic deep architecture for single image reflection removal and image smoothing. In: Proceedings of the 16th International Conference on Computer Vision (ICCV), pp. 3238–3247 (2017)
17. Fan, Q., Yang, J., Hua, G., Chen, B., Wipf, D.: Revisiting deep intrinsic image decompositions (2018)
18. Farbman, Z., Fattal, R., Lischinski, D., Szeliski, R.: Edge-preserving decompositions for multi-scale tone and detail manipulation. In: ACM Transactions on Graphics (TOG), vol. 27, p. 67. ACM (2008)

19. Fu, X., Huang, J., Ding, X., Liao, Y., Paisley, J.: Clearing the skies: a deep network architecture for single-image rain removal. IEEE Trans. Image Process. **26**(6), 2944–2956 (2017)
20. Fu, X., Huang, J., Zeng, D., Huang, Y., Ding, X., Paisley, J.: Removing rain from single images via a deep detail network. In: IEEE Conference on Computer Vision and Pattern Recognition, pp. 1715–1723 (2017)
21. Gu, S., Zhang, L., Zuo, W., Feng, X.: Weighted nuclear norm minimization with application to image denoising. In: Proceedings of the IEEE Conference on Computer Vision and Pattern Recognition, pp. 2862–2869 (2014)
22. Ha, D., Dai, A., Le, Q.V.: Hypernetworks. In: ICLR (2018)
23. He, M., Chen, D., Liao, J., Sander, P.V., Yuan, L.: Deep exemplar-based colorization. ACM Trans. Graph. **37**, 47 (2018). Proceedings of SIGGRAPH 2018
24. Karacan, L., Erdem, E., Erdem, A.: Structure-preserving image smoothing via region covariances. ACM Trans. Graph. (TOG) **32**(6), 176 (2013)
25. Kim, J., Kwon Lee, J., Mu Lee, K.: Accurate image super-resolution using very deep convolutional networks. In: Proceedings of the IEEE Conference on Computer Vision and Pattern Recognition, pp. 1646–1654 (2016)
26. Kligvasser, I., Shaham, T.R., Michaeli, T.: xUnit: learning a spatial activation function for efficient image restoration. In: CVPR (2018)
27. Ledig, C., et al.: Photo-realistic single image super-resolution using a generative adversarial network. In: CVPR, vol. 2, p. 4 (2017)
28. Li, D., He, X., Huang, Q., Sun, M.T., Zhang, L.: Generating diverse and accurate visual captions by comparative adversarial learning. arXiv preprint arXiv:1804.00861 (2018)
29. Li, Y., Dixit, M., Vasconcelos, N.: Deep scene image classification with the MFAFVNet. In: Proceedings of the IEEE Conference on Computer Vision and Pattern Recognition, pp. 5746–5754 (2017)
30. Lin, K., Li, D., He, X., Zhang, Z., Sun, M.T.: Adversarial ranking for language generation. In: Advances in Neural Information Processing Systems, pp. 3155–3165 (2017)
31. Liu, S., Pan, J., Yang, M.-H.: Learning recursive filters for low-level vision via a hybrid neural network. In: Leibe, B., Matas, J., Sebe, N., Welling, M. (eds.) ECCV 2016. LNCS, vol. 9908, pp. 560–576. Springer, Cham (2016). https://doi.org/10.1007/978-3-319-46493-0_34
32. Ma, S., Fu, J., Chen, C.W., Mei, T.: DA-GAN: instance-level image translation by deep attention generative adversarial networks
33. Mao, X., Shen, C., Yang, Y.B.: Image restoration using very deep convolutional encoder-decoder networks with symmetric skip connections. In: Advances in Neural Information Processing Systems, pp. 2802–2810 (2016)
34. Osher, S., Rudin, L.I.: Feature-oriented image enhancement using shock filters. SIAM J. Numer. Anal. **27**(4), 919–940 (1990)
35. Qi, G.J., Zhang, L., Hu, H., Edraki, M., Wang, J., Hua, X.S.: Global versus localized generative adversarial nets. In: Proceedings of IEEE Conference on Computer Vision and Pattern Recognition (CVPR) (2018)
36. Schmidhuber, J.: Learning to control fast-weight memories: an alternative to dynamic recurrent networks. Neural Comput. **4**(1), 131–139 (1992)
37. Sun, J., Xu, Z., Shum, H.Y.: Image super-resolution using gradient profile prior. In: IEEE Conference on Computer Vision and Pattern Recognition, CVPR 2008, pp. 1–8. IEEE (2008)

38. Tai, Y., Yang, J., Liu, X., Xu, C.: MemNet: A persistent memory network for image restoration. In: Proceedings of the IEEE Conference on Computer Vision and Pattern Recognition, pp. 4539–4547 (2017)
39. Tipping, M.E., Bishop, C.M.: Bayesian image super-resolution. In: Advances in Neural Information Processing Systems, pp. 1303–1310 (2003)
40. Ulyanov, D., Vedaldi, A., Lempitsky, V.: Improved texture networks: maximizing quality and diversity in feed-forward stylization and texture synthesis. In: Proceedings of the CVPR (2017)
41. Wichrowska, O., et al.: Learned optimizers that scale and generalize. In: International Conference on Machine Learning (2017)
42. Xu, L., Lu, C., Xu, Y., Jia, J.: Image smoothing via L 0 gradient minimization. In: ACM Transactions on Graphics (TOG), vol. 30, p. 174. ACM (2011)
43. Xu, L., Lu, C., Xu, Y., Jia, J.: Image smoothing via l0 gradient minimization. ACM Trans. Graph. **30**, 174 (2011). SIGGRAPH Asia
44. Xu, L., Ren, J., Yan, Q., Liao, R., Jia, J.: Deep edge-aware filters. In: International Conference on Machine Learning, pp. 1669–1678 (2015)
45. Xu, L., Yan, Q., Xia, Y., Jia, J.: Structure extraction from texture via relative total variation. ACM Trans. Graph. (TOG) **31**(6), 139 (2012)
46. Yang, J., Wright, J., Huang, T.S., Ma, Y.: Image super-resolution via sparse representation. IEEE Trans. Image Process. **19**(11), 2861–2873 (2010)
47. Yu, F., Koltun, V.: Multi-scale context aggregation by dilated convolutions. In: ICLR (2016)
48. Zhang, D., Dai, X., Wang, X., Wang, Y.F.: S3D: Single shot multi-span detector via fully 3D convolutional network. In: British Machine Vision Conference (BMVC) (2018)
49. Zhang, H., Patel, V.M.: Density-aware single image de-raining using a multi-stream dense network. In: CVPR (2018)
50. Zhang, Q., Shen, X., Xu, L., Jia, J.: Rolling guidance filter. In: Fleet, D., Pajdla, T., Schiele, B., Tuytelaars, T. (eds.) ECCV 2014. LNCS, vol. 8691, pp. 815–830. Springer, Cham (2014). https://doi.org/10.1007/978-3-319-10578-9_53
51. Zhang, Q., Xu, L., Jia, J.: 100+ times faster weighted median filter (WMF). In: Proceedings of the IEEE Conference on Computer Vision and Pattern Recognition, pp. 2830–2837 (2014)
52. Zoran, D., Weiss, Y.: From learning models of natural image patches to whole image restoration. In: 2011 IEEE International Conference on Computer Vision (ICCV), pp. 479–486. IEEE (2011)

Triplet Loss in Siamese Network
for Object Tracking

Xingping Dong[1] and Jianbing Shen[1,2(✉)]

[1] Beijing Lab of Intelligent Information Technology, School of Computer Science,
Beijing Institute of Technology, Beijing, China
{dongxingping,shenjianbing}@bit.edu.cn
[2] Inception Institute of Artificial Intelligence, Abu Dhabi, UAE
http://github.com/shenjianbing/TripletTracking

Abstract. Object tracking is still a critical and challenging problem with many applications in computer vision. For this challenge, more and more researchers pay attention to applying deep learning to get powerful feature for better tracking accuracy. In this paper, a novel triplet loss is proposed to extract expressive deep feature for object tracking by adding it into Siamese network framework instead of pairwise loss for training. Without adding any inputs, our approach is able to utilize more elements for training to achieve more powerful feature via the combination of original samples. Furthermore, we propose a theoretical analysis by combining comparison of gradients and back-propagation, to prove the effectiveness of our method. In experiments, we apply the proposed triplet loss for three real-time trackers based on Siamese network. And the results on several popular tracking benchmarks show our variants operate at almost the same frame-rate with baseline trackers and achieve superior tracking performance than them, as well as the comparable accuracy with recent state-of-the-art real-time trackers.

Keywords: Siamese network · Triplet loss · Object tracking
Real-time

1 Introduction

Object tracking containing single object tracking [8,9] and multi-object tracking [24,25] remains an important problem with many applications, such as automated surveillance, and vehicle navigation [34]. In single object tracking, powerful feature selecting is one of the key step to improve tracking accuracy. In the recent years, this strategy has been widely used for many correlation filter (CF) based trackers. For example, Henriques et al. [12] applied the Histogram of Oriented Gradients (HOG) feature instead of gray feature in [11] to achieve more robust tracking performance. Danelljan et al. [5] tried to use the color name to process color sequence. More recently, the pre-trained deep networks are applied to extract feature from raw image for improving accuracy, such as

V. Ferrari et al. (Eds.): ECCV 2018, LNCS 11217, pp. 472–488, 2018.
https://doi.org/10.1007/978-3-030-01261-8_28

DeepSRDCF [6], CCOT [7], MCPF [36], and ECO [4]. Besides CF trackers, some deep learning based trackers focus on designing an end-to-end network to achieve more powerful and suitable feature for its tracking system. MDNet [20] used a multi-domain convolutional neural network to extract common feature inside various samples during the off-line training phase. Then, the trained network is refined frame by frame in different sequences through online training. This tracker achieved excellent performance on OTB-2013 [32] and won the main challenge in VOT-2015 [18]. However, its running speed is less than 1 frame-per-second (fps), which is far below the real-time requirement for processing videos (30 fps). The slow speed is caused by the online training. Thus, in order to satisfy the real-time requirement in practical application, recent work like SiamFC [2] still uses the deep network for off-line training to achieve powerful feature while try to avoid online training for acceleration.

Although SiamFC utilizes deep network to extract powerful feature, it does not take full advantage of the relationship among the input samples. SiamFC addresses the tracking task as similarity learning in an embedding space. The similarity function is constructed with a Siamese network trained in off-line phase. The inputs include an exemplar image enclosing the object and a larger search image where the sliding-windows with the same size of exemplar can be viewed as instances, i.e. candidate object bounding boxes. According to the distance between the location of object and an instance, it is labeled as positive when its distance is less than a threshold, otherwise, it is labeled as negative. The logistic loss is applied to maximize the similarity scores on exemplar-positive pairs and minimize them on exemplar-negative pairs. This training method only utilizes the pairwise relationship on samples and ignores the underlying connections inside the triplet: exemplar, positive instance and negative instance.

In this paper, we try to make the best of the triplet inputs to achieve more powerful features by adding a novel triplet loss into the Siamese framework. For each triplet, we define a matching probability to measure the possibility assigning positive instance to exemplar compared with the negative instance. Then, our goal is to maximize the joint probability among all triplets during training. The proposed triplet loss not only can further mine the potential relationship among exemplar, positive instance and negative instance, but also contains more elements for training at most situation. Here, we give an intuitive example. In object tracking, the number of exemplar is 1 since only one object bounding box is given in the first frame. While the numbers of positive and negative instance usually are more than 1. We can set them in a batch as M and N, respectively. In SiamFC, at most $M+N$ pairwise elements (M exemplar-positive pairs $+$ N exemplar-negative pairs) can be applied for training. However, our method can produce MN triplet-wise elements (the combination of M exemplar-positive pairs and N exemplar-negative pairs). If $M > 2$ and $N > 2$, then $MN > M + N$. It indicates our method will get more elements for training to enhance the performance. In the other situation, we can also get approximate number of elements. This example illustrates our loss is able to make better use of the combination of samples to achieve more powerful features. For clearer explanation, the training framework of triplet loss is shown in Fig. 1.

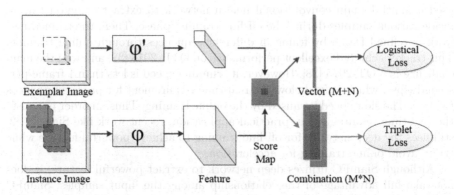

Fig. 1. Training framework of the triplet loss in Siamese network. We also give the original logistic loss for comparison. Given the same feature extraction in baselines [2], [28], we can apply the triplet loss to the score map. In contrast to use the vectorization of score map in logistic loss, we utilize the combination between positive scores (red) and negative scores (blue). The red rectangle means a positive score matrix produced by repeating M positive scores N times and the blue rectangle is a negative score matrix by repeating N negative scores M times. In fact, our loss is suitable for the network with same branches ($\phi' = \phi$ in SiamFC [2]) or different branches ($\phi' \neq \phi$ in CFnet [28]). (Color figure online)

Furthermore, we give the theoretical analysis between the original logistic loss and the proposed triplet loss to prove the effectiveness of our method. Firstly, the logistic loss is reformulated to be comparable with our triplet loss. Then we analyze their difference by comparing their gradients on various inputs. We find the triplet loss can offer larger absolute gradient when the similarity score of exemplar-positive pair vp is not more than the one of exemplar-negative pair vn. It means that the triplet loss will give stronger feedback for back-propagation when the network gives wrong similarities ($vp \leq vn$). This advantage will improve the tracking accuracy since if $vp \leq vn$, the tracking system will produce tracking error by labeling the negative instance as the object.

In fact, our triplet loss is suitable for the Siamese network with different structures. In our experiments, we applied the triplet loss to three existing trackers based on Siamese networks: SiamFC [2], CFnet2 [28], and SiamImp [28]. The experimental results on the famous tracking benchmark OTB-2013 have shown that all variants with our loss outperform original trackers and achieve similar high speed (55 - 86 fps) beyond real-time requirement. In three tracking benchmarks: OTB-2013 [32], OTB-100 [33] and VOT-2017 [15], our trackers achieve comparable results compared with recent state-of-the-art real-time trackers.

2   Related Works

Trackers with Siamese network: With the development of deep learning in recent years, many classical networks are introduced into object tracking, such as Siamese network [27], [2], [28]. Tao *et al.* [27] trained a Siamese network to learn a matching function in the off-line phase. In the online tracking phase, the learned matching function is applied to find the most similar patch in new frame compared with the initial patch of object in the first frame. This Siamese Instance search Tracker (SINT) performs well in OTB-2013 [32] while its speed is only 2 fps. In order to improve running speed, Bertinetto *et al.* [2] omitted the fully connected layers to reduce computation and only apply 5 fully convolutional layers to train an end-to-end Siamese network (SiamFC) for similarity function. Then, the similarity function is directly applied to online track without complex fine-tuning strategies. Therefore, SiamFC achieves high frame-rates beyond real-time, nearly at 86 fps with GPU. Another related tracker CFnet [28] regards the correlation filter as a network layer to compute the similarity between the generating convolutional features of Siamese network. It enables the learning deep features to be tightly coupled to the correlation filter. The experimental results show that 2 convolutional layers with CF layer in Siamese network (CFnet2) will achieve comparable performance and speed (75 fps) compared with SiamFC containing 5 convolutional layers. Otherwise, CFnet proposes an improved Siamese network (SiamImp) by modifying the structure in some convolutional layers of SiamFC [2]. SiamImp outperforms SiamFC in tracking accuracy on OTB-2013 and OTB-100 while it operates at lower speed, nearly 52 fps.

To prove the generality of the proposed triplet loss for network structure, we apply it to three real-time trackers SiamFC, CFnet2 and SiamImp, which own similar Siamese frameworks but different network structures.

Triplet loss in computer vision: Triplet loss has been widely applied for numerous applications in computer vision, such as face recognition [23], image retrieval [14], [37], [26], and person re-identification [3], [30], [13]. Here we illustrate some works for reference. Schroff *et al.* [23] proposed a FaceNet for face recognition and clustering by combining the triplet loss [31] and the deep convolutional network. To ensure fast convergence, an online triplet mining method is proposed by selecting hardest sample pairs (face patch pairs) on each batch. In order to further mine the underlying connection among triplets, Song *et al.* [26] applied a structured loss for training by lifting the vector of pairwise distances within the batch to the matrix of pairwise distances. Hermans *et al.* [13] systematically evaluated several variants of classic triplet loss and proposed a novel batch hard loss with the soft margin for person re-identification. Their method randomly sampled some instances to construct small set as a batch and selected some hardest instances to compute the loss. In contrast to most existing approaches with margin-based triplet loss above, our method uses a probability-based triplet loss to avoid manually selecting the suitable margin.

3   Revisiting the Siamese Network for Tracking

Bertinetto *et al.* [2] proposed a Siamese network with fully convolutional layers for object tracking (SiamFC) by transferring tracking task to exemplar matching in an embedding space. The tacking object patch is usually given in the first frame of a sequence and it can be viewed as an exemplar. The goal is to find a most similar patch (instance) from each frame in the semantic embedding space. How to learn a powerful embedding function is the key step for this matching problem. The authors of SiamFC apply a fully convolution Siamese deep network to represent this embedding function. Two network branches are designed to process the special inputs in the tracking task. One input is the object bounding box in the first frame, which is called as exemplar input. The other instance input is the searching region in each subsequent frame including the candidate patches to be matched. These two network branches can be seen as an identical transformation ϕ for different inputs, since they share the same parameters. Denote the exemplar as z and the instance as x, then the similar function is defined as

$$f(z, x) = g(\phi(z), \phi(x)), \tag{1}$$

where g is a simple similarity metric such as vectorial angle and cross correlation.

In SiamFC, the cross correlation function is applied for g, and the formulation of function f is transferred as follows:

$$f(z, x) = \phi(z) * \phi(x) + b. \tag{2}$$

Then, a logistic loss is applied to define the pairwise loss function for training, which is formulated as follows:

$$L_l(\mathcal{Y}, \mathcal{V}) = \sum_{x_i \in \mathcal{X}} w_i \log(1 + e^{-y_i \cdot v_i}). \tag{3}$$

where $\mathcal{Y}$, $\mathcal{V}$, $\mathcal{X}$ are respectively the sets of ground-truth label, similarity score, instance input. $y_i \in \{+1, -1\}$ is the ground-truth label of a single exemplar-instance pair (z, x_i). v_i is the similarity score of (z, x_i) i.e. $v_i = f(z, x_i)$. w_i is the weight for an instance x_i, and $\sum_{x_i \in \mathcal{X}} w_i = 1, w_i > 0, x_i \in \mathcal{X}$. In SiamFC, the balance weights are used for loss according to the number of positive and negative instances. The formulation of balance weights is defined as follows:

$$w_i = \begin{cases} \frac{1}{2M}, & y_i = 1 \\ \frac{1}{2N}, & y_i = -1 \end{cases} \tag{4}$$

where M, N are the number of positive instance set $\mathcal{X}_p$ and negative instance set $\mathcal{X}_n$ i.e. $M = |\mathcal{X}_p|$, $N = |\mathcal{X}_n|$. (In SiamFC, $M = 13$, $N = 212$.)

4   Siamese Network with Triplet Loss

As mentioned before, we can split the instances set $\mathcal{X}$ in SiamFC [2] to positive instances set $\mathcal{X}_p$ and negative instances set $\mathcal{X}_n$. Considering the other exemplar input, we can construct triplet tuples using the inputs of SiamFC i.e. a tuple contains exemplar, positive instance and negative instance. However, SiamFC only utilizes the pairwise loss and ignores the underlying relation between the positive instance and the negative instance. Based on this consideration, we design a new triplet loss to mine the potential relation among the inputs as much as possible. As splitting the instances set $\mathcal{X}$, the similarity score set $\mathcal{V}$ of exemplar-instance pairs can also be split as a positive score set $\mathcal{V}_p$ and a negative score set $\mathcal{V}_n$. Then, we can directly define the triplet loss on these score-pairs. To measure each score-pair, we apply a matching probability i.e. the probability assigning positive instance to exemplar by using a soft-max function. The formulation of this matching probability is defined as follows.

$$prob(vp_i, vn_j) = \frac{e^{vp_i}}{e^{vp_i} + e^{vn_j}}. \tag{5}$$

In the explanation of probability theory, our goal is to maximize the joint probability among all score-pairs i.e. the product of all probabilities. By using its negative logarithm, we can get the loss formulation as follows.

$$L_t(\mathcal{V}_p, \mathcal{V}_n) = -\frac{1}{MN} \sum_i^M \sum_j^N \log prob(vp_i, vn_j), \tag{6}$$

where the balance weight $\frac{1}{MN}$ is used to keep the loss with the same scale for different number of instance sets.

Compared with the original pairwise logistic loss L_l in Eq. 3, our triplet loss L_t will capture more underlying information to achieve more powerful representation with little extra computation during training. Firstly, our triplet loss contains more elements (i.e. single losses), which can mine more underlying relationship among exemplar, positive instance, and negative instance. In more detail, L_l only includes $M + N$ varied losses while our L_t is the weighted average of MN variates. The more variates in the loss function means the more powerful representation, since it can capture more information by these variates. More detailed analysis is shown in next section. Secondly, our loss is defined on the original scores by using their combination between positive scores and negative scores. Thus, we use the same inputs to feed the network. It means we do not need extra computation for feature extraction with deep network during training. The only adding time cost is taken for computing the new loss, which is occupied small part of time cost during training.

5   Relationship Between Logistic Loss and Triplet Loss

As mentioned before, our triplet loss in Eq. 6 contains MN elements while the number in the logistic loss in Eq. 3 is $M + N$. If we want to compare these two losses, we have to keep the number consistent. Therefore, we manage to transform Eq. 3 for comparison. To keep the same input of instances, no additional instance is imported for increasing element number during the transformation. The only change is the increased frequency of usage of exemplar-instance pairs. We also add constant weight to make it become equivalent transformation. For a set of instances $\mathcal{X}$, the logistic loss can be reformulated as follows.

$$
\begin{aligned}
L_l &= \sum_i^M \frac{1}{2M} \log(1 + e^{-vp_i}) + \sum_j^N \frac{1}{2N} \log(1 + e^{vn_j}) \\
&= \frac{1}{N} \sum_j^N \sum_i^M \frac{1}{2M} \log(1 + e^{-vp_i}) + \frac{1}{M} \sum_i^M \sum_j^N \frac{1}{2N} \log(1 + e^{vn_j}) \quad (7) \\
&= \frac{1}{MN} \sum_i^M \sum_j^N \frac{1}{2} \left(\log(1 + e^{-vp_i}) + \log(1 + e^{vn_j}) \right).
\end{aligned}
$$

This equation is similar with Eq. 6. We need to simplify Eq. 6 for further analysis. By submitting Eq. 5 to Eq. 6, we can get the following formulation.

$$
L_t = -\frac{1}{MN} \sum_i^M \sum_j^N \log \frac{e^{vp_i}}{e^{vp_i} + e^{vn_j}} = \frac{1}{MN} \sum_i^M \sum_j^N \log(1 + e^{vn_j - vp_i}). \quad (8)
$$

From Eqs. 7 and 8, we can find the main difference is their terms inside summation. Thus, we only need to further analyze these two terms to achieve the difference between two losses. Their formulation can be denoted as follows.

$$
T_l = \frac{1}{2} \left(\log(1 + e^{-vp}) + \log(1 + e^{vn}) \right), \quad T_t = \log(1 + e^{vn - vp}). \quad (9)
$$

For simplification, we omit the subscripts i and j to focus on the difference on these terms.

5.1   Comparison on the Gradients

The gradients play important role during deep learning training since they are directly involved in the back-propagation stage. Thus, they are used to point out the characteristics of different terms. Firstly, we give their gradients. For the logistic term, the gradients are derived as:

$$
\frac{\partial T_l}{\partial vp} = -\frac{1}{2(1 + e^{vp})}, \quad \frac{\partial T_l}{\partial vn} = \frac{1}{2(1 + e^{-vn})}. \quad (10)
$$

For our triplet loss, the gradients of its term are given as:

$$
\frac{\partial T_t}{\partial vp} = -\frac{1}{1 + e^{vp - vn}}, \quad \frac{\partial T_t}{\partial vn} = \frac{1}{1 + e^{vp - vn}}. \quad (11)
$$

From Eq. 10, we can find $\partial T_l / \partial vp$ and $\partial T_l / \partial vn$ in logistic term only depend on vp and vn respectively, while our $\partial T_t / \partial vp$ considers both vp and vn. It means the logistic term can not take full advantage of information offered by vp and vn. In the other words, $\partial T_l / \partial vp$ can not utilize the information from vn and

$\partial T_l/\partial vn$ fails to make use of the information of vp. For further analysis, visual comparison is shown in Fig. 2 by using the color maps of different gradients. Figure 2(a) and (d) also show that $\partial T_l/\partial vp$ and $\partial T_l/\partial vn$ are independent for vn and vp, respectively.

In the tracking task, we should keep the important constraint condition $vp > vn$ to reduce the tracking error. $vp \leq vn$ means the similarity score of positive instance is less than or equal to the negative instance, and the negative instance will be regarded as the object leading to tracking failure. Thus, we should pay more attention for $vp \leq vn$ during training. Now we will analyze the gradients of positive instance of two losses.

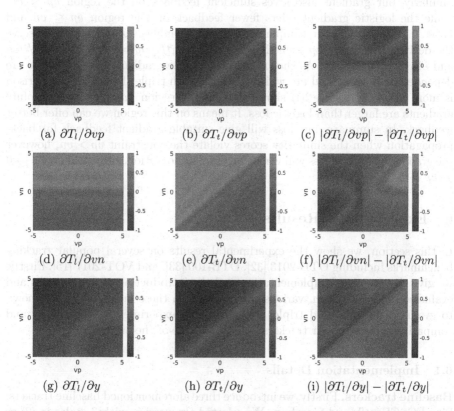

Fig. 2. Comparison of gradients for logistic loss and triplet loss. (a) and (b) are the gradients on positive instance of logistic loss and triplet loss, respectively. (c) is the differences between their absolute values. Similarly, (d), (e), and (f) are corresponding to the negative instance. (g), (h), and (i) are corresponding to their difference $y = vp - vn$.

As shown in Fig. 2(a) and (b), when $vp \leq vn$ (i.e. up-left-triangle region), our gradient $\partial T_t/\partial vp$ has relatively large absolute value ($|\partial T_t/\partial vp| \geq 0.5$) in this situation. While the absolute gradient $|\partial T_l/\partial vp|$ will be close to 0 even on

$vp < vn$ when vp is approaching a big value like 5. It means the gradient $\partial T_l/\partial vp$ only offers little feedback for back-propagation even vn violates the constraint $vp > vn$, when vp is large. However, our gradient $\partial T_t/\partial vp$ can give more feedback for this situation by offering larger absolute gradient. For further comparison, the color map of difference between absolute gradients $|\partial T_l/\partial vp| - |\partial T_t/\partial vp|$ is shown in Fig. 2(c). It indicates that inside the region $vp \leq vn$ and $vp > 0$, our absolute gradient is larger than logistic absolute gradient, which means our loss can offer better feedback for back-propagation in this region. In most of the resident region of $vp \leq vn$, our gradient is approximately equal to the logistic gradient. Secondly, the comparison of negative instance gradients is shown in Fig. 2(d), (e), and (f). Similarly, our gradient also gives sufficient feedback on the region $vp \leq vn$, while the logistic gradient offers fewer feedback on the region $vp \leq vn$ and $vn < 0$. For more direct comparison on two variables vp and vn, we observe the derivatives on $y = vp - vn$. It is easy to get $\partial T_l/\partial y = \partial T_l/\partial vp - \partial T_l/\partial vn$ and $\partial T_t/\partial y = \partial T_t/\partial vp$. As shown in Fig. 2(g), the gradients of logistic loss are depended on both vp and vn, which is similar with triplet loss. This comparison is more intuitive. Figure 2(i) shows that on the region $vp \leq vn$, our absolute gradients are larger than logistic loss. It means on this region we can offer better feedback. In summary, our loss will give suitable gradient feedback for back-propagation when the similarity scores violate the constraint $vp > vn$, however the gradient of logistic loss will vanish on extreme condition, such as $\partial T_l/\partial vp \to 0$ at $vp \to 5$.

6   Experimental Results

In this section, we show the experimental results on several popular tracking benchmarks including OTB-2013 [32], OTB-100 [33], and VOT-2017 [15]. Firstly, we give the details of implementation and the introduction of benchmarks and evaluation metrics. Then, various comparisons on these benchmarks are shown to evaluate the proposed triplet loss, including experiments on baselines and comparisons between our trackers and other state-of-the-art trackers.

6.1   Implementation Details

Baseline trackers. Firstly, we introduce three aforementioned baseline trackers: SiamFC, CFnet2, and SiamImp. We selected the version with 3 scales in [2] as baseline tracker denoted as SiamFC, since this version runs faster than the one with 5 scales and only performs slightly lower. In [28], a lot of variants of CFnet are proposed for experimental comparison. The one with 2 convolutional layers (CFnet2) obtains high speed and slightly lower performance than the best. Thus, it is selected as the representative of CFnet structure. This work also proposes an improved Siamese network (SiamImp) as baseline, by reducing the total stride and the number of final CNN output channels in SiamFC. The training method and training dataset are similar with the ones in [2,28] except the training loss.

Training. The deep learning toolbox MatConvNet [29] is applied to train the parameters of the shared network by minimizing the loss with SGD. The initial weights of the shared networks are set with the pre-trained models in SiamFC [2] and CFnet [28]. We randomly sample 53,200 pairs from the dataset ILSVRC15 [22] as a training epoch and perform training over 10 epochs. 10% pairs are chosen as the validation set at each epoch. And we decide the final network used for testing from the trained models at the end of each epoch, by the minimal mean error of distance (presented in [2]) on the validation set. The gradients for each iteration are estimated using mini-batches of size 8, and the learning rate is decayed geometrically after epoch from 10^{-4} to 10^{-5}. To handle the gray videos in benchmarks like [2,28], 25% of the pairs are converted to grayscale during training for SiamFC. For CFnet2 and SiamImp, a gray network is trained with all grayscale pairs to process gray videos. Similarly, all color pairs are applied to train a color network.

Tracking. In the tracking phase, we only replace the pre-trained networks with the models trained by triplet loss. The others inside online tracking, such as tracking approaches, and hyper-parameters setting, are the same with the original papers. Thus, the improved trackers can run at very similar high speed with baseline trackers. In more details, our variants: SiamFC-tri, CFnet2-tri, and SiamImp-tri achieve speeds at 86.3 fps, 55.3 fps and 55.8 fps on OTB-2013, respectively. The corresponding baseline trackers run respectively at 86.5 fps, 55.1 fps, and 55.4 fps. Our machine is equipped with a single NVIDIA GeForce 1080 and an Intel Core i7-6700 at 3.4 GHz, and our software platform is Matlab 2017a + CUDA 8.0 + cudnn v7.0.5.

6.2   Tracking Benchmarks

Our improved trackers are evaluated with recent state-of-the-art trackers in popular benchmarks: OTB-2013 [32], OTB-50, OTB-100 [33], and VOT-2017 [15].

The OTB-2013 benchmark proposes several metrics to evaluate trackers on 51 challenging sequences. OTB-100 including 100 sequences is the extension of OTB-2013 where 50 more challenging sequences are selected as a small benchmark denoted as OTB-50. In this paper, the overlap success rate and distance precision metrics [32] are used to evaluate trackers on OTB-2013, OTB-50, and OTB-100. Overlap success rate measures the intersection over union (IoU) of ground truth and predicted bounding boxes. The success plot shows the rate of bounding boxes whose IoU score is larger than a given threshold. We apply the overlap success rate in terms of Area Under Curve (AUC) to rank the trackers. The precision metric means the percentage of frame locations within a certain threshold distance from those of the ground truth. The threshold distance is set as 20 for all the trackers. VOT-2017 is the 2017 edition of Visual Object Tracking challenge [17] evaluating the short-term tracking performance. In this challenge, a tracker is restarted in the case of a failure, where there is no overlap between the predicted bounding box and ground truth. VOT-2017 updated the sequences in VOT-2016 [16] by replacing 10 easily tracking sequences with 10 more challenging videos. A new real-time challenge was proposed to evaluate trackers with the limit of real-time speed i.e. the tracker should update the tracking result for each frame at frequency higher than or equal to the video frame rate. If a new frame is available before the tracker responds, the last updated bounding box is assumed as the reported tracker output at the available frame. For this dataset, we evaluated the tracking performance under the real-time challenge in terms of Expected Average Overlap (EAO). EAO is a principled combination of accuracy (overlap with the ground-truth) and robustness (failure rate) [15].

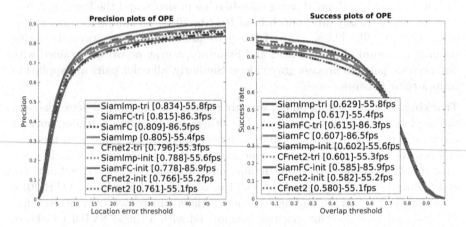

Fig. 3. Self-comparisons with variants of baseline trackers. The plots show precision and overlap success rate with AUC on OTB-2013 [32] in terms of OPE.

6.3   Experiments on Baseline Trackers

To validate the effectiveness of our triplet loss, we compare the baseline trackers (SiamFC [2], CFnet2, and SiamImp [28]) against their different variants: SiamFC-init, CFnet2-init, SiamImp-init, SiamFC-tri, CFnet2-tri, and SiamImp-tri. The postfix '-init' means the variant is initialized with the original pre-trained model and trained again with original logistic loss over 10 epochs with the aforementioned hyper-parameters. Similarly, the '-tri' represents it is trained with our triplet loss over 10 epochs with the same initialization and hyper-parameters.

These trackers are evaluated with one-pass evaluation (OPE) on OTB-2013, via running them throughout a test sequence with initialization from the ground truth position in the first frame. As shown in Fig. 3, directly training more epochs using logistic loss will reduce the precision and AUC of most baseline trackers excepting CFnet2. It indicates that the logistic loss can not enhance the representation power of original networks by training more iterations. However, the proposed triplet loss can further mine the potential of original networks to achieve more powerful representation. The corresponding results in Fig. 3 show it improves the performance in terms of both precision and overlap success rate in all the baseline trackers. It is worth mentioning all of the variants with triplet loss operate at almost the same high speed with baselines.

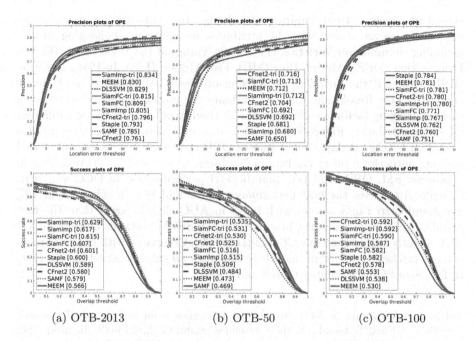

(a) OTB-2013   (b) OTB-50   (c) OTB-100

Fig. 4. Precision and success plots with AUC for OPE on OTB-2013 [32], OTB-50 and OTB-100 [33] benchmark. Only 10 best ranked trackers are shown.

6.4   Comparisons on OTB Benchmarks

On OTB-2013 [32], OTB-50, and OTB-100 [33] benchmarks, we compare improved trackers: SiamFC-tri, CFnet2-tri and SiamImp-tri against several state-of-the-art real-time trackers: SiamFC [2], CFnet2, SiamImp [28], Staple [1], CN [5], and KCF [12]. For reference, we also compare with recent trackers: DSST [5], MEEM [35], SAMF [19], and DLSSVM [21].

Overall comparison. Both precision and success metrics are reported for OPE. Figure 4 shows that all of our improved trackers SiamFC-tri, SiamImp-tri, and CFnet2 achieve improvement compared with their baselines in these three benchmarks in terms of both precision and success metrics. Especially on OTB-50 with success metric, SiamImp-tri achieves 3.9% improvement compared with its baseline SiamImp. In success metric, our trackers perform better than all other trackers on these three benchmarks, where our variants (SiamImp-tri and CFnet2-tri) occupy top two ranks. In precision metric, SiamImp-tri achieves the best performance on OTB-2013 as well as CFnet2-tri ranks first on OTB-50.

On OTB-100, our tracker SiamFC-tri ranks third (0.781) slightly lower than the second MEEM (0.781) and the first Staple (0.784) in precision while increases the success rate from 0.530 (MEEM) and 0.582 (Staple) to 0.590, respectively.

Attribute-based Performance Analysis. In OTB-100 benchmark, the sequences are annotated with 11 attributes for different challenging factors including Illumination Variation (IV), Scale Variation (SV), Occlusion (OCC), Deformation (DEF), Motion Blur (MB), Fast Motion (FM), In-Plane Rotation (IPR), Out-of-Plane Rotation (OPR), Out-of-View (OV), Background Clutters (BC), and Low Resolution (LR). To evaluate the proposed method in terms of each challenging factor, we compare our method to other trackers with different dominate attributes. Figure 5 shows the results of 9 main challenging attributes evaluated by the overlap success rate of OPE in terms of AUC. Our improved trackers outperform other trackers in 7 subsets, where SiamFC-tri rank first in 3 subsets: FM, OPR, and OV, SiamImp-tri performs best in OCC and IPR, CFnet2-tri achieves the best performance in SV and BC. In other subset LR, our SiamFC-tri ranks second with 0.615 in AUC slightly lower than the first SiamFC with 0.619. Similarly, in subset MB, DLSSVM performs best with 0.571 AUC slightly higher than our CFnet2-tri (0.568). Compared with baseline trackers, our trackers outperform than them in almost all subsets except for one case. In LR, SiamFC ranks higher than SiamFC-tri.

Table 1. EAO scores of VOT-2017 real-time challenge for our improved trackers: SiamFCT, CFnet2T, SiamImT, their baselines: SiamFC [2], CFnet2, SiamImp [28], recent tracker PTAV [10], and the other top 9 trackers in VOT-2017 [15].

	SiamFCT	SiamImT	CFnet2T	PTAV	DACF	ECOhc	Staple	KFebT	ASMS
EAO	**0.2125**	0.1833	0.1080	0.0654	0.2120	0.1767	0.1696	0.1693	0.1678
	SiamFC	SiamImp	CFnet2	sskcf	csrf	UCT	mosse_ca	SiamDCF	KCF
EAO	0.1966	0.1728	0.0963	0.1638	0.1585	0.1447	0.1395	0.1347	0.1336

6.5   Results on VOT-2017

Real-time challenge: We compare our improved trackers: SiamFC-tri, CFnet2-tri, SiamImp-tri, their baselines: SiamFC [2], CFnet2, SiamImp [28], recent tracker PTAV [10], and the top 9 trackers in VOT-2017 by using real-time evaluation. For simplicity, we shortened the names of our improved trackers as SiamFCT, CFnet2T and SiamImT. As shown in Table 1, all of our trackers also outperform their baseline trackers on VOT-2017 in terms of Expected Average Overlap (EAO). Especially, our SiamFCT achieves the best EAO among all these compared trackers. Another variant with our triplet loss SiamImT also occupies top position at the 4th ranking among all the trackers.

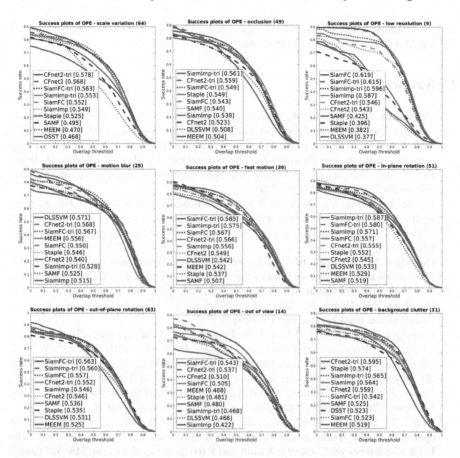

Fig. 5. Overlap success plots of OPE with AUC for 9 tracking challenges on OTB-100.

7   Conclusions

In this paper, we have proposed a novel triplet loss to achieve more powerful feature for object tracking by applying it into Siamese network. In contrast to original logistic loss, our triplet loss can further mine potential relationships among samples and utilize more elements for better training performance. We have shown the effectiveness of the proposed triplet loss in theory and experiments. In theoretical analysis, we found that when the network outputs wrong similarity scores, it gives more absolute gradients for feedback in back-propagation. We added this triplet loss into three baseline trackers based on Siamese network for experiments. The results on popular tracking benchmarks show that our triplet loss can improve the performance without reducing speed for these baselines.

Acknowledgements. This work was supported in part by the Beijing Natural Science Foundation under Grant 4182056, and the Fok Ying-Tong Education Foundation for

Young Teachers under Grant 141067. Specialized Fund for Joint Building Program of Beijing Municipal Education Commission.

References

1. Bertinetto, L., Valmadre, J., Golodetz, S., Miksik, O., Torr, P.H.: Staple: complementary learners for real-time tracking. In: IEEE CVPR, pp. 1401–1409 (2016)
2. Bertinetto, L., Valmadre, J., Henriques, J.F., Vedaldi, A., Torr, P.H.S.: Fully-convolutional siamese networks for object tracking. In: Hua, G., Jégou, H. (eds.) ECCV 2016. LNCS, vol. 9914, pp. 850–865. Springer, Cham (2016). https://doi.org/10.1007/978-3-319-48881-3_56
3. Cheng, D., Gong, Y., Zhou, S., Wang, J., Zheng, N.: Person re-identification by multi-channel parts-based cnn with improved triplet loss function. In: Proceedings of the IEEE Conference on Computer Vision and Pattern Recognition, pp. 1335–1344 (2016)
4. Danelljan, M., Bhat, G., Khan, F.S., Felsberg, M.: Eco: efficient convolution operators for tracking. In: Proceedings of the 2017 IEEE Conference on Computer Vision and Pattern Recognition (CVPR), Honolulu, HI, USA, pp. 21–26 (2017)
5. Danelljan, M., Häger, G., Khan, F., Felsberg, M.: Accurate scale estimation for robust visual tracking. In: BMVC (2014)
6. Danelljan, M., Häger, G., Khan, F.S., Felsberg, M.: Learning spatially regularized correlation filters for visual tracking. In: IEEE ICCV, pp. 4310–4318 (2015)
7. Danelljan, M., Robinson, A., Shahbaz Khan, F., Felsberg, M.: Beyond correlation filters: learning continuous convolution operators for visual tracking. In: Leibe, B., Matas, J., Sebe, N., Welling, M. (eds.) ECCV 2016. LNCS, vol. 9909, pp. 472–488. Springer, Cham (2016). https://doi.org/10.1007/978-3-319-46454-1_29
8. Dong, X., Shen, J., Wang, W., Liu, Y., Shao, L., Porikli, F.: Hyperparameter optimization for tracking with continuous deep q-learning. In: Proceedings of the IEEE Conference on Computer Vision and Pattern Recognition, pp. 518–527 (2018)
9. Dong, X., Shen, J., Yu, D., Wang, W., Liu, J., Huang, H.: Occlusion-aware real-time object tracking. IEEE Trans. Multimedia 19(4), 763–771 (2017)
10. Fan, H., Ling, H.: Parallel tracking and verifying: a framework for real-time and high accuracy visual tracking. In: Proceedings of the IEEE International Conference on Computer Vision, Venice, Italy (2017)
11. Henriques, J.F., Caseiro, R., Martins, P., Batista, J.: Exploiting the circulant structure of tracking-by-detection with Kernels. In: Fitzgibbon, A., Lazebnik, S., Perona, P., Sato, Y., Schmid, C. (eds.) ECCV 2012. LNCS, vol. 7575, pp. 702–715. Springer, Heidelberg (2012). https://doi.org/10.1007/978-3-642-33765-9_50
12. Henriques, J.F., Rui, C., Martins, P., Batista, J.: High-speed tracking with kernelized correlation filters. IEEE Trans. Pattern Anal. Mach. Intell. 37(3), 583–596 (2015)
13. Hermans, A., Beyer, L., Leibe, B.: In defense of the triplet loss for person re-identification. arXiv preprint arXiv:1703.07737 (2017)
14. Hoffer, E., Ailon, N.: Deep metric learning using triplet network. In: Feragen, A., Pelillo, M., Loog, M. (eds.) SIMBAD 2015. LNCS, vol. 9370, pp. 84–92. Springer, Cham (2015). https://doi.org/10.1007/978-3-319-24261-3_7
15. Kristan, M., Leonardis, A., Matas, J., Felsberg, M., Pflugfelder, R., Čehovin Zajc, L., et al.: The visual object tracking VOT2017 challenge results. In: Visual Object Tracking Workshop 2017 at ICCV 2017 (2017)

16. Kristan, M., et al.: The visual object tracking VOT2016 challenge results. In: Hua, G., Jégou, H. (eds.) ECCV 2016. LNCS, vol. 9914, pp. 777–823. Springer, Cham (2016). https://doi.org/10.1007/978-3-319-48881-3_54

17. Kristan, M., et al.: A novel performance evaluation methodology for single-target trackers. IEEE Trans. Pattern Anal. Mach. Intell. **38**(11), 2137–2155 (2016)

18. Kristan, M., Matas, J., Leonardis, A., Felsberg, M., Čehovin, L., et al.: The visual object tracking VOT2015 challenge results. In: Visual Object Tracking Workshop 2015 at ICCV 2015 (2015)

19. Li, Y., Zhu, J.: A scale adaptive kernel correlation filter tracker with feature integration. In: Agapito, L., Bronstein, M.M., Rother, C. (eds.) ECCV 2014. LNCS, vol. 8926, pp. 254–265. Springer, Cham (2015). https://doi.org/10.1007/978-3-319-16181-5_18

20. Nam, H., Han, B.: Learning multi-domain convolutional neural networks for visual tracking. In: IEEE CVPR (2016)

21. Ning, J., Yang, J., Jiang, S., Zhang, L., Yang, M.H.: Object tracking via dual linear structured SVM and explicit feature map. In: IEEE CVPR, pp. 4266–4274 (2016)

22. Russakovsky, O., et al.: ImageNet large scale visual recognition challenge. Int. J. Comput. Vis. (IJCV) **115**(3), 211–252 (2015). https://doi.org/10.1007/s11263-015-0816-y

23. Schroff, F., Kalenichenko, D., Philbin, J.: Facenet: a unified embedding for face recognition and clustering. In: Proceedings of the IEEE Conference on Computer Vision and Pattern Recognition, pp. 815–823 (2015)

24. Shen, J., Liang, Z., Liu, J., Sun, H., Shao, L., Tao, D.: Multiobject tracking by submodular optimization. IEEE Trans. Cybern. (2018, in press). https://doi.org/10.1109/TCYB.2018.2803217

25. Shen, J., Yu, D., Deng, L., Dong, X.: Fast online tracking with detection refinement. IEEE Trans. Intell. Transp. Syst. **19**(1), 162–173 (2017)

26. Song, H.O., Xiang, Y., Jegelka, S., Savarese, S.: Deep metric learning via lifted structured feature embedding. In: 2016 IEEE Conference on Computer Vision and Pattern Recognition (CVPR), pp. 4004–4012. IEEE (2016)

27. Tao, R., Gavves, E., Smeulders, A.W.: Siamese instance search for tracking. In: 2016 IEEE Conference on Computer Vision and Pattern Recognition (CVPR), pp. 1420–1429. IEEE (2016)

28. Valmadre, J., Bertinetto, L., Henriques, J.F., Vedaldi, A., Torr, P.H.S.: End-to-end representation learning for correlation filter based tracking. In: IEEE CVPR, pp. 5000–5008 (2017)

29. Vedaldi, A., Lenc, K.: Matconvnet: Convolutional neural networks for matlab. In: Proceedings of the 23rd ACM International Conference on Multimedia, pp. 689–692. ACM (2015)

30. Wang, F., Zuo, W., Lin, L., Zhang, D., Zhang, L.: Joint learning of single-image and cross-image representations for person re-identification. In: Proceedings of the IEEE Conference on Computer Vision and Pattern Recognition, pp. 1288–1296 (2016)

31. Weinberger, K.Q., Blitzer, J., Saul, L.K.: Distance metric learning for large margin nearest neighbor classification. In: Advances in Neural Information Processing Systems, pp. 1473–1480 (2006)

32. Wu, Y., Lim, J., Yang, M.H.: Online object tracking: A benchmark. In: IEEE CVPR, pp. 2411–2418 (2013)

33. Yi, W., Jongwoo, L., Yang, M.H.: Object tracking benchmark. IEEE Trans. Pattern Anal. Mach. Intell. **37**(9), 1834–1848 (2015)

34. Yilmaz, A., Javed, O., Shah, M.: Object tracking: a survey. ACM Comput. Surv. (CSUR) **38**(4), 13 (2006)
35. Zhang, J., Ma, S., Sclaroff, S.: MEEM: robust tracking via multiple experts using entropy minimization. In: Fleet, D., Pajdla, T., Schiele, B., Tuytelaars, T. (eds.) ECCV 2014. LNCS, vol. 8694, pp. 188–203. Springer, Cham (2014). https://doi. org/10.1007/978-3-319-10599-4_13
36. Zhang, T., Xu, C., Yang, M.H.: Multi-task correlation particle filter for robust object tracking. In: Proceedings of the IEEE Conference on Computer Vision and Pattern Recognition, vol. 1, p. 3 (2017)
37. Zhuang, B., Lin, G., Shen, C., Reid, I.: Fast training of triplet-based deep binary embedding networks. In: Proceedings of the IEEE Conference on Computer Vision and Pattern Recognition, pp. 5955–5964 (2016)

Point-to-Point Regression PointNet for 3D Hand Pose Estimation

Liuhao Ge[1]💿, Zhou Ren[2], and Junsong Yuan[3(✉)]

[1] Institute for Media Innovation, Interdisciplinary Graduate School,
Nanyang Technological University, Singapore, Singapore
ge0001ao@e.ntu.edu.sg
[2] Snap Inc., 64 Market Street, Venice, CA, USA
zhou.ren@snapchat.com
[3] Department of Computer Science and Engineering,
State University of New York at Buffalo, Buffalo, NY, USA
jsyuan@buffalo.edu

Abstract. Convolutional Neural Networks (CNNs)-based methods for
3D hand pose estimation with depth cameras usually take 2D depth
images as input and directly regress holistic 3D hand pose. Different
from these methods, our proposed *Point-to-Point Regression PointNet*
directly takes the 3D point cloud as input and outputs point-wise estimations, *i.e.*, heat-maps and unit vector fields on the point cloud, representing the closeness and direction from every point in the point cloud
to the hand joint. The point-wise estimations are used to infer 3D joint
locations with weighted fusion. To better capture 3D spatial information
in the point cloud, we apply a stacked network architecture for PointNet
with intermediate supervision, which is trained end-to-end. Experiments
show that our method can achieve outstanding results when compared
with state-of-the-art methods on three challenging hand pose datasets.

Keyword: 3D hand pose estimation

1 Introduction

A key technology for human-computer interaction in virtual reality and augmented reality applications is accurate and real-time 3D hand pose estimation,
which allows direct hand interaction with virtual objects. Despite the recent
progress of 3D hand pose estimation with depth cameras [11,13,17,22,23,35,36,
38,43,45,51,54], it remains challenging to achieve accurate and robust results
due to the high dimensionality and large variations of 3D hand pose, high similarity among fingers, severe self-occlusion, and noisy depth images.

Electronic supplementary material The online version of this chapter (https://
doi.org/10.1007/978-3-030-01261-8_29) contains supplementary material, which is
available to authorized users.

V. Ferrari et al. (Eds.): ECCV 2018, LNCS 11217, pp. 489–505, 2018.
https://doi.org/10.1007/978-3-030-01261-8_29

Most of the recently proposed 3D hand pose estimation methods [4,5,10–12,19,22,45,53] are based on convolutional neural networks (CNNs) and have achieved drastic performance improvement on large hand pose datasets [35,36, 43,55]. Many methods directly regress 3D coordinates of hand joints or hand pose parameters using CNNs [4,5,7,9,11,12,19,21,22,45,56]. However, the direct mapping from input representation to 3D hand pose is highly non-linear and difficult to learn, which makes these direct regression methods difficult to achieve high accuracy [42]. An alternative way is to generate a set of heat-maps representing the probability distributions of joint locations on 2D image plane [8,10,43], which has been successfully applied in 2D human pose estimation [18,49]. However, it is non-trivial to lift 2D heat-maps to 3D joint locations [24,30,41]. One straightforward solution is to generate volumetric heat-maps using 3D CNNs, but it is computationally inefficient. Wan et al. [46] recently propose a dense pixel-wise estimation method. Apart from generating 2D heat-maps, this method estimates 3D offsets of hand joints for each pixel of the 2D image. However, this method suffers from two limitations. First, as it regresses pixel-wise 3D estimations from 2D images, the proposed method may not fully exploit the 3D spatial information in depth images. Second, generating 3D estimations for background pixels of the 2D image may distract the deep neural network from learning effective features in the hand region.

To tackle these problems, we aim at regressing point-wise estimations directly from 3D point cloud, since the depth image is intrinsically composed of a set of 3D points on the visible object surface. We take advantages of PointNet [25,27] to learn features directly from 3D point cloud. Compared with [46], our method can better utilize the 3D spatial information in the depth image in an efficient way and concentrate on learning effective features of the hand point cloud in a natural way, since both the input and the output of our network directly take the form of hand point cloud. In addition, this point-to-point regression scheme also allows us to expand the single hierarchical PointNet module [27] to a stacked network architecture as in [18] to further improve the estimation accuracy.

As illustrated in Fig. 1, we propose a point-to-point regression method for 3D hand pose estimation in single depth images. Hand is first segmented from the depth image and is converted to a set of 3D points. The downsampled and normalized 3D points are then fed into a hierarchical PointNet [27] with two-stacked network architecture. The outputs of the network are heat-maps and unit vector fields on the 3D point cloud, reflecting the closeness and directions from 3D points to the target hand joints, respectively. Point-wise offsets to hand joints are inferred from the network outputs and are used to vote for 3D hand joint locations. With post-processing steps to alleviate other limitations, the estimation accuracy is further improved.

Our main contributions are summarized as follows:

- We propose to directly take the 3D point cloud as network input and generate heat-maps as well as unit vector fields on the input point cloud, which reflect the per-point closeness and directions to hand joints, respectively. With such a point-to-point regression network, our method is able to better utilize the

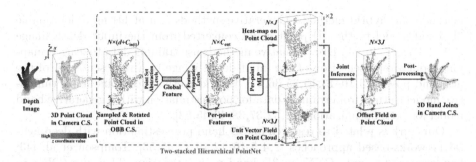

Fig. 1. Overview of our proposed point-to-point regression method for 3D hand pose estimation from single depth images. We propose to directly take N sampled and normalized 3D hand points as network input and output a set of heat-maps as well as unit vector fields on the input point cloud, reflecting the closeness and directions from input points to J hand joints, respectively. From the network outputs, we can infer point-wise offsets to hand joints and estimate the 3D hand pose with post-processing. We apply the hierarchical PointNet [27] with two-stacked network architecture which feeds the output of one module as input to the next. For illustration purpose, we only visualize the heat-map, unit vector field and offset field of one hand joint. 'C.S.' stands for coordinate system; 'MLP' stands for multi-layer perceptron network.

3D spatial information in the depth image and capture local structure of the 3D point cloud for accurate 3D hand pose estimation.

- We propose to apply the stacked network architecture [18] to the hierarchical PointNet [27] for point-to-point regression, which is the first stacked PointNet architecture, to our best knowledge. Similar to [18], the stacked PointNet architecture, feeding the output of one module as input into the next, allows repeated bottom-up and top-down inference on 3D point cloud and is able to boost the estimation accuracy in our experiments.

- We analyze the limitations of our point-to-point regression method and propose to use results of direct regression method as the alternative when the divergence among candidate estimations of point-to-point regression method is too large. Experiments show that the direct regression method is complementary with the point-to-point regression method and their combination can further improve the estimation accuracy.

We conduct extensive experiments on three challenging hand pose datasets: NYU dataset [43], ICVL dataset [36] and MSRA datasets [35]. Experimental results on these three datasets show that our proposed point-to-point regression method can achieve superior performance with runtime speed of 41.8 fps and network model size of 17.2 MB.

2   Related Work

Hand Pose Estimation. The methods for 3D hand pose estimation from depth images can be classified into three categories: generative methods, discriminative methods and hybrid methods. Generative methods aim at fitting a deformable 3D hand model to the 3D point cloud converted from the input depth image [1,14,23,28,31,40,44]. Discriminative methods use training data to learn a mapping from a representation of the input depth image to a representation of the 3D hand pose [4,5,10–13,19,35,36,51]. Hybrid methods combine a discriminative model learned from training data for pose estimation with a generative hand model for pose optimization [22,32,37,38,43,45,53].

Our work is related to research on 3D hand pose estimation with deep neural networks-based approaches [2,4,5,10–12,19,22,45,53]. Tompson et al. [43] first propose to apply CNNs in 3D hand pose estimation. They use CNNs to generate heat-maps representing the 2D probability distributions of hand joints in the depth image, and recover 3D hand pose from estimated heat-maps and corresponding depth values using model-based inverse kinematics. Ge et al. [10] solve the problem of lacking 3D information in 2D heat-maps [43] by projecting the depth image onto multiple views and estimating 3D hand pose from multi-view heat-maps. Oberweger et al. [19,21] instead directly regress 3D coordinates of hand joints or a lower dimensional embedding of 3D hand pose from depth images. They also propose a feedback loop [22] to iteratively refine the 3D hand pose. Zhou et al. [56] propose to directly regress hand model parameters from depth images. Ge et al. [11] encode the hand depth images as 3D volumes and use 3D CNNs to directly regress 3D hand pose from 3D volumes. Guo et al. [12] propose a region ensemble network that directly regresses 3D hand pose from depth images. Chen et al. [4] improve [12] through iterative refinement. Although many 3D hand pose estimation methods directly regress 3D hand pose, Wan et al. [46] recently propose a dense pixel-wise estimation method that applies an hourglass network to generate 2D and 3D heat-maps as well as 3D unit vector fields, from which the 3D hand joint locations can be inferred. Our method is inspired by this work [46], but is essentially different from it. Firstly, the network proposed in [46] takes 2D images as input, while our method takes 3D point cloud as the network input, thus is able to better utilize 3D spatial information in the depth image. Secondly, the network proposed in [46] outputs estimations for each pixel in the original image which may contain large useless background regions, while our proposed point-to-point regression network outputs estimations for each point in the hand point cloud, thus is able to concentrate on learning effective features from the hand point cloud instead of background regions.

3D Deep Learning. 3D data usually are not suitable to be directly processed by conventional CNNs that work on 2D images. Methods in [3,10,26,34] project 3D points into 2D images on multiple views and process them with multi-view CNNs. Methods in [11,16,26,33,50] rasterize 3D points into 3D voxels and apply 3D CNNs to extract features. But the time and space complexities of 3D CNNs are high. Octree-based 3D CNNs [29,48] are then proposed for efficient computation on 3D volumes with high resolution, but still suffer from voluminous input data.

PointNet [25,27] is a recently proposed method that directly takes an unordered point set as input and is able to learn features on the point set.

In the basic PointNet [25], each input point is mapped into a feature vector via multi-layer perceptron networks (MLP), of which the weights are shared across all the input points. Then, a vector max operator aggregates per-point features into a global feature that is invariant to different permutations of input points. The extracted global feature and per-point features can be used for various tasks. The basic PointNet [25] cannot capture local structures of the point cloud. To tackle this issue, a hierarchical PointNet [27] is proposed to extract local features in a hierarchical way. We refer readers to [27] for the details of hierarchical Point-Net. Deep Kd-networks [15], similar to PointNet, directly consumes point cloud by adopting a Kd-tree structure. Although these methods have shown promising performance on 3D classification and segmentation tasks, none of them has been applied to 3D hand pose estimation in a point-to-point regression manner.

3 Methodology

Our proposed method aims at estimating 3D hand pose from single depth images. The input is a depth image containing a hand, and the output is a set of 3D hand joint locations $\mathbf{\Phi}^{cam} = \left\{ \phi_j^{cam} \right\}_{j=1}^{J} \in \mathbf{\Lambda}$ in the camera Coordinate System (C.S.), where J is the number of hand joints, $\mathbf{\Lambda}$ is the $3 \times J$ dimensional hand joint space.

3.1 Point Cloud Preprocessing

The hand depth image is first converted to a set of 3D points using the depth camera's intrinsic parameters. The 3D point set is then downsampled to N points. To make our method robust to various hand orientations, we create an oriented bounding box (OBB) from the 3D point cloud and transform the 3D points into the OBB C.S., as shown in Fig. 1. The coordinates of 3D points are normalized between -0.5 and 0.5 by subtracting the centroid of point cloud and dividing by L_{obb}, which is the maximum edge length of OBB. We denote the downsampled and normalized 3D point set in OBB C.S. as $\mathcal{P}^{obb} = \left\{ p_i^{obb} \right\}_{i=1}^{N}$. In our implementation, we set the number of sampled points N as 1024. Since we process the point set in OBB C.S., we will omit the superscript 'obb' in symbols of points and joint locations in the following sections for simplicity.

3.2 Point Cloud Based Representation for 3D Hand Pose

Most existing CNN-based methods for 3D hand pose estimation directly regress 3D coordinates of hand joints [4,11,12,22,45] or hand pose parameters [5,19, 21,56]. In contrast to direct regression approaches that require to learn a highly non-linear mapping, our method aims at generating point-wise estimations of hand joint locations from the point cloud, which is able to better utilize the local evidence. The point-wise estimations can be defined as the offsets from points to hand joint locations. However, estimating offsets for all points in the point set is unnecessary and may make the per-point votes noisy. Thus, we only estimate offsets for the neighboring points of the hand joint, as shown in Fig. 2. We define the element in the target offset fields V for point p_i $(i = 1, \cdots, N)$ and ground truth hand joint location ϕ_j^* $(j = 1, \cdots, J)$ as:

$$V\left(p_i, \phi_j^*\right) = \begin{cases} \phi_j^* - p_i & p_i \in \mathcal{P}_K\left(\phi_j^*\right) \text{ and } \left\|\phi_j^* - p_i\right\| \leq r, \\ 0 & \text{otherwise;} \end{cases} \quad (1)$$

where $\mathcal{P}_K\left(\phi_j^*\right)$ is a set of K nearest neighboring points (KNN) of the ground truth hand joint location ϕ_j^* in the point set $\mathcal{P}^{obb}$; r is the maximum radius of ball for nearest neighbor search; in our implementation, we set K as 64 and r as $80 \, \text{mm}/L_{obb}$. We combine KNN with ball query for nearest neighbor search in order to guarantee that both the number of neighboring points and the scale of neighboring region are controllable.

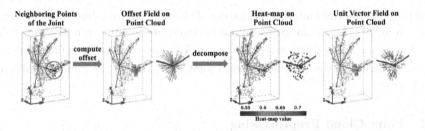

Fig. 2. An illustration of the ground truth of the point cloud based representation for 3D hand pose. We visualize the neighboring points, offset field, heat-map and unit vector field on 3D point cloud for the root joint of the thumb finger. For illustration propose, we enlarge the region of neighboring points of the hand joint location on the right of each complete point cloud.

However, it is difficult to train a neural network that directly generates the offset field due to the large variance of offsets. Similar to [46], we decompose the target offset fields V into heat-maps H reflecting per-point closeness to hand joint locations:

$$H\left(p_i, \phi_j^*\right) = \begin{cases} 1 - \left\|\phi_j^* - p_i\right\|/r & p_i \in \mathcal{P}_K\left(\phi_j^*\right) \text{ and } \left\|\phi_j^* - p_i\right\| \leq r, \\ 0 & \text{otherwise;} \end{cases} \quad (2)$$

and unit vector fields U reflecting per-point directions to hand joint locations:

$$U\left(p_i, \phi_j^*\right) = \begin{cases} \left(\phi_j^* - p_i\right)/\left\|\phi_j^* - p_i\right\| & p_i \in \mathcal{P}_K\left(\phi_j^*\right) \text{ and } \left\|\phi_j^* - p_i\right\| \leq r, \\ 0 & \text{otherwise.} \end{cases} \quad (3)$$

Different from [46] that generates heat-maps and unit vector fields on 2D images, our proposed method generates heat-maps and unit vector fields on the 3D point cloud, as shown in Fig. 2, which can better utilize the 3D spatial information in the depth image. In addition, generating heat-maps and unit vector fields on 2D images with large blank background regions may distract the neural network from learning effective features in the hand region. Although this problem can be alleviated by multiplying a binary hand mask in the loss function, our method is able to concentrate on learning effective features of the hand point cloud in a natural way without using any mask, since the output heat-maps and unit vector fields are represented on the hand point cloud.

3.3 Network Architecture

In this work, we exploit the hierarchical PointNet [27] for learning heat-maps and unit vector fields on 3D point cloud. Different from the hierarchical PointNet for point set segmentation adopted in [27], our proposed point-to-point regression network has a two-stacked network architecture in order to better capture the 3D spatial information in the 3D point cloud.

We first describe the network architecture of a single hierarchical PointNet module. As illustrated in Fig. 3, the input of the network is a set of d-dim coordinates with C_{in}-dim input features, $i.e.$, 3D surface normals that are approximated by fitting a local plane for the nearest neighbors of the query point in the point cloud ($d = 3$ and $C_{in} = 3$ in this work). Similar to the network architecture for set segmentation proposed in [27], a single module of our network extracts a global feature vector from point cloud using three set abstraction levels and propagates the global feature to point features for original points using three feature propagation levels, as shown in Fig. 3. In the feature propagation level, we use nearest neighbors of the interpolation point in N_l points to interpolate features for N_{l-1} points [27]. The interpolated C_l-dim features of N_{l-1} points are concatenated with the corresponding point features in the set abstraction level and are mapped to C_{l-1}-dim features using per-point MLP, of which the weights are shared across all the points ($l = 1, 2, 3; N_0 = N, C_0 = C_{out}, N_3 = 1$). The heat-map and the unit vector field are generated from the point features for the original point set using per-point MLP. In our implementation, we set $N = 1024$, $N_1 = 512$, $N_2 = 128$, $C_1 = 128$, $C_2 = 256$ and $C_{out} = 128$.

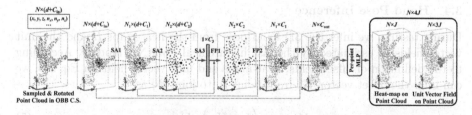

Fig. 3. An illustration of a single network module which is based on the hierarchical PointNet [27]. Here, 'SA' stands for point set abstraction layers; 'FP' stands for feature propagation layers; 'MLP' stands for multi-layer perceptron network. The dotted shortcuts denote skip links for feature concatenation.

Inspired by the stacked hourglass networks for human pose estimation [18], we stack two hierarchical PointNet modules end-to-end to boost the performance of the network. The two hierarchical PointNet modules have the same network architecture and the same hyper-parameters, except for the hyper-parameter in the input layer. As shown in Fig. 4, the output heat-map and unit vector field of the first module are concatenated with the input and output point features of the first module as the input into the second hierarchical PointNet module. For real-time consideration, we only stack two hierarchical PointNet modules.

We apply intermediate supervision when training the two-stacked hierarchical PointNet. The loss function for each training sample is defined as:

$$\mathcal{L} = \sum_{t=1}^{T} \sum_{j=1}^{J} \sum_{i=1}^{N} \left[\left(\hat{H}_{ij}^{(t)} - H\left(\boldsymbol{p}_i, \boldsymbol{\phi}_j^*\right) \right)^2 + \left\| \hat{\boldsymbol{U}}_{ij}^{(t)} - \boldsymbol{U}\left(\boldsymbol{p}_i, \boldsymbol{\phi}_j^*\right) \right\|^2 \right], \qquad (4)$$

where T is the number of stacked network modules, in this work $T = 2$; $\hat{H}_{ij}^{(t)}$ and $\hat{\boldsymbol{U}}_{ij}^{(t)}$ are elements in the heat-maps and unit vector fields estimated by the t-th network module, respectively; $H\left(\boldsymbol{p}_i, \boldsymbol{\phi}_j^*\right)$ and $\boldsymbol{U}\left(\boldsymbol{p}_i, \boldsymbol{\phi}_j^*\right)$ are elements in the ground truth heat-maps and ground truth unit vector fields defined in Eqs. 2 and 3, respectively.

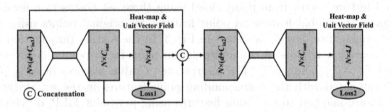

Fig. 4. An illustration of the two-stacked hierarchical PointNet architecture with intermediate supervision. The input feature dimension of the 2nd network module is $C_{in2} = C_{in1} + C_{out} + 4J$.

3.4 Hand Pose Inference

During testing, we infer the 3D hand pose from the heat-maps $\hat{H}$ and the unit vector fields $\hat{U}$ estimated by the last hierarchical PointNet module. According to the definition of offset fields, heat-maps and unit vector fields in Eq. 1–3, we can infer the offset vector $\hat{\boldsymbol{V}}_{ij}$ from point $\boldsymbol{p}_i$ to joint $\hat{\boldsymbol{\phi}}_j$ as:

$$\hat{\boldsymbol{V}}_{ij} = r \cdot \left(1 - \hat{H}_{ij} \right) \cdot \hat{\boldsymbol{U}}_{ij}. \qquad (5)$$

According to Eq. 1, only the offset vectors for the neighboring points of the hand joint are used for hand pose inference, which can be found from the estimated heat-map reflecting the closeness of points to the hand joint. We denote the estimated heat-map for the j-th hand joint as $\hat{H}_j$ that is the j-th column of $\hat{H}$. We determine the neighboring points of the j-th hand joint as the points corresponding to the largest M values of the heat-map $\hat{H}_j$. The indices of these points in the point set are denoted as $\{i_m\}_{m=1}^{M}$. The hand joint location $\hat{\phi}_j$ can be simply inferred from the corresponding offset vectors $\hat{V}_{i_m j}$ and 3D points p_{i_m} ($m = 1, \cdots, M$) using weighted average:

$$\hat{\phi}_j = \sum_{m=1}^{M} w_m \left(\hat{V}_{i_m j} + p_{i_m} \right) / \sum_{m=1}^{M} w_m, \tag{6}$$

where w_m is the weight of the candidate estimation. In our implementation, we set the weight w_m as the corresponding heat-map value $\hat{H}_{i_m j}$, and set M as 25.

3.5   Post-processing

There are two issues in our point-to-point regression method. The first issue is that the estimation is unreliable when the divergence of the M candidate estimations are large in 3D space, as shown in Fig. 5(a). This is usually caused by missing depth data near the hand joint. The second issue is that there is no explicit constraint on the estimated 3D hand pose, although the neural network may learn joint constraints in the output heat-maps and unit vector fields.

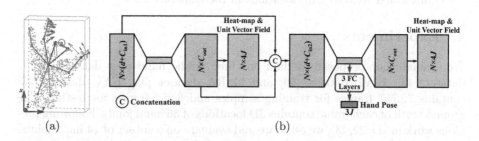

Fig. 5. (a) A failure case in which the candidate estimations of the middle fingertip can not converge to a small local region in 3D space due to missing depth data near the hand joint. The ground truth hand joint locations are plotted in this figure. (b) An illustration of the two-stacked hierarchical PointNet architecture in which we add three fully-connected layers to directly regress the 3D coordinates of hand joints from the global feature extracted by the second hierarchical PointNet module.

To tackle the first issue, when the divergence of the M candidate estimations is larger than a threshold, we replace the estimation result with the result of the direct regression method that directly regresses 3D coordinates of hand joints, since the direct regression method does not have this issue. In order to save the inference time, instead of training a separate PointNet for direct hand pose regression, we add three fully-connected layers for direct hand pose regression to the pre-trained two-stacked hierarchical PointNet, as shown in Fig. 5(b). The three fully-connected layers are trained to directly regress the 3D coordinates of hand joints from the features extracted by the second hierarchical PointNet module. The divergence of the M candidate estimations is defined as the sum of standard deviations of x, y and z coordinates of candidate estimations. In our implementation, we set the divergence threshold as $7.5\,\mathrm{mm}/L_{obb}$. Experimental results in Sect. 4.1 will show that although only a small portion of the hand joint estimations requires to be replaced by the direct regression results, this replacement strategy can improve the estimation accuracy to some extent.

To tackle the second issue, we explicitly constrain the estimated 3D hand pose $\hat{\Phi}$ on a lower dimensional space learned by principal component analysis (PCA). By performing PCA on the ground truth 3D joint locations in the training dataset, we can obtain the principal components $E = [e_1, e_2, \cdots, e_H]$ ($H < 3J$) and the empirical mean u. The constrained 3D hand pose can be calculated using the following formula:

$$\hat{\Phi}_{cons} = E \cdot E^T \cdot \left(\hat{\Phi} - u\right) + u. \tag{7}$$

In our implementation, we set the number of principle components H as 30. Experimental results in Sect. 4.1 will show that adding PCA constraint will improve the accuracy slightly, which shows that the neural network may have already learned joint constraints in the output heat-maps and unit vector fields.

Finally, the estimated 3D hand joint locations in the normalized OBB C.S. are transformed back to joint locations in the camera C.S. $\hat{\Phi}^{cam}$.

4   Experiments

We evaluate our proposed method on three public hand pose datasets: NYU dataset [43], ICVL dataset [36] and MSRA dataset [35]. NYU dataset [43] contains 72,757 frames for training samples and 8,252 frames for testing. The ground truth of each frame contains 3D locations of 36 hand joints. Following previous work in [11,22,43], we estimate and evaluate on a subset of 14 hand joints. Since the frames in this dataset are original depth images containing human body and background, we use a single hourglass network [18] to detect 2D hand joint locations and use the corresponding depth information for hand segmentation. We augment the training data with random arm lengths due to various lengths of hand arm in the segmented images. ICVL dataset [36] contains 22,059 frames for training and 1,596 frames for testing. The ground truth of each frame contains 3D locations of 16 hand joints. We use the same method as that used on NYU dataset for hand segmentation. The training data is randomly augmented with various arm lengths and stretch factors. MSRA dataset [35] contains nine subjects, each subject contains 17 hand gestures and each hand gesture contains about 500 frames with segmented hand depth image. The ground truth of each frame contains 3D locations of 21 hand joints. In the experiments, we train on eight subjects and test on the remaining one. This is repeated nine times for all subjects. We do not perform any data augmentation on this dataset.

We adopt two metrics to evaluate the performance of 3D hand pose estimation methods. The first metric is the per-joint mean error distance over all test frames as well as the overall mean error distance for all joints on all test frames. The second metric is the proportion of good frames in which the worst joint error is below a threshold [39]. This metric is more strict.

We train and evaluate our proposed deep neural network models on a workstation with two Intel Core i7 5930K, 64 GB of RAM and an Nvidia TITAN Xp GPU. The deep neural network models are implemented within the PyTorch framework. When training the deep neural network models, we use Adam [14] optimizer with initial learning rate 0.001, batch size 32, momentum 0.5 and weight decay 0.0005. The learning rate is divided by 10 after 30 epochs. The training is stopped after 60 epochs to prevent overfitting.

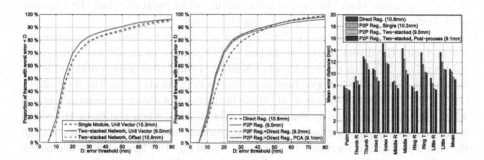

Fig. 6. Self-comparison of different methods on NYU dataset [43]. **Left:** the impacts of the stacked network architecture and different network outputs on the proportion of good frames. **Middle:** the impacts of our point-to-point regression method and post-processing methods on the proportion of good frames. We use two-stacked network for point-to-point regression in this figure. **Right:** the impact of point-to-point regression method, stacked network architecture and post-processing methods on the per-joint mean error distance (R: root, T: tip). 'P2P Reg.' stands for point-to-point regression. The overall mean error distances are shown in parentheses.

Table 1. The impacts of the number of candidate estimations M and weighted average on the overall mean error distance on NYU dataset [43].

# Candidate estimations M	5	15	25	35	45	55
Unweighted average	9.50 mm	9.47 mm	9.48 mm	9.57 mm	9.70 mm	9.84 mm
Weighted average	9.50 mm	9.47 mm	9.46 mm	9.53 mm	9.61 mm	9.71 mm

4.1 Self-comparisons

We first evaluate the impact of the stacked network architecture for hierarchical PointNet. As shown in Fig. 6 (left and right), the two-stacked network evidently performs better than the single network module, which indicates the importance of the stacked network architecture on our point-to-point regression method.

We also evaluate the impact of different network outputs. In our method, we train the network to output heat-maps and unit vector fields for hand joints, then use them to recover the offset fields, as described in Sect. 3. In this experiment, we compare our method with a baseline method in which a network is trained to generate offset fields instead of unit vector fields. The network also outputs heat-maps which are only used to find neighboring points of hand joints. As shown in Fig. 6 (left), when adopting the two-stacked network architecture, the network generating unit vector fields performs better than the network generating offset fields. This result shows that the network regressing unit vectors of offsets may be easier to learn than the network regressing offset vectors, since the variance of the offset vectors is larger than the unit vectors.

To evaluate our proposed point-to-point regression method, we compare our method with the direct regression method. In this experiment, we use a hierarchical PointNet [27] with three set abstraction levels and three full-connected levels to directly regress the 3D coordinates of hand joints. As shown in Fig. 6 (middle), our point-to-point regression method outperforms the direct regression method when the error threshold is smaller than 45 mm. But when the error threshold is larger than 45 mm, our point-to-point regression method performs worse than the direct regression method. This may be caused by the large divergence of the candidate estimations in some results, as described in Sect. 3.5. By combining the point-to-point method with the direct regression method as described in Sect. 3.5, the estimation accuracy can be further improved, as shown in Fig. 6 (middle). Furthermore, the performance of the combination method is superior to or on par with the direct regression method over all the error thresholds. In this experiment, only 7.9% of joint locations estimated by point-to-point regression method are replaced by the results of direct regression method, which indicates that the estimation results are dominated by the point-to-point regression method, and the direct regression method is complementary with the point-to-point regression method. In addition, adding the PCA constraint can further improve the estimation accuracy slightly.

We further study the influence of the number of candidate estimations M used in Eq. 7 and the weighted average on the overall mean error distance. As shown in Table 1, the mean error distance is the smallest when the number of candidate estimations M is between 15 and 25. When M is larger than 25, the mean error distance will become larger. In addition, when M is smaller than 25, the weighted average will not improve the mean error distance. But when M becomes larger, the improvement of the weighted average on the mean error distance is more and more evident. Thus, the weighted average is able to make the estimation more robust to noisy candidate estimations. We set M as 25 and use weighted average with post-processing in the following experiments.

4.2   Comparisons with State-of-the-arts

We compare our proposed point-to-point regression method with 16 state-of-the-art methods: latent random forest (LRF) [36], hierarchical regression with random forest (RDF, Hierarchical) [35], local surface normal based random forest (LSN) [47], collaborative filtering [6], 2D heat-map regression using 2D CNNs (Heat-map) [43], feedback loop based 2D CNNs (Feedback Loop) [22], hand model parameter regression using 2D CNNs (DeepModel) [56], Lie group based 2D CNNs (Lie-X) [52], improved direct regression with a pose prior using 2D CNNs (DeepPrior++) [19], hallucinating heat distribution using 2D CNNs (Hallucination Heat) [5], multi-view CNNs [10], 3D CNNs [11], crossing nets using deep generative models (Crossing Nets) [45], region ensemble network (REN) [12], pose guided structured REN (Pose-REN) [4] and dense 3D regression using 2D CNNs (DenseReg) [46]. We evaluate the proportion of good frames over different error thresholds and the per-joint mean error distances as well as the overall mean error distance on NYU [43], ICVL [36] and MSRA [35] datasets, as presented in Figs. 7 and 8, respectively.

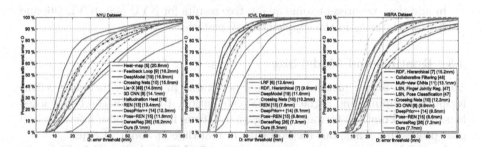

Fig. 7. Comparison with state-of-the-art methods on NYU [43] (left), ICVL [36] (middle) and MSRA [35] (right) datasets. The proportions of good frames and the overall mean error distances (in parentheses) are presented in this figure.

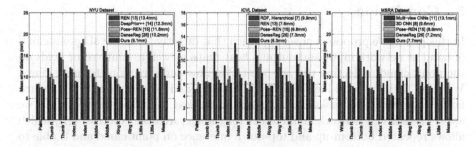

Fig. 8. Comparison with state-of-the-art methods on NYU [43] (left), ICVL [36] (middle) and MSRA [35] (right) datasets. The per-joint mean error distances and the overall mean error distances are presented in this figure (R: root, T: tip).

As can be seen in Figs. 7 and 8, our method can achieve superior performance on these three datasets. On NYU [43] and ICVL [36] datasets, our method outperforms other methods over almost all the error thresholds and achieves the smallest overall mean error distances on these two datasets. Specifically, on NYU dataset [43], when the error threshold is between 15 mm and 20 mm, the proportions of good frames of our method is about 15% better than DenseReg [46] and 20% batter than Pose-REN [4]; on ICVL dataset [36], when the error threshold is between 10 mm and 15 mm, the proportions of good frames of our method is more than 10% better than DenseReg [46] and Pose-REN [4] methods. On MSRA dataset [35], our method outperforms other methods over almost all the error thresholds, except for the DenseReg [46] method. Although our method is about 10% better than DenseReg [46] when the error threshold is 10 mm and the overall mean error distance of our method is only 0.5 mm worse than that of DenseReg [46], our method is worse than the DenseReg [46] method when the error threshold is larger 15 mm. As mentioned in [20] and shown in the qualitative results, some of the 3D hand joint annotations in MSRA dataset [35] exhibit significant errors, which may make the evaluation on this dataset less meaningful and may limit the learning ability of our deep neural network.

In addition, we present some qualitative results for NYU [43], ICVL [36] and MSRA [35] datasets in the supplementary material.

4.3   Runtime and Model Size

The runtime of our method is 23.9 ms per frame in average, including 8.2 ms for point sampling and surface normal calculation, 15.1 ms for the two-stacked hierarchical PointNet forward propagation, 0.6 ms for hand pose inference and post-processing. Thus, our method runs in real-time at about 41.8 fps.

In addition, the model size our network is 17.2 MB, including 11.1 MB for the point-to-point regression network which is a two-stacked hierarchical PointNet and 6.1 MB for the additional direct regression module which consists of three fully-connected layers. Compared with the model size of the 3D CNNs proposed in [11] which is about 420 MB, our model size is smaller.

5   Conclusion

In this paper, we propose a novel approach that directly takes the 3D point cloud of hand as network input and outputs heat-maps as well as unit vector fields on the point cloud, reflecting the per-point closeness and directions to hand joints. We infer 3D hand joint locations from the estimated heat-maps and unit vector fields using weighted fusion. Similar to the stacked hourglass network [18], we apply the stacked network architecture for the hierarchical PointNet [27], which allows repeated bottom-up and top-down inference on point cloud and is able to further boost the performance. Our proposed point-to-point regression method can also be easily combined with direct regression method to achieve more robust performance. Experimental results on three challenging hand pose datasets show that our method achieves superior accuracy performance in real-time.

Acknowledgment. This research is supported by the BeingTogether Centre, a collaboration between NTU Singapore and UNC at Chapel Hill. The BeingTogether Centre is supported by the National Research Foundation, Prime Minister's Office, Singapore under its International Research Centres in Singapore Funding Initiative. This work is also supported in part by Singapore Ministry of Education Academic Research Fund Tier 2 MOE2015-T2-2-114, start-up grants from University at Buffalo, and a gift grant from Snap Inc.

References

1. Ballan, L., Taneja, A., Gall, J., Van Gool, L., Pollefeys, M.: Motion capture of hands in action using discriminative salient points. In: Fitzgibbon, A., Lazebnik, S., Perona, P., Sato, Y., Schmid, C. (eds.) ECCV 2012. LNCS, vol. 7577, pp. 640–653. Springer, Heidelberg (2012). https://doi.org/10.1007/978-3-642-33783-3_46
2. Cai, Y., Ge, L., Cai, J., Yuan, J.: Weakly-supervised 3D hand pose estimation from monocular RGB images. In: ECCV (2018)
3. Cao, Z., Huang, Q., Ramani, K.: 3D object classification via spherical projections. In: 3DV (2017)
4. Chen, X., Wang, G., Guo, H., Zhang, C.: Pose guided structured region ensemble network for cascaded hand pose estimation. arXiv preprint arXiv:1708.03416 (2017)
5. Choi, C., Kim, S., Ramani, K.: Learning hand articulations by hallucinating heat distribution. In: ICCV (2017)
6. Choi, C., Sinha, A., Hee Choi, J., Jang, S., Ramani, K.: A collaborative filtering approach to real-time hand pose estimation. In: ICCV (2015)
7. Ge, L., Liang, H., Yuan, J., Thalmann, D.: Real-time 3D hand pose estimation with 3D convolutional neural networks. IEEE Trans. Pattern Anal. Mach. Intell. 1–15 (2018). https://doi.org/10.1109/TPAMI.2018.2827052. ISSN: 0162-8828
8. Ge, L., Liang, H., Yuan, J., Thalmann, D.: Robust 3D hand pose estimation from single depth images using multi-view CNNs. IEEE Trans. Image Process. **27**(9), 4422–4436 (2018)
9. Ge, L., Cai, Y., Weng, J., Yuan, J.: Hand pointnet: 3D hand pose estimation using point sets. In: Proceedings of the IEEE Conference on Computer Vision and Pattern Recognition, pp. 8417–8426 (2018)
10. Ge, L., Liang, H., Yuan, J., Thalmann, D.: Robust 3D hand pose estimation in single depth images: from single-view CNN to multi-view CNNs. In: CVPR (2016)
11. Ge, L., Liang, H., Yuan, J., Thalmann, D.: 3D convolutional neural networks for efficient and robust hand pose estimation from single depth images. In: CVPR (2017)
12. Guo, H., Wang, G., Chen, X., Zhang, C., Qiao, F., Yang, H.: Region ensemble network: improving convolutional network for hand pose estimation. In: ICIP (2017)
13. Keskin, C., Kıraç, F., Kara, Y.E., Akarun, L.: Hand pose estimation and hand shape classification using multi-layered randomized decision forests. In: Fitzgibbon, A., Lazebnik, S., Perona, P., Sato, Y., Schmid, C. (eds.) ECCV 2012. LNCS, vol. 7577, pp. 852–863. Springer, Heidelberg (2012). https://doi.org/10.1007/978-3-642-33783-3_61
14. Khamis, S., Taylor, J., Shotton, J., Keskin, C., Izadi, S., Fitzgibbon, A.: Learning an efficient model of hand shape variation from depth images. In: CVPR (2015)
15. Klokov, R., Lempitsky, V.: Escape from cells: deep Kd-networks for the recognition of 3D point cloud models. In: ICCV (2017)

16. Maturana, D., Scherer, S.: Voxnet: a 3D convolutional neural network for real-time object recognition. In: IROS (2015)
17. Moon, G., Chang, J.Y., Lee, K.M.: V2V-PoseNet: Voxel-to-voxel prediction network for accurate 3D hand and human pose estimation from a single depth map. In: CVPR (2018)
18. Newell, A., Yang, K., Deng, J.: Stacked hourglass networks for human pose estimation. In: Leibe, B., Matas, J., Sebe, N., Welling, M. (eds.) ECCV 2016. LNCS, vol. 9912, pp. 483–499. Springer, Cham (2016). https://doi.org/10.1007/978-3-319-46484-8_29
19. Oberweger, M., Lepetit, V.: Deepprior++: improving fast and accurate 3D hand pose estimation. In: ICCV Workshop (2017)
20. Oberweger, M., Riegler, G., Wohlhart, P., Lepetit, V.: Efficiently creating 3D training data for fine hand pose estimation. In: CVPR (2016)
21. Oberweger, M., Wohlhart, P., Lepetit, V.: Hands deep in deep learning for hand pose estimation. In: CVWW (2015)
22. Oberweger, M., Wohlhart, P., Lepetit, V.: Training a feedback loop for hand pose estimation. In: ICCV (2015)
23. Oikonomidis, I., Kyriazis, N., Argyros, A.: Efficient model-based 3D tracking of hand articulations using Kinect. In: BMVC (2011)
24. Pavlakos, G., Zhou, X., Derpanis, K.G., Daniilidis, K.: Coarse-to-fine volumetric prediction for single-image 3D human pose. In: CVPR (2017)
25. Qi, C.R., Su, H., Mo, K., Guibas, L.J.: PointNet: deep learning on point sets for 3D classification and segmentation. In: CVPR (2017)
26. Qi, C.R., Su, H., Nießner, M., Dai, A., Yan, M., Guibas, L.J.: Volumetric and multi-view CNNs for object classification on 3D data. In: CVPR (2016)
27. Qi, C.R., Yi, L., Su, H., Guibas, L.J.: PointNet++: deep hierarchical feature learning on point sets in a metric space. In: NIPS (2017)
28. Remelli, E., Tkach, A., Tagliasacchi, A., Pauly, M.: Low-dimensionality calibration through local anisotropic scaling for robust hand model personalization. In: ICCV (2017)
29. Riegler, G., Ulusoy, A.O., Geiger, A.: Octnet: learning deep 3D representations at high resolutions. In: CVPR (2017)
30. Rogez, G., Weinzaepfel, P., Schmid, C.: Lcr-net: Localization-classification-regression for human pose. In: CVPR (2017)
31. Romero, J., Tzionas, D., Black, M.J.: Embodied hands: modeling and capturing hands and bodies together. ACM Trans. Graph. (TOG) 36(6), 245 (2017)
32. Sharp, T., et al.: Accurate, robust, and flexible real-time hand tracking. In: CHI (2015)
33. Song, S., Xiao, J.: Deep sliding shapes for amodal 3D object detection in RGB-D images. In: CVPR (2016)
34. Su, H., Maji, S., Kalogerakis, E., Learned-Miller, E.: Multi-view convolutional neural networks for 3D shape recognition. In: ICCV (2015)
35. Sun, X., Wei, Y., Liang, S., Tang, X., Sun, J.: Cascaded hand pose regression. In: CVPR (2015)
36. Tang, D., Chang, H.J., Tejani, A., Kim, T.K.: Latent regression forest: structured estimation of 3D articulated hand posture. In: CVPR (2014)
37. Tang, D., Taylor, J., Kohli, P., Keskin, C., Kim, T.K., Shotton, J.: Opening the black box: hierarchical sampling optimization for estimating human hand pose. In: ICCV (2015)

38. Taylor, J., et al.: Efficient and precise interactive hand tracking through joint, continuous optimization of pose and correspondences. ACM Trans. Graph. **35**(4), 143 (2016)
39. Taylor, J., Shotton, J., Sharp, T., Fitzgibbon, A.: The vitruvian manifold: inferring dense correspondences for one-shot human pose estimation. In: CVPR (2012)
40. Tkach, A., Tagliasacchi, A., Remelli, E., Pauly, M., Fitzgibbon, A.: Online generative model personalization for hand tracking. ACM Trans. Graph. (TOG) **36**(6), 243 (2017)
41. Tome, D., Russell, C., Agapito, L.: Lifting from the deep: convolutional 3D pose estimation from a single image. In: CVPR (2017)
42. Tompson, J., Jain, A., LeCun, Y., Bregler, C.: Joint training of a convolutional network and a graphical model for human pose estimation. In: NIPS (2014)
43. Tompson, J., Stein, M., Lecun, Y., Perlin, K.: Real-time continuous pose recovery of human hands using convolutional networks. ACM Trans. Graph. **33**(5), 169 (2014)
44. Tzionas, D., Ballan, L., Srikantha, A., Aponte, P., Pollefeys, M., Gall, J.: Capturing hands in action using discriminative salient points and physics simulation. Int. J. Comput. Vis. **118**(2), 172–193 (2016)
45. Wan, C., Probst, T., Van Gool, L., Yao, A.: Crossing nets: dual generative models with a shared latent space for hand pose estimation. In: CVPR (2017)
46. Wan, C., Probst, T., Van Gool, L., Yao, A.: Dense 3D regression for hand pose estimation, pp. 5147–5156 (2018)
47. Wan, C., Yao, A., Van Gool, L.: Hand pose estimation from local surface normals. In: Leibe, B., Matas, J., Sebe, N., Welling, M. (eds.) ECCV 2016. LNCS, vol. 9907, pp. 554–569. Springer, Cham (2016). https://doi.org/10.1007/978-3-319-46487-9_34
48. Wang, P.S., Liu, Y., Guo, Y.X., Sun, C.Y., Tong, X.: O-CNN: Octree-based convolutional neural networks for 3D shape analysis. ACM Trans. Graph. (TOG) **36**(4), 72 (2017)
49. Wei, S.E., Ramakrishna, V., Kanade, T., Sheikh, Y.: Convolutional pose machines. In: CVPR (2016)
50. Wu, Z., et al.: 3D shapenets: a deep representation for volumetric shapes. In: CVPR (2015)
51. Xu, C., Cheng, L.: Efficient hand pose estimation from a single depth image. In: ICCV (2013)
52. Xu, C., Govindarajan, L.N., Zhang, Y., Cheng, L.: Lie-X: Depth image based articulated object pose estimation, tracking, and action recognition on lie groups. Int. J. Comput. Vis. **123**(3), 454–478 (2017)
53. Ye, Q., Yuan, S., Kim, T.-K.: Spatial attention deep net with partial PSO for hierarchical hybrid hand pose estimation. In: Leibe, B., Matas, J., Sebe, N., Welling, M. (eds.) ECCV 2016. LNCS, vol. 9912, pp. 346–361. Springer, Cham (2016). https://doi.org/10.1007/978-3-319-46484-8_21
54. Yuan, S., et al.: Depth-based 3D hand pose estimation: from current achievements to future goals. In: CVPR (2018)
55. Yuan, S., Ye, Q., Stenger, B., Jain, S., Kim, T.K.: BigHand2.2m benchmark: hand pose dataset and state of the art analysis. In: CVPR (2017)
56. Zhou, X., Wan, Q., Zhang, W., Xue, X., Wei, Y.: Model-based deep hand pose estimation. In: IJCAI (2016)

DOCK: Detecting Objects by Transferring Common-Sense Knowledge

Krishna Kumar Singh[1,3](✉)(iD), Santosh Divvala[2,3](iD), Ali Farhadi[2,3](iD), and Yong Jae Lee[1](iD)

[1] University of California, Davis, USA
krsingh@ucdavis.edu
[2] University of Washington, Seattle, USA
[3] Allen Institute for AI, Seattle, USA
https://dock-project.github.io

Abstract. We present a scalable approach for Detecting Objects by transferring Common-sense Knowledge (DOCK) from source to target categories. In our setting, the training data for the source categories have bounding box annotations, while those for the target categories only have image-level annotations. Current state-of-the-art approaches focus on image-level visual or semantic similarity to adapt a detector trained on the source categories to the new target categories. In contrast, our key idea is to (i) use similarity not at the image-level, but rather at the region-level, and (ii) leverage richer common-sense (based on attribute, spatial, etc.) to guide the algorithm towards learning the correct detections. We acquire such common-sense cues automatically from readily-available knowledge bases without any extra human effort. On the challenging MS COCO dataset, we find that common-sense knowledge can substantially improve detection performance over existing transfer-learning baselines.

1 Introduction

Object detection has witnessed phenomenal progress in recent years, where *fully-supervised* detectors have produced amazing results. However, getting large volumes of bounding box annotations has become an Achilles heel of this setting. To address this scalability concern, transfer-learning methods that transform knowledge from source categories (with bounding boxes) to *similar* target classes (with only image labels) have evolved as a promising alternative [17,32,37,39].

While recent works [17,18,39] have demonstrated the exciting potential of transfer-learning on *object-centric* datasets like ImageNet, it has not yet been thoroughly explored on more complex *scene-centric* datasets like MS COCO. Why is it so?

Electronic supplementary material The online version of this chapter (https://doi.org/10.1007/978-3-030-01261-8_30) contains supplementary material, which is available to authorized users.

ⓒ Springer Nature Switzerland AG 2018
V. Ferrari et al. (Eds.): ECCV 2018, LNCS 11217, pp. 506–522, 2018.
https://doi.org/10.1007/978-3-030-01261-8_30

We hypothesize three key challenges:

(i) Existing transfer learning methods rely only on similarity knowledge between the source and target categories to compute the transformations that need to be transferred. Unfortunately, using similarity alone is often insufficient. For example, can you guess the orange-colored region proposal in the masked image using only the provided similarity cues (Fig. 1)? (ii) Existing methods depend on having a robust image-level object classifier for transferring knowledge, which

Fig. 1. Guess the object? (Color figure online)

for object-centric datasets like ImageNet is easy to obtain, but is challenging for scene-centric datasets like MS COCO (where multiple and potentially small objects like 'toothbrush' exist in each image). If the image classifier does not perform well, then transforming it into a detector will not perform well either. (iii) Finally, if instances of the target classes frequently co-occur with the source classes, then the target class regions can end up being undesirably learned as 'background' while training the detector for the source classes.

In this paper, we overcome the above limitations by proposing a new approach for Detecting Objects by transferring Common-sense Knowledge (DOCK). To overcome the first limitation, our key idea is to leverage multiple sources of *common-sense* knowledge. Specifically, we encode: (1) *similarity*, (2) *spatial*, (3) *attribute*, and (4) *scene*. For example, if 'spoon' is one of the target objects and 'fork', 'table', and 'kitchen' are among the source categories, we can learn to better detect the 'spoon' by leveraging the fact that it is usually '*similar* to fork', '*on* a table', '*is* metallic', and '*seen* in kitchens'. Figure 2 shows another scenario, which builds upon the Fig. 1 example.

Fig. 2. Using the multiple common-sense cues, can you now guess the object corresponding to the orange box? (For answer, see [1]) (Color figure online)

In this way, even if a target class does not have a visually/semantically *similar* class among the source classes, the other common-sense can help in obtaining a better detector. All the common-sense knowledge we use is freely-acquired from readily-available external knowledge bases [19,23,27,29,38,44]. Further, our approach learns all the required common-sense models using source-class bounding box annotations only and does not require *any* bounding box annotations for the target categories.

To address the latter limitations, our idea is to directly model objects at the region-level rather than at the image-level. To this end, any detection framework that learns using region proposals with image-level labels for the target object categories is applicable. In this paper, we use an object proposal classification and ranking detection framework based upon [5] for its simplicity and competitive performance. It learns an object detector by minimizing an image classification loss based on object proposals' class probabilities. We inject common-sense into this framework by modulating the object proposals' class probabilities with our proposed common-sense prior probabilities. The proposed priors give higher preference to regions that are more likely (under common-sense) to belong to the object-of-interest. Interestingly, since the common-sense cues are encoded only as *priors*, our algorithm can choose to ignore them when they are not applicable. This is particularly helpful to alleviate the concern when frequently co-occurring target classes are incorrectly learned as 'background'.

We evaluate our approach on the challenging MS COCO dataset [22]. We find that transferring common-sense knowledge substantially improves object detection performance for the target classes that lack bounding box annotations, compared to other contemporary transfer-learning methods [17,18,39]. We also perform ablation analyses to inspect the contribution of our proposed idea of encoding common sense. Finally, we explore the potential of our proposed framework in the context of webly-supervised object detection.

2   Related Work

Transfer learning for scalable object detection. Existing transfer learning approaches can be roughly divided into two groups: one that learns using bounding box annotations for both source and target categories [3,11,21,36,40,43], and another that learns using bounding box annotations for source categories but only image-level annotations for target categories [17,18,32,37,39]. In this paper, we are interested in the latter setting, which is harder but likely to be more scalable. In particular, the recent state-of-the-art deep learning approaches of [17,18,39] adapt an image classifier into an object detector by learning a feature transformation between classifiers and detectors on the source classes, and transfer that transformation to related target classes based on visual or semantic similarity for which only classifiers exist. While our approach also leverages pre-trained object detectors for encoding visual and semantic similarity, we explore additional common-sense cues such as spatial and attribute knowledge. Moreover, both [17,39] use similarity information at the image-level (which works well on only object-centric datasets like ImageNet), while our approach uses similarity at the region-level. All these contributions together help us achieve a significant performance boost on the scene-centric MS COCO dataset.

Use of context. Our use of common-sense is related to previous works on context which leverage additional information beyond an object's visual appearance. Context has been used for various vision tasks including object detection [4,8,9,15,31,33], semantic segmentation [28], and object discovery [10,20]. As context by definition is something that frequently co-occurs with the object-of-interest, without bounding box annotations the contextual regions can easily be confused with the object-of-interest (e.g., a piece of 'road' context with a 'car'). Our approach tries to address this issue by using external common-sense knowledge to model context for a target object in terms of its spatial relationship with

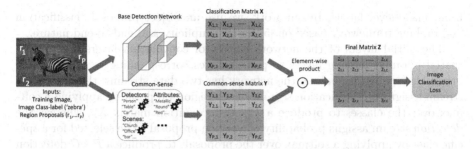

Fig. 3. Proposed framework for transferring common-sense knowledge for object detection. The base detection network computes a classification matrix $X_{P \times C}$ without any bounding box annotations (Sect. 3.1). We introduce a common-sense matrix $Y_{P \times C}$ that modulates the probabilities of region proposals belonging to various classes based on common-sense knowledge (Sect. 3.2). The common-sense matrix is computed using readily-available knowledge base resources (Sect. 3.3).

previously-learned source objects. This idea is related to [20], which makes use of already known objects to discover new categories from unlabeled images.

Using external knowledge for vision tasks. Our field has witnessed the rise of several interesting knowledge bases, including ConceptNet [23], BabelNet [29], WordNet [27], WebChild [38], Visual Genome [19], ImSitu [44], etc. While resources like WebChild [38] and BabelNet [29] are created automatically by crawling the web, others are generated with crowd-sourced effort. The key advantage of these resources is that they contain freely-available rich knowledge.

Such external knowledge bases have been used in several vision tasks including image classification [7,25], VQA [41,47], visual relationship detection [24,30], and modeling object affordances [46]. However, there has been very limited work on using external knowledge for object detection [13], especially in the transfer learning setting in which bounding box annotations for the target classes are lacking. Tang et al. [39] use word2vec semantic similarity between classes to perform domain transfer between a classifier and a detector. In contrast, we go beyond using semantic similarity and explore spatial, scene, and attribute cues.

3   Proposed Approach

In this section, we first briefly describe the base detection network used in our framework and then explain our proposed approach for injecting common-sense knowledge into it. Finally, we describe our process for automatically gathering the different types of common-sense knowledge from existing resources.

3.1   Base Detection Network

Our idea of transferring common-sense knowledge to improve object detection is generic and could be incorporated into any detection approach that learns from image-level labels. In our work, we use an object proposal classification and ranking framework based on [5] for its simplicity and end-to-end nature.

The initial layers of the network consist of convolution layers followed by spatial pyramid pooling layers to pool features corresponding to image region proposals (r_i). After pooling, the network has two data streams: the *recognition* stream assigns a classification score for each region proposal by applying a softmax over the classes to produce a $P \times C$ recognition matrix X_r, whereas the *detection* stream assigns probability of a region proposal to be selected for a specific class by applying a softmax over the proposals to produce a $P \times C$ detection matrix X_d. The final probability for each proposal to belong to different classes is computed by taking their element-wise dot product $X = X_r \odot X_d$. The network takes P proposals of a training image as input and outputs the probability for each of them to belong to C classes. This is shown as a $P \times C$ classification matrix X in Fig. 3. Note that the network learns to detect objects while being trained for the image classification task. The image-level class probabilities are obtained by summing the probabilities of each class (c_i) over the proposals:

$$Prob(c_i) = \sum_{n=1}^{P} X_{r_n,c_i}, i \in (1, C),$$

where X_{r_n,c_i} is the probability of proposal r_n belonging to class c_i. A binary cross-entropy loss is applied over the probabilities to learn the detection models.

3.2   Transferring Common-Sense

In order to transfer common-sense knowledge from the source categories with both image and bounding box annotations to the target categories with only image-level annotations, we augment the above base detection network with a novel *common-sense* matrix Y of size $P \times C$ (analogous to the classification matrix $X_{P \times C}$). Each element of Y_{r_n,c_i} can be thought of as representing a 'prior' probability of a proposal r_n belonging to class c_i according to common-sense knowledge (see Fig. 3). We will maintain a separate common-sense matrix for each type of common-sense (*similarity, attribute*, etc.) and later (Sect. 3.3) describe the details for acquiring and merging these matrices.

Assuming we have access to this common-sense matrix Y, we utilize this information by taking an element-wise dot product of it with the classification matrix (X) to create a resultant matrix $Z_{P \times C}$:

$$Prob(c_i) = \sum_{n=1}^{P} Y_{r_n,c_i} * X_{r_n,c_i} = \sum_{n=1}^{P} Z_{r_n,c_i}, i \in (1, C),$$

which now will be used for obtaining the image-level class probabilities over which a binary cross-entropy loss is applied.

For example, in Fig. 3, the *attribute* common-sense matrix (which would encode the common-sense that a 'zebra' is *striped*) would have a low prior probability $(Y_{r_P,zebra})$ for the proposal r_P to be a 'zebra'. And, the *class-similarity*

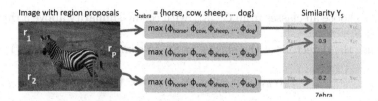

Fig. 4. Similarity Common-sense: For computing the $Y_s(., zebra)$ values, all the proposals of the input image are scored by the detectors of zebra's semantically similar classes S_{zebra}. Observe that proposal r_2, which contains the zebra's full-body gets the highest Y_s value.

common-sense (which would encode the common-sense that a 'zebra' is similar to a 'horse') would have a low value for the zebra head proposal ($Y_{r_1,zebra}$) compared to the zebra full-body proposal ($Y_{r_2,zebra}$).

Intuitively, the common-sense matrix Y influences the values of the classification matrix X during training and over time the common-sense priorities are transferred from Y to X. To drive home this intuition, we take the example in Fig. 3. The $Prob_{zebra}$ should be high for this training image as it contains a 'zebra', i.e., $\sum_{n=1}^{P} Z_{r_n,zebra} = \sum_{n=1}^{P} Y_{r_n,zebra} * X_{r_n,zebra}$ should be high. This can be easily achieved if both $Y_{r_n,zebra}$ and $X_{r_n,zebra}$ are high. In this case $Y_{r_2,zebra}$ is high according to common-sense which in turn encourages the network to have high value for $X_{r_2,zebra}$. At the same time, due to a low value for $Y_{r_1,zebra}$ and $Y_{r_P,zebra}$, the network is discouraged to have a high value for $X_{r_1,zebra}$ and $X_{r_P,zebra}$. Therefore, during training itself, the network learns to incorporate the common-sense prior information of the Y matrix into the X matrix.

3.3   Acquiring Common-Sense

Now that we have seen how we transfer common-sense information (i.e., matrix Y) into the base detection framework, we next explain our approach for automatically gathering this matrix using existing knowledge resources.

Class Similarity Common-sense. Our goal here is to leverage the semantic similarity of a new target class to previously-learned source classes. For example, as a 'zebra' is semantically similar to a 'horse', the proposals that are scored higher by a 'horse' detector should be more probable of being a 'zebra'. More generally, for any class c_i, the proposals looking similar to its semantically similar classes should receive higher prior for c_i.

To construct the class-similarity common-sense matrix Y_s, we tap into the readily-available set of pre-trained detectors (ϕ) for the source object classes (C_{source}) in the PASCAL VOC [12] knowledge base. Let c_i be one of the new target object classes for which we are trying to learn a detector with just image-level labels. To find the set of semantically similar source classes (i.e., $S_{c_i} \subset C_{source}$) to c_i, we represent all the classes (c_i as well as C_{source}) using their word2vec textual feature representation [26] and then compute the cosine-similarity between them. We choose all classes from C_{source} with cosine-similarity above a threshold (0.35) as S_{c_i}.

We use the detectors of the classes in S_{c_i} to compute the values in Y_s as:

$$Y_s(r_n, c_i) = \max_{c_j \in S_{c_i}} \phi_{c_j}(r_n), n \in (1, P).$$

Specifically, we set the value $Y_s(r_n, c_i)$ for a proposal r_n to be of class c_i as being equal to the maximum detection probability of the classes similar to c_i. Figure 4 illustrates how the class-similarity common-sense Y_s is assigned in case of the target 'zebra' object class, where S_{zebra} consists of the source object classes {'horse','cow','sheep','dog','cat','bird'}. Observe that a correct proposal (i.e., r_2 containing the 'zebra' full-body) gets the highest similarity common-sense probability as it is scored higher by the object detectors in S_{zebra}.

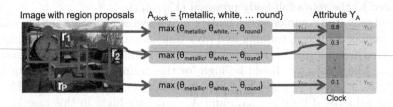

Fig. 5. Attribute Common-sense: For computing $Y_a(., clock)$ values, we apply the attribute classifiers for the common attributes of 'clock' on the proposals. Observe that r_1 containing a 'clock' with *white & round* attributes gets the highest Y_a value.

Attribute Common-sense. Attributes are mid-level semantic visual concepts (e.g., *furry, red, round*, etc.,) that are shareable across object categories [14]. For example, an 'apple' is usually *red*, a 'clock' is typically *round*, etc. Therefore region proposals that possess the characteristic attributes of a specific class should be more probable to belong to that class.

To build the attribute common-sense matrix Y_a, we leverage the pre-trained set of attribute classifiers (θ) from the ImageNet Attribute [35] knowledge base and the readily-available set of object-attribute relationships from the Visual Genome [19] knowledge base. Let c_i be one of the new target classes for which we are trying to learn a detector and A_{c_i} be its set of common attributes (determined by the frequency by which it is used to described c_i). The classifiers of the attributes in A_{c_i} are used to compute the values of the matrix Y_a as

$$Y_a(r_n, c_i) = \max_{a_j \in A_{c_i}} \theta_{a_j}(r_n), n \in (1, P).$$

As the attributes in ImageNet [35] knowledge base (that we use in this work) have been additionally grouped into sets of *color* A^{col}, *shape* A^{shape}, and *texture* A^{text} attributes, we adopt this information by updating $Y_a(r_n, c_i)$ as: $Y_a(r_n, c_i) = mean(Y_a^{col}(r_n, c_i), Y_a^{shape}(r_n, c_i), Y_a^{text}(r_n, c_i))$, where Y^{col}, Y^{shape}, Y^{text} have been computed over the A^{col}, A^{shape}, A^{text} domains. In Fig. 5, for the 'clock'

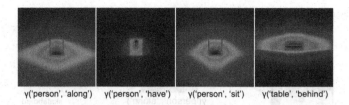

γ('person', 'along')   γ('person', 'have')   γ('person', 'sit')   γ('table', 'behind')

Fig. 6. Spatial common-sense distribution: We model the relative location distributions $\gamma^L_{c_j,rel}$ encoding the pixel-wise probability γ of all other source objects for a given object c_j (shown as a red box) under a given relation rel. (Color figure online)

class, the proposal r_1 containing its attributes, i.e., *white/black* and *round*, get the highest Y value, while the other proposals (r_2, r_P) get lower values as they lack the characteristic 'clock' attributes.

Spatial Common-sense. In our day-to-day experience objects often appear in characteristic spatial relations with other objects. For example, a 'bowl' is typically *on* a 'table', a 'backpack' is typically *behind* a 'person', etc. Therefore region proposals that have the characteristic spatial relation of a target class to other source classes should be more probable of belonging to that target class.

To obtain the spatial-relation common-sense matrix Y_{sp}, we utilize the information about relative locations and sizes of *source* object classes C_{source} in the Visual Genome [19] knowledge base that contains visually-grounded triplets {object1, relation, object2}.

For each class c_j in C_{source}, we model the relative location distributions $\gamma^L_{c_j,rel}$ encoding the pixel-wise probability of all other source objects under a given relation rel. For example, Fig. 6 shows the distribution of objects with respect to the 'along' relationship for the source 'person' object class. In a similar way, for each class c_j in C_{source} and a given relation rel, we also model the relative size distributions $\gamma^S_{c_j,rel}$. Note that these distributions need to be learned just once using *only the source classes* and then can be reused for any of the target classes (i.e., without bounding box annotations for C_{target} classes).

For a new target class c_i from C_{target}, we first gather its most common relation with respect to source classes c_j in C_{source} using the {object1, relation, object2} triplet information from [19][1] and then compute the Y_{sp} matrix as:

$$Y_{sp}(r_n, c_i) = \max_{c_j \in C_{vis}} \frac{1}{2}(\gamma^L_{c_j,rel}(\mathbf{x}^{center}_{r_n}) + \gamma^S_{c_j,rel}(area_{r_n})),$$

where $\mathbf{x}^{center}$ and $area$ denote the center coordinate and the size of a proposal, and C_{vis} are the subset of classes from C_{source} that are visible in the given image with their locations determined by running the pre-trained detectors ϕ.

In Fig. 7, the proposal r_P gets a higher Y_{sp} value for the 'skateboard' class as it is in sync with the 'along' relation under the $\gamma^L_{person,along}$ distribution.

---

[1] For any target class, we gather this information from existing knowledge bases [19,38] by analyzing the *rel* that is commonly used to associate it with the source classes.

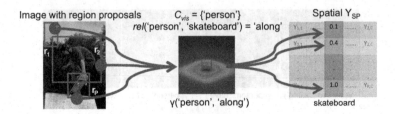

Fig. 7. Spatial Common-sense: The $Y_{sp}(., skateboard)$ values are computed by measuring the spatial relationship of proposals with respect to the source 'person' class. Based on our knowledge base [19], 'along' is the most common relation between the 'skateboard' and 'person' class. Observe that the proposal r_P gets the highest Y_{sp} value.

Scene Common-sense. Some objects appear more in certain scenes than others; e.g., a 'surfboard' is more likely to be found on a *beach*. Hence, images depicting scenes associated with class c_i are more likely to contain instances of c_i.

To obtain the scene common-sense matrix Y_{sc}, we leverage the SceneUNderstanding (SUN) [42] and Places [45] knowledge bases. These databases not only contain information about commonly occurring scene labels for the different object classes but also provide access to pre-trained scene classifiers (β). Let SC_{c_i} denote the set of scene labels associated with a new target object class c_i, and I be the given image containing the proposals, then Y_{sc} can be computed as: $Y_{sc}(r_n, c_i) = \sum_{s_j \in SC_{c_i}} \beta_{s_j}(I), n \in (1, P)$. All proposals r_n in image I get high prior for class c_i if I depicts the scene that frequently contains instances of class c_i. Note that this scene common-sense knowledge would be helpful in case of noisy image-level labels (e.g., in the webly-supervised setting), and may not be relevant when we already have clean human-annotated labels that indicate the presence/absence of objects in images.

4   Experimental Results and Analysis

In this section, we report quantitative and qualitative analyses for validating the benefit of transferring common-sense knowledge for object detection. We also conduct ablation studies to dissect the various components of our approach.

Dataset. Recent state-of-the-art transfer learning approaches for object detection [17,39] have limited their analysis to ImageNet [34]. While this dataset has enabled substantial progress in this domain, we believe the time is ripe for advancing the transfer-learning paradigm to the next level, i.e., the more complex MS COCO [22] benchmark. The MS COCO dataset is challenging not only in terms of its diversity (non-iconic views, varying sizes, etc.) but also in number of classes, and thus poses a tough challenge for methods that do not have access to bounding box annotations for the target classes. We believe our idea of leveraging multiple common-sense would be more relevant to address this challenge.

Recall that, in our framework, we use the PASCAL VOC object detectors as one of our sources of common-sense knowledge (i.e., for similarity and spatial). Hence, we avoid using the 20 VOC classes (C_{source}) within the MS COCO dataset and focus our analysis on the remaining 60 object classes (C_{target}). We train our network with MS COCO 2015 training images, evaluate on the validation images, and use the standard performance metrics (mAP with 50% IoU threshold).

Implementation details. Our base network of [4] is initialized with VGG-CNN-F [6]. We train the network with a learning rate of 10^{-5} for the first 20 epochs and 10^{-6} for the next 10 epochs. During training, the images are randomly flipped horizontally and scaled to one of 5 scales: 800×608, 656×496, 544×400, 960×720, and 1152×864. During testing, we average the corresponding 10 detection scores and apply NMS with an overlap threshold of 0.4 after filtering out proposals with probability less than 10^{-4}. We use MCG [2] object proposals. In order to combine the common-sense matrices (Y_a, Y_{sp}, Y_s), we take the average of the three matrices and obtain Y_{all}, which is used to train the base network. Although our approach involves a few task-specific insights to effectively leverage common-sense knowledge, we found our approach to be robust to a wide range of choices when constructing these common-sense matrices (e.g. number of similar known classes for similarity common-sense, number of common relations between known/unknown classes for spatial common-sense, etc). For similarity common-sense, we represent each class name using a 300-d word2vec representation (obtained using pre-trained model on Google news dataset [26]).

Table 1. Detection results on MS COCO validation set. Our proposed approach substantially improves over existing transfer-learning methods.

Methods	AP	AP^S	AP^M	AP^L
Classification Network ('No Adapt' [17])	3.4	0.9	2.9	6.1
LSDA [17]	4.6	1.2	5.1	7.8
LSDA+Semantic [39]	4.7	1.1	5.1	8.0
LSDA+MIL [18]	5.9	1.5	8.3	10.7
Fine-tuned Detection Network	10.8	1.2	8.9	18.6
Proposed Approach	**14.4**	**2.0**	**12.8**	**24.9**
Oracle: Full Detection Network [16]	25.2	5.8	26.0	41.6

4.1 Quantitative Results

Table 1 presents the results obtained using our approach and compares it to other relevant approaches. As an upper-bound, we also include the fully-supervised Fast-RCNN [16] detection result (using VGG-CNN-F and trained with bounding box annotations for the target classes) obtaining 25.2% mAP. While our approach falls well short of this upper bound, it reveals to us the possibility of using common-sense for bridging the gap to fully-supervised methods.

Comparison to Transfer-learning. The most relevant state-of-the-art transfer learning methods are LSDA [17], [18] and [39]. However, as [17,18,39] neither report results on the challenging MS COCO dataset nor provide their training code, we re-implemented LSDA [17][2]. Running this baseline on the 60 MS COCO C_{target} classes yields 4.6% mAP, which is substantially inferior than our proposed approach (14.4%). We hypothesize the poor performance of the LSDA frameworks on the MS COCO dataset to the following reasons:

(i)   LSDA approaches [17,18,39] are inherently limited to exploiting only *similarity* common-sense. While similarity suffices in case of object-centric datasets, more richer common-sense (such as *attribute, spatial*, etc., that we use) needs to be leveraged when dealing with complex scene-centric datasets. Further when the size of C_{source} is small (e.g., set of 20 classes in our MS COCO experiments), similarity fails to work well in gathering meaningful neighbors between C_{target} and C_{source} classes. As a result, LSDA methods cannot transform the classifier successfully. Particularly, the class-invariant transformation of the weights from conv1 to fc7 layers in LSDA will not generalize well when the similarity overlap between the classes in C_{source} and C_{target} is poor. Our approach alleviates this concern by explicitly using detection probabilities of the C_{source} classes for each image (rather than doing a weight transformation), and also by using other common-sense knowledge (*attribute, spatial*, etc., which would weigh more in the absence of similar C_{source} classes).

(ii) As MS COCO has images with multiple categories and small objects, the initial classifier network learned in the LSDA methods is poor (giving only 3.4% mAP, see Table 1 top-row) and therefore transforming it results in a poor detector. Our approach alleviates this concern by employing a proposal classification and ranking detection network (11.7% mAP, see Table 2, 'Base network').

(iii) Finally, class co-occurrences in images poses a formidable challenge for the LSDA methods. For example, in case of the target class 'spoon', the top nearest neighbor (among the 20 C_{source} classes) is 'dining-table', which often co-occurs with it and thus transferring its detection knowledge will cause confusion to the detector. Our approach is robust to such cases of incorrect similarities as the similarity information is only used as a 'prior' during our base detection network training.

Transfer learning by fine-tuned detection network. We also explored an alternate transfer-learning strategy, where we initialize our base detection network (Sect. 3.1) with pre-trained Fast-RCNN weights from the source categories and

---

[2] Similar setting as ours: use image-level labels for all training images of MS COCO and VOC, use bounding box for only 20 VOC classes, and VGG-CNN-F as base network.

then fine-tune it on the target classes using only image-level labels. While this method produces a relatively higher mAP of 10.8% than LSDA, it is still lower than our approach. We believe this is due to the network weights getting overfit to the 20 C_{source} classes and subsequently failing to generalize well to the 60 C_{target} classes. In contrast, our approach does not have this overfitting issue as we initialize our base detection network with the weights from a more general network (trained on 1000 ImageNet classes) and then use the 20 C_{source} classes pre-trained detection models only for computing similarity common-sense.

Alternate approaches for leveraging common-sense. To analyze the significance of our proposed approach for leveraging common-sense, we also studied alternative strategies for leveraging common sense cues that use exactly the same external knowledge/bounding box information as our approach.

The first strategy uses common-sense as a contextual post-processing tool [9]. Specifically, for a test image, we compute the common-sense matrix Y, and then modulate its classification matrix X via element-wise multiplication to produce the final score matrix: $Z_{test} = X_{test} \cdot Y_{test}$. Table 2 ('Post-process') displays the result obtained using this post-processing strategy, which obtains 11.8% (and 14.1% when common-sense matrix Y is also used during training). Observe that the post-processing result is lower compared to our approach, which transfers common-sense during training only and not during testing. This indicates that X has already incorporated the common-sense knowledge during training, and thus using Y is redundant at test time. When Y is introduced during testing, it is difficult for common sense to fix any incorrect biases that the detector may have learned (e.g., focusing only on the most discriminative part of an object). It may even hurt as any mistakes in common-sense information Y cannot be circumvented when used directly at test time. In contrast, by transferring common sense during training, it can guide the algorithm to *learn* to focus on the correct image regions.

The second alternate strategy for leveraging common-sense analyzes the possibility of improving detection performance by simply having access to pre-trained object/spatial/attribute classifiers. In this case, we trivially append a 45-dimensional feature to the fc7 appearance feature of each proposal during training. The first 20 dimensions correspond to the detection probabilities of the

Table 2. Analysis on the MS COCO dataset: 'Base network' is the result obtained by using our base detection network using no common-sense. 'Alternatives' are the alternate strategies for leveraging common-sense knowledge. Their performance is lower than our model demonstrating the benefit of our proposed approach. 'Ablations' show the improvement obtained using each common-sense cue over the base network. Combining all common-sense cues produces the best result indicating their complementarity.

Method	Base network	Alternatives		Ablations				Ours
		Post-process	Feature	Attr	Spatial	Sim	Joint	+Sim(Bbox)
mAP	11.7	11.8/14.1	12.7	12.2	13.0	13.7	14.1	**14.4**

20 C_{source} classes and the remaining 25 dimensions correspond to the attribute probabilities of the classifiers (θ) pre-trained on the ImageNet attribute knowledge base. While this model yields a boost of 1.0% mAP compared to the base detection network (see Table 2 'Feature'), it is 1.7% lower than our proposed model. This reveals that merely concatenating external knowledge features to visual appearance features is insufficient.

4.2   Ablation and Qualitative Analysis

We also analyzed the importance of the various common-sense cues in our proposed approach. Table 2 'Ablations' shows that each common sense gives a boost over the base network, which only relies on appearance cues. Among the individual cues, we see that similarity helps the most. (Scene cue was not explored in this scenario and its influence will be analyzed in the webly-supervised setting.) Combining attribute, spatial, and similarity common sense ('Joint') leads to a greater boost of 2.4% mAP, which shows their complementarity. Finally, we also borrow the bounding box regressors trained on the similar C_{source} classes and apply them to the C_{target} classes, which further boosts performance to 14.4%.

Taking a closer look at individual classes, we find that using the attribute common-sense for 'oven' (that is usually *white/black*) results in a boost of 7.3% AP. By using the spatial common-sense for 'frisbee' with respect to the source object 'person', we get an improvement of 10.5% in AP, whereas using the spatial relation for a 'bowl' with respect to the source object 'table' gives a boost of 2.2%. For 'giraffe' and 'bed', we use the common-sense that they are semantically similar to {'sheep', 'horse', 'dog', 'cow', 'bird', 'cat'}, and 'couch' respectively, which leads to an improvement of 28.7% and 12.1% AP, respectively.

We next analyze the importance of using word2vec for similarity common-sense. For this, we replace word2vec similarity with visual similarity, which results in 12.1% compared to our 13.7%. Word2vec similarity is more robust than visual similarity (used in LSDA [17]), particularly for challenging dataset like MS COCO (with small objects and co-occurring objects from different classes). We also tried WordNet [27] treepath based similarity which also gives an inferior result of 13.1%.

Figure 8 shows some qualitative detections (for each of the common-sense) produced by our approach (green box) and compares them to competing baselines. We can observe that using common-sense helps improve performance. For example, by using spatial common-sense, our approach gets rid of the co-occurring background for 'frisbee' and 'surfboard' (person and water, respectively). Interestingly, for 'frisbee', our approach uses the spatial common-sense that a 'frisbee' often spatially-overlaps with a 'person' in order to learn its appearance during training. It is then able to detect a 'frisbee' at test time even when a 'person' is not present (see 'frisbee' image in the second column). This indicates that while our approach leverages common-sense as a prior during training to learn about the object's appearance, at the same time, our network is not dependent on common-sense during testing. Figure 9 shows some failure cases.

Fig. 8. Qualitative detection results on MS COCO (Ours: green boxes; Base network: red; LSDA+Semantic [39]: Yellow): Observe that our approach produces better detections than the base network for all three common-sense. For 'giraffe' and 'elephant', by using similarity common-sense (i.e., being similar to other animal categories in C_{source}), our approach detects the full body extent rather than localizing a discriminative body part. By using spatial and attribute common-sense, e.g., 'clock' being *round*, 'spoon' being *metallic*, and 'microwave' being *white/black*, we get better detections. (Color figure online)

Fig. 9. Example failures: Our approach fails when the object-of-interest is hardly-visible ('handbag') or when source objects with similar attribute (*metallic*) are cluttered together ('spoon'). For 'wine glass', we falsely detect the 'bottle' because during training we provided the common-sense that wine-glass is semantically similar to a bottle.

Towards webly-supervised detection using common-sense supervision. What happens when we apply our method in cases when we do not even have explicit human-annotated image labels for the target class? This is exactly the setting studied in the webly-supervised domain where images retrieved from the web are used for training detection models.

We conducted a preliminary investigation wherein we ran our proposed approach on training images retrieved from the web (i.e., instead of the MS COCO training imageset). As images retrieved from web are potentially noisy, common-sense knowledge should be particularly useful in mitigating the noise. Our preliminary results indicate that our proposed idea is promising even in the webly setting (Base network [5]: 6.8%, vs. Ours: 8.3%).

Further, to analyze potential concerns about the generalizability of our acquired common-sense knowledge, we also tested these webly+commonsense models on the ImageNet 200 detection valset [34]. Even in this case, our approach yields interesting performance gains (Base network [5]: 6.2%, vs. Ours: 8.8%).

5   Conclusion

In this paper, we presented DOCK, a novel approach for transferring common-sense knowledge from a set of categories with bounding box annotations to a set of categories that only have image-level annotations for object detection. We explored how different common-sense cues based on similarity, attributes, spatial relations, and scene could be jointly used to guide the algorithm towards improved object localization. Our experiments showed that common-sense knowledge can improve detection performance on the challenging MS COCO dataset. We hope our work will spur further exciting research in this domain.

Acknowledgements. This work is in part supported by ONR N00014-13-1-0720, NSF IIS-1338054, NSF IIS-1748387, NSF IIS-1751206, NSF-1652052, NRI-1637479, ARO YIP W911NF-17-1-0410, Allen Distinguished Investigator Award, Allen Institute for AI, Microsoft Azure Research Award and the GPUs donated by NVIDIA. A part of this work was done while Krishna Kumar Singh was an intern at Allen Institute for AI.

References

1. Toothbrush. http://cocodataset.org#explore?id=315486
2. Arbeláez, P., Pont-Tuset, J., Barron, J., Marques, F., Malik, J.: Multiscale combinatorial grouping. In: CVPR (2014)
3. Aytar, Y., Zisserman, A.: Tabula rasa: model transfer for object category detection. In: ICCV (2011)
4. Bilen, H., Pedersoli, M., Namboodiri, V., Tuytelaars, T., Gool, L.V.: Object classification with adaptable regions. In: CVPR (2014)
5. Bilen, H., Vedaldi, A.: Weakly supervised deep detection networks. In: CVPR (2016)

6. Chatfield, K., Simonyan, K., Vedaldi, A., Zisserman, A.: Return of the devil in the details: delving deep into convolutional nets. In: BMVC (2014)
7. Chowdhury, S.N., Tandon, N., Ferhatosmanoglu, H., Weikum, G.: VISIR: visual and semantic image label refinement. In: WSDM (2018)
8. Desai, C., Ramanan, D., Fowlkes, C.: Discriminative models for multi-class object layout. IJCV 95(1), 1–12 (2011)
9. Divvala, S.K., Hoiem, D., Hays, J.H., Efros, A.A., Hebert, M.: An empirical study of context in object detection. In: CVPR (2009)
10. Doersch, C., Gupta, A., Efros, A.A.: Context as supervisory signal: discovering objects with predictable context. In: Fleet, D., Pajdla, T., Schiele, B., Tuytelaars, T. (eds.) ECCV 2014. LNCS, vol. 8691, pp. 362–377. Springer, Cham (2014). https://doi.org/10.1007/978-3-319-10578-9_24
11. Donahue, J., Hoffman, J., Rodner, E., Saenko, K., Darrell, T.: Semi-supervised domain adaptation with instance constraints. In: CVPR (2013)
12. Everingham, M., Van Gool, L., Williams, C.K.I., Winn, J., Zisserman, A.: The PASCAL Visual Object Classes Challenge 2012 (VOC2012) Results. http://www.pascal-network.org/challenges/VOC/voc2012/workshop/index.html
13. Fang, Y., Kuan, K., Lin, J., Tan, C., Chandrasekhar, V.: Object detection meets knowledge graphs. In: IJCAI (2017)
14. Farhadi, A., Endres, I., Hoiem, D., Forsyth, D.: Describing objects by their attributes. In: CVPR (2009)
15. Gidaris, S., Komodakis, N.: Object detection via a multi-region and semantic segmentation-aware CNN model. In: ICCV (2015)
16. Girshick, R.: Fast R-CNN. In: ICCV (2015)
17. Hoffman, J., et al.: LSDA: Large scale detection through adaptation. In: NIPS (2014)
18. Hoffman, J., Pathak, D., Darrell, T., Saenko, K.: Detector discovery in the wild: joint multiple instance and representation learning. In: CVPR (2015)
19. Krishna, R., et al.: Visual genome: connecting language and vision using crowd-sourced dense image annotations. IJCV 123(1), 32–73 (2017)
20. Lee, Y.J., Grauman, K.: Object-graphs for context-aware visual category discovery. TPAMI 34(2), 346–358 (2012)
21. Lim, J.J., Salakhutdinov, R.R., Torralba, A.: Transfer learning by borrowing examples for multiclass object detection. In: NIPS (2011)
22. Lin, T.-Y., et al.: Microsoft COCO: common objects in context. In: Fleet, D., Pajdla, T., Schiele, B., Tuytelaars, T. (eds.) ECCV 2014. LNCS, vol. 8693, pp. 740–755. Springer, Cham (2014). https://doi.org/10.1007/978-3-319-10602-1_48
23. Liu, H., Singh, P.: ConceptNet - a practical commonsense reasoning tool-kit. BT Technol. J. 22(4), 211–226 (2004)
24. Lu, C., Krishna, R., Bernstein, M., Fei-Fei, L.: Visual relationship detection with language priors. In: Leibe, B., Matas, J., Sebe, N., Welling, M. (eds.) ECCV 2016. LNCS, vol. 9905, pp. 852–869. Springer, Cham (2016). https://doi.org/10.1007/978-3-319-46448-0_51
25. Marino, K., Salakhutdinov, R., Gupta, A.: The more you know: using knowledge graphs for image classification. In: CVPR (2017)
26. Mikolov, T., Sutskever, I., Chen, K., Corrado, G.S., Dean, J.: Distributed representations of words and phrases and their compositionality. In: NIPS (2013)
27. Miller, G.A.: WordNet: a lexical database for English. Commun. ACM 38(11), 39–41 (1995)
28. Mottaghi, R., et al.: The role of context for object detection and semantic segmentation in the wild. In: CVPR (2014)

29. Navigli, R., Ponzetto, S.P.: BabelNet: the automatic construction, evaluation and application of a wide-coverage multilingual semantic network. Artif. Intell. **193**, 217–250 (2012)

30. Plummer, B.A., Mallya, A., Cervantes, C.M., Hockenmaier, J., Lazebnik, S.: Phrase localization and visual relationship detection with comprehensive linguistic cues. In: ICCV (2017)

31. Rabinovich, A., Vedaldi, A., Galleguillos, C., Wiewiora, E., Belongie, S.: Objects in context. In: ICCV (2007)

32. Rochan, M., Wang, Y.: Weakly supervised localization of novel objects using appearance transfer. In: CVPR (2015)

33. Russakovsky, O., Lin, Y., Yu, K., Fei-Fei, L.: Object-centric spatial pooling for image classification. In: Fitzgibbon, A., Lazebnik, S., Perona, P., Sato, Y., Schmid, C. (eds.) ECCV 2012. LNCS, pp. 1–15. Springer, Heidelberg (2012). https://doi.org/10.1007/978-3-642-33709-3_1

34. Russakovsky, O., et al.: ImageNet large scale visual recognition challenge. IJCV **115**, 211–252 (2015)

35. Russakovsky, O., Fei-Fei, L.: Attribute learning in large-scale datasets. In: Kutulakos, K.N. (ed.) ECCV 2010. LNCS, vol. 6553, pp. 1–14. Springer, Heidelberg (2012). https://doi.org/10.1007/978-3-642-35749-7_1

36. Salakhutdinov, R., Torralba, A., Tenenbaum, J.: Learning to share visual appearance for multiclass object detection. In: CVPR (2011)

37. Shi, Z., Siva, P., Xiang, T.: Transfer learning by ranking for weakly supervised object annotation. In: BMVC (2012)

38. Tandon, N., de Melo, G., Suchanek, F., Weikum, G.: WebChild: Harvesting and organizing commonsense knowledge from the web. In: WSDM (2014)

39. Tang, Y., Wang, J., Gao, B., Dellandréa, E., Gaizauskas, R., Chen, L.: Large scale semi-supervised object detection using visual and semantic knowledge transfer. In: CVPR (2016)

40. Wang, Y.X., Hebert, M.: Model recommendation: generating object detectors from few samples. In: CVPR (2015)

41. Wu, Q., Wang, P., Shen, C., Dick, A., van den Hengel, A.: Ask me anything: free-form visual question answering based on knowledge from external sources. In: CVPR (2016)

42. Xiao, J., Ehinger, K.A., Hays, J., Torralba, A., Oliva, A.: Sun database: exploring a large collection of scene categories. IJCV **119**, 3–22 (2016)

43. Xu, J., Ramos, S., Vázquez, D., López, A.M.: Domain adaptation of deformable part-based models. PAMI **36**, 2367–2380 (2014)

44. Yatskar, M., Zettlemoyer, L., Farhadi, A.: Situation recognition: visual semantic role labeling for image understanding. In: CVPR (2016)

45. Zhou, B., Lapedriza, A., Xiao, J., Torralba, A., Oliva, A.: Learning deep features for scene recognition using places database. In: NIPS (2014)

46. Zhu, Y., Fathi, A., Fei-Fei, L.: Reasoning about object affordances in a knowledge base representation. In: Fleet, D., Pajdla, T., Schiele, B., Tuytelaars, T. (eds.) ECCV 2014. LNCS, vol. 8690, pp. 408–424. Springer, Cham (2014). https://doi.org/10.1007/978-3-319-10605-2_27

47. Zhu, Y., Zhang, C., Ré, C., Fei-Fei, L.: Building a large-scale multimodal knowledge base system for answering visual queries. arXiv preprint (2015)

Multi-scale Spatially-Asymmetric Recalibration for Image Classification

Yan Wang[1], Lingxi Xie[2], Siyuan Qiao[2], Ya Zhang[1(✉)],
Wenjun Zhang[1], and Alan L. Yuille[2]

[1] Cooperative Medianet Innovation Center,
Shanghai Jiao Tong University, Shanghai, China
tiffany940107@gmail.com,
{ya_zhang,zhangwenjun}@sjtu.edu.cn

[2] Department of Computer Science, The Johns Hopkins University, Baltimore, USA
198808xc@gmail.com, siyuan.qiao@jhu.edu, alan.l.yuille@gmail.com

Abstract. Convolution is *spatially-symmetric*, *i.e.*, the visual features are independent of its position in the image, which limits its ability to utilize contextual cues for visual recognition. This paper addresses this issue by introducing a *recalibration* process, which refers to the surrounding region of each neuron, computes an importance value and multiplies it to the original neural response. Our approach is named **multi-scale spatially-asymmetric recalibration** (MS-SAR), which extracts visual cues from surrounding regions at *multiple scales*, and designs a weighting scheme which is *asymmetric in the spatial domain*. MS-SAR is implemented in an efficient way, so that only small fractions of extra parameters and computations are required. We apply MS-SAR to several popular building blocks, including the residual block and the densely-connected block, and demonstrate its superior performance in both CIFAR and ILSVRC2012 classification tasks.

Keywords: Large-scale image classification
Convolutional Neural Networks
Multi-Scale Spatially Asymmetric Recalibration

1 Introduction

In recent years, deep learning has been dominating in the field of computer vision. As one of the most important models in deep learning, the convolutional neural networks (CNNs) have been applied to various vision tasks, including image classification [19], object detection [7], semantic segmentation [23], boundary

Y. Wang and L. Xie—Two authors contributed equally. This work was supported by the High Tech R&D Program of China 2015AA015801, NSFC 61521062, STCSM 18DZ2270700 and 2018 CSC-IBM Future Data Scientist Scholarship Program (Y-100), the NSF award CCF-1317376, and ONR N00014-15-1-2356. We thank Huiyu Wang for discussions.

© Springer Nature Switzerland AG 2018
V. Ferrari et al. (Eds.): ECCV 2018, LNCS 11217, pp. 523–539, 2018.
https://doi.org/10.1007/978-3-030-01261-8_31

detection [41], *etc.* The fundamental idea is to stack a number of linear operations (*e.g.*, convolution) and non-linear activations (*e.g.*, ReLU [24]), so that a deep network has the ability to fit very complicated distributions. There are two prerequisites in training a deep network, namely, the availability of large-scale image data, and the support of powerful computational resources.

Convolution is the most important operation in a deep network. A window is slid across the image lattice, and a number of small convolutional kernels are applied to capture local visual patterns. This operation suffers from a weakness of being *spatially-symmetric*, which assumes that visual features are independent of their spatial position. This limits the network's ability to learn from contextual cues (*e.g.*, an object is located upon another) which are often important in visual recognition. Conventional networks capture such spatial information by stacking a number of convolutions and gradually enlarging the receptive field, but we propose an alternative solution which equips *each* neuron with the ability to refer to its contexts at multiple scales efficiently.

Our approach is named **multi-scale spatially asymmetric recalibration** (MS-SAR). It quantifies the importance of each neuron by a score, and multiplies it to the original neural response. This process is named *recalibration* [13]. Two features are proposed to enhance the effect of recalibration. First, the importance score of each neuron is computed from a local region (named a *coordinate set*) covering that neuron. This introduces the factor of spatial position into recalibration, leading to the desired *spatially-asymmetric* property. Second, we relate each neuron to multiple coordinate sets of different sizes, so that the importance of that neuron is evaluated by incorporating *multi-scale* information. The conceptual flowchart of our approach is illustrated in Fig. 1.

In practice, the recalibration function (taking inputs from the coordinate sets and outputting the importance score) is the combination of two linear operations and two non-linear activations, and we allow the parameters to be learned from training data. To avoid heavy computational costs as well as a large amount of extra parameters to be introduced, we first perform a regional pooling over the coordinate set to reduce the spatial resolution, and use a smaller number of outputs in the first linear layer to reduce the channel resolution. Consequently, our approach only requires small fractions of extra parameters and computations beyond the baseline building blocks.

We integrate MS-SAR into two popular building blocks, namely, the residual block [11] and the densely-connected block [15], and empirically evaluate its performance in two image classification tasks. In the CIFAR datasets [18], our approach outperforms the baseline networks, the ResNets [11] and the DenseNets [15]. In the ILSVRC2012 dataset [29], we also compare with SENet [13], a special case of our approach with single-scale spatially-symmetric recalibration and demonstrate the superior performance of MS-SAR. In all cases, the extra computational overhead brought by MS-SAR does not exceed 1%.

The remainder of this paper is organized as follows. Section 2 briefly reviews the previous literatures on image classification based on deep learning, and Sect. 3 illustrates the MS-SAR approach and describes how we apply it to different building blocks. After extensive experimental results are shown in Sect. 4, we conclude this work in Sect. 5.

2 Related Work

2.1 Convolutional Neural Networks for Visual Recognition

Deep convolutional neural networks (CNNs) have been widely applied to computer vision tasks. These models are based on the same motivation to learn and organize visual features in a hierarchical manner. In the early years, CNNs were verified successful in simple classification problems, in which the input image is small yet simple (*e.g.*, MNIST [20] and CIFAR [18]) and the network is shallow (*i.e.* with 3–5 layers). With the emerge of large-scale image datasets [4,22] and powerful computational resources such as GPUs, it is possible to design and train deep networks for recognizing high-resolution natural images [19]. Important technical advances involve using the piecewise-linear ReLU activation [24] to prevent under-fitting, and applying Dropout [32] to regularize the training process and avoid over-fitting.

Modern deep networks are built upon a handful of building blocks, including convolution, pooling, normalization, activation, element-wise operation (sum [11] or product [36]), *etc.* Among them, convolution is considered the most important module to capture visual patterns by template matching (computing the inner-product between the input data and the learned templates), and most often, we refer to the depth of a network by the maximal number of convolutional layers along any path connecting the input to the output. It is believed that increasing the depth leads to better recognition performance [3,11,15,31,34]. In order to train these very deep networks efficiently, researchers proposed batch normalization [17] to improve numerical stability, and highway connections [11,33] to facilitate visual information to be propagated faster. The idea of automatically learning network architectures was also explored [38,47].

Image classification lays the foundation of other vision tasks. The pre-trained networks can be used to extract high-quality visual features for image classification [5], instance retrieval [27], fine-grained object recognition [39,45] or object detection [8], surpassing the performance of conventional handcraft features. Another way of transferring knowledge learned in these networks is to fine-tune them to other tasks, including object detection [7,28], semantic segmentation [1,23], boundary detection [41], pose estimation [25,35], *etc.* A network with stronger classification results often works better in other tasks.

2.2 Spatial Enhancement for Deep Networks

One of the most important factor of deep networks lies in the spatial domain. Although the convolution operation is naturally invariant to spatial translation, there still exist various approaches aimed at enhancing the ability of visual recognition by introducing different *priors* into deep networks.

In an image, the relationship between two features is often tighter when their spatial locations are closer to each other. An efficient way of modeling such distance-sensitive information is to perform spatial pooling [10], which explicitly splits the image lattice into several groups, and ignores the diversity of features in the same group. This idea is also widely used in object detection to summarize visual features given a set of regional proposals [7, 28].

On the other hand, researchers also noticed that spatial importance (saliency) is not uniformly distributed in the spatial domain. Thus, various approaches were designed to discriminate the important (salient) features from others. Typical examples include using gradient back-propagation to find the neurons that contribute most to the classification result [39, 43], introducing saliency [26, 30] or attention [2] into the network, and investigating local properties (*e.g.*, smoothness [37]). We note that a regular convolutional layer also captures local patterns in the spatial domain, but (i) it performs linear template matching and so cannot capture non-linear properties (*e.g.*, smoothness), meanwhile (ii) it often needs a larger number of parameters and heavier computational overheads.

In this work, we consider a *recalibration* approach [13], which aims at revising the response of each neuron by a spatial weight. Unlike [13], the proposed approach utilizes multi-scale visual information and allows different weights to be added at different spatial positions. This brings significant accuracy gains.

3   Our Approach

3.1   Motivation: Why Spatial Asymmetry Is Required?

Let $\mathbf{X}$ be the output of a convolutional layer. This is a 3D cube with $W \times H \times D$ entries, where W and H are the width and height, indicating the spatial resolution, and D is the depth, indicating the number of convolutional kernels. According to the definition of convolution, each element in $\mathbf{X}$, denoted by $x_{w,h,d}$, represents the intensity of the d-th visual pattern at the coordinate (w, h), which is obtained from the inner-product of the d-th convolutional kernel and the input region corresponding to the coordinate (w, h).

Here we notice that convolution performs *spatially-symmetric* template matching, in which the intensity $x_{w,h,d}$ is independent of the spatial position (w, h). We argue that this is not the optimal choice. In visual recognition, we often hope to learn contextual information (*e.g.*, feature d_1 often appears upon feature d_2), and so the *spatially-asymmetric* property is desired. To this end, we define $\mathcal{S}_{w,h}$ to be the *coordinate set* containing the neighboring coordinates of (w, h) (detailed in the next subsection). We aim at computing a new response $\tilde{x}_{w,h,d}$ by taking into consideration all neural responses in $\mathcal{S}_{w,h} \times \{1, 2, \ldots, D\}$, where $\times$ denotes the Cartesian product. Our approach is related but different from several existing approaches.

- First, we note that a standard convolution can learn contexts in a small local region, *e.g.*, $\mathcal{S}_{w,h}$ is a 3×3 square centered at (w, h). Our approach can refer to multiple $\mathcal{S}_{w,h}$'s at different scales, capturing richer information and being more computationally efficient than convolution.

– The second type works in the spatial domain, which uses the responses in the set $\mathcal{S}_{w,h} \times \{d\}$ to compute $\tilde{x}_{w,h,d}$. Examples include the Spatial Pyramid Pooling (SPP) [10] layer which set regular pooling regions and ignored feature diversity within each region, and the Geometric Neural Phrase Pooling (GNPP) [37] layer which took advantage of the spatial relationship of neighboring neurons (it also assumed that spatially closer neurons have tighter connections) to capture feature co-occurrence. But, both of them are non-parameterized and work in each channel individually, which limited their ability to adjust feature weights.

– Another related approach is called feature recalibration [13], which computed $\tilde{x}_{w,h,d}$ by referring to the visual cues in the entire image lattice, i.e., the set $\{(w,h)\}_{w=1,h=1}^{W,H} \times \{1, 2, \ldots, D\}$ was used. This is still a spatially-symmetric operation. As we shall see later, our approach is a generalized version and produces better visual recognition performance.

3.2   Formulation: Spatially-Asymmetric Recalibration

Given the neural responses cube $\mathbf{X}$ and the coordinate set $\mathcal{S}_{w,h}$ at (w,h), the goal is to compute a revised intensity $\tilde{x}_{w,h,d}$ with spatial information taken into consideration. We formulate it as a weighting scheme $\tilde{x}_{w,h,d} = x_{w,h,d} \times z_{w,h,d}$, in which $z_{w,h,d} = f_d(\mathbf{X}, \mathcal{S}_{w,h})$ and $f_d(\cdot)$ is named the *recalibration function* [13]. This creates a weighting cube $\mathbf{Z}$ with the same size as $\mathbf{X}$ and propagate $\tilde{\mathbf{X}} = \mathbf{X} \odot \mathbf{Z}$ to the next network layer. We denote the D-dimensional feature vector of $\mathbf{X}$ at (w,h) by $\mathbf{x}_{w,h} = [x_{w,h,1}; \ldots ; x_{w,h,D}]^{\top}$, and similarly for $\tilde{\mathbf{x}}_{w,h}$ and $\mathbf{z}_{w,h}$.

Let the set of all spatial positions be $\mathcal{P} = \{(w,h)\}_{w=1,h=1}^{W,H}$. The coordinate set of each position is a subset of $\mathcal{P}$, i.e., $\mathcal{S}_{w,h} \in 2^{\mathcal{P}}$ where $2^{\mathcal{P}}$ is the power set of $\mathcal{P}$. Each coordinate set $\mathcal{S}_{w,h}$ defines a corresponding feature set $\mathbf{X}_{\mathcal{S}_{w,h}} = [\mathbf{x}_{w',h'}]_{(w',h') \in \mathcal{S}_{w,h}}$, and we abbreviate $\mathbf{X}_{\mathcal{S}_{w,h}}$ as $\mathfrak{X}_{w,h}$. Thus, $z_{w,h,d} = f_d(\mathbf{X}, \mathcal{S}_{w,h})$ can be rewritten as $z_{w,h,d} = f_d(\mathfrak{X}_{w,h})$. This means that, for two spatial positions (w_1, h_1) and (w_2, h_2), $\mathbf{z}_{w_1,h_1}$ can be impacted by $\mathbf{x}_{w_2,h_2}$ if and only if $(w_2, h_2) \in \mathcal{S}_{w_1,h_1}$, and vice versa. It is common knowledge that if two positions (w_1, h_1) and (w_2, h_2) are close in the image lattice, i.e., $\|(w_1, h_1) - (w_2, h_2)\|_1$ is small[1], the relationship of their feature vectors is more likely to be tight. Therefore, we define each $\mathcal{S}_{w,h}$ to be a continuous region[2] that covers (w,h) itself.

We provide two ways of defining $\mathcal{S}_{w,h}$, both of which are based on a scale parameter K. The first one is named the *sliding* strategy, in which $\mathcal{S}_{w,h} = \{(w', h') \mid \|(w,h) - (w', h')\|_1 \leqslant T\}$, where $T = \sqrt{WH}/K$ is the threshold of distance. The second one is named the *regional* strategy, which partitions the image lattice into $K \times K$ equally-sized regions, and $\mathcal{S}_{w,h}$ is composed of all positions falling in the same region with it. The former is more flexible, i.e.,

---

[1] Constraining $\|(w_1, h_1) - (w_2, h_2)\|_1$ results in a square region which is more friendly in implementation than constraining $\|(w_1, h_1) - (w_2, h_2)\|_2$.

[2] By continuous we mean that $\mathcal{S}_{w,h}$ equals to the smallest convex hull that contains it, i.e., there are no holes in this region.

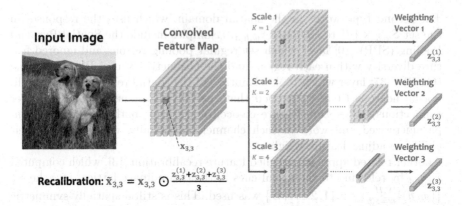

Fig. 1. Illustration of multi-scale spatially-asymmetric recalibration (MS-SAR). The feature vector for recalibration is marked in red, and the spatial coordinate sets at different scales are marked in yellow, and the weighting vectors are marked in green. For the first and second scales, for better visualization, we copy the neural responses used for recalibration. This figure is best viewed in color. (Color figure online)

each position has a unique spatial region set, and so there are $W \times H$ different sets, while the latter reduces this number to K^2, which slightly reduces the computational costs (see Sect. 3.5).

It remains to determine the form of the recalibration function $f_d(\mathcal{X}_{w,h})$. The major consideration is to reduce the number of parameters to alleviate the risk of over-fitting, and reduce the computational costs (FLOPs) to prevent the network from being much slower. We borrow the idea of adding both spatial and channel bottlenecks for this purpose [13]. $\mathcal{X}_{w,h}$ is first down-sampled into a single vector using average pooling, $i.e.$, $\mathbf{y}_{w,h} = |\mathcal{S}_{w,h}|^{-1} \sum_{(w,h)\in\mathcal{S}_{w,h}} \mathbf{x}_{w,h}$, and passed through two fully-connected layers: $z_{w,h,d} = \sigma_2[\boldsymbol{\Omega}_{2,d} \cdot \sigma_1[\boldsymbol{\Omega}_1 \cdot \mathbf{y}_{w,h}]]$. Here, both $\boldsymbol{\Omega}_1$ and $\boldsymbol{\Omega}_{2,d}$ are learnable weight matrices, and $\sigma_1[\cdot]$ and $\sigma_2[\cdot]$ are activation functions which add non-linearity to the recalibration function. The dimension of $\boldsymbol{\Omega}_1$ is $D' \times D$ ($D' < D$), and that of $\boldsymbol{\Omega}_{2,d}$ is $1 \times D'$. This idea is similar to using channel bottleneck to reduce computations [11]. $\sigma_1[\cdot]$ is a composite function of batch normalization [17] followed by ReLU activation [24], and $\sigma_2[\cdot]$ replaces ReLU with sigmoid so as to output a floating point number in $(0, 1)$.

We share $\boldsymbol{\Omega}_1$ over all $f_d(\mathcal{X}_{w,h})$'s, but use an individual $\boldsymbol{\Omega}_{2,d}$ for each output channel. Let $\boldsymbol{\Omega}_2 = \left[\boldsymbol{\Omega}_{2,1}^\top; \ldots; \boldsymbol{\Omega}_{2,D}^\top\right]^\top$, and thus the recalibration function is:

$$\mathbf{z}_{w,h} = \mathbf{f}(\mathcal{X}_{w,h}) = \sigma_2\left[\boldsymbol{\Omega}_2 \cdot \sigma_1\left[\boldsymbol{\Omega}_1 \cdot \frac{1}{|\mathcal{S}_{w,h}|} \cdot \sum_{(w,h)\in\mathcal{S}_{w,h}} \mathbf{x}_{w,h}\right]\right]. \tag{1}$$

3.3   Multi-scale Spatially Asymmetric Recalibration

In Eq. (1), the coordinate set $\mathcal{S}_{w,h}$ determines the region-of-interest (ROI) that can impact $\mathbf{z}_{w,h}$. There is the need of using different scales to evaluate the importance of each feature. We achieve this goal by defining multiple coordinate sets for each spatial position.

Let the total number of scales be L. For each $l = 1, 2, \ldots, L$, we define the scale factor $K^{(l)}$, construct the coordinate set $\mathcal{S}_{w,h}^{(l)}$ and the feature set $\mathfrak{X}_{w,h}^{(l)}$, and compute $\mathbf{z}_{w,h}^{(l)}$ using Eq. (1). The weights from different scales are averaged: $\mathbf{z}_{w,h} = \frac{1}{L}\sum_{l=1}^{L}\mathbf{z}_{w,h}^{(l)}$. Using the matrix notation, we write **multi-scale spatially-asymmetric recalibration** (MS-SAR) as:

$$\tilde{\mathbf{X}}_{w,h} = \mathbf{X} \odot \mathbf{Z} = \mathbf{X} \odot \frac{1}{L}\sum_{l=1}^{L}\mathbf{Z}^{(l)}. \tag{2}$$

The configuration of this an MS-SAR is denoted by $\mathcal{L} = \left\{K^{(l)}\right\}_{l=1}^{L}$. When $\mathcal{L} = \{1\}$, MS-SAR degenerates to the recalibration approach used in the Squeeze-and-Excitation Network (SENet) [13], which is single-scaled and spatially-symmetric, i.e., each pair of spatial positions can impact each other, and $\mathbf{z}_{w,h}$ is the same at all positions. We will show in experiments that MS-SAR produces superior performance than this degenerated version.

3.4   Applications to Existing Building Blocks

MS-SAR can be applied to each convolutional layer individually. Here we consider two examples, which integrate MS-SAR into a residual block [11] and a densely-connected block [15], respectively. The modified blocks are shown in Fig. 2. In a residual block, we only recalibrate the second convolutional layer, while in a densely-connected block, this operation is performed before each convolved feature vector is concatenated to the main feature vector.

Another difference lies in the input of the recalibration function. In the residual block, we simply use the convolved response map for "self recalibration", but in the densely-connected block, especially in the late stages, we note that the main vector is of a much higher dimensionality and thus contains multi-stage visual information. Therefore, we compute the recalibration function using the main vector. We name this option as *multi-stage recalibration*. In comparison to *single-stage recalibration* (input the convolved vector to the recalibration function), it requires more parameters as well as computations, but also leads to better classification performance (see Sect. 4.2).

3.5   Computational Costs

Let $\mathbf{X}$ be a $W \times H \times D$ cube, and the input of convolution also have D channels, then the number of parameters of convolution is $9D^2$ (assuming the convolution

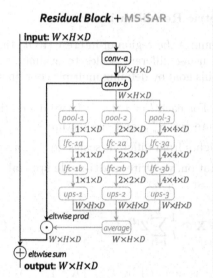
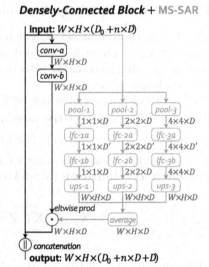

Fig. 2. Applying MS-SAR (green parts) to a residual block (left) or one single step in a densely-connected block (right). In both examples we set $\mathcal{L} = \{1, 2, 4\}$. Here, *pool* indicates a $\frac{W}{K} \times \frac{H}{K}$ regional pooling, *lfc* is a local fully-connected layer (1×1 convolution), and *ups* performs up-sampling by duplicating each element for $\frac{W}{K} \times \frac{H}{K}$ times. The feature map size is labeled for each cube. This figure is best viewed in color.

kernel size is 3×3). Given that MS-SAR is configured by $\mathcal{L} = \{K^{(l)}\}_{l=1}^{L}$, the learnable parameters come from two weight matrices $\boldsymbol{\Omega}_1$ ($D' \times D$) and $\boldsymbol{\Omega}_2$ ($D \times D'$), and so there are $2DD'$ extra parameters for each scale, and $2LDD'$ for all L scales. We set $D' = D/L$ so that using multiple scales does not increase the total number of parameters.

The extra computations (FLOPs) brought by MS-SAR is related to the strategy of defining the coordinate sets. We first consider the *sliding* strategy, in which each position (w, h) has a different feature set $\mathfrak{X}_{w,h}$. The spatial average pooling over the feature sets of all positions takes around WHD FLOPs[3]. Then, each D-dimensional vector $\mathbf{y}_{w,h}$ is passed through two matrix-vector multiplications, and the total FLOPs is $2WHDD'$. For the *regional* strategy, the difference lies in that the number of unique feature sets is $K^{(l)2}$ at the l-th scale. By sharing computations, the total FLOPs of the fully-connected layers is decreased to $2K^{(l)2}DD'$. For all L scales, the extra FLOPs is $2LWHDD'$ for the *sliding* strategy and $2DD'\sum_{l=1}^{L} K^{(l)2}$ for the *regional* strategy, respectively.

---

[3] This is implemented by the idea of *partial sum*. For each channel, we compute $T_{w,h} = \sum_{w'=1}^{w}\sum_{h'=1}^{h}\sum_{d=1}^{D} x_{w',h',d}$ for each position (w, h) – using a gradual accumulation process, this takes WHD sum operations for all D channels. Then we have $\sum_{w=w_1}^{w_2}\sum_{h=h_1}^{h_2}\sum_{d=1}^{D} x_{w,h,d} = T_{w_2,h_2} - T_{w_1-1,h_2} - T_{w_2,h_1-1} + T_{w_1-1,h_1-1}$, which takes $O(WH)$ sum operations for all spatial position (w, h)'s.

Table 1. Comparison of classification error rates (%) on the CIFAR10 and CIFAR100 datasets. The left three columns list several recent work, and the right part compares our approach with the baselines. "RN" and "DN" denotes "ResNet" and "DenseNet". An asterisk sign (*) indicates that MS-SAR is added. For all ResNets, the error rates are averaged from 3 individual runs. All FLOPs and numbers of parameters are computed on the experiments on CIFAR10. The difference in these numbers between the CIFAR10 and CIFAR100 experiments are ignorable.

Approach	C10	C100	Network	C10	C100	FLOPs	Params
Lee et al. [21]	7.97	34.57	RN-20	8.61	31.87	40.8M	0.27M
He et al. [11]	6.61	27.22	RN-20*	**7.61**	**31.09**	40.9M	0.28M
Huang et al. [16]	5.23	24.58	RN-32	7.51	30.63	69.1M	0.46M
He et al. [12]	4.62	22.71	RN-32*	**6.68**	**29.41**	69.3M	0.48M
Zagoruyko et al. [42]	4.17	20.50	RN-56	6.97	29.07	125.7M	0.85M
Han et al. [9]	3.48	17.01	RN-56*	**6.04**	**27.71**	126.0M	0.89M
Huang et al. [14]	3.40	17.40	DN-100	4.67	22.45	252.5M	0.80M
Zhang et al. [46]	3.25	19.25	DN-100*	**4.16**	**21.13**	253.3M	0.99M
Gastaldi et al. [6]	2.86	15.85	DN-190	3.46	17.34	7.95G	25.8M
Zhang et al. [44]	2.70	16.80	DN-190*	**3.32**	**16.92**	7.98G	32.7M

Note that in both ResNets and DenseNets, MS-SAR is applied to half of convolutional layers, and so the fractions of extra parameters and FLOPs are relatively small. We will report the detailed numbers in experiments.

4 Experiments

4.1 The CIFAR Datasets

We first evaluate MS-SAR on the CIFAR datasets [18] which contain tiny RGB images with a fixed spatial resolution of 32×32. There are two subsets with 10 and 100 object classes, referred to as CIFAR10 and CIFAR100, respectively. Each set has 50,000 training samples and 10,000 testing samples, both of which are evenly distributed over all (10 or 100) classes.

We choose different baseline network architectures, including the deep residual networks (ResNets) [11] with 20, 32 and 56 layers and the densely-connected networks (DenseNets) [15] with 100 and 190 layers. MS-SAR is applied to *each* residual block and densely-connected block, as illustrated in Fig. 2. We choose the *regional* strategy to construct coordinate sets, use $\mathcal{L} = \{1, 2, 4\}$ and set $D' = D/3$. For other options, see ablation studies in the next subsection.

We follow the conventions to train these networks from scratch. The standard SGD with a weight decay of 0.0001 and a Nesterov momentum of 0.9 are used. In the ResNets, we train the network for 160 epochs with mini-batch size of 128. The base learning rate is 0.1, and is divided by 10 after 80 and 120 epochs. In

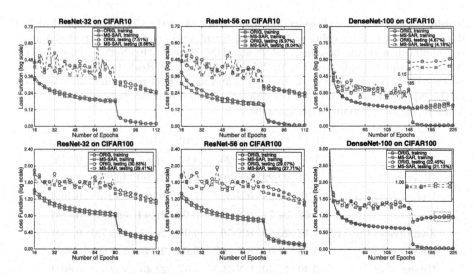

Fig. 3. The curves of different networks, with and without MS-SAR. All the curves on ResNet-32 and ResNet-56 are averaged over 3 individual runs.

the DenseNets, we train the network for 300 epochs with a mini-batch size of 64. The base learning rate is 0.1, and is divided by 10 after 150 and 225 epochs. Adding MS-SAR does not require any of these settings to be modified. In the training process, the standard data-augmentation is used, *i.e.*, each image is padded with a 4-pixel margin on each of the four sides. In the enlarged 40×40 image, a subregion with 32×32 pixels is randomly cropped and flipped with a probability of 0.5. No augmentation is used at the testing stage.

Classification results are summarized in Table 1. One can observe that MS-SAR improves the baseline classification accuracy consistently and significantly. In particular, in terms of the relative drop in error rates, almost all these numbers are higher than 10% on CIFAR10 (except for DenseNet-190), and higher than 4% on CIFAR100 (except for ResNet-20 and DenseNet-190). The highest drop is over 10% on CIFAR10 and over 5% on CIFAR100. We note that these improvements are produced at the price of higher model complexities. The additional computational costs are very small for both the ResNets (*e.g*, ~0.3% extra FLOPs) and DenseNets (*e.g*, ~0.3% and ~0.4% extra FLOPs for DenseNet-100 and DenseNet-190, respectively), and the fractions of extra parameters are moderate (~5% for the ResNets and ~25% for the DenseNets, respectively).

We also compare our results with the state-of-the-arts (listed in the left part of Table 1). Although some recent approaches reported much higher accuracies in the CIFAR datasets, we point out that they often used larger spatial resolutions [9], complicated network modules [46] or complicated regularization methods [6,44], and thus the results are not directly comparable to ours. In addition, we believe that MS-SAR can be applied to these networks towards better classification performance.

Table 2. Comparison of classification error rates (%) on the CIFAR10 and CIFAR100 datasets with different scale combinations. Other specifications remain the same as in Fig. 1. All results of ResNet-56 are averaged over 3 individual runs. See Sect. 3.5 for the reason that different scale configurations have the same number of parameters.

Scale			ResNet-56			DenseNet-100			
1	2	4	C10 (±std)	C100 (±std)	FLOPs	C10	C100	FLOPs	Params
			6.97 ± 0.05	29.07 ± 0.14	125.7M	4.67	22.45	252.5M	0.80M
✓			6.80 ± 0.06	28.99 ± 0.15	125.7M	4.45	21.83	252.6M	0.99M
	✓		6.55 ± 0.05	28.31 ± 0.17	125.8M	4.35	21.33	253.0M	0.99M
		✓	6.48 ± 0.06	28.74 ± 0.18	126.3M	4.39	21.79	254.3M	0.99M
✓	✓		6.38 ± 0.07	28.28 ± 0.19	125.8M	4.29	21.42	252.8M	0.99M
✓		✓	6.11 ± 0.14	28.05 ± 0.22	126.0M	4.32	21.27	253.5M	0.99M
	✓	✓	6.35 ± 0.09	28.87 ± 0.27	126.1M	4.33	21.23	253.7M	0.99M
✓	✓	✓	**6.04 ± 0.11**	**27.71 ± 0.21**	126.0M	**4.06**	**21.13**	253.3M	0.99M

In Fig. 3, we plot the training/testing curves of different networks on the CIFAR datasets. We find that MS-SAR effectively decreases the testing losses (and consequently, error rates) in all cases. On CIFAR10, due to the simplicity of the recognition task (10 classes), the training losses of both approaches, with and without MS-SAR, are very close to 0, but MS-SAR produces lower testing losses, giving evidence for its ability to alleviate over-fitting.

4.2 Ablation Study and Analysis

We first investigate the impacts of incorporating multi-scale visual information. To this end, we set $\mathcal{L}$ to be a non-empty subset of $\{1, 2, 4\}$ (7 possibilities), and summarize the results in Table 2. Compared with using a single scale, incorporating multi-scale information often leads to better classification performance (the only exception is that on DenseNet-100, $\mathcal{L} = \{2, 4\}$ works worse than $\mathcal{L} = \{2\}$, which may be caused by random noise as DenseNet-100 experiments are performed only once). Combining all three scales is always produces the best recognition performance. Provided that the extra computational costs brought by multi-scale recalibration are almost ignorable, we will use $\mathcal{L} = \{1, 2, 4\}$ in all the remaining experiments.

Next, we compare the two ways of defining coordinate sets (*sliding* vs. *regional*, see Sect. 3.2). In the experiments on CIFAR100, in both ResNets and DenseNets, the *regional* strategy outperforms the *sliding* strategy by ~0.2%. The *training* accuracy using the *sliding* strategy is also decreased, giving evidence that it is less capable of fitting training data. This reveals that, although spatial asymmetry is a nice property, its degree of freedom should be controlled, so that MS-SAR, containing a limited number of parameters, does not need to fit an over-complicated distribution. Considering that the *regional* strategy requires fewer computational costs (see Sect. 3.5), we set it to be the default option.

Table 3. Comparison of top-1 and top-5 classification error rates (%) produced by different recalibration approaches (none, SE and MS-SAR) on the ILSVRC2012 dataset. All these numbers are based on our own implementation. See Sect. 3.5 for the reason that different scale configurations have the same number of parameters.

Approach	Scale			Top-1	Top-5	FLOPs	Params
	1	2	4				
ResNet-18				30.50	11.07	1.81G	10.9M
ResNet-18+SE	✓			29.78	10.27	1.81G	13.8M
ResNet-18+MS-SAR	✓	✓	✓	**29.43**	**10.19**	1.81G	13.8M
ResNet-34				27.02	8.77	3.66G	21.7M
ResNet-34+SE	✓			26.67	8.43	3.66G	27.3M
ResNet-34+MS-SAR	✓	✓	✓	**26.15**	**8.35**	3.67G	27.4M
ResNeXt-50				22.20	6.12	3.86G	25.0M
ResNeXt-50+SE	✓			21.95	5.93	3.87G	27.5M
ResNeXt-50+MS-SAR	✓	✓	✓	**21.64**	**5.78**	3.89G	27.6M

Finally, we compare the *single-level* and *multi-level* recalibration methods on DenseNet-100. Detailed descriptions are in Sect. 3.4. Note that this is independent of the comparison between *multi-scale* and *single-scale* methods – they work on the spatial domain and the channel domain, and are complementary to each other. In the 100-layer DenseNet, *multi-level* recalibration produces 4.06% and 21.13% error rates on CIFAR10 and CIFAR100, and these numbers are 4.45% and 21.83% for *single-level* recalibration, respectively. *Multi-level* recalibration reduces the relative errors by 7.77% and 5.12%, at the price of 23.75% extra parameters and 0.3% additional FLOPs.

4.3   The ILSVRC2012 Dataset

The ILSVRC2012 dataset [29] is a subset of the ImageNet database [4], created for a large-scale visual recognition competition. It contains $1,000$ categories located at different levels of the WordNet hierarchy. The training and testing sets have ~ 1.3M and 50K images, roughly uniformly distributed over all classes.

The baseline network architectures include two ResNets [11] with 18 and 34 layers, and a ResNeXt [40] with 50 layers. We also compare with the Squeeze-and-Excitation (SE) module [13], which is a special case of our approach ($\mathcal{L} = \{1\}$: single-scale and spatially-symmetric). As illustrated in Fig. 2, both SE and MS-SAR modules are appended after each residual block.

All these networks are trained from scratch. We follow [13] in configuring the following parameters. SGD with a weight decay of 0.0001 and a Nesterov momentum of 0.9 is used. There are a total of 100 epochs in the training process, and the mini-batch size is 1024. The learning rate starts with 0.6, and is divided by 10 after 30, 60 and 90 epochs. Again, adding MS-SAR does not require

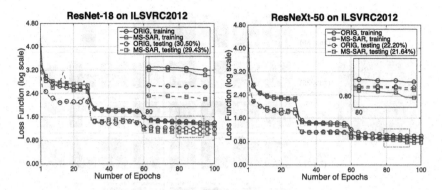

Fig. 4. The curves of different networks with and without MS-SAR on the ILSVRC2012 dataset. We zoom-in on a small part of each curve for better visualization.

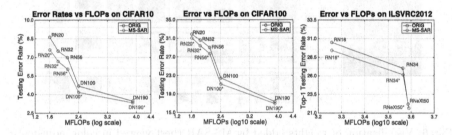

Fig. 5. The relationship between classification accuracy and computation (in FLOPs) on three datasets. RN, DN and RNeXt denote ResNet, DenseNet and ResNeXt, respectively. An asterisk sign (*) indicates that MS-SAR is added.

any of these settings to be modified. In the training process, we apply a series of data-augmentation techniques, including rescaling and cropping the image, randomly mirroring and rotating (slightly) the image, changing its aspect ratio and performing pixel jittering, which is same with SENet [13]. In the testing process, we use the standard single-center-crop on each image.

Results are summarized in Table 3. In all cases, MS-SAR works better than the baseline (no recalibration) and SE (single-scale spatially-symmetric recalibration). For example, based on ResNeXt-50, MS-SAR reduces the top-5 error of the baseline by an absolute value of 0.34% or a relative value of 5.56%, using ~1% extra FLOPs and 10% extra parameters. On top of SE, the error rate drops are 0.15% (absolute) and 2.53% (relative) and the extra FLOPs and parameters are merely ~0.5% and ~0.4%, respectively. The training/testing curves in Fig. 4 show similar phenomena as in CIFAR experiments.

We also investigate the relationship between classification accuracy and computation on these three datasets. In Fig. 5, we plot the testing error as the function of FLOPs, which reveals the trend that MS-SAR can achieve higher recognition accuracy under the same computational complexity.

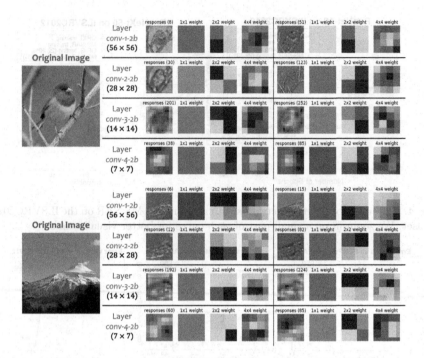

Fig. 6. Visualization of weights added by MS-SAR (best viewed in color, adjusted to the spatial resolution in each layer) to a 18-layer ResNet. The response/weight is higher if the color is closer to yellow. Each number in parentheses indicates the filter index. (Color figure online)

Last but not least, we visualize spatial weights added by the MS-SAR layer in Fig. 6. We present two input images containing an object (a *bird*) and a scene (a *mountain*), respectively. One can observe that, in comparison to the 1×1 weight, both 2×2 and 4×4 weights are more flexible to capture semantically meaningful regions and add higher weights. In each layer, we see some filters focus on the foreground, *e.g.*, the characteristic patterns of the *bird* and the *mountain*, while some others focus on the background, *e.g.*, the tree branch or the sky. High-level layers have low-resolution feature maps, but this property is preserved. We argue that it is the spatial asymmetry that allows the recalibration module to capture different visual information (foreground vs. background), which allows the weighted neural response ($x_{w,h,d}$) to be *dependent* to its spatial location (w, h).

5   Conclusions

In this paper, we present a module named MS-SAR for image classification. This is aimed at assigning eacg convolutional layer with the ability to incorporate spatial contexts to "recalibrate" neural responses, *i.e.*, summarizing regional information into an importance factor and multiplying it to the original response. We implement each recalibration function as the combination of a multi-scale pooling operation in the spatial domain and a linear model in the channel domain. Experiments on CIFAR and ILSVRC2012 demonstrate the superior performance of MS-SAR over several baseline network architectures.

Our work delivers two messages. First, it is not the best choice to rely on a gradually increasing receptive field (via local convolution, pooling or down-sampling) to capture spatial information – MS-SAR is a light-weighted yet specifically designed module which deals with this issue more efficiently. Second, there exists a tradeoff between diversity and simplicity – this is why *regional* pooling works better than *sliding* pooling. In its current form, MS-SAR is able to add a weight factor to each neural response (unary or linear terms), but unable to explicitly model the co-occurrence of multiple features (binary or higher-order terms). We leave this topic for future research.

References

1. Chen, L.C., Papandreou, G., Kokkinos, I., Murphy, K., Yuille, A.L.: DeepLab: semantic image segmentation with deep convolutional nets, atrous convolution, and fully connected CRFs. In: International Conference on Learning Representations (2016)
2. Chen, L.C., Yang, Y., Wang, J., Xu, W., Yuille, A.L.: Attention to scale: scale-aware semantic image segmentation. In: Computer Vision and Pattern Recognition (2016)
3. Chen, Y., Li, J., Xiao, H., Jin, X., Yan, S., Feng, J.: Dual path networks. In: Advances in Neural Information Processing Systems (2017)
4. Deng, J., Dong, W., Socher, R., Li, L., Li, K., Fei-Fei, L.: ImageNet: a large-scale hierarchical image database. In: Computer Vision and Pattern Recognition (2009)
5. Donahue, J., et al.: DeCAF: a deep convolutional activation feature for generic visual recognition. In: International Conference on Machine Learning (2014)
6. Gastaldi, X.: Shake-shake regularization. arXiv preprint arXiv:1705.07485 (2017)
7. Girshick, R.: Fast R-CNN. In: Computer Vision and Pattern Recognition (2015)
8. Girshick, R., Donahue, J., Darrell, T., Malik, J.: Rich feature hierarchies for accurate object detection and semantic segmentation. In: Computer Vision and Pattern Recognition (2014)
9. Han, D., Kim, J., Kim, J.: Deep pyramidal residual networks. In: Computer Vision and Pattern Recognition (2017)
10. He, K., Zhang, X., Ren, S., Sun, J.: Spatial pyramid pooling in deep convolutional networks for visual recognition. In: Fleet, D., Pajdla, T., Schiele, B., Tuytelaars, T. (eds.) ECCV 2014. LNCS, vol. 8691, pp. 346–361. Springer, Cham (2014). https://doi.org/10.1007/978-3-319-10578-9_23
11. He, K., Zhang, X., Ren, S., Sun, J.: Deep residual learning for image recognition. In: Computer Vision and Pattern Recognition (2016)
12. He, K., Zhang, X., Ren, S., Sun, J.: Identity mappings in deep residual networks. In: Leibe, B., Matas, J., Sebe, N., Welling, M. (eds.) ECCV 2016. LNCS, vol. 9908, pp. 630–645. Springer, Cham (2016). https://doi.org/10.1007/978-3-319-46493-0_38
13. Hu, J., Shen, L., Sun, G.: Squeeze-and-excitation networks. arXiv preprint arXiv:1709.01507 (2017)

14. Huang, G., Li, Y., Pleiss, G., Liu, Z., Hopcroft, J.E., Weinberger, K.Q.: Snapshot ensembles: train 1, get M for free. In: International Conference on Learning Representations (2017)
15. Huang, G., Liu, Z., Weinberger, K.Q., van der Maaten, L.: Densely connected convolutional networks. In: Computer Vision and Pattern Recognition (2017)
16. Huang, G., Sun, Y., Liu, Z., Sedra, D., Weinberger, K.Q.: Deep networks with stochastic depth. In: Leibe, B., Matas, J., Sebe, N., Welling, M. (eds.) ECCV 2016. LNCS, vol. 9908, pp. 646–661. Springer, Cham (2016). https://doi.org/10.1007/978-3-319-46493-0_39
17. Ioffe, S., Szegedy, C.: Batch normalization: accelerating deep network training by reducing internal covariate shift. In: International Conference on Machine Learning (2015)
18. Krizhevsky, A., Hinton, G.: Learning multiple layers of features from tiny images (2009)
19. Krizhevsky, A., Sutskever, I., Hinton, G.: Imagenet classification with deep convolutional neural networks. In: Advances in Neural Information Processing Systems (2012)
20. LeCun, Y., Bottou, L., Bengio, Y., Haffner, P.: Gradient-based learning applied to document recognition. Proc. IEEE 86(11), 2278–2324 (1998)
21. Lee, C., Xie, S., Gallagher, P., Zhang, Z., Tu, Z.: Deeply-supervised nets. In: Artificial Intelligence and Statistics (2015)
22. Lin, T.-Y., et al.: Microsoft COCO: common objects in context. In: Fleet, D., Pajdla, T., Schiele, B., Tuytelaars, T. (eds.) ECCV 2014. LNCS, vol. 8693, pp. 740–755. Springer, Cham (2014). https://doi.org/10.1007/978-3-319-10602-1_48
23. Long, J., Shelhamer, E., Darrell, T.: Fully convolutional networks for semantic segmentation. In: Computer Vision and Pattern Recognition (2015)
24. Nair, V., Hinton, G.E.: Rectified linear units improve restricted boltzmann machines. In: International Conference on Machine Learning (2010)
25. Newell, A., Yang, K., Deng, J.: Stacked hourglass networks for human pose estimation. In: Leibe, B., Matas, J., Sebe, N., Welling, M. (eds.) ECCV 2016. LNCS, vol. 9912, pp. 483–499. Springer, Cham (2016). https://doi.org/10.1007/978-3-319-46484-8_29
26. Noh, H., Hong, S., Han, B.: Learning deconvolution network for semantic segmentation. In: International Conference on Computer Vision (2015)
27. Razavian, A.S., Azizpour, H., Sullivan, J., Carlsson, S.: CNN features off-the-shelf: an astounding baseline for recognition. In: Computer Vision and Pattern Recognition (2014)
28. Ren, S., He, K., Girshick, R., Sun, J.: Faster R-CNN: towards real-time object detection with region proposal networks. In: Advances in Neural Information Processing Systems (2015)
29. Russakovsky, O., et al.: Imagenet large scale visual recognition challenge. Int. J. Comput. Vis. 115(3), 211–252 (2015)
30. Simonyan, K., Vedaldi, A., Zisserman, A.: Deep inside convolutional networks: Visualising image classification models and saliency maps. arXiv preprint arXiv:1312.6034 (2013)
31. Simonyan, K., Zisserman, A.: Very deep convolutional networks for large-scale image recognition. In: International Conference on Learning Representations (2015)
32. Srivastava, N., Hinton, G.E., Krizhevsky, A., Sutskever, I., Salakhutdinov, R.: Dropout: a simple way to prevent neural networks from overfitting. J. Mach. Learn. Res. 15(1), 1929–1958 (2014)

33. Srivastava, R.K., Greff, K., Schmidhuber, J.: Highway networks. arXiv preprint arXiv:1505.00387 (2015)
34. Szegedy, C., et al.: Going deeper with convolutions. In: Computer Vision and Pattern Recognition (2015)
35. Toshev, A., Szegedy, C.: DeepPose: human pose estimation via deep neural networks. In: Computer Vision and Pattern Recognition (2014)
36. Wang, Y., Xie, L., Liu, C., Qiao, S., Zhang, Y., Zhang, W., Tian, Q., Yuille, A.: SORT: second-order response transform for visual recognition. In: International Conference on Computer Vision (2017)
37. Xie, L., Tian, Q., Flynn, J., Wang, J., Yuille, A.: Geometric neural phrase pooling: modeling the spatial co-occurrence of neurons. In: European Conference on Computer Vision (2016)
38. Xie, L., Yuille, A.: Genetic CNN. In: International Conference on Computer Vision (2017)
39. Xie, L., Zheng, L., Wang, J., Yuille, A., Tian, Q.: Interactive: inter-layer activeness propagation. In: Computer Vision and Pattern Recognition (2016)
40. Xie, S., Girshick, R., Dollar, P., Tu, Z., He, K.: Aggregated residual transformations for deep neural networks. In: Computer Vision and Pattern Recognition (2017)
41. Xie, S., Tu, Z.: Holistically-nested edge detection. In: International Conference on Computer Vision (2015)
42. Zagoruyko, S., Komodakis, N.: Wide residual networks. arXiv preprint arXiv:1605.07146 (2016)
43. Zeiler, M.D., Fergus, R.: Visualizing and understanding convolutional networks. In: Fleet, D., Pajdla, T., Schiele, B., Tuytelaars, T. (eds.) ECCV 2014. LNCS, vol. 8689, pp. 818–833. Springer, Cham (2014). https://doi.org/10.1007/978-3-319-10590-1_53
44. Zhang, H., Cisse, M., Dauphin, Y.N., Lopez-Paz, D.: mixup: Beyond empirical risk minimization. arXiv preprint arXiv:1710.09412 (2017)
45. Zhang, N., Donahue, J., Girshick, R., Darrell, T.: Part-based R-CNNs for fine-grained category detection. In: Fleet, D., Pajdla, T., Schiele, B., Tuytelaars, T. (eds.) ECCV 2014. LNCS, vol. 8689, pp. 834–849. Springer, Cham (2014). https://doi.org/10.1007/978-3-319-10590-1_54
46. Zhang, T., Qi, G.J., Xiao, B., Wang, J.: Interleaved group convolutions. In: Computer Vision and Pattern Recognition (2017)
47. Zoph, B., Le, Q.V.: Neural architecture search with reinforcement learning. In: International Conference on Learning Representations (2017)

Choose Your Neuron: Incorporating Domain Knowledge Through Neuron-Importance

Ramprasaath R. Selvaraju[1(✉)], Prithvijit Chattopadhyay[1],
Mohamed Elhoseiny[2], Tilak Sharma[2], Dhruv Batra[1,2], Devi Parikh[1,2],
and Stefan Lee[1]

[1] Georgia Institute of Technology, Atlanta, USA
{ramprs,prithvijit3,dbatra,parikh,steflee}@gatech.edu
[2] Facebook, Menlo Park, USA
{elhoseiny,tilaksharma,dbatra,dparikh}@fb.com

Abstract. Individual neurons in convolutional neural networks supervised for image-level classification tasks have been shown to implicitly
learn semantically meaningful concepts ranging from simple textures
and shapes to whole or partial objects – forming a "dictionary" of concepts acquired through the learning process. In this work we introduce a
simple, efficient zero-shot learning approach based on this observation.
Our approach, which we call Neuron Importance-Aware Weight Transfer (NIWT), learns to map domain knowledge about novel *"unseen"*
classes onto this dictionary of learned concepts and then optimizes for
network parameters that can effectively combine these concepts – essentially learning classifiers by discovering and composing learned semantic
concepts in deep networks. Our approach shows improvements over previous approaches on the CUBirds and AWA2 generalized zero-shot learning
benchmarks. We demonstrate our approach on a diverse set of semantic
inputs as external domain knowledge including attributes and natural
language captions. Moreover by learning inverse mappings, NIWT can
provide visual and textual explanations for the predictions made by the
newly learned classifiers and provide neuron names. Our code is available
at https://github.com/ramprs/neuron-importance-zsl.

Keywords: Zero Shot Learning · Interpretability · Grad-CAM

1 Introduction

Deep neural networks have pushed the boundaries of standard classification tasks
in the past few years, with performance on many challenging benchmarks reach-
ing near human-level accuracies. One caveat however is that these deep models require massive labeled datasets – failing to generalize from few examples

---

R. R. Selvaraju and P. Chattopadhyay—Equal Contribution.
R. R. Selvaraju—Work done partly at Facebook.

© Springer Nature Switzerland AG 2018
V. Ferrari et al. (Eds.): ECCV 2018, LNCS 11217, pp. 540–556, 2018.
https://doi.org/10.1007/978-3-030-01261-8_32

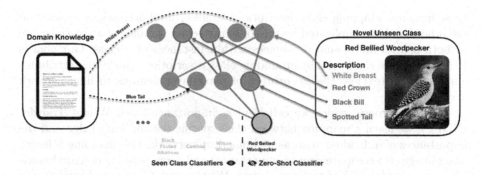

Fig. 1. We present our Neuron Importance-Aware Weight Transfer (NIWT) approach which maps free-form domain knowledge about unseen classes to relevant concept-sensitive neurons within a pretrained deep network. We then optimize the weights of a novel classifier such that the activation of this set of neurons results in high output scores for the unseen classes in the generalized zero-shot learning setting.

or descriptions of unseen classes like humans can. To close this gap, the task of learning deep classifiers for unseen classes from external domain knowledge alone – termed zero-shot learning (ZSL) – has been the topic of increased interest within the community [2,3,5,10,11,14,16,17,21,25,28,30,35].

As humans, much of the way we acquire and transfer knowledge about novel concepts is in reference to or via composition of concepts which are already known. For instance, upon hearing that *"A Red Bellied Woodpecker is a small, round bird with a white breast, red crown, and spotted wings."*, we can compose our understanding of colors and birds to imagine how we might distinguish such an animal from other birds. However, applying a similar compositional learning strategy for deep neural networks has proven challenging.

While individual neurons in deep networks have been shown to learn localized, semantic concepts, these units lack referable groundings – *e.g.* even if a network contains units sensitive to *"white breast"* and *"red crown"*, there is no explicit mapping of these neurons to the relevant language name or description. This observation encouraged prior work in interpretability to crowd-source "neuron names" to discover these groundings [4]. However, this annotation process is model dependent and needs to be re-executed for each model trained, which makes it expensive and impractical. Moreover, even if given perfect "neuron names", it is an open question how to leverage this neuron-level descriptive supervision to train novel classifiers. This question is at the heart of our approach.

Many existing zero-shot learning approaches make use of deep features (*e.g.* vectors of activations from some late layer in a network pretrained on some large-scale task) to learn joint embeddings with class descriptions [1,3,5,7–9,23,31]. These higher-level features collapse many underlying concepts in the pursuit of class discrimination; consequentially, accessing lower-level concepts and recombining them in new ways to represent novel classes is difficult with these features. Mapping class descriptions to lower-level activations directly on the other hand is complicated by the high intra-class variance of activations due to both spatial and visual differences within instances of a class. Our goal is to address these challenges by grounding class descriptions (including attributes and free-form text) to the *importance* of lower-layer neurons to final network decisions [26].

In our approach, which we call Neuron Importance-based Weight Transfer (NIWT), we learn a mapping between class-specific domain knowledge and the importances of individual neurons within a deep network. This mapping is learnt using images (to compute neuron-importance) and corresponding domain knowledge representation(s) of training classes. We then use this learned mapping to predict neuron importances from knowledge about unseen classes and optimize classification weights such that the resulting network aligns with the predicted importances. In other words, based on domain-knowledge of the unseen categories, we can predict which low-level neurons should matter in the final classification decision. We can then learn network weights such that the neurons predicted to matter actually do contribute to the final decision. In this way, we connect the description of a previous unseen category to weights of a classifier that can predict this category at test time – all without having seen a single image from this category. To the best of our knowledge, this is the first zero-shot learning approach to align domain knowledge to intermediate neurons within a deep network. As an additional benefit, the learned mapping from domain knowledge to neuron importances grounds the neurons in interpretable semantics; automatically performing neuron naming.

We focus on the challenging generalized zero-shot (GZSL) learning setting. Unlike standard ZSL settings which evaluate performance only on unseen classes, GZSL considers both unseen and seen classes to measure the performance. In effect, GZSL is made more challenging by dropping the unrealistic assumption that test instances are known a priori to be from unseen classes in standard ZSL. We validate our approach across two standard datasets - Caltech-UCSD Birds (CUB) [29] and Animals with Attributes 2 (AWA2) [31] - showing improved performance over existing methods. Moreover, we examine the quality of our grounded explanations for classifier decisions through textual and visual examples.

Contributions. Concretely, we make the following contributions in this work:

○ We introduce a zero-short learning approach based on mapping unseen class descriptions to neuron importance within a deep network and then optimizing unseen classifier weights to effectively combine these concepts. We demonstrate the effectiveness of our approach by reporting improvements on the generalized zero-shot benchmark on CUB and AWA2. We also show our approach can handle arbitrary forms of domain knowledge including attributes and captions.

○ In contrast to existing approaches, our method is capable of explaining its zero-shot predictions with human-interpretable semantics from attributes. We show how inverse mappings from neuron importance to domain knowledge can also be learned to provide interpretable visual and textual explanations for the decisions made by newly learned classifiers for seen and unseen classes.

2 Related Work

Model Interpretability. Our method aligns human interpretable domain knowledge to neurons within deep neural networks, instilling these neurons with understandable semantic meanings. There has been significant recent interest in building machine learning models that are transparent and interpretable in their decision making process. For deep networks, several works propose explanations based on internal states or structures of the network [12,26,33,36]. Most related to our work is the approach of Selvaraju et al. [26] which computes neuron importance as part of a visual explanation pipeline. In this work, we leverage these importance scores to embed free-form domain knowledge to individual neurons in a deep network and train new classifiers based on this information. In contrast, Grad-CAM [26] simply visualizes the importance of input regions.

Attribute-based Zero-Shot Learning. One long-pursued approach for zero-shot learning is to leverage knowledge about common attributes and shared parts (e.g., furry, in addition to being simpler and more efficient [2,3,25,31].

Text-Based Zero-Shot Learning (ZSL). In parallel research, pure text articles extracted from the web have been leveraged instead of attributes to design zero-shot visual classifiers [8]. The description of a new category is purely textual (avoiding the use of attributes) and could be extracted easily by just mining article(s) about the class of interest from the web (e.g., Wikipedia). Recent approaches have adopted deep neural network based classifiers, leading to a noticeable improvement on zero-shot accuracy (Bo et al. [18]). The proposed approaches mainly rely on learning a similarity function between text descriptions and images (either linearly [8,25] or non-linearly via deep neural networks [18] or kernels [7]). At test-time, classification is performed by associating the image to the class with the highest similarity to the corresponding class-level text. Recently, Reed et al. [24] showed that by collecting 10 sentences per-image, their sentence-based approach can outperform attribute-based alternatives on CUB.

In contrast to these approaches, we directly map external domain knowledge (text-based or otherwise) to internal components (neurons) of deep neural networks rather than learning associative mappings between images and text – providing interpretability for our novel classifiers.

3 Neuron Importance-Aware Weight Transfer (NIWT)

In this section, we describe our Neuron Importance-Aware Weight Transfer (NIWT) approach to zero-shot learning. At a high level, NIWT maps free-form domain knowledge to neurons within a deep network and then learns classifiers based on novel class descriptions which respect these groundings. Concretely,

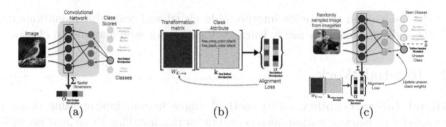

Fig. 2. Our Neuron Importance-Aware Weight Transfer (NIWT) approach can be broken down in to three stages. (a) class-specific neuron importances are extracted for seen classes at a fixed layer, (b) a linear transform is learned to project free-form domain knowledge to these extracted importances, and (c) weights for new classifiers are optimized such that neuron importances match those predicted by this mapping for unseen classes.

NIWT consists of three steps: (1) estimating the importance of individual neuron(s) at a fixed layer w.r.t. the decisions made by the network for the seen classes (see Fig. 2a), (2) learning a mapping between domain knowledge and these neuron-importances (see Fig. 2b), and (3) optimizing classifier weights with respect to predicted neuron-importances for unseen classes (see Fig. 3c). We discuss each stage in the following sections.

3.1 Preliminaries: Generalized Zero-Shot Learning (GZSL)

Consider a dataset $\mathcal{D} = \{(x_i, y_i)\}_{i=1}^N$ comprised of example input-output pairs from a set of *seen classes* $\mathcal{S} = \{1, \ldots, s\}$ and *unseen classes* $\mathcal{U} = \{s+1, \ldots, s+u\}$. For convenience, we use the subscripts $\mathcal{S}$ and $\mathcal{U}$ to indicate subsets corresponding to seen and unseen classes respectively, e.g. $\mathcal{D}_S = \{(x_i, y_i) \mid y_i \in \mathcal{S}\}$. Further, assume there exists domain knowledge $\mathcal{K} = \{k_1, \ldots, k_{s+u}\}$ corresponding to each class (e.g. class level attributes or natural language descriptions). Concisely, the goal of generalized zero-shot learning is then to learn a mapping $f : \mathcal{X} \to \mathcal{S} \cup \mathcal{U}$ from the input space $\mathcal{X}$ to the combined set of seen and unseen class labels using only the domain knowledge $\mathcal{K}$ and instances $\mathcal{D}_S$ belonging to the seen classes.

3.2 Class-Dependent Neuron Importance

Class descriptions capture salient concepts about the content of corresponding images – for example, describing the coloration and shape of a bird's head. Similarly, a classifier must also learn discriminative visual concepts in order to succeed; however, these concepts are not grounded in human interpretable language. In this stage, we identify neurons corresponding to these discriminative concepts before aligning them with domain knowledge in Sect. 3.3.

Consider a deep neural network $\text{NET}_S(\cdot)$ trained for classification which predicts scores $\{o_c \mid c \in \mathcal{S}\}$ for seen classes $\mathcal{S}$. One intuitive measure of a neuron

n's importance to the final score o_c is simply the gradient of o_c with respect to the neuron's activation a^n (where n indexes the channel dimension). For networks containing convolutional units (which are replicated spatially), we follow [26] and simply compute importance as the mean gradient (along spatial dimensions), writing the neuron importance α_c^n as

$$\alpha_c^n = \overbrace{\frac{1}{HW} \sum_{i=1}^{H} \sum_{j=1}^{W}}^{\text{global average pooling}} \underbrace{\frac{\partial o_c}{\partial a_{ij}^n}}_{\text{gradients via backprop}} \tag{1}$$

where $a_{i,j}^n$ is the activation of neuron n at spatial position i, j. For a given input, the importance of every neuron in the network can be computed for a given class via a single backward pass followed by a global average pooling operation for convolutional units. In practice, we focus on α's from single layers in the network in our experiments. We note that other measures of neuron importance have been proposed [15,32] in various contexts; however, this simple gradient-based importance measure has some notable properties which we leverage.

Firstly, we find gradient-based importance scores to be quite consistent across images of the same class despite the visual variation between instances, and likewise to correlate poorly across classes. To assess this quantitatively, we computed α's for neurons in the final convolutional layer of a convolutional neural network trained on a fine-grained multi-class task (conv5-3 of VGG-16 [27] trained on AWA2 [31]) for 10,000 randomly selected images. We observed an average rank correlation of 0.817 for instances within the same class and 0.076 across pairs of classes. This relative invariance of α's to intra-class input variation may be due in part to the piece-wise linear decision boundaries in networks using ReLU [20] activations. As shown in [22], transitions between these linear regions are much less frequent between same-class inputs than across classes. Within the same linear region, activation gradients (and hence α's) are trivially identical.

Secondly, this measure is fully differentiable with respect to model parameters which we use to learn novel classifiers with gradient methods (see Sect. 3.4).

3.3   Mapping Domain Knowledge to Neurons

Without loss of generality, consider a single layer L within $\text{NET}_\mathcal{S}(\cdot)$. Given an instance $(x_i, y_i) \in \mathcal{D}_\mathcal{S}$, let $\mathbf{a}_c = \{\alpha_c^n \mid n \in L\}$ be a vector of importances computed for neurons in L with respect to class c when x_i is passed through the network. In this section, we learn a simple linear mapping from domain knowledge to these importance vectors – aligning interpretable semantics with individual neurons.

We first compute the importance vector $\mathbf{a}_{y_i}$ for each seen class instance (x_i, y_i) and match it with the domain knowledge representation k_{y_i} of the corresponding class. Given this dataset of $(\mathbf{a}_{y_i}, k_{y_i})$ pairs, we learn a linear transform $W_{\mathcal{K} \to a}$ to map domain knowledge to importances. As importances are gradient based, we penalize errors in the predicted importances based on cosine distance – emphasizing alignment over magnitude. We minimize the cosine distance loss as

$$\mathcal{L}(\mathbf{a}_{y_i}, \mathbf{k}_{y_i}) = 1 - \frac{(W_{\mathcal{K} \to a} \cdot \mathbf{k}_{y_i}) \cdot \mathbf{a}_{y_i}}{\|W_{\mathcal{K} \to a} \cdot \mathbf{k}_{y_i}\| \, \|\mathbf{a}_{y_i}\|}, \qquad (2)$$

via gradient descent to estimate $W_{\mathcal{K} \to a}$. We stop training when average rank-correlation of predicted and true importance vectors stabilizes for a set of held out validation classes from $\mathcal{S}$.

Notably, this is a many-to-one mapping with the domain knowledge of one class needing to predict many different importance vectors. Despite this, this mapping achieves average rank correlations of 0.2 to 0.5 for validation class instances. We explore the impact of error in importance vector prediction on weight optimization in Sect. 3.4. We also note that this simple linear mapping can also be learned in an inverse fashion, mapping neuron importances back to semantic concepts within the domain knowledge (which we explore in Sect. 6).

3.4 Neuron Importance to Classifier Weights

In this section, we use predicted importances to learn classifiers for the unseen classes. As these new classifiers will be built atop the trained seen-class network $\text{NET}_{\mathcal{S}}$, we modify $\text{NET}_{\mathcal{S}}$ to extend the output space to include the unseen class – expanding the final fully-connected layer to include additional neurons with weight vectors $\mathbf{w}^1, \ldots, \mathbf{w}^u$ for the unseen classes such that the network now additionally outputs scores $\{o_c \mid c \in \mathcal{U}\}$. We refer to this expanded network as $\text{NET}_{\mathcal{S} \cup \mathcal{U}}$. At this stage, the weights for the unseen classes are sampled randomly from a multivariate normal distribution with parameters estimated from the seen class weights and as such the output scores are uncalibrated and uninformative.

Given the learned mapping $W_{\mathcal{K} \to A}$ and unseen class domain knowledge $\mathcal{K}_{\mathcal{U}}$, we can predict unseen class importances $A_{\mathcal{U}} = \{\mathbf{a}_1, \ldots, \mathbf{a}_u\}$ with the importance vector for unseen class c predicted as $\mathbf{a}_c = W_{\mathcal{K} \to a} \mathbf{k}_c$. For a given input, we can compute importance vectors $\hat{a}_c$ for each unseen class c. As $\hat{a}^c$ is a function of the weight parameters $\mathbf{w}_c$, we can simply supervise $\hat{a}_c$ with the predicted importances $\mathbf{a}_c$ and optimize w^c with gradient descent – minimizing the cosine distance loss between predicted and observed importance vectors. However, the cosine distance loss does not account for scale and without regularization the scale of weights (and as consequence the outputs) of seen and unseen classes might vary drastically, resulting in bias towards one set or the other.

To address this problem, we introduce a L_2 regularization term which constrains the learned unseen weights to be a similar scale as the mean of seen weights $\overline{\mathbf{w}}_{\mathcal{S}}$. We write the final objective as

$$\mathcal{L}(\hat{\mathbf{a}}_c, \mathbf{a}_c) = 1 - \frac{\hat{\mathbf{a}}_c \cdot \mathbf{a}_c}{\|\hat{\mathbf{a}}_c\| \, \|\mathbf{a}_c\|} + \lambda \|\mathbf{w}_c - \overline{\mathbf{w}}_{\mathcal{S}}\|, \qquad (3)$$

where λ is controls the strength of this regularization. We examine the effect of this trade-off in Sect. 5.1, finding training to be robust to a wide range of

λ values. We note that as observed importances $\mathbf{a}^c$ are themselves computed from network gradients, updating weights based on this loss requires computing a Hessian-vector product; however, this is relatively efficient as the number of weights for each unseen class is small and independent of those for other classes.

Training Images. Note that to perform the optimization described above, we need to pass images through the network to compute importance vectors. We observe importances to be only weakly correlated with image features and find they can be computed for any of the unseen classes irrespective of the input image class – as such, we find simply inputting images with natural statistics to be sufficient. Specifically, we pair random images from ImageNet [6] with random tuples $(\hat{\mathbf{a}}_c, \mathbf{k}_c)$ to perform the importance to weight optimization.

4   Experiments

In this section, we evaluate our approach on generalized zero-shot learning (GZSL) (Sect. 4.1) and present analysis for each stage of NIWT (Sect. 5).

4.1   Experimental Setting

Datasets and Metrics. We conduct our GZSL experiments on the

- **Animals with Attributes 2 (AWA2)** [31] – The AWA2 dataset consists of 37,322 images of 50 animal species (on average 764 per class but with a wide range). Each class is labeled with 85 binary and continuous attributes.
- **Caltech-UCSD Birds 200 (CUB)** [29] – The CUB dataset consists of 11788 images corresponding to 200 species of birds. Each image and each species has been annotated with 312 binary and continuous attribute labels respectively. These attributes describe fine-grained physical bird features such as the color and shape of specific body parts. Additionally, each image is associated with 10 human captions [24].

For both datasets, we use the GZSL splits proposed in [31] which ensure that no unseen class occurs within the ImageNet [6] dataset which is commonly used for training classification networks for feature extraction. As in [30], we evaluate our approach using class-normalized accuracy computed over both seen and unseen classes (e.g. 200-way for CUB) – breaking the results down into unseen accuracy $\text{Acc}_{\mathcal{U}}$, seen accuracy $\text{Acc}_{\mathcal{S}}$, and the harmonic mean between them H.

Models. We experiment with ResNet101 [13] and VGG16 [27] models pretrained on ImageNet [6] and fine-tuned on the seen classes. For each, we train a version by finetuning all layers and another by updating only the final classification weights. Compared to ResNet, where we see sharp declines for fixed models (60.6% finetuned vs 28.26% fixed for CUB and 90.10% vs 70.7% for AWA2), VGG achieves similar accuracies for both finetuned and fixed settings (74.84% finetuned vs 66.8% fixed for CUB and 92.32% vs 91.44% for AWA2). We provide more training details in the Appendix.

NIWT Settings. To train the domain knowledge to importance mapping we hold out five seen classes and stop optimization when rank correlation between observed and predicted importances is highest. For attribute vectors, we use the class level attributes directly and for captions on CUB we use average word2vec embeddings [19] for each class. When optimizing for weights given importances, we stop when the loss fails to improve by 1% over 40 iterations. We choose values of λ (between $1e^{-5}$ to $1e^{-2}$), learning rate ($1e^{-5}$ to $1e^{-2}$) and the batch size ($\{16, 32, 64\}$) by grid search on H for a disjoint set of validation classes sampled from the seen classes of the proposed splits [31] based (see Table 1).

Baselines. We compare NIWT with a number of well-performing zero-shot learning approaches based on learning joint embeddings of image features and class information. Methods like ALE [2] focus on learning compatibility functions for class labels and visual features using some form of ranking loss. In addition to comparing with ALE as reported in [31], we also compare with settings where the hyper-parameters have been directly tuned on the test-set.

We also compare against the recent Deep Embedding approach of [34] which also leverages deep networks, jointly aligning domain knowledge with deep features end-to-end. For both of the mentioned baselines, we utilize code provided by the authors and report results by directly tuning hyper-parameters on the test-set so as to convey an upper-bound of performance.

4.2   Results

We show results in Table 1 for AWA2 and CUB using all model settings. There are a number of interesting trends to observe:

1. **NIWT sets the state of the art in generalized zero-shot learning.** For both datasets, NIWT-Attributes based on VGG establishes a new state of the art for harmonic mean (48.1% for AWA2 and 37.0% for CUB). For AWA2, this corresponds to a $\sim 10\%$ improvement over prior state-of-the-art which is based on deep feature embeddings. These results imply that mapping domain knowledge to internal neurons can lead to improved results.
2. **Seen-class finetuning yields improved harmonic mean H.** For CUB and AWA2, finetuning the VGG network on seen class images offers significant gains for NIWT (26.7%→37.0% H and 36.1%→48.1% H respectively); finetuning ResNet sees similar gains (17.3%→27.7% H on CUB and 27.5%→40.5 %H on AWA2). Notably, these trends seem inconsistent for the compared methods.
3. **NIWT effectively grounds both attributes and free-form language.** We see strong performance both for attributes and captions across both networks (37.0% and 23.6% H for VGG and 27.7% and 23.8% H for ResNet). We note that we use relatively simple, class-averaged representations for captioning which may contribute to the lower absolute performance.

Table 1. Generalized Zero-Shot Learning performances on the proposed splits [31] for AWA2 and CUB. We report class-normalized accuracies on seen and unseen classes and harmonic mean. [1]reproduced from [31]. [2]based on code provided by the authors by tuning hyper-parameters on the test-set to convey an upper-bound of performance.

		Method	AWA2 [32]			CUB [30]		
			$Acc_{\mathcal{U}}$	$Acc_{\mathcal{S}}$	H	$Acc_{\mathcal{U}}$	$Acc_{\mathcal{S}}$	H
ResNet101 [13]	Fixed	ALE [2][1]	14.0	81.8	23.9	23.7	**62.8**	**34.4**
		ALE [2][2]	20.9	**88.8**	33.8	**24.7**	62.3	**34.4**
		Deep Embed. [35][2]	**28.5**	82.3	**42.3**	22.3	45.1	29.9
		NIWT-Attributes	21.6	37.8	27.5	10.2	57.7	17.3
	FT	ALE [2][2]	22.7	**75.1**	34.9	24.1	**60.8**	34.5
		Deep Embed. [35][2]	21.5	59.6	31.6	**24.7**	57.4	34.5
		NIWT-Attributes	**42.3**	38.8	**40.5**	20.7	41.8	27.7
		NIWT-Caption	N/A			22.1	25.7	23.8
VGG16 [28]	Fixed	ALE [2][2]	17.9	**84.3**	29.5	22.2	**54.8**	**31.6**
		Deep Embed. [35][2]	**28.8**	81.7	**42.6**	**24.1**	45.2	31.5
		NIWT-Attributes	43.8	30.7	36.1	17.0	54.6	26.7
	FT	ALE [2][2]	16.9	**91.5**	28.5	25.3	**62.6**	36.0
		Deep Embed. [35][2]	26.6	83.3	38.2	27.0	49.7	35.0
		NIWT-Attributes	**35.3**	75.5	**48.1**	**31.5**	44.9	**37.0**
		NIWT-Caption	N/A			15.9	46.5	23.6

5   Analysis

To better understand the different stages of NIWT, we perform a series of experiments to analyze and isolate individual components in our approach.

5.1   Effect of Regularization Coefficient λ

One key component to our importance to weight optimization is the regularizer which enforces that learned unseen weights be close to the mean seen weight – avoiding arbitrary scaling of the learned weights and the bias this could introduce. To explore the effect of the regularizer, we vary the coefficient λ from 0 to $1e^{-2}$. Figure 3b shows the final seen and unseen class-normalized accuracy for the AWA2 dataset at convergence for different λ's.

Without regularization ($\lambda = 0$) the unseen weights tend to be a bit too small and achieve an unseen accuracy of only 33.9% on AWA2. As λ is increased the unseen accuracy grows until peaking at $\lambda = 1e^{-5}$ with an unseen accuracy of 41.3% – an improvement of over 8% from the unregularized version! Of course, this improvement comes with a trade-off in seen accuracy of about 3% over the same interval. As λ grows larger $>1e^{-4}$, the regularization constraint becomes too strong and NIWT has trouble learning anything for the unseen classes.

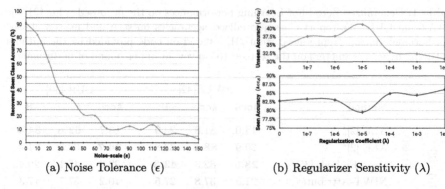

(a) Noise Tolerance (ϵ)   (b) Regularizer Sensitivity (λ)

Fig. 3. Analysis of the importance vector to weight optimization for VGG-16 trained on AWA2 (a). We find that ground-truth weights can be recovered for a pre-trained network even in the face of high magnitude noise. (b) We also show the importance of the regularization term to final model performance.

5.2 Noise Tolerance in Neuron Importance to Weight Optimization

One important component of NIWT is the ability to ground concepts learnt by a convolutional network in some referable domain. Due to the inherent noise involved in this mapping $W_{\mathcal{K} \to A}$, the classifiers obtained for unseen classes in the expanded network $\text{NET}_{\mathcal{S} \cup \mathcal{U}}$ are not perfect. In order to judge the capacity of the optimization procedure, we experiment with a toy setting where we initialize an unseen classifier head with the same dimensionality as the seen classes and try to explicitly recover the seen class weights with supervision only from the *oracle* $\mathbf{a}_c$ obtained from the seen classifier head for the seen classes. To simulate for the error involved in estimating $\mathbf{a}_c$, we add increasing levels of zero-centered gaussian noise and study recovery performance in terms of accuracy of the recovered classifier head on the seen-test split. That is, the supervision from importance vectors is constructed as follows:

$$\tilde{\mathbf{a}}_c = \mathbf{a}_c + \epsilon \overline{||\mathbf{a}_c||}_1 \mathcal{N}(0, I) \qquad (4)$$

We operate at different values of ϵ, characterizing different levels of corruption of the supervision from $\mathbf{a}_c$ and observe recovery performance in terms of accuracy of the recovered classifier head. Figure 3a shows the effect of noise on the ability to recover seen classifier weights (fc7) for a VGG-16 network trained on 40 seen classes of AWA2 dataset with the same objective as the one used for unseen classes.

In the absence of noise over $\mathbf{a}_c$ supervision, we find that we are exactly able to recover the seen class weights and are able to preserve the pre-trained accuracy on seen classes. Even with a noise-level of $\epsilon = 10$ (or adding noise with a magnitude 10x the average norm of $\mathbf{a}_c$), we observe only minor reduction in the accuracy of the recovered seen class weights. As expected, this downward trend continues as we increase the noise-level until we reach almost chance-level performance on the recovered classifier head. This experiment shows that the importance vector to weights optimization is quite robust even to fairly extreme noise.

5.3 Network Depth of Importance Extraction

In this section, we explore the sensitivity of NIWT with respect to the layer from which we extract importance vectors in the convolutional network. As an experiment (in addition to Table 1) we evaluate NIWT on AWA2 with importance vectors extracted at different convolutional layers of VGG-16. We observe that out of those we experimented with conv5_3 performs the best with H = 48.1 followed by conv4_3 (H = 39.3), conv3_3 (H = 35.5), conv2_2 (H = 23.8) and conv2_2 (H = 20.8). We also experimented with the fully-connected layers fc6 and fc7 resulting in values of H being 40.2 and 1 respectively.

Note that performing NIWT on importance vectors extracted from the penultimate layer fc7 is equivalent to learning the unseen head classifier weights directly from the domain space representation ($\mathbf{k}_c$). Consistent with our hypothesis, this performs very poorly across all the metrics with almost no learning involved for the unseen classes at all. Though we note that this may be due to the restricted capacity of the linear transformation $W_{\mathcal{K} \to A}$ involved in the process.

5.4 Importance to Weight Input Images

We evaluate performance with differing input images during weight optimization (random noise images, ImageNet images, and seen class images). We show results of each in Table 2. As expected, performance improves as input images more closely resemble the unseen classes; however, we note that learning occurs even with random noise images.

6 Explaining NIWT

In this section we demonstrate how we can use NIWT to provide visual and textual explanations for the decisions made by the newly learned classifiers on the unseen classes. In addition to the visual explanations provided by Grad-CAM [26], we utilize a mapping (similar to the one in Sect. 3.3) learned in the inverse direction – $W_{a \to \mathcal{K}}$, i.e., neuron-importance(s) $\mathbf{a}_c$ to domain knowledge

Table 2. Results by sampling images from different sets for NIWT-Attributes on VGG-CUB.

Sampling mode	$Acc_{\mathcal{U}}$	$Acc_{\mathcal{S}}$	H
Random normal	23.9	41.0	30.2
ImageNet	31.5	44.9	37.0
Seen-classes	36.4	40.0	38.1

$\mathcal{K}$ to ground the predictions made in the textual domain used as external knowledge. Since this mapping explicitly grounds the *important* neurons in the interpretable domain, we automatically obtain neuron names.

Visual Explanations. Since NIWT learns the classifier associated with the unseen classes as an extension to the existing deep network for the seen classes, it preserves the end-to-end differentiable pipeline for the novel classes as well. This allows us to directly use any of the existing deep network interpretability mechanisms to visually explain the decisions made at inference. We use Grad-CAM [26] on instances of unseen classes to visualize the support for decisions (see Fig. 4) made by the network with NIWT learnt classification weights.

Evaluating Visual Explanations. Quantitatively, we evaluate the generated maps for both seen and unseen classes by the mean fraction of the Grad-CAM activation present inside the bounding box annotations associated with the present objects. On seen classes, we found this number to be 0.80 ± 0.008 versus 0.79 ± 0.005 for the unseen classes on CUB – indicating that the unseen classifier learnt via NIWT is indeed capable of focusing on relevant regions in the input image while making a prediction.

Textual Explanations. In Sect. 3.3, we learned a mapping $W_{\mathcal{K} \to a}$ to embed the external domain knowledge (attributes or captions) into the neurons of a specific layer of the network. Similarly, by learning an inverse mapping from the neuron importances to the attributes (or captions), we can ground the former associated with a prediction in a human-interpretable domain. We utilize such a inverse mapping to obtain scores in the attribute-space (given $\mathbf{a}_c$) and retrieve the top-k attributes as explanations. A high scoring $\mathbf{k}_c$ retrieved via $W_{a \to \mathcal{K}}$ from a certain $\mathbf{a}_c$ emphasizes the relevance of that attribute for the corresponding class c. This helps us ground the class-score decisions made by the learnt unseen classifier head in the attribute space, thus, providing an explanation for the decision.

Evaluating Textual Explanations. We evaluate the fidelity of such textual explanations by the percentage of associated ground truth attributes captured in the top-k generated explanations on a per instance level – 83.9% on CUB using a VGG-16 network. Qualitative results in Fig. 4 show visual and textual explanation(s) demonstrating the discriminative attributes learned by the model for predicting the given target category.

Neuron Names and Focus. Neuron names are referable groundings of concepts captured by a deep convolutional network. Unlike previous approaches, we obtain neuron names in an automatic fashion (without the use of any extra annotations) by feeding a one-hot encoded vector corresponding to a neuron being activated to $W_{a \to \mathcal{K}}$ and performing a similar process of top-1 retrieval (as the textual explanations) to obtain the corresponding *'neuron name'*.

Figure 4 provides qualitative examples for named neurons and their activation maps. The green block shows instances where the unseen class images were correctly classified by $\mathrm{NET}_{S \cup U}$. Conversely, those in red correspond to errors. The columns correspond to the class-labels, images, Grad-CAM visualizations for the class, textual explanations in the attribute space and top-3 neuron names responsible for the target class and their corresponding activation maps. For instance, notice that in the second row, for the image – correctly classified as a yellow-headed blackbird – the visualizations for the class focus specifically at the union of attributes that comprise the class. In addition, the textual explanations also filter out these attributes based on the neuron-importance scores - *has throat*

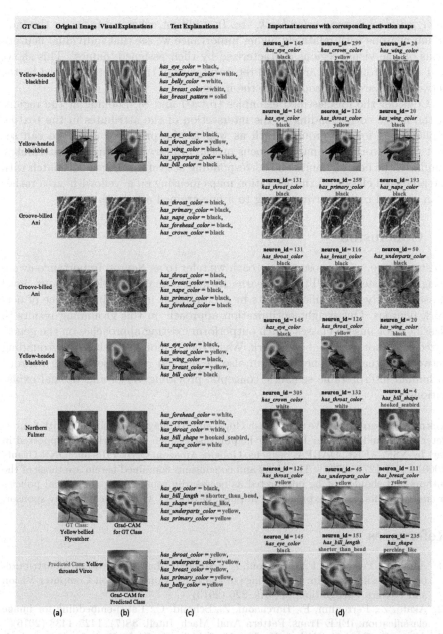

Fig. 4. Success and failure cases for unseen classes using explanations for NIWT: Success cases: (a) the ground truth class and image, (b) Grad-CAM visual explanations for the GT category, (c) textual explanations obtained using the inverse mapping from a_c to domain knowledge, (d) most important neurons for this decision, their names and activation maps. The last 2 rows show failure cases, where the model predicted a wrong category. We show Grad-CAM maps and textual explanations for both the ground truth and predicted category. By looking at the explanations for the failure cases we can see that the model's mistakes are not completely unreasonable.

color yellow, has wing color black, etc. In addition, when we focus on the individual neurons with relatively higher importance we see that individual neurons focus on the visual regions characterized by their assigned 'names'. This shows that our neuron names are indeed representative of the concepts learned by the network and are well grounded in the image.

Consider the misclassified examples (rows 7 and 8). Looking at the regions in the image corresponding to the intersection of the attributes in the textual explanations for the ground truth as well as the predicted class, we can see that the network was unable to focus on the primary discriminative attributes. Similarly, the neuron names and corresponding activations have a mismatch with the predicted class with the activation maps focusing on a 'yellowish' area rather than a visual region corresponding to a fine-grained attribute.

7   Conclusion

To summarize, we propose an approach we refer to as Neuron Importance-aware Weight Transfer (NIWT), that learns to map domain knowledge about novel classes directly to classifier weights by grounding it into the importance of network neurons. Our weight optimization approach on this grounding results in classifiers for unseen classes which outperform existing approaches on the generalized zero-shot learning benchmark. We further demonstrate that this grounding between language and neurons can also be learned in reverse, linking neurons to human interpretable semantic concepts, providing visual and textual explanations.

Acknowledgements. We thank Yash Goyal and Nirbhay Modhe for help with figures; Peter Vajda and Manohar Paluri for helpful discussions. This work was supported in part by NSF, AFRL, DARPA, Siemens, Google, Amazon, ONR YIPs and ONR Grants N00014-16-1-{2713,2793}. The views and conclusions contained herein are those of the authors and should not be interpreted as necessarily representing the official policies or endorsements, either expressed or implied, of the U.S. Government, or any sponsor.

References

1. Akata, Z., Perronnin, F., Harchaoui, Z., Schmid, C.: Label-embedding for attribute-based classification. In: Proceedings of the IEEE Conference on Computer Vision and Pattern Recognition, pp. 819–826 (2013)
2. Akata, Z., Perronnin, F., Harchaoui, Z., Schmid, C.: Label-embedding for image classification. IEEE Trans. Pattern Anal. Mach. Intell. **38**(7), 1425–1438 (2016)
3. Akata, Z., Reed, S., Walter, D., Lee, H., Schiele, B.: Evaluation of output embeddings for fine-grained image classification. In: Proceedings of the IEEE Conference on Computer Vision and Pattern Recognition, pp. 2927–2936 (2015)
4. Bau, D., Zhou, B., Khosla, A., Oliva, A., Torralba, A.: Network dissection: quantifying interpretability of deep visual representations. In: Computer Vision and Pattern Recognition (2017)
5. Changpinyo, S., Chao, W.L., Gong, B., Sha, F.: Synthesized classifiers for zero-shot learning. In: CVPR (2016)

6. Deng, J., Dong, W., Socher, R., Li, L.J., Li, K., Fei-Fei, L.: ImageNet: a large-scale hierarchical image database. In: CVPR (2009)

7. Elhoseiny, M., Elgammal, A., Saleh, B.: Write a classifier: predicting visual classifiers from unstructured text. IEEE Trans. Pattern Anal. **PP**(99), 1 (2017)

8. Elhoseiny, M., Saleh, B., Elgammal, A.: Write a classifier: zero-shot learning using purely textual descriptions. In: Proceedings of the IEEE International Conference on Computer Vision, pp. 2584–2591 (2013)

9. Elhoseiny, M., Zhu, Y., Zhang, H., Elgammal, A.: Link the head to the "beak": zero shot learning from noisy text description at part precision. In: The IEEE Conference on Computer Vision and Pattern Recognition (CVPR), July 2017

10. Farhadi, A., Endres, I., Hoiem, D., Forsyth, D.: Describing objects by their attributes. In: IEEE Conference on Computer Vision and Pattern Recognition, CVPR 2009, pp. 1778–1785. IEEE (2009)

11. Frome, A., et al.: DeViSE: a deep visual-semantic embedding model. In: Advances in Neural Information Processing Systems (2013)

12. Goyal, Y., Mohapatra, A., Parikh, D., Batra, D.: Interpreting visual question answering models. CoRR abs/1608.08974 (2016). http://arxiv.org/abs/1608.08974

13. He, K., Zhang, X., Ren, S., Sun, J.: Deep residual learning for image recognition. In: CVPR (2016)

14. Kodirov, E., Xiang, T., Gong, S.: Semantic autoencoder for zero-shot learning. In: The IEEE Conference on Computer Vision and Pattern Recognition (CVPR), July 2017

15. Konam, S., Quah, I., Rosenthal, S., Veloso, M.: Understanding convolutional networks with apple : automatic patch pattern labeling for explanation. In: First AAAI/ACM Conference on AI, Ethics, and Society (2018)

16. Lampert, C.H., Nickisch, H., Harmeling, S.: Attribute-based classification for zeroshot visual object categorization. IEEE Trans. Pattern Anal. Mach. Intell. **36**(3), 453–465 (2014)

17. Larochelle, H., Erhan, D., Bengio, Y.: Zero-data learning of new tasks. In: AAAI, vol. 1, p. 3 (2008)

18. Lei Ba, J., Swersky, K., Fidler, S., et al.: Predicting deep zero-shot convolutional neural networks using textual descriptions. In: Proceedings of the IEEE International Conference on Computer Vision, pp. 4247–4255 (2015)

19. Mikolov, T., Sutskever, I., Chen, K., Corrado, G.S., Dean, J.: Distributed representations of words and phrases and their compositionality. In: NIPS (2013)

20. Nair, V., Hinton, G.E.: Rectified linear units improve restricted boltzmann machines. In: ICML, pp. 807–814 (2010)

21. Norouzi, M., et al.: Zero-shot learning by convex combination of semantic embeddings. In: ICLR (2014)

22. Novak, R., Bahri, Y., Abolafia, D.A., Pennington, J., Sohl-Dickstein, J.: Sensitivity and generalization in neural networks: an empirical study. arXiv preprint arXiv:1802.08760 (2018)

23. Qiao, R., Liu, L., Shen, C., Hengel, A.V.D.: Less is more: zero-shot learning from online textual documents with noise suppression. In: 2016 IEEE Conference on Computer Vision and Pattern Recognition (CVPR) (2016)

24. Reed, S., Akata, Z., Lee, H., Schiele, B.: Learning deep representations of finegrained visual descriptions. In: Proceedings of the IEEE Conference on Computer Vision and Pattern Recognition, pp. 49–58 (2016)

25. Romera-Paredes, B., Torr, P.: An embarrassingly simple approach to zero-shot learning. In: Proceedings of The 32nd International Conference on Machine Learning, pp. 2152–2161 (2015)

26. Selvaraju, R.R., Das, A., Vedantam, R., Cogswell, M., Parikh, D., Batra, D.: Grad-CAM: why did you say that? visual explanations from deep networks via gradient-based localization. In: ICCV (2017)
27. Simonyan, K., Zisserman, A.: Very deep convolutional networks for large-scale image recognition. In: ICLR (2015)
28. Socher, R., Ganjoo, M., Manning, C.D., Ng, A.: Zero-shot learning through cross-modal transfer. In: Advances in Neural Information Processing Systems (2013)
29. Wah, C., Branson, S., Welinder, P., Perona, P., Belongie, S.: The Caltech-UCSD Birds-200-2011 Dataset. Technical report CNS-TR-2011-001. California Institute of Technology (2011)
30. Xian, Y., Akata, Z., Sharma, G., Nguyen, Q., Hein, M., Schiele, B.: Latent embeddings for zero-shot classification. In: Proceedings of the IEEE Conference on Computer Vision and Pattern Recognition (2016)
31. Xian, Y., Schiele, B., Akata, Z.: Zero-shot learning - the good, the bad and the ugly. In: The IEEE Conference on Computer Vision and Pattern Recognition (CVPR), July 2017
32. Yu, R., et al.: NISP: pruning networks using neuron importance score propagation. In: CVPR (2018)
33. Zeiler, M.D., Fergus, R.: Visualizing and understanding convolutional networks. In: Fleet, D., Pajdla, T., Schiele, B., Tuytelaars, T. (eds.) ECCV 2014. LNCS, vol. 8689, pp. 818–833. Springer, Cham (2014). https://doi.org/10.1007/978-3-319-10590-1_53
34. Zhang, L., Xiang, T., Gong, S.: Learning a deep embedding model for zero-shot learning. In: CVPR (2017)
35. Zhang, Z., Saligrama, V.: Zero-shot learning via semantic similarity embedding. In: Proceedings of the IEEE International Conference on Computer Vision (2015)
36. Zhou, B., Khosla, A., Lapedriza, À., Oliva, A., Torralba, A.: Object detectors emerge in deep scene CNNs. CoRR abs/1412.6856 (2014)

Fully Motion-Aware Network for Video Object Detection

Shiyao Wang[1], Yucong Zhou[2], Junjie Yan[2], and Zhidong Deng[1(✉)]

[1] State Key Laboratory of Intelligent Technology and Systems, Beijing National Research Center for Information Science and Technology, Department of Computer Science, Tsinghua University, Beijing 100084, China
sy-wang14@mails.tsinghua.edu.cn, michael@tsinghua.edu.cn
[2] SenseTime Research Institute, Beijing, China
{zhouyucong,yanjunjie}@sensetime.com

Abstract. Video objection detection is challenging in the presence of appearance deterioration in certain video frames. One of typical solutions is to enhance per-frame features through aggregating neighboring frames. But the features of objects are usually not spatially calibrated across frames due to motion from object and camera. In this paper, we propose an end-to-end model called fully motion-aware network (MANet), which jointly calibrates the features of objects on both pixel-level and instance-level in a unified framework. The pixel-level calibration is flexible in modeling detailed motion while the instance-level calibration captures more global motion cues in order to be robust to occlusion. To our best knowledge, MANet is the first work that can jointly train the two modules and dynamically combine them according to the motion patterns. It achieves leading performance on the large-scale ImageNet VID dataset.

Keywords: Video object detection · Feature calibration · Pixel-level Instance-level · End-to-end

1 Introduction

Object detection is a fundamental problem in image understanding. Deep convolutional neural networks have been successfully applied to this task, including [2,18–22,29]. Although they have achieved great success in object detection from static image, video object detection remains a challenging problem. Frames in videos are usually deteriorated by motion blur or video defocus, which are extremely difficult for single-frame detectors.

To tackle the challenges in deteriorated frames, one of straightforward solutions is to consider the spatial and temporal coherence in videos and leverage information from nearby frames. Following this idea, [5,8,14,15] explore hand-crafted bounding box association rules to refine the final detection results. As post-processing methods, those rules are not jointly optimized. As contrast,

© Springer Nature Switzerland AG 2018
V. Ferrari et al. (Eds.): ECCV 2018, LNCS 11217, pp. 557–573, 2018.
https://doi.org/10.1007/978-3-030-01261-8_33

FGFA [30] attempts to leverage temporal coherence on feature level by aggregating features of nearby frames along the motion paths. They use flow estimation to predict per-pixel motion which is hereinafter referred to as pixel-level feature calibration. However, such pixel-level feature calibration approach would be inaccurate when appearance of objects dramatically changes, especially as objects are occluded. With inaccurate flow estimation, the flow-guided warping may undesirably mislead the feature calibration, failing to produce ideal results. Thus, the robustness of feature calibration is of great importance.

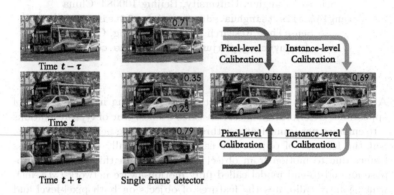

Fig. 1. Examples of occlusion in video object detection. When the bus is occluded by a passing car, the single frame detector fails to produce an accurate box. Pixel-level calibration can help improve the results but it is still influenced due to occlusions. Instance-level calibration performs the best among these results.

In this paper, our philosophy is that accurate and robust feature calibration across frames plays an important role in video object detection. Besides existing pixel-level methods, we propose an instance-level feature calibration method. It estimates the motion of each object along time in order to accurately aggregate features. Specifically, for each proposal in the reference frame, the corresponding motion features are extracted to predict the relative movements between nearby frames and the current frame. According to the predicted relative movements, the features of the same object in nearby frames are RoI-pooled and aggregated for better representation. Compared to the pixel-level calibration, the instance-level calibration is more robust to large temporal appearance variations such as occlusions. As shown in Fig. 1, when the bus in the reference frame is occluded, the flow estimation fails to predict such detailed motion. The warped features of nearby frames can be used to improve the current result, but they are still affected by occluded pixels. In contrast to the pixel-level calibration, the instance-level calibration considers an object as a whole and estimate the motion of the entire object. We argue that such high-level motion is more reliable to use especially when the object is occluded.

Moreover, taking a closer look at above two calibration, we find the pixel-level and instance-level calibration can work collaboratively depending on different motion patterns. The former one is more flexible for modeling non-rigid motion, particularly for some tiny animals. And high-level motion estimation can well describe regular motion trajectory (*e.g.* car). On the basis of observation, we develop a motion pattern reasoning module. If the motion pattern is more likely to be non-rigid and any occlusion does not occur, the final result relies more on the pixel-level calibration. Otherwise, it depends more on the instance-level calibration. All above modules are integrated in a unified framework that can be trained end-to-end.

In terms of the baseline model R-FCN, the proposed instance-level calibration and the MANet improve the mAP 3.5% and 4.5%, respectively, on ImageNet VID dataset.

In summary, the contributions of this paper include:

- We propose an instance-level feature calibration method by learning instance movements through time. The instance-level calibration is more robust to occlusions and outperforms pixel-level feature calibration.
- By visualizing typical samples and conducting statistical experiments, we develop a motion pattern reasoning module to dynamically combine pixel-level and instance-level calibration according to the motion. We show how to jointly train them in an end-to-end manner.
- We demonstrate the MANet on the large-scale ImageNet VID dataset [23] with state-of-the-art performance. Our code is available at: https://github. com/wangshy31/MANet_for_Video_Object_Detection.git.

2 Related Work

2.1 Object Detection from Still Images

Existing state-of-the-art methods for general object detection are mainly based on deep CNNs [1,10,11,16,25–27]. Based on such powerful networks, a lot of works [2,3,6,7,18,22,24] have been done for further improvement in performance of detection. [7] is a typical proposal based CNN detector by using Selective Search [28] to extract proposals. Different from the above multi-stage pipeline, [6] develops an end-to-end training method through applying spatial pyramid pooling [9]. Faster R-CNN [22] further incorporates proposal generation procedure into CNNs with most parameters shared, leading to much higher proposal quality as well as computation speed. R-FCN [2] is another fully convolutional detector. To address the lack of position sensitivity, R-FCN introduces position-sensitive score maps and a position-sensitive RoI pooling layer. We use R-FCN as our baseline and further extend it for video object detection.

2.2 Object Detection in Videos

Unlike those methods of object detection in still images, detectors for videos should take the temporal information into account. One of the main-stream approaches aims to explore bounding box association rules and apply heuristic post-processing. And the other stream of previous work is to leverage temporal coherence on feature level and seek to improve the detection quality in a principled way.

For post-processing, the main idea is to use high-scoring objects from nearby frames to boost scores of weaker detections within the same video. The major difference among these methods is the mapping strategy of linking still image detections to cross-frame box sequences. [8] links cross-frame bounding boxes iff their IoU is beyond a certain threshold and generate potential linkages across the entire clip. Then they propose a heuristic method for re-ranking bounding boxes called "Seq-NMS". [14,15] focus on tubelet rescoring. Tubelets are bounding boxes of an object over time. They apply an offline tracker to revisit the detection results and then associate still-image object detections around the tubelets. [15] presents a re-scoring method to improve the tubelets in terms of temporal consistency. Moreover, [14] proposes multi-context suppression (MCS) to suppress false positive detections and motion-guided propagation (MGP) to recover false negatives. D&T [5] is the first work to jointly learn ROI tracker along with detector. The cross-frame tracker is used to boost the scores for positive boxes. All above approaches focus on post-processing that can be further collaborated with feature-level methods. We will prove it by combining Seq-NMS [8] with our model to reinforce each other and further improve performance.

For feature-level learning, [13,30,31] propose end-to-end learning frameworks to enhance the feature of individual frames in videos. [30] presents flow-guided feature aggregation to leverage temporal coherence on feature level. In order to spatially calibrate the features across frames, they apply an optical flow network [4] to estimate the per-pixel motion between the nearby frames and the reference frame. All the feature maps from nearby frames are then warped to the reference frame so as to enhance the current representations. Similar to this work, [31] also utilizes an optical flow network to model the correspondences in raw pixels. The difference is that they use it to achieve significant speedup. However, the low-level motion prediction is lack of robustness especially in the presence of occlusion [12]. Such individual pixel-wise prediction without considering context may suffer from local consistency [17]. Different from still image proposals, [13] provides a novel tubelet proposal network to efficiently generate spatiotemporal proposals. The tubelet starts from static proposals, and extracts multi-frame features, in order to predict the object motion patterns relative to the spatial anchor. The detector extends 2-D proposals to spatiotemporal tubelet proposals. All those methods will be our strong baselines.

3   Fully Motion-Aware Network

3.1   Overview

We first briefly overview the entire pipeline. Table 1 summarizes the main notations used in this paper. The proposed model is built on standard still image

Table 1. Notations.

$t - \tau, t, t + \tau$	Video frames index
i	Proposal index
(x, y, w, h)	Proposal location described by center (x, y), height and width
$(\Delta_x, \Delta_y, \Delta_w, \Delta_h)$	normed proposal movements
I	Video frame
p, q	2D location
f, s	Output feature maps and score maps
$\mathcal{N}_{feat}, \mathcal{N}_{rpn}, \mathcal{N}_{rfcn}$	CNNs for feature extractor, RPN and R-FCN
$\mathcal{F}$	Functions of flow estimation
$\mathcal{W}, G$	Bi-linear interpolation $\mathcal{W}$ with its kernel function G
ϕ, ψ	ROI pooling and position-sensitive ROI pooling

detector which consists of the feature extractor $\mathcal{N}_{feat}$, the region proposal network $\mathcal{N}_{rpn}$ [22] and the region-based detector $\mathcal{N}_{rfcn}$ [2]. The key idea of the proposed model is to aggregate neighboring frames through feature calibration.

First, $\mathcal{N}_{feat}$ will simultaneously receive three frames $I_{t-\tau}$, I_t and $I_{t+\tau}$ as input, and produce the intermediate features $f_{t-\tau}$, f_t and $f_{t+\tau}$. As shown in Fig. 2, the horizontal line running through the middle of the diagram produces the reference features f_t. The top and bottom lines are nearby features $f_{t-\tau}$ and $f_{t+\tau}$. These single frame features will be spatially calibrated through the following two steps.

Second, the pixel-level calibration will be first applied to calibrate $f_{t-\tau}$ and $f_{t+\tau}$, generating $f_{t-\tau \to t}$ and $f_{t+\tau \to t}$. These features are then aggregated as f_{pixel}. The elaborated formulations are in Sect. 3.2. f_{pixel} is subsequently delivered to $\mathcal{N}_{rpn}$ to produce proposals, as well as $\mathcal{N}_{rfcn}$, waiting to be further combined with instance-level calibrated features.

Third, the instance-level calibration is conducted on the position-sensitive score maps in $\mathcal{N}_{rfcn}$. Specialized convolutional layers are applied on $f_{t-\tau}$, f_t and $f_{t+\tau}$ to produce a bank of k^2 position-sensitive score maps $s_{t-\tau}, s_t$ and $s_{t+\tau}$. For the i-th proposal $(x_t^i, y_t^i, w_t^i, h_t^i)$ of s_t, we introduce a procedure to regress the corresponding proposal location $(x_{t-\tau}^i, y_{t-\tau}^i, w_{t-\tau}^i, h_{t-\tau}^i)$ for $s_{t-\tau}$ and $(x_{t+\tau}^i, y_{t+\tau}^i, w_{t+\tau}^i, h_{t+\tau}^i)$ for $s_{t+\tau}$. As formulated in Sect. 3.3, with these predicted proposal, features in nearby frames are RoI-pooled and aggregated as s_{insta}^i.

At last, motion pattern reasoning is carried out to decide how to combine the different calibrated features. Since f_{pixel} is also fed into $\mathcal{N}_{rfcn}$, it produces s_{pixel}^i for the i-th proposal. Such module is designed to combine s_{insta}^i and s_{pixel}^i according to dynamic motion pattern. It is described in Sect. 3.4.

In our method, all the modules, including feature extractor $\mathcal{N}_{feat}$, $\mathcal{N}_{rpn}$, $\mathcal{N}_{rfcn}$, pixel-level calibration, instance-level calibration and motion pattern reasoning are trained end-to-end.

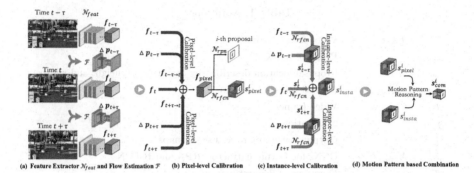

(a) Feature Extractor $\mathcal{N}_{feat}$ and Flow Estimation $\mathcal{F}$ (b) Pixel-level Calibration   (c) Instance-level Calibration   (d) Motion Pattern based Combination

Fig. 2. (Better viewed in color) The overall framework of the proposed fully motion-aware network (MANet). It composes the four steps below: (a) single frame feature extraction and flow estimation whose results are fed to the next two steps; (b) the pixel-level calibration by per-pixel warping; (c) the instance-level calibration through predicting instance movements; (d) the motion pattern based feature combination.

3.2 Pixel-Level Calibration

As motivated by [30,31], given a reference frame I_t and a neighbor frame $I_{t-\tau}$ (or $I_{t+\tau}$), we can model the pixel-level calibration through optical flow estimation. Let $\mathcal{F}$ be a flow estimation algorithm, such as FlowNet [4], and $\mathcal{F}(I_{t-\tau}, I_t)$ indicates the flow field estimated through such network from frame I_t to $I_{t-\tau}$. Then we can warp the feature maps from the neighbor frames to the current frame as follows:

$$\begin{aligned}
\boldsymbol{f}_{t-\tau} &= \mathcal{N}_{feat}(\boldsymbol{I}_{t-\tau}) \\
\boldsymbol{f}_{t-\tau \to t} &= \mathcal{W}(\boldsymbol{f}_{t-\tau}, \mathcal{F}(\boldsymbol{I}_{t-\tau}, \boldsymbol{I}_t))
\end{aligned} \tag{1}$$

where $\boldsymbol{f}_{t-\tau}$ denotes feature maps extracted by $\mathcal{N}_{feat}$ and $\boldsymbol{f}_{t-\tau \to t}$ is the warped features from time $t - \tau$ to time t. The warping operation $\mathcal{W}$ is implemented by bi-linear function which is applied on each location for all the feature maps. It projects a location $\boldsymbol{p} + \Delta\boldsymbol{p}$ in the nearby frame $t - \tau$ to the location $\boldsymbol{p}$ in the current frame. We formulate it as:

$$\begin{aligned}
\Delta\boldsymbol{p} &= \mathcal{F}(\boldsymbol{I}_{t-\tau}, \boldsymbol{I}_t)(\boldsymbol{p}) \\
\boldsymbol{f}_{t-\tau \to t}(\boldsymbol{p}) &= \sum_{\boldsymbol{q}} G(\boldsymbol{q}, \boldsymbol{p} + \Delta\boldsymbol{p}) \boldsymbol{f}_{t-\tau}(\boldsymbol{q})
\end{aligned} \tag{2}$$

where $\Delta\boldsymbol{p}$ is the output of flow estimation at location $\boldsymbol{p}$. $\boldsymbol{q}$ enumerates all spatial locations in the feature maps $\boldsymbol{f}_{t-\tau}$, and $G(\cdot)$ denotes bi-linear interpolation kernel as follow:

$$G(\boldsymbol{q}, \boldsymbol{p} + \Delta\boldsymbol{p}) = max(0, 1 - ||\boldsymbol{q} - (\boldsymbol{p} + \Delta\boldsymbol{p})||) \tag{3}$$

After obtaining calibrated features of nearby frames, we average these features as the low-level aggregation for the updated reference features:

$$\boldsymbol{f}_{pixel} = \frac{\sum_{j=t-\tau}^{t+\tau} \boldsymbol{f}_{j \to t}}{2\tau + 1} \tag{4}$$

where $\boldsymbol{f}_{pixel}$ is generated by the nearby frames from time $t - \tau$ to time $t + \tau$. [30] proposes an adaptive weight to combine those nearby features. But we find that averaging motion guided features has the similar performance with less computation cost. As a result, we adopt average operation in our model.

Through the pixel-wise calibration, the features of nearby frames are spatially-temporally calibrated so as to provide diverse information for the reference frame. It alleviates several challenges in videos such as motion blur and video defocus.

3.3   Instance-Level Calibration

The pixel-level feature calibration is flexible for modeling non-rigid motion, which needs precise per-pixel correspondence. But the low-level calibration may be inaccurate when object is occluded. In this subsection, we extend it to instance-level motion modeling which has much more tolerance of occlusions.

The instance-level calibration is conducted on score maps of R-FCN. R-FCN uses specialized convolutional layers to produce position-sensitive score maps $\boldsymbol{s}_t$. In order to aggregate scores for the i-th proposal $\boldsymbol{s}_t^i$, we should obtain the $\boldsymbol{s}_{t-\tau}$, $\boldsymbol{s}_{t+\tau}$ and proposal movements. $\boldsymbol{s}_{t-\tau}$ and $\boldsymbol{s}_{t+\tau}$ can be easily yielded by feeding $\boldsymbol{f}_{t-\tau}$ and $\boldsymbol{f}_{t+\tau}$ to the R-FCN. The problem is how to learn the relative movements of the i-th proposal, which is the prerequisites for calibrating instance-level features.

We employ the flow estimation and proposals of reference frame as input, and produce movements of each proposal between the neighboring frame and the current frame. The relative movements require motion information. Although per-pixel motion prediction by FlowNet is not accurate due to occlusion, it is capable of describing the motion tendency. We use this motion tendency as input, and output the movements of the entire object. Similar to the Sect. 3.2, we only formulate the relationship between $\boldsymbol{I}_{t-\tau}$ and $\boldsymbol{I}$, and $\boldsymbol{I}_{t+\tau}$ is in a similar way.

First, we utilize the RoI pooling operation to generate the pooled features $\boldsymbol{m}_{t-\tau}^i$ of the i-th proposal at location $(x_t^i, y_t^i, h_t^i, w_t^i)$:

$$\boldsymbol{m}_{t-\tau}^i = \phi(\mathcal{F}(\boldsymbol{I}_{t-\tau}, \boldsymbol{I}_t), (x_t^i, y_t^i, h_t^i, w_t^i)) \tag{5}$$

where $\phi(\cdot)$ indicates the RoI pooling [6] and $\mathcal{F}(\boldsymbol{I}_{t-\tau}, \boldsymbol{I}_t)$ is the flow estimation produced by shared FlowNet in Sect. 3.2. RoI pooling uses max pooling to convert the features inside any valid region of interest into a small feature map with fixed spatial extent.

Then regression network $R(\cdot)$ is exploited to estimate the movement of the i-th proposal between the frame $t - \tau$ and t according to the $\boldsymbol{m}_{t-\tau}^i$:

$$(\Delta_{x_{t-\tau}}^i, \Delta_{y_{t-\tau}}^i, \Delta_{w_{t-\tau}}^i, \Delta_{h_{t-\tau}}^i) = R(\boldsymbol{m}_{t-\tau}^i) \tag{6}$$

where $(\Delta_{x_{t-\tau}}^i, \Delta_{y_{t-\tau}}^i, \Delta_{w_{t-\tau}}^i, \Delta_{h_{t-\tau}}^i)$ is relative movements and $R(\cdot)$ is implemented by a fully connected layer. The remaining problem is how to design proper supervisions for learning the relative movements. Since we have the track-id of each object within a video, we are able to generate the relative movements in terms of the ground-truth bounding boxes. We believe that the proposals should have consistent movement with the ground-truth objects. Thus, the above regression target is assigned the ground-truth box movement if the proposal overlaps with a ground-truth at least by 0.5 in intersection-over-union (IoU). In other word, only the positive proposals will learn to regress the movements among consecutive frames. We use the normed relative movements as regression targets.

Once we obtain the relative movements, we are able to calibrate the features across time and aggregate them to enhance the feature of the current frame. The proposal of frame $I_{t-\tau}$ can be inferred as:

$$
\begin{aligned}
x_{t-\tau}^i &= \Delta_{x_{t-\tau}}^i \times w_t^i + x_t^i & y_{t-\tau}^i &= \Delta_{y_{t-\tau}}^i \times h_t^i + y_t^i \\
w_{t-\tau}^i &= exp(\Delta_{w_{t-\tau}}^i) \times w_t^i & h_{t-\tau}^i &= exp(\Delta_{h_{t-\tau}}^i) \times h_t^i
\end{aligned}
\tag{7}
$$

Based on the estimated proposal locations for nearby frames, the aggregated feature of the i-th proposal can be calculated as:

$$
s_{insta}^i = \frac{\sum_{j=t-\tau}^{t+\tau} \psi(s_j, (x_j^i, y_j^i, h_j^i, w_j^i))}{2\tau + 1}
\tag{8}
$$

where s_j denotes the neighboring score maps, ψ indicates position-sensitive pooling layer introduced by [2], and s_{insta}^i is the instance-level calibrated feature of the i-th proposal.

Discussion about the regression of relative movements. In [13], they have the similar movement regression problem when generating tubelets. They utilize pooled multi-frame visual features from the same spatial location of proposals to regress the movements of the objects. However, these features within the same location across time without explicit motion information make the regression difficult for training. In our instance-level movements learning, we use flow estimation as input to predict movements. It can regress the movements of all the proposals simultaneously without any extra initialization tricks. [5] proposes a correlation based regression. Compared to this additional correlation operation, we adopt a shared FlowNet to model two kinds of motions (both pixel-level and instance-level) simultaneously. This brings two advantages: (1) the feature sharing saves computation cost (shown in Sect. 4.6). (2) the supervision for instance-level movement regression provides additional motion information and improves flow estimation as well.

3.4   Motion Patten Reasoning and Overall Learning Objective

Sections 3.2 and 3.3 give two motion estimation methods. Since they have respective advantages on different motion, the key issue of combination is to measure the non-rigidity of the motion pattern. Intuitively, when the boundingbox's aspect ratio $\frac{x_t^i}{y_t^i}$ changes rapidly across time, the motion pattern is more likely to be non-rigid. Thus, we use the central-difference $\delta(\frac{x_t^i}{y_t^i})$ to express the change rate of aspect ratio at current time. In order to provide more stable estimates, we use average operation over a short snippet to produce the final descriptor of motion pattern:

$$\delta(\frac{x_t^i}{y_t^i}) = (\frac{x_{t+1}^i}{y_{t+1}^i} - \frac{x_{t-1}^i}{y_{t-1}^i})/2$$

$$p_{nonri}^i = \frac{\sum_{j=t-\tau+1}^{t+\tau-1}\delta(\frac{x_j^i}{y_j^i})}{2\tau - 1} \tag{9}$$

where p_{nonri}^i is the motion pattern descriptor for the i-th proposal. The corresponding proposals in the nearby frames can be obtained from Sect. 3.3.

Additionally, occlusion is another important factor when combining these two calibrations. We exploit the visual feature within the proposal to predict the probability of the object being occluded:

$$p_{occlu}^i = R(\phi(\boldsymbol{f}_t, (x_t^i, y_t^i, h_t^i, w_t^i))) \tag{10}$$

where $R(\cdot)$ is also implemented by a fully connected layer and p_{occlu}^i is the probability of occlusion for the i-th proposal. Notice that Eq. 10 is similar to Eq. 6, but Eq. 6 uses motion features from FlowNet to regress movements while Eq. 10 adopts visual features to predict occlusion. It is mainly due to the fact that occlusion is more related to appearance.

Considering these two factors, we use learnable soft weights to combine the two calibrated features:

$$s_{com}^i = s_{insta}^i \times \alpha(\frac{p_{occlu}^i}{p_{nonri}^i}) + s_{pixel}^i \times (1 - \alpha(\frac{p_{occlu}^i}{p_{nonri}^i})) \tag{11}$$

where $\alpha(\cdot) : \mathbb{R} \to [0,1]$ is the mapping function that controls the adjustment range for the weight.

The overall learning objective function is given as:

$$\mathcal{L}(I) = \frac{1}{N}\sum_{i=1}^{N}\mathcal{L}_{cls}(p^i, c_{gt}^i)+$$

$$\frac{1}{N_{fg}}\sum_{i=1}^{N}\mathbf{1}\{c_i^{gt} > 0\}(\mathcal{L}_{reg}(b^i, b_{gt}^i) + \mathcal{L}_{cls}(p_{occlu}^i, c_{o\_gt}^i))+ \tag{12}$$

$$\lambda\frac{1}{N_{tr}}\sum_{i=1}^{N_{tr}}\mathcal{L}_{tr}(\Delta^i, \Delta_{gt}^i)$$

where c_{gt}^i is the ground-truth class label. p^i and b^i stand for the predicted category-wise softmax score and bounding box regression based on s_{com}^i. p_{occlu}^i and Δ^i are occlusion probability and relative movement. $\mathbf{1}\{c_{gt}^i > 0\}$ denotes that we only regress the foreground proposals and N_{tr} indicates that only positive proposals will learn to regress the movement targets. $\mathcal{L}_{cls}$ is the cross-entropy loss while $\mathcal{L}_{reg}$ and $\mathcal{L}_{tr}$ are defined as the smooth $L1$ function. The FlowNet is supervised by both the movement targets and the final detection targets.

Given the overall objective function, the whole architecture, including pixel-level calibration, instance-level calibration, motion pattern reasoning, bounding box classification and regression, is learned in an end-to-end way.

4   Experiments

4.1   Dataset Sampling and Evaluation Metrics

We evaluate the proposed framework on the ImageNet [23] object detection from video (VID) dataset that contains 30 classes. It is split into 3862 training videos and 555 validation videos. The 30 categories are labeled with ground-truth bounding boxes and track IDs on all the video frames. We report all results on the validation set and use the mean average precision (mAP) as the evaluation metric by following the protocols in [13,30,31].

The 30 object categories in ImageNet VID are a subset of the 200 categories in the ImageNet DET dataset. Although there are more than 112,000 frames in VID training set, the redundancy among video frames make the training procedure less efficient. Moreover, the quality of frames in video is much poorer than the still images in DET dataset. Thus we follow previous approaches and train our model on an intersection of ImageNet VID and DET set - 30 categories. To sum up, we sample 10 frames from each video in VID dataset and at most 2 K images per class from DET dataset as our training samples.

4.2   Training and Evaluation

Our model is trained by SGD optimization with momentum of 0.9. During the training, we use a batch size of 4 on 4GPUs, where each GPU holds one mini-batch. The two-phase training is performed. In the first phase, the model is trained on the mixture of DET and VID for 12 K iterations, with learning rates of 2.5×10^{-4} and 2.5×10^{-5} in the first 80 K and 40 K iterations, respectively. In the second phase, the movement regression along with the R-FCN are learned for another 30K iteration on VID dataset in order to be more adapted to VID domain. The feature extractor ResNet101 model is pre-trained for ImageNet classification as default. FlowNet (the "Simple" version) is also pre-trained on synthetic Flying Chairs dataset in [4] in order to provide motion information. They are jointly learned during the above procedure. In both training and testing, we use single scale images with shorter dimension of 600 pixels. For testing we aggregate in total of 12 frames nearby to enhance the feature of the current frame by using the Eqs. 4 and 9. Non-maximum suppression (NMS) is applied with intersection-over-union (IoU) threshold 0.7 in RPN and 0.4 on the scored and regressed proposals.

4.3   Ablation Study

In this section, we conduct an ablation study so as to validate the effectiveness of the proposed network. To make better analysis, we follow the evaluation protocols in [30] where the ground-truth objects are divided into three groups in

Table 2. Accuracy of different methods on ImageNet VID validation, using ResNet-101 feature extraction networks.

Feature extractor	ResNet-101				
Methods	(a)	(b)	(c)	(d)	(e)
Multi-frame feature aggregation?		✓	✓	✓	✓
Pixel-level Calibration?			✓		✓
Instance-level Calibration?				✓	✓
mAP(%)	73.6	73.4 $\downarrow_{0.2}$	76.5 $\uparrow_{2.9}$	77.1 $\uparrow_{3.5}$	**78.1** $\uparrow_{\mathbf{4.5}}$
mAP(%)(slow)	81.8	83.8 $\uparrow_{2.0}$	85.0 $\uparrow_{3.2}$	85.5 $\uparrow_{3.7}$	**86.9** $\uparrow_{\mathbf{5.1}}$
mAP(%)(medium)	71.3	75.7 $\uparrow_{4.4}$	74.9 $\uparrow_{3.6}$	76.1 $\uparrow_{4.8}$	**76.8** $\uparrow_{\mathbf{5.5}}$
mAP(%)(fast)	52.2	45.2 $\downarrow_{7.0}$	56.6 $\uparrow_{4.4}$	55.4 $\uparrow_{3.2}$	**56.7** $\uparrow_{\mathbf{4.5}}$

accordance with? their motion speed. They use object' averaged intersection-over-union(IoU) scores with its corresponding instances in the nearby frames as measurement. It means that the lower the motion IoU(< 0.7) is , the faster the object moves. Otherwise, the larger Motion IoU ($score > 0.9$) expresses the object moves slowly. The rest is medium speed.

Method (a) is the single-frame baseline. It achieves 73.6% mAP by using ResNet-101. All the other experiments keep the same setting as this baseline. Note that we only use the single model and do not add bells and whistles.

Method (b) is carried out conducted by averaging multi-frame features. Even we use the same feature extractor in an end-to-end training manner, the model is even worse than our baseline result. It indicates the importance of motion guidance.

Method (c) incorporates the pixel-level feature calibration. The pixel-wise motion information effectively enhances the information from nearby frames in feature aggregation.

Method (d) is the proposed the instance-level calibration. It aligns the proposal features by predicting the movements among consecutive frames, and finally aggregate them across time. It improve the overall performance by 3.5%, even better than the pixel-wise motion guided features in Method (c).

Method (e) is conducted to prove the pixel-wise motion guided(Method (c)) and the instance-wise motion guided features (Method (d)) are complementary and they are able to collaboratively improve the model. We utilize the motion pattern reasoning (introduced by Sect. 3.4) to adaptively combine these two kinds of calibrated features, and it helps to further enhance the performance from 77.1% to 78.1%.

To sum up, aggregating the multi-frame features by explicitly modeling the motion is quite necessary, and the combination of these two calibration modes is capable of promoting the final feature representations collaboratively. Through the above modules, the overall mAP is improved from 73.6% to 78.1%.

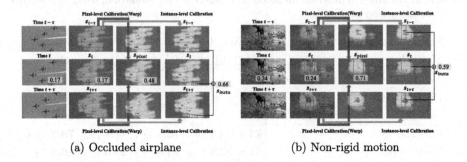

(a) Occluded airplane   (b) Non-rigid motion

Fig. 3. (Better viewed in color) Visualization of two typical examples: occluded and non-rigid objects. They show respective strengths of the two calibration methods.

Table 3. Statistical analysis on different validation sets. The instance-level calibration is better when objects are occluded or move more regularly while the pixel-level calibration performs well on non-rigid motion. Combination of these two module can achieve best performance.

Motion pattern	Pixel-level	Instance-level	Combine
Occlusion	73.0	74.1	75.3
Rigid	81.0	81.9	82.3
Non-rigid	52.8	51.6	53.2

4.4 Case Study and Motion Pattern Analysis

We attempt to take a deeper look at detection results. In order to prove that two calibrated features have respective strengths, we split the validation dataset into different subsets that include different typical samples. The first row in Table 3 shows the performance of occluded samples. We select 87,195 images from validation, where more than half bounding boxes are occluded. The instance-level calibration achieves better performance (74.1%) than pixel-level calibration (73.0%). In terms of motion pattern, we use p_{nonri} to divide the dataset. The objects in a snippet whose p_{nonri} are greater than pre-define $thresh$ will be considered as non-rigid motion, otherwise the rigid motion. $Thresh$ is set to 0.02 in our experiments. From the second and third rows of Table 3, the instance-level calibration is better for modeling rigid motion while pixel-level calibration has advantages of modeling non-rigid patterns. In particular, the adaptive combination distills their advantages and obtain the best performance.

We visualize the learned feature maps in order to better understand the two calibration methods. Figure 3(a) show an occluded airplane which is at the bottom of the current frame. When using a single frame detector, the confidence of category *"airplane"* is 0.17. When applying pixel-level calibrated features, it can be improved to 0.48 (the third column). However, due to the occluded part, the quality of warped feature is undesirably reduced. The last column is instance-level calibration. Since it uses original feature maps of nearby frames, the confidence of category *"airplane"* achieves 0.66. For non-rigid objects in Fig. 3(b), both of the direction and trajectory are changed through the time, and the parts of dogs may have different motion tendencies. So it is difficult for instance-level module to produce correct movements of the whole dog. The corresponding locations in the nearby frames are not accurate, leading to the unsatisfactory score 0.59. By contrast, the pixel-level calibration is flexible of modeling dog's motion and appearance, so it can achieve higher confidence 0.71.

4.5   Comparison with State-of-the-art Systems

We compare our model to the existing state-of-the-art methods which can be divided into two groups: end-to-end learned feature methods [2,13,30,31] and post-processing based methods [5,14,15]. In terms of feature-level comparison, the proposed MANet achieves the best performance among these methods. [13] has the similar regression target with our instance movements learning. But it is much inferior to our calibrated features. [30,31] are pixel-level feature aggregation and our model is better than these methods mainly due to the robustness of motion prediction. It has been analysed in Sect. 4.4.

Since the MANet aims to improve the feature quality in video frames, it can further incorporate bounding-box post-processing techniques to improve the recognition accuracy. Thus using post-processing based methods and combined with [8], the MANet achieves better performance (from 78.1% to 80.3%) that still outperforms other strong baselines [5,14,15].

To sum up, the comparison among feature based methods is more related to our motivation. Our model focuses on the end-to-end feature learning and has obvious advantages among these methods. In addition, we also demonstrate that the MANet can be further improved by post processing and achieves the state-of-the art performance.

4.6   Performance and Time-Consuming Evaluation

Assume that $O(\cdot)$ is denoted as the time spent for the main model $\mathcal{N}$ ($\mathcal{N}_{feat} + \mathcal{N}_{rpn} + \mathcal{N}_{rfcn}$), $\mathcal{F}$ as the flow estimation, $\mathcal{W}$ as the pixel-level feature warping, Ins as the instance-level regression and Ocu as the occlusion predicting. When aggregating 1 adjacent frame, we have:

$$O(\mathcal{N}) = (82.8ms) \gg O(\mathcal{F}) = (6.8\text{ms}) > $$
$$O(Ocu) = (2\text{ms}) > O(Ins) = (1.5\text{ms}) > O(\mathcal{W}) = (0.8\text{ms}) \tag{13}$$

where the aggregation modules take negligible time-consuming compared to $\mathcal{N}$.

For testing, we aggregate k nearby frames to enhance the reference frame. The performance and time for varying k are listed in Table 5. Notice that aggregating nearby 4 frames, our model can achieve 77.58% mAP, which exceeds the performance of [30] where nearby 20 frames are aggregated.

Table 4. Performance comparison with state-of-the-art systems on the ImageNet VID validation set. The average precision (in %) for each class and the mean average precision over all classes are provided.

Methods	airplane	antelope	bear	bicycle	bird	bus	car	cattle	dog	d_cat	elephant	fox	g-panda	hamster	horse	lion
R-FCN[2]	90.5	80.1	83.0	69.6	73.4	72.4	57.2	62.5	69.0	81.6	77.3	85.0	80.7	87.0	72.5	41.6
TPN+LSTM[13]	84.6	78.1	72.0	67.2	68.0	80.1	54.7	61.2	61.6	78.9	71.6	83.2	78.1	91.5	66.8	21.6
D (& T loss)[5]	89.4	80.4	83.8	70.0	71.8	82.6	56.8	71.0	71.8	76.6	79.3	89.9	83.3	91.9	76.8	57.3
DFF[31]	84.6	82.1	84.1	67.1	71.1	76.1	56.5	67.8	65.0	82.3	76.3	87.8	81.9	91.3	70.3	47.7
FGFA[30]	89.4	85.1	83.9	69.8	73.5	79.0	60.6	70.7	72.5	84.3	79.9	89.8	81.0	93.3	72.3	50.5
MANet	90.1	87.3	83.4	70.9	73.0	75.6	62.0	74.0	73.3	85.3	79.6	91.6	83.5	96.5	74.5	70.5
TCN [15]	72.7	75.5	42.2	39.57	25.0	64.1	36.3	51.1	24.4	48.6	65.6	73.9	61.7	82.4	30.8	34.4
TCNN[14]	83.7	85.7	84.4	74.5	73.8	75.7	57.1	58.7	72.3	69.2	80.2	83.4	80.5	93.1	84.2	67.8
D (& T loss)($\tau=1$)[5]	90.2	82.3	87.9	70.1	73.2	87.7	57.0	80.6	77.3	82.6	83.0	97.8	85.8	96.6	82.1	66.7
MANet (+[8])	88.7	88.4	86.9	71.4	73.0	78.9	59.3	78.5	77.8	90.6	79.1	96.3	84.8	98.5	77.4	75.5

Methods	lizard	monkey	motor	rabbit	r-panda	sheep	snake	squirrel	tiger	train	turtle	watercraft	whale	zebra	mAP(%)
R-FCN[2]	78.0	52.2	81.2	66.6	81.5	57.3	70.5	53.1	90.8	82.3	79.1	64.6	75.0	91.2	73.6
TPN+LSTM[13]	74.4	36.6	76.3	51.4	70.6	64.2	61.2	42.3	84.8	78.1	77.2	61.5	66.9	88.5	68.4
D (& T loss)[5]	79.0	54.1	80.3	65.3	85.3	56.9	74.1	59.9	91.3	84.9	81.9	68.3	68.9	90.9	75.8
DFF[31]	76.5	45.7	78.1	62.8	77.8	55.8	74.5	50.5	90.2	81.7	77.9	65.8	66.2	89.5	72.8
FGFA[30]	80.8	52.3	83.0	72.7	84.0	57.8	77.1	55.8	91.9	83.8	83.3	68.7	75.9	91.1	76.5
MANet	82.0	54.4	81.6	67.0	89.3	73.3	77.4	54.3	91.9	82.9	80.3	69.3	75.4	92.4	**78.1**
TCN[15]	54.2	1.6	61.0	36.6	19.7	55.0	38.9	2.6	42.8	54.6	66.1	69.2	26.5	68.6	47.5
TCNN[14]	80.3	54.8	80.6	63.7	85.7	60.5	72.9	52.7	89.7	81.3	73.7	69.5	33.5	90.2	73.8
D (& T loss)($\tau=1$)[5]	83.4	57.6	86.7	74.2	91.6	59.7	76.4	68.4	92.6	86.1	84.3	69.7	66.3	95.2	79.8
MANet(+[8])	84.8	55.1	85.8	76.7	95.3	76.2	75.7	59.0	91.5	81.7	84.2	69.1	72.9	94.6	**80.3**

Table 5. Results obtained by using different k in inference. The runtime contains data processing which is measured on an NVIDIA Titan X Pascal GPU.

k	0	4	8	12	16	18
mAP(%)	73.57	77.58	77.96	78.09	78.08	78.07
Runtime(ms)	87.4	126.8	161.3	201.8	241.1	269.7

5   Conclusions

We propose an end-to-end learning framework for video object detection by aggregating multi-frame features in a principled way. We model the motion among consecutive frames in two different ways and combine them to further improve the performance of the model. We conduct extensive ablation study to prove the effectiveness of each module in our model. In addition, we also give in-depth analysis of their respective strengths on modeling different motion. The proposed model achieves 80.3% mAP on the large-scale ImageNet VID dataset with backbone network ResNet101, which outperforms existing state-of-the-art results.

Acknowledgments. This work was supported in part by the National Key R&D Program of China under Grant No. 2017YFB1302200 and by Joint Fund of NORINCO Group of China for Advanced Research under Grant No. 6141B010318.

References

1. Chen, Y., Li, J., Xiao, H., Jin, X., Yan, S., Feng, J.: Dual path networks. CoRR abs/1707.01629 (2017)
2. Dai, J., Li, Y., He, K., Sun, J.: R-FCN: object detection via region-based fully convolutional networks. In: Advances in Neural Information Processing Systems, pp. 379–387 (2016)
3. Dai, J., et al.: Deformable convolutional networks. In: IEEE International Conference on Computer Vision, ICCV 2017, Venice, Italy, pp. 764–773, 22–29 October 2017
4. Dosovitskiy, A., et al.: FlowNet: Learning optical flow with convolutional networks. In: Proceedings of the IEEE International Conference on Computer Vision, pp. 2758–2766 (2015)
5. Feichtenhofer, C., Pinz, A., Zisserman, A.: Detect to track and track to detect. In: International Conference on Computer Vision (ICCV) (2017)
6. Girshick, R.: Fast R-CNN. In: Proceedings of the IEEE International Conference on Computer Vision, pp. 1440–1448 (2015)
7. Girshick, R.B., Donahue, J., Darrell, T., Malik, J.: Rich feature hierarchies for accurate object detection and semantic segmentation. In: 2014 IEEE Conference on Computer Vision and Pattern Recognition, CVPR 2014, Columbus, OH, USA, pp. 580–587, 23–28 June 2014
8. Han, W., et al.: Seq-NMS for video object detection. arXiv preprint arXiv:1602.08465 (2016)

9. He, K., Zhang, X., Ren, S., Sun, J.: Spatial pyramid pooling in deep convolutional networks for visual recognition. IEEE Trans. Pattern Anal. Mach. Intell. **37**(9), 1904–1916 (2015)

10. He, K., Zhang, X., Ren, S., Sun, J.: Deep residual learning for image recognition. In: Proceedings of the IEEE Conference on Computer Vision and Pattern Recognition, pp. 770–778 (2016)

11. Huang, G., Liu, Z., van der Maaten, L., Weinberger, K.Q.: Densely connected convolutional networks. In: 2017 IEEE Conference on Computer Vision and Pattern Recognition, CVPR 2017, Honolulu, HI, USA, pp. 2261–2269, 21–26 July 2017

12. Hur, J., Roth, S.: MirrorFlow: exploiting symmetries in joint optical flow and occlusion estimation. In: IEEE International Conference on Computer Vision, ICCV 2017, Venice, Italy, pp. 312–321, 22–29 October 2017

13. Kang, K., et al.: Object detection in videos with tubelet proposal networks. In: CVPR (2017)

14. Kang, K., et al.: T-CNN: tubelets with convolutional neural networks for object detection from videos. IEEE Trans. Circuits Syst. Video Technol. (2017)

15. Kang, K., Ouyang, W., Li, H., Wang, X.: Object detection from video tubelets with convolutional neural networks. In: Proceedings of the IEEE Conference on Computer Vision and Pattern Recognition, pp. 817–825 (2016)

16. Krizhevsky, A., Sutskever, I., Hinton, G.E.: ImageNet classification with deep convolutional neural networks. In: Advances in Neural Information Processing Systems, pp. 1097–1105 (2012)

17. Li, Y., Min, D., Do, M.N., Lu, J.: Fast guided global interpolation for depth and motion. In: Leibe, B., Matas, J., Sebe, N., Welling, M. (eds.) ECCV 2016. LNCS, vol. 9907, pp. 717–733. Springer, Cham (2016). https://doi.org/10.1007/978-3-319-46487-9_44

18. Lin, T., Dollár, P., Girshick, R.B., He, K., Hariharan, B., Belongie, S.J.: Feature pyramid networks for object detection. In: 2017 IEEE Conference on Computer Vision and Pattern Recognition, CVPR 2017, Honolulu, HI, USA, pp. 936–944, 21–26 July 2017

19. Lin, T., Goyal, P., Girshick, R.B., He, K., Dollár, P.: Focal loss for dense object detection. In: IEEE International Conference on Computer Vision, ICCV 2017, Venice, Italy, pp. 2999–3007, 22–29 October 2017

20. Liu, W., et al.: SSD: single shot multibox detector. In: Leibe, B., Matas, J., Sebe, N., Welling, M. (eds.) ECCV 2016. LNCS, vol. 9905, pp. 21–37. Springer, Cham (2016). https://doi.org/10.1007/978-3-319-46448-0_2

21. Redmon, J., Divvala, S., Girshick, R., Farhadi, A.: You only look once: unified, real-time object detection. In: Proceedings of the IEEE Conference on Computer Vision and Pattern Recognition, pp. 779–788 (2016)

22. Ren, S., He, K., Girshick, R., Sun, J.: Faster R-CNN: towards real-time object detection with region proposal networks. In: Advances in Neural Information Processing Systems, pp. 91–99 (2015)

23. Russakovsky, O., et al.: Imagenet large scale visual recognition challenge. Int. J. Comput. Vis. **115**(3), 211–252 (2015)

24. Shrivastava, A., Gupta, A., Girshick, R.B.: Training region-based object detectors with online hard example mining. In: 2016 IEEE Conference on Computer Vision and Pattern Recognition, CVPR 2016, Las Vegas, NV, USA, pp. 761–769, 27–30 June 2016

25. Simonyan, K., Zisserman, A.: Very deep convolutional networks for large-scale image recognition. arXiv preprint arXiv:1409.1556 (2014)

26. Szegedy, C., Ioffe, S., Vanhoucke, V., Alemi, A.A.: Inception-v4, inception-ResNet and the impact of residual connections on learning. In: Proceedings of the Thirty-First AAAI Conference on Artificial Intelligence, San Francisco, California, USA, pp. 4278–4284, 4–9 February 2017
27. Szegedy, C., et al.: Going deeper with convolutions. In: Proceedings of the IEEE Conference on Computer Vision and Pattern Recognition, pp. 1–9 (2015)
28. Uijlings, J.R.R., van de Sande, K.E.A., Gevers, T., Smeulders, A.W.M.: Selective search for object recognition. Int. J. Comput. Vis. **104**(2), 154–171 (2013)
29. Zeng, X., Ouyang, W., Yang, B., Yan, J., Wang, X.: Gated bi-directional CNN for object detection. In: Leibe, B., Matas, J., Sebe, N., Welling, M. (eds.) ECCV 2016. LNCS, vol. 9911, pp. 354–369. Springer, Cham (2016). https://doi.org/10.1007/978-3-319-46478-7_22
30. Zhu, X., Wang, Y., Dai, J., Yuan, L., Wei, Y.: Flow-guided feature aggregation for video object detection. In: ICCV (2017)
31. Zhu, X., Xiong, Y., Dai, J., Yuan, L., Wei, Y.: Deep feature flow for video recognition. In: CVPR (2017)

Generative Semantic Manipulation
with Mask-Contrasting GAN

Xiaodan Liang[1]([✉]), Hao Zhang[1], Liang Lin[2], and Eric Xing[1]

[1] Carnegie Mellon University, Pittsburgh, USA
{xiaodan1,hao,epxing}@cs.cmu.edu
[2] Sun Yat-sen University, Guangzhou, China
linliang@ieee.org

Abstract. Despite the promising results on paired/unpaired image-to-image translation achieved by Generative Adversarial Networks (GANs), prior works often only transfer the low-level information (e.g. color or texture changes), but fail to manipulate high-level semantic meanings (e.g., geometric structure or content) of different object regions. On the other hand, while some researches can synthesize compelling real-world images given a class label or caption, they cannot condition on arbitrary shapes or structures, which largely limits their application scenarios and interpretive capability of model results. In this work, we focus on a more challenging semantic manipulation task, aiming at modifying the semantic meaning of an object while preserving its own characteristics (e.g. viewpoints and shapes), such as cow→sheep, motor→bicycle, cat→dog. To tackle such large semantic changes, we introduce a contrasting GAN (contrast-GAN) with a novel adversarial contrasting objective which is able to perform all types of semantic translations with one category-conditional generator. Instead of directly making the synthesized samples close to target data as previous GANs did, our adversarial contrasting objective optimizes over the distance comparisons between samples, that is, enforcing the manipulated data be semantically closer to the real data with target category than the input data. Equipped with the new contrasting objective, a novel mask-conditional contrast-GAN architecture is proposed to enable disentangle image background with object semantic changes. Extensive qualitative and quantitative experiments on several semantic manipulation tasks on ImageNet and MSCOCO dataset show considerable performance gain by our contrast-GAN over other conditional GANs.

Keywords: Generative Adversarial Network
Image semantic manipulation

1 Introduction

Arbitrarily manipulating image content given either a target image, class or caption has recently attracted a lot of research interests and would advance a

© Springer Nature Switzerland AG 2018
V. Ferrari et al. (Eds.): ECCV 2018, LNCS 11217, pp. 574–590, 2018.
https://doi.org/10.1007/978-3-030-01261-8_34

wide range of applications, e.g. image editing and unsupervised representation learning. Recent generative models [4,13,15,17,36,42,43,46] have achieved great progress on modifying low-level content, such as transferring color and texture from a holistic view. However, these models often tend to ignore distinct semantic information (e.g. background or objects) conveyed at distinct image regions and directly render the whole image with one holistic color/texture. This largely limits the application potential of image generation/translation tasks where large semantic changes (e.g. cat → dog, motor → bicycle) are more appealing and essential to bridge the gap between high-level concepts and low-level image processing.

Fig. 1. Some example semantic manipulation results by our model, which takes one image and the desired object category (e.g. *cat, dog*) as inputs and then learns to automatically change the object semantics by modifying their appearance or geometric structure. We show the original image (left) and manipulated result (right) in each pair.

On the other hand, compelling conditional image synthesis given a specific object category (e.g. "bird") [29,41], a textual description ("a yellow bird with a black head") [33], or locations [34] has already been demonstrated using variants of Generative Adversarial Networks (GANs) [9,32] and Variational Autoencoders [10]. However, existing approaches have so far only used fixed and simple conditioning variables such as a class or location that can be conveniently formatted as inputs, but failed to control more complex variables (e.g. shapes and viewpoints). It is thus desirable to endow the unsupervised generation models with the interpretive and controllable capability.

In this paper, we take a further step towards image semantic manipulation in the absence of any paired training examples. It not only generalizes image-to-image translation research by enabling manipulate high-level object semantics but also pushes the boundary of controllable image generation research by retaining intrinsic characteristics conveyed in the original image as much as possible. Figure 1 shows some example semantic manipulation results by our model. Our model can successfully change the semantic meaning of the objects into desired ones, such as cat→dog by manipulating the original shape, geometric or texture of objects in the original image. Note that our model often manipulates the object shapes and structures of target regions to make them more likely be the target semantic.

To tackle such large semantic changes, we propose a novel contrasting GAN (contrast-GAN) in the spirit of learning by comparisons [11,37]. Different from the objectives used in previous GANs that often directly compare the target values with the network outputs, the proposed contrast-GAN introduces an adversarial distance comparison objective for optimizing one conditional generator and several semantic-aware discriminators. This contrasting objective enforces that the features of synthesized samples are much closer to those of real data with the target semantic than the input data. In addition, distinguished from existing GANs [8,26,45,46] that require training distinct generators and discriminators for each type of semantic/style translation, our contrast-GAN only needs to train one single conditional generator for all types of semantic translations benefiting from the category-conditional network structure.

In order to transform object semantics while keeping their original charismatics as much as possible (e.g. only manipulating animal faces for translating dog to cat), exploiting the distinct characteristics that depict different object semantics is thus very critical. Distinguished from the commonly used ranking loss, the new contrasting objective has two merits: (a) the approximated feature center by considering a set of randomly selected instances with target semantic, can statistically learn the crucial characteristics determining each semantic; (b) The competition between two distance pairs of the desired object with original features and approximated feature center of target semantic enables to learn a good balance between semantic manipulation and characteristic-preserving, leading to a controllable system. Compared to simple object replacement, the controllable manipulation is critical for some applications (e.g. image editing). Such competition objective also alleviates the model collapse into average object appearance, like that other GANs suffer from.

In order to disentangle image background from semantic object regions, we further propose a novel mask-conditional contrast-GAN architecture for realizing the attentive semantic manipulation on the whole image by conditioning on masks of object instances. A category-aware local discriminator is employed to examine the fidelity and manipulated semantics of generated object regions, while a whole-image discriminator is responsible for the appearance consistency of the manipulated object regions and image backgrounds. Note that our model is general for taking any mask resources as inputs for each image, such as human specified masks or mask results by any segmentation methods [2,20–23,27,40].

We demonstrate the promising semantic manipulation capability of the proposed contrast-GAN on labels↔photos on Cityscape dataset [3], apple↔orange and horse↔zebra on Imagenet [5] and ten challenging semantic manipulation tasks (e.g. cat↔dog, bicycle↔motorcycle) on MSCOCO dataset [24], as illustrated in Fig. 1. We further quantitatively show its superiority compared to existing GAN models [8,15,26,38,46] on unpaired image-to-image translation task and more challenging semantic manipulation tasks.

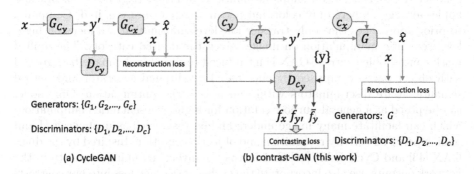

Fig. 2. An overview of the proposed contrast-GAN. c_y and c_x indicate the object categories (semantics) of domain X and Y, respectively. G_{c_y} translates samples into domain Y and D_{c_y} distinguishes between the manipulated result y' and real ones y, and vice verse for G_{c_x} and D_{c_x}. (a) shows the original CycleGAN in [46] where separate generators and discriminators for each mapping are optimized using the cycle-consistency loss. (b) presents the workflow of our contrast-GAN that optimizes one conditional generator G and several semantic-aware discriminators $D_1, D_2, \ldots, D_C$, where C is the total number of object categories. We introduce an adversarial contrasting loss into GAN that encourages the features $f_{y'}$ of generated sample y' are much closer to the feature center $\bar{f}_y$ of target domain Y than those of input x.

2   Related Work

Generative Adversarial Networks (GANs). There have been ever-growing GAN-family methods since the seminal work by Goodfellow et al. [9]. Impressive progresses have been achieved on a wide variety of image generation [6,7,29,34, 35,44], image editing [45], text generation [12,18] and conditional image generation such as text2image [33], image inpainting [30], and image translation [13,19] tasks. The key to GANs' success is the variants of adversarial loss that forces the synthesized images to be indistinguishable from real data distribution. To handle the well-known mode collapse issue of GAN and make its training more stable, diverse training objectives have been developed, such as Earth Mover Distance in WGAN [1], feature matching loss [35], loss-sensitive GAN [31]. However, unlike existing GAN objectives that seek an appropriate criterion between synthesized samples and target outputs, we propose a tailored adversarial contrasting objective for image semantic manipulation. Our contrast-GAN is inspired by the strategy of learning by comparison, that is, aiming to learn the mapping function such that the semantic features of manipulated images are much closer to feature distributions of target domain than those of the original domain.

Generative Image-conditional Models. GANs have shown great success on a variety of image-conditional models such as style transfer [15,39] and general-purpose image-to-image translation [13]. More recent approaches [25,26,43,46] have tackled the unpaired setting for cross-domain image translation and also conducted experiments on simple semantic translation (e.g. horse→zebra and apple→orange), where only color and texture changes are required. Compared to prior approaches that only transfer low-level information, we focus on high-level semantic manipulation on images given the desired category. The unified mask-controllable contrast-GAN is introduced to disentangle image background with object parts, comprised by one shared conditional generator and several semantic-aware discriminators within an adversarial optimization. Our model can be posed as a general-purpose solution for high-level semantic manipulation, which can facilitate many image understanding task, such as unsupervised and semi-supervised activity recognition and object recognition. Inspired by the dual-GAN [43] and Cycle-GAN [46] that learns the inverse mapping to constrain the network outputs, we also incorporate the cycle-consistency loss into our contrast-GAN architecture.

3   Semantic Manipulation with Contrasting GAN

The goal of semantic manipulation is to learn mapping functions for manipulating input images into target domains specified by various object semantics $\{c_k\}_{k=1}^{C}$, where C is the total number of target categories. For each semantic c_k, we have a set of images $\{I_{c_k}\}$. For notation simplicity, we denote the input domain as X with semantic c_x and output domain as Y with semantic c_y in each training/testing step. As illustrated in Fig. 2, our contrast-GAN learns a conditional generator G, which takes a desired semantic c_y and an input image x as inputs, and then manipulates x into y'. The semantic-aware adversarial discriminators D_{c_y} aims to distinguish between images $y \in Y$ and manipulated results $y' = G(x, c_y)$. Our new adversarial contrasting loss forces the representations of y' be closer to those of images $\{y\}$ in target domain Y than those of input image x.

In the following sections, we first describe our contrast-GAN architecture and then present the mask-conditional contrast-GAN for disentangling image background and object semantics.

3.1   Adversarial Contrasting Objective

The adversarial loss introduced in Generative Adversarial Networks (GANs) [9] consists of a generator G and a discriminator D that compete in a two-player min-max game. The objective of vanilla GAN is to make the discriminator correctly classify its inputs as either real or synthetic and the generator synthesize images that the discriminator will classify as real. In practice, we can replace the negative log-likelihood objective by a least square loss [28], which performs more stable during training and generates higher quality results. Thus, the GAN objective becomes:

$$\mathcal{L}_{\mathrm{LSGAN}}(G, D_{c_y}, c_y) = \mathbb{E}_{y \sim p_{\mathrm{data}}(y)}[(D_{c_y}(y) - 1)^2] \\ + \mathbb{E}_{x \sim p_{\mathrm{data}}(x)}[D_{c_y}(G(x, c_y))^2]. \tag{1}$$

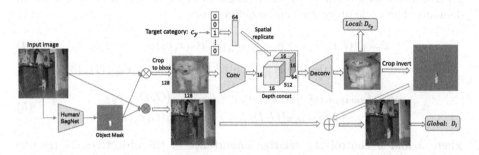

Fig. 3. The proposed mask-conditional contrast-GAN for semantic manipulation by taking an input image, an object mask and a target category as input. Any segmentation methods can be used to produce the object masks with input categories.

In this work, in order to tackle large semantic changes, we propose a new adversarial contrasting objective in the spirit of learning by comparison. Using a comparative measure of the neural network to learn embedding space was introduced in the "Siamese network" [11,37] with triple samples. The main idea is to optimize over distance comparisons between generated samples and those from the source domain X and target domain Y. We consider the feature representation of manipulated result y' should be closer to those of real data $\{y\}$ in target domain Y than that of x in input domain X under the background of object semantic c_y. Formally, we can produce semantic-aware features by feeding the samples into D_{c_y}, resulting in $f_{y'}$ for y' served as an anchor sample, f_x for the input x as a contrasting sample and $\{f_y\}_N$ for samples $\{y\}_N$ in the target domain as positive samples. Note that, at each training step, we compare the anchor $f_{y'}$ with the approximated feature center $\bar{f}_y$ computed as the average of all features $\{f_y\}_N$ rather than that of one randomly sampled y in each step, in order to reduce model oscillation. The generator aims to minimize the contrasting distance $Q(\cdot)$:

$$Q(f_{y'}, f_x, \bar{f}_y) = -\log \frac{e^{-||f_{y'} - \bar{f}_y||_2}}{e^{-||f_{y'} - \bar{f}_y||_2} + e^{-||f_{y'} - f_x||_2}}. \tag{2}$$

Similar to the target of $D_{c_y(y)}$ in Eq.(1) that tries to correctly classify its inputs as either real or fake, our discriminator aims to maximize the contrasting distance $Q(f_{y'}, f_x, \bar{f}_y)$. The adversarial contrasting objective for GAN can be defined as:

$$\mathcal{L}_{\text{contrast}}(G, D_{c_y}, c_y) = \mathbb{E}_{y \sim p_{\text{data}}(y), x \sim p_{\text{data}}(x)}$$
$$[Q(D_{c_y}(G(x, c_y)), D_{c_y}(x), D_{c_y}(\{y\}))]. \tag{3}$$

To further reduce the space of possible mapping functions by the conditional generator, we also use the cycle-consistency loss in [46] which constrains the mappings (induced by the generator G) between two object semantics should be inverses of each other. Notably, different from [46] which used independent generators for each domain, we use a single shared conditional generator for all domains. The cycle objective can be defined as:

$$\mathcal{L}_{\text{cycle}}(G, c_y, c_x) = \mathbb{E}_{x \sim p_{\text{data}}(x)}[|||G(G(x, c_y), c_x) - x||_1]. \tag{4}$$

Therefore, our full objective is computed by combining Eqs. (1), (3) and (4):

$$\mathcal{L}_{\text{contrast-GAN}}(G, D_{c_y}, c_y) = \mathcal{L}_{\text{contrast}}(G, D_{c_y}, c_y)$$
$$+ \lambda \mathcal{L}_{\text{LSGAN}}(G, D_{c_y}, c_y) + \beta \mathcal{L}_{\text{cycle}}(G, c_y, c_x), \tag{5}$$

where λ and β control the relative importance of the objectives. G tries to minimize this objective against a set of adversarial discriminators $\{D_{c_y}\}$ that try to maximize them, i.e. $G^* = \arg\min_G(\frac{1}{C}\sum_{c_y}\max_{D_{c_y}}\mathcal{L}_{\text{contrast-GAN}}(G, D_{c_y}, c_y))$. Our extensive experiments show that each of objectives plays a critical role in arriving at high-quality manipulation results.

3.2   Mask-Conditional Contrast-GAN

Figure 3 shows a sketch of our model, which starts from an input image x, an object mask M and target category c_y and outputs the manipulated image. Note that the whole model is fully differential for back-propagation. For clarity, the full cycle architecture (i.e. the mapping $y' \to \hat{x}$ via $G(y, c_x)$) is omitted. Below we walk through each step.

First, a masking operation and subsequent spatial cropping operation are performed to obtain the object region with the size of 128×128. The background image is calculated by functioning the inverse mask map on an input image. The object region is then fed into several convolutional layers to get 16×16 feature maps with 512 dimension. Second, we represent the target category c_y using a one-hot vector which is then passed into a linear layer to get a feature embedding with 64 dimension. This feature is replicated spatially to form a $16 \times 16 \times 64$ feature maps, and then concatenated with image feature maps via the depth concatenation. Third, several deconvolution layers are employed to obtain target region with 128×128. We then wrap the manipulated region back into the original image resolution, which is then combined with the background image via an additive operation to get the final manipulated image. We implement the spatial masking and cropping modules using spatial transformers [14].

To enforce the semantic manipulation results be semantically consistent with both the target semantic and the background appearance of the input image,

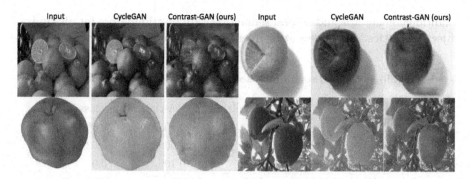

Fig. 4. Result comparison by our contrast-GAN with CycleGAN [46] for translating orange→apple (first row) and apple→orange (second row) on ImageNet, which demonstrates the advantage of leveraging adversarial contrasting objective in GAN.

we adopt both local discriminators $\{D_{c_y}\}$ defined in our contrast-GAN and a global image discriminator D_I. Each local discriminator D_{c_y} is responsible for verifying whether the high-level semantic of outputs is semantically coherent with the input target while the global one D_I evaluates the visual fidelity of the whole manipulated image. The global discriminator D_I takes the combined image of the transformed regions and background, and randomly sampled image as inputs, then employ the same patch-level network as local discriminator, which is jointly trained with local discriminators.

3.3   Implementation Details

Network Architecture. To make a fair comparison, We adopt similar architectures from [46] which have shown impressive results for unpaired image translation. This generator contains three stride-2 convolutions, six residual blocks, and three fractionally stridden convolutions. For the architecture of mask-conditional contrast-GAN in Fig. 3, the residual blocks are employed after concatenating convolutional feature maps with maps of the target category. In terms of the target category input for generator G, we specify a different number of categories C for each dataset, such as $C = 10$ for ten semantic manipulation tasks on MSCOCO dataset. We use the same patch-level discriminator used in [46] for local discriminators $\{D_{c_y}\}$ and the global discriminator D_I. By using the patch-level discriminator network, f(y) is a vector with 14*14 dimension.

Training Details. To compute the approximate feature center $\bar{f}_y$ in Eq.(2) for the contrasting objective, we keep an image buffer with randomly selected $N = 50$ samples in target domain Y. For all the experiments, we set $\lambda = 10$ and $\beta = 10$ in Eq. (5) to balance each objective. We use the Adam solver [16] with a batch size of 1. All networks were trained from scratch and trained with a learning rate of 0.0002 for the first 100 epochs and a linearly decaying rate that goes to zero over the next 100 epochs. Our algorithm only optimizes over one conditional generator and several semantic-aware discriminators for all kinds of object semantics. All models are implemented on Torch framework.

Table 1. Comparison of FCN-scores on Cityscapes labels→photos.

Method	Per-pixel acc.	Per-class acc.	Class IOU
CoGAN [26]	0.40	0.10	0.06
BiGAN [8]	0.19	0.06	0.02
Pixel loss + GAN [38]	0.20	0.10	0.0
Feature loss + GAN [15]	0.07	0.04	0.01
CycleGAN [46]	0.52	0.17	0.11
Contrast alone	0.53	0.13	0.12
Contrast + classify	0.55	0.15	0.11
Contrast + Cycle	0.57	0.22	0.13
Contrast-GAN (separate G)	0.57	**0.22**	**0.17**
Contrast-GAN (ours)	**0.58**	0.21	0.16

4 Experiments

4.1 Experimental Settings

Datasets. First, we quantitatively compare the proposed contrast-GAN against recent state-of-the-arts on the task of labels↔photos on the Cityscape dataset [3]. The labels↔Photos dataset uses images from Cityscape training set for training and validation set for testing. Following [46], we use the unpaired setting during training and the ground truth input-output pairs for evaluation. Second, we compare our contrast-GAN with CycleGAN [46] on unpaired translation, evaluating on the task of horse↔zebra and apple↔orange from ImageNet. The images for each class are downloaded from ImageNet [5] and scaled to 128×128, consisting of 939 images for the horse, 1177 for zebra, 996 for apple and 1020 for orange. Finally, we apply contrast-GAN into ten more challenging semantic manipulation tasks, i.e. dog↔cat, cow↔sheep, bicycle↔motorcycle, horse↔giraffe, horse↔zebra. To disentangle image background with the object semantic information, we test the performance of mask-conditional architecture. The mask annotations for each image are obtained from MSCOCO dataset [24]. For each object category, the images in MSCOCO train set are used for training and those in MSCOCO validation set for testing. The output realism of manipulated results by different methods is quantitatively compared by AMT perception studies described below.

Evaluation Metrics. We adopt the "FCN score" from [13] to evaluate Cityscapes labels→photo task, which evaluates how interpretable the generated photos are according to an off-the-shelf semantic segmentation algorithm.

Table 2. Comparison of classification performance on Cityscapes photos→ labels dataset.

Method	Per-pixel acc	Per-class acc	Class IOU
CoGAN [26]	0.45	0.11	0.08
BiGAN [8]	0.41	0.13	0.07
Pixel loss + GAN [38]	0.47	0.11	0.07
Feature loss + GAN [15]	0.50	0.10	0.06
CycleGAN [46]	0.58	0.22	0.16
Contrast alone Contrast + classify	0.55	0.13	0.11
Contrast + Cycle	0.60	0.19	0.15
Contrast-GAN (separate G)	0.60	0.23	0.17
Contrast-GAN (ours)	**0.61**	**0.23**	**0.18**

To evaluate the performance of photo→labels, we use the standard "semantic segmentation metrics" from Cityscapes benchmark, including per-pixel accuracy, per-class accuracy, and mean class Intersection-Over-Union [3]. For semantic manipulation tasks on ImageNet and MSCOCO datasets (e.g. cat→dog), we run real vs.fake AMT perceptual studies to compare the realism of outputs from different methods under the background of a specific object semantic (e.g. dog), similar to [46]. For each semantic manipulation task, we collect 10 annotations for randomly selected 100 manipulated images by each method and all methods perform manipulation results on the same set of images.

4.2 Result Comparisons

Labels↔photos on Cityscape. Tables 1 and 2 report the performance comparison on the labels→photos task and photos→labels task on Cityscape, respectively. In both cases, the proposed contrast-GAN with a new adversarial contrasting objective outperforms the state-of-the-arts [8,15,26,38,46] on unpaired image-to-image translation. Note that we adopt the same baselines [8,15,26,38] for fair comparison in [46].

Apple ↔orange and horse↔zebra on ImageNet. Figure 4 shows some example results by the baseline CycleGAN [46] and our contrast-GAN on the apple↔orange semantic manipulation. It can be seen that our method successfully transforms the semantic of objects while CycleGAN only tends to modify low-level characteristics (e.g. color and texture). We also perform real vs. fake AMT perceptual studies on both apple↔orange and horse↔zebra tasks. Our contrast-GAN can fool participants much better than CycleGAN [46] by comparing the number of manipulated images that Turkers labeled real, that is 14.3% vs 12.8% on average for apple↔orange and 10.9% vs 9.6% on average for horse↔zebra.

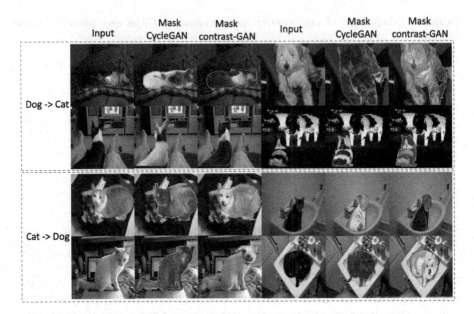

Fig. 5. Result comparison between our mask contrast-GAN with mask CycleGAN [46] for translating dog→cat and cat→dog on the MSCOCO dataset with provided object masks. It shows the superiority of adversarial contrasting objectiveness over the objectiveness used in CycleGAN [46].

4.3   Semantic Manipulation Tasks on MSCOCO

We further demonstrate the effectiveness of our method on ten challenging semantic manipulation applications with large semantic changes.

Contrasting objective vs. other GAN objectives. Figure 5 visualizes the comparisons of our mask-conditional architecture using cycle-consistency loss in [46] and our contrasting objective, that is, mask CycleGAN vs mask contrast-GAN. The baseline method often tries to translate very low-level information (e.g. color changes) and fails to edit the shapes and key characteristic (e.g. structure) that truly convey a specific high-level object semantic. However, our contrast-GAN tends to perform trivial yet critical changes on object shapes and textures to satisfy the target semantic while preserving the original object characteristics. In Table 3, we report quantitative comparison results with the state-of-the-art CoGAN [26], BiGAN [8] and CycleGAN [46] on the AMT perceptual realism measure for eight semantic manipulation tasks. It can be observed that our method substantially outperforms the baseline on all tasks, especially on those requiring large semantic changes (e.g. cat↔dog and bicycle↔motorcycle). In Fig. 6, we show more qualitative results. Our model shows the promising capability of manipulating object semantics while retaining original shapes, viewpoints, and interactions with the background.

Fig. 6. Example results by our mask contrast-GAN for manipulating a variety of object semantics on MSCOCO dataset. For each image pair, we show the original image (left) and manipulated image (right) by specifying a desirable object semantic.

4.4 The Effectiveness of Mask-Conditional Architecture

As observed from Fig. 7, the original GAN networks often renders the whole image with the target texture and ignores the particular image content at different locations/regions. It may result in wrongly translating the unrelated objects (e.g. person, building) and background as the stripe texture in the horse→zebra case. On the contrary, our mask-conditional framework shows appealing results with the capability of selectively manipulating objects of interest (e.g. horse) into the desired semantic (e.g. zebra). It should be noted that our mask-conditional is general enough that can support any mask resources, e.g. human-provided masks and segmentation regions produced by any segmentation methods [2].

4.5 The Effectiveness of Each Objective

In Tables 1 and 2, we report the results by different variants of our full model on Cityscape labels↔photos task. "Contrast alone" indicates the model only uses $\mathcal{L}_{contrast}$ as the final objective in Eq.(5) while "Contrast + classify" represents the usage of combining of $\mathcal{L}_{contrast}$ and $\mathcal{L}_{LSGAN}$ as the final objective. "Contrast + cycle" is the variant that removes $\mathcal{L}_{LSGAN}$. CycleGAN [46] can also be regarded as one simplified version of our model that removes the contrasting objective. Table 3 shows the ablation studies on mask-conditional semantic manipulation tasks on MSCOCO dataset. It can be seen that "Contrast alone" and "Mask

Table 3. Result comparison of AMT perception test on eight mask-conditional semantic-manipulation tasks on the MSCOCO dataset. The numbers indicate % images that Turkers labeled real.

Method	cat→dog	dog→cat	bicycle→motor	motor→bicycle
Mask CoGAN [26]	1.1%	2.0%	7.6%	12.1%
Mask BiGAN [8]	1.9%	2.1%	8.2%	11.4%
Mask CycleGAN [46]	2.5%	4.1%	10.9%	15.6%
Mask Contrast alone	3.7%	5.0%	9.3%	13.1%
Mask Contrast-GAN w/o D_I	4.3%	6.0%	12.8%	15.7%
Mask Contrast-GAN (gt)	**4.8%**	6.2%	13.0%	**16.7%**
Mask Contrast-GAN (predict)	4.5%	**6.5%**	**13.1%**	15.8%
Method	horse→ giraffe	giraffe→ horse	cow→sheep	sheep→cow
Mask CoGAN [26]	0.1%	0.9%	11.2%	15.3%
Mask BiGAN [8]	1.2%	1.5%	12.5%	16.8%
Mask CycleGAN [46]	1.5%	2.3%	16.3%	18.9%
Mask Contrast alone	1.6%	1.8%	17.1%	15.5%
Mask Contrast-GAN w/o D_I	1.9%	4.5%	18.3%	19.1%
Mask Contrast-GAN (gt)	**1.9%**	5.4%	18.7%	20.5%
Mask Contrast-GAN (predict)	1.7%	**6.3%**	**18.9%**	**21.6%**

Contrast alone" achieve comparable results with the state-of-the-arts. Removing the original *classification*-like objective $\mathcal{L}_{LSGAN}$ degrades results compared to our full model, as does removing the cycle-consistency objective $\mathcal{L}_{Cycle}$. Therefore, we can conclude that all three objectives are critical for performing the semantic manipulation. $\mathcal{L}_{LSGAN}$ can be complementary with our contrasting objective $\mathcal{L}_{contrast}$ on validating the visual fidelity of manipulated results. We also validate the advantage of using an auxiliary global discriminator D_I by comparing "Mask Contrast-GAN w/o D_I" and our full model in Table 3.

4.6   One Conditional Generator vs. Separate Generators

Note that instead of using separate generators for each semantic as in previous works [8,15,26,38,46], we propose to employ a conditional generator shared for all object semantics. Using one conditional generator has two advantages: first, it can lead to more powerful and robust feature representation by learning over more diverse samples of different semantics; second, the model size can be effectively reduced by only feeding different target categories as inputs to achieve different semantic manipulations. Tables 1 and 2 also report the results of using separate generators for each semantic task in our model, that is, "Contrast-GAN (separate G)". We can see that our full model using only one conditional generator shows slightly better results than "Contrast-GAN (separate G)".

Fig. 7. Result comparisons between our mask contrast-GAN with CycleGAN [46] for translating horse→zebra and zebra→horse on the MSCOCO dataset. It shows the effectiveness of incorporating object masks to disentangle image background and object semantics.

4.7   The Effect of Different Mask Resources

Our mask-conditional architecture is able to manipulate any input images by firstly obtaining rough object masks of input categories using any segmentation methods [2], which is demonstrated by comparing "Mask Contrast-GAN (predict)" with "Mask Contrast-GAN (gt)" in Table 3. "Mask Contrast-GAN (predict)" indicates the results of using predicted masks by the segmentation model [2] as the network input. We can observe that no significant difference in visualization quality of manipulated images can be observed. The reason is that our model only needs a rough localization of objects with input categories and then generates the manipulated regions with new shapes and structures conditioned on the input object regions. Thus the inaccurate input masks will not significantly affect the manipulation performance.

5   Discussion and Future Work

This paper presents a novel adversarial contrasting objective and mask-conditional architecture, which together achieve compelling results in many semantic manipulation tasks. However, it still shows unsatisfactory results for some cases which require very large geometric changes, such as car↔truck and car↔bus. Integrating spatial transformation layers for explicitly learning pixel-wise offsets may help resolve very large geometric changes. To be more general, our model can be extended to automatically learned attentive regions via attention modeling. This paper pushes forward the research of unsupervised setting by demonstrating the possibility of manipulating high-level object semantics rather than the low-level color and texture changes as previous works did. In addition, it would be more interesting to develop techniques that are able to manipulate object interactions and activities in images/videos.

References

1. Arjovsky, M., Chintala, S., Bottou, L.: Wasserstein GAN. In: ICLR (2017)
2. Chen, L.C., Papandreou, G., Kokkinos, I., Murphy, K., Yuille, A.L.: DeepLab: semantic image segmentation with deep convolutional nets, atrous convolution, and fully connected CRFs. arXiv preprint arXiv:1606.00915 (2016)
3. Cordts, M., et al.: The cityscapes dataset for semantic urban scene understanding. In: CVPR, pp. 3213–3223 (2016)
4. Dai, W., et al.: Scan: structure correcting adversarial network for chest x-rays organ segmentation. arXiv preprint arXiv:1703.08770 (2017)
5. Deng, J., Dong, W., Socher, R., Li, L.J., Li, K., Fei-Fei, L.: ImageNet: a large-scale hierarchical image database. In: CVPR, pp. 248–255 (2009)
6. Deng, Z., et al.: Structured generative adversarial networks. In: Advances in Neural Information Processing Systems, pp. 3899–3909 (2017)
7. Donahue, J., Krähenbühl, P., Darrell, T.: Adversarial feature learning. arXiv preprint arXiv:1605.09782 (2016)
8. Dumoulin, V., et al.: Adversarially learned inference. arXiv preprint arXiv:1606.00704 (2016)
9. Goodfellow, I., et al.: Generative adversarial nets. In: NIPS, pp. 2672–2680 (2014)
10. Gregor, K., Danihelka, I., Graves, A., Rezende, D.J., Wierstra, D.: Draw: a recurrent neural network for image generation. arXiv preprint arXiv:1502.04623 (2015)
11. Hoffer, E., Hubara, I., Ailon, N.: Deep unsupervised learning through spatial contrasting. arXiv preprint arXiv:1610.00243 (2016)
12. Hu, Z., Yang, Z., Liang, X., Salakhutdinov, R., Xing, E.P.: Controllable text generation. arxiv preprint. arXiv preprint arXiv:1703.00955, p. 7 (2017)
13. Isola, P., Zhu, J.Y., Zhou, T., Efros, A.A.: Image-to-image translation with conditional adversarial networks. arXiv preprint arXiv:1611.07004 (2016)
14. Jaderberg, M., Simonyan, K., Zisserman, A., et al.: Spatial transformer networks. In: NIPS, pp. 2017–2025 (2015)
15. Johnson, J., Alahi, A., Fei-Fei, L.: Perceptual losses for real-time style transfer and super-resolution. In: ECCV, pp. 694–711 (2016)
16. Kingma, D., Ba, J.: Adam: A method for stochastic optimization. arXiv preprint arXiv:1412.6980 (2014)
17. Li, J., Liang, X., Wei, Y., Xu, T., Feng, J., Yan, S.: Perceptual generative adversarial networks for small object detection. In: CVPR (2017)
18. Liang, X., Hu, Z., Zhang, H., Gan, C., Xing, E.P.: Recurrent topic-transition GAN for visual paragraph generation. In: ICCV (2017)
19. Liang, X., Lee, L., Dai, W., Xing, E.P.: Dual motion GAN for future-flow embedded video prediction. In: IEEE International Conference on Computer Vision (ICCV), vol. 1 (2017)
20. Liang, X., Shen, X., Feng, J., Lin, L., Yan, S.: Semantic object parsing with graph LSTM. In: Leibe, B., Matas, J., Sebe, N., Welling, M. (eds.) ECCV 2016. LNCS, vol. 9905, pp. 125–143. Springer, Cham (2016). https://doi.org/10.1007/978-3-319-46448-0_8
21. Liang, X., et al.: Reversible recursive instance-level object segmentation. In: Proceedings of the IEEE Conference on Computer Vision and Pattern Recognition, pp. 633–641 (2016)
22. Liang, X., Zhou, H., Xing, E.: Dynamic-structured semantic propagation network. In: Proceedings of the IEEE Conference on Computer Vision and Pattern Recognition, pp. 752–761 (2018)

23. Lin, L., Wang, G., Zhang, R., Zhang, R., Liang, X., Zuo, W.: Deep structured scene parsing by learning with image descriptions. In: Proceedings of the IEEE Conference on Computer Vision and Pattern Recognition, pp. 2276–2284 (2016)
24. Lin, T.-Y., et al.: Microsoft COCO: common objects in context. In: Fleet, D., Pajdla, T., Schiele, B., Tuytelaars, T. (eds.) ECCV 2014. LNCS, vol. 8693, pp. 740–755. Springer, Cham (2014). https://doi.org/10.1007/978-3-319-10602-1_48
25. Liu, M.Y., Breuel, T., Kautz, J.: Unsupervised image-to-image translation networks. arXiv preprint arXiv:1703.00848 (2017)
26. Liu, M.Y., Tuzel, O.: Coupled generative adversarial networks. In: NIPS, pp. 469–477 (2016)
27. Long, J., Shelhamer, E., Darrell, T.: Fully convolutional networks for semantic segmentation. In: CVPR, pp. 3431–3440 (2015)
28. Mao, X., Li, Q., Xie, H., Lau, R.Y., Wang, Z.: Multi-class generative adversarial networks with the l2 loss function. arXiv preprint arXiv:1611.04076 (2016)
29. Mirza, M., Osindero, S.: Conditional generative adversarial nets. arXiv preprint arXiv:1411.1784 (2014)
30. Pathak, D., Krahenbuhl, P., Donahue, J., Darrell, T., Efros, A.A.: Context encoders: feature learning by inpainting. In: CVPR, pp. 2536–2544 (2016)
31. Qi, G.J.: Loss-sensitive generative adversarial networks on lipschitz densities. arXiv preprint arXiv:1701.06264 (2017)
32. Radford, A., Metz, L., Chintala, S.: Unsupervised representation learning with deep convolutional generative adversarial networks. arXiv preprint arXiv:1511.06434 (2015)
33. Reed, S., Akata, Z., Yan, X., Logeswaran, L., Schiele, B., Lee, H.: Generative adversarial text to image synthesis. In: ICML (2016)
34. Reed, S.E., Akata, Z., Mohan, S., Tenka, S., Schiele, B., Lee, H.: Learning what and where to draw. In: NIPS, pp. 217–225 (2016)
35. Salimans, T., Goodfellow, I., Zaremba, W., Cheung, V., Radford, A., Chen, X.: Improved techniques for training GANs. arXiv preprint arXiv:1606.03498 (2016)
36. Sangkloy, P., Lu, J., Fang, C., Yu, F., Hays, J.: Scribbler: controlling deep image synthesis with sketch and color. In: CVPR (2017)
37. Schroff, F., Kalenichenko, D., Philbin, J.: FaceNet: a unified embedding for face recognition and clustering. In: CVPR, pp. 815–823 (2015)
38. Shrivastava, A., Pfister, T., Tuzel, O., Susskind, J., Wang, W., Webb, R.: Learning from simulated and unsupervised images through adversarial training. In: CVPR (2017)
39. Wang, H., Liang, X., Zhang, H., Yeung, D.Y., Xing, E.P.: ZM-Net: real-time zero-shot image manipulation network. arXiv preprint arXiv:1703.07255 (2017)
40. Wei, Y., Feng, J., Liang, X., Cheng, M.M., Zhao, Y., Yan, S.: Object region mining with adversarial erasing: a simple classification to semantic segmentation approach. In: IEEE CVPR, vol. 1, p. 3 (2017)
41. Yan, X., Yang, J., Sohn, K., Lee, H.: Attribute2Image: conditional image generation from visual attributes. In: Leibe, B., Matas, J., Sebe, N., Welling, M. (eds.) ECCV 2016. LNCS, vol. 9908, pp. 776–791. Springer, Cham (2016). https://doi.org/10.1007/978-3-319-46493-0_47
42. Yang, L., Liang, X., Xing, E.: Unsupervised real-to-virtual domain unification for end-to-end highway driving. arXiv preprint arXiv:1801.03458 (2018)
43. Yi, Z., Zhang, H., Gong, P.T., et al.: DualGAN: unsupervised dual learning for image-to-image translation. In: ICCV (2017)

44. Zhang, H., Xu, T., Li, H., Zhang, S., Huang, X., Wang, X., Metaxas, D.: Stack-Gan: text to photo-realistic image synthesis with stacked generative adversarial networks. In: ICCV (2017)
45. Zhu, J.-Y., Krähenbühl, P., Shechtman, E., Efros, A.A.: Generative visual manipulation on the natural image manifold. In: Leibe, B., Matas, J., Sebe, N., Welling, M. (eds.) ECCV 2016. LNCS, vol. 9909, pp. 597–613. Springer, Cham (2016). https://doi.org/10.1007/978-3-319-46454-1_36
46. Zhu, J.Y., Park, T., Isola, P., Efros, A.A.: Unpaired image-to-image translation using cycle-consistent adversarial networks. In: ICCV (2017)

Interpolating Convolutional Neural Networks Using Batch Normalization

Gratianus Wesley Putra Data$^{(\boxtimes)}$ (iD), Kirjon Ngu(iD), David William Murray(iD), and Victor Adrian Prisacariu(iD)

Active Vision Laboratory, Department of Engineering Science, University of Oxford, Oxford, UK
gwpd@robots.ox.ac.uk

Abstract. Perceiving a visual concept as a mixture of learned ones is natural for humans, aiding them to grasp new concepts and strengthening old ones. For all their power and recent success, deep convolutional networks do not have this ability. Inspired by recent work on universal representations for neural networks, we propose a simple emulation of this mechanism by purposing batch normalization layers to discriminate visual classes, and formulating a way to combine them to solve new tasks. We show that this can be applied for 2-way few-shot learning where we obtain between 4% and 17% better accuracy compared to straightforward full fine-tuning, and demonstrate that it can also be extended to the orthogonal application of style transfer.

Keywords: Neural network interpolation · Batch normalization
Few-shot learning · Style transfer

1 Introduction

Human visual cognition is remarkable. One of the many things humans do naturally is linking visual concepts to a combination of other concepts. For example, after being shown images of a dog, a cat, and a fox, a child could say that the fox looks like a cross between a cat and a dog (Fig. 1). Furthermore, the child will understand much about the concept of a fox given prior knowledge of what cats and dogs look like. A loose mathematical analogy can be expressed as follows: if visual representations of cats and dogs can be encapsulated in the form of functions ϕ_{cat} and ϕ_{dog}, respectively, it should also be possible to build from them a representation for foxes $\phi_{fox} = f(\phi_{cat}, \phi_{dog}, \alpha)$, where f represents how the functions should be combined as parameterized by α. Additionaly, it should be easier to deduce the value of α than ϕ_{fox} directly.

In this paper we ask if the same ideas can be adapted to deep convolutional neural networks to enable more efficient learning. This is desirable as, despite generally being powerful state-of-the-art models [11,16,22], deep networks require a tremendous amount of data to tune millions of parameters that

© Springer Nature Switzerland AG 2018
V. Ferrari et al. (Eds.): ECCV 2018, LNCS 11217, pp. 591–606, 2018.
https://doi.org/10.1007/978-3-030-01261-8_35

allow it to work so well, limiting its application to tasks where data is plenty or inexpensive.

Recent works [3, 20] have reported that it is possible to prepare a single network that is able to perform visual recognition in multiple domains. This is achieved by training the network to produce universal image representations, relying on (i) the convolutional kernels to extract domain-agnostic information about the world and on (ii) the batch normalization (BN) layers to transform the internal representations to the relevant target domains. Analogously, within the application domain of style transfer, [6] shows that a single network can be equipped with multiple distinct styles by encoding the style information in the network's instance normalization (IN) layers, after which each style can selectively be applied to a target image. These discoveries seem to provide evidence for the ability of normalization layers to encode transforms that can be used to express visual concepts.

In line with our opening exposition, we propose and wish to test the following intuition in this paper: given that normalization layers (e.g. BN) can be trained to discriminate specific visual classes, it should be possible to combine these normalization layers and interpolate within them to efficiently learn new, unseen classes. In particular, since we will only be manipulating the normalization layers within a network, the number of parameters that we need to tweak will be much lower than full fine-tuning. Fewer parameters also means less tendency to overfit, enabling training with smaller amounts of data. Focusing on binary classification tasks, we summarize our contributions in this paper as follows:

1. Defining a procedure that specifies how component networks that discriminate specific classes are generated and interpolated to discriminate new, unseen classes.
2. Demonstrating how interpolation of component BN layers can be applied to the problem of few-shot visual recognition.
3. Showing that the same interpolation process (using IN) can be adapted to the orthogonal task of style transfer.

Fig. 1. The fox can be seen as a mix between this cat and this dog.

The remainder of the paper proceeds as follows: we first mention several works that are related to our method in Sect. 2. Afterwards, we describe and elaborate procedures for creating and interpolating between component BNs in

Sect. 3. We validate the key idea of interpolating BNs on CIFAR10 [15], apply the same procedures to few-shot learn ImageNet32 [5] using CIFAR10-trained kernels, and also apply it to the orthogonal task of style transfer (by replacing BNs with INs) in Sect. 4. Finally, we conclude our paper in Sect. 5.

2   Related Work

To our knowledge, we are the first to tackle the problem of neural network interpolation. Our main reason for attempting this is to reduce the number of parameters required to train the neural network and to achieve faster convergence with fewer images. We therefore believe our approach is most related to other works that (i) try to reduce the number of trained/tested parameters, (ii) dictionary learning, and (iii) few-shot learning/meta-learning approaches.

Parameter Reduction. Within the realm of parameter reduction, there have been attempts to compress and distill knowledge in neural networks [12], and novel designs for efficient architectures which reduce the number of parameters during inference [4,9]. These assume the neural network is trained in a traditional way and provide methods by which the post-training parameters can be reduced, e.g. through some form of sparsity. Reduction of training parameters is however much less studied, with the traditional approach looking at training only a subset of the complete network, e.g. the last few layers. However, recent work has shown an alternative strategy of training a neural network (rather than just retuning the last layers): to adapt the network's batch normalization parameters. This proved to be effective when training and adapting domain-agnostic neural networks in [3,20] and, relatedly, when aiming to adapt existing neural networks to new types of style transfer as in [6].

Dictionary Learning. The aim of dictionary learning [21] is to learn fundamental representations from data that can be combined linearly to construct sparse codings of the data. A collection of these fundamental representations (*atoms*) form a *dictionary*. A few well-known algorithms that perform dictionary learning include the method of optimal directions [7] and K-SVD [1].

Few-Shot Learning/Meta-Learning. The application of deep convolutional networks for few-shot learning has recently seen a resurgence. Naming just a few methods, Koch *et al.* [14] used Siamese networks to quantify distances between samples, and then used a non-parametric classifier such as k-nearest neighbours to perform one-shot learning. Bertinetto *et al.* [2] modified the Siamese architecture to enable the first network to predict suitable weights for the other in the one-shot regime. Hariharan and Girschick [10] proposed the SGM loss and hallucination as data augmentation to perform n-way few-shot learning where n is large. Luo *et al.* [18] suggested a network framework that is able to learn transferrable representations in a label-efficient manner.

Within the framework of meta-learning, Vinyals *et al.* [25] introduced the concept of episodic training to ensure few-shot training and testing conditions match, and used a cosine similarity metric on network embeddings to peform the classification. Ravi and Larochelle [19] used an LSTM meta-learner to directly perform episodic weight updates on a few-shot learner network, made possible by the similarity between LSTM and gradient descent update formulation. Snell *et al.* [23] utilized a network to learn embeddings which cluster classes around prototypes, which then classifies new examples by proximity to learned prototypes. Finn *et al.* [8] proposed a simple meta-learning training algorithm that aims to generate good initialization parameters for a classifier network, which was then able to achieve good performance after a single parameter update step.

3   Method

First, we briefly review the batch normalizing (BN) transform [13]. Let x_i be the activations of a single example i inside a mini-batch of size m. The BN transform is defined as the operation

$$\mathrm{BN}(x_i) \equiv \gamma \widehat{x}_i + \beta, \tag{1}$$

given the mean $\mu_{\mathcal{B}} = \frac{1}{m} \sum_{i=1}^{m} x_i$, variance $\sigma_{\mathcal{B}}^2 = \frac{1}{m} \sum_{i=1}^{m} (x_i - \mu_{\mathcal{B}})^2$, and the normalized input $\widehat{x}_i = (x_i - \mu_{\mathcal{B}})/\sqrt{\sigma_{\mathcal{B}}^2 + \epsilon}$. The scale γ and shift β parameters are learnable, while ϵ is a small positive constant to prevent division by zero.

Next, we will show how component BNs are constructed, and detail two ways of combining them for the purpose of interpolating new classes. This section focuses on the binary classification scenario, but the principles presented can translate to other application domains, as we show later in Sect. 4.

3.1   Component Generation

Given that component BNs are purposed to be discriminative towards a particular object class, a straightforward way to generate them for that object class would be to extract BNs from a network trained on a corresponding binary classification task.

More specifically, we start from a base pretrained network which we refer to as the template network. To create BN layers that detect the concept of e.g. cat, we fine-tune the network on a dataset containing examples of cats and non-cats by adjusting only the BN and last classification layer parameters. This fine-tuned network is now a component network that detects cats. We repeat this procedure for other object classes, always starting from the same template network, until the desired number of component networks is obtained.

The number of component networks is a function of the task at hand and the quantity of available data and classes. For example, for our experiments, we create 9 component networks for CIFAR10 and 200 for ImageNet.

3.2   Binary Dataset Creation

It is beneficial to generate a number of component BNs so that a good coverage of the target task is achievable. Large multiclass datasets are naturally a suitable source. However, they need to be binarized before they can be used for component generation.

We formalize this as follows. Suppose we have a set of N labelled images $\mathcal{D} = \{(x_1, y_1), \ldots, (x_N, y_N)\}$ where $y_n \in \{1, \ldots, K\}$ are the labels. Binarizing $\mathcal{D}$ for class k means randomly copying $S/2$ elements of $\mathcal{D}$ where $y_n = k$ and another $S/2$ where $y_n \neq k$ to form a new set $\mathcal{D}_k = \{(x_1, y_1), \ldots, (x_S, y_S)\}$ where $y_s \in \{0, 1\}$ after applying the binary label transform

$$\phi(y_n) = y_s = \begin{cases} 1 & \text{if } y_n = k, \\ 0 & \text{if } y_n \neq k. \end{cases} \tag{2}$$

3.3   Component Selection

Once a number of component BNs have been generated, it is important to select the components that will be relevant for the task at hand (e.g. airplanes are probably not a good component to include when trying to detect foxes). Although there may exist sophisticated selection methods, we propose two straightforward criteria which we demonstrate in more detail in Sect. 4.2. The first criterion involves selecting m component networks with the lowest cross-entropy loss on the target binary task. The second criterion does the same thing, except that it ranks based on highest accuracy on the target binary task. Naturally, the first criterion is more amenable to tasks with few examples to evaluate.

3.4   Interpolating Component Networks

After the BN components have been computed and selected for a specific novel target class, we propose two approaches for interpolation:

1. Composite Batch Normalization (ComBN), providing a linear combination of BN components.
2. Principal Component Batch Normalization (PCBN), providing a PCA-based latent space interpolation.

The interpolation weights for both approaches are learned through standard neural network optimization techniques, i.e. backpropagation and stochastic gradient descent (SGD).

Other methods could be used to interpolate the BN components, such as more complex non-linear dimensionality reduction techniques like Gaussian Process Latent Variable Models [17], but, as we show in the results section, the simpler linear models already achieve very good results.

Composite Batch Normalization (ComBN). Using a similar notation to the one above, we propose the ComBN transform as a linear combination of generated BN components,

$$\text{ComBN}_\alpha(x_i) \equiv \sum_{j=1}^{J} \alpha_j \text{BN}_j(x_i), \tag{3}$$

where J is the number of BN components that make up a ComBN, and α_j are learnable scalar coefficients that represent the interpolation weights, all initialized to $1/J$.

In practice, after the component networks have been generated, each BN layer in the original template network is replaced with a ComBN, which is constructed from BN layers of selected component networks originating from the same depth-wise layer position. Afterwards, we train the ComBN network by optimizing α_j and the last layer to the target task using standard techniques (i.e. backpropagation and SGD).

Note that the component BNs in the ComBN network are always utilized in inference mode; i.e. their γ, β, running mean, and running variance are frozen, and the running mean and variance are used in place of the mini-batch mean μ_B and variance σ_B^2 when evaluating Eq. 1.

Additionally, this formulation typically enables a large reduction of the number of parameters, which is helpful in reducing overfitting when the training data is scarce.

Principal Component Batch Normalization (PCBN). An alternative way to exploit information contained in BN components is to first use them to learn a latent space mapping for its parameters, and then perform optimization in the latent space.

To achieve this using PCA, we first stack row vectors of γ and β parameters that originate from each BN component j to form $J \times C$ matrices $\boldsymbol{\Gamma}$ and $\mathbf{B}$, respectively, where J is the number of components and C is the number of channels in each component BN layer. We then mean-center $\boldsymbol{\Gamma}$ and $\mathbf{B}$ by subtracting from them their column-wise mean vectors μ_γ and μ_β, resulting in $\mathbf{X}_\gamma = \boldsymbol{\Gamma} - \mu_\gamma$ and $\mathbf{X}_\beta = \mathbf{B} - \mu_\beta$. Afterwards, we apply singular value decomposition to obtain principal axes matrices $\mathbf{V}_\gamma^\top$ and $\mathbf{V}_\beta^\top$,

$$\mathbf{U}_\gamma \mathbf{S}_\gamma \mathbf{V}_\gamma^\top \leftarrow \mathbf{X}_\gamma, \tag{4}$$

$$\mathbf{U}_\beta \mathbf{S}_\beta \mathbf{V}_\beta^\top \leftarrow \mathbf{X}_\beta. \tag{5}$$

The number of dimensions of our latent space is set to the maximum possible, i.e. $\min(J, C)$. We then train latent space parameter vectors g and b (initialized by transforming existing BN weights of the template network to latent space), and transform these back to parameter space using the principal axes matrices,

$$\gamma = g\mathbf{V}_\gamma^\top + \mu_\gamma, \tag{6}$$

$$\beta = b\mathbf{V}_\beta^\top + \mu_\beta. \tag{7}$$

This is then finally applied in a similar fashion to ComBN by replacing BN layers in the original template network with PCBN (*i.e.* substituting Eqs. 6 and 7 into Eq. 1). In essence, this is like using standard BN except for the optimization of parameters in latent space.

In contrast to ComBN where interpolation is directly performed in the parameter space of the original component class (in the form of frozen BN components), here we attempt to first distill the concepts of class into principal classes in latent space before optimizing them.

4   Experiments

In this section, we show results for two application domains: visual classification and style transfer.

We choose to constrain our experiments to binary classification so that the same protocol can be used for both component generation and evaluation. To highlight the contribution of BN layers, we utilize a template network trained on a different dataset to the one we are testing with; first using ImageNet for the template and CIFAR10 for the testing of our approach, and second using CIFAR10 to train the template network and ImageNet32 for testing.

We chose style transfer because (i) we view this as an orthogonal (i.e. related but highly distinct) task to binary classification since it requires utilization of full encoder-decoder networks and replacement of batch normalization with instance normalization, and (ii) it allows us to produce qualitative results.

4.1   Learning CIFAR10 from ImageNet Template

Here we validate the idea of using BN components for training networks on new, unseen tasks. Lastly, for the experiments in this section, we base our template network on an ILSVRC2012-pretrained ResNet34 [11], and use binarized CIFAR10 datasets to generate our BN components and evaluate the performance of ComBN and PCBN networks.

We begin by creating master training/validation/test splits. These master training/validation splits are created by partitioning the original CIFAR10 training set 40,000/10,000, while the master test split is the same as the original CIFAR10 test set. Afterwards, we generate binarized splits by applying the method in Sect. 3.2 to each of the master splits. Specifically, for each target class, the binary training split is formed by sequentially sampling 1000 positive and 1000 negative examples from the master split, while the binary validation/test splits are formed by sequentially and exhaustively sampling all available examples from their respective master splits such that a balanced dataset is obtained.

Table 1. Percentage test accuracies on binary CIFAR10 datasets. Asterix (*) indicates results that were based on a random template network. Best results are in bold.

Positive class	Last	Full	BN	ComBN	PCBN	BN*	ComBN*	PCBN*
airplane	90.1	**96.1**	95.8	81.9	93.8	76.8	77.2	95.4
car	92.0	**98.0**	97.3	97.7	97.4	77.7	79.8	97.1
bird	87.5	**95.5**	94.5	93.8	91.4	66.7	68.3	93.5
cat	84.3	91.7	89.6	**91.9**	90.3	70.6	69.8	88.9
deer	86.0	**96.6**	94.8	94.3	94.0	71.7	73.1	93.5
dog	89.1	93.1	93.3	**93.9**	93.7	71.4	70.9	93.1
frog	92.3	97.3	95.9	**97.4**	96.0	77.6	77.8	97.0
horse	91.2	**96.8**	96.0	96.2	95.3	67.4	68.5	95.1
ship	91.2	**97.3**	96.9	97.0	95.8	77.8	78.7	96.0
truck	92.9	**97.3**	96.5	90.1	96.2	76.4	73.7	95.9

All experiments pertaining to a particular target class use identical binary training/validation/test splits.

All networks (except the template, which naturally follows [11]) are trained on random batches of size of 8 using SGD with a momentum of 0.9 for 30 epochs. The learning rate is set initially to 10^{-3} and decayed by 0.1 after epoch 20. Images fed into the networks are upscaled to 224 by 224 using bilinear interpolation and normalized without any additional augmentation. We did not perform hyperparameter tuning and while this choice of hyperparameters is arbitrary, we believe it suffices for the tasks at hand as all networks were able to converge.

To generate and evaluate a component network pertaining to a target class, we fine-tune the BN and last layers (BN) of the template network on its binary training set. We then select the network that has the best validation accuracy and finally report on the test set accuracy. This is repeated for each target class in CIFAR10, resulting in 10 component networks. To generate and evaluate the ComBN/PCBN networks, we replace the BN layers in the template network with ComBN/PCBN layers built from the BNs of the 9 component networks that were not trained on the target class, and then apply the same evaluation procedure. One might object to the fact that the 9 component networks might have seen a few examples of the target class as negative examples during their original training, but we find the difference to be negligible even after carefully omitting them. Finally, for completeness, we also report on results of performing full (Full) and last layer (Last) fine-tuning on the same tasks. The results are summarized in Table 1.

For this initial set of experiments, we find that in comparison with other methods, fine-tuning just the last layer results in the lowest accuracy. We also find that results obtained by ComBN and PCBN were comparable, if not just slightly worse, with BN and full fine-tuning, suggesting that ComBN and PCBN are potentially valid methods for training networks.

To better understand the role of BN components, we also performed the Comp, ComBN and PCBN experiments using a template network that has randomized (according to [11]) convolutional layer weights. Surprisingly, this configuration still manages to achieve respectable accuracies, suggesting that random weights can still manage to map the inputs to representations which can be discriminated by the BN tranformations, while also attesting the representational power of BN layers. Even more surprising is the performance that random PCBN obtained, which we leave for future investigation.

4.2   Few-Shot Learning ImageNet32 from CIFAR10 Template

Motivated by the results in Sect. 4.1, we now attempt the more challenging task of evaluating ComBN and PCBN on ImageNet using a CIFAR10-pretrained template network. Owing to constraints on computational resources, we switch to testing on ImageNet32 [5] (which is ImageNet downsampled to 32×32 images) and use ResNet32 [11] as the template network. Additionally, to align ourselves with the original goal, we will perform the evaluations in terms of 2-way few-shot tasks.

Unlike the previous experiments, we forego the creation of a test split and will instead report on validation accuracy. We use the original ImageNet training/validation sets as our master training/validation splits, and then create binarized splits from the master splits using the same procedure outlined in Sect. 3.2. In order to ensure evaluation is performed on unseen classes, we first randomly sample 200 target classes to construct our component networks and reserve the remaining 800 for few-shot tuning and evaluation. The training/validation splits of these 200 binary datasets exhaust all available positive and negative examples from the master splits that result in a balanced dataset (i.e. about 2000 examples in the training split, and exactly 100 in the validation split). The remaining 800 binary datasets will have training/validation splits that respectively possess $2n/100$ examples per split, where n refers to a particular n-shot task.

Unless stated otherwise, all results are trained on random batches of size 128 ($2n$ during few-shot) using SGD with a momentum of 0.9 for 60 epochs and weight decay of 10^{-4}. The learning rate is set initially to 0.01, and is decayed by 0.1 after epochs 30 and 45. The model with the best validation accuracy during the training procedure is selected. No data augmentation is performed, and this choice of hyperparameters is again not optimized. The template network was trained following [11].

The following discussions refer to Table 2, where we report the mean validation accuracy of various networks trained in the few-shot training regime on the 800 binary datasets (except for Max, which uses all training data and is therefore not few-shot; we include this to illustrate a peformance upper bound). As in Sect. 4.1, we also report on the results of fine-tuning the last layer (Last), all layers (Full), and only BN + last layers (BN) of the template network to serve as baselines.

Table 2. Mean percentage validation accuracies μ on the 800 binary ImageNet32 datasets and their differences relative to full fine-tuning $\Delta = \mu - \mu_{Full}$. Asterix (*) indicates evaluation towards a subset (of about 400) of the 800 binary datasets that fulfill the 75% threshold criterion.

Setup	Component selection	No. of components	1-shot		5-shot	
			μ	Δ	μ	Δ
Max	—	—	87.6	25.1	87.6	17.6
Last	—	—	63.0	0.5	69.3	−0.7
Full	—	—	62.5	—	70.1	—
BN	—	—	62.9	0.4	69.6	−0.5
PCBN	—	200	58.2	−4.3	65.3	−4.8
ComBN	Few-shot loss	3	66.3	3.8	73.6	3.5
ComBN	Few-shot loss	5	65.8	3.3	73.3	3.2
ComBN	Few-shot loss	10	65.7	3.2	71.5	1.4
ComBN	Max-shot accuracy	3	77.2	14.7	78.3	8.3
ComBN	Max-shot accuracy	5	76.3	13.8	78.0	7.9
ComBN	Max-shot accuracy	10	72.2	9.7	75.0	4.9
ComBN	Max-shot accuracy	75% threshold*	80.0	17.5	81.6	11.5
PCBN	Few-shot loss	3	64.5	2.0	71.3	1.3
PCBN	Few-shot loss	5	63.3	0.7	70.6	0.5
PCBN	Few-shot loss	10	62.8	2.6	68.4	−1.7
PCBN	Max-shot accuracy	3	71.2	8.7	74.4	4.4
PCBN	Max-shot accuracy	5	70.8	8.3	74.5	4.4
PCBN	Max-shot accuracy	10	67.5	5.0	71.4	1.3
PCBN	Max-shot accuracy	75% threshold*	73.0	10.5	77.5	7.4
SGM	—	—	64.8	2.3	70.6	0.5
L2	—	—	57.0	−5.5	59.7	−10.4

Afterwards, we proceed to generating the 200 component networks by fine-tuning the BN and last layers of the template network using the aforementioned 200 binary datasets, and use all 200 components to construct a PCBN network. However, as we can see from the results, this construction performs worse than the baselines in both 1-shot and 5-shot tasks. This drop in performance might be attributed to the presence of components that are irrelevant for the target task. Furthermore, it is not feasible to create a ComBN network using 200 components due to memory constraints, making it apparent that we need to selectively reduce the number of components used in ComBN/PCBN.

To do so, and as previously hinted in Sect. 3.3, we propose to evelute the cross-entropy loss of each component network on the training split of one of the 800 datasets that correspond to the unknown target class. We then rank and select m component networks with the lowest loss and use these m networks to construct our ComBN/PCBN networks (i.e. few-shot loss component selection). The results from Table 2 seem to indicate that this strategy works, with both ComBN and PCBN outpeforming the baselines by about 4%, and $m = 3$ leading to the best results overall.

Furthermore, we also considered the case of having an ideal selection of components by assuming we were able to binarize all available training data from the master split for component selection (i.e. max-shot accuracy component selection). From here, we (i) selected m component networks with the highest validation accuracy on the target task and (ii) selected 3–10 component networks that perform above 75% in terms of validation accuracy on the target task. This resulted in a marked performance increase of about 14–17% when compared to the baseline, suggesting that component selection is an important procedure that warrants further study. Again, $m = 3$ seems to lead to the best results overall. An illustration of (i) for 3-component ComBN in the 1-shot regime for other as a function of dataset size is plotted in Fig. 2.

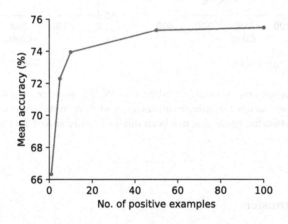

Fig. 2. Mean 1-shot validation accuracy of 3-component ComBN as a function of number of positive examples in training split used in 1-shot loss component selection.

Additionally if we plot the validation accuracies of 75% threshold components and ComBN/PCBN networks constructed from them (Fig. 3), we notice that for some classes ComBN/PCBN does worse than any of the components. This seems odd given that we know for ComBN, a solution consisting of $\alpha_j = 1$ if $j = 1$, and $\alpha_j = 0$ if $j \neq 1$ should result in an accuracy above 75%. This anomaly might be caused by the tendency of SGD to avoid this particular solution, although further work is necessary to better understand this.

As an extra benchmark, we also attempted to compare our results to [10], which is one of the few works which attempted to tackle few-shot tasks without resorting to meta-learning. We do this by training two additional template networks using SGM and L2 loss functions as described in that work, which are theorized to create features better suited for few-shot learning. As before, we then subjected the two template networks to fine-tuning in the few-shot regime, and reported their mean validation accuracies. Set up this way, our best-performing method (3-component ComBN) outperformed theirs (SGM) by a margin of 2–3% with the few-shot loss selection, which could go up to 8–13% assuming ideal component selection.

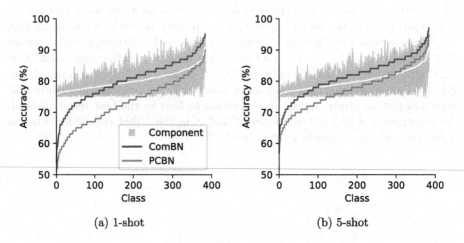

(a) 1-shot   (b) 5-shot

Fig. 3. 75% threshold component, ComBN, and PCBN network validation accuracies. The filled plot represents the minimum, mean, and maximum accuracies for each set of component networks. Each plot has been independently sorted by mean accuracy to aid visualization.

4.3   Style Transfer

To demonstrate a completely orthogonal application of our framework and generate qualitative results, we took the network proposed by [6] and used it as a template. As the network uses instance normalization (IN) layers [24], we will need to replace BNs in our method formulation with INs, resulting in composite instance normalization (ComIN) and principal component instance normalization (PCIN). The bases are formed by 32 IN parameters that were already present in the original network, and are used to learn new styles, some of which are shown in Fig. 4.

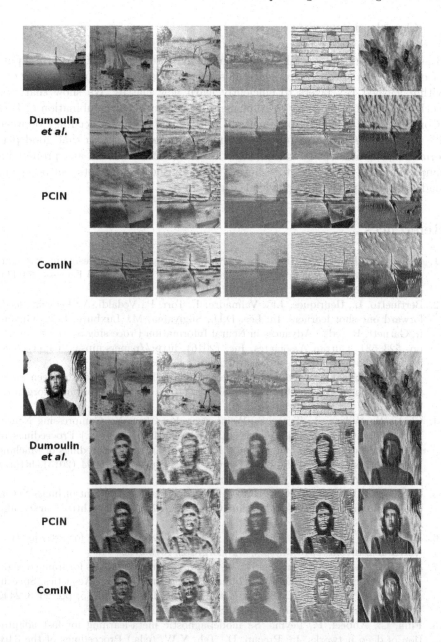

Fig. 4. Results on style transfer. Images on the top row are styles that are applied on the leftmost content image. Images on each consecutive row below are stylized images obtained from utilizing the original training procedure of Dumoulin *et al.* [6], PCIN, and ComIN, respectively.

5   Conclusions

Based on a recent idea that batch normalization modules could transform inputs to encode class-specific representations, we propose an interpolation method within learned BN layers to efficiently learn new classes. We show that this works for few-shot learning by implementing it as a linear combination of BNs (ComBN) or PCA on BN paramaters (PCBN), obtaining an accuracy between 4% to 17% over standard full fine-tuning. We have also shown that good performance is dependent on careful selection of the BN modules, and proposed a simple criterion to achieve this. Source code for the experiments can be downloaded from http://bninterp.avlcode.org/.

References

1. Aharon, M., Elad, M., Bruckstein, A.: K-SVD: an algorithm for designing overcomplete dictionaries for sparse representation. IEEE Trans. Signal Process. **54**(11), 4311–4322 (2006). https://doi.org/10.1109/TSP.2006.881199
2. Bertinetto, L., Henriques, J.F., Valmadre, J., Torr, P., Vedaldi, A.: Learning feed-forward one-shot learners. In: Lee, D.D., Sugiyama, M., Luxburg, U.V., Guyon, I., Garnett, R. (eds.) Advances in Neural Information Processing Systems, vol. 29, pp. 523–531. Curran Associates, Inc. (2016). http://papers.nips.cc/paper/6068-learning-feed-forward-one-shot-learners.pdf
3. Bilen, H., Vedaldi, A.: Universal representations: the missing link between faces, text, planktons, and cat breeds. CoRR abs/1701.0 (2017). http://arxiv.org/abs/1701.07275
4. Chen, W., Wilson, J., Tyree, S., Weinberger, K., Chen, Y.: Compressing Neural Networks with the Hashing Trick. In: Bach, F., Blei, D. (eds.) Proceedings of the 32nd International Conference on Machine Learning, Proceedings of Machine Learning Research, PMLR, Lille, France, vol. 37, pp. 2285–2294 (2015). http://proceedings.mlr.press/v37/chenc15.html
5. Chrabaszcz, P., Loshchilov, I., Hutter, F.: A downsampled variant of ImageNet as an alternative to the CIFAR datasets. CoRR abs/1707.0 (2017). http://arxiv.org/abs/1707.08819
6. Dumoulin, V., Shlens, J., Kudlur, M.: A learned representation for artistic style. CoRR abs/1610.0 (2016). http://arxiv.org/abs/1610.07629
7. Engan, K., Aase, S.O., Husoy, J.H.: Method of optimal directions for frame design. In: Proceedings of the 1999 IEEE International Conference on Acoustics, Speech, and Signal Processing, ICASSP99 (Cat. No. 99CH36258). vol. 5, pp. 2443–2446 (1999). https://doi.org/10.1109/ICASSP.1999.760624
8. Finn, C., Abbeel, P., Levine, S.: model-agnostic meta-learning for fast adaptation of deep networks. In: Precup, D., Teh, Y.W. (eds.) Proceedings of the 34th International Conference on Machine Learning, Proceedings of Machine Learning Research, PMLR, vol. 70, pp. 1126–1135. International Convention Centre, Sydney (2017). http://proceedings.mlr.press/v70/finn17a.html
9. Gao, Y., She, Q., Ma, J., Zhao, M., Liu, W., Yuille, A.L.: NDDR-CNN: layer-wise feature fusing in multi-task CNN by neural discriminative dimensionality reduction. CoRR abs/1801.0 (2018). http://arxiv.org/abs/1801.08297

10. Hariharan, B., Girshick, R.: Low-shot visual recognition by shrinking and hallucinating features. In: The IEEE International Conference on Computer Vision (ICCV), pp. 3018–3027, October 2017
11. He, K., Zhang, X., Ren, S., Sun, J.: Deep residual learning for image recognition. In: The IEEE Conference on Computer Vision and Pattern Recognition (CVPR), pp. 770–778, June 2016
12. Hinton, G., Vinyals, O., Dean, J.: Distilling the knowledge in a neural network. In: NIPS Deep Learning and Representation Learning Workshop (2015)
13. Ioffe, S., Szegedy, C.: Batch normalization: accelerating deep network training by reducing internal covariate shift. In: Bach, F., Blei, D. (eds.) Proceedings of the 32nd International Conference on Machine Learning, Proceedings of Machine Learning Research, PMLR, Lille, France, vol. 37, pp. 448–456 (2015). http://proceedings.mlr.press/v37/ioffe15.html
14. Koch, G., Zemel, R., Salakhutdinov, R.: Siamese neural networks for one-shot image recognition. In: ICML Deep Learning Workshop (2015)
15. Krizhevsky, A.: Learning multiple layers of features from tiny images. Technical report (2009)
16. Krizhevsky, A., Sutskever, I., Hinton, G.: ImageNet classification with deep convolutional neural networks. In: Pereira, F., Burges, C.J.C., Bottou, L., Weinberger, K.Q. (eds.) Advances in Neural Information Processing Systems, vol. 25, pp. 1097–1105. Curran Associates, Inc. (2012). http://papers.nips.cc/paper/4824-imagenet-classification-with-deep-convolutional-neural-networks.pdf
17. Lawrence, N.: Probabilistic non-linear principal component analysis with Gaussian process latent variable models. J. Mach. Learn. Res. **6**, 1783–1816 (2005). http://dl.acm.org/citation.cfm?id=1046920.1194904
18. Luo, Z., Zou, Y., Hoffman, J., Fei-Fei, L.: Label efficient learning of transferable representations acrosss domains and tasks. In: Guyon, I., Luxburg, U.V., Bengio, S., Wallach, H., Fergus, R., Vishwanathan, S., Garnett, R. (eds.) Advances in Neural Information Processing Systems, vol. 30, pp. 165–177. Curran Associates, Inc. (2017). http://papers.nips.cc/paper/6621-label-efficient-learning-of-transferable-representations-acrosss-domains-and-tasks.pdf
19. Ravi, S., Larochelle, H.: Optimization as a model for few-shot learning. In: International Conference on Learning Representations (2017)
20. Rebuffi, S.A., Bilen, H., Vedaldi, A.: Learning multiple visual domains with residual adapters. In: Guyon, I., et al. (eds.) Advances in Neural Information Processing Systems, vol. 30, pp. 506–516. Curran Associates, Inc. (2017). http://papers.nips.cc/paper/6654-learning-multiple-visual-domains-with-residual-adapters.pdf
21. Rubinstein, R., Bruckstein, A.M., Elad, M.: Dictionaries for sparse representation modeling. Proc. IEEE **98**(6), 1045–1057 (2010). https://doi.org/10.1109/JPROC.2010.2040551
22. Simonyan, K., Zisserman, A.: Very deep convolutional networks for large-scale image recognition. In: International Conference on Learning Representations (2015)
23. Snell, J., Swersky, K., Zemel, R.S.: Prototypical networks for few-shot learning. CoRR abs/1703.0 (2017). http://arxiv.org/abs/1703.05175

24. Ulyanov, D., Vedaldi, A., Lempitsky, V.S.: Instance normalization: the missing ingredient for fast stylization. CoRR abs/1607.0 (2016). http://arxiv.org/abs/1607.08022
25. Vinyals, O., Blundell, C., Lillicrap, T., Kavukcuoglu, K., Wierstra, D.: Matching networks for one shot learning. In: Lee, D.D., Sugiyama, M., Luxburg, U.V., Guyon, I., Garnett, R. (eds.) Advances in Neural Information Processing Systems, vol. 29, pp. 3630–3638. Curran Associates, Inc. (2016). http://papers.nips.cc/paper/6385-matching-networks-for-one-shot-learning.pdf

Toward Characteristic-Preserving Image-Based Virtual Try-On Network

Bochao Wang[1,2], Huabin Zheng[1,2], Xiaodan Liang[1(✉)], Yimin Chen[2], Liang Lin[1,2], and Meng Yang[1]

[1] Sun Yat-sen University, Guangzhou, China
{wangboch,zhhuab}@mail2.sysu.edu.cn
[2] SenseTime Group Limited, Beijing, China
xdliang328@gmail.com, chenyimin@sensetime.com, linliang@ieee.org,
yangm6@mail.sysu.edu.cn

Abstract. Image-based virtual try-on systems for fitting a new in-shop clothes into a person image have attracted increasing research attention, yet is still challenging. A desirable pipeline should not only transform the target clothes into the most fitting shape seamlessly but also preserve well the clothes identity in the generated image, that is, the key characteristics (e.g. texture, logo, embroidery) that depict the original clothes. However, previous image-conditioned generation works fail to meet these critical requirements towards the plausible virtual try-on performance since they fail to handle large spatial misalignment between the input image and target clothes. Prior work explicitly tackled spatial deformation using shape context matching, but failed to preserve clothing details due to its coarse-to-fine strategy. In this work, we propose a new fully-learnable Characteristic-Preserving Virtual Try-On Network (CP-VTON) for addressing all real-world challenges in this task. First, CP-VTON learns a thin-plate spline transformation for transforming the in-shop clothes into fitting the body shape of the target person via a new Geometric Matching Module (GMM) rather than computing correspondences of interest points as prior works did. Second, to alleviate boundary artifacts of warped clothes and make the results more realistic, we employ a Try-On Module that learns a composition mask to integrate the warped clothes and the rendered image to ensure smoothness. Extensive experiments on a fashion dataset demonstrate our CP-VTON achieves the state-of-the-art virtual try-on performance both qualitatively and quantitatively.

Keywords: Virtual try-on · Characteristic-preserving
Thin plate spline · Image alignment

1 Introduction

Online apparel shopping has huge commercial advantages compared to traditional shopping (e.g. time, choice, price) but lacks physical apprehension. To

© Springer Nature Switzerland AG 2018
V. Ferrari et al. (Eds.): ECCV 2018, LNCS 11217, pp. 607–623, 2018.
https://doi.org/10.1007/978-3-030-01261-8_36

create a shopping environment close to reality, virtual try-on technology has attracted a lot of interests recently by delivering product information similar to that obtained from direct product examination. It allows users to experience themselves wearing different clothes without efforts of changing them physically. This helps users to quickly judge whether they like a garment or not and make buying decisions, and improves sales efficiency of retailers. The traditional pipeline is to use computer graphics to build 3D models and render the output images since graphics methods provide precise control of geometric transformations and physical constraints. But these approaches require plenty of manual labor or expensive devices to collect necessary information for building 3D models and massive computations.

VITON   CP-VTON   VITON   CP-VTON   VITON   CP-VTON

Fig. 1. The proposed CP-VTON can generate more realistic image-based virtual try-on results that preserve well key characteristics of the in-shop clothes, compared to the state-of-the-art VITON [10].

More recently, the image-based virtual try-on system [10] without resorting to 3D information, provides a more economical solution and shows promising results by reformulating it as a conditional image generation problem. Given two images, one of a person and the other of an in-shop clothes, such pipeline aims to synthesize a new image that meets the following requirements: (a) the person is dressed in the new clothes; (b) the original body shape and pose are retained; (c) the clothing product with high-fidelity is warped smoothly and seamlessly connected with other parts; (d) the characteristics of clothing product, such as texture, logo and text, are well preserved, without any noticeable artifacts and distortions. Current research and advances in conditional image generation (e.g. image-to-image translation [5,6,12,20,34,38]) make it seem to be a natural approach of facilitating this problem. Besides the common pixel-to-pixel losses (e.g.

L1 or L2 losses) and perceptual loss [14], an adversarial loss [12] is used to alleviate the blurry issue in some degree, but still misses critical details. Furthermore, these methods can only handle the task with roughly aligned input-output pairs and fail to deal with large transformation cases. Such limitations hinder their application on this challenging virtual try-on task in the wild. One reason is the poor capability in preserving details when facing large geometric changes, e.g. conditioned on unaligned image [23]. The best practice in image-conditional virtual try-on is still a two-stage pipeline VITON [10]. But their performances are far from the plausible and desired generation, as illustrated in Fig. 1. We argue that the main reason lies in the imperfect shape-context matching for aligning clothes and body shape, and the inferior appearance merging strategy.

To address the aforementioned challenges, we present a new image-based method that successfully achieves the plausible try-on image syntheses while preserving cloth characteristics, such as texture, logo, text and so on, named as Characteristic-Preserving Image-based Virtual Try-On Network (CP-VTON). In particular, distinguished from the hand-crafted shape context matching, we propose a new learnable thin-plate spline transformation via a tailored convolutional neural network in order to align well the in-shop clothes with the target person. The network parameters are trained from paired images of in-shop clothes and a wearer, without the need of any explicit correspondences of interest points. Second, our model takes the aligned clothes and clothing-agnostic yet descriptive person representation proposed in [10] as inputs, and generates a pose-coherent image and a composition mask which indicates the details of aligned clothes kept in the synthesized image. The composition mask tends to utilize the information of aligned clothes and balances the smoothness of the synthesized image. Extensive experiments show that the proposed model handles well the large shape and pose transformations and achieves the state-of-art results on the dataset collected by Han et al. [10] in the image-based virtual try-on task.

Our contributions can be summarized as follows:

- We propose a new Characteristic-Preserving image-based Virtual Try-On Network (CP-VTON) that addresses the characteristic preserving issue when facing large spatial deformation challenge in the realistic virtual try-on task.
- Different from the hand-crafted shape context matching, our CP-VTON incorporates a full learnable thin-plate spline transformation via a new Geometric Matching Module to obtain more robust and powerful alignment.
- Given aligned images, a new Try-On Module is performed to dynamically merge rendered results and warped results.
- Significant superior performances in image-based virtual try-on task achieved by our CP-VTON have been extensively demonstrated by experiments on the dataset collected by Han et al. [10].

2   Related Work

2.1   Image Synthesis

Generative adversarial networks (GANs) [9] aim to model the real image distribution by forcing the generated samples to be indistinguishable from the real images. Conditional generative adversarial networks (cGANs) have shown impressive results on image-to-image translation, whose goal is to translate an input image from one domain to another domain [5,12,18,19,34,35,38]. Compared L1/L2 loss, which often leads to blurry images, the adversarial loss has become a popular choice for many image-to-image tasks. Recently, Chen and Koltun [3] suggest that the adversarial loss might be unstable for high-resolution image generation. We find the adversarial loss has little improvement in our model. In image-to-image translation tasks, there exists an implicit assumption that the input and output are roughly aligned with each other and they represent the same underlying structure. However, most of these methods have some problems when dealing with large spatial deformations between the conditioned image and the target one. Most of image-to image translation tasks conditioned on unaligned images [10,23,37], adopt a coarse-to-fine manner to enhance the quality of final results. To address the misalignment of conditioned images, Siarohit et al. [31] introduced a deformable skip connections in GAN, using the correspondences of the pose points. VITON [10] computes shape context thin-plate spline (TPS) transformation [2] between the mask of in-shop clothes and the predicted foreground mask. Shape context is a hand-craft feature for shape and the matching of two shapes is time-consumed. Besides, the computed TPS transformations are vulnerable to the predicted mask. Inspired by Rocco et al. [27], we design a convolutional neural network (CNN) to estimate a TPS transformation between in-shop clothes and the target image without any explicit correspondences of interest points.

2.2   Person Image Generation

Lassner et al. [17] introduced a generative model that can generate human parsing [8] maps and translate them into persons in clothing. But it is not clear how to control the generated fashion items. Zhao et al. [37] addressed a problem of generating multi-view clothing images based on a given clothing image of a certain view. PG2 [23] synthesizes the person images in arbitrary pose, which explicitly uses the target pose as a condition. Siarohit et al. [31] dealt the same task as PG2, but using the correspondences between the target pose and the pose of conditional image. The generated fashion items in [23,31,37], kept consistent with that of the conditional images. FashionGAN [39] changed the fashion items on a person and generated new outfits by text descriptions. The goal of virtual try-on is to synthesize a photo-realistic new image with a new piece of clothing product, while leaving out effects of the old one. Yoo et al. [36] generated in shop clothes conditioned on a person in clothing, rather than the reverse.

2.3   Virtual Try-On System

Most virtual try-on works are based on graphics models. Sekine et al. [30] introduced a virtual fitting system that captures 3D measurements of body shape. Chen et al. [4] used a SCAPE [1] body model to generate synthetic people. Pons-Moll et al. [26] used a 3D scanner to automatically capture real clothing and estimate body shape and pose. Compared to graphics models, image-based generative models are more computationally efficient. Jetchev and Bergmann [13] proposed a conditional analogy GAN to swap fashion articles, without other descriptive person representation. They didn't take pose variant into consideration, and during inference, they required the paired images of in-shop clothes and a wearer, which limits their practical scenarios. The most related work is VITON [10]. We all aim to synthesize photo-realistic image directly from 2D images. VITON addressed this problem with a coarse-to-fine framework and expected to capture the cloth deformation by a shape context TPS transformation. We propose an alignment network and a single pass generative framework, which preserving the characteristics of in-shop clothes.

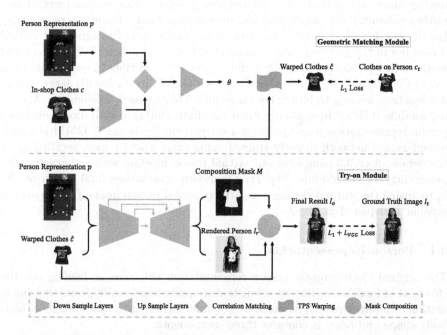

Fig. 2. An overview of our CP-VTON, containing two main modules. (a) Geometric Matching Module: the in-shop clothes c and input image representation p are aligned via a learnable matching module. (b) Try-On Module: it generates a composition mask M and a rendered person I_r. The final results I_o is composed by warped clothes $\hat{c}$ and the rendered person I_r with the composition mask M.

3   Characteristic-Preserving Virtual Try-On Network

We address the task of image-based virtual try-on as a conditional image generation problem. Generally, given a reference image I_i of a person wearing in clothes c_i and a target clothes c, the goal of CP-VTON is to synthesize a new image I_o of the wearer in the new cloth c_o, in which the body shape and pose of I_i are retained, the characteristics of target clothes c are reserved and the effects of the old clothes c_i are eliminated.

Training with sample triplets (I_i, c, I_t) where I_t is the ground truth of I_o and c is coupled with I_t wearing in clothes c_t, is straightforward but undesirable in practice. Because these triplets are difficult to collect. It is easier if I_i is same as I_t, which means that c, I_t pairs are enough. These paris are in abundance from shopping websites. But directly training on (I_t, c, I_t) harms the model generalization ability at testing phase when only decoupled inputs (I_i, c) are available. Prior work [10] addressed this dilemma by constructing a clothing-agnostic person representation p to eliminate the effects of source clothing item c_i. With (I_t, c, I_t) transformed into a new triplet form (p, c, I_t), training and testing phase are unified. We adopted this representation in our method and further enhance it by eliminating less information from reference person image. Details are described in Sect. 3.1. One of the challenges of image-based virtual try-on lies in the large spatial misalignment between in-shop clothing item and wearer's body. Existing network architectures for conditional image generation (e.g. FCN [21], UNet [28], ResNet [11]) lack the ability to handle large spatial deformation, leading to blurry try-on results. We proposed a Geometric Matching Module (GMM) to explicitly align the input clothes c with aforementioned person representation p and produce a warped clothes image $\hat{c}$. GMM is a end-to-end neural network directly trained using pixel-wise L1 loss. Sect. 3.2 gives the details. Sect. 3.3 completes our virtual try-on pipeline with a characteristic-preserving Try-On Module. The Try-On module synthesizes final try-on results I_o by fusing the warped clothes $\hat{c}$ and the rendered person image I_r. The overall pipeline is depicted in Fig. 2.

3.1   Person Representation

The original cloth-agnostic person representation [10] aims at leaving out the effects of old clothes c_i like its color, texture and shape, while preserving information of input person I_i as much as possible, including the person's face, hair, body shape and pose. It contains three components:

- Pose heatmap: an 18-channel feature map with each channel corresponding to one human pose keypoint, drawn as an 11×11 white rectangle.
- Body shape: a 1-channel feature map of a blurred binary mask that roughly covering different parts of human body.
- Reserved regions: an RGB image that contains the reserved regions to maintain the identity of a person, including face and hair.

These feature maps are all scaled to a fixed resolution 256×192 and concatenated together to form the cloth-agnostic person representation map p of k channels, where $k = 18 + 1 + 3 = 22$. We also utilize this representation in both our matching module and try-on module.

3.2 Geometric Matching Module

The classical approach for the geometry estimation task of image matching consists of three stages: (1) local descriptors (e.g. shape context [2], SIFT [22]) are extracted from both input images, (2) the descriptors are matched across images form a set of tentative correspondences, (3) these correspondences are used to robustly estimate the parameters of geometric model using RANSAC [7] or Hough voting [16,22].

Rocco et al. [27] mimics this process using differentiable modules so that it can be trainable end-to-end for geometry estimation tasks. Inspired by this work, we design a new Geometric Matching Module (GMM) to transform the target clothes c into warped clothes $\hat{c}$ which is roughly aligned with input person representation p. As illustrated in Fig. 2, our GMM consists of four parts: (1) two networks for extracting high-level features of p and c respectively. (2) a correlation layer to combine two features into a single tensor as input to the regressor network. (3) the regression network for predicting the spatial transformation parameters θ. (4) a Thin-Plate Spline (TPS) transformation module T for warping an image into the output $\hat{c} = T_\theta(c)$. The pipeline is end-to-end learnable and trained with sample triplets (p, c, c_t), under the pixel-wise L1 loss between the warped result $\hat{c}$ and ground truth c_t, where c_t is the clothes worn on the target person in I_t:

$$\mathcal{L}_{GMM}(\theta) = ||\hat{c} - c_t||_1 = ||T_\theta(c) - c_t||_1 \tag{1}$$

The key differences between our approach and Rocco et al. [27] are threefold. First, we trained from scratch rather than using a pretrained VGG network. Second, our training ground truths are acquired from wearer's real clothes rather than synthesized from simulated warping. Most importantly, our GMM is directly supervised under pixel-wise L1 loss between warping outputs and ground truth.

3.3 Try-On Module

Now that the warped clothes $\hat{c}$ is roughly aligned with the body shape of the target person, the goal of our Try-On module is to fuse $\hat{c}$ with the target person and for synthesizing the final try-on result.

One straightforward solution is directly pasting $\hat{c}$ onto target person image I_t. It has the advantage that the characteristics of warped clothes are fully preserved, but leads to an unnatural appearance at the boundary regions of clothes and undesirable occlusion of some body parts (e.g. hair, arms). Another solution widely adopted in conditional image generation is translating inputs to outputs by a single forward pass of some encoder-decoder networks, such as UNet [28], which is desirable for rendering seamless smooth images. However, It is impossible to perfectly align clothes with target body shape. Lacking explicit spatial deformation ability, even minor misalignment could make the UNet-rendered output blurry.

Our Try-On Module aims to combine the advantages of both approaches above. As illustrated in Fig. 2, given a concatenated input of person representation p and the warped clothes $\hat{c}$, UNet simultaneously renders a person image I_r and predicts a composition mask M. The rendered person I_r and the warped clothes $\hat{c}$ are then fused together using the composition mask M to synthesize the final try-on result I_o:

$$I_o = M \odot \hat{c} + (1 - M) \odot I_r \tag{2}$$

where $\odot$ represents element-wise matrix multiplication.

At training phase, given the sample triples (p, c, I_t), the goal of Try-On Module is to minimize the discrepancy between output I_o and ground truth I_t. We adopted the widely used strategy in conditional image generation problem that using a combination of L1 loss and VGG perceptual loss [14], where the VGG perceptual loss is defined as follows:

$$\mathcal{L}_{\mathrm{VGG}}(I_o, I_t) = \sum_{i=1}^{5} \lambda_i \|\phi_i(I_o) - \phi_i(I_t)\|_1 \tag{3}$$

where $\phi_i(I)$ denotes the feature map of image I of the i-th layer in the visual perception network ϕ, which is a VGG19 [32] pre-trained on ImageNet. The layer $i \geq 1$ stands for 'conv1_2', 'conv2_2', 'conv3_2', 'conv4_2', 'conv5_2', respectively.

Towards our goal of characteristic-preserving, we bias the composition mask M to select warped clothes as much as possible by applying a L1 regularization $\|1 - M\|_1$ on M. The overall loss function for Try-On Module (TOM) is:

$$\mathcal{L}_{\mathrm{TOM}} = \lambda_{L1}\|I_o - I_t\|_1 + \lambda_{vgg}\mathcal{L}_{\mathrm{VGG}}(\hat{I}, I) + \lambda_{mask}\|1 - M\|_1. \tag{4}$$

4 Experiments and Analysis

4.1 Dataset

We conduct our all experiments on the datasets collected by Han et al. [10]. It contains around 19,000 front-view woman and top clothing image pairs. There are 16253 cleaned pairs, which are split into a training set and a validation set with 14221 and 2032 pairs, respectively. We rearrange the images in the validation set into unpaired pairs as the testing set.

4.2 Quantitative Evaluation

We evaluate the quantitative performance of different virtual try-on methods via a human subjective perceptual study. Inception Score (IS) [29] is usually used as to quantitatively evaluate the image synthesis quality, but not suitable for evaluating this task for that it cannot reflect whether the details are preserved as described in [10]. We focus on the clothes with rich details since we are interested in characteristic-preservation, instead of evaluating on the whole testing set. For simplicity, we measure the detail richness of a clothing image by its total variation (TV) norm. It is appropriate for this dataset since the background is in pure color and the TV norm is only contributed by clothes itself, as illustrated in Fig. 3. We extracted 50 testing pairs with largest clothing TV norm named as **LARGE** to evaluate characteristic-preservation of our methods, and 50 pairs with smallest TV norm named as **SMALL** to ensure that our methods perform at least as good as previous state-of-the-art methods in simpler cases.

Fig. 3. From top to bottom, the TV norm values are increasing. Each line shows some clothes in the same level.

We conducted pairwise A/B tests on Amazon Mechanical Turk (AMT) platform. Specifically, given a person image and a target clothing image, the worker is asked to select the image which is more realistic and preserves more details of the target clothes between two virtual try-on results from different methods. There is no time limited for these jobs, and each job is assigned to 4 different workers. Human evaluation metric is computed in the same way as in [10].

4.3   Implementation Details

Training Setup. In all experiments, we use $\lambda_{L1} = \lambda_{vgg} = 1$. When composition mask is used, we set $\lambda_{mask} = 1$. We trained both Geometric Matching Module and Try-on Module for 200 K steps with batch size 4. We use Adam [15] optimizer with $\beta_1 = 0.5$ and $\beta_2 = 0.999$. Learning rate is first fixed at 0.0001 for 100 K steps and then linearly decays to zero for the remaining steps. All input images are resized to 256×192 and the output images have the same resolution.

Geometric Matching Module. Feature extraction networks for person representation and clothes have the similar structure, containing four 2-strided down-sampling convolutional layers, succeeded by two 1-strided ones, their numbers of

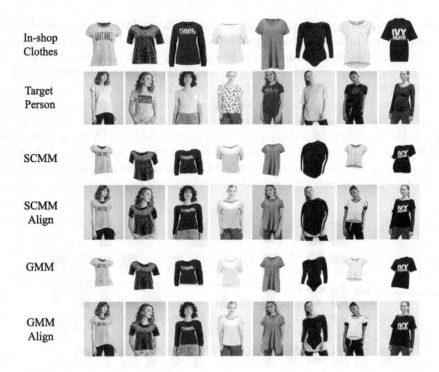

Fig. 4. Matching results of SCMM and GMM. Warped clothes are directly pasted onto target persons for visual checking. Our method is comparable with SCMM and produces less weird results.

filters being 64, 128, 256, 512, 512, respectively. The only difference is the number of input channels. Regression network contains two 2-strided convolutional layers, two 1-strided ones and one fully-connected output layer. The numbers of filters are 512, 256, 128, 64. The fully-connected layer predicts the x- and y-coordinate offsets of TPS anchor points, thus has an output size of $2 \times 5 \times 5 = 50$.

Try-On Module. We use a 12-layer UNet with six 2-strided down-sampling convolutional layers and six up-sampling layers. To alleviate so-called "checkerboard artifacts", we replace 2-strided deconvolutional layers normally used for up-sampling with the combination of nearest-neighbor interpolation layers and 1-strided convolutional layers, as suggested by [25]. The numbers of filters for down-sampling convolutional layers are 64, 128, 256, 512, 512, 512. The numbers of filters for up-sampling convolutional layers are 512, 512, 256, 128, 64, 4. Each convolutional layer is followed by an Instance Normalization layer [33] and Leaky ReLU [24], of which the slope is set to 0.2.

4.4   Comparison of Warping Results

Shape Context Matching Module (SCMM) uses hand-crafted descriptors and explicitly computes their correspondences using an iterative algorithm, which is time-consumed, while GMM runs much faster. In average, processing a sample pair takes GMM 0.06 s on GPU, 0.52 s on CPU, and takes SCMM 2.01 s on CPU.

Qualitative Results. Figure 4 demonstrates a qualitative comparison of SCMM and GMM. It shows that both modules are able to roughly align clothes with target person pose. However, SCMM tends to overly shrink a long sleeve into a "thin band", as shown in the 6-th column in Fig. 4. This is because SCMM merely relies on matched shape context descriptors on the boundary of cloths shape, while ignores the internal structures. Once there exist incorrect correspondences of descriptors, the warping results will be weird. In contrast, GMM takes full advantages of the learned rich representation of clothes and person images to determinate TPS transformation parameters and more robust for large shape differences (Fig. 5).

Quantitative Results. It is difficult to evaluate directly the quantitative performance of matching modules due to the lack of ground truth in the testing phase. Nevertheless, we can simply paste the warped clothes onto the original person image as a non-parametric warped synthesis method in [10]. We conduct a perceptual user study following the protocol described in Sect. 4.2, for these two warped synthesis methods. The synthesized by GMM are rated more realistic in 49.5% and 42.0% for **LARGE** and **SMALL**, which indicates that GMM is comparable to SCMM for shape alignment.

4.5   Comparison of Try-On Results

Qualitative Results. Figure 2 shows that our pipeline performs roughly the same as VITON when the patterns of target clothes are simpler. However, our pipeline preserves sharp and intact characteristic on clothes with rich details (e.g. texture, logo, embroidery) while VITON produces blurry results.

We argue that the failure of VITON lies in its coarse-to-fine strategy and the imperfect matching module. Precisely, VITON learns to synthesis a coarse person image at first, then to align the clothes with target person with shape context matching, then to produce a composition mask for fusing UNet rendered person with warped clothes and finally producing a refined result. After extensive training, the rendered person image has already a small VGG perceptual loss with respect to ground truth. On the other hand, the imperfect matching module introduces unavoidable minor misalignment between the warped clothes and ground truth, making the warped clothes unfavorable to perceptual loss. Taken together, when further refined by truncated perceptual loss, the composition mask will be biased towards selecting rendered person image rather than warped clothes, despite the regularization of the composition mask (Eq. 4). The VITON's "ragged" masks shown in Fig. 6 confirm this argument.

Our pipeline doesn't address the aforementioned issue by improving matching results, but rather sidesteps it by simultaneously learning to produce a UNet rendered person image and a composition mask. Before the rendered person image becomes favorable to loss function, the central clothing region of composition mask is biased towards warped clothes because it agrees more with ground

Fig. 5. Qualitative comparisons of VITON and CP-VTON. Our CP-VTON successfully preserve key details of in-shop clothes.

Table 1. Results of pairwise comparisons of images synthesized with **LARGE** and **SMALL** clothes by different models. Each column compares our approach with one of the baselines. Higher is better. The random chance is at 50%.

Data	VITON	CP-VTON (w/o mask)	CP-VTON (w/o L1 Loss)
LARGE	67.5%	72.5%	84.5%
SMALL	55.0%	42%	38.5%

truth in the early training stage. It is now the warped clothes rather than the rendered person image that takes the early advantage in the competition of mask selection. After that, the UNet learns to adaptively expose regions where UNet rendering is more suitable than directly pasting. Once the regions of hair and arms are exposed, rendered and seamlessly fused with warped clothes.

Quantitative Results. The first column of Table 1 shows that our pipeline surpasses VITON in the preserving the details of clothes using identical person representation. According to the table, our approach performs better than other methods, when dealing with rich details clothes.

In-shop Clothes   Target Person   Coarse Result   Warped Clothes   Composition Mask   Refined Result

Fig. 6. An example of VITON stage II. The composition mask tends to ignore the details of coarsely aligned clothes.

4.6   Discussion and Ablation Studies

Effects of Composition Mask. To empirically justify the design of composition mask and mask L1 regularization (Eq. 4) in our pipeline, we compare it with two variants for ablation studies: (1): mask composition is also removed and the final results are directly rendered by UNet as CP-VTON (w/o mask). (2): the mask composition is used but the mask L1 regularization is removed as CP-VTON (w/o L1 Loss);

As shown in Fig. 6, even though the warped clothes are roughly aligned with target person, CP-VTON (w/o mask) still loses characteristic details and produces blurry results. This verifies that encoder-decoder network architecture like UNet fails to handle even minor spatial deformation.

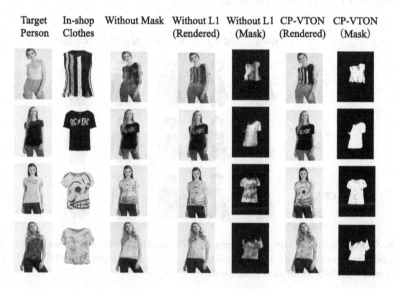

| Target Person | In-shop Clothes | Without Mask | Without L1 (Rendered) | Without L1 (Mask) | CP-VTON (Rendered) | CP-VTON (Mask) |

Fig. 7. Ablation studies on composition mask and mask L1 loss. Without mask composition, UNet cannot handle well even minor misalignment and produces undesirable try-on results. Without L1 regularization on mask, it tends to select UNet-rendered person, leading to blurry results as well.

Though integrated with mask composition, CP-VTON (no L1) performs as poorly as variant CP-VTON (w/o mask. Figure 7 shows that composition mask tends to select rendered person image without L1 regularization. This verifies that even minor misalignment introduces large perceptual disagreement between warped clothes and ground truth.

Robustness Against Minor Misalignment. In Sect. 4.5 we argue that VITON is vulnerable to minor misalignment due to its coarse-to-fine strategy, while our pipeline sidesteps imperfect alignment by simultaneously producing rendered person and composition mask. This is further clarified below in a controlled condition with simulated warped clothes.

Specifically, rather than real warped clothes produced by matching module, we use the wore clothes collected from person images to simulate perfect alignment results. We then train VITON stage II, our proposed variant CP-VTON (w/o mask) and our pipeline. For VITON stage II, we synthesize coarse person image with its source code and released model checkpoint.

It is predictable that with this "perfect matching module", all the three methods could achieve excellent performance in training and validation phase, where input samples are paired. Next is the interesting part: what if the perfect alignment is randomly perturbed within a range of N pixels, to simulate an imperfect matching module? With the perturbation getting greater $(N = 0, 5, 10, 15, 20)$, how fast will the try-on performance decay?

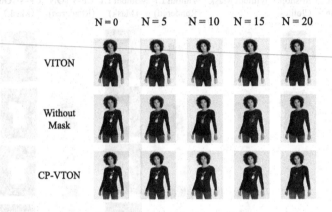

Fig. 8. Comparisons on the robustness of three methods against minor misalignment simulated by random shift within radius N. As N increasing, results of CP-VTON decays more slightly than other methods.

These questions are answered in Fig. 8. As we applying greater perturbation, the performance of both VITON stage II and CP-VTON (w/o mask) decays quickly. In contrast, our pipeline shows robustness against perturbation and manages to preserve detailed characteristic.

Fig. 9. Some failure cases of our CP-VTON.

Failure Cases. Figure 9 shows three failure cases of our CP-VTON method caused by (1) improperly preserved shape information of old clothes, (2) rare poses and (3) inner side of the clothes undistinguishable from the outer side, respectively.

5 Conclusions

In this paper, we propose a fully learnable image-based virtual try-on pipeline towards the characteristic-preserving image generation, named as CP-VTON, including a new geometric matching module and a try-on module with the new merging strategy. The geometric matching module aims at aligning in-shop clothes and target person body with large spatial displacement. Given aligned clothes, the try-on module learns to preserve well the detailed characteristic of clothes. Extensive experiments show the overall CP-VTON pipeline produces high-fidelity virtual try-on results that retain well key characteristics of in-shop clothes. Our CP-VTON achieves state-of-the-art performance on the dataset collected by Han et al. [10] both qualitatively and quantitatively.

References

1. Anguelov, D., Srinivasan, P., Koller, D., Thrun, S., Rodgers, J., Davis, J.: SCAPE: shape completion and animation of people. In: ACM Transactions on Graphics (TOG), vol. 24, pp. 408–416. ACM (2005)
2. Belongie, S., Malik, J., Puzicha, J.: Shape matching and object recognition using shape contexts. IEEE Trans. Pattern Anal. Mach. Intell. **24**(4), 509–522 (2002)
3. Chen, Q., Koltun, V.: Photographic image synthesis with cascaded refinement networks. In: The IEEE International Conference on Computer Vision (ICCV), vol. 1 (2017)
4. Chen, W., et al.: Synthesizing training images for boosting human 3D pose estimation. In: 2016 Fourth International Conference on 3D Vision (3DV), pp. 479–488. IEEE (2016)
5. Choi, Y., Choi, M., Kim, M., Ha, J.W., Kim, S., Choo, J.: Stargan: Unified generative adversarial networks for multi-domain image-to-image translation. arXiv preprint arXiv:1711.09020 (2017)
6. Deng, Z., et al.: Structured generative adversarial networks. In: Advances in Neural Information Processing Systems, pp. 3899–3909 (2017)
7. Fischler, M.A., Bolles, R.C.: Random sample consensus: a paradigm for model fitting with applications to image analysis and automated cartography. In: Readings in computer vision, pp. 726–740. Elsevier (1987)
8. Gong, K., Liang, X., Shen, X., Lin, L.: Look into person: self-supervised structure-sensitive learning and a new benchmark for human parsing. arXiv preprint arXiv:1703.05446 (2017)
9. Goodfellow, I., et al.: Generative adversarial nets. In: Advances in Neural Information Processing Systems, pp. 2672–2680 (2014)
10. Han, X., Wu, Z., Wu, Z., Yu, R., Davis, L.S.: Viton: an image-based virtual try-on network. arXiv preprint arXiv:1711.08447 (2017)

11. He, K., Zhang, X., Ren, S., Sun, J.: Deep residual learning for image recognition. In: CVPR, pp. 770–778 (2016)
12. Isola, P., Zhu, J.Y., Zhou, T., Efros, A.A.: Image-to-image translation with conditional adversarial networks. arXiv preprint (2017)
13. Jetchev, N., Bergmann, U.: The conditional analogy GAN: swapping fashion articles on people images. arXiv preprint arXiv:1709.04695 (2017)
14. Johnson, J., Alahi, A., Fei-Fei, L.: Perceptual losses for real-time style transfer and super-resolution. In: Leibe, B., Matas, J., Sebe, N., Welling, M. (eds.) ECCV 2016. LNCS, vol. 9906, pp. 694–711. Springer, Cham (2016). https://doi.org/10.1007/978-3-319-46475-6_43
15. Kinga, D., Adam, J.B.: A method for stochastic optimization. In: International Conference on Learning Representations (ICLR) (2015)
16. Lamdan, Y., Schwartz, J.T., Wolfson, H.J.: Object recognition by affine invariant matching. In: Proceedings of Computer Society Conference on Computer Vision and Pattern Recognition, CVPR 1988, pp. 335–344. IEEE (1988)
17. Lassner, C., Pons-Moll, G., Gehler, P.V.: A generative model of people in clothing. arXiv preprint arXiv:1705.04098 (2017)
18. Li, J., Liang, X., Wei, Y., Xu, T., Feng, J., Yan, S.: Perceptual generative adversarial networks for small object detection. In: IEEE CVPR (2017)
19. Liang, X., Lee, L., Dai, W., Xing, E.P.: Dual motion GAN for future-flow embedded video prediction. In: IEEE International Conference on Computer Vision (ICCV), vol. 1 (2017)
20. Liang, X., Zhang, H., Xing, E.P.: Generative semantic manipulation with contrasting GAN. arXiv preprint arXiv:1708.00315 (2017)
21. Long, J., Shelhamer, E., Darrell, T.: Fully convolutional networks for semantic segmentation. In: CVPR, pp. 3431–3440 (2015)
22. Lowe, D.G.: Distinctive image features from scale-invariant keypoints. Int. J. Comput. Vis. 60(2), 91–110 (2004)
23. Ma, L., Jia, X., Sun, Q., Schiele, B., Tuytelaars, T., Van Gool, L.: Pose guided person image generation. In: Advances in Neural Information Processing Systems, pp. 405–415 (2017)
24. Maas, A.L., Hannun, A.Y., Ng, A.Y.: Rectifier nonlinearities improve neural network acoustic models. In: Proceedings of ICML, vol. 30, p. 3 (2013)
25. Odena, A., Dumoulin, V., Olah, C.: Deconvolution and checkerboard artifacts. Distill 1(10), e3 (2016)
26. Pons-Moll, G., Pujades, S., Hu, S., Black, M.J.: Clothcap: seamless 4D clothing capture and retargeting. ACM Trans. Graph. (TOG) 36(4), 73 (2017)
27. Rocco, I., Arandjelovic, R., Sivic, J.: Convolutional neural network architecture for geometric matching. In: Proceedings of CVPR, vol. 2 (2017)
28. Ronneberger, O., Fischer, P., Brox, T.: U-Net: convolutional networks for biomedical image segmentation. In: Navab, N., Hornegger, J., Wells, W.M., Frangi, A.F. (eds.) MICCAI 2015. LNCS, vol. 9351, pp. 234–241. Springer, Cham (2015). https://doi.org/10.1007/978-3-319-24574-4_28
29. Salimans, T., Goodfellow, I., Zaremba, W., Cheung, V., Radford, A., Chen, X.: Improved techniques for training GANs. In: NIPS, pp. 2234–2242 (2016)
30. Sekine, M., Sugita, K., Perbet, F., Stenger, B., Nishiyama, M.: Virtual fitting by single-shot body shape estimation. In: International Conference on 3D Body Scanning Technologies, pp. 406–413. Citeseer (2014)
31. Siarohin, A., Sangineto, E., Lathuiliere, S., Sebe, N.: Deformable GANs for pose-based human image generation. arXiv preprint arXiv:1801.00055 (2017)

32. Simonyan, K., Zisserman, A.: Very deep convolutional networks for large-scale image recognition. arXiv preprint arXiv:1409.1556 (2014)
33. Ulyanov, D., Vedaldi, A., Lempitsky, V.: Improved texture networks: maximizing quality and diversity in feed-forward stylization and texture synthesis. In: Proceedings of CVPR (2017)
34. Wang, T.C., Liu, M.Y., Zhu, J.Y., Tao, A., Kautz, J., Catanzaro, B.: High-resolution image synthesis and semantic manipulation with conditional GANs. arXiv preprint arXiv:1711.11585 (2017)
35. Yang, L., Liang, X., Xing, E.: Unsupervised real-to-virtual domain unification for end-to-end highway driving. arXiv preprint arXiv:1801.03458 (2018)
36. Yoo, D., Kim, N., Park, S., Paek, A.S., Kweon, I.S.: Pixel-level domain transfer. In: Leibe, B., Matas, J., Sebe, N., Welling, M. (eds.) ECCV 2016. LNCS, vol. 9912, pp. 517–532. Springer, Cham (2016). https://doi.org/10.1007/978-3-319-46484-8_31
37. Zhao, B., Wu, X., Cheng, Z.Q., Liu, H., Feng, J.: Multi-view image generation from a single-view. arXiv preprint arXiv:1704.04886 (2017)
38. Zhu, J.Y., Park, T., Isola, P., Efros, A.A.: Unpaired image-to-image translation using cycle-consistent adversarial networks. arXiv preprint arXiv:1703.10593 (2017)
39. Zhu, S., Fidler, S., Urtasun, R., Lin, D., Loy, C.C.: Be your own prada: fashion synthesis with structural coherence. arXiv preprint arXiv:1710.07346 (2017)

Deep Cross-Modality Adaptation via Semantics Preserving Adversarial Learning for Sketch-Based 3D Shape Retrieval

Jiaxin Chen[1,2] and Yi Fang[1,2(✉)]

[1] NYU Multimedia and Visual Computing Lab,
Department of Electrical and Computer Engineering,
New York University Abu Dhabi, Abu Dhabi, UAE
chenjiaxinX@gmail.com, yfang@nyu.edu
[2] Department of Electrical and Computer Engineering,
NYU Tandon School of Engineering, New York, USA

Abstract. Due to the large cross-modality discrepancy between 2D sketches and 3D shapes, retrieving 3D shapes by sketches is a significantly challenging task. To address this problem, we propose a novel framework to learn a discriminative deep cross-modality adaptation model in this paper. Specifically, we first separately adopt two metric networks, following two deep convolutional neural networks (CNNs), to learn modality-specific discriminative features based on an importance-aware metric learning method. Subsequently, we explicitly introduce a cross-modality transformation network to compensate for the divergence between two modalities, which can transfer features of 2D sketches to the feature space of 3D shapes. We develop an adversarial learning based method to train the transformation model, by simultaneously enhancing the holistic correlations between data distributions of two modalities, and mitigating the local semantic divergences through minimizing a cross-modality mean discrepancy term. Experimental results on the SHREC 2013 and SHREC 2014 datasets clearly show the superior retrieval performance of our proposed model, compared to the state-of-the-art approaches.

Keywords: Sketch-based 3D shape retrieval
Cross-modality transformation · Adversarial learning
Importance-aware metric learning

1 Introduction

In the last few years, there has been an explosive growth of 3D shape data, due to increasing demands from real industrial applications, such as virtual reality, LiDAR based autonomous vehicles. 3D shape related techniques have emerged as extremely hot research topics recently. Retrieving a certain category of 3D shapes from a given database is one of the fundamental problems for 3D shape

© Springer Nature Switzerland AG 2018
V. Ferrari et al. (Eds.): ECCV 2018, LNCS 11217, pp. 624–640, 2018.
https://doi.org/10.1007/978-3-030-01261-8_37

based applications. A lot of efforts have been devoted to 3D shape retrieval by 3D models [29, 31], which are intuitively straightforward, but difficult to acquire. Alternatively, freehand sketch is a more convenient way for human to interact with data collection and processing systems, especially with the sharply increased use of touch-pad devices such as smart phones and tablet computers. As a consequence, sketch-based 3D shape retrieval, *i.e.*, searching 3D shapes queried by sketches, has attracted more and more attentions [3, 15, 28, 30].

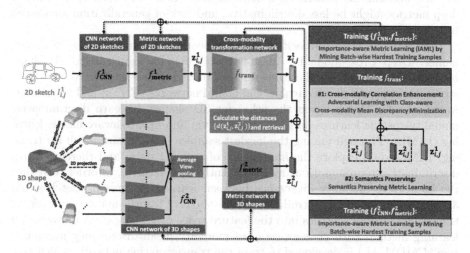

Fig. 1. Framework of our proposed method. Our model consists of the CNN network f_{CNN}^1 and metric network f_{metric}^1 of 2D sketches, the CNN network f_{CNN}^2 and metric network f_{metric}^2 of rendered images of 3D shapes, together with the cross-modality transformation network f_{trans}. The CNN and metric networks for each single modality (*i.e.*, 2D sketches or 3D shapes) is trained by importance-aware metric learning through mining the hardest training samples. The cross transformation network f_{trans} is trained by enforcing features of sketches to be semantics preserving after adaptation. Simultaneously, an adversarial learning with cross-modality mean discrepancy minimization is employed to enhance both the local and holistic correlations between data distributions of transformed features of sketches and features of 3D shapes.

Despite of its succinctness and convenience to acquire, freehand sketches remain two disadvantages in the application of 3D shape retrieval, making the sketch-based 3D shape retrieval an extremely challenging task. Firstly, sketches are usually drawn subjectively in uncontrolled environments, resulting in *severe intra-class variations* as shown in Fig. 3. Secondly, sketches and 3D shapes have heterogenous data structures, which leads to *large cross-modality divergences*.

A variety of models have been proposed to address the aforementioned two issues, which can be roughly divided into two categories, *i.e.*, representation based methods and matching based methods. The first category aims to extract robust features for both sketches and 3D shapes [3, 4, 12, 15, 28, 30, 35, 36]. However, due to the heterogeneity of sketches and 3D shapes, it is quite difficult to achieve modality-invariant discriminative representations. On the other hand, matching based methods focus on developing effective models for calculating similarities or distances between sketches and 3D shapes, among which deep metric learning based models [2,28,30] have achieved the state-of-the-art performance. Nevertheless, these methods fail to explore the varying importance of different training samples. Besides, they can merely enhance local cross-modality correlations, by selecting data pairs or triplets across modalities, while not taking into account the holistic data distributions. As a consequence, the learned deep metrics might be less discriminative, and lack of generalization for unseen test data.

To overcome the drawbacks of existing works, we propose a novel model, namely Deep Cross-modality Adaptation (DCA), for sketch-based 3D shape retrieval. Figure 1 shows the framework of our proposed model. We first construct two separate deep convolutional neural networks (CNNs) and metric networks, one for sketches and the other for 3D shapes, to learn discriminative modality-specific features for each modality via importance-aware metric learning (IAML). Through mining the hardest samples in each mini-batch for training, IAML could explore the importance of training data, and therefore learn discriminative representations more efficiently. Furthermore, in order to reduce the large cross-modality divergence between learned features of sketches and 3D shapes, we explicitly introduce a cross-modality transformation network, to transfer features of sketches into the feature space of 3D shapes. An adversarial learning method with class-aware cross-modality mean discrepancy minimization (CMDM-AL) is developed to train the transformation network, which acts as a generator. Since CMDM-AL is able to enhance correlations between distributions of transferred data of sketches and data of 3D shapes, our model can compensate for the cross-modality discrepancy in a holistic way. IAML is also applied to the transformed data, in order to further preserve semantic structures of sketch data after adaptation. The main contributions of this paper are three-fold:

(1) We propose a novel deep cross-modality adaptation model via semantics preserving adversarial learning. To our best knowledge, this work is the first one that incorporates adversarial learning into sketch-based 3D shape retrieval.
(2) We develop a new adversarial learning based method for training the deep cross-modality adaptation network, which simultaneously reduces the holistic cross-modality discrepancy of data distributions, and enhances semantic correlations of local data batches across modalities.
(3) We significantly boost the performance of existing state-of-the-art sketch-based 3D shape retrieval methods on two large benchmark datasets.

2   Related Work

In the literature, most of existing works on sketch-based 3D shape retrieval mainly concentrate on building modality-invariant representations for sketches and 3D shapes, and developing discriminative matching models. Various hand-craft features are employed, such as Zernike moments, coutour-based Fourier descriptor, eccentricity feature and circularity feature [16], the chordal axis transform based shape descriptor [32], HoG-SIFT features [33], the local improved Pyramid of Histograms of Orientation Gradients (iPHOG) [14], the sparse coding spatial pyramid matching feature (ScSPM), local depth scale-invariant feature transform (LD-SIFT) [36]. Besides, many learning-based features are developed, including bag-of-features (BoF) with Gabor local line based features (GALIF) [13], dense SIFT with BOF [4]. Meanwhile, tremendous matching approaches have also been developed, such as manifold ranking [4], dynamic time warping [32], sparse coding based matching [33] and adaptive view clustering [12,14].

Recently, various deep models have been developed for both feature extraction and matching, which are closely related to our proposed method. In [28], two Siamese CNNs were employed to learn discriminative features of sketches and 3D shapes by minimizing within-modality and cross-modality losses. In [36], the pyramid cross-domain neural networks were utilized to compensate for cross-domain divergences. In [2,31], Siamese metric networks were applied to minimize both within-modality and cross-modality intra-class distances whilst maximizing inter-class distances. In [31], the Wasserstein barycenters were additionally employed to aggregate multi-view deep features of rendered images from 3D models. However, these methods only reduced the local cross-modality divergence. They failed to remove the shift of data distributions across modalities. In contrast, our proposed model employs an adversarial learning based method to mitigate the discrepancy between distributions of two modalities in a holistic way, whilst addressing the local divergence issues by introducing a class-aware mean discrepancy term. Moreover, we apply IAML to mine importance of different training samples, which has also been ignored by current works.

Another branch of works related to our work is the cross-domain adaptation [1,5,20,27], especially the supervised discriminative adversarial learning for domain adaptation. In [5,17,18,27], a variety of adversarial discriminative models were developed for domain adaptation. The basic idea of these methods is to remove the domain shift between the source and target domains, by employing a domain discriminator and an adversarial loss. However, these works concentrate on scenarios where few labeled data are available in the target domain (despite abundant labeled data in the source domain), and are unable to jointly explore local discriminative semantic structures for both domains, making them unsuitable for our task. In [34], the authors also explicitly adopted a transformation network to transfer data from source domain to the target domain, where the cross-domain divergence is mitigated by an adversarial loss. However, they used hand crafted features, while our model employs deep CNNs to learn discriminative modality-specific features, and integrates them with the transformation network as a whole. Moreover, we introduce a class-aware cross-modality mean discrepancy term to the original adversarial loss. This term can enhance semantic correlations of data distributions across modalities as well as remove domain shift, which is largely neglected by existing works.

3   Deep Cross-Modality Adaptation

As illustrated in Fig. 1, our proposed framework mainly consists of five components, including the CNN networks for 2D sketches (denoted by f^1_{CNN}) and for 3D shapes (denoted by f^2_{CNN}), fully connected metric networks for 2D sketches (denoted by f^1_{metric}) and for 3D shapes (denoted by f^2_{metric}), together with the cross-modality transformation network f_{trans}, of which the parameters are $\theta^1_{\text{CNN}}, \theta^2_{\text{CNN}}, \theta^1_{\text{metric}}, \theta^2_{\text{metric}}$ and θ_{trans}, respectively.

Similar to most existing deep learning methods, we train our model by mini-batches. In order to depict our own method more conveniently, we build image batches from the whole training data in a slightly different way from random sampling. Specifically, for 2D sketches, we first select C classes randomly, and then collect K images for each class. The selected images finally comprise a mini-batch $\mathcal{I}^1 = \{I^1_{1,1}, \cdots, I^1_{1,K}, \cdots, I^1_{C,1}, \cdots, I^1_{C,K}\}$ of size $C \times K$, of which the corresponding class labels are denoted by $\mathbf{Y}^1 = \{y_1, \cdots, y_1, \cdots, y_C, \cdots, y_C\}$. Following the same way, a batch of 3D shapes $\mathcal{O} = \{O_{1,1}, \cdots, O_{1,K}, \cdots, O_{C,1}, \cdots, O_{C,K}\}$ is constructed, together with labels $\mathbf{Y}^2 = \{y_1, \cdots, y_1, \cdots, y_C, \cdots, y_C\}$. To characterize a 3D shape, we utilize the widely used multi-view representation as in [2, 24, 30], i.e., projecting a 3D shape to N_v grayscale images from N_v rendered views that are evenly divided around the 3D shape. The pixel color of the grayscale image is determined by interpolating the reflected intensity of polygon vertices of a 3D shape, via the Phong reflection model [19]. Thereafter, we can represent $\mathcal{O}$ as a batch of images $\mathcal{I}^2 = \{\mathbf{I}^2_{1,1}, \cdots, \mathbf{I}^2_{1,K}, \cdots, \mathbf{I}^2_{C,1}, \cdots, \mathbf{I}^2_{C,K}\}$, where $\mathbf{I}^2_{i,j} = \{I^2_{i,j,v}\}^{N_v}_{v=1}$ consists of N_v ($N_v = 12$ is used in our paper) 2D rendered images of the 3D shape $O_{i,j}$.

As demonstrated in Fig. 1, we train the CNN and metric networks for sketches, i.e., f^1_{CNN} and f^1_{metric}, jointly by adopting an importance-aware metric learning (IAML). This method could explore hardest training samples within a mini-batch. The CNN and metric networks for 3D shapes, i.e., f^2_{CNN} and f^2_{metric}, are also trained in the same way. The cross-modality transformation network θ_{trans} is learned by preserving semantic structures of transformed features, and employing an adversarial learning based training strategy with class-aware cross-modality mean discrepancy minimization.

In the rest of this paper, we will elaborate the training details about the proposed method, including the importance-aware metric learning, the semantic adversarial learning, and the optimization algorithm. Without loss of generality, all loss functions are formulated based on image batches $\mathcal{I}^1$ and $\mathcal{I}^2$ throughout this paper, which can be easily extended to the whole training data.

3.1   Importance-Aware Feature Learning

Given a mini-batch $\mathcal{I}^m$, after successively passing $\mathcal{I}^m$ through the CNN network f^m_{CNN} and the metric network f^m_{metric}, we can obtain a set of feature vectors:

$$\mathbf{Z}^m = \{\mathbf{z}^m_{1,1}, \cdots, \mathbf{z}^m_{1,K}, \cdots, \mathbf{z}^m_{C,1}, \cdots, \mathbf{z}^m_{C,K}\},$$

where $m \in \{\mathbf{1}, \mathbf{2}\}$, and for $i = 1, \cdots, C$, $j = 1, \cdots, K$

$$\mathbf{z}_{i,j}^1 = f_{\mathbf{metric}}^1 \left(f_{\mathbf{CNN}}^1 (I_{i,j}^1) \right), \mathbf{z}_{i,j}^2 = f_{\mathbf{metric}}^2 \left(f_{\mathbf{CNN}}^2 (\mathbf{I}_{i,j}^2) \right).$$

Ideally, in order to learn discriminative features for each modality (*i.e.*, the 2D sketches or the 3D shapes), the inter-class distances within the batch $\mathbf{Z}^m$ need to be larger than the intra-class distances. To achieve this, we adopt the following loss function for importance-aware metric learning [8]:

$$L_{IAML}^m (\{\boldsymbol{\theta}_{\mathbf{CNN}}^m, \boldsymbol{\theta}_{\mathbf{metric}}^m\}; \mathbf{Z}^m)$$
$$= \sum_i^C \sum_{j=1}^K \max \left(0, \eta - \left[\left\| \mathbf{z}_{i,j}^m - \mathbf{z}_{i^*,n^*}^m \right\|_2 - \left\| \mathbf{z}_{i,j}^m - \mathbf{z}_{i,p^*}^m \right\|_2 \right] \right), \quad (1)$$

where

$$\mathbf{z}_{i^*,n^*}^m = \underset{i' \in \{1,\cdots,C\}, y_{i'} \neq y_i, n \in \{1,\cdots,K\}}{\operatorname{argmin}} \left\| \mathbf{z}_{i,j}^m - \mathbf{z}_{i',n}^m \right\|_2, \quad (2)$$

$$\mathbf{z}_{i,p^*}^m = \underset{p \in \{1,\cdots,K\}, p \neq j}{\operatorname{argmax}} \left\| \mathbf{z}_{i,j}^m - \mathbf{z}_{i,p}^m \right\|_2, \quad (3)$$

and $\eta > 0$ is a constant.

As can be seen from Eq. (2), for a certain anchor point $\mathbf{z}_{i,j}^m$, $\mathbf{z}_{i^*,n^*}^m \in \mathbf{Z}^m$ is the sample that has the minimal Euclidean distance to $\mathbf{z}_{i,j}^m$ among those samples from different classes. And from Eq. (3), we can see that $\mathbf{z}_{i,p^*}^m$ is the sample that has the maximal Euclidean distance to $\mathbf{z}_{i,j}^m$, among samples belonging to the same class as $\mathbf{z}_{i,j}^m$. In other words, $\left\| \mathbf{z}_{i,j}^m - \mathbf{z}_{i^*,n^*}^m \right\|_2$ and $\left\| \mathbf{z}_{i,j}^m - \mathbf{z}_{i,p^*}^m \right\|_2$ indicate the largest inter-class Euclidean distance and the minimal intra-class Euclidean distance with respect to $\mathbf{z}_{i,j}^m$ within the batch $\mathbf{Z}^m$, respectively. Therefore, $\mathbf{z}_{i,p^*}^m$ and $\mathbf{z}_{i^*,n^*}^m$ are the batch-wise *"hardest positive"* and the *"hardest negative"* samples w.r.t. $\mathbf{z}_{i,j}^m$, and should be given higher importance during training. Existing deep metric learning based models [2,31] equally treat all training samples. In contrast, we apply IAML to explore the hardest positive and negative training samples within a mini-batch, whilst enforcing them to be consistent with semantics. As a result, our method can learn discriminative features more efficiently.

By minimizing L_{IAML}^m in Eq. (1), $\left\| \mathbf{z}_{i,j}^m - \mathbf{z}_{i^*,n^*}^m \right\|_2 - \left\| \mathbf{z}_{i,j}^m - \mathbf{z}_{i,p^*}^m \right\|_2$ are forced to be greater than η, *i.e.*, $\left\| \mathbf{z}_{i,j}^m - \mathbf{z}_{i^*,n^*}^m \right\|_2 - \left\| \mathbf{z}_{i,j}^m - \mathbf{z}_{i,p^*}^m \right\|_2 > \eta$. That is to say, by minimizing L_{IAML}^m, the minimal inter-class distance is compelled to be larger than the maximal intra-class distance in the feature space, whilst keeping a certain margin η. Consequently, we can train the CNN network $f_{\mathbf{CNN}}^m$ and the metric network $f_{\mathbf{metric}}^m$ to generate discriminative features for each modality.

3.2   Cross-Modality Transformation Based on Adversarial Learning

By applying the importance-aware metric learning via minimizing the losses L_{IAML}^1 and L_{IAML}^2, we can learn discriminative features for sketches and shapes, *i.e.*, $\{\mathbf{z}^1_{i,j}\}$ and $\{\mathbf{z}^2_{i,j}\}$, respectively. However, due to the large discrepancy between data distributions of different modalities, directly using $\{\mathbf{z}^1_{i,j}\}$ and $\{\mathbf{z}^2_{i,j}\}$ for cross-modality retrieval will result in extremely poor performance.

To address this problem, we propose a cross-modality transformation network $f_{\mathbf{trans}}$, in order to adapt the learnt features of 2D sketches to the feature space of 3D shapes with cross-modality discrepancies removal.

Suppose $\mathbf{Z}^t = \{\mathbf{z}^t_{i,j}\}$ is the transformed features of sketches $\mathbf{Z}^1 = \{\mathbf{z}^1_{i,j}\}$ with class labels $\mathbf{Y}^t = \{y_1, \cdots, y_1, \cdots, y_C, \cdots, y_C\}$, where $\mathbf{z}^t_{i,j} = f_{\mathbf{trans}}(\mathbf{z}^1_{i,j}|\boldsymbol{\theta}_{\mathbf{trans}})$ for $\forall i \in \{1, \cdots, C\}$, and $j \in \{1, \cdots, K\}$. Ideally, the transformed features $\{\mathbf{z}^t_{i,j}\}$ are expected to have the following properties, in order to guarantee good performance for the cross-modality retrieval task:

(1) $\{\mathbf{z}^t_{i,j}\}$ should be *semantics preserving*, *i.e.*, maintaining small intra-class distances and large inter-class distances.
(2) $\{\mathbf{z}^t_{i,j}\}$ should have *correlated data distribution* with $\{\mathbf{z}^2_{i,j}\}$, *i.e.*, the learnt features of 3D shapes.

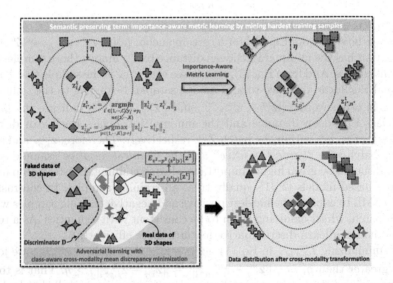

Fig. 2. Illustration on training the cross-modality transformation network. Importance-aware Metric Learning is applied to the transformed features of sketches to preserve semantic structures. An adversarial learning based method is developed to reduce the divergence between distributions of two modalities (*i.e.*, sketches and 3D shapes). A class-aware mean discrepancy term is simultaneously minimized to further strengthened correlations between local batch-wise features across modalities. Here, shapes with solid (dashed) bounding boxes indicate faked data of 3D shapes (transformed sketch data). Shapes without bounding boxes indicate real data of 3D shapes.)

The first property aims to compel the transformed features to preserve semantics, whilst the second attempts to remove the cross-modality discrepancy through strengthening correlations between data distributions of two modalities.

As shown in Fig. 2, we introduce a semantics preserving term by repeatedly utilizing the importance-aware metric learning to accomplish (1). And in order to achieve (2), we employ a cross-modality correlation enhancement term based on adversarial learning with class-aware cross-modality mean discrepancy minimization. We will provide details about the aforementioned two terms in the rest of this section.

Semantics Preserving Term. In order to preserve semantic structures, *i.e.*, keeping small (large) intra-class (inter-class) distances, we apply the loss of Importance-aware Metric Learning previously introduced to transformed data:

$$L_{SeP}\left(\boldsymbol{\theta_{\mathbf{trans}}}\right) = \sum_{i=1}^{C}\sum_{j=1}^{K}\max\left(0, \eta - \left[\left\|\mathbf{z}_{i,j}^{t} - \mathbf{z}_{i^*,n^*}^{t}\right\|_{2} - \left\|\mathbf{z}_{i,j}^{t} - \mathbf{z}_{i,p^*}^{t}\right\|_{2}\right]\right), \quad (4)$$

where

$$\mathbf{z}_{i^*,n^*}^{t} = \operatorname*{argmin}_{i' \in \{1,\cdots,C\}, y_{i'} \neq y_i, n \in \{1,\cdots,K\}} \left\|\mathbf{z}_{i,j}^{t} - \mathbf{z}_{i',n}^{t}\right\|_{2}, \quad (5)$$

$$\mathbf{z}_{i,p^*}^{t} = \operatorname*{argmax}_{p \in \{1,\cdots,K\}, p \neq j} \left\|\mathbf{z}_{i,j}^{t} - \mathbf{z}_{i,p}^{t}\right\|_{2}, \quad (6)$$

and $\eta > 0$ is a constant.

Cross-Modality Correlation Enhancement Term. Generative adversarial networks (GANs) have recently emerged as an effective method to generate synthetic data [6]. The basic idea is to train two competing networks, a generator G and a discriminator D, based on game theory. The generator G is trained to sample from the data distribution $p_{\mathbf{x}}(\mathbf{x})$ from the vector of noise $\mathbf{v}$. The discriminator D is trained to distinguish synthetic data generated by G and real data sampled from $p_{\mathbf{x}}(\mathbf{x})$. The problem of training GANs is formulated as follows:

$$\min_{G}\max_{D} L_{GAN} := E_{\mathbf{x} \sim p_{\mathbf{x}}(\mathbf{x})}\left[\log(D(\mathbf{x}))\right] + E_{\mathbf{v} \sim p_{\mathbf{v}}(\mathbf{v})}\left[\log(1 - D(G(\mathbf{v})))\right], \quad (7)$$

where $p_{\mathbf{v}}(\mathbf{v})$ is a prior distribution over $\mathbf{v}$. It has been pointed out in [6] that the global equilibrium of the two-player game in Eq. (7) achieves if and only if $p_{\mathbf{x}}(\mathbf{x}) = p_g(\mathbf{x})$, where $p_g(\mathbf{x})$ is the distribution of generated data.

In our model, we treat the transformation network $f_{\mathbf{trans}}$ as the generator G. Suppose $p^1(\mathbf{z}^1)$, $p^2(\mathbf{z}^2)$ and $p^t(\mathbf{z}^t)$ are distributions of learnt features of sketches, 3D shapes and transformed data (denoted by $\mathbf{z}^1$, $\mathbf{z}^2$ and $\mathbf{z}^t$), respectively. By solving the following problem

$$\min_{f_{\mathbf{trans}}}\max_{D} E_{\mathbf{z}^2 \sim p^2(\mathbf{z}^2)}\left[\log(D(\mathbf{z}^2))\right] + E_{\mathbf{z}^1 \sim p^1(\mathbf{z}^1)}\left[\log(1 - D(f_{\mathbf{trans}}(\mathbf{z}^1)))\right], \quad (8)$$

we can expect that $p^t(\mathbf{z}^t) = p^t(f_{\mathbf{trans}}(\mathbf{z}^1)) = p^2(\mathbf{z}^2)$, *i.e.*, the transformed data $\mathbf{z}^t$ has the same data distribution as $\mathbf{z}^2$ of 3D shapes, if problem (8) reaches the global equilibrium. Consequently, the cross-modality discrepancy can be reduced.

Conventionally, problem (8) is solved by alternatively optimizing f_{trans} and D through minimizing the following two loss functions:

$$L_G = E_{\mathbf{z}^1 \sim p^1(\mathbf{z}^1)} \left[\log(1 - D(\mathbf{z}^t))) \right], \tag{9}$$

$$L_D = -E_{\mathbf{z}^2 \sim p^2(\mathbf{z}^2)} \left[\log(D(\mathbf{z}^2)) \right] - E_{\mathbf{z}^1 \sim p^1(\mathbf{z}^1)} \left[\log(1 - D(\mathbf{z}^t)) \right]. \tag{10}$$

So far, we have trained a transformation network f_{trans} such that $p^t(\mathbf{z}^t) \approx p^2(\mathbf{z}^2)$ by minimizing L_G and L_D. Albeit the divergence between the distributions for transformed features of sketches and for features of 3D models can be diminished by adversarial learning, the cross-modality semantic structures are not taken into account. To address this problem, we further introduce the following term, namely the class-aware cross-modality mean discrepancy

$$L_{CMD} = \sum_y \left\| E_{\mathbf{z}^t \sim p^t(\mathbf{z}^t|y)} \left[\mathbf{z}^t \right] - E_{\mathbf{z}^2 \sim p^2(\mathbf{z}^2|y)} \left[\mathbf{z}^2 \right] \right\|_2, \tag{11}$$

to adversarial learning, where y is the class label. By minimizing L_{CMD}, the mean feature vector of class y from the sketch modality is compelled to be close to the mean feature vector of the same class from the 3D shape modality.

In practice, provided a mini-batch $\mathbf{Z}^q = \{\mathbf{z}^q_{i,j}\}_{i=1,j=1}^{C,K}$ ($q \in \{2, t\}$), the term $E_{\mathbf{z}^q \sim p^q(\mathbf{z}^q|y)} \left[\mathbf{z}^q \right]$ can be approximated by the batch-wise mean feature vector, i.e., $E_{\mathbf{z}^q \sim p^q(\mathbf{z}^q|y)} \left[\mathbf{z}^q \right] \approx \frac{1}{K} \sum_{j=1,c_i=y}^K \mathbf{z}^q_{i,j}$.

Through minimizing the loss $L_{AL} = L_G + L_{CMD}$, we can obtain the adversarial learning method with cross-modality mean discrepancy minimization (CMDM-AL), which could enhance the semantic correlations across modalities.

By combing the semantics preserving loss L_{SeP} and the cross-modality correlation enhancing loss L_{AL}, we finally get the loss function for training f_{trans}:

$$L_T(\theta_{trans}) = L_{SeP} + (L_G + L_{CMD}). \tag{12}$$

3.3   Optimization

In Eq. (1), we defined the loss function L^1_{IAML} for jointly training $\{f^1_{CNN}(\theta^1_{CNN}), f^1_{metric}(\theta^1_{metric})\}$, and the loss function L^2_{IAML} for training $\{f^2_{CNN}(\theta^2_{CNN}), f^2_{metric}(\theta^2_{metric})\}$ of 3D shapes. We also developed a loss function L_T for training the cross-modality transformation network $f_{trans}(\theta_{trans})$ in Eq. (12).

In order to learn parameters of the proposed model, we optimize different networks in an alternating iterative way. Specifically, we first pre-train the CNN and metric networks of sketches and 3D shapes based on the loss L^m_{IAML} in Eq. (1), and pre-train the cross-modality transformation network by minimizing L_T and L_D. After initialization, we then alternatively update $\{\theta^1_{CNN}, \theta^1_{metric}\}$, $\{\theta^1_{CNN}, \theta^1_{metric}\}$, θ_{trans}, and the adversarial discriminator D, by minimizing $L^1_{IAML}, L^2_{IAML}, L_T$, and L_D, respectively. Throughout the whole training process, we use the Adam stochastic gradient method [9] as the optimizer.

4   Experimental Results and Analysis

In order to evaluate the performance of our method, we conduct experiments on two widely used benchmark datasets for sketch-based 3D shape retrieval: *i.e.*, **SHREC 2013** and **SHREC 2014**.

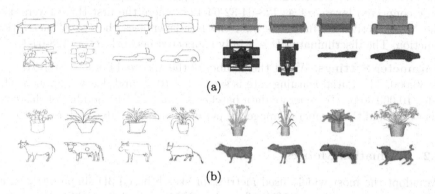

(a)

(b)

Fig. 3. Samples from two benchmarks: (a) the **SHREC 2013** dataset, (b) the **SHREC 2014** dataset. Images in the first four columns are sketches, whilst images in the last four columns are 3D shapes. Samples in the same row belong to the same class.

SHREC 2013 [12,13] is a large-scale dataset for sketch-based 3D shape retrieval. This dataset consists of 7,200 sketches and 1,258 shapes from 90 classes, by collecting human-drawn sketches [3] and 3D shapes from the Princeton Shape Benchmark (PSB) [21] that share common categories. For each class, there are totally 80 sketches, where 50 images are used for training and 30 images for test. The numbers of 3D shapes are different for distinct classes, about 14 on average. **SHREC 2014** [15,16] is a sketch track benchmark larger than SHREC 2013. It totally contains 13,680 sketches and 8,987 3D shapes, grouped into 171 classes. The 3D shapes are collected from various datasets, including SHREC 2012 [11] and the Toyohashi Shape Benchmark (TSB) [26]. Similar to SHREC 2013, there are 80 images for sketches, and about 53 3D shapes on average for each class. The sketches are further split into 8,550 training data and 5,130 test data, where for each class, 50 images are used for training and the rest 30 images for test.

Figure 3 shows some samples from the two datasets. As illustrated, retrieving 3D shapes by sketches is quite challenging, due to large intra-class variations and cross-modality discrepancies between sketches and 3D shapes.

4.1   Implementation Details

In this subsection, we provide implementation details about the proposed method.

Network Structures. For CNN networks of both sketches and shapes, *i.e.*, f_{CNN}^1 and f_{CNN}^2, we utilize the ResNet-50 network [7]. Specifically, we use the layers of ResNet-50 before the *"pooling5"* layer (inclusive). As for metric networks of sketches and 3D shapes, *i.e.*, $f^1_{\mathbf{metric}}$ and $f^2_{\mathbf{metric}}$, both of them consist of four fully connected layers set as 2048-1024-512-256-128. We utilize the *"relu"* activation functions and batch normalization for all layers in the metric networks, except that the last layer uses the *"tanh"* activation function. As to the cross-modality transformation model $f_{\mathbf{trans}}$, we adopt a network with four fully connected layers set as 128-64-32-64-128, where the first three layers uses the *"relu"* activation functions, and the last layer uses the *"tanh"* activation function. The discriminator D is a fully connected network set as 128-64-1.

Parameter Settings. We set the number of the maximal iterative step $Iter_{\max}$ as 30,000. The initial learning rate is set to 1×10^{-4}, and decays exponentially after 10,000 steps. To generate data batches $\boldsymbol{\mathcal{I}^1}$ and $\boldsymbol{\mathcal{I}^2}$, the number of classes C per batch and the number of images K per class are set as 16 and 4, respectively.

4.2   Evaluation Metrics

We adopt the most widely used metrics for sketch-based 3D shape retrieval as follows: nearest neighbor (**NN**), first tier (**FT**), second tier (**ST**), E-measure (**E**), discounted cumulated gain (**DCG**) and mean average precision (**mAP**) [2,13,30]. We also report the **precision-recall curve**.

4.3   Evaluation of the Proposed Method

In this section, we will evaluate the effect of the proposed adversarial learning with class-aware cross-modality mean discrepancy minimization (CMDM-AL), together with the semantics preserving (SeP) term.

As a baseline, we apply the importance-aware metric learning to separately train $\{f^1_{\mathbf{CNN}}, f^1_{\mathbf{metric}}\}$, and $\{f^2_{\mathbf{CNN}}, f^2_{\mathbf{metric}}\}$, where the cross-modality transformation network $f_{\mathbf{trans}}$ is trained by only using the semantics preserving loss L_{SeP}. This baseline method, denoted by **DCA (SeP)**, merely learns discriminative features without considering the cross-modality issues. Different from DCA (SeP), another baseline approach, denoted by **DCA (CMDM-AL)**, trains $f_{\mathbf{trans}}$ via minimizing the loss L_{AL} for adversarial learning. By further adding the semantics preserving term L_{SeP}, *i.e.*, training $f_{\mathbf{trans}}$ by $L_T = L_{AL}+L_{SeP}$, we can obtain the complete model of our proposed method denoted by **DCA (CMDM-AL+SeP)**. By comparing the performance of DCA (SeP), DCA (CMDM-AL) and DCA (CMDM-AL+SeP), we can evaluate the effects of the proposed adversarial learning method and semantics preserving term.

The results are summarized in Tables 1 and 2. As can be seen, the baseline method DCA (SeP) yields a rather poor performance, due to its weakness in dealing with cross-modality discrepancies. By introducing the adversarial learning method, DCA (CMDM-AL) significantly boosts the performance of the baseline, implying that the adversarial learning can largely enhance the correlation between data distributions of different modalities. Moreover, we can see a consistent improvements of DCA (CMDM-AL+SeP) on two benchmarks, compared to DCA (CMDM-AL). This indicates that the semantics preserving term can help learn more discriminative cross-modality transformation network.

Moreover, we also evaluate the performance of DCA by using different base networks, rather than ResNet-50. We select AlexNet [10] and VGG-16 [22], of which the corresponding methods are denoted by **AlexNet-DCA** and **VGG-16-DCA**, respectively. As shown in Table 2, DCA using ResNet-50 yields much better performance than AlexNet-DCA and VGG-16-DCA.

4.4 Comparison with the State-of-the-art Methods

Retrieval Performance on SHREC 2013. Here we report experimental results of the proposed method on SHREC 2013, by comparing with the state-of-the-art methods, including the cross domain manifold ranking method (**CDMR**) [4], sketch-based retrieval method with view clustering (**SBR-VC**) [12], spatial proximity method (**SP**) [23], Fourier descriptors on 3D model silhouettes (**FDC**) [12], edge-based Fourier spectra descriptor (**EFSD**) [12], Siamese network (**Siamese**) [28], chordal axis transform with dynamic time warping (**CAT-DTW**), deep correlated metric learning (**DCML**) [2], and the learned Wasserstein barycentric representation method (**LWBR**) [30].

Table 1. Performance on **SHREC 2013**, compared with the state-of-the-art methods.

Methods	NN	FT	ST	E	DCG	mAP
CDMR [4]	0.279	0.203	0.296	0.166	0.458	0.250
SBR-VC [12]	0.164	0.097	0.149	0.085	0.348	0.114
SP [23]	0.017	0.016	0.031	0.018	0.240	0.026
FDC [12]	0.110	0.069	0.107	0.061	0.307	0.086
Siamese [28]	0.405	0.403	0.548	0.287	0.607	0.469
CAT-DTW [32]	0.235	0.135	0.198	0.109	0.392	0.141
KECNN [25]	0.320	0.319	0.397	0.236	0.489	-
DCML [2]	0.650	0.634	0.719	0.348	0.766	0.674
LWBR [30]	0.712	0.725	0.785	0.369	0.814	0.752
DCA (SeP)	0.009	0.015	0.027	0.014	0.231	0.034
DCA (CMDM-AL)	0.762	0.776	0.812	0.370	0.842	0.795
DCA (CMDM-AL+SeP)	**0.783**	**0.796**	**0.829**	**0.376**	**0.856**	**0.813**

Figure 4 demonstrates the precision-recall curves of the proposed method and compared approaches. As illustrated, the precision rate of our method is significantly higher than those of compared models, when the recall rate is smaller than 0.8. Considering that the top retrieved results are preferable, our method therefore performs significantly better than the state-of-the-art approaches.

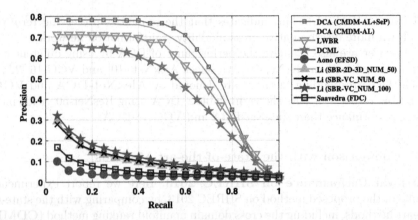

Fig. 4. The precision-recall curves of various methods on **SHREC 2013**.

Table 2. Performance on **SHREC 2014**, compared with the state-of-the-art methods

Methods	NN	FT	ST	E	DCG	mAP
CDMR [4]	0.109	0.057	0.089	0.041	0.328	0.054
SBR-VC [12]	0.095	0.050	0.081	0.037	0.319	0.050
DB-VLAT [26]	0.160	0.115	0.170	0.079	0.376	0.131
CAT-DTW [32]	0.137	0.068	0.102	0.050	0.338	0.060
Siamese [28]	0.239	0.212	0.316	0.140	0.496	0.228
DCML [2]	0.272	0.275	0.345	0.171	0.498	0.286
LWBR [30]	0.403	0.378	0.455	0.236	0.581	0.401
AlexNet-DCA	0.498	0.464	0.513	0.294	0.627	0.502
VGG-16-DCA	0.682	0.698	0.723	0.375	0.783	0.711
DCA (SeP)	0.018	0.020	0.028	0.007	0.266	0.030
DCA (CMDM-AL)	0.745	0.766	0.808	0.392	0.845	0.782
DCA (CMDM-AL+SeP)	**0.770**	**0.789**	**0.823**	**0.398**	**0.859**	**0.803**

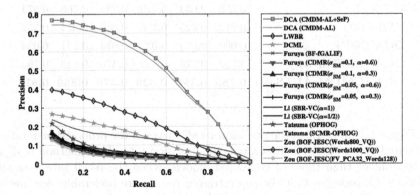

Fig. 5. The precision-recall curves of various methods on **SHREC 2014**.

We also report NN, FT, ST, E, DCG and mAP of various methods, including CDMR, SBR-VC, SP, FDC, Siamese, DCML, LWBR and the proposed method. As summarized in Table 1, our approach yields the best retrieval performance w.r.t. all evaluation metrics. Among all compared approaches, Siamese, DCML and LWBR are deep metric learning based models. They directly map data from different modalities into a common embedding subspace, where both the single-modality and cross-modality intra-class Euclidean distances are decreased, and the inter-class distances are simultaneously enlarged. However, they equally treat each training data, and fail to explore varying importance of distinct samples. Besides, they only reduce the local cross-modality divergences between data pairs or triplets, without considering the correlation between data distributions in a holistic way. In contrast, our method learns features by mining the batch-wise hardest positive and hardest negative samples. Through automatically selecting the most important training samples, we can learn discriminative features more efficiently. Moreover, we explicitly introduce a cross-modality transformation network, in order to transfer the feature from the sketch modality to the feature space of 3D shapes. By leveraging the semantics preserving adversarial learning, we simultaneously reduce holistic divergences between data distributions from two modalities, and enhance the semantic correlations. As a consequence, our method achieves better retrieval performance. For instance, the mAP of our method reaches 0.813, which is 34.4%, 13.9% and 6.1% higher than Siamese, DCML and LWBR, respectively.

Retrieval Performance on SHREC 2014. On this dataset, we compared our proposed model to the following state-of-the-art methods: the BoF with Gabor local line based feature (**BF-fGALIF**) [3], **CDMR** [4], **SBR-VC** [12], depth-buffered vector of locally aggregated tensors (**DB-VLAT**) [26], **SCMR-OPHOG** [16], BOF junction-based extended shape context (**BOFJESC**) [16], **Siamese** [28], **DCML** [2], and **LWBR** [30].

Figure 5 provides precision-recall curves for BF-fGALIF, CDMR, SBR-VC, SCMR-OPHOG, OPHOG, DCML, LWBR and the proposed model. As shown, the precision rate of our proposed method is remarkably higher than compared approaches, when the recall rate is less than 0.8.

Besides the precision-recall curves, we additionally report NN, FT, ST, E, DCG and mAP of CDMR, SBR-VC, DB-VLAT, Siamese, DCML, LWBR in Table 2. As can be seen, the performance of existing deep metric learning based methods including Siamese, DCML and LWBR drops sharply on SHREC 2014. For example, the mAP of LWBR on SHREC 2014 is 0.401, around 35% lower than the mAP that it has achieved on SHREC 2013. The reason might lie in that SHREC 2014 has much more class categories (90 classes on SHREC 2013 versus 171 classes on SHREC 2014) and larger scale 3D shapes (1,258 3D shapes on SHREC 2013 versus 8,987 3D shapes on SHREC 2014) with more severe intra-class and cross-modality variations, making SHREC 2014 more challenging than SHREC 2013. As a comparison, the mAP of our proposed model merely drops about 1%, and reaches 0.803 on SHREC 2014. This result is 40.2%, 51.7%

and 57.5% higher than that of LWBR, DCML and Siamese, indicating that our method are much more scalable than existing deep models.

5   Conclusions

In this paper, we proposed a novel cross-modality adaptation model for sketch-based 3D shape retrieval. We firstly learnt modality-specific discriminative features, by employing the importance-aware metric learning through mining the batch-wise hardest samples. To remove the cross-modality discrepancy, we proposed a transformation network, aiming to transfer the features of sketches into the feature space of 3D shapes. We developed an adversarial learning based method for training the network, by enhancing correlations between holistic data distributions and preserving local semantic structures across modalities. Extensive experimental results on two benchmark datasets demonstrated the superiority of the propose method, compared to the state-of-the-art approaches.

References

1. Chen, J., Wang, Y., Qin, J., Liu, L., Shao, L.: Fast person re-identification via cross-camera semantic binary transformation. In: IEEE Conference on Computer Vision and Pattern Recognition (2017)
2. Dai, G., Xie, J., Zhu, F., Fang, Y.: Deep correlated metric learning for sketch-based 3D shape retrieval. In: AAAI, pp. 4002–4008 (2017)
3. Eitz, M., Richter, R., Boubekeur, T., Hildebrand, K., Alexa, M.: Sketch-based shape retrieval. ACM Trans. Graph. 31(4), 1–10 (2012)
4. Furuya, T., Ohbuchi, R.: Ranking on cross-domain manifold for sketch-based 3D model retrieval. In: 2013 International Conference on Cyberworlds (CW), pp. 274–281. IEEE (2013)
5. Ganin, Y., et al.: Domain-adversarial training of neural networks. J. Mach. Learn. Res. 17(1), 2096–2030 (2016)
6. Goodfellow, I., et al.: Generative adversarial nets. In: Advances in Neural Information Processing Systems, pp. 2672–2680 (2014)
7. He, K., Zhang, X., Ren, S., Sun, J.: Deep residual learning for image recognition. arXiv preprint arXiv:1512.03385 (2015)
8. Hermans, A., Beyer, L., Leibe, B.: In defense of the triplet loss for person re-identification. arXiv preprint arXiv:1703.07737 (2017)
9. Kingma, D.P., Ba, J.: Adam: a method for stochastic optimization. In: International Conference on Learning Representations (2015)
10. Krizhevsky, A., Sutskever, I., Hinton, G.E.: Imagenet classification with deep convolutional neural networks. In: Advances in Neural Information Processing Systems, pp. 1097–1105 (2012)
11. Li, B., et al.: Shrec'12 track: generic 3D shape retrieval. In: 3DOR, vol. 6 (2012)
12. Li, B., et al.: SHREC'13 track: large scale sketch-based 3D shape retrieval (2013)
13. Li, B., et al.: A comparison of methods for sketch-based 3D shape retrieval. Comput. Vis. Image Underst. 119, 57–80 (2014)
14. Li, B., Lu, Y., Johan, H., Fares, R.: Sketch-based 3D model retrieval utilizing adaptive view clustering and semantic information. Multimed. Tools Appl. 76(24), 26603–26631 (2017)

15. Li, B., et al.: A comparison of 3D shape retrieval methods based on a large-scale benchmark supporting multimodal queries. Comput. Vis. Image Underst. **131**, 1–27 (2015)
16. Li, B., et al.: SHREC'14 track: extended large scale sketch-based 3D shape retrieval. In: Eurographics Workshop on 3D Object Retrieval, vol. 2014 (2014)
17. Liu, Z., Qin, J., Li, A., Wang, Y., Van Gool, L.: Adversarial binary coding for efficient person re-identification. arXiv preprint arXiv:1803.10914 (2018)
18. Motiian, S., Jones, Q., Iranmanesh, S., Doretto, G.: Few-shot adversarial domain adaptation. In: Advances in Neural Information Processing Systems, pp. 6673–6683 (2017)
19. Phong, B.T.: Illumination for computer generated pictures. Commun. ACM **18**(6), 311–317 (1975)
20. Qin, J., Liu, L., Yu, M., Wang, Y., Shao, L.: Fast action retrieval from videos via feature disaggregation. Comput. Vis. Image Underst. **156**, 104–116 (2017)
21. Shilane, P., Min, P., Kazhdan, M., Funkhouser, T.: The princeton shape benchmark. In: Proceedings of Shape Modeling Applications 2004, pp. 167–178. IEEE (2004)
22. Simonyan, K., Zisserman, A.: Very deep convolutional networks for large-scale image recognition. arXiv preprint arXiv:1409.1556 (2014)
23. Sousa, P., Fonseca, M.J.: Sketch-based retrieval of drawings using spatial proximity. J. Vis. Lang. Comput. **21**(2), 69–80 (2010)
24. Su, H., Maji, S., Kalogerakis, E., Learned-Miller, E.: Multi-view convolutional neural networks for 3D shape recognition. In: Proceedings of the IEEE International Conference on Computer Vision, pp. 945–953 (2015)
25. Tabia, H., Laga, H.: Learning shape retrieval from different modalities. Neurocomputing **253**, 24–33 (2017)
26. Tatsuma, A., Koyanagi, H., Aono, M.: A large-scale shape benchmark for 3D object retrieval: Toyohashi shape benchmark. In: Signal & Information Processing Association Annual Summit and Conference (APSIPA ASC), 2012 Asia-Pacific, pp. 1–10. IEEE (2012)
27. Tzeng, E., Hoffman, J., Saenko, K., Darrell, T.: Adversarial discriminative domain adaptation. In: Computer Vision and Pattern Recognition (CVPR), vol. 1, p. 4 (2017)
28. Wang, F., Kang, L., Li, Y.: Sketch-based 3D shape retrieval using convolutional neural networks. In: 2015 IEEE Conference on Computer Vision and Pattern Recognition (CVPR), pp. 1875–1883. IEEE (2015)
29. Wang, P.S., Liu, Y., Guo, Y.X., Sun, C.Y., Tong, X.: O-CNN: octree-based convolutional neural networks for 3D shape analysis. ACM Trans. Graph. (TOG) **36**(4), 72 (2017)
30. Xie, J., Dai, G., Zhu, F., Fang, Y.: Learning barycentric representations of 3D shapes for sketch-based 3D shape retrieval. In: 2017 IEEE Conference on Computer Vision and Pattern Recognition (CVPR), pp. 3615–3623. IEEE (2017)
31. Xie, J., Dai, G., Zhu, F., Wong, E.K., Fang, Y.: Deepshape: deep-learned shape descriptor for 3D shape retrieval. IEEE Trans. Pattern Anal. Mach. Intell. **39**(7), 1335–1345 (2017)
32. Yasseen, Z., Verroust-Blondet, A., Nasri, A.: View selection for sketch-based 3D model retrieval using visual part shape description. Vis. Comput. **33**(5), 565–583 (2017)
33. Yoon, G.J., Yoon, S.M.: Sketch-based 3D object recognition from locally optimized sparse features. Neurocomputing **267**, 556–563 (2017)

34. Zhang, Y., Barzilay, R., Jaakkola, T.: Aspect-augmented adversarial networks for domain adaptation. arXiv preprint arXiv:1701.00188 (2017)

35. Zhu, F., Xie, J., Fang, Y.: Heat diffusion long-short term memory learning for 3D shape analysis. In: Leibe, B., Matas, J., Sebe, N., Welling, M. (eds.) ECCV 2016. LNCS, vol. 9911, pp. 305–321. Springer, Cham (2016). https://doi.org/10.1007/978-3-319-46478-7_19

36. Zhu, F., Xie, J., Fang, Y.: Learning cross-domain neural networks for sketch-based 3D shape retrieval. In: AAAI, pp. 3683–3689 (2016)

RIDI: Robust IMU Double Integration

Hang Yan[1]([✉]), Qi Shan[2], and Yasutaka Furukawa[3]

[1] Washington University in St. Louis, St. Louis, USA
yanhang@wustl.edu
[2] Zillow Group, Seattle, USA
qis@zillowgroup.com
[3] Simon Fraser University, Burnaby, Canada
furukawa@sfu.ca

Abstract. This paper proposes a novel data-driven approach for inertial navigation, which learns to estimate trajectories of natural human motions just from an inertial measurement unit (IMU) in every smartphone. The key observation is that human motions are repetitive and consist of a few major modes (e.g., standing, walking, or turning). Our algorithm regresses a velocity vector from the history of linear accelerations and angular velocities, then corrects low-frequency bias in the linear accelerations, which are integrated twice to estimate positions. We have acquired training data with ground truth motion trajectories across multiple human subjects and multiple phone placements (e.g., in a bag or a hand). The qualitatively and quantitatively evaluations have demonstrated that our simple algorithm outperforms existing heuristic-based approaches and is even comparable to full Visual Inertial navigation to our surprise. As far as we know, this paper is the first to introduce supervised training for inertial navigation, potentially opening up a new line of research in the domain of data-driven inertial navigation. We will publicly share our code and data to facilitate further research (Project website: https://yanhangpublic.github.io/ridi).

1 Introduction

Accurate position estimation from an Inertial Measurement Unit (IMU) has long been a dream in academia and industry. IMU double integration is an approach with a simple principle: given a device rotation (e.g., from IMU), one measures an acceleration, subtracts the gravity, integrates the residual acceleration once to get velocities, and integrates once more to get positions. Dead-reckoning or step counting is another approach, which detects foot-steps to estimate the distance of travel and utilizes device rotations to estimate motion directions. IMU is in every smart-phone, is very energy-efficient (i.e., capable of running 24 h a day), and works anywhere even inside a bag or a pocket. A robust inertial navigation would be an ultimate anytime anywhere navigation system.

Electronic supplementary material The online version of this chapter (https://doi.org/10.1007/978-3-030-01261-8_38) contains supplementary material, which is available to authorized users.

© Springer Nature Switzerland AG 2018
V. Ferrari et al. (Eds.): ECCV 2018, LNCS 11217, pp. 641–656, 2018.
https://doi.org/10.1007/978-3-030-01261-8_38

Unfortunately, the current state-of-the-art suffers from severe limitations. First, IMU double integration does not work unless one uses a million dollar military-grade IMU unit in a submarine, because small sensor errors and biases explode quickly in the double integration process. Second, dead-reckoning typically assumes that device rotations are exactly aligned with motion directions. This assumption almost always breaks in daily activities, as we move around devices from a hand to a pocket to a bag.

This paper proposes a simple data-driven approach that learns to estimate natural human motions only from IMU. Our key idea is that human motions are repetitive and consist of a small number of major modes. Our algorithm, dubbed Robust IMU Double Integration (RIDI), learns to regress walking velocities from IMU signals, while compensating for arbitrary device rotations with respect to the body. More precisely, RIDI regresses a velocity vector from the history of linear accelerations and angular velocities, then corrects low-frequency errors in the linear accelerations such that their integration matches the regressed velocities. A standard double integration is then used to estimate the trajectory from the corrected linear accelerations.

We have acquired IMU sensor data across 10 human subjects with 4 popular smartphone placements. The ground truth trajectories are obtained by a Visual Inertial Odometry system (i.e., a Google Tango phone, Lenovo Phab2 Pro) [12]. Our datasets consist of various motion trajectories over 150 min at 200 Hz. Our experiments have shown that RIDI produces motion trajectories comparable to the ground truth, with mean positional errors below 3%.

To our knowledge, this paper is the first to introduce supervised training for inertial navigation. Our algorithm is surprisingly simple, yet outperforms existing heuristic-based algorithms, and is even comparable to Visual Inertial Odometry. This paper could start a new line of research in data-driven Inertial Navigation. Commercial implications of the proposed research are also significant. IMUs are everywhere on the market, inside smartphones, tablets, or emerging wearable devices (e.g., Fitbit or Apple Watch). Almost everybody always carries one of these devices, for which RIDI could provide precise motion information with minimal additional energy consumption, a potential to enable novel location-aware services in broader domains. We will publicly share our code and data to facilitate further research.

2 Related Work

Motion tracking has long been a research focus in the Computer Vision and Robotics communities. Visual SLAM (V-SLAM) has made remarkable progress in the last decade [5,7,8,16,22,23], enabling a robust real-time system for indoors or outdoors up to a scale ambiguity. Visual-inertial SLAM (VI-SLAM) combines V-SLAM and IMU sensors, resolving the scale ambiguity and making the system further robust [13,18]. VI-SLAM has been used in many successful products such as Google Project Tango [12], Google ARCore [10], Apple ARKit [2] or Microsoft Hololens [21]. While being successful, the system suffers from two

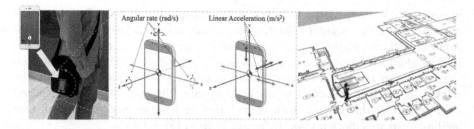

Fig. 1. Smartphones with motion sensors are ubiquitous in modern life. This paper proposes a novel data-driven approach for inertial navigation, which uses Inertial Measurement Unit (IMU) in every smartphone to estimate trajectories of natural human motions. IMU is energy-efficient and works anytime anywhere even for smartphones in your pockets or bags.

major drawbacks: (1) a camera must have a clear light-of-sight under well-lit environments all the time, and (2) the recording and processing of video data quickly drain a battery (Fig. 1).

IMU-only motion tracking has been successful in 3 DOF rotation estimation and been used in many recent Virtual Reality applications, such as Google Cardboard VR [11] or Samsung Gear VR [25]. While position estimation from IMU sensors has been a challenge due to sensor bias in the accelerometers, successful approaches exist for pedestrian motion tracking. The first family of these methods count foot-steps from accelerometers and multiply predefined step-lengths to estimate the translation [4,27]. Most these methods assume that the device orientation is aligned with the walking direction. Several methods seek to loosen this assumption by principal component analysis [15], forward-lateral modeling [6], or frequency domain analysis [17]. However, as shown in our experiments, these methods are based on heuristics and cannot handle more complex and varying motions in our database. Our approach is data-driven with supervised learning and makes significant improvements over these methods with a simple algorithm.

Another family of IMU-only pedestrian tracking methods use a foot-mounted IMU sensor and rely on the fact that the foot comes to a complete stop at every step [28]. The sensor drifts are eliminated through a zero-velocity constraint at each foot-step, producing impressive results. Our approach shares the idea of enforcing velocity constraints, but does not require a foot-mounted sensor.

WiFi signals are another information source for motion tracking without cameras in indoor environments [3,9,14,20]. A particle filter is applied on IMU, WiFi, and the map data to enable reliable motion tracking [19,24]. Inertial navigation is a critical component of WiFi based tracking. Our research is orthogonal and directly benefits these techniques.

3   Inertial Motion Trajectory Database

One contribution of the paper is a database of IMU sensor measurements and motion trajectories across multiple human subjects and multiple device placements. We have used a Google Tango phone, Lenovo Phab2 Pro, to record linear accelerations, angular velocities, gravity directions, device orientations (via Android APIs), and 3D camera poses. The camera poses come from the Visual Inertial Odometry system on Tango, which is accurate enough for our purpose (less than 1 m positional error after 200 m tracking). We make sure that the camera has a clear field-of-view all the time (See Fig. 2). This is only required when recording the ground truth trajectories for training and evaluation. Our method estimates motion trajectories solely from IMU data.

Fig. 2. We place a Tango phone in four popular configurations to collect training data. The ground truth motions come from Visual Inertial Odometry, and we have carefully designed the placements to make the camera always visible. From left to right: (1) in a leg pocket, (2) in a bag, (3) held by a hand, or (4) on a body (e.g., for officers).

We have collected more than 150 min of data at 200 Hz from ten human subjects under four popular smartphone placements with various motion types including walking forward/backward, side motion, or acceleration/deceleration. Asynchronous signals from various sources are synchronized into the time-stamps of Tango poses via linear interpolation. At total, our database consists of approximately two million samples.

4 Algorithm

The proposed algorithm, dubbed Robust IMU Double Integration (RIDI), consists of two steps. First, it regresses velocity vectors from angular velocities and linear accelerations (i.e., accelerometer readings minus gravity). Second, it estimates low-frequency corrections in the linear accelerations so that their integrated velocities match the regressed values. Corrected linear accelerations are double-integrated to estimate positions. We assume subjects walk on a flat floor. The regression and the position estimation are conducted on a 2D horizontal plane. We now explain a few coordinate frames and the details of the two steps.

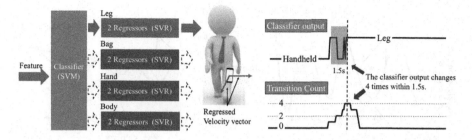

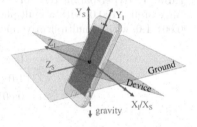

Fig. 3. Left: our cascaded regression model consists of one SVM and eight SVRs. SVM classifies the phone placement from the four types. Two type-specific SVRs predict a 2D velocity vector in the stabilized-IMU frame, ignoring the vertical direction. Right: we leverage the classifier output to handle transition periods. For the sample marked with the vertical dash line, the classifier output changes 4 times in the past 1.5 s, thus is identified to be within the transition period.

4.1 Coordinate Frames

The arbitrary device orientations with respect to the body makes it hard to infer the motion direction, being one of the core challenges of heuristic-based methods. Such arbitrariness also poses challenges to the regression task. With the assumption that the subject walks on a horizontal plane, we eliminate the device pitch and roll ambiguities by utilizing gravity estimations. We define a rectified coordinate frame, in which we train a velocity regressor to handle the remaining yaw ambiguity.

More precisely, we consider three coordinate frames in our algorithm. The first one is the world coordinate frame W, in which the output positions are estimated. W is set to be the global coordinate frame from the Android API at the first sample. The second one is the IMU/device coordinate frame I (marked with blue arrows in the right figure) in which IMU readings are provided by the Android APIs. Lastly, we leverage the gravity direction from the system to define our stabilized-IMU frame S, where the device pitch and roll are eliminated from I by aligning its y-axis with the gravity vector (see the green arrows in the right figure). This coordinate frame makes our regression task easier, since the regression becomes independent of the device pitching and rolling.

4.2 Learning to Regress Velocities

We learn to regress velocities in the stabilized IMU frame S. For each training sequence, we transform device poses (in W), and IMU readings (angular velocities and linear accelerations, in I) into S. The central difference generates velocity vectors from the transformed device poses (ignoring the vertical direction). To suppress high-frequency noise, we apply Gaussian smoothing with $\sigma = 2.0$ samples to 6 IMU channels, and with $\sigma = 30.0$ samples to 2 velocity

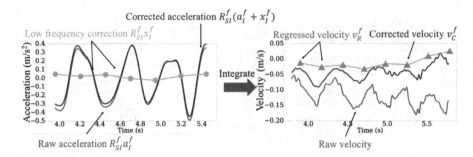

Fig. 4. Robust IMU double integration process. Our approach directly models the errors (green on the left) in the linear acceleration as a piecewise linear (thus low-frequency) function. We estimate parameters of this correction function so that the integration of the corrected linear accelerations (blue on the right) matches the regressed velocities (brown on the right). (Color figure online)

Table 1. Hyper-parameters for SVRs are found by the grid search: (1) C within a range of $[0.1, 100.0]$ with a multiplicative increment of 10; and (2) ϵ within a range of $[0.001, 1.0]$ with a multiplicative increment of 10.

	Leg	Bag	Hand	Body
C	1.0	10.0	10.0	1.0
ϵ	0.001	0.01	0.001	0.001

channels, respectively. We concatenate smoothed angular velocities and linear accelerations from the past 200 samples (i.e., 1 s) to construct a 1200 dimensional feature vector (Fig. 4).

People carry smartphones in different ways, exhibiting different IMU signal patterns. We assume that a phone is either (1) in a leg pocket, (2) in a bag, (3) held by a hand, or (4) on a body, and exploit this knowledge to propose a cascaded regression model (See Fig. 3). More precisely, a Support Vector Machine (SVM) first classifies the placement to be one of the above four types, then two type-specific ϵ-insensitive Support Vector Regression (SVR) [26] models estimate two velocity values independently (ignoring the vertical direction). The hyper-parameters for each model are tuned independently by the grid search and 3-fold cross validation, based on the mean squared error on the regressed velocities. The grid-search finds the soft-margin parameter $C = 10.0$ for SVM. Table 1 summarizes the chosen parameters for SVR models.

The above model assumes a phone being in the same placement all the time. To handle users switching a phone from one placement to another (e.g., picking up a phone from a leg pocket to a hand), we use a simple heuristic to identify *transition* periods, during which we specify the target velocity to be 0 without regression. Our observation is that the classifier makes near random predictions during transition periods. We inspect 10 contiguous classifier outputs in the past

1.5 s (i.e., one classification per 0.15 s) and declare the current sample to be in a transition if the classification results changed more than twice in the period (See Fig. 3 right).

4.3 Correcting Acceleration Errors

Predicted velocities provide effective cues in removing sensor noises and biases.[1] The errors come from various sources (e.g., IMU readings, system gravities, or system rotations) and interact in a complex way. We make a simplified assumption and model all the errors as a low-frequency bias in the linear acceleration. This approach is not physically grounded, but bypasses explicit noise/bias modeling and turns our problem into simple linear least squares.

We model the bias in the linear acceleration in the IMU/device coordinate frame I. To enforce the low-frequency characteristics, we represent the bias as linear interpolation of correction terms x_I^f at sub-sampled samples ($\mathcal{F}_1$), in particular, one term every 50 samples [29]. With abuse of notation, we also use x_I^f to denote interpolated acceleration correction (e.g., $x_I^{11} = 0.8 x_I^1 + 0.2 x_I^{51}$).

Our goal is to estimate $\{x_I^f\}$ at $\mathcal{F}_1$ by minimizing the discrepancy between the corrected velocities (v_C^f) and the regressed velocities (v_R^f) at sub-sampled samples $\mathcal{F}_2$ (once every 50 samples, to avoid evaluating SVRs at every sample for efficiency). The discrepancy is measured in the stabilized IMU frame S.

$$
\min_{\{x_I^1, x_I^{51}, \cdots\}} \sum_{f \in \mathcal{F}_2} \left\| v_C^f - v_R^f \right\|^2 + \lambda \sum_{f \in \mathcal{F}_1} \left\| x_I^f \right\|^2,
$$

$$
v_C^f = \mathcal{R}_{SW}^f \sum_{f'=1}^{f} \mathcal{R}_{WI}^{f'} \left(a_I^{f'} + x_I^{f'} \right) \Delta t.
$$

(1)

a_I^f denotes the raw linear acceleration in I. $\mathcal{R}_{AB}$ denotes the rotation that transforms a vector from coordinate frame B to A. $\mathcal{R}_{WI}$ is the IMU orientation provided by the Android API. Suppose $\mathcal{R}_{SI}$ is the rotation that aligns the gravity vector to $(0, 1, 0)$, $\mathcal{R}_{SW}$ can be then computed by left-multiplying $\mathcal{R}_{SI}$ to $\mathcal{R}_{IW}$. Δt is the time interval between samples, which is roughly 0.005 s under 200 Hz sampling rate.

The first term minimizes the discrepancy between the regressed (v_R^f) and the corrected (v_C^f) velocities. The corrected velocity (V_C^f) in the stabilized coordinate frame S is computed by (1) transforming each corrected linear acceleration into frame W by $\mathcal{R}_{WI}$; (2) integrating them in W; and (3) transforming to S by $\mathcal{R}_{SW}$.[2] Note that our regressor estimates the horizontal velocity, namely only the two entries in v_R^f without the vertical direction. We assume that subjects walk on the flat surface, and hence, fix the vertical component of v_R^f to be 0.

---

[1] Direct integration of the predicted velocities would produce positions but perform worse (See Sect. 6 for comparisons).

[2] We assume zero-velocity at the first sample, which is the case for our datasets. Relaxing this assumption is our future work.

The second term enforces l_2 regularization on the correction terms, which allows us to balance the velocity regression and the raw IMU signals. When λ is 0, the system simply integrates the regressed velocities without using raw IMU data. When λ is infinity, the system ignores the regressed velocities and performs the naive IMU double integration. We have used $\lambda = 0.1$ in our experiments. Double integration of the corrected accelerations produces our position estimations.

5   Implementation Details

We have implemented the proposed system in C++ with third party libraries including OpenCV, Eigen and Ceres Solver [1]. Note that our optimization problem (1) has a closed form solution, but we use Ceres for the ease of implementation. We have used a desktop PC with a Intel I7-4790 CPU and 32 GB RAM.

We have presented the algorithm as an offline batch method for clarity. It is fairly straightforward to implement an online algorithm, which has been used in all our experiments. Given sample i, the system returns the position at i by using corrected linear acceleration up to $i - 1$. It also initializes the correction term for i as 0. Meanwhile, a second thread is launched once per 200 samples to solve for corrections within the last 1000 samples (with overlapping). In this way, the error is accumulated for no more than 1 s. The two expensive steps are the velocity regression and the optimization, which takes 26 ms and 17 ms on average, respectively. Our system processes 10,000 samples within 10 s, effectively achieving 1,000 fps on a desktop PC.

6   Experimental Results

We have acquired 74 motion sequences over 8 human subjects (marked as S1–S8), 4 different phone placements, and a variety of motion types. We have randomly selected 49 sequences for training and the remaining 25 sequences for testing. We have created one training/testing sample per 10 IMU samples, resulting in 109,365 training samples and 46,173 testing samples. We have also acquired 8 sequences from two unseen human subjects (S9, S10) and 4 sequences from an unseen device (Google Pixel XL) for testing.

6.1   Position Evaluations

Baseline Comparisons: Table 2 summarizes the quantitative evaluations on the accuracy of the final positions over 8 testing sequences (marked as T1–T8). We compared our method against 5 competing methods:

- **RAW** denotes the naive double integration with uncorrected linear accelerations (with system-level calibration and filtering).
- **STEP-ENH** denotes a recent step counting method [27]. The step length is set to the average of the ground truth step lengths over the whole training set.

- **STEP-FRQ** denotes another recent step counting method that uses frequency domain analysis to infer misalignment between the device orientation and the motion direction [17].[3] The step detection is provided by the Android API. The ground truth is used to set the step length as in STEP-ENH.
- **RIDI-MAG** is a variant of the proposed method. The regressed velocity vector consists of the magnitude and direction information. RIDI-MAG keeps the velocity magnitude, while replacing its direction by the system rotation through the Android API. RIDI-MAG cannot compensate for the device rotations with respect to the body.
- **RIDI-ORI** is another variant of RIDI that keeps the regressed velocity direction, while replacing the regressed velocity magnitude by the average of the ground truth values for each sequence.

Table 2. Positional accuracy evaluations. Each entry shows the mean positional error (in meters) and its percentage (inside parentheses) with respect to the trajectory length. The blue and the brown numbers show the best and the second best results.

Seq.	Place.	RAW	STEP-ENH	STEP-FRQ	RIDI-MAG	RIDI-ORI	RIDI
T1	Leg	15.43(23.41)	2.78(4.22)	6.64(10.08)	1.26(1.91)	1.93(2.93)	1.12(1.71)
T2	Leg	36.95(54.19)	3.91(5.74)	4.89(7.17)	1.03(1.52)	3.65(5.35)	1.00(1.47)
T3	Bag	55.35(35.73)	4.43(2.86)	10.67(6.89)	5.26(3.39)	9.74(6.29)	3.97(2.56)
T4	Bag	20.78(27.41)	2.10(2.76)	3.08(4.07)	1.32(1.74)	3.20(4.22)	1.14(1.51)
T5	Hand	172.8(112.2)	4.22(2.74)	14.98(9.73)	2.72(1.76)	10.36(6.73)	2.80(1.82)
T6	Hand	13.58(28.67)	4.38(9.25)	4.93(10.40)	4.88(10.30)	2.72(5.75)	1.22(2.57)
T7	Body	45.42(56.85)	15.17(18.98)	2.01(2.51)	10.78(13.49)	4.56(5.70)	1.71(2.14)
T8	Body	17.09(25.36)	0.94(1.40)	1.88(2.78%)	1.87(2.77)	2.66(3.94)	1.11(1.65)

For all the experiments, we align each motion trajectory to the ground truth by computing a 2D rigid transformation that minimizes the sum of squared distances for the first 10 s (2,000 samples). Table 2 shows that RIDI outperforms all the other baselines in most sequences, and achieves mean positional errors (MPE) less than 3.0% of the total travel distance, that is, a few meters after 150 m of walking. Figure 5 illustrates a few representative examples with regressed velocities. In T1, the phone is mounted over the leg pocket, where STEP-FRQ fails to infer correct motion direction due to abrupt leg movements. T5 is a case, in which the subject frequently changes the walking speeds. Both STEP-FRQ and RIDI-ORI fail for assuming a constant step frequency or velocity. In T7, the subject mixes different walking patterns, including backward motions. Only RIDI, STEP-FRQ and RIDI-ORI, which infer motion directions, perform well. Please visit our project website for more results and visualizations.

---

[3] Their algorithm has a heuristic to resolve the 180° ambiguity in the frequency analysis, but did not work well with our data. Our implementation favors this method by resolving the 180° ambiguity with the ground truth direction.

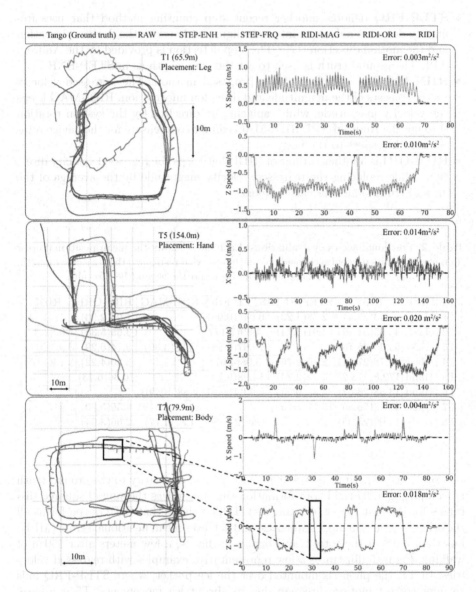

Fig. 5. Left: Motion trajectories from Tango, competing methods and RIDI. Short green segments indicate headings of device's X axis. Right: Regressed velocity vectors and their mean squared errors (MSE). In T1 (top row), the device is in a leg pocket and STEP-FRQ fails to infer correct orientation. In T5 (middle row), the subject frequently changes the speed, where STEP-FRQ and RIDI-ORI produce large errors for inaccurate motion frequencies and speed magnitudes. In T7 (bottom row), the subject mixes different walking patterns including 4 backward motions (the black rectangle is one place), where STEP-ENH and RIDI-MAG fails for not inferring velocity directions. Trajectories from the naive double integration(RAW) quickly diverge in all examples.

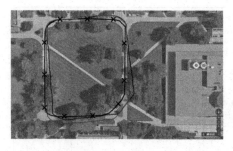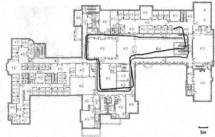

Fig. 6. Overlaying the trajectories with the online digital map (from Google Maps) or the floorplan image with the estimated scale. The red line marks the trajectory given by the Tango system and the blue line marks the trajectory given by our system. The accuracy of the Tango system degrades at outdoors in our experiments, so we manually drew the actual walking path with the black line at the left. (Color figure online)

Scale Consistency: One of the key advantages of the inertial or visual-inertial navigation is that the reconstruction is up to a metric-scale, which is not the case for image-only techniques such as visual-SLAM. Figure 6 shows that our trajectories are well aligned over a satellite or a floorplan image. We adjusted the scales (meters per pixel) based on the scale rulers, and manually specified the starting point and the initial orientation.

Parameter λ: Table 3 shows the impact of the parameter λ in Eq. 1, suggesting that it is important to integrate the velocity regression with the raw IMU acceleration data. Neither the regressed velocities (small λ) nor the naive double integration (large λ) performs well alone. We set $\lambda = 0.1$ in all experiments.

Table 3. The average MPE (as a ratio against the trajectory distance) over the testing sequences with different λ.

λ	0.0001	0.001	0.1	1.0	10,000
MPE	11.62%	1.49%	1.45%	1.47%	33.98%

Real-World Evaluation: we have qualitatively evaluated our system in a real world setting. A subject starts walking with the phone held by the hand. Along the route inside a large building, the subject performs several complex motions including putting the phone inside a bag, resting at a table, walking sideways and putting the phone into the leg pocket. Our method is able to estimate the trajectory under nature motions. The camera is blocked inside bag or pocket, therefore we omit the ground truth trajectory. See Fig. 7. Please visit our project website for detailed visualization.

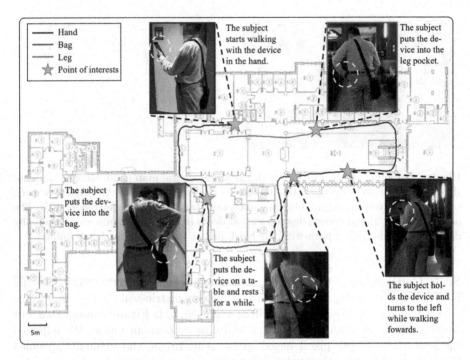

Fig. 7. Real-world example with natural motions. The subject carries the phone with different placements (marked with colored lines) and performs several complex motions (marked with stars) along the route. Our method is able to estimate accurate trajectory only from IMU data. (Color figure online)

6.2   Velocity Evaluations

Our cascaded velocity regression achieves the mean squared errors of 0.017 $[m^2/s^2]$ and 0.017 $[m^2/s^2]$ on the X and Z axes on the testing set, respectively. We have also calculated the accuracy of the SVM classifier on the placement types, where the training and the testing accuracies are 97.00% and 96.22%, respectively. Lastly, we have evaluated the SVR regression model without the placement classification. The mean squared errors on the X and Z axes are 0.028 $[m^2/s^2]$ and 0.032 $[m^2/s^2]$, respectively, which are worse than our cascaded model. Acquiring more training data and evaluating the accuracy of more data-hungry methods such as deep neural networks is one of our future works.

6.3   Generalization

Unseen Devices: Considering the impact to commercial applications, the generalization capability to unseen devices is of great importance. We have used another device (Google Pixel XL) to acquire additional testing sequences. The subjects also carried the Tango phone to obtain ground truth trajectories. The sequence contains a quick rotation motion at the beginning to generate distinctive peaks in the gyroscope signals, which are used to synchronize data from the two devices. We register the estimated trajectories to the ground truth by the same process as before. Figure 8 shows that our system generalizes reasonably well under all placement types, in particular, still keeping the mean positional errors below 3%.

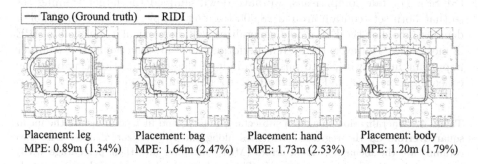

Placement: leg   Placement: bag   Placement: hand   Placement: body
MPE: 0.89m (1.34%)   MPE: 1.64m (2.47%)   MPE: 1.73m (2.53%)   MPE: 1.20m (1.79%)

Fig. 8. Generalization to an unseen device (Google Pixel XL).

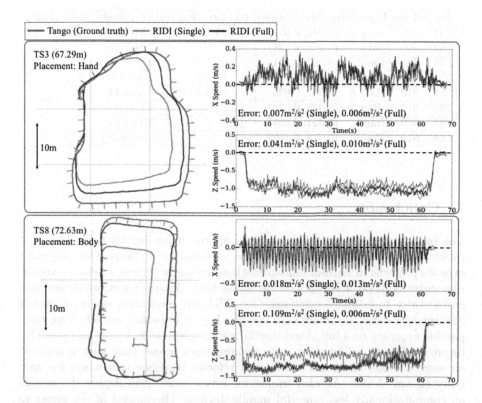

Fig. 9. Generalization to unseen subjects. We varied the number of human subjects in the training data and evaluated two RIDI models for unseen testing subjects. RIDI (single) uses training data only from 1 subject, while RIDI (Full) uses training data from the 8 subjects.

Unseen Subjects: The last experiment evaluates the generalization capability to unseen subjects (marked as S9 and S10). These two subjects have no prior knowledge of our project and we asked them to walk in their own ways. We have trained two RIDI models with different training sets. RIDI (Single) is trained on data only from 1 subject (S1). RIDI (Full) is trained on data from the 8 subjects (S1–S8). For fair comparisons, we have down-sampled the larger training set so that both sets contain around 28,000 training samples. Figure 9 and Table 4 demonstrate that the Full model generalizes well, in particular, below 4% MPE in most cases. However, the system performs worse in some sequences. Another important future work is to push the limit of the generalization capability by collecting more data and designing better regression machineries.

Table 4. Generalization to unseen subjects. The forth and fifth columns are the mean squared errors on the regressed velocities along the two horizontal axes. Last two columns are the mean positional errors (MPE) in meter and their percentage w.r.t. trajectory lengths (inside parentheses). The model trained on more subjects generalizes better.

Seq.	Subject	Place.	Reg. Err. (Single)	Reg. Err. (Full)	MPE (Single)	MPE (Full)
TS1	S9	Leg	(0.041, 0.072)	(0.023, 0.023)	3.51(4.83)	2.65(3.65)
TS2	S9	Bag	(0.108, 0.128)	(0.053, 0.009)	5.34(7.06)	2.88(3.80)
TS3	S9	Hand	(0.007, 0.041)	(0.006, 0.010)	2.35(3.49)	1.37(2.03)
TS4	S9	Body	(0.021, 0.053)	(0.011, 0.023)	8.43(12.42)	2.89(4.26)
TS5	S10	Leg	(0.031, 0.026)	(0.018, 0.018)	4.48(3.14)	3.22(2.26)
TS6	S10	Bag	(0.045, 0.024)	(0.013, 0.014)	2.71(1.94)	1.92(1.37)
TS7	S10	Hand	(0.021, 0.027)	(0.009, 0.008)	2.33(1.67)	1.25(0.89)
TS8	S10	Body	(0.018, 0.109)	(0.013, 0.006)	4.450(6.19)	1.35(1.86)

7   Conclusion

The paper proposes a novel data-driven approach for inertial navigation that robustly integrates linear accelerations to estimate motions. Our approach exploits patterns in natural human motions, learns to regress a velocity vector, then corrects linear accelerations via simple linear least squares, which are integrated twice to estimate positions. Our IMU-only navigation system is energy efficient and works anywhere even inside a bag or a pocket, yet achieving comparable accuracy to a full visual inertial navigation system to our surprise. Our future work is to collect a lot more training data across more human subjects on more devices, and learn a universal velocity regressor that works for anybody on any device. Another important future work is to deploy the system on computationally less powerful mobile devices. The impact of the paper to both scientific and industrial communities could be profound. This paper has a potential to open up a new line of learning based inertial navigation research. Robust anytime-anywhere navigation system could immediately benefit a wide range of industrial applications through location-aware services including online advertisements, digital mapping, navigation, and more.

Acknowledgement. This research is partially supported by National Science Foundation under grant IIS 1540012 and IIS 1618685, Google Faculty Research Award, and Zillow gift fund.

References

1. Agarwal, S., Mierle, K., et al.: Ceres solver. http://ceres-solver.org
2. Apple: Apple arkit. https://developer.apple.com/arkit/
3. Bahl, P., Padmanabhan, V.N.: RADAR: An in-building RF-based user location and tracking system. In: Proceedings of Nineteenth Annual Joint Conference of the IEEE Computer and Communications Societies, INFOCOM 2000, vol. 2, pp. 775–784. IEEE (2000)
4. Brajdic, A., Harle, R.: Walk detection and step counting on unconstrained smartphones. In: Proceedings of the 2013 ACM International Joint Conference on Pervasive and Ubiquitous Computing, pp. 225–234. ACM (2013)
5. Cadena, C., et al.: Past, present, and future of simultaneous localization and mapping: toward the robust-perception age. IEEE Trans. Robot. **32**(6), 1309–1332 (2016)
6. Chowdhary, M., Sharma, M., Kumar, A., Dayal, S., Jain, M.: Method and apparatus for determining walking direction for a pedestrian dead reckoning process. US Patent App. 13/682,684, 22 May 2014
7. Davison, A.J., Reid, I.D., Molton, N.D., Stasse, O.: Monoslam: real-time single camera slam. IEEE Trans. Pattern Anal. Mach. Intell. **29**(6), 1052–1067 (2007)
8. Engel, J., Koltun, V., Cremers, D.: Direct sparse odometry. IEEE Trans. Pattern Anal. Mach. Intell. **40**(3), 611–625 (2018)
9. Ferris, B., Fox, D., Lawrence, N.: WiFi-SLAM using Gaussian process latent variable models. In: Proceedings of IJCAI 2007, pp. 2480–2485 (2007)
10. Google: Arcore. https://developers.google.com/ar/
11. Google: Cardboard. https://vr.google.com/cardboard/
12. Google: Project tango. https://get.google.com/tango/
13. Hesch, J.A., Kottas, D.G., Bowman, S.L., Roumeliotis, S.I.: Camera-IMU-based localization: observability analysis and consistency improvement. Int. J. Robot. Res. **33**(1), 182–201 (2014)
14. Huang, J., Millman, D., Quigley, M., Stavens, D., Thrun, S., Aggarwal, A.: Efficient, generalized indoor wifi graphslam. In: IEEE International Conference on Robotics and Automation, pp. 1038–1043 (2011)
15. Janardhanan, J., Dutta, G., Tripuraneni, V.: Attitude estimation for pedestrian navigation using low cost mems accelerometer in mobile applications, and processing methods, apparatus and systems. US Patent 8,694,251, 8 April 2014
16. Klein, G., Murray, D.: Parallel tracking and mapping for small AR workspaces. In: ISMAR, pp. 225–234. IEEE (2007)
17. Kourogi, M., Kurata, T.: A method of pedestrian dead reckoning for smartphones using frequency domain analysis on patterns of acceleration and angular velocity. In: 2014 IEEE/ION Position, Location and Navigation Symposium-PLANS 2014, pp. 164–168. IEEE (2014)

18. Leutenegger, S., Lynen, S., Bosse, M., Siegwart, R., Furgale, P.: Keyframe-based visual–inertial odometry using nonlinear optimization. Int. J. Robot. Res. **34**(3), 314–334 (2015)

19. Li, F., Zhao, C., Ding, G., Gong, J., Liu, C., Zhao, F.: A reliable and accurate indoor localization method using phone inertial sensors. In: Proceedings of the 2012 ACM Conference on Ubiquitous Computing, pp. 421–430. ACM (2012)

20. Lim, C.H., Wan, Y., Ng, B.P., See, C.M.S.: A real-time indoor WiFi localization system utilizing smart antennas. IEEE Trans. Consum. Electron. **53**(2), 618–622 (2007)

21. Microsoft: Hololens. https://www.microsoft.com/microsoft-hololens/en-us

22. Mur-Artal, R., Montiel, J.M.M., Tardos, J.D.: ORB-SLAM: a versatile and accurate monocular slam system. IEEE Trans. Robot. **31**(5), 1147–1163 (2015)

23. Newcombe, R.A., Lovegrove, S.J., Davison, A.J.: DTAM: dense tracking and mapping in real-time. In: ICCV. pp. 2320–2327. IEEE (2011)

24. Racko, J., Brida, P., Perttula, A., Parviainen, J., Collin, J.: Pedestrian dead reckoning with particle filter for handheld smartphone. In: 2016 International Conference on Indoor Positioning and Indoor Navigation (IPIN), pp. 1–7. IEEE (2016)

25. Samsung: Samsung gear VR. http://www.samsung.com/global/galaxy/gear-vr/

26. Smola, A.J., Schölkopf, B.: A tutorial on support vector regression. Stat. Comput. **14**(3), 199–222 (2004)

27. Tian, Q., Salcic, Z., Kevin, I., Wang, K., Pan, Y.: An enhanced pedestrian dead reckoning approach for pedestrian tracking using smartphones. In: 2015 IEEE Tenth International Conference on Intelligent Sensors, Sensor Networks and Information Processing (ISSNIP), pp. 1–6. IEEE (2015)

28. Yun, X., Bachmann, E.R., Moore, H., Calusdian, J.: Self-contained position tracking of human movement using small inertial/magnetic sensor modules. In: 2007 IEEE International Conference on Robotics and Automation, pp. 2526–2533. IEEE (2007)

29. Zhou, Q.Y., Koltun, V.: Simultaneous localization and calibration: self-calibration of consumer depth cameras. In: Proceedings of the IEEE Conference on Computer Vision and Pattern Recognition, pp. 454–460 (2014)

Training Binary Weight Networks via Semi-Binary Decomposition

Qinghao Hu[1,2] , Gang Li[1,2] , Peisong Wang[1,2] , Yifan Zhang[1,2] ,
and Jian Cheng[1,2,3](✉)

[1] National Laboratory of Pattern Recognition, Institute of Automation, Chinese
Academy of Sciences, Beijing, China
{qinghao.hu,gang.li,peisong.wang,yfzhang,jcheng}@nlpr.ia.ac.cn
[2] University of Chinese Academy of Sciences, Beijing, China
[3] Center for Excellence in Brain Science and Intelligence Technology, Beijing, China

Abstract. Recently binary weight networks have attracted lots of attentions due to their high computational efficiency and small parameter size. Yet they still suffer from large accuracy drops because of their limited representation capacity. In this paper, we propose a novel semi-binary decomposition method which decomposes a matrix into two binary matrices and a diagonal matrix. Since the matrix product of binary matrices has more numerical values than binary matrix, the proposed semi-binary decomposition has more representation capacity. Besides, we propose an alternating optimization method to solve the semi-binary decomposition problem while keeping binary constraints. Extensive experiments on AlexNet, ResNet-18, and ResNet-50 demonstrate that our method outperforms state-of-the-art methods by a large margin (5% higher in top1 accuracy). We also implement binary weight AlexNet on FPGA platform, which shows that our proposed method can achieve $\sim 9\times$ speed-ups while reducing the consumption of on-chip memory and dedicated multipliers significantly.

Keywords: Deep neural networks · Binary weight networks
Deep network acceleration and compression

1 Introduction

Deep convolutional neural networks have become more and more popular since AlexNet [16] made a success in ILSVRC2012. After that, convolutional neural networks have shown significant improvements on a variety of computer vision tasks such as image classification [16], object detection [24], image segmentation [21], and so on. However, the great performance of deep networks comes at the cost of large parameter size and high computational complexity. For applications on mobile phones or embedded devices, it's difficult to deploy deep networks on them due to their limited computation and storage resources.

To alleviate these problems, a lot of methods have been proposed, such as pruning [10,11,19], low-rank decomposition [6,13,15,17,25,30] and fixed-point

© Springer Nature Switzerland AG 2018
V. Ferrari et al. (Eds.): ECCV 2018, LNCS 11217, pp. 657–673, 2018.
https://doi.org/10.1007/978-3-030-01261-8_39

quantization [8,9,20,22,28]. Binary quantization, a special case of fixed-point quantization, represents the weights of deep networks via only binary values. As there are only binary values in the quantized weights, multiplication operations can be replaced with addition operations. Thus binary quantization can not only achieve high (32×) compression ratio, but also speed up the deep networks. Besides, binary weight networks are more efficient on field-programmable gate array (FPGA), digital signal processor (DSP), and the deep learning accelerator (DLA). On these architectures, binary weight networks usually can achieve higher speed-ups and save more hardware resources. Due to the appealing properties of binary quantization, many binary weight networks have been proposed, such as BC [4], BWN [23], SQ-BWN [7], and so on.

However, state-of-the-art binary weight networks suffer from significant accuracy drop due to their limited representation capacity. Convolutional kernels in BC [4] have only binary patterns, and all the parameters' magnitude equals to 1. This severely lowers down the diversity of convolutional kernels. BWN [23] multiplies each binary convolutional kernel by a different scale factor to approximate the full-precision convolutional kernel, then each convolutional kernel has a different magnitude. But parameters in the same convolutional kernel still share the same magnitude, which limits the representation power of convolutional kernels.

In order to increase the representation capacity of binary weight networks, we propose a novel semi-binary decomposition method which decomposes a matrix into two binary matrices and a diagonal matrix. Besides, we propose an alternating optimization method to learn the decomposition factors with binary constraints. Extensive experiments on ImageNet show that our proposed method outperforms state-of-the-art algorithms. Our main contributions can be summarized as the follows:

- Inspired by that the matrix product of binary matrices has more numerical possibilities than binary matrix, we propose a novel semi-binary decomposition method to train binary weight networks. By using proposed semi-binary decomposition, our binary weight networks have more representation capacity than state-of-the-art methods.
- Since learning the semi-binary decomposition factors is difficult, here we propose an alternating optimization method to solve semi-binary factors while still keeping the binary constraints.
- Extensive experiments are conducted on ImageNet to evaluate our methods. The experiments results on AlexNet, ResNet-18, and ResNet-50 demonstrate that our proposed method outperforms state-of-the-art algorithms by a large margin. In addition, we implement binary weight AlexNet on FPGA platform, and the experiment result shows that our binary weight networks can achieve ∼9× speed-ups using less on-chip memory and hardware multipliers.

2   Related Work

In recent years, a lot of methods [3] have been proposed to compress or accelerate deep networks. Most of these methods fall into three categories: pruning-based methods, low-rank decomposition based methods, and quantization-based methods.

2.1 Pruning-Based Methods

Pruning-based methods compress the deep networks by removing unimportant connections. Early works of pruning [11,19] use the second derivative of loss functions to determine which connections are unimportant. Recently Han *et al.* [10] propose a three-step method to compress the deep networks. They first prune those unimportant connections, then quantize the remaining weights via K-means, and finally encode the quantized weights using Huffman coding. During the inference phase, a decoder is required to reconstruct the weights, which makes their method inconvenient. Besides, above methods can hardly utilize the Basic Linear Algebra Subprograms (BLAS) since they prune weights in an unstructured way. To cure this problem, Lebedev *et al.* [18] propose the Group-wise Brain Damage. By imposing the group-sparsity regularizer, the weights are pruned in a group-wise fashion. As a result, convolutions can be reduced to multiplications of thinned dense matrices, and they still can use BLAS library to get higher speed-ups.

2.2 Low-Rank Decomposition Based Methods

Low-rank decomposition based methods [5,6,13] mainly use matrix or tensor decomposition methods to decompose convolutional kernels into several small matrices or tensors. Denton *et al.* propose to use Singule Value Decomposition (SVD) to reduce the computational complexity [6]. Instead of directly approximating the weights, Zhang *et al.* [30] propose to approximate the layer response via a low-rank matrix. Besides, their method also takes the non-linear layers' responses into account. Lebedev *et al.* [17] propose to use CANDE-COMP/PARAFAC (CP) decomposition to approximate the convolutional kernels. They only apply their method on a single layer of AlexNet. Similar like CP-decomposition, Tucker decomposition is also used to accelerate the convolutional layers [15]. Differently, Tucker decomposition can be used to compress the whole network while CP decomposition can not. Wang *et al.* [25] propose to use Block Term Decomposition to speed up the convolutional layers. The Block Term Decomposition can be regarded as a compromise between CP-decomposition and Tucker decomposition. Novikov *et al.* propose to use the Tensor-Train format to compress the fully-connected layers of deep networks. Their method can achieve up to 7× compression ratio on VGG16 network.

2.3 Quantization Based Methods

Vector quantization has a long history in data compression. This technique is introduced into network compression by Gong *et al.* They [8] propose to use vector quantization to compress the fully-connected layers of CNNs. Following this line, Wu *et al.* [2,28] propose an product quantization based algorithm to simultaneously speed up the computation and reduce the parameter size. Another kind of quantization method is low-bit fixed-point quantization. Gupta *et al.* [9] propose to quantize the weights to fixed-point format via a stochastic rounding scheme instead of deterministic rounding scheme. By using this method, deep networks can be quantized with 16-bit fixed-point numbers with little degradation of accuracy. Wang *et al.* [26] proposed the fixed-point factorized network which decomposes the weights into two fixed-point matrix and one diagonal matrix. As a special case of fixed-point quantization, binary quantization aims to quantize the weights into binary values. Courbariaux *et al.* [4] proposed BinaryConnect to train binary weight networks. Like [9], they used a stochastic binarization scheme instead of deterministic scheme. Since binary values have limited representation capacity, Rastegari *et al.* [23] propose to approximate full-precision convolutioal kernels with binary kernels and a scaling factor. By multiplying a scaling factor, binary kernels have lower quantization loss than directly binary quantization. Dong *et al.* [7] propose a stochastic quantization scheme. In each iteration, they only quantize a portion of parameters to low-bit with a stochastic probability inversely proportional to the quantization error and the remaining parameters stay unchanged with full-precision. Hu *et al.* [12] proposed to train binary weight network from the view of hashing, which learns binary weights using inner-product preserving hashing methods. Wang *et al.* [27] proposed a two-step quantization methods which decomposing the network quantization problem into code learning and transformation function learning step.

3   Our Method

In this section, we propose the semi-binary decomposition to increase the representation capacity of binary weight networks. Then an alternating optimization method is proposed to solve the semi-binary decomposition problem. Finally, we analyse the time and space complexity of the proposed binary weight networks in the inference phase.

3.1   Preliminary

Given an L-layer pre-trained CNN model, let $\mathbf{W} \in \mathbb{R}^{T \times S}$ be the full-precision weights of lth layer. To quantize the weights $\mathbf{W}$ into a binary matrix $\mathbf{B}$, a simple binarization method [4] is:

$$\mathbf{B} = sgn(\mathbf{W}) \tag{1}$$

where sgn denotes the sign function, and $sgn(x) = 1$ for $x > 0$ and -1 otherwise. Simple binarization has limited representation capacity because $\mathbf{B}$ has only *binary patterns*. Thus direct binarization will result in significant quantization loss. Rastegari *et al.* [23] propose to multiply a scale factor α_i for each binary convolutioal kernel $\mathbf{B_i} \in \mathbb{R}^{1 \times S}$, and the objective function is:

$$\min L(\varLambda, \mathbf{B}) = \|\mathbf{W} - \varLambda \mathbf{B}\|_F^2$$
$$s.t. \quad \mathbf{B} \in \{+1, -1\}^{T \times S} \tag{2}$$

where $\varLambda \in \mathbb{R}^{T \times T}$ is a diagonal matrix and $\alpha_i = \varLambda_{ii}$ is the scaling factor for $\mathbf{B_i}$. Different convolutional kernels in [23] have different magnitudes, thus it has better representation power. Yet multiplying a scaling factor for each binary convolutional kernels still suffers from large quantization loss because parameters in the same convolutional kernels has the same magnitude α_i.

3.2 Semi-Binary Decomposition

Since current binary quantization methods have limited representation capacity, here we aims to find better quantization methods to increase the parameter's diversity. In this paper, we propose a novel semi-binary decomposition method which approximates a matrix by the matrix product of two binary matrices and a diagonal matrix, thus the diversity of approximate matrix is higher than binary matrix. Specifically, the proposed semi-binary decomposition can be formulated as:

$$\min L(\mathbf{U}, \mathbf{D}, \mathbf{V}) = \|\mathbf{W} - \mathbf{U}\mathbf{D}\mathbf{V}^{\mathrm{T}}\|_F^2$$
$$s.t. \quad \mathbf{U} \in \{+1, -1\}^{T \times K} \tag{3}$$
$$\mathbf{V} \in \{+1, -1\}^{S \times K}$$

where $\mathbf{D} \in \mathbb{R}^{K \times K}$ is a diagonal matrix, $K \leq min(S, T)$, $\mathbf{U}$ and $\mathbf{V}$ are binary matrix. The proposed semi-binary decomposition is quite suitable for compressing the deep networks because $\mathbf{D}$ has lower computational complexity and $\mathbf{U}$ and $\mathbf{V}$ are still binary matrix. Besides, by using semi-binary decomposition, the representation capacity of binary weight networks is enhanced. Let $\mathbf{W'}$ be the approximate matrix of $\mathbf{W}$ via semi-binary decomposition, then $\mathbf{W'} = \mathbf{U}\mathbf{D}\mathbf{V}^{\mathrm{T}} = \sum_{k=1}^{K} d_k \mathbf{U_k}\mathbf{V_k}^{\mathrm{T}}$ where $d_k = \mathbf{D_{kk}}$, $\mathbf{U_k}$ and $\mathbf{V_k}$ are the kth column of matrix $\mathbf{U}$ and $\mathbf{V}$ respectively. For any parameter $\mathbf{W'_{i,j}}$ in $\mathbf{W'}$, its magnitude has 2^K possibilities while parameter in BC [4] and BWN-like methods [1,7,23] has only 2 and T possibilities respectively. Thus the proposed semi-binary decomposition method can improve the representation capacity.

Equation (3) is hard to solve due to the binary constraints, here we learn the components in a greedy way. Let $\mathbf{W_k}$ be k-term approximation of semi-binary decomposition, then $\mathbf{W_k} = \sum_{i=1}^{k} d_i \mathbf{U_i}\mathbf{V_i}^{\mathrm{T}}$. Let $\mathbf{R_k}$ be the residual matrix after $k-1$ terms of approximation, then $\mathbf{R_k} = \mathbf{W} - \mathbf{W_{k-1}}$ and $\mathbf{R_1} = \mathbf{W}$. In each step, we learn the kth term via approximating the residual matrix $\mathbf{R_k}$, the objective function is formulated as:

$$\min \; L(\mathbf{U_k}, d_k, \mathbf{V_k}) = \|\mathbf{R_k} - d_k \mathbf{U_k}\mathbf{V_k}^T\|_F^2$$
$$s.t. \quad \mathbf{U_k} \in \{+1, -1\}^{T \times 1} \tag{4}$$
$$\mathbf{V_k} \in \{+1, -1\}^{S \times 1}$$

To solve Eq. (4), we propose an alternating optimization method i.e. iteratively update one decomposition factor with other factors fixed.

Update d_k with Fixed $\mathbf{U_k}$ and $\mathbf{V_k}$: Given fixed $\mathbf{U_k}$ and $\mathbf{V_k}$, the objective function can be reformulated as:

$$\min \; L(d_k) = -2d_k \mathbf{U_k}^T \mathbf{R_k} \mathbf{V_k} + TS \cdot d_k^2 \tag{5}$$

The optimal solution of above equation is:

$$d_k = \frac{1}{T*S} \mathbf{U_k}^T \mathbf{R_k} \mathbf{V_k} \tag{6}$$

Update $\mathbf{U_k}$ with Fixed $\mathbf{V_k}$ and d_k: Given fixed $\mathbf{V_k}$, we replace d_k with its optimal solution, then the objective function is transformed as:

$$\max \; L(\mathbf{U_k}) = \frac{(\mathbf{U_k}^T \mathbf{R_k} \mathbf{V_k})^2}{\|\mathbf{U_k}\|_F^2 \|\mathbf{V_k}\|_F^2} = (\mathbf{U_k}^T \mathbf{R_k} \mathbf{V_k})^2$$
$$s.t. \quad \mathbf{U_k} \in \{+1, -1\}^{T \times 1} \tag{7}$$

The optimal solution for above equation is

$$\mathbf{U_k} = sgn(\mathbf{R_k} \mathbf{V_k}) \tag{8}$$

Update $\mathbf{V_k}$ with Fixed $\mathbf{U_k}$ and d_k: similar like updating $\mathbf{U_k}$, the optimal solution for $\mathbf{V_k}$ is:

$$\mathbf{V_k} = sgn(\mathbf{R_k}^T \mathbf{U_k}) \tag{9}$$

Until now, we have described the optimization algorithm of semi-binary decomposition for one layer. For the whole network quantization, we use the semi-binary decomposition for each layer's weights. This method is denoted as SBD-Direct and the overall training algorithm is summarized in Algorithm 1.

3.3   Featuremap-Oriented Semi-Binary Factors

Directly decomposing $\mathbf{W}$ for all layers of deep networks via semi-binary decomposition has two drawbacks. First, because the weights is multiplied by the input featuremap in the forward propagation, the binary quantization error will be amplified by the input featuremap. Second, directly applying semi-binary decomposition for the whole network can cause large accuracy drop since the quantization error accumulates across multiple layers.

To cure these problems, here we learn the semi-binary components via minimizing the output featuremap's quantization loss. Let $\mathbf{X}^l \in \mathbb{R}^{S \times N}$ be the lth-layer's input featuremap of full-precision network. Similarly, let l^{th}-layer's input

---

Algorithm 1. Training Binary Weight Networks via SBD-Direct

Input: Pre-trained convolutional neural networks weights $\{\mathbf{W}^l\}_{l=1}^L$ and
     Max_Iter
Output: Learned binary components $\{\mathbf{U}^l\}_{l=1}^L, \{\mathbf{V}^l\}_{l=1}^L$ and $\{\mathbf{D}^l\}_{l=1}^L$
for $l = 1; l \leq L$ **do**
   for $k = 1; k \leq K$ **do**
      Update residual matrix R_k
      Initialize $\mathbf{V_k}$ with all-ones matrix
      while *iter $\leq$ Max_Iters* **do**
         Update $\mathbf{U_k}$ with Eq. (8)
         Update $\mathbf{V_k}$ with Eq. (9)
      end
      Update d_k with Eq. (6)
   end
end
return $\{\mathbf{U}^l\}_{l=1}^L$, $\{\mathbf{V}^l\}_{l=1}^L$ and $\{\mathbf{D}^l\}_{l=1}^L$;

---

featuremap of quantized network be $\tilde{\mathbf{X}}^l$. Here quantized network means that
the first $l-1$ layers have been quantized via semi-binary decomposition, thus
$\tilde{\mathbf{X}}^l = \mathbf{U}^{l-1}\mathbf{D}^{l-1}(\mathbf{V}^{l-1})^T\tilde{\mathbf{X}}^{l-1}$. The objective function is formulated as:

$$\min \; L(\mathbf{U}^l, \mathbf{D}^l, \mathbf{V}^l) = \|\mathbf{W}^l\mathbf{X}^l - \mathbf{U}^l\mathbf{D}^l(\mathbf{V}^l)^T\tilde{\mathbf{X}}^l\|_F^2 = \|\mathbf{Y}^l - \sum_{k=1}^K d_k^l\mathbf{U_k}^l(\mathbf{V_k}^l)^T\tilde{\mathbf{X}}^l\|_F^2$$

$$s.t. \quad \mathbf{U} \in \{+1, -1\}^{T \times K}$$
$$\mathbf{V} \in \{+1, -1\}^{S \times K}$$
$$(10)$$

where $\mathbf{Y}^l = \mathbf{W}^l\mathbf{X}^l$ is the lth-layer's output featuremap. In what follows, we omit
the superscript l for convenience. Solving Eq. (10) is difficult due to the binary
constraints, here we learn the semi-binary components in a greedy way. Let $\mathbf{Y_k}$ be
the k-term approximation of output featuremap, then $\mathbf{Y_k} = \sum_{i=1}^k d_i\mathbf{U_i}\mathbf{V_i}^T\tilde{\mathbf{X}}$. Let
$\mathbf{Z_k}$ be the featuremap's residual matrix after $k-1$ terms of approximation, thus
$\mathbf{Z_k} = \mathbf{Y} - \mathbf{Y_{k-1}}$ and $\mathbf{Z_1} = \mathbf{W}$. Then we learn the kth term via approximating
the residual matrix $\mathbf{Z_k}$, the objective function is formulated as:

$$\min \; L(\mathbf{U_k}, d_k, \mathbf{V_k}) = \|\mathbf{Z_k} - d_k\mathbf{U_k}\mathbf{V_k}^T\tilde{\mathbf{X}}\|_F^2$$

$$s.t. \quad \mathbf{U_k} \in \{+1, -1\}^{T \times 1}$$
$$\mathbf{V_k} \in \{+1, -1\}^{S \times 1}$$
$$(11)$$

To solve Eq. (11), we propose an alternating optimization method to update the
semi-binary components iteratively.

Update d_k with Fixed $\mathbf{U_k}$ and $\mathbf{V_k}$: Given fixed $\mathbf{U_k}$ and $\mathbf{V_k}$, the objective function can be formulated as:

$$\min L(d_k) = -2d_k \mathbf{V_k}^T \tilde{\mathbf{X}} \mathbf{Z_k}^T \mathbf{U_k} + d_k^2 \|\mathbf{U_k} \mathbf{V_k}^T \tilde{\mathbf{X}}\|_F^2 \tag{12}$$

The optimal solution of d_k for Eq. (12) is:

$$d_k = \frac{\mathbf{V_k}^T \tilde{\mathbf{X}} \mathbf{Z_k}^T \mathbf{U_k}}{\|\mathbf{U_k} \mathbf{V_k}^T \tilde{\mathbf{X}}\|_F^2} \tag{13}$$

Update $\mathbf{U_k}$ with Fixed $\mathbf{V_k}$ and d_k: Given $\mathbf{V_k}$ fixed, we get the following objective by substituting the d_k's optimal solution:

$$max \ L(\mathbf{U_k}) = \frac{(\mathbf{V_k}^T \tilde{\mathbf{X}} \mathbf{Z_k}^T \mathbf{U_k})^2}{\|\mathbf{U_k} \mathbf{V_k}^T \tilde{\mathbf{X}}\|_F^2} = (\mathbf{V_k}^T \tilde{\mathbf{X}} \mathbf{Z_k}^T \mathbf{U_k})^2 \tag{14}$$

Thus the optimal $\mathbf{U_k}$ for above equation is:

$$\mathbf{U_k} = sgn(\mathbf{Z_k} \tilde{\mathbf{X}}^T \mathbf{V_k}) \tag{15}$$

Update $\mathbf{V_k}$ with Fixed $\mathbf{U_k}$ and d_k: Given $\mathbf{U_k}$ and d_k fixed, we get the following objective function:

$$\min L(\mathbf{V_k}) = -2Tr(\mathbf{V_k}^T \mathbf{q}) + \alpha \|\mathbf{V_k}^T \tilde{\mathbf{X}}\|_F^2 \tag{16}$$

where $\mathbf{q} = d_k \tilde{\mathbf{X}} \mathbf{Z_k}^T \mathbf{U_k}$ and $\alpha = d_k^2 \|\mathbf{U_k}\|_F^2$.

Optimizing $\mathbf{V_k}$ for Eq. (16) is still difficult, here we solve $\mathbf{V_k}$ by discrete cyclic coordinate descent method. Specifically, we solve one row of $\mathbf{V_k}$ each time while fixing all other rows. Let v be the jth row of $\mathbf{V_k}$, and $\mathbf{V_k}'$ the column vector of $\mathbf{V_k}$ excluding v. Similarly we denote the jth element of $\mathbf{q}$ as $\mathbf{q_j}$, and let $\mathbf{q}'$ as the $\mathbf{q}$ excluding $\mathbf{q_j}$. Let $\mathbf{x}^T$ be the jth row of matrix $\tilde{\mathbf{X}}$ and $\tilde{\mathbf{X}}'$ be matrix $\tilde{\mathbf{X}}$ excluding $\mathbf{x}^T$. Then problem can be written as:

$$\min L(\mathbf{V_k}) = -2vq + 2\alpha \mathbf{V_k}'^T \tilde{\mathbf{X}}' xv \tag{17}$$

Thus the jth row of $\mathbf{V_k}$ can be updated by:

$$v = sgn(q - \alpha \mathbf{V_k}'^T \tilde{\mathbf{X}}' \mathbf{x}) \tag{18}$$

So far, we have given details of learning semi-binary components by minimizing the featuremap's quantization loss, we denote this method as SBD-FQ and the overall training algorithm of SBD-FQ is summarized in Algorithm 2.

3.4   Fine-Tuning

After direct semi-binary decomposition or minimizing the featuremap's quantization loss, we get the $\mathbf{U}$, $\mathbf{V}$ and $\mathbf{D}$ for each layer. For a convolutional layer

---

Algorithm 2. Training Binary Weight Networks via SBD-FQ

Input: Pre-trained convolutional neural networks weights $\{\mathbf{W}^l\}_{l=1}^{L}$ and
    Max_Iter
Output: Learned binary components $\{\mathbf{U}^l\}_{l=1}^{L}, \{\mathbf{V}^l\}_{l=1}^{L}$ and $\{\mathbf{D}^l\}_{l=1}^{L}$
for $l = 1; l \leq L$ **do**
    Sampling a mini-batch images
    Forward propagation to get $\tilde{\mathbf{X}}^l$ and $\mathbf{X}^l$
    Calculate $\mathbf{Y}$ with $\mathbf{X}^l$ and $\mathbf{W}^l$
    for $i = 1; i \leq N$ **do**
        Update residual matrix $\mathbf{Z_k}$
        Initialize $\mathbf{V_k}$ with all-ones matrix
        while $iter \leq Max\_Iters$ **do**
            Update $\mathbf{U_k}$ with Eq. (15)
            Update d_k with Eq. (13)
            for $j = 1; j \leq S$ **do**
                | Update j^{th} element of $\mathbf{V_k}$ with Eq. (18)
            end
        end
    end
end
Fine-tune the binarized CNN model
return $\{\mathbf{U}^l\}_{l=1}^{L}$, $\{\mathbf{V}^l\}_{l=1}^{L}$ and $\{\mathbf{D}^l\}_{l=1}^{L}$;

---

with T covolutional kernels of size $c * d * d$. After semi-binary decomposition, we replace the original layer with three layers: a convolutional layer *conv_v*, one scale layer *scale_d*, and a convolutional layer *conv_u*. Layer *conv_v* has K covolutional kernels of size $c * d * d$, layer *conv_u* has T covolutional kernels of size $K * 1 * 1$ and layer *scale_d* has only K parameters.

For the fine-tune stage, we adopt a similar scheme as [4] to maintain the binary values in *conv_v* and *conv_u*. Take *conv_u* layer for example, we adopt a full-precision (32-bit floating) weight matrix $\mathbf{U_f}$ as the proxy of $\mathbf{U}$. $\mathbf{U_f}$ is initialized with $\mathbf{U}$ in the beginning of fine-tuning. In the forward propagation, $\mathbf{U}$ is updated by directly quantizing $\mathbf{U_f}$ to binary value, then $\mathbf{U}$ is used for the forward computation. In the backward propagation, gradients is calculated based on $\mathbf{U}$. The full-precision $\mathbf{U_f}$ is used to accumulate the gradients of weights $\mathbf{U}$.

3.5 Complexity Analysis

In this subsection, we analyse the time and space complexity of our binary weight network in the inference phase. For a convolutional layer with T kernels of size $c * d * d$, let H and W be the height and width of output featuremap respectively, and let $S = c * d * d$. Let T_m be the time for one multiplication operation, and let T_a be the time for one addition operation. Normally speaking, multiplication operation consumes more time than addition operation, especially for FPGA architecture, thus $T_a \ll T_m$. Since the time and space complexity is highly dependent on K, here we use a hyper-parameter β to control the value of K i.e. let $K = \frac{S*T}{\beta*(S+T)}$. For the experiments in the paper, $\beta = 1$ if not specified.

Time Complexity. After semi-binary decomposition, the time complexity of layer $conv\_v$, $scale\_d$, and $conv\_u$ is $H * W * S * K * T_a$, $H * W * K * T_m$ and $H * W * K * T * T_a$ respectively.

Thus the speed up ratio is:

$$\frac{S * T * (T_m + T_a)}{K(S+T) * T_a + K * T_m} \approx \frac{S * T * (T_m + T_a)}{K(S+T) * T_a} = \frac{\beta(T_m + T_a)}{T_a} \quad (19)$$

Space Complexity. After semi-binary decomposition, the space complexity of layer $conv\_v$, $scale\_d$, and $conv\_u$ is $S * K$, $32K$ and $K * T$ bits respectively. The compression ratio is:

$$\frac{S * T * 32}{K(S+T) + K * 32} \approx \frac{32 * S * T}{K(S+T)} = 32\beta. \quad (20)$$

For $\beta = 1$, our binary weight networks can achieve $\geq 2\times$ speed-ups and $32\times$ compression ratio. On FPGA platforms, our binary weight networks can achieve higher speed-ups since $T_a \ll T_m$. Table 1 shows that the space and time complexity of our method is less than [1,7,23] and nearly equals to [4].

Table 1. Time and Space complexity of state-of-the-art binary weight networks

Method	Time complexity	Speed-ups	Space complexity	Compress ratio
Full-Precision	$S * T * (T_m + T_a)$	1	$32 * S * T$	1
BinaryConnect [4]	$S * T * T_a$	$\frac{T_m + T_a}{T_a}$	$S * T$	32
BWN-like [1,7,23]	$S * T * T_a + T * T_m$	$\approx \frac{T_m + T_a}{T_a}$	$S * T + 32T$	≈ 32
Ours ($\beta = 1$)	$S * T * T_a + K * T_m$	$\approx \frac{T_m + T_a}{T_a}$	$S * T + 32K$	≈ 32

4   Experiments

In this section, we first give details about training settings, then we compare different methods in terms of quantization loss and classification accuracy. We also implement binary weight AlexNet on FPGA platform, and finally we discuss the effect of different β for semi-binary decomposition.

4.1   Experiment Settings

We implement our method based on the Caffe [14] framework, and experiments are mainly conducted on a GPU Server with 8 Nvidia Titan Xp GPUs.

We evaluate our proposed methods on ImageNet2012 with three deep networks i.e. AlexNet, ResNet-18, and ResNet-50. In the proposed alternating optimization method, we set the maximum iterations to 20. For all the experiments in this paper, we train the networks with a SGD solver with momentum = 0.9, weight decay = 0.0005. As in [1,23,31], the first and last layer in the deep networks are still in floating-number format. Following [7,23], batch normalization layers are used in the AlexNet. We fine-tune AlexNet for 200k iterations with batch-size equals to 256. We set the learning rate to 0.0001 in the beginning, and divide it by 10 after 100k, 150k, and 180k iterations. For ResNet-18, the learning rate starts at 0.0005, and is divided by 10 every 200k iterations. We fine-tune ResNet-18 for 650k iterations with batch size equal to 100. Since fine-tuning ResNet-50 is quite time-consuming, we fine-tune ResNet-50 for only 450K iterations with batchsize = 140 by using 7 GPUs. The learning rate is initialized with 0.0001 and divided by 10 every 200k iterations.

4.2 Comparison on Quantization Loss

In this subsection, we compare different binary quantization methods in terms of quantization loss. The quantization loss is defined by Frobenius norm of residual weights between approximate weights and full-precision weights. Here we compare the proposed SBD-Direct with BC [4] and BWN [23]. Figure 1 shows the binary quantization loss of different methods on AlexNet's *conv2* and *fc6* layer. It shows that the proposed method has lower quantization loss than BC [4] and BWN [23], which benefits from the higher representation capacity of semi-binary decomposition.

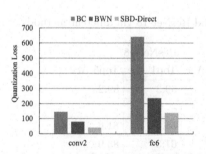

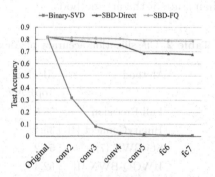

Fig. 1. Binary quantization loss via different methods

Fig. 2. Top5 accuracy of AlexNet by different quantization methods without fine-tuning

4.3 Comparison on Learning Methods

In the previous subsection, we have shown that semi-binary decomposition can achieve lower quantization loss than other binary quantization methods, but which method can learn better semi-binary components has not been discussed.

In this subsection, we compare different methods for learning the semi-binary components. Since semi-binary decomposition has a similar form as Singular Vector Decomposition (SVD), a naive method to get the semi-binary components is quantizing the left and right singular vectors to binary values after using SVD for original weight matrix. We denote this method as Binary-SVD.

Figure 2 shows the top5 accuracy of AlexNet after learning semi-binary components via different methods. Here we binarize the weights of AlexNet layer by layer, i.e. *conv4* in the horizontal axis of Fig. 2 means that *conv2, conv3, conv4* are all quantized to binary values. Figure 2 shows that Binary-SVD performs worst among three methods, which means that simply binarizing the singular vectors of SVD can hardly achieve good performance. SBD-Direct still maintains the accuracy after binarizing one or two layers, but it performs worse as more layers are quantized. SBD-FQ aims to minimize the output featuremap's quantization loss, and it performs well even for multiple layers.

4.4 Comparison on Network's Accuracy

To evaluate our proposed method in terms of classification accuracy, we compare our method with BC [4], BWN [23], SQ-BWN [7], and HWGQ-BWN [1]. Table 2 shows the Top1 and Top5 classification accuracy of AlexNet and ResNet-18 on ImageNet2012 dataset. It's clear that both SBD-Direct and SBD-FQ outperform state-of-the-art methods with a large margin in Top1 and Top5 accuracy. Specifically, our binary ResNet-18 achieves 66.2% top1 accuracy which is 5% higher than state-of-the-art methods.

Table 2. Classification accuracy of AlexNet and ResNet-18 via different methods

Method	AlexNet		ResNet-18	
	Top1 Acc	Top5 Acc	Top1 Acc	Top5 Acc
Full-Precision	58.5	81.5	69.3	89.2
BinaryConnect [4]	35.4	61.0	-	-
SQ-BWN [7]	51.2	75.1	58.3	81.6
HWGQ-BWN [1]	52.4	75.9	61.3	83.9
BWN [23]	56.8	79.4	60.8	83.0
SBD-Direct (Ours)	**58.0**	**80.3**	**64.9**	**86.4**
SBD-FQ (Ours)	**58.5**	**80.6**	**66.2**	**87.1**

We also evaluate our methods on a more challenging network i.e. ResNet-50. ResNet-50 is deeper than AlexNet and ResNet-18, and it has more 1×1 convolutional kernels. Table 3 reports the Top1 and Top5 accuracy of ResNet-50. After fine-tuning, both SBD-Direct and SBD-FQ outperforms state-of-the-art methods by a large margin (5% in top1 accuracy).

From Tables 2 and 3, we can find that SBD-FQ achieves higher accuracy than SBD-Direct, which shows that minimizing the featuremap's quantization loss is better than direct semi-binary decomposition. But SBD-Direct is faster than SBD-FQ because minimizing the featuremap's quantization loss takes more training time than direct semi-binary decomposition.

Table 3. Classification accuracy of ResNet-50 via different methods

Method	Classification accuracy	
	Top1	Top5
Full-Precision	75.2	92.2
BWN [23]	63.9	85.1
SBD-Direct (Ours)	**67.7**	**87.8**
SBD-FQ (Ours)	**68.9**	**88.7**

4.5 Experiments on FPGA

In order to demonstrate the efficiency of our proposed method on hardware acceleration of CNN, we further implement the binary-weight AlexNet on Xilinx Virtex-7 VX485T FPGA platform. The microarchitecture design is based on [29], which is a state-of-the-art CNN accelerator. We quantize the activations of binary-weight AlexNet to 8-bit for the consideration of energy and resource efficiency, and the top1 and top5 accuracy after activation quantization is 58.46% and 80.7% respectively. For fair comparison, we adopt the same platform and working frequency, and restrict the usage of on-chip computing resources (LUTs and FFs) as the same level as in [29].

Table 4 shows the results of our evaluation on the binary-weight AlexNet. It is obvious that our accelerator is 8.78× faster than the floating point counterpart with nearly the same usage of LUTs and FFs. In addition, the consumption of on-chip memory and DSP blocks are drastically reduced due to the weight binarization and low precision representation of activations.

Table 4. Experiment result on FPGA

	Activation	Weight	Resource utilization				Latency	Speed-ups
			DSP	BRAM	LUT	FF		
Zhang et al. [29]	32 bits	32 bits	2240	1024	186251	205704	21.6 ms	1×
Ours	8 bits	1 bit	0	261	211554	303642	2.46 ms	**8.78×**

4.6   The Effect of Different β

Figure 3 shows the top5 accuracy of AlexNet after using the proposed SBD-Direct method with different values of β. With β increasing, we get higher compression ratio but lower accuracy. Besides, we notice that fully-connected layers is insensitive to the values of β, which means that we can choose larger β for fully-connected layers to achieve higher compression ratio.

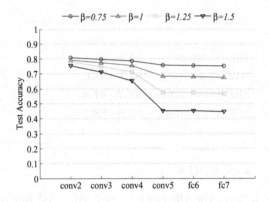

Fig. 3. Top5 accuracy of AlexNet for different β without fine-tuning

5   Conclusion

In this paper, we propose a novel semi-binary quantization method to train the binary weight networks, and we also propose an alternating optimization method to solve the semi-binary decomposition factors under binary constraints. Extensive experiments on ImageNet2012 dataset demonstrate that our methods outperform state-of-the-art methods with a large margin. Experiments on FPGA platform demonstrates that our proposed binary weight networks can achieve nearly 9× speed-ups using less on-chip memory and hardware resources.

Acknowledgements. This work was supported in part by National Natural Science Foundation of China (No. 61332016, and No. 61572500), the Scientific Research Key Program of Beijing Municipal Commission of Education (KZ201610005012), and the Strategic Priority Research Program of Chinese Academy of Science (Grant No. XDBS01000000).

References

1. Cai, Z., He, X., Sun, J., Vasconcelos, N.: Deep learning with low precision by half-wave Gaussian quantization. In: 2017 IEEE Conference on Computer Vision and Pattern Recognition. pp. 5406–5414. IEEE Computer Society, Honolulu (2017). https://doi.org/10.1109/CVPR.2017.574
2. Cheng, J., Wu, J., Leng, C., Wang, Y., Hu, Q.: Quantized CNN: a unified approach to accelerate and compress convolutional networks. IEEE Trans. Neural Netw. Learn. Syst., 1–14 (2017). https://doi.org/10.1109/TNNLS.2017.2774288
3. Cheng, J., Wang, P., Li, G., Hu, Q., Lu, H.: Recent advances in efficientcomputation of deep convolutional neural networks. Front. IT EE **19**(1), 64–77 (2018). https://doi.org/10.1631/FITEE.1700789
4. Courbariaux, M., Bengio, Y., David, J.: Binaryconnect: training deep neural networks with binary weights during propagations. In: Cortes, C., Lawrence, N.D., Lee, D.D., Sugiyama, M., Garnett, R. (eds.) Advances in Neural Information Processing Systems 28, Montreal, Quebec, Canada, pp. 3123–3131 (2015)
5. Denil, M., Shakibi, B., Dinh, L., de Freitas, N.: Predicting parameters in deep learning. In: Burges, C.J.C., Bottou, L., Ghahramani, Z., Weinberger, K.Q. (eds.) Advances in Neural Information Processing Systems 26, pp. 2148–2156. Curran Associates Inc., Lake Tahoe (2013)
6. Denton, E.L., Zaremba, W., Bruna, J., LeCun, Y., Fergus, R.: Exploiting linear structure within convolutional networks for efficient evaluation. In: Ghahramani, Z., Welling, M., Cortes, C., Lawrence, N.D., Weinberger, K.Q. (eds.) Advances in Neural Information Processing Systems 27, pp. 1269–1277. Curran Associates Inc., Montreal (2014)
7. Dong, Y., Ni, R., Li, J., Chen, Y., Zhu, J., Su, H.: Learning accurate low-bit deep neural networks with stochastic quantization. CoRR abs/1708.01001 (2017). http://arxiv.org/abs/1708.01001
8. Gong, Y., Liu, L., Yang, M., Bourdev, L.: Compressing deep convolutional networks using vector quantization. arXiv preprint arXiv:1412.6115 (2014)
9. Gupta, S., Agrawal, A., Gopalakrishnan, K., Narayanan, P.: Deep learning with limited numerical precision. In: Bach, F., Blei, D. (eds.) Proceedings of the 32nd International Conference on Machine Learning. Proceedings of Machine Learning Research, vol. 37, pp. 1737–1746. PMLR, Lille (2015)
10. Han, S., Pool, J., Tran, J., Dally, W.J.: Learning both weights and connections for efficient neural network. In: Cortes, C., Lawrence, N.D., Lee, D.D., Sugiyama, M., Garnett, R. (eds.) Advances in Neural Information Processing Systems 28, Montreal, Quebec, Canada, pp. 1135–1143 (2015)
11. Hassibi, B., Stork, D.G.: Second order derivatives for network pruning: optimal brain surgeon. In: Hanson, S.J., Cowan, J.D., Giles, C.L. (eds.) Advances in Neural Information Processing Systems 5, pp. 164–171. Morgan Kaufmann, Denver (1992)
12. Hu, Q., Wang, P., Cheng, J.: From hashing to CNNs: training binary weight networks via hashing. In: McIlraith, S.A., Weinberger, K.Q. (eds.) Proceedings of the Thirty-Second AAAI Conference on Artificial Intelligence. AAAI Press, New Orleans (2018)
13. Jaderberg, M., Vedaldi, A., Zisserman, A.: Speeding up convolutional neural networks with low rank expansions. In: Valstar, M.F., French, A.P., Pridmore, T.P. (eds.) BMVC 2014. BMVA Press, Nottingham (2014)
14. Jia, Y., et al.: Caffe: convolutional architecture for fast feature embedding. In: Proceedings of the 22nd ACM International Conference on Multimedia, MM 2014, pp. 675–678. ACM, New York (2014). https://doi.org/10.1145/2647868.2654889

15. Kim, Y., Park, E., Yoo, S., Choi, T., Yang, L., Shin, D.: Compression of deep convolutional neural networks for fast and low power mobile applications. CoRR abs/1511.06530 (2015). http://arxiv.org/abs/1511.06530
16. Krizhevsky, A., Sutskever, I., Hinton, G.E.: Imagenet classification with deep convolutional neural networks. Commun. ACM **60**(6), 84–90 (2017). https://doi.org/10.1145/3065386
17. Lebedev, V., Ganin, Y., Rakhuba, M., Oseledets, I.V., Lempitsky, V.S.: Speeding-up convolutional neural networks using fine-tuned CP-decomposition. CoRR abs/1412.6553 (2014). http://arxiv.org/abs/1412.6553
18. Lebedev, V., Lempitsky, V.S.: Fast convnets using group-wise brain damage. In: 2016 IEEE Conference on Computer Vision and Pattern Recognition, pp. 2554–2564. IEEE Computer Society, Las Vegas (2016). https://doi.org/10.1109/CVPR.2016.280
19. LeCun, Y., Denker, J.S., Solla, S.A.: Optimal brain damage. In: Touretzky, D.S. (ed.) Advances in Neural Information Processing Systems 2, pp. 598–605. Morgan Kaufmann, Denver (1989)
20. Lin, D., Talathi, S., Annapureddy, S.: Fixed point quantization of deep convolutional networks. In: Balcan, M.F., Weinberger, K.Q. (eds.) Proceedings of the 33rd International Conference on Machine Learning. Proceedings of Machine Learning Research, vol. 48, pp. 2849–2858. PMLR, New York (2016)
21. Long, J., Shelhamer, E., Darrell, T.: Fully convolutional networks for semantic segmentation. In: IEEE Conference on Computer Vision and Pattern Recognition, CVPR 2015, Boston, MA, USA, 7–12 June 2015, pp. 3431–3440. IEEE Computer Society (2015). https://doi.org/10.1109/CVPR.2015.7298965
22. Qiu, J., et al.: Going deeper with embedded FPGA platform for convolutional neural network. In: Chen, D., Greene, J.W. (eds.) Proceedings of the 2016 ACM/SIGDA International Symposium on Field-Programmable Gate Arrays, FPGA 2016, pp. 26–35. ACM, New York (2016). https://doi.org/10.1145/2847263.2847265
23. Rastegari, M., Ordonez, V., Redmon, J., Farhadi, A.: XNOR-Net: imagenet classification using binary convolutional neural networks. In: Leibe, B., Matas, J., Sebe, N., Welling, M. (eds.) ECCV 2016. LNCS, vol. 9908, pp. 525–542. Springer, Cham (2016). https://doi.org/10.1007/978-3-319-46493-0_32
24. Ren, S., He, K., Girshick, R.B., Sun, J.: Faster R-CNN: towards real-time object detection with region proposal networks. IEEE Trans. Pattern Anal. Mach. Intell. **39**(6), 1137–1149 (2017). https://doi.org/10.1109/TPAMI.2016.2577031
25. Wang, P., Cheng, J.: Accelerating convolutional neural networks for mobile applications. In: Proceedings of the 2016 ACM on Multimedia Conference, MM 2016, pp. 541–545. ACM, New York (2016). https://doi.org/10.1145/2964284.2967280
26. Wang, P., Cheng, J.: Fixed-point factorized networks. In: 2017 IEEE Conference on Computer Vision and Pattern Recognition, CVPR 2017, Honolulu, HI, USA, 21–26 July 2017, pp. 3966–3974. IEEE Computer Society (2017). https://doi.org/10.1109/CVPR.2017.422
27. Wang, P., Hu, Q., Zhang, Y., Zhang, C., Liu, Y., Cheng, J.: Two-step quantization for low-bit neural networks. In: The IEEE Conference on Computer Vision and Pattern Recognition (CVPR). IEEE Computer Society (2018)
28. Wu, J., Leng, C., Wang, Y., Hu, Q., Cheng, J.: Quantized convolutional neuralnetworks for mobile devices. In: IEEE Conference on Computer Vision and Pattern Recognition (CVPR), pp. 4820–4828. IEEE Computer Society, LasVegas (2016). https://doi.org/10.1109/CVPR.2016.521

29. Zhang, C., Li, P., Sun, G., Guan, Y., Xiao, B., Cong, J.: Optimizing FPGA-based accelerator design for deep convolutional neural networks. In: Constantinides, G.A., Chen, D. (eds.) Proceedings of the 2015 ACM/SIGDA International Symposium on Field-Programmable Gate Arrays, pp. 161–170. ACM, Monterey (2015). https://doi.org/10.1145/2684746.2689060

30. Zhang, X., Zou, J., He, K., Sun, J.: Accelerating very deep convolutional networks for classification and detection. IEEE Trans. Pattern Anal. Mach. Intell. **38**(10), 1943–1955 (2016). https://doi.org/10.1109/TPAMI.2015.2502579

31. Zhou, S., Ni, Z., Zhou, X., Wen, H., Wu, Y., Zou, Y.: DoReFa-Net: training low bitwidth convolutional neural networks with low bitwidth gradients. CoRR abs/1606.06160 (2016). http://arxiv.org/abs/1606.06160

Focus, Segment and Erase: An Efficient Network for Multi-label Brain Tumor Segmentation

Xuan Chen[1](✉)(iD), Jun Hao Liew[1](iD), Wei Xiong[2], Chee-Kong Chui[1](iD), and Sim-Heng Ong[1](iD)

[1] National University of Singapore, Singapore, Singapore
{xuan.chen,liewjunhao}@u.nus.edu,
{mpecck,eleosh}@nus.edu.sg
[2] Institute for Infocomm Research, Singapore, Singapore
wxiong@i2r.a-star.edu.sg

Abstract. In multi-label brain tumor segmentation, class imbalance and inter-class interference are common and challenging problems. In this paper, we propose a novel end-to-end trainable network named FSENet to address the aforementioned issues. The proposed FSENet has a tumor region pooling component to restrict the prediction within the tumor region ("focus"), thus mitigating the influence of the dominant non-tumor region. Furthermore, the network decomposes the more challenging multi-label brain tumor segmentation problem into several simpler binary segmentation tasks ("segment"), where each task focuses on a specific tumor tissue. To alleviate inter-class interference, we adopt a simple yet effective idea in our work: we erase the segmented regions before proceeding to further segmentation of tumor tissue ("erase"), thus reduces competition among different tumor classes. Our single-model FSENet ranks 3rd on the multi-modal brain tumor segmentation benchmark 2015 (BraTS 2015) without relying on ensembles or complicated post-processing steps.

Keywords: Brain tumor segmentation
Convolutional neural network · Class imbalance
Inter-class interference

1 Introduction

Brain tumor, though not a common disease, severely harms the health of patients and causes high mortality. Automatic brain tumor segmentation would greatly assist medical diagnosis and treatment planning, since manual segmentation is time-consuming and requires a high degree of professional expertise. The segmentation task is very challenging due to the diversity of the tumors in terms of

---

X. Chen and J. H. Liew—Equally contributed.

© Springer Nature Switzerland AG 2018
V. Ferrari et al. (Eds.): ECCV 2018, LNCS 11217, pp. 674–689, 2018.
https://doi.org/10.1007/978-3-030-01261-8_40

their location, shape, size and contrast, which restrict the application of strong priors. Hence, researchers have spent much time and effort in studying this topic.

The approaches for brain tumor segmentation can be generally categorized into two classes, *i.e.*, generative methods and discriminative methods. Generative methods [19,23], which model tumor anatomy and appearance statistics explicitly, usually have better generalization ability, but require more professional knowledge and elaborate pre-processing steps. Discriminative methods [1,4,7,11,22], though relying heavily on the quality of training data, can learn task-relevant demands from human-labeled data directly.

An example of discriminative methods is machine learning, which has been successfully applied in this field. Before the advent of the deep learning era, traditional machine learning approaches typically rely on the dedicated selection of hand-crafted features, for example, first-order textures [1], histogram and spatial location [4], and a mixture of high dimensional multi-scale features [7] to achieve good performance. However, searching exhaustively for the best combination of features by trial-and-error is not feasible. Deep convolutional neural networks (DCNNs), on the other hand, are able to extract more suitable features for the task on their own by updating the networks gradually with gradient backpropagation, and thus have gained popularity in the medical image processing community [2,5,6,10,11,14,20,22,24,25].

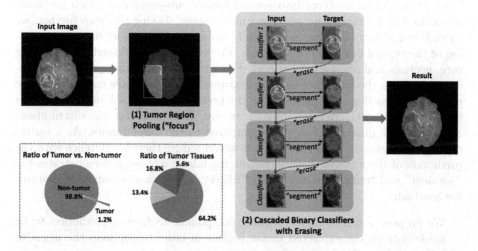

Fig. 1. Overview of FSENet. The operations are shown on the input image for illustrative purpose. (1) The tumor region pooling first extracts the tumor region ("focus"). (2) Within the tumor region, each classifier sequentially segments a target tissue ("segment"), and erases it before proceeding to the next classifier ("erase"), forming a cascaded framework. Finally, all segmented tissues are combined to produce the multi-label result. Blue, green, red and yellow indicate edema, enhancing core, necrosis and non-enhancing core respectively. The darkened regions represent the erased areas. The pie charts illustrate the class imbalance problem (Better viewed in color) (Color figure online)

Common problems faced in multi-label brain tumor segmentation are class imbalance and inter-class interference. The class imbalance problem exhibits two aspects. First, the non-tumor region may be tens, or even hundreds of times the size of a tumor lesion. Second, some tumor tissues are much larger compared to others, for example, edema *vs.* necrotic core. We plot the statistics of each class in the training set of BraTS 2015 [15,18] as pie charts in Fig. 1 to show the class imbalance problem. The inter-class interference is caused by similar features shared among different tumor tissues, leading to difficulties in differentiating each class and also interfering with their predictions.

In this paper, we propose a novel network named FSENet that aims to address these problems. Fig. 1 shows an overview of the proposed FSENet. While segmenting each tumor tissue is highly challenging, separating the entire tumor from the non-tumor region is relatively easy. Thus, we first identify the tumor region with a whole-tumor classifier and then extract features of the tumor region with a tumor region pooling component, such that the influence of the large non-tumor region can be alleviated by discarding a large portion of negative sample features. This step tells the network where it should pay attention to, demonstrating the "focus" feature of our FSENet.

In order to reduce the inter-class interference, a simple yet effective idea is adopted: the previously segmented tumor tissues are erased before proceeding to the segmentation of the next tumor label. We first decompose the multi-label segmentation problem into several binary sub-problems, which are more specialized in discriminating specific tumor tissues. Taking this step further, we cascade our binary classifiers sequentially in an "outer-to-inner" manner according to the typical brain tumor structure, *i.e.,* edema first, followed by enhancing core, necrosis and non-enhancing core. Furthermore, an erasing process is introduced between the classifiers to erase features from the feature maps if they are confidently classified as foreground by the previous classifiers. Usually, the inner tissues, like necrosis, are more irregular in size, shape, contrast and distribution, and thus more difficult to segment compared to the outer tissues. As a result, erasing the segmented outer tissue class would reduce their interference with the prediction of the remaining more challenging labels. This step demonstrates the "segment" and "erase" features of our FSENet. To summarize, our contributions are fourfold:

- We propose a tumor region pooling component to force a prediction to be made only on the extracted tumor region, in order to suppress the negative influence from the dominant non-tumor region.
- We propose to replace one-stage multi-label segmentation with a component that consists of cascaded binary classifiers with erasing to simplify and specialize the problem, and to avoid inter-class interference.
- We develop an end-to-end training pipeline which achieves significantly performance boost over the baseline (without the proposed components) with only ~1.7% overhead.

– Our single-model FSENet achieves 3rd place performance on the BraTS 2015 leaderboard without heavy model ensembles or complicated post-processing steps.

2   Related Work

Class imbalance is a common problem in medical image analysis. For example, in liver computed tomography (CT) images, the lesions are several times smaller than the liver, and may only occupy a few pixels.

Various approaches have been proposed to address the class imbalance problem. One approach is to keep a reasonable ratio of positive samples and negative samples by manual oversampling or undersampling [2,9,22]. However, as in multi-label segmentation, this method is only applicable to a patch-based framework, but not to one that takes the entire image as input. Another typical approach is to modify the loss function [5,20], such that the network is less sensitive to the class imbalance problem. Although [20] claims the effectiveness of using the Dice loss, it is only suitable for a binary segmentation problem. The weighted cross-entropy loss [5], unlike the Dice loss, is more flexible in that it is suitable for both binary and multi-label segmentation. However, it suffers from the elaborate selection of weighting factors.

In our approach, we use the coarse binary segmentation result to locate the tumor region, and then extract the region for fine multi-label segmentation. By extracting the tumor region, the non-tumor samples are naturally reduced and hence have less influence on the fine-grained prediction. The proposed method is implemented as a region pooling component, which is able to work within an image-based framework and requires no hyperparameter.

Sequential prediction is also one plausible way to deal with the class imbalance problem, as well as simplifying difficult one-stage multi-label segmentation by using several specialized classifiers. Its effectiveness in multi-label segmentation has been widely reported. Sequential prediction is usually implemented by cascading multiple models [2,3,5,8,10,11,25]. The first model performs a similar function to our proposed region pooling component, which is to identify the region of interest (RoI). The following models are trained to handle more difficult tasks with the help of the identified RoI. For example, in [2], one 3D-UNet that is used to separate the whole tumor from the non-tumor region is cascaded with a second 3D-UNet which discriminates the different brain tumor tissues. One obvious disadvantage of cascading multiple models is that the overall framework may be sub-optimal since end-to-end training is inapplicable. In addition, the deep convolution features extracted by each CNN could not be fully utilized, thus reducing computational efficiency.

In our paper, we implement sequential prediction by cascading classifiers, rather than cascading models, in such a way that the proposed FSENet can perform end-to-end training. All classifiers share features that are first extracted by a fully convolutional network, instead of having their own networks as in the case of cascading models, so that the deep convolutional features can be well

678   X. Chen et al.

utilized. Similarly, the cascaded classifiers solve the difficult multi-label segmentation problem in a more specialized and effective way. The main difference lies in the novel erasing operation introduced between classifiers, which is able to alleviate the inter-class interference that is common in medical images due to the similar features shared by different tissues. This erasing operation suppresses the responses of regions that correspond to the confident foreground prediction produced by the previous classifiers. The classifiers are cascaded in an "outer-to-inner" manner according to the typical brain tumor structure, and this is done in such a way that the outer tissues would not interfere with the segmentation of the inner tissues.

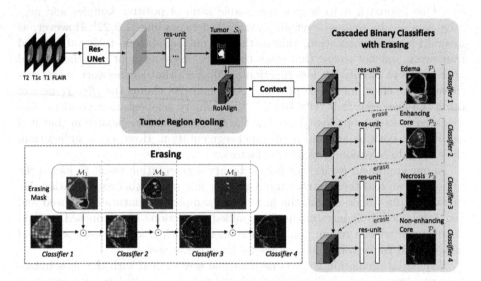

Fig. 2. Architecture of the proposed FSENet. The input goes through Res-UNet for the extraction of deep convolutional features. A whole-tumor classifier produces binary tumor/non-tumor segmentation to locate the tumor, and then the tumor region pooling component extracts the valid region from the feature maps accordingly. The extracted feature maps pass through the cascaded binary classifiers with erasing component for the segmentation of each tumor tissue in an "outer-to-inner" order. An example of the erasing process is visualized in the bottom left box. Feature multiplying the erasing mask with Hadamard product gives the erased feature maps.

3   FSENet

The proposed FSENet includes two novel components, *i.e.*, tumor region pooling and cascaded binary classifiers with erasing. The architecture of FSENet is shown in Fig. 2.

Following convention, the input of the proposed network is the concatenation of all four available channels, *i.e.*, contrast-enhanced T1-weighted (T1c) image, T1-weighted (T1) image, T2-weighted (T2) image and FLuid-Attenuated Inversion Recovery (FLAIR) image of each brain magnetic resonance (MR) slice to fully utilize the multi-modal information. We feed forward the input to a fully-convolutional network to extract deep convolutional features. The feature maps pass through a whole-tumor classifier, which separates the tumor and non-tumor regions. According to the binary tumor/non-tumor segmentation result, the tumor region pooling module knows where to focus to extract the tumor region from the feature maps, such that the negative influence from the dominant non-tumor region can be alleviated in the subsequent predictions. The extracted feature maps are sequentially fed to the cascaded binary classifiers with erasing component such that more discriminative representation related to a specific tissue is emphasized, thus favors more accurate pixel-wise classification. The erasing operation helps to suppress inter-class interference, and hence assists the prediction of the latter class to improve overall performance. The final multi-label segmentation result is the fusion of the predictions given by the four binary classifiers, as well as the whole-tumor classifier.

3.1   Res-UNet

UNet [24] has wide applications in medical image processing [5,6,14]. Features and ground truth information of small and scattered tissues can totally disappear in a network whose output stride is larger than 1. Thus, UNet is an appropriate choice since the generated feature maps share the size of the input image. In order to increase the network capability without hindering the gradient back-propagation, we replace each convolution layer in UNet with a residual convolution block (res-conv) (Fig. 3) as proposed in [13], which turns UNet into its residual counterpart (Res-UNet). Res-UNet is adopted as our backbone architecture to extract deep convolutional features. However, the proposed components can be generalized to any fully convolutional network easily, and is not limited to this specific Res-UNet.

A whole-tumor binary classifier is attached to the Res-UNet to segment the entire tumor from the non-tumor region. By thresholding the prediction $\mathcal{P}_0 \in$

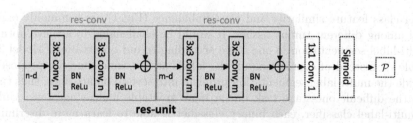

Fig. 3. Configuration of the residual unit and the classifier in the FSENet. The parts inside the green rectangle are the residual convolution block (res-conv). A residual unit (res-unit) consists of two res-convs. The parts indicated in dash line are only included in the classifier (Color figure online)

$\mathbb{R}^{H \times W}$ of the whole-tumor classifier with a constant value of 0.5, the binary tumor/non-tumor segmentation result $\mathcal{S}_0 \in \mathbb{R}^{H \times W}$ can be obtained. The feature maps extracted with Res-UNet and the binary tumor/non-tumor segmentation result $\mathcal{S}_0$ are further utilized in the following components of the FSENet, which are discussed in detail below.

3.2 Tumor Region Pooling

Brain tumor tissues usually occupy a small number of pixels in the MR image, while the non-tumor region is several times larger than the tumor (Fig. 1), which causes a severe class imbalance problem and hence leads to difficulties in learning. To address this problem, we propose to use RoIAlign [12] to extract the features of the tumor region from the original feature maps, so that the following classifiers only need to focus on the tumor region for subsequent fine-grained segmentation. Extracting the tumor region has two benefits. First, since the non-tumor region contains a large no-measurement area (the black region), computational resources can be saved on its segmentation since this is a relatively easy task. Second, the following fine-grained multi-label segmentation would not be hindered by the presence of the large non-tumor region.

RoIAlign locates the tumor region according to an RoI proposal, and then converts the valid region in the feature maps into RoI feature maps with fixed spatial extent $H_{\mathrm{RoI}} \times W_{\mathrm{RoI}}$. The RoI proposal is produced based on the binary tumor/non-tumor segmentation result $\mathcal{S}_0$ generated by the whole-tumor classifier. To avoid the warping problem, the RoI proposal is set to the smallest square bounding box that contains the tumor region. With the consideration of not losing too much detail during the pooling operation from a large spatial dimension to a small one, we empirically set both H_{RoI} and W_{RoI} equal to 100 in our experiments.

The RoI feature maps, which mainly contain features related to the tumor region, are then fed to the four cascaded binary classifiers with erasing to classify each pixel to its correct target class.

3.3 Cascaded Binary Classifiers with Erasing

Inter-class feature similarity and class imbalance (Fig. 1) are commonly exhibited among different tumor tissues. It would be challenging to achieve optimal multi-label segmentation in one stage according to our observation (Model 2 in Table 1). Instead of considering all the labels at the same time, we propose to divide the multi-label segmentation problem into several binary ones, thus turning the difficult one-stage task into a more tractable multi-stage task. Unlike a multi-label classifier, each binary classifier is able to learn more discriminative task-relevant representation of the target class for more accurate binary segmentation. The configuration of a binary classifier is shown in Fig. 3.

However, simply decomposing a multi-label classifier into several binary counterparts may not necessarily lead to improvement in performance. This is because the prediction of relatively small and scattered tissues, like necrotic tissue, would still be difficult due to the scarcity of positive samples and competition from other classes. Therefore, the overall performance is sub-optimal and should be improved. To address the problem, we first cascade the classifiers in an "outer-to-inner" fashion according to the typical brain tumor structure, *i.e.*, edema first, followed by enhancing core, necrosis and non-enhancing core. We introduce an erasing process between the classifiers to erase the responses of previously segmented tissues, such that the remaining classes, which are usually more irregular in sizes, shapes, contrast and distributions, are free from the competition and interference of the earlier class. The erasing operation is multiplying, element-wise, the RoI feature maps with an erasing mask:

$$\mathcal{F}' = \mathcal{F} \odot \mathcal{M} \tag{1}$$

where $\mathcal{F}$ and $\mathcal{F}'$ are the RoI feature maps and the erased RoI feature maps respectively, $\mathcal{M}$ the erasing mask, and $\odot$ the Hadamard product.

An example demonstrating the erasing process is shown in the bottom left box in Fig. 2. The responses in the RoI feature maps are gradually erased after each binary segmentation stage, thus leading to fewer features and hence less competition and interference in subsequent segmentation of more difficult tumor tissues.

Suppose the prediction produced by each binary classifier is denoted as $\mathcal{P}_i \in \mathbb{R}^{H_{\mathrm{RoI}} \times W_{\mathrm{RoI}}}$, $i \in \{1, \dots, 4\}$ with its value in the range $[0, 1]$, indicating the confidence of classifying the corresponding pixel to a target class. The erasing mask $\mathcal{M}_i$ is generated based on the prediction $\mathcal{P}_i$:

$$\mathcal{M}_i(x, y) = 1 - \mathcal{P}_i(x, y) \tag{2}$$

where $\mathcal{M}_i(x, y) \in [0, 1]$. The erasing mask is a reverse attention mask that focuses on the unsegmented regions, while suppressing the responses of the confident foreground regions predicted by previous classifiers.

Instead of totally removing the segmented region by thresholding the prediction with a specific constant value, the proposed erasing mask only suppresses their response to a certain extent according to the prediction confidence. This avoids the selection of the threshold value, and allows regions with not very high prediction confidence (usually along the boundary) to partially pass through the mask as supporting context in the following segmentations.

To provide the classifiers with a better understanding of the overall tumor structure, we introduce a context branch in our FSENet (Fig. 2), which contains the pyramid pooling module proposed in [26]. The multi-scale context information is concatenated with the erased RoI feature maps as the input of the classifier, thus providing additional reference to assist the segmentation.

3.4   Loss and Final Result

The network contains one whole-tumor classifier to identify the tumor region and four class-specific classifiers to segment different tumor tissues. For each classifier, we adopt both cross-entropy loss and Dice loss. Dice loss, which is widely used in the medical image processing community [20], can be defined as:

$$\mathcal{L}_{\text{dice}} = 1 - \frac{2\sum_{k=1}^{K} p_k g_k}{\sum_{k=1}^{K} p_k + \sum_{k=1}^{K} g_k} \tag{3}$$

where p_k is the prediction of a pixel, g_k, the corresponding ground truth, and K, the total number of pixels. The total loss is the weighted sum of all the losses:

$$\mathcal{L}_{\text{total}} = \sum_i \alpha_i \mathcal{L}^i + \sum_i \beta_i \mathcal{L}^i_{\text{dice}} \tag{4}$$

where $i \in \{0, \dots, 4\}$ refers to the whole-tumor classifier and the four class-specific classifiers respectively, $\mathcal{L}^i$ the cross-entropy loss of the ith classifier, and α_i and β_i the hyperparameters to emphasize or mitigate a certain loss. We assign equal importance to all losses, and hence α_i and β_i, $\forall i \in \{0, \dots, 4\}$ are set to 1.

To generate the final multi-label segmentation result, the prediction $\mathcal{P}_i \in \mathbb{R}^{H_{\text{RoI}} \times W_{\text{RoI}}}, i \in \{1, \dots, 4\}$ is first projected to have its original scale $\mathcal{P}'_i \in \mathbb{R}^{H \times W}, i \in \{1, \dots, 4\}$, which represents the probability of each pixel belonging to the class. As for the non-tumor class, we have $\mathcal{P}'_0 = J - \mathcal{P}_0$, where $J \in \mathbb{R}^{H \times W}$ is an all-one matrix. Fusing the five predictions by the argmax function gives us the final multi-label segmentation result.

4   Experiment

4.1   Dataset and Experiment Settings

Dataset and Evaluation Metrics. We evaluate the proposed FSENet on the multi-label brain tumor segmentation benchmark 2015 (BraTS 2015) [15,18], which includes 4 tumor tissue categories and one non-tumor category (label = 0). The 4 types of tumor tissues are necrosis (label = 1), edema (label = 2), non-enhancing core (label = 3) and enhancing core (label = 4). BraTS 2015 contains 220 high-grade glioma (HGG) cases and 54 low-grade glioma (LGG) cases in the training set, and 110 mixture cases of HGG and LGG in the test set. Each case includes four volumes, which correspond to the four modalities, i.e., T1, T1c, T2 and FLAIR. A volume consists of 155 MR images of size 240×240. The performance is evaluated in terms of the Dice similarity score (Dice), positive prediction value (PPV), and sensitivity (Sens) over three predefined regions, i.e. whole tumor (label 1 + 2 + 3 + 4), tumor core (label 1 + 3 + 4) and active tumor (label 4). Dice score, PPV and sensitivity are defined respectively as:

$$\text{Dice}(P,T) = \frac{2|P_1 \cap T_1|}{|P_1| + |T_1|}$$

$$\text{PPV}(P,T) = \frac{|P_1 \cap T_1|}{|P_1|} \tag{5}$$

$$\text{Sens}(P,T) = \frac{|P_1 \cap T_1|}{|T_1|}$$

where $P \in \{0, 1\}$ is the prediction, $T \in \{0, 1\}$ the ground truth, P_1 and T_1 the sets of pixels where $P = 1$ and $T = 1$ respectively, and $|\cdot|$ the size of the set.

Training/Testing Settings. In the training phase, only the slices that contain tumor tissue labels are used (19676 slices). We train our FSENet from scratch with mini-batch size equals to 2. The T1, T1c, T2 and FLAIR images that correspond to the same brain MR slice are concatenated, forming a 4-channel input to the model. All patient cases in the training and test sets are pre-processed to correct for intensity inhomogeneity with a learning based two-step standardization [21]. In the test phase, for each patient case, all 155 slices are fed into the network for inference.

Our implementation is based on the PyTorch[1] platform using a NVIDIA GeForce TITAN Xp GPU with 12GB memory. The initial learning rate is set to 1×10^{-3} and decreased by a factor of 10 after 15 epochs. We train the FSENet for 25 epochs in total before deployment. To facilitate learning, we use ground truth to generate RoI proposal during training. However, the masks are always generated based on the predictions of the network stated in Eq. (2). We use stochastic gradient descent (SGD) with momentum and weight decay set as 0.9 and 0.0005 respectively. The input images are horizontally flipped with probability of 0.5 during training. No other data augmentation is used.

In the test phase, we adopt horizontal flip as data augmentation. Simple connected component analysis is applied as the post-processing step to remove noise. We also experimented with more complicated post-processing steps such as 3D denseCRF [16] but only observe a marginal improvement. In the consideration of trade-off between marginal gain and heavy computational cost, we do not use any complicated post-processing techniques in the remaining experiments. It is also worth mentioning that all experimental results presented are generated by a single model without heavy model ensembles.

4.2 Ablation Analysis

We conducted a systematic ablation study using 220 out of the 274 patient cases (220 HGG cases and 54 LGG cases) from the training set for training and the remaining 54 cases for validation.

We present quantitative and qualitative analysis in Table 1 and Fig. 4 respectively. To better demonstrate the effectiveness of the cascaded classifier with erasing module in mitigating the inter-class interference and benefiting the prediction of the difficult class, we additionally report the mean intersection over union (IoU) score over the non-enhancing core category, which is the most difficult class to predict because of its irregularity and dispersibility.

Tumor Region Pooling. We first study the effect of the tumor region pooling component in the FSENet. As discussed previously, tumor region pooling helps to ease the class imbalance problem, so that the model can focus on learning useful task-relevant representations for multi-label segmentation without the

---

[1] http://pytorch.org/.

interference of the dominant non-tumor region. Firstly, we notice that Model 1 without the region pooling component fails to learn and predict almost all pixels as non-tumor category, if normal cross-entropy loss is applied. Instead, we use a weighted cross-entropy loss, where the weighting factor for each class is the normalized inverse frequency of the corresponding class.

Table 1. Quantitative comparison among baselines and our models

Model	Methods				Dice			PPV			Sens			mean
No.	TRP	MultiS	Context	Erase	W	T	A	W	T	A	W	T	A	IoU
1					0.744	0.686	0.721	0.616	0.577	0.689	**0.982**	**0.910**	**0.805**	22.1
2	✓				0.751	0.735	0.688	0.628	0.686	0.774	0.965	0.837	0.659	24.6
					↑ 9.4%	↑ 7.1%	↓ 4.6%	↑ 1.9%	↑ 18.9%	↑ 12.3%	↓ 1.7%	↓ 8.0%	↓ 18.1%	↑ 11.3%
3	✓	✓			0.890	0.776	0.708	0.897	0.831	0.788	0.892	0.768	0.677	28.1
					↑ 19.6%	↑ 13.1%	↓ 1.8%	↑ 45.6%	↑ 44.0%	↑ 14.4%	↓ 9.2%	↓ 15.6%	↓ 15.9%	↑ 27.1%
4	✓	✓		✓	0.891	0.775	0.711	**0.912**	**0.843**	**0.792**	0.878	0.763	0.675	**28.3**
					↑ 19.8%	↑ 13.0%	↓ 1.4%	↑ 48.1%	↑ 46.1%	↑ 14.9%	↓ 10.6%	↓ 16.2%	↓ 16.2%	↑ 28.1%
5	✓	✓	✓	✓	**0.892**	**0.782**	**0.734**	0.902	0.817	0.766	0.891	0.790	0.745	**28.3**
					↑ 19.9%	↑ 14.0%	↑ 1.8%	↑ 46.4%	↑ 41.6%	↑ 11.2%	↓ 9.3%	↓ 13.2%	↓ 7.5%	↑ 28.1%

We apply the same weighted cross entropy loss to Model 2 for fair comparison. Obviously, even with a weighted cross-entropy loss function, Model 1 still gives unsatisfactory results (second row in Fig. 4). Despite its high sensitivity score due to excessively predicting pixels as foreground classes, the generated result is undesirable. Model 2 generates more accurate segmentation results, and hence outperforms Model 1 in most of the evaluation categories as shown in Table 1. This shows the effectiveness of the "focus" step.

One-stage vs. Multi-stage. To simplify multi-label segmentation task, we propose to decompose the one-stage multi-label segmentation problem into several binary segmentations. We expect these more specialized classifiers would perform better in differentiating each class, and hence boost overall results. To examine this, we additionally train a model which feeds the RoI feature map to 4 binary classifiers for individual tumor tissue segmentation (Model 3) as opposed to Model 2 that applies a softmax layer for one-stage multi-label segmentation. We find that Model 3 significantly outperforms Model 2 in most categories of the metrics, which endorses our assumption.

Erasing and Contextual Compensation. In Model 3, the inter-class interference problem remains unsolved. Taking this one step further, we introduce the proposed erasing process to Model 4 to study its effectiveness. However, Model 4 only achieves slightly better performance compared to Model 3 which may due to the loss of context information. Therefore, a context branch is added to form Model 5. The additional context information provides reference for the classifiers to understand the structure of the tumor. Together with the context branch and the erase process, Model 5 outperforms Model 3 in most evaluation metrics.

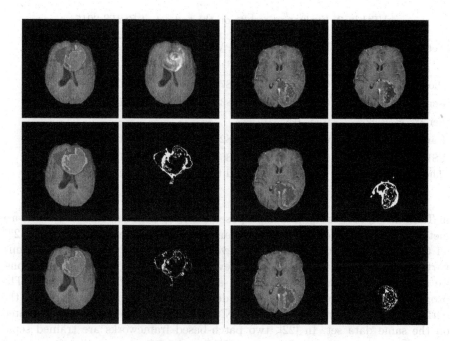

Fig. 4. Qualitative comparison among baselines and FSENet. The ground truths and T1c images of two examples are shown in the first row. The segmentation results generated by the baseline model (Model 1) and their corresponding error images are shown in the second row. The segmentation results produced by FSENet (Model 5) and their corresponding error images are shown in the third row. Color code is the same as that in Fig. 1 (Better viewed in color) (Color figure online)

The Proposed FSENet. The proposed FSENet achieves top performance in terms of the Dice similarity score which is a very important evaluation metric in medical image segmentation, and the prediction of the most difficult non-enhancing core class (Table 1). On top of Res-UNet ($\sim$65.5 million parameters), the FSENet only introduces $\sim$1.1 million extra parameters ($\sim$1.7% overhead) to achieve this significant boost in performance compared to the baseline (Model 1). We find that our FSENet can accurately identify and segment each tumor tissue (Fig. 4). The error images in the third row of Fig. 4 indicate that the prediction errors usually occur along the boundary.

A noteworthy advantage of our FSENet is that no hyperparameter is required. On the whole, the proposed pipeline is simple yet effective in dealing with problems of class imbalance and inter-class interference in multi-label brain tumor segmentation.

4.3   Comparison with State-of-the-art Methods

We evaluate the performance of our FSENet by submitting our test set results to the official BraTS 2015 online evaluation platform. The results are reported

Table 2. Evaluation results on the test set of BraTS 2015

Network	Dice			PPV			Sens			Rank[a]
	W	T	A	W	T	A	W	T	A	
zhouc1 [17]	0.87	0.75	0.64	0.87	0.81	0.61	0.89	0.75	0.72	1
isenf1 [17]	0.85	0.74	0.64	0.83	0.80	0.63	0.91	0.73	0.72	2
Pereira et al. [22]	0.78	0.65	0.75	-	-	-	-	-	-	-
Kamnitsas et al. [14]	0.84	0.63	0.63	0.82	0.85	0.64	0.89	0.62	0.66	-
FSENet	0.85	0.72	0.61	0.86	0.83	0.66	0.86	0.68	0.63	3

[a]The rank is according to the leader-board by the time of paper submission.

in Table 2. We also compare our proposed FSENet with several state-of-the-art methods. The two methods "zhouc1" and "isenf1" currently rank 1st and 2nd on the leader-board respectively. However, since BraTS 2015 does not require participants to substantiate their achievements in peer-reviewed publications, we are unable to identify the authors and the details of their methods. The proposed FSENet ranks 3rd on the learder-board. In addition, we also show the performance of two state-of-the-art CNN-based approaches that are evaluated on the same data set. In [22], two patch-based frameworks are trained separately for multi-label segmentation of HGG and LGG case respectively, considering their different characteristics. A multi-scale 3D CNN named DeepMedic proposed by [14] has two convolutional pathways, in order to better utilize multi-scale features for prediction. As shown in Table 2, the proposed FSENet achieve competitive single-model performance.

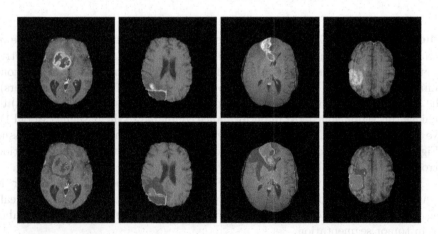

Fig. 5. Examples of the multi-label segmentation results produced by the proposed FSENet. First row shows T1c images from the test set of BraTS 2015. Results generated by the our FSENet are shown in the second row. Color code is the same as that in Fig. 1 (Better viewed in colors) (Color figure online)

We also present several examples of the segmentation results generated by our FSENet in Fig. 5, showing the effectiveness of the proposed pipeline.

We are currently unable to report the performance of FSENet on the BraTS 2017 challenge, since access to the dataset is restricted to the challenge participants. A performance analysis based on the BraTS 2017 dataset will be conducted in future when the dataset is publicly available.

5   Conclusion

In this paper, we propose an end-to-end pipeline named FSENet for the challenging multi-label brain tumor segmentation task, which follows the "focus, segment and erase" approach. To address the common class imbalance and inter-class interference problems, two novel components are introduced, which are tumor region pooling and cascaded binary classifiers with erasing. We demonstrate the effectiveness of the tumor region pooling component, and also discuss its advantages compared to other techniques in terms of its flexibility for image-based multi-label segmentation framework and no restriction by the elaborate selection of hyperparameter. The cascaded binary classifiers with erasing component divides difficult one-stage multi-label segmentation into multiple binary ones for capturing more discriminative task-relevant features. In addition, to suppress the competition and interference from easier to be segmented categories in the prediction of tougher ones, the binary classifiers are cascaded in the "outer-to-inner" manner and possess an erasing processing in between. We show the advantages of the proposed FSENet over the baseline models, demonstrating the effectiveness of the proposed pipeline. Besides, our FSENet achieves 3rd place single-model performance on the BraTS 2015 leader-board without relying on heavy model ensembles or complicated post-processing techniques.

Other applications, like liver tumor segmentation and whole heart segmentation, share similar characteristics and challenges to that of multi-label brain tumor segmentation. We intend to investigate the performance of FSENet to these applications in future.

Acknowledgment. We appreciate the support of NVIDIA Corporation with the donation of the Pascal Titan Xp GPU used in this study.

References

1. Bauer, S., Fejes, T., Slotboom, J., Wiest, R., Nolte, L.P., Reyes, M.: Segmentation of brain tumor images based on integrated hierarchical classification and regularization. In: 2012 International Conference on Medical Image Computing and Computer-Assisted Intervention (MICCAI) BraTS Workshop (2012)
2. Beers, A., et al.: Sequential 3D U-Nets for biologically-informed brain tumor segmentation. arXiv preprint arXiv:1709.02967 (2017)
3. Casamitjana, A., Català, M., Sánchez, I., Combalia, M., Vilaplana, V.: Cascaded V-Net using ROI masks for brain tumor segmentation. In: Crimi, A., Bakas, S., Kuijf, H., Menze, B., Reyes, M. (eds.) BrainLes 2017. LNCS, vol. 10670, pp. 381–391. Springer, Cham (2018). https://doi.org/10.1007/978-3-319-75238-9_33

4. Chen, X., Nguyen, B.P., Chui, C.K., Ong, S.H.: Automated brain tumor segmentation using kernel dictionary learning and superpixel-level features. In: IEEE International Conference on Systems, Man, and Cybernetics (SMC), pp. 2547–2552 (2016)
5. Christ, P.F., et al.: Automatic liver and lesion segmentation in CT using cascaded fully convolutional neural networks and 3D conditional random fields. In: Ourselin, S., Joskowicz, L., Sabuncu, M.R., Unal, G., Wells, W. (eds.) MICCAI 2016. LNCS, vol. 9901, pp. 415–423. Springer, Cham (2016). https://doi.org/10.1007/978-3-319-46723-8_48
6. Çiçek, Ö., Abdulkadir, A., Lienkamp, S.S., Brox, T., Ronneberger, O.: 3D U-Net: learning dense volumetric segmentation from sparse annotation. In: Ourselin, S., Joskowicz, L., Sabuncu, M.R., Unal, G., Wells, W. (eds.) MICCAI 2016. LNCS, vol. 9901, pp. 424–432. Springer, Cham (2016). https://doi.org/10.1007/978-3-319-46723-8_49
7. Cobzas, D., Birkbeck, N., Schmidt, M., Jagersand, M., Murtha, A.: 3D variational brain tumor segmentation using a high dimensional feature set. In: IEEE International Conference on Computer Vision (ICCV), pp. 1–8. IEEE (2007)
8. Rodríguez Colmeiro, R.G., Verrastro, C.A., Grosges, T.: Multimodal brain tumor segmentation using 3D convolutional networks. In: Crimi, A., Bakas, S., Kuijf, H., Menze, B., Reyes, M. (eds.) BrainLes 2017. LNCS, vol. 10670, pp. 226–240. Springer, Cham (2018). https://doi.org/10.1007/978-3-319-75238-9_20
9. Feng, X., Meyer, C.: Patch-based 3D U-Net for brain tumor segmentation. In: International Conference on Medical Image Computing and Computer-Assisted Intervention (MICCAI) (2017)
10. Gadermayr, M., Dombrowski, A.K., Klinkhammer, B.M., Boor, P., Merhof, D.: CNN cascades for segmenting whole slide images of the kidney. arXiv preprint arXiv:1708.00251 (2017)
11. Havaei, M., et al.: Brain tumor segmentation with deep neural networks. Med. Image Anal. **35**, 18–31 (2017)
12. He, K., Gkioxari, G., Dollár, P., Girshick, R.: Mask R-CNN. In: IEEE International Conference on Computer Vision (ICCV) (2017)
13. He, K., Zhang, X., Ren, S., Sun, J.: Deep residual learning for image recognition. In: IEEE Conference on Computer Vision and Pattern Recognition (CVPR), pp. 770–778 (2016)
14. Kamnitsas, K., et al.: Efficient multi-scale 3D CNN with fully connected CRF for accurate brain lesion segmentation. Med. Image Anal. **36**, 61–78 (2017)
15. Kistler, M., Bonaretti, S., Pfahrer, M., Niklaus, R., Büchler, P.: The virtual skeleton database: an open access repository for biomedical research and collaboration. J. Med. Internet Res. **15**(11), e245 (2013). https://doi.org/10.2196/jmir.2930. http://www.jmir.org/2013/11/e245/
16. Krähenbühl, P., Koltun, V.: Efficient inference in fully connected CRFs with Gaussian edge potentials. In: Advances in Neural Information Processing Systems, pp. 109–117 (2011)
17. Menze, B.H., et al.: BraTS 2015 online evaluation platform. https://www.virtualskeleton.ch/BRATS/Start2015
18. Menze, B.H., et al.: The multimodal brain tumor image segmentation benchmark (brats). IEEE Trans. Med. Imaging **34**(10), 1993–2024 (2015)

19. Menze, B.H., van Leemput, K., Lashkari, D., Weber, M.-A., Ayache, N., Golland, P.: A generative model for brain tumor segmentation in multi-modal images. In: Jiang, T., Navab, N., Pluim, J.P.W., Viergever, M.A. (eds.) MICCAI 2010. LNCS, vol. 6362, pp. 151–159. Springer, Heidelberg (2010). https://doi.org/10.1007/978-3-642-15745-5_19

20. Milletari, F., Navab, N., Ahmadi, S.A.: V-Net: fully convolutional neural networks for volumetric medical image segmentation. In: Fourth International Conference on 3D Vision, pp. 565–571. IEEE (2016)

21. Nyúl, L.G., Udupa, J.K., Zhang, X.: New variants of a method of MRI scale standardization. IEEE Trans. Med. Imaging 19(2), 143–150 (2000)

22. Pereira, S., Pinto, A., Alves, V., Silva, C.A.: Brain tumor segmentation using convolutional neural networks in MRI images. IEEE Trans. Med. Imaging 35(5), 1240–1251 (2016)

23. Prastawa, M., Bullitt, E., Ho, S., Gerig, G.: A brain tumor segmentation framework based on outlier detection. Med. Image Anal. 8(3), 275–283 (2004)

24. Ronneberger, O., Fischer, P., Brox, T.: U-Net: convolutional networks for biomedical image segmentation. In: Navab, N., Hornegger, J., Wells, W.M., Frangi, A.F. (eds.) MICCAI 2015. LNCS, vol. 9351, pp. 234–241. Springer, Cham (2015). https://doi.org/10.1007/978-3-319-24574-4_28. arxiv.org/abs/1505.04597

25. Wang, G., Li, W., Ourselin, S., Vercauteren, T.: Automatic brain tumor segmentation using cascaded anisotropic convolutional neural networks. arXiv preprint arXiv:1709.00382 (2017)

26. Zhao, H., Shi, J., Qi, X., Wang, X., Jia, J.: Pyramid scene parsing network. In: IEEE Conference on Computer Vision and Pattern Recognition (CVPR) (2017)

X2Face: A Network for Controlling Face Generation Using Images, Audio, and Pose Codes

Olivia Wiles$^{(\boxtimes)}$, A. Sophia Koepke, and Andrew Zisserman

Visual Geometry Group, University of Oxford, Oxford, UK
{ow,koepke,az}@robots.ox.ac.uk

Abstract. The objective of this paper is a neural network model that controls the pose and expression of a given face, using another face or modality (e.g. audio). This model can then be used for lightweight, sophisticated video and image editing.

We make the following three contributions. First, we introduce a network, X2Face, that can control a *source* face (specified by one or more frames) using another face in a *driving* frame to produce a *generated* frame with the identity of the *source* frame but the pose and expression of the face in the *driving* frame. Second, we propose a method for training the network fully self-supervised using a large collection of video data. Third, we show that the generation process can be driven by other modalities, such as audio or pose codes, without any further training of the network.

The generation results for driving a face with another face are compared to state-of-the-art self-supervised/supervised methods. We show that our approach is more robust than other methods, as it makes fewer assumptions about the input data. We also show examples of using our framework for video face editing.

1 Introduction

Being able to animate a still image of a face in a controllable, lightweight manner has many applications in image editing/enhancement and interactive systems (e.g. animating an on-screen agent with natural human poses/expressions). This is a challenging task, as it requires representing the face (e.g. modelling in 3D) in order to control it and a method of mapping the desired form of control (e.g. expression or pose) back onto the face representation. In this paper we investigate whether it is possible to forgo an explicit face representation and instead implicitly learn this in a self-supervised manner from a large collection

---

O. Wiles and A. S. Koepke—Equally contributed.

Electronic supplementary material The online version of this chapter (https://doi.org/10.1007/978-3-030-01261-8_41) contains supplementary material, which is available to authorized users.

© Springer Nature Switzerland AG 2018
V. Ferrari et al. (Eds.): ECCV 2018, LNCS 11217, pp. 690–706, 2018.
https://doi.org/10.1007/978-3-030-01261-8_41

of video data. Further, we investigate whether this implicit representation can then be used directly to control a face with another modality, such as audio or pose information.

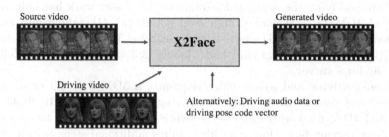

Fig. 1. Overview of X2Face: a model for controlling a *source* face using a *driving* frame, audio data, or specifying a pose vector. X2Face is trained without expression or pose labels.

To this end, we introduce X2Face, a novel self-supervised network architecture that can be used for face puppeteering of a *source* face given a *driving vector*. The *source* face is instantiated from a single or multiple *source* frames, which are extracted from the same face track. The *driving vector* may come from multiple modalities: a *driving* frame from the same or another video face track, pose information, or audio information; this is illustrated in Fig. 1. The *generated* frame resulting from X2Face has the identity, hairstyle, etc. of the *source* face but the properties of the *driving vector* (e.g. the given pose, if pose information is given; or the *driving* frame's expression/pose, if a *driving* frame is given).

The network is trained in a self-supervised manner using pairs of *source* and *driving* frames. These frames are input to two subnetworks: the *embedding network* and the *driving network* (see Fig. 2). By controlling the information flow in the network architecture, the model learns to factorise the problem. The *embedding network* learns an *embedded* face representation for the *source* face – effectively face frontalisation; the *driving network* learns how to map from this *embedded* face representation to the *generated* frame via an embedding, named the *driving vector*.

The X2Face network architecture is described in Sect. 3.1, and the self-supervised training framework in Sect. 3.2. In addition we make two further contributions. First, we propose a method for linearly regressing from a set of labels (e.g. for head pose) or features (e.g. from audio) to the *driving vector*; this is described in Sect. 4. The performance is evaluated in Sect. 5, where we show (i) the robustness of the generated results compared to state-of-the-art self-supervised [45] and supervised [1] methods; and (ii) the controllability of the network using other modalities, such as audio or pose. The second contribution, described in Sect. 6, shows how the *embedded* face representation can be used for video face editing, e.g. adding facial decorations in the manner of [31] using multiple or just a single *source* frame.

2   Related Work

Explicit Modelling of Faces for Image Generation. Traditionally facial animation (or puppeteering) given one image was performed by fitting a 3DMM and then modifying the estimated parameters [3]. Later work has built on the fitting of 3DMMs by including high level details [34,41], taking into account additional images [33] or 3D scans [4], or by learning 3DMM parameters directly from RGB data without ground truth labels [2,39]. Please refer to Zollhöfer et al. [46] for a survey.

Given a driving and source video sequence, a 3DMM or 3D mesh can be obtained and used to model both the driving and source face [10,40,43]. The estimated 3D is used to transform the expression of the source face to match that of the driving face. However, this requires additional steps to transfer the hidden regions (e.g. the teeth). As a result, a neural network conditioned on a single driving image can be used to predict higher level details to fill in these hidden regions [25].

Motivated by the fact that a 3DMM approach is limited by the components of the corresponding morphable model, which may not model the full range of required expressions/deformations and the higher level details, [1] propose a 2D warping method. Given only one source image, [1] use facial landmarks in order to warp the expression of one face onto another. They additionally allow for fine scale details to be transferred by monitoring changes in the driving video.

An interesting related set of works consider how to frontalise a face in a still image using a generic reference face [14], transferring expressions of an actor to an avatar [35] and swapping one face with another [20,24].

Learning Based Approaches for Image Generation. There is a wealth of literature on supervised/self-supervised approaches; here we review only the most relevant work. Supervised approaches for controlling a given face learn to model factors of variation (e.g. lighting, pose, etc.) by conditioning the generated image on known ground truth information which may be head pose, expression, or landmarks [5,12,21,30,42,44]. This requires a training dataset with known pose or expression information which may be expensive to obtain or require subjective judgement (e.g. in determining the expression). Consequently, self-supervised and unsupervised approaches attempt to automatically learn the required factors of variation (e.g. optical flow or pose) without labelling. This can be done by maximising mutual information [7] or by training the network to synthesise future video frames [11,29].

Another relevant self-supervised method is CycleGAN [45] which learns to transform images of one domain into those of another. While not explicitly devised for this task, as CycleGAN learns to be cycle-consistent, the transformed images often bear semantic similarities to the original images. For example, a CycleGAN model trained to transform images of one person's face (domain A) into those of another (domain B), will often learn to map the pose/position/expression of the face in domain A onto the generated face from domain B.

Using Multi-modal Setups to Control Image Generation. Other modalities, such as audio, can control image generation by using a neural network that learns the relationship between audio and correlated parts in corresponding images. Examples are controlling the mouth with speech [8,38], controlling a head with audio and a known emotional state [16], and controlling body movement with music [36].

Our method has the benefits of being self-supervised and the ability to control the generation process from other modalities without requiring explicit modelling of the face. Thus it is applicable to other domains.

3   Method

This section introduces the network architecture in Sect. 3.1, followed by the curriculum strategy used to train the network in Sect. 3.2.

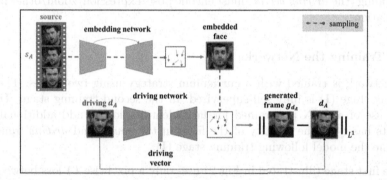

Fig. 2. An overview of X2Face during the initial training stage. Given multiple frames of a video (here 4 frames), one frame is designated the *source* frame and another the *driving* frame. The *source* frame is input to the *embedding network*, which learns a sampler to map pixels from the *source* frame to the *embedded* face. The *driving* frame is input to the *driving network*, which learns to map pixels from the *embedded* face to the *generated* frame. The *generated* frame should have the identity of the *source* frame and the pose/expression of the *driving* frame. In this training stage, as the frames are from the same video, the *generated* and *driving* frames should match. However, at test time the identities of the *source* and *driving* face can differ.

3.1   Architecture

The network takes two inputs: a *driving* and a *source* frame. The *source* frame is input to the *embedding network* and the *driving* frame to the *driving network*. This is illustrated in Fig. 2. Precise architectural details are given in the supplementary material.

Embedding Network. The *embedding network* learns a bilinear sampler to determine how to map from the *source* frame to a face representation, the *embedded* face. The architecture is based on U-Net [32] and pix2pix [15]; the output is a 2-channel image (of the same dimensions as the *source* frame) that encodes the flow $\delta x, \delta y$ for each pixel.

While the *embedding network* is not explicitly forced to frontalise the *source* frame, we observe that it learns to do so for the following reason. Because the *driving network* samples from the *embedded* face to produce the *generated* frame without knowing the pose/expression of the *source* frame, it needs the *embedded* face to have a common representation (e.g. be frontalised) across *source* frames with differing poses and expressions.

Driving Network. The *driving network* takes a *driving* frame as input and learns a bilinear sampler to transform pixels from the *embedded* face to produce the *generated* frame. It has an encoder-decoder architecture. In order to sample correctly from the *embedded* face and produce the *generated* frame, the latent embedding (the *driving vector*) must encode pose/expression/zoom/other factors of variation.

3.2   Training the Network

The network is trained with a curriculum strategy using two stages. The first training stage (**I**) is fully self-supervised. In the second training stage (**II**), we make use of a CNN pre-trained for face identification to add additional constraints based on the identity of the faces in the *source* and *driving* frames to finetune the model following training stage (**I**).

I. The first stage (illustrated in Fig. 2) uses only a pixelwise $L1$ loss between the *generated* and the *driving* frames. Whilst this is sufficient to train the network such that the *driving* frame encodes expression and pose, we observe that some face shape information is leaked through the *driving vector* (e.g. the *generated* face becomes fatter/longer depending on the face in the *driving* frame). Consequently, we introduce additional loss functions – called identity loss functions – in the second stage.

II. In the second stage, the identity loss functions are applied to enforce that the identity is the same between the *generated* and the *source* frames irrespective of the identity of the *driving* frame. This loss should mitigate against the face shape leakage discussed in stage **I**. In practice, one *source* frame s_A of identity A, and two *driving* frames d_A, d_R are used as training inputs; d_A is of identity A and d_R a random identity. This gives two generated frames g_{d_A}, g_{d_R} respectively, which should both be of identity A. Two identity loss functions are then imposed: $\mathcal{L}_{\text{identity}}(d_A, g_{d_A})$ and $\mathcal{L}_{\text{identity}}(s_A, g_{d_R})$. $\mathcal{L}_{\text{identity}}$ is implemented using a network pre-trained for identity to measure the similarity of the images in feature space by comparing appropriate layers of the network (i.e. a content loss as in [6,13]). The precise layers are chosen based on whether we are considering g_{d_A} or g_{d_R}:

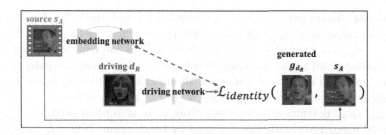

Fig. 3. The identity loss function when the *source* and *driving* frames are of different identities. This loss enforces that the *generated* frame has the same identity as the *source* frame.

1. $\mathcal{L}_{identity}(d_A, g_{d_A})$. g_{d_A} should have the same identity, pose and expression as d_A so we use the photometric $L1$ loss and a $L1$ content loss on the Conv2-5 and Conv7 layers (i.e. layers that encode both lower/higher level information such as pose/identity) between g_{d_A} and d_A.
2. $\mathcal{L}_{identity}(s_A, g_{d_R})$ (Fig. 3). g_{d_R} should have the identity of s_A but the pose and expression of d_R. Consequently, we cannot use the photometric loss but only a content loss. We minimise a $L1$ content loss on the Conv6-7 layers (i.e. layers encoding higher level identity information) between g_{d_A} and s_A.

The pre-trained network used for these losses is the 11-layer VGG network (configuration A) [37] trained on the VGG-Face Dataset [26].

4   Controlling the Image Generation with Other Modalities

Given a trained X2Face network, the *driving vector* can be used to control the *source* face with other modalities such as audio or pose.

4.1   Pose

Instead of controlling the generation with a *driving* frame, we can control the head pose of the *source* face using a pose code such that when varying the code's pitch/yaw/roll angles, the *generated* frame varies accordingly. This is done by learning a forward mapping $f_{p \to v}$ from head pose p to the *driving vector* v such that $f_{p \to v}(p)$ can serve as a modified input to the *driving network's* decoder. However, this is an ill-posed problem; directly using this mapping loses information, as the *driving vector* encodes more than just pose.

As a result, we use vector arithmetic. Effectively we drive a *source* frame with itself but modify the corresponding *driving vector* v_{emb}^{source} to remove the pose of the *source* frame p_{source} and incorporate the new driving pose $p_{driving}$. This gives:

$$v_{emb}^{driving} = v_{emb}^{source} + v_{emb}^{\Delta pose} = v_{emb}^{source} + f_{p \to v}(p_{driving} - p_{source}). \qquad (1)$$

However, VoxCeleb [23] does not contain ground truth head pose, so an additional mapping $f_{v\to p}$ is needed to determine $p_{source} = f_{v\to p}(v_{emb}^{source})$.

$f_{v\to p}$. $f_{v\to p}$ is trained to regress p from v. It is implemented using a fully connected layer with bias and trained using an L1 loss. Training pairs (v, p) are obtained using an annotated dataset with image to pose labels p; v is obtained by passing the image through the encoder of the *driving network*.

$f_{p\to v}$. $f_{p\to v}$ is trained to regress v from p. It is implemented using a fully-connected linear layer with bias followed by batch-norm. When $f_{v\to p}$ is known, this function can be learnt directly on VoxCeleb by passing an image through X2Face to get the *driving vector* v and $f_{v\to p}(v)$ gives the pose p.

4.2   Audio

Audio data from the videos in the VoxCeleb dataset can be used to drive a *source* face in a manner similar to that of pose by driving the *source* frame with itself but modifying the *driving vector* using the audio from another frame. The forward mapping $f_{a\to v}$ from audio features a to the corresponding *driving vector* v is trained using pairs of audio features a and driving vectors v. These can be directly extracted from VoxCeleb (so no backward mapping $f_{v\to a}$ is required). a is obtained by extracting the 256D audio features from the neural network in [9] and the 128D v by passing the corresponding frame through the *driving network*'s encoder. Ordinary least squares linear regression is then used to learn $f_{a\to v}$ after first normalising the audio features to $\sim N(0, 1)$. No normalisation is used when employing the mapping to drive the frame generation; this amplifies the signal, visually improving the generated results.

As learning the function $f_{a\to v} : \mathbb{R}^{1\times 256} \to \mathbb{R}^{1\times 128}$ is under-constrained, the embedding learns to encode some pose information. Therefore, we additionally use the mappings $f_{p\to v}$ and $f_{v\to p}$ described in Sect. 4.1 to remove this information. Given driving audio features $a_{driving}$ and the corresponding, non-modified *driving vector* v_{emb}^{source}, the new *driving vector* $v_{emb}^{driving}$ is then

$$v_{emb}^{driving} = v_{emb}^{source} + f_{a\to v}(a_{driving}) - f_{a\to v}(a_{source}) + f_{p\to v}(p_{audio} - p_{source}),$$

where $p_{source} = f_{v\to p}(v_{emb}^{source})$ is the head pose of the frame input to the *driving network* (i.e. the *source* frame), $p_{audio} = f_{v\to p}(f_{a\to v}(a_{driving}))$ is the pose information contained in $f_{a\to v}(a_{driving})$, and a_{source} is the audio feature vector corresponding to the *source* frame.

5   Experiments

This section evaluates X2Face by first performing an ablation study in Sect. 5.1 on the architecture and losses used for training, followed by results for controlling a face with a *driving* frame in Sect. 5.2, pose information in Sect. 5.3, and audio information in Sect. 5.4.

Training. X2Face is trained on the VoxCeleb video dataset [23] using dlib [18] to crop the faces to 256 × 256. The identities are randomly split into train/val/test identities (with a split of 75/15/10) and frames extracted at one fps to give 900,764 frames for training and 125,131 frames for testing.

The model is trained in PyTorch [27] using SGD with momentum 0.9 and batchsize of 16. First, it is trained just with $L1$ loss, and a learning rate of 0.001. The learning rate is decreased by a factor of 10 when the loss plateaus. Once the loss converges, the identity losses are incorporated and are weighted as follows: (i) for same identities to be as strong as the photometric $L1$ loss at each layer; (ii) for different identities to be 1/10 the size of the photometric loss at each layer. This training phase is started with a learning rate of 0.0001.

Testing. The model can be tested using either a single or multiple source frames. The reasoning for this is that if the *embedded* face is stable (e.g. different facial regions always map to the same place on the *embedded* face), we expect to be able to combine multiple *source* frames by averaging over the *embedded* faces.

5.1   Architecture Studies

To quantify the utility of using additional views at *test* time and the benefit of the curriculum strategy for training the network (i.e. using the identity losses explained in Sect. 3.2), we evaluate the results for these different settings on a left-out test set of VoxCeleb. We consider 120K *source* and *driving* pairs where the *driving* frame is from the same video as the *source* frames; thus, the *generated* frame should be the same as the *driving* frame. The results are given in Table 1.

Table 1. $L1$ reconstruction error on the test set, comparing the *generated* frame to the ground truth frame (in this case the *driving* frame) for different training/testing setups. Lower is better for $L1$ error. Additionally, we give the percentage improvement over the $L1$ error for the model trained with only training stage **I** and tested with a single *source* frame. In this case, higher is better

Training strategy	# of *source* Frames at test time	$L1$ error	% Improvement
Training stage **I**	1	0.0632	0%
Training stage **II**	1	0.0630	0.32%
Training stage **I**	3	0.0524	17.14%
Training stage **II**	3	0.0521	17.62%

The results in Table 1 confirm that both training with the curriculum strategy and using additional views at *test* time improve the reconstructed image. The supplementary material includes qualitative results and shows that using additional *source* frames when testing is especially useful if a face is seen at an extreme pose in the initial *source* frame.

Source frames
for X2Face

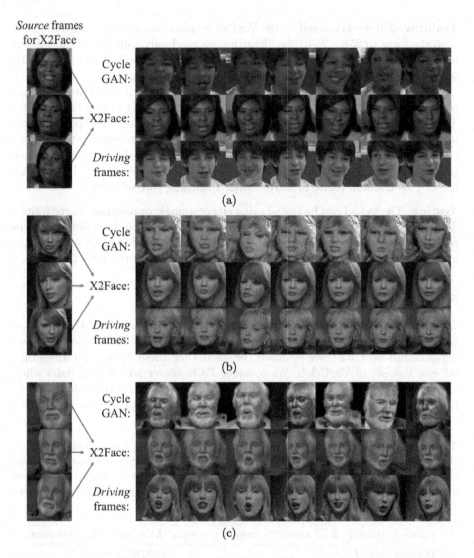

Cycle
GAN:

X2Face:

Driving
frames:

(a)

Cycle
GAN:

X2Face:

Driving
frames:

(b)

Cycle
GAN:

X2Face:

Driving
frames:

(c)

Fig. 4. Comparison of X2Face's *generated* frames to those of CycleGAN given a driving video sequence. Each example shows from bottom to top: the *driving* frame, our *generated* result and CycleGAN's generated result. To the left, *source* frames for X2Face are shown (at test time CycleGAN does not require *source* frames, as it is has been trained to map between the given *source* and *driving* identities). These examples demonstrate multiple benefits of our method. *First*, X2Face is capable of preserving the face shape of the source identity (top row) whilst driving the pose and expression according to the *driving* frame (bottom row); CycleGAN correctly keeps pose and expression but loses information about face shape and geometry when given too few training images as in example (a) (whereas X2Face requires no training samples for new identities). *Second*, X2Face has temporal consistency. CycleGAN samples from the latent space, so it sometimes samples from different videos resulting in jarring changes between frames (e.g. in example (c)).

5.2   Controlling Image Generation with a *Driving Frame*

The motivation of our architecture is to be able to map the expression and pose of a *driving* frame onto a *source* frame *without* any annotations on expression or pose. This section demonstrates that X2Face does indeed achieve this, as a set of *source* frames can be controlled with a driving video and generate realistic results. We compare to two methods: CycleGAN [45] which uses *no* labels and [1] which is designed top down and demonstrates impressive results. Additional qualitative results are given in the supplementary material and video.

Comparison to CycleGAN [45]. CycleGAN learns a mapping from a given domain (in this case a given identity A) to another domain (in this case another identity B). To compare to their method for a given pair of identities, we take all images of the given identities (so images may come from different video tracks) to form two sets of images: one set corresponding to identity A and the other to B. We then train their model using these sets. To compare, for a given *driving* frame of identity A, we visualise their *generated* frame from identity B which is compared to that of X2Face.

The results in Fig. 4 illustrate multiple benefits. First, X2Face generalises to unseen pairs of identities at test time given only a *source* and *driving* frame. CycleGAN is trained on pairs of identities, so if there are too few example images, it fails to correctly model the shape and geometry of the *source* face, producing unrealistic results. Additionally, our results have better temporal coherence (i.e. consistent background/hair style/etc. across *generated* frames), as X2Face transforms a given frame whereas CycleGAN samples from a latent space.

Comparison to Averbuch-Elor et al. [1]. We compare to [1] in Fig. 5. There are two significant advantages of our formulation over theirs: first, we can handle more significant pose changes in the driving video and *source* frame (Fig. 5b, c). Second, ours has fewer assumptions: (1) [1] assumes that the first frame of the driving video is in a frontal pose with a neutral expression and that the *source* frame also has a neutral expression (Fig. 5d). (2) X2Face can be used when given a single *driving* frame whereas their method requires a video so that the face can be tracked and the tracking used to expand the number of correspondences and to obtain high level details.

While this is not the focus of this paper, our method can be augmented with the ideas from these methods. For example, as inspired by [1], we can perform simple post-processing to add higher level details (Fig. 5a, X2Face+p.p.) by transferring hidden regions using Poisson editing [28].

5.3   Controlling the Image Generation with Pose

Before reporting results on controlling the *driving vector* using pose, we validate our claim that the *driving vector* does indeed learn about pose. To do this, we evaluate how accurately we can predict the three head pose angles – yaw, pitch and roll – given the 128D *driving vector*.

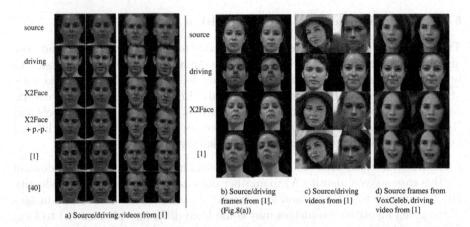

Fig. 5. Comparison of X2Face to supervised methods. In comparison to [1]: X2Face matches (b) pitch, and (c) roll and yaw; and X2Face can handle non-neutral expressions in the *source* frame (d). As with other methods, post-processing (X2Face + p.-p.) can be applied to add higher level details (a).

Pose Predictor. To train the pose predictor which also serves as $f_{v \to p}$ (Sect. 4.1), the 25,993 images in the AFLW dataset [19] are split into train/val set, leaving out the 1,000 test images from [22] as test set. The results on the test set are reported in Table 2 confirming that the *driving vector* learns about head pose without having been trained on pose labels, as the results are comparable to those of a network directly trained for this task.

We then use $f_{v \to p}$ to train $f_{p \to v}$ (Sect. 4.1) and present generated frames for different, unseen test identities using the learnt mappings in Fig. 6. The *source* frame corresponds to p_{source} in Sect. 4.1 while $p_{driving}$ is used to vary one head pose angle while keeping the others fixed.

Table 2. MAE in degrees using the *driving vector* for head pose regression (lower is better). Note that the linear pose predictor from the *driving vector* performs only slightly worse than a supervised method [22], which has been trained for this task

Method	Roll	Pitch	Yaw	MAE
X2Face	5.85	7.59	14.62	9.36
KEPLER [22] (supervised)	8.75	5.85	6.45	7.02

5.4   Controlling the Image Generation with Audio Input

This section presents qualitative results for using audio data from videos in the VoxCeleb dataset to drive the *source* frames. The VoxCeleb dataset consists of videos of interviews, suggesting that the audio should be especially correlated

Source
frame

Source   Generated frames with varying yaw, pitch and roll angle for different source identities using
frame   pose code vectors to drive the frame generation.

Fig. 6. Controlling image generation with pose code vectors. Results are shown for a single *source* frame which is controlled using each of the three head pose angles for the same identity (top three rows) and for different identities (bottom three rows). For further results and a video animation, we refer to the supplementary material. Whilst some artefacts are visible, the method allows the head pose angles to be controlled separately.

with the movements of the mouth. [9]'s model, trained on the BBC-Oxford 'Lip Reading in the Wild' dataset (LRW), is used to extract audio features. We use the 256D vector activations of the last fully connected layer of the audio stream (FC7) for a 0.2s audio signal centred on the *driving* frame (the frame occurs half way through the 0.2s audio signal).

A potential source of error is the domain gap between the LRW dataset and VoxCeleb, as [9]'s model is not fine-tuned on the VoxCeleb dataset which contains much more background noise than the LRW dataset. Thus, their model has not necessarily learnt to become indifferent to this noise. However, our model is relatively robust to this problem; we observe that the mouth movements in the *generated* frames are reasonably close to what we would expect from the sounds of the corresponding audio, as demonstrated in Fig. 7. This is true even if the person in the video is not speaking and instead the audio is coming from an interviewer. However, there is some jitter in the generation.

6   Using the Embedded Face for Video Editing

We consider how the *embedded* face can be used for video editing. This idea is inspired by the concept of an unwrapped mosaic [31]. We expect the *embedded* face to be pose and expression invariant, as can be seen qualitatively across the example *embedded* faces shown in the paper. Therefore, the *embedded* face can be considered as a UV texture map of the face and drawn on directly.

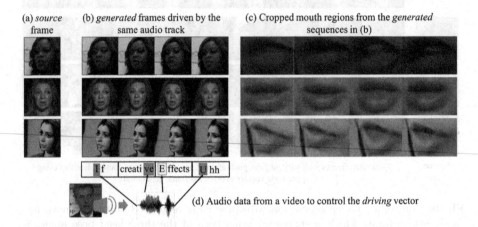

(a) *source* frame   (b) *generated* frames driven by the same audio track   (c) Cropped mouth regions from the *generated* sequences in (b)

I f   creati ve   E ffects   U hh

(d) Audio data from a video to control the *driving* vector

Fig. 7. Controlling image generation with audio information. We show how the same sounds affect various *source* frames; if our model is working well then the *generated* mouths should behave similarly. (a) shows the *source* frames. (b) shows the *generated* frames for a given audio sound which is visualised in (d) by the coloured portion of the word being spoken. As most of the change is expected to be in the mouth region, the cropped mouth regions are additionally visualised in (c). The audio comes from a native British speaker. As can be seen, in all generated frames, the mouths are more closed at the "ve" and "I" and more open at the "E" and "U". Another interesting point is that for the "Effects" frame, the audio is actually coming from an interviewer, so while the frame corresponding to the audio has a closed mouth, the *generated* results still open the mouth. (Color figure online)

This task is executed as follows. A *source* frame (or set of *source* frames) is extracted and input to the *embedding network* to obtain the *embedded* face. The *embedded* face can then be drawn on using an image or other interactive tool. A video is reconstructed using the modified *embedded* face which is driven by a set of *driving* frames. Because the *embedded* face is stable across different identities, a given edit can be applied across different identities. Example edits are shown in Fig. 8 and in the supplementary material.

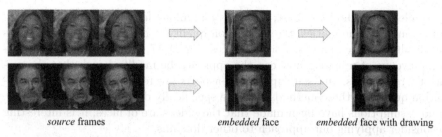

source frames   embedded face   embedded face with drawing

(a) *Source* frames are input to extract the *embedded* face which is drawn on. The modified *embedded* face is used to *generate* the frames below.

(b) An example sequence of *generated* frames (top row) from the modified *embedded* face controlled using a sequence of *driving* frames (bottom row).

Fig. 8. Example results of the video editing application. (a) For given *source* frames, the *embedded* face is extracted and modified. (b) The modified *embedded* face is used for a sequence of *driving* frames (bottom) and the result is shown (top). Note how for the second example, the blue tattoo disappears behind the nose when the person is seen in profile and how, as above, the modified *embedded* face can be driven using the same or another identity's pose and expression. Best seen in colour. Zoom in for details. Additional examples using the blue tattoo and Harry Potter scar are given in the supplementary video and pdf. (Color figure online)

7   Conclusion

We have presented a self-supervised framework X2Face for driving face generation using another face. This framework makes no assumptions about the pose, expression, or identity of the input images, so it is more robust to unconstrained settings (e.g. an unseen identity). The framework can also be used with minimal alteration *post* training to drive a face using audio or head pose information. Finally, the trained model can be used as a video editing tool. Our model has achieved all this without requiring annotations for head pose/facial landmarks/depth data. Instead, it is trained self-supervised on a large collection of videos and learns itself to model the different factors of variation.

While our method is robust, versatile, and allows for generation to be conditioned on other modalities, the generation quality is not as high as approaches specifically designed for transforming faces (e.g. [1,17,40]). This opens an interesting avenue of research: how can the approach be modified such that the versatility, robustness, and self-supervision aspects are retained but with the generation quality of these methods that are specifically designed for faces. Finally, as no assumptions have been made that the videos are of faces, it is interesting to consider applying our approach to other domains.

Acknowledgements. The authors are grateful to Hadar Averbuch-Elor for helpfully running their model on our data and to Vicky Kalogeiton for suggestions/comments. This work was funded by an EPSRC studentship and EPSRC Programme Grant Seebibyte EP/M013774/1.

References

1. Averbuch-Elor, H., Cohen-Or, D., Kopf, J., Cohen, M.F.: Bringing portraits to life. ACM Trans. Graph. (Proceeding of SIGGRAPH Asia 2017) **36**(6), 196 (2017)
2. Bas, A., Smith, W.A.P., Awais, M., Kittler, J.: 3D morphable models as spatial transformer networks. In: Proceedings of ICCV Workshop on Geometry Meets Deep Learning (2017)
3. Blanz, V., Vetter, T.: A morphable model for the synthesis of 3D faces. In: Proceedings of ACM SIGGRAPH (1999)
4. Booth, J., Roussos, A., Ponniah, A., Dunaway, D., Zafeiriou, S.: Large scale 3D morphable models. IJCV **126**(2–4), 233–254 (2018)
5. Cao, J., Hu, Y., Yu, B., He, R., Sun, Z.: Load balanced GANs for multi-view face image synthesis. arXiv preprint arXiv:1802.07447 (2018)
6. Chen, Q., Koltun, V.: Photographic image synthesis with cascaded refinement networks. In: Proceedings of ICCV (2017)
7. Chen, X., Duan, Y., Houthooft, R., Schulman, J., Sutskever, I., Abbeel, P.: Infogan: interpretable representation learning by information maximizing generative adversarial nets. In: NIPS (2016)
8. Chung, J.S., Senior, A., Vinyals, O., Zisserman, A.: Lip reading sentences in the wild. In: Proceedings of CVPR (2017)
9. Chung, J.S., Zisserman, A.: Out of time: automated lip sync in the wild. In: Chen, C.-S., Lu, J., Ma, K.-K. (eds.) ACCV 2016. LNCS, vol. 10117, pp. 251–263. Springer, Cham (2017). https://doi.org/10.1007/978-3-319-54427-4_19
10. Dale, K., Sunkavalli, K., Johnson, M.K., Vlasic, D., Matusik, W., Pfister, H.: Video face replacement. ACM Trans. Graph. (TOG) **30**(6), 130 (2011)
11. Denton, E.L., Birodkar, V.: Unsupervised learning of disentangled representations from video. In: NIPS (2017)
12. Ding, H., Sricharan, K., Chellappa, R.: ExprGAN: facial expression editing with controllable expression intensity. In: Proceedings of AAAI (2018)
13. Gatys, L.A., Ecker, A.S., Bethge, M.: Image style transfer using convolutional neural networks. In: Proceedings of CVPR (2016)
14. Hassner, T., Harel, S., Paz, E., Enbar, R.: Effective face frontalization in unconstrained images. In: Proceedings of CVPR (2015)
15. Isola, P., Zhu, J.Y., Zhou, T., Efros, A.A.: Image-to-image translation with conditional adversarial networks. In: Proceedings of CVPR (2017)

16. Karras, T., Aila, T., Laine, S., Herva, A., Lehtinen, J.: Audio-driven facial animation by joint end-to-end learning of pose and emotion. ACM Trans. Graph. (TOG) **36**(4), 94 (2017)
17. Kim, H., et al.: Deep video portraits. In: Proceedings of ACM SIGGRAPH (2018)
18. King, D.E.: Dlib-ml: a machine learning toolkit. J. Mach. Learn. Res. **10**, 1755–1758 (2009)
19. Koestinger, M., Wohlhart, P., Roth, P.M., Bischof, H.: Annotated facial landmarks in the wild: a large-scale, real-world database for facial landmark localization. In: Proceedings of First IEEE International Workshop on Benchmarking Facial Image Analysis Technologies (2011)
20. Korshunova, I., Shi, W., Dambre, J., Theis, L.: Fast face-swap using convolutional neural networks. In: Proceedings of ICCV (2017)
21. Kulkarni, T.D., Whitney, W.F., Kohli, P., Tenenbaum, J.: Deep convolutional inverse graphics network. In: NIPS (2015)
22. Kumar, A., Alavi, A., Chellappa, R.: KEPLER: keypoint and pose estimation of unconstrained faces by learning efficient H-CNN regressors. In: Proceedings of the International Conference on Automatic Face and Gesture Recognition (2017)
23. Nagrani, A., Chung, J.S., Zisserman, A.: VoxCeleb: a large-scale speaker identification dataset. In: INTERSPEECH (2017)
24. Nirkin, Y., Masi, I., Tran, A.T., Hassner, T., Medioni, G.: On face segmentation, face swapping, and face perception. In: Proceedings of International Conference on Automatic Face and Gesture Recognition (2018)
25. Olszewski, K., et al.: Realistic dynamic facial textures from a single image using GANs. In: Proceedings of ICCV (2017)
26. Parkhi, O.M., Vedaldi, A., Zisserman, A.: Deep face recognition. In: Proceedings of BMVC (2015)
27. Paszke, A., et al.: Automatic differentiation in PyTorch (2017)
28. Pérez, P., Gangnet, M., Blake, A.: Poisson image editing. ACM Trans. Graph. (TOG) **22**(3), 313–318 (2003)
29. Pătrăucean, V., Handa, A., Cipolla, R.: Spatio-temporal video autoencoder with differentiable memory. In: NIPS (2016)
30. Qiao, F., Yao, N., Jiao, Z., Li, Z., Chen, H., Wang, H.: Geometry-contrastive generative adversarial network for facial expression synthesis. arXiv preprint arXiv:1802.01822 (2018)
31. Rav-Acha, A., Kohli, P., Rother, C., Fitzgibbon, A.: Unwrap mosaics: a new representation for video editing. ACM Trans. Graph. (TOG) **27**(3), 17 (2008)
32. Ronneberger, O., Fischer, P., Brox, T.: U-Net: convolutional networks for biomedical image segmentation. In: Navab, N., Hornegger, J., Wells, W.M., Frangi, A.F. (eds.) MICCAI 2015. LNCS, vol. 9351, pp. 234–241. Springer, Cham (2015). https://doi.org/10.1007/978-3-319-24574-4_28
33. Roth, J., Tong, Y., Liu, X.: Adaptive 3D face reconstruction from unconstrained photo collections. In: Proceedings of CVPR (2016)
34. Saito, S., Wei, L., Hu, L., Nagano, K., Li, H.: Photorealistic facial texture inference using deep neural networks. In: Proceedings of CVPR (2017)
35. Saragih, J.M., Lucey, S., Cohn, J.F.: Real-time avatar animation from a single image. In: Proceedings of International Conference on Automatic Face and Gesture Recognition (2011)
36. Shlizerman, E., Dery, L., Schoen, H., Kemelmacher-Shlizerman, I.: Audio to body dynamics. In: Proceedings of CVPR (2018)

37. Simonyan, K., Zisserman, A.: Very deep convolutional networks for large-scale image recognition. In: International Conference on Learning Representations (2015)
38. Suwajanakorn, S., Seitz, S.M., Kemelmacher-Shlizerman, I.: Synthesizing Obama: learning lip sync from audio. ACM Trans. Graph. (TOG) $36(4)$, 95 (2017)
39. Tewari, A., et al.: Mofa: model-based deep convolutional face autoencoder for unsupervised monocular reconstruction. In: Proceedings of ICCV (2017)
40. Thies, J., Zollhöfer, M., Stamminger, M., Theobalt, C., Nießner, M.: Face2Face: real-time face capture and reenactment of RGB videos. In: Proceedings of CVPR (2016)
41. Tran, A.T., Hassner, T., Masi, I., Paz, E., Nirkin, Y., Medioni, G.: Extreme 3D face reconstruction: Seeing through occlusions. In: Proceedings of CVPR (2018)
42. Tran, L., Yin, X., Liu, X.: Disentangled representation learning GAN for pose-invariant face recognition. In: Proceedings of CVPR (2017)
43. Vlasic, D., Brand, M., Pfister, H., Popović, J.: Face transfer with multilinear models. ACM Trans. Graph. (TOG) $24(3)$, 426–433 (2005)
44. Worrall, D.E., Garbin, S.J., Turmukhambetov, D., Brostow, G.J.: Interpretable transformations with encoder-decoder networks. In: Proceedings of ICCV (2017)
45. Zhu, J.Y., Park, T., Isola, P., Efros, A.A.: Unpaired image-to-image translation using cycle-consistent adversarial networks. In: Proceedings of ICCV (2017)
46. Zollhöfer, M., Thies, J., Garrido, P., Bradley, D., Beeler, T., Pérez, P., Stamminger, M., Nießner, M., Theobalt, C.: State of the art on monocular 3D face reconstruction, tracking, and applications. In: Proceedings of Eurographics (2018)

Model Adaptation with Synthetic and Real Data for Semantic Dense Foggy Scene Understanding

Christos Sakaridis[1]([✉]), Dengxin Dai[1], Simon Hecker[1], and Luc Van Gool[1,2]

[1] ETH Zürich, Zürich, Switzerland
[2] KU Leuven, Leuven, Belgium
{csakarid,dai,heckers,vangool}@vision.ee.ethz.ch

Abstract. This work addresses the problem of semantic scene understanding under dense fog. Although considerable progress has been made in semantic scene understanding, it is mainly related to clear-weather scenes. Extending recognition methods to adverse weather conditions such as fog is crucial for outdoor applications. In this paper, we propose a novel method, named Curriculum Model Adaptation (CMAda), which *gradually* adapts a semantic segmentation model from light synthetic fog to dense real fog in multiple steps, using both synthetic and real foggy data. In addition, we present three other main stand-alone contributions: (1) a novel method to add synthetic fog to real, clear-weather scenes using semantic input; (2) a new fog density estimator; (3) the *Foggy Zurich* dataset comprising 3808 real foggy images, with pixel-level semantic annotations for 16 images with dense fog. Our experiments show that (1) our fog simulation slightly outperforms a state-of-the-art competing simulation with respect to the task of semantic foggy scene understanding (SFSU); (2) CMAda improves the performance of state-of-the-art models for SFSU significantly by leveraging unlabeled real foggy data. The datasets and code will be made publicly available.

Keywords: Semantic foggy scene understanding · Fog simulation Synthetic data · Curriculum Model Adaptation · Curriculum learning

1 Introduction

Adverse weather conditions create visibility problems for both people and the sensors that power automated systems [25,37,48]. While sensors and the down-streaming vision algorithms are constantly getting better, their performance is mainly benchmarked with clear-weather images. Many outdoor applications, however, can hardly escape from bad weather. One typical example of adverse weather conditions is fog, which degrades the visibility of a scene significantly [36, 52]. The denser the fog is, the more severe this problem becomes.

During the past years, the community has made a tremendous progress on image dehazing (defogging) to increase the visibility of foggy images [24,40,56].

© Springer Nature Switzerland AG 2018
V. Ferrari et al. (Eds.): ECCV 2018, LNCS 11217, pp. 707–724, 2018.
https://doi.org/10.1007/978-3-030-01261-8_42

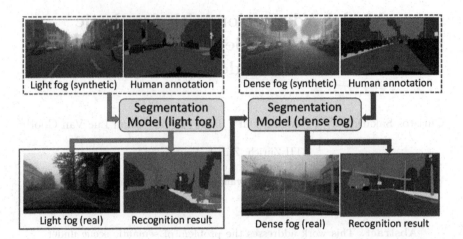

Fig. 1. The illustrative pipeline of our approach for semantic scene understanding under dense fog

The last few years have also witnessed a leap in object recognition. The semantic understanding of foggy scenes, however, has received little attention, despite its importance in outdoor applications. For example, an automated car still needs to detect other traffic agents and traffic control devices in the presence of fog. This work investigates the problem of semantic foggy scene understanding (SFSU).

The current "standard" policy for addressing semantic scene understanding is to train a neural network with many annotations of real images [11,47]. Applying the same protocol to diverse weather conditions seems to be problematic, as the manual annotation part is hard to scale. The difficulty of data collection and annotation increases even more for adverse weather conditions. To overcome this problem, two streams of research have gained extensive attention: (1) transfer learning [9] and (2) learning with synthetic data [46,48].

Our method falls into the middle ground, and aims to combine the strength of these two kinds of methods. In particular, our method is developed to learn from (1) a dataset with high-quality synthetic fog and corresponding human annotations, and (2) a dataset with a large number of images with real fog. The goal of our method is to improve the performance of SFSU without requiring extra human annotations.

To this aim, this work proposes a novel fog simulator to generate high-quality synthetic fog into real images that contain clear-weather outdoor scenes, and then leverage these partially synthetic foggy images for SFSU. The new fog simulator builds on the recent work in [48], by introducing a semantic-aware filter to exploit the structures of object instances. We show that learning with our synthetic data improves the performance for SFSU. Furthermore, we present a novel method, dubbed Curriculum Model Adaptation (CMAda), which is able to *gradually* adapt a segmentation model from light synthetic fog to dense real fog in multiple steps, by using both synthetic and real foggy data. CMAda improves upon direct adaptation significantly on two datasets with dense real fog.

The main contributions of the paper are: (1) a new automatic and scalable pipeline to generate high-quality synthetic fog, with which new datasets are generated; (2) a novel curriculum model adaptation method to learn from both synthetic and (unlabeled) real foggy images; (3) a new real foggy dataset with 3808 images, including 16 finely annotated images with dense fog. A visual overview of our approach is presented in Fig. 1.

2   Related Work

Our work is relevant to image defogging (dehazing), foggy scene understanding, and domain adaptation.

2.1   Image Defogging/Dehazing

Fog fades the color of observed objects and reduces their contrast. Extensive research has been conducted on image defogging (dehazing) to increase the visibility of foggy scenes [5,15,16,24,36,40,52]. Certain works focus particularly on enhancing foggy road scenes [38,54]. Recent approaches also rely on trainable architectures [53], which have evolved to end-to-end models [34,59]. For a comprehensive overview of dehazing algorithms, we point the reader to [32,57]. Our work is complementary and focuses on semantic foggy scene understanding.

2.2   Foggy Scene Understanding

Typical examples in this line include road and lane detection [3], traffic light detection [28], car and pedestrian detection [19], and a dense, pixel-level segmentation of road scenes into most of the relevant semantic classes [7,11]. While deep recognition networks have been developed [20,33,45,58,60] and large-scale datasets have been presented [11,19], that research mainly focused on clear weather. There is also a large body of work on fog detection [6,17,42,51]. Classification of scenes into foggy and fog-free has been tackled as well [43]. In addition, visibility estimation has been extensively studied for both daytime [22,35,55] and nighttime [18], in the context of assisted and autonomous driving. The closest of these works to ours is [55], in which synthetic fog is generated and foggy images are segmented to *free-space area* and *vertical objects*. Our work differs in that our semantic understanding task is more complex and we tackle the problem from a different route by learning jointly from synthetic fog and real fog.

2.3   Domain Adaptation

Our work bears resemblance to transfer learning and model adaptation. Model adaptation across weather conditions to semantically segment simple road scenes

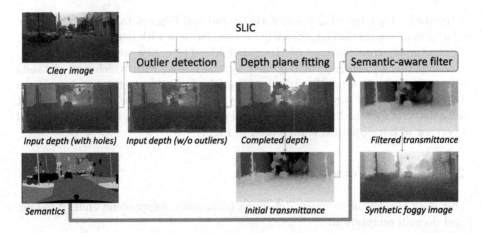

SLIC

Outlier detection   Depth plane fitting   Semantic-aware filter

Clear image

Input depth (with holes)   *Input depth (w/o outliers)*   *Completed depth*   *Filtered transmittance*

Semantics   *Initial transmittance*   *Synthetic foggy image*

Fig. 2. The pipeline of our fog simulation using semantics

is studied in [31]. More recently, domain adversarial based approaches were proposed to adapt semantic segmentation models both at pixel level and feature level from simulated to real environments [27,49]. Our work closes the domain gap by generating synthetic fog and by using the policy of *gradual* adaptation. Combining our method and the aforementioned transfer learning methods is a promising direction. The concurrent work in [13] on adaptation of semantic models from daytime to nighttime solely with real data is closely related to ours.

3   Fog Simulation on Real Scenes Using Semantics

3.1   Motivation

We drive our motivation for fog simulation on real scenes using semantic input from the pipeline that was used in [48] to generate the Foggy Cityscapes dataset, which primarily focuses on depth denoising and completion. This pipeline is denoted in Fig. 2 with thin gray arrows and consists of three main steps: depth outlier detection, robust depth plane fitting at the level of SLIC superpixels [2] using RANSAC, and postprocessing of the completed depth map with guided image filtering [23]. Our approach adopts the general configuration of this pipeline, but aims to improve its postprocessing step by leveraging the semantic annotation of the scene as additional reference for filtering, which is indicated in Fig. 2 with the thick blue arrow.

The guided filtering step in [48] uses the clear-weather color image as guidance to filter depth. However, as previous works on image filtering [50] have shown, guided filtering and similar joint filtering methods such as cross-bilateral filtering [14,44] transfer the structure that is present in the guidance/reference image to the output target image. Thus, any structure that is specific to the reference image but irrelevant for the target image is also transferred to the latter erroneously.

Whereas previous approaches such as mutual-structure filtering [50] attempt to estimate the common structure between reference and target images, we identify this common structure with the structure that is present in the ground-truth *semantic labeling* of the image. In other words, we assume that edges which are shared by the color image and the depth map generally coincide with *semantic edges*, *i.e.* locations in the image where the semantic classes of adjacent pixels are different. Under this assumption, the semantic labeling can be used directly as the reference image in a classical cross-bilateral filtering setting, since it contains exactly the mutual structure between the color image and the depth map. In practice, however, the boundaries drawn by humans in the semantic annotation are not pixel-accurate, and using the color image as additional reference helps to capture the precise shape of edges better. As a result, we formulate the postprocessing step of the completed depth map in our fog simulation as a *dual-reference* cross-bilateral filter, with color and semantic reference.

3.2 Dual-reference Cross-Bilateral Filter Using Color and Semantics

Let us denote the RGB image of the clear-weather scene by $\mathbf{R}$ and its CIELAB counterpart by $\mathbf{J}$. We consider CIELAB, as it has been designed to increase perceptual uniformity and gives better results for bilateral filtering of color images [41]. The input image to be filtered in the postprocessing step of our pipeline constitutes a scalar-valued transmittance map $\hat{t}$. We provide more details on this transmittance map in Sect. 3.3. Last, we are given a labeling function

$$h : \mathcal{P} \rightarrow \{1, \ldots, C\} \tag{1}$$

which maps pixels to semantic labels, where $\mathcal{P}$ is the discrete domain of pixel positions and C is the total number of semantic classes in the scene. We define our dual-reference cross-bilateral filter with color and semantic reference as

$$t(\mathbf{p}) = \frac{\displaystyle\sum_{q\in\mathcal{N}(\mathbf{p})} G_{\sigma_s}(\|\mathbf{q}-\mathbf{p}\|)\left[\delta(h(\mathbf{q})-h(\mathbf{p}))+\mu G_{\sigma_c}(\|\mathbf{J}(\mathbf{q})-\mathbf{J}(\mathbf{p})\|)\right]\hat{t}(\mathbf{q})}{\displaystyle\sum_{q\in\mathcal{N}(\mathbf{p})} G_{\sigma_s}(\|\mathbf{q}-\mathbf{p}\|)\left[\delta(h(\mathbf{q})-h(\mathbf{p}))+\mu G_{\sigma_c}(\|\mathbf{J}(\mathbf{q})-\mathbf{J}(\mathbf{p})\|)\right]}, \tag{2}$$

where $\mathbf{p}$ and $\mathbf{q}$ denote pixel positions, $\mathcal{N}(\mathbf{p})$ is the neighborhood of $\mathbf{p}$, δ denotes the Kronecker delta, G_{σ_s} is the spatial Gaussian kernel, G_{σ_c} is the color-domain Gaussian kernel and μ is a positive constant. The novel dual reference is demonstrated in the second factor of the filter weights, which constitutes a sum of the terms $\delta(h(\mathbf{q}) - h(\mathbf{p}))$ for semantic reference and $G_{\sigma_c}(\|\mathbf{J}(\mathbf{q}) - \mathbf{J}(\mathbf{p})\|)$ for color reference, weighted by μ. The formulation of the semantic term implies that only pixels $\mathbf{q}$ with the same semantic label as the examined pixel $\mathbf{p}$ contribute to the output at $\mathbf{p}$ through this term, which prevents blurring of semantic edges. At the same time, the color term helps to better preserve true depth edges that do not coincide with any semantic boundary but are present in $\mathbf{J}$.

The formulation of (2) enables an efficient implementation of our filter based on the bilateral grid [41]. More specifically, we construct two separate bilateral grids that correspond to the semantic and color domains and operate separately on each grid to perform filtering, combining the results in the end. In this way, we handle a 3D bilateral grid for the semantic domain and a 5D grid for the color domain instead of a single joint 6D grid that would dramatically increase computation time [41].

In our experiments, we set $\mu = 5$, $\sigma_s = 20$, and $\sigma_c = 10$.

3.3   Remaining Steps

Here we outline the rest parts of our fog simulation pipeline of Fig. 2. For more details, we refer the reader to [48], with which most parts of the pipeline are common. The standard optical model for fog that forms the basis of our fog simulation was introduced in [29] and is expressed as

$$\mathbf{I}(\mathbf{x}) = \mathbf{R}(\mathbf{x})t(\mathbf{x}) + \mathbf{L}(1 - t(\mathbf{x})), \tag{3}$$

where $\mathbf{I}(\mathbf{x})$ is the observed foggy image at pixel $\mathbf{x}$, $\mathbf{R}(\mathbf{x})$ is the clear scene radiance and $\mathbf{L}$ is the atmospheric light, which is assumed to be globally constant. The transmittance $t(\mathbf{x})$ determines the amount of scene radiance that reaches the camera. For homogeneous fog, transmittance depends on the distance $\ell(\mathbf{x})$ of the scene from the camera through

$$t(\mathbf{x}) = \exp\left(-\beta\ell(\mathbf{x})\right). \tag{4}$$

The attenuation coefficient β controls the density of the fog: larger values of β mean denser fog. Fog decreases the meteorological optical range (MOR), also known as visibility, to less than 1 Km by definition [1]. For homogeneous fog MOR $= 2.996/\beta$, which implies

$$\beta \geq 2.996 \times 10^{-3} \text{ m}^{-1}, \tag{5}$$

where the lower bound corresponds to the lightest fog configuration. In our fog simulation, the value that is used for β always obeys (5).

The required inputs for fog simulation with (3) are the image $\mathbf{R}$ of the original clear scene, atmospheric light $\mathbf{L}$ and a complete transmittance map t. We use the same approach for atmospheric light estimation as that in [48]. Moreover, we adopt the stereoscopic inpainting method of [48] for depth denoising and completion to obtain an initial complete transmittance map $\hat{t}$ from a noisy and incomplete input disparity map D, using the recommended parameters. We filter $\hat{t}$ with our dual-reference cross-bilateral filter (2) to compute the final transmittance map t, which is used in (3) to synthesize the foggy image $\mathbf{I}$.

Results of the presented pipeline for fog simulation on example images from Cityscapes [11] are provided in Fig. 3 for $\beta = 0.02$, which corresponds to visibility of ca. 150 m. We specifically leverage the instance-level semantic annotations that are provided in Cityscapes and set the labeling h of (1) to a different value for each distinct instance of the same semantic class in order to distinguish adjacent instances. We compare our synthetic foggy images against the respective images

(a) Cityscapes   (b) Foggy Cityscapes   (c) Our foggy image

Fig. 3. Comparison of our synthetic foggy images against Foggy Cityscapes [48]. This figure is better seen on a screen and zoomed in

of Foggy Cityscapes that were generated with the approach of [48]. Our synthetic foggy images generally preserve the edges between adjacent objects with large discrepancy in depth better than the images in Foggy Cityscapes, because our approach utilizes semantic boundaries, which usually encompass these edges. The incorrect structure transfer of color textures to the transmittance map, which deteriorates the quality of Foggy Cityscapes, is also reduced with our method.

4 Semantic Segmentation of Scenes with Dense Fog

In this section, we first present a standard supervised learning approach for semantic segmentation under dense fog using our synthetic foggy data with the novel fog simulation of Sect. 3, and then elaborate on our novel curriculum model adaptation approach using both synthetic and real foggy data.

4.1 Learning with Synthetic Fog

Generating synthetic fog from real clear-weather scenes grants the potential of inheriting the existing human annotations of these scenes, such as those from the Cityscapes dataset [11]. This is a significant asset that enables training of standard segmentation models. Therefore, an effective way of evaluating the merit of a fog simulator is to adapt a segmentation model originally trained on clear weather to the synthesized foggy images and then evaluate the adapted model against the original one on real foggy images. The goal is to verify that the standard learning methods for semantic segmentation can benefit from our simulated fog in the challenging scenario of real fog. This evaluation policy has been proposed in [48]. We adopt this policy and fine-tune the RefineNet model [33] on synthetic foggy images generated with our simulation. The performance of our adapted models on dense real fog is compared to that of the original clear-weather model as well as the models that are adapted on Foggy Cityscapes [48], providing an objective comparison of our simulation method against [48].

4.2   Curriculum Model Adaptation with Synthetic and Real Fog

While adapting a standard segmentation model to our synthetic fog improves its performance as shown in Sect. 6.2, the paradigm still suffers from the domain discrepancy between synthetic and real foggy images. This discrepancy becomes more accentuated for denser fog. We present a method which can learn from our synthetic fog plus unlabeled real foggy data.

The method, which we term Curriculum Model Adaptation (CMAda), uses two versions of synthetic fog —one with light fog and another with dense fog— and a large dataset of unlabeled real foggy scenes with variable, unknown fog density, and works as follows:

1. generate a synthetic foggy dataset with multiple versions of varying fog density;
2. train a model for fog density estimation on the dataset of step 1;
3. rank the images in the real foggy dataset with the model of step 2 according to fog density;
4. generate a dataset with light synthetic fog, and train a segmentation model on it;
5. apply the segmentation model from step 4 to the light-fog images of the real dataset (ranked lower in step 3) to obtain "noisy" semantic labels;
6. generate a dataset with dense synthetic fog;
7. adapt the segmentation model from step 4 to the union of the dense synthetic foggy dataset from step 6 and the light real foggy one from step 5.

CMAda adapts segmentation models from light synthetic fog to dense real fog and is inspired by curriculum learning [4], in the sense that we first solve easier tasks with our synthetic data, i.e. fog density estimation and semantic scene understanding under light fog, and then acquire new knowledge from the already "solved" tasks in order to better tackle the harder task, i.e. scene understanding under dense real fog. CMAda also exploits the direct control of fog density for synthetic foggy images. Figure 1 provides an overview of our method. Below we present details on our fog density estimation, i.e. step 2, and the training of the model, i.e. step 7.

Fog Density Estimation. Fog density is usually determined by the visibility of the foggy scene. An accurate estimate of fog density can benefit many applications, such as image defogging [10]. Since annotating images in a fine-grained manner regarding fog density is very challenging, previous methods are trained on a few hundreds of images divided into only two classes: foggy and fog-free [10]. The performance of the system, however, is affected by the small amount of training data and the coarse class granularity.

In this paper, we leverage our fog simulation applied to Cityscapes [11] for fog density estimation. Since simulated fog density is directly controlled through β, we generate several versions of Foggy Cityscapes with varying $\beta \in \{0, 0.005, 0.01, 0.02\}$ and train AlexNet [30] to regress the value of β for each image, lifting the need to handcraft features relevant to fog as [10] did. The predicted fog density using our method correlates well with human judgments of fog density taken in a subjective study on a large foggy image database on Amazon Mechanical Turk (cf. Sect. 6.1 for results). The fog density estimator is used to rank our new *Foggy Zurich* dataset, to select light foggy images for usage in CMAda, and to select dense foggy images for manual annotation.

Curriculum Model Adaptation. We formulate CMAda for semantic segmentation as follows. Let us denote a clear-weather image by $\mathbf{x}$, the corresponding image under light synthetic fog by $\mathbf{x}'$, the corresponding image under dense synthetic fog by $\mathbf{x}''$, and the corresponding human annotation by $\mathbf{y}$. Then, the training data consist of labeled data with light synthetic fog $\mathcal{D}_l' = \{(\mathbf{x}_i', \mathbf{y}_i)\}_{i=1}^l$, labeled data with dense synthetic fog $\mathcal{D}_l'' = \{(\mathbf{x}_i'', \mathbf{y}_i)\}_{i=1}^l$ and unlabeled images with light real fog $\bar{\mathcal{D}}_u' = \{\bar{\mathbf{x}}_j'\}_{j=l+1}^{l+u}$, where $\mathbf{y}_i^{m,n} \in \{1, ..., C\}$ is the label of pixel (m, n), and C is the total number of classes. l is the number of labeled training images with synthetic fog, and u is the number of unlabeled images with light real fog. The aim is to learn a mapping function $\phi'' : \mathcal{X}'' \mapsto \mathcal{Y}$ from $\mathcal{D}_l'$, $\mathcal{D}_l''$ and $\bar{\mathcal{D}}_u'$, and evaluate it on images with dense real fog $\bar{\mathcal{D}}'' = \{\bar{\mathbf{x}}_1'', ..., \bar{\mathbf{x}}_k''\}$, where k is the number of images with dense real fog.

Since $\bar{\mathcal{D}}_u'$ does not have human annotations, we generate the supervisory labels as previously described in step 5. In particular, we first learn a mapping function $\phi' : \mathcal{X}' \mapsto \mathcal{Y}$ with $\mathcal{D}_l'$ and then obtain the labels $\bar{\mathbf{y}}_j' = \phi'(\bar{\mathbf{x}}_j')$ for $\bar{\mathbf{x}}_j'$, $\forall j \in \{l+1, ..., l+u\}$. $\bar{\mathcal{D}}_u'$ is then upgraded to $\bar{\mathcal{D}}_u' = \{(\bar{\mathbf{x}}_j', \bar{\mathbf{y}}_j')\}_{j=l+1}^{l+u}$. The proposed scheme for training semantic segmentation models for dense foggy image $\bar{\mathbf{x}}''$ is to learn a mapping function ϕ'' so that human annotations for dense synthetic fog and the generated labels for light real fog are both taken into account:

$$\min_{\phi''} \frac{1}{l} \sum_{i=1}^l L(\phi''(\mathbf{x}_i''), \mathbf{y}_i) + \lambda \frac{1}{u} \sum_{j=l+1}^{l+u} L(\phi''(\bar{\mathbf{x}}_j'), \bar{\mathbf{y}}_j'), \quad (6)$$

where $L(., .)$ is the cross entropy loss function and $\lambda = \frac{u}{l} \times w$ is a hyper-parameter balancing the weights of the two data sources, with w serving as the relative weight of each real weakly labeled image compared to each synthetic labeled one. We empirically set $w = 1/3$ in our experiment, but an optimal value can be obtained via cross-validation if needed. The optimization of (6) is implemented by mixing images from $\mathcal{D}_l''$ and $\bar{\mathcal{D}}_u'$ in a proportion of $1 : w$ and feeding the stream of hybrid data to a CNN for standard supervised training.

This learning approach bears resemblance to model distillation [21, 26] or imitation [8, 12]. The underpinnings of our proposed approach are the following: (1) in light fog objects are easier to recognize than in dense fog, hence models trained on synthetic data are more generalizable to real data in case both data sources contain light rather than dense fog; (2) dense synthetic fog and light real fog reflect different and complementary characteristics of the target domain of dense real fog. On the one hand, dense synthetic fog features a similar overall visibility obstruction to dense real fog, but includes artifacts. On the other hand, light real fog captures the true nonuniform and spatially varying structure of fog, but at a different density than dense fog.

5   The Foggy Zurich Dataset

5.1   Data Collection

Foggy Zurich was collected during multiple rides with a car inside the city of Zurich and its suburbs using a GoPro Hero 5 camera. We recorded four large video sequences, and extracted video frames corresponding to those parts of the sequences where fog is (almost) ubiquitous in the scene at a rate of one frame per second. The extracted images are manually cleaned by removing the duplicates (if any), resulting in 3808 foggy images in total. The resolution of the frames is 1920×1080 pixels. We mounted the camera inside the front windshield, since we found that mounting it outside the vehicle resulted in significant deterioration in image quality due to blurring artifacts caused by dew.

5.2   Annotation of Images with Dense Fog

We use our fog density estimator presented in Sect. 4.2 to rank all images in *Foggy Zurich* according to fog density. Based on the ordering, we manually select 16 images with *dense* fog and diverse visual scenes, and construct the test set of *Foggy Zurich* therefrom, which we term *Foggy Zurich-test*. We annotate these images with fine pixel-level semantic annotations using the 19 evaluation classes of the Cityscapes dataset [11]. In addition, we assign the *void* label to pixels which do not belong to any of the above 19 classes, or the class of which is uncertain due to the presence of fog. Every such pixel is ignored for semantic segmentation evaluation. Comprehensive statistics for the semantic annotations of *Foggy Zurich-test* are presented in Fig. 4. We also distinguish the semantic classes that occur frequently in *Foggy Zurich-test*. These "frequent" classes are: *road, sidewalk, building, wall, fence, pole, traffic light, traffic sign, vegetation, sky*, and *car*. When performing evaluation on *Foggy Zurich-test*, we occasionally report the average score over this set of frequent classes, which feature plenty of examples, as a second metric to support the corresponding results.

Despite the fact that there exists a number of prominent large-scale datasets for semantic road scene understanding, such as KITTI [19], Cityscapes [11] and Mapillary Vistas [39], most of these datasets contain few or even no foggy scenes,

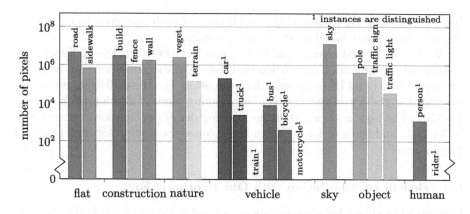

Fig. 4. Number of annotated pixels per class for *Foggy Zurich-test*

which can be attributed partly to the rarity of the condition of fog and the difficulty of annotating foggy images. To the best of our knowledge, the only previous dataset for semantic foggy scene understanding whose scale exceeds that of *Foggy Zurich-test* is Foggy Driving [48], with 101 annotated images. However, we found that most images in Foggy Driving contain relatively light fog and most images with dense fog are annotated *coarsely*. Compared to Foggy Driving, *Foggy Zurich* comprises a much greater number of high-resolution foggy images. Its larger, unlabeled part is highly relevant for unsupervised or semi-supervised approaches such as the one we have presented in Sect. 4.2, while the smaller, labeled *Foggy Zurich-test* set features *fine* semantic annotations for the particularly challenging setting of dense fog, making a significant step towards evaluation of semantic segmentation models in this setting.

In order to ensure a sound training and evaluation, we manually filter the unlabeled part of *Foggy Zurich* and exclude from the resulting training sets those images which bear resemblance to any image in *Foggy Zurich-test* with respect to the depicted scene.

6   Experiments

6.1   Fog Density Estimation with Synthetic Data

We conduct a user study on Amazon Mechanical Turk (AMT) to evaluate the ranking results of our fog density estimator. In order to guarantee high quality, we only employ AMT Masters in our study and verify the answers via a Known Answer Review Policy. Each human intelligence task (HIT) comprises five image pairs to be compared: three pairs are the true query pairs; the rest two pairs contain synthetic fog of different densities and are used for validation. The participants are shown two images at a time, side by side, and are simply asked to choose the one which is more foggy. The query pairs are sampled based on the ranking results of our method. In order to avoid confusing cases, *i.e.* two images of similar fog densities, the two images of each pair need to be at least 20 percentiles apart based on the ranking results.

We have collected answers for 12000 pairs in 4000 HITs. The HITs are only considered for evaluation only when both the validation questions are correctly answered. 87% of all HITs are valid for evaluation. For these 10400 annotations, we find that the agreement between our ranking method and human judgment is 89.3%. The high accuracy confirms that fog density estimation is a relatively easier task, and the solution to it can be exploited for solving high-level tasks of foggy scenes.

6.2   Benefit of Adaptation with Our Synthetic Fog

Our model of choice for experiments on semantic segmentation is the state-of-the-art RefineNet [33]. We use the publicly available *RefineNet-res101-Cityscapes* model, which has been trained on the clear-weather training set of Cityscapes. In all experiments of this section, we use a constant learning rate of 5×10^{-5} and mini-batches of size 1. Moreover, we compile all versions of our synthetic foggy dataset by applying our fog simulation (which is denoted by "Stereo-DBF" in the following for short) on the same *refined* set of Cityscapes images that was used in [48] to compile Foggy Cityscapes-refined. This set comprises 498 training and 52 validation images; we use the former for training. We considered dehazing as a preprocessing step as in [48] but did not observe a gain against *no* dehazing and thus omit such comparisons from the following presentation.

Our first segmentation experiment shows that our semantic-aware fog simulation performs competitively compared to the fog simulation of [48] (denoted by "Stereo-GF") for generating synthetic data to adapt RefineNet to dense real fog. *RefineNet-res101-Cityscapes* is fine-tuned on the version of Foggy Cityscapes-refined that corresponds to each simulation method for 8 epochs. We experiment with two synthetic fog densities. For evaluation, we use *Foggy Zurich-test* as well as a subset of Foggy Driving [48] containing 21 images with dense fog, which we term Foggy Driving-dense, and report results in Tables 1 and 2 respectively. Training on lighter synthetic fog helps to beat the baseline clear-weather model in all cases and yields consistently better results than denser synthetic fog, which verifies the first motivating assumption of CMAda at the end of Sect. 4.2. In addition, Stereo-DBF beats Stereo-GF in most cases by a small margin and is consistently better at generating denser synthetic foggy data. On the other hand, Stereo-GF with light fog is slightly better for *Foggy Zurich-test*. This motivates us to consistently use the model that has been trained with Stereo-GF in steps 4 and 5 of CMAda for the experiments of Sect. 6.3, assuming that its merit for dense real fog extends to lighter fog. However, Stereo-DBF is still fully relevant for step 6 of CMAda based on its favorable comparison for denser synthetic fog.

6.3   Benefit of Curriculum Adaptation with Synthetic and Real Fog

Our second segmentation experiment showcases the effectiveness of our CMAda pipeline, using Stereo-DBF and Stereo-GF as alternatives for generating

Table 1. Performance comparison on *Foggy Zurich-test* of RefineNet and fine-tuned versions of it using Foggy Cityscapes-refined, rendered with different fog simulations and attenuation coefficients β

Mean IoU over *all* classes (%)			Mean IoU over *frequent* classes (%)		
RefineNet [33]	32.0		RefineNet [33]	48.8	
Fog simulation	$\beta = 0.005$	$\beta = 0.01$	Fog simulation	$\beta = 0.005$	$\beta = 0.01$
Stereo-GF [48]	**33.9**	30.2	Stereo-GF [48]	**49.3**	45.8
Stereo-DBF	33.4	**31.2**	Stereo-DBF	49.0	**46.6**

Table 2. Performance comparison on Foggy Driving-dense of RefineNet and fine-tuned versions of it using Foggy Cityscapes-refined, rendered with different fog simulations and attenuation coefficients β

Mean IoU over *all* classes (%)			Mean IoU over *frequent* classes (%)		
RefineNet [33]	30.4		RefineNet [33]	57.6	
Fog simulation	$\beta = 0.005$	$\beta = 0.01$	Fog simulation	$\beta = 0.005$	$\beta = 0.01$
Stereo-GF [48]	32.5	32.4	Stereo-GF [48]	60.4	58.7
Stereo-DBF	**32.8**	**32.8**	Stereo-DBF	**60.8**	**59.2**

Table 3. Performance comparison on *Foggy Zurich-test* of the two adaptation steps of CMAda using Foggy Cityscapes-refined and *Foggy Zurich-light* for training

Mean IoU over *all* classes (%)			Mean IoU over *frequent* classes (%)		
Fog simulation	CMAda-4	CMAda-7	Fog simulation	CMAda-4	CMAda-7
Stereo-GF [48]	33.9	34.7	Stereo-GF [48]	49.3	53.3
Stereo-DBF	33.4	**37.9**	Stereo-DBF	49.0	**56.7**

synthetic Foggy Cityscapes-refined in steps 4 and 6 of the pipeline. *Foggy Zurich* serves as the real foggy dataset in the pipeline. We use the results of our fog density estimation to select 1556 images with light fog and name this set *Foggy Zurich-light*. The models which are obtained after the initial adaptation step that uses Foggy Cityscapes-refined with $\beta = 0.005$ are further fine-tuned for 6k iterations on the union of Foggy Cityscapes-refined with $\beta = 0.01$ and *Foggy Zurich-light* setting $w = 1/3$, where the latter set is noisily labeled by the aforementioned initially adapted models. Results for the two adaptation steps (denoted by "CMAda-4" and "CMAda-7") on *Foggy Zurich-test* and *Foggy Driving-dense* are reported in Tables 3 and 4 respectively. The second adaptation step CMAda-7, which involves dense synthetic fog and light real fog, consistently improves upon the first step CMAda-4. Moreover, using our fog simulation to simulate dense synthetic fog for CMAda-7 gives the best result on *Foggy Zurich-test*, improving the clear-weather baseline by 5.9% and 7.9% in terms of mean IoU over all classes and frequent classes respectively. Figure 5 supports this result with visual comparisons. The real foggy images of *Foggy Zurich-light* used in CMAda-7 additionally provide a clear generalization benefit on Foggy Driving-dense, which involves different camera sensors than *Foggy Zurich*.

Table 4. Performance comparison on Foggy Driving-dense of the two adaptation steps of CMAda using Foggy Cityscapes-refined and *Foggy Zurich-light* for training

Mean IoU over *all* classes (%)			Mean IoU over *frequent* classes (%)		
Fog simulation	CMAda-4	CMAda-7	Fog simulation	CMAda-4	CMAda-7
Stereo-GF [48]	32.5	34.1	Stereo-GF [48]	60.4	**61.6**
Stereo-DBF	32.8	**34.3**	Stereo-DBF	60.8	61.5

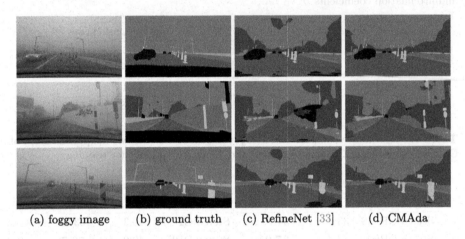

(a) foggy image   (b) ground truth   (c) RefineNet [33]   (d) CMAda

Fig. 5. Qualitative results for semantic segmentation on *Foggy Zurich-test*. "CMAda" stands for RefineNet [33] fine-tuned with our full CMAda pipeline on the union of Foggy Cityscapes-refined using our simulation and *Foggy Zurich-light*

7   Conclusion

In this paper, we have shown the benefit of using partially synthetic as well as unlabeled real foggy data in a curriculum adaptation framework to progressively improve performance of state-of-the-art semantic segmentation models in dense real fog. To this end, we have proposed a novel fog simulation approach on real scenes, which leverages the semantic annotation of the scene as input to a novel dual-reference cross-bilateral filter, and applied it to the Cityscapes dataset. We have presented *Foggy Zurich*, a large-scale dataset of real foggy scenes, including pixel-level semantic annotations for 16 scenes with dense fog. Through detailed evaluation, we have evidenced clearly that our curriculum adaptation method exploits both our synthetic and real data and significantly boosts performance on dense real fog without using any labeled real foggy image and that our fog simulation performs competitively to state-of-the-art counterparts.

Acknowledgements. This work is funded by Toyota Motor Europe via the research project TRACE-Zürich.

References

1. Federal Meteorological Handbook No. 1: Surface Weather Observations and Reports. U.S, Department of Commerce/National Oceanic and Atmospheric Administration (2005)
2. Achanta, R., Shaji, A., Smith, K., Lucchi, A., Fua, P., Süsstrunk, S.: SLIC superpixels compared to state-of-the-art superpixel methods. IEEE Trans. Pattern Anal. Mach. Intell. **34**(11), 2274–2282 (2012)
3. Bar Hillel, A., Lerner, R., Levi, D., Raz, G.: Recent progress in road and lane detection: a survey. Mach. Vision Appl. **25**(3), 727–745 (2014)
4. Bengio, Y., Louradour, J., Collobert, R., Weston, J.: Curriculum learning. In: International Conference on Machine Learning, pp. 41–48 (2009)
5. Berman, D., Treibitz, T., Avidan, S.: Non-local image dehazing. In: IEEE Conference on Computer Vision and Pattern Recognition (CVPR) (2016)
6. Bronte, S., Bergasa, L.M., Alcantarilla, P.F.: Fog detection system based on computer vision techniques. In: IEEE International Conference on Intelligent Transportation Systems (ITSC) (2009)
7. Brostow, G.J., Shotton, J., Fauqueur, J., Cipolla, R.: Segmentation and recognition using structure from motion point clouds. In: Forsyth, D., Torr, P., Zisserman, A. (eds.) ECCV 2008, Part I. LNCS, vol. 5302, pp. 44–57. Springer, Heidelberg (2008). https://doi.org/10.1007/978-3-540-88682-2_5
8. Buciluă, C., Caruana, R., Niculescu-Mizil, A.: Model compression. In: International Conference on Knowledge Discovery and Data Mining (SIGKDD) (2006)
9. Chen, Y., Li, W., Sakaridis, C., Dai, D., Van Gool, L.: Domain adaptive faster R-CNN for object detection in the wild. In: IEEE Conference on Computer Vision and Pattern Recognition (CVPR) (2018)
10. Choi, L.K., You, J., Bovik, A.C.: Referenceless prediction of perceptual fog density and perceptual image defogging. IEEE Trans. Image Process. **24**(11), 3888–3901 (2015)
11. Cordts, M., et al.: The Cityscapes dataset for semantic urban scene understanding. In: IEEE Conference on Computer Vision and Pattern Recognition (CVPR) (2016)
12. Dai, D., Kroeger, T., Timofte, R., Van Gool, L.: Metric imitation by manifold transfer for efficient vision applications. In: IEEE Conference on Computer Vision and Pattern Recognition (CVPR) (2015)
13. Dai, D., Van Gool, L.: Progressive model adaptation and knowledge transfer from daytime to nighttime for semantic road scene understanding. In: IEEE International Conference on Intelligent Transportation Systems (2018)
14. Eisemann, E., Durand, F.: Flash photography enhancement via intrinsic relighting. In: ACM SIGGRAPH (2004)
15. Fattal, R.: Single image dehazing. ACM Trans. Graph. **27**(3), 72 (2008)
16. Fattal, R.: Dehazing using color-lines. ACM Trans. Graph. **34**(1), 1–14 (2014)
17. Gallen, R., Cord, A., Hautière, N., Aubert, D.: Towards night fog detection through use of in-vehicle multipurpose cameras. In: IEEE Intelligent Vehicles Symposium (IV) (2011)
18. Gallen, R., Cord, A., Hautière, N., Dumont, É., Aubert, D.: Nighttime visibility analysis and estimation method in the presence of dense fog. IEEE Trans. Intell. Transp. Syst. **16**(1), 310–320 (2015)

19. Geiger, A., Lenz, P., Urtasun, R.: Are we ready for autonomous driving? The KITTI vision benchmark suite. In: IEEE Conference on Computer Vision and Pattern Recognition (CVPR) (2012)

20. Girshick, R.: Fast R-CNN. In: International Conference on Computer Vision (ICCV) (2015)

21. Gupta, S., Hoffman, J., Malik, J.: Cross modal distillation for supervision transfer. In: The IEEE Conference on Computer Vision and Pattern Recognition (CVPR) (2016)

22. Hautière, N., Tarel, J.P., Lavenant, J., Aubert, D.: Automatic fog detection and estimation of visibility distance through use of an onboard camera. Mach. Vis. Appl. **17**(1), 8–20 (2006)

23. He, K., Sun, J., Tang, X.: Guided image filtering. IEEE Trans. Pattern Anal. Mach. Intell. **35**(6), 1397–1409 (2013)

24. He, K., Sun, J., Tang, X.: Single image haze removal using dark channel prior. IEEE Trans. Pattern Anal. Mach. Intell. **33**(12), 2341–2353 (2011)

25. Hecker, S., Dai, D., Van Gool, L.: Learning driving models with a surround-view camera system and a route planner. In: European Conference on Computer Vision (ECCV) (2018, to appear)

26. Hinton, G., Vinyals, O., Dean, J.: Distilling the knowledge in a neural network. arXiv preprint arXiv:1503.02531 (2015)

27. Hoffman, J., Tzeng, E., Park, T., Zhu, J.Y., Isola, P., Saenko, K., Efros, A., Darrell, T.: CyCADA: Cycle-consistent adversarial domain adaptation. In: International Conference on Machine Learning (2018)

28. Jensen, M.B., Philipsen, M.P., Møgelmose, A., Moeslund, T.B., Trivedi, M.M.: Vision for looking at traffic lights: Issues, survey, and perspectives. IEEE Trans. Intell. Transp. Syst. **17**(7), 1800–1815 (2016)

29. Koschmieder, H.: Theorie der horizontalen Sichtweite. Beitrage zur Physik der freien Atmosphäre (1924)

30. Krizhevsky, A., Sutskever, I., Hinton, G.E.: ImageNet classification with deep convolutional neural networks. In: NIPS (2012)

31. Levinkov, E., Fritz, M.: Sequential bayesian model update under structured scene prior for semantic road scenes labeling. In: IEEE International Conference on Computer Vision (2013)

32. Li, Y., You, S., Brown, M.S., Tan, R.T.: Haze visibility enhancement: A survey and quantitative benchmarking, coRR abs/1607.06235 (2016)

33. Lin, G., Milan, A., Shen, C., Reid, I.: Refinenet: Multi-path refinement networks with identity mappings for high-resolution semantic segmentation. In: IEEE Conference on Computer Vision and Pattern Recognition (CVPR) (2017)

34. Ling, Z., Fan, G., Wang, Y., Lu, X.: Learning deep transmission network for single image dehazing. In: IEEE International Conference on Image Processing (ICIP) (2016)

35. Miclea, R.C., Silea, I.: Visibility detection in foggy environment. In: International Conference on Control Systems and Computer Science (2015)

36. Narasimhan, S.G., Nayar, S.K.: Contrast restoration of weather degraded images. IEEE Trans. Pattern Anal. Mach. Intell. **25**(6), 713–724 (2003)

37. Narasimhan, S.G., Nayar, S.K.: Vision and the atmosphere. Int. J. Comput. Vis. **48**(3), 233–254 (2002)

38. Negru, M., Nedevschi, S., Peter, R.I.: Exponential contrast restoration in fog conditions for driving assistance. IEEE Trans. Intell. Transp. Syst. **16**(4), 2257–2268 (2015)

39. Neuhold, G., Ollmann, T., Rota Bulò, S., Kontschieder, P.: The Mapillary Vistas dataset for semantic understanding of street scenes. In: The IEEE International Conference on Computer Vision (ICCV) (2017)
40. Nishino, K., Kratz, L., Lombardi, S.: Bayesian defogging. Int. J. Comput. Vis. 98(3), 263–278 (2012)
41. Paris, S., Durand, F.: A fast approximation of the bilateral filter using a signal processing approach. Int. J. Comput. Vis. 81, 24–52 (2009)
42. Pavlić, M., Belzner, H., Rigoll, G., Ilić, S.: Image based fog detection in vehicles. In: IEEE Intelligent Vehicles Symposium (2012)
43. Pavlić, M., Rigoll, G., Ilić, S.: Classification of images in fog and fog-free scenes for use in vehicles. In: IEEE Intelligent Vehicles Symposium (IV) (2013)
44. Petschnigg, G., Szeliski, R., Agrawala, M., Cohen, M., Hoppe, H., Toyama, K.: Digital photography with flash and no-flash image pairs. In: ACM SIGGRAPH (2004)
45. Ren, S., He, K., Girshick, R., Sun, J.: Faster R-CNN: Towards real-time object detection with region proposal networks. In: Advances in Neural Information Processing Systems, pp. 91–99 (2015)
46. Ros, G., Sellart, L., Materzynska, J., Vazquez, D., Lopez, A.M.: The SYNTHIA dataset: A large collection of synthetic images for semantic segmentation of urban scenes. In: The IEEE Conference on Computer Vision and Pattern Recognition (CVPR), June 2016
47. Russakovsky, O., et al.: Imagenet large scale visual recognition challenge. Int. J. Comput. Vis. 115(3), 211–252 (2015)
48. Sakaridis, C., Dai, D., Van Gool, L.: Semantic foggy scene understanding with synthetic data. Int. J. Comput. Vis. 126, 973–992 (2018)
49. Sankaranarayanan, S., Balaji, Y., Jain, A., Nam Lim, S., Chellappa, R.: Learning from synthetic data: Addressing domain shift for semantic segmentation. In: IEEE Conference on Computer Vision and Pattern Recognition (CVPR), June 2018
50. Shen, X., Zhou, C., Xu, L., Jia, J.: Mutual-structure for joint filtering. In: The IEEE International Conference on Computer Vision (ICCV) (2015)
51. Spinneker, R., Koch, C., Park, S.B., Yoon, J.J.: Fast fog detection for camera based advanced driver assistance systems. In: IEEE International Conference on Intelligent Transportation Systems (ITSC) (2014)
52. Tan, R.T.: Visibility in bad weather from a single image. In: IEEE Conference on Computer Vision and Pattern Recognition (CVPR) (2008)
53. Tang, K., Yang, J., Wang, J.: Investigating haze-relevant features in a learning framework for image dehazing. In: IEEE Conference on Computer Vision and Pattern Recognition (2014)
54. Tarel, J.P., Hautière, N., Caraffa, L., Cord, A., Halmaoui, H., Gruyer, D.: Vision enhancement in homogeneous and heterogeneous fog. IEEE Intell. Transp. Syst. Mag. 4(2), 6–20 (2012)
55. Tarel, J.P., Hautière, N., Cord, A., Gruyer, D., Halmaoui, H.: Improved visibility of road scene images under heterogeneous fog. In: IEEE Intelligent Vehicles Symposium, pp. 478–485 (2010)
56. Wang, Y.K., Fan, C.T.: Single image defogging by multiscale depth fusion. IEEE Trans. Image Process. 23(11), 4826–4837 (2014)
57. Xu, Y., Wen, J., Fei, L., Zhang, Z.: Review of video and image defogging algorithms and related studies on image restoration and enhancement. IEEE Access 4, 165–188 (2016)

58. Yu, F., Koltun, V.: Multi-scale context aggregation by dilated convolutions. In: International Conference on Learning Representations (2016)
59. Zhang, H., Sindagi, V.A., Patel, V.M.: Joint transmission map estimation and dehazing using deep networks, coRR abs/1708.00581 (2017)
60. Zhao, H., Shi, J., Qi, X., Wang, X., Jia, J.: Pyramid scene parsing network. In: IEEE Conference on Computer Vision and Pattern Recognition (CVPR) (2017)

Deep Adaptive Attention for Joint Facial Action Unit Detection and Face Alignment

Zhiwen Shao[1], Zhilei Liu[2](✉), Jianfei Cai[3], and Lizhuang Ma[1,4](✉)

[1] Department of Computer Science and Engineering, Shanghai Jiao Tong University,
Shanghai, China
shaozhiwen@sjtu.edu.cn, ma-lz@cs.sjtu.edu.cn
[2] College of Intellengence and Computing, Tianjin University, Tianjin, China
zhileiliu@tju.edu.cn
[3] School of Computer Science and Engineering, Nanyang Technological University,
Singapore, Singapore
asjfcai@ntu.edu.sg
[4] School of Computer Science and Software Engineering, East China Normal
University, Shanghai, China

Abstract. Facial action unit (AU) detection and face alignment are
two highly correlated tasks since facial landmarks can provide precise
AU locations to facilitate the extraction of meaningful local features for
AU detection. Most existing AU detection works often treat face alignment as a preprocessing and handle the two tasks independently. In this
paper, we propose a novel end-to-end deep learning framework for joint
AU detection and face alignment, which has not been explored before.
In particular, multi-scale shared features are learned firstly, and high-
level features of face alignment are fed into AU detection. Moreover, to
extract precise local features, we propose an adaptive attention learning module to refine the attention map of each AU adaptively. Finally,
the assembled local features are integrated with face alignment features
and global features for AU detection. Experiments on BP4D and DISFA
benchmarks demonstrate that our framework significantly outperforms
the state-of-the-art methods for AU detection.

Keywords: Joint learning · Facial AU detection · Face alignment
Adaptive attention learning

1 Introduction

Facial action unit (AU) detection and face alignment are two important face
analysis tasks in the fields of computer vision and affective computing [13]. In
most of face related tasks, face alignment is usually employed to localize certain distinctive facial locations, namely landmarks, to define the facial shape or
expression appearance. Facial action units (AUs) refer to a unique set of basic

© Springer Nature Switzerland AG 2018
V. Ferrari et al. (Eds.): ECCV 2018, LNCS 11217, pp. 725–740, 2018.
https://doi.org/10.1007/978-3-030-01261-8_43

facial muscle actions at certain facial locations defined by Facial Action Coding System (FACS) [5], which is one of the most comprehensive and objective systems for describing facial expressions. Considering facial AU detection and face alignment are coherently related to each other, they should be beneficial for each other if putting them in a joint framework. However, in literature it is rare to see such joint study of the two tasks.

Although most of the previous studies [3,31] on facial AU detection only make use of face detection, facial landmarks have been adopted in the recent works since they can provide more precise AU locations and lead to better AU detection performance. For example, Li et al. [10] proposed a deep learning based approach named EAC-Net for facial AU detection by enhancing and cropping the regions of interest (ROIs) with facial landmark information. However, they just treat face alignment as a pre-processing to determine the region of interest (ROI) of each AU with a fixed size and a fixed attention distribution. Wu et al. [23] tried to exploit face alignment and facial AU detection simultaneously with the cascade regression framework, which is a pioneering work for the joint study of the two tasks. However, this cascade regression method only uses handcrafted features and is not based on the prevailing deep learning technology, which limits its performance.

In this paper, we propose a novel deep learning based joint AU detection and face alignment framework called JAA-Net to exploit the strong correlations of the two tasks. In particular, multi-scale shared features for the two tasks are learned firstly, and high-level features of face alignment are extracted and fed into AU detection. Moreover, to extract precise local features, we propose an adaptive attention learning module to refine the attention map of each AU adaptively, which is initially specified by the predicted facial landmarks. Finally, the assembled local features are integrated with face alignment features and global facial features for AU detection. The entire framework is end-to-end without any post-processing operation, and all the modules are optimized jointly.

The contributions of this paper are threefold. First, we propose an end-to-end multi-task deep learning framework for joint facial AU detection and face alignment. To the best of our knowledge, jointly modeling these two tasks with deep neural networks has not been done before. Second, with the aid of face alignment results, an adaptive attention network is learned to determine the attention distribution of the ROI of each AU. Third, we conduct extensive experiments on two benchmark datasets, where our proposed joint framework significantly outperforms the state-of-the-art, particularly on AU detection.

2   Related Work

Our proposed framework is closely related to existing landmark aided facial AU detection methods as well as face alignment with multi-task learning methods, since we combine both AU detection models and face alignment models.

Landmark Aided Facial AU Detection: The first step in most of the previous facial AU recognition works is to detect the face with the help of face detection or face alignment methods [1,10,13]. In particular, considering it is robust to measure the landmark-based geometry changes, Benitez-Quiroz et al. [1] proposed an approach to fuse the geometry and local texture information for AU detection, in which the geometry information is obtained by measuring the normalized facial landmark distances and the angles of Delaunay mask formed by the landmarks. Valstar et al. [21] analyzed Gabor wavelet features near 20 facial landmarks, and these features were then selected and classified by Adaboost and SVM classifiers for AU detection. Zhao et al. [29,30] proposed a joint patch and multi-label learning (JPML) method for facial AU detection by taking into account both patch learning and multi-label learning, in which the local regions of AUs are defined as patches centered around the facial landmarks obtained using IntraFace [20]. Recently, Li et al. [10] proposed the EAC-Net for facial AU detection by enhancing and cropping the ROIs with roughly extracted facial landmark information.

All these researches demonstrate the effectiveness of utilizing facial landmarks on feature extraction for AU detection task. However, they all treat face alignment as a single and independent task and make use of the existing well-designed facial landmark detectors.

Face Alignment with Multi-task Learning: The correlation of facial expression recognition and face alignment has been leveraged in several face alignment works. For example, recently, Wu et al. [22] combined the tasks of face alignment, head pose estimation, and expression related facial deformation analysis using a cascade regression framework. Zhang et al. [27,28] proposed a Tasks-Constrained Deep Convolutional Network (TCDCN) to optimize the shared feature map between face alignment and other heterogeneous but subtly correlated tasks, e.g. head pose estimation and the inference of facial attributes including expression. Ranjan et al. [17] proposed a deep multi-task learning framework named HyperFace for simultaneous face detection, face alignment, pose estimation, and gender recognition. All these works demonstrate that related tasks such as facial expression recognition are conducive to face alignment.

However, in TCDCN and HyperFace, face alignment and other tasks are just simply integrated with the first several layers shared. In contrast, besides sharing feature layers, our proposed JAA-Net also feeds high-level representations of face alignment into AU detection, and utilizes the estimated landmarks for the initialization of the adaptive attention learning.

Joint Facial AU Detection and Face Alignment: Although facial AU recognition and face alignment are related tasks, their interaction is usually one way in the aforementioned methods, i.e. facial landmarks are used to extract features for AU recognition. Li et al. [11] proposed a hierarchical framework with Dynamic Bayesian Network to capture the joint local relationship between facial landmark tracking and facial AU recognition. However, this framework requires an offline facial activity model construction and an online facial motion measurement and inference, and only local dependencies between facial landmarks and AUs are considered. Inspired by [11], Wu et al. [23] tried to exploit global AU relationship, global facial shape patterns, and global dependencies between

AUs and landmarks with a cascade regression framework, which is a pioneering work for the joint process of the two tasks.

In contrast with these conventional methods using handcrafted local appearance features, we employ an end-to-end deep framework for joint learning of facial AU detection and face alignment. Moreover, we develop a deep adaptive attention learning method to explore the feature distributions of different AUs in different ROIs specified by the predicted facial landmarks.

3   JAA-Net for Facial AU Detection and Face Alignment

The framework of our proposed JAA-Net is shown in Fig. 1, which consists of four modules (in different colors): hierarchical and multi-scale region learning, face alignment, global feature learning, and adaptive attention learning. Firstly, the hierarchical and multi-scale region learning is designed as the foundation of JAA-Net, which extracts features of each local region with different scales. Secondly, the face alignment module is designed to estimate the locations of facial landmarks, which will be further utilized to generate the initial attention maps for AU detection. The global feature learning module is to capture the structure and texture features of the whole face. Finally, the adaptive attention learning is designed as the central part for AU detection with a multi-branch network, which learns the attention map of each AU adaptively so as to capture local AU features at different locations. The three modules, face alignment, global feature learning, and adaptive attention learning, are optimized jointly, which share the layers of the hierarchical and multi-scale region learning.

As illustrated in Fig. 1, by taking a color face of $l \times l \times 3$ as input, JAA-Net aims to achieve AU detection and face alignment simultaneously, and refine the attention maps of AUs adaptively. We define the overall loss of JAA-Net as

$$E = E_{au} + \lambda_1 E_{align} + \lambda_2 E_r, \tag{1}$$

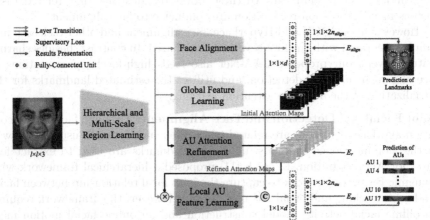

Fig. 1. The proposed JAA-Net framework, where "C" and "×" denote concatenation and element-wise multiplication, respectively

where E_{au} and E_{align} denote the losses of AU detection and face alignment, respectively, E_r measures the difference before and after the attention refinement, which is a constraint to maintain the consistency, and λ_1 and λ_2 are trade-off parameters.

3.1 Hierarchical and Multi-scale Region Learning

Considering different AUs in different local facial regions have various structure and texture information, each local region should be processed with independent filters. Instead of employing plain convolutional layers with weights shared across the entire spatial domain, the filter weights of the region layer proposed by DRML [31] are shared only within each local facial patch and different local patches use different filter weights, as shown in Fig. 2(b). However, all the local patches have identical sizes, which is unable to adapt multi-scale AUs. To address this issue, we propose the hierarchical and multi-scale region layer to learn features of each local region with different scales, as illustrated in Fig. 2(a). Let $R_{hm}(l_1, l_2, c_1)$, $R(l_1, l_2, c_1)$, and $P(l_1, l_2, c_1)$ respectively denote the blocks of our proposed hierarchical and multi-scale region layer, the region layer [31], and the plain stacked convolutional layers, where the expression of $l_1 \times l_2 \times c_1$ indicates that the height, width, and channel of a layer are l_1, l_2, and c_1 respectively. The expression of $3 \times 3/1/1$ in Fig. 2 means that the height, width, stride, and padding of the filter for each convolutional layer are 3, 3, 1, and 1, respectively.

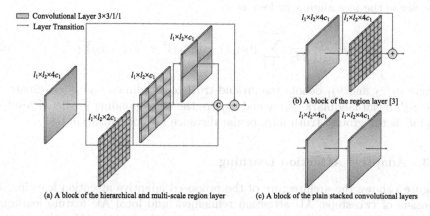

(a) A block of the hierarchical and multi-scale region layer

(b) A block of the region layer [3]

(c) A block of the plain stacked convolutional layers

Fig. 2. Architectures of different blocks for region learning, where "C" and "+" denote concatenation and element-wise sum, respectively

As shown in Fig. 2(a), one block of our proposed hierarchical and multi-scale region layer contains one convolutional layer and another three hierarchical convolutional layers with different sizes of weight sharing regions. Specifically, the uniformly divided 8×8, 4×4, and 2×2 patches of the second, third, and fourth convolutional layers are the results of convolution on corresponding patches in the previous layer, respectively. By concatenating the outputs of the second, third, and fourth convolutional layers, we extract hierarchical and multi-scale features with the same number of channels as the first convolutional layer. In addition, a residual structure is also utilized to sum the hierarchical and multi-scale maps with those of the first convolutional layer element-wisely for learning over-complete features and avoiding the vanishing gradient problem. Different from the region layer of DRML, our proposed hierarchical and multi-scale region layer uses multi-scale partitions, which are beneficial for covering all kinds of AUs in the ROIs of different sizes with less parameters.

In JAA-Net, the module of the hierarchical and multi-scale region learning is composed by $R_{hm}(l, l, c)$ and $R_{hm}(l/2, l/2, 2c)$, each of which is followed by a max-pooling layer. The output of this module is named as "pool2", which will be fed into the rest three modules. In JAA-Net, the size of the filter for each max-pooling layer is $2 \times 2/2/0$, and each convolutional layer is operated with Batch Normalization (BN) [7] and Rectified Linear Unit (ReLU) [16].

3.2 Face Alignment

The face alignment module includes three successive convolutional layers of $P(l/4, l/4, 3c)$, $P(l/8, l/8, 4c)$, and $P(l/16, l/16, 5c)$, each of which connects with a max-pooling layer. As shown in Fig. 1, the output of this module is fed into a landmark prediction network with two fully-connected layers with the dimension of d and $2n_{align}$, respectively, where n_{align} is the number of facial landmarks. We define the face alignment loss as

$$E_{align} = \frac{1}{2d_o^2} \sum_{j=1}^{n_{align}} [(y_{2j-1} - \hat{y}_{2j-1})^2 + (y_{2j} - \hat{y}_{2j})^2], \tag{2}$$

where y_{2j-1} and y_{2j} denote the ground-truth x-coordinate and y-coordinate of the j-th facial landmark, $\hat{y}_{2j-1}$ and $\hat{y}_{2j}$ are the corresponding predicted results, and d_o is the ground-truth inter-ocular distance for normalization [18].

3.3 Adaptive Attention Learning

Figure 3 shows the architecture of the proposed adaptive attention learning. It consists of two steps: AU attention refinement and local AU feature learning, where the first step is to refine the attention map of a certain AU with a branch respectively and the second step is to learn and extract local AU features.

The inputs and outputs of the AU attention refinement step are initialization and refined results of attention maps, respectively. Each AU has an attention map corresponding to the whole face with size $l/4 \times l/4 \times 1$, where the attention distributions of predefined ROI and remaining regions are both refined. The predefined ROI of each AU has two AU centers due to the symmetry, each of which is the central point of a subregion. In particular, the locations of AU centers are predefined by the estimated facial landmarks using the rule proposed

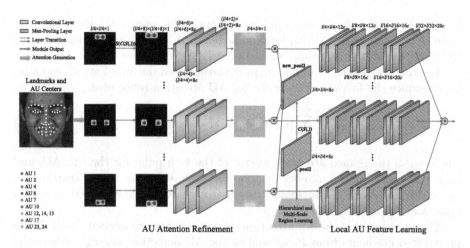

Fig. 3. Architecture of the proposed adaptive attention learning. "×" and "+" denote element-wise multiplication and sum operations, respectively

by [10]. For the i-th AU, if the k-th point of the attention map is in a subregion of the predefined ROI, its attention weight is initialized as

$$v_{ik} = \max\{1 - \frac{d_{ik}\xi}{(l/4)\zeta}, 0\}, \quad i = 1, \cdots, n_{au}, \tag{3}$$

where d_{ik} is the Manhattan distance of this point to the AU center of the subregion, ζ is the ratio between the width of the subregion and the attention map, $\xi \geq 0$ is a coefficient, and n_{au} is the number of AUs. Equation (3) essentially suggests that the attention weights are decaying when the ROI points are moving away from the AU center. The maximization operation in Eq. (3) is to ensure $v_{ik} \in [0, 1]$. If a point belongs to the overlap of two subregions, it is set to be the maximum value of all its associated initial attention weights. Note that, when $\xi = 0$, the attention weights of points in the subregions become 1. The attention weight of any point beyond the subregions is initialized to be 0.

Considering that padding is used in each convolutional layer of the hierarchical and multi-scale region learning module, the output "pool2" could do harm to the local AU feature learning. To eliminate the influence of padding, we propose a padding removal process $C(S(M, \alpha), \beta)$, where $S(M, \alpha)$ is a function scaling a feature map M with the scaling coefficient α using bilinear interpolation [2], and $C(M, \beta)$ is a function cropping a feature map M around its center with the ratio β to preserve its original width. The padding removal process first zooms the feature map with $\alpha > 1$ and then crops it. Specifically, the initial attention maps and "pool2" are performed with $C(S(\cdot, (l/4 + 6)/(l/4)), (l/4)/(l/4 + 6))$, where the resulting output of "pool2" is named "new_pool2" as shown in Fig. 3. To avoid the effect of the padding of the convolutional layers in the AU attention refinement step, the initial attention maps are further zoomed with $S(\cdot, (l/4 + 8)/(l/4))$. Following three convolutional layers with the filter size of

$3 \times 3/1/0$, the fourth convolutional layer outputs the refined AU attention map. Note that except for the convolutional layers in this attention refinement step, the filters for all the convolutional layers in JAA-Net are set as $3 \times 3/1/1$.

To avoid the refined attention maps deviating from the initial attention maps, we introduce the following constraint for AU attention refinement:

$$E_r = -\sum_{i=1}^{n_{au}} \sum_{k=1}^{n_{am}} [v_{ik} \log \hat{v}_{ik} + (1 - v_{ik}) \log(1 - \hat{v}_{ik})], \tag{4}$$

where $\hat{v}_{ik}$ is the refined attention weight of the k-th point for the i-th AU, and $n_{am} = l/4 \times l/4$ is the number of points in each attention map. Equation (4) essentially measures the sigmoid cross entropy between the refined attention maps and the initial attention maps.

The parameters of the AU attention refinement step are learned via the back-propagated gradients from E_r as well as the AU detection loss E_{au}, where the latter plays a critical role. To enhance the supervision from the AU detection, we propose a back-propagation enhancement method, formulated as

$$\frac{\partial E_{au}}{\partial \hat{V}_i} \leftarrow \lambda_3 \frac{\partial E_{au}}{\partial \hat{V}_i}, \tag{5}$$

where $\hat{V}_i = \{\hat{v}_{ik}\}_{k=1}^{n_{am}}$, and $\lambda_3 \geq 1$ is the enhancement coefficient. By enhancing the gradients from E_{au}, the attention maps are performed stronger adaptive refinement.

Finally, after multiplying "new_pool2" with each attention map to extract local AU features, each branch of the local AU feature learning is performed with a network consisting of three max-pooling layers, each of which follows a stack of two convolutional layers with the same size. The local features with respect to the ROI of each AU are learned, and the output feature maps of all AUs are summed element-wisely, where the assembled local feature representations will then contribute to the final AU detection.

3.4 Facial AU Detection

As illustrated in Fig. 1, the output feature maps of the three modules of face alignment, global feature learning, and adaptive attention learning are concatenated together and fed into a network of two fully-connected layers with the dimension of d and $2n_{au}$, respectively. In this way, landmark related features, global facial features, and local AU features are integrated together for facial AU detection. Finally, a softmax layer is utilized to predict the probability of occurrence of each AU. Note that the module of global feature learning has the same structure as the face alignment module.

Facial AU detection can be regarded as a multi-label binary classification problem with the following weighted multi-label softmax loss:

$$E_{softmax} = -\frac{1}{n_{au}} \sum_{i=1}^{n_{au}} w_i [p_i \log \hat{p}_i + (1 - p_i) \log(1 - \hat{p}_i)], \tag{6}$$

where p_i denotes the ground-truth probability of occurrence for the i-th AU, which is 1 if occurrence and 0 otherwise, and $\hat{p}_i$ denotes the corresponding predicted probability of occurrence. The weight w_i introduced in Eq. (6) is to alleviate the data imbalance problem. For most facial AU detection benchmarks, the occurrence rates of AUs are imbalanced [12,13]. Since AUs are not mutually independent, imbalanced training data has a bad influence on this multi-label learning task. Particularly, we set $w_i = \frac{(1/r_i)n_{au}}{\sum_{i=1}^{n_{au}}(1/r_i)}$, where r_i is the occurrence rate of the i-th AU in the training set.

In some cases, some AUs appear rarely in training samples, for which the softmax loss often makes the network prediction strongly biased towards absence. To overcome this limitation, we further introduce a weighted multi-label Dice coefficient loss [15]:

$$E_{dice} = \frac{1}{n_{au}} \sum_{i=1}^{n_{au}} w_i(1 - \frac{2p_i\hat{p}_i + \epsilon}{p_i^2 + \hat{p}_i^2 + \epsilon}), \qquad (7)$$

where ϵ is the smooth term. Dice coefficient is also known as F1-score: $F1 = 2pr/(p + r)$, the most popular metric for facial AU detection, where p and r denote precision and recall respectively. With the help of the weighted Dice coefficient loss, we also take into account the consistency between the learning process and the evaluation metric. Finally, the AU detection loss is defined as

$$E_{au} = E_{softmax} + E_{dice}. \qquad (8)$$

4   Experiments

4.1   Datasets and Settings

Datasets: Our JAA-Net is evaluated on two widely used datasets for facial AU detection, i.e. DISFA [14] and BP4D [26], in which both AU labels and facial landmarks are provided.

- **BP4D** contains 41 participants with 23 females and 18 males, each of which is involved in 8 sessions captured with both 2D and 3D videos. There are about $140,000$ frames with AU labels of occurrence or absence. Each frame is also annotated with 49 landmarks detected by SDM [24]. Similar to the settings of [10,31], 12 AUs are evaluated using subject exclusive 3-fold cross validation with the same subject partition rule, where two folds are used for training and the remaining one is used for testing.
- **DISFA** consists of 27 videos recorded from 12 women and 15 men, each of which has $4,845$ frames. Each frame is annotated with AU intensities from 0 to 5 and 66 landmarks detected by AAM [4]. To be consistent with BP4D, we use 49 landmarks, a subset of 66 landmarks. Following the settings of [10,31], our network is initialized with the well-trained model from BP4D, and is further fine-tuned to 8 AUs using subject exclusive 3-fold cross validation on DISFA. The frames with intensities equal or greater than 2 are considered as positive, while others are treated as negative.

Implementation Details: For each face image, we perform similarity transformation including rotation, uniform scaling, and translation to obtain a $200 \times 200 \times 3$ color face. This transformation is shape-preserving and brings no change to the expression. In order to enhance the diversity of training data, transformed faces are randomly cropped into 176×176 and horizontally flipped. Our JAA-Net is trained using Caffe [8] with stochastic gradient descent (SGD), a mini-batch size of 9, a momentum of 0.9, a weight decay of 0.0005, and $\epsilon = 1$. The learning rate is multiplied by a factor of 0.3 at every 2 epoches. The structure parameters of JAA-Net are chosen as $l = 176$, $c = 8$, $d = 512$, $n_{align} = 49$, and n_{au} is 12 for BP4D and 8 for DISFA. $\zeta = 0.14$ and $\xi = 0.56$ are used in Eq. (3) for generating approximate Gaussian attention distributions for subregions of predefined ROIs of AUs.

The hyperparameters λ_1, λ_2, and λ_3 are obtained by cross validation. In our experiments, we set $\lambda_2 = 10^{-7}$ and $\lambda_3 = 2$. JAA-Net is firstly trained with all the modules optimized with 8 epoches, an initial learning rate of 0.01 for BP4D and 0.001 for DISFA, and $\lambda_1 = 0.5$. Next, we fix the parameters of the three modules of hierarchical and multi-scale region learning, global AU feature learning, and adaptive attention learning, and train the module of face alignment with $\lambda_1 = 1$. Finally, only the modules of global AU feature learning and adaptive attention learning are trained while fixing the parameters of the other modules. The number of epoches and the initial learning rate for both of the last two steps are set to 2 and 0.001, respectively. Although the two tasks of facial AU detection and face alignment are optimized stepwise, the gradients of the losses for the two tasks are back-propagated mutually in each step.

Evaluation Metrics: The evaluation metrics for the two tasks are chosen as follows.

- **Facial AU Detection:** Similar to the previous methods [9,10,31], the frame-based F1-score (F1-frame, %) is reported. To conduct a more comprehensive comparison, we also evaluate the performance with accuracy (%) used by EAC-Net [10]. In addition, we compute the average results over all AUs (Avg). In the following sections, we omit % in all the results for simplicity.
- **Face Alignment:** We report the mean error normalized by inter-ocular distance, and treat the mean error larger than 10% as a failure. In other words, we evaluate different methods on the two popular metrics [19,28]: mean error (%) and failure rate (%), where % is also omitted in the results.

4.2   Comparison with State-of-the-Art Methods

We compare our method JAA-Net against state-of-the-art single-image based AU detection works under the same 3-fold cross validation setting. These methods include both traditional methods, LSVM [6], JPML [30], APL [32], and CPM [25], and deep learning methods, DRML [31], EAC-Net [10], and ROI [9]. Note that LSTM-extended version of ROI [9] is not compared due to its input of a sequence of images instead of a single image. For a fair comparison, we use the results of LSVM, JPML, APL, and CPM reported in [3,10,31].

Table 1. F1-frame and accuracy for 12 AUs on BP4D. Since CPM and ROI do not report the accuracy results, we just show their F1-frame results

AU	F1-Frame							Accuracy				
	LSVM	JPML	DRML	CPM	EAC-Net	ROI	JAA-Net	LSVM	JPML	DRML	EAC-Net	JAA-Net
1	23.2	32.6	36.4	43.4	39.0	36.2	**47.2**	20.7	40.7	55.7	68.9	**74.7**
2	22.8	25.6	41.8	40.7	35.2	31.6	**44.0**	17.7	42.1	54.5	73.9	**80.8**
4	23.1	37.4	43.0	43.3	48.6	43.4	**54.9**	22.9	46.2	58.8	78.1	**80.4**
6	27.2	42.3	55.0	59.2	76.1	77.1	**77.5**	20.3	40.0	56.6	78.5	**78.9**
7	47.1	50.5	67.0	61.3	72.9	73.7	**74.6**	44.8	50.0	61.0	69.0	**71.0**
10	77.2	72.2	66.3	62.1	81.9	**85.0**	84.0	73.4	75.2	53.6	77.6	**80.2**
12	63.7	74.1	65.8	68.5	86.2	**87.0**	86.9	55.3	60.5	60.8	84.6	**85.4**
14	64.3	**65.7**	54.1	52.5	58.8	62.6	61.9	46.8	53.6	57.0	60.6	**64.8**
15	18.4	38.1	33.2	36.7	37.5	**45.7**	43.6	18.3	50.1	56.2	78.1	**83.1**
17	33.0	40.0	48.0	54.3	59.1	58.0	**60.3**	36.4	42.5	50.0	70.6	**73.5**
23	19.4	30.4	31.7	39.5	35.9	38.3	**42.7**	19.2	51.9	53.9	81.0	**82.3**
24	20.7	**42.3**	30.0	37.8	35.8	37.4	41.9	11.7	53.2	53.9	82.4	**85.4**
Avg	35.3	45.9	48.3	50.0	55.9	56.4	**60.0**	32.2	50.5	56.0	75.2	**78.4**

Table 1 reports the F1-frame and accuracy results of different methods on BP4D. It can be seen that our JAA-Net outperforms all these previous works on the challenging BP4D dataset. JAA-Net is superior to all the conventional methods, which demonstrates the strength of deep learning based methods. Compared to the state-of-the-art ROI and EAC-Net methods, JAA-Net brings significant relative increments of 6.38% and 7.33% respectively for average F1-frame. In addition, our method obtains high accuracy without sacrificing F1-frame, which is attributed to the integration of the softmax loss and the Dice coefficient loss.

Table 2. F1-frame and accuracy for 8 AUs on DISFA

AU	F1-Frame					Accuracy				
	LSVM	APL	DRML	EAC-Net	JAA-Net	LSVM	APL	DRML	EAC-Net	JAA-Net
1	10.8	11.4	17.3	41.5	**43.7**	21.6	32.7	53.3	85.6	**93.4**
2	10.0	12.0	17.7	26.4	**46.2**	15.8	27.8	53.2	84.9	**96.1**
4	21.8	30.1	37.4	**66.4**	56.0	17.2	37.9	60.0	79.1	**86.9**
6	15.7	12.4	29.0	**50.7**	41.4	8.7	13.6	54.9	69.1	**91.4**
9	11.5	10.1	10.7	**80.5**	44.7	15.0	64.4	51.5	88.1	**95.8**
12	70.4	65.9	37.7	**89.3**	69.6	93.8	**94.2**	54.6	90.0	91.2
25	12.0	21.4	38.5	**88.9**	88.3	3.4	50.4	45.6	80.5	**93.4**
26	22.1	26.9	20.1	15.6	**58.4**	20.1	47.1	45.3	64.8	**93.2**
Avg	21.8	23.8	26.7	48.5	**56.0**	27.5	46.0	52.3	80.6	**92.7**

Experimental results on DISFA dataset are shown in Table 2, from which it can be observed that our JAA-Net outperforms all the state-of-the-art works with even more significant improvements. Specifically, JAA-Net increases the average F1-frame and accuracy relatively by 15.46% and 15.01% over EAC-Net, respectively. Due to the serious data imbalance issue in DISFA, performances of different AUs fluctuate severely in most of the previous methods. For instance, the accuracy of AU 12 is far higher than that of other AUs for LSVM and APL. Although EAC-Net processes the imbalance problem explicitly, its detection result for AU 26 is much worse than others. In contrast, our method weights the loss of each AU, which contributes to the balanced and high detection precision of each AU.

4.3   Ablation Study

To investigate the effectiveness of each component in our framework, Table 3 presents the average F1-frame for different variants of JAA-Net on BP4D benchmark, where "w/o" is the abbreviation of "without". Each variant is composed by different components of our framework.

Table 3. Average F1-frame for different variants of JAA-Net on BP4D. **R**: Region layer [31]. **HMR**: Hierarchical and multi-scale region layer. **S**: Multi-label softmax loss. **D**: Multi-label Dice coefficient loss. **W**: Weighting the loss of each AU. **FA**: Face alignment module. **GF**: Global feature learning module. **LF**: Local AU feature learning. **AR**: AU attention refinement. **BE**: Back-propagation enhancement. **GA**: Approximate Gaussian attention distributions for subregions of predefined ROIs. **UA**: Uniform attention distributions for subregions of predefined ROIs with $\xi = 0$

Method	R	HMR	S	D	W	FA	GF	LF	AR	BE	GA	UA	Avg
R-Net	√		√				√						54.9
HMR-Net	√	√	√				√						55.8
HMR-Net+D	√	√	√	√			√						56.6
HMR-Net+DW	√	√	√	√	√		√						57.4
HMR-Net+DWA	√	√	√	√	√	√	√						58.0
JAA-Net	√	√	√	√	√	√	√	√	√	√	√		**60.0**
JAA-Net w/o AR	√	√	√	√	√	√	√	√		√	√		57.4
JAA-Net w/o BE	√	√	√	√	√	√	√	√	√		√		59.1
JAA-Net w/o GA	√	√	√	√	√	√	√	√	√			√	57.3

Hierarchical and Multi-scale Region Learning: Comparing the results of HMR-Net with R-Net, we can observe that our proposed hierarchical and multi-scale region layer improves the performance of AU detection, since it can adapt multi-scale AUs and obtain larger receptive fields than the region layer [31]. In addition to the stronger feature learning ability, the hierarchical and multi-scale region layer utilizes less parameters. Specifically, except for the common first convolutional layer, the parameters of $R(l_1, l_2, c_1)$ is $(3 \times 3 \times 4c_1 + 1) \times 4c_1 \times 8 \times 8 = 9216c_1^2 + 256c_1$, while the parameters of $R_{hm}(l_1, l_2, c_1)$ is $(3 \times 3 \times 4c_1 + 1) \times 2c_1 \times$

$8 \times 8 + (3 \times 3 \times 2c_1 + 1) \times c_1 \times 4 \times 4 + (3 \times 3 \times c_1 + 1) \times c_1 \times 2 \times 2 = 4932c_1^2 + 148c_1$,
where adding 1 corresponds to the biases of convolutional filters.

Integration of Softmax Loss and Dice Coefficient Loss: By integrating the softmax loss with the Dice coefficient loss, HMR-Net+D achieves higher F1-frame result than HMR-Net. This profits from the Dice coefficient loss which optimizes the network from the perspective of F1-score. Softmax loss is very effective for classification, but facial AU detection is a binary classification problem which focuses on both precision and recall.

Weighting of Loss: After weighting the loss of each AU, HMR-Net+DW attains higher average F1-frame than HMR-Net+D. Benefiting from the weighting to address the data imbalance issue, our method obtains more significant and balanced performance.

Contribution of Face Alignment to AU Detection: Compared to HMR-Net+DW, HMR-Net+DWA achieves better result by directly adding the face alignment task. When integrating the two tasks deeper by combining with the adaptive attention learning module, our JAA-Net improves the performance with a larger gap. This demonstrates that the joint learning with face alignment contributes to AU detection.

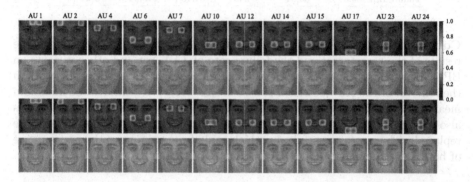

Fig. 4. Visualization of attention maps of JAA-Net. The first and third rows show the predefined attention maps, and the second and fourth rows show the refined attention maps. Attention weights are visualized with different colors as shown in the color bar (Color figure online)

Adaptive Attention Learning: In Table 3, JAA-Net w/o AR, JAA-Net w/o BE, and JAA-Net w/o GA are variants of adaptive attention learning of JAA-Net. It can be observed that JAA-Net achieves the best performance compared to other three variants. The predefined attention map of each AU uses fixed size and attention distribution for subregions of the predefined ROI and ignores regions beyond the ROI completely, which makes JAA-Net w/o AR fail to adapt AUs with different scales and exploit correlations among different facial parts. JAA-Net w/o GA gives predefined ROIs with a uniform initialization, which makes the constraint of E_r more difficult to be traded off with back-propagated gradients from E_{au}. In addition, the performance of JAA-Net w/o BE can be further improved with the back-propagation enhancement.

The attention maps before and after the adaptive refinement of JAA-Net are visualized in Fig. 4. The refined attention map of each AU adjusts the size and attention distribution of the ROI adaptively, where the learned ROI has irregular shape and integrates smoothly with the surrounding area. Moreover, the low attentions in other facial regions contribute to exploiting correlations among different facial parts. With the adaptively localized ROIs, local features with respect to AUs can be well captured. Although different persons have different facial shapes and expressions, our JAA-Net can detect the ROI of each AU accurately and adaptively.

Table 4. Comparison of the results of the mean error and the failure rate of different methods on BP4D

Method	JAA-Net w/o AU	HMR-Net + DWA	JAA-Net w/o AR	JAA-Net w/o BE	JAA-Net w/o GA	**JAA-Net**
Mean error	12.23	11.86	12.32	9.21	14.14	**6.38**
Failure rate	66.85	65.84	53.48	34.46	76.04	**3.27**

Contribution of AU Detection to Face Alignment: Table 4 shows the results of the mean error and the failure rate of JAA-Net and other variants on BP4D benchmark. JAA-Net w/o AU denotes the single face alignment task with the removal of the AU detection. It is seen that JAA-Net achieves the minimum mean error and failure rate. It can be concluded that the AU detection task is also conducive to face alignment. Note that the face alignment module can be replaced with a more powerful one, which could further improve the performance of both face alignment and AU detection.

5   Conclusions

In this paper, we have developed a novel end-to-end deep learning framework for joint AU detection and face alignment. Joint learning of the two tasks contributes to each other by sharing features and initializing the attention maps with the face alignment results. In addition, we have proposed the adaptive attention learning module to localize ROIs of AUs adaptively so as to extract better local features. Extensive experiments have demonstrated the effectiveness of our method for both AU detection and face alignment. The proposed framework is also promising to be applied for other face analysis tasks and other multi-task problems.

Acknowledgments. This work was supported by the National Natural Science Foundation of China (No. 61503277 and No. 61472245), the Science and Technology Commission of Shanghai Municipality Program (No. 16511101300), and Data Science & Artificial Intelligence Research Centre@NTU (DSAIR) and SINGTEL-NTU Cognitive & Artificial Intelligence Joint Lab (SCALE@NTU).

References

1. Benitez-Quiroz, C.F., Srinivasan, R., Martinez, A.M., et al.: Emotionet: an accurate, real-time algorithm for the automatic annotation of a million facial expressions in the wild. In: IEEE Conference on Computer Vision and Pattern Recognition, pp. 5562–5570. IEEE (2016)
2. Chen, L.C., Papandreou, G., Kokkinos, I., Murphy, K., Yuille, A.L.: Deeplab: semantic image segmentation with deep convolutional nets, atrous convolution, and fully connected crfs. IEEE Trans. Pattern Anal. Mach. Intell. 40(4), 834–848 (2017)
3. Chu, W.S., De la Torre, F., Cohn, J.F.: Learning spatial and temporal cues for multi-label facial action unit detection. In: IEEE International Conference on Automatic Face & Gesture Recognition, pp. 25–32. IEEE (2017)
4. Cootes, T.F., Edwards, G.J., Taylor, C.J.: Active appearance models. IEEE Trans. Pattern Anal. Mach. Intell. 23(6), 681–685 (2001)
5. Ekman, P., Rosenberg, E.L.: What the Face Reveals: Basic and Applied Studies of Spontaneous Expression Using the Facial Action Coding System (FACS). Oxford University Press, USA (1997)
6. Fan, R.E., Chang, K.W., Hsieh, C.J., Wang, X.R., Lin, C.J.: Liblinear: a library for large linear classification. J. Mach. Learn. Res. 9(Aug), 1871–1874 (2008)
7. Ioffe, S., Szegedy, C.: Batch normalization: accelerating deep network training by reducing internal covariate shift. In: International Conference on Machine Learning, pp. 448–456 (2015)
8. Jia, Y., Shelhamer, E., Donahue, J., Karayev, S., Long, J., Girshick, R., Guadarrama, S., Darrell, T.: Caffe: Convolutional architecture for fast feature embedding. In: ACM International Conference on Multimedia, pp. 675–678. ACM (2014)
9. Li, W., Abtahi, F., Zhu, Z.: Action unit detection with region adaptation, multi-labeling learning and optimal temporal fusing. In: IEEE Conference on Computer Vision and Pattern Recognition, pp. 6766–6775. IEEE (2017)
10. Li, W., Abtahi, F., Zhu, Z., Yin, L.: EAC-Net: A region-based deep enhancing and cropping approach for facial action unit detection. In: IEEE International Conference on Automatic Face & Gesture Recognition, pp. 103–110. IEEE (2017)
11. Li, Y., Wang, S., Zhao, Y., Ji, Q.: Simultaneous facial feature tracking and facial expression recognition. IEEE Trans. Image Process. 22(7), 2559–2573 (2013)
12. Liu, Z., Song, G., Cai, J., Cham, T.J., Zhang, J.: Conditional adversarial synthesis of 3D facial action units. arXiv preprint arXiv:1802.07421 (2018)
13. Martinez, B., Valstar, M.F., Jiang, B., Pantic, M.: Automatic analysis of facial actions: a survey. IEEE Trans. Affect. Comput. PP(99), 1 (2017)
14. Mavadati, S.M., Mahoor, M.H., Bartlett, K., Trinh, P., Cohn, J.F.: Disfa: A spontaneous facial action intensity database. IEEE Trans. Affect. Comput. 4(2), 151–160 (2013)
15. Milletari, F., Navab, N., Ahmadi, S.A.: V-net: Fully convolutional neural networks for volumetric medical image segmentation. In: International Conference on 3D Vision, pp. 565–571. IEEE (2016)
16. Nair, V., Hinton, G.E.: Rectified linear units improve restricted boltzmann machines. In: International Conference on Machine Learning, pp. 807–814 (2010)
17. Ranjan, R., Patel, V.M., Chellappa, R.: Hyperface: A deep multi-task learning framework for face detection, landmark localization, pose estimation, and gender recognition. IEEE Trans. Pattern Anal. Mach. Intell. PP(99), 1 (2017)

18. Shao, Z., Ding, S., Zhao, Y., Zhang, Q., Ma, L.: Learning deep representation from coarse to fine for face alignment. In: IEEE International Conference on Multimedia and Expo, pp. 1–6. IEEE (2016)
19. Shao, Z., Zhu, H., Hao, Y., Wang, M., Ma, L.: Learning a multi-center convolutional network for unconstrained face alignment. In: IEEE International Conference on Multimedia and Expo, pp. 109–114. IEEE (2017)
20. la Torre, F.D., Chu, W.S., Xiong, X., Vicente, F., Ding, X., Cohn, J.: Intraface. In: IEEE International Conference on Automatic Face & Gesture Recognition, pp. 1–8. IEEE (2015)
21. Valstar, M., Pantic, M.: Fully automatic facial action unit detection and temporal analysis. In: IEEE Conference on Computer Vision and Pattern Recognition Workshop, pp. 149–149. IEEE (2006)
22. Wu, Y., Gou, C., Ji, Q.: Simultaneous facial landmark detection, pose and deformation estimation under facial occlusion. In: IEEE Conference on Computer Vision and Pattern Recognition, pp. 3471–3480. IEEE (2017)
23. Wu, Y., Ji, Q.: Constrained joint cascade regression framework for simultaneous facial action unit recognition and facial landmark detection. In: IEEE Conference on Computer Vision and Pattern Recognition, pp. 3400–3408. IEEE (2016)
24. Xiong, X., De la Torre, F.: Supervised descent method and its applications to face alignment. In: IEEE Conference on Computer Vision and Pattern Recognition, pp. 532–539. IEEE (2013)
25. Zeng, J., Chu, W.S., De la Torre, F., Cohn, J.F., Xiong, Z.: Confidence preserving machine for facial action unit detection. In: IEEE International Conference on Computer Vision, pp. 3622–3630. IEEE (2015)
26. Zhang, X., Yin, L., Cohn, J.F., Canavan, S., Reale, M., Horowitz, A., Liu, P.: A high-resolution spontaneous 3D dynamic facial expression database. In: IEEE International Conference and Workshops on Automatic Face and Gesture Recognition, pp. 1–6. IEEE (2013)
27. Zhang, Z., Luo, P., Loy, C.C., Tang, X.: Facial landmark detection by deep multi-task learning. In: Fleet, D., Pajdla, T., Schiele, B., Tuytelaars, T. (eds.) ECCV 2014, Part VI. LNCS, vol. 8694, pp. 94–108. Springer, Cham (2014). https://doi.org/10.1007/978-3-319-10599-4_7
28. Zhang, Z., Luo, P., Loy, C.C., Tang, X.: Learning deep representation for face alignment with auxiliary attributes. IEEE Trans. Pattern Anal. Mach. Intell. **38**(5), 918–930 (2016)
29. Zhao, K., Chu, W.S., De la Torre, F., Cohn, J.F., Zhang, H.: Joint patch and multi-label learning for facial action unit detection. In: IEEE Conference on Computer Vision and Pattern Recognition, pp. 2207–2216. IEEE (2015)
30. Zhao, K., Chu, W.S., De la Torre, F., Cohn, J.F., Zhang, H.: Joint patch and multi-label learning for facial action unit and holistic expression recognition. IEEE Trans. Image Process. **25**(8), 3931–3946 (2016)
31. Zhao, K., Chu, W.S., Zhang, H.: Deep region and multi-label learning for facial action unit detection. In: IEEE Conference on Computer Vision and Pattern Recognition, pp. 3391–3399. IEEE (2016)
32. Zhong, L., Liu, Q., Yang, P., Huang, J., Metaxas, D.N.: Learning multiscale active facial patches for expression analysis. IEEE Trans. Cybern. **45**(8), 1499–1510 (2015)

Deep Pictorial Gaze Estimation

Seonwook Park[⊠], Adrian Spurr, and Otmar Hilliges

AIT Lab, Department of Computer Science, ETH Zurich, Zürich, Switzerland
{seonwook.park,adrian.spurr,otmar.hilliges}@inf.ethz.ch

Abstract. Estimating human gaze from natural eye images only is a challenging task. Gaze direction can be defined by the pupil- and the eyeball center where the latter is unobservable in 2D images. Hence, achieving highly accurate gaze estimates is an ill-posed problem. In this paper, we introduce a novel deep neural network architecture specifically designed for the task of gaze estimation from single eye input. Instead of directly regressing two angles for the pitch and yaw of the eyeball, we regress to an intermediate pictorial representation which in turn simplifies the task of 3D gaze direction estimation. Our quantitative and qualitative results show that our approach achieves higher accuracies than the state-of-the-art and is robust to variation in gaze, head pose and image quality.

Keywords: Appearance-based gaze estimation · Eye tracking

1 Introduction

Accurately estimating human gaze direction has many applications in assistive technologies for users with motor disabilities [4], gaze-based human-computer interaction [19], visual attention analysis [16], consumer behavior research [34], AR, VR and more. Traditionally this has been done via specialized hardware, shining infrared illumination into the user's eyes and via specialized cameras, sometimes requiring use of a headrest. Recently deep learning based approaches have made first steps towards fully unconstrained gaze estimation under free head motion, in environments with uncontrolled illumination conditions, and using only a single commodity (and potentially low quality) camera. However, this remains a challenging task due to inter-subject variance in eye appearance, self-occlusions, and head pose and rotation variations. In consequence, current approaches attain accuracies in the order of 6° only and are still far from the requirements of many application scenarios. While demonstrating the feasibility of purely image based gaze estimation and introducing large datasets, these

Electronic supplementary material The online version of this chapter (https://doi.org/10.1007/978-3-030-01261-8_44) contains supplementary material, which is available to authorized users.

© Springer Nature Switzerland AG 2018
V. Ferrari et al. (Eds.): ECCV 2018, LNCS 11217, pp. 741–757, 2018.
https://doi.org/10.1007/978-3-030-01261-8_44

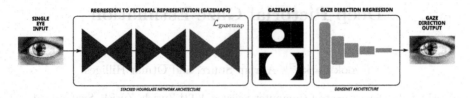

Fig. 1. Our sequential neural network architecture first estimates a novel pictorial representation of 3D gaze direction, then performs gaze estimation from the minimal image representation to yield improved performance on MPIIGaze, Columbia and EYEDIAP.

learning-based approaches [14,43,44] have leveraged convolutional neural network (CNN) architectures, originally designed for the task of image classification, with minor modifications. For example, [43,45] simply append head pose orientation to the first fully connected layer of either LeNet-5 or VGG-16, while [14] proposes to merge multiple input modalities by replicating convolutional layers from AlexNet. In [44] the AlexNet architecture is modified to learn so-called spatial-weights to emphasize important activations by region when full face images are provided as input. Typically, the proposed architectures are only supervised via a mean-squared error loss on the gaze direction output, represented as either a 3-dimensional unit vector or pitch and yaw angles in radians.

In this work we propose a network architecture that has been specifically designed with the task of gaze estimation in mind. An important insight is that regressing first to an abstract but gaze specific representation helps the network to more accurately predict the final output of 3D gaze direction. Furthermore, introducing this gaze representation also allows for intermediate supervision which we experimentally show to further improve accuracy. Our work is loosely inspired by recent progress in the field of human pose estimation. Here, earlier work directly regressed joint coordinates [32]. More recently the need for a more task specific form of supervision has led to the use of confidence maps or heatmaps, where the position of a joint is depicted as a 2-dimensional Gaussian [20,31,35]. This representation allows for a simpler mapping between input image and joint position, allows for intermediate supervision, and hence for deeper networks. However, applying this concept of heatmaps to regularize training is not directly applicable to the case of gaze estimation since the crucial eyeball center is not observable in 2D image data. We propose a conceptually similar representation for gaze estimation, called *gazemaps*. Such a gazemap is an abstract, pictorial representation of the eyeball, the iris and the pupil at it's center (see Fig. 1).

The simplest depiction of an eyeball's rotation can be made via a circle and an ellipse, the former representing the eyeball, and the latter the iris. The gaze direction is then defined by the vector connecting the larger circle's center and the ellipse. Thus 3D gaze direction can be (pictorially) represented in the form of an image, where a spherical eyeball and circular iris are projected onto the image plane, resulting in a circle and ellipse. Hence, changes in gaze direction result in changes in ellipse positioning (cf. Fig. 2a). This pictorial representation can be easily generated from existing training data, given known gaze direction annotations. At inference time recovering gaze direction from such a pictorial representation is a much simpler task than regressing directly from raw pixel values. However, adapting the input image to fit our pictorial representation is non-trivial. For a given eye image, a circular eyeball and an ellipse must be fitted, then centered and rescaled to be in the expected shape. We experimentally observed that this task can be performed well using a fully convolutional architecture. Furthermore, we show that our approach outperforms prior work on the final task of gaze estimation significantly.

Our main contribution consists of a novel architecture for appearance-based gaze estimation. At the core of the proposed architecture lies the pictorial representation of 3D gaze direction to which the network fits the raw input images and from which additional convolutional layers estimate the final gaze direction. In addition, we perform: (a) an in-depth analysis of the effect of intermediate supervision using our pictorial representation, (b) quantitative evaluation and comparison against state-of-the-art gaze estimation methods on three challenging datasets (MPIIGaze, EYEDIAP, Columbia) in the person independent setting, and a (c) detailed evaluation of the robustness of a model trained using our architecture in terms of gaze direction and head pose as well as image quality. Finally, we show that our method reduces gaze error by 18% compared to the state-of-the-art [45] on MPIIGaze.

2 Related Work

Here we briefly review the most important work in eye gaze estimation and review work touching on relevant aspects in terms of network architecture from adjacent areas such as image classification and human pose estimation.

2.1 Appearance-Based Gaze Estimation with CNNs

Traditional approaches to image-based gaze estimation are typically categorized as *feature-based* or *model-based*. Feature-based approaches reduce an eye image down to a set of features based on hand-crafted rules [11,12,24,39] and then feed these features into simple, often linear machine learning models to regress the final gaze estimate. Model-based methods instead attempt to fit a known 3D model to the eye image [28,33,37,40] by minimizing a suitable energy.

Appearance-based methods learn a direct mapping from raw eye images to gaze direction. Learning this direct mapping can be very challenging due to changes in illumination, (partial) occlusions, head motion and eye decorations. Due to these challenges, appearance-based gaze estimation methods required the introduction of large, diverse training datasets and typically leverage some form of convolutional neural network architecture.

Early works in appearance-based methods were restricted to laboratory settings with fixed head pose [1,30]. These initial constraints have become progressively relaxed, notably by the introduction of new datasets collected in everyday settings [14,43] or in simulated environments [27,36,38]. The increasing scale and complexity of training data has given rise to a wide variety of learning-based methods including variations of linear regression [7,17,18], random forests [27], k-nearest neighbours [27,38], and CNNs [14,25,36,43–45]. CNNs have proven to be more robust to visual appearance variations, and are capable of person-independent gaze estimation when provided with sufficient scale and diversity of training data. Person-independent gaze estimation can be performed without a user calibration step, and can directly be applied to areas such as visual attention analysis on unmodified devices [21], interaction on public displays [46], and identification of gaze targets [42], albeit at the cost of increased need for training data and computational cost.

Several CNN architectures have been proposed for person-independent gaze estimation in unconstrained settings, mostly differing in terms of possible input data modalities. Zhang et al. [43,44] adapt the LeNet-5 and VGG-16 architectures such that head pose angles (pitch and yaw) are concatenated to the first fully-connected layers. Despite its simplicity this approach yields the current best gaze estimation error of 5.5° when evaluating for the within-dataset cross-person case on MPIIGaze with single eye image and head pose input. In [14] separate convolutional streams are used for left/right eye images, a face image, and a 25 × 25 grid indicating the location and scale of the detected face in the image frame. Their experiments demonstrate that this approach yields improvements compared to [43]. In [44] a single face image is used as input and so-called spatial-weights are learned. These emphasize important features based on the input image, yielding considerable improvements in gaze estimation accuracy.

We introduce a novel pictorial representation of eye gaze and incorporate this into a deep neural network architecture via intermediate supervision. To the best of our knowledge we are the first to apply fully convolutional architecture to the task of appearance-based gaze estimation. We show that together these contribution lead to a significant performance improvement of 18% even when using a single eye image as sole input.

2.2 Deep Learning with Auxiliary Supervision

It has been shown [15,29] that by applying a loss function on intermediate outputs of a network, better performance can be yielded in different tasks. This technique was introduced to address the vanishing gradients problem during the training of deeper networks. In addition, such intermediate supervision allows for the network to quickly learn an estimate for the final output then learn to refine the predicted features - simplifying the mappings which need to be learned at every layer. Subsequent works have adopted intermediate supervision [20,35] to good effect for human pose estimation, by replicating the final output loss.

Another technique for improving neural network performance is the use of auxiliary data through multi-task learning. In [23,47], the architectures are formed of a single shared convolutional stream which is split into separate fully-connected layers or regression functions for the auxiliary tasks of gender classification, face visibility, and head pose. Both works show marked improvements to state-of-the-art results in facial landmarks localization. In these approaches through the introduction of multiple learning objectives, an implicit prior is forced upon the network to learn a representation that is informative to both tasks. On the contrary, we *explicitly* introduce a gaze-specific prior into the network architecture via gazemaps.

Most similar to our contribution is the work in [9] where facial landmark localization performance is improved by applying an auxiliary emotion classification loss. A key aspect to note is that their network is sequential, that is, the emotion recognition network takes only facial landmarks as input. The detected facial landmarks thus act as a manually defined representation for emotion classification, and creates a bottleneck in the full data flow. It is shown experimentally that applying such an auxiliary loss (for a different task) yields improvement over state-of-the-art results on the AFLW dataset. In our work, we learn to regress an intermediate and minimal representation for gaze direction, forming a bottleneck before the main task of regressing two angle values. Thus, an important distinction to [9] is that while we employ an auxiliary loss term, it directly contributes to the task of gaze direction estimation. Furthermore, the auxiliary loss is applied as an intermediate task. We detail this further in Sect. 3.1.

Recent work in multi-person human pose estimation [3] learns to estimate joint location heatmaps alongside so-called "part affinity fields". When combined, the two outputs then enable the detection of multiple peoples' joints with reduced ambiguity in terms of which person a joint belongs to. In addition, at the end of every image scale, the architecture concatenates feature maps from each separate stream such that information can flow between the "part confidence" and "part affinity" maps. Thus, they operate on the image representation space, taking advantage of the strengths of convolutional neural networks. Our work is similar in spirit in that it introduces a novel image-based representation.

3   Method

A key contribution of our work is a pictorial representation of 3D gaze direction - which we call *gazemaps*. This representation is formed of two boolean maps, which can be regressed by a fully convolutional neural network. In this section, we describe our representation (Sect. 3.1) then explain how we constructed our architecture to use the representation as reference for intermediate supervision during training of the network (Sect. 3.2).

3.1   Pictorial Representation of 3D Gaze

In the task of appearance-based gaze estimation, an input eye image is processed to yield gaze direction in 3D. This direction is often represented as a 3-element unit vector v [6,25,44], or as two angles representing eyeball pitch and yaw $g = (\theta, \phi)$ [27,36,43,45]. In this section, we propose an alternative to previous direct mappings to v or g.

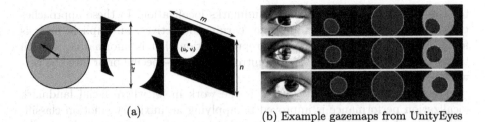

(a)   (b) Example gazemaps from UnityEyes

Fig. 2. Our pictorial representation of 3D gaze direction, essentially a projection of simple eyeball and iris models onto binary maps (a). Example-pairs are shown in (b) with (left-to-right) input image, iris map, eyeball map, and a superimposed visualization.

If we state the input eye images as x and regard regressing the values g, a conventional gaze estimation model estimates $f : x \rightarrow g$. The mapping f can be complex, as reflected by the improvement in accuracies that have been attained by simple adoption of newer CNN architectures ranging from LeNet-5 [25,43], AlexNet [14,44], to VGG-16 [45], the current state-of-the-art CNN architecture for appearance-based gaze estimation. We hypothesize that it is possible to learn an intermediate image representation of the eye, m. That is, we define our model as $g = k \circ j(x)$ where $j : x \rightarrow m$ and $k : m \rightarrow g$. It is conceivable that the complexity of learning j and k should be significantly lower than directly learning f, allowing for neural network architectures with significantly lower model complexity to be applied to the same task of gaze estimation with higher or equivalent performance.

Thus, we propose to estimate so-called *gazemaps* (m) and from that the 3D gaze direction (g). We reformulate the task of gaze estimation into two concrete tasks: (a) reduction of input image to minimal normalized form (gazemaps), and (b) gaze estimation from gazemaps.

The gazemaps for a given input eye image should be visually similar to the input yet distill only the necessary information for gaze estimation to ensure that the mapping $k : m \rightarrow g$ is simple. To do this, we consider that an average human eyeball has a diameter of ≈ 24 mm [2] while an average human iris has a diameter of ≈ 12 mm [5]. We then assume a simple model of the human eyeball and iris, where the eyeball is a perfect sphere, and the iris is a perfect circle. For an output image dimension of $m \times n$, we assume the projected eyeball diameter $2r = 1.2 n$ and calculate the iris centre coordinates (u_i, v_i) to be:

$$u_i = \frac{m}{2} - r' \sin \phi \cos \theta \tag{1}$$

$$v_i = \frac{n}{2} - r' \sin \theta \tag{2}$$

where $r' = r \cos \left(\sin^{-1} \frac{1}{2} \right)$, and gaze direction $g = (\theta, \phi)$. The iris is drawn as an ellipse with major-axis diameter of r and minor-axis diameter of $r |\cos \theta \cos \phi|$. Examples of our gazemaps are shown in Fig. 2b where two separate boolean maps are produced for one gaze direction g.

Learning how to predict gazemaps only from a single eye image is not a trivial task. Not only do extraneous factors such as image artifacts and partial occlusion need to be accounted for, a simplified eyeball must be fit to the given image based on iris and eyelid appearance. The detected regions must then be scaled and centered to produce the gazemaps. Thus the mapping $j : \boldsymbol{x} \rightarrow \boldsymbol{m}$ requires a more complex neural network architecture than the mapping $k : \boldsymbol{m} \rightarrow \boldsymbol{g}$.

3.2   Neural Network Architecture

Our neural network consists of two parts: (a) regression from eye image to gazemap, and (b) regression from gazemap to gaze direction $\boldsymbol{g}$. While any CNN architecture can be implemented for (b), regressing (a) requires a fully convolutional architecture such as those used in human pose estimation. We adapt the stacked hourglass architecture from Newell *et al.* [20] for this task. The hourglass architecture has been proven to be effective in tasks such as human pose estimation and facial landmarks detection [41] where complex spatial relations need to be modeled at various scales to estimate the location of occluded joints or key points. The architecture performs repeated multi-scale refinement of feature maps, from which desired output confidence maps can be extracted via 1×1 convolution layers. We exploit this fact to have our network predict gazemaps instead of classical confidence or heatmaps for joint positions. In Sect. 5, we demonstrate that this works well in practice.

In our gazemap-regression network, we use 3 hourglass modules with intermediate supervision applied on the gazemap outputs of the last module only. The minimized intermediate loss is:

$$\mathcal{L}_{\text{gazemap}} = -\alpha \sum_{p \in \mathcal{P}} \boldsymbol{m}(p) \log \hat{\boldsymbol{m}}(p), \tag{3}$$

where we calculate a cross-entropy between predicted $\hat{\boldsymbol{m}}$ and ground-truth gazemap $\boldsymbol{m}$ for pixels p in set of all pixels $\mathcal{P}$. In our evaluations, we set the weight coefficient α to 10^{-5}.

For the regression to $\boldsymbol{g}$, we select DenseNet which has recently been shown to perform well on image classification tasks [10] while using fewer parameters compared to previous architectures such as ResNet [8]. The loss term for gaze direction regression (per input) is:

$$\mathcal{L}_{\text{gaze}} = \|\boldsymbol{g} - \hat{\boldsymbol{g}}\|_2^2, \tag{4}$$

where $\tilde{g}$ is the gaze direction predicted by our neural network.

4   Implementation

In this section, we describe the fully convolutional (Hourglass) and regressive (DenseNet) parts of our architecture in more detail.

4.1 Hourglass Network

In our implementation of the Stacked Hourglass Network [20], we provide images of size 150×90 as input, and refine 64 feature maps of size 75×45 throughout the network. The half-scale feature maps are produced by an initial convolutional layer with filter size 7 and stride 2 as done in the original paper [20]. This is followed by batch normalization, ReLU activation, and two residual modules before being passed as input to the first hourglass module.

There exist 3 hourglass modules in our architecture, as visualized in Fig. 1. In human pose estimation, the commonly used outputs are 2-dimensional confidence maps, which are pixel-aligned to the input image. Our task differs, and thus we do not apply intermediate supervision to the output of every hourglass module. This is to allow for the input image to be processed at multiple scales over many layers, with the necessary features becoming aligned to the final output gazemap representation. Instead, we apply 1×1 convolutions to the output of the last hourglass module, and apply the gazemap loss term (Eq. 3) (Fig. 3).

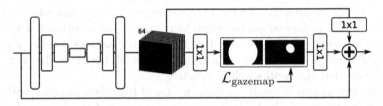

Fig. 3. Intermediate supervision is applied to the output of an hourglass module by performing 1×1 convolutions. The intermediate gazemaps and feature maps from the previous hourglass module are then concatenated back into the network to be passed onto the next hourglass module as is done in the original Hourglass paper [20].

4.2 DenseNet

As described in Sect. 3.1, our pictorial representation allows for a simpler function to be learnt for the actual task of gaze estimation. To demonstrate this, we employ a very lightweight DenseNet architecture [10]. Our gaze regression network consists of 5 dense blocks (5 layers per block) with a growth-rate of 8, bottleneck layers, and a compression factor of 0.5. This results in just 62 feature maps at the end of the DenseNet, and subsequently 62 features through global average pooling. Finally, a single linear layer maps these features to g. The resulting network is light-weight and consists of just 66 k trainable parameters.

4.3 Training Details

We train our neural network with a batch size of 32, learning rate of 0.0002 and L_2 weights regularization coefficient of 10^{-4}. The optimization method used is

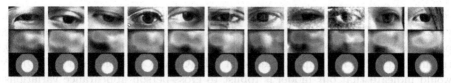

(a) Intermediate representations of training samples without (middle) and with (bottom) intermediate supervision

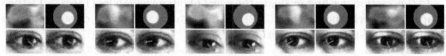

(b) Intermediate representations and predictions from test samples without (left) and with (right) intermediate supervision

Fig. 4. Example of image representations learned by our architecture in the absence or presence of $\mathcal{L}_{\text{gazemap}}$. Note that the pictorial representation is more consistent, and that the hourglass network is able to account for occlusions. Predicted gaze directions are shown in green, with ground-truth in red. (Color figure online)

Adam [13]. Training occurs for 20 epochs on a desktop PC with an Intel Core i7 CPU and Nvidia Titan Xp GPU, taking just over 2 h for one fold (out of 15) of a leave-one-person-out evaluation on the MPIIGaze dataset.

During training, slight data augmentation is applied in terms of image translation and scaling, and learning rate is multiplied by 0.1 after every 5k gradient update steps, to address over-fitting and to stabilize the final error.

5   Evaluations

We perform our evaluations primarily on the MPIIGaze dataset, which consists of images taken of 15 laptop users in everyday settings. The dataset has been used as the standard benchmark dataset for unconstrained appearance-based gaze estimation in recent years [25,36,38,43–45]. Our focus is on cross-person single-eye evaluations where 15 models are trained per configuration or architecture in a leave-one-person-out fashion. That is, a neural network is trained on 14 peoples' data (1500 entries each from left and right eyes), then tested on the test set of the left-out person (1000 entries). The mean over 15 such evaluations is used as the final error metric representing cross-person performance. As MPIIGaze is a dataset which well represents real-world settings, cross-person evaluations on the dataset is indicative of the real-world person-independence of a given model.

To further test the generalization capabilities of our method, we also perform evaluations on two additional datasets in this section: Columbia [26] and EYEDIAP [7], where we perform 5-fold cross validation. While Columbia displays large diversity between its 55 participants, the images are of high quality, having been taken using a DSLR. EYEDIAP on the other hand suffers from the low resolution of the VGA camera used, as well as large distance between camera and participant. We select screen target (CS/DS) and static head pose sequences (S) from the EYEDIAP dataset, sampling every 15 s from its VGA video streams (V). Training on moving head sequences (M) with just single eye input proved infeasible, with all models experiencing diverging test error during training. Performance improvements on MPIIGaze, Columbia, and EYEDIAP would indicate that our model is robust to cross-person appearance variations and the challenges caused by low eye image resolution and quality.

In this section, we first evaluate the effect of our gazemap loss (Sect. 5.1), then compare the performance (Sect. 5.2) and robustness (Sect. 5.3) of our approach against state-of-the-art architectures.

5.1 Pictorial Representation (*Gazemaps*)

We postulated in Sect. 3.1 that by providing a pictorial representation of 3D gaze direction that is visually similar to the input image, we could achieve improvements in appearance-based gaze estimation. In our experiments we find that applying the gazemaps loss term generally offers performance improvements compared to the case where the loss term is not applied. This improvement is particularly emphasized when DenseNet growth rate is high (eg. $k = 32$), as shown in Table 1.

Table 1. Cross-person gaze estimation errors in the absence and presence of $\mathcal{L}_{gazemap}$, with DenseNet (k=32).

Dataset	$\mathcal{L}_{\text{gazemap}}$	
	No	Yes
MPIIGaze	4.67	**4.56**
Columbia	3.78	**3.59**
EYEDIAP	11.28	**10.63**

By observing the output of the last hourglass module and comparing against the input images (Fig. 4), we can confirm that even without intermediate supervision, our network learns to isolate the iris region, yielding a similar image representation of gaze direction across participants. Note that this representation is learned only with the final gaze direction loss, $\mathcal{L}_{\text{gaze}}$, and that blobs representing iris locations are not necessarily aligned with actual iris locations on the input images. Without intermediate supervision, the learned minimal image representation may incorporate visual factors such as occlusion due to hair and eyeglases, as shown in Fig. 4a.

This supports our hypothesis that an intermediate representation consisting of an iris and eyeball contains the required information to regress gaze direction. However, due to the nature of learning, the network may also learn irrelevant details such as the edges of the glasses. Yet, by explicitly providing an intermediate representation in the form of gazemaps, we enforce a prior that helps the network learn the desired representation, without incorporating the previously mentioned unhelpful details.

5.2 Cross-Person Gaze Estimation

We compare the cross-person performance of our model by conducting a leave-one-person-out evaluation on MPIIGaze and 5-fold evaluations on Columbia and EYEDIAP. In Sect. 3.1 we discussed that the mapping k from gazemap to gaze direction should not require a complex architecture to model. Thus, our DenseNet is configured with a low growth rate ($k = 8$). To allow fair comparison, we re-implement 2 architectures for single-eye image inputs (of size 150×90): AlexNet and VGG-16. The AlexNet and VGG-16 architectures have been used in recent works in appearance-based gaze estimation and are thus suitable baselines [44,45]. Implementation and training procedure details of these architectures are provided in supplementary materials.

Table 2. Mean gaze estimation error in degrees for within-dataset cross-person k-fold evaluation. Evaluated on (a) MPIIGaze, (b) Columbia, and (c) EYEDIAP datasets.

(a) MPIIGaze (15-fold)

Model	kNN [45]	RF [45]	[43]	AlexNet	VGG-16	GazeNet [45]	ours
# params	0	-	1.8M	86M	158M	90M	0.7M
Inputs	e + h	e + h	e + h	e	e	e + h	e
Error	7.2	6.7	6.3	5.7	5.4	5.5	**4.5**

(b) Columbia (5-fold)

Model	AlexNet	VGG-16	ours
Error	4.2	3.9	**3.8**

(c) EYEDIAP (5-fold)

Model	AlexNet	VGG-16	ours
Error	11.5	11.2	**10.3**

where e: single-eye, h: head pose (pitch, yaw)

In MPIIGaze evaluations (Table 2a), our proposed approach outperforms the current state-of-the-art approach by a large margin, yielding an improvement of $1.0°$ ($5.5° \rightarrow 4.5° = 18.2\%$). This significant improvement is in spite of the reduced number of trainable parameters used in our architecture ($90\,M$ vs $0.7\,M$). Our performance compares favorably to that reported in [44] ($4.8°$) where full-face input is used in contrast to our single-eye input. While our results cannot directly be compared with those of [44] due to the different definition of gaze direction (face-centred as opposed to eye centred), the similar performance suggests that eye images may be sufficient as input to the task of gaze direction estimation. Our approach attains comparable performance to models taking face input, and uses considerably less parameters than recently introduced architectures (129x less than GazeNet).

We additionally evaluate our model on the Columbia Gaze and EYEDIAP datasets in Table 2b and c respectively. While high image quality results in all three methods performing comparably for Columbia Gaze, our approach still prevails with an improvement of $0.4°$ over AlexNet. On EYEDIAP, the mean

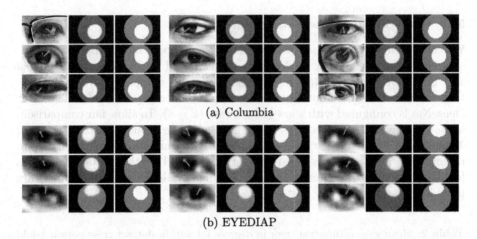

(a) Columbia

(b) EYEDIAP

Fig. 5. Gazemap predictions (middle) on Columbia and EYEDIAP datasets with ground-truth (red) and predicted (green) gaze directions visualized on input eye images (left). Ground-truth gazemaps are shown on the far-right of each triplet. (Color figure online)

error is very high due to the low resolution and low quality input. Note that there is no head pose estimation performed, with only single eye input being relied on for gaze estimation. Our gazemap-based architecture shows its strengths in this case, performing 0.9° better than VGG-16 - a 8% improvement. Sample gazemap and gaze direction predictions are shown in Fig. 5 where it is evident that despite the lack of visual detail, it is possible to fit gazemaps to yield improved gaze estimation error.

By evaluating our architecture on 3 different datasets with different properties in the cross-person setting, we can conclude that our approach provides significantly higher generalization capabilities compared to previous approaches. Thus, we bring gaze estimation closer to direct real-world applications.

5.3   Robustness Analysis

In order to shed more light onto our models' performance, we perform an additional robustness analysis. More concretely, we aim to analyze how our approach performs under difficult and challenging situations, such as extreme head pose and gaze direction. In order to do so, we evaluate a moving average on the output of our within-MPIIGaze evaluations, where the y-values correspond to the mean angular error and the x-values take *one* of the following factor of variations: head pose (pitch & yaw), gaze direction (pitch & yaw). Additionally, we also consider image quality (contrast & sharpness) as a qualitative factor. In order to isolate each factor of variation from the rest, we evaluate the moving average only on the points whose remaining factors are close to its median value. Intuitively, this corresponds to data points where the person moves only in one specific direction, while staying at rest in all of the remaining directions. This is

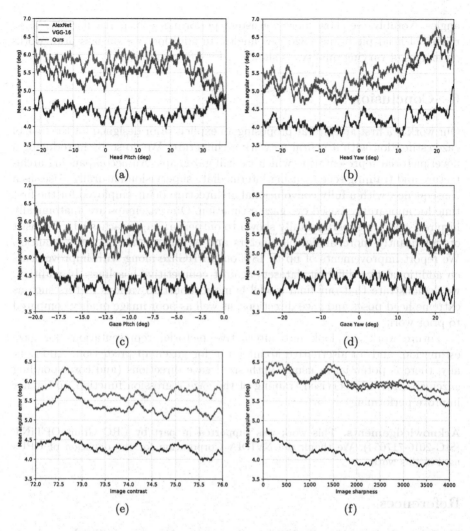

Fig. 6. Robustness of AlexNet (red), VGG-16 (green), and our approach (blue) to different head pose (top), gaze direction (middle), and image quality (bottom). The lines are a moving average. (Color figure online)

not the case for image quality analysis, where all data points are used. Figure 6 plots the mean angular error as a function of different movement variations and image qualities. The top row corresponds to variation along the head pose, the middle along gaze direction and the bottom to varying image quality. In order to calculate the image contrast, we used the RMS contrast metric whereas to compute the sharpness, we employ a Laplacian-based formula as outlined in [22]. Both metrics are explained in supplementary materials. The figure shows that we *consistently* outperform competing architectures for extreme head and gaze angles. Notably, we show more consistent performance in particular over large ranges of head pitch and gaze yaw angles. In addition, we surpass prior works on images of varying quality, as shown in Figs. 6e and f.

6 Conclusion

Our work is a first attempt at proposing an explicit prior designed for the task of gaze estimation with a neural network architecture. We do so by introducing a novel pictorial representation which we call gazemaps. An accompanying architecture and training scheme using intermediate supervision naturally arises as a consequence, with a fully convolutional architecture being employed for the first time for appearance-based eye gaze estimation. Our gazemaps are anatomically inspired, and are experimentally shown to outperform approaches which consist of significantly more model parameters and at times, more input modalities. We report improvements of up to 18% on MPIIGaze along with improvements on additional two different datasets against competitive baselines. In addition, we demonstrate that our final model is more robust to various factors such as extreme head poses and gaze directions, as well as poor image quality compared to prior work.

Future work can look into alternative pictorial representations for gaze estimation, and an alternative architecture for gazemap prediction. Additionally, there is potential in using synthesized gaze directions (and corresponding gazemaps) for unsupervised training of the gaze regression function, to further improve performance.

Acknowledgements. This work was supported in part by ERC Grant OPTINT (StG-2016-717054). We thank the NVIDIA Corporation for the donation of GPUs used in this work.

References

1. Baluja, S., Pomerleau, D.: Non-intrusive gaze tracking using artificial neural networks. Technical report, Pittsburgh, PA, USA (1994)
2. Bekerman, I., Gottlieb, P., Vaiman, M.: Variations in eyeball diameters of the healthy adults. J. Ophthalmol. **2014**, 5 (2014)
3. Cao, Z., Simon, T., Wei, S.E., Sheikh, Y.: Realtime multi-person 2D pose estimation using part affinity fields. In: CVPR, vol. 1, p. 7 (2017)
4. Chin, C.A., Barreto, A., Cremades, J.G., Adjouadi, M.: Integrated electromyogram and eye-gaze tracking cursor control system for computer users with motor disabilities. J. Rehabil. Res. Dev. **45**(1), 161–174 (2008)
5. Forrester, J.V., Dick, A.D., McMenamin, P.G., Roberts, F., Pearlman, E.: The Eye E-Book: Basic Sciences in Practice. Elsevier Health Sciences, New York (2015)
6. Funes-Mora, K.A., Odobez, J.M.: Gaze estimation in the 3D space using RGB-D sensors. Int. J. Comput. Vis. **118**(2), 194–216 (2016). https://doi.org/10.1007/s11263-015-0863-4

7. Funes Mora, K.A., Monay, F., Odobez, J.M.: Eyediap: A database for the development and evaluation of gaze estimation algorithms from RGB and RGB-D cameras. In: Proceedings of the Symposium on Eye Tracking Research and Applications, ETRA 2014, pp. 255–258. ACM, New York, USA (2014). https://doi.org/10.1145/2578153.2578190

8. He, K., Zhang, X., Ren, S., Sun, J.: Deep residual learning for image recognition. In: The IEEE Conference on Computer Vision and Pattern Recognition (CVPR), June 2016

9. Honari, S., Molchanov, P., Tyree, S., Vincent, P., Pal, C., Kautz, J.: Improving landmark localization with semi-supervised learning. In: The IEEE Conference on Computer Vision and Pattern Recognition (CVPR), June 2018

10. Huang, G., Liu, Z., van der Maaten, L., Weinberger, K.Q.: Densely connected convolutional networks. In: The IEEE Conference on Computer Vision and Pattern Recognition (CVPR), July 2017

11. Huang, M.X., Kwok, T.C., Ngai, G., Leong, H.V., Chan, S.C.: Building a self-learning eye gaze model from user interaction data. In: Proceedings of the 22nd ACM International Conference on Multimedia, MM 2014, pp. 1017–1020. ACM, New York, USA (2014). https://doi.org/10.1145/2647868.2655031

12. Huang, Q., Veeraraghavan, A., Sabharwal, A.: TabletGaze: Dataset and analysis for unconstrained appearance-based gaze estimation in mobile tablets. Mach. Vis. Appl. **28**(5–6), 445–461 (2017). https://doi.org/10.1007/s00138-017-0852-4

13. Kingma, D.P., Ba, J.: Adam: A method for stochastic optimization. CoRR abs/1412.6980 (2014)

14. Krafka, K., Khosla, A., Kellnhofer, P., Kannan, H., Bhandarkar, S., Matusik, W., Torralba, A.: Eye tracking for everyone. In: The IEEE Conference on Computer Vision and Pattern Recognition (CVPR), June 2016

15. Lee, C.Y., Xie, S., Gallagher, P., Zhang, Z., Tu, Z.: Deeply-supervised nets. In: Artificial Intelligence and Statistics, pp. 562–570 (2015)

16. Liu, H., Heynderickx, I.: Visual attention in objective image quality assessment: based on eye-tracking data. IEEE Trans. Circuits Syst. Video Technol. **21**(7), 971–982 (2011)

17. Lu, F., Okabe, T., Sugano, Y., Sato, Y.: A head pose-free approach for appearance-based gaze estimation. In: Proceedings of the British Machine Vision Conference, pp. 126.1–126.11. BMVA Press (2011). https://doi.org/10.5244/C.25.126

18. Lu, F., Sugano, Y., Okabe, T., Sato, Y.: Inferring human gaze from appearance via adaptive linear regression. In: Proceedings of the 2011 International Conference on Computer Vision, ICCV 2011, pp. 153–160. IEEE Computer Society, Washington, DC, USA (2011). https://doi.org/10.1109/ICCV.2011.6126237

19. Majaranta, P., Bulling, A.: Eye tracking and eye-based human–computer interaction. In: Fairclough, S.H., Gilleade, K. (eds.) Advances in Physiological Computing. HIS, pp. 39–65. Springer, London (2014). https://doi.org/10.1007/978-1-4471-6392-3_3

20. Newell, A., Yang, K., Deng, J.: Stacked hourglass networks for human pose estimation. In: Leibe, B., Matas, J., Sebe, N., Welling, M. (eds.) ECCV 2016, Part VIII. LNCS, vol. 9912, pp. 483–499. Springer, Cham (2016). https://doi.org/10.1007/978-3-319-46484-8_29

21. Papoutsaki, A., Sangkloy, P., Laskey, J., Daskalova, N., Huang, J., Hays, J.: Webgazer: Scalable webcam eye tracking using user interactions. In: Proceedings of the 25th International Joint Conference on Artificial Intelligence (IJCAI), pp. 3839–3845. AAAI (2016)

22. Pech-Pacheco, J.L., Cristobal, G., Chamorro-Martinez, J., Fernandez-Valdivia, J.: Diatom autofocusing in brightfield microscopy: a comparative study. In: Proceedings 15th International Conference on Pattern Recognition, ICPR-2000. vol. 3, pp. 314–317 (2000). https://doi.org/10.1109/ICPR.2000.903548

23. Ranjan, R., Patel, V.M., Chellappa, R.: Hyperface: a deep multi-task learning framework for face detection, landmark localization, pose estimation, and gender recognition. arXiv abs/1603.01249 (2016)

24. Sesma, L., Villanueva, A., Cabeza, R.: Evaluation of pupil center-eye corner vector for gaze estimation using a web cam. In: Proceedings of the Symposium on Eye Tracking Research and Applications, ETRA 2012, pp. 217–220. ACM, New York, USA (2012). https://doi.org/10.1145/2168556.2168598

25. Shrivastava, A., Pfister, T., Tuzel, O., Susskind, J., Wang, W., Webb, R.: Learning from simulated and unsupervised images through adversarial training. In: The IEEE Conference on Computer Vision and Pattern Recognition (CVPR), July 2017

26. Smith, B.A., Yin, Q., Feiner, S.K., Nayar, S.K.: Gaze locking: passive eye contact detection for human-object interaction. In: Proceedings of the 26th Annual ACM Symposium on User Interface Software and Technology, UIST 2013, pp. 271–280. ACM, New York, USA (2013). https://doi.org/10.1145/2501988.2501994

27. Sugano, Y., Matsushita, Y., Sato, Y.: Learning-by-synthesis for appearance-based 3D gaze estimation. In: 2014 IEEE Conference on Computer Vision and Pattern Recognition, pp. 1821–1828, June 2014. https://doi.org/10.1109/CVPR.2014.235

28. Sun, L., Liu, Z., Sun, M.T.: Real time gaze estimation with a consumer depth camera. Inf. Sci. **320**(C), 346–360 (2015). https://doi.org/10.1016/j.ins.2015.02.004

29. Szegedy, C., et al.: Going deeper with convolutions. In: Proceedings of the IEEE Conference on Computer Vision and Pattern Recognition (2015)

30. Tan, K.H., Kriegman, D.J., Ahuja, N.: Appearance-based eye gaze estimation. In: Proceedings of the Sixth IEEE Workshop on Applications of Computer Vision, WACV 2002, p. 191. IEEE Computer Society, Washington, DC, USA (2002)

31. Tompson, J., Jain, A., LeCun, Y., Bregler, C.: Joint training of a convolutional network and a graphical model for human pose estimation. In: Proceedings of the 27th International Conference on Neural Information Processing Systems - Volume 1, NIPS 2014, pp. 1799–1807. MIT Press, Cambridge, MA, USA (2014)

32. Toshev, A., Szegedy, C.: Deeppose: Human pose estimation via deep neural networks. In: Proceedings of the 2014 IEEE Conference on Computer Vision and Pattern Recognition, CVPR 2014, pp. 1653–1660. IEEE Computer Society, Washington, DC, USA (2014). https://doi.org/10.1109/CVPR.2014.214

33. Wang, K., Ji, Q.: Real time eye gaze tracking with 3D deformable eye-face model. In: Proceedings of the 2017 IEEE International Conference on Computer Vision (ICCV), ICCV 2017. IEEE Computer Society, Washington, DC, USA (2017)

34. Wedel, M., Pieters, R.: A review of eye-tracking research in marketing. In: Malhotra, N.K. (ed.) Review of Marketing Research, pp. 123–147. Emerald Group Publishing Limited, Bingley (2008)

35. Wei, S.E., Ramakrishna, V., Kanade, T., Sheikh, Y.: Convolutional pose machines. In: The IEEE Conference on Computer Vision and Pattern Recognition (CVPR), June 2016

36. Wood, E., Baltruaitis, T., Zhang, X., Sugano, Y., Robinson, P., Bulling, A.: Rendering of eyes for eye-shape registration and gaze estimation. In: Proceedings of the 2015 IEEE International Conference on Computer Vision (ICCV), ICCV 2015, pp. 3756–3764. IEEE Computer Society, Washington, DC, USA (2015). https://doi.org/10.1109/ICCV.2015.428

37. Wood, E., Baltrušaitis, T., Morency, L.-P., Robinson, P., Bulling, A.: A 3D morphable eye region model for gaze estimation. In: Leibe, B., Matas, J., Sebe, N., Welling, M. (eds.) ECCV 2016, Part I. LNCS, vol. 9905, pp. 297–313. Springer, Cham (2016). https://doi.org/10.1007/978-3-319-46448-0_18

38. Wood, E., Baltrušaitis, T., Morency, L.P., Robinson, P., Bulling, A.: Learning an appearance-based gaze estimator from one million synthesised images. In: Proceedings of the Ninth Biennial ACM Symposium on Eye Tracking Research & Applications, ETRA 2016, pp. 131–138. ACM, New York, USA (2016). https://doi.org/10.1145/2857491.2857492

39. Wood, E., Bulling, A.: Eyetab: Model-based gaze estimation on unmodified tablet computers. In: Proceedings of the Symposium on Eye Tracking Research and Applications, ETRA 2014, pp. 207–210. ACM, New York (2014). https://doi.org/10.1145/2578153.2578185

40. Xiong, X., Liu, Z., Cai, Q., Zhang, Z.: Eye gaze tracking using an RGBD camera: A comparison with a RGB solution. In: Proceedings of the 2014 ACM International Joint Conference on Pervasive and Ubiquitous Computing: Adjunct Publication, UbiComp 2014 Adjunct, pp. 1113–1121. ACM, New York, USA (2014). https://doi.org/10.1145/2638728.2641694

41. Zafeiriou, S., Trigeorgis, G., Chrysos, G., Deng, J., Shen, J.: The menpo facial landmark localisation challenge: a step towards the solution. In: The IEEE Conference on Computer Vision and Pattern Recognition (CVPR) Workshops, July 2017

42. Zhang, X., Sugano, Y., Bulling, A.: Everyday eye contact detection using unsupervised gaze target discovery. In: Proc. of the ACM Symposium on User Interface Software and Technology (UIST), pp. 193–203 (2017). https://doi.org/10.1145/3126594.3126614, best paper honourable mention award

43. Zhang, X., Sugano, Y., Fritz, M., Bulling, A.: Appearance-based gaze estimation in the wild. In: The IEEE Conference on Computer Vision and Pattern Recognition (CVPR), pp. 4511–4520, June 2015. https://doi.org/10.1109/CVPR.2015.7299081

44. Zhang, X., Sugano, Y., Fritz, M., Bulling, A.: It's written all over your face: fullface appearance-based gaze estimation. In: The IEEE Conference on Computer Vision and Pattern Recognition (CVPR) Workshops, pp. 2299–2308, July 2017. https://doi.org/10.1109/CVPRW.2017.284

45. Zhang, X., Sugano, Y., Fritz, M., Bulling, A.: MPIIGaze: real-world dataset and deep appearance-based gaze estimation. IEEE Trans. Pattern Anal. Mach. Intell. (2017). https://doi.org/10.1109/TPAMI.2017.2778103

46. Zhang, Y., Bulling, A., Gellersen, H.: Sideways: a gaze interface for spontaneous interaction with situated displays. In: Proceedings of the SIGCHI Conference on Human Factors in Computing Systems, CHI 2013, pp. 851–860. ACM, New York, USA (2013). https://doi.org/10.1145/2470654.2470775

47. Zhang, Z., Luo, P., Loy, C.C., Tang, X.: Facial landmark detection by deep multitask learning. In: Fleet, D., Pajdla, T., Schiele, B., Tuytelaars, T. (eds.) ECCV 2014, Part VI. LNCS, vol. 8694, pp. 94–108. Springer, Cham (2014). https://doi.org/10.1007/978-3-319-10599-4_7

Learning to Fuse Proposals from Multiple Scanline Optimizations in Semi-Global Matching

Johannes L. Schönberger[1,2]([✉]), Sudipta N. Sinha[1], and Marc Pollefeys[1,2]

[1] Microsoft, Redmond, USA
[2] Department of Computer Science, ETH Zürich, Zürich, Switzerland
jsch@inf.ethz.ch

Abstract. Semi-Global Matching (SGM) uses an aggregation scheme to combine costs from multiple 1D scanline optimizations that tends to hurt its accuracy in difficult scenarios. We propose replacing this aggregation scheme with a new learning-based method that fuses disparity proposals estimated using scanline optimization. Our proposed SGM-Forest algorithm solves this problem using per-pixel classification. SGM-Forest currently ranks 1st on the ETH3D stereo benchmark and is ranked competitively on the Middlebury 2014 and KITTI 2015 benchmarks. It consistently outperforms SGM in challenging settings and under difficult training protocols that demonstrate robust generalization, while adding only a small computational overhead to SGM.

1 Introduction

Semi-Global Matching (SGM) is a popular stereo matching algorithm proposed by Hirschmüller [15] that has found widespread use in applications ranging from 3D mapping [17,34,39,40], robot and drone navigation [19,38], and assisted driving [8]. The technique is efficient and parallelizable and suitable for real-time stereo reconstruction on FPGAs and GPUs [2,9,19]. SGM incorporates regularization in the form of smoothness priors, similar to global stereo methods but at lower computational cost. The main idea in SGM is to approximate a 2D Markov random field (MRF) optimization problem with several independent 1D scanline optimization problems corresponding to multiple canonical scanline directions in the image (typically 4 or 8). These 1D problems are optimized exactly using dynamic programming (DP) by aggregating matching costs along the multi-directional 1D scanlines. The costs of the minimum cost paths for the various directions are then summed up to compute a final aggregated cost per pixel. Finally, a winner-take-all (WTA) strategy is used to select the disparity with the minimum aggregated cost at each pixel.

Electronic supplementary material The online version of this chapter (https://doi.org/10.1007/978-3-030-01261-8_45) contains supplementary material, which is available to authorized users.

V. Ferrari et al. (Eds.): ECCV 2018, LNCS 11217, pp. 758–775, 2018.
https://doi.org/10.1007/978-3-030-01261-8_45

Summation of the aggregated costs from multiple directions and the final WTA strategy are both ad-hoc steps in SGM that lack proper theoretical justification. The summation was originally proposed to reduce 1D streaking artifacts [15] but is ineffective for weakly textured slanted surfaces and also generally inadequate when multiple scanline optimization solutions are inconsistent.

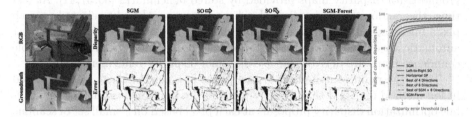

Fig. 1. Fusing Multiple Scanline Proposals. *Left:* Visualization of disparity maps from SGM, two (out of 8) scanline optimizations (SO) and our proposed SGM-Forest method. While SGM is more accurate than each SO on the whole image, each SO solution is better in some specific areas. SGM-Forest identifies the best SO proposal at each pixel and produces the best overall result. *Right:* Error plots for SGM, SO and SGM-Forest solutions (solid line) and upper bounds for oracles making optimal selections (dotted line). In this example, SGM-Forest gets close to the upper bounds.

Our main motivation in this work is to devise a better strategy to fuse 1D scanline optimization costs from multiple directions. We argue that the scanline optimization solutions should be considered as independent disparity map proposals and the WTA step should be replaced by a more general fusion step. Figure 1 shows two of the eight scanline optimization solutions for the ADIRONDACK pair from the Middlebury 2014 dataset [35]. While both solutions suffer from directional bias due to their respective propagation directions, each solution is accurate in certain image regions where the other one is inaccurate. For example, the horizontal pass produces accurate disparities near the left occlusion boundaries of the chair, whereas the diagonal pass performs better on the right occlusion edges. In those regions, the final SGM solution is slightly worse. The error plot in Fig. 1 quantifies this observation for the entire image. Whereas SGM is more accurate than each scanline optimization individually, the *joint accuracy* of all scanlines is much higher than SGM. Here, joint accuracy refers to a theoretical upper bound of the achievable accuracy of an oracle, which has access to ground truth and selects the best out of all the scanline solution proposals.

Based on this insight, we formulate the fusion step as the task of selecting the best amongst all the scanline optimization proposals at each pixel in the image. We propose to solve this task using supervised learning. Our method, named *SGM-Forest*, uses a per-pixel random forest classifier. As shown in Fig. 1, it gets close to the theoretical upper bound and significantly outperforms SGM.

The per-pixel classifier in SGM-Forest is trained on a low-dimensional input feature that encodes a sparse set of aggregated cost samples. Specifically, these cost values are sampled from the cost volumes computed during the scanline optimization passes. The sampling locations correspond to the disparity candidates for all scanline directions at each pixel. In fact, the proposals need not be limited to the usual scanline directions. Including the SGM solution and two horizontal scanline optimization solutions from the right image as additional proposals improves accuracy further. We train and evaluate the forest using ground truth disparity maps provided by stereo benchmarks [35,37,41]. At test time, the random forest predicts the disparity proposal to be selected at each pixel. Inference is fast and parallelizable and thus has small overhead. The forest automatically outputs per-pixel posterior class probabilities from which suitable confidence maps are derived, for use in a final disparity refinement step.

Thus, the main contribution in this paper is a new, efficient learning-based fusion method for SGM that directly predicts the best amongst all the 1D scanline optimization disparity proposals at each pixel based on a small set of scanline optimization costs. SGM-Forest uses this fusion method instead of SGM's sum-based aggregation and WTA steps and our results shows that it consistently outperforms SGM in many different settings. We evaluate SGM-Forest on three stereo benchmarks. Currently, it is ranked 1st on ETH3D [41] and is competitive on Middlebury 2014 [35] and KITTI 2015 [10]. We run extensive ablation studies and show that our method is extremely robust to dataset bias. It outperforms SGM even when the forests are trained on datasets from different domains.

2   Related Work

In this section, we review SGM and learning-based methods for stereo. We then compare and contrast our proposed SGM-Forest to closely related works.

SGM was built on top of earlier methods such as 1D scanline optimization [29,37,50] and dynamic programming stereo [46] with a new aggregation scheme to fix the lack of proper 2D regularization in those methods. However, a proper derivation of the aggregation step remained elusive until Drory et al. [6] showed its connection to non-loopy belief propagation on a special graph structure. Veksler [47] and Bleyer et al. [3] advanced dynamic programming stereo to tree structures connecting all pixels, but those methods have not been widely adopted. SGM has been extended to improve speed and accuracy [1,2,7,9,13,14,16,19], reduce memory usage [18,19,23], and to compute optical flow [45,49].

Scharstein and Pal [36] were one of the first to use learning in stereo. They trained a conditional random field (CRF) on Middlebury 2005–06 datasets to model the relationship between the CRF's penalty terms and local intensity gradients in the image. The KITTI and Middlebury 2014 [10,35] benchmarks encouraged much work on learning. In particular, CNNs have been trained to compute robust matching costs [5,25,48]. Zbontar and Lecun were the first; they proposed MC-CNN [48] and reported higher accuracy when using MC-CNN in conjunction with SGM for regularization and additional post-processing steps. Newer methods combined MC-CNN with better optimization but as a result are much slower. The method of Taniai et al. [44] uses iterative graph cut optimization and MC-CNN-acrt [48] and is the current state of the art on Middlebury.

End-to-end training of CNNs is nowadays popular on KITTI [11,21,27,30] but is almost never tested on Middlebury. In one rare case, moderate results were reported [22]. In contrast, our method generalizes across three benchmarks [10,35,41] on which it consistently outperforms baseline SGM. Furthermore, we train three separate models on Middlebury 2005–06, KITTI, and ETH3D. All three outperform SGM when tested on the Middlebury 2014 training set. SGM-Net [42] is a CNN-based method for improving SGM. SGM-Net performs more accurate scanline optimization by using a CNN to predict the parameters of the underlying scanline optimization objective. In contrast, we use regular scanline optimization but propose a learning-based fusion step using random forests.

Stereo matching has been solved by combining multiple disparity maps using MRF fusion moves [4,24,44]. Fusion moves are quite general, but computationally expensive and need many iterations. This makes them slow. Alternatively, multiple disparity maps can also be fused using learning, based on random forests [43] and CNNs [32]. Other methods first predict confidence maps [20], often via learning [12,26,31,33], and then use the predicted confidence values in a greedy fashion to combine multiple solutions. Drory et al. [6] proposed a different uncertainty measure for SGM but do not show how to use it. Unlike MRF fusion moves [24], our fusion method is not general. It combines a specific number and specific type of proposals but does so in a single efficient step.

Michael et al. [28] and Poggi and Mattoccia [33] (SGM-RF) proposed replacing SGM's sum-based aggregation with a weighted sum, setting smaller weights in areas with 1D streaking artifacts. The former work [28] proposes using global weights per scanline direction. SGM-RF [33] is more effective as it predicts per-pixel weights for each scanline direction using random forests based on disparity-based features. However, SGM-RF was not evaluated on the official test sets of the Middlebury 2014 and KITTI 2015 benchmarks. Mac Aodha et al. [26] also used random forests to fuse optical flow proposals using flow-based features.

Our SGM-Forest differs from these methods in several ways. First, it avoids predicting confidence separately for each proposal [26,33] but instead directly predicts the best proposal at each pixel. The forest is invoked only once at each pixel and has information from all the scanline directions. This makes inference more effective. Furthermore, the features used by our forest are directly obtained by sampling the aggregated cost volumes of each scanline optimization problem at multiple selective disparities. This is much more effective than hand-crafted disparity-based features [33,43]. Finally, our confidence maps derived from posterior class probabilities are normalized and hence better for refining the disparities during post-processing. Haeusler et al. [12] aim to detect unreliable disparities and suggest adding SGM's aggregated (summed) costs to their handcrafted disparity-based features. In contrast, we focus on fusing multiple proposals and propose to sample all the cost volumes for each independent scanline optimization at multiple disparities to better exploit contextual information.

3   Semi-Global Matching

We now review SGM as proposed by Hirschmüller [17] for approximate energy minimization of a 2D Markov Random Field (MRF)

$$E(D) = \sum_{\mathbf{p}} C_{\mathbf{p}}(d_{\mathbf{p}}) + \sum_{\mathbf{p,q} \in \mathcal{N}} V(d_{\mathbf{p}}, d_{\mathbf{q}}), \tag{1}$$

where $C_{\mathbf{p}}(d)$ is a unary data term that encodes the penalty of assigning pixel $\mathbf{p} \in \mathbb{R}^2$ to disparity $d \in \mathcal{D} = \{d_{\min}, \dots, d_{\max}\}$. The pairwise smoothness term $V(d, d')$ penalizes disparity differences between neighboring pixels $\mathbf{p}$ and $\mathbf{q}$. In SGM, the term V is chosen to have the following specific form

$$V(d, d') = \begin{cases} 0 & \text{if } d = d' \\ P_1 & \text{if } |d - d'| = 1 \\ P_2 & \text{if } |d - d'| \geq 2, \end{cases} \tag{2}$$

which favors first-order smoothness, *i.e.*, has a preference for fronto-parallel surfaces. Minimizing the 2D MRF is NP-hard. Therefore, SGM instead solves multiple scanline optimization problems, each of which involves solving the 1D version of Eq. 1 along 1D scanlines in 8 cardinal directions $\mathbf{r} = \{(0, 1), (0, -1), (1, 0), \dots\}$. For each direction $\mathbf{r}$, SGM computes an aggregated matching cost

$$L_{\mathbf{r}}(\mathbf{p}, d) = C_{\mathbf{p}}(d) + \min_{d' \in \mathcal{D}} (L_{\mathbf{r}}(\mathbf{p} - \mathbf{r}, d') + V(d, d')). \tag{3}$$

The definition of $L_{\mathbf{r}}(\mathbf{p}, d)$ is recursive and is typically started from a pixel on the image border. An aggregated cost volume $S(\mathbf{p}, d)$ is finally computed by summing up the eight individual aggregated cost volumes

$$S(\mathbf{p}, d) = \sum_{\mathbf{r}} L_{\mathbf{r}}(\mathbf{p}, d). \tag{4}$$

The final disparity map is obtained using a WTA strategy by selecting per-pixel minima in the aggregated cost volume

$$d_{\mathbf{p}} = \arg \min_{d} S(\mathbf{p}, d). \tag{5}$$

The steps in Eqs. 4 and 5 are accurate when the costs from different scanline directions are mostly consistent wrt. each other. However, these steps are likely to fail as the scanlines become more inconsistent. To overcome this problem, we propose a novel fusion method to robustly compute the disparity $d_{\mathbf{p}}$ from the multiple scanline costs $L_{\mathbf{r}}(\mathbf{p}, d)$.

4   Learning to Fuse Scanline Optimization Solutions

We start by analyzing some difficult examples for scanline optimization in order to motivate our fusion method and then describe the method in detail.

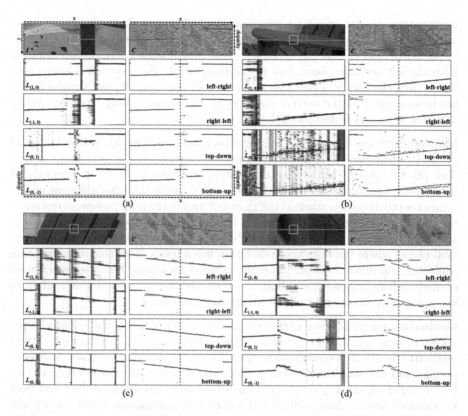

Fig. 2. 1D Scanline Optimization Costs. Each of the four subfigures shows the following – *Top Left:* Image and reference scanline section in green centered around yellow patch. *Top Right:* x–d slice of unary cost volume C along the reference scanline and ray of reference patch center in yellow. *Bottom:* Aggregated costs L_r for four scanline directions on the left and the corresponding disparities on the right. The WTA solution is shown in red whereas the ground truth disparity is in blue. (Color figure online)

4.1 Scanline Optimization Analysis

Figure 2 shows four scanlines from the left ADIRONDACK image with the corresponding x–d slices of the the unary cost C and the four horizontal and vertical aggregated scanline costs L_r alongside their respective WTA solutions. Notice the patterns in the L_r cost slices for the different passes. When the smoothness prior is effective, the noisy unary costs get filtered, producing strong minima at the correct disparities. However, when the unary costs are weak and the prior is ineffective, multiple noisy minima are present or the minimum is at an incorrect location. We now investigate these problematic cases in further detail.

Weak Texture. Figure 2(a)–(d) focus on weakly textured image patches. Whenever the unary cost is weak, the smoothness prior in the 1D optimization favors propagating several equally likely disparity estimates along the propagation direction. This effect is seen clearly on the vertical wooden plank in Fig. 2(d) in the horizontal passes. Here, the left-right propagation continues the solution from the left occlusion boundary to the right, while the right-left solution continues from the corner of the chair to the left. In contrast, the two vertical passes are in agreement at the correct disparity as the surface *along that propagation direction* is indeed fronto-parallel.

Slanted Surface. Figure 2(b), (c), (d) show examples of weakly textured slanted surfaces, where the 1D scanline solutions are typically biased and jump at random pixel locations, leading to inconsistent solutions in different scanlines. A prominent example is the arm rest in Fig. 2(b), where the left-right pass underestimates the disparity, whereas the right-left and bottom-up passes overestimate the disparity. In this case, there is no clear outlier in the solution but final cost summation leads to a biased estimate. Notice also the asymmetry in the two vertical passes where the bottom-up direction has a much more consistent solution while the top-down solution jumps at random locations. On weakly textured slanted surfaces, adjacent scanlines solutions are mostly inconsistent leading to noisy disparity maps and well-known streaking artifacts.

Occlusion. Figure 2(a) is centered around a region which is occluded in the right image. In this case, the unary cost is invalid and the only pass producing a correct prediction is the left-to-right direction. Here, the occluded surface is fronto-parallel and the smoothness prior is likely to propagate the correct disparity to the occluded region. Typically, only a small subset of scanlines results are correct in occluded areas, whereas SGM's standard cost summation is not robust and therefore produces gross outliers (see Fig. 1).

Repetitive Structure. The wooden planks on the chair's backrest in Fig. 2(c) are repetitive and produce multiple ambiguous local cost minima. In this example, the solutions of the left-right and top-down directions are incorrectly estimated, since the centered patch is almost identical to the symmetric patch on the right-most wooden plank. Notice also that the right-left and bottom-up directions are much less susceptible to this specific ambiguity problem.

These examples show that the joint distribution of aggregated costs over the disparity range at each pixel appears to provide strong clues about which scanline proposal or which subset of proposals are likely to be correct. This insight forms the basis of our fusion model which is described next.

4.2   Definition of Fusion Model

The disparities of the different scanline solutions are often inconsistent, especially in areas of weak data cost. Yet, in almost all cases there is at least one scanline that is either correct or is very close to the correct solution. The main challenge for robust and accurate scanline fusion is to identify the scanlines which agree on the correct estimate. In our proposed approach, we cast the fusion of scanlines as a classification problem that chooses the optimal estimate from the given set of candidate scanlines. Typically, the pattern at which specific scanlines perform well is consistent and repeatable. We aim to encode these patterns into rules that can identify the correct solution from a given set of candidate solutions. However, manually hand-crafting these rules is unfeasible and error-prone, which is why we resort to automatically learning these rules from training data in a supervised fashion. To facilitate the learning of these rules, we provide the model with discriminative signals that allow for a robust and efficient disparity prediction. Our proposed model takes sparse samples from a set of proposal cost volumes $K_n(\mathbf{p}, d)$ (e.g., the optimized scanline costs $L_\mathbf{r}(\mathbf{p}, d)$) and concatenates them into a per-pixel feature vector $\mathbf{f_p}$. This feature vector is then fed into a learned model that predicts a disparity estimate $\hat{d}_\mathbf{p}$ together with a posterior probability $\hat{\rho}_\mathbf{p}$, which we use as a confidence measure for further post-processing.

More specifically, our model is defined as $(\hat{d}_\mathbf{p}, \hat{\rho}_\mathbf{p}) = F(f_\mathbf{p})$ with $d_\mathbf{p} \in \mathbb{R}_0^+$, $\rho_\mathbf{p} \in [0, 1]$, and $\mathbf{f_p} \in \mathbb{R}^{N+N^2}$, where N is the number of proposal costs $K_n(\mathbf{p}, d)$. For all $n = 1...N$ proposals $K_n(\mathbf{p}, d)$, the feature $\mathbf{f_p}$ stores the location of its per-pixel WTA solution $d_\mathbf{p}^*(n) = \arg\min_d K_n(\mathbf{p}, d)$ and the corresponding costs $K_m(\mathbf{p}, d_\mathbf{p}^*(n))$ in all proposals $m = 1...N$. Overall, the feature is composed of N WTA solutions and the N^2 sparsely sampled costs. For each disparity proposal $d_\mathbf{p}^*(n)$, we thereby encode its relative significance wrt. the other proposals in a compact representation. The intuition is that when multiple proposals agree, their minima $d_\mathbf{p}^*(n)$ are close and their respective costs $K_m(\mathbf{p}, d_\mathbf{p}^*(n))$ are low.

Note that the naïve approach of concatenating the per-pixel costs of all proposals into a feature vector is not feasible for two reasons. First, we want a light-weight feature representation and model with small runtime overhead wrt. regular SGM. However, the naïve approach would result in a very high-dimensional feature representation of size $N \cdot |\mathcal{D}|$ (e.g., $8 \cdot 256 = 2048$ for 256 disparity candidates and 8 scanlines), which would require a complex model and eliminate the computational efficiency of SGM. In contrast, our proposed feature vector is only $8 + 8^2 = 72$-dimensional in case of 8 scanline proposals. Second, we strive to learn a generalizable model, which uses a fixed-size feature representation during training and inference even though the disparity range $\mathcal{D}$ may vary between scenes. In summary, our proposed feature encodes discriminative signals for our classification task without sacrificing efficiency, compactness, or accuracy.

4.3   Random Forests for Disparity and Confidence Prediction

Given ground truth disparities, there are many ways to learn the model $F(\mathbf{f_p})$ using supervised learning. The first principal design decision is whether to pose the problem as a classification or regression task. Arguably, classification problems are often considered as easier to solve. As shown in Fig. 1, at least one of the different scanline solutions is often accurate. We therefore chose to formulate a N-class classification task that predicts the best solution from the set of candidates $d_\mathbf{p}^*(n)$. This approach gave much better results than modeling the problem as a regression task. The second principal design decision is the specific type of classifier to use, e.g., k-NN, support vector machines, decision trees,

Table 1. Validation performance for non-occluded pixels on the Middlebury 2014 training set (15 half resolution pairs). Rows 1–5 show results for SGM baselines. Rows 6–14 report ablation studies for SGM-Forest. Bottom three rows show results for the best SGM-Forest setting, trained on different datasets. Letters M, K, and E refer to Middlebury 2005–06, KITTI, and ETH3D, respectively. The matching cost is always MC-CNN-acrt. Runtimes exclude matching cost and timed on same CPU.

Method	Left View Scanlines	Right View Scanlines	Filtering	Training Dataset	bad 0.5px [%]	bad 1px [%]	bad 2px [%]	bad 4px [%]	Time [s]
SGM	all			–	50.85	23.04	8.89	5.16	**3.0**
SGM – $\min_d L_r(\mathbf{p}, d)$	all			–	52.18	25.45	11.81	7.79	3.1
SGM – $\min_d \mathrm{median}_r L_r(\mathbf{p}, d)$	all			–	63.25	31.81	9.90	8.24	3.2
SGM-SVM	all			M	48.68	21.88	8.57	5.09	323.7
SGM-MLP	all			M	47.77	21.83	8.53	5.08	21.0
	horiz+vert			M	47.36	21.30	8.49	4.93	5.7
	top-down			M	47.45	21.20	8.38	4.94	5.8
	bottom-up			M	47.65	21.54	8.54	4.98	5.8
SGM-Forest	all			M	46.67	20.85	8.40	4.89	6.1
	all	•		M	46.49	20.81	8.23	4.72	6.3
	all	•	•	E	46.80	20.32	8.17	4.79	8.2
	all	•	•	K	46.48	20.45	8.09	4.81	8.2
	all	•	•	M	**46.08**	**19.99**	**7.78**	**4.41**	8.2

neural nets, etc. In our experiments, random forests provided the best trade-off between accuracy and efficiency (see Sect. 5.2 and Table 1).

At test time, we first perform 1D scanline optimization to construct the proposal cost volumes $K_n(\mathbf{p}, d)$, from which we build the per-pixel feature vectors $\mathbf{f_p}$. In the second stage, we simply feed the feature vectors $\mathbf{f_p}$ of all pixels $\mathbf{p}$ through our model to obtain a posterior probability $\rho_\mathbf{p}(n)$ for each proposal n. We select the proposal with the maximum posterior probability $n_\mathbf{p}^* = \arg\max_n \rho_\mathbf{p}(n)$ as our initial disparity estimate $d_\mathbf{p}^*(n^*)$ for pixel $\mathbf{p}$. To further refine this initial estimate, we find the subset of disparity proposals close to the initial estimate and their corresponding posteriors:

$$\mathcal{D}_\mathbf{p}^* = \{(d_\mathbf{p}^*(k), \rho_\mathbf{p}(k)) \mid k = 1...N \wedge |d_\mathbf{p}^*(k) - d_\mathbf{p}^*(n^*)| < \epsilon_d\} \qquad (6)$$

When multiple scanlines agree on a solution, the inlier set $\mathcal{D}_\mathbf{p}^*$ contains multiple elements, even for small disparity thresholds ϵ_d. The final per-pixel disparity estimate $\hat{d}_\mathbf{p}$ and confidence measure $\hat{\rho}_\mathbf{p}$ are computed as

$$\hat{d}_\mathbf{p} = \frac{\sum_k \rho_\mathbf{p}(k) \, d_\mathbf{p}^*(k)}{\sum_k \rho_\mathbf{p}(k)} \quad \text{and} \quad \hat{\rho}_\mathbf{p} = \sum_k \rho_\mathbf{p}(k) \qquad (7)$$

Note that the final disparity estimate has sub-pixel precision. Moreover, all steps are fully parallelizable on the pixel level and therefore suitable for real-time FPGA implementations (see Sects. 5.2 and 5.5). Next, we will describe our spatial edge-aware filtering scheme for disparity refinement.

4.4 Confidence-Based Spatial Filtering

The random forest produces a per-pixel estimate for disparity and confidence. In a final filtering step, we now enhance the spatial smoothness of the disparity and confidence maps. Towards this goal, we define the adaptive local neighborhood

$$\mathcal{N}_{\mathbf{p}} = \{\mathbf{q} \mid \|\mathbf{q} - \mathbf{p}\| < \epsilon_{\mathbf{p}} \wedge \hat{\rho}_{\mathbf{q}} > \epsilon_{\rho} \wedge |I(\mathbf{p}) - I(\mathbf{q})| < \epsilon_I\} \tag{8}$$

centered around each pixel $\mathbf{p}$, where $I(\mathbf{q})$ is the image intensity at pixel $\mathbf{q}$. The filtered disparity and confidence estimates are finally given as $\bar{d}_{\mathbf{p}} = \text{median}\, \hat{d}_{\mathbf{q}}$ and $\bar{\rho}_{\mathbf{p}} = \text{median}\, \hat{\rho}_{\mathbf{q}}$ with $\mathbf{q} \in \mathcal{N}_{\mathbf{p}}$. The filter essentially computes a median on the selective set of neighborhood pixels $\mathcal{N}_{\mathbf{p}}$ which have high confidence and similar color as the center pixel $\mathbf{p}$.

5 Experiments

We report a thorough evaluation of SGM-Forest on three stereo benchmarks – Middlebury 2014, KITTI 2015, and ETH3D 2017 [10,35,41]. Our evaluation protocol contrasts to most top-ranked stereo methods which often evaluate only on one benchmark [11,21,27,30,42,44]. In all our experiments, SGM-Forest outperforms SGM by a significant margin and ranks competitively against the state-of-the-art learning-based and global stereo methods, which are computationally more expensive. It also robustly generalizes across different dataset domains.

5.1 Implementation Details

Scanline Optimization and SGM. To facilitate an unbiased comparison, we use the same SGM implementation throughout all experiments. We compare three different matching costs (NCC, MC-CNN-fast [48], MC-CNN-acrt [48]) as the unary term C, which is quantized to 8 bits for reduced memory usage using linear rescaling to the range $[0, 255]$. Image intensities are given in the range $[0, 255]$. For NCC, we use a patch size of 7×7. We follow standard procedure and improve the right image rectification using sparse feature matching before computing the matching cost. The smoothness term $V(d, d')$ uses the constant parameters $P_1 = 100$ and $P_2 = P_1(1 + \alpha e^{-|\Delta I|/\beta})$, where $\alpha = 8$, $\beta = 10$, and ΔI is the intensity difference between neighboring pixels.

SGM-Forest. In all our experiments, we train random forests with 128 trees, a maximum depth of 25, and the Gini impurity measure to decide on the optimal data split. We set $\epsilon_d = 2$, $\epsilon_\rho = 0.1$, $\epsilon_{\mathbf{p}} = 5$, and $\epsilon_I = 10$. These optimal parameters were decided using parameter grid search and 3-fold cross validation on the Middlebury 2014 training scenes. For generalization across different disparity ranges between training and test datasets, we normalize to relative disparities prior to the extraction of the feature $\mathbf{f}_{\mathbf{p}}$ using the average of the input disparity proposals $d_{\mathbf{p}}^*(n)$. The relative disparity estimates are then denormalized to achieve absolute disparities. To showcase the generalization robustness of our approach, we train and evaluate our SGM-Forest on different dataset combinations. In all settings, the training and test scenes are non-overlapping and we provide a detailed list of training/test splits in the supplementary material. For learning our SGM-Forest model, we sample a maximum of 500 K random pixels with ground-truth disparity uniformly in each training image.

5.2   Ablation Study

We now evaluate several aspects of our algorithm using an extensive ablation study summarized in Tables 1 and 2 (full tables in the supplementary material).

Table 2. This table shows the validation performance for non-occluded pixels using 3-fold cross-validation for different matching costs and datasets at different error thresholds. Our method (SGM-F.) outperforms baseline SGM in all settings.

Datacost	Method	Middlebury 2014				KITTI 2015				ETH3D 2017			
		0.5px	1px	2px	4px	0.5px	1px	2px	4px	0.5px	1px	2px	4px
NCC	SGM	54.15	28.59	15.23	10.14	59.70	32.28	13.09	6.17	30.94	14.78	8.62	5.67
	SGM-F.	50.06	25.29	12.55	8.08	51.61	24.74	9.22	4.17	21.14	10.28	5.59	3.67
MC-CNN-fast	SGM	51.22	23.49	10.58	6.85	57.53	29.82	11.28	4.80	24.70	8.56	4.14	2.57
	SGM-F.	48.73	22.24	9.55	5.91	50.25	22.98	7.88	3.28	16.31	6.08	3.04	1.94
MC-CNN-acrt	SGM	50.85	23.04	8.89	5.16	56.27	26.90	7.41	3.00	37.46	14.44	7.17	4.72
	SGM-F.	46.08	19.99	7.78	4.41	46.16	18.82	5.76	2.56	26.26	11.05	6.56	4.71

SGM Baseline. We compare our SGM baseline against two simple methods that robustify Eqs. 4 and 5 (see Table 1): SGM $-$ $\min_d L_\mathbf{r}(\mathbf{p}, d)$ selects the scanline solution with minimum cost as the disparity estimate, while SGM $-$ $\min_d \text{median}_\mathbf{r} L_\mathbf{r}(\mathbf{p}, d)$ uses the robust median instead of summation for aggregating the costs from multiple scanlines. Both methods perform worse than baseline SGM, underlining the need for a more sophisticated fusion approach.

Input Proposals. The input to our algorithm is a set of proposal cost volumes $K_n(\mathbf{p}, d)$. As demonstrated in Fig. 1, a single scanline performs worse than SGM while the best of multiple scanlines is significantly better. In fact, our method is general and the input proposals to our system need not be limited to the canonical 1D scanline optimizations. We always consider the regular SGM cost volume $S(\mathbf{p}, d)$ as a proposal. Using only this proposal leads to a trivial 1-class classification problem and is equivalent to running baseline SGM (see Table 1). Adding the four horizontal and vertical scanlines from the left image as proposals improves the accuracy significantly, which is further boosted by adding the remaining 4 diagonal scanlines. Using only scanlines that propagate in the five top-down or five bottom-up directions degrades performance slightly but is still much better than regular SGM and enables real-time implementation of our algorithm on an FPGA [19]. We also experimented with running two horizontal scanline optimizations on the right image and warping the results to the left view to be used as two additional proposals. This is because the occluded pixels in the left image are invisible in the right image and the left occlusion edges are usually more accurately recovered in the right disparity map. These additional proposals provide a small but consistent improvement.

Classification Model. In Sect. 4.3, we argued that, for our task, random forests provide the best trade-off in terms of accuracy and efficiency. We experimented with many different classification models, including k-NN search, SVMs, (gradient boosted) decision trees, AdaBoost, neural nets, etc. In Table 1, we show results for two other well-performing models: SGM-SVM uses a linear SVM classifier and SGM-MLP is a multi-layer perceptron using 3 hidden layers with ReLU activation and twice the neurons after each layer followed by a final softmax layer for classification. SGM-MLP outperforms the SGM baseline but has slightly lower accuracy and efficiency on the CPU than SGM-Forest.

Table 3. Middlebury Benchmark. *Left:* Official results for the top 10 performing methods using MC-CNN-acrt for our SGM-Forest. Our method achieves the best runtime among the top performing methods. *Right:* Inofficial results on the training scenes trained on Middlebury 2005–06 using MC-CNN-fast. SGM-Forest with MC-CNN-fast outperforms baseline SGM with MC-CNN-acrt but is an order of magnitude faster.

Middlebury 2014 (MC-CNN-acrt)					Middlebury 2014 (MC-CNN-fast)				
Method	non-occl.		all	Time	Method	non-occl.		all	Time
LocalExp	5.43%	#1	11.7% #1	881s	LocalExp	6.52 %	#1	12.1% #1	846s
3DMST	5.92%	#2	12.5% #3	174s	3DMST	7.08 %	#2	12.9% #2	167s
MC-CNN+TDSR	6.35%	#2	12.1% #3	657s	APAP-Stereo	7.53%	#3	14.3% #6	117s
PMSC	6.71%	#4	13.6% #4	599s	FEN-D2DRR	7.89%	#4	14.1% #4	73s
LW-CNN	7.04%	#5	17.8% #15	314s	...				
MeshStereoExt	7.08%	#6	15.7% #9	161s	MC-CNN-acrt	10.1%	#12	19.7% #20	106s
FEN-D2DRR	7.23%	#7	16.0% #11	121s	...				
APAP-Stereo	7.26%	#8	13.7% #5	131s	**SGM-Forest**	**11.1%**	**#19**	**17.8% #14**	**9s**
SGM-Forest	**7.37%**	**#9**	**15.5% #8**	**88s**	...				
NTDE	7.44%	#10	15.3% #7	152s	MC-CNN-fast	11.7%	#21	21.5% #27	1s

Filtering. The final step in our algorithm is the confidence-based spatial filtering of the disparity and confidence maps. While the biggest accuracy improvement stems from the initial fusion step (see Table 1), the final filtering further improves the results by eliminating spatially inconsistent outliers.

Efficiency. The reported runtimes in Table 1 show only a small computational overhead of SGM-Forest and our proposed filtering over baseline SGM, enabling a potential real-time implementation on the GPU or FPGA (see Sect. 5.5). Note that the runtimes exclude the matching cost computation, *i.e.*, the overhead of SGM-Forest becomes negligible if, for example, MC-CNN-acrt is used.

Generalization and Robustness. All results in Table 1 were obtained by training on Middlebury 2005–06 and evaluating on Middlebury 2014, which already demonstrates good generalization properties. Note that Middlebury 2014 images are much more challenging than those in Middlebury 2005–06. Moreover, we also evaluate cross-domain generalization by training on KITTI (outdoors) and ETH3D (outdoors and indoors) and evaluating on Middlebury 2014 (indoors). In both cases, our approach achieves almost the same performance as compared to training on Middlebury. Table 2 shows that SGM-Forest improves over baseline SGM in every single metric irrespective of matching cost and dataset. In contrast to most learning-based methods, we demonstrate that our learned fusion approach is general and extremely robust across different domains and settings: SGM-Forest performs well outdoors when trained on indoor scenes, handles different image resolutions, disparity ranges and diverse matching costs, and consistently outperforms baseline SGM by a large margin.

5.3   Benchmark Results

Unlike most existing methods, we evaluate SGM-Forest on three benchmarks and achieve competitive performance wrt. the state of the art. For all benchmark submissions, we use the best setting found in our ablation study, *i.e.*, we include 8 (and 2) proposals from the left (and right) view and run disparity refinement.

Table 4. KITTI and ETH3D Benchmarks. *Left:* KITTI results over all pixels for all ranked SGM variants. Our SGM-Forest uses MC-CNN-fast as matching cost and achieves high accuracy at comparatively low runtime. *Right:* ETH3D results over non-occluded and all pixels for all ranked methods. Our SGM-Forest uses MC-CNN-fast as matching cost and achieves the best accuracy at comparatively low runtime.

KITTI 2015		
Method	Error	Time
CNNF+SGM	3.60% (#9)	71.0s
SGM-Net	3.66% (#11)	67.0s
MC-CNN-acrt	3.89% (#12)	67.0s
SGM-Forest	**4.38% (#14)**	**6.0s**
MC-CNN-WS	4.97% (#18)	1.4s
SGM_ROB [17]	6.38% (#27)	0.1s
SGM+C+NL	6.84% (#31)	270.0s
SGM+LDOF	6.84% (#32)	86.0s
SGM+SF	6.84% (#33)	2700.0s
CSCT+SGM+MF	8.24% (#35)	6.4ms

ETH3D 2017			
Method	non-occl.	all	Time
SGM-Forest	**5.40%**	**4.96%**	**5.21s**
SGM_ROB [17]	10.08%	10.77%	0.15s
MeshStereo	11.94%	11.52%	159.24s
SPS-Stereo	15.83%	15.04%	1.59s
ELAS	17.99%	16.72%	0.13s

Middlebury. Table 3 reports our results on Middlebury 2014. For the benchmark submission, we use MC-CNN-acrt matching costs and jointly train on Middlebury 2005–06 and the training scenes of Middlebury 2014. Our method ranks competitively among the top ten methods in terms of accuracy but is significantly faster. In addition to our official submission, we also report unofficial results for MC-CNN-fast evaluated on the training scenes[1]. The models for this submission were trained only on the Middlebury 2005–06 scenes. Using MC-CNN-fast, SGM-Forest outperforms SGM by two percentage points on non-occluded pixels. Evaluated on all pixels, SGM-Forest with MC-CNN-fast outperforms baseline SGM with MC-CNN-acrt by two percentage points but SGM-Forest is an order of magnitude faster.

KITTI. Table 4 lists all SGM-based methods evaluated on KITTI. We use MC-CNN-fast for this submission and are ranked right behind the original MC-CNN-acrt method [48], CNNF+SGM [51], and SGM-Net [42]. However, our method

---

[1] Only one submission per method is allowed on Middlebury 2014.

is an order of magnitude faster even though our scanline optimization and the proposed additional steps are implemented on the CPU while MC-CNN-WS runs on the GPU. Note that CNNF+SGM and SGM-Net report results only on KITTI whereas our method generalizes across domains and datasets.

ETH3D. On this fairly new benchmark with diverse indoor and outdoor images, SGM-Forest is currently ranked 1st with competitive running times (see Table 4). Our submission uses MC-CNN-fast which was surprisingly more accurate than MC-CNN-acrt on ETH3D (also see Table 2). Here, our SGM-Forest submission has almost half the error as the original SGM method [17].

5.4 Qualitative Results

Figure 3 shows qualitative results for Middlebury. Compared to baseline SGM, our SGM-Forest produces less streaking artifacts and performs significantly better in occluded areas. High confidence regions in general correspond to low errors. This is further confirmed by the monontonically decreasing precision-recall curves, which were produced by thresholding on the predicted confidences. For further qualitative results, *e.g.*, comparisons between raw predictions and filtered results, we refer the reader to the supplementary material.

5.5 Limitations and Future Work

Our current SGM and random forest implementation is CPU-based and is not real-time capable since we buffer all scanline cost volumes before fusion. The learned forests in this paper use 128 trees, so our method could be sped up easily by using fewer trees. In our experiments, even a single decision tree improved upon baseline SGM. An implementation of our method on the GPU would be straightforward, where SGM-MLP would probably outcompete SGM-Forest in

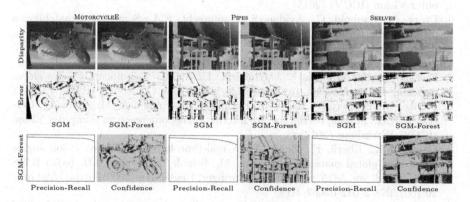

Fig. 3. Qualitative Middlebury results for SGM and SGM-Forest. Absolute error maps clipped to [0px, 8px]. Precision (Y) and Recall (X) in [0, 1]. Confidence maps log-scaled.

efficiency at the cost of a small degradation in accuracy. Real-time implementation on embedded systems [19] requires a one-pass, buffer-less algorithm prohibiting the use of all 8 scanline directions. In Table 1, we demonstrated that our idea also works well for top-down/bottom-up directions only.

6   Conclusion

We proposed a learning-based approach to fuse scanline optimization proposals in SGM, replacing the brittle and heuristic scanline aggregation steps in standard SGM. Our method is efficient and accurate and ranks 1st on the ETH3D benchmark while being competitive on Middlebury and KITTI. We have demonstrated consistent improvements over SGM on three stereo benchmarks. The learning appears to be extremely robust and generalizes well across datasets. Our method can be readily integrated into existing SGM variants and allows for real-time implementation in practical, high-quality stereo systems.

References

1. Semi-global stereo matching with surface orientation priors. In: International Conference on 3D Vision (3DV) (2017)
2. Banz, C., Blume, H., Pirsch, P.: Real-time semi-global matching disparity estimation on the GPU. In: International Conference on Computer Vision (ICCV) Workshops (2011)
3. Bleyer, M., Gelautz, M.: Simple but effective tree structures for dynamic programming-based stereo matching. In: International Conference on Computer Vision Theory and Applications (VISAPP) (2008)
4. Bleyer, M., Rother, C., Kohli, P., Scharstein, D., Sinha, S.: Object stereo—joint stereo matching and object segmentation. In: Conference on Computer Vision and Pattern Recognition (CVPR) (2011)
5. Chen, Z., Sun, X., Wang, L., Yu, Y., Huang, C.: A deep visual correspondence embedding model for stereo matching costs. In: International Conference on Computer Vision (ICCV) (2015)
6. Drory, A., Haubold, C., Avidan, S., Hamprecht, F.A.: Semi-global matching: a principled derivation in terms of message passing. In: Jiang, X., Hornegger, J., Koch, R. (eds.) GCPR 2014. LNCS, vol. 8753, pp. 43–53. Springer, Cham (2014). https://doi.org/10.1007/978-3-319-11752-2_4
7. Facciolo, G., De Franchis, C., Meinhardt, E.: MGM: a significantly more global matching for stereovision. In: British Machine Vision Conference (BMVC) (2015)
8. Franke, U., Pfeiffer, D., Rabe, C., Knoeppel, C., Enzweiler, M., Stein, F., Herrtwich, R.G.: Making bertha see. In: International Conference on Computer Vision (ICCV) Workshops (2013)
9. Gehrig, S.K., Eberli, F., Meyer, T.: A real-time low-power stereo vision engine using semi-global matching. In: Fritz, M., Schiele, B., Piater, J.H. (eds.) ICVS 2009. LNCS, vol. 5815, pp. 134–143. Springer, Heidelberg (2009). https://doi.org/10.1007/978-3-642-04667-4_14
10. Geiger, A., Lenz, P., Urtasun, R.: Are we ready for autonomous driving? the kitti vision benchmark suite. In: Conference on Computer Vision and Pattern Recognition (CVPR) (2012)

11. Gidaris, S., Komodakis, N.: Detect, replace, refine: Deep structured prediction for pixel wise labeling. In: Conference on Computer Vision and Pattern Recognition (CVPR) (2017)
12. Haeusler, R., Nair, R., Kondermann, D.: Ensemble learning for confidence measures in stereo vision. In: Conference on Computer Vision and Pattern Recognition (CVPR) (2013)
13. Hermann, S., Klette, R.: Iterative semi-global matching for robust driver assistance systems. In: Lee, K.M., Matsushita, Y., Rehg, J.M., Hu, Z. (eds.) ACCV 2012, Part III. LNCS, vol. 7726, pp. 465–478. Springer, Heidelberg (2013). https://doi.org/10.1007/978-3-642-37431-9_36
14. Hermann, S., Klette, R., Destefanis, E.: Inclusion of a second-order prior into semi-global matching. In: Wada, T., Huang, F., Lin, S. (eds.) PSIVT 2009. LNCS, vol. 5414, pp. 633–644. Springer, Heidelberg (2009). https://doi.org/10.1007/978-3-540-92957-4_55
15. Hirschmüller, H.: Accurate and efficient stereo processing by semi-global matching and mutual information. In: Conference on Computer Vision and Pattern Recognition (CVPR) (2005)
16. Hirschmuller, H.: Stereo vision in structured environments by consistent semi-global matching. In: Conference on Computer Vision and Pattern Recognition (CVPR) (2006)
17. Hirschmüller, H.: Stereo processing by semiglobal matching and mutual information. Trans. Pattern Anal. Mach. Intell. **30**, 328–341 (2008)
18. Hirschmüller, H., Buder, M., Ernst, I.: Memory efficient semi-global matching. In: ISPRS Annals of Photogrammetry, Remote Sensing and Spatial Information Sciences (2012)
19. Honegger, D., Oleynikova, H., Pollefeys, M.: Real-time and low latency embedded computer vision hardware based on a combination of FPGA and mobile CPU. In: International Conference on Intelligent Robots and Systems (IROS) (2014)
20. Hu, X., Mordohai, P.: A quantitative evaluation of confidence measures for stereo vision. Trans. Pattern Anal. Mach. Intell. **34**, 2121–2133 (2012)
21. Kendall, A., et al.: End-to-end learning of geometry and context for deep stereo regression. In: International Conference on Computer Vision (ICCV) (2017)
22. Knöbelreiter, P., Reinbacher, C., Shekhovtsov, A., Pock, T.: End-to-end training of hybrid CNN-CRF models for stereo. In: Conference on Computer Vision and Pattern Recognition (CVPR) (2017)
23. Lee, Y., Park, M.G., Hwang, Y., Shin, Y., Kyung, C.M.: Memory-efficient parametric semiglobal matching. Signal Process. Lett. **25**, 194–198 (2018)
24. Lempitsky, V., Rother, C., Roth, S., Blake, A.: Fusion moves for markov random field optimization. Trans. Pattern Anal. Mach. Intell. **32**, 1392–1405 (2010)
25. Luo, W., Schwing, A.G., Urtasun, R.: Efficient deep learning for stereo matching. In: Conference on Computer Vision and Pattern Recognition (CVPR) (2016)
26. Mac Aodha, O., Humayun, A., Pollefeys, M., Brostow, G.J.: Learning a confidence measure for optical flow. Trans. Pattern Anal. Mach. Intell. **35**, 1107–1120 (2013)
27. Mayer, N., et al.: A large dataset to train convolutional networks for disparity, optical flow, and scene flow estimation. In: Conference on Computer Vision and Pattern Recognition (CVPR) (2016)
28. Michael, M., Salmen, J., Stallkamp, J., Schlipsing, M.: Real-time stereo vision: Optimizing semi-global matching. In: Intelligent Vehicles Symposium (2013)
29. Ohta, Y., Kanade, T.: Stereo by intra-and inter-scanline search using dynamic programming. Trans. Pattern Anal. Mach. Intell. **2**, 139–154 (1985)

30. Pang, J., Sun, W., Ren, J., Yang, C., Yan, Q.: Cascade residual learning: A two-stage convolutional neural network for stereo matching. In: International Conference on Computer Vision (ICCV) Workshops (2017)
31. Park, M.G., Yoon, K.J.: Leveraging stereo matching with learning-based confidence measures. In: Conference on Computer Vision and Pattern Recognition (CVPR) (2015)
32. Poggi, M., Mattoccia, S.: Deep stereo fusion: combining multiple disparity hypotheses with deep-learning. In: International Conference on 3D Vision (3DV) (2016)
33. Poggi, M., Mattoccia, S.: Learning a general-purpose confidence measure based on O(1) features and a smarter aggregation strategy for semi global matching. In: International Conference on 3D Vision (3DV) (2016)
34. Rothermel, M., Wenzel, K., Fritsch, D., Haala, N.: SURE: Photogrammetric surface reconstruction from imagery. In: LC3D Workshop (2012)
35. Scharstein, D., et al.: High-resolution stereo datasets with subpixel-accurate ground truth. In: Jiang, X., Hornegger, J., Koch, R. (eds.) GCPR 2014. LNCS, vol. 8753, pp. 31–42. Springer, Cham (2014). https://doi.org/10.1007/978-3-319-11752-2_3
36. Scharstein, D., Pal, C.: Learning conditional random fields for stereo. In: Conference on Computer Vision and Pattern Recognition (CVPR) (2007)
37. Scharstein, D., Szeliski, R.: A taxonomy and evaluation of dense two-frame stereo correspondence algorithms. Int. J. Comput. Vis. **47**, 7–42 (2002)
38. Schmid, K., Tomic, T., Ruess, F., Hirschmüller, H., Suppa, M.: Stereo vision based indoor/outdoor navigation for flying robots. In: International Conference on Intelligent Robots and Systems (IROS) (2013)
39. Schönberger, J.L., Radenović, F., Chum, O., Frahm, J.M.: From Single Image Query to Detailed 3D Reconstruction. In: Conference on Computer Vision and Pattern Recognition (CVPR) (2015)
40. Schönberger, J.L., Zheng, E., Frahm, J.-M., Pollefeys, M.: Pixelwise view selection for unstructured multi-view stereo. In: Leibe, B., Matas, J., Sebe, N., Welling, M. (eds.) ECCV 2016. LNCS, vol. 9907, pp. 501–518. Springer, Cham (2016). https://doi.org/10.1007/978-3-319-46487-9_31
41. Schöps, T., Schönberger, J.L., Galliani, S., Sattler, T., Schindler, K., Pollefeys, M., Geiger, A.: A multi-view stereo benchmark with high-resolution images and multi-camera videos. In: Conference on Computer Vision and Pattern Recognition (CVPR) (2017)
42. Seki, A., Pollefeys, M.: Sgm-nets: Semi-global matching with neural networks. In: Conference on Computer Vision and Pattern Recognition (CVPR) (2017)
43. Spyropoulos, A., Mordohai, P.: Ensemble classifier for combining stereo matching algorithms. In: International Conference on 3D Vision (3DV) (2015)
44. Taniai, T., Matsushita, Y., Sato, Y., Naemura, T.: Continuous 3D label stereo matching using local expansion moves. Trans. Pattern Anal. Mach. Intell. (2017). https://ieeexplore.ieee.org/document/8081755/
45. Taniai, T., Sinha, S.N., Sato, Y.: Fast multi-frame stereo scene flow with motion segmentation. In: Conference on Computer Vision and Pattern Recognition (CVPR) (2017)
46. Van Meerbergen, G., Vergauwen, M., Pollefeys, M., Van Gool, L.: A hierarchical symmetric stereo algorithm using dynamic programming. Int. J. Comput. Vis. **47**, 275–285 (2002)
47. Veksler, O.: Stereo correspondence by dynamic programming on a tree. In: Conference on Computer Vision and Pattern Recognition (CVPR) (2005)
48. Žbontar, J., LeCun, Y.: Stereo matching by training a convolutional neural network to compare image patches. J. Mach. Learn. Res. **17**, 1–32 (2016)

49. Yamaguchi, K., McAllester, D., Urtasun, R.: Efficient joint segmentation, occlusion labeling, stereo and flow estimation. In: Fleet, D., Pajdla, T., Schiele, B., Tuytelaars, T. (eds.) ECCV 2014, Part V. LNCS, vol. 8693, pp. 756–771. Springer, Cham (2014). https://doi.org/10.1007/978-3-319-10602-1_49

50. Zach, C., Sormann, M., Karner, K.: Scanline optimization for stereo on graphics hardware. In: 3DPVT (2006)

51. Zhang, F., Wah, B.W.: Fundamental principles on learning new features for effective dense matching. Trans. Image Process. **27**, 822–836 (2018)

Incremental Non-Rigid Structure-from-Motion with Unknown Focal Length

Thomas Probst[1(✉)], Danda Pani Paudel[1], Ajad Chhatkuli[1],
and Luc Van Gool[1,2]

[1] Computer Vision Lab, ETH Zürich, Zürich, Switzerland
{probstt,paudel,ajad.chhatkuli,vangool}@vision.ee.ethz.ch
[2] VISICS, ESAT/PSI, KU Leuven, Leuven, Belgium

Abstract. The perspective camera and the isometric surface prior have recently gathered increased attention for Non-Rigid Structure-from-Motion (NRSfM). Despite the recent progress, several challenges remain, particularly the computational complexity and the unknown camera focal length. In this paper we present a method for incremental Non-Rigid Structure-from-Motion (NRSfM) with the perspective camera model and the isometric surface prior with unknown focal length. In the template-based case, we provide a method to estimate four parameters of the camera intrinsics. For the template-less scenario of NRSfM, we propose a method to upgrade reconstructions obtained for one focal length to another based on local rigidity and the so-called Maximum Depth Heuristics (MDH). On its basis we propose a method to simultaneously recover the focal length and the non-rigid shapes. We further solve the problem of incorporating a large number of points and adding more views in MDH-based NRSfM and efficiently solve them with Second-Order Cone Programming (SOCP). This does not require any shape initialization and produces results orders of times faster than many methods. We provide evaluations on standard sequences with ground-truth and qualitative reconstructions on challenging YouTube videos. These evaluations show that our method performs better in both speed and accuracy than the state of the art.

1 Introduction

Given images of a rigid object from different views, Structure-from-Motion (SfM) [1–3] allows the computation of the object's 3D structure. However, many such objects of interest are non-rigid and the rigidity constraints of SfM do not hold. The ever increasing number of monocular videos with deforming objects

Electronic supplementary material The online version of this chapter (https://doi.org/10.1007/978-3-030-01261-8_46) contains supplementary material, which is available to authorized users.

V. Ferrari et al. (Eds.): ECCV 2018, LNCS 11217, pp. 776–793, 2018.
https://doi.org/10.1007/978-3-030-01261-8_46

means provides a large incentive for being able to reconstruct such scenes. Such reconstruction problems can be solved with Non-Rigid Structure-from-Motion (NRSfM) which uses multiple images of a deforming object to reconstruct its 3D from a single camera. Another related approach computes the shape based on the object's template shape and its deformed image, also termed as Shape-from-Template (SfT). While SfM is well-posed and has already seen several applications in commercial software [4,5], non-rigid reconstruction has inherent theoretical problems. It is severely under-constrained without prior knowledge of the deformation or the shapes. In fact given a number of images, infinite possibilities of deformations exist that provide the same image projections. Therefore, one of the major challenges in NRSfM is to efficiently combine a realistic deformation constraint and the camera projection model to reduce the solution ambiguity.

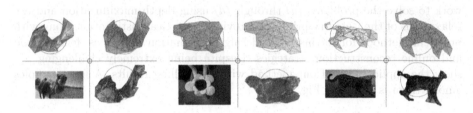

Fig. 1. Qualitative Results. Comparison of our dense NRSfM method (bottom-right) to Ji et al. [6] (top-left) and Dai et al. [7] (top-right) on three different sequences.

A large majority of previous methods tackle NRSfM with an affine camera model and a low rank approximation of the deforming shapes [7–14]. However, such methods do not handle perspective effects and nonlinear deformations very well. In this paper we study the use of the uncalibrated perspective camera and the isometric deformation prior for non-rigid reconstruction. Isometry is a geometric prior which implies that the geodesic distances on the surface are preserved with the deformations. This is a good approximation for many real objects such as a human body, paper-like surfaces, or cloth. In SfT, the use of the isometric deformation prior with the perspective camera is considered to be the state-of-the-art [15–17] among the parameter-free approaches. In particular, [15,18] also estimate the focal length while recovering the deformation. In NRSfM, some recent methods [6,19] provide a convex formulation with the inextensible deformation for a calibrated perspective camera setup. The reconstruction is achieved by maximizing depth along the sightlines introduced in [20,21] for template-based reconstruction. Although the methods use the perspective camera model and geometric priors for non-rigid reconstruction, their computational complexity does not allow reconstructing a large number of points. On the other hand, some recent dense methods using the perspective camera model have shown promising results, but they rely on piecewise rigidity constraints [22,23] and shape initialization; this may be too constraining for several applications.

Furthermore, methods using the perspective camera either rely on known intrinsics or cannot handle significant nonrigidity [28]. To the best of our knowledge, estimation of the unknown focal length has not been investigated in NRSfM for deforming surfaces.

In this paper we address the aforementioned issues with methods based on the convex relaxation of isometry. More precisely, we provide the following contributions: *(a)* a method to 'upgrade' the non-rigid reconstruction obtained using incorrect camera intrinsics to the reconstruction of the correct one, *(b)* a method to estimate intrinsics - all five entries in the case of SfT and the unknown focal length in the case template-less NRSfM *(c)* an incremental method to add more points to the sparse 3D point-sets for consistent and semi-dense reconstruction *(d)* online method of reconstruction by adding images. Besides being of immense practical concern and theoretical value, questions *(a)* and *(b)* have not been attempted for NRSfM for deforming objects. We provide a unified framework to solve the problems *(a)* through *(d)* using depth maximization and the relaxations of the isometry prior. We provide theoretical justification along with practical methods for intrinsics/focal length estimation as well as densification and online reconstruction strategies. Despite being extremely challenging, we show the applicability of our method with compelling results. A few examples among them is shown in Fig. 1.

1.1 Related Work

We discuss briefly the methods based on the isometry prior and the perspective camera model. This has been widely explored in the template-based methods [20,21,24]. In particular, [21] uses the inextensibility as a relaxation of the isometry prior in order to formulate non-rigid reconstruction as a convex problem by maximizing the depth point-wise. Several recent NRSfM methods [6,19,25–27] also use isometry or inextensibility with the perspective camera model. [26,27] require the correspondence mapping function with its first and second-order derivatives limiting their application in practice. [19] improved upon [25] by providing a convex solution to NRSfM. They achieve this by maximizing point-wise depth in all views under the inextensibility cone constraints of [21] while also computing the template geodesics. Very recently a method [6] improving upon [19] suggested the use of maximization of sightlines rather than the point-wise depth. Both these methods have shown that moving the surface away from the camera under the inextensibility constraints can be formulated as a convex problem effectively reconstructing non-rigid as well as rigid objects. A different class of methods that use energy minimization approach on an initial solution also use the perspective camera model but with a piece-wise rigidity prior [22,23]. However, all of these methods discussed here require the calibrated camera for reconstruction and do not provide any insights on how they can be extended to an uncalibrated camera. One notable exception is given by [28], however this approach is limited to dynamic scenes featuring a few independently moving objects [29,30]. Yet another problem that has not been addressed in [6,19] is the incremental reconstruction of a large number of points. Semi-dense or dense reconstruction as such is not possible here due to the high computational complexity of these methods.

2   Problem Modelling

We pose the NRSfM problem as that of finding point-wise depth in each view. We write the unknown depth as λ_i^l and the known homogeneous image coordinates as u_i^l, for the point i in the l-th image. A set of neighboring points of i is denoted by $\mathcal{N}(i)$. d_{ij} represents the template geodesic distance between point i and j, which is an unknown quantity for the NRSfM problem and a known quantity for the SfT problem. We define a nearest neighborhood graph as a set of fixed number of neighbors for each point i [19]. To represent the exact isometric NRSfM problem, we also introduce a geodesic distance function between two 3D points on the surface $\mathcal{S}$, $g_{\mathcal{S}}(x,y): \mathbb{R}^3 \times \mathbb{R}^3 \to \mathbb{R}$. Given the camera intrinsics K, the isometric NRSfM problem can be written as:

$$\text{Find} \quad \mathsf{K}, \; \lambda_i^l$$
$$\text{s.t.} \quad g\left(\mathsf{K}^{-1}\lambda_i^l u_i^l, \; \mathsf{K}^{-1}\lambda_j^l u_j^l\right) = d_{ij}, \; \forall i, \forall j. \tag{1}$$

(1) defines a non-convex problem and is also not tractable in its given form. It has been shown that with various relaxations [6,19,25], problem (1) can be solved for a known K when different views and deformations are observed. In order to tackle the NRSfM problem with an unknown focal length we start with the observation that not all such solutions provide isometrically consistent shapes through all the views. We formulate our methods in the following sections.

3   Uncalibrated NRSfM

Given a known object template and a calibrated camera the NRSfM problem in (1) can be formulated as a convex problem by relaxing the isometry constraint with an inextensibility constraint [21] as below:

$$\max_{\lambda_i^l} \; \sum_l \sum_i \lambda_i^l,$$
$$\text{s.t.} \quad \left\| \mathsf{K}^{-1}(\lambda_i^l u_i^l - \lambda_j^l u_j^l) \right\| \leq d_{ij}, \quad \forall j \in \mathcal{N}(i). \tag{2}$$

We are, however, interested on solving the same problem when both d_{ij} and K are unknown. Unfortunately, this problem is not only non-convex, but also unbounded. Therefore, we use two extra constraints on the variables K and d_{ij} such that the problem of (2), for unknown d_{ij} and K, becomes bounded.

$$\sum_i \sum_{j \in \mathcal{N}(i)} d_{ij} = 1, \; \mathsf{K} \leq \overline{\mathsf{K}}. \tag{3}$$

Despite being bounded with the addition of (3), the reconstruction problem is still non-convex. More importantly, the maximization of the objective function favors the solution when K is as close as possible to $\overline{\mathsf{K}}$. Therefore, we instead solve the reconstruction problem in (2) with a fixed initial guess $\hat{\mathsf{K}}$ and seek for the upgrade of both intrinsics and reconstruction later. Note that fixing the intrinsics makes the problem convex and identical to that in [19].

$$
\begin{aligned}
\max_{\lambda_i^l, d_{ij}} \quad & \sum_l \sum_i \lambda_i^l, \\
\text{s.t.} \quad & \left\| \hat{\mathsf{K}}^{-1} (\lambda_i^l u_i^l - \lambda_j^l u_j^l) \right\| \le d_{ij}, \quad j \in \mathcal{N}(i), \\
& \sum_i \sum_{j \in \mathcal{N}(i)} d_{ij} = 1.
\end{aligned}
\tag{4}
$$

Now, we are interested to upgrade the solution of (4) such that the upgraded reconstruction correctly describes the deformed object in the 3D-space. In this work, the upgrade is carried out using a pointwise upgrade equation. In the following, we first derive this upgrade equation assuming that the correct focal length is known and then provide the theory and practical approaches to recover the unknown focal length.

3.1   Upgrade Equation

Let us consider, λ_i^l and $\hat{\lambda}_i^l$ are depths, of the point represented by u_i^l, obtained from (2) and (4), respectively. The following proposition is the key ingredient of our work that relates $\hat{\lambda}_i^l$ to λ_i^l for the reconstruction upgrade.

Proposition 1. *For $u_i^l \approx u_{\mathcal{N}(i)}^l$, $\hat{\lambda}_i^l$ can be upgraded to λ_i^l with the known K using,*

$$
\lambda_i^l \approx \frac{\hat{\lambda}_i^l \left\| \hat{\mathsf{K}}^{-1} u_i^l \right\|}{\left\| \mathsf{K}^{-1} u_i^l \right\|}.
\tag{5}
$$

Proof. It is sufficient to show that every $j \in \mathcal{N}(i)$ satisfies $\left\| \hat{\mathsf{K}}^{-1} (\hat{\lambda}_i^l u_i^l - \hat{\lambda}_j^l u_j^l) \right\| \approx \left\| \mathsf{K}^{-1} (\lambda_i^l u_i^l - \lambda_j^l u_j^l) \right\|$. From (5), for any $u_i^l \approx u_{\mathcal{N}(i)}^l$, $\left\| \hat{\mathsf{K}}^{-1} (\hat{\lambda}_i^l u_i^l - \hat{\lambda}_j^l u_j^l) \right\|^2$ can be expressed as,

$$
\begin{aligned}
& \approx \left\| \mathsf{K}^{-1} u_i^l \right\|^2 \left\| \hat{\mathsf{K}}^{-1} (\lambda_i^l - \lambda_j^l) u_i^l \right\|^2 / \left\| \hat{\mathsf{K}}^{-1} u_i^l \right\|^2, \\
& = (\lambda_i^l - \lambda_j^l)^2 \left\| \mathsf{K}^{-1} u_i^l \right\|^2 \approx \left\| \mathsf{K}^{-1} (\lambda_i^l u_i^l - \lambda_j^l u_j^l) \right\|^2.
\end{aligned}
\tag{6}
$$

$\square$

Note that the condition $u_i^l \approx u_{\mathcal{N}(i)}^l$ is valid for any two sufficiently close neighbors. Such neighbors can be chosen using only the image measurements. More importantly, the assumption $u_i^l \approx u_{\mathcal{N}(i)}^l$ still allows depths λ_i^l and $\lambda_{\mathcal{N}(i)}^l$ to be different. This plays a vital role especially when the close neighboring points differ distinctly in depth, either due to camera perspective or high frequency structural changes. Although, (5) is only a close approximation for the reconstruction upgrade, its upgrade quality in practice was observed to be accurate. The following remark concerns Proposition 1.

Remark 1. As the guess on intrinsics $\hat{K}$ tends to the real intrinsics K, the upgrade equation (5) holds true for exact equality even when $u_i^l \not\approx u_{\mathcal{N}(i)}^l$. In other words,

$$\lim_{\hat{K} \to K} \lambda_i^l = \hat{\lambda}_i^l. \tag{7}$$

3.2   Upgrade Strategies

The upgrade equation presented in Proposition 1 assumes that the exact intrinsics K is known. However, for uncalibrated NRSfM, K is unknown. While the principal point can be assumed to be at the center of the image for most cameras [31], nothing can be said about the focal length. We henceforth, present strategies to estimate K in two different scenarios of known and unknown shape template. We rely on the fact that isometric deformation, to a large extent, preserves local rigidity. This is reflected somewhat in the reconstruction obtained from (4). However, due to changes in the perspective and the extension of points along incorrect sightlines, the use of incorrect intrinsics produces reconstructions that are very less likely to remain isometric across different views. Similarly, an upgrade towards the correct intrinsics in that case produces reconstructions which satisfy the isometry better. This is also supported by the results in Sect. 6. There are various ways one can use isometry of the reconstructed surfaces to determine the correct intrinsics. A very simple method would be to use the fact that given reconstructed points that are dense enough, the correct intrinsics must preserve the local euclidean distance. For $\hat{a}_i = \hat{\lambda}_i \left\| \hat{K}^{-1} u_i \right\|$, the euclidean distance between two upgraded neighboring 3D points, in any view as a function of intrinsics, can be expressed as,

$$\hat{d}_{ij}(K) = \left\| \frac{\hat{a}_i K^{-1} u_i}{\|K^{-1} u_i\|} - \frac{\hat{a}_j K^{-1} u_j}{\|K^{-1} u_j\|} \right\|. \tag{8}$$

Now, we present techniques to estimate K when the shape template is known (SfT), followed by a method to estimate the focal length for template-less case of NRSfM.

Template-Based Calibration. For the sake of simplicity, we present the calibration theory using only one image. This is also the sufficient condition for reconstruction when the shape template is known [21]. Recall that for SfT, d_{ij} in (4) are already known during the reconstruction process. For known template distance d_{ij} and the estimated euclidean distance after reconstruction upgrade $\hat{d}_{ij}(K)$, the intrinsics K can be estimated by minimizing,

$$\Phi_T(K) = \sum_i \sum_{j \in \mathcal{N}(i)} \left(d_{ij} - \hat{d}_{ij}(K) \right)^2. \tag{9}$$

Alternatively, one can also derive polynomial equations on the entries of the so-called Image of the Absolute Conic (IAC), defined as $\Omega = \mathsf{K}^{-\mathsf{T}}\mathsf{K}^{-1}$.

Proposition 2. *As long as the rigidity between any pair $\{u_i, u_j\}$ is maintained, either for any $\hat{\mathsf{K}}$ and $u_i \approx u_j$ or for any pair $\{u_i, u_j\}$ as $\hat{\mathsf{K}} \to \mathsf{K}$, the IAC can be approximated by solving,*

$$u_i^{\mathsf{T}}\Omega u_i u_j^{\mathsf{T}}\Omega u_j = \gamma_{ij}\left(u_i^{\mathsf{T}}\Omega u_j\right)^2, \tag{10}$$

for sufficiently many pairs, where,

$$\gamma_{ij} = \left(\frac{2\hat{a}_i\hat{a}_j}{\hat{a}_i^2 + \hat{a}_j^2 - d_{ij}^2}\right)^2. \tag{11}$$

We provide the proof in the supplementary material.

Note that (10) is a degree 2 polynomial on the entries of Ω. Since, Ω has 5 degrees of freedom, it can be estimated from 5 pairs of image points, using numerical methods.

The core idea of our template-based calibration consists of three steps: (i) a fixed number of hypothesis generation, (ii) hypothesis validation using the upgraded reconstruction quality, (iii) refinement of the best hypothesis.

Hypothesis Generation: Given the template-based uncalibrated reconstruction from (4), we generate a set of hypotheses for camera intrinsics from randomly selected sets of minimal closest-point pairs. For every minimal set, we solve (10) for Ω to obtain these hypotheses. Then, the camera intrinsics K is recovered by performing the Cholesky-decomposition on Ω.

Hypothesis Validation: Each hypothesis is validated by computing its 3D reconstruction error. To do so, we first upgrade the initial reconstruction using the upgrade (5) for current hypothesis. Then, the reconstruction error is computed using (9). The hypothesis that results into minimum reconstruction error is chosen for further refinement.

Intrinsics Refinement: Starting from the best hypothesis, we refine the intrinsics by minimizing the following objective function:

$$\mathcal{E}(\mathsf{K}) = \Phi_T(\mathsf{K}) + k_{(1,3)}^2 + k_{(2,3)}^2 + \left(1 - \frac{k_{(1,1)}}{k_{(2,2)}}\right)^2, \tag{12}$$

where, $k_{(i,j)}$ is the ith-row and j^{th}-column entry of the normalized intrinsic matrix K. Note that, we regularize the 3D reconstruction error $\Phi_T(\mathsf{K})$ by the expected structure of K (i.e. principal point close to the center and unit aspect ratio). Our regularization term is often the main objective for existing autocalibration methods [31,32]. The minimization of objective $\mathcal{E}(\mathsf{K})$ can be carried out efficiently using locally optimal iterative refinement methods.

Now, we summarize our calibration method in Algorithm 1.

Algorithm 1 [K] = calibrateWithTemplate($\hat{\mathsf{K}}$)

---

1. Reconstruct 3D using (4) for known d_{ij} and the guess $\hat{\mathsf{K}}$.
2. Select multiple sets of minimal closest-point pairs $\{\mathsf{u}_i, \mathsf{u}_j\}$.
3. For each set,
   (i) Generate hypothesis $\tilde{\mathsf{K}}$ by solving (10).
   (ii) Upgrade the reconstruction for $\tilde{\mathsf{K}}$ using (5).
   (iii) Compute the reconstruction error for $\tilde{\mathsf{K}}$ using (9).
4. Among all sets, choose $\tilde{\mathsf{K}}$ with best reconstruction error.
5. Refine the best hypothesis $\tilde{\mathsf{K}}$ using (12) to obtain K.

Template-Less Calibration. As the self-calibration with the unknown template is extremely challenging, we relax it by considering that the principal point is at the center of the image and that the two focal lengths are equal. We assume that the intrinsics are constant across views. We then measure the consistency of the upgraded local euclidean distances, defined by (8), across different views. More precisely, we wish to estimate the focal length in K by minimizing the following objective function,

$$\Phi(\mathsf{K}) = \sum_k \sum_{l \neq k} \sum_i \sum_{j \in \mathcal{N}(i)} \left(\hat{d}_{ij}^k(\mathsf{K}) - \hat{d}_{ij}^l(\mathsf{K}) \right)^2. \tag{13}$$

Ideally, it is also possible to derive polynomials on Ω, analogous to (10). This can be done by eliminating the unknown variable d_{ij} from two equations for two views of the same pair. Unfortunately, the equation derived in this manner does not turn out to be easily tractable. Alternatively, one can also attempt to solve the polynomials without eliminating variables d_{ij} – on both variables Ω and d_{ij}. However for practical reasons[1], we design a method assuming only one entry of Ω, corresponding to the focal length, is unknown. Under such assumption, we show in the supplementary materials that a polynomial of degree 4, one variable, equivalent to (10), can also be derived.

In this paper, we avoid making hypothesis on the focal length, since it is not really necessary. Unlike the case of template-based calibration, we address the problem of template-less calibration iteratively in two steps: (i) focal length refinement, (ii) focal length validation. Henceforth for the template-less calibration, we make a slight abuse of notation by using K even for the intrinsics with only unknown focal length, unless mentioned otherwise.

Focal Length Refinement: Given an initial guess on focal length, its refinement is carried out by minimizing the objective function $\Phi(\mathsf{K})$ of (13) (optionally, on the full intrinsics). This refinement process finds a refined K which results a better isometric consistency of the reconstructions across views.

Focal Length Validation: The main problem of template-less calibration is to obtain the validity for the given pair of intrinsics and the reconstruction. In other

---

[1] For most of the cameras, it is safe to assume that their intrinsics have no skew, unit aspect ratio, and a principal point close to the image center.

words, if one is given all reconstructions from all possible focal lengths, it is not trivial to know the correct reconstruction. Especially when reconstructing using overestimated intrinsics with MDH, K allows the average depths to dominate the objective, while preserving the isometry. This usually leads to a flat and small scaled reconstruction [17]. Therefore an overestimated guess $\hat{K}$ favors its own reconstruction over any upgraded one, while minimizing $\Phi(K)$. Relying on this observation, *we seek for the isometrically consistent reconstruction with the smallest focal length,* which works very well in practice. An algebraic analysis of our reasoning is provided in the supplementary material.

While searching for focal length, we use a sweeping procedure. On the one hand, if a reconstruction with the given focal length does not favor any upgrade, the sweeping is performed towards the lower focal length with a predefined step size, unless it starts favoring the upgrade. On the other hand, if the reconstruction favors the upgrade, we follow the suggested focal length update, until it suggests no more upgrade. The sought focal length is the one below which the upgrade is favorable, whereas above which it is not. Let $\delta(K_1, K_2)$ be gap in focal lengths of two intrinsics K_1 and K_2, ΔK be a small step size which when added to an intrinsic matrix K increases its focal length by that step size. Our template-less calibration method is summarized in Algorithm 2.

Algorithm 2 [K] = calibrateWithoutTemplate($\hat{K}$)

---

0. Set sweep direction $flag = 0$.
1. Reconstruct 3D using (4) for the guess $\hat{K}$.
2. Starting from $\hat{K}$, minimize $\Phi(K)$ in (13) to obtain K^*.
3. IF $\delta(K^*, \hat{K}) \leq \epsilon$,
      IF $flag == 0$, set $\hat{K} = K^* - \Delta K$ and goto step 1.
      ELSE, return K^*.
   ELSE, set and $flag = 1$, $\hat{K} = K^*$ and goto step 1.

We show in the experiment section, that the Algorithm 2 converges in very few iterations. In every iteration, beside the reconstruction itself, the major computation is only required while minimizing $\Phi(K)$. Recall that, $\Phi(K)$ is minimized iteratively using a local method. During local search, the reconstruction for every update is required to compute $\Phi(K)$. Thanks to the upgrade equation, the cost $\Phi(K)$ can be computed instantly, without going through the computationally expensive reconstruction process.

3.3   Intrinsics Recovery in Practice

Although our reconstruction method makes inextensible shape assumption, the upgrade strategies use the piece-wise rigidity constraint. Despite the fact that the piece-wise rigid assumption is mostly true for inextensible shapes, it could be problematic in certain cases, for example, when the reconstructed points are too sparse. Therefore, some special care need to taken for a robust calibration.

Distance Normalization and Geodesics: Recall that the upgrade equation (5) is an approximation under the assumption that either the neighboring image points are sufficiently close to each other or a good guess $\hat{\mathsf{K}}$ is provided. When neither of these conditions are satisfied, the intrinsics obtained from energy minimization may not be sufficiently accurate. While a larger focal length may reduce the residual error, it also reduces individual distances creating disparities in the reconstruction scale of different views. Therefore, during each iteration of refinement, we fix the scale by enforcing,

$$\sum_i \sum_{j \in \mathcal{N}(i)} \hat{d}^l_{ij}(\mathsf{K}) = 1, \forall l. \tag{14}$$

Another important practical aspect here is the use of geodesics $\hat{g}^l(i,j)$ instead of $\hat{d}^l_{ij}$ in Eq. (13) or Eq. (9). When the scene points are sparse, using geodesics instead of the local euclidean distances may be necessary. We therefore choose to use geodesics computed from Dijkstra's algorithm [33] instead of the local euclidean distances for stability.

Re-reconstruction and Re-calibration: For a better calibration accuracy, especially when the initial guess $\hat{\mathsf{K}}$ is largely inaccurate, we iteratively perform re-reconstruction and re-calibration, starting from newly estimated intrinsics, until convergence. This has already been included in Algorithm 2, which we also included on top of Algorithm 1 in our implementation. In practice, only a few such iterations are sufficient to converge, even when the initial guess on intrinsics is very arbitrary.

4 Incremental Semi-dense NRSfM

The SOCP problem of (4) has the time complexity of $O(n^3)$. Therefore in practice, only a sparse set of points can be reconstructed in this manner. Here, we present a method to iteratively densify the initial sparse reconstruction, followed by online new view/camera addition strategy. Besides many obvious importance of incremental reconstruction, it is also necessary in our context: (a) to allow the selection of the closest image point pairs for camera calibration, (b) to compute 3D Geodesic distances for single view reconstruction.

4.1 Adding New Points

Let $\mathcal{P}$ represents a set of sparse points reconstructed using (4). We would like to reconstruct a set of new points $\mathcal{Q}$ with depths ζ^l_i, such that $\mathcal{Q} \cap \mathcal{P} = \emptyset$, consistent to the existing reconstruction. This can be achieved by solving the following convex optimization problem,

$$\max_{\zeta_i^l, e_{ij}, \alpha} \quad \alpha \Lambda + \sum_l \sum_{i \in Q} \zeta_i^l,$$

$$\text{s.t.} \quad \left\| \hat{K}^{-1}(\zeta_i^l u_i^l - \alpha \lambda_j^l u_j^l) \right\| \le e_{ij}, \quad j \in \mathcal{N}_p(i),$$

$$\left\| \hat{K}^{-1}(\zeta_i^l u_i^l - \zeta_j^l u_j^l) \right\| \le e_{ij}, \quad j \in \mathcal{N}_q(i), \tag{15}$$

$$\sum_i \sum_{j \in \mathcal{N}_q(i)} e_{ij} = 1 - \alpha,$$

where, $\Lambda = \sum_l \sum_{i \in P} \lambda_i^l$, $\mathcal{N}_p(i) = \mathcal{N}(i) \cap \mathcal{P}$, and $\mathcal{N}_q(i) = \mathcal{N}(i) \cap \mathcal{Q}$. The scalars α and $1 - \alpha$ represent the contributions of initial reconstruction $\mathcal{P}$ and new reconstruction $\mathcal{Q}$, respectively. Note that the newly reconstructed points respect the inextensible criteria not only among themselves but also with respect to the initial reconstruction. This maintains the consistency between reconstructions $\mathcal{P}$ and $\mathcal{Q}$. The incremental dense reconstruction process iteratively adds disjoint sets $\mathcal{Q}_1, \mathcal{Q}_2, \dots \mathcal{Q}_r$ to the initial reconstruction $\mathcal{P}$, where $\mathcal{P}$ encodes the overall shape and $\mathcal{Q}_r$ represents the details.

4.2 Adding New Cameras

Adding a new camera to the NRSfM reconstruction is fundamentally a template-based reconstruction problem. If the camera is calibrated, one can obtain the reconstruction directly from (2). For the uncalibrated case, the camera can be calibrated first using (10), and the reconstruction upgraded from (4) using (5). It is important to note that the computation of accurate template geodesic distances d_{ij}, as required for template-based reconstruction, is possible only when the reconstruction is dense enough. This is not really a problem, thanks to the proposed incremental reconstruction method.

5 Discussion

Initial Guess $\hat{K}$: In all our experiments, we choose the initial guess $\hat{K}$ by setting both focal lengths to the half of the mean image size and principal point to the image center.

Missing Features: Feature points may be missing from some images due to occlusion or matching failure. This problem can be addressed during reconstruction by discarding all the variables corresponding to missing points together with all the inextensible constraints involving them as done in [19, 25].

Reconstruction Consistency: Alternative to (15), one can also think of reconstructing two overlapping sets $\mathcal{P}$ and $\mathcal{Q}$ such that $\mathcal{P} \cap \mathcal{Q} = \mathcal{R}$ independently. Then, the registration between them can be done with the help of $\mathcal{R}$ from two sides. However, this is not only computationally inefficient due to the overlap, but also geometrically inconsistent.

6   Experimental Results

We conduct extensive experiments in order to validate the presented theory and to evaluate the performance, run time and practicality of the proposed methods.

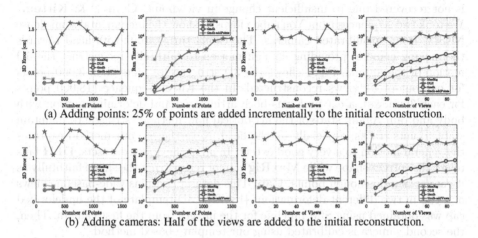

(a) Adding points: 25% of points are added incrementally to the initial reconstruction.

(b) Adding cameras: Half of the views are added to the initial reconstruction.

Fig. 2. Incremental Semi-dense NRSfM. Comparison of reconstruction error and run time on the *Hand* dataset. Left: varying number of points (number of views = 88). Right: varying number of views (number of points = 751). Run time shown in log scale.

Datasets. We first provide a brief descriptions of the datasets we use to analyze our algorithms. **KINECT Paper.** This VGA resolution image sequence shows a textured paper deforming smoothly [34]. The tracks contain about 1500 semi-dense but noisy points. **Hulk & T-Shirt.** The datasets contain a comic book cover in 21 different deformations, and a textured T-Shirt with 10 different deformations [35], in high resolution images. Although the number of points is low (122 and 85, resp.), the tracks have very little noise and therefore we obtain a very accurate auto-calibration. **Flag.** This semi-synthetic dataset is created from mocap recordings of deforming cloth [36]. We generate 250 points in 30 views using a virtual 640 × 480 perspective camera. **Newspaper.** This sequence[2] contains the deformation and tearing of a double-page newspaper, recorded with KINECT in HD resolution [19]. **Hand.** The Hand dataset [19] features medium resolution images. Dense tracking [37] of image points yield up to 1500 tracks in 88 views. The dataset consists of ground-truth 3D for the first and the last image of the sequence. **Minion & Sunflower.** These sequences are recorded with a static Kinect sensor [38]. Minion contains a stuffed animal undergoing folding and squeezing deformations. Sunflower however features only small translation w.r.t. the camera. We incrementally reconstruct more than

---

[2] The dataset was provided by the authors.

10,000 points for Minion, and 5,000 for Sunflower, as shown in Fig. 1. We are able to reconstruct the global deformation, and mid-level details such as the glasses of Minion. Unfortunately, due to the failure of optical flow tracking, we fail to reconstruct homogeneous areas and fine details. In Sunflower we can capture the deformation of the outside leafs, whereas finer details in the center of the blossom is not recovered due to insufficient change in viewpoint. **Camel**[3] **& Kitten.**[4] We took two sequences from YouTube videos to show the incremental semi-dense NRSfM from uncalibrated cameras. The camel turns around its head towards the moving camera, providing enough motion to faithfully reconstruct the 3D motion of the animal. Fig. 1 shows the 3D structure of more than 3,000 points for one out of 61 views reconstructed. In the Kitten sequence (18,000 points for each 36 views), a cat performs both articulated and deforming motion with body and tail. Again, state-of-the-art optical flow methods struggle to maintain stable points tracks, especially on the head. Nevertheless, our method captures the general motion to a very good extent. In all of the above datasets, **DLH** fails to get the correct shape while **MaxRig** cannot reconstruct the shape faithfully as it cannot handle enough points. **Cap.** This dataset contains wide-baseline views of a cap in two different deformations [18]. The 3D template of the undeformed cap was obtained using SfM pipeline for the images from the first camera. Then, the second camera is calibrated using our template-based method.

6.1   Camera Calibration from a Non-rigid Scene

To measure the quality of our calibration results, we report the 3D root mean square error (RMSE), the relative focal length and principal point estimation error. Furthermore, we provide the number of iterations and the corresponding run times in Table 1.

Template-Based Camera Calibration. In the first part of Algorithm 1 we generate hypotheses for K and choose the one with best isometric match with the template. We perform experiments on the KINECT Paper, Hulk and Flag dataset and report the results in Table 1. We observe a consistent improvement in reconstruction accuracy with the estimated intrinsics. The second part of Algorithm 1 involves gradient-based refinement on the intrinsics by minimizing Eq. (12). To analyze this part, we conduct two experiments: First, we perform refinement on the initially estimated intrinsics f_{poly}. Here we can consistently improve reconstruction errors with the refined intrinsics. In the Hulk and Flag dataset, we also get a better estimate of the focal length. On KINECT Paper however, the focal length deteriorates, while reconstruction accuracy improves. This is most probably due to the noisy tracks in the sequence. Due to the effective regularization, the error in principal point is consistently low. In the second experiment, we gauge the robustness of our refinement method. To this end, we simulate initial intrinsics by adding ±20% uniform noise independently on each of the entries of K_{GT}, and compare reconstruction error and the refined

---

[3] https://www.youtube.com/watch?v=PhpeadpZsa4.
[4] https://www.youtube.com/watch?v=DIZM2OMNc7c.

Table 1. Focal Length Estimation from a Non-Rigid Scene. We report the run-time, reconstruction error and relative focal length estimation error of our template-based and template-less NRSfM calibration methods. T_{orig} is the time needed to reconstruct with a given focal length, T_{total} the run time including calibration. For the template-less case, N_{iter} iterations were performed until convergence.

Dataset	Number of		Run time [s]			Focal Estimation				Reconstruction Error E_{rec}	
	Points	Views	T_{orig}	N_{iter}	T_{total}	f_{init}	f_{GT}	f_{est}	Error %	f_{GT}	f_{est}
Template-based focal length estimation											
KINECT Paper	301	23	2.3	–	16.8	–	528	590	11.74	3.00	0.54%	**2.83**	0.50%
Hulk	122	21	0.4	–	4.2	–	3784	4300	13.61	5.73	1.43%	**5.53**	1.37%
Flag	250	30	1.3	–	178.2	–	384	420	9.38	4.74	0.58%	**4.54**	0.56%
Cap	137	1	0.3	–	11.0	–	2039	2300	12.8	**1.13**	4.80%	**1.13**	4.80%
Template-less focal length estimation											
KPaper	301	23	5.8	3	110.1	280	528	540	2.27	4.44	0.80%	**4.28**	0.77%
Hulk	122	21	1.9	5	36.5	1641	3784	3800	0.40	2.76	0.67%	**2.75**	0.66%
T-Shirt	85	10	0.6	10	24.1	2000	3787	4000	5.63	3.52	1.10%	**3.42**	1.07%
Flag	250	30	2.6	6	185.4	280	384	400	4.17	5.24	0.64%	**5.05**	0.62%
Newspaper	441	19	24.5	5	523.6	750	1055	870	16.6	**7.79**	1.09%	9.27	1.30%

intrinsics shown in Table 2. We compare to Bartoli et al. [18] on the Cap dataset directly from the paper, since it is non-trivial to implement the method itself. We observed an error E_f of about 13% with our method, compared to 3.8%–7.3% reported by [18]. The slightly higher error in the Cap dataset can be partly attributed to the repeating texture that makes our image matches non-ideal. Overall we can observe a consistent improvement in almost all metrics, validating the robustness of the method and the assumptions it is based on.

Table 2. Calibration Refinement. We compute the full calibration K by initializing with the template-based calibration f_{poly}, and test the robustness by adding synthetic noise on the K_{GT}. Reconstruction errors E_{rec} are in mm, others in %.

Dataset	f_{GT}	Template-based			Refined				Simulated initial K (10^3 samples avg.)					
		f_{poly}	E_f	E_{rec}	f_{ref}	E_f	E_{PP}	E_{rec}	E_f	ΔE_f	E_{PP}	ΔE_{PP}	E_{rec}	ΔE_{rec}
KINECT Paper	528	590	**11.74**	2.83	604	14.45	0.04	**2.73**	8.87	-0.37	0.05	-10.96	3.82	-0.25
Hulk	3784	4300	13.61	5.53	4119	**8.85**	1.74	**5.53**	7.30	-2.36	1.77	-8.84	6.52	-0.01
Flag	384	420	9.38	4.54	414	**7.98**	0.05	**4.34**	8.61	-1.05	0.08	-10.45	6.05	+0.08
Cap	2039	2300	**12.8**	**1.13**	2360	13.1	2.33	**1.13**	9.18	-0.10	2.33	-8.42	1.48	-0.00

Template-Less Camera Calibration. To visualize the dynamics of Algorithm 2, we plot the error in isometry $\Phi(K)$ over focal length for each iteration on the Hulk dataset in Fig. 3(a). Typically, less than 10 iterations are necessary for the method to converge. As we hypothesized above, Fig. 3(b) empirically verifies that we can find the termination criterion for our sweeping strategy by thresholding the focal length change $\delta(K^*, \hat{K})$. Our method consistently recovers a correct estimate of the intrinsics as reported in Table 1. Moreover, the fact that we obtain better reconstruction accuracy in almost all datasets validates our approach of using the isometric consistency $\Phi(\mathsf{K})$.

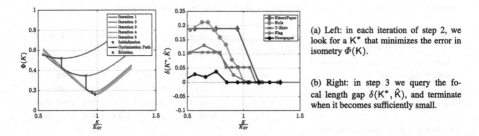

(a) Left: in each iteration of step 2, we look for a K^* that minimizes the error in isometry $\Phi(\mathsf{K})$.

(b) Right: in step 3 we query the focal length gap $\delta(\mathsf{K}^*, \hat{\mathsf{K}})$, and terminate when it becomes sufficiently small.

Fig. 3. Template-less Calibration (Algorithm 2). We iteratively search the smallest K that maximizes isometry.

6.2   Incremental Reconstruction

We first present experiments on the dense Hand dataset in Fig. 2. We compare to two state-of-the-art NRSfM approaches, **MaxRig** [6] and **DLH** [7], as well as the to batch version of our approach **tlmdh** [19]. In the first row, we plot the performance of **tlmdh-addPoints**: we start by reconstructing a random subset of $\max\{150, \frac{N}{4}\}$ points, and incrementally add the remaining points in subsequent iterations according to Eq. (15). While achieving competitive reconstruction accuracy on par with **tlmdh**, we observe remarkable advantages in run time compared to all other methods. **MaxRig** shows good accuracy, but suffers from serious run time and memory problems. **DLH** on the other hand is slow and exhibits poor accuracy on this dataset, due to perspective and non-linear deformations. The second row of Fig. 2 shows the same experimental setup with **tlmdh-addViews**. Here, we reconstruct all points at once, but incrementally add the remaining 50% of views to the reconstruction of the first half. To this

Table 3. Comparison of NRSfM methods. Mean 3D errors in mm and run time comparison for batch and incremental reconstruction in real datasets.

Datasets	incr-tlmdh		tlmdh		p-isomet	p-isolh	DLH	o-kfac
KPaper	**4.64**	**176.16s**	5.41	605.06s	7.63	13.64	14.66	13.93
Hulk	2.99	**0.80s**	**2.76**	1.99s	10.76	14.54	22.98	–
T-Shirt	3.83	**0.23s**	**3.53**	0.47s	10.60	8.94	–	–
Cardboard	**13.22**	**18.94s**	14.56	34.35s	–	12.95	–	–
Rug	**26.40**	**205.89s**	26.60	542.39s	26.15	38.26	31.01	–
Table mat	15.99	**5.54s**	14.36	7.65s	**14.21**	20.71	17.51	16.24
Newspaper	**10.79**	**89.27s**	11.63	190.96s	18.40	37.21	24.94	30.74

end, we compute the template from the first reconstruction and employ SfT. The graphs clearly show that **tlmdh-addViews** exhibits a favorable run time complexity without impairing the reconstruction accuracy. We provide more results in the supplementary material. Furthermore, we perform extensive experiments on a variety of additional datasets, and compare with the reconstructions of **p-isomet** [27], **p-isolh** [35], **DLH** [7], and **o-kfc** [39] in Table 3 obtained from [40]. Overall, we observe a significant advantage in accuracy and run time in particular compared to the best performing baseline **tlmdh**.

7   Conclusions

In this paper we formulated a method addressing the unknown focal-length in NRSfM and unknown intrinsics in SfT. Despite the computational complexity of convex NRSfM, we formulated an incremental framework to obtain semi-dense reconstruction and reconstruct new views. We developed our theory based on the surface isometry prior in the context of the perspective camera. We developed and verified our approach for intrinsics/focal-length recovery for both template-based and template-less non-rigid reconstruction. Essential to our method is a novel upgrade equation, that analytically relates reconstructions for different intrinsics. We performed extensive quantitative and qualitative analysis of our methods on different datasets which shows the proposed methods perform well despite addressing very challenging problems.

Acknowledgements. Research was funded by the EU's Horizon 2020 programme under grant No. 645331– EurEyeCase and grant No. 687757– REPLICATE, and the Swiss Commission for Technology and Innovation (CTI, Grant No. 26253.1 PFES-ES, EXASOLVED).

References

1. Longuet-Higgins, H.: A computer algorithm for reconstructing a scene from two projections. Nature **293**, 133–135 (1981)
2. Nistér, D.: An efficient solution to the five-point relative pose problem. IEEE Trans. Pattern Anal. Mach. Intell. **26**(6), 756–777 (2004)
3. Hartley, R.I., Zisserman, A.: Multiple View Geometry in Computer Vision, 2nd edn. Cambridge University, New York Press (2004). ISBN 0521540518
4. Agisoft PhotoScan: Agisoft PhotoScan User Manual Professional Edition, Version 1.2 (2017)
5. Autodesk ReCap: ReCap 360 - Advanced Workflows (2015)
6. Ji, P., Li, H., Dai, Y., Reid, I.: "Maximizing Rigidity" revisited: a convex programming approach for generic 3D shape reconstruction from multiple perspective views. In: ICCV (2017)
7. Dai, Y., Li, H., He, M.: A simple prior-free method for non-rigid structure-from-motion factorization. In: CVPR (2012)
8. Bregler, C., Hertzmann, A., Biermann, H.: Recovering non-rigid 3D shape from image streams. In: CVPR (2000)

9. Torresani, L., Hertzmann, A., Bregler, C.: Nonrigid structure-from-motion: estimating shape and motion with hierarchical priors. IEEE Trans. Pattern Anal. Mach. Intell. **30**(5), 878–892 (2008)

10. Del Bue, A.: A factorization approach to structure from motion with shape priors. In: CVPR (2008)

11. Garg, R., Roussos, A., Agapito, L.: Dense variational reconstruction of non-rigid surfaces from monocular video. In: CVPR (2013)

12. Fayad, J., Agapito, L., Del Bue, A.: Piecewise quadratic reconstruction of nonrigid surfaces from monocular sequences. In: Daniilidis, K., Maragos, P., Paragios, N. (eds.) ECCV 2010. LNCS, vol. 6314, pp. 297–310. Springer, Heidelberg (2010). https://doi.org/10.1007/978-3-642-15561-1_22

13. Agudo, A., Montiel, J., Agapito, L., Calvo, B.: Online dense non-rigid 3D shape and camera motion recovery. In: BMVC (2014)

14. Taylor, J., Jepson, A.D., Kutulakos, K.N.: Non-rigid structure from locally-rigid motion. In: CVPR (2010)

15. Bartoli, A., Pizarro, D., Collins, T.: A robust analytical solution to isometric shape-from-template with focal length calibration. In: ICCV (2013)

16. Ngo, T.D., Östlund, J.O., Fua, P.: Template-based monocular 3D shape recovery using Laplacian meshes. IEEE Trans. Pattern Anal. Mach. Intell. **38**(1), 172–187 (2016)

17. Chhatkuli, A., Pizarro, D., Bartoli, A., Collins, T.: A stable analytical framework for isometric shape-from-template by surface integration. IEEE Trans. Pattern Anal. Mach. Intell. **39**(5), 833–850 (2017)

18. Bartoli, A., Collins, T.: Template-based isometric deformable 3D reconstruction with sampling-based focal length self-calibration. In: CVPR (2013)

19. Chhatkuli, A., Pizarro, D., Collins, T., Bartoli, A.: Inextensible non-rigid shape-from-motion by second-order cone programming. In: CVPR (2016)

20. Perriollat, M., Hartley, R., Bartoli, A.: Monocular template-based reconstruction of inextensible surfaces. Int. J. Comput. Vis. **95**(2), 124–137 (2011)

21. Salzmann, M., Fua, P.: Linear local models for monocular reconstruction of deformable surfaces. IEEE Trans. Pattern Anal. Mach. Intell. **33**(5), 931–944 (2011)

22. Kumar, S., Dai, Y., Li, H.: Monocular dense 3D reconstruction of a complex dynamic scene from two perspective frames. In: ICCV (2017)

23. Russell, C., Yu, R., Agapito, L.: Video pop-up: monocular 3D reconstruction of dynamic scenes. In: Fleet, D., Pajdla, T., Schiele, B., Tuytelaars, T. (eds.) ECCV 2014. LNCS, vol. 8695, pp. 583–598. Springer, Cham (2014). https://doi.org/10.1007/978-3-319-10584-0_38

24. Bartoli, A., Gérard, Y., Chadebecq, F., Collins, T., Pizarro, D.: Shape-from-template. IEEE Trans. Pattern Anal. Mach. Intell. **37**(10), 2099–2118 (2015)

25. Vicente, S., Agapito, L.: Soft inextensibility constraints for template-free non-rigid reconstruction. In: Fitzgibbon, A., Lazebnik, S., Perona, P., Sato, Y., Schmid, C. (eds.) ECCV 2012. LNCS, vol. 7574, pp. 426–440. Springer, Heidelberg (2012). https://doi.org/10.1007/978-3-642-33712-3_31

26. Chhatkuli, A., Pizarro, D., Bartoli, A.: Stable template-based isometric 3D reconstruction in all imaging conditions by linear least-squares. In: CVPR (2014)

27. Parashar, S., Pizarro, D., Bartoli, A.: Isometric non-rigid shape-from-motion in linear time. In: CVPR (2016)

28. Xiao, J., Kanade, T.: Uncalibrated perspective reconstruction of deformable structures. In: Tenth IEEE International Conference on Computer Vision (ICCV 2005), vol. 1, 2, pp. 1075–1082 (2005)

29. Salzmann, M., Hartley, R., Fua, P.: Convex optimization for deformable surface 3-D tracking. In: ICCV (2007)
30. Akhter, I., Sheikh, Y., Khan, S., Kanade, T.: Trajectory space: a dual representation for nonrigid structure from motion. IEEE TPAMI **33**(7), 1442–1456 (2011)
31. Nistér, D.: Untwisting a projective reconstruction. Int. J. Comput. Vis. **60**(2), 165–183 (2004)
32. Chandraker, M., Agarwal, S., Kahl, F., Nistér, D., Kriegman, D.: Autocalibration via rank-constrained estimation of the absolute quadric. In: IEEE Conference on Computer Vision and Pattern Recognition, CVPR 2007, pp. 1–8. IEEE (2007)
33. Dijkstra, E.W.: A note on two problems in connexion with graphs. Numer. Math. **1**(1), 269–271 (1959)
34. Varol, A., Salzmann, M., Fua, P., Urtasun, R.: A constrained latent variable model. In: CVPR (2012)
35. Chhatkuli, A., Pizarro, D., Bartoli, A.: Non-rigid shape-from-motion for isometric surfaces using infinitesimal planarity. In: BMVC (2014)
36. White, R., Crane, K., Forsyth, D.: Capturing and animating occluded cloth. In: SIGGRAPH (2007)
37. Sundaram, N., Brox, T., Keutzer, K.: Dense point trajectories by GPU-accelerated large displacement optical flow. In: Daniilidis, K., Maragos, P., Paragios, N. (eds.) ECCV 2010. LNCS, vol. 6311, pp. 438–451. Springer, Heidelberg (2010). https://doi.org/10.1007/978-3-642-15549-9_32
38. Innmann, M., Zollhöfer, M., Nießner, M., Theobalt, C., Stamminger, M.: VolumeDeform: real-time volumetric non-rigid reconstruction. In: Leibe, B., Matas, J., Sebe, N., Welling, M. (eds.) ECCV 2016. LNCS, vol. 9912, pp. 362–379. Springer, Cham (2016). https://doi.org/10.1007/978-3-319-46484-8_22
39. Gotardo, P.F., Martinez, A.M.: Computing smooth time trajectories for camera and deformable shape in structure from motion with occlusion. IEEE Trans. Pattern Anal. Mach. Intell. **33**(10), 2051–2065 (2011)
40. Chhatkuli, A., Pizarro, D., Collins, T., Bartoli, A.: Inextensible non-rigid structure-from-motion by second-order cone programming. IEEE Trans. Pattern Anal. Mach. Intell. **1**(99), PP (2017)

R2P2: A ReparameteRized Pushforward Policy for Diverse, Precise Generative Path Forecasting

Nicholas Rhinehart[1,2](✉) ⓘ, Kris M. Kitani[1] ⓘ, and Paul Vernaza[2] ⓘ

[1] Carnegie Mellon University, Pittsburgh, PA 15213, USA
nrhineha@cs.cmu.edu
[2] NEC Labs America, Cupertino, CA 95014, USA

Abstract. We propose a method to forecast a vehicle's ego-motion as a distribution over spatiotemporal paths, conditioned on features (*e.g.*, from LIDAR and images) embedded in an overhead map. The method learns a policy inducing a distribution over simulated trajectories that is both "diverse" (produces most of the likely paths) and "precise" (mostly produces likely paths). This balance is achieved through minimization of a symmetrized cross-entropy between the distribution and demonstration data. By viewing the simulated-outcome distribution as the *pushforward* of a simple distribution under a simulation operator, we obtain expressions for the cross-entropy metrics that can be efficiently evaluated and differentiated, enabling stochastic-gradient optimization. We propose concrete policy architectures for this model, discuss our evaluation metrics relative to previously-used degenerate metrics, and demonstrate the superiority of our method relative to state-of-the-art methods in both the KITTI dataset and a similar but novel and larger real-world dataset explicitly designed for the vehicle forecasting domain.

Keywords: Trajectory forecasting · Imitation learning
Generative modeling · Self-driving vehicles

1 Introduction

We consider forecasting a vehicle's trajectory (*i.e.*, predicting future paths). Forecasts can be used to foresee and avoid dangerous scenarios, plan safe paths, and model driver behavior. Context from the environment informs prediction, *e.g.* a map populated with features from imagery and LIDAR. We would like to learn a context-conditioned *distribution* over spatiotemporal trajectories to

Electronic supplementary material The online version of this chapter (https:// doi.org/10.1007/978-3-030-01261-8_47) contains supplementary material, which is available to authorized users.

V. Ferrari et al. (Eds.): ECCV 2018, LNCS 11217, pp. 794–811, 2018.
https://doi.org/10.1007/978-3-030-01261-8_47

represent the many possible outcomes of the vehicle's future. With this distribution, we can perform inference tasks such as *sampling* a set of plausible paths, or *assigning a likelihood* to a particular observed path. Sampling suggests routes and visualizes the model; assigning likelihood helps measure the model's quality.

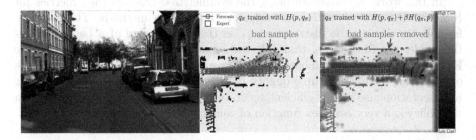

Fig. 1. *Left:* Natural image input. *Middle:* generated trajectories (red circles) and true, expert future (blue squares) overlaid on LIDAR map. *Right:* Generated trajectories respect approximate prior, here a "cost function," overlaid as a heatmap. Making the expert paths likely corresponds to $\min_\pi H(p, q_\pi)$. Only producing likely paths corresponds to steering the trajectories away from unlikely territory via $\min_\pi H(q_\pi, \tilde{p})$. Doing both, *i.e.* producing most of the likely paths while mostly producing likely paths corresponds to $\min_\pi H(p, q_\pi) + \beta H(q_\pi, \tilde{p})$. (Color figure online)

Our key motivation is to learn a trajectory forecasting model that is simultaneously "diverse"—covering all the modes of the data distribution—and "precise" in the sense that it rarely generates bad trajectories, such as trajectories that intersect obstacles. Covering the modes ensures the model can generate samples similar to human behavior. High "precision" ensures the model rarely generates samples very different from human behavior, which is important when samples are used for a downstream task. Figure 1 contrasts a model trained to cover modes, versus a model trained to cover modes *and* generate good samples, which generates less samples that hit perceived obstacles. To these ends, we define our model q_π as the trajectory distribution induced by *rolling out* (simulating) a stochastic one-step policy π for T steps to produce a trajectory sample x, and we propose choosing π to minimize the following symmetrized cross-entropy objective, where ϕ denotes the scene context:

$$\min_\pi \underbrace{\mathbb{E}_{x \sim p} - \log q_\pi(x|\phi)}_{H(p, q_\pi)} + \beta \underbrace{\mathbb{E}_{x \sim q_\pi} - \log \tilde{p}(x|\phi)}_{H(q_\pi, \tilde{p})}. \tag{1}$$

The $H(p, q_\pi)$ term encourages the model q_π to cover all the modes of the distribution of true driver behavior p, by heavily penalizing q for assigning a low density to any observed example from p. However, $H(p, q_\pi)$ *is insensitive to samples from* q, so optimizing it alone can yield a model that generates some "low-quality" samples. The $H(q_\pi, \tilde{p})$ term penalizes q_π for generating "low-quality" samples (where an approximate data density $\tilde{p}$ is low). However, $H(q_\pi, \tilde{p})$ *is insensitive* to *mode loss* of $\tilde{p}$. Therefore, *we optimize them simultaneously to collect the complementary benefits and mitigate the complementary shortcomings of each term*. This motivation is illustrated in Fig. 2. As the *true* density function, p, is unavailable, we cannot evaluate $H(q_\pi, p)$. Instead, we substitute a learned approximation, $\tilde{p}$, that is simple and visually interpretable as a "cost map."

In this work, we advocate using the symmetrized cross-entropy metrics *for both training and evaluation* of trajectory forecasting methods. This is made feasible by viewing the distribution q_π as the *pushforward* of a base distribution under the function g_π that *rolls-out* (simulates) a stochastic policy π (see Fig. 3b). This idea (also known as the *reparameterization trick*, [9,22]) enables optimization of model-sample quality metrics such as $H(q_\pi, \tilde{p})$ with SGD. Our representation also admits efficient accurate computation of $H(p, q_\pi)$, even when the policy is a very complex function of context and past state, such as a CNN.

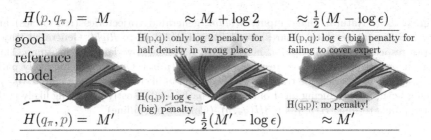

$$H(p, q_\pi) = M \qquad\qquad \approx M + \log 2 \qquad \approx \tfrac{1}{2}(M - \log \epsilon)$$

good reference model

H(p,q): only log 2 penalty for half density in wrong place

H(p,q): log ϵ (big) penalty for failing to cover expert

H(q,p): log ϵ (big) penalty

H($\overline{\text{q}}$,p): no penalty!

$$H(q_\pi, p) = M' \qquad\qquad \approx \tfrac{1}{2}(M' - \log \epsilon) \qquad \approx M'$$

Fig. 2. Illustration of the complementarity of cross-entropies $H(p, q_\pi)$ (top) and $H(q_\pi, p)$ (bottom). Dashed lines show past vehicle path. Light blue lines delineate samples from the data (expert) distribution p. Samples from the model q_π are depicted as red lines. Green areas represent obstacles (areas with low p). The left figure shows cross-entropy values for a reference model. Other figures show poor models and their effects on each metric. ϵ is a very small nonnegative number. (Color figure online)

We present the following novel contributions: (1) recognize and address the diversity-precision trade-off of generative forecasting models and formulating a symmetrized cross-entropy training objective to address it; (2) propose to train a policy to induce a roll-out distribution minimizing this objective; (3) use the pushforward parameterization to render inference and learning in this model efficient; (4) refine an existing deep imitation learning method (GAIL) based on our parameterization; (5) illuminate deficiencies of previously-used trajectory forecasting metrics; (6) outperform state-of-the-art forecasting and imitation learning methods, including our improvements to GAIL; (7) present CALIFORE-CASTING, a novel large scale dataset designed specifically for vehicle ego-motion forecasting.

2   Related Work

Trajectory Forecasting prior work spans two primary domains: trajectories of vehicles, and trajectories of people. The method of [26] predicts future trajectories of wide-receivers from surveillance video. In [5,23,28,50] future pedestrian trajectories are predicted from surveillance video. Deterministic vehicle predictions are produced in [18], and deterministic pedestrian trajectories are produced in [3,30,34]. However, non-determinism is a key aspect of forecasting: the future is generally uncertain, with many plausible outcomes. While several approaches forecast distributions over trajectories [12,25], global sample quality and likelihood have not been considered or measured, hindering performance evaluation.

Activity Forecasting is distinct from trajectory forecasting, as it predicts categorical activities. In [17,24,35,36], future activities are predicted via classification-based approaches. In [33], a first-person camera wearer's future goals are forecasted with Inverse Reinforcement Learning (IRL). IRL has been applied to predict and control robot, taxi, and pedestrian behavior [23,31,52].

Imitation Learning can be used to frame our problem: learn a model to mimic an agent's behavior from a set of demonstrations [2]. One subtle difference is that in forecasting, we are not required to actually execute our plans in the real world. IRL is a form of imitation learning in which a reward function is learned to model demonstrated behavior. In the IRL method of [49], a cost map representation is used to plan vehicle trajectories. However, no time-profile is represented in the predictions, preventing use of time-profiled metrics and modeling. GAIL [16,27] is also a form of IRL, yet its adversarial framework and policy optimization are difficult to tune and lead to slow convergence. By adding the assumption of model dynamics, we derive a new differentiable GAIL training approach, supplanting the noisy, inefficient policy gradient search procedure. We show this easier-to-train approach achieves better performance in our domain.

Image Forecasting methods generate full image or video representations of predictions, endowing their samples with interpretability. In [43–45], unsupervised model are learned to generate sequences and representations of future images. In [46], surveillance image predictions of vehicles are formed by smoothing a patch across the image. [42,47] also predict future video frames with an intermediate pose prediction. In [10], predictions inform a robot's behavior, and in [40], policy representations for imitation and reinforcement learning are guided by a future observation forecasting objective. In [7], image boundaries are predicted. One drawback to image-based forecasting methods is difficulty in measurement, a drawback shared by many popular generative models.

Generative models have surged in popularity [9,13,14,16,25,44,51]. However, one major difficulty is *performance evaluation*. Most popular models are quantified through heuristics that attempt to measures the "quality" of model samples [25]. In image generation, the Inception score is a popular heuristic [38]. These fail to measure the learned distribution's likelihood, the gold standard of evaluating probabilistic models. Notable exceptions include [9,20], which also leverage invertible pushforward models to perform exact likelihood inference.

3   Approach

We approach the forecasting problem from an *imitation learning* perspective, learning a *policy* (state-to-action mapping) π that mimics the actions of an expert

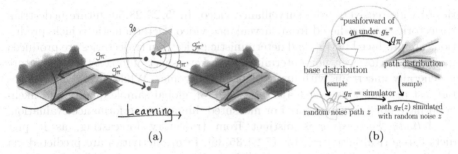

Fig. 3. (a) Consider making trajectories inside the yellow region on the road likelier by increasing $\log q_\pi(x)$ for the demonstration $x \sim p$ inside the region. This is achieved by making an infinitesimal region around $g_\pi^{-1}(x)$ more likely under q_0 by moving the region (yellow parallelogram, size proportional to $|\det J_{g_\pi}|^{-1}$) towards a mode of q_0 (here, the center of a Gaussian), and making the region bigger. Increasing $\log \tilde{p}(x)$ for some sample $x \sim q_\pi$ is equivalent to sampling a (red) point z from q_0 and adjusting π so as to increase $\log \tilde{p}(q_0(z))$. (b) Pushing forward a base distribution to a trajectory distribution. (Color figure online)

in varying contexts. We are given a set of training episodes (a short car path trajectory) $\{(x, \phi)_n\}_{n=1}^N$. Each episode $(x, \phi)_n$ has $x \in \mathbb{R}^{T \times 2}$ as a sequence of T two-dimensional future vehicle locations and ϕ as an associated set of side information. In our implementation, ϕ contains the past path of the car and a feature grid derived from LIDAR and semantic segmentation class scores. The grid is centered on the vehicle's position at $t = 0$ and is aligned with its heading.

Repeatedly applying the policy π from a start state with the context ϕ results in a distribution $q_\pi(x|\phi)$ over trajectories x, since our policy is stochastic. Similarly, the training set is drawn from a *data distribution* $p(x|\phi)$. We therefore train π so as to minimize a divergence between q_π and p. This divergence consists of a weighted combination of the cross-entropies $H(p, q_\pi)$ and $H(q_\pi, \tilde{p})$. We precisely describe forms of $\tilde{p}$ in Sect. 3.1, for now, conceptualize it as a distribution that assigns low likelihood to trajectories passing through obstacles. In the following, Φ denotes the distribution of ground-truth features:

$$\min_\pi \mathbb{E}_{\phi \sim \Phi} \left[-\mathbb{E}_{x \sim p(\cdot|\phi)} \log q_\pi(x|\phi) - \beta \mathbb{E}_{x \sim q_\pi(\cdot|\phi)} \log \tilde{p}(x|\phi) \right]. \qquad (2)$$

The motivation for this objective is illustrated in Fig. 2. The two factors are complementary. $H(p, q_\pi)$ is intuitively similar to *recall* in binary classification, in that it is very sensitive to the model's ability to produce all of the examples in the dataset, but is relatively insensitive to whether the model produces examples that are unlikely under the data. $H(q_\pi, \tilde{p})$ is intuitively similar to *precision* in that it is very sensitive to whether the model produces samples likely under $\tilde{p}$, but is insensitive to q_π's likelihood to produce *all* samples in the dataset.

3.1   Pushforward Distribution Modeling

Optimizing Eq. (2) presents at least two challenges: we must be able to evaluate $q_\pi(x|\phi)$ at arbitrary x in order to compute $H(p, q_\pi)$, and we must be able to differentiate the expression $\mathbb{E}_{x \sim q_\pi(\cdot|\phi)} \log \tilde{p}(x|\phi)$. We address these issues by constructing a learnable bijection, g_π between samples from q_π and samples from a simple noise distribution q_0, as illustrated in Fig. 3b; in our construction, the bijection is interpreted as a simulator mapping noise to simulated outcomes. This assumption allows us to evaluate the required expressions and derivatives via the change-of-variables formula and the *reparameterization trick*.

Specifically, let $g_\pi(z; \phi)$: $\mathbb{R}^{T \times 2} \to \mathbb{R}^{T \times 2}$ be a simulator mapping noise sequences $z \sim q_0$ and scene context ϕ to forecasted outcomes x. Then the distribution of forecasted outcomes $q_\pi(x|\phi)$ is fully determined by q_0 and g_π: this distribution, q_π, is known as the *pushforward* of q_0 under g_π in measure theory. If g_π is differentiable and invertible ($z = g_\pi^{-1}(x; \phi)$), then q_π is obtained by the change-of-variables formula for multivariate integration:

$$q_\pi(x|\phi) = q_0\big(g_\pi^{-1}(x; \phi)\big)\big|\det J_{g_\pi}(g_\pi^{-1}(x; \phi))\big|^{-1}, \qquad (3)$$

where $J_{g_\pi}(g_\pi^{-1}(x; \phi))$ is the Jacobian of g_π evaluated at $g_\pi^{-1}(x; \phi)$. This resolves both of the aforementioned issues: we can evaluate q_π and we can rewrite $\mathbb{E}_{x \sim q_\pi} \log \tilde{p}(x)$ as $\mathbb{E}_{z \sim q_0} \log \tilde{p}(g_\pi(z; \phi))$, since $g_\pi(z; \phi) \sim q_\pi$. The latter allows us to move derivatives w.r.t. π inside the expectation, as q_0 does not depend on π. Figure 3a illustrates how this aids learning. Equation (2) can then be rewritten as:

$$\min_\pi - \mathop{\mathbb{E}}_{\phi \sim \Phi} \mathop{\mathbb{E}}_{x \sim p(\cdot|\phi)} \log \frac{q_0(g_\pi^{-1}(x; \phi))}{\big|\det J_{g_\pi}(g_\pi^{-1}(x; \phi))\big|} - \beta \mathop{\mathbb{E}}_{z \sim q_0} \log \tilde{p}(g_\pi(z; \phi)|\phi). \qquad (4)$$

We note ours is not the only way to represent q_π and optimize Eq. (2). As long as q_π is analytically differentiable in the parameters, we may also apply REINFORCE [48] to obtain the required parameter derivatives. However, empirical evidence and some theoretical analysis suggests that the reparameterization-based gradient estimator typically yields lower-variance gradient estimates than REINFORCE [11]. This is consistent with the results we obtained in Sect. 4.

An Invertible, Differentiable Simulator. In order to exploit the pushforward density formula (3), we must ensure g_π is invertible and differentiable. Inspired by [9,21], we define g_π as an autoregressive map, representing the evolution of a controlled, discrete-time stochastic dynamical system with additive noise. Denoting $[x_1, \ldots, x_{t-1}]$ as $x_{1:t-1}$, and $[x_{1:t-1}, \phi]$ as ψ_t, the system is:

$$x_t \triangleq \mu_t^\pi(\psi_t; \theta) + \sigma_t^\pi(\psi_t; \theta)z_t, \qquad (5)$$

where $\mu_t^\pi(\psi_t; \theta) \in \mathbb{R}^2$ and $\sigma_t^\pi(\psi_t; \theta) \in \mathbb{R}^{2 \times 2}$ represent the stochastic one-step *policy*, and θ its parameters. The context, ϕ, is given in the form of a past trajectory $x_{\text{past}} = x_{-H_{\text{past}}+1:0} \in \mathbb{R}^{2H_{\text{past}}}$, and overhead feature map $M \in \mathbb{R}^{H_{\text{map}} \times W_{\text{map}} \times C}$:

$\phi = (x_{\text{past}}, M)$. Note that the case $\sigma^\pi = 0$ would correspond to simply evolving the state by repeatedly applying μ^π—though this case is not allowed, as then g_π would not be invertible. However, as long as σ_t^π is invertible for all x, then g_π is invertible, and it is differentiable in x as long as μ^π and σ^π are differentiable in x. Since x_{τ_1} is not a function of x_{τ_2} for $\tau_1 < \tau_2$, the determinant of the Jacobian of this map is easily computed, because it is triangular (see supplement). Thus, we can easily compute terms in Eq. 4 via the following:

$$[g_\pi^{-1}(x)]_t = z_t = \sigma_t^\pi(\psi_t; \theta)^{-1}(x_t - \mu_t^\pi(\psi_t; \theta)), \tag{6}$$

$$\log \left| \det J_{g_\pi}(g_\pi^{-1}(x; \phi)) \right| = \sum_t \log \left| \det(\sigma_t^\pi(\psi_t; \theta)) \right|. \tag{7}$$

We note that q_π can also be computed via the chain rule of probability. For instance, if $z_t \sim$ is standard normal, then the marginal distributions are

$$q_\pi(x_t | \psi_t) = \mathcal{N}(x_t; \mu = \mu_t^\pi(\psi_t; \theta), \Sigma = \sigma_t^\pi(\psi_t; \theta)\sigma_t^\pi(\psi_t; \theta)^\top). \tag{8}$$

However, since it is still necessary to compute g_π in order to optimize $H(q_\pi, \tilde{p})$, we find it simplifies the implementation to compute q_π in terms of g_π.

Prior Approximation of the Data Distribution. Evaluating $H(q_\pi, p)$ directly is unfortunately impossible, since we cannot evaluate the data distribution p's PDF. We therefore propose approximating it with a very simple density estimator $\tilde{p} \approx p$ trained independently and then fixed while training q_π. Simplicity reduces sample-induced variance in fitting $\tilde{p}$—crucial, because if $\tilde{p}$ severely underestimates p in some region R due to sampling error, then $H(q_\pi, \tilde{p})$ will erroneously assign a large penalty to samples from q_π landing in R.

We consider two options for $\tilde{p}$—first, simply using a kernel density estimator with a relatively large bandwidth. Since we have only one training sample per episode, this reduces to a single-kernel model. Choosing an isotropic Gaussian kernel, $H(q_\pi, \tilde{p})$ becomes $\mathbb{E}_{\hat{x} \sim q_\pi(\cdot | \phi)} \|x - \hat{x}\|^2 / \sigma^2$, where (x, ϕ) constitutes an episode from the data. The net objective (2) in this case corresponds to $H(p, q_\pi)$ plus a mean squared distance penalty between model samples and data samples.

The second possibility is making an i.i.d. approximation; *i.e.*, parameterizing $\tilde{p}$ as $\tilde{p}(x \mid \phi) = \prod_t \tilde{p}_c(x_t \mid \phi)$. We proceed by discretizing x_t in a large finite region centered at the vehicle's start location; $\tilde{p}_c$ then corresponds to a categorical distribution with L classes representing the L possible locations. Training the i.i.d. model can then be reduced to training $\tilde{p}_c$ via logistic regression:

$$\min_{\tilde{p}} -\mathbb{E}_{x \sim p} \log \tilde{p}(x) = \max_\theta \mathbb{E}_{x \sim p} \sum_t -C_\theta(x_t, \phi) - \log \sum_{y=1}^L \exp -C_\theta(y, \phi), \tag{9}$$

where $C_\theta = -\log \tilde{p}_c$ can be thought of as a *spatial cost function* with parameters θ. We found it useful to decompose $C_\theta(y)$ as a sum $C_\theta^0(y) + C_\theta^1(y, \phi)$, where $C_\theta^0 \in \mathbb{R}^L$ is thought of as a non-contextual location prior, and $C_\theta^1(y, \phi)$ has the form of a convolutional neural network acting on the spatial feature grid in ϕ and producing a grid of scores $\in \mathbb{R}^L$. Figure 4 shows example learned $C_\theta^1(\cdot, \phi)$.

3.2   Policy Modeling

We turn to designing learnable functions μ_t^π and σ_t^π. Across our three models, we use the following expansion: $\mu_t^\pi(\psi_t) = 2x_t - x_{t-1} + \hat{\mu}_t^\pi(\psi_t)$. The first terms correspond to a *constant velocity step* $(x_t + (x_t - x_{t-1}))$, and let us interpret $\hat{\mu}_t^\pi$ as a *deterministic acceleration*. Altogether, the update equation (Eq. 5) mimics Verlet integration [41], used to integrate Newton's equations of motion.

"Linear": The simplest model uses $\hat{\mu}_t^\pi, S_t$ linear in ψ_t:

$$\hat{\mu}_t^\pi(\psi_t) = Ah_t + b_0, \quad S_t(\psi_t) = Bh_t + b_1, \tag{10}$$

with $A \in \mathbb{R}^{2\times 2H}$, $h_t = x_{t-H:t-1} \in \mathbb{R}^{2H}$, $B \in \mathbb{R}^{4\times 2H}$, $b_i \in \mathbb{R}^{2H}$, and $S_t(\psi_t) \in \mathbb{R}^{2\times 2}$. To produce $\sigma_t^\pi \in \text{PD}$, we use the matrix exponential [29]: $\sigma_t^\pi = \text{expm}(S_t + S_t^\top)$, which we found to optimize more efficiently than $\sigma_t^\pi = S_t S_t^\top$.

(a) CALIFORECASTING Prior Examples   (b) KITTI Prior Examples

Fig. 4. The prior penalizes positions corresponding to obstacles (white: high cost, black: low cost). The demonstrated expert trajectory is shown in each scene.

"Field": The Linear model ignores M: it has no environment perception. We designed a CNN model that takes in M and outputs $O \in \mathbb{R}^{H_{\text{map}} \times W_{\text{map}} \times 6}$. The 6 channels in O are used to form the 6 components of μ_t^π and S_t in the following way. To ensure differentiability, the values in O are bilinearly interpolated at the current rollout position, x_t in the spatial dimensions (H_{map} and W_{map}) of O.

"RNN": The Linear and Field models reason with different contextual inputs: Linear uses the past, and CNN uses the feature map M. We developed a joint

model to reason with both. M is passed through a CNN similar to Field's. The past is encoded with a GRU-RNN. Both featurizations inform a GRU-RNN that produces μ_t^π, S_t. See Fig. 5 and the supplementary material for details.

3.3 GAIL and Differentiable GAIL

As a deep generative approach to imitation learning, our method is comparable to Generative Adversarial Imitation Learning (GAIL [16]). GAIL is model-free: it is agnostic to model dynamics. However, this flexibility requires an expensive model-free policy gradient method, whereas the approach we have proposed is fully differentiable. The model-free approach is significantly disadvantaged in sample complexity [19,32] in theory and practice. By assuming the dynamics are known and differentiable, as described in Sect. 3.1, we can also derive a version of GAIL that does not require model-free RL, since we can apply the reparameterization trick to differentiate the generator objective with respect to the policy parameters. A similar idea was explored for general imitation learning in [6]. We refer to this method as **R2P2 GAIL**. As our experiments show, R2P2 GAIL significantly outperforms standard GAIL, and our main model (R2P2) significantly outperforms and is easier to train than both GAIL and R2P2 GAIL.

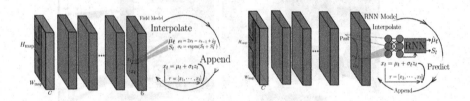

Fig. 5. RNN and CNN Policy models. The Field model produces a map of values to use for producing μ^π, σ^π through interpolation. The RNN model uses the same base as the Field model as well as information from the past trajectory to decode a featurized context representation and previous state to next μ^π, σ^π.

4 Experiments

We implemented R2P2 and baselines with the primary aim of testing the following hypotheses. (1) The ability to exactly evaluate the model PDF should help R2P2 obtain better solutions than methods that do not use exact PDF inference (which includes GAIL). (2) The optimization of $H(p, q_\theta)$ should be correlated with the model's ability to cover the training data, in analogy to recall in binary classification. (3) Including $H(q_\theta, \tilde{p})$ in our objective should improve sample quality relative to methods without this term, as it serves a purpose analogous to precision in binary classification. (4) R2P2 GAIL will outperform GAIL through its more efficient optimization scheme.

4.1   The CaliForecasting Dataset

Current public datasets such as KITTI are suboptimal for the purpose of validating these hypotheses. KITTI is relatively small and was not designed with forecasting in mind. It contains relatively few episodes of subjectively interesting, nonlinear behavior. For this reason, we collected a novel dataset specifically designed for the ego-motion forecasting task, which we make public. The data is similar to KITTI in sensor modalities, but the data was collected so as to maximize the number of intersections, turning, and other subjectively interesting episodes. The data was collected with a sensor platform consisting of a Ford Transit Connect van with two Point Grey Flea3 cameras mounted on the roof in a wide-baseline configuration, in addition to a roof-mounted Velodyne VLP16 LIDAR unit and an IMU. The initial version of the dataset consists of three continuous driving sequences, each about one hour long, collected in mostly suburban areas of northern California (USA). The data was post-processed to produce a collection of episodes in the previously described format. The overhead feature map was populated by pretraining a semantic segmentation network [39], evaluating it on the sequences, correlating them with the LIDAR point cloud, and binning the resulting semantic segmentation scores in addition to a height-above-ground plane feature. With a subsampling scheme of 2 Hz, CALIFORECASTING consists of over 10,000 training, 1,200 validation and 1,200 testing examples. The KITTI splits, in comparison, are about 3,100 training, 140 validation, and slightly less than 500 test examples with a subsampling scheme of 1 Hz.

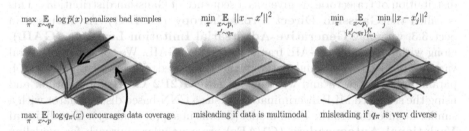

$$\max_{\pi} \; \mathbb{E}_{x \sim q_{\pi}} \log \tilde{p}(x) \; \text{penalizes bad samples} \qquad \min_{\substack{\pi \\ x' \sim q_{\pi}}} \; \mathbb{E}_{x \sim p,} \; ||x - x'||^2 \qquad \min_{\pi} \; \mathbb{E}_{\substack{x \sim p, \\ \{x'_i \sim q_{\pi}\}_{i=1}^K}} \; \min_{j} ||x - x'_j||^2$$

$$\max_{\pi} \; \mathbb{E}_{x \sim p} \log q_{\pi}(x) \; \text{encourages data coverage} \qquad \text{misleading if data is multimodal} \qquad \text{misleading if } q_{\pi} \text{ is very diverse}$$

Fig. 6. Possible objectives and their attributes. $\min_{\theta} H(p, q_{\theta})$ encourages data coverage, $\min_{\theta} H(q_{\theta}, \tilde{p})$ penalizes bad samples. Measuring mean squared error is misleading when the data is multimodal, and measuring mean squared error of the best sample fails to measure quality of samples far from the demonstrations.

4.2   Metrics and Baselines

Metrics Our primary metrics are the cross-entropy distribution metrics $H(p, q_{\theta})$ and $H(q_{\theta}, \tilde{p})$. Note that $H(p, q_{\theta})$ is lower-bounded by the entropy of p, $H(p)$, by Gibbs' inequality. Subtracting this quantity (computing KL) would be ideal; unfortunately, since $H(p)$ is unknown, we simply report $H(p, q_{\theta})$. We also note that cross-entropy is *not* coordinate-invariant: we use path coordinates in an ego-centric frame that is a rotation and translation away from UTM coordinates (in meters) and report cross-entropy values for path distributions in this frame.

A subtle related issue is that $H(p, q_\theta)$ may be unbounded below since $H(p)$ may be arbitrarily negative. This phenomenon arises when the support of p is restricted to a submanifold—for example, if for $x \sim p$ and $x_1 - x_2 = b$, the distribution $q(x) \propto \exp(-\|x_1 - x_2 - b\|^2/\epsilon^2 + \|x\|^2/2)$ achieves arbitrarily low values of $H(p, q_\theta)$. We resolve this by slightly perturbing training and testing samples from p: *i.e.* instead of computing $H(p, q_\theta)$, we compute $-\mathbb{E}_{\eta \sim \mathcal{N}(0, \epsilon I)} \mathbb{E}_{x \sim p} \log q(x + \eta)$ for $\epsilon = 0.001$. This is lower-bounded by $H(\mathcal{N}(0, \epsilon I))$, which resolves the issue.

We include two commonly used sample metrics [3,8,15,25,37], despite the shortcomings illustrated in Fig. 6. We measure the quality of the "best" sample from K samples from q_θ: $\hat{X}$, relative to the demonstrated sample x via $\mathbb{E}_{\hat{X}_k \sim q_\theta} \min_{\hat{x} \in \hat{X}_k} \|x - \hat{x}\|^2$ (known as "minMSD"). This metric fails to measure the quality of *all* of the samples, and thus can be exploited by an approach that predicts samples that are mostly poor. Additionally, we measure the mean distance to the demonstration of all samples in $\hat{X}$: $\frac{1}{K} \sum_{k=1}^{K} \|x - \hat{x}_k\|^2$ (known as "meanMSD"). This metric is misleading if the data is multimodal, as the metric rewards predicting the mean, as opposed to covering multiple outcomes. *Due to the deficiencies of these common sample-based metrics for measuring the quality of multimodal predictions, we advocate supplementing sample-based metrics with the complementary cross-entropy metrics used in this work.*

Baselines. We construct a simple a unimodal baseline: given the context, the distribution of trajectories is given as a sequence of Gaussian distributions. This is called the **Gaussian Direct Cross-Entropy (DCE-G)**. As discussed in Sect. 3.3, we apply **Generative Adversarial Imitation Learning (GAIL)**, along with our modified GAIL framework, R2P2 GAIL. We constructed several variants of GAIL: with and without the (improved) Wasserstein-GAN [4,14] parameterization, with and without our novel **R2P2 GAIL** formulation, and using the standard MLP discriminator, versus a CNN-based discriminator with a similar architecture to the Field model (details in supplementary). **Conditional Variational Autoencoders (CVAEs)** are a popular approach for modeling generative distributions conditioned on context. We follow the CVAE construction of [25] in our implementation. One key distinguishing factor is that CVAEs cannot perform *exact inference* by construction: given an arbitrary sample, a CVAE cannot produce a PDF value. Quantification of CVAE performance is thus required to be approximation-based, or sample-based. Our approaches are implemented in Tensorflow [1]. Architectural details are given in the supplement.

4.3   Cross Trimodal Experiments

Our first set of experiments is designed to test the multimodal modeling capability of each approach in an easy domain. The contextual information is fixed – a single four-way intersection, along with three demonstrated outcomes: turning left, turning right, and going straight. Figure 7 shows qualitative and quantitative

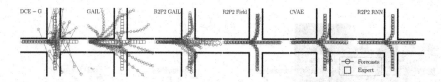

Fig. 7. CROSS Trimodal Evaluation. *Top:* Qualitative results. *Bottom:* Quantitative results. A * indicates R2P2, and a † indicates using a WGAN Discriminator.

results. We see that several approaches fail to model multimodality well in this scenario. RNN. The models that can perform exact inference (all except CVAE) cover the modes with different success, as measured by Test $-H(p, q_\theta)$. We observe the models minimizing $H(p, q_\theta)$ cover the data well, supporting hypothesis 2 (coverage hypothesis), and outperform both GAIL approaches, supporting hypothesis 1 (exact inference hypothesis). We observer R2P2 GAIL outperforms GAIL in this scenario, supporting hypothesis 4 (optimization hypothesis). We also note the failure of DCE-G: its unimodal model is too restrictive for covering the diverse demonstrated behavior.

Table 1. CALIFORECASTING and KITTI evaluation, $K = 12$

CALIFORECASTING approach	Test $-H(p, q_\theta)$	Test minMSD	Test meanMSD	Test $-H(q_\theta, \tilde{p})$
DCE-G	-1.604 ± 0.02	4.953 ± 0.18	11.66 ± 0.27	-129.2 ± 0.43
GAIL-WG [16]	27.43 ± 0.03	9.117 ± 0.27	36.77 ± 2.50	-221.5 ± 2.40
CVAE [25]	$\approx 10.1 \pm 0.9$	1.680 ± 0.12	9.961 ± 0.25	-122.2 ± 0.48
R2P2 GAIL-WG	45.55 ± 0.07	5.529 ± 0.33	25.12 ± 0.80	-152.1 ± 1.00
R2P2 GAIL-WG CNN	43.55 ± 0.08	4.937 ± 0.26	26.59 ± 0.96	-154.3 ± 1.20
R2P2 Linear	64.02 ± 0.11	2.339 ± 0.14	10.51 ± 0.39	-144.5 ± 1.00
R2P2 Linear $\beta = 0.1$	61.57 ± 0.10	2.387 ± 0.13	11.27 ± 0.44	-134.1 ± 0.76
R2P2 Field	54.56 ± 0.11	2.171 ± 0.13	11.59 ± 0.39	-142.5 ± 0.75
R2P2 Field $\beta = 0.1$	53.88 ± 0.11	2.162 ± 0.11	10.87 ± 0.39	-132.8 ± 0.54
R2P2 RNN	$\mathbf{70.20} \pm 0.11$	$\mathbf{1.530} \pm 0.12$	11.25 ± 0.29	-125.0 ± 0.53
R2P2 RNN $\beta = 0.1$	66.89 ± 0.12	1.860 ± 0.14	10.68 ± 0.30	$\mathbf{-119.0} \pm 0.44$
R2P2 RNN $\gamma = 1.0$	65.12 ± 0.12	1.661 ± 0.11	$\mathbf{8.542} \pm 0.22$	-124.8 ± 0.48
KITTI approach	Test $-H(p, q_\theta)$	Test minMSD	Test meanMSD	Test $-H(q_\theta, \tilde{p})$
DCE-G	-1.884 ± 0.03	6.217 ± 0.30	15.20 ± 0.62	-137.0 ± 0.72
GAIL-WG [16]	39.53 ± 0.11	5.517 ± 0.34	20.08 ± 2.00	-188.8 ± 1.76
CVAE [25]	$\approx 9.22 \pm 0.9$	1.436 ± 0.15	9.593 ± 0.52	-133.8 ± 1.21
R2P2 GAIL-WG	47.45 ± 0.16	4.062 ± 0.25	13.80 ± 1.10	-168.9 ± 1.50
R2P2 GAIL-WG CNN	42.49 ± 0.12	4.601 ± 0.30	19.87 ± 1.34	-164.2 ± 1.43
R2P2 Linear	62.39 ± 0.14	2.438 ± 0.16	16.16 ± 1.26	-163.4 ± 1.50
R2P2 Linear $\beta = 0.1$	63.82 ± 0.16	2.587 ± 0.15	28.33 ± 1.40	-151.1 ± 1.40
R2P2 Field	64.71 ± 0.18	1.717 ± 0.13	10.34 ± 0.59	-139.2 ± 1.10
R2P2 Field $\beta = 0.1$	62.79 ± 0.29	1.639 ± 0.13	10.92 ± 0.59	$\mathbf{-126.9} \pm 0.77$
R2P2 RNN	$\mathbf{67.70} \pm 0.20$	1.574 ± 0.15	10.46 ± 0.57	-131.6 ± 0.91
R2P2 RNN $\beta = 0.3$	65.80 ± 0.21	$\mathbf{1.282} \pm 0.09$	$\mathbf{9.352} \pm 0.55$	-130.8 ± 0.87

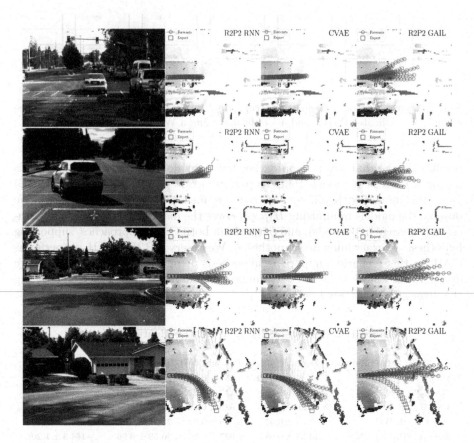

Fig. 8. CALIFORECASTING Results. Comparison of R2P2 RNN (middle-left), CVAE (middle-right), and R2P2 GAIL (right). Trajectory samples are overlaid on overhead LIDAR map, colored by height. *Bottom two rows:* Comparison of $\beta = 0$ (top) and $\beta = 0.1$ (bottom), overlaid on $\tilde{p}$ cost map. The cost map improves sample quality. (Color figure online)

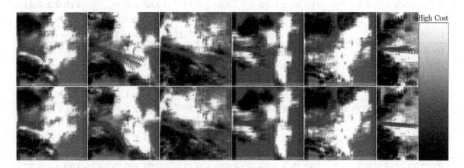

Fig. 9. Comparison of using β on CALIFORECASTING test data. *Top row:* With $\beta = 0$, some trajectories are forecasted into obvious obstacles. *Bottom row:* With $\beta \neq 0$, many forecasted trajectories do not hit obstacles.

4.4 CaliForecasting Experiments and KITTI Experiments

We conducted larger-scale experiments designed to test our hypotheses. First, we trained $\tilde{p}$ on each dataset by the procedure described in Sect. 3.1. As discussed, our goal was to develop a simple model to minimize overfitting: we used a 3-layer Fully Convolutional NN. In the resulting spatial "cost" maps, we observe the model's ability to perceive obstacles in its assignment of low cost to on-road regions, and high-cost to clearly visible obstacles (*e.g* Fig. 4). We performed hyperparameter search for each method, and report the mean and its standard error of test set metrics corresponding to each method's best validation loss in Table 1. These results provide us with a rich set of observations. Of the three baselines, none catastrophically failed, with CVAE most often generating the cleanest samples. Across datasets and metrics, our approach achieves performance superior to the three baselines and our improved GAIL approach. By minimizing $H(p, q_\theta)$, our approach results in higher Test $-H(p, q_\theta)$ than all GAIL approaches, supporting the coverage and optimization hypotheses. We find that by incorporating our prior with nonzero β, hypothesis 3 is supported: our model architectures can improve the quality of its samples as measured by the Test $-H(q_\theta, \tilde{p})$. We observe that our GAIL optimization approach yields higher Test $-H(p, q_\theta)$, supporting hypothesis 4. We plot means and its standard error of the minMSD metrics as a function of K in Fig. 10 for all 3 datasets.

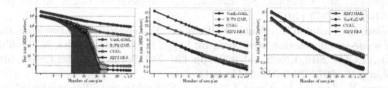

Fig. 10. Test $\min_k$ MSD vs. K on CROSS, CALIFORECASTING, and KITTI.

We also find that qualitatively, our approach usually generates the best samples with diversity along multiple paths and precision in its tendency to avoid obstacles. Figure 8 illustrates results on our dataset for our method, CVAE, and our improved GAIL approach. Figure 9 illustrates qualitative examples for how incorporating nonzero β can improve sample quality.

5 Conclusions

This work has raised the previously under-appreciated issue of balancing diversity and precision in probabilistic trajectory forecasting. We have proposed a training a policy to induce a simulated-outcome distribution that minimizes a symmetrized cross-entropy objective. The key technical step that made this possible was a parameterizing the model distribution as the pushforward of a simple base distribution under the simulation operator. The relationship of this method to deep generative models was noted, and we showed that part of our full model enhances an existing deep imitation learning method. Empirically, we demonstrated that the pushforward parameterization enables reliable optimization of the objective, and that the optimized model has the desired characteristics of both covering the training data and generating high-quality samples. Finally, we introduced a novel large-scale, real-world dataset designed specifically for the vehicle ego-motion forecasting problem.

Acknowledgment. This work was sponsored in part by JST CREST (JPMJCR14E1) and IARPA (D17PC00340).

References

1. Abadi, M., et al.: Tensorflow: a system for large-scale machine learning. OSDI **16**, 265–283 (2016)
2. Abbeel, P., Ng, A.Y.: Apprenticeship learning via inverse reinforcement learning. In: Proceedings of the Twenty-First International Conference on Machine Learning, p. 1. ACM (2004)
3. Alahi, A., Goel, K., Ramanathan, V., Robicquet, A., Fei-Fei, L., Savarese, S.: Social LSTM: human trajectory prediction in crowded spaces. In: Proceedings of the IEEE Conference on Computer Vision and Pattern Recognition, pp. 961–971 (2016)
4. Arjovsky, M., Chintala, S., Bottou, L.: Wasserstein GAN. arXiv preprint arXiv:1701.07875 (2017)
5. Ballan, L., Castaldo, F., Alahi, A., Palmieri, F., Savarese, S.: Knowledge transfer for scene-specific motion prediction. In: Leibe, B., Matas, J., Sebe, N., Welling, M. (eds.) ECCV 2016. LNCS, vol. 9905, pp. 697–713. Springer, Cham (2016). https://doi.org/10.1007/978-3-319-46448-0_42
6. Baram, N., Anschel, O., Caspi, I., Mannor, S.: End-to-end differentiable adversarial imitation learning. In: International Conference on Machine Learning, pp. 390–399 (2017)
7. Bhattacharyya, A., Malinowski, M., Schiele, B., Fritz, M.: Long-term image boundary prediction. In: Thirty-Second AAAI Conference on Artificial Intelligence, AAAI (2017)
8. Bhattacharyya, A., Schiele, B., Fritz, M.: Accurate and diverse sampling of sequences based on a "best of many" sample objective. In: Proceedings of the IEEE Conference on Computer Vision and Pattern Recognition, pp. 8485–8493 (2018)
9. Dinh, L., Sohl-Dickstein, J., Bengio, S.: Density estimation using real nvp. arXiv preprint arXiv:1605.08803 (2016)
10. Finn, C., Levine, S.: Deep visual foresight for planning robot motion. In: IEEE International Conference on Robotics and Automation (ICRA), pp. 2786–2793. IEEE (2017)
11. Gal, Y.: Uncertainty in deep learning. Ph.D. thesis, University of Cambridge (2016)
12. Galceran, E., Cunningham, A.G., Eustice, R.M., Olson, E.: Multipolicy decision-making for autonomous driving via changepoint-based behavior prediction. In: Robotics: Science and Systems XI, Sapienza University of Rome, Rome, 13–17 July 2015. http://www.roboticsproceedings.org/rss11/p43.html

13. Grover, A., Dhar, M., Ermon, S.: Flow-GAN: bridging implicit and prescribed learning in generative models. arXiv preprint arXiv:1705.08868 (2017)
14. Gulrajani, I., Ahmed, F., Arjovsky, M., Dumoulin, V., Courville, A.C.: Improved training of Wasserstein GANs. In: Advances in Neural Information Processing Systems, pp. 5769–5779 (2017)
15. Gupta, A., Johnson, J.: Social GAN: socially acceptable trajectories with generative adversarial networks (2018)
16. Ho, J., Ermon, S.: Generative adversarial imitation learning. In: Advances in Neural Information Processing Systems, pp. 4565–4573 (2016)
17. Hoai, M., De la Torre, F.: Max-margin early event detectors. Int. J. Comput. Vis. 107(2), 191–202 (2014)
18. Jain, A., Singh, A., Koppula, H.S., Soh, S., Saxena, A.: Recurrent neural networks for driver activity anticipation via sensory-fusion architecture. In: IEEE International Conference on Robotics and Automation (ICRA), pp. 3118–3125. IEEE (2016)
19. Kakade, S.M., et al.: On the sample complexity of reinforcement learning. Ph.D. thesis (2003)
20. Kingma, D.P., Dhariwal, P.: Glow: generative flow with invertible 1 × 1 convolutions. arXiv preprint arXiv:1807.03039 (2018)
21. Kingma, D.P., Salimans, T., Jozefowicz, R., Chen, X., Sutskever, I., Welling, M.: Improved variational inference with inverse autoregressive flow. In: Advances in Neural Information Processing Systems, pp. 4743–4751 (2016)
22. Kingma, D.P., Welling, M.: Auto-encoding variational bayes. arXiv preprint arXiv:1312.6114 (2013)
23. Kitani, K.M., Ziebart, B.D., Bagnell, J.A., Hebert, M.: Activity forecasting. In: Fitzgibbon, A., Lazebnik, S., Perona, P., Sato, Y., Schmid, C. (eds.) ECCV 2012. LNCS, vol. 7575, pp. 201–214. Springer, Heidelberg (2012). https://doi.org/10.1007/978-3-642-33765-9_15
24. Lan, T., Chen, T.-C., Savarese, S.: A hierarchical representation for future action prediction. In: Fleet, D., Pajdla, T., Schiele, B., Tuytelaars, T. (eds.) ECCV 2014. LNCS, vol. 8691, pp. 689–704. Springer, Cham (2014). https://doi.org/10.1007/978-3-319-10578-9_45
25. Lee, N., Choi, W., Vernaza, P., Choy, C.B., Torr, P.H., Chandraker, M.: Desire: Distant future prediction in dynamic scenes with interacting agents (2017)
26. Lee, N., Kitani, K.M.: Predicting wide receiver trajectories in American football. In: IEEE Winter Conference on Applications of Computer Vision (WACV), pp. 1–9. IEEE (2016)
27. Li, Y., Song, J., Ermon, S.: Infogail: interpretable imitation learning from visual demonstrations. In: Advances in Neural Information Processing Systems, pp. 3815–3825 (2017)
28. Ma, W.C., Huang, D.A., Lee, N., Kitani, K.M.: Forecasting interactive dynamics of pedestrians with fictitious play. In: IEEE Conference on Computer Vision and Pattern Recognition (CVPR), pp. 4636–4644. IEEE (2017)
29. Najfeld, I., Havel, T.F.: Derivatives of the matrix exponential and their computation. Adv. Appl. Math. 16(3), 321–375 (1995)
30. Park, H.S., Hwang, J.J., Niu, Y., Shi, J.: Egocentric future localization. In: CVPR, vol. 2, p. 4 (2016)
31. Ratliff, N.D., Bagnell, J.A., Zinkevich, M.A.: Maximum margin planning. In: Proceedings of the 23rd International Conference on Machine Learning, pp. 729–736. ACM (2006)

32. Recht, B.: The policy of truth (2018). http://www.argmin.net/2018/02/20/reinforce/

33. Rhinehart, N., Kitani, K.M.: First-person activity forecasting with online inverse reinforcement learning. In: The IEEE International Conference on Computer Vision (ICCV), October 2017

34. Robicquet, A., Sadeghian, A., Alahi, A., Savarese, S.: Learning social etiquette: human trajectory understanding in crowded scenes. In: Leibe, B., Matas, J., Sebe, N., Welling, M. (eds.) ECCV 2016. LNCS, vol. 9912, pp. 549–565. Springer, Cham (2016). https://doi.org/10.1007/978-3-319-46484-8_33

35. Ryoo, M.S., Fuchs, T.J., Xia, L., Aggarwal, J.K., Matthies, L.H.: Robot-centric activity prediction from first-person videos: what will they do to me'. In: Proceedings of the Tenth Annual ACM/IEEE International Conference on Human-Robot Interaction, HRI 2015, Portland, 2–5 March 2015, pp. 295–302 (2015). https://doi.org/10.1145/2696454.2696462

36. Ryoo, M.S.: Human activity prediction: early recognition of ongoing activities from streaming videos. In: IEEE International Conference on Computer Vision (ICCV), pp. 1036–1043. IEEE (2011)

37. Sadeghian, A., Kosaraju, V., Gupta, A., Savarese, S., Alahi, A.: TrajNet: towards a benchmark for human trajectory prediction. arXiv preprint (2018)

38. Salimans, T., Goodfellow, I., Zaremba, W., Cheung, V., Radford, A., Chen, X.: Improved techniques for training GANs. In: Advances in Neural Information Processing Systems, pp. 2234–2242 (2016)

39. Szegedy, C., et al.: Going deeper with convolutions. In: CVPR (2015)

40. Venkatraman, A., et al.: Predictive-state decoders: encoding the future into recurrent networks. In: Advances in Neural Information Processing Systems, pp. 1172–1183 (2017)

41. Verlet, L.: Computer "experiments" on classical fluids. I. Thermodynamical properties of Lennard-Jones molecules. Phys. Rev. **159**(1), 98 (1967)

42. Villegas, R., Yang, J., Zou, Y., Sohn, S., Lin, X., Lee, H.: Learning to generate long-term future via hierarchical prediction. In: Proceedings of the 34th International Conference on Machine Learning, ICML 2017, Sydney, 6–11 August 2017, pp. 3560–3569 (2017). http://proceedings.mlr.press/v70/villegas17a.html

43. Vondrick, C., Pirsiavash, H., Torralba, A.: Anticipating visual representations from unlabeled video. In: Proceedings of the IEEE Conference on Computer Vision and Pattern Recognition, pp. 98–106 (2016)

44. Vondrick, C., Pirsiavash, H., Torralba, A.: Generating videos with scene dynamics. In: Advances in Neural Information Processing Systems, pp. 613–621 (2016)

45. Vondrick, C., Torralba, A.: Generating the future with adversarial transformers. In: IEEE Conference on Computer Vision and Pattern Recognition, CVPR 2017, Honolulu, 21–26 July 2017, pp. 2992–3000 (2017). https://doi.org/10.1109/CVPR.2017.319

46. Walker, J., Gupta, A., Hebert, M.: Patch to the future: unsupervised visual prediction. In: Proceedings of the IEEE Conference on Computer Vision and Pattern Recognition, pp. 3302–3309 (2014)

47. Walker, J., Marino, K., Gupta, A., Hebert, M.: The pose knows: video forecasting by generating pose futures. In: IEEE International Conference on Computer Vision (ICCV), pp. 3352–3361. IEEE (2017)

48. Williams, R.J.: Simple statistical gradient-following algorithms for connectionist reinforcement learning. Reinf. Learn. 5–32 (1992)

49. Wulfmeier, M., Rao, D., Wang, D.Z., Ondruska, P., Posner, I.: Large-scale cost function learning for path planning using deep inverse reinforcement learning. Int. J. Robot. Res. **36**(10), 1073–1087 (2017)
50. Xie, D., Todorovic, S., Zhu, S.C.: Inferring "dark matter" and "dark energy" from videos. In: IEEE International Conference on Computer Vision (ICCV), pp. 2224–2231. IEEE (2013)
51. Zhu, J., Park, T., Isola, P., Efros, A.A.: Unpaired image-to-image translation using cycle-consistent adversarial networks. In: IEEE International Conference on Computer Vision, ICCV 2017, Venice, 22–29 October 2017, pp. 2242–2251 (2017). https://doi.org/10.1109/ICCV.2017.244
52. Ziebart, B.D., Maas, A.L., Bagnell, J.A., Dey, A.K.: Maximum entropy inverse reinforcement learning. In: Proceedings of the Twenty-Third AAAI Conference on Artificial Intelligence, AAAI 2008, Chicago, 13–17 July 2008, pp. 1433–1438 (2008). http://www.aaai.org/Library/AAAI/2008/aaai08-227.php

Eliminating the Blind Spot: Adapting 3D Object Detection and Monocular Depth Estimation to 360° Panoramic Imagery

Grégoire Payen de La Garanderie$^{(\boxtimes)}$ ⓘ, Amir Atapour Abarghouei ⓘ,
and Toby P. Breckon ⓘ

Department of Computer Science, Durham University, Durham, UK
{gregoire.p.payen-de-la-garander,amir.atapour-abarghouei,
toby.breckon}@durham.ac.uk

Abstract. Recent automotive vision work has focused almost exclusively on processing forward-facing cameras. However, future autonomous vehicles will not be viable without a more comprehensive surround sensing, akin to a human driver, as can be provided by 360° panoramic cameras. We present an approach to adapt contemporary deep network architectures developed on conventional rectilinear imagery to work on equirectangular 360° panoramic imagery. To address the lack of annotated panoramic automotive datasets availability, we adapt contemporary automotive dataset, via style and projection transformations, to facilitate the cross-domain retraining of contemporary algorithms for panoramic imagery. Following this approach we retrain and adapt existing architectures to recover scene depth and 3D pose of vehicles from monocular panoramic imagery without any panoramic training labels or calibration parameters. Our approach is evaluated qualitatively on crowd-sourced panoramic images and quantitatively using an automotive environment simulator to provide the first benchmark for such techniques within panoramic imagery.

Keywords: Object detection · Panoramic imagery
Monocular 3D object detection · Style transfer · Monocular depth
Panoramic depth · 360 depth

1 Introduction

Recent automotive computer vision work (object detection [50,51], segmentation [3], stereo vision [38,49], monocular depth estimation [1,26,41]) has focused almost exclusively on the processing of forward-facing rectified rectilinear vehicle mounted cameras. Indeed by sharp contrast to the abundance

Electronic supplementary material The online version of this chapter (https://doi.org/10.1007/978-3-030-01261-8_48) contains supplementary material, which is available to authorized users.

V. Ferrari et al. (Eds.): ECCV 2018, LNCS 11217, pp. 812–830, 2018.
https://doi.org/10.1007/978-3-030-01261-8_48

of common evaluation criteria and datasets for the forward-facing camera case [2,4,16,18,19,39,48], there are no annotated evaluation datasets or frameworks for any of these tasks using 360° view panoramic cameras.

Fig. 1. Our monocular panoramic image approach. A: 3D object detection. B: depth recovery.

However, varying levels of future vehicle autonomy will require full 360° situational awareness, akin to that of the human driver of today, in order to be able to function across complex and challenging driving environments. One popularly conceived idea of capturing this awareness is to use active sensing in the form of 360°LIDAR, however this is currently an expensive, low-resolution method which does not encompass the richness of visual information required for high fidelity semantic scene understanding. An alternative is to fuse the information from multiple cameras surrounding the vehicle [29] and such methods have been used to fuse between a forward-facing camera and LIDAR [10,27]. However, here opportunities are lost to share visual information in early stages of the pipeline with further computational redundancy due to overlapping fields of view. Alternatively the imagery from a multiview setup can be stitched into a 360°panorama [5]. A roof mounted on-vehicle panoramic camera offers superior angular resolution compared to any LIDAR, is 1–2 orders of magnitude lower cost and provides rich scene colour and texture information that enables full semantic scene understanding [35].

Panoramic images are typically represented using an equirectangular projection (Fig. 1A); in contrast a conventional camera uses a rectilinear projection. In this projection, the image-space coordinates are proportional to latitude and longitude of observed points rather than the usual projection onto a focal plane as shown in Fig. 1A.

Recent work on panoramic images has largely focused on indoor scene understanding [61,63], panoramic to rectilinear video conversion [34,42,57] and dual camera 360° stereo depth recovery [30,46]. However, no work to date has explicitly tackled contemporary automotive sensing problems.

By contrast, we present an approach to adapt existing deep architectures, such as convolutional neural networks (CNN) [6,26], developed on rectilinear imagery to operate on equirectangular panoramic imagery. Due to the lack of explicit annotated panoramic automotive training datasets, we show how to reuse existing non-panoramic datasets such as KITTI [18,19] using style and projection transformations, to facilitate the cross-domain retraining of contemporary algorithms for panoramic imagery. We apply this technique to estimate the dense monocular depth (see example in Fig. 1B) and to recover the full 3D pose of vehicles (Fig. 1B) from panoramic imagery. Additionally, our work provides the first performance benchmark for the use of these techniques on 360° panoramic imagery acting as a key driver for future research on this topic. Our technique is evaluated qualitatively on crowd-sourced 360° panoramic images from Mapillary [45] and quantitatively using ground truth from the CARLA [13] high fidelity automotive environment simulator[1].

2   Related Work

Related work is considered within panoramic imagery (Sect. 2.1), monocular 3D object detection (Sect. 2.2), monocular depth recovery (Sect. 2.3) and domain adaptation (Sect. 2.4).

2.1   Object Detection Within Panoramic Imagery

Even though significant strides have been made in rectilinear image object proposal [33] and object detection methods utilizing deep networks [6,24,25,31,51, 55], comparatively limited literature exists within panoramic imagery.

Deng *et al.* [11] adapted, trained and evaluated Faster R-CNN [51] on a new dataset of 2,000 indoor panoramic images for 2D object detection. However their approach does not handle the special case of object wrap-around at the equirectangular image boundaries.

Recently object detection and segmentation has been applied directly to equirectangular panoramic images to provide object detection and saliency in the context of virtual cinematography [34,42] using pre-trained detectors such as Faster R-CNN [51]. Su and Grauman [56] introduce a Flat2Sphere technique to train a spherical CNN to imitate the results of an existing CNN facilitating large object detection at any angle.

In contemporary automotive sensing problems, the required vertical field of view is small as neither the view above the horizon nor the view directly underneath the camera have any useful information for those problems. Therefore, the additional complexity of the spherical CNN introduced by [56] is not needed in the specific automotive context. Instead we show how to reuse existing deep architectures without requiring any significant architectural changes.

---

[1] For future comparison our code, models and evaluation data is publicly available at: https://gdlg.github.io/panoramic.

2.2   Monocular 3D Object Detection

Prior work on 3D pose regression in panorama is mostly focused on indoor scene reconstruction such as PanoContext by Zhang *et al.* [63] and Pano2CAD by Xu *et al.* [61]. The latter retrieves the object poses by regression using a bank of known CAD (Computer-Aided Design) models. In contrast, our method does not require any *a priori* knowledge of the object geometry.

Contemporary end-to-end CNN driven detection approaches are based on the R-CNN architecture introduced by Girshick [23]. Successive improvements from Fast-RCNN [22] and Faster-RCNN [51] increased the performance by respectively sharing feature maps across proposals and generating the proposals using a Region Proposal Network (RPN) instead of traditional techniques based on sliding window. This allowed a unified end-to-end training of the network to solve the combined detection and classification tasks. More recently, Yang *et al.* [62] and Cai *et al.* [6] introduced a multi-scale approach by pooling the region proposals from multiple layers in order to reduce the number of proposals needed as well as to improve performance on smaller objects such as distant objects.

While most of the work has focused on 2D detection, the work of Chen *et al.* [9,10] leverages 3D pointcloud information gained either from stereo on LIDAR modalities to generate 3D proposals which are pruned using Fast R-CNN. Whereas these works use complex arrangements using stereo vision, handcrafted features or 3D model regression, recent advances [7,8,47] show that it is actually possible to recover the 3D pose from monocular imagery. Chen *et al.* [8] uses post-processing of the proposals within an energy minimization framework assuming that the ground plane is known. Chabot *et al.* [7] use 3D CAD models as templates to regress the 3D pose of an object given part detections; while Mousavian *et al.* [47] show the 3D pose can be recovered without any template assumptions using carefully-expressed geometrical constraints. In this work, we propose a new approach, similar to [47], however without explicitly-expressed geometrical constraints, which performs on both rectilinear and equirectangular panoramic imagery without any knowledge of the ground plane position with respect to the camera.

2.3   Monocular Depth Estimation

Traditionally dense scene depth is recovered using multi-view approaches such as structure-from-motion and stereo vision [54], relying on an explicit handling of geometrical constraints between multiple calibrated views. However recently with the advance of deep learning, it has been shown that dense scene depth can also be recovered from monocular imagery.

After the initial success of classical learning-based techniques such as [52,53], depth recovery was first approached as a supervised learning problem by the depth classifier of Ladický *et al.* [41] and deep learning-based approaches such as [15,43]. However, these techniques are based on the availability of high-quality ground truth depth maps, which are difficult to obtain. In order to combat the ground truth data issue, the method in [1] relies on readily-available high-resolution synthetic depth maps captured from a virtual environment and domain transfer to resolve the problem of domain bias.

On the other hand, other monocular depth estimation methods have recently emerged that are capable of performing depth recovery without the need for large quantities of ground truth depth data. Zhou et al. [64] estimate monocular depth and ego-motion using depth and pose prediction networks that are trained via view synthesis. The approach proposed in [40] utilizes a deep network semi-supervised by sparse ground truth depth and then reinforced within a stereo framework to recover dense depth information.

Godard et al. [26] train their model based on left-right consistency inside a stereo image pair during training. At inference time, however, the model solely relies on a single monocular image to estimate a dense depth map. Even though said approach is primarily designed to deal with rectilinear images, in this work we further adapt this model to perform depth estimation on equirectangular panoramic images.

2.4   Domain Adaptation and Style Transfer

Machine learning architectures trained on one dataset do not necessarily transfer well to a new dataset – a problem known as dataset bias [58] or covariate shift [28]. A simple solution to dataset bias would be fine-tuning the trained model using the new data but that often requires large quantities of ground truth, which is not always readily-available.

While many strategies have been proposed to reduce the feature distributions between the two data domains [12,21,44,59], a novel solution was recently proposed in [1] that uses image style transfer as a means to circumvent the data domain bias.

Image style transfer was first proposed by Gatys et al. [17] but since then remarkable advances have been made in the field [14,20,36,60]. In this work, we attempt to transform existing rectilinear training images (such as KITTI [18,19]) to share the same style as our panoramic destination domain (Mapillary [45]). However, these two datasets have been captured in different places and share no registration relationship. As demonstrated in [1,32], unpaired image style transfer solved by CycleGAN [65], can be used to transfer the style between two data domains that possess approximately similar content.

2.5   Proposed Contributions

Overall the main contributions, against the state of the art [6,13,18,19,26,26,47], presented in this work are:

- a novel approach to convert deep network architectures [6,26] operating on rectilinear images for equirectangular panoramic images based on style and projection transformations;
- a novel approach to reuse and adapt existing datasets [18,19] in order to train models for panoramic imagery;

- the subsequent application of these approaches for monocular 3D object detection using a simpler formulation than earlier work [47], additionally operable on conventional imagery without modification;
- further application of these techniques to monocular depth recovery using an adaptation of the rectilinear imagery approach of Godard *et al.* [26];
- provision of the first performance benchmark based on a new synthetic evaluation dataset (based on CARLA [13]) for this new challenging task of automotive panoramic imagery depth recovery and object detection evaluation.

3   Approach

We first describe the mathematical projections underlining rectilinear and equirectangular projections and the relationship between the two required to enable our approach within panoramic imagery (Sect. 3.1). Subsequently we describe the dataset adaptation (Sect. 3.2), its application to monocular 3D pose recovery (Sect. 3.3) and depth estimation (Sect. 3.4) and finally the architectural modifications required for inference within panoramic imagery (Sect. 3.5).

3.1   Rectilinear and Equirectangular Projections

Projection using a classical rectified rectilinear camera is typically defined in terms of its camera matrix P. Given the Cartesian coordinates (x, y, z) of a 3D scene point in camera space, its projection (u_{lin}, v_{lin}) is defined as:

$$\begin{bmatrix} u_{lin} \\ v_{lin} \end{bmatrix} = \left\lfloor P \cdot \begin{bmatrix} x \\ y \\ z \end{bmatrix} \right\rfloor \tag{1}$$

where $\lfloor \cdot \rfloor$ denotes the homogeneous normalization of the vector by its last component. The camera matrix P is conventionally defined as:

$$P = \begin{bmatrix} f & 0 & c_x \\ 0 & f & c_y \\ 0 & 0 & 1 \end{bmatrix} \tag{2}$$

where f and (c_x, c_y) are respectively the focal length and the principal point of the camera.

The rectilinear projection as defined in Eq. 1 is advantageous because the camera matrix P can be combined with further image and object space transformations into a single linear transformation followed by an homogeneous normalization. However, this transformation can also be written as:

$$\begin{bmatrix} u_{lin} \\ v_{lin} \end{bmatrix} = P \cdot \begin{bmatrix} x/z \\ y/z \\ 1 \end{bmatrix} \tag{3}$$

This formulation (Eq. 3) is convenient because the image-space coordinates are expressed in terms of the ratio x/z and y/z which are the same regardless of the distance from the 3D scene point to the camera.

In contrast, the equirectangular projection is defined in terms of the longitude and latitude of the point. The longitude and latitude, respectively (λ, ϕ), are defined as:

$$\lambda = \arctan x/z \qquad (4)$$

$$\phi = \arcsin y/r \quad \text{where } r = (x^2 + y^2 + z^2)^{\frac{1}{2}} \qquad (5)$$

The latitude definition in Eq. 5 can be conveniently rewritten in terms of the ratios x/z and y/z as in Eq. 3 for rectilinear projections:

$$\phi = \arcsin \frac{y/z}{r} \quad \text{where } r = (x/z^2 + y/z^2 + 1^2)^{\frac{1}{2}} \qquad (6)$$

For the sake of simplicity, this computation of the latitude and longitude from the Cartesian coordinates can be represented as a function Γ:

$$\begin{bmatrix} \lambda \\ \phi \end{bmatrix} = \Gamma \left(\begin{bmatrix} x \\ y \\ z \end{bmatrix} \right) = \Gamma \left(\begin{bmatrix} x/z \\ y/z \\ 1 \end{bmatrix} \right) \qquad (7)$$

Finally we define an image transformation matrix T_{equi} which transforms the longitude and latitude to image space coordinates (u_{equi}, v_{equi}):

$$\begin{bmatrix} u_{equi} \\ v_{equi} \\ 1 \end{bmatrix} = T_{equi} \cdot \begin{bmatrix} \lambda \\ \phi \\ 1 \end{bmatrix} = T_{equi} \cdot \Gamma \left(\begin{bmatrix} x/z \\ y/z \\ 1 \end{bmatrix} \right) \qquad (8)$$

The matrix T_{equi} can be defined as:

$$T_{equi} = \begin{bmatrix} \alpha & 0 & c_\lambda \\ 0 & \alpha & c_\phi \\ 0 & 0 & 1 \end{bmatrix} \qquad (9)$$

where α is an angular resolution parameter akin to the focal length. Like the focal length, it can be defined in terms of the field of view:

$$\alpha = \text{fov}_\lambda / w = \text{fov}_\phi / h \qquad (10)$$

where $\text{fov}_\lambda, \text{fov}_\phi, w, h$ are respectively the image horizontal field of view, vertical field of view; width and height. In contrast to rectilinear imagery where the focal length is difficult to determine without any kind of camera calibration, the equirectangular imagery, commonly generated by panoramic cameras from the raw dual-fisheye pair, can be readily used without any prior calibration because the angular resolution $\alpha = 2\pi / w$ depends only on the image width. Therefore, approaches that would require some knowledge of the camera intrinsics of rectilinear images (*e.g.* monocular depth estimation) can be readily used on any 360° panoramic image without any prior calibration.

By coupling the definitions of both the rectilinear and equirectangular projections in terms of the ratios x/z and y/z (Eqs. 3 and 8), we establish the relationship between the coordinates in the rectilinear projection and equirectangular projection for the given matrices P and T_{equi}:

$$\begin{bmatrix} u_{equi} \\ v_{equi} \\ 1 \end{bmatrix} = T_{equi} \cdot \Gamma \left(P^{-1} \cdot \begin{bmatrix} u_{lin} \\ v_{lin} \\ 1 \end{bmatrix} \right) \tag{11}$$

This enables us to reproject an image from one projection to another, such as from the rectilinear image (Fig. 2A) to an equirectangular image (Fig. 2C) and vice versa—a key enabler for the application of our approach within panoramic imagery.

3.2 Dataset Adaptation

In our approach, the source domain is the KITTI [18,19] dataset of rectilinear images captured using a front-facing camera rig (1242 × 375 image resolution; 82.5° horizontal FoV and 29.7° vertical FoV); while our target domain consist of 30,000 images from the Mapillary [45] crowd-sourced street-level imagery (2048 × 300 image resolution; 360° × 52.7° FoV). These latter images are cropped vertically from 180° down to 52.7° which is more suitable for automotive problems. This reduced panorama has an angular coverage 7.7 times larger than our source KITTI imagery. Due to the lack of annotated labels for our target domain, we adapt the source domain dataset to train deep architectures for panoramic imagery via a methodology based on projection and style transformations.

Due to dataset bias [58], training on the original source domain is unlikely to perform well on the target domain. Furthermore our target is relatively low resolution and has numerous compression artefacts not present in the source domain

Fig. 2. Output of each step of the adaptation of an image from the KITTI dataset: A: No transformation, B: Style-transfer, C: Projection-transfer, D: Style and projection

– present due to the practicality of 360° image transmission and storage. To improve generalization to the target domain, we transform the source domain to look similar to imagery from our target domain via a two-step process.

The first step transfers the style of our target domain (reprojected as rectilinear images) onto each image from the source domain (Fig. 2A); resulting images are shown in Fig. 2B. We use the work of Zhu *et al.* on CycleGAN [65] to learn a transformation back and forth between the two unpaired domains. Subsequently, this transformation model is used to transfer the style of our target domain onto all the images from our source domain. In essence, the style transfer introduces a tone mapping and imitates compression artifacts present in most panoramic images while preserving the actual geometry. Without the use of style transfer, the weights are biased toward high-quality imagery and perform poorly on low-quality images.

The second step reprojects the style-transferred images (Fig. 2B) and annotations from the source domain rectilinear projection to an equirectangular projection (Fig. 2D). The transformed images represent small subregions (FoV: 82.5° × 29.7°) of a larger panorama. While this set of transformed images does not cover the full panorama, we find that they are sufficient to train deep architectures that perform well on full size panoramic imagery.

3.3   3D Object Detection

For 3D detection, we use a network by Cai *et al.* [6] based on Faster R-CNN [51]. This network generates a sequence of detection proposals using a Region Proposal Network (RPN) and then pools a subregion around each proposal to further regress the proposal 2D location. We extend this network to support 3D object pose regression. Uniquely, our extended network can be used on either rectilinear or equirectangular imagery without any changes to the network itself, instead only requiring a change to the interpretation of the output for subsequent rectilinear or equirectangular imagery use.

While Mousavian *et al.* [47] shows that 3D pose can be estimated without any assumptions of known 3D templates, their algorithm relies on geometrical properties. In contrast, we regress the 3D pose directly, simplifying the computation and making it easier to adapt to equirectangular images.

Here, we directly regress the 3D dimensions (width, length and height) in meters of each object using a fully-connected layer as well as the orientation as per [47]. Moreover, instead of relying on geometrical assumptions, we also regress the object disparity $d_{lin} = \frac{r}{f}$ which is the inverse of the distance r multiplied by the focal length f. For equirectangular imagery, we use a similar definition $d_{equi} = \frac{r}{\alpha}$ substituting the angular resolution for the focal length. Using a fully-connected layer connected to the last common layer defined in [6], we learn coefficients a, b such that the disparity d can be expressed as:

$$d = ah_{roi} + b \tag{12}$$

where h_{roi} is the height of the region proposal generated by the RPN. To simplify the computation, we also learn the 2D projection of the centre of the object onto the image (u, v) using another fully-connected layer. As a result, we can recover the actual 3D position (x, y, z) using:

$$[x, y, z]^T = r \cdot u[P^{-1} \cdot [u_{lin}, v_{lin}, 1]^T] \qquad rectilinear\ case \qquad (13)$$

$$[x, y, z]^T = r \cdot u[\Gamma^{-1}(T_{equi}^{-1} \cdot [u_{equi}, v_{equi}, 1]^T)] \quad equirectangular\ case \qquad (14)$$

where $u[v] = \frac{v}{\|v\|}$ is the unit vector in the direction of v.

For network training of our model, we additionally use data augmentation including image cropping and resizing as defined by [6]. Any of those operations on the image must be accompanied by the corresponding transformation of the corresponding camera matrix P or T_{equi} in order to facilitate effective training.

As noted by Mousavian et al. [47], distant objects (far) pose a significant challenge for reliable detection of the absolute orientation (i.e. relative front to back directional pose). Confronted with such an ambiguity (absolute directional orientation), a naive regression using the mean-square error would choose the average of the two extremas rather than the most likely extrema. To circumvent this problem, given the object yaw θ (orientation on the ground plane), we instead learn $c = \cos^2 \theta$ an $s = \sin^2 \theta$ which are both independent of the directionality. Noting that $\cos^2 \theta + \sin^2 \theta = 1$, c and s can be very conveniently learned with a fully-connected layer followed by a *Softmax()* layer. For each pair (s, c), there are four possible angles each in a different quadrant depending on the sign of the sine and cosine:

$$\hat{\theta} = \operatorname{atan2}(\pm\sqrt{s}, \pm\sqrt{c}) \qquad (15)$$

We further discriminate between the four quadrants:

$$\{(-1, -1), (-1, 1), (1, -1), (1, 1)\} \qquad (16)$$

using a separate classifier consisting of a fully-connected layer followed by a *Softmax()* classification layer.

Our entire network, comprising the architecture of [6] and our 3D pose regression extension, is fine-tuned end-to-end using a multi-task loss over 6 sets of heterogeneous network outputs: *class* and *quadrant classification* are learned via cross entropy loss while *bounding-box position, object centre, distance, orientation* are dependent on a mean-square loss. As a result, it would be time-consuming to manually tune via multi-task loss weights, therefore we use the methodology of [37] to dynamically adjust the multi-task weights during training based on homoscedastic uncertainty without any use of manual hyperparameters.

3.4   Monocular Depth Recovery

We rely on the approach of Godard et al. [26] which was originally trained and tested on the rectilinear stereo imagery of the KITTI dataset [19]. We reuse the same architecture and retrain it on our domain-adapted KITTI dataset constructed using the methodology of Sect. 3.2.

Following from the original work [26], the loss function is based on a left-right consistency check between a pair of stereo images. In our new dataset, both stereo images have been warped to an equirectangular projection as well as depth smoothness constraints. While Godard *et al.* uses the stereo disparity $d_{stereo} = \frac{fB}{zw}$ where f is the focal length, B the stereo baseline and w the width of the image, we replace the focal length with the angular resolution: $d_{equi} = \frac{\alpha B}{rw}$.

Given a point $p_l = (u_l, v_l)^T$, the corresponding point $p_r = (u_r, v_r)^T$ for a given disparity d can be calculated as:

$$p_r = T_{equi} \cdot \Gamma \left[u \left[\Gamma^{-1}(T_{equi}^{-1} \cdot p_l) \right] + \left[\frac{d_{equi} w}{\alpha}, 0, 0 \right]^T \right] \tag{17}$$

with definitions as per Sect. 3.1. The corresponding point p_r in Eq. 17 is differentiable w.r.t. d_{equi} and is used for the left/right consistency check instead of the original formulation presented in [26]. This alternative formulation explicitly takes into account that the epipolar lines in a conventional rectilinear stereo setup are transformed to epipolar curves within panoramic imagery, hence enabling the adaptation of monocular depth prediction [26] to this case.

3.5   360° Network Adaptation

While the trained network can be used as is [11,34] without any further modification, objects overlapping the left and right extremities of the equirectangular image would be split into two objects; one of the left, and one on the right (as depicted in Fig. 3(a), bottom left). Moreover information would not flow from one side of the image to the other side of the image—at least in the early feature detection layers. As a result, the deep architecture would "see" those objects as if heavily occluded. Therefore, it is more difficult to detect objects overlapping the image boundary leading to decreased overall detection accuracy and recall.

A cropped equirectangular panorama can be folded into a 360° ring shown in Fig. 3(a) by stitching the left and right edges together. A 2D convolution on this

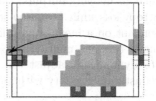

(a) A 360° equirectangular image can be folded over itself until the ends meet.

(b) A 3 × 3 convolution kernel, a column of padding copied from the other side is added at each extremity

Fig. 3. Convolutions are computed seamlessly across horizontal image boundaries using our proposed padding approach.

ring is equivalent to padding the left and right side of the equirectangular image with respective pixels from the right and left side as if the image was tiled (as illustrated on Fig. 3(b) for 3×3 convolutions). This horizontal ring-padding is hence used on all convolutional layers instead of the conventional zero-padding to eliminate these otherwise undesirable boundary effects.

For 3D detection, our proposed approached based on Faster R-CNN [51] generates a sequence of detection proposals and subsequently pools a subregion around each proposal to further regress the final proposal location, class and 3D pose. To adapt this operation, instead of clamping subregion coordinates by the equirectangular image extremities, we instead wrap horizontally the coordinates of each pixel within the box:

$$u_{wrap} \equiv u \ (\mathrm{mod} \ w) \tag{18}$$

where u is the horizontal coordinate of the pixel, u_{wrap} the wrapped horizontal coordinate within the image and w the image width.

As a result of this approach, we are hence able to hide the image boundary, as a result, enabling a true 360° processing of the equirectangular imagery.

4 Evaluation

We evaluate our approach both qualitatively on panoramic images from the crowd-sourced street-level imagery of Mapillary [45] as well as quantitatively using synthetic data generated using the CARLA [13] automotive environment simulator[2].

4.1 Qualitative Evaluation

As discussed in Sect. 2.4, we qualitatively evaluate our method using 30,000 panoramic images (Miami, USA) from the crowd-sourced street-level imagery of Mapillary [45]. Figure 4 shows our depth recovery and 3D object detection results on a selection of images of representative scenes from the data. Ring-padding naturally enforces continuity across the right/left boundary, for instance, zero-padding can prevent detection of vehicles crossing the image boundary (Fig. 5A) whereas ring-padding seamlessly detect such vehicle (Fig. 5C). Similarly zero-padding introduces depth discontinuities on the boundary (Fig. 5B) whereas ring-padding enforces depth continuity (Fig. 5D).

The algorithm is able to successfully estimate the 3D pose of vehicles and recover scene depth. However the approach fails on vehicles which are too close to the camera, almost underneath the camera. Indeed those view angles from above are not available in the narrow vertical field of view of the KITTI benchmark. Following the conventions of the KITTI dataset, any vehicles less than 25 pixels in image height were ignored during training. Due to the lower resolutions of the

---

[2] For future comparison our code, models and evaluation data is publicly available at: https://gdlg.github.io/panoramic.

panoramic images, an average-size vehicle (about 2 m height) with an apparent height of 25 pixels in KITTI is approximately at a distance of 56.6 m, whereas the same vehicle in a panoramic image will stand at 26 m. As a result, the range of the algorithm is reduced even though this is not a fundamental limitation of the approach itself. Rather, we expect this maximum distance to be increased as the resolution of the panoramic imagery is increased.

Further results are available in the supplementary video.

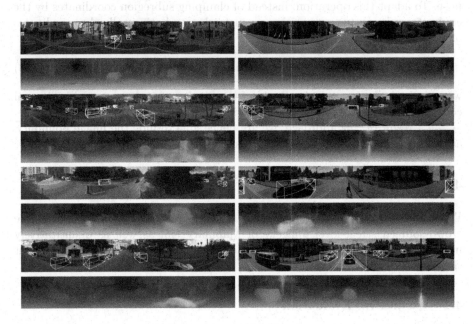

Fig. 4. Monocular depth recovery and 3D object detection with our approach. Left: Real-world images. Right: Synthetic images.

4.2 Quantitative Evaluation Methodology

Due to the lack of available annotated automotive panoramic imagery dataset, we evaluate our algorithm on synthetic data generated using the CARLA automotive environment simulator [13] adapted for panoramic imagery rendering

Fig. 5. Right/left boundary effect. A, B: Zero-padding; C, D: Ring-padding.

using the same format as our qualitative dataset. Due to lack of variety, our dataset based on CARLA is not suitable for training purposes, while it is suitable for cross-dataset validation. Following KITTI conventions, we filtered out vehicles less than 25 pixels in height from our detection results.

Table 1. 3D Object detection (mAP) results; and depth recovery results using metrics defined by [15]. Training dataset: C: CARLA, M: Mapillary, K: KITTI

Transformation	Dataset	Detection[a]	Depth Error Metrics[b]				Depth Acc.[a]
		mAP	Abs. rel.	Sq. rel.	RMSE	RMSE log	$\delta < 1.25$
none	K	0.336	0.247	7.652	3.484	0.465	0.697
proj	K	0.244	0.251	7.381	3.451	0.445	0.732
style	C	0.355	0.262	7.668	3.601	0.480	0.686
style	M	0.359	0.257	7.937	3.634	0.474	0.682
style	M+C	0.378	0.230	6.338	3.619	0.474	0.679
style & proj.	C	0.259	0.292	9.649	3.660	0.469	0.723
style & proj.	M	0.308	0.300	10.467	3.798	0.473	0.719
style & proj.	M+C	0.344	0.231	6.377	3.598	0.463	0.716

[a]Higher, better
[b]Lower, better

Table 1 shows the *mean average precison* (mAP) using an *intersection over union* (IoU) of 0.5 across variations of our algorithm on 8,000 images. Overall, the projection transformation during training impairs the results by about 10% points. Our best results come from the combined style-transferred training dataset consisting of both Mapillary and CARLA (4% points increased compared to original) whilst training on the CARLA-adapted dataset alone increases the performance by 2% points. This is due to the simplistic rendering and lack of variety of the synthetic dataset which impairs the style transfer. As a result, the CARLA-adapted dataset significantly boosts the accuracy for very low recall; however, it also reduces the recall ability of the network (Fig. 6(a)). The model trained on the CARLA-adapted dataset achieves a mAP of 0.82 on our evaluation set of the adapted images but only 0.35 on the actual CARLA dataset which shows that the style transfer is somewhat limited. Qualitatively, style transfer toward the Mapillary dataset, which is of similar scene complexity to KITTI, is significantly better than CARLA. By contrast, the combined dataset is able to outperform on both metrics (Fig. 6(a)).

The monocular depth estimation results are shown in Table 1 for 200 images (for distances <50 m). Similar to our detection result, using CARLA-adapted imagery impairs the performance. Using projection transformation, we see an increase of about 2.5% points in accuracy. Overall, those differences are smaller than those on object detection across the different transformations (Table 1).

From our results, we can clearly see that we have identified a new and challenging problem within the automotive visual sensing space (Table 1) when compared to the rectilinear performance of contemporary benchmarks [18,19].

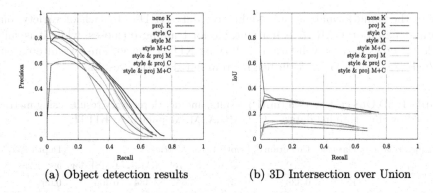

(a) Object detection results   (b) 3D Intersection over Union

Fig. 6. Object detection results

5   Conclusion

We have adapted existing deep architectures and training datasets, proven on forward-facing rectilinear camera imagery, to perform on panoramic images. The approach is based on domain adaptation using geometrical and style transforms and novel updates to training loss to accommodate panoramic imagery. Our approach is able to recover the monocular depth and the full 3D pose of vehicles.

We have identified panoramic imagery has a new set of challenging problems in automotive visual sensing and provide the first performance benchmark for the use of these techniques on 360° panoramic imagery, with a supporting dataset, hence acting as a key driver for future research on this topic.

References

1. Atapour-Abarghouei, A., Breckon, T.P.: Real-time monocular depth estimation using synthetic data with domain adaptation. In: Proceedings of the Computer Vision and Pattern Recognition. IEEE (2018)
2. Austrian Institute of Technology: WildDash benchmark (2018). http://www.wilddash.cc/
3. Badrinarayanan, V., Kendall, A., Cipolla, R.: SegNet: a deep convolutional encoder-decoder architecture for image segmentation. IEEE Trans. Pattern Anal. Mach. Intell. **39**(12), 2481–2495 (2015). https://doi.org/10.1109/TPAMI.2016.2644615
4. Brostow, G.J., Fauqueur, J., Cipolla, R.: Semantic object classes in video: a high-definition ground truth database. Pattern Recognit. Lett. **30**, 88–97 (2009). https://doi.org/10.1016/j.patrec.2008.04.005
5. Brown, M., Szeliski, R., Winder, S.: Multi-image matching using multi-scale oriented patches. In: IEEE Computer Society Conference on Computer Vision and Pattern Recognition (CVPR 2005), vol. 1, pp. 510–517, June 2005. https://doi.org/10.1109/CVPR.2005.235

6. Cai, Z., Fan, Q., Feris, R.S., Vasconcelos, N.: A unified multi-scale deep convolutional neural network for fast object detection. In: Leibe, B., Matas, J., Sebe, N., Welling, M. (eds.) ECCV 2016. LNCS, vol. 9908, pp. 354–370. Springer, Cham (2016). https://doi.org/10.1007/978-3-319-46493-0_22
7. Chabot, F., Chaouch, M., Rabarisoa, J., Teulière, C., Chateau, T.: Deep MANTA: a coarse-to-fine many-task network for joint 2D and 3D vehicle analysis from monocular image. In: IEEE Conference on Computer Vision and Pattern Recognition (CVPR), pp. 1827–1836 (2017). https://doi.org/10.1109/CVPR.2017.198
8. Chen, X., Kundu, K., Zhang, Z., Ma, H., Fidler, S., Urtasun, R.: Monocular 3D object detection for autonomous driving. In: Proceedings of the IEEE Conference on Computer Vision and Pattern Recognition, pp. 2147–2156 (2016)
9. Chen, X., et al.: 3D object proposals for accurate object class detection. In: Advances in Neural Information Processing Systems, pp. 424–432 (2015)
10. Chen, X., Ma, H., Wan, J., Li, B., Xia, T.: Multi-view 3D object detection network for autonomous driving. In: IEEE Conference on Computer Vision and Pattern Recognition (CVPR), pp. 6526–6534 (2017). https://doi.org/10.1109/CVPR.2017.691
11. Deng, F., Zhu, X., Ren, J.: Object detection on panoramic images based on deep learning. In: 3rd International Conference on Control, Automation and Robotics (ICCAR), pp. 375–380, April 2017. https://doi.org/10.1109/ICCAR.2017.7942721
12. Donahue, J., Krähenbühl, P., Darrell, T.: Adversarial feature learning. CoRR abs/1605.09782 (2016)
13. Dosovitskiy, A., Ros, G., Codevilla, F., Lopez, A., Koltun, V.: CARLA: an open urban driving simulator. CoRL (2017)
14. Dumoulin, V., Shlens, J., Kudlur, M.: A learned representation for artistic style. arXiv:1610.07629 [cs], October 2016
15. Eigen, D., Puhrsch, C., Fergus, R.: Depth map prediction from a single image using a multi-scale deep network. In: Proceedings of the 27th International Conference on Neural Information Processing Systems, NIPS 2014, vol. 2. pp. 2366–2374. MIT Press (2014)
16. Fisher, Y.: Berkeley data drive (2018). http://data-bdd.berkeley.edu/
17. Gatys, L.A., Ecker, A.S., Bethge, M.: Image style transfer using convolutional neural networks. In: IEEE Conference on Computer Vision and Pattern Recognition, pp. 2414–2423, June 2016. https://doi.org/10.1109/CVPR.2016.265
18. Geiger, A., Lenz, P., Stiller, C., Urtasun, R.: Vision meets robotics: the KITTI dataset. Int. J. Robot. Res. **32**(11), 1231–1237 (2013). https://doi.org/10.1177/0278364913491297
19. Geiger, A., Lenz, P., Urtasun, R.: Are we ready for autonomous driving? The KITTI vision benchmark suite. In: IEEE Conference on Computer Vision and Pattern Recognition, pp. 3354–3361, June 2012. https://doi.org/10.1109/CVPR.2012.6248074
20. Ghiasi, G., Lee, H., Kudlur, M., Dumoulin, V., Shlens, J.: Exploring the structure of a real-time, arbitrary neural artistic stylization network. In: BMVC (2017)
21. Ghifary, M., Kleijn, W.B., Zhang, M., Balduzzi, D., Li, W.: Deep reconstruction-classification networks for unsupervised domain adaptation. In: Leibe, B., Matas, J., Sebe, N., Welling, M. (eds.) ECCV 2016. LNCS, vol. 9908, pp. 597–613. Springer, Cham (2016). https://doi.org/10.1007/978-3-319-46493-0_36
22. Girshick, R.: Fast R-CNN. In: IEEE International Conference on Computer Vision (ICCV), pp. 1440–1448, December 2015. https://doi.org/10.1109/ICCV.2015.169

23. Girshick, R., Donahue, J., Darrell, T., Malik, J.: Rich feature hierarchies for accurate object detection and semantic segmentation. In: IEEE Conference on Computer Vision and Pattern Recognition, pp. 580–587, June 2014. https://doi.org/10.1109/CVPR.2014.81
24. Girshick, R.: Fast R-CNN. In: IEEE International Conference on Computer Vision (ICCV) (2015)
25. Girshick, R., Donahue, J., Darrell, T., Malik, J.: Rich feature hierarchies for accurate object detection and semantic segmentation, pp. 580–587 (2014)
26. Godard, C., Mac Aodha, O., Brostow, G.J.: Unsupervised monocular depth estimation with left-right consistency. In: IEEE Conference on Computer Vision and Pattern Recognition (CVPR), pp. 6602–6611 (2017). https://doi.org/10.1109/CVPR.2017.699
27. González, A., Vázquez, D., López, A.M., Amores, J.: On-board object detection: multicue, multimodal, and multiview random forest of local experts. IEEE Trans. Cybern. 47(11), 3980–3990 (2017). https://doi.org/10.1109/TCYB.2016.2593940
28. Gretton, A., Smola, A., Huang, J., Schmittfull, M., Borgwardt, K., Schölkopf, B.: Covariate shift by kernel mean matching (2008). https://doi.org/10.1.1.165.8929
29. Hamilton, O.K., Breckon, T.P.: Generalized dynamic object removal for dense stereo vision based scene mapping using synthesised optical flow. In: IEEE International Conference on Image Processing (ICIP), pp. 3439–3443, September 2016. https://doi.org/10.1109/ICIP.2016.7532998
30. Häne, C., Heng, L., Lee, G.H., Sizov, A., Pollefeys, M.: Real-time direct dense matching on Fisheye images using plane-sweeping stereo. In: 2nd International Conference on 3D Vision, vol. 1, pp. 57–64, December 2014. https://doi.org/10.1109/3DV.2014.77
31. He, K., Gkioxari, G., Dollár, P., Girshick, R.: Mask R-CNN. In: IEEE International Conference on Computer Vision (ICCV), pp. 2980–2988. IEEE (2017)
32. Hoffman, J., et al.: CyCADA: cycle-consistent adversarial domain adaptation. arXiv:1711.03213 [cs], November 2017
33. Hosang, J., Benenson, R., Dollár, P., Schiele, B.: What makes for effective detection proposals? IEEE Trans. Pattern Anal. Mach. Intell. 38(4), 814–830 (2016)
34. Hu, H.N., Lin, Y.C., Liu, M.Y., Cheng, H.T., Chang, Y.J., Sun, M.: Deep 360 pilot: learning a deep agent for piloting through 360° sports video. In: IEEE Conference on Computer Vision and Pattern Recognition (CVPR), pp. 1396–1405, May 2017. https://doi.org/10.1109/CVPR.2017.153
35. Janai, J., Güney, F., Behl, A., Geiger, A.: Computer vision for autonomous vehicles: problems, datasets and state-of-the-art. arXiv:1704.05519 [cs], April 2017
36. Johnson, J., Alahi, A., Fei-Fei, L.: Perceptual losses for real-time style transfer and super-resolution. arXiv:1603.08155 [cs], March 2016
37. Kendall, A., Gal, Y., Cipolla, R.: Multi-task learning using uncertainty to weigh losses for scene geometry and semantics. arXiv:1705.07115 [cs], May 2017
38. Kendall, A., et al.: End-to-end learning of geometry and context for deep stereo regression. In: IEEE International Conference on Computer Vision (ICCV), pp. 66–75 (2017)
39. Kondermann, D., et al.: The HCI benchmark suite: stereo and flow ground truth with uncertainties for urban autonomous driving. In: IEEE Conference on Computer Vision and Pattern Recognition Workshops (CVPRW), pp. 19–28, June 2016. https://doi.org/10.1109/CVPRW.2016.10
40. Kuznietsov, Y., Stückler, J., Leibe, B.: Semi-supervised deep learning for monocular depth map prediction. In: Proceedings of IEEE Conference on Computer Vision and Pattern Recognition, pp. 6647–6655 (2017)

41. Ladický, L., Shi, J., Pollefeys, M.: Pulling things out of perspective. In: IEEE Conference on Computer Vision and Pattern Recognition, pp. 89–96, June 2014. https://doi.org/10.1109/CVPR.2014.19
42. Lai, W.S., Huang, Y., Joshi, N., Buehler, C., Yang, M.H., Kang, S.B.: Semantic-driven generation of hyperlapse from 360° video. IEEE Trans. Vis. Comput. Graph. (2018). https://doi.org/10.1109/TVCG.2017.2750671
43. Liu, F., Shen, C., Lin, G., Reid, I.: Learning depth from single monocular images using deep convolutional neural fields. IEEE Trans. Pattern Anal. Mach. Intell. **38**(10), 2024–2039 (2016). https://doi.org/10.1109/TPAMI.2015.2505283
44. Long, M., Cao, Y., Wang, J., Jordan, M.I.: Learning transferable features with deep adaptation networks. arXiv:1502.02791 [cs], February 2015
45. Mapillary: Mapillary research. https://research.mapillary.com/
46. Matzen, K., Cohen, M.F., Evans, B., Kopf, J., Szeliski, R.: Low-cost 360 stereo photography and video capture. ACM Trans. Graph. **36**(4), 148:1–148:12 (2017). https://doi.org/10.1145/3072959.3073645
47. Mousavian, A., Anguelov, D., Flynn, J., Kosecka, J.: 3D bounding box estimation using deep learning and geometry. In: IEEE Conference on Computer Vision and Pattern Recognition (CVPR), pp. 5632–5640, December 2016. https://doi.org/10.1109/CVPR.2017.597
48. Neuhold, G., Ollmann, T., Bulò, S.R., Kontschieder, P.: The Mapillary Vistas dataset for semantic understanding of street scenes. In: IEEE International Conference on Computer Vision (ICCV), pp. 5000–5009, October 2017. https://doi.org/10.1109/ICCV.2017.534
49. Pang, J., Sun, W., Ren, J.S., Yang, C., Yan, Q.: Cascade residual learning: a two-stage convolutional neural network for stereo matching. In: IEEE International Conference on Computer Vision Workshops (ICCVW), pp. 878–886 (2017). https://doi.org/10.1109/ICCVW.2017.108
50. Ren, J., et al.: Accurate single stage detector using recurrent rolling convolution. In: IEEE Conference on Computer Vision and Pattern Recognition (CVPR), pp. 752–760 (2017). https://doi.org/10.1109/CVPR.2017.87
51. Ren, S., He, K., Girshick, R., Sun, J.: Faster R-CNN: towards real-time object detection with region proposal networks. In: Cortes, C., Lawrence, N.D., Lee, D.D., Sugiyama, M., Garnett, R. (eds.) Advances in Neural Information Processing Systems, vol. 28, pp. 91–99. Curran Associates Inc., New York (2015)
52. Saxena, A., Chung, S.H., Ng, A.Y.: Learning depth from single monocular images. In: NIPS, pp. 1161–1168 (2006)
53. Saxena, A., Sun, M., Ng, A.Y.: Make3D: learning 3D scene structure from a single still image. IEEE Trans. Pattern Anal. Mach. Intell. **31**(5), 824–840 (2009)
54. Scharstein, D., Szeliski, R.: A taxonomy and evaluation of dense two-frame stereo correspondence algorithms. Int. J. Comput. Vis. **47**(1), 7–42 (2002). https://doi.org/10.1109/SMBV.2001.988771
55. Sermanet, P., Eigen, D., Zhang, X., Mathieu, M., Fergus, R., LeCun, Y.: Overfeat: integrated recognition, localization and detection using convolutional networks. arXiv preprint arXiv:1312.6229 (2013)
56. Su, Y.C., Grauman, K.: Flat2Sphere: learning spherical convolution for fast features from 360° imagery. arXiv:1708.00919 [cs], August 2017
57. Su, Y.-C., Jayaraman, D., Grauman, K.: Pano2Vid: automatic cinematography for watching 360° videos. In: Lai, S.-H., Lepetit, V., Nishino, K., Sato, Y. (eds.) ACCV 2016. LNCS, vol. 10114, pp. 154–171. Springer, Cham (2017). https://doi.org/10.1007/978-3-319-54190-7_10

58. Torralba, A., Efros, A.A.: Unbiased look at dataset bias. In: IEEE Conference on Computer Vision and Pattern Recognition, pp. 1521–1528, June 2011. https://doi.org/10.1109/CVPR.2011.5995347

59. Tzeng, E., Hoffman, J., Saenko, K., Darrell, T.: Adversarial discriminative domain adaptation. In: IEEE Conference on Computer Vision and Pattern Recognition (CVPR), pp. 2962–2971, July 2017. https://doi.org/10.1109/CVPR.2017.316

60. Ulyanov, D., Lebedev, V., Vedaldi, A., Lempitsky, V.: Texture networks: feed-forward synthesis of textures and stylized images. arXiv:1603.03417 [cs], March 2016

61. Xu, J., Stenger, B., Kerola, T., Tung, T.: Pano2CAD: room layout from a single panorama image. In: IEEE Winter Conference on Applications of Computer Vision (WACV), pp. 354–362, March 2017. https://doi.org/10.1109/WACV.2017.46

62. Yang, F., Choi, W., Lin, Y.: Exploit all the layers: fast and accurate CNN object detector with scale dependent pooling and cascaded rejection classifier. In: IEEE International Conference on Computer Vision and Pattern Recognition (2016)

63. Zhang, Y., Song, S., Tan, P., Xiao, J.: PanoContext: a whole-room 3D context model for panoramic scene understanding. In: Fleet, D., Pajdla, T., Schiele, B., Tuytelaars, T. (eds.) ECCV 2014. LNCS, vol. 8694, pp. 668–686. Springer, Cham (2014). https://doi.org/10.1007/978-3-319-10599-4_43

64. Zhou, T., Brown, M., Snavely, N., Lowe, D.G.: Unsupervised learning of depth and ego-motion from video. In: Proceedings of IEEE Conference on Computer Vision and Pattern Recognition, pp. 6612–6619 (2017)

65. Zhu, J.Y., Park, T., Isola, P., Efros, A.A.: Unpaired image-to-image translation using cycle-consistent adversarial networks. In: IEEE International Conference on Computer Vision (ICCV), pp. 2242–2251 (Unpaired Image-to-Image Translation using Cycle-Consistent Adversarial). https://doi.org/10.1109/ICCV.2017.244

Cross-Modal Ranking with Soft Consistency and Noisy Labels for Robust RGB-T Tracking

Chenglong Li[1,2] , Chengli Zhu[2] , Yan Huang[1] , Jin Tang[2] ,
and Liang Wang[1(✉)]

[1] Center for Research on Intelligent Perception and Computing (CRIPAC),
National Laboratory of Pattern Recognition (NLPR), Institute of Automation,
Chinese Academy of Sciences (CASIA), Beijing, China
{yhuang,wangliang}@nlpr.ia.ac.cn, lcl1314@foxmail.com
[2] School of Computer Science and Technology, Anhui Univeristy, Hefei, China
zcl912@foxmail.com, jtang99029@foxmail.com

Abstract. Due to the complementary benefits of visible (RGB) and thermal infrared (T) data, RGB-T object tracking attracts more and more attention recently for boosting the performance under adverse illumination conditions. Existing RGB-T tracking methods usually localize a target object with a bounding box, in which the trackers or detectors is often affected by the inclusion of background clutter. To address this problem, this paper presents a novel approach to suppress background effects for RGB-T tracking. Our approach relies on a novel cross-modal manifold ranking algorithm. First, we integrate the *soft cross-modality consistency* into the ranking model which allows the sparse inconsistency to account for the different properties between these two modalities. Second, we propose an *optimal query learning* method to handle label noises of queries. In particular, we introduce an intermediate variable to represent the optimal labels, and formulate it as a l_1-optimization based sparse learning problem. Moreover, we propose a single unified optimization algorithm to solve the proposed model with stable and efficient convergence behavior. Finally, the ranking results are incorporated into the patch-based object features to address the background effects, and the structured SVM is then adopted to perform RGB-T tracking. Extensive experiments suggest that the proposed approach performs well against the state-of-the-art methods on large-scale benchmark datasets.

Keywords: Visual tracking · Information fusion · Manifold ranking
Soft cross-modality consistency · Label optimization

Electronic supplementary material The online version of this chapter (https://doi.org/10.1007/978-3-030-01261-8_49) contains supplementary material, which is available to authorized users.

© Springer Nature Switzerland AG 2018
V. Ferrari et al. (Eds.): ECCV 2018, LNCS 11217, pp. 831–847, 2018.
https://doi.org/10.1007/978-3-030-01261-8_49

1 Introduction

The goal of RGB-T tracking is to estimate the states of the target object in videos by fusing RGB and thermal (corresponds the visible and thermal infrared spectrum data, respectively) information, given the initial ground truth bounding box. Recently, researchers pay more and more attention on RGB-T tracking [1–5] partly due to the following reasons. (i) The imaging quality of visible spectrum is limited under bad environmental conditions (e.g., low illumination, rain, haze and smog, etc.). (ii) The thermal information can provide the complementary benefits for visible spectrum, especially in adverse illumination conditions. (iii) The thermal sensors have many advantages over others, such as the long-range imaging ability, the insensitivity to lighting conditions and the strong ability to penetrate haze and smog. Figure 1 shows some examples.

(a)   (b)

Fig. 1. Typically complementary benefits of RGB and thermal data [5]. (a) Benefits of thermal sources over RGB ones, where visible spectrum is disturbed by low illumination, high illumination and fog. (b) Benefits of RGB sources over thermal ones, where thermal spectrum is disturbed by glass and thermal crossover.

Most of RGB-T tracking methods focus on the sparse representation because of its capability of suppressing noises and errors [2–4]. These approaches, however, only adopt pixel intensities as feature representation, and thus be difficult to handle complex scenarios. Li et al. [5] extend the spatially ordered and weighted patch descriptor [6] to a RGB-T one, but this approach may be affected by the inaccurate initialization to their model. Deep learning based trackers [7–9] adopt powerful deep features or networks to improve tracking performance, but extending them to multi-modal ones has the following issues: (i) Regarding thermal as one channel of RGB or directly concatenating their features might not make the best use of the complementary benefits from multiple modalities [4]. For example, if one modality is malfunction, fusing it equals to adding noises, which might disturb tracking performance [4]. (ii) Designing multi-modal networks usually leads to the time-consuming procedures of network training and testing, especially for multiple input videos.

In this paper, we propose a novel cross-modal ranking algorithm for robust RGB-T tracking. Given one bounding box of the target object, we first partition it into non-overlapping patches, which are characterized by RGB and thermal features (such as color and gradient histograms). The bounding box can thus be represented with a graph with image patches as nodes. Motivated by [5,6], we assign each patch with a weight to suppress background information, and propose a cross-modal ranking algorithm to compute the patch weights. The patch weights are then incorporated into the RGB-T patch features, and the object location is finally predicted by applying the structured SVM [10]. Figure 2 shows the pipeline of our approach. In particular, our cross-modal ranking algorithm advances existing ones in the following aspects.

First, we propose a general scheme for effective multimodal fusion. The RGB and thermal modalities are heterogeneous with different properties, and the hard consistency [4,11] between these two modalities may be difficult to perform effective fusion. Therefore, we propose a *soft cross-modality consistency* to enforce ranking consistency between modalities while allowing sparse inconsistency exists.

Second, we propose a novel method to mitigate the effects of ranking noises. In conventional manifold ranking models, the query quality is very important for ranking accuracy, and thus how to set good queries need to be designed manually [12–14]. In visual tracking, the setting of initial patch weights (i.e., queries) is not always reasonable due to noises of tracking results and irregular object shapes [6]. To handle this problem, we introduce an intermediate variable to represent the optimal labels of initial patches, and optimize it in a semi-supervised way based on the observation that *visually similar patches tend to have same labels or weights*. We formulate it as a l_1-optimization based sparse learning problem to promote sparsity of the inconsistency between inferred queries and initial ones (because most of the initial queries should be correct and the remaining ones are noises). We call this process as *optimal query learning* in this paper.

Finally, we present an efficient solver for the objective. Instead of individual consideration for each problem, we propose a single unified optimization framework to learn the patch weights and the optimal queries at a same time, which can be beneficial to boosting their respective performance. In particular, an efficient ADMM (alternating direction method of multipliers) [15] is adopted, and a linearized operation [16] is also employed to avoid matrix inversion for efficiency. By this way, our algorithm has a stable convergence behavior, and each iteration has small computational complexity.

In summary, we make the following contributions to RGB-T tracking and related applications. (i) We integrate a soft consistency into the cross-modal ranking process to model the interdependency between two modalities while allowing sparse inconsistency exists to account for their heterogeneous properties. The proposed cross-modality consistency is general, and can be applied to other multimodal fusion problems. (ii) To mitigate noise effects of initial patches, we introduce an intermediate variable to represent the optimal labels of the initial patches, and formulate it as a l_1-optimization based sparse learning problem. It is also general and applicable to other semi-supervized tasks, such as saliency detection and interactive object segmentation. (iii) We present a unified ADMM-based optimization framework to solve the objective with stable and efficient convergence behavior, which makes our tracker very efficient. (iv) To demonstrate the efficiency and superior performance of the proposed approach over the state-of-the-art methods, we conduct extensive experiments on two large-scale benchmark datasets, i.e., GTOT [4] and RGBT210 [5].

2   Related Work

The methods of visual tracking are vast, we only discuss the most related to us.

RGB-T tracking has drawn much attention in the computer vision community with the popularity and affordability of thermal infrared sensors [17]. Works on RGB-T tracking mainly focus on sparse representation because of its capability of suppressing noises and errors [2–4,18]. Wu et al. [2] concatenate the intensity features of image patches from RGB and thermal sources into a one-dimensional vector, which is sparsely represented in the target template space. The RGB-T tracking is performed in Bayesian filtering framework by defining reconstruction residues as the likelihood. Liu et al. [3] perform joint sparse representation on both RGB and thermal modalities, and fuse the resultant tracking results using min operation on the sparse representation coefficients. A Laplacian sparse representation is proposed to learn a multi-modal features using the reconstruction coefficients that encode both the spatial local information and occlusion handling [18]. Li et al. [4] propose a collaborative sparse representation based trackers to adaptively fuse RGB and thermal modalities by assigning each modality with a reliability weight. These approaches, however, only adopt pixel intensities as feature representation, and thus be difficult to handle complex scenarios. Kim et al. [6] propose a Spatially Ordered and Weighted Patch (SOWP) descriptor for target object based on the random walk algorithm, and achieve excellent performance for tracking. Li et al. [19] extend SOWP by optimizing a dynamic graph, and an another extension is further proposed to integrate multimodal information adaptively for RGB-T tracking [5].

Different from these works, we propose a novel cross-modal ranking algorithm for RGB-T tracking from a new perspective. In particular, our approach has the following advantages. (i) **Generality**. The proposed model and schemes are general and applicable, including soft cross-modality consistency and optimal query learning, and can be easily extended to other vision problems. (ii) **Effectiveness**. Our approach performs well against the state-of-the-art RGB and RGB-T trackers on two large-scale benchmark datasets. (iii) **Efficiency**. The proposed optimization algorithm is with a fast and stable convergence behavior, which makes our tracker very efficient.

3   Cross-Modal Ranking Algorithm

Our cross-modal ranking algorithm aims to compute patch weights to suppress background effects in the bounding box description of target object. This section will introduce the details of our cross-modal ranking model and the associated optimization algorithm. The weighted patch feature construction and object tracking will be described in detail in the next section. For clarity, we present the pipeline of our tracking approach in Fig. 2.

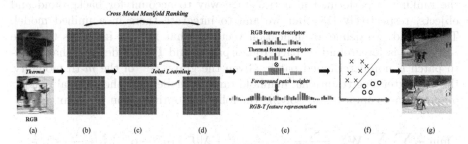

Fig. 2. Pipeline of our approach. (a) Cropped regions, where the red bounding box represents the region of initial patches. (b) Patch initialization indicated by red color. (c) Optimized results from initial patches. (d) Ranking results with the soft cross-modality consistency. (e) RGB-T feature representation. (f) Structured SVM. (g) Tracking results. (Color figure online)

3.1   Model Formulation

The graph-based manifold ranking problem is described as follows: given a graph and a node in this graph as query, the remaining nodes are ranked based on their affinities to the given query. The goal is to learn a ranking function that defines the relevance between unlabelled nodes and queries [12]. We employ the graph-based manifold ranking model to solve our problem.

Given the target bounding box, we first partition it into a set of non-overlapping patches, which are described with RGB and thermal features (e.g., color, thermal and gradient histograms). To mitigate the effects of background information, we assign each patch with a weight that describes its importance belonging to target, and compute these weights via the cross-modal ranking algorithm. Given a patch feature set $\mathbf{X}^m = \{\mathbf{x}_1^m, ..., \mathbf{x}_n^m\}$, some patches are labelled as queries and the rest need to be ranked according to their affinities to the queries. Here, $m \in \{1, 2, ..., M\}$ indicates the m-th modality, and M denotes the number of modalities. Note that RGB-T data is the special case with $M = 2$, and we discuss its general form from the applicable perspective. Let $\mathbf{s}^m : \mathbf{X}^m \rightarrow \mathbb{R}^n$ denotes a ranking function which assigns a ranking value s_i^m to each patch $\mathbf{x}_i^m$ in the m-th modality, and $\mathbf{s}^m$ can be viewed as a vector $\mathbf{s}^m = [s_1^m, ..., s_n^m]^T$. In this work, we regard the initial patch weights as query labels, and $\mathbf{s}^m$ is thus a patch weight vector.

Let $\mathbf{q}^m = [q_1^m, ..., q_n^m]^T$ denote an indication vector, in which $q_i^m = 1$ if $\mathbf{x}_i^m$ is target object patch, and $q_i^m = 0$ if $\mathbf{x}_i^m$ is the background patch. $\mathbf{q}^m$ is computed by the initial ground truth (for the first frame) or tracking results (for the subsequent frames) as follows. For i-th patch, if it belongs to the shrunk region of the bounding box then $\mathbf{q}_i^m = 1$, and if it belongs to the expanded region of the bounding box then $\mathbf{q}_i^m = 0$, as shown in Fig. 3(a). The remaining patches are non-determined, and will be diffused by other patches. In general, the ranking is performed in a two-stage way to account for background and objects, respectively [13], but we aim to integrate them in a unified model. To this end, we define an indication vector $\boldsymbol{\Gamma}$ that $\boldsymbol{\Gamma}_i = 1$ indicates that the i-th patch is foreground or background patch, and $\boldsymbol{\Gamma}_i = 0$ denotes that the i-th patch is non-determined patch. Given the graph G^m of the m-th modality, through extending traditional manifold ranking model [12], the optimal ranking of queries are computed by solving the following optimization problem:

$$\min_{\{\mathbf{s}^m\}} \frac{1}{2} \sum_{m=1}^{M} \sum_{i,j=1}^{n} \mathbf{W}_{ij}^m \|\frac{\mathbf{s}_i^m}{\sqrt{\mathbf{D}_{ii}^m}} - \frac{\mathbf{s}_j^m}{\sqrt{\mathbf{D}_{jj}^m}}\|^2 + \lambda \|\boldsymbol{\Gamma} \circ (\mathbf{s}^m - \mathbf{q}^m)\|_F^2 + \frac{\lambda_2}{2} \|\mathbf{s}^m\|_F^2, \tag{1}$$

where λ is a parameter to balance the smoothness term and fitting term, and λ_2 is a regularization parameter. $\circ$ indicates the element-wise product. $\mathbf{D}^m$ is the degree matrix of the graph affinity matrix $\mathbf{W}^m$, whose computation is as follows. In the m-th modality, if graph nodes v_i and v_j are adjacent with 8-neighbors, they are connected by an edge e_{ij}, which is assigned a weight $\mathbf{W}_{ij}^m = \exp^{(-\gamma \|\mathbf{x}_i^m - \mathbf{x}_j^m\|)}$, where γ is the scaling parameter, which is set to 5 in this paper.

In (1), it inherently indicates that the available modalities are independent, which may significantly limit the performance in dealing with occasional perturbation or malfunction of individual sources. In addition, the settings of initial patch weights (i.e., queries) are not always reasonable due to noises of tracking results and irregular object shapes, as shown in Fig. 3(a). In this paper, we integrate the *soft cross-modality consistency* and the *optimal query learning* into (1) to handle above problems, respectively.

Soft Cross-Modality Consistency. To take advantage of the complementary benefits of RGB and thermal data, we need impose the modality consistency on the ranking process. Wang et al. [11] propose a multi-graphs regularized manifold ranking method to integrate different protein domains using hard constraints, i.e., employing multiple graphs to regularize the same ranking score. It is not suitable for our problem, as RGB and thermal sources are heterogeneous with different properties. Therefore, we introduce a *soft cross-modality consistency* to enforce ranking consistency between modalities while allowing sparse inconsistency exists to account for their heterogeneous properties. To this end, we propose the *soft cross-modality consistency* as a l_1-optimization based sparse learning problem as follows:

$$\min_{\{\mathbf{s}^m\}} \lambda_1 \sum_{m=2}^{M} \|\mathbf{s}^m - \mathbf{s}^{m-1}\|_1 = \min_{\mathbf{s}^m} \lambda_1 \|\mathbf{CS}\|_1, \tag{2}$$

where λ_1 is a regularization parameter, and $\mathbf{S} = [\mathbf{s}^1; \mathbf{s}^2; ...; \mathbf{s}^M]$. $\mathbf{C}$ is the cross-modal consistency matrix, which is defined as:

$$
\mathbf{C} = \begin{bmatrix} \mathbf{I}^1 & -\mathbf{I}^2 & 0 & & 0 \\ 0 & \mathbf{I}^2 & -\mathbf{I}^3 & & \\ & & ... & ... & \\ 0 & & & \mathbf{I}^{M-1} & -\mathbf{I}^M \end{bmatrix}
$$

where $\mathbf{I}$ is the identity matrix.

Optimal Query Learning. To mitigate noise effects of initial patch weights, we introduce an intermediate variable to represent the optimal ones, and optimize it in a semi-supervised way. The details are presented below.

Denoting the intermediate variable as $\hat{\mathbf{q}}^m = [\hat{\mathbf{q}}_1^m, ..., \hat{\mathbf{q}}_n^m]^T$, we first introduce two constraints for inferring $\hat{\mathbf{q}}^m$, i.e., *visual similarity constraint* and *inconsistency sparsity constraint*. The first constraint assumes that visually similar patches should have same labels and weights, and vice versa. Therefore, we add a smoothness term $\sum_{i,j=1}^n \mathbf{W}_{ij}^m (\hat{\mathbf{q}}_i^m - \hat{\mathbf{q}}_j^m)^2$ that can make visual similarity become a graph smoothness constraint. The second constraint aiming to compel sparsity in $\hat{\mathbf{q}}^m - \mathbf{q}^m$ is enlightened by the common use of l_1-norm sparsity regularization term in data noise, which has been proven to be effective even when the data noise is not sparse [20,21]. Therefore, we formulate it as $||\hat{\mathbf{q}}^m - \mathbf{q}^m||_1$, where l_1-norm is used to promote sparsity on the inconsistency between inferred labels and initial ones (because most of the initial labels should be correct and the remaining ones are noises). Figure 3 shows the superiority of the l_1 norm over the l_2 norm. By combining these two constraints, the proposed l_1-optimization problem is formulated as follows:

$$
\min_{\{\hat{\mathbf{q}}^m\}} \alpha \sum_{i,j=1}^n \mathbf{W}_{ij}^m (\hat{\mathbf{q}}_i^m - \hat{\mathbf{q}}_j^m)^2 + \beta ||\hat{\mathbf{q}}^m - \mathbf{q}^m||_1, \tag{3}
$$

where α and β are the balance parameters. Integrating the *soft cross-modality consistency* (2) and the *optimal query learning* (3) into (1), the final cross-modal ranking model is written as:

$$
\min_{\{\mathbf{s}^m\},\{\hat{\mathbf{q}}^m\}} \frac{1}{2} \sum_{m=1}^M (\sum_{i,j=1}^n \mathbf{W}_{ij}^m || \frac{s_i^m}{\sqrt{\mathbf{D}_{ii}^m}} - \frac{s_j^m}{\sqrt{\mathbf{D}_{jj}^m}} ||^2 + \lambda ||\Gamma \circ (\mathbf{s}^m - \hat{\mathbf{q}}^m)||_F^2
$$
$$
+ \frac{\lambda_2}{2} ||\mathbf{s}^m||_F^2 + \alpha \sum_{i,j=1}^n \mathbf{W}_{ij}^m (\hat{\mathbf{q}}_i^m - \hat{\mathbf{q}}_j^m)^2 + \beta ||\hat{\mathbf{q}}^m - \mathbf{q}^m||_1) + \lambda_1 ||\mathbf{CS}||_1. \tag{4}
$$

Although (4) seems complex, as demonstrated in the experiments, the tracking performance is insensitive to parameter variations.

3.2 Optimization Algorithm

Although the variables of (4) are not joint convex, the subproblem to each variable with fixing others is convex and has a closed-form solution. The ADMM

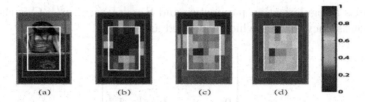

Fig. 3. Comparison of l_1-norm and l_2-norm in learning the optimal queries. (a) Target bounding box (red color), shrink bounding box (white color) and expand bounding box (green color). (b) Heatmap optimized by l_1-norm. (c) Heatmap optimized by l_2-norm. (d) Heatmap without optimal query learning. Herein, the heatmap represents the ranking results. (Color figure online)

(alternating direction method of multipliers) algorithm [15] is efficient and effective solver for the problems like (4). To apply ADMM to our problem, we introduce two auxiliary variables $\mathbf{P} = \mathbf{CS}$ and $\mathbf{f}^m = \hat{\mathbf{q}}^m$ to make (4) separable. With some algebra, we have

$$
\begin{aligned}
\min_{\{\mathbf{s}^m\},\{\hat{\mathbf{q}}^m\},\mathbf{P},\{\mathbf{f}^m\}} \sum_{m=1}^{M} & ((\mathbf{s}^m)^T \mathbf{L}^m \mathbf{s}^m + \lambda ||\mathbf{\Gamma} \circ (\mathbf{s}^m - \hat{\mathbf{q}}^m)||_F^2 + \frac{\lambda_2}{2}||\mathbf{s}^m||_F^2 \\
& + 2\alpha(\mathbf{f}^m)^T (\mathbf{D}^m - \mathbf{W}^m)\mathbf{f}^m + \beta||\hat{\mathbf{q}}^m - \mathbf{q}^m||_1) + \lambda_1||\mathbf{P}||_1, \\
s.t. \quad \mathbf{P} &= \mathbf{CS}, \mathbf{f}^m = \hat{\mathbf{q}}^m,
\end{aligned}
\tag{5}
$$

where $\mathbf{L}^m = \mathbf{I} - (\mathbf{D}^m)^{-\frac{1}{2}} \mathbf{W}^m (\mathbf{D}^m)^{-\frac{1}{2}}$ is the normalized Laplacian matrix of m-th modality. The augmented Lagrange function of (5) is:

$$
\begin{aligned}
\mathbb{L}(\{\mathbf{s}^m\}&, \{\hat{\mathbf{q}}^m\}, \mathbf{P}, \{\mathbf{f}^m\}, \mathbf{Y}_1, \mathbf{Y}_2) \\
= \sum_{m=1}^{M} & ((\mathbf{s}^m)^T \mathbf{L}^m \mathbf{s}^m + \lambda ||\mathbf{\Gamma} \circ (\mathbf{s}^m - \hat{\mathbf{q}}^m)||_F^2 + \frac{\lambda_2}{2}||\mathbf{s}^m||_F^2 \\
& + 2\alpha(\mathbf{f}^m)^T (\mathbf{D}^m - \mathbf{W}^m)\mathbf{f}^m + \beta||\hat{\mathbf{q}}^m - \mathbf{q}^m||_1) + \lambda_1||\mathbf{P}||_1 \\
& + \frac{\mu}{2}(||\mathbf{P} - \mathbf{CS} + \frac{\mathbf{Y}_1}{\mu}||_F^2 + \sum_{m=1}^{M} ||\hat{\mathbf{q}}^m - \mathbf{f}^m + \frac{\mathbf{y}_2^m}{\mu}||_F^2) \\
& - \frac{1}{2\mu}(||\mathbf{Y}_1||_F^2 + ||\mathbf{Y}_2||_F^2),
\end{aligned}
\tag{6}
$$

where $\mathbf{Y}_1$ and $\mathbf{Y}_2 = [\mathbf{y}_2^1, \mathbf{y}_2^2, ..., \mathbf{y}_2^M]$ are the Lagrangian multipliers, and μ is the Lagrangian parameter. Due to space limitation, we present the detailed derivations in the **supplementary file**. ADMM alternatively updates one variable by minimizing (6) with fixing other variables. Besides the Lagrangian multipliers, there are four variables, including $\mathbf{S}$, $\hat{\mathbf{q}}^m$, $\mathbf{P}$ and $\mathbf{f}^m$ to solve. Note that the $\mathbf{S}$-subproblem includes the inversion operation of a matrix with size of $Mn \times Mn$, which is time consuming. To handle this problem, we adopt a linearized operation [16] to avoid matrix inversion for efficiency. Due to space limitation, we only present the solutions of these subproblems as follows:

$$\mathbf{f}^m = (4\alpha(\mathbf{D}^m - \mathbf{W}^m) + \mu\mathbf{I})^{-1}(\mu\hat{\mathbf{q}}^m + \mathbf{y}_2^m)$$

$$\hat{\mathbf{q}}^m = soft\_thr_1(\mathbf{s}^m, \mathbf{f}^m - \frac{\mathbf{y}_2^m}{\mu}, \mathbf{q}^m, \lambda \circ \mathbf{\Gamma} \circ \mathbf{\Gamma}, \frac{\mu}{2}, \beta)$$

$$\mathbf{P} = soft\_thr(\mathbf{CS} - \frac{\mathbf{Y}_1}{\mu}, \frac{\lambda_1}{\mu}) \tag{7}$$

$$\mathbf{S}_{k+1} = \mathbf{S}_k - \frac{1}{\eta\mu}\nabla_{\mathbf{S}_k}J_k,$$

where $soft\_thr$ is a soft thresholding operator and $soft\_thr_1$ is also a soft thresholding operator with different inputs to $soft\_thr$, see the **supplementary file** for detailed definitions. k indicates the k-th iteration, and J_k is the abbreviation of $J(\mathbf{S}_k, \hat{\mathbf{Q}}_k^m, \mathbf{P}_k, \mathbf{Y}_{1,k}, \mu_k) = \mathbf{S}_k^T\mathbf{L}\mathbf{S}_k + \lambda\|\mathbf{\Gamma}\circ(\mathbf{S}_k - \hat{\mathbf{Q}}_k)\|_F^2 + \frac{\mu_k}{2}\|\mathbf{P}_k - \mathbf{CS}_k + \frac{\mathbf{Y}_{1,k}}{\mu_k}\|_F^2 + \frac{\lambda_2}{2}\|\mathbf{S}_k\|_F^2$, where $\hat{\mathbf{Q}} = [\hat{\mathbf{q}}^1; \hat{\mathbf{q}}^2; ...; \hat{\mathbf{q}}^M]$, and

$$\mathbf{L} = \begin{bmatrix} \mathbf{L}^1 & 0 & 0 \\ 0 & \mathbf{L}^2 & \\ & & ... & \\ 0 & & \mathbf{L}^M \end{bmatrix}$$

$\nabla_{\mathbf{S}}J$ is the partial differential of J with respect to $\mathbf{S}$, and $\eta = \frac{1}{M}\sum_{m=1}^M \|\mathbf{X}^m\|_F^2$. Please refer to the **supplementary file** for the detailed derivations.

4   RGB-T Object Tracking

This section first imposes the optimized patch weights on the extracted multi-spectral features for more robust feature representation, and then present the tracker's details.

4.1   Feature Representation

We perform cross-modal ranking to obtain the patch weights, i.e., $\mathbf{s}^1, \mathbf{s}^2, ..., \mathbf{s}^M$. Let $\mathbf{x}_i = [\mathbf{x}_i^1; ...; \mathbf{x}_i^M] \in \mathbb{R}^{dM \times 1}$ be the RGB-T feature vector of i-th patch. Then, we construct the final collaborative feature representation by incorporating the patch weights. Specifically, for the i-th patch, we compute its final weight $\hat{\mathbf{s}}_i$ by combining all modal weights as follows:

$$\hat{\mathbf{s}}_i = \frac{1}{1 + \exp(-\sigma\frac{\sum_{m=1}^M \mathbf{s}_i^m}{M})}, \tag{8}$$

where σ is a scaling parameter fixed to 35 in this work. The collaborative feature representation is thus obtained by $\hat{\mathbf{x}} = [\hat{\mathbf{s}}_1\mathbf{x}_1; ...; \hat{\mathbf{s}}_n\mathbf{x}_n] \in \mathbb{R}^{dMn \times 1}$.

4.2 Tracking

We adopt the structured SVM (S-SVM) [10] to perform object tracking in this paper, and other tracking algorithm, such as correlation filters [22], can also be utilized.

Instead of using binary-labeled samples, S-SVM employs the structured sample that consists of a target bounding box and nearby boxes in the same frame to prevent the labelling ambiguity in training the classifier. Specifically, it constrains that the confidence score of an target bounding box y_t is larger than that of nearby box y by a margin determined by the intersection over union overlap ratio (denoted as $IoU(y_t, y)$) between two boxes:

$$\mathbf{h}^* = \arg\min_{\mathbf{h}} \; \xi ||\mathbf{h}||^2 + \sum_y \max\{0, \triangle(y_t, y) - \mathbf{h}^T \epsilon(y_t, y)\}, \qquad (9)$$

where $\triangle(y_t, y) = 1 - IoU(y_t, y)$, $\epsilon(y_t, y) = \Psi(y_t) - \Psi(y)$, and $\xi = 0.0001$ is a regularization parameter. $\Psi(y_t)$ denotes the object descriptor representing a bounding box y_t at the t-th frame, and $\mathbf{h}$ is the normal vector of a decision plane. In this paper, we employ the stochastic variance reduced gradient (SVRG) technique [23] to optimize (9). By this way, S-SVM can reduce adverse effects of false labelling.

Given the bounding box of the target object in previous frame $(t-1)$, we first set a searching window in current frame t, and sample a set of candidates within the searching window. S-SVM selects the optimal target bounding box y_t^* in the t-th frame by maximizing a classification score:

$$y_t^* = \arg\max_{y_t} \; (\omega \mathbf{h}_{t-1}^T \Psi(y_t) + (1 - \omega) \mathbf{h}_0^T \Psi(y_t)), \qquad (10)$$

where ω is a balancing parameter, and $\mathbf{h}_{t-1}$ is the normal vector of a decision plane of $(t-1)$-th frame. $\mathbf{h}_0$ is learnt in the initial frame, which can prevent it from learning drastic appearance changes. To prevent the effects of unreliable tracking results, we update the classifier only when the confidence score of tracking result is larger than a threshold θ, where the confidence score of tracking result in t-th frame is defined as the average similarity between the weighted descriptor of the tracked bounding box and the positive support vectors: $\frac{1}{|\mathbb{V}_t|} \sum_{\mathbf{v} \in \mathbb{V}_t} \mathbf{v}^T \Psi(y_t^*)$, where $\mathbb{V}_t$ is the set of the positive support vectors at time t. In addition, we update object scales with three frames interval using the method from [24].

5   Performance Evaluation

5.1   Evaluation Settings

Data. There are only two large RGB-T tracking datasets, i.e., GTOT [4] and RGBT210 [5]. They are large and challenging enough, and we evaluate our approach on them for comprehensive validations. GTOT includes 50 RGB-T video clips with ground truth object locations under different scenarios and conditions. RGBT210 is another larger dataset for RGB-T tracking evaluation. It is highly-aligned, and contains 210 video clips with both RGB and thermal data. This dataset takes many challenges into consideration, such as camera moving, different occlusion levels, large scale variations and environmental challenges. The precision rate (PR) and success rate (SR) are employed to measure quantitative performance of various trackers.

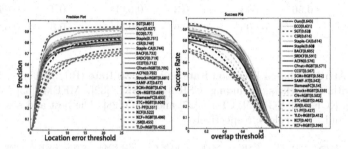

Fig. 4. Success Rate (SR) on the public GTOT benchmark dataset.

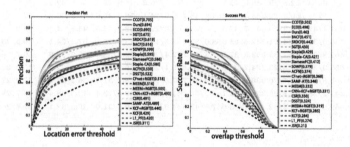

Fig. 5. The evaluation results on the public RGBT210 benchmark dataset. The representative score of PR/SR is presented in the legend.

Parameters. We fix all parameters and other settings in our experiments. We partition all bounding box into 64 non-overlapping patches to balance accuracy-efficiency trade-off [6], and extract RGB-T features for each patch, including color, thermal and gradient histograms, where the dimensions of gradient and each color channel are set to be 8. To improve the efficiency, each frame is scaled so that the minimum side length of a bounding box is 32 pixels, and the side length of a searching window is fixed to be $2\sqrt{WH}$, where W and H are the width and height of the scaled bounding box, respectively. We shrink and expand the tracked bounding box (lx, ly, W, H) as $(lx+0.1W, ly+0.1H, 0.8W, 0.8H)$ and $(lx - W', ly - H', W + 2W', H + 2H')$, respectively, where (lx, ly) denotes the

Table 1. Success Rate (SR) of the proposed method with different parameters on the GTOT dataset.

Param	Setting	SR	Param	Setting	SR	Param	Setting	SR
α	0.325	0.624	β	0.0002	0.615			
	0.65	0.643		0.002	0.643			
	1.3	0.59		0.02	0.633			
λ	0.28	0.62	λ_1	0.15	0.628	λ_2	0.2	0.602
	0.56	0.643		0.3	0.643		0.4	0.643
	1.12	0.605		0.6	0.628		0.8	0.632

Table 2. Attribute-based Precision Rate and Success Rate (PR/SR %) on RGBT210 dataset with 9 trackers, including CSR [4], DSST [32], MEEM [33], CNN [22], SOWP [6], KCF [22], SGT [5], CFnet [27] and ECO [28]. The best and second results are in red and green colors, respectively.

	ECO	SOWP	DSST	CSR	SGT	KCF+RGBT	MEEM+RGBT	CNN+KCF+RGBT	CFnet+RGBT	Ours
NO	87.7/64.3	75.0/46.1	70.2/41.4	68.1/45.2	82.4/50.7	56.6/36.3	64.7/41.2	63.7/42.9	69.7/52.2	86.1/59.4
PO	72.2/52.5	61.3/39.5	57.0/35.1	52.7/36.6	/48.3	49.6/31.6	57.4/35.5	56.0/36.4	57.2/38.4	77.1/52.2
HO	58.3/41.3	52.0/32.8	39.4/25.7	37.1/24.3	53.1/34.1	33.0/22.2	37.2/24.2	36.6/25.9	39.3/27.3	54.3/34.6
LI	66.6/45.6	48.3/30.7	47.8/29.0	47.3/31.1	71.6/44.7	48.3/30.4	39.2/25.6	52.8/34.5	49.8/33.6	71.4/46.4
LR	64.1/38.1	51.0/29.1	52.8/29.1	46.0/23.1	65.8/37.5	42.6/26.2	44.9/23.4	54.6/32.5	45.2/27.7	64.8/37.4
TC	82.1/58.8	70.0/44.9	50.9/32.2	43.2/29.3	64.9/40.7	39.0/24.1	58.2/35.6	49.6/33.2	42.8/29.4	65.8/43.0
DEF	61.2/45.0	61.4/41.7	46.5/33.0	44.7/33.0	65.3/45.9	40.6/29.5	48.7/33.5	44.8/34.4	48.9/35.2	65.2/45.8
FM	58.2/39.2	56.0/32.3	34.4/21.2	42.6/25.0	58.0/33.1	33.3/19.1	43.5/26.8	37.1/24.1	36.5/23.0	58.8/34.9
SV	74.5/55.4	62.8/37.7	58.7/33.5	53.3/37.5	67.4/41.7	42.4/27.5	52.8/33.0	50.3/32.6	56.7/40.6	72.5/49.2
MB	67.8/49.9	55.2/38.3	32.3/23.2	34.7/23.8	58.6/39.6	29.1/20.7	46.2/31.4	30.4/22.0	30.3/22.4	58.4/40.5
CM	61.7/45.0	55.8/36.9	38.7/26.9	38.9/27.4	59.0/40.7	37.5/26.0	48.7/31.9	36.2/27.0	37.2/27.9	59.7/41.8
BC	52.9/35.2	47.2/28.6	43.8/26.3	38.4/23.7	58.6/35.5	41.0/25.6	40.5/23.4	42.3/28.4	43.7/28.1	57.9/35.2
ALL	69.0/49.8	59.9/37.9	52.2/32.4	49.1/33.0	67.5/43.0	44.0/28.5	50.5/31.9	49.3/33.1	51.8/36.0	69.4/46.3

top-left coordinate of the tracked bounding box, and W' and H' indicate the patch width and height, respectively.

The proposed model involves several parameters in (6), including α, β, λ, λ_1 and λ_2, and the tracking sensitivity with different parameters are shown in Table 1. The results show the robustness of the proposed model to parameters' variations, and we set α, β, λ, λ_1 and λ_2 to be 0.65, 0.002, 0.56, 0.3 and 0.4, respectively. In S-SVM, we empirically set $\{\omega, \theta\} = \{0.598, 0.3\}$, and employ a linear kernel.

Baselines. For comprehensive evaluation, we compare ours method with 23 popular trackers, some of which are from GTOT and RGBT210 benchmarks. Since there are few RGB-T trackers [2–5,18], we extend some RGB tracking methods to RGB-T ones by concatenating RGB and thermal features into a single vector or regarding the thermal as an extra channel, such as KCF [22], Struck [25], SCM [26] and CFnet [27]. In addition, we also select recently proposed state-of-the-art trackers for comparison, such as C-COT [9], ECO [28], ACFnet [29], SiameseFC [30] and Staple-CA [31], see Figs. 4 and 5 for details.

5.2 Comparison Results

GTOT Evaluation. We present the evaluation results on the GTOT dataset in Fig. 4. Overall, the proposed algorithm performs favorably against the state-of-the-art methods. In particular, our approach outperforms the state-of-the-art methods using deep features with a clear margin, e.g., 5.0%/1.2% over ECO [28] and 11.5%/7.6% over C-COT [9] in PR/SR score. It is beneficial to the effective fusion of visible and thermal information in our method. Note that the methods based on deep features have weak performance on GTOT, including ECO and C-COT. It may be partly due to the weakness of deep features in representing the target objects with low resolution (many targets are small in GTOT). Our approach can handle this challenging factor. Figure 4 shows that our tracker performs well against the state-of-the-art RGB-T methods, which suggest that the proposed fusion approach is effective. SGT [5] is better than our tracker in PR mainly due to adaptive fusion of different modalities by introducing modality weights, but performs weaker than ours in SR.

RGBT210 Evaluation. We further evaluate our method on the RGBT210 dataset in Fig. 5 and Table 2. The comparison curves show that our tracker also performs well against the state-of-the-art methods on RGBT210. In particular, our approach outperforms the state-of-the-art RGB-T tracking methods, e.g., 1.9%/3.3% over SGT [5] and 20.3%/13.3% over CSR [4] in PR/SR score. It justifies the effectiveness of the proposed method in fusing multimodal information for visual tracking. For the state-of-the-art methods using deep features, the proposed tracker performs well against the SiameseFC [30] and CFnet [27] methods in all aspects. The proposed tracker performs equally well against the C-COT [9] and ECO [28] schemes in terms of PR and slightly worse in terms of SR. Furthermore, the proposed algorithm advances the C-COT and ECO methods in several aspects.

- It does not require laborious pre-training or a large training set, and also does not need to save a large pre-trained deep model. We initialize the proposed model using the ground truth bounding box in the first frame, and update it in subsequent frames.
- It is easy to implement as each subproblem of the proposed model has a closed-form solution.
- It performs favorably against the state-of-the-art deep tracking methods in terms of efficiency on a cheaper hardware setup (Ours: 8 FPS on 4.0 GHz CPU, ECO: 8 FPS on 3.4 GHz CPU and NVIDIA Tesla K40m GPU, C-COT: 1 FPS).
- It performs more robustly than the ECO and C-COT methods in some situations. In particular, it outperforms the ECO method on sequences with partial occlusion, low illumination, object deformation and background clutters in terms of PR and SR, which suggests the effectiveness of our approach

in fusing the multimodal information and suppressing the background effects during tracking.

In addition, the example visual results on RGBT210 and GTOT are presented in the **supplementary file**, which further qualitatively verify the effectiveness of our method.

Table 3. PR/SR (%) of the proposed method with the different versions on the GTOT dataset.

	Ours-noC	Ours-noĝ	Ours-noS	Ours
PR	78.7	78.0	71.1	82.7
SR	61.2	63.1	57.6	64.3

5.3   Ablation Study

To justify the significance of the main components, we implement 3 versions of our approach for empirical analysis on GTOT. The 3 versions are: (1) Ours-noC, that computes the patch weights without the constraint of cross-modal consistency. (2) Ours-noĝ, that removes the optimal query learning operation in ranking model. (3) Ours-noS, that removes the patch weights in the feature presentation.

From the evaluation results reported in Table 3, we can draw the following conclusions. (1) The patch weights in collaborative object representation plays critical roles in RGB-T tracking by observing that Ours outperforms Ours-noS. (2) The improvements of Ours over Ours-noĝ demonstrate the effectiveness of the introduced optimal query learning. (3) The soft consistency is important for cross-modal ranking from the observation that Ours-noC is much lower than Ours.

5.4   Runtime Performance

The experiments are carried out on a PC with an Intel i7 4.0 GHz CPU and 32 GB RAM, and implemented in C++. The proposed tracker performs at about 8 frames per second. In particular, our ranking algorithm converges within 30 iterations, and costs about 20 ms per frame (tested on all datasets). Note that our codes do not include any optimization and parallel operation, and the feature extraction and the structured SVM take most of time per frame (above 80%).

6   Conclusion

In this paper, we propose a graph-based cross-modal ranking algorithm to learn robust RGB-T object features for visual tracking. In the ranking process, we introduce the soft cross-modality consistency between modalities and the optimal query learning to improve the robustness. The solver to the proposed model is fast makes the tracker efficient. Extensive experiments on two large-scale benchmark datasets demonstrate the effectiveness and efficiency of the proposed approach against the state-of-the-art trackers.

However, our approach has the following two major limitations. First, the tracking performance is affected by the imaging limitation of some individual source, as shown in Table 2 (TC). Second, the runtime does not meet the demand of real-time applications. In future work, we will introduce the modality weights [4,5] in our model to address the first limitation, and implement our approach using parallel computation to improve the efficiency, such as multi-thread based multimodal feature extraction and GPU based structured SVM [34].

Acknowledgment. This work is jointly supported by National Key Research and Development Program of China (2016YFB1001000), National Natural Science Foundation of China (61702002, 61472002, 61525306, 61633021, 61721004, 61420102015), Beijing Natural Science Foundation (4162058), Capital Science and Technology Leading Talent Training Project (Z181100006318030), China Postdoctoral Science Foundation, Natural Science Foundation of Anhui Province (1808085QF187), Natural Science Foundation of Anhui Higher Education Institution of China (KJ2017A017), and Co-Innovation Center for Information Supply & Assurance Technology, Anhui University.

References

1. Cvejic, N., et al.: The effect of pixel-level fusion on object tracking in multi-sensor surveillance video. In: Proceedings of IEEE Conference on Computer Vision and Pattern Recognition (2007)
2. Wu, Y., Blasch, E., Chen, G., Bai, L., Ling, H.: Multiple source data fusion via sparse representation for robust visual tracking. In: Proceedings of International Conference on Information Fusion (2011)
3. Liu, H., Sun, F.: Fusion tracking in color and infrared images using joint sparse representation. Inf. Sci. **55**(3), 590–599 (2012)
4. Li, C., Cheng, H., Hu, S., Liu, X., Tang, J., Lin, L.: Learning collaborative sparse representation for grayscale-thermal tracking. IEEE Trans. Image Process. **25**(12), 5743–5756 (2016)
5. Li, C., Zhao, N., Lu, Y., Zhu, C., Tang, J.: Weighted sparse representation regularized graph learning for RGB-T object tracking. In: Proceedings of ACM International Conference on Multimedia (2017)
6. Kim, H.U., Lee, D.Y., Sim, J.Y., Kim, C.S.: SOWP: spatially ordered and weighted patch descriptor for visual tracking. In: Proceedings of IEEE International Conference on Computer Vision (2015)
7. Ma, C., Huang, J.B., Yang, X., Yang, M.H.: Hierarchical convolutional features for visual tracking. In: Proceedings of IEEE International Conference on Computer Vision (2015)
8. Wang, L., Ouyang, W., Wang, X., Lu, H.: Visual tracking with fully convolutional networks. In: Proceedings of IEEE International Conference on Computer Vision (2015)

9. Danelljan, M., Robinson, A., Shahbaz Khan, F., Felsberg, M.: Beyond correlation filters: learning continuous convolution operators for visual tracking. In: Leibe, B., Matas, J., Sebe, N., Welling, M. (eds.) ECCV 2016. LNCS, vol. 9909, pp. 472–488. Springer, Cham (2016). https://doi.org/10.1007/978-3-319-46454-1_29

10. Tsochantaridis, I., Joachims, T., Hofmann, T., Altun, Y.: Large margin methods for structured and interdependent output variables. J. Mach. Learn. Res. **6**, 1453–1484 (2005)

11. Wang, J., Bensmail, H., Gao, X.: Multiple graph regularized protein domain ranking. In: BMC Bioinformatics (2012)

12. Zhou, D., Weston, J., Gretton, A., Bousquet, O., Scholkopf, B.: Ranking on data manifolds. In: Proceedings of Neural Information Processing Systems (2004)

13. Zhang, L., Yang, C., Lu, H., Ruan, X., Yang, M.H.: Ranking saliency. IEEE Trans. Pattern Anal. Mach. Intell. **39**(9), 1892–1904 (2017)

14. Wang, L., Lu, H., Yang, M.H.: Constrained superpixel tracking. IEEE Trans. Cybern. **48**(3), 1030–1041 (2017)

15. Boyd, S., Parikh, N., Chu, E., Peleato, B., Eckstein, J.: Distributed optimization and statistical learning via the alternating direction method of multipliers. Found. Trends Mach. Learn. **3**, 1–122 (2011)

16. Lin, Z., Liu, R., Su, Z.: Linearized alternating direction method with adaptive penalty for low rank representation. In: Proceedings of Annual Conference on Neural Information Processing Systems (2011)

17. Gade, R., Moeslund, T.B.: Thermal cameras and applications: a survey. Mach. Vis. Appl. **25**, 245–262 (2014)

18. Li, C., Hu, S., Gao, S., Tang, J.: Real-time grayscale-thermal tracking via Laplacian sparse representation. In: Tian, Q., Sebe, N., Qi, G.-J., Huet, B., Hong, R., Liu, X. (eds.) MMM 2016. LNCS, vol. 9517, pp. 54–65. Springer, Cham (2016). https://doi.org/10.1007/978-3-319-27674-8_6

19. Li, C., Lin, L., Zuo, W., Tang, J.: Learning patch-based dynamic graph for visual tracking. In: Proceedings of the AAAI Conference on Artificial Intelligence, pp. 4126–4132 (2017)

20. Wright, J., Yang, A.Y., Ganesh, A., Sastry, S.S., Ma, Y.: Robust face recognition via sparse representation. IEEE Trans. Pattern Anal. Mach. Intell. **31**(2), 210–227 (2009)

21. Fu, Y., et al.: Robust subjective visual property prediction from crowdsourced pairwise labels. IEEE Trans. Pattern Anal. Mach. Intell. **38**(3), 563–577 (2016)

22. Henriques, J.F., Caseiro, R., Martins, P., Batista, J.: High-speed tracking with kernelized filters. IEEE Trans. Pattern Anal. Mach. Intell. **37**(3), 583–596 (2015)

23. Johnson, R., Zhang, T.: Accelerating stochastic gradient descent using predictive variance reduction. In: Proceedings of Annual Conference on Neural Information Processing Systems (2013)

24. Ma, C., Yang, X., Zhang, C., Yang, M.H.: Long-term tracking. In: Proceedings of IEEE Conference on Computer Vision and Pattern Recognition (2015)

25. Hare, S., Saffari, A., Torr, P.H.S.: Struck: structured output tracking with kernels. In: Proceedings of IEEE International Conference on Computer Vision (2011)

26. Zhong, W., Lu, H., Yang, M.H.: Robust object tracking via sparsity-based collaborative model. In: Proceedings of IEEE Conference on Computer Vision and Pattern Recognition (2012)

27. Valmadre, J., et al.: End-to-end representation learning for correlation filter based tracking. In: Proceedings of IEEE Conference on Computer Vision and Pattern Recognition (2017)

28. Danelljan, M., Bhat, G., Khan, F.S., Felsberg, M.: Eco: efficient convolution operators for tracking. In: Proceedings of IEEE Conference on Computer Vision and Pattern Recognition (2017)
29. Choi, J., Chang, H.J., Yun, S., Fischer, T., Demiris, Y., Choi, J.Y., et al.: Attentional filter network for adaptive visual tracking. In: Proceedings of the IEEE Conference on Computer Vision and Pattern Recognition (2017)
30. Bertinetto, L., Valmadre, J., Henriques, J.F., Vedaldi, A., Torr, P.H.: Fully-convolutional Siamese networks for object tracking. arXiv preprint arXiv:1606.09549 (2016)
31. Mueller, M., Smith, N., Ghanem, B.: Context-aware correlation filter tracking. In: Proceedings of the IEEE Conference on Computer Vision and Pattern Recognition (2017)
32. Danelljan, M., Hager, G., Khan, F., Felsberg, M.: Accurate scale estimation for robust visual tracking. In: Proceedings of British Machine Vision Conference (2014)
33. Zhang, J., Ma, S., Sclaroff, S.: MEEM: robust tracking via multiple experts using entropy minimization. In: Fleet, D., Pajdla, T., Schiele, B., Tuytelaars, T. (eds.) ECCV 2014. LNCS, vol. 8694, pp. 188–203. Springer, Cham (2014). https://doi.org/10.1007/978-3-319-10599-4_13
34. Hare, S., Saffari, A., Torr, P.H.S.: Struck: structured output tracking with kernels. IEEE Trans. Pattern Anal. Mach. Intell. **38**(10), 2096–2109 (2016)

Author Index

Printed in the United States
By Bookmasters

Printed in the United States
By Bookmasters